December 12–15, 2016
Irvine, CA, USA

Association for
Computing Machinery

Advancing Computing as a Science & Profession

CoNEXT'16

Proceedings of the 12th International
Conference on emerging Networking EXperiments and Technologies

Sponsored by:

ACM SIGCOMM

Supported by:

NSF, Google, Ciena & Barefoot Networks

Association for
Computing Machinery

Advancing Computing as a Science & Profession

The Association for Computing Machinery
2 Penn Plaza, Suite 701
New York, New York 10121-0701

ISBN: 978-1-4503-4292-6 (Digital)

ISBN: 978-1-4503-4889-8 (Print)

Additional copies may be ordered prepaid from:

ACM Order Department
PO Box 30777
New York, NY 10087-0777, USA

Phone: 1-800-342-6626 (USA and Canada)
+1-212-626-0500 (Global)
Fax: +1-212-944-1318
E-mail: acmhelp@acm.org
Hours of Operation: 8:30 am – 4:30 pm ET

Printed in the USA

Welcome Message from the General Chairs

It is our great pleasure to welcome you to ACM CoNEXT 2016, one of ACM's flagship conferences in networking, taking place in Irvine in Southern California.

CoNEXT 2016 is a single-track event over three days, preceded by three one-day of workshops, and enhanced by several social events to foster interactions. The Technical Program Co-Chairs, Dejan Kostic and Vyas Sekar, together with an outstanding Technical Program Committee, have put together an exciting technical program of 30 full-length and 5 short papers. We defer to the TPC Chairs' message for details. Vyas Sekar is also the recipient of the SIGCOMM Rising Star Award 2016 and will give the keynote speech in the main conference.

There are also three workshops taking place on the day before the main conference. The Cloud Assisted Networking (CAN) is co-chaired by Mural Yuksel and Tim Wood, and features a keynote by Anees Shaikh. The CoNEXT Student Workshop is a unique event collocated with CoNEXT, addressed specifically to and free for students. This year, it is co-chaired by Rocky K. C. Chang, Hulya Seferoglu, and Laurent Vanbever, and features a keynote speech by Lixia Zhang, several presentations and posters. Finally, GENI NICE is an NSF sponsored workshop also collocated with CoNEXT 2016, and features presentations and demos; we would especially like to thank Vicraj Thomas for coordinating the GENI NICE effort with us.

We would like to recognize and thank so many people that made this conference possible. In addition to the aforementioned chairs, we would like to especially recognize the efforts of our dedicated Local Arrangements Chair, Jiasi Chen, who handled and coordinated a heavy load and wide range of local arrangements. Taylor Garrett from UCI has also been invaluable in making things happen. Our diligent Publications Chair, George Smaragdakis, has been on top of deadlines to make sure the program is published on time and in coordination with the Sheridan folks. Minas Gjoka has been our reliable Webmaster, who also stepped in to help with all kind of tasks whenever needed, from setting up the travel grants site to shooting the non-copyright photos needed for the website. Vyas Sekar has contributed his broad experience from organization of past CoNEXTs. Cristina Nita-Rotaru served as the Travel Grants Chair, including handling the NSF grant and evaluating the applications. Konstantinos Pelechrinis did a great job as the Publicity Chair (while becoming a father, congratulations Konstantinos), and Hamed Haddadi helped with SIGCOMM publicity. David Choffnes and Minaxi Gupta served as Workshops co-chairs. The ACM Conference Management Team and their affiliates in MeetGreen have been a pleasure to work with. We would like to thank the Steering Committee for being resourceful and responsive. CoNEXT has always encouraged and supported student participation, a tradition that successfully continues this year, thanks to the efforts of the travel grants and student workshop chairs, the volunteering and participation of local students, as well as to the generosity of our sponsors. We are grateful to our Sponsors, both institutional (ACM, SIGCOMM, NSF) and industrial (Google, Ciena, Barefoot Networks), and especially to the individuals in those organizations that made it happen.

We encourage you to consider taking a few days before or after the conference to enjoy the location and surrounding areas. Irvine is located at the heart of Orange County in Southern California, next to major surf destinations (e.g., Huntington Beach, Newport Beach - the conference hotel is located walking distance from Balboa Island and Balboa Peninsula), the scenic Pacific coastline (e.g., the Crystal Cove State Park), Disneyland (for those with kids, or simply young at heart), and the major metropolitan cities of Los Angeles and San Diego (within an hour's drive). Additional suggestions will be posted on the conference website.

We hope that you will enjoy the Technical Program and that you will find CoNEXT 2016 a great stimulating event from a scientific and a social point of view. Looking forward to seeing you in Southern California in December!

Athina Markopoulou and Michalis Faloutsos
CoNEXT'16 General Chairs

TPC Chairs' Message

It is our pleasure to welcome you to the 12th edition of the ACM Conference on Emerging Networking Experiments and Technologies (ACM CoNEXT '16). Networking continues to be one of the key building blocks of vital societal services, and we are all proud to be participating in the ongoing quest for even higher performance and reliability, ease of programming and management, new technologies, and lower power consumption in networks.

We have composed a single-track program that consists of a keynote by Prof. Vyas Sekar (winner of this year's ACM SIGCOMM "Rising Star" Award), followed by 30 long and 5 short paper presentations. These papers were chosen from the initial batch of 160 long papers (18.75% acceptance rate) and 39 short papers (12.8%). Overall, the acceptance rate was 17.6%.

Our primary goal was to conduct the selection in a fair and transparent manner, and we are happy to share with you some details about the process. In all stages of the review process we respected the conflicts of interest. As chairs, we made a conscious decision not to submit any papers ourselves, and we would like to thank our students for agreeing not to submit to CoNEXT.

There were 199 papers submitted, but a small number were either removed for formatting guidelines or withdrawn. The remaining papers proceeded through rounds, and in round one the papers received three reviews. We largely followed Remzi Arpaci-Dusseau's guidelines of promoting a paper to round two if it received at least one positive review (score of 3 or more in our case). After a discussion, this led to 101 papers advancing to round two where each paper received at least two additional reviews. For this round we manually checked and adjusted the review assignments produced by the conference management system (HotCRP). With the round two complete, we held detailed discussions to decide which papers to bring to the meeting, and requested external reviews in several situations.

We discussed 60 papers at the single-day meeting in Pittsburgh on September 9, with a vast majority of the committee physically attending the meeting. All accepted papers were discussed at the meeting. During the PC meeting, we almost always achieved consensus on the fate of the papers, and used excellence as our guiding principle. Short papers were judged according to the published guidelines in the call for papers. The discussions were detailed, and respectful. We hope that the program that was selected will have lasting impact on our field.

It is a phrase that is often repeated, but we are very grateful to all authors who submitted their papers. We would also like to extend our warmest thanks to the program committee members who have faithfully followed our guidelines of providing thorough and objective reviews. We would also like to thank the organizers, led by the co-General chairs Athina Markopoulou and Michalis Faloutsos.

We sincerely hope that you will enjoy the ACM CoNEXT '16 program.

Dejan Kostic and Vyas Sekar
CoNEXT'16 Technical Program Committee Chairs

Table of Contents

Session 9: Measurement and Diagnosis 1

Session 10: Wireless 3

Session 11: Measurement and Diagnosis 2

Co-Located Workshops Summaries

ACM CoNEXT 2016 Conference Organization

General Chairs: Athina Markopoulou *(University of California, Irvine, USA)*
Michalis Faloutsos *(University of California, Riverside, USA)*

Program Chairs: Vyas Sekar *(Carnegie Mellon University, USA)*
Dejan Kostic *(KTH Royal Institute of Technology, Sweden)*

Workshop Chairs: David Choffnes *(Northeastern University, USA)*
Minaxi Gupta *(Indiana University)*

Student Workshop Chairs: Laurent Vanbever *(ETH Zurich, Switzerland)*
Rocky K. C. Chang *(The Hong Kong Polytechnic University, Hong Kong)*
Hulya Seferoglu *(University of Illinois at Chicago, USA)*

Travel Grants Chair: Cristina Nita-Rotaru *(Northeastern University, USA)*

Local Arrangement Chairs: Jiasi Chen *(University of California, Riverside, USA)*
Taylor Garrett *(University of California, Irvine, USA)*

Publicity Chair: Konstantinos Pelechrinis *(University of Pittsburg, USA)*

Publications Chair: Georgios Smaragdakis *(Massachusetts Institute of Technology, USA)*

Webmaster: Minas Gjoka *(Google, USA)*

Steering Committee: Hamed Haddadi *(QMUL, UK)*
Vishal Misra *(Columbia University, USA)*
Max Ott *(NICTA, Australia)*
Dina Papagiannaki *(Google, USA)*
Luigi Rizzo *(Università di Pisa, Italy)*
Patrick Thiran *(EPFL, Switzerland)*

Program Committee: Rachit Agarwal *(University of California, Berkeley, USA)*
Mohammad Alizadeh *(Massachusetts Institute of Technology, USA)*
Ganesh Ananthanarayanan *(Microsoft Research, USA)*
Sujata Banerjee *(Hewlett Packard Labs, USA)*
Chadi Barakat *(Inria Sophia-Antipolis Research Center, France)*
Theo Benson *(Duke University, USA)*
Olivier Bonaventure *(Universite Catholique de Louvain, Belgium)*
Marco Canini *(KAUST, Saudi Arabia)*
David Choffnes *(Northeastern University, USA)*
Mosharaf Chowdhury *(University of Michigan, USA)*
Nicolas Christin *(Carnegie Mellon University, USA)*

Program Committee (continued):

Paolo Costa *(Microsoft Research, UK)*
Italo Cunha *(Universidade Federal de Minas Gerais, Brazil)*
Samir Das *(Stony Brook University, USA)*
Colin Dixon *(Brocade, USA)*
Roya Ensafi *(Princeton University, USA)*
Christian Esteve Rothenberg *(University of Campinas, Brazil)*
Alessandro Finamore *(Telefonica Research, Spain)*
Monia Ghobadi *(Microsoft Research, USA)*
Sergey Gorinsky *(IMDEA Networks Institute, Spain)*
Dongsu Han *(KAIST, Korea)*
Wenjun Hu *(Yale University, USA)*
Mohammad Dali Kaafar *(CSIRO New South Wales, Australia)*
Swarun Kumar *(Carnegie Mellon University, USA)*
Aleksandar Kuzmanovic *(Northwestern University, USA)*
Franck Le *(Thomas J. Watson Research Center, USA)*
Harsha Madhyastha *(University of Michigan, USA)*
Alan Mislove *(Northeastern University, USA)*
Vishal Misra *(Columbia University, USA)*
Michael Mitzenmacher *(Harvard University, USA)*
Dan Pei *(Tsinghua University, USA)*
Adrian Perrig *(ETH Zurich, Switzerland)*
Ihsan Ayyub Qazi *(Lahore University of Management Sciences, Pakistan)*
Costin Raiciu *(University Politehnica of Bucharest, Romania)*
Michael Schapira *(Hebrew University of Jerusalem, Israel)*
Siddhartha Sen *(Microsoft Research, USA)*
Ramesh Sitaraman *(University of Massachusetts & Akamai Tech, USA)*
Vijay Sivaraman *(University of New South Wales, Australia)*
Robert Soulé *(Università della Svizzera italiana, Switzerland)*
Neil Spring *(University of Maryland, USA)*
Kannan Srinivasan *(The Ohio State University, USA)*
Patrick Thiran *(EPFL, Switzerland)*
Laurent Vanbever *(ETH Zurich, Switzerland)*
Matteo Varvello *(Telefonica Research, Spain)*
Nedeljko Vasic *(Swisscom, Switzerland)*
Walter Willinger *(NIKSUN, USA)*
Keith Winstein *(Stanford University, USA)*
Xiaowei Yang *(Duke University, USA)*
Haifeng Yu *(National University of Singapore, Singapore)*
Minlan Yu *(University of Southern California, USA)*
Ben Zhao *(University of California, Santa Barbara, USA)*

Additional reviewers:

Omid Alipourfard *(Yale University, USA)*
Daniele Asoni *(ETH Zurich, Switzerland)*
Ayon Chakraborty *(Stony Brook, USA)*
Chen Chen *(ETH Zurich, Switzerland)*
Laurent Chuat *(ETH Zurich, Switzerland)*
Quentin De Coninck *(UCL, Belgium)*
Eduardo Cuervo *(Microsoft, USA)*
Prabal Dutta *(University of Michigan, USA)*
Vasileios Giotsas *(UCSD/CAIDA, USA)*
Vijay Gopalakrishnan *(AT&T Labs – Research, USA)*
Junchen Jiang *(Carnegie Mellon University, USA)*
Srikanth Kandula *(University of Washington, USA)*
Tae-Ho Lee *(ETH Zurich, Switzerland)*
Yuliang Li *(Yale University, USA)*
Martina Lindorfer *(University of California, Santa Barbara, USA)*
Rui Miao *(University of Southern California, USA)*
Vasudevan Nagendra *(Stony Brook, USA)*
Chris Pappas *(ETH Zurich, Switzerland)*
Simon Peter *(University of Texas Austin,USA)*
Raphael Reischuk *(ETH Zurich, Switzerland)*
Laurent Schumacher *(U Namur, Belgium)*
Vamsi Talla *(University of Washington, USA)*
Olivier Tilmans *(UCL, Belgium)*
Bolun Wang *(University of California, Santa Barbara, USA)*
Gang Wang *(Virginia Tech, USA)*
Xia Zhou *(Dartmouth, USA)*

ACM CoNEXT 2016 Sponsors & Supporters

Sponsors:

Platinum Supporters:

Silver Supporter:

Bronze Supporter:

Enabling Software-Defined Network Security for Next-Generation Networks

Vyas Sekar
Carnegie Mellon University
Pittsburgh, PA, USA
vsekar@andrew.cmu.edu

ABSTRACT

The state of network security today is quite abysmal. Security breaches and downtime of critical infrastructures continue to be the norm rather than the exception, despite the dramatic rise in spending on network security.

Attackers today can easily leverage a distributed and programmable infrastructure of compromised machines (or botnets) to launch large-scale and sophisticated attack campaigns. In contrast, the defenders of our critical infrastructures are fundamentally crippled as they rely on fixed capacity, inflexible, and expensive hardware appliances deployed at designated "chokepoints". These primitive defense capabilities force defenders into adopting weak and static security postures configured for simple and known attacks, or otherwise risk user revolt, as they face unpleasant tradeoffs between false positives and false negatives. Unfortunately, attacks can easily evade these defenses; e.g., piggybacking on popular services (e.g., drive-by-downloads) and by overloading the appliances. Continuing along this trajectory means that attackers will always hold the upper hand as defenders are stifled by the inflexible and impotent tools in their arsenal.

An overarching goal of my work is to change the dynamics of this attack-defense equation. Instead of taking a conventional approach of developing attack-specific defenses, I argue that we can leverage recent trends in software-defined networking and network functions virtualization to better empower defenders with the right tools and abstractions to tackle the constantly evolving attack landscape. To this end, I envision a new software-defined approach to network security, where we can rapidly develop and deploy novel in-depth defenses and dynamically customize the networkâĂŹs security posture to the current operating context.

In this talk, I will give an overview of our recent work on the basic building blocks to enable this vision as well as some early security capabilities we have developed. Using anecdotes from this specific exercise, I will also try to highlight lessons and experiences in the overall research process (e.g., how to pick and formulate problems, the role of serendipity, and the benefits of finding "bridges" to other subdomains).

Keywords

Networking; Network Security; Software-defined Networks

Bio

Vyas Sekar is an Assistant Professor in the ECE Department at Carnegie Mellon University, where he is part of CyLab. His research interests lie at the intersection of networking, security, and systems. He received his Ph.D. from the Computer Science Department at Carnegie Mellon University in 2010. He earned his bachelor's degree from the Indian Institute of Technology Madras, where he was awarded the President of India Gold Medal. His work has been recognized with the NSF CAREER award, the ACM SIGCOMM Rising Star Award, the NSA Best Scientific Cybersecurity Paper Award, the CSAW Applied Security Research Prize, and multiple best paper awards (ACM SIGCOMM, ACM CoNext, and ACM Multimedia).

CoNEXT '16, December 12-15, 2016, Irvine, CA, USA
ACM 978-1-4503-4292-6/16/12.
http://dx.doi.org/10.1145/2999572.2999573

Flurries: Countless Fine-Grained NFs for Flexible Per-Flow Customization

Wei Zhang
The George Washington University
District of Columbia, USA
zhangwei1984@gwu.edu

Jinho Hwang
IBM T.J. Watson Research Center
Yorktown Heights, NY, USA
jinho@us.ibm.com

Shriram Rajagopalan
IBM T.J. Watson Research Center
Yorktown Heights, NY, USA
shriram@us.ibm.com

K. K. Ramakrishnan
University of California, Riverside
California, USA
kk@cs.ucr.edu

Timothy Wood
The George Washington University
District of Columbia, USA
timwood@gwu.edu

Abstract

The combination of Network Function Virtualization (NFV) and Software Defined Networking (SDN) allows flows to be flexibly steered through efficient processing pipelines. As deployment of NFV becomes more prevalent, the need to provide fine-grained customization of service chains and flow-level performance guarantees will increase, even as the diversity of Network Functions (NFs) rises. Existing NFV approaches typically route wide classes of traffic through preconfigured service chains. While this aggregation improves efficiency, it prevents flexibly steering and managing performance of flows at a fine granularity.

To provide both efficiency and flexibility, we present Flurries, an NFV platform designed to support large numbers of short-lived lightweight NFs, potentially running a unique NF for each flow. Flurries maintains a pool of Docker container NFs–several thousand on each host–and resets NF memory state between flows for fast reuse. Flurries uses a hybrid of polling and interrupts to improve throughput and latency while allowing multiple NFs to efficiently share CPU cores. By assigning each NF an individual flow or a small set of flows, it becomes possible to dynamically manage the QoS and service chain functionality for flows at a very fine granularity. Our Flurries prototype demonstrates the potential for this approach to run as many as *80,000 Flurry NFs during a one second interval*, while forwarding over 30Gbps of traffic, dramatically increasing data plane customizability.

CoNEXT '16, December 12-15, 2016, Irvine, CA, USA

DOI: http://dx.doi.org/10.1145/2999572.2999602

Keywords

Cloud Computing, Network Function Virtualization, Scheduling, Resource Management

1. INTRODUCTION

Network Function Virtualization (NFV) runs in-network services in software, as virtual machines or containers on commodity servers. NFV combined with Software Defined Networking (SDN) seeks to transform networks from purpose-built hardware appliances to a predominantly software base, increasing flexibility and providing a path for the evolution of network capabilities, possibly at lower cost. NFV promises to support a rapidly evolving network with dynamic instantiation of network services as needed in the path of a flow [1].

However, existing NFV platforms do not fully bring the per-flow customization supported by SDNs to the data plane layer. NFs are still often deployed as monolithic processing entities that process a queue of packets from many different flows. This prevents per-flow customization of processing since NFV platforms must multiplex a small number of NFs for thousands of different flows. This aggregation limits flexibility and prevents the deployment of diverse processing pipelines customized for each customer [2].

A further challenge for NFV is providing flow-level performance management and isolation. Hardware-based middleboxes implement complex queueing structures to provide per class service. The holy-grail is to offer per-flow queuing and service to provide true isolation at large scale. When network functions are implemented in a software platform, providing the same level of isolation is more challenging because of dynamic bottlenecks exacerbated by complex service chains where processing times vary by function and flow. A system that provides a high degree of isolation across flows in a scalable manner, while incorporating appropriate scheduling mechanisms is very desirable. This would allow for the platform to provide in-network services dynamically placed with little concern on the impact on the flows in the network. At a minimum, this needs to be provided to each service class of flows, yet current NFV platforms take a function-centric view on scheduling and isolation–they do not focus on the flows themselves.

When we look at the application ecosystem in cloud environments, it is undergoing dramatic changes with the goal of increasing the flexibility and efficiency with which services can be deployed and isolated from one another. Technologies such as Docker and LXC containers are gaining popularity as an alternative to heavier weight server virtualization platforms. The shift towards microservices breaks applications down into modular components that can be more flexibly developed, deployed, and customized based on a user's needs. This can be taken to the extreme with cloud platforms such as Amazon Lambda, which allow microservices to be further divided into functions that are instantiated and executed on demand for each incoming request. This form of "transient computing" transforms the provisioning time of cloud services from hours to milliseconds.

These approaches are eminently suitable to be used in a NFV environment as a way to increase flexibility while providing fine grained isolation [3, 4]. Breaking network functions down into their component pieces allows for more flexible service chaining depending on the precise needs of a flow. From a network service provider or an enterprise administrator's perspective, being able to download and instantly deploy a container image of a network service dramatically simplifies manageability when compared to past approaches that relied on specialized hardware or monolithic software middlebox implementations. The elasticity of light-weight container-based NFs has the potential to extend this even further by allowing a vast array of NFs to be instantiated and customized on demand for different customer flows.

The challenge in bringing these concepts to an NFV platform is that network services have strict performance requirements so as to function essentially as a 'bump in the wire' [5–7]. Scalability is also a major challenge since current NFV platforms achieve high performance only by dedicating resources (i.e., CPU cores and memory) to a small number of functions running on each server. Current approaches are simply unable to offer high throughput, low latency, and efficient resource usage when running a large number of NFs.

We have developed a NFV platfrom called Flurries to tackle these challenges. Akin to flurries in the real world, NFs in Flurries are extremely transient. They last for the lifetime of a flow, and the platform is carefully architected to support thousands of unique Flurry NF containers executing at the same time. Flurries allows network operators to extend the flow-level routing customization provided by SDNs to the data plane layer. This provides greater flexibility in how processing pipelines are deployed and improves QoS management by making flows a first class scheduling entity. Our transient NF approach also enables entirely new functionality such as zero-downtime NF upgrades. Our contributions include:

- A Docker Container-based NFV platform that uses Intel's DPDK [8] and shared memory between NFs for efficient packet processing.
- A novel hybrid software architecture that uses polling to rapidly retrieve packets from the NIC and interrupt driven NF processing to allow a large number of functions to share each CPU core.
- Fine grained mappings of flows to NFs that allow per-flow customization of processing and scheduling.
- An adaptive scheduling scheme that dynamically adjusts batching to improve latency for interactive flows and reduces context switch overheads.

We have developed Flurries on top of our DPDK-based OpenNetVM platform [9]. Our evaluation shows how Flurries improves performance of service chains and allows customizable priority for different customer flows. Our prototype demonstrates the potential for this approach to run nearly 80,000 unique NFs over a one second interval, while maintaining 30 Gbps throughput for real web traffic.

2. MOTIVATION

In this section, we highlight the recent trends in the industry that motivated the design of Flurries. We then outline how the current advances in the NFV community is lagging behind these industry trends and is sometimes at odds with the enterprise requirements.

2.1 Industry Trends

The following trends in the industry have dramatically changed the way in which organizations design, deliver and operate their services in the cloud.

Docker. Container-based process isolation has existed for a long time in mainline Linux distributions. However, Docker and similar emerging technologies have taken the concept one level further. The application, its configurations, software dependencies, and the filesystem are packaged and distributed as one single unit. Traditional enterprises and startups alike are shifting away from using heavy-weight virtual machines and towards packaging their applications as light-weight containers that can be scaled and distributed much more efficiently than VM images.

Microservices. Driven by the need to quickly respond to market needs, enterprises and startups alike have adopted modern software practices such as DevOps and Microservices [10, 11] . Applications are no longer delivered as monolithic pieces of software that are updated once or twice a year. The microservice architecture breaks an application into a collection of small components, each implementing a single service, that communicate over the network to provide the end-to-end application functionality.

The microservices architecture approach eenables enterprises to deliver software updates to or or more components immediately and continuously. When combined with the packaging ease of Docker containers, these practices have enabled even traditional enterprises to update and deploy their cloud deployments hundreds of times a day [12–14].

Extensive automation. The key enabling factor behind such frequent deployments is automation. The "infrastructure as code" approach to automation has enabled the entire data center deployment to be expressed and controlled through software. The goal is to create an immutable infrastructure, i.e., one where automation and modularity allow any component of the infrastructure to be fully replaced by a new version. When one or more components misbehave or fail, their associated Docker containers are simply thrown away and restarted or upgraded. This is in contrast to past approaches where systems organically evolved over time, often leading to overly complex and unwieldy components.

2.2 Making the Data Plane Agile

Given the agility and automation that is prevalent throught the industry, we posit that NFV environments should be equally agile and automated. In fact, NFV solution providers have already begun movining in this direction [3, 4]. Despite recent advances in NFV, much of the ecosystem requires careful tuning, setup and configuration and professional services to manage the systems. None of these characteristics suit the modern enterprise infrastructure.

While container based NFs cannot provide as strong isolation as virtual machines since they rely on OS-level process address space protection, we posit that this is a small tradeoff, especially in NFV environments where applications are likely to be trusted or thoroughly vetted.

Currently, SDN enables fine grained routing by allowing traffic to be steered at the flow level. Each flow can be flexibly routed based on the particular needs of the user or the application being accessed. Unfortunately, the flexibility of flow routing cannot fully extend to the network function layer because NFV platforms are ill-equipped to support large numbers of unique functions: *they provide neither the abstractions necessary to isolate and process flows with fine granularity nor the resource efficiency to effectively run large numbers of distinct NFs.*

Many NFV platforms, such as those based on the popular DPDK library rely on polling to recieve and process packets, meaning that each NF must be dedicated CPU cores [15, 16]. Our evaluation reveals that even interrupt-driven I/O libraries such as netmap perform poorly when a modest number of NFs, e.g., five or more, share a CPU core. As a result, the number of NFs that can be safely run on a single server is approximately equal to its number of cores. This is far less than the number of flows or even traffic classes likely to be seen by a server. Therefore, NFV servers typically run a small number of general purpose functions. Each NF receives packets from many different flows, and it is typically the NF's responsibility to divide those packets into flows. This leaves the onus on the NF to prioritize processing of packets at the flow level (e.g., handling video traffic first) and to maintain a state table with data for each flow (e.g., a TCP state machine for each flow), as illustrated at the top of Figure 1.

Flurries takes the fine grained *routing* flexibility offered by SDNs and extends it to *processing* at the network function layer. This allows unique data plane processing entities to be

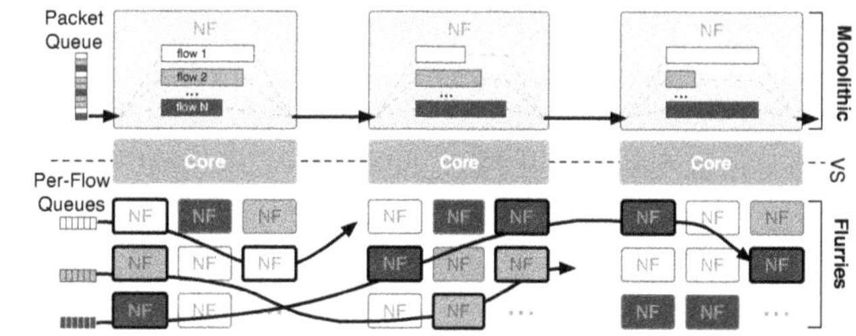

Figure 1: Flurries splits monolithic NFs (top) into light weight, flow-specific functions (bottom). This simplifies NF logic, since they don't need to differentiate flow types, and enables more flexible chaining and resource management.

spawned and customized for each flow, enabling far greater diversity in the number and types of NFs that can be run on each server, as shown at the bottom of Figure 1. Deploying a unique NF for each flow provides many benefits. Some of these are:

Application-specific Networking: Our approach allows for more flexible and powerful customization of flow processing, since a particular middlebox function may want to distinguish how it processes different flows based on their characteristics. For example a flow classified as malicious may be treated differently than a benign flow, or 'elephant' flows may be treated differently than 'mice'. Flurries vastly expands the number of different processing pipelines that can be run on a server, making it feasible to carefully customize processing for each destination application, customer sending traffic, or n-tuple in general. While current NFV platforms are designed to run a handful of different NFs over the time scale of hours, our evaluation shows how Flurries can run tens of thousands of different NFs *each second.*

Multi-Tenant Isolation: A cloud or network provider may wish to host network functions from a variety of vendors or for a variety of customer flows. In either case, it is important for NFs to be kept cleanly isolated since different vendors may be unwilling to have their proprietary functions be combined with code from other vendors. Similarly, clients whose flows are being processed by NFs may demand that their packet data be kept isolated from other flows and functions they do not trust. Supporting this type of isolation is impractical and inefficient unless many distinct NFs can be run on each server.

Simplified NF development: The use of single flow-specific NFs that last only as long as the flows they process can simplify their state management and application logic. This approach moves complex flow tables outside of the NF and into the management layer, allowing the NF to focus only on packet processing.

Flow-Level Performance Management: By dedicating a logical processing 'entity' to each flow, it becomes easier for the management system to prioritize and schedule NFs to achieve flow-level performance goals. For example, when service times for packets of different flows are different at each of the NFs, and the processing of a flow on the platform involves a service chain of multiple NFs, bottlenecks may dynamically form within the chain. Such dynamic variability can be difficult to provision against. This results in interference between flows, with the potential for excessive delay and potential packet loss for flows being processed in the service chain. Having isolation on a per-flow basis, provided by having flow-specific NFs can significantly mitigate the effect of such dynamic bottlenecks. Flurries changes the object being scheduled from a heavy-weight network function, to a light-weight flow at a particular stage of its execution.

3. DESIGN

To support a large number of NFs, the Flurries system design strikes a healthy balance between the two polar opposites of packet processing system designs: busy polling and interrupts. To achieve performance isolation across flows, we resort to containerization and leverage the Linux scheduler to appropriate resources across NFs. In addition, Flurries adopts a simple thread pool design pattern in order to minimize the launch time per container by "recycling" NFs. We describe each of these design concepts in detail in the following subsections.

3.1 Hybrid Polling-Interrupt Processing

Poll-based platforms like DPDK [17] provide the ability to quickly receive large numbers of packets from the wire into the system. Such platforms have been known to scale to extremely high bandwidth systems on the order of 40Gbps. Such scalability also comes at a cost: the CPU performing the polling is at 100% usage at all times. To support a large number of NFs running simultaneously, a poll-based approach would restrict the concurrency to the number of cores available in the system.

Interrupt based packet processing [18, 19] allows for a large number of NFs to be active simultaneously, while only a handful are actually processing packets. However, interrupt based approaches cannot scale to extremely high throughput environments (e.g., 40Gbps).

Flurries design marries the processing capacity of poll-based techniques and the resource efficiency of interrupt-based techniques to achieve the best of both worlds. Polling at the NIC-level lets us get large numbers of packets quickly into the system. Interrupt based NF management lets us divide up those packets and only wake up the NFs that actually need to process them.

3.2 An NF per Flow

A distinguishing feature of Flurries platform is its *NF per flow* processing model, in addition to the *NF per traffic class* model. In the *NF per flow* mode, each NF runs as a transient process managing a single flow at a time. When packets are received from the NIC, a flow table lookup determines if this is the start of a new flow. If it is, then a free NF is allocated out of an idle pool of NFs to handle the flow. If the packet matches an existing flow, then it is directed from the management layer to the correct NF.

The lifetime of an NF is that of its respective flow. For TCP-based flows, when a flow terminates, the NF is recycled back into the idle pool. To identify the NFs that can be recycled, Flurries tracks the state of TCP flow using lightweight state tracking. As flows terminate, Flurries invokes a cleanup callback handler provided by the NF, wherein the NF is expected to cleanup any residual state associated with the flow. Flurries defers responsibility of state management to the NF itself. Such functionality can be achieved using state management frameworks for middlebox applications [20].

3.3 NF Containers

In order to run a large number of NFs (on the order of 1000s), while keeping the design lightweight, we utilize process-based NFs, where each process handles a network flow. While the lifetime of a process transcends that of a flow, the processes themselves are expected to voluntarily yield the CPU between batches of packets, and to reset themselves when the flow finishes.

Flurries uses containerized NFs to support manageability. We assume that a set of trusted NF providers package NF container images with all necessary dependencies, file system layers, etc., as a Docker container that can simply be installed and run on the provider's platform with minimal configuration and management effort.

Flurries chooses to use containers because they provide NF developers a way to combine code and dependencies with a lightweight execution environment. This is in contrast to approaches such as Click [21], Cisco's VPP [22] and Bess [23] in which the NFV management framework contains the execution environment in the form of a set of worker threads, and NFs are simply code libraries that are called by the framework. We believe our approach is more flexible for NF developers since they have greater control over the environment that will process their functions and get greater isolation from other NFs.

Unlike the traditional Docker containers, our security model does not enforce complete memory isolation between NF containers. The address space within each NF process is restricted, protecting their code and private data, but all NFs map in a shared memory region from the manager that hosts packet data. This enables zero-copy I/O across NF service chains as described in the next section.

4. ARCHITECTURE & IMPLEMENTATION

The Flurries architecture is split between the Flurries Manager that interfaces with the NIC and moves packets, and the set of Flurry NFs, which wait in the idle pool until they have a flow to process, as illustrated in Figure 2. We first provide a high level overview of our architecture and then discuss the implementation details of the key components.

When packets arrive at the NIC, the RX threads in the Flurries Manager use DPDK's poll mode driver to bypass the operating system and read packets into a memory region shared with all NFs. The RX thread then performs a lookup in the Flow Table to determine if this is a new flow; if so, the

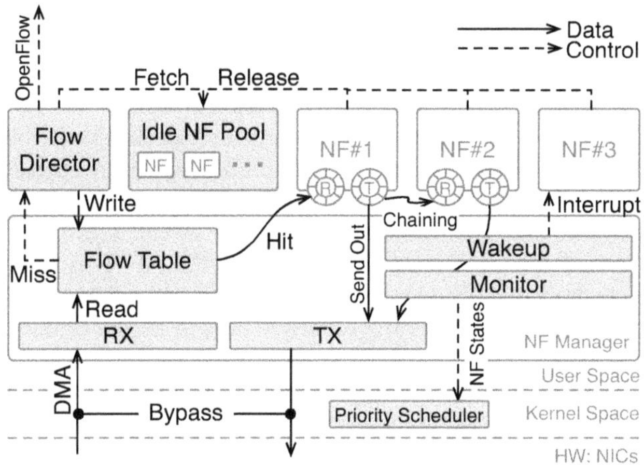

Figure 2: The Flurries architecture bypasses the OS and uses polling for high performance I/O. RX threads do Flow Table lookups to route existing flows, and new flows are assigned an NF by the Flow Director. The Wakeup system alerts NFs when they have packets available, allowing many NFs to efficiently share the CPU.

packet is directed to the special Flow Director NF that is responsible for finding an Idle NF to handle processing. Once a flow is matched to an NF, packet descriptors are copied into the NF's receive ring buffer and the Wakeup subsystem decides whether to transition the NF process into the runnable state.

Each NF is compiled together with libFlurry, which handles the interface with the manager for sending and receiving packets. libFlurry also keeps track of TCP state to detect when the current flow ends so the NF can be recycled. When the NF is scheduled to run, libFlurry will check for new packets in its receive ring and call the designated handler function (e.g., an intrusion detection function) for each one. When its receive ring is empty (or it has watchdog timer expire), libFlurry puts the NF to sleep so that another process can use the CPU. When libFlurry detects the last packet in a TCP flow, it notifies the Flow Director NF that it has become idle, resets its state, and goes to sleep.

Flurries Manager Initialization: When the Flurries Manager starts, it initializes the DPDK EAL (Environment Abstraction Layer), allocates the shared memory pool used to store packets, and preallocates a set of RX and TX rings for the first batch of NFs added to the idle pool. The Manager is also responsible for configuring the NIC ports to initialize one queue for each RX and TX thread.

Wherever possible, Flurries preallocates memory buffers to avoid any dynamic memory allocations within the critical packet processing path. The memory pools used to store packets as well as the receive and transmit ring buffers created for each NF are all stored in a shared memory region backed by huge pages. This allows the Manager to provide zero-copy packet movement between NFs since only a small packet descriptor needs to be copied into the ring of an NF for it to be able to access a packet. Flurries, like the OpenNetVM platform it is based on [9], relies on lock-free ring buffers for all inter-thread and most inter-process communication. This eliminates expensive mutual exclusion and system call overheads.

Once memory is allocated and the NIC has been configured, the Manager starts the RX, TX, Monitor, and Wakeup threads, which are described in detail below. Multiple RX or TX threads can be used if necessary—we have found that one RX thread and one TX threads are sufficient to handle a 10 Gbps arrival rate that is distributed across several thousand individual NFs. When using multiple RX threads, Flurries enables Receive Side Scaling (RSS) in the NIC using a symmetric hash to ensure that all packets for a given TCP flow will be sent to the same RX thread for processing.

RX and TX Threads: RX threads use polling to pull batches of packets from the NIC into the shared memory pool. The RX thread then does a flow table lookup for each packet to determine if it is for a new or old flow. As part of this lookup, the RX thread updates statistics for the flow which are used by Flurries to differentiate between long versus short flows. Since we use RSS, flows are consistently distributed across RX threads. This allows us to partition the flow table across RX threads to avoid contention since two RX threads will never need to perform lookups for packets from the same flow.

An optimization we add is for the RX thread to check for FIN or RST flags that indicate the end of a TCP flow. If either of these flags are observed, the RX thread updates the meta data for the flow so that it will be woken up immediately. We add this optimization in order to avoid the case where packets for the end of a flow arrive at an NF, but it is not immediately scheduled to handle them, delaying when sockets can close and when the NF can be recycled. Having RX threads perform full TCP state tracking would incur too high a cost since they are on the critical path, but checking for these flags is a low overhead way to schedule the NF so that libFlurries can determine if the flow is really ending.

TX threads read a batch of packets from an NF's transmit ring and do flow table lookups on each packet to determine whether they should be sent to another NF or out a NIC port. To minimize cache contention and avoid locks, TX threads only read from the flow table, and never make updates to the table or packet meta data. Like RX threads, TX threads use polling and are dedicated a core. This is necessary since a small number of TX threads are used to move millions of packets per second between the different NFs that make up the processing pipelines. NFs are partitioned across TX threads using *NF_ID % number of TX threads*; this keeps a consistent mapping since the number of TX threads is static but the number of NFs may fluctuate. Since Flurry NFs are so transient and lightweight, we have found that this leads to a reasonably even workload distribution.

Wakeup Thread and Monitor: Although the Flurries Manager relies on polling and dedicated CPUs to achieve high overall performance, individual NFs need to be carefully woken up and put to sleep so that they can efficiently share CPU cores. The Manager's Wakeup thread is responsible

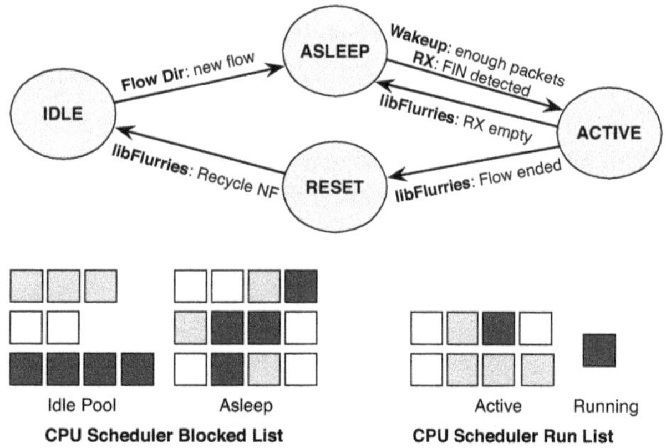

Figure 3: Flurry NFs transition between states depending on whether they are currently in use and the number of packets in their queues. The mapping at bottom shows how NFs for different service types (colors) are mapped to different states, and states are mapped to the CPU scheduler queues.

for checking the receive queues of each NF to determine if there are sufficient packets to warrant waking up the NF. We use an adaptive threshold on the number of packets to decide whether to wake up, and a timeout to avoid starvation, as described in Section 5.1.

While one can think of Flurry NFs as being "interrupt driven," that is not completely accurate since interrupts are not sent for each packet. Instead, Flurry NFs go to sleep by waiting on a linux semaphore used specifically for that NF. When the Wakeup thread finds that the number of packets in the receive queue for an NF exceeds the threshold or the NF's timeout has expired, it marks a flag in the flow entry to indicate the NF is being woken up and signals the semaphore. This transitions the NF to the ACTIVE state, as shown in Figure 3, which means it will be moved from the CPU scheduler's blocked list to the run queue. Once the NF is selected as the running process, libFlurries will update a flag in the NF meta data to indicate it has woken up. This prevents any further signals from the Wakeup thread until the NF empties its queue and transitions back to the ASLEEP state. This protocol ensures that only one semaphore signal will be performed between the time when the queue size first exceeds its threshold and when that batch is fully processed.

The Monitor periodically gathers aggregate statistics about NFs for display on the console and to provide to an NF resource management system. This thread does not need to be dedicated a core since it only runs periodically.

Flow Director: The Flow Director is a special NF that maps incoming flows to new NFs. When an RX thread has a flow table miss for a packet, it sends the packet to the Flow Director to determine how it should be processed. The Flow Director can use an internal rule set, or communicate with an SDN controller using OpenFlow to decide what service chain of NFs a new flow should be sent through. It then adds a new entry to the flow table and initializes the statistics for the flow. The flow table is shared with the RX and TX threads. To avoid locks, only the Flow Director adds or removes entries, while only the RX and Wakeup Threads update the statistics within a flow entry.

If Flurries is used with an NF for each flow, then the TCP handshake ensures that only the very first packet in a flow will go to the Flow Director. By the time the second packet in the flow (the server's SYN-ACK) arrives, the flow table rule will have been installed and the RX thread will deliver it and all subsequent packets directly to the NF. This minimizes the work done by the Flow Director, although we still run it in polling mode on a dedicated core to ensure efficient flow startup.

The Flow Director is responsible for tracking the pool of idle NFs. As shown in Figure 3, it maintains a list of idle NFs for each service type (e.g., IDS, proxy, VPN gateway, router, etc.); NFs are added to the appropriate list when their flow terminates, and NFs are recycled in FIFO order. Idle NFs are "blocked" processes that will not be scheduled on the CPU. They consume relatively little memory since the majority of the memory needed by an NFV platform is for the packet buffer pools, which are shared across all NFs by the NF manager. In order to run thousands of processes concurrently, some Linux and Docker configuration parameters need to be adjusted, e.g., to increase the number of open file descriptors and process IDs. While concurrently running thousands of processes is generally ill-advised when they are contending for resources such as the Linux networking stack, our approach alleviates these issues since NFs typically use entirely user-space processing, and only interact with the network via libFlurries which provides efficient zero-copy I/O to the management layer.

libFlurries and Container-based NFs: Each NF is a process that can be encapsulated within a container. NFs are implemented with the help of libFlurries, by registering call backs that NF developers define to handle a packet and clear their state at the end of a flow. The libFlurries API provides functions for NFs to perform common packet operations such as manipulating the header and forwarding packets out NIC ports or to other NFs. After initialization, NFs enter the libFlurries main loop, which checks the receive queue for a batch of packets, issues call backs to process them if available, and then sleeps on the NF's semaphore if the queue is empty.

In order to access the receive/transmit queues and packet buffer pools, the NF uses the DPDK library to map the shared huge page region at start up. This is achieved even in container environments by granting the container access to the Linux huge page file system (hugetlbfs), which exposes a file-based API to map the memory. The NF will map the huge pages with the exact same address mappings as the Flurries Manager by reading the configuration of virtual and physical addresses from the /var/run/.rte_config file. This ensures that the manager and all NFs can use identical addresses when referencing packets and ring buffers, eliminating the need to translate addresses when moving between the host and containers.

After each packet is processed by the NF's packet handler code, libFlurries checks the header bits in the packet to maintain a lightweight TCP state machine for the flow. Flurries only needs to detect the end of a flow by watching for FIN and RST flags, although we also have it track SYN flags at the start of each flow for debugging purposes. Accurately finding the end of a flow within the NF is critical, since otherwise NFs will not be able to free themselves. Once the end of a connection is found, libFlurries calls the NF's reset callback to ensure that relevant memory is cleared before it is recycled for a new flow.

Correctly tracking the end of a TCP connection can be a challenge, especially since occasionally extraneous RST, FIN, or ACK packets may be retransmitted. If such packets arrive after an NF has been reset, Flurries currently drops the packets since it views the connection as closed. This could be avoided by adding a delay before NFs are reset. A timeout could also be used to detect the end of flows that do not cleanly shut down, similar to how SDN switches use timeouts to expire flow rules.

API and Extensibility The libFlurries API is designed to abstract most platform management functions away from the NF developer. The primary functions used in libFlurries are listed below:

Function Name	Description
register_pkt_handler	register NF-specific packet handler
register_state_cleaner	register NF-specific state cleaner
sleep_nf	wait for interrupt message from wakeup thread
flow_close	detect flow close based on FIN and RST flags
adjust_prio	adjust NF priority based on flow characteristic

The two key functions which a developer must implement are the `pkt_handler` and `state_cleaner` functions, which are then registered with the functions listed above. The first function is called for each new packet that arrives, while the latter is used to clean up any NF-specific state when the flow ends and the NF must be decommissioned. While the other functions listed here are not currently exposed to NF developers, they could be extended to add new features to the platform, for example to allow NFs to request changes to their own priority or to define alternative triggers to close a flow for non-TCP traffic.

The Flurries Management layer includes the following:

Function Name	Description
wakeup_nf	determine if an NF must be woken up
adjust_thresh	adjust the wakeup threshold based on the current flow type and the algorithm in §5.1
sem_post	send the interrupt message to wake up the NF
start_nf	start a new NF of specified type
destroy_nf	Destroy an NF of specified type

The `wakeup_nf` and matching `sleep_nf` function in libFlurries are currently implemented using semaphores, however, other communication mechanisms could be considered, as discussed in [24]. Flurries currently assumes NFs of the appropriate type for any new flows are already running (although possibly busy). The `start` and `destroy_nf` functions could be extended to automatically instantiate the appropriate type of NFs based on requests from an SDN controller, or to build a more dynamic NF management system that adjusts the number of idle NFs at runtime, as discussed in the following section.

5. OPTIMIZATIONS

This section describes some of the performance optimizations that enable Flurries to handle thousands of flows/NFs per second. Specifically, we describe how the Flurries platform manages wake up messages for large numbers of NFs to improve both latency and throughput, and how the per-flow NF abstraction allows for fine grained prioritization.

5.1 Adaptive Wakeup Batching

Waking an NF whenever at least one packet is in its receive queue can become very inefficient if it prevents batching of packets. In the worst case, an NF might be scheduled to handle a packet and then descheduled just when another packet arrives for it to be processed. On the other hand, holding a packet until more arrive can incur high latency, especially during TCP startup and for interactive flows where a packet must be processed and sent out before a new one will arrive.

To balance latency and context switch overhead, the Flurries Wakeup system classifies flows as latency or bandwidth sensitive. It then adjusts a wakeup threshold for each NF to determine how many packets must arrive before it is woken up. The Wakeup system also maintains a timer for each flow that is started when its queue becomes non-empty; if the timer expires before the NF is woken up, then the NF will be preemptively scheduled to avoid starvation.

Since all TCP flows are latency sensitive during the handshake phase, and short flows tend to be latency sensitive, Flurries considers any flow that has received less than T_{short} packets to be a latency sensitive flow. In our evaluation we configure $T_{short} = 36$ packets. These latency sensitive flows are always woken up when at least one packet arrives, allowing them to quickly finish the TCP handshake and handle short, interactive flows such as HTTP requests.

Once a flow has received more than T_{short} packets over its lifetime, we use an additive increase, multiplicative decrease controller to automatically adapt the wakeup threshold, T_{adapt}. Whenever the flow's queue contains at least T_{adapt} packets, the NF is woken up and T_{adapt} is updated to $T_{adapt}+1$. If further packets do not arrive and the NF is scheduled because of the flow timeout, then we adjust the threshold to $T_{adapt} = T_{adapt}/2$.

System administrators can tune these parameters and set maximum or minimum wakeup thresholds on a per-flow basis. The wakeup parameters and statistics for each flow are maintained inside the flow table.

5.2 NF Priority Management

Tuning the parameters for the adaptive wakeup algorithm described above provides an indirect way to adjust performance, but Flurries also provides direct prioritization of NFs. Since each Flurry NF handles traffic for a single flow or traffic class, this provides fine grained performance management.

In the early stages of our research we explored sharing NF performance statistics (e.g., queue lengths) with a custom CPU scheduler in order to have NF-aware process scheduling. However, we found that even when using shared memory between user space and kernel space, it was costly and difficult to keep fine grained statistics up to date in the kernel due to the high speed of packet arrivals. Further, since Flurries NFs run for only a short time before switching to a new NF, having a more complex scheduling algorithm actually hurt performance and limited the scalability.

Instead, Flurries uses coarser grained scheduling priorities to increase or decrease the performance of flows. To minimize the context switches, we use the Linux Real Time scheduler with the Round Robin policy. This is because RT scheduler limits context switches, especially when a woken up process has the same priority with the current process. The standard Completely Fair Scheduler (CFS) allows a newly awoken process to preempt the current one, which can lead to poor batching and more context switches since Flurries frequently wakes up NFs. When an idle NF is assigned a new flow, Flurries sets the scheduler priority for the NF. This priority is retained until the flow finishes. The scheduler maintains a queue for each priority and selects processes from a queue in round robin order. This allows Flurries to provide a total performance ordering for different flows, for example ensuring that latency sensitive voice chat flows will be scheduled before bulk data transfer flows. However, adaptive wakeups and flow prioritization are not enough to provide strict performance guarantees, especially for service chains. Our future work will explore how monitoring data from multiple NFs in a chain can be used to automatically adapt priorities to meet target SLAs.

5.3 Minimizing Startup Times

Creating a new NF process for each arriving flow would result in high latency due to the process setup delay. Consequently, Flurries maintains a sufficiently large idle pool of NFs from which NFs are assigned to new incoming flows. The wait time experienced by an incoming flow depends on the availability of idle NFs in the pool. When the workload consists of short connections, as is usually the case for web-based workloads, new flows are less likely to experience any wait time. Even in complex web applications that initiate multiple flows, individual flows are typically short-lived. When the majority of connections are long-lived, there is a higher chance of new flows experiencing longer delays.

To handle highly dynamic workloads whose characteristics vary dramatically within short periods of time, the idle pool size can be dynamically resized based factors like the flow arrival rate, average lifetime of a flow, etc. Our current implementation does not support the dynamic idle pool resizing feature.

6. EVALUATION

In this section, we evaluate Flurries to:

- Show the hybrid approach of interrupt and polling provides better throughput and resource utilization than purely interrupt or purely polling solutions (§6.1)
- Demonstrate the benefits of Flurries (§6.2)
- Analyze the impact of the adaptive wakeup threshold (§6.3)
- Show the scalability of Flurries when using up to six 10Gbps NICs (§6.4)

In our experimental setup, we use seven severs. Six workload generator servers have dual Xeon X5650 @ 2.67GHz CPUs (2x6 cores), 384KB of L1 cache, 1536KB of L2 cache per core, and a shared 12MB L3 cache, an Intel 82599EB 10G Dual Port NIC and 48GB memory. One server used to host Flurries has an Intel(R) Xeon(R) CPU E5-2697 v3 @ 2.60GHz (2x14 cores), three Dual Port NICs (Intel 10G X520-DA2) and 164GB memory. Every server runs Ubuntu 14.04.4 with kernel 4.2.0-36-generic for Flurries testing and kernel 3.13.0 when using Netmap. We use MoonGen as a high speed packet generator, apache bench (ab) for generating latency-sensitive TCP flows, and iperf for bandwidth-sensitive TCP flows. On the web servers, we run haproxy 1.4.24 and nginx 1.4.6 which are capable of sustaining 10Gbps rates when ab requests 32KB files.

6.1 Hybrid Interrupt & Polling

The hybrid notification mechanism of Flurries is designed to provide high performance at the NIC-layer, while allowing multiple NFs to share one core. This allows NFs to efficiently use CPU resources when the workload is low, and for a larger number of NFs than cores to run on a server. To show that Flurries can provide high performance when multiple NFs share a single core, we measure the achieved throughput when increasing the number of NFs.

We measure the throughput in Mbits/sec for three cases: Flurries, Polling, and Netmap. The first two cases are based on our OpenNetVM platform, so the RX and TX threads use polling to efficiently receive and send packets from the NIC; Flurries then uses NFs that sleep between batches, while the Polling case runs NFs that spin looking for packets in their receive queues. For netmap, we run the load distributor (lb) to receive the packets from the NIC on a dedicated core (similar to Flurries' RX thread), then distribute packets to pkt-gen receiver NFs that share a different core. Unlike the Flurries and Polling cases, the netmap NFs simply drop all packets that are received rather than forwarding them back out the NIC, so we expect netmap to have better performance all else being equal.

The experiment uses MoonGen with a 64 byte packet size. Since MoonGen only sends a single large packet flow, we use round robin to distribute packets evenly across the configured number of NFs and we do not recycle them. This setup mimics the case where you have N different traffic classes that each need to be processed by their own NF.

In this scenario, Flurries consistently achieves 9.4Gbps for up to $N = 45$ NFs, as shown in Figure 4(a). In contrast, polling quickly drops to 5.5Gbps even when just two NFs share one core. This is because a polling NF may hog CPU cycles even when there are no packets available, causing other waiting NFs to drop packets from their overflowing queues. Netmap performs better than the Polling NFs, but its performance drops as the number of NFs rises over five since

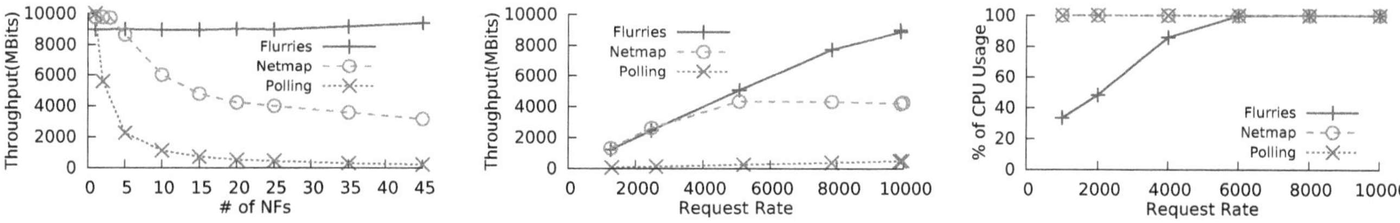

(a) Throughput vs # of NFs (b) Throughput with 20 NFs (c) CPU Usage with 20 NFs

Figure 4: Flurries provides high throughput and scalable CPU usage, even when running multiple NFs on each core.

it is not well optimized to run many NFs per core.

When the workload is low, Flurries avoids wasteful polling to get good performance and CPU utilization. Figure 4(b) and 4(c) respectively show the throughput and CPU usage vs. request rate for the three systems when one core runs 20 NFs. The throughput of Flurries linearly increases as the request rate goes up. With an arrival rate of 1270 Mbps, the 20 Flurries NFs consume a total of 33% of the CPU, whereas the other approaches consistently consume all available CPU resources with that many NFs. Even the interrupt driven netmap system uses 100% of the CPU if there are 20 NFs running, although with only a single NF it can meet the line rate using 20% of the CPU, similar to Flurries.

NF Complexity: The above experiments use light-weight NFs that only perform forwarding, not complex packet analysis or processing. To evalute how Flurries reacts differently when facing complex NFs compared to simple NFs, we create a more heavy-weight NF that uses about three times as many CPU cycles for each packet processed (incurring a 162 ns processing cost compared to 67 ns in our simple NF). We then run either a single NF of the given type, or a group of 45 Flurry NFs, all of the same type. This allows us to see the overhead of Flurries when running different types of NFs.

The throughput of simple NF vs complex NF is shown in figure 5. For a simple forwarding NF, we see about 10.3% performance drop when we run 45 Flurry NFs instead of a single NF that is dedicated the CPU. The primary cause of this overhead is the context switch cost to cycle between the different Flurry NFs servicing the packet stream. With more complex NFs, the maximum throughput that can be achieved drops since the CPU becomes the primary bottleneck; however, the overhead of Flurries falls to only 2.8%. This is because in a more complex NF, the context switch overhead becomes relatively smaller compare against lighter NF. This suggests that as NFs become more complex, it may be necessary to use more resources (e.g., CPU cores) to host them in order to meet a target throughput, but that the amount of extra resources required to run Flurry NFs as opposed to traditional, monolithic NFs will continue to fall.

NF Scalability: Figure 6 shows the throughput and latency when scaling to up to 900 Flurry NFs, well beyond the capacity of Netmap or our Polling system. The "Flurries-Single" case is identical to that described above, so the 900 NFs can be thought of as 900 different traffic classes that each are sent to their own NF. The "Flurries-Chain 4" case means

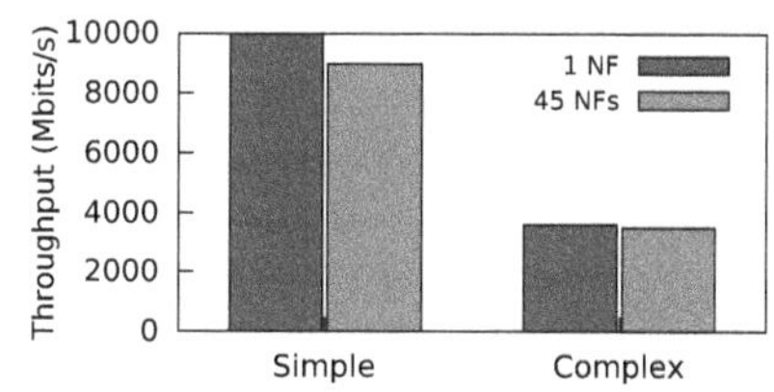

Figure 5: The overhead incurred by Flurries falls as NFs become more complex.

that packets are sent through a chain of four NFs before being sent out. In the latter case, we use two cores to split the NFs across, so each core runs at most 450 NFs. Note that a chain of four NFs puts four times as much pressure on the NFs and requires the management layer to do four times as many packet transfer operations to maintain the same rate as a single NF.

When having a single NF process each traffic class, Flurries is able to maintain a throughput over 9Gbps and latency under 1ms when running 240 NFs (i.e., 240 traffic classes) on just one core. With 900 NFs, Flurries can still meet a 6Gbps rate and a 6ms latency, running almost one hundred times as many NFs per core as netmap while meeting the same throughput. With a chain of 4 NFs per traffic class, Flurries initially gets even better performance since the NFs are spread across two cores instead of one. Even with 900 NFs (i.e., $900/4 = 225$ different traffic class chains), Flurries achieves a throughput of over 5Gbps for 64 byte packets. Latency rises when there are a large number of chains, but we discuss ways to mitigate this issue by scheduling NFs in a service chain-aware manner later in our evaluation.

Port Scalability: We next evaluate the scalability of each approach when using two NIC ports instead of one. Here we focus on performance of the I/O layer in each system, so we use a single core to receive packets from both NIC ports. In Flurries and Polling we run a single RX thread on the core. In netmap we run two of its interrupt driven load balancer programs (one per port) on the same core since each can only read from one NIC port. The RX threads and load balancers distribute packets in a round robin fashion to a pair of NFs running together on a second core.

We measure the throughput of each approach when sending 128 byte packets. Flurries achieves 15Gbps, which is the maximum our hardware supports when using two ports on the same NIC, even for the minimalist L2fwd DPDK code.

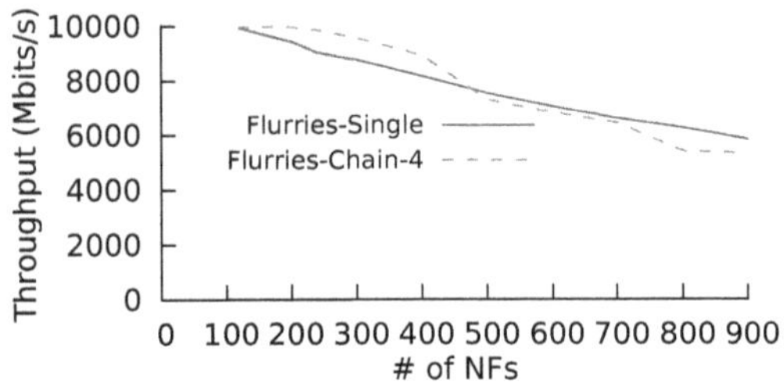

(a)

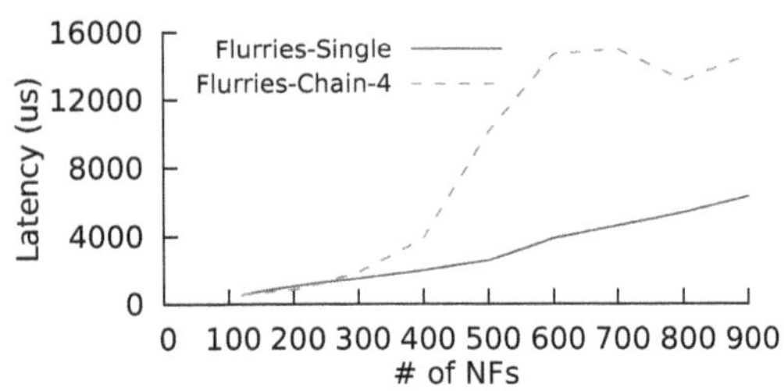

(b)

Figure 6: Even with hundreds of NFs on two cores, Flurries can achieve over 5Gbps when processing 64 byte packets through a chain of 4 FNs

Netmap can only get 10.3Gbps in this setup, illustrating the limitations of an interrupt-driven I/O architecture. Polling achieves 9.3Gbps with two NFs, an improvement over the single port case since it is more likely that a spinning NF will find packets from one of the ports to process.

6.2 Benefits of Flurries

Given the high performance potential of Flurries, we now investigate some of the benefits of our architecture for fine-grained scheduling, flow affinity, and performance isolation.

Fine-grained Flow Priority: To illustrate the potential for traffic prioritization in Flurries, we first setup a scenario where two tenants, Tenant 1 and Tenant 2, send traffic through NFs of the same type of service. Tenant 2 is a VIP customer (high priority), thus expects better performance for her flows than the non-VIP user, Tenant 1. If the system is unable to differentiate traffic at the flow level, flows from both tenants will be assigned to NFs with equal shares of resources, and thus will receive similar throughput and latency. However, since Flurries assigns NFs to individual traffic classes (one per tenant in this case), it can easily achieve differentiated levels of service.

We demonstrate this in Figure 7(a) and 7(b), where HTTP requests from two clients are sent through a middlebox system that is either oblivious of the tenant priorities ("Unaware") or priority-aware ("Flurries"). In the priority-aware version of Flurries, a common idle pool is used for NFs from both tenants, all running identical forwarding functions. When the Flow Director assigns a new flow to an NF, it also sets the scheduler priority for that NF, increasing or decreasing the likelihood it will run for the length of that flow. As a result, Tenant 2 achieves substantially higher throughput and lower latency compared to the priority un-

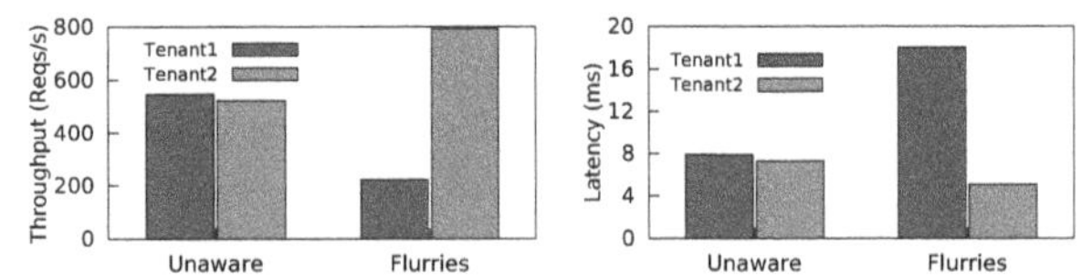

(a) Throughput (b) Latency

Figure 7: Flurries dynamically sets the priority of NFs based on tenant flow characteristics.

aware case. This illustrates how Flurries provides the basic mechanisms that can be used to dynamically tune NF performance on a per-flow basis.

Service Chain-Aware Scheduling: Next we consider how adjusting priorities of NFs in a service chain can improve performance by avoiding wasted work. We configure a three NF service chain, where each NF in the chain has an increasing computation cost with ratio 1:3:7 across the chain. For simplicity, we send a single large UDP flow with MoonGen through the service chain without recycling NFs.

Since, for example, the 3rd NF has seven times higher computation cost than the first, we would expect it to receive approximately seven times as much CPU time. However, this is not the case, and NF 1, despite having the lowest cost per packet, ends up receiving the most CPU as shown in Figure 8(b). The reason for this is that since packets are arriving into the NFV platform at a high fixed rate, the RX threads are constantly receiving packets for NF 1 and marking it as runnable. This makes it more likely for NF 1 to run and process a full batch of packets. However, when these packets are sent on through the chain, it becomes increasingly likely that they will arrive at an NF that already has a full receive queue and is waiting for NF 1 to relinquish the CPU. In Figure 8(a), this causes a large number of drops at the input queue for NF 2, essentially causing it to become a rate limiter before packets can reach NF 3. However, having packets dropped at NF 2 is wasteful since it means we have already paid the cost of partially processing them through the chain; it would be far preferable to drop packets when they first arrive at the service chain if there is insufficient capacity. Such a problem is exacerbated with even longer chains.

To prevent this form of wasted work in service chains, Flurries can assign an increasing scheduler priority to each NF in the chain. This ensures that if the system becomes overloaded, the extra workload will be dropped as early as possible. Figure 8(c) shows that when Flurries is service chain-aware and assigns priorities to NFs in increasing order, it achieves a more appropriate CPU usage assignment and improves throughput by over 2.5 times.

Flow Affinity: Flurries can provide NF affinity at the flow or traffic class level, meaning that all of the requests and responses of the same type go through the same set of NFs. In this experiment, we use apache bench to send realistic traffic and vary the number of NFs, then measure performance when Flurries uses three different NF-assignment algorithms: Round Robin, RSS, and Per-Flow. The first simply assigns batches of incoming packets to NFs in a round

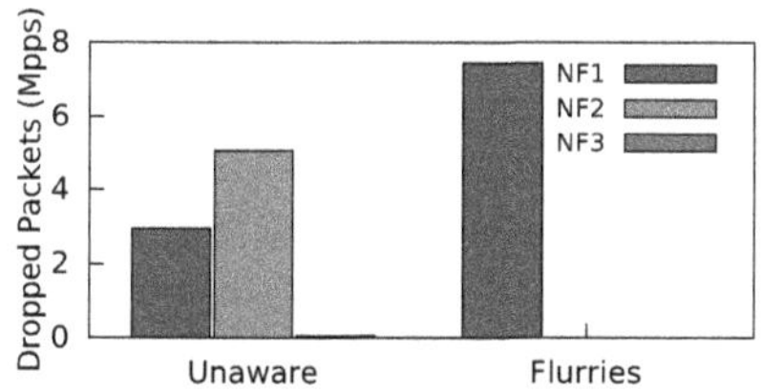

(a) Drop Rate

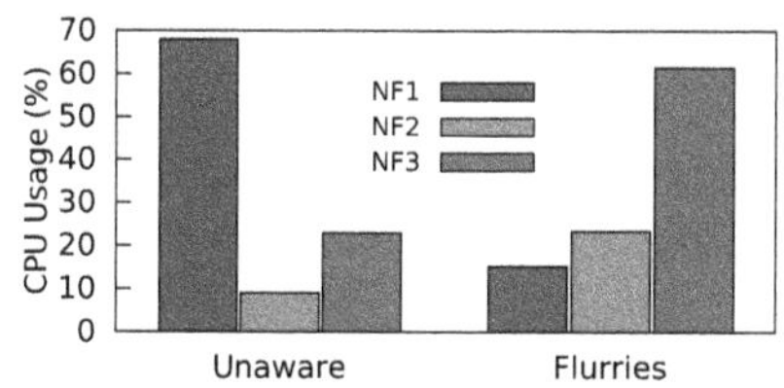

(b) CPU Usage

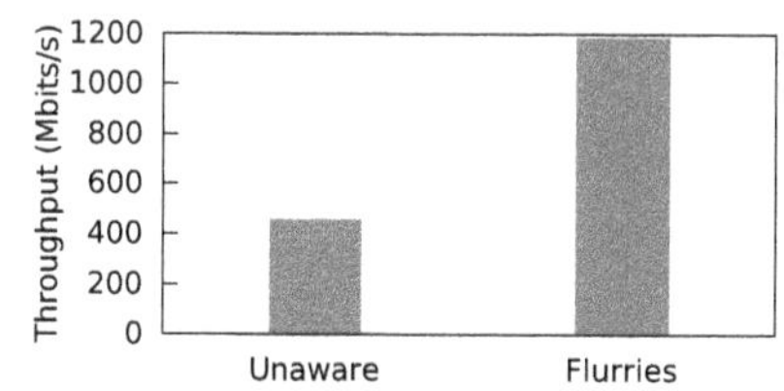

(c) Throughput

Figure 8: Using service chain position to set NF priority helps throughput by dropping packets early to avoid wasted work.

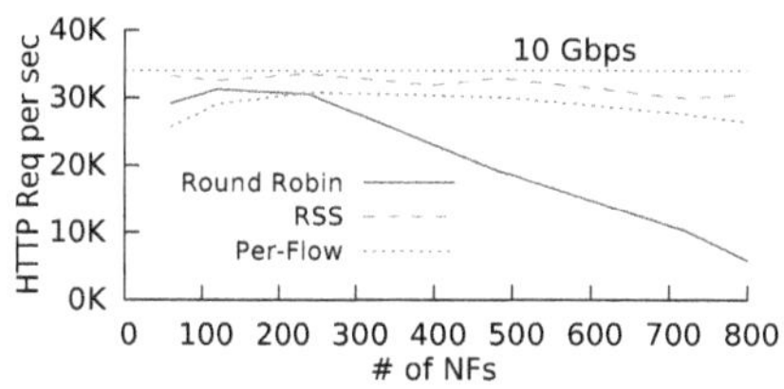

(a) Throughput

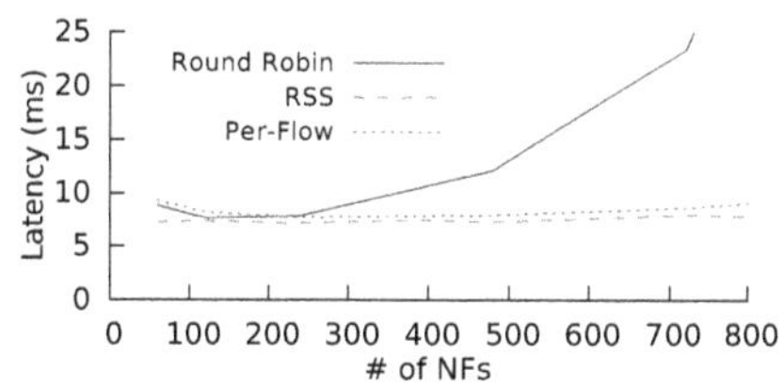

(b) Latency

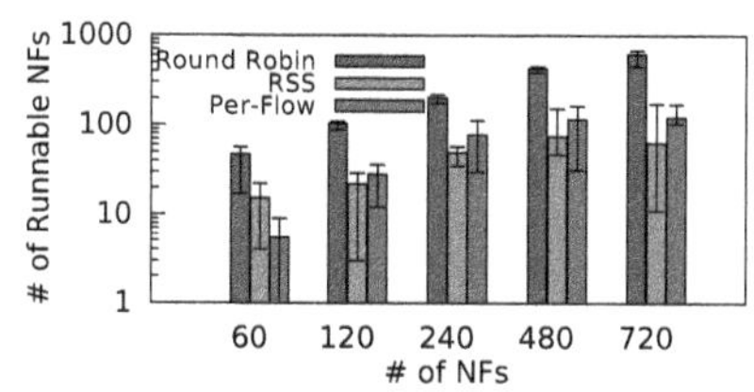

(c) Runnable NFs

Figure 9: Using RSS or Per-Flow assignment of NFs allows Flurries to maintain close to 10Gbps even with hundreds of NFs.

robin fashion, potentially causing out of order problems since packets from the same flow may be delivered to different NFs. The RSS approach provides flow affinity by assigning flows to NFs based on the packet header's *RSS value mod number of NFs*. While this prevents out of order packets, it does not guarantee a unique NF is assigned to each flow, so this multiplexing can cause interference as shown in the next section. Finally, the Per-Flow case represents the standard Flurries deployment where each incoming flow is matched to its own private NF which is recycled for a different flow once it completes.

We fix the HTTP workload concurrency to 240 flows and adjust the number of available NFs. When the number of NFs increases, the throughput of Round Robin decreases significantly as shown in Figure 9(a), and the request latency quickly rises up from 9*ms* to 25*ms* as shown in Figure 9(b). This is due to two factors: first, the rate of packets arriving out of order reaches up to 4.5% since round robin is not flow-aware, and second, round robin spreads incoming packets across all NFs, causing more NFs to be in the Runnable state contending for the CPU, but having fewer packets in their queues, reducing the benefits of batching. Figure 9(c) shows the average number of runnable NFs for each approach; the error bars indicate the 25th and 75th percentiles. When the number of available NFs is lower than the workload concurrency, the Per-Flow case performs worse since it does not have enough NFs to assign one for each flow. Otherwise, it is able to perform similarly to the RSS case, maintaining a throughput close to 33K requests per second which utilizes the full 10Gbps bandwidth. RSS performs the best since it does not incur NF recycling overheads and it tends to multiplex a smaller number of NFs (leading to better batching) than the Per-Flow case.

Performance Isolation: While RSS-based flow direction provides the highest performance, it does not offer any way to carefully control which flows are delivered to which NFs. As a result, if different flows have different traffic characteristics, they may be assigned to the same NF causing interference. In Table 1, we compare the performance when latency-sensitive web traffic and bandwidth-sensitive iperf traffic need to go through the same type of NF. Using RSS, iperf uses up almost all the bandwidth and incurs high interference to web traffic. While Flurries can schedule to steer the web flows and iperf flows to different NFs and control the resource allocation in a fine-grained fashion, the web throughput doubles, the web latency drops by 50%. Therefore, Flurries can achieve the comparable iperf throughput compared to RSS.

	Web Reqs/s	**Web Latency**	**Iperf Tput**
RSS	3378	11.8ms	9.3BGbps
Flurries	6650	6.0ms	8.8Gbps

Table 1: Impact of flow direction on mixed workloads

Per-Flow Overheads: Running Flurries with Per-Flow NFs puts more stress on the Flow Director since it must assign NFs to each incoming flow recycle them when they are finished. To evaluate the minimum cost of flow setup we maintain a large pool of idle NFs and measure the latency between when a packet arrives to Flurries and when the new NF is allocated for the flow. We find that this takes an average of 708*ns*, including the time for the Flow Director to find an idle NF of the appropriate service type, establish a new flow table rule, initialize the flow entry statistics, and enqueue the packet for the new NF.

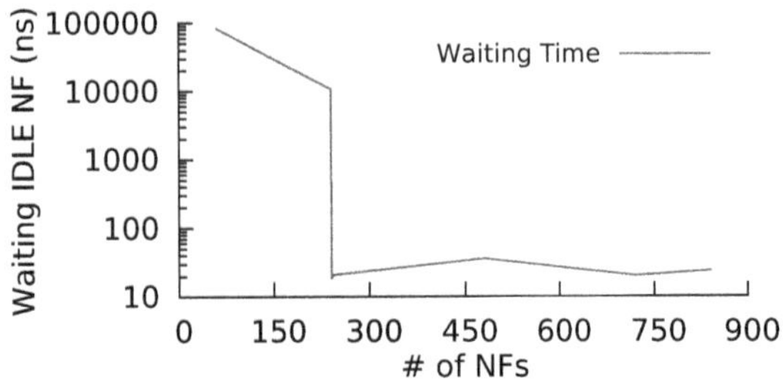

Figure 10: Waiting times are small if there are enough NFs to meet the concurrency level (240 flows)

To show how the size of the idle pool affects performance, we vary the number of NFs and measure the cost to find an idle NF. We fix the flow concurrency to 240 and use apache bench to send requests through Flurries. Figure 10 shows that the time to find a free idle NF is linearly decreased as the number of NFs increases up to 240. After that, the waiting time becomes stable since there is always an NF available.

6.3 Adaptive Wakeup Threshold

The Flurries adaptive wakeup threshold algorithm is designed to balance the needs of latency and throughput focused flows. We evaluate its effectiveness by comparing against several simpler wakeup strategies. *Min* tries to minimize the latency of flows by always transitioning an NF to the runnable state once it has at least one packet in its queue. *Naive-100us* represents a simple approach to balance latency and throughput: it requires at least 32 packets to be in the queue before waking an NF and uses a timeout of 100 microseconds to avoid starvation. The *Naive-1ms* is similar, but uses a 1 millisecond timeout in order to further reduce the number of context switches. Finally, we run *Adaptive*, which uses a dynamic approach: during flow startup it mimics the Min technique, but once flows are established it uses an adaptive threshold and a 1ms timeout. We run a mix of web flows, which are particularly sensitive to TCP handshake latency, and iperf flows, which are throughput focused.

	Web Req/s	**Web Latency**	**Iperf Tput**	**CPU**	**Context Switches**
Min	4002	3.7ms	6.0 Gbps	80%	258K/s
Naive-100us	3899	3.8ms	5.8 Gbps	99%	237K/s
Naive-1ms	2694	5.6ms	4.7 Gbps	67%	136K/s
Adaptive	5022	4.0ms	6.9 Gbps	99%	217K/s

Table 2: Wakeup algorithm effect on mixed workloads

The table shows that the Min approach incurs the highest number of context switches, while keeping the minimum web latency. The Naive approaches both perform relatively poorly, with high latency and low throughput when using a timeout of 1ms. This approach leaves the CPU idle about 33% of the time. Flurries' Adaptive algorithm provides the best overall performance, getting the highest web and iperf throughput with only a small latency degradation.

6.4 Multi-NIC Scalability

Finally, we investigate the scalability of Flurries when using web traffic across multiple NIC ports and a large number of NFs. We setup our Flurries server with three dual port NICs as a "bump in the wire" between three client generator servers and three web servers as shown in Figure 11(a). Flurries is used to bridge ports between the two servers, and we use Per-NF flow allocation to dedicate a distinct NF to each flow. We use one thread each for RX, TX, and Wakeup.

First, we show how Flurries' performance changes as we adjust the number of flows on one core and with one NIC (i.e., only client 1 and web server 1). Figure 11(b) shows the throughput and latency vs. # of flows on one core (the number of flows is equal to the number of NFs). We use apache bench to request a file (32KB), and adjust the concurrency of the clients so the total concurrency is equal to the number of NFs in each test. As the number of flows goes up, the throughput increases until the full NIC bandwidth is used. Using 32KB files for this test results in Flurries seeing a large number of relatively short flows–as of September 2016, the average size of web page content is 2.4MB [25], although this may be split over several HTTP connections. For flows larger than 32KB, we expect Flurries' performance to improve, since relatively less time will be spent on assigning idle NFs and generating the flow entry.

Note that since Flurries is bridging two ports that each support 10Gbps in both directions, the total data rate being sent and received through the NFV platform is well over 20Gbps—approximately 10Gbps of server responses are received and sent out each port plus client requests are also being transmitted. Increasing the number of flows causes a minimal increase in latency because there are more flows contending for the CPU, however, the majority of the latency rise is because there is simply more load on all the client and server machines–running the two machines directly connected gives a baseline latency that is consistently within 2ms of Flurries, as shown in the figure.

Next we measure the scalability when using multiple NIC ports and multiple cores. In each stage of the experiment we add one more core hosting 720 NFs and one more dual port 10Gbps NIC, until all three NICs (6 ports) are in use and there is a total of 2,160 NFs in the idle pool. We keep the management configuration the same in all cases, with one thread each for RX, TX, and Wakeup. We measure the number of "active NFs" within each one second interval, i.e., the number of NFs that are selected when a new flow arrives and then recycled for a subsequent flow. Figure 11(c) shows that over the course of the experiment, three cores can support an average of nearly 80,000 active NFs each second. This is about 2.6 times greater than when only a single core and a single port are used. At this scale, each of the 80,000 NFs could be assigned different priorities based on the needs of each flow, and since the active NFs are drawn from a pool of over 2,000 unique NFs, it would be possible to host a vast variety of different types of functions each being flexibly assigned on a per-flow basis.

In the three core case, Flurries saturates all three of the

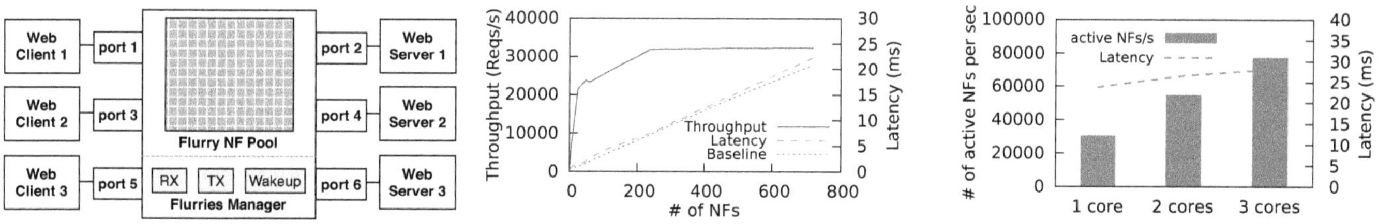

(a) Multi NIC Testbed (b) Single NIC (c) Multi NIC

Figure 11: Testing Flurries with 6 NIC ports shows its capacity to run up to 80,000 NFs in a one second interval, while meeting a 30Gbps traffic rate and incurring minimal added latency to web traffic.

dual port NICs, so adding additional cores of NFs does not affect the scalability results. We believe that adding more NICs and cores should continue this trend, while maintaining a relatively flat latency. Latency rises in part due to the increasing load on the RX thread, but our current implementation only supports running one RX thread, so we are not able to evaluate scalability further.

7. RELATED WORK

Several NFV platforms have demonstrated high-speed networking virtualization on commodity off-the-shelf servers [9, 18, 23, 26]. In 2009, Greenhalgh et. al. [27] first proposed Flowstream, an architecture designed to enable flexible flow processing and forwarding, and leading to a growing interest in managing network functions in a more fine-grained fashion. More recently, the Superfluid cloud [28] project sought to increase and manage the number of concurrently running network functions up to 10,000 using an optimized platform plus lightweight network functions; their focus was on fast startup of NFs, and they do not provide performance results. Cerrato [29] also considers running large numbers of tiny NFs, and faces many performance problems that our platform overcomes with our hybrid polling-interrupt I/O scheme. The ClickOS platform [30] builds on top of netmap to provide a lightweight Click router based operating system with high speed network processing. Our evaluation compares against netmap directly since our testing suggests it generally has higher performance. Their work, and others such as Jitsu [31] and Miniproxy [32], illustrate the potential of unikernels to reduce NF startup time to the 20 *ms* range. Flurries relies on an idle pool of NFs and we have not yet explored ways to reduce the startup delay of our NFs (approximately 500ms).

Managing a large number of network functions at fine-grained granularity requires maximizing the parallelism and efficiency of hardware resources. E2 [33] is an NFV management platform, which includes NF placement across the cluster, dynamic scaling and migration avoidance for flow affinity. Our work focuses on a different scale: running large number of NFs on a small number of cores. Especially, for a service chain [34, 35] spanning multiple NFs requires good resource schedulability in order to not increase latency or drop packets. The RouteBricks project [36] increases the speed of software routers by exploiting parallelism both across multiple servers and across multiple cores within a single server. Li et. al. [37] sought to provide timing guarantees in network function virtualization environment, and enable a set of service chains that each consist of some network functions. Cao et. al. [38] characterized the performance of virtual network functions.

Flurries makes use of a mix of polling and interrupts, a concept which has been explored in prior work. Dovrolis et. al. [39] proposed the hybrid approach for the network interface to benefit merits of both. Deri et. al. [40] proposes a new approach to passive packet capture that combines with device polling to allow packets to be captured and analyzed using the NetFlow protocol at (almost) wire speed on Gbit networks. Liu et. al. [41] significantly accelerates the I/O virtualization by using the dedicated cores to poll the network interfaces. Also, Yang et. al. [42] investigated cases where polling is better than interrupt. To our knowledge, we are the first NFV platform to try to balance these two approaches to maximize performance at the I/O layer while efficiently using resources at the application layer.

8. CONCLUSION

NFV offers unprecedented power to manipulate and analyze traffic as it flows through the network. Existing NFV platforms have been designed to maximize performance of a small number of NFs, but this prevents truly exploiting the flexible per-flow routing provided by SDNs. Flurries draws from recent trends such as containerization and transient microservices to build an NFV platform optimized for running thousands of distinct NFs per server, each of which can be flexibly assigned to a single flow or traffic class. We believe that this can dramatically expand the diversity of functionality and performance management in the network. Our prototype has shown that Flurries can run 100 times as many NFs as netmap while meeting the same throughput, and that over 2000 distinct NFs can share 3 CPU cores while fully utilizing six 10Gbps NIC ports. This provides a substantial increase in performance, flexibility, and isolation compared to the state of the art.

Acknowledgements: This work was supported in part by NSF grants CNS-1422362 and CNS-1522546. We would like to thank the anonymous reviewers and our shepherd, Ihsan Ayyub Qazi, for their comments and feedback.

References

[1] Wei Zhang, Guyue Liu, Ali Mohammadkhan, Jinho Hwang, K. K. Ramakrishnan, and Timothy Wood. Sdnfv: Flexible and dynamic software defined control of an application- and flow-aware data plane. In *Middleware*, 2016.

[2] T. Wood, K. K. Ramakrishnan, J. Hwang, G. Liu, and W. Zhang. Toward a software-based network: integrating software defined networking and network function virtualization. *IEEE Network*, 29(3):36–41, May 2015.

[3] Ciena Toolkit Applies DevOps To Control SDN/NFV Networks. https://virtualizationreview.com/articles/2016/05/27/ciena-devops.aspx, May 2016. [ONLINE].

[4] Achieving DevOps for NFV Continuous Delivery on Openstack - Verizon Case Study. https://www.openstack.org/videos/video/achieving-devops-for-nfv-continuous-delivery-on-/openstack-verizon-case-study. [ONLINE].

[5] Anirudh Sivaraman, Suvinay Subramanian, Mohammad Alizadeh, Sharad Chole, Shang-Tse Chuang, Anurag Agrawal, Hari Balakrishnan, Tom Edsall, Sachin Katti, and Nick McKeown. Programmable packet scheduling at line rate. In *Proceedings of the 2016 Conference on ACM SIGCOMM 2016 Conference*, SIGCOMM '16, pages 44–57, New York, NY, USA, 2016. ACM.

[6] Radhika Mittal, Rachit Agarwal, Sylvia Ratnasamy, and Scott Shenker. Universal packet scheduling. In *13th USENIX Symposium on Networked Systems Design and Implementation (NSDI 16)*, pages 501–521, Santa Clara, CA, March 2016. USENIX Association.

[7] Wei Zhang, Timothy Wood, Jinho Hwang, Shriram Rajagopalan, and K. K. Ramakrishnan. Performance management challenges for virtual network functions. In *Proc. NetSoft*. IEEE, 2016.

[8] Intel Corporation. Intel data plane development kit: Getting started guide. 2013.

[9] Wei Zhang, Guyue Liu, Wenhui Zhang, Neel Shah, Phillip Lopreiato, Gregoire Todeschi, K.K. Ramakrishnan, and Timothy Wood. Opennetvm: A platform for high performance network service chains. In *Proceedings of the 2016 ACM SIGCOMM Workshop on Hot Topics in Middleboxes and Network Function Virtualization*. ACM, 2016.

[10] Sam Neuman. *Building Microservices: Designing Fine-Grained Systems*. O'Reilly Media, February 2015.

[11] Martin Fowler and James Lewis. Microservices. http://martinfowler.com/articles/microservices.html, 2014. [ONLINE].

[12] Jez Humble and David Farley. *Continuous Delivery: Reliable Software Releases through Build, Test, and Deployment Automation*. Addison-Wesley Professional, 1 edition, July 2010.

[13] ORBITZ. Enabling Microservices at Orbitz. *DockerCon (2015)*.

[14] HUBSPOT. How We Deploy 300 Times a Day. http://product.hubspot.com/blog/how-we-deploy-300-times-a-day, November 2013. [ONLINE].

[15] Wei Zhang, Timothy Wood, and Jinho Hwang. Netkv: Scalable, self-managing, load balancing as a network function. In *IEEE International Conference on Autonomic Computing*. IEEE, 2016.

[16] Wei Zhang, Timothy Wood, K.K. Ramakrishnan, and Jinho Hwang. Smartswitch: Blurring the line between network infrastructure & cloud applications. In *6th USENIX Workshop on Hot Topics in Cloud Computing (HotCloud 14)*, Philadelphia, PA, June 2014. USENIX Association.

[17] Intel Corporation. Intel data plane development kit: Intel 64 and ia-32 architectures software developer's manual. 2013.

[18] Luigi Rizzo. Netmap: a novel framework for fast packet i/o. In *21st USENIX Security Symposium (USENIX Security 12)*, pages 101–112, 2012.

[19] Radu Stoenescu, Vladimir Olteanu, Matei Popovici, Mohamed Ahmed, Joao Martins, Roberto Bifulco, Filipe Manco, Felipe Huici, Georgios Smaragdakis, Mark Handley, et al. In-net: in-network processing for the masses. In *Proceedings of the Tenth European Conference on Computer Systems*, page 23. ACM, 2015.

[20] Shriram Rajagopalan, Dan Williams, Hani Jamjoom, and Andrew Warfield. Split/merge: System support for elastic execution in virtual middleboxes. In *Proceedings of the 10th USENIX Conference on Networked Systems Design and Implementation*, nsdi'13, pages 227–240, Berkeley, CA, USA, 2013. USENIX Association.

[21] Eddie Kohler, Robert Morris, Benjie Chen, John Jannotti, and M Frans Kaashoek. The click modular router. *ACM Transactions on Computer Systems (TOCS)*, 18(3):263–297, 2000.

[22] VPP. https://fd.io/, 2016. [ONLINE].

[23] Sangjin Han, Keon Jang, Aurojit Panda, Shoumik Palkar, Dongsu Han, and Sylvia Ratnasamy. Softnic: A software nic to augment hardware. Technical Report UCB/EECS-2015-155, EECS Department, University of California, Berkeley, May 2015.

[24] I. Cerrato, M. Annarumma, and F. Risso. Supporting Fine-Grained Network Functions through Intel DPDK. In *2014 Third European Workshop on Software Defined Networks*, pages 1–6, September 2014.

[25] HTTP Archive - Interesting Stats. http://httparchive.org/interesting.php. [ONLINE].

[26] Jinho Hwang, K. K. Ramakrishnan, and Timothy Wood. Netvm: High performance and flexible networking using virtualization on commodity platforms. In *Proc. NSDI*, NSDI'14, pages 445–458, Berkeley, CA, USA, 2014. USENIX Association.

[27] Adam Greenhalgh, Felipe Huici, Mickael Hoerdt, Panagiotis Papadimitriou, Mark Handley, and Laurent

Mathy. Flow processing and the rise of commodity network hardware. *SIGCOMM Comput. Commun. Rev.*, 39(2):20–26, March 2009.

[28] Filipe Manco, Joao Martins, Kenichi Yasukata, Jose Mendes, Simon Kuenzer, and Felipe Huici. The case for the superfluid cloud. In *7th USENIX Workshop on Hot Topics in Cloud Computing (HotCloud 15)*, 2015.

[29] Ivano Cerrato, Mauro Annarumma, and Fulvio Risso. Supporting fine-grained network functions through intel dpdk. In *EWSDN*, pages 1–6. IEEE, 2014.

[30] Joao Martins, Mohamed Ahmed, Costin Raiciu, Vladimir Olteanu, Michio Honda, Roberto Bifulco, and Felipe Huici. Clickos and the art of network function virtualization. In *11th USENIX Symposium on Networked Systems Design and Implementation (NSDI 14)*, pages 459–473, Seattle, WA, April 2014. USENIX Association.

[31] Anil Madhavapeddy, Thomas Leonard, Magnus Skjegstad, Thomas Gazagnaire, David Sheets, Dave Scott, Richard Mortier, Amir Chaudhry, Balraj Singh, Jon Ludlam, Jon Crowcroft, and Ian Leslie. Jitsu: Just-in-time summoning of unikernels. In *Proc. NSDI*, pages 559–573, Oakland, CA, May 2015. USENIX Association.

[32] Giuseppe Siracusano, Roberto Bifulco, Simon Kuenzer, Stefano Salsano, Nicola Blefari Melazzi, and Felipe Huici. On-the-fly tcp acceleration with miniproxy. In *Proceedings of the 2016 ACM SIGCOMM Workshop on Hot Topics in Middleboxes and Network Function Virtualization*, 2016.

[33] Shoumik Palkar, Chang Lan, Sangjin Han, Keon Jang, Aurojit Panda, Sylvia Ratnasamy, Luigi Rizzo, and Scott Shenker. E2: A framework for nfv applications. In *Proceedings of the 25th Symposium on Operating Systems Principles*, SOSP '15, pages 121–136, New York, NY, USA, 2015. ACM.

[34] Seungik Lee, Myung-Ki Shin, EunKyoung Paik, and Sangheon Pack. Resource Management in Service Chaining. Internet-Draft draft-lee-nfvrg-resource-management-service-chain-01, Internet Engineering Task Force, October 2015. Work in Progress.

[35] ETSI. Network functions virtualization (nfv); architectural framework. *ETSI GS NFV V002*, 2013.

[36] Mihai Dobrescu, Norbert Egi, Katerina Argyraki, Byung-Gon Chun, Kevin Fall, Gianluca Iannaccone, Allan Knies, Maziar Manesh, and Sylvia Ratnasamy. Routebricks: exploiting parallelism to scale software routers. In *Proceedings of the ACM SIGOPS 22nd symposium on Operating systems principles*, pages 15–28. ACM, 2009.

[37] Y. Li, L. T. X. Phan, and B. T. Loo. Network functions virtualization with soft real-time guarantees. In *IEEE International Conference on Computer Communications (INFOCOM)*, 2016.

[38] L. Cao, P. Sharma, S. Fahmy, and V. Saxena. Nfv-vital: A framework for characterizing the performance of virtual network functions. In *Network Function Virtualization and Software Defined Network (NFV-SDN), 2015 IEEE Conference on*, pages 93–99, Nov 2015.

[39] Constantinos Dovrolis, Brad Thayer, and Parameswaran Ramanathan. Hip: Hybrid interrupt-polling for the network interface. *SIGOPS Oper. Syst. Rev.*, 35(4):50–60, October 2001.

[40] Luca Deri, Netikos S. P. A, Via Del Brennero Km, and Loc La Figuretta. Improving passive packet capture: Beyond device polling. In *In Proceedings of SANE 2004*, 2004.

[41] Jiuxing Liu and Bulent Abali. Virtualization polling engine (vpe): Using dedicated cpu cores to accelerate i/o virtualization. In *Proceedings of the 23rd International Conference on Supercomputing*, ICS '09, pages 225–234, New York, NY, USA, 2009. ACM.

[42] Jisoo Yang, Dave B Minturn, and Frank Hady. When poll is better than interrupt. In *Proceedings of the 10th USENIX conference on File and Storage Technologies*, pages 3–3. USENIX Association, 2012.

Mind the Gap: Monitoring the Control-Data Plane Consistency in Software Defined Networks

Peng Zhang, Hao Li, Chengchen Hu, Liujia Hu, Lei Xiong, Ruilong Wang, and Yuemei Zhang
Department of Computer Science and Technology
Xi'an Jiaotong University
{p-zhang,hao.li,chengchenghu}@xjtu.edu.cn; {liujia-hu,hbxgxiong,wangruilongy,zym665456}@stu.xjtu.edu.cn

ABSTRACT

How to debug large networks is always a challenging task. Software Defined Network (SDN) offers a centralized control platform where operators can *statically* verify network policies, instead of checking configuration files device-by-device. While such a static verification is useful, it is still not enough: due to data plane faults, packets may not be forwarded according to control plane policies, resulting in network faults at *runtime*. To address this issue, we present VeriDP, a tool that can continuously monitor what we call *control-data plane consistency*, defined as the consistency between control plane policies and data plane forwarding behaviors. We prototype VeriDP with small modifications of both hardware and software SDN switches, and show that it can achieve a verification speed of 3 μs per packet, with a false negative rate as low as 0.1%, for the Stanford backbone and Internet2 topologies. In addition, when verification fails, VeriDP can localize faulty switches with a probability as high as 96% for fat tree topologies.

CCS Concepts

•**Networks** → **Network measurement;** •**Hardware** → **Error detection and error correction;**

Keywords

Software Defined Network; consistency; verification

1. INTRODUCTION

Networks are prone to faults. Meanwhile, most operators still debug network faults in an ad-hoc way: checking configurations device-by-device with simple tools like ping, traceroute, SNMP, etc. As a result, it is highly-demanding and time-consuming for operators to pinpoint the root causes. A network debugging toolkit that can automatically detect, locate, and repair network faults is highly desired [57].

Software Defined Network (SDN) decouples control functions away from the data plane, so that operators can configure/program the network from a centralized point. This centralized control offers new opportunities for automating the network debugging process. Many tools have been developed to verify the correctness of network configuration in SDN [36, 37, 35, 58]. Since these tools generally debug network configurations at the controller side, we will term them as control plane verification tools.

Though the above tools are useful for reducing errors in the configuration process, they assume these configurations will be reflected in packet forwarding behaviors. As will be shown later, even if configurations are error-free at the control plane, packets forwarding can still be faulty at the data plane. Reasons for these faults include: lack of acknowledgement from switches [50, 46, 40], switch software bugs [57, 34], premature switch implementation [46], external modification [18, 47], etc (see Section 2.2).

To detect such faults, data plane verification tools have been developed. ATPG [57] sends probe packets to test the data plane, while it solely checks reception of probe packets, without inspecting the paths took by the probe packets. This prevents ATPG from verifying policies (*e.g.*, waypoint, access control) that are dependent on paths. Monocle [41] generates probe packets to test the existence of rules at switches. However, due to the slow probe generation process (at a scale of seconds), Monocle can only check a relatively steady network configuration and cannot work under frequent network updates or reconfigurations. In addition, probe packets may be treated differently from real traffic, thereby leading to inaccurate judgements (see Section 3.1).

Given the limitations of both control plane and data plane verification tools, we think a missing part in the current SDN architecture is a tool that can ensure the operator's configurations will correctly reflect at packet forwarding behaviors. To this end, this paper proposes VeriDP, a tool that can continuously monitor the control-data plane consistency, *i.e.*, whether packet forwarding behaviors agree with the network configurations. By ensuring such consis-

CoNEXT '16, December 12-15, 2016, Irvine, CA, USA
© 2016 ACM. ISBN 978-1-4503-4292-6/16/12. . . $15.00
DOI: http://dx.doi.org/10.1145/2999572.2999605

tency, VeriDP enables operators to focus on configuration correctness.

VeriDP uses *path table* as the abstract of control plane configurations, and tests whether packet forwarding behaviors are conforming to the path table. A path table is a data structure that records forwarding paths between any two ports in the network. Each path entry consists of (1) a forwarding path, which consists of a sequence of hops, in the form of $\langle input\_port, switch\_ID, output\_port\rangle$, (2) a set of all packets, which can be forwarded along the path, and (3) a tag, which is a compression of the path information. VeriDP generates the path table based on the network topologies and rules installed by the controller. When a packet traverses through the network, each switch generates/updates the tag of the packet the same way as the tag in the path table is computed. Before the packet leaves the network, a report encapsulating the header and tag of the packet is sent to the controller for verification. If the forwarding path is correct, the reported header will match an entry in the path table, and the reported packet tag should be the same with the one of the matched entry.

We face the following two challenges when realizing VeriDP. First, we need an efficient method to construct the path table, so that (1) it should allow fast lookups in order to scale to large networks, (2) it can be updated incrementally to accommodate frequent rule updates, and (3) it should encode packet headers with efficient methods without consuming too much memory. Second, we need a tag compression method which allows localization of faulty switches, when inconsistency is detected. Thus, simple hash-based tag compression is not possible.

To address the above challenges, we leverage Binary Decision Diagram (BDD) to encode packet headers, and use Bloom filter for tag compression. In addition, we design an incremental path table update algorithm that only updates a small portion of path table. In summary, our contribution is two-fold:

- We propose VeriDP, the first tool (to the best of our knowledge) that can monitor the control-data plane consistency in SDN. VeriDP can achieve a false negative rate as low as 0.1% for inconsistency detection, and an accuracy as high as 96% for faulty switch localization. The verification speed is as fast as 3 μs per packet for the Stanford backbone and Internet2 topologies.
- We prototype VeriDP with small modifications of both hardware and software SDN switches. We use extensive experiments to show that VeriDP incurs a minimal overhead on data-plane packet processing.

As a first step towards monitoring control-data plane consistency, VeriDP is limited in the following aspects: (1) it cannot handle packet rewrites that will change headers of packets when they are forwarded, (2) it cannot detect packet drops due to hardware failures, and (3) it requires modification (even small) of switches.

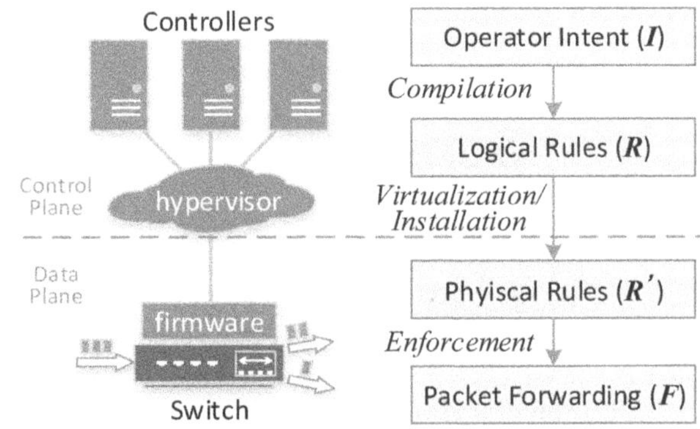

Figure 1: The translation process from operator intent to packet forwarding in SDN.

In the rest of this paper, we will first give more background on the control-data plane consistency issue (§2), and present an overview of VeriDP (§3). Then, we give details on the design and implementation of VeriDP (§4 and §5), and evaluate its performance (§6). After discussing some related work (§7), we conclude the paper (§8).

2. BACKGROUND AND MOTIVATION

In this section, we will first present some background on SDN. Specifically, we clearly define how an operator's intent is mapped to packet forwarding behaviors in SDN. Then, we show some cases under which the data plane becomes inconsistent with the control plane. Following that, we show the consequences that can be caused by such inconsistency. The reason that we separately discuss the causes and consequences of control-data inconsistency is that a single case of inconsistency can result in multiple consequences. For example, a missing rule at a switch may cause blackholes, loops, or access violation.

2.1 All the Way from Operator Intent to Forwarding Behavior

The purpose of an SDN is to translate a network operator's intent into packet forwarding behaviors [30]. Figure 1 illustrates such a translation process, which consists of four stages: operator intent (I), logical rules (R), physical rules (R'), and packet forwarding (F).

At the first stage, an operator specifies her *intent (I)* in terms of high-level policies (we will use intent and policy interchangeably in the rest of paper). For example, she may want packets from hosts inside a department directly reach a database server, while packets from hosts outside the department should go through a firewall before reaching the server. Many SDN programming languages (Frenetic [28], Pyretic [44], Merlin [53], etc.) and controllers (Ryu [9], ONOS [21], etc.) allow operators to specify such high-level intent. Though the operator's intent could be quite diverse, some intent is invariant, including pairwise reachability, backhole-freedom, loop-freedom, etc.

At the second stage, a compiler (often a built-in component of a controller) should be used to translate the high-level operator intent into device-specific *logical rules (R)* that can be understood by forwarding devices (*i.e.*, switches). By logical, we mean that these rules are complied based on a logic view of the network by the controller, and have not yet been installed at switches.

At the third stage, the controller will install the compiled rules through some southbound protocols like OpenFlow. The network may use virtualization platforms (*e.g.*, FlowVisor [52], OpenVirtex [15], etc.) to translate the rules, before they are sent to switches. We will term the rules installed by switches as *physical rules* (R'). Note that $R = R'$ may not hold, due to reasons like switch software bugs.

At the fourth stage, switches process and forward incoming packets according to the installed rules R'. At this point, the operator intent finally translates into packet *forwarding (F)*. Assuming everything goes well, the packet forwarding behaviors should exactly reflect the operator's intent, *i.e.*, $I = R = R' = F$.

Most previous tools try to verify whether $I = R$, assuming I as a set of basic invariants, *i.e.*, $I \leftarrow$ {*reachability, blackhole-freedom, loop-freedom*}. We will refer to them as control plane verification tools. For other tools, ATPG verifies $I = F$ (also assuming I as set of basic invariants), and Monocle verifies whether $R = R'$. In contrast, VeriDP checks whether $R = F$.

2.2 Control-Data Plane Inconsistency: The Causes

There could be many reasons that data plane forwarding behaviors deviate from the operator intent at the control plane. The following lists four possible reasons.

Lack of data plane acknowledgement. SDN advocates a fine-grained dynamic control over switches, meaning controllers have to frequently update the data plane states. Currently, update in SDN is "open-loop" in nature, without effective data plane acknowledgement mechanisms. Then, network updates may be out of order, or even fail to take effect, without being noticed by the controller. This will result in that the controller and switches can have inconsistent views, where the controller thinks a rule has taken effect, while the switch fails to install it [41]. Note that it is challenging to design such an acknowledgement mechanism [40]. The `Barrier` command provided by OpenFlow attempts to enable controllers to confirm when switches have installed rules [8]. However, measurements show that switches may respond to `Barrier` too early before the rules are actually installed in the flow table, in order to save cost [50, 46].

Switch software bugs. According to a survey among network operators, switch/router software bug is one of the most possible reasons for network failures [57]. For example, [34] provides a concrete bug where switches wrongly manages hardware-software-hybrid flow tables. Since the size of hardware flow table is relatively small, most SDN switches use software flow tables. However, rule placement strategies are prone to faults, due to cross-rule dependency [34]. The authors showed that the Pronto-Pica8 3290 switch, which can hold up to 2000 rules in hardware flow table, simply placed all extra rules at software flow table. This simple placement strategy respects no dependency across rules, and was shown to cause forwarding behaviors that are inconsistent with controller's policies [34].

Premature switch implementation. Currently, the implementation of SDN switches is quite premature, with some mandatory features not supported by some switches. Without noting that, rules complied by the controller may not translate into the forwarding behaviors. For example, according to a recent measurement, the HP ProCurve 5406zl switch lacks support for rule priority [46]. If two rules with different priorities have overlapped matching fields but different actions, the packet may be wrongly forwarded according to the low-priority rule.

External rule modifications. Besides the SDN controller, a rule can also be modified by an external source. For example, a careless operator may install a new rule that overrides previous one through data plane configuration tools like `dpctl` [2]. An attacker can gain the access to the switch OS and modify a forwarding rule to redirect traffic elsewhere [18]. These actions may not be noticed by the controller, resulting in a faulty data plane configuration. Worse still, [47] showed that ONIE [6], the boot loader for 3rd-party switch OS, can be exploited by an attacker to gain persistent control over SDN switches, even after OS re-installation.

In sum, apart from misconfigurations, faults can also come from the data plane. These faults are out of the scope of many existing verification tools (*e.g.*, Veriflow [37]) that function at the control plane. Note that we are not considering inconsistency caused by network updates [49], as they only cause transient failures.

2.3 Control-Data Plane Inconsistency: The Consequences

In the following, we show how control-data plane inconsistency may break the operator's intent. We will list some common intent, including basic invariants, access control, waypoint traversal, and traffic engineering.

Basic Invariants. As mentioned earlier, all networks should satisfy some basic invariants including reachability, blackhole-freedom, loop-freedom, etc [37]. Due to control-data plane inconsistency, even these invariants are satisfied at the control layers, they may be violated when packets are forwarded. For example, when a forwarding rule is not successfully installed, or wrongly modified by an external source, the corresponding hosts may no longer be reached. These invariants can be checked by sending probe packets in the network, as in ATPG [57].

Access control. Besides basic invariants, there are also

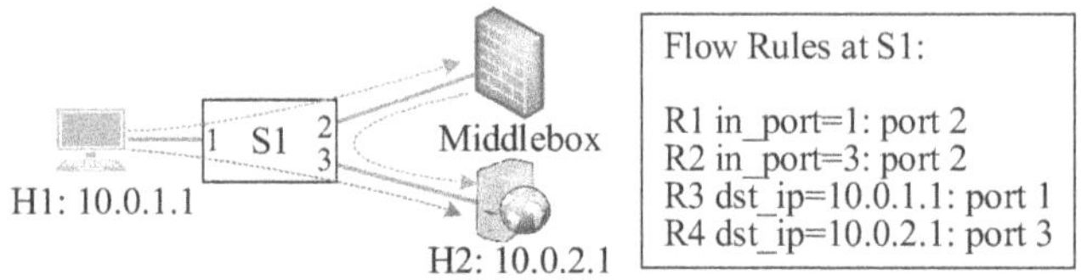

Figure 2: Middlebox traversal. The security policy of $H1 \rightarrow Middlebox \rightarrow H2$ is violated.

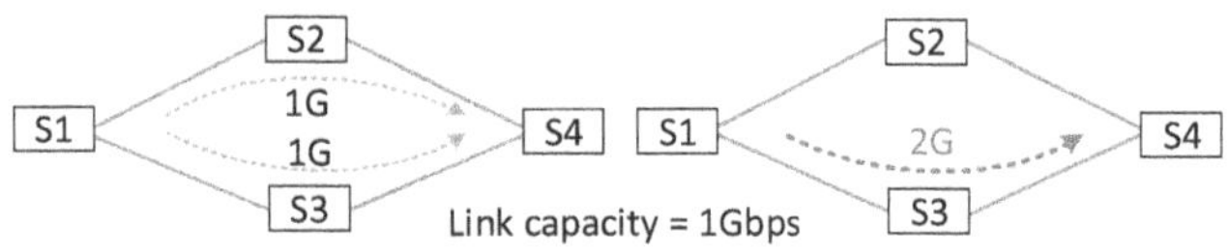

Figure 3: Traffic engineering. Path $S1 \rightarrow S3 \rightarrow S4$ can be congested if traffic engineering rules fail at $S1$.

custom policies that may vary from network to network. For example, an operator may specify some access control policies to prevent some set of hosts from talking with each other. These policies will translate into ACL rules that are installed by switches. If these ACL rules are missing in the flow table, say due to bad rule replacement strategies, the access control intent will be violated.

Waypoint traversal. An operator may also require some packets to traverse a set of middleboxes in sequence when being forwarded inside the network. Take Figure 2 as an example, where rules at switch $S1$ indicate that traffic from the client $H1$ to the server $H2$ must go through the middlebox. Now, consider the high-priority rules $R1$ and/or $R2$ fail. Then the middlebox chaining policy is violated, and the firewall is bypassed.

Traffic engineering. A traffic engineering policy may require packets to be forwarded over multiple links or tunnels according to some specific distribution. As shown in Figure 3, rules at switch $S1$ evenly distribute traffic from $S1$ to $S4$ between two paths $S1 \rightarrow S2 \rightarrow S4$ and $S1 \rightarrow S3 \rightarrow S4$. Now, consider that the rules fail at switch $S1$, resulting in that all traffic goes through the second path. Then, this traffic engineering policy is violated, resulting in sub-optimal performance.

3. DESIGN OVERVIEW

In this section, we will first discuss several design options, and then present the design of VeriDP.

3.1 Design Options

First, we consider the following two approaches for checking control-data plane consistency.

Checking flow tables. For this approach, the controller can periodically check the healthy of rules at switches' flow tables. Frequently dumping all rules from switches is clearly inefficient, and will place burden on switches. To address this problem, Monocle [41] generates probe packets to test the existence of rules. However, the probe generation is too slow (at a scale of several seconds) to keep up with frequent network updates.

Checking packet forwarding behaviors. Instead of checking flow tables, ATPG [57] directly looks at packet forwarding behaviors. Specifically, ATPG lets end hosts send probe packets into the network, and checks whether they are correctly received. Violation of reachability policies like black holes and loops can thus be detected. However, ATPG cannot detect violation of the other three types of inconsistency as listed in Section 2.3. Checking them requires we inspect not only the correct reception of packets, but also the paths traversed by packets.

Given the limitations of checking flow tables or packet receptions, we decide to check whether packet forwarding paths are consistent with control-plane configurations. With this decision made, a remaining question is should we inject probe packets and verify their forwarding paths, or should we sample real traffic from the data plane for verification? In the following, we will discuss this issue.

Probes or real traffic. First, using probe packets, we can only verify whether the forwarding paths of probe packets agree with the configurations. However, it does not necessarily mean that the real traffic will also follow the same paths. For example, consider an ACL rule $R1$ that only permits HTTP traffic from IP address 10.0.0.1:

$$R1 \;\; src\_ip = 10.0.0.1, dst\_port = 80 : \text{ Allow}$$

A probe packet with source address 10.0.0.1 and destination port 80 can trigger this rule. However, even the packet is successfully received, it may not mean the rule is correctly configured at the switch. For example, consider the above rule is prioritized by an ill-inserted rule $R2$:

$$R2 \;\; src\_ip = 10.0.0.1, dst\_port = * : \text{ Allow}$$

The probe packet can still be received, while non-HTTP traffic, *e.g.*, SSH, from 10.0.0.1 will also be allowed, violating the controller's policy. The reason that the probe packet cannot detect such violation is that it can only verify the control-data plane consistency with respect to a single packet. To capture all possible inconsistency, we need to exhaust all possible packets, which is clearly infeasible. *Given the limitations of probe packets, we decide to sample real traffic from the data plane for verification.*

3.2 VeriDP Architecture

As shown in Figure 4, VeriDP consists of a server alongside the SDN controller, and a pipeline for each switch in the network. The server intercepts the bidirectional OpenFlow messages exchanged between the controller and switches, in order to construct the *path table*, which records all paths for each input and output port pair. The pipeline is responsible for *sampling*, *tagging*, and *reporting* packets to the server. With the path table, the server *verifies* the reported packets sent from switches, and when the verification fails, it tries to

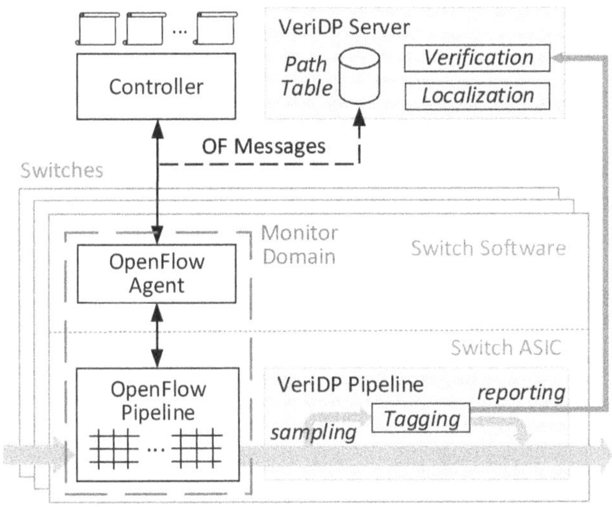

Figure 4: System architecture. The shaded components belong to VeriDP; those within the dashed rectangle are the components that VeriDP monitors.

localize the faulty switches. The dashed rectangle represents the domain that VeriDP monitors, *i.e.*, VeriDP is expected to detect the faults caused by the components inside the domain. The monitor domain includes: (1) the OpenFlow agent that terminates the OpenFlow channel, and (2) the OpenFlow pipeline that manages the hardware flow table and forwards packets based on table lookups.

3.3 VeriDP Pipeline

VeriDP distinguishes among three different types of switches: entry switches, exit switches, and internal switches. Entry and exit switches are edge switches that are directly connected with end hosts or middleboxes, and internal switches are aggregate and core switches that sit inside the network, interconnecting edge switches.

The VeriDP pipeline is responsible for generating tags for packets at entry switches, updating tags for packets at internal switches, and reporting packet headers and tags to the controller at exit switches. Entry switches' pipelines will perform sampling and all other switches are maintained stateless; exit switches' pipelines should report packets to the server (some internal switches should also conditionally report packets); all switches should tag packets that are sampled by entry switches.

The pipeline is implemented in a switch's fast path, separated from the OpenFlow pipeline. The reason for such separation is to prevent faults caused by flow tables from propagating into the tagging module. Since a typical switch can contain a cascade of flow tables, each of which may hold thousands of flow entries, flow entries used for tagging may be overridden by other rules, replaced when flow table is full, and even incorrectly modified/deleted by applications.

The pipeline processing is shown in Algorithm 1. The entry switch initializes the packet tag to zero, and the TTL

Algorithm 1: $\texttt{Tag}(s, x, y, p)$

Input: s: the switch ID; x/y: the local input/output port ID of packet p, which is received from the OpenFlow pipeline.

1 **if** $\langle s, x \rangle$ *is an edge port* **then**
2     $p.tag \leftarrow 0$; // initialize the tag
3     $p.ttl \leftarrow$ MAX_PATH_LENGTH; // initialize the ttl
4 $p.tag \leftarrow p.tag \sqcup \texttt{BF}(x||s||y)$; // update the tag
5 $p.TTL \leftarrow p.TTL - 1$; // decrement the ttl
6 **if** $\langle s, y \rangle$ *is an edge port or* $y = \perp$ *or* $p.TTL = 0$ **then**
7   SendReport(*inport*, $\langle s, y \rangle$, $p.header$, $p.tag$);

---

to the maximum path length (Line 1-3). Each switch updates the tag as:

$$tag \leftarrow tag \sqcup \texttt{BF}(input\_port||switch\_ID||output\_port)$$

, where $switch\_ID$ is the identifer of the switch; $input\_port$ /$output\_port$ is the local input/output port ID of the packet; $\texttt{BF}(x)$ is a k-bit Bloom filter holding a single element x; $\sqcup$ represents the bit-by-bit OR operation.

Initially, we were tempted to use hash-based tagging, *i.e.*, replace the BF with a hash function, and use the bit-by-bit OR instead of bit-by-bit XOR. Later, we found that this tagging method prevents us from localizing the faulty switch. On the other hand, by exploiting the information contained in Bloom filter, we can achieve a high localization probability (refer to Section 4.3 for details).

Besides tag updating, the switch also decrements the TTL by one (Line 4-5). When the packet is output to an edge port connected with an end host, or output to the dropping port $\perp$, or its TTL value hits zero, the switch sends a *tag report* to the server (Line 6-7). A tag report is a 4-tuple $\langle inport, outport, header, tag \rangle$, where $inport/outport$ is the entry/exit port of the packet; $header$ is a portion of packet header (*e.g.*, TCP 5-tuple); tag is the tag of the packet. Besides sending tag reports, the exit switch should also pop the tag from the packet, and deliver the packet to its destination host.

One thing to note is that switches should send tag reports for dropped packets. This is necessary to ensure the visibility of verification server into blackholes and loops. Here, we consider two cases of packet drops: (1) the packet does not match any forwarding entry, and (2) the packet matches some forwarding entries, but the entries do not specify any output ports. On the other hand, we do not consider packet drops due to hardware failures, which will totally prevent the failed switch from sending any tag reports.

3.4 VeriDP Server

The VeriDP server is responsible for parsing and verifying tag reports sent by switches. Central to the VeriDP server is the *path table*, which maps a pair of $\langle inport, outport \rangle$ to a list of paths that enter the network at $inport$ and exit at $outport$. Each path is again a pair of $\langle headers, tag \rangle$, where $headers$ is a set of headers allowed for the path, and tag is the tag representing the path.

Table 1: Part of the path table for Figure 5. $[\cdot]$ represents $\texttt{BF}(\cdot)$, and $\sqcup$ represents bit-by-bit OR.

inport	outport	headers	tag
$\langle S_1, 1\rangle$	$\langle S_3, 2\rangle$	$src\_ip = 10.0.1.1, dst\_ip = 10.0.2.1, dst\_port = 22$	$[1\|\|S_1\|\|3] \sqcup [1\|\|S_2\|\|3] \sqcup [3\|\|S_2\|\|2] \sqcup [1\|\|S_3\|\|2]$
		$src\_ip = 10.0.1.1, dst\_ip = 10.0.2.1, dst\_port \neq 22$	$[1\|\|S_1\|\|4] \sqcup [3\|\|S_3\|\|2]$
$\langle S_1, 2\rangle$	$\langle S_3, \perp\rangle$	$src\_ip = 10.0.1.2, dst\_ip = 10.0.2.1, dst\_port = 22$	$[2\|\|S_1\|\|3] \sqcup [1\|\|S_2\|\|3] \sqcup [2\|\|S_2\|\|2] \sqcup [1\|\|S_3\|\|\perp]$
		$src\_ip = 10.0.1.2, dst\_ip = 10.0.2.1, dst\_port \neq 22$	$[2\|\|S_1\|\|4] \sqcup [3\|\|S_3\|\|\perp]$

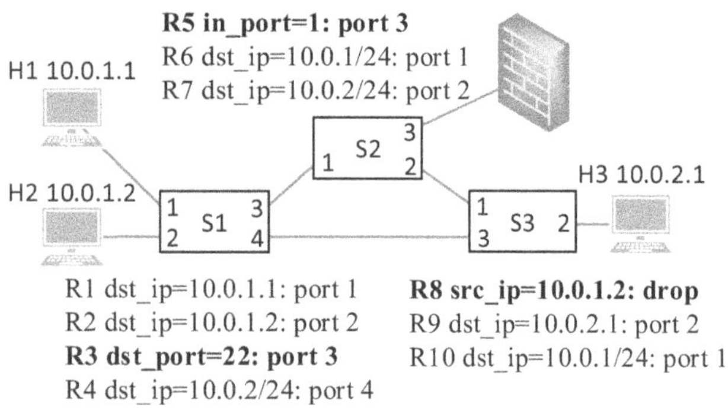

Figure 5: A simple example for path table construction. The network consists of three switches and a total of 10 rules.

Algorithm 2: $\texttt{Traverse}(inport, \langle s, x\rangle, h, p, t)$

Input: *inport*: the entry port tuple; $\langle s, x\rangle$: the current port tuple; h: the current header set; p: the current path; t: the current tag; $P_{x,y}$: the predicate for admitted packets from port x to port y;

1 **foreach** *port* $y \in \{1, 2, \ldots, n, \perp\}$ **do**
2 $\quad h' \leftarrow h \wedge P_{x,y}$ // packets forwarded to port y
3 $\quad$ **if** $h' \neq \emptyset$ **then**
4 $\quad\quad p' \leftarrow p || \langle x, s, y\rangle$ // update the path
5 $\quad\quad t' \leftarrow t \sqcup \texttt{BF}(x||s||y)$ // update the tag
6 $\quad\quad$ **if** $\langle s, y\rangle$ *is an edge port* **then**
7 $\quad\quad\quad \texttt{PathTable}(inport, \langle s, y\rangle).\texttt{AddPath}(h', p', t')$;
8 $\quad\quad$ **else**
9 $\quad\quad\quad \langle s', y'\rangle \leftarrow \texttt{Link}(\langle s, y\rangle)$ // go to next hop
10 $\quad\quad\quad \texttt{Traverse}(inport, \langle s', y'\rangle, h', p', t')$;

For a concrete example, consider the toy network in Figure 5. Rule 3 redirects all SSH traffic to $S2$, and Rule 4 forwards all other packets towards 10.0.2/24 to $S3$. Rule 5 directs all traffic from port 1 to the middlebox. Rule 8 at switch $S3$ drops all traffic from $H2$. Other rules are plain forwarding rules ensuring connectivity. Table 1 shows a part of the path table for this network.

Here, we assume there are no packet rewrites, *i.e.*, packet headers remain the same when packets are forwarded in the network. In this way, when a packet is about to exit the network, the VeriDP server can verify the packet's forwarding path against its header. We acknowledge this is a limitation of the current design, and may be resolved in the future.

4. DESIGN DETAILS

4.1 Path Table Construction

A first problem for constructing path table is how to represent header sets. A straightforward way is to use wildcard expressions, just as in Header Space Analysis [36]. However, even wildcard expressions are widely used for representing suffix, they are very inefficient for representing arbitrary header sets. For example, the header set for $dst\_port \neq 22$ in the second row of Table 1 is a union of 16 wildcard expressions. In addition, wildcard expressions have a poor support of set operation like union, conjunction, and complement. For a typical network consisting of tens of switches, each of which has thousands of flow rules, a huge number of wildcard expressions will be needed to represent the whole packet sets. According to [33], characterizing the Stanford backbone network (16 switches) needs 652 million wildcard expressions.

Inspired by the previous work [56], we decide to use the Binary Decision Diagram (BDD) [22] to represent header sets. BDD is an efficient data structure for Boolean expressions, and has a better support of set operations. With BDD, we can expect to significantly reduce the size of path table.

In the following, we will show how to construct the path table from a network configuration. First, we show how to specify the configuration of a single switch in the network. A switch s with ports numbered from 1 to n can be specified by a bunch of *transfer predicates* $P_{x,y}$, where $x \in \{1, 2, \ldots, n\}$ and $y \in \{1, 2, \ldots, n, \perp\}$. Only those packets with headers satisfying predicate $P_{x,y}$ can transfer (*i.e.*, be forwarded) from port x to port y. Transfer predicate is a general abstraction of switch configuration, which can be parsed from both traditional and OpenFlow switches.

For now, we will assume transfer predicates of all switches are already computed, and show how to construct the path table. Later on, we will come back and explain how to generate the transfer predicates from switch configurations. Algorithm 2 summarizes the process of path table construction. From each port, denoted as *inport*, of each switch, we inject a header set h initialized to all-match (*i.e.*, a BDD of $\texttt{True}$), and a tag t initialized to zero. Then, we call $\texttt{Traverse}(inport, h, p, t)$, with the current path p being empty. When the header h is received at a port $\langle s, x\rangle$, we intersect h with the transfer predicate $P_{x,y}$ (Line 2). If the intersection is non-empty, we update the path p and the tag t (Line 4-5). If y is an edge port, we insert a new entry into the path table (Line 6-7); otherwise, we move on to the next-

Algorithm 3: `Verify`$(inport, outport, header, tag)$

```
Input: inport/outport: the input/output port of the packet;
       header: the header of the packet; tag: the tag of the packet.
Output: True (pass), or False (fail).
1 foreach p ∈ PathTable(inport, outport) do
2     if header ≺ p.headers then
3         if tag = p.tag then
4             return True; // the path is correct
5         return False; // the path is wrong
6 return False; // the packet should not reach here
```

hop, and recursively call the algorithm with the new header and tag (Line 8-10).

Now we go back and show how to generate transfer predicates from switch configuration files. Specifically, we consider the Cisco configuration files for the Stanford backbone network [36]. The configuration files specify forwarding rules, in-bound ACLs, out-bound ACLs, VLAN, etc.

First, we use Algorithm 1 and 2 in [56] to transform the configuration files into *port predicates* for each switch. The port predicates consist of: (1) in-bound ACL predicate P_x^{in} for each port x: only packets satisfying P_x^{in} are allowed to be received from port x, (2) out-bound ACL predicate P_y^{out} for each port y: only packets satisfying P_y^{out} are allowed to be output to port y, and (3) forwarding predicate P_y^{fwd} for each port y: only packets satisfying P_y^{fwd} will be forwarded to port y. Then, we can compute the transfer predicates as:

$$P_{x,y} = P_x^{in} \wedge P_y^{fwd} \wedge P_y^{out},\ y \neq \bot$$

$$P_{x,\bot} = \neg P_x^{in} \vee \left(P_x^{in} \wedge P_\bot^{fwd}\right) \vee \left(P_x^{in} \wedge \vee_y \left(P_y^{fwd} \wedge \neg P_y^{out}\right)\right)$$

, where $P_\bot^{fwd} = \neg\left(\vee_y P_y^{fwd}\right)$

Intuitively, the three terms of $P_{x,\bot}$ represent three reasons that a packet is dropped: (1) filtered by the in-bound ACL, (2) not forwarded to any port, and (3) filtered by the out-bound ACL.

4.2 Tag Verification

The tag verification process is quite simple, as shown in Algorithm 3. On receiving a tag report of the form $\langle inport, outport, header, tag\rangle$, the server looks up in the path table with index $\langle inport, outport\rangle$, and possibly finds a list of paths. For each path p, it tries to match $header$ with the header set of path p (Line 1-2). If matched, tag is compared with the tag of path p. The verification succeeds if these tags are equal (meaning that the packet followed the right path), or fails otherwise (Line 3-6). If no matched path is found (meaning that the packet should not have reached here), then the verification also fails (Line 7).

Let us turn back to Figure 5, and assume H_1 sends a packet to port 22 of H_3. The packet should take the path of $S_1 \rightarrow S_2 \rightarrow Middlebox \rightarrow S_2 \rightarrow S_3$, and the tag should be $[1||S_1||3] \sqcup [1||S_2||3] \sqcup [3||S_2||2] \sqcup [1||S_3||2]$. With

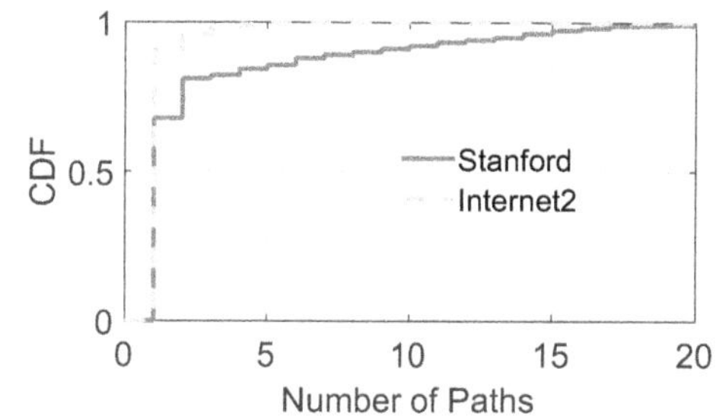

Figure 6: Distribution of the number of paths per inport-outport pair in the Stanford backbone and Internet2 networks.

$(\langle S_1, 1\rangle, \langle S_3, 2\rangle)$ as the index, the server would find two paths: one for $dst\_port = 22$ and the other for $dst\_port \neq 22$. The header of the packet would match the packet set of the first path. If the tag of the packet is the same with that of that path, the verification succeeds. Now consider that $R3$ fails, the packet will take the path of $S_1 \rightarrow S_3$. The tag would then be $[1||S_1||4] \sqcup [3||S_3||2]$, disagreeing with that of the path, and the verification fails.

Note that there may be multiple paths for an inport-outport pair, and each path corresponds to a specific header set. Thus, we should assume that the number of paths for an inport-outport pair should not be too large, so that the linear search used in Algorithm 3 is feasible. To validate this assumption, we construct the path table with the configuration files of the Stanford backbone network [4] and Internet2 [11]. As shown in Figure 6, the number of paths per inport-outport pair is relatively small, thereby validating the feasibility of linear search for these two networks.

4.3 Fault Localization

When the tag is different from the one in the path table, we know the path took by the corresponding packet is inconsistent with the control plane configuration. We are interested in which switches are to blame for such inconsistency, that is, localizing those switches that have faults in flow tables.

Take Figure 7 as an example, where Src sends a packet to Dst. Each switch has four ports numbered 1 through 4, and a "drop" port $\bot$. The correct path is $\langle 1, S1, 2\rangle$, $\langle 1, S2, 2\rangle$, $\langle 1, S4, 3\rangle$, while switch $S1$ is faulty and outputs the packet to a wrong port 4 instead of the right one 2, resulting in the actual path being $\langle 1, S1, 4\rangle, \langle 1, S3, 3\rangle, \langle 1, S6, \bot\rangle$. Even $S6$ drops the packet, we cannot simply blame $S6$ since the fault occurs at an upstream switch, *i.e.*, S_1.

To localize the faulty switches, we will first present a strawman approach, outline its limitation, and finally introduce the fault localization algorithm used by VeriDP.

Strawman Approach. Define a *hop* as a 3-tuple of the form $\langle input\_port, switch\_ID, output\_port\rangle$. That is, a hop encodes the forwarding behavior of a switch on a packet, including from which port the packet is received, and to which port the packet is forwarded. A path is then a ordered

```
Algorithm 4: PathInfer(header, inport, outport, tag)
  Input: inport/outport: the input/output port of the packet;
         header: the header of the packet; tag: the tag of the packet.
  Output: pathset: the set of all possible paths for the packet.
  pathset ← {}; // all possible paths
  path ← GetPath(inport, header); // the original path
  com_path ← {}; // common part with original path
  foreach hop ∈ path do
      com_path.push_hop(hop);
      if BF(hop) ⊓ tag ≠ BF(hop) then
          break; // the path deviates from hop
  while ¬com_path.is_empty() do
      dev_hop ← com_path.pop_hop();
      s ← dev_hop.switch;
      x ← dev_hop.input_port;
      foreach output port y of switch s do
          dev_path ← {⟨x, s, y⟩};
          inport' ← Link(⟨s, y⟩);
          path' ← GetPath(inport', header);
          foreach hop ∈ path' do
              if BF(hop) ⊓ tag ≠ BF(hop) then
                  break; // dismiss this path
              dev_path.push_hop(hop);
              if hop.output_port = outport then
                  pathset ← pathset ∪ (com_path + dev_path);
                  break; // found a valid path
```

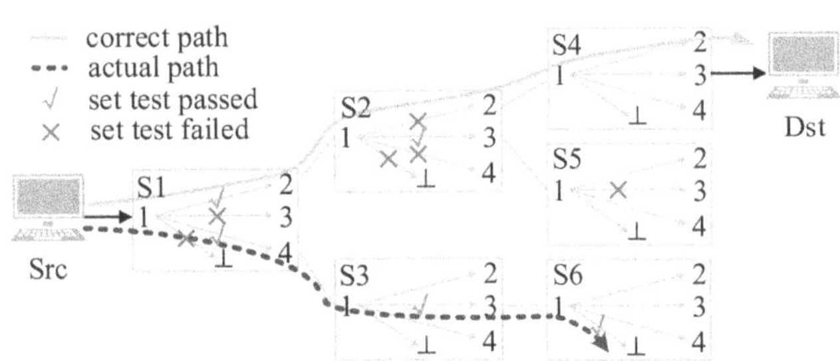

Figure 7: An example for fault localization. Each switch has four ports, and a port "⊥" representing packet drops. The path configured by the controller is $S1 \rightarrow S2 \rightarrow S4$. $S1$ falsely forwards the packet to port 4, and the path actually took by the packet is $S1 \rightarrow S3 \rightarrow S6$.

list of hops. We refer to the path computed according to network policies as the *correct path*, and the one actually traversed by the packet as the *real path*. The idea of our strawman approach is to first compute the correct path, and then for each hop of the correct path, test whether it also belongs to the real path. The test is based on the tag of the packet, which is a Bloom filter encoding all hops of the real path. If the switch has no faults, then the hop will forward the packet correctly, and this hop will pass the test; otherwise the switch should have forwarded the packet to a wrong port, and this hop will fail the test with large probability. Finally, the first hop that fails the test can be identified as a faulty switch.

One problem with the above strawman approach is that the false positives of Bloom filter may raise high localization error. Returning to the example in Figure 7, the hop $\langle 1, S1, 2\rangle$ may falsely pass the set test due to false positives of Bloom filter, and the next hop $\langle 1, S2, 2\rangle$ may fail the test. Then, we will falsely identify $S2$ as the faulty switch. Indeed, this problem can be mitigated if we reduce the false positive of Bloom filter by using more bits for Bloom filter. However, this would incur a large overhead on the header space.

The fault localization algorithm. To reduce the localization error without increasing header space overhead, we leverage the fact that most switches in the network are functioning well except some faulty ones. Thus, if a switch is identified as faulty, then we are expected to find a valid path from this switch towards the destination by looking up in downstream switches' flow tables. Specifically, we enumerate all possible output ports of the faulty switch, and from each of these output ports, we continue to test whether the next hops can pass the set testing.

Let us return to the example in Figure 7 and suppose we suspect that $S2$ is faulty. First, we enumerate all its output ports and know that only $\langle 1, S2, 3\rangle$ can pass the test. Then, we continue to look up in $S5$'s flow table, and know the next hop is $\langle 1, S5, 3\rangle$. However, this hop fails the test, meaning that $S2$ cannot be the faulty switch since there is no valid path from it to the destination. Then, we backtrace to the last hop of $S2$, *i.e.*, $S1$, and perform a similar process. This time, we can successfully find a valid path, which is just the real path of the packet.

The above method is summarized as Algorithm 4, which consists of two phases: (1) constructing the first half of the real path that is common with the correct one, and (2) constructing the second half of the real path that is different from the correct one. The first phase puts as many hops as possible into the common path *com_path*. The second phase backtraces to a previous hop in *com_path* each time, and tries to construct a valid path *dev_path* from one of its outports. When a valid *dev_path* is found, the concatenation of *com_path* and *dev_path* is put into the list of all possible paths *pathset*. This process continues until the *com_path* becomes empty. Section 6 will evaluate the probability that Algorithm 4 can find the real path.

4.4 Path Table Update

When the controller adds, deletes, or modifies a rule at a switch, we need to update the path table to reflect that change, in order to keep synchronized with the data plane. Rather than re-compute the whole path table, we show how to update the path table incrementally, such that only a small portion of the path table needs to be updated.

For simplicity, we only consider forwarding rules matching IP prefixes, while neglecting the in-bound and out-bound ACL rules, However, note that the incremental update can also be performed with ACL rules. Then, the transfer predicate $P_{x,y}$ can be reduced to $P_y = P_y^{fwd}$, where P_y^{fwd} is the port predicate for output port y. In addition, we only

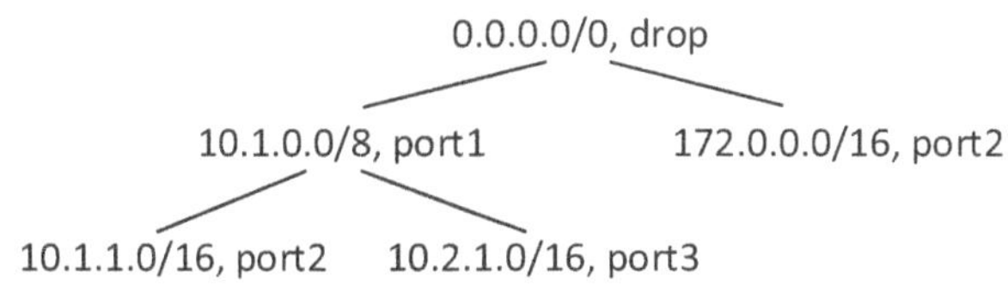

Figure 8: An example of forwarding rules organized as a tree.

consider rule addition and deletion, since rule modification can be regarded as deleting the old rule and then adding a new rule. The incremental path table update process consists of two phases: port predicate update and path entry update.

Port predicate update. This stage is an adaption of the port predicate update algorithm in [56]. It takes the newly added or deleted rule as input, and updates the port predicates accordingly.

First, define an IP forwarding rule as a 3-tuple $R = \langle prefix, match, outport \rangle$, where $prefix$ is the IP prefix to be matched, $match$ is the IP addresses that will actually be matched, and $outport$ is the output port of the matched packets. The difference between $prefix$ and $match$ will manifest in the following.

Similar to [56], we organize the forwarding rules as a forest: a rule R_j is a child of another rule R_i, if $R_i.prefix$ contains $R_j.prefix$. Figure 8 gives an example of such a forest. By longest match, the rule R with prefix $R.prefix =$ 10.1.0.0/8 will match $R.match =$ 10.1.0.0/8$\backslash$(10.1.1.0/16 $\vee$10.2.1.0/16).

Different from [56], we add a virtual drop rule with zero prefix length, *i.e.*, 0.0.0.0/0, and transform the forest into a tree, as shown in Figure 8. This will greatly simplify our treatment of transfer predicates for drop ports.

Then, the transfer predicate for output port x, *i.e.*, P_x, can be calculated as:

$$R_i.match = R_i.prefix \wedge (\vee_{R_j \text{ is a child of } R_i} \neg R_j.prefix)$$
$$P_x = \vee_{R_i.outport=x} R_i.match$$

Suppose a rule R_i with $R_i.outport = x$ is added, and let R_j be its parent with $R_j.outport = y$. Then, two port predicates need to be updated as:

$$P_x \leftarrow P_x \vee R_i.match$$
$$P_y \leftarrow P_y \wedge \neg R_i.match$$

Similarly, if R_i is deleted, two port predicates need to be updated as:

$$P_x \leftarrow P_x \wedge \neg R_i.match$$
$$P_y \leftarrow P_y \vee R_i.match$$

Path entry update. With port predicates updated, we are ready to update the path table. We only consider the addition of a new rule R_i, and deletion is much the same. Let $\Delta = R_i.match$, and view a transfer predicate as a set of headers. When R_i is added, P_x grows by adding Δ, and P_y shrinks by subtracting Δ. Then the path table update naturally consists of two parts:

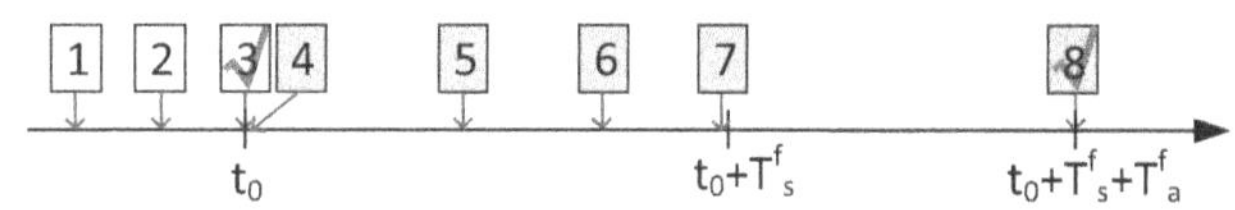

Figure 9: An example for sampling.

- For each path that passes port y, we should update its header set by subtracting Δ. Let the path be p, then its header set should be updated by $p.headers \leftarrow p.headers \backslash \Delta$, If $p.headers$ becomes `False`, then we delete the path from the path table.

- This part is a little more complicated since we need to not only update existing paths, but also add new paths if there are. Let S be the switch where the rule is to be added, then we need to consider each header set that has reached the switch S in the recursive search of Algorithm 2. Let h be such a header set, and $p = (hop_1, hop_2, \ldots, hop_n)$ be the path traversed by this header set before reaching switch S. Then, we should first compute $h \leftarrow h \wedge \Delta$, then output h to port x of switch S, and continue the recursive search. If h reaches an edge port without being `False`, then we check whether the resultant path is already in the path table. If there is such a path q, then we update its header set by $q.header \leftarrow q.headers \vee h$; otherwise, we create a new path with header set h, and add it into the path table.

4.5 Traffic Sampling

Tagging and verifying every packet in the network can incur a large overhead. In this paper, we use a simple method which samples packets based on flows at entry switches. Each flow f is associated with a parameter $T_s^f > 0$, termed the *sampling interval*. The entry switch S of f maintains the last sampling instant t^f. For each packet received by S at time t, if $t - t^f > T_s^f$, S marks the packet and updates $t^f \leftarrow t$.

In order to determine the sampling interval, we introduce another per-flow parameter T_a^f, defined as the maximum inter-packet-arrival time for flow f. We aim to have a detection latency (from the time that a fault occurs and that it is detected) less than a threshold τ. To achieve this goal, T_s^f should be set to satisfy $T_s^f \leq \tau - T_a^f$. To see why, consider the worst-case example in Figure 9. Packet 3 is sampled at time t_0, then a fault is experienced by the next back-to-back Packet 4 and all the following packets. Packet 7 arrives just before time $t_0 + T_s^f$, and is thus not sampled. After maximum inter-packet-arrival time T_a^f, Packet 8 arrives and is sampled, and the fault can be detected. By now, $T_s^f + T_a^f$ has elapsed since fault is first experienced by Packet 4. This is just the longest possible elapsed time to detect a fault.

5. IMPLEMENTATION

Bloom filter. For Bloom filter operations, we use the approaches described by Kirsch and Mitzenmacher [38]. First, three hashes are constructed as $g_i(x) = h_1(x)+ih_2(x)$ for $i = 0, 1, 2$, where $h_1(x)$ and $h_2(x)$ are the two halves of a 32-bit Murmur3 hash of x [12]. Then, we use the first 4 bits of $g_i(x)$ to set the 16-bit Bloom filter for $i = 0, 1, 2$. A similar approach is used by Cassandra [10].

Packet format. For each data packet, VeriDP inserts three additional fields: `marker`, `tag`, and `inport`. Here, `marker` is a single bit carried in the IP TOS field, indicating whether the packet is sampled for verification; `tag` is a 16-bit Bloom filter encoding the path traversed by the packet, which is carried in the first VLAN tag; `inport` is a 14-bit identifier of the entry port (8 for switch ID and 6 for port ID), which is carried in the second VLAN tag[1]. Tag reports (sent by destination switches) are encapsulated with plain UDP packets.

VeriDP server. The VeriDP server is responsible for constructing the path table based on network configurations, verifying tag reports and localizing faulty switches based on the path table. For path table construction, we first generate transfer predicates (represented with BDDs) from OpenFlow rules. Then, we run Algorithm 2 to generate all possible paths, and calculate a tag for each path. We implement the tag verification based on Algorithm 3. When iterating over possible paths for the inport-outport pair of a packet, we need to determine whether the header of the packet belongs to the header set of the path (*i.e.*, $header \prec p.headers$, Line 2). To test this, we first generate a BDD representation for the packet header, and then intersect this BDD with the header set (which is also a BDD). The packet header belongs to the header set if the intersection is not `False`.

VeriDP pipeline (Software). We implement the VeriDP pipeline with Open vSwitch [7]. The VeriDP pipeline functions after all actions have been executed on a packet, and before the packet is sent to the output port. We currently use the TCP 5-tuple to identify a flow, and associate with each flow a sampling instant (refer to Section 4.5). We simply use a hash table to store the sampling instants of all active flows.

VeriDP pipeline (Hardware). We implement the VeriD-P pipeline with ONetSwitch [32, 31], a hardware programmable switch that we built (available online at [13]). As shown in Figure 10, we implement both the VeriDP and OpenFlow pipeline with the FPGA resource. Due to the limited resource of FPGA, we use an array to record a limited number of active flows. Besides a sampling instant, each flow entry also contains a last-hit instant, which helps us identify active flows.

6. EVALUATION

[1]Double VLAN tags are supported by 802.1ad [1]; each tag has a 2-byte Tag Control Information (TCI), which is used to carry our data.

Table 2: Path table statistics.

Setup	# entries	# paths	avg. path len.	time (s)
Stanford	26K	77K	4.85	4.32
Internet2	43K	50K	2.89	3.22
FT($k = 4$)	448	448	3.79	0.10
FT($k = 6$)	4176	4176	4.23	0.26

6.1 Experiment Setup

We use both emulated and real switches for experiments. Otherwise specified, we emulate networks with Mininet [5], consisting of Open vSwitch (OVS [7]) instances, and use Floodlight as the controller [3]. The verification server runs on a desktop with an Intel Core i7 CPU 3.6GHz and 32GB Memory. We use the following four topologies for experiments.

- Stanford backbone. The Stanford backbone network [4] consists of 16 Cisco routers and 10 layer-2 switches. A portion of the topology is shown in Figure 11. Overall, there are 757,170 forwarding rules and 1,584 ACL rules.
- Internet2. The Internet2 topology [11] consists of 9 Juniper routers. As the ACL rules are not publicly available, we only use the 126,017 IPv4 forwarding rules.
- Fat tree. We emulate fat tree topologies which represent medium-sized networks. In prior to experiments, we let the emulated hosts ping each other in order to populate the switches' flow tables with shortest-path forwarding rules.
- Single ONetSwitch. We use a single ONetSwitch that implements both OpenFlow and VeriDP to test the overhead of VeriDP on data plane.

For Stanford and Internet2, we translate the configuration files to equivalent OpenFlow rules, and install them at Open vSwitches with Floodlight. The translation algorithm is customized based on [57], which was originally written for the Beacon controller.

Since there are loops in the Stanford and Internet2 topologies, we remove all the loops in prior to generating the path table. Specifically, when searching for all paths using Algorithm 2, if a port is visited for the second time for a path, we will not continue to search that path. Thus, initially the control plane and data plane are inconsistent: the control plane is loop-free, while the data plane contains loops. The path table statistics are summarized as Table 2.

6.2 Function Test

For function test, we generate faults in the emulated Stanford backbone network, and test whether VeriDP can detect these faults and pinpoint the faulty switches.

Black hole. In Figure 11, there is a flow (red solid line) from *boza* to *coza* with destination address 172.20.10.33. Similar

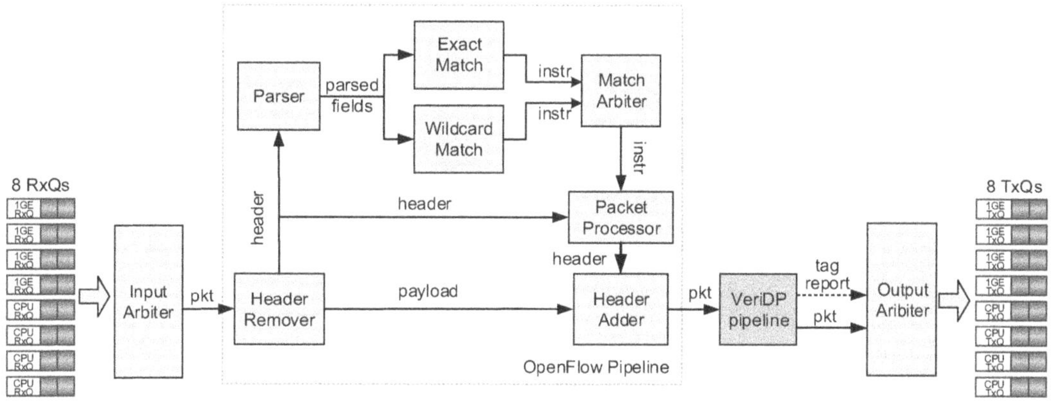

Figure 10: Hardware implementation of the VeriDP pipeline based on ONetSwitch.

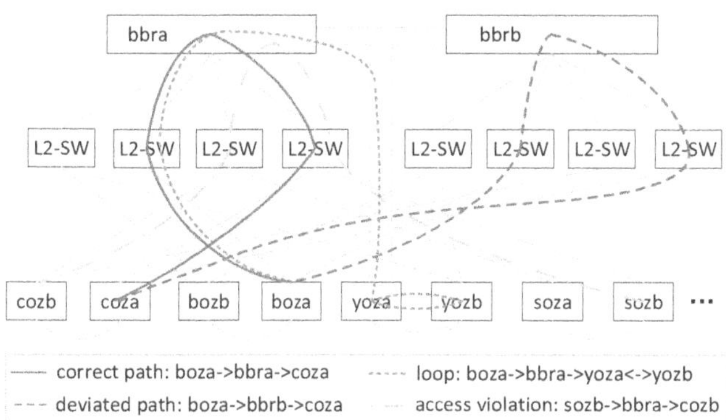

Figure 11: Function test on the Stanford backbone network (only part of the topology is shown).

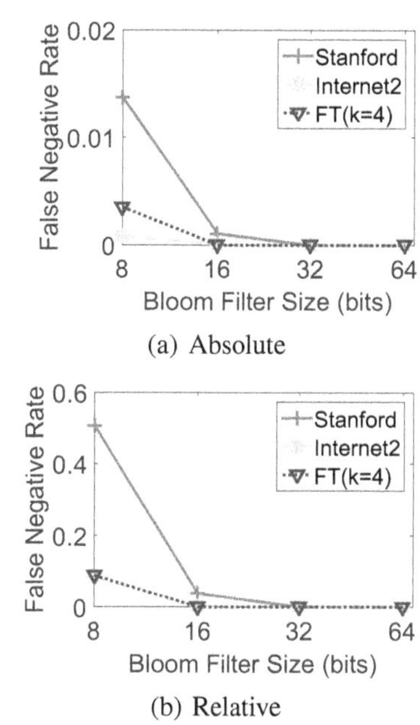

Figure 12: False positive rate vs. Bloom filter size.

to ATPG, we deliberately create a fault by modifying the action of the forwarding rule in $boza$ that matched $dst\_ip = 172.20.10.32/27$ with a drop action. Then, the flow will be dropped at $boza$. VeriDP immediately detects the fault, and localizes the faulty switch $boza$.

Path deviation. We continue to create a fault that causes the previous flow to deviate from the original path, by modifying the same rule. This time, we replace the action to forward towards $bbrb$, resulting in another path from $boza$ to $coza$ (red dash line). VeriDP immediately detects the fault, and recover the real path, thereby localizing the faulty switch $boza$.

Access violation. To simulate an access violation, we delete an ACL rule in $sozb$ that denies all packets with destination address 10.0.0.0/8. Then, we send packets with destination address 10.63.16.0/20 from $sozb$, and they are received at $cozb$ (the yellow dash dot line). VeriDP successfully detects the fault and reconstructs the path took by the flow.

Loop. Recall that we removed all loops when generating the path table at the control plane, while the data plane still uses the original configuration that contains loops. We will test whether VeriDP can detect these loops. We inject a flow with destination address 172.26.4.152 from $boza$, which loops between $yoza$ and $yozb$ (green dash line). Since the host with address 172.26.4.152 is connected to a port of $yoza$, then each time $yoza$ receives the packet, it will forward the packet to that port. Since the port is an edge port (connected with non-routers), then multiple tag reports would be sent to the VeriDP server. Only the first tag report passes the verification, while all others fail.

6.3 Detection and Localization Performance

Detection accuracy. The inconsistency detection of VeriDP has no false positives. The reason is simple: if the forwarding path of a packet is the same with that in the path table, then the tag will be exactly the same, and the verification will pass. False negatives happen when a packet traverses a path different from the one in the path table, while satisfying two conditions: (1) the packet arrives at the destination port,

Table 3: Probability of successful fault localization when verification fails for fat tree $k = 4$ and $k = 6$.

Setup	# failed verif.	# recovered paths	localization prob.
FT ($k = 4$)	2,527	2,505	99.2%
FT ($k = 6$)	7,148	6,902	96.6%

and (2) the tag of the packet is the same with the one in the path table. The reason why condition (1) is necessary is that if the packet arrives at a wrong port (including drop ports), the packet header will definitely not match the header set of any path for the input-output pair, and thus the verification will fail.

To evaluate the detection accuracy, we randomly select paths in the path table, and generate a packet for each path. Then, for each packet we randomly select a switch on its forwarding path, and output the packet to a port different from the original one, in order to simulate a fault. Let n be the number of total packets we select, $n1$ be the number of packets that arrive at the destination port, and $n2$ be the number of packets that arrive at the destination port and the tag is same with that in the path table. Then, we define the *absolute false negative rate* as $n2/n$, and the *relative false negative rate* as $n2/n1$. To evaluate the impact of Bloom filter size on false negative rate, we vary the Bloom filter size from 8 bits to 64 bits, and measure the false negative rate for Stanford, Internet2, and fat trees ($k = 4$).

As shown in Figure 12, the absolute false negative rate is rather small for $k = 6$. Specifically, the absolute false negative rate is only around 0.1% for Stanford backbone network. The relative false negative rate is higher, but also decreases to zero for k larger than 32.

Localization accuracy. We continue to evaluate the localization accuracy using fat tree topologies. First, we select a random rule from a random switch, and change its output port to a different one. Then, we let all hosts ping each other, collect the tag reports, and perform tag verification. If the verification fails, we try to recover the actual path took by the ping packet. Table 3 reports the number of failed verifications, the number of recovered paths, and the localization probability. We can see that our fault localization algorithm can recover the real paths took by packets with a high probability when verification fails: 99.2% and 96.6% for fat tree $k = 4$ and $k = 6$, respectively.

6.4 Verification Time

We measure the time to verify a tag report, with the Stanford backbone and Internet2 topology. For each topology, we generate a test packet for each path in the path table. Then, we inject these test packets into the network and collect the tag reports. After that, we run the verification algorithm for each tag report for 10^4 times, and record the time. Figure 13 shows the verification time for a single tag report, which is calculated by taking an average over the 10^4 verifications. We can see that the verification time is

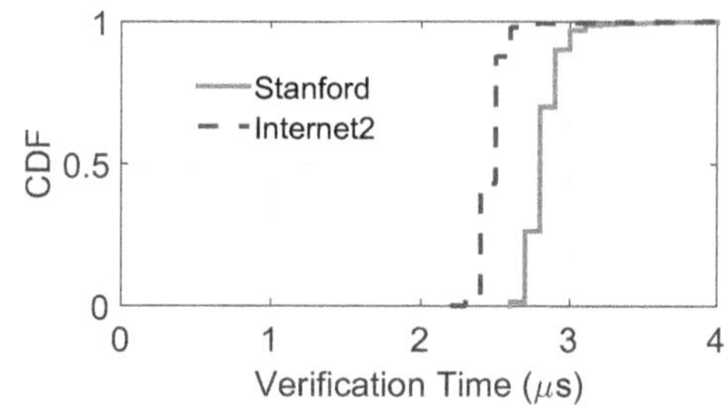

Figure 13: The time to verify a tag report on VeriDP server.

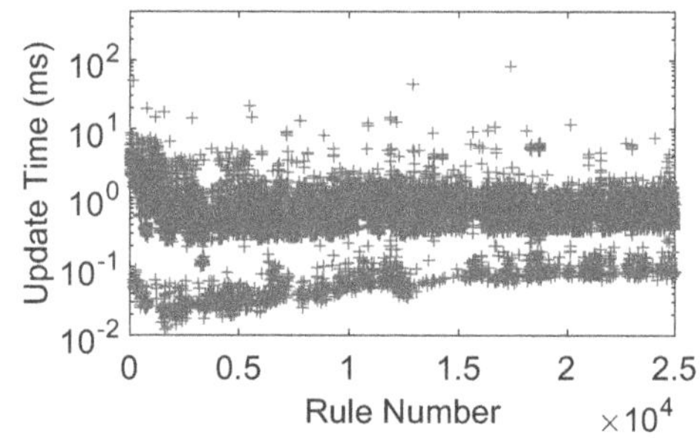

Figure 14: The time to add a new rule to a router of Internet2.

in-between 2 and 3 μs, which translates into a verification throughput of up to 5×10^5 per second. Since the verification is still single-threaded without optimization, we expect a higher throughput with multi-threading in the future.

6.5 Path Table Update Time

We continue to evaluate the incremental update algorithm using the Internet2 topology, which consists of 9 switches. First, we populate the flow tables of 8 switches with OpenFlow rules. For the remaining switch, we install rules into its flow table one-by-one, and measure the time to update the path table. There are more than 28,000 rules for this switch in total. The update time for each rule is shown in Figure 14. We can see that for most rules, the time to update the path table is less than 10ms. This update time should be sufficient, considering the time to update the data plane is at a scale of several milliseconds [34, 50].

6.6 Dataplane Overhead

Our implementation of VeriDP on the FPGA-based hardware switch (*i.e.*, ONetSwitch) can process packets at a line speed (1Gbps). To measure the processing delay, we send packets to one port of the switch, receive them from another one, and record the CPU cycles c used in this process. As the FPGA has a frequency of 125MHz, the delay can be calculated as $T = c \times 0.008\mu s$.

Table 4 reports the delay of the native OpenFlow pipeline (T_1), the delay of the VeriDP sampling module (T_2) and its overhead (T_2/T_1), the delay of the VeriDP tagging module (T_3) and its overhead (T_3/T_1). We can see that the delay of

Table 4: Processing delay of the VeriDP pipeline and native OpenFlow pipeline on the hardware SDN switch.

	Packet Size (Bytes)				
	128	256	512	1024	1500
Native (μs)	4.32	7.33	19.89	26.21	36.68
Sampling (μs)	0.15	0.14	0.14	0.14	0.15
Overhead	3.52%	1.96%	0.74%	0.55%	0.41%
Tagging (μs)	0.27	0.26	0.27	0.26	0.27
Overhead	6.29%	3.60%	1.37%	1.01%	0.74%

VeriDP sampling and tagging modules are around $0.15\mu s$ and $0.27\mu s$, respectively. For packet size of 512 Bytes, the overhead of these two modules is 0.74% and 1.37%, respectively. Note that tagging is necessary for each hop, while sampling is only performed by entry switches. Thus, non-entry switches only incur the tagging overhead.

7. RELATED WORK

Recently there have been many verification tools proposed for SDN. Some tools debug controller softwares or applications [24, 51, 55, 20, 26, 19], while others check the correctness of network policies [16, 43, 36, 35, 37, 56, 60, 58, 17, 42, 27, 48]. A limitation with these tools is that they can only ensure network correctness (*i.e.*, controller softwares or network policies) at the controller side, while cannot guarantee the correctness of switch configurations (*i.e.*, rules at flow tables), or data plane behaviors (*i.e.*, packet forwarding). As shown in previous work [46, 41], data plane configurations may deviate from those on the control plane.

Data plane testing tools [57, 41] try to check the correctness of rules at switches' flow tables. ATPG [57] generates the minimum number of probe packets that can trigger all rules in the network, and verifies whether all these probe packets can be sent and received by end hosts. Since ATPG only checks packet receptions, it can only verify that pairwise reachability are ensured by rules of switches, while cannot verify other properties like middlebox traversals that require inspections on packet trajectories. Moreover, real packets may experience different forwarding behaviors with probe packets, making the verification results less convincing. Monocle [41] tests whether a rule is in a switch's flow table by sending a probe packet to the switch and checking which port the packet is output to. The probe packet should be constructed in such a way that it can only trigger the rule under test, while not being affected by other rules in the switch. A similar approach, RuleScope [23], also monitors the flow table integrity by sending probes. The difference is that it can detect priority swaps of rules as well. There are several problems with Monocle and RuleScope. First, the probe generation process is slow: Monocle costs around 43 seconds to generate probes for 10K real rules; RuleScope uses more than 300 seconds to generate probes for 320 synthetic rules. As a result, they can only verify relatively steady configurations and would have issues tracking down frequent data-planes updates or reconfigurations. In addition, similar to ATPG, the probe packets may experience different forwarding behaviors with real production packets.

Packet trajectory tracers [59, 45, 54, 14] try to record packet trajectories by letting switches imprint specific information into packet headers. However, packet trajectories by themselves are not very useful unless we know whether they are correct. In contrast, VeriDP not only traces packet trajectories, but also enables the controller to reason about whether the trajectories are compliant with high-level policies. Moreover, they either require a large number of rules at switches [59, 45], or highly depend on the datacenter structures [54]. Different from the above approaches, NetSight [29] records detailed forwarding information of real packets using postcards. However, since each packet will trigger a postcard at each hop, NetSight will incur a huge volume of postcards traffic on the data plane.

Switch software debuggers [39, 25] use symbolic execution to test the software components of SDN switches. They only carry out static testing of switch software codes, while cannot detect hidden bugs that only show at runtime, *i.e.*, flow table or packet forwarding faults. In contrast, VeriDP can potentially capture these runtime bugs by constantly monitoring the policy incompliance of switches.

8. CONCLUSION AND FUTURE WORK

This paper presented VeriDP, a new tool to monitor the consistency of control plane and data plane in SDN. VeriDP used the path table abstraction at the control plane and packet tagging at the data plane, in order to detect inconsistency. The Bloom-filter-based tagging method allowed VeriDP to pinpoint the faulty switches that caused the inconsistency. We implemented VeriDP on both software and hardware switches to demonstrate its feasibility, and used real network topologies and policies to test its functions.

Our future work includes: (1) incorporating header rewrites into the current VeriDP framework, in order to support actions that need to modify packet headers, and (2) designing a method that can automatically repair the flow table of a faulty switch, in order to resolve the inconsistency with minimal human interaction.

Acknowledgements

We would like to thank our shepherd Laurent Vanbever for helping us revise the paper, and all the CoNEXT reviewers for their valuable comments. We also thank Hongkun Yang from Google for inspiring discussions with him, and Jiamin Liu, Peng Zheng, Zhimin Gong for their work at the early stage. This work is supported by the NSFC (No. 61402357, 61272459, and 61672425), the China Postdoctoral Science Foundation, the Program for New Century Excellent Talents in University (NCET-13-0450), and the Fundamental Research Funds for the Central Universities.

9. REFERENCES

[1] 802.1ad - Provider Bridges. http://www.ieee802.org/1/pages/802.1ad.html.

[2] Dpctl Documentation. https://github.com/CPqD/ofsoftswitch13/wiki/Dpctl-Documentation.

[3] Floodlight OpenFlow Controller. http://floodlight.openflowhub.org/.

[4] Hassel, the header space library. https://bitbucket.org/peymank/hassel-public.

[5] Mininet. http://mininet.org/.

[6] Open Network Install Environment (ONIE). http://onie.org/.

[7] Open vSwitch. http://openvswitch.org/.

[8] OpenFlow Switch Specification Version 1.5.1. https://www.opennetworking.org/sdn-resources/technical-library.

[9] Ryu OpenFlow Controller. http://osrg.github.io/ryu/.

[10] The Apache Cassandra Project. http://cassandra.apache.org/.

[11] The Internet2 Observatory. http://www.internet2.edu/research-solutions/research-support/observatory/.

[12] The Murmur3 hash function. https://code.google.com/p/smhasher/wiki/MurmurHash3.

[13] The ONetSwitch SDN platform. http://onetswitch.org.

[14] K. Agarwal, E. Rozner, C. Dixon, and J. Carter. SDN traceroute: Tracing SDN forwarding without changing network behavior. In *HotSDN*, 2014.

[15] A. Al-Shabibi, M. De Leenheer, M. Gerola, A. Koshibe, G. Parulkar, E. Salvadori, and B. Snow. Openvirtex: Make your virtual sdns programmable. In *HotSDN*, 2014.

[16] E. Al-Shaer and S. Al-Haj. Flowchecker: Configuration analysis and verification of federated openflow infrastructures. In *ACM workshop on Assurable and usable security configuration*, 2010.

[17] V. Altukhov, V. Podymov, V. Zakharov, and E. Chemeritskiy. Vermont-a toolset for checking sdn packet forwarding policies on-line. In *IEEE Modern Networking Technologies (MoNeTeC)*, 2014.

[18] M. Antikainen, T. Aura, and M. Särelä. Spook in Your Network: Attacking an SDN with a Compromised OpenFlow Switch. In *Secure IT Systems*. 2014.

[19] T. Ball, N. Bjørner, A. Gember, S. Itzhaky, A. Karbyshev, M. Sagiv, M. Schapira, and A. Valadarsky. Vericon: Towards verifying controller programs in software-defined networks. In *ACM PLDI*, 2014.

[20] R. Beckett, X. K. Zou, S. Zhang, S. Malik, J. Rexford, and D. Walker. An assertion language for debugging sdn applications. In *HotSDN*, 2014.

[21] P. Berde, M. Gerola, J. Hart, Y. Higuchi, M. Kobayashi, T. Koide, B. Lantz, B. OConnor, P. Radoslavov, W. Snow, et al. ONOS: towards an open, distributed SDN OS. In *HotSDN*, 2014.

[22] R. E. Bryant. Graph-based algorithms for boolean function manipulation. *IEEE Transactions on Computers*, 100(8):677–691, 1986.

[23] K. Bu, X. Wen, B. Yang, Y. Chen, L. E. Li, and X. Chen. Is every flow on the right track?: Inspect SDN forwarding with RuleScope. In *IEEE INFOCOM*, 2016.

[24] M. Canini, D. Venzano, P. Peresini, D. Kostic, and J. Rexford. A NICE way to test OpenFlow applications. In *USENIX NSDI*, 2012.

[25] M. Dobrescu and K. Argyraki. Software dataplane verification. In *USENIX NSDI*, 2014.

[26] R. Durairajan, J. Sommers, and P. Barford. Controller-agnostic sdn debugging. In *ACM CoNEXT*, 2014.

[27] A. Fogel, S. Fung, L. Pedrosa, M. Walraed-Sullivan, R. Govindan, R. Mahajan, and T. Millstein. A general approach to network configuration analysis. In *USENIX NSDI*, 2015.

[28] N. Foster, R. Harrison, M. J. Freedman, C. Monsanto, J. Rexford, A. Story, and D. Walker. Frenetic: A network programming language. In *ACM SIGPLAN Notices*, volume 46, pages 279–291, 2011.

[29] N. Handigol, B. Heller, V. Jeyakumar, D. Mazieres, and N. McKeown. I know what your packet did last hop: Using packet histories to troubleshoot networks. In *USENIX NSDI*, 2014.

[30] B. Heller, C. Scott, N. McKeown, S. Shenker, A. Wundsam, H. Zeng, S. Whitlock, V. Jeyakumar, N. Handigol, J. McCauley, et al. Leveraging SDN layering to systematically troubleshoot networks. In *HotSDN*, 2013.

[31] C. Hu, J. Yang, Z. Gong, S. Deng, and H. Zhao. Desktopdc: setting all programmable data center networking testbed on desk. *ACM SIGCOMM Computer Communication Review*, 44(4):593–594, 2015.

[32] C. Hu, J. Yang, H. Zhao, and J. Lu. Design of all programmable innovation platform for software defined networking. In *Open Networking Summit*, 2014.

[33] T. Inoue, T. Mano, K. Mizutani, S.-i. Minato, and O. Akashi. Rethinking packet classification for global network view of software-defined networking. In *IEEE ICNP*, 2014.

[34] N. Katta, O. Alipourfard, J. Rexford, and D. Walker. CacheFlow: Dependency-aware rule-caching for software-defined networks. In *ACM SOSR*, 2016.

[35] P. Kazemian, M. Chan, H. Zeng, G. Varghese, N. McKeown, and S. Whyte. Real time network policy checking using header space analysis. In *USENIX NSDI*, 2013.

[36] P. Kazemian, G. Varghese, and N. McKeown. Header space analysis: Static checking for networks. In *USENIX NSDI*, 2012.

[37] A. Khurshid, W. Zhou, M. Caesar, and P. Godfrey. Veriflow: Verifying network-wide invariants in real time. In *USENIX NSDI*, 2013.
[38] A. Kirsch and M. Mitzenmacher. Less hashing, same performance: Building a better Bloom filter. In *Algorithms–ESA 2006*, pages 456–467. Springer, 2006.
[39] M. Kuzniar, P. Peresini, M. Canini, D. Venzano, and D. Kostic. A SOFT way for openflow switch interoperability testing. In *ACM CoNEXT*, 2012.
[40] M. Kuzniar, P. Peresini, and D. Kostić. Providing reliable fib update acknowledgments in sdn. In *ACM CoNEXT*, 2014.
[41] M. Kuzniar, P. Peresini, and D. Kostic. Monocle: Dynamic, fine-grained data plane monitoring. In *ACM CoNEXT*, 2015.
[42] N. P. Lopes, N. Bjørner, P. Godefroid, K. Jayaraman, and G. Varghese. Checking beliefs in dynamic networks. In *USENIX NSDI*, 2015.
[43] H. Mai, A. Khurshid, R. Agarwal, M. Caesar, P. Godfrey, and S. T. King. Debugging the data plane with Anteater. In *ACM SIGCOMM*, 2011.
[44] C. Monsanto, J. Reich, N. Foster, J. Rexford, D. Walker, et al. Composing software defined networks. In *USENIX NSDI*, 2013.
[45] S. Narayana, J. Rexford, and D. Walker. Compiling path queries in software-defined networks. In *HotSDN*, 2014.
[46] P. Peresini, M. Kuzniar, and D. Kostic. What You Need to Know About SDN Flow Tables. In *PAM*, 2015.
[47] G. Pickett. Staying persistent in software defined networks. In *Black Hat Briefings*, 2015.
[48] G. D. Plotkin, N. Bjørner, N. P. Lopes, A. Rybalchenko, and G. Varghese. Scaling network verification using symmetry and surgery. In *ACM POPL*, 2016.
[49] M. Reitblatt, N. Foster, J. Rexford, C. Schlesinger, and D. Walker. Abstractions for network update. In *ACM SIGCOMM*, 2012.
[50] C. Rotsos, N. Sarrar, S. Uhlig, R. Sherwood, and A. W. Moore. OFLOPS: An open framework for OpenFlow switch evaluation. In *Passive and Active Measurement*, pages 85–95, 2012.
[51] C. Scott, A. Wundsam, B. Raghavan, A. Panda, A. Or, J. Lai, E. Huang, Z. Liu, A. El-Hassany, S. Whitlock, et al. Troubleshooting blackbox SDN control software with minimal causal sequences. In *ACM SIGCOMM*, 2014.
[52] R. Sherwood, G. Gibb, K.-K. Yap, G. Appenzeller, M. Casado, N. McKeown, and G. M. Parulkar. Can the production network be the testbed? In *OSDI*, 2010.
[53] R. Soulé, S. Basu, P. J. Marandi, F. Pedone, R. Kleinberg, E. G. Sirer, and N. Foster. Merlin: A language for provisioning network resources. In *ACM CoNEXT*, 2014.
[54] P. Tammana, R. Agarwal, and M. Lee. CherryPick: Tracing packet trajectory in software-defined datacenter networks. In *SOSR*, 2015.
[55] A. Wundsam, D. Levin, S. Seetharaman, A. Feldmann, et al. OFRewind: Enabling record and replay troubleshooting for networks. In *USENIX Annual Technical Conference*, 2011.
[56] H. Yang and S. S. Lam. Real-time verification of network properties using atomic predicates. In *IEEE ICNP*, 2013.
[57] H. Zeng, P. Kazemian, G. Varghese, and N. McKeown. Automatic test packet generation. In *ACM CoNEXT*, 2012.
[58] H. Zeng, S. Zhang, F. Ye, V. Jeyakumar, M. Ju, J. Liu, N. McKeown, and A. Vahdat. Libra: Divide and conquer to verify forwarding tables in huge networks. In *USENIX NSDI*, 2014.
[59] H. Zhang, C. Lumezanu, J. Rhee, N. Arora, Q. Xu, and G. Jiang. Enabling layer 2 pathlet tracing through context encoding in software-defined networking. In *HotSDN*, 2014.
[60] S. Zhang and S. Malik. Sat based verification of network data planes. In *Automated Technology for Verification and Analysis*. 2013.

HyPer4: Using P4 to Virtualize the Programmable Data Plane

David Hancock
University of Utah
School of Computing
Salt Lake City, Utah, USA
dhancock@cs.utah.edu

Jacobus van der Merwe
University of Utah
School of Computing
Salt Lake City, Utah, USA
kobus@cs.utah.edu

ABSTRACT

Through virtualization, single physical data planes can logically support multiple networking contexts. We propose HyPer4 as a portable virtualization solution. HyPer4 provides a general purpose program, written in the P4 dataplane programming language, that may be dynamically configured to adopt behavior that is functionally equivalent to other P4 programs. HyPer4 extends, through software, the following features to diverse P4-capable devices: the ability to logically store multiple programs and either run them in parallel (network slicing) or as hot-swappable snapshots; and virtual networking between programs (supporting program composition or multi-tenant service interaction). HyPer4 permits modifying the set of programs, as well as the virtual network connecting them, at runtime, without disrupting currently active programs. We show that realistic ASICs-based hardware would be capable of running HyPer4 today.

CCS Concepts

•**Networks** → **Programmable networks;** *Network manageability;*

Keywords

Software Defined Networking; P4; network virtualization

1. INTRODUCTION

Recent advances in Software Defined Networking have paved the way for *dataplane programmability*, which results in network devices, including hardware, that may be reprogrammed in the field to parse custom protocols and execute custom functionality. The full potential of dataplane programmability, however, (1) remains untapped, and (2) efforts to exploit this feature are at risk of fragmentation among a proliferating collection of software and hardware devices that provide programmable dataplanes. To the first point, we believe virtualization opens up attractive possibilities, and to the second point, an ideal virtualization solution should be portable across many platforms.

OpenFlow[35] has provided a standard for programmability of the network *control plane* and has been instrumental to network operators seeking more freedom and flexibility. It leaves the network *data plane*, however, "fixed" in the sense that operators are still restricted to working with those protocols identified in the OpenFlow specification. In response to the demand for OpenFlow support for novel protocols, the specification has continually expanded [11]. A truly *programmable data plane* is free from such restrictions, permitting operators to reconfigure the data plane according to *completely custom* protocol syntax and semantics. Recent work on a reconfigurable match table (RMT) architecture proved that a programmable data plane is possible even in ASICs hardware [12]. This result inspires tools such as the P4 domain specific language [11] to make this programmable data plane easily accessible in a uniform way on a variety of switches, from ASICs with RMT, to FPGA-based switches, to software switches like PISCES [40], behavioral models [5], and the network data planes on edge servers [21].

Ordinarily, each programmable data plane provided by a P4-capable device represents a single networking context, within which one P4 program defines (1) the collection of protocol headers and the corresponding state machine by which all traffic is *parsed*; and (2) matches and actions by which all traffic is *processed*. In order to support diverse sets of customers or to flexibly compose virtual functions together for complex packet processing, in many cases operators might desire more than one context for a given network device even if this

CoNEXT '16, December 12–15, 2016, Irvine, CA, USA
© 2016 ACM. ISBN 978-1-4503-4292-6/16/12...$15.00
DOI: http://dx.doi.org/10.1145/2999572.2999607

device has only one physical data plane. One answer is virtualization. This technique permits the illusion of multiple programmable data planes and greater flexibility as to how they are used. For example, with data plane virtualization we gain the ability to deploy multiple network functions to the device simultaneously in various configurations, permitting:

- network *slicing*, to isolate sets of customers and/or equipment (e.g., legacy vs. modern, or insecure vs. secure), in which each slice (i.e., isolated networking context) may be unique with respect to supported protocol types and functionality;
- network *snapshotting*, storing multiple network or device configurations while a single configuration is active at a time, and permitting quick transitions between configurations;
- virtual networking *within* the device, providing a solution for both:
  - complex compositions of packet processing programs, allowing modular development; and
  - supporting multiple tenants on the switch that may wish to provide services to each other in a controlled way;
- providing standard high level features such as program profiling, traffic monitoring, and other functions.

Such an environment calls for isolation mechanisms (§4.5) to prevent one program from posing security threats to other programs, to protect the device itself from potentially dangerous programs, and to prevent one program from consuming more than a fair share of resources.

We are focused on the feasibility of virtualization implemented as a user-level program so that the result may work on top of a diverse mix of underlying system stacks. That is, we are intrigued by the possibility that a specially designed P4 program itself may provide the benefits of programmable data plane virtualization by *emulating other P4 programs*. Of the many ways to pursue programmable data plane virtualization, our approach is highly *dynamic*, such that the features listed above may be employed and reconfigured without interrupting the operation of the network device. Our approach is also highly *portable*.

One concern is that virtualization in the application layer comes at a cost. The cost, however, may be amortized over many programs (i.e., functions) sharing the same physical substrate. A second concern is that our prototype is only portable to the extent that sufficient hardware resources are available. Even for the most constrained high performance ASICs-based hardware, however, our analysis (§6) shows that a simple configuration of HyPer4 could be run in a modified version of RMT [12] today.

In the remainder of this paper, first we provide some background (§2) on the rise of data plane programmability. We then make the following contributions:

- **Context:** We provide the operational concept for HyPer4 and present some example use cases for a virtualized programmable data plane (§3).
- **Design:** We explain the design that allows HyPer4 to emulate various aspects of P4 programs and enforce program isolation (§4).
- **Implementation:** We describe the implementation of our prototype which is deployable on an unmodified software P4 switch (§5).
- **Evaluation:** We illuminate the performance and memory costs of HyPer4 and justify our claim that it could be deployed on RMT-like ASICs hardware (§6).

2. BACKGROUND

In this section we provide background material on data plane programmability and P4.

2.1 Data Plane Programmability

The concept of network progammability has a long history [22]. It begins with *active networking* [47] [9] [42] research, and continues with the separation of the control and data planes [49] [39] [16]. The term Software Defined Networking is commonly understood to describe an architecture in which the control plane and data plane are separate, and furthermore, that the control plane is *centralized*, exerting control over a *distributed* data plane [22]. The most well known example is the widely adopted OpenFlow, which provides an open API and thereby defines a standard for *control plane* programmability [30].

The OpenFlow model allows operators to write applications that run on a centralized controller, interacting with devices throughout the network to insert, modify, or remove data plane table entries in response to significant events. The community was energized by this ability to define new network functionality as software running in the controller. Previously operators had to choose between high performing but difficult to modify hardware devices, or low performing but easy to modify software devices. OpenFlow-capable hardware allowed high performance and easily modifiable functionality.

The data plane itself, however, is relatively fixed in this model, by which we mean the supported protocol headers are explicitly identified by each version of the OpenFlow specification [11]. Demand for extending the flexibility of OpenFlow architecture to an ever larger set of protocol header types has led to successive expansions of the OpenFlow specification. Clearly, this approach cannot easily respond to protocol innovation. Attention has therefore turned toward extending programmability to the *data plane*.

The presentation of the Reconfigurable Match Table architecture [12] proved that a constrained but powerful form of data plane programmability could be achieved in the fastest ASICs-based network hardware.

2.2 The P4 language

P4, a language for Programming Protocol Independent Packet Processors, is a recent innovation providing an abstract model suitable for programming the network data plane [11]. A P4-enabled device is *protocol independent* in the sense that no inherent support for any protocols is assumed. Rather, programs written in P4 define packet headers and specify packet parsing and processing behaviors.

P4 programs include these elements: (i) **header definitions** that specify the field names and widths for protocol headers on which the program is intended to operate; (ii) **metadata**, providing packet-specific state; (iii) **registers, meters, and counters**, for state independent of packets; (iv) packet **parser** specification; (v) **match-action table** specification, identifying the packet and metatdata fields to be read and the possible actions to execute in response; (vi) **actions** - functions that may be parameterized and that invoke one or more primitives; (vii) **control flow** indicating the table execution sequence, with support for conditional branching.

Figure 1 depicts the basic operation of a P4-enabled environment. Conceptually, a P4-capable device starts with a clean-slate as in Figure 1(b). Operators *configure* the device with operational functionality by first compiling P4 code (e.g., `foo.p4` in the figure) to produce the binary or equivalent artifact suitable for loading on a P4 target. Once configured with the `foo` "persona", the tables in the switch can be *populated* via a `foo` specific controller at runtime as in Figure 1(c). Loading a different program changes the persona of the P4 target and thereby changes the device functionality itself. Such *reconfigurability in the field* is one of the goals of the P4 environment.

Figure 1(a) depicts the compilation process as typically involving two steps: first, a front-end component (such as the open source p4-hlir [7]) parses the p4 source code to produce a high-level intermediate representation (HLIR). A compiler back-end converts the HLIR into a target-specific form (e.g., binary or JSON). Examples of current P4 compiler back-end offerings include p4c-bmv2 [8] from Barefoot Networks for the software-based "simple switch" [6] or other targets using the behavioral model framework [5], SDNet [14] for Xilinx FPGAs, a P4 back end for Netronome's Network Flow C Compiler and NFP product line [34], and two efforts LLVM_P4 [21] and P4-to-EBPF [15] that compile to EBPF programs for the Linux network plane.

3. EXAMPLES

This section demonstrates some of the use cases for virtualizing the programmable data plane to provide context for the design of HyPer4 presented in §4, with a brief explanation of HyPer4's operational concept first.

3.1 HyPer4 Operational Concept

First, we explain the basic HyPer4 concept for virtualizing the programmable data plane, which involves a P4 program that emulates other P4 programs. This special program is itself a new P4 target to add to the set depicted in Figure 1(a). Figure 2 illustrates the process for deploying and working with foo.p4 within a HyPer4 environment. As shown in Figure 2(a), we configure the P4 target with the HyPer4 persona.

This persona program is itself configurable, endowed with the ability to perform many distinct behaviors, but made to execute specific behaviors through the entries in its tables. This program now becomes the target for configuration by foo.p4. In Figure 2(b), the HyPer4 compiler produces a set of commands for populating a set of HyPer4 tables.

These table entries direct the persona to carry out the behavior expressed in foo.p4. When the controller needs to perform the equivalent of populating *foo's* tables, in order to avoid modifying existing controllers we can send the commands through a Data Plane Management Unit (DPMU) as in Figure 2(c). The name of the DPMU is inspired by the Memory Management Unit in common computer architecture that translates virtual memory addresses to physical addresses and enforces program isolation. Similarly, the DPMU translates virtual table operations (intended for foo.p4) into HyPer4 table operations.

We have written some simple network functions in P4 and converted them into the table population commands necessary to make HyPer4 emulate them:

1. A layer 2 ethernet switch;
2. An IPv4 router;
3. An ARP proxy that responds to ARP requests on behalf of the IPv4 hosts for which the requests are intended; and
4. A firewall that can filter traffic based on IPv4, TCP, and UDP sources and destinations.

Using these functions, we have constructed three examples of various possibilities enabled by virtualizing the programmable data plane.

3.2 Snapshots and Simple Composition

The first (Figure 3) demonstrates network snapshots and composition. The network consists of three connected P4 targets s1, s2, and s3, each running HyPer4 (the state of these is as in Figure 2(a)), two hosts h1 and h2 connected to s1, and two hosts h3 and h4 connected to s3.

At the start, HyPer4 tables are empty and the devices are devoid of functionality. We then populate the HyPer4 tables in each device such that each logically stores all of the programs required for three network configurations (as in Figure 2(b)).

In the first configuration, s1 and s3 each run an arp proxy, while s2 runs a layer 2 switch. Inside s1 and s3 in Figure 3, the dotted-outlined rectangles labeled "A" represent the arp proxy function, while the rectangle labeled "A" within s2 represents the layer 2 switch function.

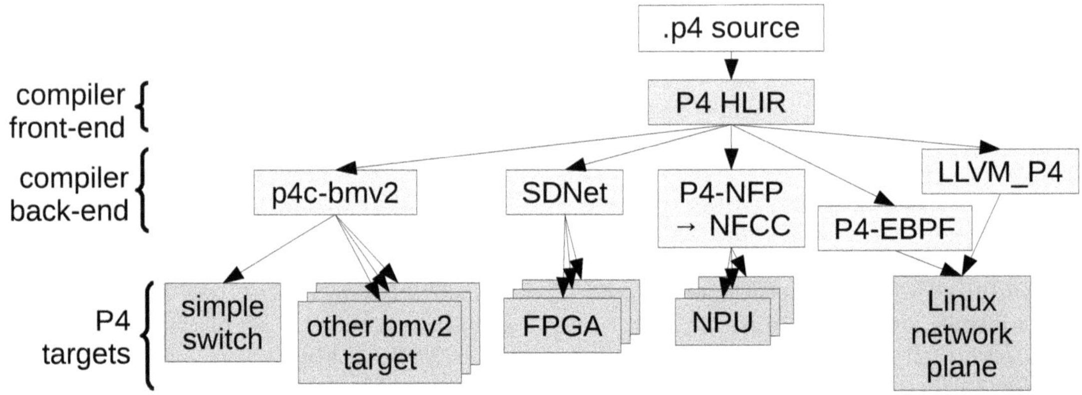

(a) Compiling a p4 program for various targets

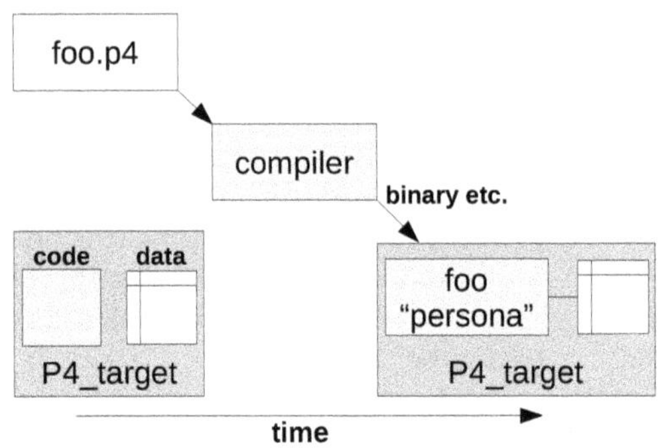

(b) Configuring a p4 target with foo.p4

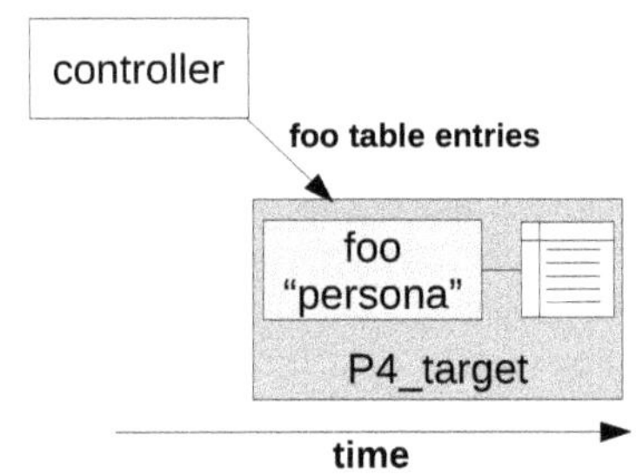

(c) Populating the tables defined by foo.p4

Figure 1: P4 operational environment

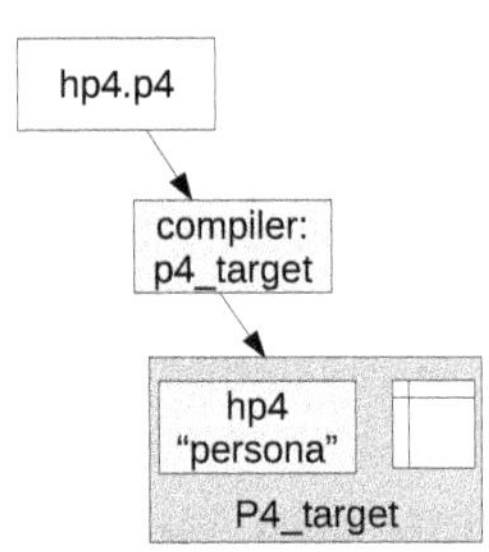

(a) Configuring a P4 target with HyPer4

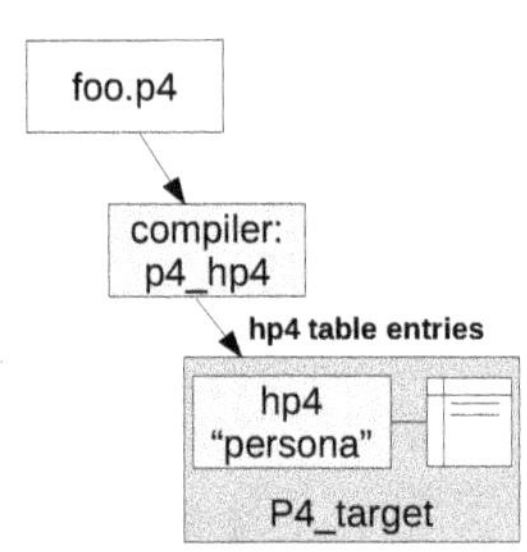

(b) Configuring HyPer4 with foo.p4

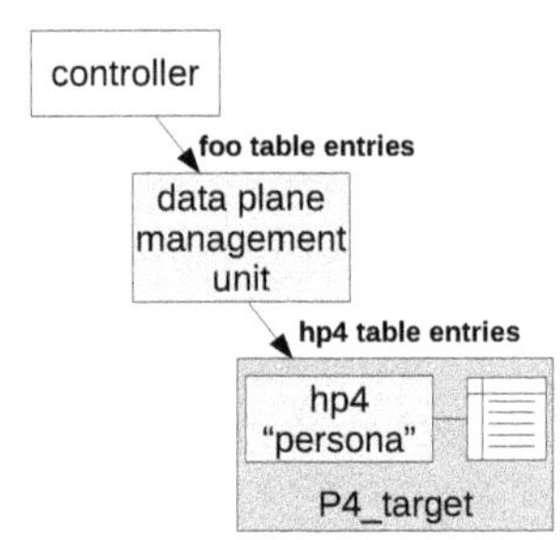

(c) Populating foo's tables within HyPer4

Figure 2: HyPer4 operational environment

In the second configuration, s1 and s3 each run a layer 2 switch, while s2 runs a firewall. These functions are labeled "B" in Figure 3.

In the third configuration, s1 and s3 run the same layer 2 switch as in the second configuration, while s2 runs a composition (labeled "C" in Figure 3). Traffic arriving at s2 is first handled by an arp proxy, which responds to arp requests. All other traffic is passed to the next virtual function in s2, a firewall, and any traffic allowed through the firewall is handled by a router function.

We also logically populate the tables of the virtual functions running within the HyPer4 devices (as in Figure 2(c)):

- MAC and destination port pairs for the layer 2 switches
- IPv4 and MAC pairs for the arp proxies
- IPv4 destination address and next hop IP and MAC address pairs for the router
- In the firewalls, we add rules to filter traffic with a certain TCP destination port

At any given time, a single configuration is active for each device. Changing from one active configuration to

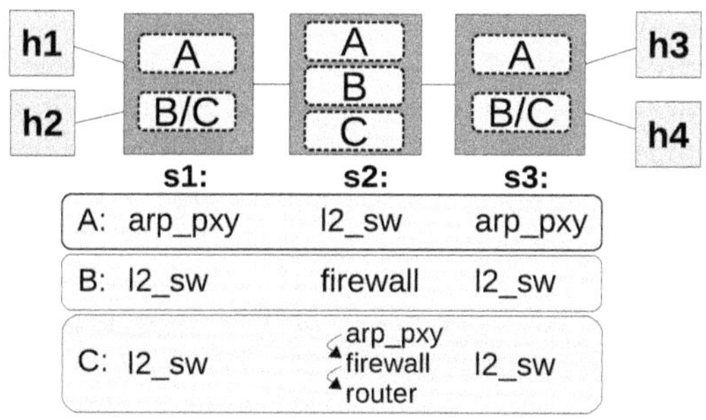

Figure 3: Example One: Network Snapshots and Composition

another is a matter of the controller sending a single table entry modification to each HyPer4 device.

3.3 Network Slicing and Composition

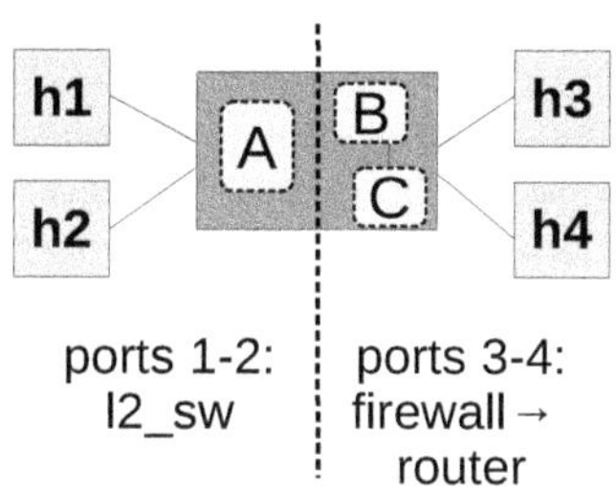

Figure 4: Example Two: Network Slicing and Composition

The second example includes network slicing and composition. Figure 4 depicts a single P4 target s1 running HyPer4, and four hosts h1, h2, h3, and h4 connected to it. IP address and subnet masks are assigned such that h3 and h4 are in separate logical networks.

We use HyPer4 to "slice" s1 such that ports 1 and 2 (for h1 and h2) appear to belong to one device, while ports 3 and 4 (for h3 and h4) belong to another.

At start, HyPer4 tables in s1 are empty, and s1 is devoid of functionality. We then populate the HyPer4 tables such that s1 logically stores three programs:

- Traffic on s1's ports 1 and 2 is handled by a layer 2 switch (program A)
- Traffic on s1's ports 3 and 4 is handled first by a firewall (program B), and secondly, for any traffic that passes through, by a router (program C).

We also logically populate the tables for the layer 2 switch (MAC destination and egress port pairs), the firewall (as in the first example, filtering traffic with a specific TCP destination port), and the router (IPv4 destination address and next hop IP and MAC address pairs).

3.4 Virtual Networking

The third example exhibits virtual networking between virtual devices. The network consists of a single

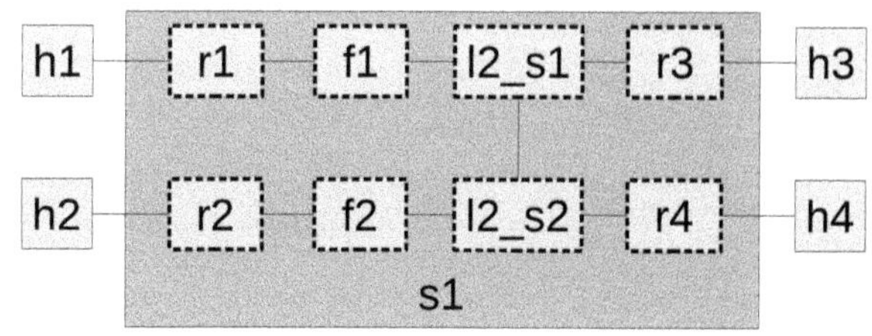

Figure 5: Example Three: Slicing and Composition

P4 target, s1, with four hosts h1, h2, h3, and h4 connected to it. Each host is assigned to a different IPv4 network.

We load eight programs into HyPer4 on s1, creating eight virtual devices:

- a router r1 and a firewall f1 for h1
- a router r2 and a firewall f2 for h2
- a router r3 for h3
- a router r4 for h4
- two layer 2 switches l2_s1 and l2_s2 facilitating connectivity in the internal network

We then populate the tables for each virtual device. This example illustrates how s1, through HyPer4, can support multiple tenants that may wish to provide service to each other but apply security controls.

4. HYPER4 PERSONA DESIGN

At a high level, HyPer4 involves the *persona* (the P4 program running on the network device), a compiler, and a data plane management unit (DPMU). Section 3.1 and Figure 2 provide an overview. In this section, we focus on how the P4 program forming the core of HyPer4 can be made to emulate other P4 programs and virtualize some of the physical resources of the programmable dataplane.

4.1 Design Overview

A P4 program defines the packet-processing *structure*, but during execution, runtime-changeable *state* in the form of table match entries affects how packets are processed within that structure. The aim for HyPer4 is to define a structure general enough that we can permit state changes that change packet processing in arbitrary ways.

Figure 6 depicts an overview of the HyPer4 persona. Conceptually, HyPer4 has three phases. First, the *parsing and setup* phase receives packets and prepares HyPer4 state process packets as specified by the emulated P4 program. In the second phase, HyPer4 emulates the target program's sequence of *match-action stages*. Finally, the *egress* phase handles any egress-specific primitives and prepares the packet for transmission.

In the following paragraphs we identify key tasks the HyPer4 persona must handle in order to properly represent arbitrary P4 programs, and briefly describe the techniques employed to carry out these tasks.

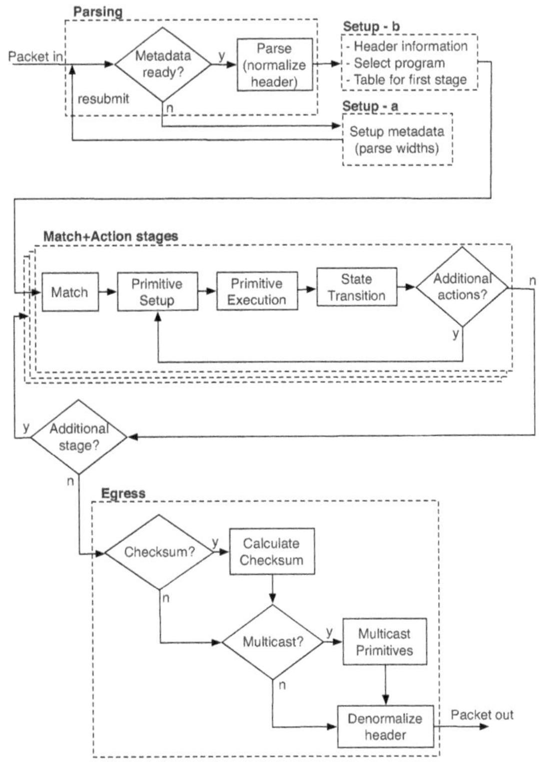

Figure 6: HyPer4 persona

Programmable parsing. The persona must be able to extract an arbitrary number of bytes based on values found in the packet, and it does so by traversing a parse tree, in which each node extracts some portion of the total requirement and branches on a metadata field `numbytes_to_extract` that stores this requirement. The HyPer4 parser is described in more detail in §4.2, but the bottom line is that to achieve the flexibility we need, we implement some aspects of the parser in the setup phase in the ingress pipeline and return to the parser as necessary. Specifically, `numbytes_to_extract` depends on the virtual device associated with the packet. We employ P4's `resubmit` primitive to return the packet back to the parser as necessary. This primitive is powerful because we can pass to it a list of fields that should retain their values (such as `numbytes_to_extract`). Ultimately, the parser extracts a stack of bytes. The `resubmit` primitive could be invoked multiple times for a given packet to accommodate the multiple headers a given virtual device might deal with.

Field representation. The persona uses very wide metadata fields to represent collections of fields used by a virtual device. We define one such field to logically store all of the data extracted from a packet (the stack of bytes extracted by the parser), and another such field to represent all of a virtual device's metadata fields.

Matching. Arbitrary P4 programs match on arbitrary fields. The task for HyPer4 is to support arbitrary matches by isolating the relevant parts of the single wide metadata fields representing a P4 program's defined fields. To this end HyPer4 makes heavy use of P4's ternary matching facility, which permits masks to be supplied with table entries along with match values. These masks are applied to the specified matching field before comparing the result to the match value.

Actions. Matches in P4 programs invoke actions, which may be complex collections of primitives. For each supported P4 primitive, HyPer4 provides a set of tables that collectively carry out the required behavior as discussed in more detail in §4.3. In short, we use a collection of metadata fields to redirect HyPer4 control flow as necessary at every stage of packet processing. Various match-action stages in HyPer4 read (match), write, or read and write these metadata fields. Specifying the values used for these reads and writes by supplying the entries for these tables is how the operator can invoke the relevant behaviors provided by HyPer4 required to carry out arbitrary functionality.

Virtual Networking. HyPer4 relies on P4's `recirculate` primitive to pass packets from one virtual device to another. This primitive marks a packet for sending back to the parser after completing the egress pipeline. It accepts a list of fields as a parameter. Any fields in this list retain their values when the packet reappears at the parser.

The HyPer4 *structure* is anchored by the concept of general purpose match-action stages, in which HyPer4 *state* determines the type of match to peform, the sequences of primitives to execute in response to matches, and the parameters to supply to each primitive. To emulate another P4 program, HyPer4 requires that the target of emulation be transformed into table operations that affect HyPer4 state accordingly. By representing P4 programs as state, HyPer4 enables *live updating* of P4 programs.

4.2 Parsing

The role of the parser in a P4 program is to identify the structure of the first N bits of the packet as a series of bitfields, and associate labels with each of these bitfields. The collection of labeled bitfields is known as the "Parsed Representation" of the packet. The programmer defines header types, indicating the names, widths, and position of bitfields within the header type, and declares header instances of these types to use when extracting bits from the packet. To "extract" a header is to add a collection of bitfields, structured and named according to the header's type, to the Parsed Representation. Enabling the parser to decide which headers to extract is done by making the parse graph branch according to values found in the packet or values of metadata fields.

HyPer4 must parse in a way that is reconfigurable at runtime to extract sufficient data to meet the needs of the various programs HyPer4 is emulating. In HyPer4, we define a header type with a single field that is one byte wide, and declare an array of these one-byte headers to accommodate a variable number of bytes to extract from the packet. We also declare a metadata field (e.g., `numbytes_to_extract`). Upon receiving a packet, the parser examines this field. A value of zero indicates it is not prepared to guide parsing. In this case, a default number of bytes are extracted (typically, 20), and control flow is directed to an initial setup function (Setup - a in Figure 6), which, if necessary, updates `numbytes_to_extract` and *resubmits* the packet. The resubmitted packet returns to the parser, but this time, `numbytes_to_extract` has a meaningful value. HyPer4 traverses the parse tree by branching on this field, where each node extracts some portion of the total.

After completing parsing, HyPer4 concatenates all extracted bytes into a single, very wide metadata field that represents the extracted data throughout the remainder of the pipeline. The setup function (Setup - b in Figure 6) then configures the pipeline for packet processing. Specifically, this function sets a metadata field indicating which of possibly several emulated programs within HyPer4 should be executed. It also sets another field identifying the initial table to execute (according to the type of matching required by the first match-action stage of the emulated program) as the packet enters the HyPer4 match-action stage.

4.3 Match-Action

Each emulated match-action stage requires several HyPer4 tables: one to carry out the match, and three for every primitive that must execute in response to a table match.

To carry out the match, we define one table for every combination of match type (exact, ternary, valid, etc.) and data type for every stage. HyPer4 branches on the value of the metadata field `next_table` (set either in an initial setup phase or at the end of the preceding match-action stage) to execute the correct table from this set.

Exact matching against extracted packet data is one match type, for which HyPer4 employs a ternary match against the single, very wide field representing extracted packet data. The ternary match is useful for isolating the bits of this field that are relevant to the match (i.e., to identify which of fields defined in *foo.p4* are involved in the match).

In general, ternary matching helps emulate a variety of match types against a variety of data types because it permits bitmasks to be supplied with table entries at runtime (though comes at a high cost, in unit TCAM cost and power consumption, see §6.3).

In every case, a match triggers an action that sets a variety of metadata fields. These fields force a branch to a control function representing the first primitive of the emulated action. Executing a primitive involves at least three tables: one to set the stage for primitive execution, another to execute the primitive, and another to perform a state transition, which includes indicating to HyPer4 whether the action (and therefore the match-action stage) is complete, or that more primitives must be carried out.

4.4 Deparsing

In P4, throughout packet processing, changes may occur to the packet's Parsed Representation, including not only header field values, but the structure of the packet itself: headers may be removed from or added to the packet. Because of this, *deparsing* is a necessary step that identifies the sequence of headers to serialize for transmission. Deparsers, however, do not appear in P4 source code; rather, the graph specified for the *parser* is once again leveraged for deparsing the packet.

Because HyPer4 uses a metadata field as a proxy for the Parsed Representation throughout packet processing, at the end of the egress pipeline it must perform a "write back" to the actual Parsed Representation to prepare the packet for deparsing. The Parsed Representation consists of a stack of single-byte headers, so preparing for deparsing involves repeatedly masking the proxy metadata field, copying the lowest order byte to the next header in the stack, and shifting the metadata field to the right by one byte.

4.5 Isolation

The current design of HyPer4 isolates programs in the sense that it prevents one program from overwriting the code of another. It also supports memory isolation. We explain these first and then describe how future versions HyPer4 can also support other forms of resource isolation.

Code isolation is achieved by assigning each program a uniquely identifying number at compile time (this could be hash of the .p4 code or downstream compilation artifact). When a packet is received, some operator-controllable criteria (e.g., ingress port, time, network security posture, or a value within the packet itself) determines which program should handle it and accordingly the metadata field `program` is set to the corresponding program ID. This field is one of the match fields for every match-action emulation table in the persona and thereby distinguishes one program's table entries from another's within the same shared physical table. We refer to the emulated program as a *virtual device*. The program ID functions similarly to a VLAN ID, though the mechanism for assigning a program ID to a packet is more dynamic. The DPMU monitors requests for adding table entries to virtual devices and ensures the program IDs in the entries are authorized for the requester.

At the same time, the DPMU can enforce limits for the number of table entries used by each virtual device, assisting partially with the requirement for memory isolation. Other memory requirements include support for stateful memory objects (counters, meters, and registers). HyPer4 design calls for preallocation of sets of such objects, where the number of sets is equal to the number of virtual devices that can be simultaneously supported. It is the role of the HyPer4 *compiler* to assign these sets to virtual devices.

CPU isolation for our purposes means that no program incurs an action that cannot be completed in a single clock cycle. If one virtual device employs an action that does not fit within a single clock cycle, then for any packet it processes it will introduce stalls in the pipeline that also delay packets behind it (which may belong to other virtual devices). HyPer4 is not currently designed to ensure this kind of isolation. Some of its actions include multiple interdependent primitives. Future designs of HyPer4 will split these actions across multiple tables to keep packets flowing steadily through the pipeline regardless of which functionality is employed by any given virtual device.

The ingress buffer is yet another resource that can lead to interference between virtual devices. In the current HyPer4 design, it is possible that one virtual device might repeatedly trigger primitives that send a packet back to the input buffer, at the possible expense of other packets trying to enter the buffer. Such packets might be coming from external connections or internally from other virtual devices using the same type of primitives. One way to address this issue would be to rely on a meter in HyPer4 at the beginning of the ingress pipeline that drops traffic above a threshold for a given virtual device.

4.6 Virtual Networking

HyPer4 is designed with a virtual network to control traffic exchange between virtual devices running within the persona. Space does not permit a detailed discussion, but we create *virtual* ports with unique IDs and allot them to virtual devices. We can map these virtual ports directly to physical ports or connect them to virtual links, on the other end of which is a virtual port for another virtual device.

For a packet destined for other virtual devices, HyPer4 invokes P4's `recirculate` primitive to send the packet back to the parser after changing the program ID.

We support *virtual multicasting* with a combination of P4's `clone` and `recirculate` primitives. Briefly, the program ID is updated according to a programmable sequence. Then one of the packet clones is sent back to the parser and ultimately processed by the relevent virtual device. The other packet clone is sent back to the start of the egress pipeline, with the program ID serving as a loop counter and triggering a packet drop once it reaches the end of the multicast sequence.

4.7 Design Consequences

This section illuminates the resource and performance consequences of design choices for HyPer4 as well as for the P4 language specification. These consequences for overhead are evaluated in §6.

First, HyPer4's use of ternary matching to emulate a variety of match types against arbitrary data fields increases TCAM pressure, resulting in increased power consumption as well as a potential TCAM scarcity obstacle to deploying HyPer4 on current hardware. See §6.3.

Second, to permit HyPer4 to emulate behaviors from a *behavioral set* in *arbitrary sequences* of maximum length K, HyPer4 source must declare K copies of the tables carrying out a given behavior from the set. This is because P4 restricts a program from using a table more than once in the processing of a specific packet. This design choice of P4 is sensible to ensure programs are compatible with hardware architectures like RMT [12], which opted to connect tables in a pipeline instead of using a crossbar due to physical wiring constraints and because packet processing algorithms naturally involve sequential dependencies.

Next, the use of the `resubmit` primitive to permit a dynamically programmable parser cuts the throughput. HyPer4 could avoid these `resubmits` with a P4 target that implements parser exceptions by repeatedly extracting bytes until an exception occurred indicating no more bytes available, up to a certain maximum number. Interestingly, Protocol Oblivious Forwarding [43], unlike P4, has a parse-as-needed approach which would also eliminate the HyPer4's need for resubmission.

The use of recirculation for virtual networking also incurs a throughput penalty, but this is a natural consequence of making one physical device do the work of multiple devices.

Finally, HyPer4 can send packets that are, in effect, completely different than what it can effectively receive, which normally is not the case for P4 programs. P4 serializes the parsed representation with the rest of the packet for transmission by using the same graph specified by the parser functions in .p4 code. The result is that a P4 program can only send packets conforming to a structure that it can also parse. HyPer4, however, moves most of the parsing decision logic into the ingress pipeline, and the actual parse graph for HyPer4 simply extracts a specified number of bytes without any higher level structure. Thus, HyPer4 makes an end run around a restriction normally imposed by P4, for better or for worse.

5. IMPLEMENTATION

This section provides implementation details. All source code is available at our git repository [23].

5.1 Configuration

As noted in §4.7, HyPer4 must declare many copies of the tables carrying out a specific behavior, differing in name only, such that one copy exists for every position in a sequence of behaviors. This results in a large codebase with numerous examples of functionally redundant code. As an example, in the source for HyPer4 one might find two tables, `t1_exact_extracted` and `t2_exact_extracted`. They both do the same thing:

exact matching against extracted packet data. The first table is callable in the first emulated match-action stage, while the second table is callable in the second stage.

This redundancy in the code lends itself to using configuration scripts to produce the P4 source for HyPer4. This approach simplifies HyPer4 development and allows us to tailor HyPer4 according to need and resource availability. Configurable parameters include:

- the maximum number of match-action stages HyPer4 must be capable of emulating
- the max number of primitives per compound action
- default, maximum, and step values for the number of bytes HyPer4 should be capable of parsing.

The configuration script (900 LoC in Python) produced the P4 source for a configuration of HyPer4 capable of executing the demonstrations in §3, supporting four emulated match-action stages with up to nine primitives per action, and supporting five of P4's 21 distinct P4 primitives. This configuration of HyPer4 is approximately 6400 LoC. Figure 7 shows the how the P4 codebase grows linearly in the maximum number of match-action stages emulated and the maximum number of primitives allowed per stage. Figure 7(a) charts the growth of the entire HyPer4 codebase, while Figure 7(b) is focused on the code required to support the `drop` primitive, and Figure 7(c) pertains solely to the code supporting the `modify_field` primitive. The average P4 LoC for the five primitives currently supported by HyPer4 ranges from 128, at one stage and one primitive, to 539, at five stages and nine primitives per stage. Extrapolating for the 16 additional primitives (of P4's set of 21), a version of HyPer4 supporting every primitive would require, in addition to the numbers reported in Figure 7(a), from 2000 more LoC at one stage and one primitive, to 8600 more LoC at five stages and nine primitives per stage.

5.2 Compiling

The HyPer4 compiler is a work in progress. In the meantime, we have manually produced files consisting of the table commands necessary to induce HyPer4 to emulate each of the network functions described in §3.1.

These "commands" files consist entirely of command line interface commands in the style of bmv2 [5]. Before producing the final commands file for a given network function, however, it is conducive to produce an intermediate artifact, which for the most part looks like the final commands file, with two key differences:

- the *intermediate* commands file permits comments and vertical whitespace for readability;
- it uses human readable tokens in the place of numbers wherever possible. This is partly for readability, and partly for operational reasons. For example, the virtual program ID as well as the numbers for the assigned virtual ports are not known at compile time and will be supplied at load time.

At load time, we employ a script to convert the intermediate commands file to the HyPer4-ready commands file, substituting numbers for tokens and eliminating comments and whitespace. Script parameters include the program ID and virtual port assignments.

5.3 Limitations

Some of the P4 language features are not currently covered by HyPer4, but will be in time, though the level of coverage may vary by feature. A long term goal is to one day support popular P4 applications like NetPaxos [18] and In-band Network Telemetry [26].

Stateful memory (registers, counters, meters). It is difficult for HyPer4 to anticipate the needs of a wide variety of programs, with respect to registers, counters, and meters, and meet them within the limited amount of physical resources available. The problem is compounded by the fact that P4 permits different modes of declaration for stateful memories. A stateful memory object may be globally accessible, or statically bound to a specific table, or furthermore statically bound to a specific table entry. HyPer4 can preemptively declare statically bound registers, counters, and meters for every table that emulates the "match" piece of a match-action stage, but this approach is likely to prove infeasible for many hardware P4 targets. In particular, registers can vary in width, which for the preemptive approach would require HyPer4 registers be declared with sufficient width to cover the maximum need, resulting in a lot of wasted register memory for the average case.

Match types: lpm, range. The single wide `extracted_data` field employed by HyPer4 to represent extracted packet fields complicates implementation of lpm matching, but we have at least two options. We can insert a preparatory match-action stage that takes the `extracted_data` field and copies, to a separate metadata field, only the bits pertaining to the represented field of interest. The lpm match is then done against this metadata field, which is made wide enough to accommodate a variety of needs. The second option is to use ternary matching, but have the DPMU identify and manage the priorities of match entries.

Range matching implementation may involve a preparatory copy step to break out the field of interest as in the first option for `lpm` matching.

Arbitrary checksums. HyPer4 cannot easily handle arbitrary checksums, by which we mean applying a checksum algorithm to an unpredictable number of fields. Though we can arbitrarily create a field list by using copies, shifts, and masks to access the emulated fields and concatenate them together into another field, we cannot predict how wide that new field must be, and if wider than the field list defined in the original program, the leading (or trailing) zeros will affect the output of many checksum algorithms, which are often designed to distinguish between messages that are in all ways equivalent except that one message has leading (or trailing) zeros and the other does not [29]. We could, however, declare one such field list-emulating field for each of many different widths we anticipate needing to

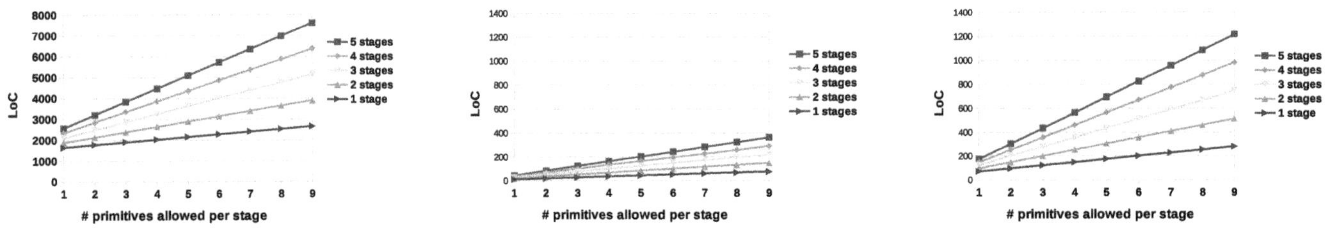

(a) Total Lines of Code (b) Drop Lines of Code (c) Modify_Field Lines of Code

Figure 7: HyPer4 Lines of Code by Number of Stages and Primitives per Stage

support, allow the user to indicate the required width via table entry, and direct control flow accordingly to make use of the correct field. In the meantime, we can "cheat" by directly adding support for the checksum requirements of well known protocols. This is what we have done with the IPv4 checksum field.

Field lists. A P4 program may define *field lists*. A field list is passed as a parameter to `clone`, `resubmit`, and `recirculate` primitives and identifies those fields whose values must be retained when the packet reappears at the start of the appropriate pipeline. Because HyPer4 represents all of the virtualized program's extracted data fields in one wide field and all of the metadata fields in another, we can construct a universal field list that includes the consolidated extracted data field e, the consolidated metadata field m, and bitmasks for each, b_e and b_m. At the start of each pipeline, we replace e with $e \,\&\, b_e$ and m with $m \,\&\, b_m$.

Expressions and **action profiles** likely will never be covered by HyPer4.

6. EVALUATION AND ANALYSIS

Our development environment for HyPer4 does not include a P4-capable hardware device. Therefore, to evaluate HyPer4 we examine resource and performance differences in terms that may be used to estimate performance impacts or realizability on any P4-capable device. Specifically, we compare selected native P4 programs with these same programs emulated by HyPer4 in terms of the number of table match-action stages incurred during operation (impacting latency), the space requirements for tables, data, and actions (impacting memory), and the width and frequency of ternary matches (impacting TCAM and power).

We also directly evaluated HyPer4 performance in terms of latency and bandwidth with the use of Barefoot Networks' bmv2 software switch [5], and explain results with discussion about the number of resubmits and recirculations involved (impacting throughput).

Finally, we analyze the difference between RMT [12] specifications and the hardware required to run HyPer4.

6.1 Match-action Stages

Table 1 shows the cost of HyPer4 emulation in terms of the number of match action stages required. Each

	No. Matches	
Program	Native	HyPer4
L2 switch	2	13
Firewall	3	22
Router	4	28
Arp Proxy	4	48

Table 1: Number of matches for most complex processing per function natively vs. in HyPer4

row of Table 1 involves a switch running a single function. Of these, HyPer4 emulation typically requires 6x to 7x as many match-action stages, except the arp_proxy, which requires 12x as many. This is because one of the actions of arp_proxy involves nine primitives in order to build an arp response. Note, this 12x penalty is only incurred when an arp request is received.

6.2 Space

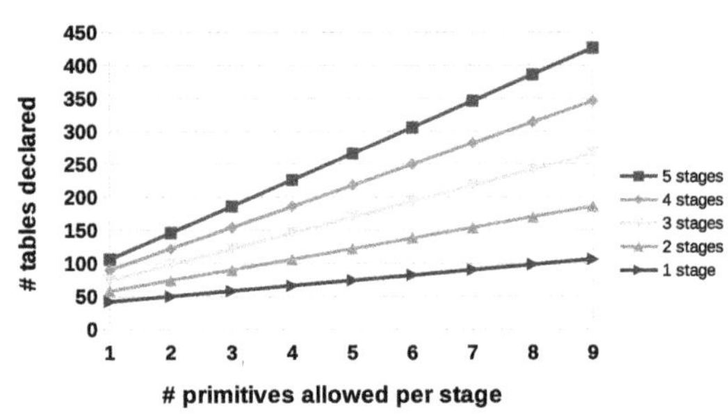

Figure 8: HyPer4 Tables by Number of Stages and Primitives per Stage

Figure 8 charts the number of tables declared in HyPer4 with different numbers of emulated match-action stages and numbers of primitives allowed per stage. Most of these tables will have no entries but exist to meet arbitrary emulation requirements. But these empty tables still occupy space; we expect most implementations of tables include code or function pointers for carrying out the match, and function pointers for actions associated with the table. In most cases, each HyPer4 table references a single action, but for some (e.g., tables that carry out the `modify_field` primitive) this can range up to 14.

The configuration used throughout HyPer4 testing permits four match-action stages and nine primitives per stage, and declares 346 tables.

	No. Tables Shared			
	l2_sw	arp_proxy	router	firewall
l2_sw	19	14	17	14
arp_proxy		57	23	30
router			33	21
firewall				35

Table 2: Number of tables referenced by both programs

During execution, if HyPer4 hosts multiple programs, many of the tables are shared. For each pair of programs, Table 2 shows the number of shared tables. The diagonal indicates the total number of tables referenced by each program. Not all of these tables are in the same branch for any given program, and hence these numbers differ from those reported in Table 1.

	No. Tables Uniquely Referenced			
	l2_sw	arp_proxy	router	firewall
l2_sw	-	5	2	5
arp_proxy	43	-	34	27
router	16	10	-	12
firewall	21	5	14	-

Table 3: Number of tables referenced uniquely in the program named at the left

Table 3 reveals the number of tables that do not share entries for each pair of programs. Clearly, `arp_proxy` has the most unique tables. This is accounted for by the fact that this program is alone in terms of executing a nine-primitive action in one of its stages.

In eight out of twelve cases, more tables are shared between programs than not, suggesting that table declarations is one area where the overhead of HyPer4 is amortized over multiple emulated programs.

Storage required for table entries, however, is much higher within HyPer4 in return for flexibility. Because each match involving extracted packet data is done against a single 800-bit-wide field, each match entry requires at least 1600 bits of storage: 800 for the value and 800 for the mask bits. Similarly, matches involving emulated metadata are done against a single 256-bit-wide field and require at least 512 bits per entry. The program ID adds a few more to the required number of bits for each entry. This is the price we pay for allowing a single table to be used to match against any of the first 800 bits of a packet, or 256 bits of metadata.

With respect to action storage, the current incarnation of HyPer4 includes 130 actions, many of which are functionally redundant, differing only in a certain constant that cannot be replaced by a variable (field). For example, HyPer4 includes 80 actions that each resize the parsed representation to the correct size between 20 and 100 bytes (accounting for packet structure changes, such as adding or removing headers) prior to writing back any changes to extracted data and deparsing. With few exceptions, most HyPer4 actions use between one and four primitives. The 130 tally does not change with different configurations of HyPer4; it only changes as we add or remove fundamental functionality to HyPer4 such as support for more primitives or revisions to virtual networking.

6.3 Ternary Matches

The increased reliance on ternary matching increases power consumption. Many efforts discuss the TCAM power issue, including [31], [4], [44], [3]. In the future we plan to evaluate this aspect of HyPer4 more closely, but in the meantime provide a few numbers to give an idea of HyPer4's increased pressure on TCAM.

	bits matched per packet		
program	total	active	no. ternary matches
l2_sw	808	56	2
router	1224	80	4
arp_proxy	1848	66	5
firewall	1928	59	6

Table 4: Ternary Match Usage in HyPer4

Table 4 shows how many bits are ternary matched for packets incurring the most complex processing for each program. The "total" column includes "don't care" or wildcard bits while the "active" column shows only the number of bits actively involved in the match. The number of ternary matches, resulting in the totals for these columns, is provided in the fourth column.

6.4 Latency and Bandwidth Measurements

Here we report the results of bandwidth and latency tests using iperf3 [19] and ping floods. We ran all tests using bmv2 software switch [5]. All evaluations were carried out in an Ubuntu 14.04 virtual machine running Mininet [1]. The VM was allocated three 2.2 GHz Intel Core i7-4770HQ CPUs and 6.15 GB of memory.

	native Mbps		hp4 Mbps		native ms		hp4 ms	
	μ	σ	μ	σ	μ ms	σ	μ ms	σ
l2_sw	110.3	4.81	18.7	0.43	451	81.4	1540	31.0
firewall	63.7	3.53	7.2	0.11	483	63.0	2277	38.7
Ex. 1 B	37.7	1.24	6.3	0.10	1454	113.2	5011	90.7
Ex. 1 C	26.3	1.06	3.1	0.15	2247	235.1	8736	63.3

Table 5: Bandwidth (iperf3) and Latency (ping -f -c 1000)

Table 5 shows the mean and standard deviation of 10 runs of each test. HyPer4 emulation incurs an 83% bandwidth penalty for the L2 switch as measured with `iperf3`, and an 89% bandwidth penalty for the firewall.

For the latency test, we sent 1000 pings using the `-f` option for "flood," in which each successive ping is sent immediately after a response is received for the previous ping. HyPer4-emulated L2 switch takes 3.4x as long as the native L2 switch, while for the firewall the difference is 4.7x.

The emulated L2 switch never invokes the `resubmit` primitive, so all performance penalty is due to the increased number of match-action stages. The emulated firewall performs one `resubmit` for each ping, and two `resubmits` for each TCP packet sent in the iperf3 test.

The next two rows involve multiple switches. "Ex. 1 B" is described in §3.2 and Figure 3: three switches (L2 switch, firewall, L2 switch) between two hosts. "Ex. 1 C" has the same topology but the middle switch runs the sequentially composed arp proxy, firewall, and router. When HyPer4 is loaded on each switch, the performance drop is similar to the previous two cases: 83% bandwidth penalty for "Ex. 1 B" and 88% penalty for "Ex. 1 C". The latency test also has similar results: HyPer4 switches take 3.4x as long in "Ex. 1 B" and 3.9x as long in "Ex. 1 C".

For "Ex. 1 B", each ping triggers one `resubmit`, while each TCP packet requires two `resubmits`. For the composition on the middle switch of "Ex. 1 C", pings incur a total of two `recirculations` and two `resubmits`, while TCP packets result in a total of two `recirculations` and three `resubmits`.

6.5 Deploying on RMT

Implementation details for RMT [12] that determine ability to run HyPer4 include the width of the packet header vector (which is made available to each match-action stage and includes bits extracted from the packet as well as all bits used for metadata), the number of physical match action stages available, and the maximum number of bits each stage can match against.

RMT supports a 4096-bit packet header vector. This meets the requirement for the HyPer4 configuration evaluated here, which uses 3312 bits: 800 bits of extracted packet data, 256 bits of metadata, and 2256 bits of overhead. This overhead includes scratch space supporting manipulations on packet data, which affects any decision regarding how to make use of the remaining packet header vector bits available, whether for extracting more bytes from the packet or representing more metadata.

RMT includes 32 match-action stages in the ingress pipeline and another 32 in egress. The single program evaluated in this section requiring the most match-action stages is the `arp proxy`, which uses 46 match action stages in the ingress pipeline (and two in egress). RMT cannot support this requirement, but for more precision, we compare the number of bits each RMT match-action stage supports to the number of bits HyPer4 match-action stages require, to know in which cases we need multiple physical stages to support a given HyPer4 match-action stage. RMT stages support matches of up to 640 bits in SRAM and 640 bits in TCAM. Of `arp proxy`'s 46 ingress stages, 44 of these can each be covered by one RMT physical stage. The other two stages involve ternary matches against the 800 bit-wide field representing extracted packet data, and each require 1600 bits of TCAM memory (800 for the value, 800 for the mask). Therefore, three RMT physical stages are required for each of these two HyPer4 stages. The final total is 51 physical stages, or 60% more than RMT's capacity. Note that this would meet not only `arp proxy`, but arbitrary compositions including `arp proxy` and any simpler programs. A variant of RMT that shifted 19 of the 32 egress match action stages to the ingress pipeline could meet the requirement today.

7. DISCUSSION OF ALTERNATIVES

The performance penalties incurred by HyPer4 illuminated in § 6 warrant consideration of alternative approaches. This section discusses alternatives to the "full" HyPer4 solution.

7.1 Partial Virtualization

In an environment in which high performance network hardware is too costly to consider spending on HyPer4's capabilities, it may yet be attractive to employ *partial* virtualization. This approach requires fewer physical resources, or may boost performance by sacrificing a portion of flexibility, or compensate for HyPer4's inability to emulate some P4 language feature.

The P4 programming model provides mechanisms to program a packet parser as well as match-action tables (§2.2). For these program elements, various combinations of virtualization and direct implementation are possible to satisfy various use cases.

Figure 9(a) depicts the "full" virtualization, in which each column runs its own program. Each column could be active simultaneously (network slicing), and packets are sent to specific columns by some criteria.

Figure 9(b) illustrates the possibility of separate virtual parsers attached to the same directly implemented match-action pipeline. This pipeline will not be as dynamically flexible as the pipeline in the full virtualization solution, yet may offer limited flexibility by permitting runtime selectable criteria to invoke different directly-implemented functionality based on which packet headers have been extracted.

Conversely, as shown in Figure 9(c), a single directly implemented parser can pass traffic to different virtual match-action pipelines. This "fixes" the set of protocol headers supported, but permits different, dynamically modifiable behaviors as responses to these headers.

Figure 9(d) suggests the match-action pipeline itself could be partially virtualized. This may be attractive for environments in which we are willing to sacrifice dynamic flexibility in one layer of the protocol stack (perhaps L2 or L3) for performance, but still need dynamic flexibility in other layers.

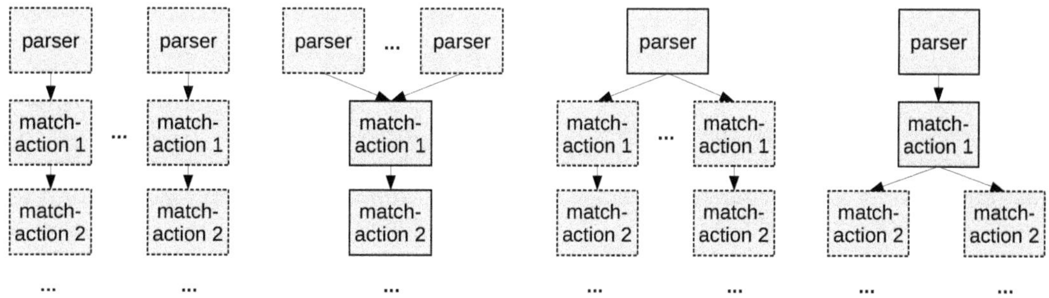

(a) Full virtualization (b) Parser only (c) Match-action only (d) Mixed match-action

Figure 9: Possible mixes of programmable data plane virtualization

7.2 Other Alternatives

Other approaches for increasing data plane flexibility:

1. A compiler for composing functions written in P4. This tool would produce a program with functionality merged from more than one P4 project. Compiler flags could allow the operator to indicate control flow across the set of included functions using parallel, sequential, and branch composition operators, in the same spirit as Pyretic [32]. This approach should result in high performance, but cannot provide the runtime reconfigurability provided by our approach.

2. Virtualization implemented below the application layer. This approach could offer runtime reconfigurability along with high performance, but requires non-portable implementation aspects specific to each platform.

3. Directly embedding P4 programs in the network. This technique entails loading different P4-capable switches with different programs, and another switch that selects the appropriate target for processing the traffic according to the criteria that marks a packet as belonging to one virtual network or another. This approach should offer high performance and the possibility of runtime reconfigurability (if spare hardware is available) at the cost of additional switches.

8. RELATED WORK

HyPer4 builds on the P4 language [11, 46]. Perhaps most closely related to our efforts is the P4 parser for OpenvSwitch, to enable flexible packet parsing in OVS, such that supported protocols and fields can be reconfigured without recompiling [37]. This effort focuses on the header and parser elements of P4 programs and is specific to extending OVS.

HyPer4 is also related to earlier work on data plane programmability [27, 45, 28, 10, 33, 25, 13, 36]. This includes the Click modular router [27] and active networks [45]. NetFPGA also represents earlier work that provided data plane programmability [28]. While not fully programmable, efforts that enabled stateful openflow applications to be realized also formed part of the current move towards fully programmable switch data planes [10, 33]. More recent efforts more closely related to P4 include Protocol Oblivious Forwarding [43], tiny packet programs [25] and work on programmable hardware platforms [13, 36].

More broadly, HyPer4 remains related to earlier SDN efforts such as work enabling portability in the SDN control plane [50], and the creation of a control plane virtualization layer [41].

HyPer4 is also related to network function virtualization research [38, 2, 48, 20], particularly concerning efficient data plane realizations [48, 24, 17].

9. CONCLUSIONS

We have described the concept, design, implementation, and evaluation of a hypervisor-like P4 program called HyPer4. It is as yet only capable of emulating a small subset of possible P4 programs, and typically incurs 80% to 90% penalties in terms of performance, in exchange for a portable solution for programmable data plane virtualization that permits reconfigurability *at runtime*. It facilitates useful modes for running network functions in parallel or virtually networked in complex compositions, and is a platform onto which we can add useful modules for features like monitoring and program verification.

Future work includes expanding HyPer4's coverage of P4 language features, improving HyPer4 efficiency, completing the HyPer4 compiler, and providing a data plane management unit.

10. ACKNOWLEDGMENTS

We are grateful to the anonymous reviewers for their valuable feedback, and our shepherd for his guidance and encouragement. This material is supported by the National Science Foundation under grant number 1302688.

11. REFERENCES

[1] Mininet. http://mininet.org/.

[2] OPNFV: An Open Platform to Accelerate NFV. https://www.opnfv.org/sites/opnfv/files/pages/files/opnfv_whitepaper_092914.pdf.

[3] B. Agrawal and T. Sherwood. Modeling tcam power for next generation network devices. In *Performance Analysis of Systems and Software, 2006 IEEE International Symposium on*, pages 120–129. IEEE, 2006.

[4] S. I. Ali and M. Islam. An energy efficient design of high-speed ternary cam using match-line segmentation and resistive feedback in sense amplifier. *Journal of Computers*, 7(3):567–577, 2012.

[5] Barefoot Networks. Behavioral Model Repository. https://github.com/p4lang/behavioral-model.

[6] Barefoot Networks. Bmv2 Simple Switch. https://github.com/p4lang/behavioral-model/tree/master/targets/simple_switch.

[7] Barefoot Networks. P4-hlir. https://github.com/p4lang/p4-hlir.

[8] Barefoot Networks. P4c-bm. https://github.com/p4lang/p4c-bm.

[9] S. Bhattacharjee, K. L. Calvert, and E. W. Zegura. An architecture for active networking. In *Proceedings of the IFIP TC6 Seventh International Conference on High Performance Netwoking VII*, HPN '97, pages 265–279, London, UK, UK, 1997. Chapman & Hall, Ltd.

[10] G. Bianchi, M. Bonola, A. Capone, and C. Cascone. Openstate: Programming platform-independent stateful openflow applications inside the switch. *SIGCOMM Comput. Commun. Rev.*, 44(2):44–51, Apr. 2014.

[11] P. Bosshart, D. Daly, G. Gibb, M. Izzard, N. McKeown, J. Rexford, and C. Schlesinger. P4: Programming protocol-independent packet processors. *SIGCOMM Computer Communication Review*, 44(3):87–95, 2014.

[12] P. Bosshart, G. Gibb, H.-S. Kim, G. Varghese, N. McKeown, M. Izzard, F. Mujica, and M. Horowitz. Forwarding metamorphosis: Fast programmable match-action processing in hardware for sdn. In *ACM SIGCOMM Computer Communication Review*, volume 43, pages 99–110. ACM, 2013.

[13] P. Bosshart, G. Gibb, H.-S. Kim, G. Varghese, N. McKeown, M. Izzard, F. Mujica, and M. Horowitz. Forwarding metamorphosis: Fast programmable match-action processing in hardware for sdn. In *Proceedings of the ACM SIGCOMM 2013 Conference on SIGCOMM*, SIGCOMM '13, pages 99–110, New York, NY, USA, 2013. ACM.

[14] Brebner, Gordon. P4 for an FPGA target. http://schd.ws/hosted_files/p4workshop2015/33/GordonB-P4-Workshop-June-04-2015.pdf.

[15] Budiu, Mihai. Compiling P4 to EBPF. https://github.com/iovisor/bcc/tree/master/src/cc/frontends/p4.

[16] M. Caesar, D. Caldwell, N. Feamster, J. Rexford, A. Shaikh, and J. van der Merwe. Design and implementation of a routing control platform. In *Proceedings of the 2nd conference on Symposium on Networked Systems Design & Implementation-Volume 2*, pages 15–28. USENIX Association, 2005.

[17] I. Cerrato, M. Annarumma, and F. Risso. Supporting fine-grained network functions through intel dpdk. In *Software Defined Networks (EWSDN), 2014 Third European Workshop on*, pages 1–6, Sept 2014.

[18] H. T. Dang, D. Sciascia, M. Canini, F. Pedone, and R. Soulé. Netpaxos: Consensus at network speed. In *Proceedings of the 1st ACM SIGCOMM Symposium on Software Defined Networking Research*, page 5. ACM, 2015.

[19] ESnet, Lawrence Berkeley National Laboratory. iperf3. http://software.es.net/iperf/.

[20] ETSI. Network Functions Virtualisation (NFV); Architectural Framework. ETSI GS NFV 002 V1.1.1 (2013-10).

[21] Fastabend, John. P4 on the Edge. http://p4.org/p4-workshop-2016/.

[22] N. Feamster, J. Rexford, and E. Zegura. The road to sdn: an intellectual history of programmable networks. *ACM SIGCOMM Computer Communication Review*, 44(2):87–98, 2014.

[23] Flux Research Group, University of Utah. HyPer4 Repository. https://gitlab.flux.utah.edu/hp4/src.git.

[24] J. Hwang, K. K. Ramakrishnan, and T. Wood. Netvm: High performance and flexible networking using virtualization on commodity platforms. In *11th USENIX Symposium on Networked Systems Design and Implementation (NSDI 14)*, pages 445–458, Seattle, WA, Apr. 2014. USENIX Association.

[25] V. Jeyakumar, M. Alizadeh, C. Kim, and D. Mazières. Tiny packet programs for low-latency network control and monitoring. In *Proceedings of the Twelfth ACM Workshop on Hot Topics in Networks*, HotNets-XII, pages 8:1–8:7, New York, NY, USA, 2013. ACM.

[26] C. Kim, A. Sivaraman, N. Katta, A. Bas, A. Dixit, and L. J. Wobker. In-band network telemetry via programmable dataplanes. In *ACM SIGCOMM Symposium on SDN Research (SOSR)*, 2015.

[27] E. Kohler, R. Morris, B. Chen, J. Jannotti, and

M. F. Kaashoek. The click modular router. *ACM Trans. Comput. Syst.*, 18(3):263–297, Aug. 2000.

[28] J. Lockwood, N. McKeown, G. Watson, G. Gibb, P. Hartke, J. Naous, R. Raghuraman, and J. Luo. Netfpga–an open platform for gigabit-rate network switching and routing. In *Microelectronic Systems Education, 2007. MSE '07. IEEE International Conference on*, pages 160–161, June 2007.

[29] H. McKee. Improved {CRC} techniques detects erroneous leading and trailing 0âĂŹs in transmitted data blocks. *Computer Design*, 14(10):102–4, 1975.

[30] N. McKeown, T. Anderson, H. Balakrishnan, G. Parulkar, L. Peterson, J. Rexford, S. Shenker, and J. Turner. Openflow: Enabling innovation in campus networks. *SIGCOMM Comput. Commun. Rev.*, 38(2), Mar. 2008.

[31] N. Mohan, W. Fung, D. Wright, and M. Sachdev. A low-power ternary cam with positive-feedback match-line sense amplifiers. *Circuits and Systems I: Regular Papers, IEEE Transactions on*, 56(3):566–573, 2009.

[32] C. Monsanto, J. Reich, N. Foster, J. Rexford, D. Walker, et al. Composing software defined networks. In *NSDI*, pages 1–13, 2013.

[33] M. Moshref, A. Bhargava, A. Gupta, M. Yu, and R. Govindan. Flow-level state transition as a new switch primitive for sdn. In *Proceedings of the Third Workshop on Hot Topics in Software Defined Networking*, HotSDN '14, pages 61–66, New York, NY, USA, 2014. ACM.

[34] Netronome Systems, Inc. Programming NFP with P4 and C. https://netronome.com/media/redactor_files/WP_Programming_with_P4_and_C%20.pdf.

[35] Open Networking Foundation. OpenFlow Switch Specifications. https://www.opennetworking.org/sdn-resources/onf-specifications/openflow.

[36] R. Ozdag. Intel Ethernet Switch FM6000 Series - Software Defined Networking. http://www.intel.com/content/dam/www/public/us/en/documents/white-papers/ethernet-switch-fm6000-sdn-paper.pdf.

[37] Pfaff, Ben. P4 Parsing in Open vSwitch. http://p4.org/p4-workshop/.

[38] A. Rajan, S. Gobriel, C. Maciocco, K. Ramia, S. Kapury, A. Singhy, J. Ermanz, V. Gopalakrishnanz, and R. Janaz. Understanding the bottlenecks in virtualizing cellular core network functions. In *Local and Metropolitan Area Networks (LANMAN), 2015 IEEE International Workshop on*, pages 1–6, April 2015.

[39] J. Salim, H. Khosravi, A. Kleen, and A. Kuznetsov. Linux netlink as an ip services protocol. *RFC3549, July*, 13, 2003.

[40] M. Shahbaz, S. Choi, B. Pfaff, C. Kim, N. Feamster, N. McKeown, and J. Rexford. Pisces: A programmable, protocol-independent software switch. *AT&T Research Academic Summit, Bedminster, NJ, USA*, 2016.

[41] R. Sherwood, G. Gibb, K.-K. Yap, G. Appenzeller, M. Casado, N. McKeown, and G. Parulkar. Flowvisor: A network virtualization layer. *OpenFlow Switch Consortium, Tech. Rep*, 2009.

[42] J. M. Smith, D. J. Farber, C. A. Gunter, S. M. Nettles, D. Feldmeier, and W. D. Sincoskie. Switchware: accelerating network evolution (white paper). Technical Report MS-CIS-96-38, CIS Department, University of Pennsylvania, 1996.

[43] H. Song. Protocol-oblivious forwarding: Unleash the power of sdn through a future-proof forwarding plane. In *Proceedings of the second ACM SIGCOMM workshop on Hot topics in software defined networking*, pages 127–132. ACM, 2013.

[44] S. Tabassum, F. Parveen, H.-u. Rashid, et al. Low power high speed ternary content addressable memory design using 8 mosfets and 4 memristors-hybrid structure. In *Electrical and Computer Engineering (ICECE), 2014 International Conference on*, pages 168–171. IEEE, 2014.

[45] D. Tennenhouse, J. Smith, W. Sincoskie, D. Wetherall, and G. Minden. A survey of active network research. *Communications Magazine, IEEE*, 35(1):80–86, Jan 1997.

[46] The P4 Language Consortium. The P4 Language Specification. http://p4.org/spec/.

[47] D. J. Wetherall, J. V. Guttag, and D. L. Tennenhouse. Ants: A toolkit for building and dynamically deploying network protocols. In *Open Architectures and Network Programming, 1998 IEEE*, pages 117–129. IEEE, 1998.

[48] T. Wood, K. Ramakrishnan, J. Hwang, G. Liu, and W. Zhang. Toward a software-based network: integrating software defined networking and network function virtualization. *Network, IEEE*, 29(3):36–41, May 2015.

[49] L. Yang, R. Dantu, T. Anderson, and R. Gopal. Forwarding and control element separation (forces) framework. Technical report, RFC 3746, April, 2004.

[50] M. Yu, A. Wundsam, and M. Raju. Nosix: A lightweight portability layer for the sdn os. *SIGCOMM Comput. Commun. Rev.*, 44(2):28–35, Apr. 2014.

EMPoWER Hybrid Networks: Exploiting Multiple Paths over Wireless and ElectRical Mediums

Sébastien Henri†, Christina Vlachou†, Julien Herzen‡*, Patrick Thiran†
† EPFL, Switzerland ‡ Swisscom, Switzerland
† firstname.lastname@epfl.ch ‡ julien.herzen@swisscom.com

ABSTRACT

Several technologies, such as WiFi, Ethernet and power-line communications (PLC), can be used to build residential and enterprise networks. These technologies often co-exist; most networks use WiFi, and buildings are readily equipped with electrical wires that can offer a capacity up to 1 Gbps with PLC. Yet, current networks do not exploit this rich diversity and often operate far below the available capacity.

We design, implement, and evaluate EMPoWER, a system that exploits simultaneously several potentially-interfering mediums. It operates at layer 2.5, between the MAC and IP layers, and combines routing (to find multiple concurrent routes) and congestion control (to efficiently balance traffic across the routes). To optimize resource utilization and robustness, both components exploit the heterogeneous nature of the network. They are fair and efficient, and they operate only within the local area network, without affecting remote Internet hosts. We demonstrate the performance gains of EMPoWER, by simulations and experiments on a 22-node testbed. We show that PLC/WiFi, benefiting from the diversity offered by wireless and electrical mediums, provides significant throughput gains (up to 10x) and improves coverage, compared to multi-channel WiFi.

Keywords

Hybrid networks; Power-line communications; Multipath routing; Multipath congestion-control; Multi-channel WiFi.

1. INTRODUCTION

Today's residential and enterprise networks often rely on heterogeneous link technologies. WiFi is used nearly everywhere as a means of providing easy access to mobile clients. It is typically completed by wired links that serve as a backbone, provide access to fixed clients, or are used as range-extenders for WiFi. Traditional wired architectures usually rely on Ethernet, but power-line communications (PLC) are becoming increasingly popular as a means of providing wired connections with no additional cabling infrastructure. In fact, as of 2014, more than 100M PLC devices have been sold worldwide, and the branch is expecting a growth of over 30% by 2017.[1] This trend is well embodied in commercial solutions, such as Qualcomm HyFi[2] that proposes products that combine WiFi and PLC. In parallel, significant efforts have been devoted to the development of new standards for hybrid networks. In particular, the IEEE 1905.1 standard [2] was proposed to provide an abstraction layer (between the data link and network layers) that combines several link technologies, which brings numerous benefits: When the technologies do not interfere with each other, it is possible to aggregate their capacity, thus enabling immediate throughput improvements. Moreover, using different technologies such as PLC and WiFi, as opposed to multi-channel WiFi, has the potential for additional performance improvements. With multi-channel WiFi, the medium quality is similar in all channels, even if they are orthogonal, as fading or other channel characteristics have a similar impact in all channels. Thus, link capacities or link failures in different channels are correlated. Combining PLC and WiFi brings spatial and temporal diversity, which enables further performance improvements in terms of throughput, coverage, and reliability. In Section 6, we show that compared to using two non-interfering WiFi channels, using hybrid PLC/WiFi yields significant throughput improvements. Achieving these benefits is not trivial and calls for the careful development of new algorithms.

Despite the commercial success and standardization efforts, there has been little research on how to design such efficient algorithms in practice.[3] Moreover, to the best of our knowledge, there is no published work on the algorithms used in commercial products. In Section 7, we review related work on distributed and centralized algorithms, and on

*Work done while at EPFL.

CoNEXT '16, December 12 - 15, 2016, Irvine, CA, USA

 ISBN 978-1-4503-4292-6/16/12... $15.00

DOI: http://dx.doi.org/10.1145/2999572.2999574

[1] http://www.qca.qualcomm.com/products/qualcomm-powerline

[2] http://www.qca.qualcomm.com/networking/connected-home/hybrid

[3] The IEEE 1905.1 standard and the corresponding *nVoy* certification focus on establishing an abstraction layer, without specifying routing or load-balancing algorithms.

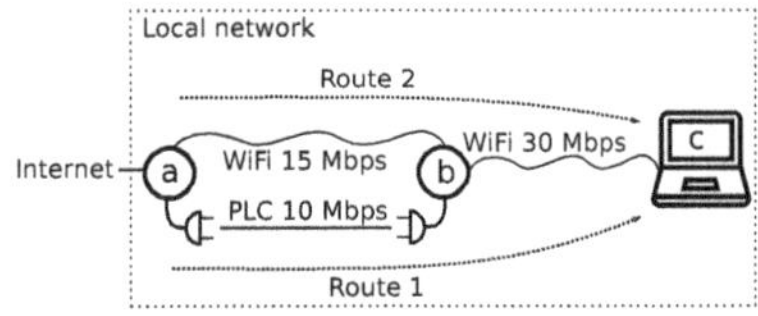

Figure 1: Scenario with a PLC/WiFi gateway (a), a PLC/ WiFi range extender (b), and a WiFi client (c). Optimal load balancing yields 10 Mbps on Route 1 and 6.6 Mbps on Route 2.

hybrid networks. The design of efficient and practical algorithms for hybrid networks raises the following questions:

1. How can these algorithms optimally exploit all mediums?
2. How can they be implemented in practice?
3. Which features of the underlying PHY and MAC layers should and can they take into account?

We propose EMPoWER, a system that includes a *multipath-routing algorithm* and a *congestion-control algorithm*, and that achieves gains close to optimum. EMPoWER is technology independent and can be deployed in any hybrid network, in particular, in PLC/WiFi networks, which are the topic of this paper. Our algorithms are based on existing works designed for a single path in wireless networks or for wired networks. We extend these works to achieve practical multipath-routing and congestion-control with self-interfering technologies. One of the main contributions of our work is the real-world implementation of EMPoWER in a hybrid PLC/WiFi network. We show that combining PLC with WiFi can yield significant performance improvements.

We now describe how we solve the above questions.

Challenge 1: (i) Hybrid algorithms should take interference into account: The absence of interference across different links (e.g., using non-interfering technologies) means that multiplexing gains are possible, whereas the presence of interference can reduce throughput. In both cases, interference needs to be accounted for when choosing the routes and when load-balancing traffic. Similarly to WiFi, PLC links are subject to interference,[4] which therefore needs to be accounted for in different technologies, and not only in wireless links. (ii) For performance to be maximized and technologies to be fully exploited, hybrid algorithms should be able to simultaneously employ multiple paths.

For example, take the network of Figure 1, with a hybrid PLC/WiFi gateway (node a), a PLC/WiFi range extender (node b), and a laptop with WiFi (node c). Node c downloads a file from the Internet (i.e., through a): Because PLC and WiFi do not interfere with each other, 10 Mbps can be sent over the hybrid PLC-WiFi Route 1, as per requirement (i) above. This is what would happen with a typical PLC/WiFi extender, but would consume only $1/3$ of WiFi resources. To maximize throughput, *some* traffic can be sent over the two-hop WiFi Route 2, to meet requirement (ii) above. The amount of traffic needs to be carefully calibrated, as it is

[4]To avoid collisions, IEEE 1901 (the *HomePlug* MAC/PHY standard used by the vast majority of PLC devices) employs a CSMA/CA scheme relatively similar to that of 802.11 [40].

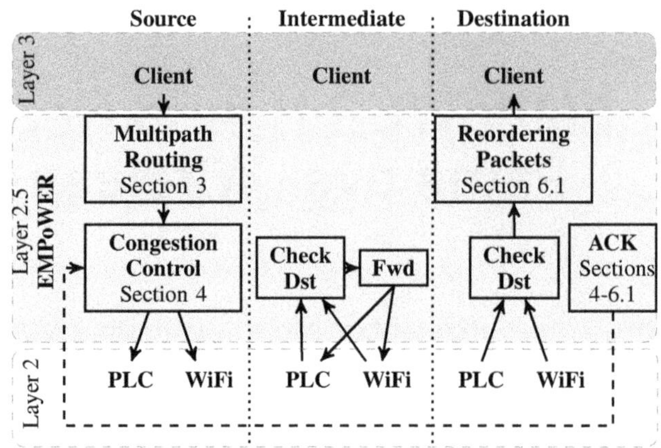

Figure 2: The main components of EMPoWER at layer 2.5. The source determines the routes (Multipath Routing) and the rates at which data is sent on each route (Congestion Control). Congestion control is separated from route selection for the sake of practical implementation. Using the header of our EMPoWER protocol, intermediate nodes simply check whether they are the destination (Check Dst) and, if needed, forward packets to the next hop (Fwd). Finally, the destination reorders the packets based on a sequence number included in their EMPoWER header. Acknowledgements (ACK) are sent by the destination every 100 ms.

well known that saturating multihop paths is inefficient and can lead to congestion collapse with packet losses and instabilities [11, 33]. This amount depends on the characteristics of the two WiFi links $a \to b$ and $b \to c$ (these links cannot transmit simultaneously and need to share the capacity). In this simple case (see Section 4 for general cases), a back-of-the-envelope computation gives us the rate x to send over Route 2 as the solution of $x/15 + x/30 = 2/3$, i.e., $x \simeq 6.6$ Mbps. Hence using both Route 1 and Route 2 provides a 66% improvement, compared to using Route 1 alone. Even in this simple example, optimally balancing traffic is not trivial.

Challenge 2: Algorithms should operate in a distributed fashion, be transparent to other network protocols, and make an optimal use of the network in terms of throughput and fairness among the different flows.

EMPoWER follows a scheme (described in Sections 3 and 4) that maximizes a global utility function. Practical and distributed, it achieves a global performance close to optimal-but-impractical schemes. Practicality is achieved, in particular, by performing congestion control on preselected routes, thus separating routing from congestion control. Figure 2 summarizes the main components of EMPoWER. EMPoWER operates at layer 2.5, between the MAC and IP layers; it is hence confined to the local network and transparent to other IP hosts and protocols. In contrast, solutions such as Multipath TCP (MPTCP) act at layer 4 and target end-to-end paths. Both end-hosts have to handle MPTCP connections. In practice, if a client has only one interface (e.g., the laptop in Figure 1), MPTCP is not supported. We further discuss MPTCP in Section 7. We evaluate the performance of EMPoWER: in Section 5, by simulations; and in Section 6, with an implementation on a testbed with both hybrid PLC/WiFi and multi-channel WiFi.

Challenge 3: Although the algorithms should be oblivious of underlying technologies, they should take into account crucial features of the PHY and MAC layers to make their implementation practical. For instance, link metrics for routing and queue-occupancy measurements for congestion control need to consider recent amendments of communication technologies (e.g., frame aggregation); recent works on WiFi and PLC link-metrics point out this requirement [31, 38]. EMPoWER employs accurate capacity link-metrics that are specific to each technology, making the estimation of link-metrics the only technology-dependent feature. We introduce a network model and a routing algorithm that use only capacities in Sections 2 and 3, and a technology-independent congestion controller in Section 4.

In summary, our contributions are the following:

- A multipath-routing algorithm that finds efficient paths in terms of total throughput. Its goal is to find paths that yield the highest total throughput when used simultaneously. Its novelty is to optimize specifically *total throughput* for *multiple self-interfering technologies.*
- A distributed congestion-control algorithm designed for *multipath use* and *self-interfering technologies*, that performs very close to an optimal, centralized scheduler, with significantly shorter convergence times.
- To the best of our knowledge, *the first published implementation and evaluation of congestion-control and multipath-routing algorithms in hybrid PLC/WiFi networks*, provably improving performance of both single-path and routing without congestion control.
- Evidence that, despite comparable aggregate capacities, *PLC/WiFi can improve throughput and coverage significantly compared to multi-channel WiFi* that has been widely studied and deployed, due to medium diversity.

2. NETWORK MODEL

In this section, we provide some necessary definitions and modeling assumptions. As explained in Section 1, we express our model only in terms of link capacities.

We consider a setting where N nodes compose a local network with K different technologies. This network can be seen as a *multigraph* $G(V, \{E_1, \dots, E_K\})$, where V is the set of nodes, and E_k the set of links available with technology k. A link is present whenever its two endpoints can communicate with nonzero capacity with the corresponding technology. $\mathcal{L}$ is the set of all links ($\mathcal{L} = \cup_k E_k$). For a link $l \in \mathcal{L}$, we write c_l for the capacity of l, and we define $d_l = 1/c_l$. We write I_l for the *interference domain* of link l. It is defined as the set that contains l itself and all the links that cannot transmit simultaneously with l (because doing so would cause a collision at one of the links). A *route* (or, equivalently, a *path*) from a source $s \in V$ to a destination $d \in V$ is a set of links that join (without loop) s to d.

We define the *airtime* μ_l of a link l as the *fraction of time* during which l is active. When a link l is not saturated, we assume that its airtime is given by

$$\mu_l = \frac{x_l}{c_l} = x_l \cdot d_l, \tag{1}$$

where x_l denotes the traffic rate at link l. In Section 3, we show how this formulation can be exploited for finding efficient combinations of paths to be employed simultaneously. Then, in Section 4, we show how expressing interference in terms of the airtimes of the links can yield a simple constraint that can be used for distributed load balancing.

3. MULTIPATH ROUTING

In this section, we present our novel multipath-routing algorithm for hybrid networks. Its purpose is to obtain *combinations of paths* that can be efficiently employed *simultaneously* by a given flow. The multipath procedure is described in Section 3.2. It aims at finding the combination of paths yielding the highest total throughput in the presence of interference, as opposed to procedures that only focus on finding maximally disjoint paths [e.g., 6, 10, 21, 36]: In our protocol, a same link can, and should if useful, be used by several paths. As this multipath procedure is fairly computation-intensive, it needs in order to be practical to be applied on a limited number of paths. These paths are computed by an efficient single-path procedure, described in Section 3.1. This single-path procedure is based on an algorithm for multi-channel wireless networks, proposed by Yang et al. [44].

3.1 Single-Path Procedure

The single-path procedure applies an efficient shortest-path algorithm (e.g., Dijkstra's algorithm, that we use for EMPoWER) on the multigraph. A weight $W(l)$ is assigned to each link. In addition, because contiguous links using the same technology necessarily interfere for both WiFi and PLC, we want to favor paths whose contiguous links use different technologies, which mitigates intra-path interference. Similarly to Yang et al. [44], we add a *channel-switching cost* (CSC). The CSC is an *extra* weight assigned to each node u, equal to $w_s(u)$ when a path switches interface at node u, and to $w_{ns}(u)$ when a path does not switch interface. The weight of a path is the sum of the weights of its links and of the CSCs of its intermediate nodes. Requiring $w_s(u) < w_{ns}(u)$ at each node u favors paths with alternating technologies. To make the CSC compatible with Dijkstra's algorithm, we perform the shortest-path computations on the virtual graph of the network *interfaces* [44].

In EMPoWER, at any link l, we set $W(l) = d_l$ in order to favor the paths of higher capacities; up to a constant factor, d_l is equivalent to the ETT metric [7], used by many schemes [7, 20]. If the weights w_{ns} and w_s can be chosen differently for each path, it is easy to show (see our Tech. Report [15]) that the optimal CSC for adjacent links is $w_{ns} = 0$ and $w_s = -\min(d_{l_i}, d_{l_e})$, with l_i the ingress link and l_e the egress link. But to guarantee that Dijkstra's algorithm converges to the shortest path, w_{ns} and w_s need to be chosen globally for a node and to be non-negative. For these reasons, we choose at any node u, based on the optimal CSC and because a link is more likely to be used in a path if it has high capacity (i.e., small d_l), $w_{ns}(u) = \min_{l \in L(u)} d_l$ and $w_s(u) = 0$, with $L(u)$ the set of egress links for node u. The link-metric W is different from the metric, called IRU, of Yang et al.: Our routing protocol focuses on intra-flow interference (*via* the CSC), whereas IRU also accounts for inter-flow interference. With EMPoWER, the congestion controller is responsible for handling inter-flow interference.

To guarantee that Dijkstra's algorithm returns the shortest path, the link-metric W must be isotone [32], which explains our choices above. Although the single-path procedure is not necessarily optimal, as the shortest path is not always the route with highest throughput, the evaluation in Section 5 nevertheless shows that the procedure succeeds in finding good routes. In addition, we account for this non-optimality in the multipath procedure presented next.

3.2 Finding Efficient Combinations of Paths

We now introduce our novel multipath-routing protocol. We start with a useful lemma that follows from the model described in Section 2.

LEMMA 1. *If λ links $l_1, \dots, l_\lambda$ are all contending for the same medium in a single collision domain ($\forall i, j, I_{l_i} = I_{l_j}$), then the rate R_{max}, defined as the maximum rate simultaneously achievable by each link (i.e., each individual link transmits at rate R_{max}), is given by $R_{max} = \left(\sum_{i=1}^{\lambda} d_{l_i}\right)^{-1}$.*

PROOF. This is equivalent to solving $\sum_{i=1}^{\lambda} \mu_{l_i} = 1$ (all links contend for the same medium) and $\mu_{l_i} c_{l_i} = \mu_{l_1} c_{l_1}$ for all $i \geq 2$ (all links send at same throughput). The solution to this linear problem yields the result. □

We now describe our procedure for finding efficient combinations of hybrid paths. To quantify the effect of employing several paths simultaneously, we define a procedure $\widetilde{G} = \texttt{update}(P, G)$ for a multigraph G and a path P. $\widetilde{G}$ is a view of the multigraph G where the capacities of the links have been updated to reflect the consumption of resources when traffic is sent over P. Let $R(P)$ be the maximum rate achievable (end-to-end) on path P. Once the procedure $\texttt{update}(P, G)$ has been applied, the capacities of all the links in the network $\widetilde{G}$ are the available capacities if P is fully loaded, i.e., if traffic is sent on P at rate $R(P)$. $R(P)$ is the maximal rate supported simultaneously by all the links of the path, and can thus be computed as follows. From Lemma 1, the maximal traffic rate $R(l, P)$ on path P supported by a link $l \in P$ is given by $\left(\sum_{l' \in I_l \cap P} d_{l'}\right)^{-1}$. A traffic rate R is supported by P if and only if $R \leq R(l, P)$ for all $l \in P$, hence $R(P) = \min_{l \in P} R(l, P)$, or, equivalently,

$$R(P) = \left(\max_{l \in P} \sum_{l' \in I_l \cap P} d_{l'}\right)^{-1}.$$

We use (1) to find the airtime of a link $l \in P$ when data is sent on P at rate $R(P)$: $\mu_l = R(P) \cdot d_l$. For each link l of the network, the remaining proportion of idle time when data is

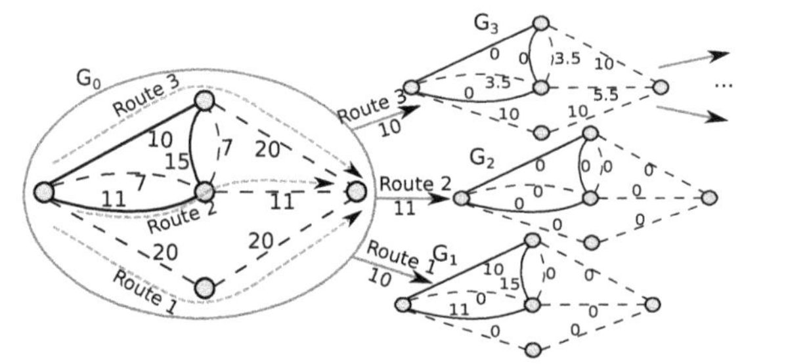

Figure 3: Illustration of the tree construction, with $n = 3$. G_0 consists of two mediums (resp. solid and dashed lines); all links using the same medium interfere. Link capacities are in Mbps. G_1, G_2 and G_3 are multigraphs with capacities updated to reflect the consumption of resources by resp. Routes 1, 2, and 3. Only G_3 has some spare capacity, therefore, the construction process continues only from G_3, after which all links have 0 capacity.

sent on path P at rate $R(P)$ is

$$r(l, P) = \left(1 - \sum_{l' \in I_l \cap P} R(P) \cdot d_{l'}\right).$$

By definition of $R(P)$, for $l \in P$, we have $r(l, P) \geq 0$, and there is at least one link l_0 of P for which $r(l_0, P) = 0$ (namely, the bottleneck link $l_0 = \arg\min_{l \in P} R(l, P)$). The procedure $\texttt{update}$ is then defined as follows.

Procedure $\widetilde{G} = \texttt{update}(P, G)$

For each link $l \in \bigcup_{l' \in P} I_{l'}$, update the capacity by:

$$C_{\widetilde{G}}(l) \leftarrow \max\{0, C_G(l) \cdot r(l, P)\},$$

where $C_G(l)$ denotes the capacity of link l in multigraph G.

The procedure $\texttt{update}$ assumes that when a path P is used, traffic is sent on it at the maximum rate $R(P)$. This choice is optimal for topologies like the typical example of Figure 1. For general networks, this assumption makes the computation much faster, which enables the procedure to be used in practice, while yielding performance very close to optimal-but-impractical schemes (see Section 5.2). To compute efficient combinations of paths, we recursively apply the procedure $\texttt{update}$, along with the single-path procedure of Section 3.1. Observe that the best path is not necessarily part of the best *combination* of paths: Consider for example the network G_0 of Figure 3. Route 2 can accommodate a traffic rate of 11 Mbps, whereas Routes 1 and 3 can both accommodate only 10 Mbps: Route 2 is the best *isolated* route. However, the best *combination* of two routes is given by Routes 1 and 3: With Lemma 1, we compute that they can accommodate together $5 + 10 = 15$ Mbps. To avoid being constrained to always using the best isolated route, we compute in G the n shortest paths of our single-path procedure described above. We denote this step by $n\texttt{-shortest}(G)$. Considering the n shortest paths also enables us to account for the potential non-optimality of the single-path procedure.

To obtain the final combination of paths, we build an *exploration tree* $\mathcal{T}$ in which the root G_0 is the initial multigraph. Each edge represents a path, and each vertex a multigraph with updated link capacities. The tree is built recursively; its construction is illustrated in Figure 3. To a vertex G of $\mathcal{T}$, we add $j \leq n$ edges that are the j non-empty paths $(P_i)_{i \leq j}$ returned by n`-shortest`(G), and j children vertices that are the multigraphs `update`(P_i, G), for which link capacities have been updated to reflect the consumption of resources by P_i. After `update`(P, G), we know that at least one link $l_0 \in P$ has a zero capacity, thus the procedure for building $\mathcal{T}$ eventually terminates; but the depth of $\mathcal{T}$ can, in the worst case, be the total number of links existing in the network, in which case the number of vertices would scale exponentially in the network size. To avoid this problem, the number of paths could be limited by stopping the `update` process along a branch of $\mathcal{T}$, once this branch has reached a certain depth. In practice, this limitation is not necessary for local networks, where paths are limited to a few hops at most. Because we use shared-medium technologies, after a call to `update`, multiple links of the network get a zero-capacity, naturally limiting the depth of $\mathcal{T}$. In our simulations and testbed experiments, the depth of the tree is never more than 3, and almost always equal to 1 or 2.

To each edge P out of a vertex G, we associate a weight equal to the capacity $R(P)$ of P in G. For each leaf G_L, let $\mathcal{B}(G_L)$ be the set of edges (i.e., paths of the network) from G_0 to G_L. Then $C_{\mathcal{B}}(G_L) = \sum_{P \in \mathcal{B}(G_L)} R(P)$ is the total achievable capacity when using simultaneously all the network paths in $\mathcal{B}(G_L)$. The final paths returned by the whole routing procedure are the paths in $\mathcal{B}(G_L^M)$ of maximum associated capacity, i.e., $G_L^M = \arg\max_{\text{leafs } G_L} C_{\mathcal{B}}(G_L)$. With this method, the number of paths returned by the routing algorithm depends on the cardinality of $\mathcal{B}(G_L^M)$. This is a desirable feature, as it means that the number of paths depends on the network topology, and that additional paths are considered only if they provide additional gain.

Note that if we limit our routing protocol to returning only one route, we do *not* necessarily find the route returned by the single-path procedure described in Section 3.1 (see our Tech. Report [15] for an example). In Section 6.3, we show that our multipath-routing protocol performs much better than the single-path procedure. This comes at the cost of an increased complexity. However, our protocol remains practical: On our routers (described in Section 6), with $n = 5$, the routes are computed in about 50 ms. The routing protocol is not responsible for dealing with short-term variability, handled by the congestion controller (described in Section 4); the routes need to be recomputed only when there is a link failure or a large capacity variation, which occurs infrequently (order of minutes or hours), hence this computation time is not an issue in practice.

4. CONGESTION CONTROL

In this section, we assume that the routes for any source-destination pair are known by the source. The congestion-control algorithm decides the amount of traffic to inject over each route. Its goal is to maximize aggregate network utility (i.e., a chosen performance/fairness tradeoff), while avoiding congestion (thus keeping the queues stable). We begin by addressing the single-path case, where there is exactly one route between any source-destination pair. We then present the extension to multiple paths. To the best of our knowledge, this is the first *practical* and *interference-aware* congestion controller using link capacities designed for *multiple paths*.

4.1 Notation and Interference Constraint

We define $\mathcal{F}$ as the set of flows, where each flow is a source-destination pair (and can potentially employ several routes), and $\mathcal{R}$ as the set of all routes (across all flows). With each route $r \in \mathcal{R}$, we associate x_r, the traffic rate that the source of r sends over route r. We define the vector $\boldsymbol{x} = (x_r)_{r \in \mathcal{R}}$. The congestion controller decides the value of x_r for each r.

To avoid congestion, the rate injected on each route should be less than what can be accepted by each intermediate link (each of which might be subject to interference). We quantify this constraint in terms of airtime: From the previous section, the airtime μ_l consumed by an unsaturated link l is given by $\mu_l = d_l \sum_{r: l \in r} x_r$. Hence a sufficient constraint to keep the queues finite is to require that the traffic intensities satisfy

$$\sum_{l' \in I_l} d_{l'} \sum_{r: l' \in r} x_r \leq 1 \quad \forall l \in \mathcal{L}. \tag{2}$$

This requires that the *airtime demand* does not exceed 100% in each interference domain. In practice, when the airtime approaches 1, the delays increase rapidly; for this reason, we might want to place a more conservative constraint

$$\sum_{l' \in I_l} d_{l'} \sum_{r: l' \in r} x_r \leq 1 - \delta \quad \forall l \in \mathcal{L}, \tag{3}$$

with a *constraint margin* δ in $[0, 1]$. Constraints (2) and (3) are conservative: The airtime could be reused by some links of an interference domain if there is no pairwise interference between them. However, (2) and (3) have the crucial advantage of being formulated locally (w.r.t. each link), making it possible to use them for distributed load-balancing optimization; this is the key basis for this formulation of conservative constraints. In Section 5, we study the effect of this conservative policy and compare our scheme with optimal solutions based on perfect centralized scheduling.

4.2 Congestion Control on a Single Path

We consider here that a single route is used by each flow: There is a one-to-one mapping between routes and flows ($\mathcal{F} = \mathcal{R}$). To each route $r \in \mathcal{R}$ we attach an increasing and strictly concave utility function $U_r : \mathbb{R}^+ \to \mathbb{R}^+$; it describes the benefit that the source of r gets by sending traffic at rate x_r. We formulate an optimization problem similar to what was proposed for wired networks [17, 25]. However, because they focus on wired networks, these works do not account for interference. To address this issue, we introduce the more general interference constraint (2), and we replace the constraints on the link *capacities* with constraints on the *airtimes* of the interference domains. The problem then reads

$$\max_{\boldsymbol{x}} \sum_{r\in\mathcal{R}} U_r(x_r) \tag{4}$$

$$\text{subject to} \sum_{l'\in I_l} d_{l'} \sum_{r:l'\in r} x_r \le 1 \qquad \forall l \in \mathcal{L}, \tag{5}$$

$$x_r \ge 0 \qquad \forall r \in \mathcal{R}. \tag{6}$$

Constraints (5) and (6) are linear: The problem is the maximization of a strictly concave function over a convex set. Assuming a slotted time, this yields (see our Tech. Report [15] for computation details) the following controller for the route rates x_r, with auxiliary variables γ_l, y_l, and q_r:

$$y_l[t] = \sum_{l'\in I_l} d_{l'} \sum_{s:l'\in s} x_s[t], \tag{7}$$

$$\gamma_l[t+1] = \left[\gamma_l[t] + \alpha_t(y_l[t]-1)\right]^+, \tag{8}$$

$$q_r[t] = \sum_{l\in r} d_l \sum_{i\in I_l} \gamma_i[t], \tag{9}$$

$$x_r[t+1] = U_r'^{-1}(q_r[t]), \tag{10}$$

with $\alpha_t > 0$ a sequence of step sizes, and $[y]^+ = y$ if $y > 0$ and 0 otherwise. This controller belongs to a class of controllers with linear constraints for which it can be shown [23] that if $\alpha_t \to 0$ as $t \to \infty$, and $\sum_t \alpha_t = \infty$, then the rate allocation vector $[x_r[t], r \in \mathcal{R}]$ converges to the optimal solution of the problem given by (4)-(6). In EMPoWER, we use a fixed *step size* $\alpha_t = \alpha$ in order to continuously adapt to changes in the network. Again, it can be shown [23] that if α is small enough, the rate allocation converges to a small neighborhood of the optimizer of Problem (4)–(6).

Although the optimization objective is computed globally over the sum of all users' utilities, a practical and lightweight controller can be built in a distributed fashion. Each node in the network monitors the traffic that it forwards and measures the airtime demand $d_l \sum_{r:l\in r} x_r$ on each of its egress links l. For each technology $k \in \{1,\ldots,K\}$, the node computes (i) the aggregate airtime demand by summing the airtime demands over all egress links employing k, and (ii) the sum of the dual variables γ_l for each egress link l employing k. The node periodically broadcasts a packet that contains these two values over the medium k. All the nodes in the interference domains of the outgoing links that overhear these broadcasts compute y_l for each of their own outgoing link l of technology k. They do so by adding (i) their own airtime demands for their egress links employing k, and (ii) the airtime demands received by all their neighbors, as described by (7). Knowing y_l, the nodes then update γ_l using (8). Finally, when forwarding a packet on link l, the nodes add the current value of $d_l \sum_{i\in I_l} \gamma_i$ to a dedicated field in the packet's 2.5-layer header (see Section 6 for more details). At the destination of route r, the value of this field is thus equal to q_r (given by (9)), and the destination can send back q_r to the source, via an acknowledgement. Upon reception of q_r, the source updates the rate x_r for route r using (10). This mechanism requires only local measurement and collaboration with a small communication-overhead among the nodes. These properties enable us to implement this algorithm on a real testbed, as described in Section 6.

4.3 Multipath Congestion-Control

We present the extension of our interference-aware congestion controller to multiple paths. We now differentiate between *flows* and *routes*: Each flow can potentially employ several routes. To express the availability of route r to flow f, we write $r \in f$. The flow of route r is denoted by $f(r)$. The utility obtained by each flow f is now given by $U_f(x_f)$ with $x_f = \sum_{r\in f} x_r$. U_f is strictly concave in x_f, but the main challenge comes from the fact that the objective function is *not* strictly concave in $\boldsymbol{x} = (x_r)_{r\in\mathcal{R}}$ anymore. To overcome this problem, we adopt the approach of *proximal optimization*, introduced by Wang et al. [41] when no interference is present, and we maximize another objective function, which has the same optimizer as the original, but is strictly concave in $\boldsymbol{x}$:

$$\max_{\boldsymbol{x},\bar{\boldsymbol{x}}} \sum_{f\in\mathcal{F}} \left(U_f\left(\sum_{r\in f} x_r\right) - \frac{1}{2}\sum_{r\in f}(x_r - \bar{x}_r)^2 \right) \tag{11}$$

$$\text{subject to} \sum_{l'\in I_l} d_{l'} \sum_{r:l'\in r} x_r \le 1, \quad \forall l \in \mathcal{L} \tag{12}$$

$$x_r \ge 0, \quad \forall r \in \mathcal{R},$$

where $\bar{x}_r$ is an auxiliary variable for route r and $\bar{\boldsymbol{x}} = (\bar{x}_r)_{r\in\mathcal{R}}$. Subtracting a quadratic term strictly convex in $\boldsymbol{x}$ in (11) makes the objective function strictly concave in $\boldsymbol{x}$ [41]. The optimization is now performed over the two variables $\boldsymbol{x}$ and $\bar{\boldsymbol{x}}$. The new objective function (11) has the same optimizer $\boldsymbol{x} = \bar{\boldsymbol{x}}$ as the original one (4). We obtain the following discrete-time multipath congestion controller:

$$x_r[t+1] =$$

$$\left[(1-\alpha)x_r[t] + \alpha\left(\bar{x}_r[t] + U'_{f(r)}\left(\sum_{h\in f(r)} x_h[t]\right) - q_r[t]\right)\right]^+$$

$$\bar{x}_r[t+1] = (1-\alpha)\bar{x}_r[t] + \alpha x_r[t],$$

with $y_l[t]$, $\gamma_l[t+1]$, and $q_r[t]$ given by (7), (8), and (9).

Accounting for interference does not change the linearity of (12), and the convergence of this controller can be established using similar techniques as Lin and Shroff [24]. This controller employs the same update rules as the single-path controller for γ_l, y_l, and q_r. In addition, the update rule for x_r depends only on q_r and $\bar{x}_r$. Thus, it can be implemented in a distributed way, exactly as the single-path controller.

This controller is able to account for external interference: Nodes can measure traffic from external nodes and add the corresponding airtimes in (7); however, because it has *no control* over external nodes, EMPoWER converges to the optimal allocation *under this external load*, which means that, except during a short transition phase, non-EMPoWER clients are not affected by EMPoWER clients. Although this allocation does not affect external nodes, it is not necessarily fair: for example, if one external node saturates WiFi, EMPoWER converges to an allocation that never uses WiFi. Extending EMPoWER to support external interference in a fair way is left for future work.

The main downside of this controller is that it takes some time to converge (see Sections 5 and 6). For this reason, it is designed mostly for long-run best-effort flows (e.g., large-file download or video streaming). Yet, in Section 6.3, we show that EMPoWER helps also for short flows.

5. EVALUATION VIA SIMULATIONS

Before validating the performance gains of EMPoWER via testbed experiments, we evaluate its performance via simulations in a controlled environment, over several thousand instances of randomly generated networks. We compare it with other algorithms, including an optimal algorithm based on backpressure, proposed by Neely et al. [27]. Implementing this algorithm would be very challenging, as it includes an optimal NP-hard [13] scheduling algorithm, that (i) requires solving a centralized optimization problem at each time step, and (ii) requires modifying the underlying MAC layer.

5.1 Simulation Settings

We write a packet-level simulator in Matlab.[5]. We simulate two different network topologies. The first topology is a typical residential network: On a 50×30 m rectangle, we drop uniformly at random 10 nodes. 5 nodes have both WiFi and PLC and can typically be PLC/WiFi gateways or extenders, desktop computers, connected televisions, etc.; 5 nodes have only single-channel WiFi and can typically be mobile phones, laptops, etc. The second topology is a typical enterprise network (e.g., company, hospital): On a 100×60 m rectangle, we drop 20 nodes. 10 nodes are PLC/WiFi APs and are randomly located on a 10×10 m grid (values close to what we observe on the managed WiFi network of our building). The remaining nodes have only single-channel WiFi and are placed uniformly at random. In both scenarios, the source of a flow is chosen among the PLC/WiFi nodes, and the destination is chosen among all the nodes, in both cases uniformly at random (we consider that there is no flow between two WiFi-only nodes). Because EMPoWER focuses on long-run applications, such as large-file downloads or video streaming, typically not well supported by moving nodes, we assume all nodes to be static.

A link between two nodes u and v exists if the distance between u and v is smaller than a given connection radius R. Based on measurements from our indoor testbed (see Section 6) and reported in our Tech. Report [15], R is set to 35 m for WiFi, and to 50 m for PLC. Additionally, a PLC link exists only when two nodes are connected to the same *central coordinator* [1], in particular, when two nodes are on the same electrical panel. In our building, we have two electrical panels that distribute power over two equal parts; we assume that buildings of 100×60 m typically employ two panels. Hence, for the enterprise topology, we divide the building area in two equal parts; a PLC link exists only if both nodes are in the same part of the building. The capacities of WiFi and PLC links are then sampled from a distribution close to the capacity distributions measured on our real testbed, reported in our Tech. Report [15]. As previously noted [38], the capacities for WiFi and PLC with the technologies used, respectively 802.11n and HPAV 200,[6] are similar. When employing two non-interfering WiFi channels, we consider that the two channels have the same bandwidth, consequently the same link capacities.

In this section and Section 6, we use the proportional fairness utility function, given by $U_f(x_f) = \log(1 + x_f)$, for each flow f. This metric, extensively used in the literature, quantifies how well an algorithm tunes the "throughput vs. fairness" tradeoff. The underlying MAC scheduling is simulated through a simplified version of CSMA/CA, with perfect sensing and no back-off. Our statistics are computed over 1000 simulation runs with different random seeds, i.e., with different topologies each time.

To quantify separately the gains provided by (i) the use of two different technologies, by (ii) our multipath-routing protocol, and by (iii) the congestion-control algorithm (CC), we evaluate in Sections 5 and 6 several combinations of algorithms and scenarios:

- **EMPoWER** Multipath routing, CC, PLC/WiFi,
- **SP** Single-path routing, CC, PLC/WiFi,
- **MP-WiFi** Multipath routing, CC, single-channel WiFi,
- **SP-WiFi** Single-path routing, CC, single-channel WiFi,
- **MP-mWiFi** Multipath routing, CC, two-channel WiFi,
- **MP-w/o-CC** Multipath routing, no CC, PLC/WiFi,
- **SP-w/o-CC** Single-path routing, no CC, PLC/WiFi,
- **MP-2bp** Naive multipath routing returning two best paths (`2-shortest`), CC, PLC/WiFi.

WiFi is available in each scenario to provide access to mobile clients. SP and SP-WiFi use the single-path routing protocol presented in Section 3.1.[7] When using only WiFi, the CSC is set to 0. EMPoWER, MP-WiFi, MP-mWiFi, and MP-w/o-CC use the multipath-routing protocol presented in Section 3.2. We use $n = 5$ for n-`shortest`, which enables route diversity while limiting the number of possible combinations to be explored.

We then compare EMPoWER with the optimal backpressure algorithm [27].

5.2 Simulation Findings

We consider scenarios with one flow in Sections 5.2.1 and 5.2.2, and with several contending flows in Section 5.2.3.

[5]The source code of our simulator and of our Click implementation described in Section 6 is available at https://c4science.ch/diffusion/1252/empower.git

[6]HPAV 200 is specified by *HomePlug*, the leading alliance in PLC. It offers rates up to 150 Mbps.

[7]We also implemented other single-path procedures employing different metrics, such as IRU [44], ETT [7], and CATT [12]; all gave worse results in our experiments.

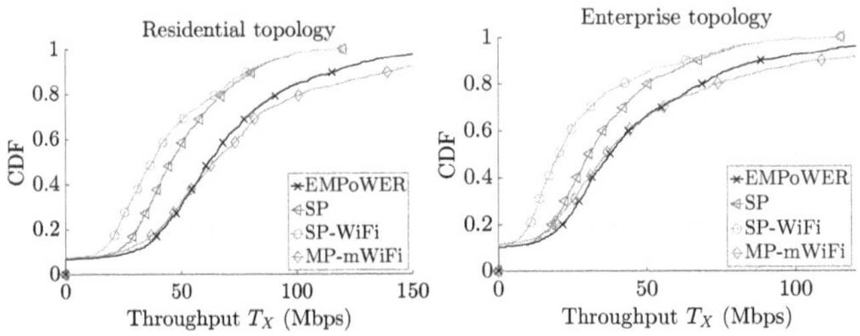

Figure 4: Distribution of T_X for different schemes X. Residential (left) and enterprise (right) topologies.

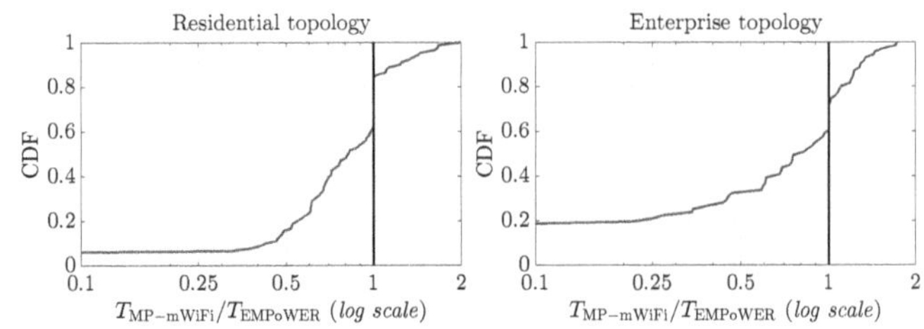

Figure 5: Distribution of $T_{\text{MP-mWiFi}}/T_{\text{EMPoWER}}$, worst flows. Residential (left) and enterprise (right) topologies.

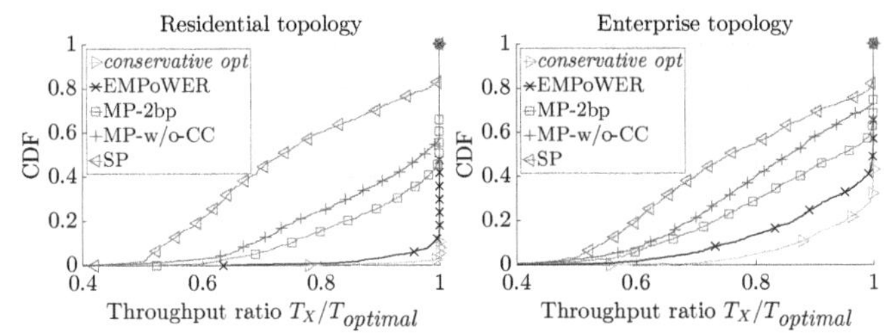

Figure 6: Distribution of $T_X/T_{optimal}$. Residential (left) and enterprise (right) topologies.

5.2.1 Hybrid vs. Single-Technology Networks

We compare the performance of EMPoWER with that of the other schemes. Here, the congestion controller is always used; the only differences are the technologies employed (WiFi with or without PLC), and the number of routes returned by the routing algorithm (one for SP, two for MP). The results are presented in Figure 4, where we show the empirical cumulative distribution of the flow throughput T_X achieved by each scheme X for both residential (left) and enterprise (right) topologies. For the sake of clarity, we do not show the results of MP-WiFi, as they coincide in all cases with those of SP-WiFi: This shows that multipath improves the throughput, only if there are two or more non-interfering technologies. Hybrid networks and multipath routing both contribute significantly to performance gains: In the residential (resp., enterprise) topology, the average gain compared to WiFi alone is 59% (resp., 68%), and it is 39% (resp., 31%) compared to single-path hybrid.

We now compare PLC/WiFi with multi-channel WiFi (two non-interfering channels). Because the two WiFi channels have the same capacities, $T_{\text{MP-mWiFi}} = 2T_{\text{SP-WiFi}}$. Figure 4 shows that on average, EMPoWER and MP-mWiFi are very close. However, it also shows that multi-channel WiFi does better primarily when the throughput is already good (the EMPoWER curve is above the MP-mWiFi curve for small throughput, and below for large throughput). This is because WiFi typically has a greater capacity than PLC at short range [38]. In contrast, PLC/WiFi performs better on flows with outage or poor connectivity. In fact, PLC/WiFi, compared to multi-channel WiFi, improves network coverage. In Figure 5, we present the cumulative distribution of the ratio $T_{\text{MP-mWiFi}}/T_{\text{EMPoWER}}$ for the *worst flows*: We call worst flows the bottom-20% of the flows w.r.t. the minimal throughput $\min(T_{\text{MP-mWiFi}}, T_{\text{EMPoWER}})$. We remove the cases where neither EMPoWER nor MP-mWiFi have connectivity. For the worst flows, EMPoWER performs better than MP-mWiFi, with about 60% of the flows having higher throughput, up to 3x (residential topology) or 4x (enterprise topology); our experiments on a real testbed (see Section 6) even show improvements up to 10x. In some cases (15% to 25%), MP-mWiFi does better, but the maximum throughput improvement over EMPoWER is only 1.7x. For about 6% of the worst flows in the residential topology, 19% in the enterprise topology, PLC/WiFi brings connectivity where multi-channel WiFi does not ($T_{\text{MP-mWiFi}} = 0$ whereas $T_{\text{EMPoWER}} > 0$).

5.2.2 EMPoWER vs. Optimal Schemes

We evaluate the performance of EMPoWER by comparing it with a backpressure scheme, shown to be optimal [27]. EMPoWER differs from the optimum for two reasons: (i) It employs preselected routes, whereas the optimal scheme finds the optimal routes using backpressure, and (ii) it uses the conservative constraint (2). For this reason, we show results of this backpressure scheme in two different scenarios

- with an optimal centralized scheduler yielding the best theoretical throughput. But this is impractical and would not be stably supported by real-world mechanisms such as CSMA/CA. This scheme is denoted by *optimal*.
- with a centralized scheduler giving the optimal result under the condition (2) used by our congestion controller. This scheme is denoted by *conservative opt*.

Comparing *conservative opt* and EMPoWER enables us to evaluate the performance of the multipath-routing protocol, as they both use the constraint (2).

For baselines, we use SP, MP-w/o-CC, and MP-2bp. In Figure 6, we show the empirical cumulative distribution of the ratio $T_X/T_{optimal}$ for different schemes X. EMPoWER achieves results very close to *conservative opt*: In the residential (resp., enterprise) topology, in 98% of the cases (resp., 85%), the performance loss of EMPoWER is less than 10%. This shows that our multipath-routing protocol succeeds in finding good routes. The performance differences with SP and MP-2bp unveil that multipath routing is beneficial, and that finding the good routes is not trivial; in addition, the performance of multipath routing strongly depends on the congestion controller. The penalty of using the condition (2) is not severe in the vast majority of the cases.

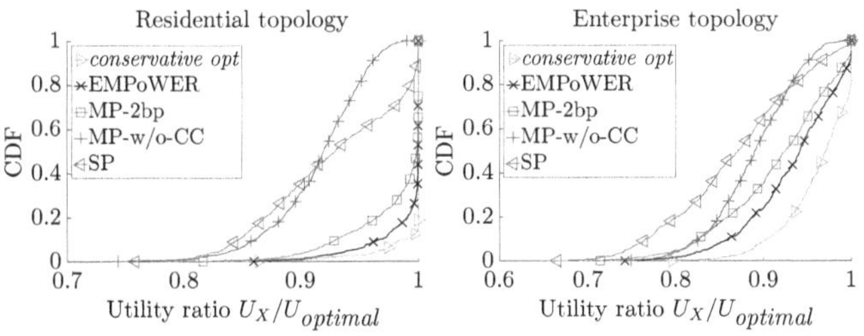

Figure 7: Distribution of $U_X/U_{optimal}$. Residential (left) and enterprise (right) topologies.

In total, in the residential topology, EMPoWER achieves optimal throughput in 88% of the cases, and in 99% of the cases, the performance loss w.r.t. *optimal* is less than 15%. In the enterprise topology, EMPoWER outperforms both SP and MP-2bp; the penalty of using (2) is a bit higher, but EMPoWER still achieves optimality in 60% of the cases, and in 83% of the cases, the performance loss w.r.t. *optimal* is less than 15%. Furthermore, EMPoWER converges drastically faster: In the residential (resp., enterprise) topology, it requires 90 time slots[8] (resp., 77) on average to reach steady-state ("steady" meaning that the throughput is within 1% of the final throughput), whereas *optimal* and *conservative opt* require more than 3 000 time slots (resp., 10 000). In fact, *optimal* and *conservative opt* suffer from symptoms of backpressure-based routing; although they are throughput-optimal at steady-state, good routes are employed only after the queues on the bad routes start to fill up.

5.2.3 Utility Maximization and Proportional Fairness

We now evaluate how EMPoWER distributes network resources among several competing flows. In Figure 7, we show the distribution of the total network utility when there are three different saturated flows between randomly chosen source-destination pairs, as a proportion of the total utility obtained with *optimal*, denoted by $U_{optimal}$. The total utility for a scheme X where each flow $1 \leq f \leq 3$ gets a throughput x_f is given by $U_X = \sum_f \log(1 + x_f)$. Clearly, the gains of employing multiple paths are conditioned on using congestion control. Note that even if our multipath-routing protocol maximizes throughput for a single flow, it also improves performance w.r.t. to MP-2bp when several flows are competing. Due to space constraints, results for the convergence time are not presented here; they are very similar to those of the single-flow case (see our Tech. Report [15]).

Overall, compared to optimal centralized schemes, EMPoWER brings significant gains in convergence and delays, and offers performance close to optimum.

[8]In EMPoWER, a time slot is the interval between two acknowledgements, and it is 100 ms in our implementation; in *optimal*, it is the time between two calls to the centralized scheduler, which causes much higher communication overhead and computation time.

6. EVALUATION ON HYBRID TESTBED

In this section, we evaluate EMPoWER on a real testbed, and demonstrate its practical usability. We first describe our testbed and some implementation details, then we show an example of how EMPoWER works. We then evaluate EMPoWER over a large number of random runs, and finally discuss its interactions with TCP.

6.1 Experimental Settings

We implement EMPoWER on a testbed of 22 nodes spread over an entire floor of an office building (see Figure 8). All the nodes have two WiFi interfaces (Atheros AR9280), and a HomePlug AV PLC interface (QCA 7420) connected to the electrical network of our building. The nodes are APU1D boards running an OpenWrt Linux distribution with the open-source ath9k wireless drivers. The PLC interfaces use a Realtek Ethernet driver. We implement EMPoWER by using the *Click Modular Router* [19] in user space. We use two non-interfering 40 MHz WiFi bands, one from 5.785 GHz to 5.825 GHz (not used by any other WiFi device), which we call Channel 1, and one from 2.412 GHz to 2.452 GHz, which we call Channel 2. To evaluate fairly our algorithm, we avoid external interference: Because Channel 2 is used by the WiFi network of the university, we run all multi-channel WiFi experiments at night, and we verify that there is no external traffic. For hybrid PLC/WiFi experiments, PLC and Channel 1 are used.[9] Link capacities with WiFi and PLC are comparable [15, 38] (the maximum link capacity is about 100 Mbps in both cases), which means that PLC/WiFi and multi-channel WiFi have comparable aggregate capacities.

When launched, the program creates a virtual tun/tap interface that, with a local IP address, can be transparently used by the applications. When a packet is received from the application, our routing protocol replaces the ARP discovery protocol and selects one or two routes. If several routes exist, each packet is sent over route r with a probability proportional to the rate x_r. We employ source routing: Route r is set by the source in a layer 2.5 header that is used by the intermediate nodes to transmit the packets to the next hop. We use short hashes of the interfaces' MAC addresses as identifiers at layer 2.5. In our current implementation, the header has a fixed size of 20 bytes, among which 12 are reserved for the route (2 bytes are used to identify each ingress interface along the route, and the total length is limited to 6 hops). 4 bytes are used to store the variable q_r along route r, as described in Section 4.2. These values are sent back to the source via dedicated acknowledgments, which are sent (at most) 10 times per second, using the best single-path. These acknowledgments use prioritized queues to minimize delays.

The header contains also a 4-byte sequence number, which is used by the destination for reordering packets that arrive from different routes. We do not use timeouts for missing packets. To identify a lost packet (because of chan-

[9]Experiments with PLC and Channel 2 yielded similar results.

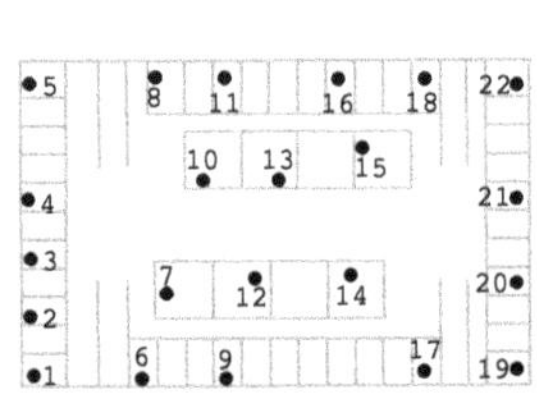

Figure 8: Map of the testbed (65×40 m).

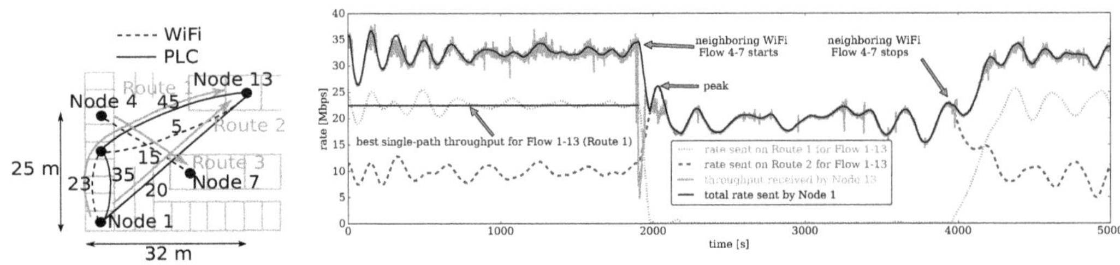

Figure 9: Left: scenario with two flows; the numbers on the figure indicate the measured link capacities in Mbps at the time of the experiment. Right: time evolution of the injected rates and measured throughput on Flow 1.

nel errors or congestion), the destination stores the last sequence number received from each route: A packet with a sequence number S is lost when it has received packets with sequence number greater than S on all routes from a certain source.

The capacities of the links are estimated for UDP traffic, using modulation information inherent in the frame header: the modulation and coding scheme (MCS) index for 802.11n, and the bit loading estimate (BLE) for PLC. In previous work, we show that these two metrics are extremely accurate when traffic is sent at a high rate [38, 39]. When no flow is active, link capacities can be estimated precisely (although not perfectly) by sending probes at a low rate (about 1 kB/s) [38, 39], which yields very low overhead. It reacts to capacity changes in a few seconds. This estimation is sufficient for our routing protocol, as it does not require high precision. The congestion controller requires higher precision, because an overestimated link capacity yields congestion. When a flow is active, the traffic sent on this flow is used for estimating the link capacities. Because traffic is sent at high rate, this estimation is extremely precise, and it is able to detect capacity changes and link failures very rapidly (to the order of hundred of milliseconds). To this end, it is possible to use the acknowledgements described above, sent every 100 ms.

For the value of the congestion controller step size α, we use a simple heuristic based on the observation that, for short paths and single-paths, the congestion controller can support a higher α to converge. α is initially set to 0.02. We multiply α by 2 when there is a single-path or when the longest route is two-hop; and by 4 when the longest route is one-hop. Finally, in order to react to a too large α, we divide α by 2 whenever we find 6 or more non-decreasing oscillations. This heuristic works well in our experiments. We leave the careful investigation of finding the optimal α for future work.

6.2 An Example

We first give an example of how EMPoWER works in practice. In the following, a flow from Node A to Node B will be denoted by Flow A-B. We propose an experiment with two flows, Flow 1-13 and Flow 4-7. The capacities of the links involved are depicted in Figure 9 (left). Our routing algorithm selects, for Flow 1-13, the two routes shown on the figure: Route 1, a two-hop WiFi-PLC route, and Route 2, a single-hop PLC route. Flow 4-7 has a single-hop WiFi route, Route 3. During the first 1950 seconds, we send UDP saturated traffic with `iperf` on Flow 1-13. In Figure 9 (right), we show the traffic rate injected over each of the two routes for Flow 1-13, along with their sum, that is, the total rate sent by Node 1, and with the throughput received at Node 13. We also show the average throughput achievable over the best possible single route (horizontal line), which is Route 1. Our congestion controller uses 100% of the capacity of Route 1. As this consumes only about 50% of the capacity of Route 2, it also injects a rate roughly equal to 50% of the available capacity on this route. Using two routes simultaneously provides an important gain in throughput (about 45% in this example) compared to a single route.

After 1950 seconds, we send UDP saturated traffic on Flow 4-7. Our congestion controller adapts to the situation by offloading all the traffic of Flow 1-13 onto Route 2 and by avoiding altogether WiFi for Flow 1-13 (leaving 100% of the WiFi capacity available to Flow 4-7). After 3950 seconds, we stop the traffic on Flow 4-7. The situation reverts back to what it was during the first 1950 seconds, with throughput gains due to multipath. Overall, the injected traffic rates match the admissible capacities of the routes: Observe the difference between the injected rate and the received throughput; when the injected rate is too large, the variance of the throughput increases (e.g., see the indicated "peak" on Figure 9). Although quite simple, this example shows that EMPoWER finds efficient routes and dynamically load-balances traffic in a way that explicitly accounts for interference.

6.3 Extensive Performance Evaluation

We now show the performance gains EMPoWER yields for an isolated flow, by broadly evaluating it on 50 randomly selected pairs of stations. As opposed to the simulations of Section 5, PHY layer conditions are not ideal: We use a small constraint margin $\delta = 0.05$ in (3). For each experiment, we send UDP saturated traffic with `iperf` during 1000 seconds.

We compare EMPoWER to four different configurations: SP-WiFi, SP, MP-mWiFi, and MP-2bp. For baselines, we show the results on the two single-paths (PLC/WiFi and WiFi-only) obtained with a brute-force approach, i.e., by

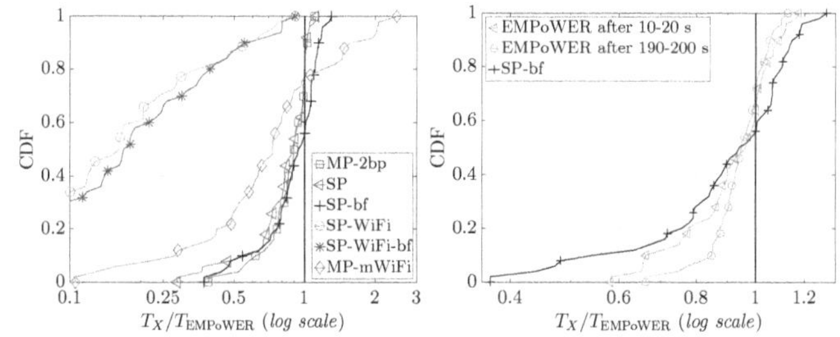

Figure 10: Distribution of T_X/T_{EMPoWER} (log scale).

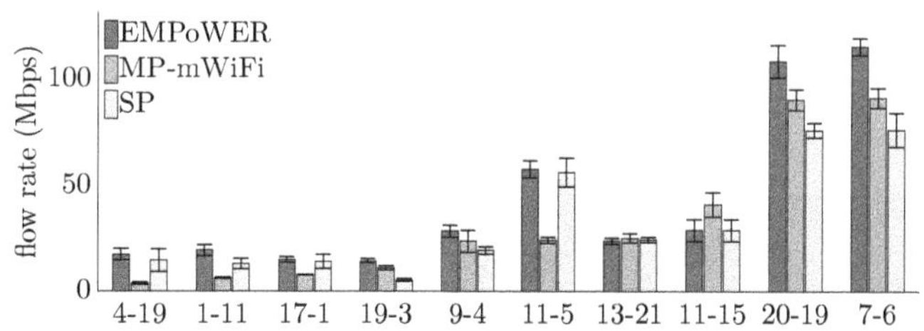

Figure 11: Average rate and standard deviation of throughput measurements during the last 100 seconds for EMPoWER, MP-mWiFi, and SP.

sending rates from 0 to the maximum possible rate with 0.25 MBps increments, and keeping the maximum rate received (denoted by SP-bf and SP-WiFi-bf). We write T_X for the final throughput of the flow for each scheme X (averaged over 10 seconds). In Figure 10 (left), we show the empirical cumulative distribution of the throughput ratio T_X/T_{EMPoWER} over the 50 runs. We make the following observations:

- Hybrid PLC/WiFi naturally yields very high throughput gains compared to single-channel WiFi: SP does much better than SP-WiFi-bf in all cases. This confirms our findings of Section 5, where we see that PLC/WiFi extends coverage by reducing the number of flows with poor connectivity.
- More interestingly, hybrid PLC/WiFi also yields gains much higher than multi-channel WiFi, despite comparable aggregate capacities. In fact, EMPoWER gives better results than MP-mWiFi in 75% of the cases. It yields throughput improvements up to 10x. In a few cases (about 25%), MP-mWiFi does better, but the maximum throughput improvement over EMPoWER is only 2.5x.
- Our multipath-routing algorithm is beneficial: EMPoWER does almost always better than MP-2bp; and in 60% of the cases, it does better than SP-bf, obtained with a brute force approach. In 70% of the cases where EMPoWER does better than SP-bf, it uses two routes; in the remaining 30% cases, our multipath-routing protocol returns only one route, which is better than the one returned by the single-path procedure. In some cases, SP-bf does better, but the difference is less than 30%, whereas EMPoWER can yield an improvement up to 2.7x over SP-bf. EMPoWER does almost always better than SP. SP employs the same route as SP-bf, which means that the difference between EMPoWER and SP-bf does not come from using multiple routes, but only from the constraint margin δ or from slight imprecisions in the link capacity estimations.

We now study the convergence time of EMPoWER. In Figure 10 (right), we plot the average throughput achieved between 10 and 20 s, and between 190 and 200 s, as a proportion of the final throughput T_{EMPoWER}. For a baseline, we plot SP-bf. EMPoWER rapidly reaches a rate close to the final one: In 80% of the cases, it is within 80% of the final rate after 10 s. This is also what we observe in our example of Section 6.2: The oscillations take some time to dampen, but their amplitude is small, and the rate is rapidly close to the final value. After only 10 s, EMPoWER already outperforms the baseline SP-bf. Still, this convergence time is quite long for bursty flows that last only a few seconds, and these flows do not get optimal rates: EMPoWER is designed mostly for long-run best-effort flows. Nevertheless, EMPoWER also improves performance for bursty flows, compared with MP-w/o-CC. To see this, we conduct four experiments: *Tiny*, *Short* and *Long*, where Flow 6-13 is a download of a file of respectively 100 kB, 5 MB and 2 GB, without concurrent traffic; and *Conc*, where Flow 6-13 is a download of a 2 GB file, and Flow 12-8 is a concurrent download of five 5 MB files, with Poisson-distributed starting times (mean 60 s) for the files. Both flows use two two-hop routes: Flow 6-13, PLC-WiFi and PLC-PLC, both through Node 7; and Flow 12-8, WiFi-PLC through Node 7 and WiFi-WiFi through Node 10. Tiny and Short are repeated 40 times, Long and Conc are repeated 10 times; mean value and standard deviation of the download times are shown in Table 1. Clearly, EMPoWER is also beneficial for short flows (Tiny and Short); but without concurrent traffic, improvement is more moderate than for long flows (24-34% vs. 60% improvement).

	EMPoWER	MP-w/o-CC
Tiny, F. 6-13 (100 kB)	0.128 s ± 0.03	0.159 s ± 0.09
Short, F. 6-13 (5 MB)	9.9 s ± 2.1	13.3 s ± 1.9
Long, F. 6-13 (2 GB)	333.2 s ± 27.7	534.5 s ± 12.6
Conc, F. 6-13 (2 GB)	416.8 s ± 30.3	581.0 s ± 61.4
Conc, F. 12-8 (25 MB)	64.9 s ± 6.5	155.2 s ± 24.3

Table 1: Download times for the four experiments.

Finally, in Figure 11, we show the average throughput after convergence for 10 randomly selected flows, along with a bar showing the standard deviation of the throughput measurements during the last 100 seconds (one measurement per second). This enables us to evaluate potential throughput variations due to packet reordering at the destination when using multiple routes. In general, multipath does not cause variations larger than single-path (see e.g., the results for Flows 20-19 and 7-6). The figure also further confirms our findings of Section 5: Compared to multi-channel WiFi, EMPoWER extends coverage by boosting performance especially for flows with poor connectivity (e.g., Flows 4-19

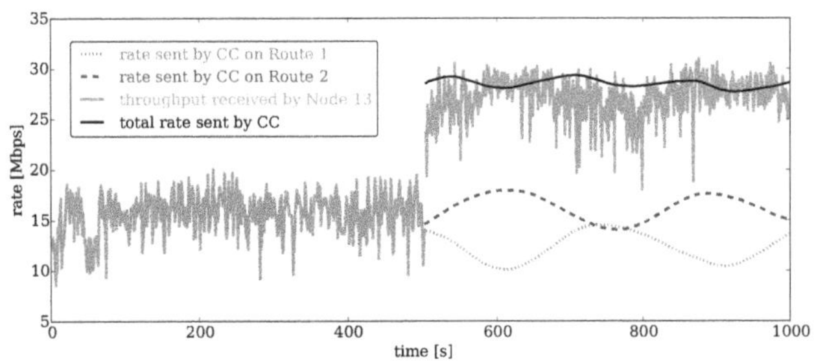

Figure 12: TCP for Flow 9-13. SP-w/o-CC from 0 s to 500 s; EMPoWER from 500 s to 1000 s.

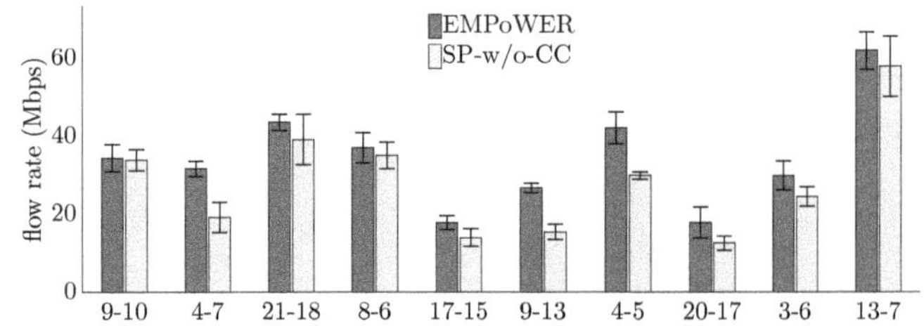

Figure 13: Average TCP rate, with standard deviation.

and 1-11). It also boosts performance for other flows in general, but not always (e.g., not for Flow 11-15), and more moderately so.

6.4 TCP Friendliness

EMPoWER interacts with TCP on two levels: First, TCP reacts to congestion (in an interference-agnostic way) and attempts to ensure fairness. This is already achieved by our congestion controller that drops packets if the rate sent by the above layers goes above the total rate for the flow. TCP will naturally adapt to the rate of our congestion control, because it will perceive the dropped packets as congestion. Because the link capacities are estimated for UDP, and to avoid being in a congested state with possible packet drops and high delays, it is possible to set a non-zero value for the constraint margin δ in (3); we discuss the impact of δ in this section. Second, TCP expects packets to be (i) in order and (ii) within some time-frame. Multipath however does not satisfy these conditions, because different delays can occur on the different routes. Our reordering algorithm addresses issue (i), but not issue (ii), and TCP timeouts might still occur, which would degrade TCP throughput. This takes place typically because one route has delays much smaller than the other one, and packets sent on the fast route timeout while waiting for packets sent on the slow route. To improve performance, we add some delay on the fast route at the destination, so that both routes have approximately the same delays (see our Tech. Report [15] for implementation details). The packets are then reordered. This procedure does not ensure that TCP timeouts do not occur; however, it reduces the number of such events, thus improving the throughput.

In Figure 12, we show how EMPoWER works with TCP for Flow 9-13. Traffic is sent during the first 500 s on Route 2 with TCP alone (SP-w/o-CC); during the next 500 s, our congestion controller is active and both Route 1 and Route 2 are used (EMPoWER). TCP acks are always sent on the best reversed route. Route 1 is a two-hop WiFi-WiFi route through Node 12. Route 2 is a three-hop PLC-PLC-WiFi route through Nodes 6 and 12. This is a "critical" case, as it uses routes of different lengths causing different delays, and both mediums have contending links. Despite this, the received throughput matches the traffic sent by our congestion controller, which means that TCP interacts well with EMPoWER. These results are obtained with $\delta = 0.3$. Results depend on the value of δ; when δ gets smaller, the performance of EMPoWER rapidly degrades, because more packets are lost due to contention. We run EMPoWER on 10 randomly selected flows that use two routes in the multipath case, and compared with single-path TCP, the value $\delta = 0.3$ is found to improve performance in all the cases, with no variance increase in general (see Figure 13).

In a practical scenario with multiple traffic types, only the nodes in the contention domain of a TCP flow should use this value of δ. If a node receives TCP messages, it informs its neighbors by piggybacking this information in the broadcasted price messages (described in Section 4.2): TCP and UDP flows can be handled efficiently at the same time.

7. RELATED WORK

We review related work on general routing and congestion control, multipath, and hybrid networks.

Congestion Control and Routing. From a theoretical point of view, several works propose routing and scheduling, building on the backpressure idea first proposed by Tassiulas and Ephremides [35]. In particular, some works propose utility maximizing schemes for wireless multi-hop networks [e.g., 5, 8, 23]. However, backpressure scheduling is NP-hard [13] and difficult to implement in practice. Furthermore, it would require changing the scheduling algorithm of the MAC layer, which we avoid in order to maintain compatibility with existing devices. These constraints are the basis for works such as *Horizon* [29], an algorithm for balancing the load over several wireless multi-hop paths. *Horizon* is based on backpressure, but simplifies the problem to implement the algorithm on existing 802.11 networks, in particular by separating congestion control from routing, an approach that we also choose in this paper. *Horizon* focuses on single-channel wireless networks and uses queue sizes to identify congestion, which might prove difficult to extend in practice to different technologies: Because of frame-aggregation amendments in both WiFi and PLC, the number of Ethernet packets in a PHY layer frame, as well as the MAC overheads, can vary significantly between technologies and for different links. Using link capacities, we explicitly account for the different interference patterns occurring in hybrid networks. Furthermore, *Horizon* assumes that the paths are fixed and given in advance, whereas we also propose a routing algorithm that discovers efficient combinations of hybrid paths. Neely et al. [27] introduce a combination of flow control, routing and scheduling for hybrid networks; it also relies on a backpressure component. These schemes require a central controller and have not been implemented in real networks. Furthermore, converging to efficient (i.e., nearly utility-optimal) steady states requires large queues and long convergence time.

Congestion control and routing have been well studied in wireless networks. Many works propose routing algorithms for multi-channel ad-hoc wireless networks [e.g., 4, 7, 12, 44], but they do not consider the use of multiple paths. Other works have considered multiple paths for multi-channel wireless networks [e.g., 6, 10, 21, 36, 43], but they merely try to build maximally disjoint paths, whereas it can be more efficient to use a same link for several paths. There is also a large body of work for congestion control in multi-hop networks. EMPoWER borrows concepts from works that study wired networks [17, 25, 41]. In order to be implemented with shared-medium technologies, it extends these concepts to consider interference. Other congestion control algorithms consider interference in multi-channel wireless networks [e.g., 14, 28], but they do not consider multiple paths involving different nodes; and they consider joint congestion control and channel assignment, whereas channel assignment is irrelevant in our hybrid PLC/WiFi networks. Moreover, these schemes are not implemented on a real testbed. The works that consider joint multipath-routing and congestion-control [3, 22, 34, 45] are challenging to implement in practice (in particular, they require centralized decisions and time sychronization) and studied only through simulations. They also include channel assignment. In contrast, EMPoWER is fully distributed, which makes it amenable to implementation on a real testbed.

Multipath TCP. Multipath TCP (MPTCP) has attracted much attention as a means to efficiently spread TCP flows over several paths across the Internet [9]. A typical use case of MPTCP concerns mobile clients that have both a 4G and a WiFi connection to the Internet; promising results have also been obtained in datacenters [30]. MPTCP relies on a window-based multipath congestion-control to efficiently balance traffic and remain fair to TCP [18, 42]. However, MPTCP acts at layer 4 and targets end-to-end paths between end-hosts. As such, it requires both end-hosts to handle MPTCP connections. In addition, MPTCP requires that either end-hosts be multi-homed (i.e., have several network interfaces directly exposing different IP sub-stacks), or that all intermediate routers employ a solution such as equal-cost multipath routing [30], that does not capture the interference phenomena mentioned above. In practice, employing MPTCP means that two endpoints in the Internet have to handle several paths, even if these paths reside only within a local network. Moreover, the endpoints themselves are often not multi-homed (e.g., the laptop client in Figure 1), even though multiple paths exist. For example, in our testbed experiments presented in Section 6, 34% of source-destination pairs (the source playing the role of the gateway, the destination the role of the client) between which multiple paths exist would not support MPTCP, because the interface used by the client is common to the different paths. Finally, very few servers currently support MPTCP (less than 0.1% of the hosts in the Alexa top-1M list [26]). Contrary to MPTCP, EMPoWER acts at layer 2.5; it is therefore confined to the local network and transparent to other Internet hosts and protocols. It can be deployed wherever multiple paths exist, independently of the end-server. In addition, although it works distributively, EMPoWER provably maximizes a global utility function, contrary to any MPTCP-like solution.

PLC and Hybrid Networks. PLC networks and hybrid PLC/WiFi networks have received little attention from the research community, despite their commercial success. A few works explore the gains of introducing PLC in local networks. In previous works [38, 39], we compare WiFi and PLC in terms of coverage and capacity variability, and we introduce capacity estimation metrics and guidelines for PLC and WiFi. Tinnakornsrisuphap et al. [37] compare the coverage and capacity among hybrid WiFi/PLC, standalone WiFi, and standalone PLC networks. The authors show via simulations (employing measurements from actual houses to model PLC capacity, because of the challenging nature of PLC channel modelling) that hybrid networks significantly improve both coverage and capacity, and that the benefits of hybrid networks are high when multi-hop topologies are used. Finally, hybrid networks can also improve reliability by using cross-link replication; this is the basis for DiversiFi [16]. DiversiFi is implemented with multi-channel WiFi; due to medium diversity, such a solution in PLC/WiFi networks could improve further reliability.

8. CONCLUSION

Today's WiFi networks benefit from additional technologies, such as PLC, to eliminate blind spots and to relieve congestion. Although many commercial products combining diverse communication technologies exist on the market, the design and performance of hybrid solutions remain largely unexplored. We introduced EMPoWER: It comprises routing and congestion-control algorithms for exploiting multiple paths in hybrid networks. To fully exploit the gains enabled by the multiple technologies, we rely on a simple interference model that describes how links that employ the same technology share the available capacity. This model enables us to devise a congestion controller that converges to utility-optimal allocations in a distributed fashion. It also enables us to design a new multipath-routing algorithm that computes efficient combinations of paths for simultaneous use. As it is implemented at layer 2.5, EMPoWER can be deployed independently by local networks.

We evaluated EMPoWER by simulations and on a testbed implementation, over WiFi and PLC stations. To the best of our knowledge, this is the first implementation of congestion-control and multipath-routing algorithms in hybrid PLC/WiFi networks. EMPoWER is practical and distributed, and it offers performance close to that of optimal-but-impractical algorithms. We also substantiated the gains of introducing PLC in local networks. In particular, we found that due to medium diversity, hybrid PLC/WiFi improves throughput and coverage compared to multi-channel WiFi.

References

[1] IEEE Standard for Broadband over Power Line Networks: Medium Access Control and Physical Layer Specifications. *IEEE Std 1901-2010*, 2010.

[2] IEEE Standard for a Convergent Digital Home Network for Heterogeneous Technologies. *IEEE Std 1905.1-2013*, 2013.

[3] M. Alicherry, R. Bhatia, and L. E. Li. Joint Channel Assignment and Routing for Throughput Optimization in Multi-radio Wireless Mesh Networks. In *ACM MobiCom*, 2005.

[4] V. C. Borges, D. Pereira, M. Curado, and E. Monteiro. Routing Metric for Interference and Channel Diversity in Multi-Radio Wireless Mesh Networks. In *AdHoc-Now*, 2009.

[5] L. Chen, S. Low, M. Chiang, and J. Doyle. Cross-Layer Congestion Control, Routing and Scheduling Design in Ad Hoc Wireless Networks. In *IEEE INFOCOM*, 2006.

[6] P. Dong, H. Qian, K. Zhou, W. Lu, and S. Lan. A Maximally Radio-disjoint Geographic Multipath Routing Protocol for MANET. *Annals of Telecommunications*, 2015.

[7] R. Draves, J. Padhye, and B. Zill. Routing in Multi-Radio, Multi-Hop Wireless Mesh Networks. In *ACM Mobicom*, 2004.

[8] A. Eryilmaz and R. Srikant. Joint Congestion Control, Routing, and MAC for Stability and Fairness in Wireless Networks. *IEEE Journal on Selected Areas in Communications*, 2006.

[9] A. Ford, C. Raiciu, M. Handley, and O. Bonaventure. TCP Extensions for Multipath Operation with Multiple Addresses, 2013. RFC 6824.

[10] J. J. Gálvez, P. M. Ruiz, and A. F. Skarmeta. Multipath Routing with Spatial Separation in Wireless Multi-hop Networks Without Location Information. *ACM Computer Networks*, 2011.

[11] V. Gambiroza, B. Sadeghi, and E. W. Knightly. End-to-end Performance and Fairness in Multihop Wireless Backhaul Networks. In *ACM Mobicom*, 2004.

[12] M. Genetzakis and V. Siris. A Contention-Aware Routing Metric for Multi-Rate Multi-Radio Mesh Networks. In *IEEE SECON*, 2008.

[13] L. Georgiadis, M. J. Neely, and L. Tassiulas. Resource Allocation and Cross-layer Control in Wireless Networks. *Foundations and Trends in Networking*, 2006.

[14] A. Giannoulis, T. Salonidis, and E. Knightly. Congestion Control and Channel Assignment in Multi-radio Wireless Mesh Networks. In *IEEE SECON*, 2008.

[15] S. Henri, C. Vlachou, J. Herzen, and P. Thiran. EMPoWER Hybrid Networks: Exploiting Multiple Paths over Wireless and ElectRical Mediums. Technical report, Infoscience EPFL, 2016. https://infoscience.epfl.ch/record/221483/files/tech_report.pdf.

[16] R. Kateja, N. Baranasuriya, V. Navda, and V. N. Padmanabhan. DiversiFi: Robust Multi-link Interactive Streaming. In *ACM CoNEXT*, 2015.

[17] F. P. Kelly, A. K. Maulloo, and D. K. Tan. Rate Control for Communication Networks: Shadow Prices, Proportional Fairness and Stability. *Journal of the Operational Research Society*, 1998.

[18] R. Khalili, N. Gast, M. Popovic, U. Upadhyay, and J.-Y. Le Boudec. MPTCP is Not Pareto-optimal: Performance Issues and a Possible Solution. In *ACM CoNEXT*, 2012.

[19] E. Kohler, R. Morris, B. Chen, J. Jannotti, and M. F. Kaashoek. The Click modular router. *ACM Transactions on Computer Systems*, 2000.

[20] P. Kyasanur and N. H. Vaidya. Routing and Link-layer Protocols for Multi-channel Multi-interface Ad-hoc Wireless Networks. *ACM SIGMOBILE Mobile Computing and Communications Review*, 2006.

[21] S. J. Lee and M. Gerla. Split Multipath Routing with Maximally Disjoint Paths in Ad-hoc Networks. In *IEEE ICC*, 2001.

[22] X. Lin and S. Rasool. A Distributed Joint Channel-Assignment, Scheduling and Routing Algorithm for Multi-Channel Ad-Hoc Wireless Networks. In *IEEE Infocom*, 2007.

[23] X. Lin and N. Shroff. Joint Rate Control and Scheduling in Multihop Wireless Networks. In *IEEE CDC*, 2004.

[24] X. Lin and N. Shroff. Utility Maximization for Communication Networks with Multipath Routing. *IEEE Transactions on Automatic Control*, 2006.

[25] S. H. Low and D. E. Lapsley. Optimization Flow Control: Basic Algorithm and Convergence. *IEEE/ACM Transactions on Networking*, 1999.

[26] O. Mehani, R. Holz, S. Ferlin, and R. Boreli. An Early Look at Multipath TCP Deployment in the Wild. In *Workshop on Hot Topics in Planet-Scale Measurement*, 2015.

[27] M. J. Neely, E. Modiano, and C.-P. Li. Fairness and Optimal Stochastic Control for Heterogeneous Networks. *IEEE/ACM Transactions on Networking*, 2008.

[28] A. H. M. Rad et al. Joint Optimal Channel Assignment and Congestion Control for Multi-channel Wireless Mesh Networks. In *IEEE ICC*, 2006.

[29] B. Radunović, C. Gkantsidis, D. Gunawardena, and P. Key. Horizon: Balancing TCP over Multiple Paths in Wireless Mesh Network. In *ACM Mobicom*, 2008.

[30] C. Raiciu, S. Barré, C. Pluntke, A. Greenhalgh, D. Wischik, and M. Handley. Improving Datacenter Performance and Robustness with Multipath TCP. In *ACM SIGCOMM*, 2011.

[31] R. K. Sheshadri and D. Koutsonikolas. Comparison of Routing Metrics in 802.11n Wireless Mesh Networks. In *IEEE INFOCOM*, 2013.

[32] J. Sobrinho. Algebra and Algorithms for QoS Path Computation and Hop-by-Hop Routing in the Internet. 2001.

[33] R. Srikant. *The Mathematics of Internet Congestion Control*. 2004.

[34] W.-H. Tam and Y.-C. Tseng. Joint Multi-Channel Link Layer and Multi-Path Routing Design for Wireless Mesh Networks. In *IEEE INFOCOM*, 2007.

[35] L. Tassiulas and A. Ephremides. Stability Properties of Constrained Queueing Systems and Scheduling Policies for Maximum Throughput in Multihop Radio Networks. *IEEE Transactions on Automatic Control*, 1992.

[36] J. Y. Teo, Y. Ha, and C. K. Tham. Interference-Minimized Multipath Routing with Congestion Control in Wireless Sensor Network for High-Rate Streaming. *IEEE Transactions on Mobile Computing*, 2008.

[37] P. Tinnakornsrisuphap, P. Purkayastha, and B. Mohanty. Coverage and Capacity Analysis of Hybrid Home Networks. In *IEEE ICNC*, 2014.

[38] C. Vlachou, S. Henri, and P. Thiran. Electri-Fi Your Data: Measuring and Combining Power-Line Communications with WiFi. In *ACM IMC*, 2015.

[39] C. Vlachou, S. Henri, and P. Thiran. Electri-Fi Your Data: Measuring and Combining Power-Line Communications with WiFi. Technical report, Infoscience EPFL, 2015. https://infoscience.epfl.ch/record/210617/files/main_1.pdf.

[40] C. Vlachou, J. Herzen, and P. Thiran. Fairness of MAC protocols: IEEE 1901 vs. 802.11. In *IEEE ISPLC*, 2013.

[41] W.-H. Wang, M. Palaniswami, and S. H. Low. Optimal Flow Control and Routing in Multi-path Networks. *Performance Evaluation*, 2003.

[42] D. Wischik, C. Raiciu, A. Greenhalgh, and M. Handley. Design, Implementation and Evaluation of Congestion Control for Multipath TCP. In *USENIX NSDI*, 2011.

[43] B. Yan and H. Gharavi. Multi-path Multi-channel Routing Protocol. In *IEEE International Symposium on Network Computing and Applications*, 2006.

[44] Y. Yang, J. Wang, and R. Kravets. Interference-aware Load Balancing for Multihop Wireless Networks. Technical report, 2005.

[45] L. Zhou, X. Wang, W. Tu, G.-M. Muntean, and B. Geller. Distributed Scheduling Scheme for Video Streaming over Multi-channel Multi-radio Multi-hop Wireless Networks. *IEEE Journal on Selected Areas in Communications*, 2010.

CPRecycle: Recycling Cyclic Prefix for Versatile Interference Mitigation in OFDM based Wireless Systems

Saravana Rathinakumar*, Bozidar Radunovic†, Mahesh K. Marina*
* The University of Edinburgh † Microsoft Research UK

ABSTRACT

OFDM is currently the most popular PHY-layer carrier modulation technique, used in the latest generations of cellular, Wi-Fi and TV standards. OFDM systems use cycle prefix to mitigate inter-symbol interference. However, most of the existing systems over-provision the size of the cycle prefix considering the worst case scenarios which rarely occur. We propose a novel OFDM PHY receiver design, called CPRecycle , that exploits the redundant cycle prefix to reduce the effects of interference from neighboring nodes. CPRecycle is based on the key observation that the starting position of the FFT window within the cyclic prefix at the OFDM receiver does not affect the received signal but can substantially reduce interference from concurrent transmissions. We further develop an algorithm that is able to find the optimal starting position of the FFT window for each subcarrier using a Gaussian kernel density function and a fixed sphere maximum likelihood detector. Through implementation and extensive evaluations using USRP and off-the-shelf IEEE 802.11g transmitters/interferers, we show the effectiveness of CPRecycle in significantly mitigating interference. CPRecycle only requires local modifications at the receiver and does not require changes in standards, making it incrementally deployable.

1. INTRODUCTION

Orthogonal Frequency Division Multiplexing (OFDM) is a spectrally efficient digital modulation method that is at the heart of almost all modern wireless systems. In OFDM, the stream of symbols (that represent the digitally modulated form of user data) are multiplexed over closely spaced sub-carriers and transmitted as parallel sub-streams. Orthogonality of sub-carriers makes them non-interfering with each other and in turn leads to other benefits including robustness to frequency-selective fading, flexible/dynamic channel-aware allocation of sub-carriers to users and ease of spectrum aggregation. For these reasons, Wi-Fi (WLANs based on IEEE 802.11) standards since 802.11a/g have adopted OFDM as the physical layer underlying a CSMA/CA multiple access scheme. 4G LTE mobile networks take this further by incorporating a multiple access scheme called OFDMA that allocates different users to different subsets of subcarriers[1]. The most recent digital audio/video broadcasting standards are also based on OFDM.

In order to maintain orthogonality between consecutive OFDM symbols, an OFDM transmitter adds a cyclic prefix in front of each symbol. This prefix is a copy of the end of each OFDM symbol whose purpose is to maintain orthogonality. The length of the prefix is adjusted to match the worst case delay spread that can occur in any deployment. This value is typically over-provisioned. The first OFDM-based Wi-Fi standard, 802.11a/g, specified 0.8μs long cyclic prefixes which corresponded to a signal path of 240m. Newer versions allowed the cyclic prefix to be halved, which is still hugely over-provisioned, give that the range of most of the Wi-Fi links is only few tens of meters. Similarly, standard LTE cyclic prefix lasts about 5μs and covers a signal path of 1.5 km.

In this paper, we present a novel receiver design called CPRecycle that leverages the over-provisioned cyclic prefix to mitigate the interference from concurrent wireless transmissions. The key observation underlying CPRecycle design is that when the receiver performs FFT with different starting points in the redundant portion of the cyclic prefix, the resulting signal component remains the same across the different FFTs but interference can vary by as much as 40dB, as we demonstrate in our measurements.

The main design challenge is how to find the optimal starting point for the FFT as it depends on the content of the interfering packet and it varies across subcarriers. This is

[1]More precisely, LTE uses OFDMA in the downlink direction. A variant called SC-FDMA is used for the uplink to suit lower cost and battery operated mobile transmitters with non-linear amplifiers.

CoNEXT '16, December 12-15, 2016, Irvine, CA, USA
© 2016 ACM. ISBN 978-1-4503-4292-6/16/12...$15.00
DOI: http://dx.doi.org/10.1145/2999572.2999577

very difficult as we cannot observe the interference signal in isolation. Instead, we create an empirical model of the interference as a function of the starting position of the FFT transformation. We then use this model to perform a maximum likelihood detection using the decoding outputs of all starting positions.

We implement CPRecycle on USRPs. An attractive aspect of CPRecycle is that it is local to the receiver and does not require any modification of the existing protocols nor changes at the transmitter, thus it can work with legacy devices. It is applicable to any OFDM/OFDMA based PHY with overprovisioned cyclic prefix. The computation complexity of CPRecycle can be tuned and it gracefully degrades to a standard OFDM receiver in the worst case.

In our evaluation we show that CPRecycle is useful in two important scenarios. The first scenario, *co-channel interference*, is a common case in real-world Wi-Fi deployments where multiple nodes access the same Wi-Fi channel at the same time. This can cause interference and packet losses, in particular in hidden-node scenarios. In the co-channel interference case we observe up to 15dB reduction in interference through the use of CPRecycle , even in case of the highest modulation rate (64QAM) and lowest coding rate (3/4).

The second important scenario is the adjacent channel interference scenario. All wireless transmitters experience RF leakage and cause interference even outside of their own channel. OFDM is able to maintain orthogonality between carriers only in perfectly synchronized systems, which rarely occurs [46]. In practice, there is a non negligible out-of-band interference and a guard-band is reserved to prevent interference between adjacent channels. We study the performance of CPRecycle interference mitigation in the adjacent channel interference scenario where we remove the guardband and tightly pack channels together. We observe that CPRecycle can remove up to 25dB of interference.

Through extensive simulation and experimental evaluations using USRP and commodity Wi-Fi hardware, we demonstrate the effectiveness of CPRecycle in significantly improving receiver side decoding in presence of interference, thereby also enabling efficient spectrum use. The network level benefits are significant due to the sharp drop in the average number of interfering neighbors in the network. In summary, the key contributions of this paper are:

- We propose CPRecycle , a novel receiver design that improves performance of existing OFDM-based wireless systems through an improved signal processing at the receiver, leveraging commonly overprovisioned OFDM cycle prefixes.
- As a part of CPRecycle , we propose a novel decoding algorithm that improves decoding performance by jointly decoding received signal over multiple FFT window positions.
- In our evaluation we show that we can reduce the effects of co-channel interference on a Wi-Fi receiver by up to 15dB and the effects of adjacent channel interference by up to 25dB by implementing only local modifications at the receiver.

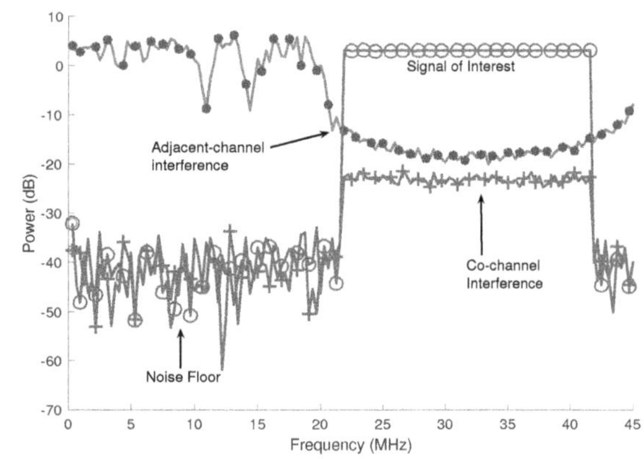

Figure 1: Illustration of Adjacent Channel Interference and Co-channel Interference.

2. BACKGROUND

This sections gives a brief overview of interference in OFDM based systems and the use of cyclic prefix for inter-symbol interference avoidance.

2.1 Interference in OFDM

Adjacent channel interference [9, 10, 34, 49, 58, 59] occurs when an interferer while transmitting in its own channels, leaks part of its power into the adjacent channels, corrupting the signal received by a receiver in those adjacent channels. This can be due to imperfect filters at the transmitters or due to intermodulation of signals. Zubow et al. [59] analyze the effects of adjacent channel interference on 802.11 WLANs and observe that adjacent channel interference causes severe problems with the carrier sensing mechanism in 802.11. It was found that the carrier sensing mechanism can be too restrictive in some cases, leading the node to mistakingly defer its transmission, and too optimistic in some cases resulting in packet losses. An illustration of adjacent channel interference is shown in Fig.1. In this example, the sender is assigned a 20MHz channel (from 24 to 44MHz) in which it transmits the signal of interest. The interferer although assigned an adjacent non-overlapping 20MHz channel (1 to 21MHz in Fig.1) leaks energy into the adjacent band interfering with the signal of interest leading to a drop in SINR by about 15dB.

Another scenario where adjacent channel interference might occur is when two neighboring transmitters use partially overlapping channels, a very common scenario in IEEE 802.11 networks due the limited number of non-overlapping channels. In this scenario, there are three main problems caused due to adjacent channel interference. (i) Incorrect determination of a busy medium: when a transmitter performs carrier sensing before transmitting a packet, it may detect a high energy level due to an interferer leaking energy into its adjacent bands. This leads the transmitter to incorrectly assume that the medium is in use and defer its transmission. (ii) Signal corruption due to power heterogeneity: a weak signal received by a receiver can be corrupted a high power interferer located close by leaking energy into the adjacent bands. (iii) Hidden terminals and exposed terminals that cause signal corruption due to adjacent channel interference cannot be handled through RTS/CTS, since the nodes are operating on a different channel, even though they are overlapping channels. One of the defining features of adjacent channel interference is the effect of interference power heterogeneity. The subcarriers closer to the channels occupied by the interferer are affected by a stronger interfering signal in relative to the other subcarriers, leading to a varying effect in different subcarriers.

Co-channel interference [13,28] occurs when multiple transmitters use the same subset of frequencies for communication. In IEEE 802.11 standards, co-channel interference is mitigated with the use of CSMA/CA, where transmitters would scan for an idle medium before transmissions. However, in dense IEEE 802.11 WLAN deployments, this situation cannot be avoided due to the limited number of non-overlapping channels in the 2.4GHz ISM band and overcrowding [12]. Gummadi et al [17], in their study of the effects of co-channel interference on 802.11 networks show how an interfering signal that is about 1000 times weaker can cause significant packet losses in a WLAN.

The presence of co-channel interference can have other indirect effects on the network performance as well. Using CSMA/CA, 802.11 nodes must scan the medium (for $4\mu s$ for 20MHz channel) and perform a clear channel assessment to determine if the channel is busy before transmission. The clear channel assessment can result in a busy medium when one of two following conditions are satisfied: (i) Carrier Sense – it is able to detect and decode an 802.11 preamble; (ii) Energy Detection – the energy detected in the channel is atleast 20dB greater than the minimum modulation and coding rate sensitivity. In the presence of co-channel interference, the transmitter would perform an exponential back-off which reduces the achievable throughput. Significant improvements in throughput [48] can be achieved by reducing this energy detection threshold.

In cellular networks, the use of femto cells can cause co-channel interference when deployed in a co-channel or hybrid configuration. In these configurations, a macrocell is overlaid with OFDM based femto cells assigned an overlapping set of channels. This can cause co-channel interference between neighboring femto cells sharing the same set of channels (co-tier interference) or between a femto cell and a macro cell (cross-tier interference) [39]. While co-tier interference can be managed through an efficient allocation of subcarriers, it is far more difficult to manage cross-tier interference due to limited availability of the wireless spectrum.

2.2 Cyclic Prefix

In OFDM based systems, the cyclic prefix (CP) or guard interval, illustrated in Fig. 2, is used primarily to prevent inter-symbol interference (ISI). ISI is a type of signal distortion that is caused when consecutively transmitted symbols interfere with each other at the receiver. This is due to the multi-path propagation characteristics of the wireless channel, where a transmitted signal may take multiple paths from the transmitter to the receiver with different propagation delays and the multiple copies of the signal may interfere with itself. The cyclic prefix acts as a guard period between successive OFDM symbols, thereby completely eliminating the ISI. The duration of the cyclic prefix is chosen to be greater than the largest delay spread expected by any user in the target environment. It is usually defined in the communication standards and cannot be changed adaptively based on the environment due to interoperability issues.

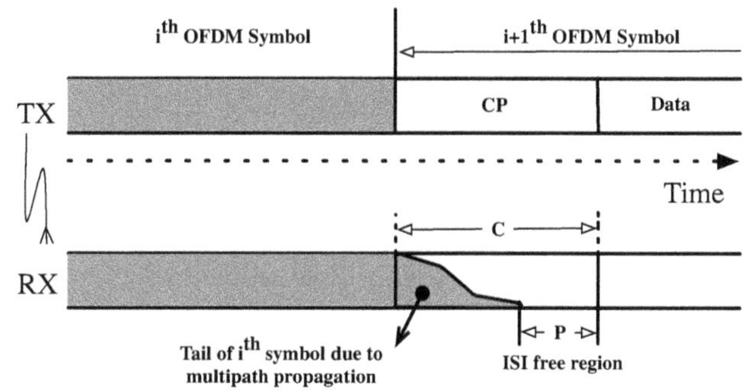

Figure 2: Illustration of Cyclic Prefix (CP) or guard interval.

In practice, cyclic prefix is a copy of a portion of the OFDM symbol towards its end, and it is inserted before the actual OFDM symbol. Because of the way cyclic prefix is constructed, only one symbol from the intended transmitter is received at any point in time during the whole course of duration spanning the cyclic prefix and actual OFDM symbol.

Standard	Bandwidth	FFT Size	CP Size	Duration
802.11a/g	20 MHz	64	16	0.8 μs
802.11n/ac	40 MHz	128	32 (16)	1.6 (0.8) μs
802.11n/ac	80 MHz	256	64 (32)	3.2 (1.6) μs
802.11n/ac	160 MHz	512	128 (64)	6.4 (3.2) μs

Table 1: Cyclic Prefix in 802.11 standards

The downside of using cyclic prefix is that it lowers the spectral efficiency since no additional information is transferred during the cyclic prefix period. Note that cyclic prefix duration is chosen based on the maximum delay spread which can result in substantial portion of the overall symbol period being consumed by the cyclic prefix. For example, in 802.11 systems about 20% of the symbol duration is allocated for the cyclic prefix.

Table 2.2 lists size and duration of cyclic prefix specified in different 802.11 standards with the default long guard interval as well as the short guard interval (in parentheses). In LTE, the normal cyclic prefix length is $4.7\mu s$, an overhead about 7% in a OFDM symbol with actual data portion of about $66.7\mu s$. There is also an extended cyclic prefix of length $16.7\mu s$ specified in LTE for broadcast services and environments with long delay spreads, increasing the cyclic prefix related overhead to 25% in this case.

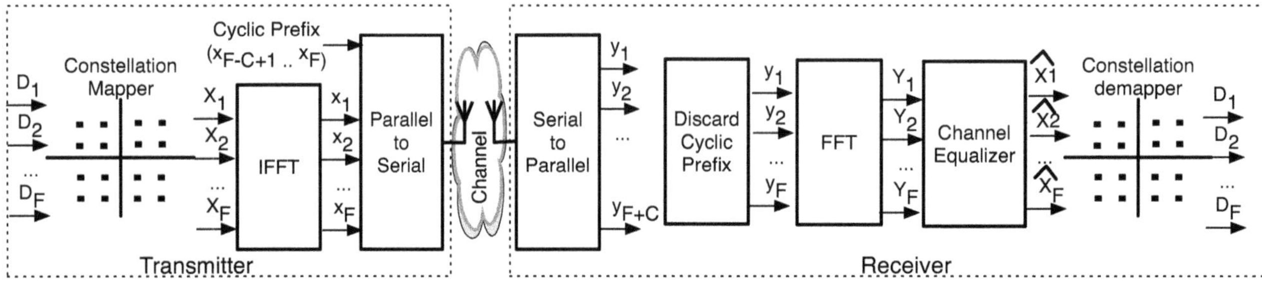

Figure 3: Schematic of a standard OFDM system.

Studies that model the indoor propagation characteristics [18,29,55] of wireless signals, however, show that in most of the cases the multi-path delay spread is in the order of nano-seconds, suggesting that cyclic prefix in practice is usually over-provisioned by a significant amount. In these measurement based studies, the power delay profile, which is the strength of the received signal plotted against time, is used to characterize the multipath channel. The time delay between the multipath arrivals is used to determine the maximum delay spread in the environment, which is in the order of nano-seconds for various environments [18, 29, 55]. Since the inter-symbol interference from an OFDM symbol on the following OFDM symbol is limited to the maximum delay spread, this suggests that the cyclic prefix is over-provisioned significantly in several environments.

Furthermore, the latest standards such as IEEE 802.11n/ac, support wider channel widths of up to 160MHz. With wider channels, as shown in Table 2.2, the duration of the cyclic prefix increases due to the increase in number of subcarriers. However, since the multipath delay spread is independent of the channel width, the number of samples that are unaffected by ISI (which is the portion of over-provisioned cyclic prefix) only increases with channel width.

3. OPPORTUNITIES IN CYCLIC PREFIX

In a standard OFDM system (illustrated in Fig. 3), the receiver discards the cyclic prefix before decoding the OFDM symbol. In this section we discuss the opportunities in retaining the cyclic prefix and using it to improve symbol decoding. We start by analyzing the effect of choosing different FFT windows on an OFDM symbol.

3.1 Sliding FFT Windows

Let us consider a discrete-time OFDM system, illustrated in Fig. 3. The system consists of F subcarriers onto which complex data symbols D_s are modulated using an inverse discrete Fourier transform (IDFT). Let vector

$$X_s = (X_s[0], \cdots, X_s[F-1]) \quad \text{where,} \quad X_s[f] \in \mathcal{L} = \{l_1, l_2, \cdots, l_k\}$$

denote, in frequency domain, a complex vector representing the sth OFDM symbol transmitted by the nth user, and $\mathcal{L}$ denotes the finite set of alphabet from the transmitter's codebook, each corresponding to a lattice point. The time-domain representation of the OFDM symbol s transmitted by the nth user is given by

$$x_s = (x_s[0], \cdots, x_s[F-1])$$

where,

$$x_s[t] = \frac{1}{F} \sum_{f=0}^{F-1} X_s[f] e^{i2\pi ft/F}, \quad 0 \le t < F$$

To eliminate the effects of dispersed channel distortion a cyclic prefix, which is a copy of a portion of the symbol, is prepended to each OFDM symbol. The time-domain signal with a cyclic prefix of size C transmitted by node n can be written as follows,

$$x'_s[t] = x_s[t \bmod F], \qquad -C \le t \le F-1$$

The received signal y_s for OFDM symbol s, contains $F+C$ samples, including the cyclic prefix of C samples. To perform DFT on the received signal, a segment of size F must be chosen with the rest of the C samples disregarded from y_s. Since there are P samples in the cyclic prefix that are not affected by ISI, as shown in Fig.2, there are P valid sampling windows which can be used to decode the data transmitted in symbol s. We refer to each of these P sampling windows as *segments*. After channel equalization, since these P segments are not affected by ISI, the signal received from the jth segment at subcarrier f in OFDM symbol s can be written as,

$$\hat{X}_s^j[f] = \frac{1}{\hat{H}} \sum_{t=0}^{F-1} y_s^i[f] e^{-i2\pi(C-P+j)f/F} + \mathcal{E}_s^i[f] \qquad (1)$$

where, $\hat{H}$ is the estimated channel matrix and $\mathcal{E}_s^i[f]$ is the cumulative noise on that subcarrier from the environment and other interferers.

In the time domain, these different segments correspond to different cyclic shifts of the data transmitted in the OFDM symbol. However, this translates to a frequency dependent phase rotation in the frequency domain which can be com-

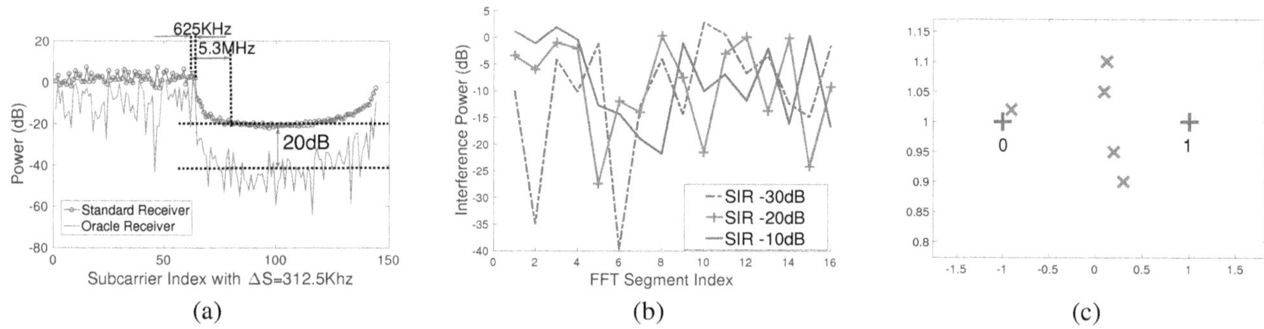

Figure 4: (a) Almost 20dB reduction in interference by choosing best FFT segment for each subcarrier; (b) Interference power in a subcarrier at different FFT segments showing significant variation; (c) Constellation plot showing two lattice points and received signal in 5 FFT segments illustrating problems with a simple metric.

puted (and easily corrected) for the segment j and subcarrier f as,

$$\theta^j[f] = e^{-i2\pi(C-P+j)f/F} \tag{2}$$

Hence, this predictable phase shift can be easily corrected to obtain P copies of the transmitted symbol.

PROPOSITION 3.1. *Choosing different FFT segments of an OFDM symbol does not affect the symbol except for a multiplicative phase shift due to the rotation in the time domain.*

3.2 Opportunities for Interference Mitigation

To understand the effects of interference in different FFT segments, we conduct real life experiments with USRPs and implement the OFDM system illustrated in Fig. 3. We consider the communication between an 802.11g access point and client in the presence of (adjacent/co-channel) interference. The transmitter is assigned a total of 64 subcarriers of 312.5KHz width and the duration of the cyclic prefix is fixed at 0.8 μs with 16 samples. To create a scenario with adjacent channel interference, contiguous subcarriers are assigned to the sender and interferer with 4 subcarriers as guardband in between. The interferer transmits the signal with a temporal offset that is greater than 0.8 μs, the duration of the cyclic prefix to create adjacent channel interference. To create co-channel interference, the interferer is assigned the same set of subcarriers used by the sender.

The key insight from analyzing the interference at the receiver is that the effect of interference varies significantly across the different FFT segments of the same OFDM symbol. For instance, an OFDM symbol received with -20dB SIR, is shown in Fig. 4a. In this scenario, the interferer occupies the subcarriers (68-132) adjacent to the sender (1 to 64) and due to a temporal offset greater than the duration of cyclic prefix, leaks energy into the adjacent bands distorting the sender's signal. The normalized interference power (obtained by muting the sender) at subcarrier 63 as seen by the receiver for different levels of SIR, over all 16 possible FFT segments of an OFDM symbol is shown in Fig.4b. It can be seen that the interference power varies significantly across the FFT segments. For instance, in the presence of adjacent channel interference with -30dB SIR, the interference power varies by almost 40dB, with the lowest at FFT segment 6.

Combining this insight with the fact that these P values for each subcarrier f have the same signal component as stated in Proposition 3.1, but are affected by a different interference component as shown in Eq. 1, it is clear that identifying the best FFT segments for each subcarrier can have significant benefits over discarding the cyclic prefix as done in existing OFDM based wireless systems.

First, minimizing interference power in each subcarrier would reduce the overall effects of interference, enabling signal decoding even in the presence of interference and it can be effective for different types of interference. In the example discussed above in Fig. 4b with SIR -30dB, a standard OFDM receiver would have discarded the cyclic prefix and selected the 16th FFT segment where the interference is almost 35dB stronger than in FFT segment 6. We refer to a scheme identifying the FFT segment yielding the lowest interference power as the Oracle scheme, which assumes perfect knowledge of the interference at the receiver. The interference power in different subcarriers with a standard OFDM receiver and an Oracle receiver are shown in Fig. 4a. The oracle scheme is able to reduce the effects of interference in the channel used by the sender by about 20dB as illustrated.

Second, the sharp spectrum mask realized by choosing the best FFT windows can reduce the number of subcarriers used as guard-band between contiguous bands assigned to neighboring transmitters. This means cognitive users can be allocated frequencies that are much closer to incumbents, improving efficiency of spectrum use. For instance, from Fig. 4a, the spectrum mask realized using the oracle scheme (shown in red) is very sharp compared to the vanilla case of not using any adjacent channel interference mitigation mechanism (shown in blue). And the required guard band is significantly reduced from 5.3MHz to just 625KHz for an adjacent channel interference threshold of about -20dB, enabling efficient use of the spectrum.

However to exploit these opportunities, we need to be able to decode the received symbol in the presence of P redun-

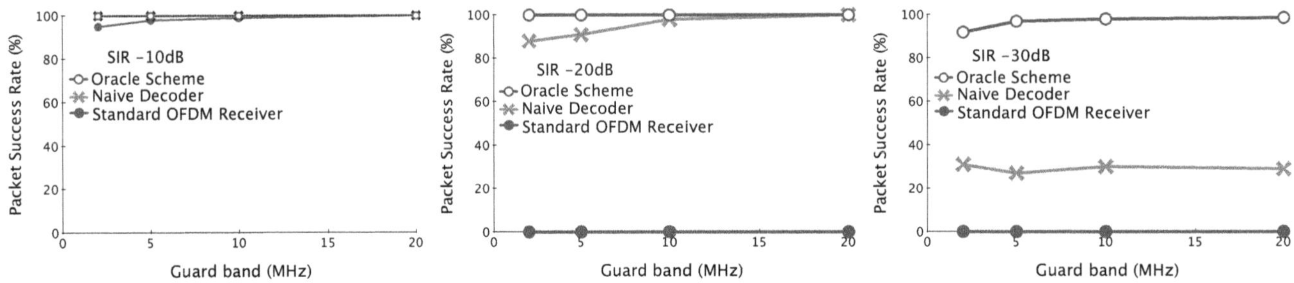

(a) SIR -10dB (b) SIR -20dB (c) SIR -30dB

Figure 5: Packet success rate using Oracle scheme and the naive decoder showing deteriorating performance when interference increases; experiment settings: single adjacent channel interferer, QPSK with 3/4 coding rate, varying guard band and SIR values.

dant copies of the signal and there are several challenges that must be overcome first.

3.3 Challenges with Decoding

It is not practical to possess perfect knowledge of interference at the receiver, without which the FFT segments with the minimum interference power cannot be identified. The Oracle scheme while it provides a clear picture of the opportunities for mitigating interference, is thus impractical.

Using simple statistical metrics to decode OFDM symbols using P redundant copies is not effective and as a result underlying opportunities for mitigating interference may be squandered using them. To understand this, we define a naive decoder to identify the closest lattice point around which the signal received in different FFT segments is scattered. For each subcarrier we compute the average deviation of the received complex vector from the various possible lattice points for the modulation scheme used, over all the FFT segments. Then the lattice point with the minimum average deviation is assumed to be the correct one [38]:

$$l* = \arg\min_{l \in \mathcal{L}} \sum_{i=1}^{P} |\hat{X}_s^i[f] - l| \tag{3}$$

To evaluate the naive decoder, we use USRPs and the same WiFi settings described above for the experiments. We vary the SIR for different modulation schemes and the packet error rates for QPSK modulation is shown in Fig. 5 for different guardband sizes. As expected, the metric performs well at lower interference power. When the SIR is about -10dB, both the Oracle scheme and the naive decoder are able to eliminate the packet errors. However, at SIR -20dB, while the Oracle scheme is able to decode all the packets successfully, using the naive decoder only results in marginal improvements. In the presence of strong interference (with SIR less than -10dB), the shortcomings of the naive decoder are apparent. The performance of the oracle scheme with strong interference shows that there are FFT segments where the received signal can be successfully decoded, however, the naive decoder is unable to find the right lattice points. In analyzing the scenarios where the naive decoder fails, we identify three main sources for these errors.

To illustrate this, we use an example scenario shown in Fig. 4c, with the set of possible lattice points of the transmitted signal (blue plus marker) and the signal received in different FFT segments (red cross marker). For simplicity, we consider only two lattice points (BPSK) and $P = 5$ (five FFT segments are used for decoding). In this instance, the transmitted signal corresponds to lattice point 1, and due to varying interference in different FFT segments, the received signal is scattered around the transmitted lattice point. To illustrate different scenarios where errors occur, we consider that one of the FFT segments suffers from strong interference and the received signal is close to lattice point 0 even though the transmitted signal corresponds to lattice point 1.

The first source of the error is the use of arithmetic mean in the naive decoder to determine the central tendency of the signal received in different FFT segments. It is well known that arithmetic mean is susceptible to outliers making it ineffective either due to a small sample size or if the underlying distribution is skewed. In the example discussed above, the received signal in four of the five FFT segments are closer to lattice point 1. However, due to a single outlier, on an average the five points are closer to lattice point 0 and hence are incorrectly identified. The small number of ISI free FFT segments further increase the proportion of these outliers.

Second the naive decoder assumes that the received signal from different FFT segments are on the correct lattice point. At the receiver, the signal corresponding to a lattice point would have been affected by fading and AWGN noise due to the wireless medium. The constellation decoders work under the assumption that of the received signal with the effects due to fading and noise perfectly removed would be exactly one of the lattice codes. However, this is not true in the presence of interference. With interference affecting each of the FFT segments apart from fading effects and channel noise, the received signal would be at a certain distance from the correct lattice point. In the example discussed above, four of the five points are at a similar distance away from the lattice point. Instead, if the received signal is expected to be at a certain distance from lattice point 1 then the decoder has a better chance of identifying the outlier.

Finally, the naive decoder completely ignores the phase errors due to interference. It only takes into account the amplitude effects of interference by computing the Euclidean distance between the lattice points. Phase noise can be introduced due to the fluctuation of the oscillators in the transmitters and the performance degradation [36, 45, 54] of OFDM systems in the presence of phase noise has been well studied. The example discussed above shows such a case, where the same phase error on the outlier would have a much larger change in the euclidean distance between the outlier and the lattice points.

4. CPRECYCLE

Considering the aforementioned issues with using simple statistical metrics for decoding, we design CPRecycle , a novel OFDM receiver that creates an interference model from the preambles to effectively utilize the opportunities provided by the redundant samples in the cyclic prefix.

4.1 Modeling the effect of interference

In OFDM based systems, the symbols with data is usually preceded by one or more training symbols of known data called preambles for channel estimation and synchronization. These preambles typically use a robust modulation scheme that can be decoded even at low SNR values. In CPRecycle receiver, using the P ISI free segments of each of the preambles, P complex values are generated for each subcarrier with every preamble symbol. These P complex values can be used to create a model of the interference effects. We now discuss the various issues that needs to be addressed in generating such a model.

The first hurdle with using the preambles to generate a model is that the modulation schemes in preambles and the data symbols could be different. Lattice codes are generated by selecting a finite number of points from a two dimensional Euclidean space $\mathcal{R}^n$ depending on the modulation scheme. Hence the received signal in the preambles cannot be directly used to create a model for the data symbols to use. To facilitate this, we compute the variations of the received signal in different FFT segments relative to the lattice point being considered. It can now be applied to a signal corresponding to any lattice point and hence used across different modulation schemes.

Another issue is the limited number of samples that are available to create and use the interference model. Most of the OFDM standards use at most two preambles for channel estimation and in each preamble the maximum number of samples for each subcarrier is the number of samples in the cyclic prefix. Furthermore, since the receiver does not possess any information about the interference, it is not accurate [28] to assume a standard probability distribution (e.g., Gaussian). Hence care has to be taken to design a non-standard probability distribution that works well with a small sample size.

Finally, there is the need to decouple the amplitude and phase effects of interference in different FFT segments, mainly because there is no correlation between them. In scenarios with strong interference, it is reasonable to expect that the interfering signal is carrying data that either amplitude or phase modulated. In such cases too it is beneficial to consider phase errors independently. Also, with amplitude and phase errors decoupled, a weighted function can be used to tune the impact of these errors to improve the accuracy of the interference model.

Based on the issues discussed above, to effectively utilize the opportunities provided by the redundant samples in the cyclic prefix, we need a non-parametric density estimation from the amplitude and phase changes in the different FFT segments that works well with a small sample set.

The simplest method to estimate the probability density of the interference is to use bins of constant or variable width in phase and amplitude and construct a bivariate histogram. However, there are two main problems with using bivariate histograms to model the effect of interference in our context: (i) with a small sample set there are discontinuities in the estimated density due to empty bins; (ii) it assumes that there is no relation between the data in adjacent bins.

So we instead employ a more effective alternative called kernel density functions [40, 42, 47] to generate a non parametric density. Unlike histograms, kernel density functions does not have discontinuities and can produce a smooth distribution with a small sample set. Furthermore, the amplitude and phase changes can be integrated using a bivariate product kernel density function where the weight for amplitude and phase variations can be tuned.

In order to generate a probability density function with the preamble data in each subcarrier, we use a bivariate gaussian product kernel density estimation function with a variable bandwidth. Let $R^j_A[f]$ and $R^j_\phi[f]$ denote the set of amplitude and phase variation values observed on a subcarrier f, $1 \leq j \leq P$, from the preambles, which can be computed as:

$$R^j_A[f] = \mathcal{A}(\hat{X}^j_s[f] - X_s[f]), \quad 1 \leq s \leq N_p, \quad 1 \leq j \leq P$$
$$R^j_\phi[f] = \Phi(\hat{X}^j_s[f] - X_s[f]), \quad 1 \leq s \leq N_p, \quad 1 \leq j \leq P$$

where N_p is the number of preambles used in modeling the interference. Then the probability density function can be written as:

$$f_m(a_{obs}, \phi_{obs}) = \frac{1}{P * N_p} \sum_{j=1}^{P*N_p} \Big[K_a\big(\frac{a_{obs} - R^j_A[f]}{B_a}\big) \times K_\phi\big(\frac{p_{obs} - R^j_\phi[f]}{B_\phi}\big) \Big]$$

where,

$$K_a(a) = \frac{1}{2\pi} e^{-a^2/2} \text{ and } K_\phi(p) = \frac{1}{2\pi} e^{-p^2/2} \tag{4}$$

B_a and B_ϕ are the kernel-bandwidths which are smoothing parameters that determine the range of amplitude and phase over which the sample points are averaged to generate the probability density.

It is well known that the choice of the kernel-bandwidths has a significant impact [21] on the accuracy of density estimation and it is crucial to identify right value. To illus-

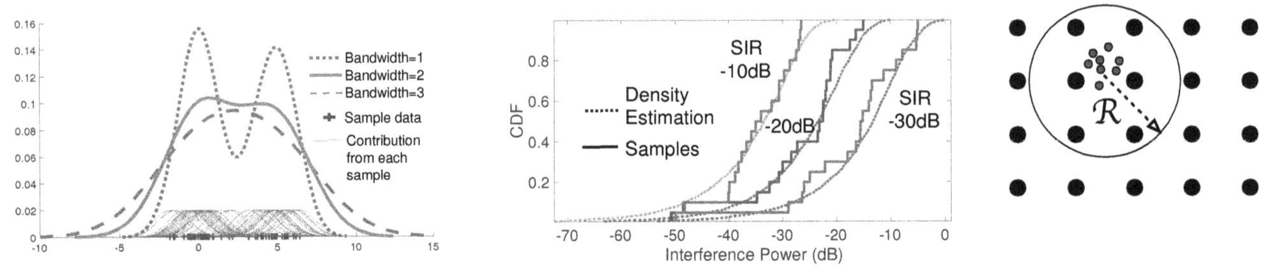

(a) (b) (c)

Figure 6: (a) Kernel density estimation with varying bandwidth; (b) Density estimates and samples of amplitude variations showing accurate modeling for different SIR scenarios; (c) Illustration of lattice points with a sphere of radius $\mathcal{R}$ centered at the centroid of signal received in 7 FFT segments.

trate this consider an example of a set of amplitude variations along with the kernel density function with three different bandwidths shown in Fig. 6(a). Larger bandwidths result in over smoothing of the density estimate and smaller bandwidths introduce large errors between the data points. In general, it is beneficial to have a larger bandwidth at low densities and a smaller bandwidth at high densities of data.

In CPRecycle , we use the data driven approach to determine the best bandwidth which is possible in the presence of at least two preambles. The Gaussian kernel density function shown above generates a smooth bivariate density function and the probability density function is recomputed each time a new set of preambles are received.

The density estimation of amplitude variations and the variations observed in the data symbols, for different SIR values are shown in Fig. 6(b). The kernel density functions accurately predict a density that is applicable for the amplitude variations in the data symbol.

4.2 Maximum likelihood decoding

To decode the received symbols $\hat{X}_s[f]$ to the correct lattice point, we use a maximum likelihood decoder that identifies the lattice point with the maximum probability of the received symbol corresponding to that point. When only one FFT segment is used, the maximum likelihood decoder reduces to a minimum Euclidean distance decoder that identifies the codeword that is closest to the received symbol. However, with CPRecycle receiver, each symbol transmitted on a subcarrier results in P received symbols, one per FFT segment.

Let the transmitted symbols $X_s[f]$ be drawn from a known finite alphabet $\mathbb{L} = \{l_1, l_2, \cdots, l_k\}$ each corresponding to a point in the lattice. The maximum likelihood decoder can be defined as:

$$l^* \triangleq \underset{X_s[f]\in\mathbb{L}}{\operatorname{argmax}} \quad \mathcal{P}(X_s[f]|\hat{X}_s[f]) \tag{5}$$

where

$$\mathcal{P}(X_s[f]|\hat{X}_s[f]) = \prod_{j=1}^{P} \frac{\mathcal{P}(\hat{X}_s^j[f]|X_s[f])}{\mathcal{P}(X_s[f])}$$

where $\mathcal{P}(X_s[f])$ sent is constant and $\mathcal{P}(\hat{X}_s^j[f]|X_s[f])$ can be computed from the probability density function defined in Eq. 4 as follows:

$$\mathcal{P}(\hat{X}_s^j[f]|X_s[f]) = f_{X_s[f]}(\mathcal{A}(\hat{X}_s^j[f]-X_s[f]), \Phi(\hat{X}_s^j[f]-X_s[f]))$$

With higher modulation schemes the search space for the decoder increases exponentially with the number of lattice points (as 2, 4, 16, 64, 256 for BPSK, QPSK, 16QAM, 64QAM, and 256QAM respectively). Hence it is essential to reduce the number of possible lattice points for comparision. In CPRecycle , to select a subset of possible lattice points we use the concept of a fixed sphere decoder.

The concept of a fixed sphere has been shown to be effective [5, 8, 50] to reduce the search space in identifying the closest lattice point. For single antenna receivers, the decoder searches through the lattice points that are located within a sphere of radius $\mathcal{R}$ centered at the received signal. However, a slight variation is required in our case since the decoder receives P signal values from which the lattice points need to be identified, instead of one.

In CPRecycle , to identify the point around which the sphere is centered, we compute the centroid of the cluster of P complex signal values. The centroid is simply the average of the real and imaginary values of all the P values. Only the subset of lattice points that fall in the sphere of radius $\mathcal{R}$ from the centroid of the P samples constitute the search space for the decoder. The choice of lattice points for a sphere decoder is illustrated in Fig. 6(c). In this instance, only the six lattice points that fall within the sphere are considered as possible transmitted codes by the decoder. This significantly reduces the number of operations required in decoding the received symbol.

4.3 Putting It All Together

Algorithm 1 shows the overall procedure followed by CPRecycle receiver from putting the above components together. When CPRecycle receiver receives a preamble, it computes the number of ISI free samples in the CP to determine P. The P segments in the preamble are used to generate a unique probability density function for each subcarrier. These prob-

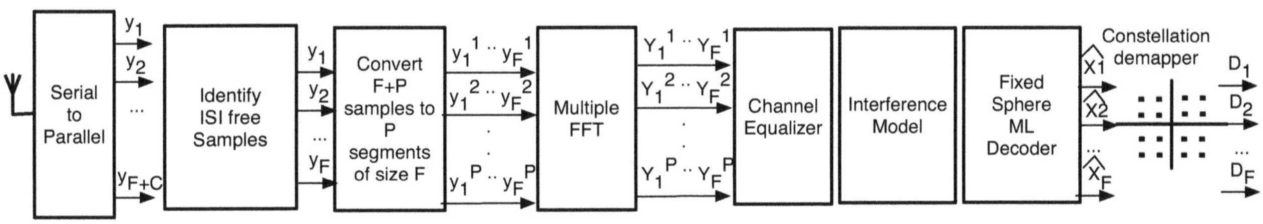

Figure 7: Block diagram of CPRecycle receiver as implemented.

ability density functions are constantly updated when subsequent preambles are received. Once the interference is modeled, the subsequent OFDM symbols are decoded using the maximum likelihood decoder. The set of lattice points over which the maximum likelihood detector searches for the transmitted symbol is computed using the radius R which is an input parameter to the CPRecycle receiver.

Algorithm 1 CPRecycle Receiver

procedure CPRECYCLE(B_a,B_ϕ,$\mathcal{R}$,$\hat{X}_s$,P)
  if OFDM Symbol s is a preamble **then**
    for each segment $j \in \{1, 2, \cdots, P\}$ **do**
      $Y_s^j = FFT(y_s^j)$
      $R_A^j[f] = \mathcal{A}(Y_s^j[f] - X_s[f])\,, \forall f \in \mathcal{F}$
      $R_\Phi^j[f] = \Phi(Y_s^j[f] - X_s[f])\,, \forall f \in \mathcal{F}$
    end for
  else
    for each subcarrier $f \in \mathcal{F}$ **do**
      $L^c \subset L$ s.t. $\forall l \in L$
      $l \in L^c$ if $\mathcal{A}(l - \text{Centroid}(\hat{X}_s[f])) < \mathcal{R}$
      $X_s[f] = \underset{l \in \mathbb{L}^c}{\text{argmax}} \;\; \mathcal{P}(l|\hat{X}_s[f])$
    end for
  end if
end procedure

Note that from the above description it is clear that CPRecycle receiver does not need to explicitly know the precise nature of interference (e.g., adjacent channel interference, co-channel interference). It can leverage the preambles used for channel estimation. The effectiveness of CPRecycle relies on the extent to which channel and interference characteristics seen from a preamble apply to the subsequent OFDM symbols with data. For rapidly varying or sporadic interference, more frequent preambles are needed to accurately model the interference.

5. EXPERIMENTAL EVALUATION

In this section, we experimentally evaluate the effectiveness of CPRecycle in mitigating different types of interference that can be mapped to practical scenarios.

5.1 Implementation

We have implemented a prototype of the CPRecycle receiver using the USRP radio platform [11], Ziria [44] an SDR programming environment, and the GNU Radio software package [3].

CPRecycle Receiver: We implement two variants of the CPRecycle receiver to run on the USRP: (i) IEEE 802.11g receiver (ii) A generic configurable OFDM baseband receiver. For the IEEE 802.11g receiver, we modify the GNU Radio based receiver [3] as shown in Fig. 7. Instead of discarding the CP, the ISI free portion of the CP is used to generate P segments that are then passed on to the FFT block to generate P values for each subcarrier corresponding to the signal transmitted on an individual subcarrier. The maximum likelihood decoder then detects the signal transmitted on the subcarrier using the interference model generated with the preambles for each subcarrier.

IEEE 802.11g Setting : The CPRecycle receiver is applicable to IEEE 802.11a/g/n radios which are based on an OFDM PHY. For our experiments we use an off-the-shelf 802.11g Linksys access point running tomato firmware. Each 20MHz channel is composed of 64 subcarriers, spaced 312.5 KHz apart, of which 52 subcarriers are used for data and 4 subcarriers for pilots. Each OFDM symbol has a duration of 4μsec. and each data payload is preceded by a long training field that contains two OFDM symbols for a duration of 8μsec, to enable synchronization and channel estimation. The variation of the signal in different segments in this long training field is used to create the interference model. For our experiments, we choose three MCS modes, QPSK 1/2 (9 Mbps), 16-QAM 1/2 (24 Mbps), and 64-QAM 2/3 (36 Mbps).

5.2 Results

We now evaluate the performance of CPRecycle in the presence of adjacent channel interference and co-channel interference.

5.2.1 *Adjacent Channel Interference*

Single Interferer. For the adjacent channel interference case, we use an off-the-shelf 802.11g access point (Linksys) that continuously transmits 400 byte packets, in channel 11 (2462MHz). To generate interference, we use a USRP (B210) to continuously transmit 802.11 traffic in an overlapping channel, in this case channel 8 (2447MHz). A CPRecycle receiver running on another USRP B210, that is capable of decoding 802.11g packets is placed in a fixed location. To choose the appropriate SNR for each MCS, the Linksys router is re-positioned from the receiver until that MCS mode has the highest throughput. Once the SNR for the MCS mode is fixed, the SIR is varied by moving the interferer that generates 802.11 packets in the adjacent channel. We transmit a total of 2000 packets for each scenario and the average values for packet success rate is shown in Fig. 8.

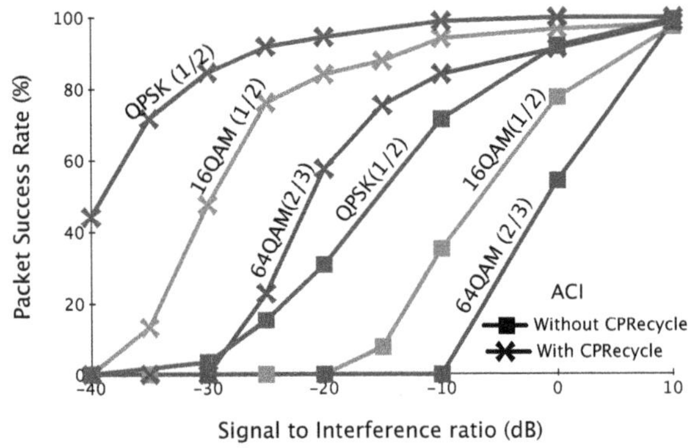

Figure 8: Packet success rates for different modulation and coding schemes with one adjacent channel interferer

The severity of the effect of adjacent channel interference on the packet success rates can be seen from the figures. At an SIR value of 0dB, where the power of the signal and the interference is the same, the success rates of packet delivery drops significantly for all MCS modes. Being the highest rate, 64QAM suffers almost 50% packet loss and is unable to transmit a packet when SIR is -10dB. This effect is slightly less pronounced for the lower modulation schemes such as QPSK, however, the increase in packet loss rate with SIR is still steep, and becomes unusable when SIR decreases to 10dB.

With the CPRecycle receiver, the packet success rates are significantly improved for all the MCS schemes with similar packet success rates achieved with atleast 15dB of adjacent channel interference and in several cases upto 25dB of adjacent channel interference for lower modulation schemes. Considering the packet success rates at -10dB, for example, it can be observed that for all MCS modes the improvement in packet success rates is significant and with higher modulation schemes communication is made possible (with almost 80% packet delivery rate) that would not have otherwise been possible without CPRecycle receiver.

Multiple Interferers. The effect of two interferers creating adjacent channel interference on either side of the channel allocated to a transmitter is shown in Fig. 9. For this experiment, the Linksys access point is allocated channel 10 (2457MHz) and the interferers are allocated channels 7 (2442MHz) and 13 (2472MHz) respectively. This is a common scenario in dense deployments of WLANs where overlapping channels has to be allocated to neighboring access points. The packet success rates is noticeably lower for all the modulation schemes, since the number of subcarriers that are affected by adjacent channel interference is almost doubled. However since the interference model is maintained independently per subcarrier, it does not have a significant impact on the performance of the CPRecycle receiver. For example, when the SIR is -10dB, CPRecycle is able to decode more than 80% of the packets successfully in most of the cases.

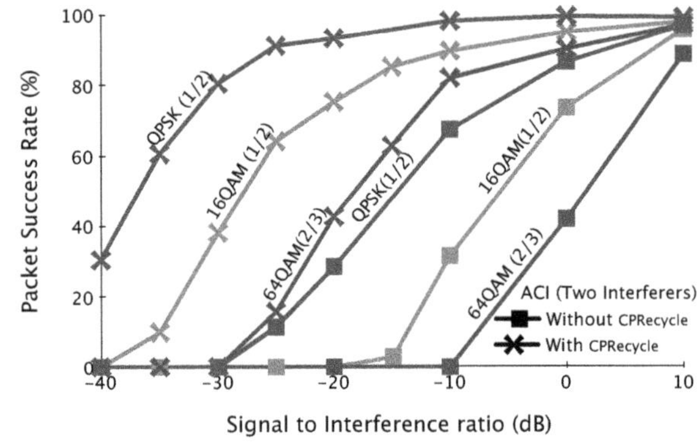

Figure 9: Packet success rates with two adjacent channel interferers

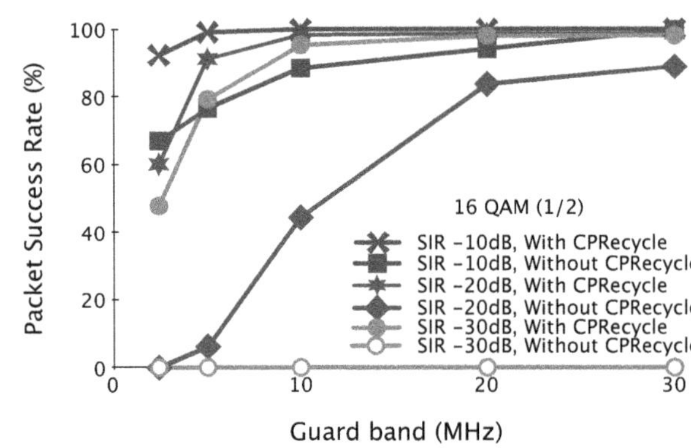

Figure 10: Packet success rates with varying guardband sizes with adjacent legacy transmitter

Guard band needed with adjacent legacy OFDM transmitter. The effect of adjacent channel interference with different sizes of guard-bands for 16QAM is shown in Fig. 10 respectively. For this experiment, the set of subcarriers assigned for the first transmitter is fixed and the set of contiguous subcarriers assigned to the second transmitter is varied to generate settings with different guard-bands between the two transmitters. It can be observed that with CPRecycle the amount of guard-bands required to achieve the same packet success rates is significantly lower for both the modulation schemes. This shows that with CPRecycle , a cognitive radio can be allocated frequencies much closer to a licensed band achieving a significantly more efficient use of the wireless spectrum. For example, considering the case with 16QAM, if a cognitive user is allocated a cluster of subcarriers adjacent to a licensed TV transmitter, whose signal is 10 times stronger, then the required guard-band would be reduced from about 15MHz to less than 5MHz to achieve a similar packet success rate.

5.2.2 *Co-Channel Interference*

Single Interferer. To generate co-channel interference, we use a setup that is similar to the adjacent channel interference scenario, except, we use a USRP 802.11 transmitter. This is so clear channel assessment can be turned off to enable simultaneous use of the same channel by both the transmitter and the interferer. Similar to the adjacent channel interference case, the SNR for each MCS mode is chosen such that any higher modulation scheme would result in a lower throughput. In total, 2000 packets of size 400 bytes, are transmitted for each scenario for each MCS mode and a given SIR setting, and the average packet success rates are computed. The results are shown in Fig. 11.

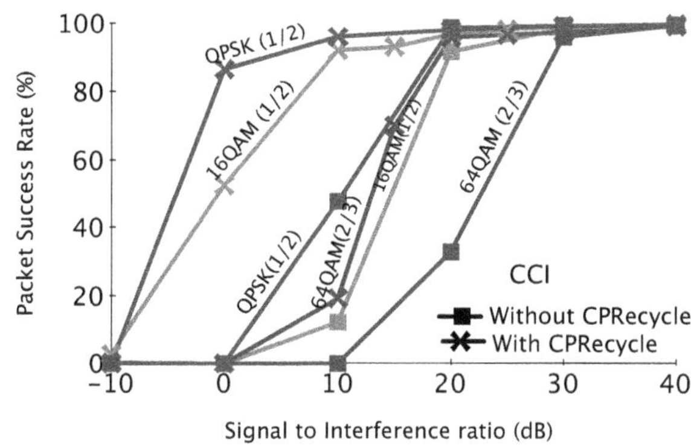

Figure 11: Packet success rates for different modulation and coding schemes with single co-channel interferer

As expected, the effect of co-channel interference on 802.11 WLANs is far more severe than adjacent channel interference, which is evident from the figures. Even with SIR 10dB, when the signal of interest is three times stronger than the interference, the packet reception rate drops steeply for all the MCS schemes. This is mainly due to two reasons. (i) Unlike adjacent channel interference, the co-channel interference is in-band. (ii) The number of subcarriers affected by interference is much higher in the co-channel interference scenario. In most cases all the subcarriers used by the transmitter is affected by strong interference.

Another observation is the steepness of the drop in packet reception rates with increasing co-channel interference. The range of co-channel interference tolerated by both with and without CPRecycle receiver is about 15dB in most cases, where as it was about 30dB of adjacent channel interference for most MCS modes. This is mainly due to the significantly higher number of subcarrier affected by interference when compared to adjacent channel interference. However, CPRecycle is able to recover most of these errors since it maintains a separate interference model for each subcarrier from the preamble data.

Multiple Interferers. The effect of multiple co-channel interferers is shown in Fig.12. For this experiment, we setup an 802.11 transmitter with carrier sensing disabled, and two interferers in the same channel, placed at the same distance from the transmitter. The SNR is chosen for each MCS mode

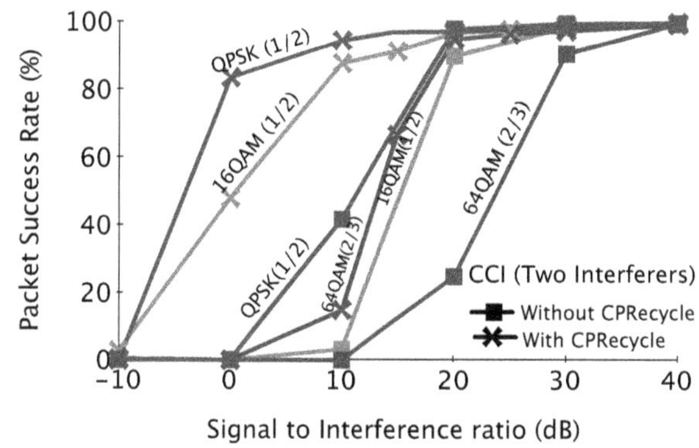

Figure 12: Packet success rates with two co-channel interferers

similar to the other experiments. The SIR is varied by increasing the transmit power in both the interferers. It can be observed that unlike in the case of adjacent channel interference, co-channel interference does not have a significant impact on packet reception. This can be attributed to the fact that the number of subcarriers affected by the higher number of interferers does not change where as it almost doubles in the case of adjacent channel interference. The improvement in packet success rate with CPRecycle is again significant even though the variance of interference is presumably higher with more interferers, while the total power of the interference remains the same. This is primarily due to the nature of the interference model that considers both amplitude and phase changes in the interference to generate the probabilistic model for each subcarrier.

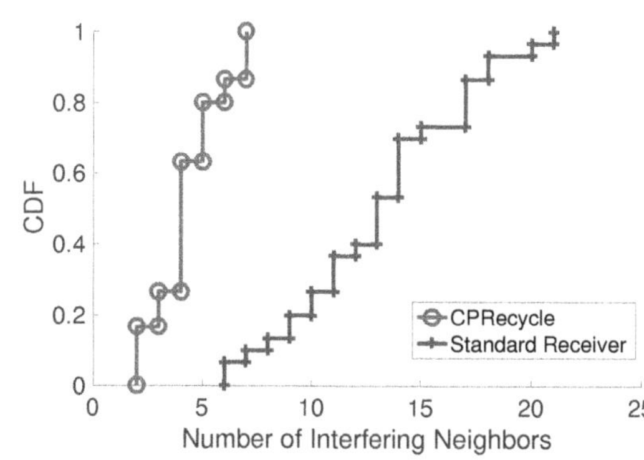

Figure 13: CDF of number of interfering neighbors for access points in a real office environment with and without CPRecycle receiver.

Network Level Improvements. While it is clear that CPRecycle can decode signals even in the presence of strong interference, the network level benefits of this are not obvious. To highlight this, we plot the CDF of number of interfering neighbors for access points in a real indoor office environment shown in Fig.13. From Fig.11, it is evident that with the CPRecycle receiver, the level of co-channel interference that can be tolerated is atleast 15dB for all the MCS modes. This is a direct measure of the increase in energy detection threshold that the CPRecycle receiver would be able to tolerate without additional packet errors.

We consider our office building [32] which has five floors with a large atirum and most of the walls are made of glass. There are 40 access points deployed in the building with mostly the same place for access points in each floor. We measure the signal strength of access points that can be detected at each of these locations and determine the number of neighbors for the access points by reducing the threshold by 15dB derived from Fig.11. It can be seen that the number of neighbors with CPRecycle is significantly reduced. For instance, with a standard receiver, more than 80% of access points have atleast 12 interfering neighbors where as with CPRecycle more than 80% of the access points have utmost 6 neighbors. This shows how CPRecycle can significantly improve the network capacity of a dense WLAN by reducing the potential interferers in the network.

6. DISCUSSION

Detecting ISI free portion of CP : Several methods [4, 37, 43, 57] have been proposed in the literature for the detection of ISI-free region in the cyclic prefix. In each of these schemes a correlation coefficient is computed between samples in a given window and a threshold is used to estimate the range of ISI free samples in the CP.

The effect of the duration of the ISI free region over the performance of CPRecycle is shown in Fig. 14, where the number of FFT segments represents the duration of the ISI free region. A key observation here is that even when a significant portion (about 60%) of the cyclic prefix is affected by ISI, CPRecycle is able recover a significant percentage of the erroneous packets. This suggests that CPRecycle can even be used in multipath environments with a significant delay spread.

Computational Complexity and Oversampling: The computational complexity of CPRecycle is O(PN_p^2f), where P is the number of ISI free samples in the CP, N_p is the number of preambles and f is the number of subcarriers. Since the number of preambles is not a configurable parameter, we study the effect of P, the number of samples. We conduct experiments for the ACI scenario with varying number of FFT samples, with five preambles to observe the behavior of CPRecycle .

The packet success rate for three different SIR conditions with 16QAM modulation is shown in Fig. 14. An interesting behavior we observe with the number of FFT segments is that, the benefits of the increasing the number of FFT segments for interference modeling saturates when P reaches about 60% of the samples even at very high interference (SIR -30dB). With lower levels of interference, even 20% of the CP is enough to reduce the packet error rates significantly. There are two advantages to this behavior with CPRecycle : (i) scenarios with high multi-path delays where the number of ISI free samples in the CP is limited, can still make use of CPRecycle to improve the performance of the

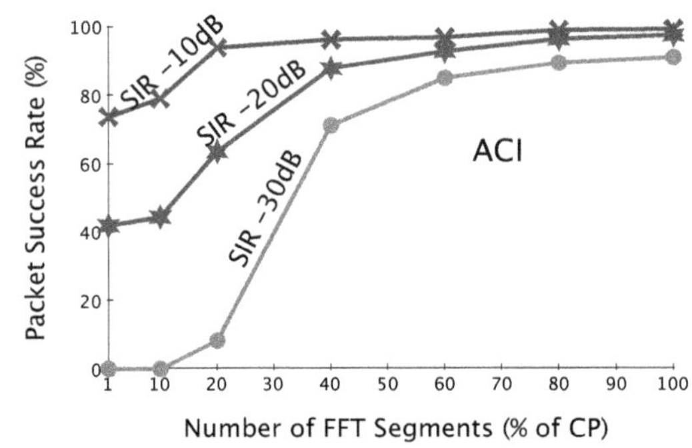

Figure 14: Packet success rates with varying number of FFT segments

receivers. (ii) on devices with limited computational capability the number of FFT segments can be tuned to the capabilities of the device, which gracefully degrades to a standard OFDM receiver with one FFT segment, in the worst case. Hence it can be used in a wide variety of hardware configurations with varying computational capabilities.

When unconstrained by computational capability, it is also beneficial to increase P beyond the number of ISI free samples available in the CP. This is possible through oversampling with new devices that support higher sampling rates.

7. RELATED WORK

Adjacent Channel Interference: OFDM systems are known to suffer from high levels of out-of-band emissions. Several techniques have been proposed to reduce this out-of-band radiation. Windowing is a time domain technique [51], where the signal is multiplied with a windowing function before transmission to reduce the energy in the side lobes. Techniques such as Subcarrier weighing [6], Multiple-choice sequences [7], Cancellation carriers [41], constellation Expansion [35], and Adaptive symbol transition [31] are some of the techniques that manipulate the frequency domain signal at the transmitter to enable out of band reduction. A comprehensive comparison of these side lobe reduction has been presented in [24]. One of the defining features of adjacent channel interference is that only the subcarriers the band assigned to a transmitter is affected. The schemes that suppress ACI are designed to mitigate the interference in the edge subcarriers and hence are not suitable to suppress other types of interference such as co-channel interference.

In LTE, fractional frequency reuse and adaptive power management techniques are used to reduce the level of interference in the network. Active interference mitigation schemes such as interference rejection combining [27], coordinated multipoint transmission (COMP) [26], and channel coding are being used to mitigate co-channel interference.

Co-Channel Interference: Co-channel interference management techniques can be grouped into two categories (i) schemes that mitigate interference by modifying the transmitted signal (ii) schemes that decode the signal of interest in the presence of interference.

Interference mitigation schemes such as [20, 52], adapt the transmissions to be more resilient to interference. Their application is limited to niche scenarios and moreover they require changes to the existing standards and are not backward compatible. Interference alignment [1, 2, 15] is a recently proposed technique that in this category. However, they require communication over the wired backbone and are not backward compatible. Similarly, Swarun et al, propose OpenRF [25] a cross-layer architecture for interference management that enables access points to cancel their interference at the clients significantly improving the network capacity and is applicable only to multiple antenna systems.

Several schemes have been proposed to decode the signal of interest in the presence of co-channel interference. Kong et al [23] propose MZig, a physical layer technique to decode simultaneous transmissions from multiple ZigBee devices to provide an m-fold increase in throughput. Gollakota et al, propose TIMO [14], an IEEE 802.11n receiver that can decode the packets in the presence of cross-technology interference. While TIMO can work even when the interference is persistent and lasts over a few seconds, unlike, CPRecycle , it can only be applied to receivers with multiple antennas. Yan et al, propose WizBee, [56], a ZigBee receiver that can decode ZigBee packets in the presence of strong interference from 802.11 nodes limiting its application.

In contrast to the interference management schemes discussed above, CPRecycle can mitigate different types of interference on single antenna systems and is also backward compatible with legacy OFDM systems.

Partial Packet Recovery: Partial packet recovery is a class of techniques that attempt to recover corrupt packets instead of retransmitting them. Several approaches [16, 19, 20, 22, 33, 53] have been proposed to address this inefficiency in retransmitting an entire packet due to a few bit errors. They can broadly be categorized into (i) co-operative packet recovery and (ii) cross-layer packet recovery.

In co-operative packet recovery schemes such as [22, 30, 33, 53] multiple access points coordinate with each other to recover partially corrupted packets by exploiting receiver diversity. SOFT and MRD use PHY layer information to identify corrupt blocks of bits that needs to be transmitted. ZipTx uses adaptive FEC codes to improve probability of repairing bit errors in co-operation with other APs in the vicinity. However, co-operative packet recovery techniques (including MRD and SOFT) demand additional constraints such as multiple coordinating APs, hardware changes, incompatible with IEEE 802.11, and hence are not useful in scenarios where CPRecycle is applicable. These techniques are useful in 802.11 mesh networks, where only the correct bits of a packet are forwarded on and the receiver combines multiple such copies to recover the entire packet, and in scenarios where these multiple APs coordinate through a wired backbone to share partial packets with the receiver.

Cross-layer partial packet recovery techniques such as [19, 20] attempt to recover partially corrupt retransmissions of the same packet and are in a way extensions of the chase combining decoder (where multiple noisy copies of a packet are combined to recover the packet). These techniques however require modification at both the transmitter and receiver to use additional parity bits to identify corrupt blocks for retransmission.

Furthermore, both categories of partial packet recovery techniques are complementary to CPRecycle and can be used in combination to improve the packet reception rate further. For example, SOFT and PPR use a confidence measure on decoding a bit as '0' or '1' cooperatively with multiple APs to improve decoding accuracy. When used in combination with CPRecycle, it would receive higher confidence measures on the decoding decision since CPRecycle exploits multiple copies of the signal in the cyclic prefix to select the FFT window with the signal that is closest to the correct lattice point.

8. CONCLUSIONS

In this paper, we have considered the problem of mitigating different types of interference experienced by OFDM based wireless systems. Exploiting the fact that OFDM based wireless standards over-provision the cyclic prefix (CP) that is meant for preventing inter-symbol interference, we presented a novel OFDM receiver design called CPRecycle that takes advantage of the redundant portion of the CP towards interference mitigation. Specifically, CPRecycle models the effect of interference in each subcarrier using a Gaussian kernel density function using the preamble symbols and uses a fixed sphere maximum likelihood detector to decode the following data carrying OFDM symbols subject to interference. Using off-the-shelf IEEE 802.11g transmitters and interferers, we experimentally show the effectiveness of CPRecycle for mitigating adjacent-channel interference and co-channel interference. We also show that two preambles and small portion of CP are sufficient to realize significant benefits in terms of packet success rate with CPRecycle . The application of CPRecycle in multiple antenna systems and evaluation of CPRecycle in the presence of different types of interference is left for future work.

9. ACKNOWLEDGMENTS

We thank our shepherd Michael Mitzenmacher and the anonymous reviewers for many helpful suggestions on improving the paper. We also thank Rik Sarkar for many helpful discussions on the statistical methods used in error correction mechanisms.

10. REFERENCES

[1] ADIB, F., KUMAR, S., ARYAN, O., GOLLAKOTA, S., AND KATABI, D. Interference alignment by motion. In *Proceedings of the ACM MobiCom* (2013), pp. 279–290.

[2] BANSAL, T., ZHOU, W., SRINIVASAN, K., AND SINHA, P. Robinhood: sharing the happiness in a wireless jungle. In *Proceedings of ACM HotMobile* (2014), p. 22.

[3] BLOESSL, B., SEGATA, M., SOMMER, C., AND DRESSLER, F. An IEEE 802.11 a/g/p OFDM receiver for GNU radio. In *Proceedings of Software radio implementation forum* (2013).

[4] CHEN, X., ZHANG, C., AND LUO, Y. Low-complexity ISI-free region detection for OFDM systems in high-mobility fading channels. In *Proceedings of IEEE HWMC* (2014).

[5] CONWAY, J. H., AND SLOANE, N. J. A. *Sphere packings, lattices and groups*, vol. 290. Springer Science & Business Media, 2013.

[6] COSOVIC, I., BRANDES, S., AND SCHNELL, M. Subcarrier weighting: a method for sidelobe suppression in OFDM systems. *Communications Letters, IEEE 10*, 6 (2006), 444–446.

[7] COSOVIC, I., AND MAZZONI, T. Suppression of sidelobes in OFDM systems by multiple-choice sequences. *European transactions on telecommunications 17*, 6 (2006), 623–630.

[8] DAMEN, M. O., EL GAMAL, H., AND CAIRE, G. On maximum-likelihood detection and the search for the closest lattice point. *Information Theory, IEEE Transactions on 49*, 10 (2003), 2389–2402.

[9] DING, Y., HUANG, Y., ZENG, G., AND XIAO, L. Channel assignment with partially overlapping channels in wireless mesh networks. In *Proceedings of ICWI* (2008), p. 38.

[10] DRAVES, R., PADHYE, J., AND ZILL, B. Routing in multi-radio, multi-hop wireless mesh networks. In *Proceedings of MobiCom* (2004), pp. 114–128.

[11] ETTUS, M. Usrp users and developers guide. *Ettus Research LLC* (2005).

[12] FARSHAD, A., MARINA, M. K., AND GARCIA, F. Urban WiFi characterization via mobile crowdsensing. In *Proceedings of NOMS IEEE* (2014), pp. 1–9.

[13] FENG, C., CUI, H., MA, M., AND JIAO, B. On statistical properties of co-channel interference in OFDM systems. *Communications Letters, IEEE 17*, 12 (2013), 2328–2331.

[14] GOLLAKOTA, S., ADIB, F., KATABI, D., AND SESHAN, S. Clearing the RF smog: making 802.11 n robust to cross-technology interference. *ACM SIGCOMM CCR 41*, 4, 170–181.

[15] GOLLAKOTA, S., PERLI, S. D., AND KATABI, D. Interference alignment and cancellation. In *ACM SIGCOMM Computer Communication Review* (2009), vol. 39, ACM, pp. 159–170.

[16] GOWDA, M., SEN, S., CHOUDHURY, R. R., AND LEE, S.-J. . J. Cooperative packet recovery in enterprise WLANs. In *INFOCOM, 2013 Proceedings IEEE* (2013), pp. 1348–1356.

[17] GUMMADI, R., WETHERALL, D., GREENSTEIN, B., AND SESHAN, S. Understanding and mitigating the impact of RF interference on 802.11 networks. *ACM SIGCOMM CCR 37*, 4 (2007), 385–396.

[18] HOLLOWAY, C. L., COTTON, M. G., AND MCKENNA, P. A model for predicting the power delay profile characteristics inside a room. *Vehicular Technology, IEEE Transactions on 48*, 4 (1999), 1110–1120.

[19] HUANG, J., XING, G., NIU, J., AND LIN, S. Coderepair: Phy-layer partial packet recovery without the pain. In *Proceedings of (INFOCOM)* (2015), pp. 1463–1471.

[20] JAMIESON, K., AND BALAKRISHNAN, H. PPR: Partial packet recovery for wireless networks. *ACM SIGCOMM Computer Communication Review 37*, 4 (2007), 409–420.

[21] JONES, M. C., MARRON, J. S., AND SHEATHER, S. J. A brief survey of bandwidth selection for density estimation. *Journal of the American Statistical Association 91*, 433 (1996), 401–407.

[22] KATTI, S., KATABI, D., BALAKRISHNAN, H., AND MEDARD, M. Symbol-level network coding for wireless mesh networks. In *ACM SIGCOMM Computer Communication Review* (2008), vol. 38, pp. 401–412.

[23] KONG, L., AND LIU, X. mzig: Enabling multi-packet reception in zigbee. 552–565.

[24] KRYSZKIEWICZ, P., BOGUCKA, H., AND WYGLINSKI, A. M. Protection of primary users in dynamically varying radio environment: practical solutions and challenges. *EURASIP Journal on Wireless Communications and Networking*, 1 (2012), 1–20.

[25] KUMAR, S., CIFUENTES, D., GOLLAKOTA, S., AND KATABI, D. Bringing cross-layer MIMO to today's wireless LANs. In *ACM SIGCOMM CCR* (2013), vol. 43, pp. 387–398.

[26] LEE, D., SEO, H., CLERCKX, B., HARDOUIN, E., MAZZARESE, D., NAGATA, S., AND SAYANA, K. Coordinated multipoint transmission and reception in LTE-advanced: deployment scenarios and operational challenges. *Communications Magazine, IEEE 50*, 2 (2012), 148–155.

[27] LÉOST, Y., ABDI, M., RICHTER, R., AND JESCHKE, M. Interference rejection combining in LTE networks. *Bell Labs Technical Journal 17*, 1 (2012), 25–49.

[28] LI, Y., WANG, X., AND MUJTABA, S. A. Cochannel interference avoidance algorithm in 802.11 wireless LANs. In *Proceedings of VTC* (2003), pp. 2610–2614.

[29] LIM, C.-P. . P., VOLAKIS, J. L., SERTEL, K., KINDT, R. W., AND ANASTASOPOULOS, A. Indoor propagation models based on rigorous methods for site-specific multipath environments. *Antennas and Propagation, IEEE Transactions on 54*, 6 (2006), 1718–1725.

[30] LIN, K. C.-J. . J., KUSHMAN, N., AND KATABI, D. Ziptx: Harnessing partial packets in 802.11 networks. In *Proceedings of the MobiCom* (2008), pp. 351–362.

[31] MAHMOUD, H., AND ARSLAN, H. Sidelobe suppression in OFDM-based spectrum sharing systems using adaptive symbol transition. *Communications Letters, IEEE 12*, 2 (2008), 133–135.

[32] MAJECKA, B. Statistical models of pedestrian behaviour in the forum. *Master's thesis, School of Informatics, University of Edinburgh* (2009).

[33] MIU, A., BALAKRISHNAN, H., AND KOKSAL, C. E. Improving loss resilience with multi-radio diversity in

wireless networks. In *Proceedings of ACM MobiCom* (2005), pp. 16–30.
[34] NACHTIGALL, J., ZUBOW, A., AND REDLICH, J.-P. . P. The impact of adjacent channel interference in multi-radio systems using IEEE 802.11. In *Proceedings of IWCMC* (2008), pp. 874–881.
[35] PAGADARAI, S., RAJBANSHI, R., WYGLINSKI, A. M., AND MINDEN, G. J. Sidelobe suppression for OFDM-based cognitive radios using constellation expansion. In *IEEE WCNC* (2008), IEEE, pp. 888–893.
[36] POLLET, T., VAN BLADEL, M., AND MOENECLAEY, M. Ber sensitivity of OFDM systems to carrier frequency offset and wiener phase noise. *Communications, IEEE Transactions on 43*, 2/3/4 (1995), 191–193.
[37] RAMASUBRAMANIAN, K., AND BAUM, K. An OFDM timing recovery scheme with inherent delay-spread estimation. In *Proceedings of IEEE GLOBECOM* (2001), vol. 5, pp. 3111–3115.
[38] RATHINAKUMAR, S. M., RADUNOVIC, B., AND MARINA, M. K. ShiftFFT: An efficient approach to mitigate adjacent channel interference in OFDM systems. In *Proceedings of the HotWireless in Conjunction with MobiCom* (2015), pp. 11–15.
[39] SAQUIB, N., HOSSAIN, E., LE, L. B., AND KIM, D. I. Interference management in OFDMA femtocell networks: issues and approaches. *Wireless Communications, IEEE 19*, 3 (2012).
[40] SCOTT, D. W. *Multivariate density estimation: theory, practice, and visualization*. John Wiley & Sons, 2015.
[41] SELIM, A., MACALUSO, I., AND DOYLE, L. Efficient sidelobe suppression for OFDM systems using advanced cancellation carriers. In *Proceedings of IEEE ICC* (2013), pp. 4687–4692.
[42] SHEATHER, S. J. Density estimation. *Statistical Science 19*, 4 (2004), 588–597.
[43] SHEU, C.-R. . R., AND HUANG, C.-C. . C. A novel guard interval based ISI-free sampling region detection method for OFDM systems. In *Proceedings of IEEE VTC 2004*, vol. 1, pp. 515–519.
[44] STEWART, G., GOWDA, M., MAINLAND, G., RADUNOVIC, B., VYTINIOTIS, D., AND PATTERSON, D. Ziria: language for rapid prototyping of wireless PHY. In *Proceedings of the 2014 ACM conference on SIGCOMM* (2014).
[45] STOTT, J. The effects of phase noise in COFDM. *EBU technical Review* (1998), 12–25.
[46] TAN, K., FANG, J., ZHANG, Y., CHEN, S., SHI, L., ZHANG, J., AND ZHANG, Y. Fine-grained channel access in wireless lan. *ACM SIGCOMM CCR 41*, 4 (2011), 147–158.
[47] TERRELL, G. R., AND SCOTT, D. W. Variable kernel density estimation. *The Annals of Statistics* (1992), 1236–1265.
[48] THORPE, C., AND MURPHY, L. A survey of adaptive carrier sensing mechanisms for IEEE 802.11 wireless networks. *Communications Surveys & Tutorials, IEEE 16*, 3 (2014), 1266–1293.
[49] VILLEGAS, E. G., LOPEZ-AGUILERA, E., VIDAL, R., AND PARADELLS, J. Effect of adjacent-channel interference in IEEE 802.11 WLANs. In *CROWNCOM* (2007), pp. 118–125.
[50] VITERBO, E., AND BOUTROS, J. A universal lattice code decoder for fading channels. *Information Theory, IEEE Transactions on 45*, 5 (1999), 1639–1642.
[51] WEISS, T., HILLENBRAND, J., KROHN, A., AND JONDRAL, F. K. Mutual interference in OFDM-based spectrum pooling systems. *IEEE Xplore 4* (5 2004), 1873–1877 Vol.4.
[52] WOO, G. R., KHERADPOUR, P., SHEN, D., AND KATABI, D. Beyond the bits: cooperative packet recovery using physical layer information. In *Proceedings ACM MobiCom* (2007), ACM, pp. 147–158.
[53] WOO, G. R., KHERADPOUR, P., SHEN, D., AND KATABI, D. Beyond the bits: cooperative packet recovery using physical layer information. In *Proceedings of ACM MobiCom* (2007), pp. 147–158.
[54] WU, S., AND BAR-NESS, Y. OFDM systems in the presence of phase noise: consequences and solutions. *Communications, IEEE Transactions on 52*, 11 (2004), 1988–1996.
[55] WYSOCKI, T. A., AND ZEPERNICK, H.-J. . J. Characterization of the indoor radio propagation channel at 2.4 GHz. *Journal of telecommunications and information technology* (2000), 84–90.
[56] YAN, Y., YANG, P., LI, X.-Y. . Y., ZHANG, Y., LU, J., YOU, L., WANG, J., HAN, J., AND XIONG, Y. Wizbee: Wise ZigBee coexistence via interference cancellation with single antenna. *Mobile Computing, IEEE Transactions on 14*, 12 (2015), 2590–2603.
[57] ZHANG, C., CHEN, X., AND LUO, Y. Threshold optimization for ISI-free region detection in high-mobility fading channels. In *Proceedings of IEEE HMWC* (2015).
[58] ZHOU, K., JIA, X., XIE, L., CHANG, Y., AND TANG, X. Channel assignment for WLAN by considering overlapping channels in SINR interference model. In *Proceedings of ICNC* (2012), IEEE, pp. 1005–1009.
[59] ZUBOW, A., AND SOMBRUTZKI, R. Adjacent channel interference in IEEE 802.11n. *WCNC 2012* (4 2012).

Mudra: User-friendly Fine-grained Gesture Recognition using WiFi Signals

Ouyang Zhang and Kannan Srinivasan
Department of Computer Science and Engineering
The Ohio State University, Columbus, OH 43210
zhang.4746@buckeyemail.osu.edu, kannan@cse.ohio-state.edu

Abstract

There has been a great interest in recognizing gestures using wireless communication signals. We are motivated in detecting extremely fine, subtle finger gestures with WiFi signals. We envision this technology to find applications in finger-gesture control, disabled-friendly devices, physical therapy etc. The requirements of mm-level sensitivity and user-friendly feature using existing WiFi signals pose great challenges. Here, we present Mudra, a fine-grained finger gesture recognition system which leverages WiFi signals to enable a near-human-to-machine interaction with finger motion.

Mudra uses a two-antenna receiver to detect and recognize finger gesture. It uses the signals received from one antenna to cancel the signal from the other. This "cancellation" is extremely sensitive to and enables us detect small variation in channel due to finger movements. Since Mudra decodes gestures with existing WiFi transmissions, Mudra enables gesture recognition without sacrificing WiFi transmission opportunities. Besides, Mudra is user-friendly with no need of user training. To demonstrate Mudra, we implement prototype on the NI-based SDR platform and use COTS WiFi adapter. We evaluate Mudra in a typical office environment. The results show that our system can achieve 96% accuracy.

Keywords

Gesture Recognition; WiFi Signals; Signal Cancellation

1. INTRODUCTION

There is recent advances in pushing gesture recognition techniques. Google Soli [2] makes a huge break-

CoNEXT '16, December 12-15, 2016, Irvine, CA, USA
© 2016 ACM. ISBN 978-1-4503-4292-6/16/12...$15.00
DOI: http://dx.doi.org/10.1145/2999572.2999582

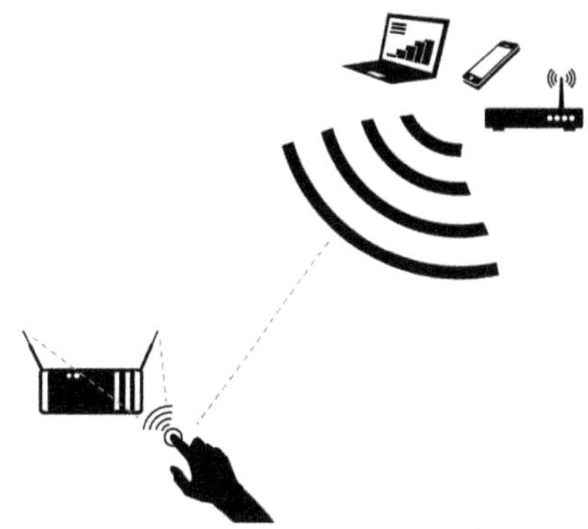

Figure 1: The system scenario of Mudra.

through pushing motion sensing to millimeter-level accuracy, enabling micro-gesture recognition. This technology enables finger control application in portable and wearable devices. Soli requires a dedicated RADAR-like chipset that needs to be integrated with the existing hardware. This motivated us to explore the following question: Can we detect fine gestures with conventional wireless signals, e.g. WiFi? If this is possible then we won't need separate hardware for communication from gesture recognition. Shown in Fig. 1, we expect users to control their portable device with finger motion nearby. We believe such a technology could enable a set of new applications [15].

One obvious application is the interaction with wearables that have limited screen space. With nine gestures, users can easily scroll through one page, click button and switch among applications. Let's imagine a reader is reading an e-book on apple watch. He can move to next page with a 'tap' and return back with 'double tap,' circling his finger to get to the bottom. It can also enable complex and in-the-air interactive games on portable devices. Users can control the action of figures with finger gestures in the air, e.g. going ahead, returning back, jumping and punching. Mobile devices increasingly appear in assisting health workers with ongoing medical education. While handling infectious medical task, e.g. blood test, touching their device would incur contamination. Now, we can enable

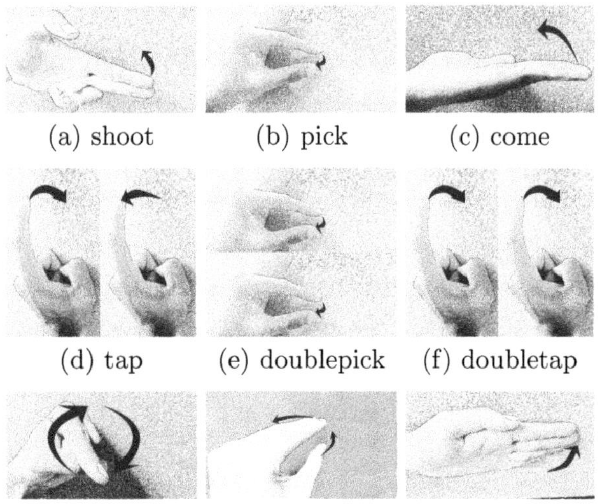

(a) shoot (b) pick (c) come (d) tap (e) doublepick (f) doubletap (g) circle (h) twist (i) go

Figure 2: Gestures considered in Mudra.

gesture recognition on the device using wireless signal eliminating the need for direct contact.

In this paper, we develop a novel finger-gesture recognition system, Mudra utilizing WiFi signals. Mudra just needs regular WiFi data transmissions either from local or remote sources. In this way, Mudra doesn't need to generate special signals (like Soli), thus, saving power for power-hungry devices [1, 19] and not hurting communication opportunities. Service of Mudra is always available as long as there are active transmissions in vicinity: Mudra can use a nearby WiFi-enabled desktop or laptop's transmissions to its access point (AP) to detect gestures. Furthermore, Mudra can use transmissions from multiple sources over time.

A key feature of Mudra is its training-free nature. This makes our system more promising in reality compared with other micro-motion technologies [9, 14, 23–25], all of which require training for specific location and user. One advantage is Mudra is not constrained by stationary scenario. That means, even if the user moves to another place, Mudra is still able to provide gesture recognition service using a WiFi transmitter at a new location without reconfiguration. Two key technologies to enable this feature are signal cancellation and gesture design and recognition principle. Signal cancellation renders us a motion indication which is highly sensitive to tiny movement and linearly relative to signal path delay. These two features together support us to apply distinct waveform shape of indication time series as recognition principle. Due to the relationship between delay and indication, those shapes could be consistent with different surrounding environments.

We implement Mudra with two receive antennas capturing signals from a COTS WiFi device. With 802.11n protocol [28], MIMO devices with multiple antennas are very commom. Thus, Mudra can be implemented on COTS receiver if manufacturers open access to the samples. Mudra tracks finger-motion by deriving motion indication with cancellation between two received signals. To make Mudra training-free, we select a set of gestures (Fig. 2) while more gestures can be added in the future. Besides, waveform consistency studies (Sec. 3.4) let us know how we can maintain waveform shapes across different users and locations. After that, Stretch Limited DTW algorithm is proposed to classify gestures with variation in duration and shape.

There are the following **challenges** in building Mudra:

- Finger-gestures are hard to detect because they result in subtle changes in the wireless channel.
- To utilize regular WiFi signals, we confront with lots of critical issues. Firstly, WiFi packets are typically not continuous. We need to implement smart packet detect/capture module in Mudra. Second, short subcarrier length and variable packet lengths in WiFi limit the tracking precision. Besides, 20MHz sampling rate poses a great computation challenge on packet alignment from two receiving antennas and real-time processing on host.
- User's movement changes the channel between the source and receiver. This makes finger-gesture recognition really hard and training for every location is not favorable for a user-friendly system.

Contributions Our contributions in this paper are as follows:

- We take the first step to look into finger-gesture recognition using conventional ISM band signals (from WiFi).
- Our system is able to utilize regular WiFi signals. To achieve this, our system needs to solve the above-mentioned challenges.
- Our system accommodates various scenarios and eliminates the need for training. Fig. 2 shows the set of gestures selected in Mudra that allows our system to be user-independent and location-independent.
- We build a prototype on NI based SDR platform. Our evaluation uses signals from COTS WiFi sources. We evaluate our system in various environmental conditions and system settings across multiple users. It shows that our system can achieve an average accuracy of 98% with a local source (2cm from Mudra) and 96% with remote source(s) (0.5-7m from Mudra).

Features: Mudra has the following features:

- It doesn't require training per user or per environment (Sec. 3.4).
- It supports both local and remote WiFi sources for gesture recognition (Sec. 3.3.2).

- It just needs conservative WiFi transmissions to perform very well (Sec. 6.1.3).
- It can combine signals from multiple WiFi sources and improve accuracy (Sec. 4.2.3).
- Multiple Mudra systems can operate simultaneously without affecting each other (Sec. 6.2.2).

2. RELATED WORK

Human tracking and motion detection have been broadly studied in the literature. We discuss existing techniques and their shortcomings in our setting.

Non-RF based micro-gesture recognition: Imaging-based systems (e.g. Xbox Kinect [4], leap motion [3] and Maestro [10]) use monochromatic infrared cameras and LEDs to build body-depth imaging. Both Radar and infrared systems require line-of-sight (LOS) operation. Sonar-based system [18] requires specially modulated sound wave and exclusive devices. Mudra, on the other hand, utilizes regular WiFi signals in the ISM band, operating in parallel with WiFi communication. Furthermore, Mudra supports both line-of-sight (LOS) and non-line-of-sight (NLOS) scenarios.

RF based micro-motion tracking: Another set of works exploit RF signals to track human's minor movements. Radar based systems (e.g. Google Soli [2]) show the ability to track minor finger movement by constructing Doppler profile using 60GHz radar signals. Such systems, however, require embedded chip to generate/capture and process radar signals. Besides, it is limited to line-of-sight (LOS) scenario due to the extra-directional feature of radar signals.

[9, 14, 23, 25] look into the keystroke detection problem. Mudra differs from them fundamentally in that Mudra is targeted at identifying finger gestures, not keystroke action. More importantly, Mudra is a user-friendly system without the need for training. Whereas, the others require location-specific or user-specific training for classification. One recent work detects minor keystroke motion by canceling two signals from two receiving antennas [9]. This system can not be applied to WiFi signals since (i) it assumed continuous signal transmissions and (ii) assumed the frequency response to be flat across the whole band. Therefore, they generate continuous wireless signal from SDR platform and only estimate the overall phase and amplitude of the channel. WiFi transmissions are not continuous and do not have a flat frequency response due to a small number of subcarriers spanning the whole band. The second issue affects cancellation quality, which is what Mudra relies on to identify finger-gestures. Mudra enables micro-gesture recognition with WiFi signals after solving those problems by implementing smart packet capture and estimating full channel state information (CSI). Mudra also resolves additional issues for WiFi signals such as variable length of packets.

[23, 25] make use of sound and electromagnetic signals emanating from keyboards, a feature unavailable with finger motion. [14] mainly use Principle Component Analysis (PCA) to remove noise based on correlated variation of CSI with different keystrokes. It is highly unlikely that such correlation still works with various finger gestures since finger movements cause subtle changes to CSI: Fig. 3 shows the amplitude and phase variation over time when the user performed the same gesture 10 times. The plot shows no periodic variations. Another line of approaches (e.g. [24]) use MIMO beamforming, using multiple antennas and step motors to project signal to target. Target locating needs 6s and 85% of accuracy greatly affects overall accuracy. Mudra, on the other hand, doesn't require such a luxurious infrastructure.

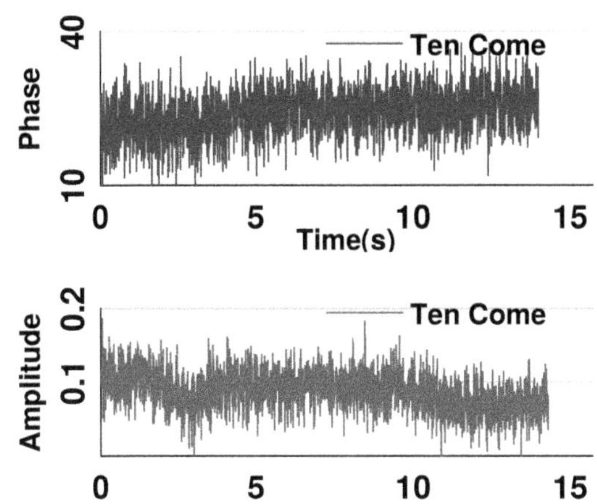

Figure 3: Phase/Amplitude variation in channel. When fingers repeat the 'Come' gesture ten times, the corresponding CSI amplitude/phase change is buried within large noise, making it infeasible for finger-gesture recognition. This is the same with other gestures while we just show 'Come' to save space, same with Fig. 4.

Coarse-grained gesture/motion detection: A large body of works track and identify larger-scale gesture motion (e.g. human limbs), which typically spans over range of several decimeters or target at the whole body, using characteristics of wireless signal. [20, 22] enables gesture recognition using Doppler profile generated from multi-second FFT to get sub-Hertz granularity. However, typical finger gestures are much shorter (e.g. tap just spans 0.5s), making this approach infeasible. To see this, we implement Wisee [20] on PXIe-1082 platform and see no observable Doppler shift with finger motion in Fig. 4. Frequency modulation was used with sound wave in [17] and carrier wave in [7] to track human breath. Mudra differs in that we don't change the regular source to generate a delicately-designed signal, which can only serve recognition purpose.

Channel CSI / RSSI-based systems [15, 26] use coarse CSI feature to extract motion information, which is not feasible in detecting slight finger motion (Fig. 3). As to antenna array based technologies (e.g. [6] and [13]), WiDeo [13] spans four-antenna infrastructure covering

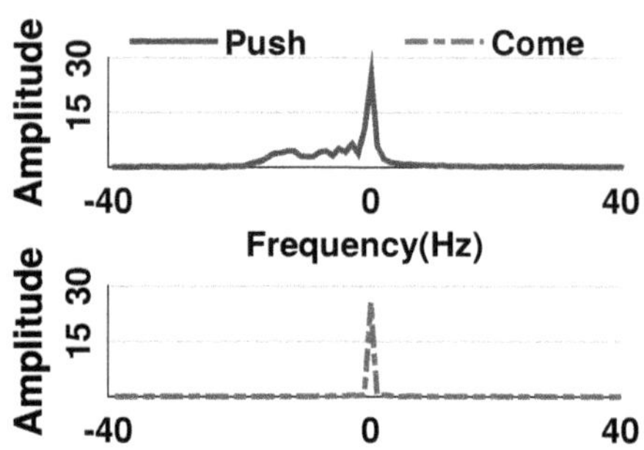

Figure 4: Doppler profile in frequency domain. Large gestures such as Limb Push produce noticeable Doppler shift (the above one) while figure gesture Come can not induce discernible shift, which is the same as no motion.

a length of 18cm, which is not available in portable devices. Wi-Vi [6] assumes a constant motion speed (1m/s) simply to identify whether the object is walking towards or away from a receiver. Another line of works get high positioning accuracy by attaching object with specific devices([16, 29, 30]). Tagoram [29] locates at a centimeter level using phase information of RFID backscatter signal. [30] tracks smartphone as a mouse by active sound wave transmission. Mudra is a user-friendly system which doesn't require such intrusive body instrumentation.

3. SYSTEM SETUP AND PRINCIPLE

To understand how exactly Mudra works, we will discuss three main issues in this section. First, we introduce the system scenario and setup. Next, we present the principle of motion tracking and then address various issues. Lastly, we explore consistency of waveform to understand how Mudra recognizes gestures without training.

3.1 System Scenario and Setup

With Mudra, we are designing a system that enables micro-gesture recognition in vicinity. As Fig. 1 shows, the hand moves roughly 7cm to the receiving antennas over 2-4cm with gestures in Fig. 2. This distance is measured as the minimum distance between the hand and the two-antenna segment. On the target device, there are two antennas capturing incoming WiFi signals. As to the distance between them, it is a critical design choice and will be studied in Sec. 6.1.2, which gives 10cm as a default setting for the best sensitivity while noting that Mudra can also work with shorter distance (Sec. 7).

Mudra can work with a remote source such as desktop, tablet and AP, and also a local source, i.e. an extra transmit antenna on the target device itself. Thus, distance between signal source and Mudra receiver could be ranging from several centimeters to a dozen meters. The motivation behind utilizing existing signals is two folds. On the one hand, it eliminates the need for special transmissions for gesture recognition. On the other hand, including distant sources allows Mudra to utilize different sources over time and provide gesture recognition service throughout.

Two directions relate to finger motion in this paper. One is the hand direction which is measured as the angle relative to the line formed by two antennas, increasing clockwise (Fig. 5). The other is the finger moving direction. User experiences show that finger moving along forearm with gestures in Fig. 2 is comfortable and adopted naturally. Note that "moving along forearm" is a 2-D description as the 'shoot' rotates the wrist while making the fingers move along forearm in horizontal plane. Thus, we measure the forearm direction relative to the two-antenna-line as moving direction while telling the users to move along forearm. In Fig. 5, moving direction is 0 degree with forearm being parallel with the two-antenna-line.

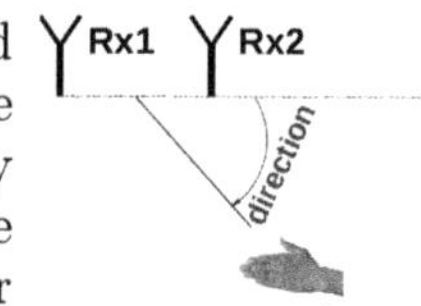

Figure 5: Direction Demonstration

3.2 Principle of Motion Tracking

In order to track minor finger motion, what indicator does Mudra use that is extra-sensitive to finger position?

3.2.1 Channel Estimation and Signal Equalization

Mudra is equipped with two receiving antennas as shown in Fig. 1. Each of the antennas captures incoming signal samples, denoted as $s_1(t)$ and $s_2(t)$ respectively. The first thing is to equalize $s_1(t)$ and $s_2(t)$ for cancellation purpose. The solution here is to estimate the relative channel response between them.

To explain this, let two channel frequency responses be $H_1(w)$ ('w' is angular frequency) and $H_2(w)$ respectively, transmitted signal be $T(w)$ and two received signals be $S_1(w)$ and $S_2(w)$. Then, $S_1(w) = T(w) * H_1(w) = T(w) * H_2(w) * \frac{H_1(w)}{H_2(w)} = S_2(w) * \frac{H_1(w)}{H_2(w)}$. As it shows, signal S_2 is equalized to S_1 by compensating for the relative channel response $\frac{H_1(w)}{H_2(w)}$. We denote the time domain signal as $\overline{s}_2(t)$ after this equalization. In Mudra, $\frac{H_1(w)}{H_2(w)}$ is transformed to time domain impulse response then put into FIR filter as coefficients to equalize S_2.

In Mudra, since WiFi signals exhibit non-flat relative channel response for two receivers, we need to estimate $\frac{H_2(w)}{H_1(w)}$ across the whole band. This is totally different from [9] which estimates just amplitude/phase difference with the flat-response assumption. In Fig. 6, the result validates the effectiveness and necessity of full channel estimation.

3.2.2 Motion Indication with Signal Cancellation

After we obtain $\overline{s}_2(t)$ from equalization, $s_1(t)$ can be canceled from $\overline{s}_2(t)$. However, we want an indication

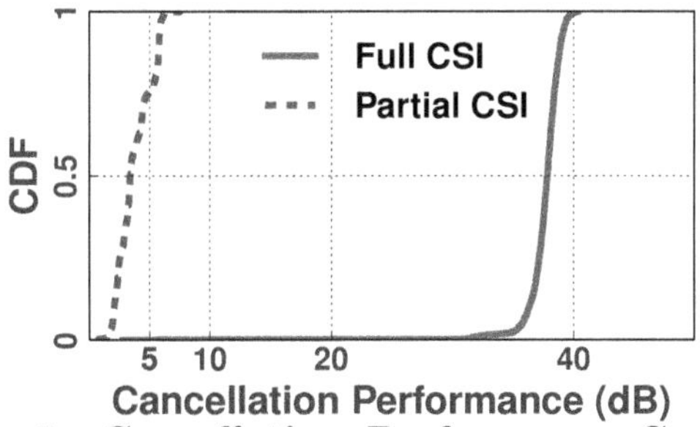

Figure 6: Cancellation Performance Comparison. We test in various scenarios. 'Full CSI' estimates on the whole band while 'Partial CSI' just calculates overall amplitude/phase difference.

which changes with finger moving. To this end, inspired by previous work [9], manual delay Δt and manual phase ϕ are introduced to $\overline{s}_2(t)$. Now, when finger moves, an extra delay $\delta\tau$ is introduced (Eq. 1a). Then, their frequency domain components ($S_1(w)$ and $\overline{S}_2(w)$) are related as shown in Eq. 1b.

$$s_1(t) = \overline{s}_2(t - \Delta t - \delta\tau)e^{-j\phi} \tag{1a}$$

$$S_1(w) = \overline{S}_2(w)e^{-jw(\Delta t + \delta\tau)}e^{-j\phi} \tag{1b}$$

Thus, as s_1 is subtracted from $\overline{s}_2$, the cancellation is perfect (i.e. zero value) only at specific frequency points where the phase shift is an integer multiple of 2π.

$$w^* = \frac{2\pi k - \phi}{\Delta t + \delta\tau}, k \in \mathbb{Z} \tag{2}$$

w^* is a set of frequencies where the cancellation will be perfect.

Since at frequencies farther away from w^* cancellation becomes worse (due to larger phase mismatch), we would get a trough at w^* shown in Fig. 8(a). Now, as the finger moves, $\delta\tau$ varies accordingly causing trough location to change. Taking 'Come' (Fig. 2(c)) for instance, when fingers move from Rx1 to Rx2 and then back from Rx2 to Rx1, $\delta\tau$ decreases first then increases to origin, which translates to increasing and decreasing of w^*. Then, we get waveform as shown in Fig. 10(c).

One could expect that a sharp trough gives us precise tracking, enabling gesture recognition with good performance. This relies both on: *perfect cancellation performance* (trough depth), which is guaranteed by our full CSI estimation, and *high sensitivity* of cancellation performance on phase mismatch (trough slope). We refer readers to [9] which has a study on sensitivity of cancellation degradation with phase mismatch.

How to select manual delay Δt and manual phase ϕ? - based on WiFi frequency structure.

In the OFDM physical layer of 802.11 protocol, there are 52 subcarriers over 20MHz band and no data at the center and edges (Fig. 7). Thus, if trough moves through these non-signal frequencies, we lose the track of finger motion. Mudra deals with this problem in two steps.

First, from Eq. 2, we can see the trough varying rate with motion drops with larger Δt. Thus, by setting a large enough Δt, we limit the varying range of trough. Second, we naturally want to make use of the maximum continuous left or right half band. Thus, manual phase ϕ is chosen as to tune the initial trough location to the center of left or right half band.

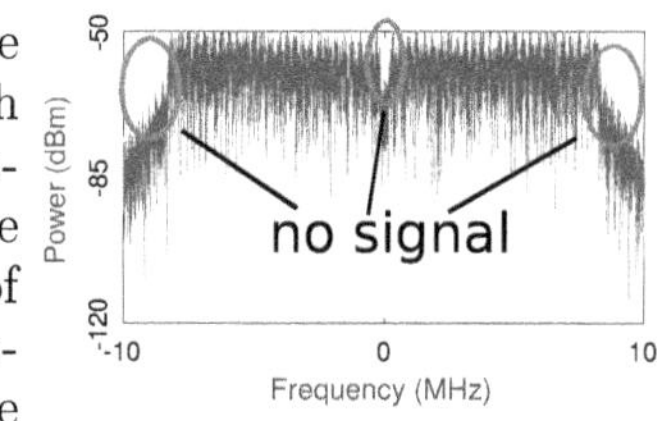

Figure 7: WiFi spectrum

3.3 Various Challenges in Practice

3.3.1 Realistic Issues with WiFi signals

1. Fewer subcarriers in WiFi and cyclic prefix (CP)

In 802.11 a/g/n protocol, an OFDM symbol has just 64 subcarriers in 20/40MHz band. This is a critical issue which is not discussed in [9] as they send special OFDM symbols with 8192 subcarriers continuously. If we just use 64 subcarriers, then the frequency resolution is too coarse to perform gesture recognition. Here, we note that WiFi signals have power over all frequency points in its band because OFDM symbols are different from each other (shown in Fig. 7). So we are safe to do a large size FFT by simply connecting multiple OFDM symbols. However, do we need to avoid CP when combining multiple symbols together? The answer is no. In Mudra, signal copies on the receive antennas are for cancellation, not decoding. Thus, CP would not affect cancellation result as it also complies to channel response. Compared with WiSee [20], which equalized and combined OFDM symbols to enable fine frequency granularity, Mudra eliminates equalization because it relies on heterogeneity among those symbols.

2. Various packet lengths in WiFi signals

Packet length decides how large the FFT could be: Larger this window better the frequency granularity. WiFi transmissions could have variable packet lengths causing the granularity to change from packet to packet. In Mudra, we utilize two signal processing properties for this issue, Zero-fill Invariance and Connect Invariance.

- **Zero-filling Invariance**

When packet length is a little less than the expected FFT length, we want to maintain the same granularity. The approach here is to use zero-filling at the end. In Eq. 3, we show the zero-filling invariance property, which means zero-filling doesn't change the value on the same frequency. **DTFT:**

$$S(w) = \sum_{n=0}^{N-1} s[n]e^{-jwn} \tag{3}$$

This is Discrete Time Fourier Transform (DTFT). $s[n]$ can be seen as the original signal samples with any length of zero-filling at the end. $S(w)$ doesn't change with those filled zeros.

• **Connect Invariance**

Zero-filling just increases samples in frequency domain while not really contributing to signal spectrum. That means, although we get more values in frequency domain with zero-filling, the precision doesn't change because the trough is smoothed at the bottom. Thus, we have to drop those packets which may frequently appear in transmission, greatly sacrificing trough tracking opportunities.

However, we note the connect invariance property, which means trough location doesn't change if we combine residual signals of two neighboring packets. In Eq. 4, $r1, r2$ are cancellation residuals from adjacent packets, which are connected to get $r[n]$. **DTFT:**

$$\begin{aligned} R(w) &= \sum_{n=0}^{N+M-1} r[n]e^{-jwn} \\ &= \sum_{n=0}^{M-1} r1[n]e^{-jwn} + \sum_{n=0}^{N-1} r2[n]e^{-jw(n+M)} \\ &= R1(w) + e^{-jwM}R2(w) \end{aligned} \quad (4)$$

If $R1(w)$ and $R2(w)$ have trough at the same frequency, then $R(w)$ will also have trough at that frequency. Thus, by connecting neighboring packets after cancellation, we get the desired precision. Since motion is continuous in space, troughs within adjacent packets would share adjacent positions.

3. Noncontinuous transmissions of WiFi signals

Transmissions in WiFi are not continuous. For this, we implement a smart packet capture module with power threshold. Inter-packet interval would affect timing resolution of motion indications. When packet's interval is smaller, we get finer motion indications and thus, the recognition performance would be better. Fig. 18 shows experimental results on the effect of inter-packet interval on recognition performance.

3.3.2 *Frequency/timing Offset, Multi-path Effect and Irritable Neighbor as well as Local Source*

1. How does Mudra deal with frequency/timing offset with remote source?

With remote source, frequency and timing offsets between transmitter and receiver ([8, 12, 21]) would impose a varying phase shift in the received signals, which can disable our system. In Mudra, however, two receiving antennas are synchronized with the same RF/sampling clock and timing offset as they are on the same device. Since our scheme obtains motion indication from cancellation of these two, we then get out of the phase shift problem.

2. Multi-path effect in received signals

In experiment, we find that multi-path effect would incur signal destruction at some frequency, causing a trough similar to the one from cancellation (shown in Fig. 8(a)). This trough will remain in the cancellation result, thus, confounding with the desired one. In Mudra, adaptive strategy is proposed to move desired trough out of confounding range. Specifically, we can detect multi-path trough from original received signals, the one without manual delay/phase. If it is in the left half band, we let the desired trough from cancellation be in the right half band by adjusting the manual phase (described earlier).

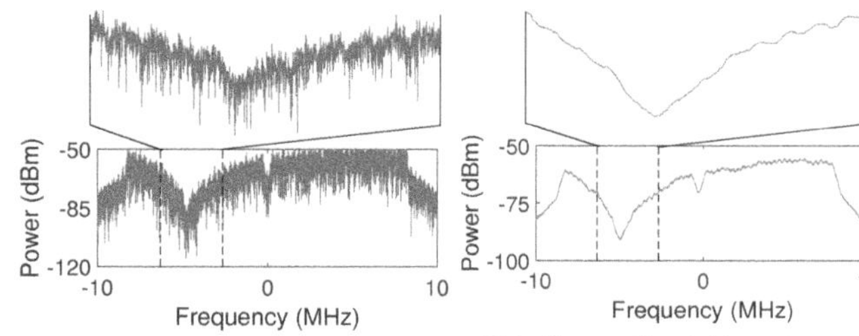

(a) Original Spectrum (b) Smoothed Spectrum

Figure 8: Canceled signal spectrum before and after smoothing over 200 neighbors. The left plot is the power spectrum across 20MHz generated by original samples and the right one is a smoothed version by averaging over adjacent 200 values. The trough in each of them is magnified in a subplot on the top.

3. Irritable neighbor around trough

Fig. 8(a) shows that the spectrum after cancellation has irritable neighboring value around trough location, which are spikes in the magnified figure, seriously deteriorating the accuracy of trough location. We use neighboring average to remedy the problem and get a smoothed curve, shown in Fig. 8(b). The effectiveness and length choice of smoothing is discussed in the evaluation part, shown in Fig. 15(a).

Mudra with a local source With a signal source on the same device, transmitting and receiving antennas are very close. Thus, the signal power over direct LOS path is much larger than reflection from hands, which means finger motion has a minor effect on received signals. Besides, due to near-field effect [27], the received signals see much noisier variation in trough recording.

Solution of Mudra: In Mudra, we deal with this problem by adding a metal plate as an electromagnetic partition between sender and receiver antennas so as to cut off the direct-path signals. Similar approach is adopted in [11] to implement absorptive shielding.

We test the effectiveness of this approach by comparing signal-to-noise ratio (SNR) in different directions with and without metal partition. We define SNR as the ratio between gesture-waveform and noisy variation amplitude. Fig. 9 validates that our method can increase SNR by 6 times on average. For fair comparison, finger moving direction is 0 for all positions.

3.4 Consistency Study of Gesture Waveforms

One of the goals of Mudra is to perform gesture recognition without any training and even when the user has moved to another environment. In this subsection, we

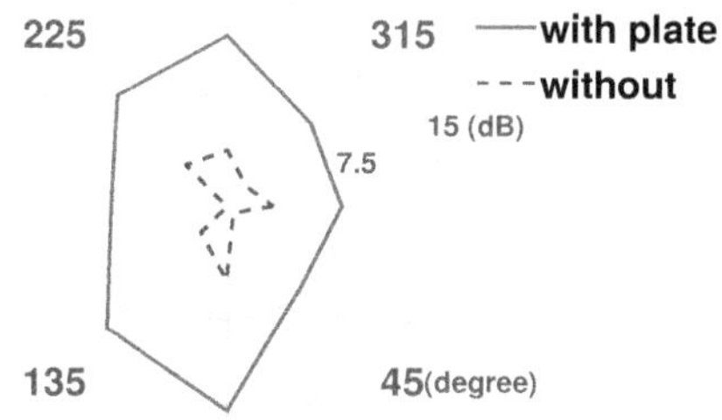

Figure 9: System SNR with and without iron plate. When signal source is very close (2cm), we test waveform-to-noise-amplitude ratio using 'Come' gesture in a circle in eight equi-angular directions.

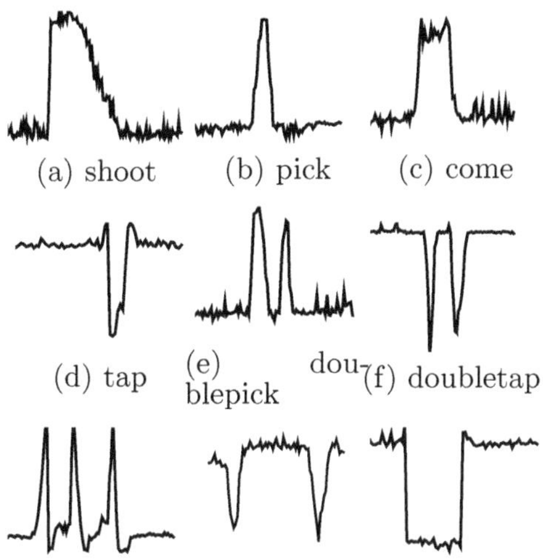

(a) shoot (b) pick (c) come

(d) tap (e) doublepick (f) doubletap

(g) circle (h) twist (i) go

Figure 10: Waveform of gestures considered in Mudra.

study how the trough variation over time can be used to identify different gestures and study how sensitive this identification is to the environment.

Fig. 10 shows the trough location (in MHz) when plotted over time for different gestures (The axes are not shown due to space issues). Do these patterns remain the same across different environments? Do they change with different users?

When user moves, the environment around him would change. We care about different directions and distances of signal source in both LOS and nLOS scenarios. Thus, we choose eight equi-angular LOS positions with 2m distance and nLOS positions 5m away. For hand positions, we put hand at 0, 45 and 90 degree respectively. Note that we can ask the users to keep their hands at an angle that gives the best accuracy for all the finger-gestures. We use this best angle in our evaluations in Sec. 6.1.2.

Five users were asked to perform nine gestures at every source and hand position in a quiet office with no other people. We combine the results of all users in Table 1. **P**1-**P**16 denotes sixteen distinct source positions with direction increasing starting from 0 degree: **P**1-**P**8 are LOS while **P**9-**P**16 are nLOS. '+' means the waveform shape is same or similar with the same gesture in first position **P**1 while '-' represents direction flip of waveform shape. '⋆' is to say the corresponding waveform shape has no similarity with **P**1. In other words, '+' or '-' is good since the shape of the pattern is retained. However, '⋆' indicates that the pattern has changed and denotes a case against Mudra.

The results in Table 1 show that hand position in 90 degree could ensure consistency in gesture waveforms (Fig. 10) across all scenarios. While this is not surprising, as we know, there exists a linear relationship between signal phase and delay, and the reflection from fingers is a combination from all point objects. In later experiments, we will adopt this setting as default.

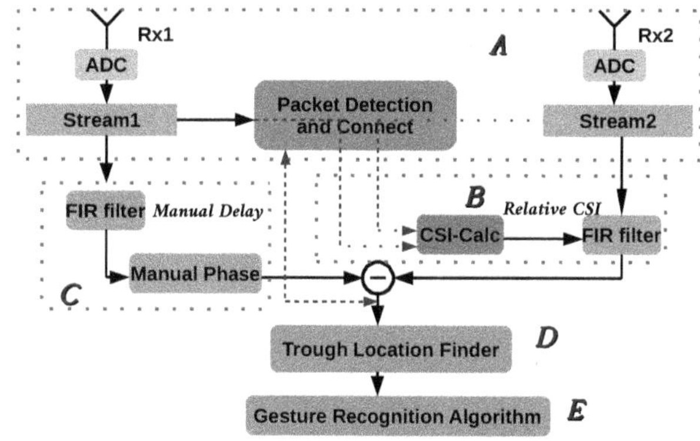

Figure 11: System model

4. SYSTEM DESIGN AND GESTURE RECOGNITION

4.1 System Design

4.1.1 System Model

Mudra has five main components (Fig. 11):

A. Packet detect/connect: This component captures packets from WiFi on two antennas. Since power level is not equal over samples, envelop of power trace is used for finding the beginning and end of continuous packet with a threshold. Mudra will discard packets shorter than 1000 samples to ensure a reasonable trough locating confidence. After that, neighboring packets will be connected together if packet length is less than 8192.

B. Channel estimator/signal equilization: As shown in Fig. 11 block **B**, channel estimator gets relative channel response between the two receiving antennas. Then, this coefficient is sent to an FIR filter, which equalizes the samples on the second antenna.

C. Manual delay/phase injector: As mentioned in Sec. 3.2.2 and 3.3.2, manual phase/delay is used to address WiFi frequency structure and multi-path issues. An FIR filter is used to inject manual delay to the captured packets followed by a manual phase addition.

D. Trough location finder: After cancellation, residual signal will be searched in the selected band and the minimum-value (frequency) position is the trough loca-

Position	**P1**	**P2**	**P3**	**P4**	**P5**	**P6**	**P7**	**P8**	**P9**	**P10**	**P11**	**P12**	**P13**	**P14**	**P15**	**P16**
0degree	+	⋆,-	+,⋆,-	+,⋆,-	⋆,-	+,⋆,-	+,⋆	+,⋆,-	+,⋆	+,-	+,⋆,-	+,⋆	+,⋆	⋆,-	+,-	+,⋆,-
45degree	+	+,⋆,-	+,⋆	+,⋆,-	+,⋆	+,⋆,-	⋆,-	⋆,-	+,⋆,-	⋆,-	+,-	+,⋆,-	+,⋆,-	+,⋆	+	⋆,-
90degree	+	+	+	+	+	+	+	+	+	+	+	+	+	+	+	+

Table 1: Consistency study of gesture waveforms with various signal source locations.

tion. Then, timing series of trough location would be sent to gesture detection/recognition module.

E. Gesture recognition algorithm: Gesture recognition module comprises of preprocessing, segmentation and classification. We implements online recognition with four gestures using simplified classification logic. To classify all nine gestures, we conduct gesture recognition off-line.

4.1.2 *Design detail*

Here, we talk about how to choose design parameters.

1. Length of FFT

Length of FFT decides the granularity we can look into in frequency domain. In 802.11 a/g/n protocol, the maximum size of PLCP Protocol Data Unit (PPDU) in physical layer is larger than 4000 bytes. Considering that one byte has 8 bits and 64-QAM modulation has 6 bits in one sample, we choose 8192 as the number of frequency points we look into, which is the length of FFT operation.

2. Manual delay $\Delta\tau$ and manual phase ϕ

As mentioned in Sec. 3.2.2, we tune the manual delay $\Delta\tau$ to avoid trough running out of the selected range. After testing all target gestures by five testers, we choose 1, which means skipping one sample, as $\Delta\tau$ to achieve largest sensitivity while satisfying this restriction, ensuring that it is feasible in almost all situations. After that, we move the trough location to the center of the range by choosing a value for ϕ. Note that ϕ is fixed after $\Delta\tau$ is decided.

4.1.3 *Authorization Key for System Access*

To avoid target device being miscontrolled by surrounding moving objects, we designed an authorization key containing multiple 'Tap' gestures as preample for users to access this system. We have test in Sec. 6.2.1 to evaluate the effectiveness of different gesture repetitions.

4.2 Gesture Recognition

4.2.1 *Preprocessing*

1. Indication prediction with linear regression

The arrival of packets is not uniform over time, thus, causing irregular sampling of the waveform. We use linear regression to estimate the missing piece of the waveform with timestamp indicating arrival time of each packet. The predicting time points are based on 50 packets/second.

2. Reduce noise variation

As wireless signals travel in the air, variations due to noise and environmental vibrations get into trough recording. We note that this variation is very random. Thus, we use averaging in small neighboring range to reduce it without affecting gesture waveform. We average 10 neighboring values when capturing at 50 packets/second.

4.2.2 *Segmentation*

In practice, we find that gesture waveform's absolute value is not consistent over time because each motion doesn't get fingers back to initial place exactly. Thus, Mudra uses derivation of indication time series for segmentation. The intuition of segmentation in Mudra is that, in derivation series, the gesture part usually holds a much larger value than non-gesture part. Thus, we use amplitude threshold to extract gesture waveform.

First, preliminary gesture waveform is located by using a conservative threshold $T1$ to get fragments belonging only to one gesture. Next, fragments in near scope will be bound together, forming a conservative range of one gesture. Then, we apply a smaller threshold $T2$ to obtain tighter gesture range with adjacent principle to existing one. Further, in order to ensure a complete waveform, we apply guard interval, which is 8 values at 50 packets/second, to expand in both sides.

4.2.3 *Classification*

For gesture recognition, the remaining issue is how to match one segment with one gesture.

1. Gesture Waveform Template

Mudra eliminates the burden of user training relying on distinct waveform shape of each gesture. Before testing, users were shown how to perform gestures. Each gesture in Fig. 10 has a typical duration, e.g. 'Tap' around 0.5s and 'Come' around 2s. Thus, we select a universal waveform template from piecewise linear function for each gesture independent with specific user.

2. Stretch Limited DTW

Without a doubt, the waveform duration and shape of gesture would have variation across different users and multiple repetitions of one user. To solve this problem, we adopt Dynamic Time Wrapping (DTW) to get the minimum distance between segment and waveform template.

However, traditional DTW is not suitable. As DTW always tries to get minimum distance by unlimited stretching, some gestures such as 'Come' and 'Tap' would be mixed up with each other. To see this, let's look at the left plots in Fig.12. By mapping parts I1, I2, I3 in waveform 1 (W1) to J1, J2, J3 in waveform 2 (W2) respectively, DTW gets a very small distance between W1 and W2 although they represent totally different shapes.

Here, we propose a novel algorithm - Stretch Limited DTW to solve this over-stretch issue. To be specific,

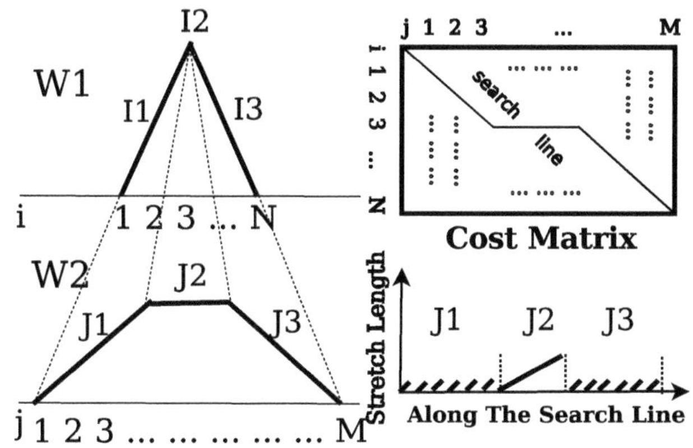

Figure 12: Stretch Limited DTW schematic diagram. The left plots show two waveform figures and how DTW map each part of them. The right plots show the walk through cost matrix and stretch length along the search line.

we introduce an additional cost proportional to stretch length. As to the algorithm, DTW first generates a cost matrix (shown in the right top of Fig.12) which contains the absolute difference between each pair of values in two arrays (which are W1 and W2 here) then walks through to find the path with least cost sum to the last. Here, we attach a penalty to the stretch through additional cost defined with stretch length (as shown in the right bottom of Fig.12). We set the scale factor to be the mean value of corresponding cost matrix.

3. Combine results from multiple sources

Our receiver system can rely on existing WiFi components on devices to fetch signal samples. In promiscuous mode, WiFi device can listen to packets from all sources. Thus, with packet decoding ability of WiFi adapter, our system could distinguish packets from different sources. To conceptually demonstrate how utilizing multiple sources could improve system performance, we simulate multiple traces using separately collected traces with sources in different locations. In classification, we use ground truth of waveform segments to include missing detection.

5. IMPLEMENTATION

We implement Mudra receiver system on the NI-based SDR platform. NI PXIe-1082 chassis is equipped with PXIe-8133 Express Controller and two NI-5791 FlexRIO adapters. Each adapter is connected with a VERT2450 3dBi gain antenna. In Virtex-5 based FPGA, DSP decimation after ADC with resolution of 14 bits generates 20MHz baseband samples. Direct Memory Access is built to transfer baseband samples from Rx1 to Rx2. Central controller is built on RTOS based PXIe-8133. We implement packet detect/connect and channel estimation on central controller.

In the FPGA of Rx2, we implement manual delay/phase injector on stream from Rx1, shown in system model Fig. 11. To equalize signal, samples from Rx2 are thrown into FIR filter with relative channel timing response as coefficients. On the central controller, two signal streams and cancellation stream are fetched from host FIFOs. Then, we use the captured packets to calculate relative channel response, sent to FIR filter in second stream pipeline with FPGA Module register map. Motion indication trace is generated online and stored to file along with timestamp indicating packet arrival time.

We design parallel architecture on central controller to solve computation challenge. First of all, we use multiple single-time ***while*** loops to distribute computation on different CPU cores. To avoid overflow of data transmission from FPGA to central controller, Mudra has a special loop assigned with highest priority dedicated for fetching data from host FIFO. Further, to maintain packet order, queue structure is used to pass data from one loop to next, forming producer-consumer structure.

We use TP-LINK TL-WN722N adapter as signal source, with output power peak at 17.8 dBm [5], and NETGEAR WNDA3100 adapter as WiFi receiver. We build an adhoc connection between these two and enable UDP stream on Windows7 system. Fig. 13 shows our testbed.

6. EVALUATION

To study various factors, we conduct a set of experiments for each and make decision of system design based on the observation. Then, we evaluate our system holistically under different conditions.

6.1 Micro-Benchmarks

We set out to look into various performance-affecting factors. First, what is the noise variation level and how it varies with changing environment. Apart from this,

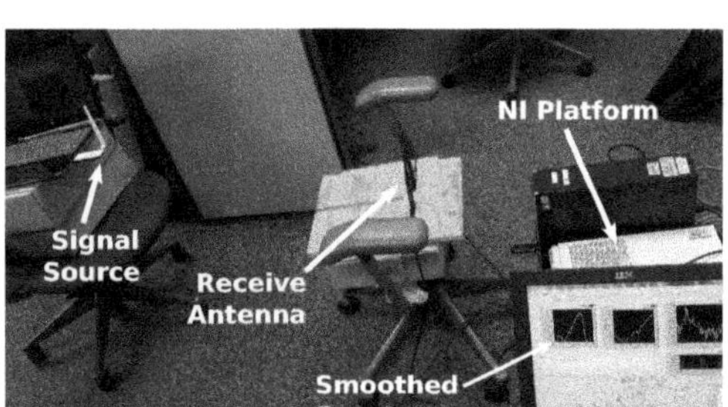

Figure 13: Testbed

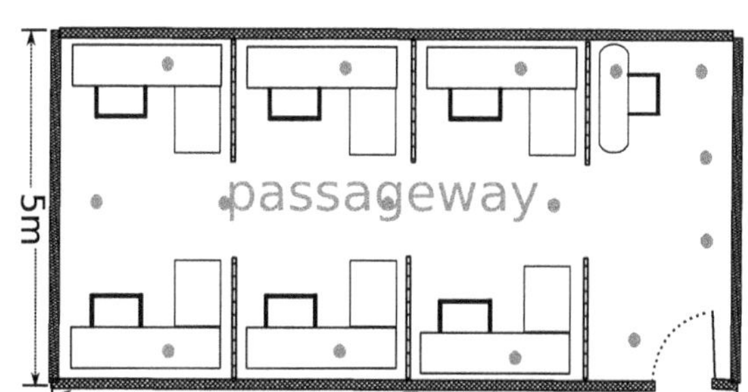

Figure 14: Floor plan

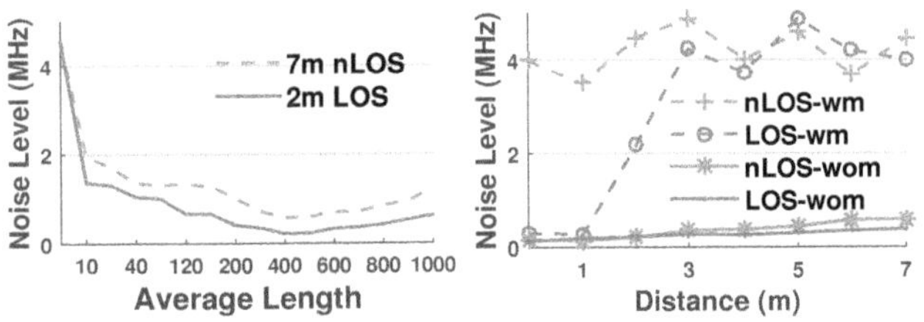

(a) Noise vs Length (b) Noise vs Distance

Figure 15: Noise Variation: 'wom' is short for "without body movement" and 'wm' is short for "with body movement" between the source and receiver.

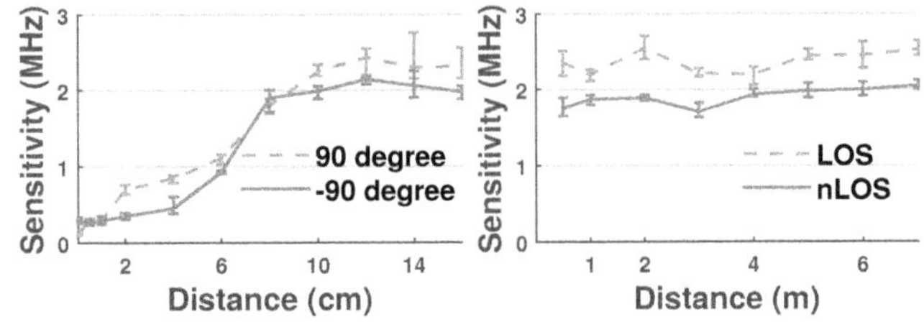

(a) Antenna Distance (b) Source Distance

Figure 16: Sensitivity Study. **Takeaway**: Sensitivity of Mudra changes with antenna distance while keeping stable with source distance.

we also care about system sensitivity, distance between the source and the receiver and orientation. After that, impact of packet length/interval will be studied.

6.1.1 Noise variation

The irritable neighbor problem introduces severe noise in trough tracking, as mentioned in Sec. 3.3.2. To study this effect, we vary the distance between two antennas in Mudra. In a quiet office with door closed (floor plan shown in Fig. 14), we put source 2m away in LOS then 7m away in nLOS at 90 degree to receiver. For fair comparison, we just let one user to be around receiver statically. We measure indication varying range shown in Fig. 15(a). We observe that the average length (for smoothing) larger than 400 samples doesn't reduce noise further. Thus, we select 400 as the default setting. We also find that noise gets even worse with more than 500. This is expected since averaging also makes the trough smoother.

Noise and environmental variation (e.g. human breath) would also induce noise variation. For this test, we choose different distances between signal source and receiver. To study the effect of moving body, another tester will move 3m away from receiver, blocking direct-path signals at some points. As indicated in Fig. 15(b), the noise increases with distance with no moving body. While, with moving body, noise gets extremely serious, disabling our system: We show how such scenarios can be detected and the corresponding samples can be avoided while performing gesture recognition in Mudra later. Another observation is that, with direct-path signal, moving body keeping 1m away from LOS generates a tolerable noise, while nLOS scenario doesn't share this feature.

6.1.2 Sensitivity

We evaluate sensitivity of our system using WiFi signal in different scenarios. First, we study the factor of distance, including antenna distance and source distance. Then, we explore the impact of orientation i.e. hand/source direction and finger moving direction. We ask the users to perform 'Come' with 6 rounds. For each round, we obtain sensitivity as the average amplitude of (trough location) waveforms.

(a) Versus distance

To study antenna distance, we put the source 2m away at 90 degree and -90 degree in LOS. The user is asked to perform 'Come' moving in 0 degree i.e. along two antennas with left hand position of 90 degree. Then, we gradually change distance between two antennas for each test. Fig. 16(a) indicates that sensitivity increases with antenna distance and stops at about 10cm. Considering that 10cm is a favorable scale for most portable devices, we select 10cm as the default setting throughout the paper.

After that, we continue to look into source distance. This time, we let the source be at 90 degree. We adjust the distance between source and receiver both in LOS and nLOS. To fairly compare sensitivity, we let user vary hand position and moving direction in eight equi-angular orientations, choosing the largest one. Fig. 16(b) shows that sensitivity with LOS is greater than nLOS. To our surprise, sensitivity almost doesn't change with distance in both scenarios. We believe the reason is that sensitivity is mainly affected by distance between hand and receiver. Those results, combined with study on noise variation (Sec. 6.1.1), also validates the feasibility of finger-gesture recognition using WiFi signals.

(b) Versus orientation

We first study the effect of finger moving direction. To this end, the user moves his fingers in eight equi-angular directions. We test with four equi-angular source positions with a distance of 2m away from receiver. For example, Fig. 17(a) represents a source at 90 degree. Hand is at 90 degree. As stated before, all directions are relative to two antennas in clockwise mode. In Fig. 17(a)-(d), we observe that moving in 0 degree guarantees at least 1MHz sensitivity for all source positions. Besides, moving in 180 degree provides comparable overall sensitivity as in 0 degree. This is expected since both directions are along two antennas. Then, we seek to evaluate the effect of hand position. We put hand in eight equi-angular positions. This time, however, the user tries to move in all directions and selects the largest one as sensitivity measurement. For example, in Fig. 17(e), with hand position at 90 degree, moving in 0 degree generates largest waveform amplitude. Fig. 17(e)-(h) show that putting hand vertical to

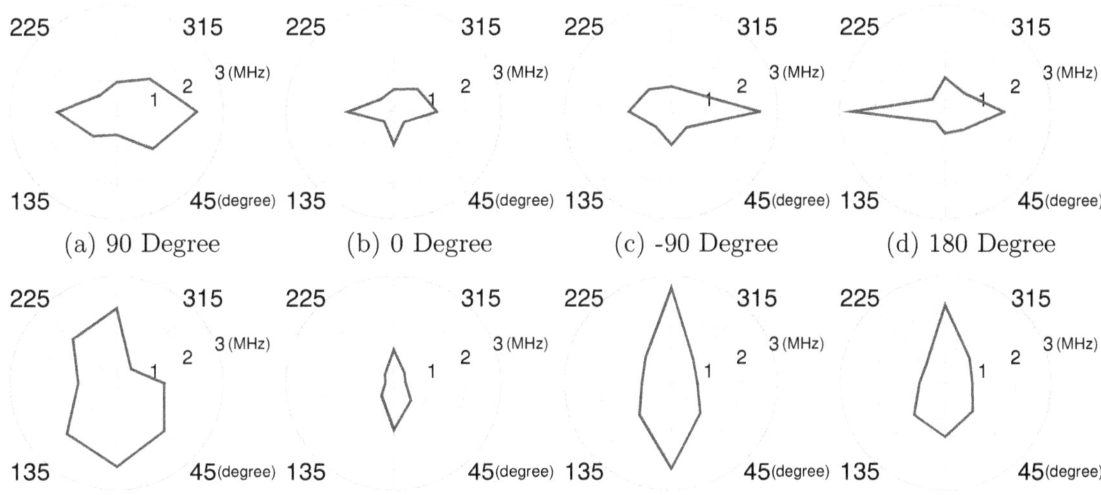

(a) 90 Degree (b) 0 Degree (c) -90 Degree (d) 180 Degree

(e) 90 Degree (f) 0 Degree (g) -90 Degree (h) 180 Degree

Figure 17: Orientation Effect. Upper four plots study moving direction; bottom ones study hand position.

antenna, in all eight positions, has the best overall sensitivity. We have roughly the same observations across other gestures, thus, pushing us to select 90 degree for hand position and 0 degree for moving direction, which means, fingers move along two antennas with hand at vertical position. With such a default setting, combing with waveform consistency study in Sec. 3.4, we desire to make our system feasible with best recognition performance.

6.1.3 Packet length/interval

We run experiments to understand the effects of these parameters on recognition performance. Specifically, we setup an ad hoc connection between two wireless adapters and enable UDP streaming on sender side. With socket programming, we can adjust the length of character string which is sent as a bunch. On both the SDR platform and Wireshark packet capturer, we validate the packet size. Inspired by this, we adjusted packet rate by tuning the while loop interval. Unfortunately, the maximum frequency we get is around 100 packets/second. If we set a lower delay, packet rate increased drastically in a burst mode, which means large portion of duration has no transmission. While, a good thing is that our system already has favorable classification accuracy with 50 packets/second. Thus, such a limitation doesn't affect our evaluation. Signal source is put 2m away at 90 degree position. We have five users perform four gestures - 'Come, Go, Tap, Pick,' each with 50 repetitions. We implement a simplified algorithm on SDR platform to recognize these gestures in real time. Specifically, a threshold is applied to derivation of the indication trace after reducing noise, where boundaries of gesture is detected. Then, we get gesture duration using the attached timestamp. Since 'Come, Go' last much longer than 'Tap' and 'Pick' (2s vs 0.5s), we can distinguish between them. Further, by utilizing the waveform direction, we come to the final decision by judging whether the first derivation is positive or negative.

To evaluate interval effect, we transmit packets at different rates. Fig. 18 shows how classification accuracy changes with packet rate. Let's first look at the resulting line with just one signal source. Here, accuracy is as high as 0.95 with just 10 packets/second - typical WiFi beacon rate, occupying 0.4% of the whole duration. This result means that our system just needs very conservative WiFi signals. We note that no gesture can be detected with rate less than 3 packets/second. This is because such low rate would miss gesture waveform. Then, we apply multiple signal sources and combine results. There are four sources located in four directions. The results indicate that with more signal sources we can get better performance. One reason is that with more sources we reduce the rate of missing detection.

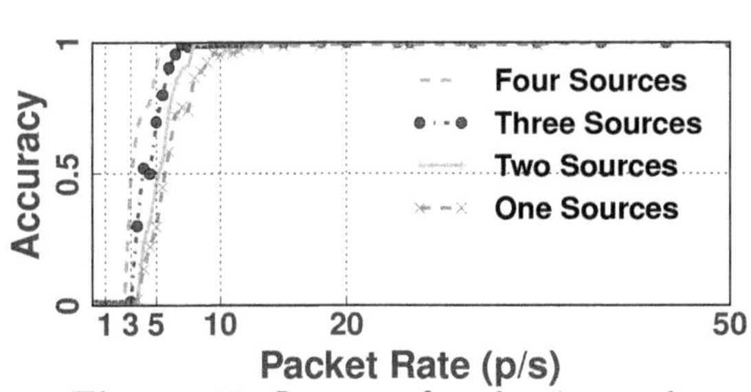

Figure 18: Impact of packet interval.

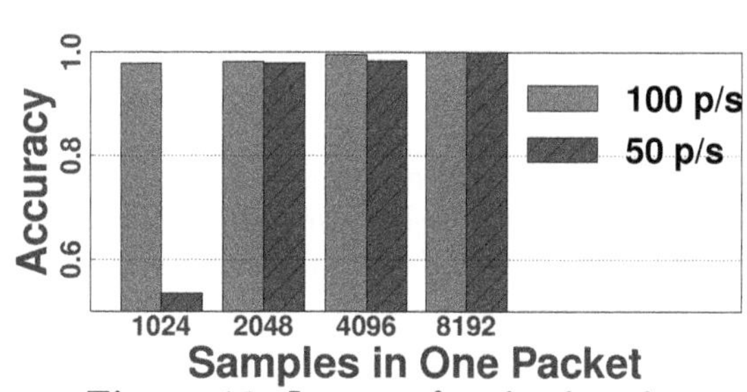

Figure 19: Impact of packet length.

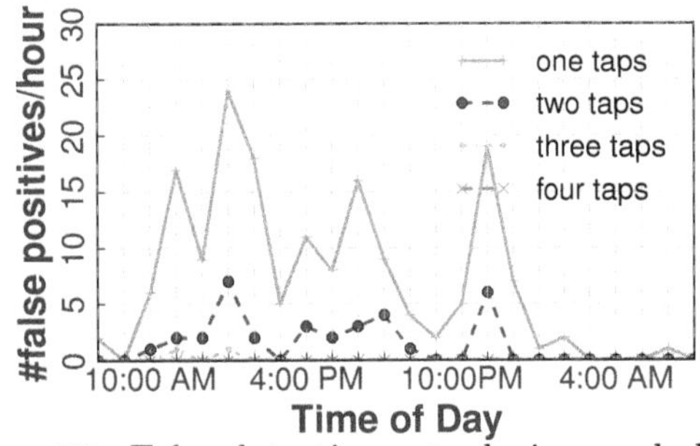

Figure 20: False detection rate during a whole day.

Another reason is that with majority voting, large errors with specific source could be avoided. Typically, with four sources, accuracy could be 0.95 same as one source while with just 5 packets/second per source.

As to the packet length, we evaluate recognition performance with four different choices. Packet rate is set to 100 packets/second and 50 packets/second. In Fig. 19, the results indicate that by connecting short packets, Mudra could be effective in gesture recognition. We note, compared with Fig. 18, that the performance is a little worse. This is because connecting packets not only reduces indication frequency but also degrades indication precision due to averaging over multiple packets. The drastic drop with 1024 at 50 p/s indicates the minimum indication length needed for good performance.

6.2 System Evaluation

6.2.1 *False Positive*

To avoid mis-detection with surrounding moving object, Mudra use multiple 'Tap' as authorization key. We evaluate its effectiveness in this section.

In our experiment, we put two antennas on one desk so that it can be affected by human regular activities. All members are free to do anything, walking, speaking or eating, in the office. We have four position settings which put source 5m away from receiver. Recording last 24 hours over a whole weekday from 8am to 8am, we get the result of false detection number per hour in Fig. 20.

The results show that when one 'Tap' is used as access key, the false detection rate over 24-hour period is 6.92 per hour. We note that this is very low. This is because 'Tap' lasts just about 0.5s, while typical human movements such as walking, eating and typing, last much longer. Besides, those large-scale motion usually push trough out of legal range. Lastly, 'Tap' waveform is special which is not easy for random motion and environmental variation to generate. We also find that with multiple repetitive gestures as the key, the false rate decreases greatly. It is reasonable since we expect gestures in one key would be in a certain range. In this way, for two repetitive 'Tap' false rate is 1.37 per hour and using three 'Tap' makes it as low as 0.08.

6.2.2 *Mudra Recognition Performance*

(a) Evaluation with Local Source: Mudra can utilize signals from the target device with solution in Sec. 3.3.2. We put source (WiFi adapter) 2cm away from the first antenna along the line with iron plate to block the direct path. Receiver is put on desks with surrounding strong reflective objects and empty space near the door shown in Fig. 14. Five users, who don't know how Mudra works, are shown how to perform each gesture. Each gesture in Fig. 2 is performed for 40 times by each user, following regulation of position and direction. During test, users sit in a chair. As to WiFi signals, we adjust packet rate to 50 per second with length of 4096, which means, indication after packet-connect would be 25 per second. We measure recognition accuracy combining detection and classification across all positions and users. Fig. 21 shows the average recognition accuracy is 98%. In this matrix, we observe that recognition has the largest error with 'shoot.' Checking the intermediate result, we find that waveform of 'shoot' is the most variable one across users.

Actual Gesture Performed \ Gesture Classified	circle	come	doublepick	doubletap	go	pick	shoot	switch	tap
circle	1	0	0	0	0	0	0	0	0
come	0	0.98	0	0	0	0.02	0	0	0
doublepick	0	0	0.97	0	0	0.02	0	0	0.01
doubletap	0	0	0	1	0	0	0	0	0
go	0	0	0	0	0.98	0.02	0	0	0
pick	0.01	0	0	0	0	0.99	0	0	0
shoot	0	0.02	0	0	0	0.03	0.95	0	0
switch	0	0	0	0.02	0	0	0	0.98	0
tap	0	0	0	0	0	0.01	0	0	0.98

Figure 21: Confusion Matrix with Local Source.

(b) Evaluation with Remote Source: To evaluate system performance with signals from remote device, we put transmitting WiFi adapter across positions in the office (dots in Fig. 14). With receiver on the walkway and on desk, we include scenarios with distances ranging from 0.5m to 7m both in LOS and nLOS. Each gesture is performed a total of 40 times. As Fig. 22 shows, the average accuracy is 96%. **Takeaway:** Mudra can deliver high accuracy with sources less than 7m away under quiet environment. The performance is worse than local source since larger distance can introduce more noisy variation. After that, we combine results of local and remote sources to look into performance with individual user (shown in Fig. 23): The accuracy is consistent across users showing that Mudra is generic and doesn't need training.

• ***Hand-held Device and Multi-source Combining:***

For portable devices, e.g. smartphone and tablet, people usually hold devices in hand when using them. It is a good utility if our system can support gesture recog-

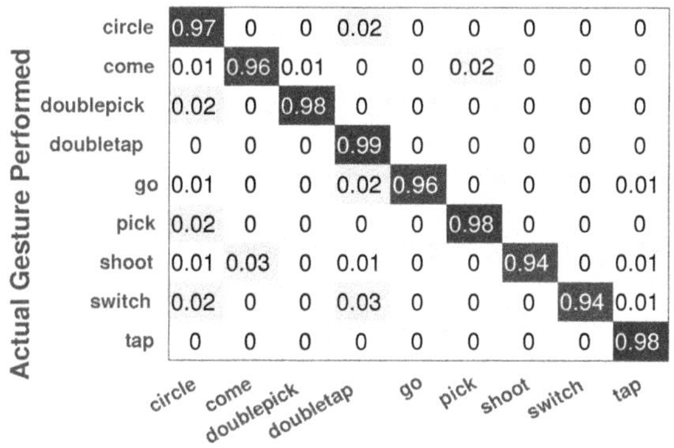

Figure 22: Confusion Matrix with Remote Source.

nition in this scenario. For this exercise, we bundle two antennas with a stick at a distance of 10cm. Users were asked to hold the stick with right hand statically and perform gestures with left hand. To test in the worst case, we put source at distances of 6m and 7m in four nLOS locations. Observation from this test is larger noisy variations due to hand-holding. However, the result shows that average recognition accuracy reaches 90% since noise is still tolerable with users sitting in a chair.

Further, to explore how multiple sources could help in such scenario, we combine recognition with traces from those sources. As a result, the overall accuracy is improved to 96%. It validates the effectiveness of utilizing multiple sources.

- ***Operating with Other Users:***

To test whether multiple users can perform gestures at the same time, we let one user operate on our system with other people nearby, also performing finger gestures. The interfering users are asked to be 2m away while facing to receiver. Also, we put the source across various locations. With three users nearby performing gestures, recognition accuracy is 94%. Thus, we are glad to show multiple users can operate simultaneously in the same room.

- ***System Adaptation:***

By tracking noise level, Mudra can enable two functions and perform better. Firstly, noise level in trace from one source indicates the link quality between the source and receiver, thus, is useful for selecting the good ones. Second, by tracking noise level, system can judge random variation around so as to avoid using such observations. Note that combining observations from multiple sources comes in handy when one or some sources are affected by significant human movements. Here, we test effectiveness of the second one. We put source 5m away. Signal would be affected by human movements between the source and receiver. During working time, i.e. 9am - 5pm, users are asked to choose 10 time slots, only depending on the system notification, to do gestures. While others can normally act in the office, our system can achieve accuracy as 90%.

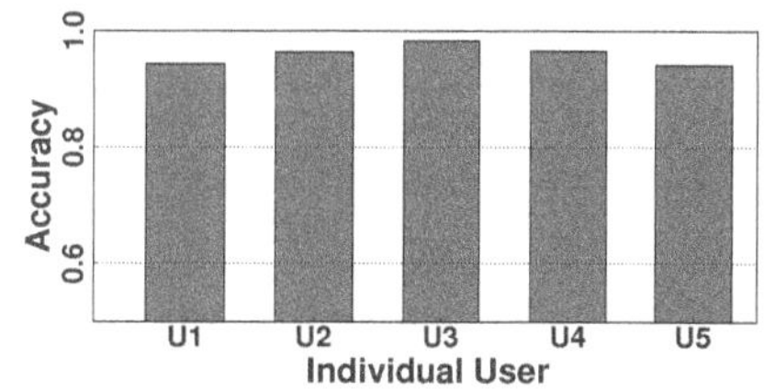

Figure 23: Recognition performance with individual user.

7. CONCLUSION AND DISCUSSION

In this paper, we take the first step towards designing a finger-gesture recognition system with WiFi signals and validate our design with COTS WiFi sources. Our system is user-friendly with no requirement of training. We believe such a technology would stimulate new applications, such as in-air interaction, untouchable-device control and disabled-friendly design. With both on-target local source and remote source, Mudra could support accuracy of at least 96%. While, our system could not support scenario with moving body nearby, we showed how such scenarios can be detected and avoided during gesture recognition.

(a) Mudra with closer antennas

There may be concern that it's hard to separate antennas on portable devices by 10 cm. Fortunately, sensitivity study in Sec. 6.1.2 reveals that shorter antenna distances still enable gesture recognition. To prove this, we test with 6 cm and 8 cm with source 2m away. In two cases, the accuracy is 86% and 93% respectively.

(b) Human interference

Surrounding human motion will incur great variation as shown in noise study Sec. 6.1.1. However, we also find that when body is far from direct path between source and receiver, noise level could be tolerant for gesture recognition. In personal spaces, such as office and living room, such requirements can be satisfied, i.e. people are separated by individual rooms with laptop/desktop nearby.

(c) Why don't we use multiple receivers?

Multiple-receiver design could solve the problem that sensitivity is low with specific position (as studied in [9]). While, in our problem, one critical issue is to ensure consistency of gesture waveforms. If we use multiple receivers, then the required position and direction couldn't be satisfied as in Sec. 3.4. However, single-receiver design doesn't suffer too much in our problem, i.e. sensitivity is favorable under various settings. We believe it is due to operating closer to receiver.

8. ACKNOWLEDGEMENTS

We thank our shepherd Ben Zhao and CoNEXT reviewers for their helpful feedback. This work was supported in part by the NSF grants CNS-1547306, CNS-1514260, CNS-1254032 and CNS-1302620.

9. REFERENCES

[1] Findlay Shearer. Power management in mobile devices, chapter Hierarchical View of Energy Conservation, pages 32-75. Newnes, 2008.

[2] Google. Soli. https://www.youtube.com/watch?v=0QNiZfSsPc0.

[3] Leap motion. https://www.leapmotion.com.

[4] Microsoft. X-box kinect. http://www.xbox.com.

[5] TPLINK. TL-WN722N. https://wikidevi.com/wiki/TP-LINK_TL-WN722N.

[6] Adib, F., and Katabi, D. Wi-Vi: See Through Walls with WiFi! In *ACM SIGCOMM*, 2013.

[7] Adib, F., Mao, H., Kabelac, Z., Katabi, D., and Miller, R. C. Smart Homes that Monitor Breathing and Heart Rate. In *ACM CHI*, 2015.

[8] Chen, B., Qiao, Y., Zhang, O., and Srinivasan, K. AirExpress: Enabling Seamless In-band Wireless Multi-hop Transmission. In *ACM MobiCom*, 2015.

[9] Chen, B., Yenamandra, V., and Srinivasan, K. Tracking Keystrokes Using Wireless Signals. In *ACM MobiSys*, 2015.

[10] Dell, N., D'Silva, K., and Borriello, G. Mobile Touch-Free Interaction for Global Health. In *ACM HotMobile*, 2015.

[11] Everett, E., Sahai, A., and Sabharwal, A. Passive self-interference suppression for full-duplex infrastructure nodes. *IEEE Transactions on Wireless Communications* (2014).

[12] Gollakota, S., and Katabi, D. Zigzag decoding: combating hidden terminals in wireless networks. In *ACM SIGCOMM*, 2008.

[13] Joshi, K., Bharadia, D., Kotaru, M., and Katti, S. Wideo: Fine-grained device-free motion tracing using RF backscatter. In *USENIX NSDI*, 2015.

[14] Kamran Ali, Alex X. Liu, W. W., and Shahzad, M. Keystroke Recognition Using WiFi Signals. In *ACM MobiCom*, 2015.

[15] Kellogg, B., Talla, V., and Gollakota, S. Bringing gesture recognition to all devices. In *USENIX NSDI*, 2014.

[16] Kotaru, M., Joshi, K., Bharadia, D., and Katti, S. Spoton: Indoor localization using commercial off-the-shelf WiFi nics. In *IPSN*, 2015.

[17] Nandakumar, R., Gollakota, S., and Watson, N. Contactless Sleep Apnea Detection on Smartphones. In *ACM MobiSys*, 2015.

[18] Nandakumar, R., Iyer, V., Tan, D., and Gollakota, S. FingerIO: Using Active Sonar for Fine-Grained Finger Tracking. In *ACM CHI*, 2016.

[19] Perrucci, G. P., Fitzek, F. H., and Widmer, J. Survey on energy consumption entities on the smartphone platform. In *IEEE Vehicular Technology Conference*, 2011.

[20] Pu, Q., Gupta, S., Gollakota, S., and Patel, S. Whole-home gesture recognition using wireless signals. In *ACM MobiCom*, 2013.

[21] Rahul, H. S., Kumar, S., and Katabi, D. JMB: scaling wireless capacity with user demands. In *ACM SIGCOMM*, 2012.

[22] Tan, B., Woodbridge, K., and Chetty, K. A real-time high resolution passive WiFi Doppler-radar and its applications. In *International Radar Conference*, 2014.

[23] Vuagnoux, M., and Pasini, S. Compromising Electromagnetic Emanations of Wired and Wireless Keyboards. In *USENIX SSYM*, 2009.

[24] Wang, G., Zou, Y., Zhou, Z., Wu, K., and Ni, L. M. We can hear you with Wi-Fi! In *ACM MobiCom*, 2014.

[25] Wang, J., Zhao, K., Zhang, X., and Peng, C. Ubiquitous keyboard for small mobile devices: harnessing multipath fading for fine-grained keystroke localization. In *ACM MobiSys*, 2014.

[26] Wang, Y., Liu, J., Chen, Y., Gruteser, M., Yang, J., and Liu, H. E-eyes: device-free location-oriented activity identification using fine-grained WiFi signatures. In *ACM MobiCom*, 2014.

[27] Wikipedia. Near and far field — wikipedia, the free encyclopedia, 2015. [Online; accessed 20-October -2015].

[28] Xiao, Y. IEEE 802.11 n: enhancements for higher throughput in wireless LANs. *IEEE Wireless Communications* (2005).

[29] Yang, L., Chen, Y., Li, X.-Y., Xiao, C., Li, M., and Liu, Y. Tagoram: Real-time tracking of mobile RFID tags to high precision using COTS devices. In *ACM MobiCom*, 2014.

[30] Yun, S., Chen, Y.-C., and Qiu, L. Turning a Mobile Device into a Mouse in the Air. In *ACM MobiSys*, 2015.

Passive Communication with Ambient Light

Qing Wang*
TU Delft
Delft, the Netherlands
q.wang-5
@tudelft.nl

Marco Zuniga
TU Delft
Delft, the Netherlands
m.a.zunigazamalloa
@tudelft.nl

Domenico Giustiniano
IMDEA Networks Institute
Madrid, Spain
domenico.giustiniano
@imdea.org

ABSTRACT

In this work, we propose a new communication system for illuminated areas, indoors and outdoors. Light sources in our environments –such as light bulbs or even the sun– are our signal emitters, but we do not modulate data at the light source. We instead propose that the environment itself modulates the ambient light signals: if mobile elements 'wear' patterns consisting of distinctive reflecting surfaces, single photodiode could decode the disturbed light signals to read *passive* information. Achieving this vision requires a deep understanding of a new type of communication channel. Many parameters can affect the performance of passive communication based on visible light: the size of reflective surfaces, the surrounding light intensity, the speed of mobile objects, the field-of-view of the receiver, to name a few. In this paper, we present our vision for a passive communication channel with visible light, the design challenges and the evaluation of an outdoor application where our receiver decodes information from a car moving at 18 km/h.

Categories and Subject Descriptors

C.2.1 [**Computer-Communication Networks**]: Network Architecture and Design—*Wireless Communication*

1. INTRODUCTION

Between the late 1960s and the late 1970s, trains and other rolling stock in North America were monitored based on the standard KarTrak [16]. This standard consisted of 'big' barcodes (≈15×45 cm) attached to wagons and readers the size

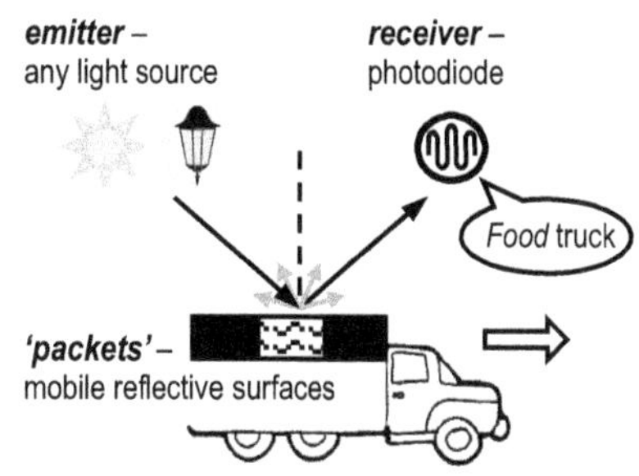

Figure 1: An application of our passive channel.

of a shoebox that had a "light source and photo-multipliers for sensing the reflected light from the barcode"[1].

In this paper, we propose to look back at the idea of KarTrak, and barcodes in general, but from a different perspective. Instead of building sophisticated lights into the reader, we exploit existing light sources such as the sun. The reader is then reduced to an inexpensive and energy-efficient 'tiny box' consisting of simple off-the-shelf photodiodes. By deploying a large number of these tiny boxes, we could gain valuable information about our environment. For example, vehicles can use distinctive reflective surfaces to encode information such as the type of cargo or id, as shown in Fig. 1. Emergency, treatment, and housekeeping trolleys could embed codes to inform their physical locations in a hospital. Furthermore, objects' intrinsic reflective surfaces, e.g., car's roof/windshield, the shape of people, etc., can be exploited by these tiny boxes for applications such as localization.

A key distinctive feature of our proposal is *sustainability*: it has a low footprint across many dimensions. First, *infrastructure*. A large part of our system builds on top of existing infrastructure: there is no need for extra light sources or electronic transmitters on objects. Second, *energy*. Cameras can also provide a passive monitoring infrastructure (by reading QR codes) and have been used for human-computer interaction [19], visual MIMO [2] and localization [8]. But cameras consume orders of magnitude more energy than simpler photodiodes: upwards of 1000 mW [3] vs 1.5 mW (power consumption of the photodiode used in our system[2]). This

*Part of the work was performed when the author was PhD student at IMDEA Networks Institute, Madrid, Spain.

CoNEXT '16, December 12-15, 2016, Irvine, CA, USA

DOI: http://dx.doi.org/10.1145/2999572.2999584

[1]KarTrak is the predecessor of the small and highly effective barcode systems that are now pervasive in supermarkets.

[2]The photodiode is TI OPT101 (https://goo.gl/TDsXS3). Its power consumption is measured in our lab.

low power requirement would enable a small solar panel –the size of a credit card– to harvest enough energy from the surrounding lights for our system to work autonomously. Third, *cost*. Cameras pose not only threats to user's privacy but can be far more expensive (depending on specific features) than single photodiodes. In order to move into higher efficiency low carbon markets, modern ICT technology should give a centric role to sustainability in the design space [1].

The performance of our system however depends on many parameters that are outside the control of the system itself. Unlike traditional barcode readers, which adopt coherent light (laser), we have no influence over the location, characteristics or illuminance power of surrounding lights. We have no influence either over the speed of passing objects: *we can not slow down an object to read its code*. All these dynamics affect the system's ability to decode data. To gain a deeper insight on our system's performance, we propose *a new passive communication channel*. In the next section, we describe the main components of our communication channel and highlight its novelty compared to related work.

2. NEW COMMUNICATION CHANNEL

The basic functional blocks of a digital communication system –the information source, the transmitter, the channel, and the receiver– are the foundation of today's wireless communication [17]. The idea behind this well-established concept is that information sources should use the transmitter to modulate data, so it can travel through the channel and be decoded by the intended receiver.

We propose a new flowchart for a *passive* communication system with low carbon footprint of electronics based on visible light, cf. Fig. 2(a). Our work differs from recent sensing systems leveraging visible light communication[3] for human motions [11, 12], mobile interaction [24], and localization [10, 8] on the basic fact that *we do not use modulated light sources*. Instead, we embed data into reflective objects for passive communication.

The system is composed of three basic block elements:

- *Emitters*, which could be any *simple unmodulated* light source such as standard luminaries or the sun.
- *Receivers*, which are tiny boxes containing at least one photodiode to measure the impinging light intensity.
- *Surfaces*, which reside at mobile objects and contain different *reflective materials*.

We *refer to these surfaces as 'packets'*. The reflective materials used to encode information could be anything, from a pure mirror (strong reflection, low power loss, perpendicular to the incident light), to a dark and rugged cloth (minimal reflection, high power loss, scattered in all directions). As the object moves, the intensity of the reflected light rays changes, altering the amount of light impinging towards a particular receiver. This disturbed reflected light can then be detected and decoded by the receiver. Note that the power

[3]In Visible Light Communication (VLC) light sources are modulated at a high speed to transmit information without affecting the illumination perceived by the user.

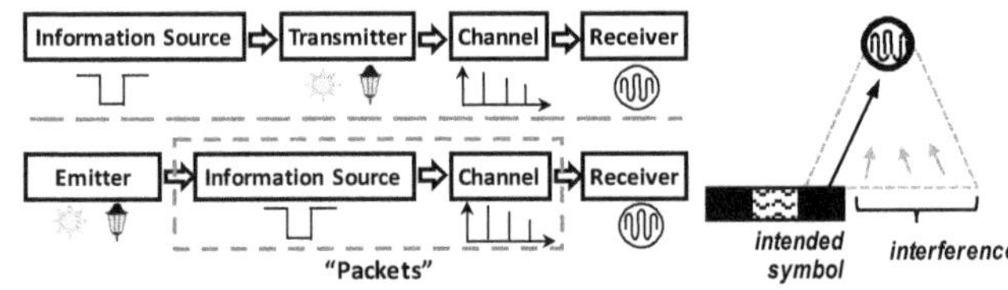

(a) Flowchart of the classic communication (top) and our passive communication system (bottom).

(b) FoV effect.

Figure 2: Communication system (a) and FoV effect (b)

loss of this communication channel is a function of the reflection coefficient of the reflective material. This simple system could *enable the monitoring of events and activities in a passive manner*.

An important aspect of our system is that light are modulated by reflective surfaces. This concept is inspired by backscatter communication, where passive tags modulate the electromagnetic waves produced by external sources. This technique has been traditionally used by RFID tags [22], and recently applied to other radio technologies, such as Wi-Fi [6] and TV signals [14]. In the same way radio-backscatter exploits the surrounding radio waves, we want to exploit visible light. However, our tags (packets) are not electronic devices and our system has to deal with visible light waves, which have completely different properties compared to radio waves. Wireless barcode [15] has been proposed to embed information into infrastructure such as building walls. The barcode was built with material (e.g., copper/cement) into a shape of square-wave. Data was modulated through the barcode's reflection of electromagnetic waves. This barcode did not have electronic devices, similar to our tag. However, [15] required expensive dedicated radio signals impinging on it (the unit cost[4] is $220,000), while ambient light is sufficient for our tag to work (our prototype costs around 50 dollars). Only recently, Retro-VLC explored backscattering with visible light communication [9]. Retro-VLC created a bidirectional link between an *active* light source and a *static* semi-passive with LCD shutters. The LCD shutters were used to change the reflected signal in time. Our work differs from Retro-VLC in two important ways, we explore backscattering for *unmodulated* light sources and *mobile* nodes. *LCD shutters however can complement our work*, at an increased carbon footprint, by enabling mobile objects to change the reflected information (code) in time.

3. CHALLENGES

Since we have no control over the location or illuminance power of light sources, the receiver's ability to decode information depends strongly on its field-of-view (FoV) and distance to the mobile object. A wide FoV provides a wider coverage but it also exposes the receiver to more interference, as shown in Fig. 2(b). A narrow FoV provides the opposite trade-off: a higher signal-to-interference ratio at the expense of having a limited coverage. Regarding the distance to the mobile object, increasing this distance is detri-

[4]See https://goo.gl/jQacLJ

Model	Description
HLMP-EG08 -YZ000	5 mm red LED (used as a receiver)
OPT101	photodiode
74HCT244N	tri-state buffer
LM358N	amplifier
MCP3008	analog-to-digital converter
ADG444	multiplexer

Figure 3: The evaluation board runs a Debian Linux and the open-source OpenVLC driver. We receive data using either the low-power LED (1) or the photodiode (PD) (2). Key used electronic devices are listed on the right.

mental for two reasons: (i) the signal strength of visible light waves decrease exponentially with distance (like radio waves), and (ii) longer distances increase the area covered by the FoV, which as stated before can add interference. With this basic understanding of the communication channel, we now describe the most relevant design challenges.

Channel capacity. Communication systems need to quantify the data rate of their channels. For us, this means understanding how different parameters –such as the FoV, distance to mobile objects, width of reflective surfaces and the speed of mobile objects– affect the capacity of the passive channel.

Channel distortions. Similar to radio systems, our channel will be exposed to distortions. For example: fog, humidity, dirt on top of the reflective surfaces and variable speeds of the mobile object will be commonplace phenomena affecting the incoming signal and making it harder to decode.

'Packet' collisions. Until now we assume that a single object moves under the FoV of a receiver. In some applications this will not hold. If several objects move under the same FoV, the incoming signal will be the sum of multiple 'overlapping' symbols. Leading in fact to the equivalent of packet collisions in traditional radio communication systems.

Noise floor. Communications based on visible light need to cope with the fact that surrounding light intensity can change significantly. These 'noise floor' changes can easily saturate a photodiode, which make links disappear abruptly.

In Section 4, we look at each of these challenges from an empirical viewpoint. We showcase the problem and present our solutions. In Section 5, we evaluate our passive system through an outdoor vehicle application.

4. DECODING INFORMATION: AN EMPIRICAL APPROACH

We empirically investigate the challenges described in Section 3. In our evaluation, we use the following components:

Emitter: we use three different types of light sources: an LED lamp, ceiling fluorescent lights, and the sun. In this section, most of our results are based on the LED lamp because it allows us to have controlled and repeatable scenarios. In Section 5, we use the sun as light source.

Receiver: we use and customize the OpenVLC platform [21]. The board is depicted in Fig. 3, highlighting the two optical receivers. Given that our channel relies on passive sources, we *only* use the OpenVLC interfaces related to reception (i.e., the optical components (1) and (2) in Fig. 3).

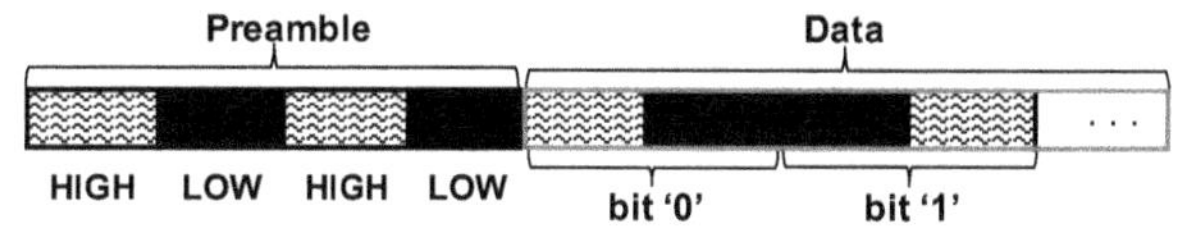

Figure 4: Packet format: Preamble + Data.

Before proceeding with our insights, we first introduce some basic information of our system: the encoding of data and the packet format.

Coding. Our encoding process is passive and is performed independently by each moving object. In the experiments, we use the following materials to encode information:

- Aluminum tape, which has a relatively high reflection coefficient and low diffused reflections (to represent the symbol `HIGH`);
- Black paper napkins, which have a lower reflection coefficient and higher diffused reflections (to represent the symbol `LOW`).

The *symbol width*, defined as the width of the material representing a symbol, remains constant within a packet, but different packets can have different symbol widths. To enable an easy and stable decoding at the receiver, we use Manchester codes: a '0'-bit is mapped to `HIGH-LOW`, and a '1'-bit is mapped to `LOW-HIGH`.

Packet format. Each packet has two fields: preamble and data, as shown in Fig. 4. The preamble is fixed and consists of four symbols `HIGH-LOW-HIGH-LOW`. The detection of the preamble requires no *a-priori* calibration, as it will be described later. The Data field comes after the preamble and includes $2N$ symbols, representing the modulated N-bit data.

4.1 Channel Capacity: The Ideal Scenario

In this subsection, we quantify the channel's capacity. All of our experiments follow the basic setup illustrated in Fig. 1, a photodiode above a passing mobile object. First we describe our decoding method. Then, we assess the impact that the symbol width and the receiver's height have on the channel's throughput.

Decoding. The receiver decodes information based on the Received Signal Strength (RSS). The RSS is perceived as a sequence of `HIGH` and `LOW` symbols. In this subsection we assume that no distortions are present (no dirt or fog) and that objects move at constant speed while passing under the FoV of the receiver. In the next subsections we propose different mechanisms to overcome signal distortion and interference.

Unless stated otherwise, we use an LED lamp as light source and the experiments are carried in an office where no other sources of light are present: the blinds are closed and light bulbs are turned off. These constraints are removed in our outdoor experiments. The ground plane where objects move is covered with black papers, to resemble tarmac. To obtain binary data out of the RSS signal, we use two thresholds: one for the magnitude of the RSS signal τ_r (to distinguish whether a symbol is `HIGH` or `LOW`) and one for the time length τ_t (to estimate the duration of a symbol). The thresholds are obtained on a per-packet basis and do not require calibration. These thresholds need to be *highly adaptive* because we do not modulate information with a common

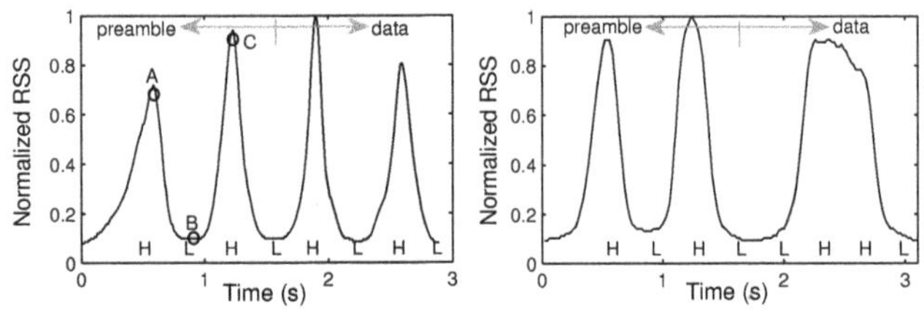

(a) Data='00' ('HLHL') (b) Data='10' ('LHHL')

Figure 5: Received signals in an ideal scenario.

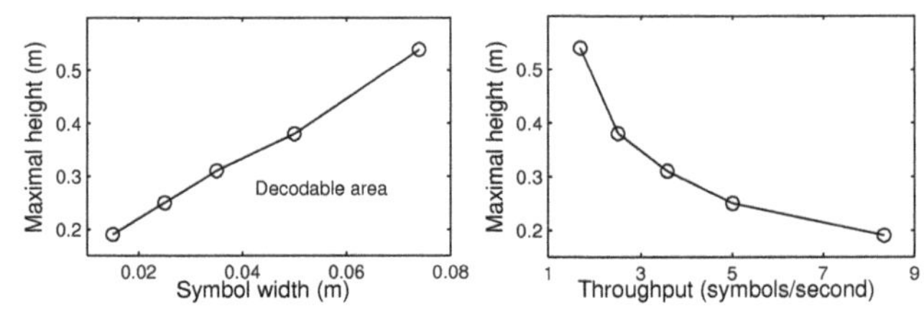

(a) Height vs. symbol width (b) Height vs. throughput

Figure 6: Maximal height vs. symbol width and system throughput. Packet's moving speed is 8cm/s.

transmitter, but we rather let each packet determine its own parameters: symbol width, materials used and speed.

We first detect the first two peaks and the first valley present in the preamble, points A, B and C in Fig. 5(a). Denoting the tuple $< r_i, t_i >$ as the RSS value and timestamp for point i, the thresholds for the magnitude and period are defined as

$$\tau_r = \frac{(r_A - r_B) + (r_C - r_B)}{2}; \ \tau_t = \frac{(t_B - t_A) + (t_C - t_B)}{2}.$$

With these thresholds, subsequent RSS measurements are grouped together in windows of length τ_t. If the maximum value in a window is above τ_r, we declare the symbol to be `HIGH`; otherwise, we declare it to be `LOW`. Figure 5 depicts the RSS for two packets carrying a two-bit (four-symbol) payload: "00" (left) and "10" (right). Both packets have the same symbol width (3 cm). The emitter and receiver are at a height of 20 cm from the workplane, and the distance between emitter and receiver is 12 cm. For this scenario, the received signals are clear. It is therefore easy for our decoding method to get accurate thresholds values (based on the preamble), and consequently, to decode information.

The symbol width and channel capacity. Our decoding method enables us to obtain binary data. But a designer willing to use this new channel would need more information to assess the feasibility of a potential application. For example, considering that the emitters (lights in buildings, streets or roads) have a fixed output power and height:

- What symbol width should the designer use on objects to be able to decode information?
- And given this symbol width, what channel capacity can the designer expect?

Depending on the symbol width and the receiver's FoV, inter-symbol interference may appear. A wider symbol width makes the system more resilient to interference, see Fig. 2(b), but it reduces the amount of information that can be encoded on the surface of the object. A narrow symbol width has the opposite trade-off. To provide some insights we gradually change the receiver's and emitter's height from 20 cm to 55 cm. For each of these heights we test packets with different symbol widths, ranging from 1.5 cm to 7.5 cm. The objects carrying the packets are moved starting from a slow speed up to the maximum speed that allows the packets to be decodable. With this basic setup we identify two important trends:

Symbol width. Fig. 6(a) shows that there is a decodable region with a linear relationship between the maximum height of the emitter/receiver and the symbol width. Assuming a constant power at the light source, there will be a height beyond which the receiver will not be able to decode information, no matter how long the symbol width is.

Throughput. For a given emitter/receiver setup, the throughput is a function of the symbol width and the speed. Fixing one of these parameters determines the other. Using a constant speed of 8 cm/s, we have identified the narrowest symbol width that makes the packet decodable. Based on these experiments, we show that the channel's capacity decreases exponentially with the receiver's height in Fig. 6(b).

Trends like the ones exposed above are important for the design of applications. Getting receivers as close as possible to moving objects would enable (i) smaller objects to be monitored (cf. the linear improvement in Fig. 6(a)), and (ii) exponentially more information (cf. Fig. 6(b)).

Impact of other light sources. We also perform experiments using standard fluorescent lights in our ceiling. The results are shown in Fig. 7. Here the lights' height is 2.3 m and the receiver's is 0.2 m. The decoding method still works in these settings but there are some important points to highlight. Note that because we have an illuminated area, the noise floor is higher, which leads to a smaller difference between the `HIGH` and `LOW` symbols compared to our dark-room experiments. There is also a larger variance in the signal, 'thicker lines' than those in Fig. 5, which is due to the AC power supply [7]. The ceiling lights are significantly further away than the LED lamp used in our prior experiments, but due to their higher output power, we can still decode information. An extreme case highlighting the relationship between high output power and coverage is presented in Section 5, where we use the sun.

This experiment exposes an important trade-off in our channel. In traditional communication systems, the transmitter and the sources creating interference are normally independent, in our case they are the same. A light source with a high output power will increase the amount of light reflected to the receiver (`HIGH` symbol) but it also increases the noise floor.

4.2 Channel Distortion: Variable Speed

Thus far we have assumed an ideal scenario leading to a clean signal. In practice many events can distort the signal, such as objects moving at variable speed. In these scenarios decoding the data may not be possible, but a plausible alternative is to transform the decoding problem into a classification problem. We could compare the distorted signal against

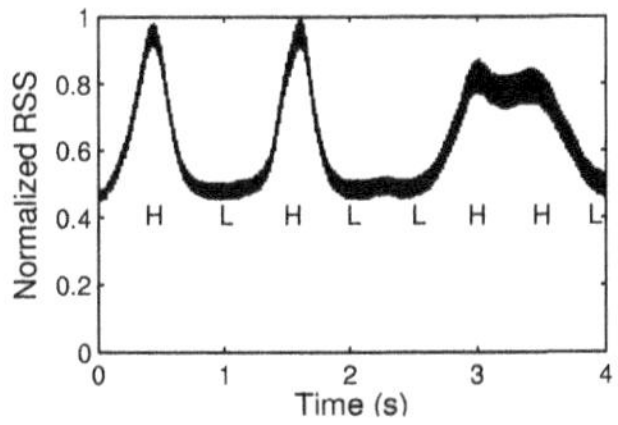

Figure 7: Signal received under incandescent bulb.

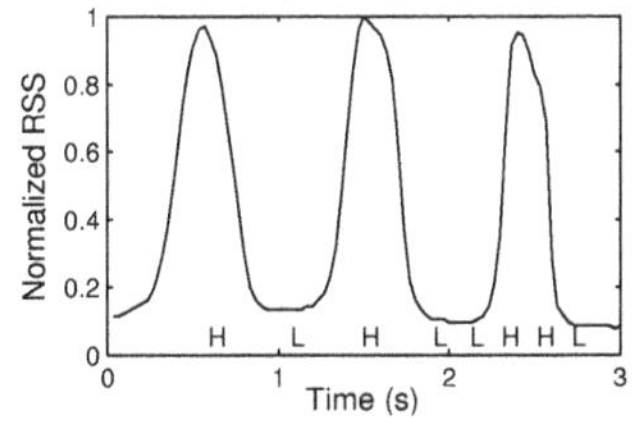

Figure 8: Signal received under variable speed.

a database of clean signals (obtained under ideal scenarios, cf. Sec. 4.1) to see which one is the best match. Clearly, in this case we will not be able to use 2^N codes. We will be constrained to use far less codes making sure that their inter-Hamming distances are maximized to have codes that are as different as possible from each other.

We now showcase a scenario where channel distortion is caused by objects moving at variable speeds. While many signal processing techniques could be used for classification problems, we use Dynamic Time Warping (DTW) to showcase our basic idea. DTW is a method used in many areas to measure the similarity of two signals. We use the two clean signals in Fig. 5 as the baselines for comparison. For the distorted signal we use the same packet as the one in Fig. 5(b), but we change its speed in the middle of the decoding process. This object moves at a certain speed when its first half (preamble) passes the receiver, and the speed is doubled when the second half (Data field) passes by. Figure 8 depicts the RSS of this distorted signal. The decoding method presented in the previous subsection leads to an erroneous symbol sequence when used on the distorted signal, "`HLHL.HL`", instead of the correct one "`HLHL.LHHL`". With DTW, the normalized distances between the signals in Fig. 8 and Fig. 5(a), and between Fig. 8 and Fig. 5(b) are 326 and 172, respectively (as a reference, the distance between the signal in Fig. 8 and itself is 131). Therefore, the distorted packet in Fig. 8 is classified as belonging to the same group as the packet in Fig. 5(b), which is correct.

4.3 'Packet' Collisions: Frequency Domain

In the previous two subsections, we assume there is only one packet moving under the FoV of the receiver. This approach works well for scenarios with 'constrained' mobility, such as car lanes or tracks, but this assumption may not hold in less structured scenarios. We now investigate the case where two packets pass through the FoV at the same time. We consider high- and low-frequency packets. A high-frequency packet is one with narrow symbol widths, so the received signal changes fast; and a low-frequency packet is one with wide symbol widths (slow-changing signal).

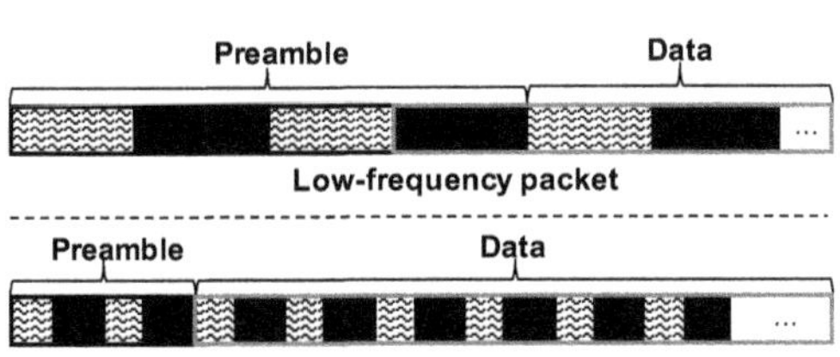

Figure 9: Illustration of the low/high-frequency packets.

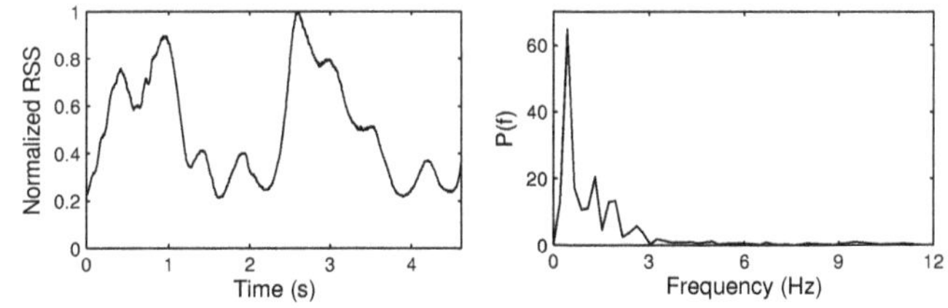

(a) `Case1`- received signal (b) `Case1`- signal after FFT

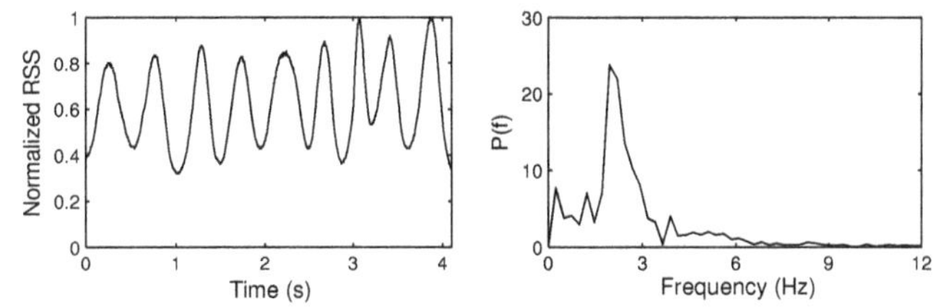

(c) `Case2`- received signal (d) `Case2`- signal after FFT

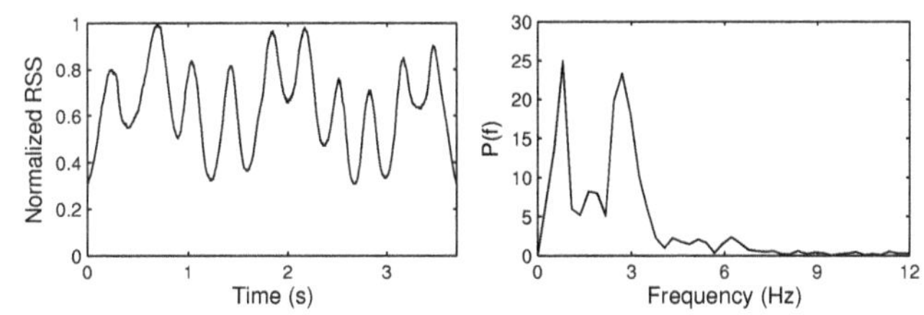

(e) `Case3`- received signal (f) `Case3`- signal after FFT

Figure 10: Overlapping signals and their FFT.

In our tests both packets have the same length, their patterns are shown in Fig. 9. We carry out three different tests:

- `Case1` – the low-frequency packet dominates the reflected light towards the FoV of the receiver;
- `Case2` – the two packets exchange their positions (the high-frequency packet becomes the dominating signal);
- `Case3` – the two packets share equally the receiver's FoV (no dominant packet).

The RSS captured at the receiver for these three cases are shown in Fig. 10(a), (c) and (e). For `Case1` and `Case2`, we can decode bits using the method presented in Sec. 4.1. For `Case3` however, we cannot get accurate information from either method, decoding or DTW.

To obtain partial information for `Case3`, we use Fast Fourier Transforms (FFT) to analyze collisions in the frequency domain. The frequency spectrums are shown in Fig. 10(b), (d) and (f). In Fig. 10(b) and (d), we can observe a single dominant frequency, which explains why it was easy to decode information in the time domain. But the undecodable signal in Fig. 10(e) also benefits from the FFT, because we can detect the presence of two different types of object.

These results however only scratch the surface of the problem. For a thorough investigation, setups such as having more than two packets under the FoV or having them pass with different speeds need to be addressed to quantify the interplay of the FoV and different collision scenarios.

	Saturation	Sensitivity
PD (G1)	450 lux	1
PD (G2)	1200 lux	0.45
PD (G3)	5000 lux	0.089
LED	35000 lux	0.013

Figure 11: Supported noise floor of the optical receivers used in this work. The sensitivities are normalized to that of the PD with gain control G1.

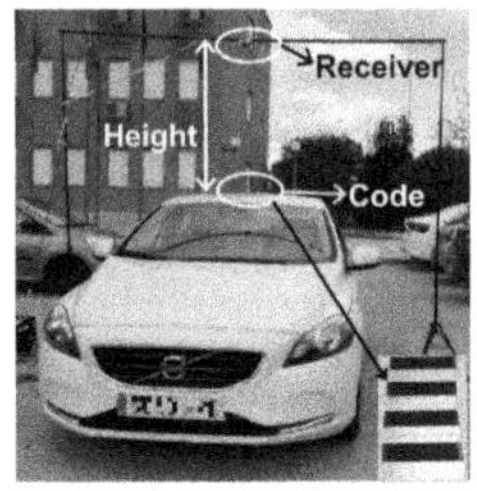

Figure 12: Setup of the outdoor application.

4.4 Noise Floor: tradeoff between PD and LED as a Receiver

Until now our focus has been on obtaining information at different levels: decoding (clean channel) and waveform mapping (distorted channel). But these evaluations do not consider explicitly the drastic changes in the noise floor, which cause photodiodes (PDs) to get easily saturated under strong light conditions, especially outdoor [13]. Given that we exploit ambient light as the 'emitter' we need a receiver that can work in a wide range of ambient illuminance conditions.

To obtain a solid receiver, we propose to use conjunctly a PD and an LED acting as a receiver (RX-LED), both shown in Fig. 3. LEDs acting as receivers have been used before in VLC systems [4, 5, 18, 20] and have different optical properties compared to PDs. In particular, we want to exploit two key properties of RX-LEDs: narrow FoV and narrow optical bandwidth. These two properties lead to lower sensitivities (which is usually not good), but they also increase the resilience to saturation. To quantify this tradeoff for the specifics of our channel we perform the following experiments. We use three different gain controls for the PD, from a high value G1 (high sensitivity and long range but easily saturated) to a low value G3 (opposite effect). To increase the sensitivity of the RX-LED we decide to operate it in photovoltaic mode (as solar cells) that minimizes the effect of dark current (current generated in the absence of ambient light). The results are shown in Fig. 11. We have two observations:

Saturation: the PD at gain control level G1 saturates at 450 lux, which maps roughly to a medium illuminated room. At G3, the PD works for noise floors up to 5000 lux. But outdoor scenarios during the day can easily go above 10 klux. The RX-LED, instead, can work when the noise floor is up to 35,000 lux and is thus more suitable for outdoor scenarios.

Sensitivity: the RX-LED is less sensitive than the PD, which will affect their ability to decode data at low RSSs, such as indoor environments with low ambient illuminance.

Concluding, a receiver with two optical components (PD and RX-LED) can alleviate the noise floor problem by properly selecting the component that provides reliable passive communication for the given ambient light conditions.

5. APPLICATION EVALUATION

We now evaluate our system with an outdoor application. We place a 'packet' on the roof of a car and attach the receiver to a pole supporting structure, cf. Fig. 12. The receiver uses two optical components: a PD and a RX-LED. The goal is to decode the packet information as the car passes by. The symbol width is 10 cm and the sampling frequency of the receiver is set to 2K samples/sec. The experiments are carried out in cloudy days at noon and late afternoon to study different sun positions and intensities.

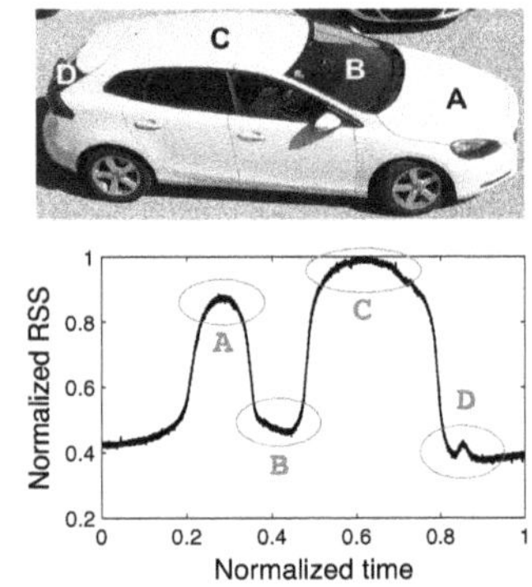

Figure 13: Top: Volvo V40; bottom: captured signal.

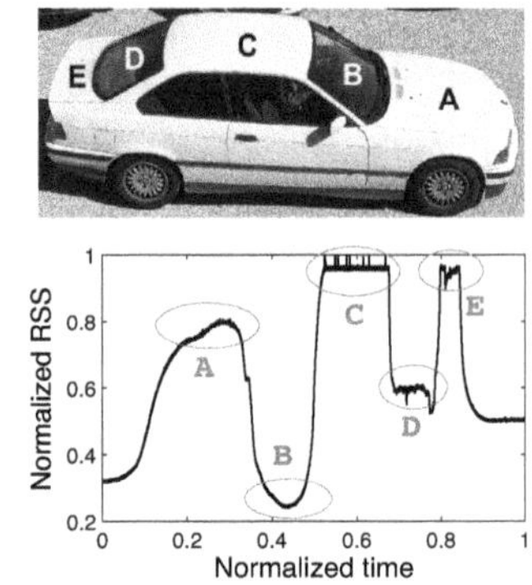

Figure 14: Top: BMW3; bottom: captured signal.

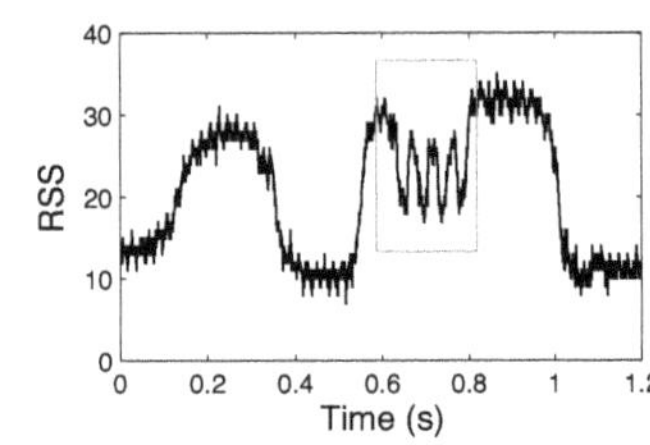

(a) Noise floor: 450 lux

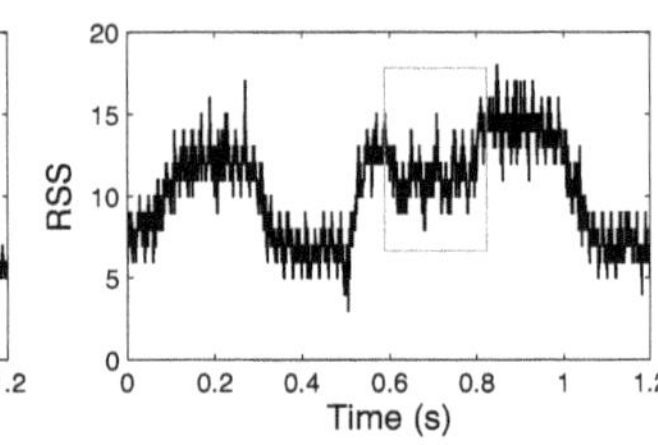

(b) Noise floor: 100 lux

Figure 15: LED as RX. Car's speed is 18 km/h, the receiver's height is 25 cm, and the code is 'HLHL.HLHL'.

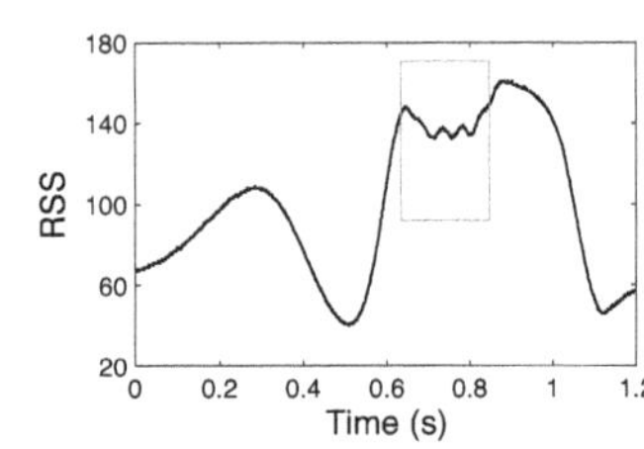

(a) Noise: 100 lux; w/o shield.

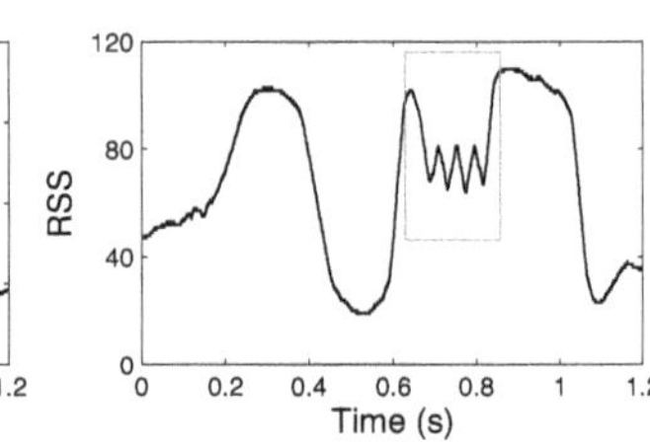

(b) Noise: 100 lux; w/ shield.

Figure 16: PD as RX. Car's speed is 18 km/h, the receiver's height is 25 cm, and the code is 'HLHL.HLHL'.

5.1 Baseline: Car's Shape Detection

We use two cars in our experiments: a Volvo V40 and a BMW series 3. As baseline experiments, we drive the cars under the receiver without any packet on the roof. The top part of the cars have two different materials, metal and glass, with different lengths and shapes. Thus, their optical signatures should be unique. Figs. 13 and 14 show the baseline signals of the cars captured with the RX-LED. We can observe that the metal parts of the cars –hoods (A), roofs (C) and trunks (E)– reflect much more light (peaks) than the front and rear windshields (B and D). The different designs of the cars are also accurately reflected by their waveforms.

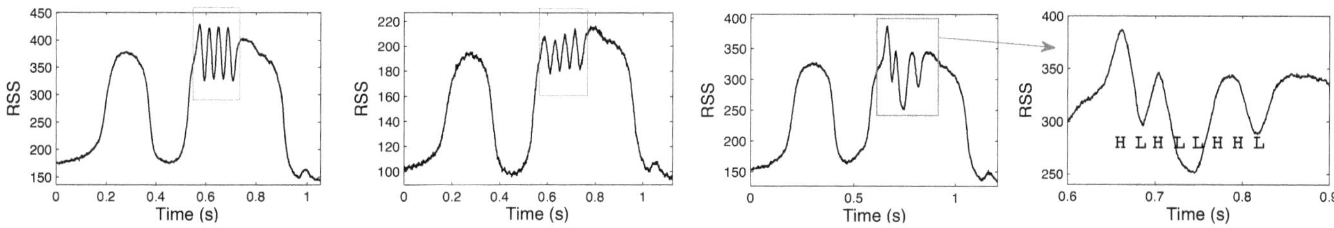

(a) Height: 75 cm; noise floor: 6200 lux; code: 'HLHL.HLHL'.
(b) Height: 100 cm; noise floor: 3700 lux; code: 'HLHL.HLHL'.
(c) Height: 100 cm; noise floor: 5500 lux; code: 'HLHL.LHHL'.

Figure 17: Car's speed is 18 km/h. Two different types of code and different distance between the car and the receiver.

The ability to detect the shape of the car with the RX-LED allows us to use the car's optical signature as a *long-duration-preamble* of the packet, indicating when the receiver needs to get ready to decode information. Due to space limitations, but without the loss of generality, we now only report the experiments with the Volvo V40 at a speed of 18 km/h.

5.2 Mild Illuminated Environment

We perform tests for various heights of the receiver and car speeds. To decode the information, we use the same method described in Section 4 but in two phases:

- We first look for the long-duration-preamble based on the car's shape (by detecting the hood 'peak' and windshield 'valley', cf. Fig. 13);
- We then perform the decoding algorithm in Sec. 4.1.

Impact of noise floor. A mild illumination requires a lower height to ensure the system works well. In Fig. 15, we observe that when the noise floor is about 450 lux, our prototype works well with the RX-LED up to a height of 25 cm. When the noise floor decreases to 100 lux, we cannot decode the information anymore, cf. Fig. 15(b). The reason behind this phenomenon is that our system harnesses the ambient light to modulate its information. If the ambient light is too weak, the modulated information can not travel too far due to the light's attenuation (cf. Section 4.4).

Since the PD is more sensitive than RX-LED (cf. Fig. 11), we use it with gain G2 to overcome the low illuminance conditions. Fig. 16(a) shows that while the signal is cleaner than the one obtained with RX-LED, the information is still not decodable. The reason is that the PD has a large FoV, thus the car's metal roof adds interference at the receiver. By reducing the PD's FoV with a small physical cap ($1.2\times1.2\times2.8$ cm), we filter out much of the interference and decode the information, as shown in Fig. 16(b), regardless of the RSS drop resulting from the smaller impinging light on the receiver.

5.3 Well Illuminated Environment

Given that the PD can easily saturate with higher noise floor (cf. Section 4.4), we evaluate the RX-LED for passive communication under well illuminated conditions.

Supported car's speed. We fix the height of the receiver to 75 cm and drive the car at 18 km/h. The noise floor is around 6200 lux during the experiments. The results are shown in Fig. 17(a). We can observe that the captured signal is very clear, and thus, the information is easy to decode. The achieved throughput is around 50 symbols/s.

Maximal height. We then increase the height of the receiver to 100 cm. The noise floor is about 3700 lux. Under these circumstances, we can decode the information easily. Note that the RSS in Fig. 17(b) is smaller than that in Fig. 17(a). This is because in Fig. 17(b), the height is higher and the ambient light is weaker compared to Fig. 17(a). Finally, the result with the car carrying a different packet code and under a different noise floor is shown in Fig. 17(c). The packet is successfully decoded in this case as well.

6. DISCUSSION AND CONCLUSION

We have presented a passive communication system that harnesses ambient light to convey information. The three block elements of our system, the emitter, the 'packet' and the receiver, are sustainable in its conception. We identified fundamental challenges and evaluated a prototype in an outdoor parking lot. While the obtained results are encouraging, more research is necessary. (1) *Encoding dynamic data.* Our system can now encode static data in each packet, targeting at low footprint. Encoding dynamic information is feasible by adopting advance materials whose reflection is adjustable (e.g. E-ink screens or LCD shutters). (3) *Maximal supported speed of an object.* This is mainly determined by the PD's response time to light changes and the receiver's sampling rate. We will exploit this in a follow-up work. (4) *Reflected light intensity.* Our system exploits reflected light to convey information, whose intensity is normally weaker than direct light. To improve the performance, we expect to benefit from next-generation optical receivers in VLC or advanced diffraction gratings (e.g., holographic gratings [23]). (5) *Networking.* If the receivers in our system are networked, then they can share the information about the tracked objects and thus could improve the system's performance. How to connect these low-end receivers efficiently is a challenge in our system. These challenges are left for future research, yet this work provides a first step for new types of passive communication with visible light.

Acknowledgement

This research work was funded in part by Ministerio de Economía y Competitividad grant TEC2014-55713-R and by the Madrid Regional Government through the TIGRE5-CM program (S2013/ICE-2919). Our sincere thanks to the reviewers and our shepherd Monia Ghobadi for all of their great comments and constructive feedbacks.

7. REFERENCES

[1] SMART 2020: Enabling the low carbon economy in the information age. *The Climate Group* (2008).

[2] ASHOK, A., GRUTESER, M., MANDAYAM, N., SILVA, J., VARGA, M., AND DANA, K. Challenge: Mobile optical networks through visual mimo. In *Proceedings of the ACM MobiCom* (2010).

[3] CHEN, X., CHEN, Y., MA, Z., AND FERNANDES, F. C. A. How is energy consumed in smartphone display applications? In *Proceedings of the ACM workshop on HotMobile* (2013), pp. 3:1–3:6.

[4] DIETZ, P., YERAZUNIS, W., AND LEIGH, D. Very low-cost sensing and communication using bidirectional LEDs. In *TR2003-35* (2003).

[5] GIUSTINIANO, D., TIPPENHAUER, N., AND MANGOLD, S. Low-complexity visible light networking with LED-to-LED communication. In *Proceedings of the IFIP Wireless Days (WD)* (2012), pp. 1–8.

[6] KELLOGG, B., PARKS, A., GOLLAKOTA, S., SMITH, J. R., AND WETHERALL, D. Wi-fi backscatter: Internet connectivity for rf-powered devices. In *Proceedings of the ACM SIGCOMM* (2014).

[7] KUO, Y.-S., PANNUTO, P., AND DUTTA, P. System architecture directions for a software-defined lighting infrastructure. In *Proceedings of the ACM workshop on VLCS* (2014).

[8] KUO, Y.-S., PANNUTO, P., HSIAO, K.-J., AND DUTTA, P. Luxapose: Indoor positioning with mobile phones and visible light. In *Proceedings of the ACM MobiCom* (2014).

[9] LI, J., LIU, A., SHEN, G., LI, L., SUN, C., AND ZHAO, F. Retro-VLC: Enabling Battery-free Duplex Visible Light Communication for Mobile and IoT Applications. In *Proceedings of the ACM Workshop on HotMobile* (2015).

[10] LI, L., HU, P., PENG, C., SHEN, G., AND ZHAO, F. Epsilon: A visible light based positioning system. In *Proceedings of the USENIX NSDI* (2014).

[11] LI, T., AN, C., TIAN, Z., CAMPBELL, A. T., AND ZHOU, X. Human sensing using visible light communication. In *Proceedings of the ACM MobiCom* (2015).

[12] LI, T., LIU, Q., AND ZHOU, X. Practical human sensing in the light. In *Proceedings of the ACM MobiSys* (2016).

[13] LIU, C. B., SADEGHI, B., AND KNIGHTLY, E. W. Enabling vehicular visible light communication (V2LC) networks. In *Proceedings of the ACM VANET* (2011), pp. 41–50.

[14] LIU, V., PARKS, A., TALLA, V., GOLLAKOTA, S., WETHERALL, D., AND SMITH, J. R. Ambient backscatter: Wireless communication out of thin air. *SIGCOMM CCR* (2013).

[15] MOSHIR, F., AND SINGH, S. Wireless barcodes for tagging infrastructure. In *Proceedings of the ACM MobiCom* (2014), pp. 103–114.

[16] NELSON, B. *Punched Cards to Bar Codes: A 200 Year Journey*. Helmers Publishing Company, 1997.

[17] PROAKIS, J., AND SALEHI, M. *Fundamentals of Communication Systems*. Pearson Education, 2007.

[18] SCHMID, S., CORBELLINI, G., MANGOLD, S., AND GROSS, T. R. LED-to-LED visible light communication networks. In *Proceedings of the ACM MobiHoc* (2013), pp. 1–10.

[19] WACHS, J. P., KÖLSCH, M., STERN, H., AND EDAN, Y. Vision-based hand-gesture applications. *Communications of the ACM* (2011).

[20] WANG, Q., GIUSTINIANO, D., AND GNAWALI, O. Low-cost, flexible and open platform for visible light communication networks. In *Proceedings of the ACM workshop on HotWireless* (2015).

[21] WANG, Q., GIUSTINIANO, D., AND PUCCINELLI, D. An open-source research platform for embedded visible light networking. *IEEE Wireless Communication* (2015).

[22] WANT, R. Enabling ubiquitous sensing with RFID. *IEEE Computer* (2004).

[23] YETISEN, A. K., BUTT, H., AND ET AL. Light-directed writing of chemically tunable narrow-band holographic sensors. *Advanced Optical Materials 2*, 3 (2014), 250–254.

[24] ZHANG, C., TABOR, J., ZHANG, J., AND ZHANG, X. Extending mobile interaction through near-field visible light sensing. In *Proceedings of the ACM MobiCom* (2015).

PI^2: A Linearized AQM for both Classic and Scalable TCP

Koen De Schepper[†] Olga Bondarenko*[‡] Ing-Jyh Tsang[†] Bob Briscoe[‡]
[†]Nokia Bell Labs, Belgium
[‡]Simula Research Laboratory, Norway
[†]{koen.de_schepper|ing-jyh.tsang}@nokia.com
[‡]{olgabo|bob}@simula.no

ABSTRACT

This paper concerns the use of Active Queue Management (AQM) to reduce queuing delay. It offers insight into why it has proved hard for a Proportional Integral (PI) controller to remain both responsive and stable while controlling 'Classic' TCP flows, such as TCP Reno and Cubic. Due to their non-linearity, the controller's adjustments have to be smaller when the target drop probability is lower. The PI Enhanced (PIE) algorithm attempts to solve this problem by scaling down the adjustments of the controller using a look-up table. Instead, we control an internal variable that is by definition linearly proportional to the load, then post-process it into the required Classic drop probability—in fact we show that the output simply needs to be squared. This allows tighter control, giving responsiveness and stability better or no worse than PIE achieves, but without all its corrective heuristics.

With suitable packet classification, it becomes simple to extend this PI^2 AQM to support coexistence between Classic and Scalable congestion controls in the public Internet. A Scalable congestion control ensures sufficient feedback at any flow rate, an example being Data Centre TCP (DCTCP). A Scalable control is linear, so we can use the internal variable directly without any squaring, by omitting the post-processing stage.

We implemented PI^2 as a Linux qdisc to extensively test our claims using Classic and Scalable TCPs.

1. INTRODUCTION

Interactive latency-sensitive applications are becoming prevalent on the public Internet, e.g. Web, voice, conversational and interactive video, finance apps, online gaming, cloud-based apps, remote desktop. It has been conjectured that there is also latent demand for more interactivity and new interactive apps would surface if there were less lag in the public Internet [10]. In the developed world, increases in access network bit-rate have been giving diminishing returns as latency has become the critical bottleneck. Recently, much has been done to reduce propagation delay, e.g. by placing caches or servers closer to users. However, latency is a multi-faceted problem [7], so other sources of delay such as queuing have become the bottleneck.

Queuing delay problems occur when a capacity-seeking (e.g. TCP) traffic flow is large enough to last long enough to build a queue in the same bottleneck as traffic from a delay-sensitive application. Therefore queuing delay only appears as an intermittent problem [17]. Nonetheless, perception of quality tends to be dominated by worst case delays and many real-time apps adapt their buffering to absorb all but worst-case delays.

To remove unnecessary queuing delays, Active Queue Management (AQM) is being deployed at bottlenecks. AQM introduces a low level of loss, to keep the queue shallow within the buffer. However, for an AQM to reduce queuing delay any further, it has to worsen drop and/or utilization. This is because the root cause of the problem is the behaviour of current TCP-friendly congestion controls (Reno, Cubic, etc.). They behave like a balloon; if the network squeezes one impairment, they make the others bulge out.

To remove one dimension from this trilemma, it would seem Explicit Congestion Notification (ECN) could be used instead of loss. However, the meaning of an ECN mark was standardized as equivalent to a loss [30], so although standard ('Classic') ECN can remove the impairment of loss itself, it cannot be used to reduce queuing delay relative to loss-based protocols.

Per-flow queuing has been used to isolate each flow from the impairments of others, but this adds a new dimension to the trilemma; the need for the network to inspect within the IP layer to identify flows, not to mention the extra complexity of multiple queues.

*The first two authors contributed equally

CoNEXT '16, December 12 - 15, 2016, Irvine, CA, USA

 ISBN 978-1-4503-4292-6/16/12...$15.00

DOI: http://dx.doi.org/10.1145/2999572.2999578

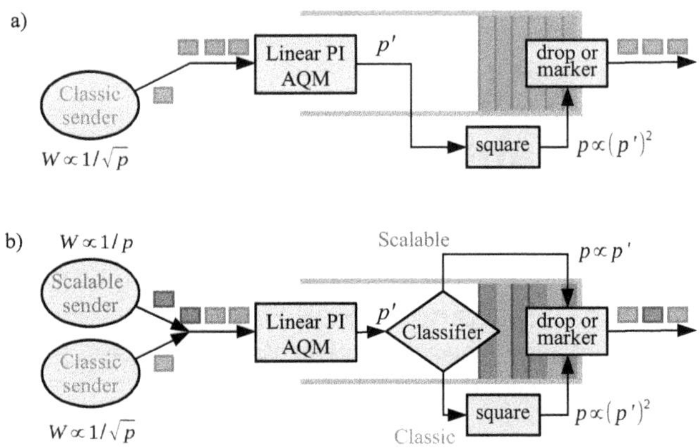

Figure 1: Controlling the window W with drop/marking probability p. a) Linearized Replacement for PIE; b) Congestion Control Coexistence

To reduce queuing delay below that achievable with state-of-the-art AQMs, and without other compromises, we decided to investigate changing TCP itself. Data Centre TCP (DCTCP [2]) is an existence proof of this approach; drastically reducing queuing delay without compromising the other factors. We shall show later that this is because, as flow-rate scales, the sawtooth variations in rate grow with TCP-friendly controls, but they do not with DCTCP, which can keep queuing delay low without compromising utilization. Thus DCTCP is an example of a 'Scalable' congestion control. In contrast, we use the term 'Classic' for unscalable controls such as Reno and Cubic.

It is a common misconception that DCTCP only works in data centres but, on its own, it works fine over wide area networks [3, 23]. However, it needs some additions for safety, which are discussed in [8]. The most critical problem is that DCTCP is too aggressive to coexist with Classic TCP. Therefore (until now) DCTCP could only be deployed in controlled environments like data centres because senders, receivers and the network all have to be updated at the same time.

During our research to make the family of Scalable congestion controls incrementally deployable on the Internet (see DualQ concepts in [13, 5]), we were interested in reusing the PIE (PI Enhanced [28]) AQM, as it can control target queuing delay and provide a reasonably stable marking probability. We modified it to separately support both Classic and Scalable congestion controls. This led us to understand that a proportional integral (PI) controller is inherently linear when controlling Scalable congestion controls, but not Classic ones.

The designers of PIE introduced scaling factors within the controller that increase stepwise as the drop/mark probability p increases, in order to keep it within its stable region. We realized that it would be much simpler to break down the structure of the AQM into two parts (Figure 1a): i) a generic part that controls a pseudo-probability p' that is, by definition, linearly proportional to the load; and ii) a congestion-control-specific part, which encodes p' into a congestion signal, p, appropriate to the congestion control that is predominant in the network.

For the case of Classic controls like TCP Reno, we shall see that the second stage should be configured to encode p as the square of p', which counterbalances the non-linear square root in the equations for the window (W) of Classic congestion controls (Figure 1a). We call this 'PI Improved with a square' or PI^2. We shall show that PI^2 can achieve similar or sometimes even better results than PIE, while using a simpler algorithm.

For Scalable controls like DCTCP, the output of the PI controller (p') can be used directly for congestion marking; no encoding is needed. This makes it feasible to solve the problem of coexistence of Scalable and Classic traffic. The PI controller can be used for the former and PI^2 for the latter (Figure 1b). This counterbalances the more aggressive response of scalable algorithms with more aggressive congestion notification (given $0 \leq p' \leq 1$, it is greater without the square).

In this paper we hold back from discussing the DualQ concept, and instead focus on restructuring PIE in single queue scenarios. The majority of the paper is about simply replacing PIE with PI^2 for Classic traffic. Nonetheless, we also test how well PI^2 would support coexistence of Scalable and Classic congestion controls.

We must emphasize that a single queue is neither the optimal nor the recommended deployment arrangement for coexistence between Scalable and Classic traffic, because the Scalable traffic suffers the high queuing delay of the Classic traffic. However, it provides interesting insights and a basis for future development of DualQ variants [12].

The paper is organized as follows. Section 2 gives background on the scalability of congestion controls and the PI AQM controller. Section 3 provides insights into related work particularly the evolution of the Proportional Integral controller. Section 4 describes how PI can be improved with a square, while Section 5 provides details of the PI^2 AQM implementation. Experimental evaluation of PI^2 in comparison with PIE is presented in Section 6. Conclusions are summarized in Section 7. Appendices A and B respectively provide steady-state throughput equations for DCTCP and a stability analysis for the PI^2 AQM.

2. BACKGROUND

Congestion Control Scaling.

A congestion control like Reno or Cubic is termed unscalable because, as flow rate scales, the number of round trips between congestion signals increases. This leads to less tight control and higher variation of queuing and/or utilization.

The number of congestion signals per round trip in the steady state is

$$c = pW, \tag{1}$$

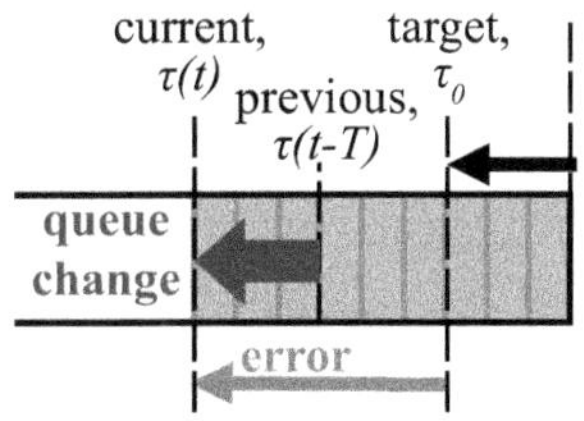

Figure 2: Basic PI algorithm

where W is the number of segments per round trip (the window) and p is the probability of congestion notification (either losses or ECN marks). Appendix A gives the formulae for the steady-state window of various congestion controls, which are all of the form

$$W \propto 1/p^B, \qquad (2)$$

where B is a characteristic constant of the congestion control.

The scalability of a congestion control can therefore be determined by substituting for p from (2) into (1):

$$c \propto W^{(1-1/B)}. \qquad (3)$$

If $B < 1$, c shrinks as W scales up, which implies fewer congestion signals per round trip (unscalable). Therefore, a congestion control is scalable if $B \geq 1$ and unscalable otherwise.

From Appendix A, Reno and Cubic in its Reno mode ('CReno') have $B = 1/2$ and pure Cubic has $B = 3/4$, so all these 'Classic' controls are unscalable. While DCTCP with probabilistic marking has $B = 1$ and with step marking it has $B = 2$. Therefore DCTCP is scalable irrespective of the type of marking.

Proportional Integral (PI) AQM.

The core of the PIE AQM is a classical Proportional Integral (PI) controller [18] that aims to keep queuing delay to a target τ_0 by updating the drop probability, p, every update interval, T. Figure 2 recaps the basic PI algorithm, which consists of a proportional and an integral part, weighted respectively by the gain factors β and α (both in units of Hz):

$$p(t) = p(t-T) + \alpha\big(\tau(t) - \tau_0\big) + \beta\big(\tau(t) - \tau(t-T)\big), \quad (4)$$

where $\tau(t)$ is the queuing delay at time t. The proportional part estimates how much load exceeds capacity by measuring how fast the queue is growing. The integral part corrects any standing queue due to the load having exceeded capacity over time, by measuring the error between the actual queuing delay and the target. Either term can be negative and the final probability is bounded between and including 0 and 1.

The proportional gain factor β can be seen as the best known correction of p to reduce the excess load. The integral gain factor α is typically smaller than the proportional, and corrects any longer term offset from the target. Note that the integral part initially calculates a proportional value, and the proportional part a

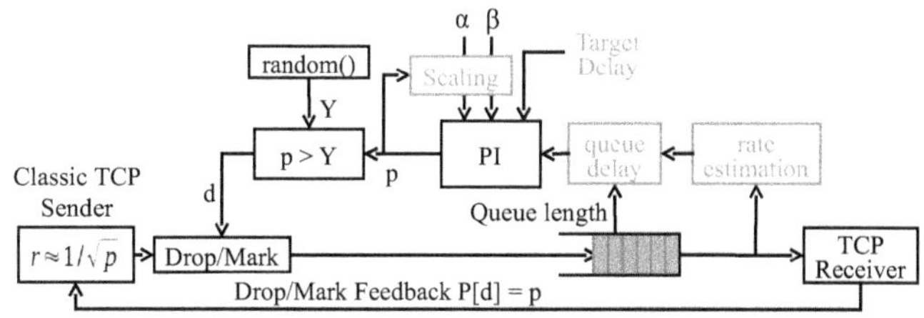

Figure 3: PIE AQM in Linux (additions to PI in green)

differential value. But these values are later integrated by adding them as a delta to the probability used in the previous update interval.

3. RELATED WORK

The evolution of the Proportional Integral controller Enhanced (PIE) AQM started with the control theoretic analysis of RED by Holot *et al* [19], which ended by pointing out that it was not necessary to adopt the approach of RED, which pushes back against higher load with higher queuing delay and higher loss. Instead, in [18], the same authors presented a Proportional Integral (PI) controller, using classical linear systems analysis with the objective of holding queuing delay to a constant target, using higher loss alone to push back against higher load.

This PI controller was used as the basis of the IEEE Data Centre Bridging (DCB) standard, 802.1Qau [15], published in 2010. Variants of the original PI AQM controller had also been proposed in the research community. In 2004, Hong *et al* claimed that the phase margin of the original PI controller could be over-conservative, leading to unnecessarily sluggish behaviour. Instead, they proposed a design [21] that would self-tune to the specified phase margin. In 2007, Hong and Yang [20] proposed to self-tune the gain margin instead, and to trigger the self-tuning process whenever it moved outside an operating range. However implementations have not adopted these self-tuning designs, probably because they require code to estimate the average (harmonic mean) round trip time of the TCP flows, which in turn depends on estimating the number of TCP flows, the link capacity and the equilibrium dropping probability, p. Of course, p is itself the output of the controller and, by definition, determining its equilibrium value is problematic when network conditions are changing, which is when self-tuning is required.

In 2013, the Proportional Integral controller Enhanced (PIE [28]) was proposed as an evolution of the original PI algorithm [18]. After extensive evaluation [32], PIE became the mandatory AQM algorithm for DOCSIS3.1 cable modems [9] and it is also being documented in an IETF specification [29].

Figure 3 shows the building blocks of the Linux PIE AQM implementation. PIE introduced three enhancements over PI. The first was to use units of time (not bytes or packets) for the queue, to hold queuing delay constant whatever the link rate. This ensures the

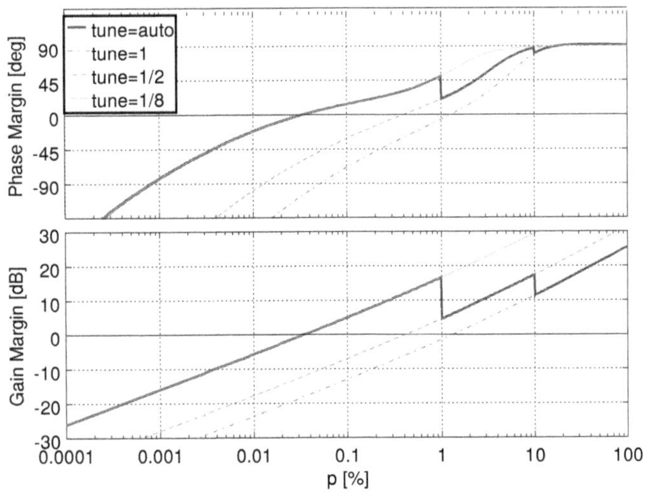

Figure 4: Bode plot margins for R=100 ms, α_{PIE}=0.125*tune, β_{PIE}=1.25*tune, T=32 ms

algorithm does not need configuring for different link rates, which could occur due to modem retraining, or if the queue serves a wireless link or it is part of a larger scheduling hierarchy. Using units of time for the queue was taught by the CoDel algorithm [27] the year before. Because PIE was designed for hardware implementation, it did not measure the service time of the queue directly using the time-stamping approach of CoDel; instead it converted queue lengths to queuing delay using a regularly updated estimate of the link rate. Actually, as far back as 2002, Kwon and Fahmy [24] had advised that the queue should be measured in units of time. Also, in 2003, Sågfors *et al* had modified the Packet Discard Prevention Counter (PDPC+ [31]) algorithm by converting queue length to queuing delay to cope with the varying link rate of 3G wireless networks.

The second main enhancement introduced in PIE was to scale α & β dependent on the magnitude of p, which was based on the stability analysis in [28] (see equation (35) in Appendix B). The Bode margin plots in Figure 4 show the gain and phase margins for loss probabilities between 0.0001% and 100%, with a fixed maximum RTT and for different α and β parameters. With fixed α and β, the gain margin evolves diagonally as p varies with load. When the gain margin and the phase margin are negative, the control loop becomes unstable, resulting in oscillating queue size and TCP throughput. On the other hand, when the gain margin becomes too high the control loop responds too sluggishly to load changes. The auto-tuned plot shows the effect of introducing scaling steps in PIE to keep the margins above zero for lower p, while keeping the gain margin low for higher p. In the original PIE paper [28], no further scaling steps were applied for $p < 1\%$. In early versions of the IETF specification, scaling did not extend below 0.1%, but following criticism during the IETF review process that a table of values inherently limits the operating range of the algorithm [6], the table of values was extended down to 0.0001% as shown in Figure 5.

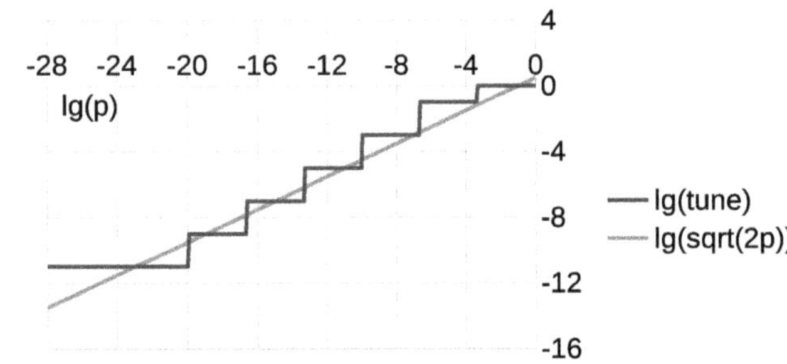

Figure 5: The factor 'tune' (stepped) that PIE uses to scale Δp from the lookup table in [29], compared against $\sqrt{2p}$ (both log scale, base 2)

Up to that point, the written justification for the scaling had been rather arbitrary. However, the extra data points confirmed suspicions that this scaling tracked the square-root law of TCP Reno, although it is not clear whether this was conscious design intent, or the outcome of empirical design iterations.

The third main enhancement introduced in PIE [28] was a burst allowance. This mechanism only allows bursts when the queue first becomes active after a period of no queuing, so it is inactive for bursts on top of a low level of queuing. The paper itself points out that the incremental evolution of drop probability p in the underlying PI algorithm already filters out anomalous bursts, but anyway adds an additional burst allowance that can be explicitly configured, if required for the deployment scenario.

The proportional-integral approach was generally considered sufficient for AQM control, with the proportional term ensuring loss increases more quickly if the queue is growing and less if it is shrinking, and the integral term returning the queue slowly enough to its target level. Nonetheless, proportional-derivative and proportional-integral-derivative controllers have been proposed. These are summarized in Adams [1], which provides a useful survey of a wide range of AQM schemes, with a particular focus on those derived from control-theoretic analysis.

As Adams [1] points out, all control theoretic approaches need to assume a model of how the traffic responds to control signals, and all known schemes (until now) assume that traffic consists predominantly of long-running TCP Reno flows.

Kühlewind *et al* [23] investigated the feasibility of using coupled AQM algorithms to deploy a scalable TCP congestion control such as Data Centre TCP [2] alongside existing TCP Reno traffic. It documented the throughput deviations between linearly coupled AQMs empirically, whereas we have derived the square relationship used in the present work analytically.

An IETF specification of a dual-queue coupled AQM has been drafted [13], to enable coexistence of 'Scalable' (e.g. DCTCP) and 'Classic' (e.g. TCP Reno) congestion controls. It requires the drop (or marking) probability of the AQM for 'Classic' traffic to be the square of that

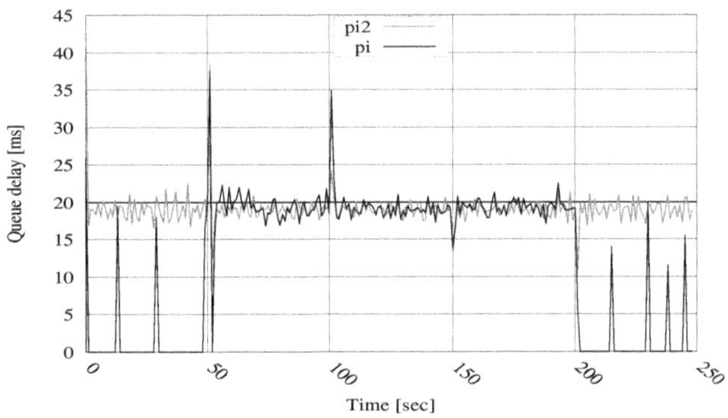

Figure 6: Performance comparison under varying traffic intensity: 10:30:50:30:10 TCP flows over durations 50:50:50:50:50 s, link capacity = 100 Mbps, RTT = 10 ms, α_{PI}=0.125, β_{PI}=1.25, α_{PI2}=0.3125, β_{PI2}=3.125, T=32ms.

for scalable traffic. It is written sufficiently generically that it covers the PI^2 approach, but the example AQM it gives is based on a RED-like AQM called Curvy RED.

The present work focuses on PI^2 in a single queue to fully evaluate it relative to existing single queue solutions before taking the next step of proposing its use in a dual-queue.

4. PI IMPROVED WITH A SQUARE

Restructuring PIE.

When the probability is small PIE tunes α and β to become smaller as well, in order to compensate for the higher sensitivity of the signal p. In Figure 6 the 'pi' curve shows what happens if the α and β parameters are not auto-tuned. For the lower load when there are 10 flows (between 0-50s and 200-250s) any onset of congestion is immediately suppressed very aggressively (p becomes too high, because β is too high), resulting in underutilization and an oscillating queue. Instead of directly PI-controlling the applied packet congestion notification probability (p), we propose to do the PI-control process on a pseudo-probability (p') in linear space and afterwards to adapt the controlled value to its non-linear form. In Figure 6 the 'pi2' curve shows what happens if constant (non-auto-tuned) α and β parameters are used, before the pseudo-probability is converted to its square and applied as a drop probability. The square ensures that the pseudo drop probability is adjusted to the right sensitivity level of the signal ($\sqrt{p}$) and it makes room for higher α and β, as we shall see.

The load that an AQM has to push back against is proportional to the number of TCP-like sources generating it. The total steady-state rate of arriving bits is not a measure of load, because all the TCP sources fit their total bit rate into the link capacity. Rather, the excess load is the rate at which each source adds packets to exceed the link capacity. For instance, TCP Reno adds one segment per RTT, so when the number of sources doubles the number of segments added per RTT doubles. TCP eventually ensures the rate of each flow halves, so load is inversely proportional to steady-state flow rate. In fact, for ACK-clocked sources like TCP, the load is proportional to $1/W$, where W is the steady-state window of each flow.

Therefore, for TCP Reno or CReno the load is proportional to $\sqrt{p}$ (from their steady-state window equations (5) and (7) in Appendix A). Therefore, we will control $p' = \sqrt{p}$. To transform the control output p' to the non-linear form needed for applying congestion notification we will simply square it ($p = (p')^2$).

Note that, even though p is smaller than p', for the same TCP load the PI^2 controller will drive the steady-state value of p' sufficiently high so that its value when squared (p) will be the same as that from PIE.

We shall now show that the heuristic table of scaling factors in PIE was actually attempting to achieve the same outcome as PI^2. We will abbreviate the main control terms in PIE (see (4) in section 2) as

$$\pi(\tau) \equiv \alpha\big(\tau(t) - \tau_0\big) + \beta\big(\tau(t) - \tau(t-T)\big)$$

Then our proposed squaring approach can be written:

$$p \leftarrow \big(p' + K\pi(\tau)\big)^2,$$

where K is a constant used later. Expanding:

$$\leftarrow (p')^2 + 2Kp'\pi(\tau) + K^2\pi^2(\tau).$$

Assuming $K\pi(\tau) \ll p'$, this approximates[1] to:

$$\leftarrow p + 2Kp'\pi(\tau).$$

As Figure 5 illustrates, PIE's stepped scaling factor 'tune' broadly fits the equation $\sqrt{2p}$. So we can say $2K_{\mathrm{PIE}}p' \approx \sqrt{2p}$ or $K_{\mathrm{PIE}} \approx 1/\sqrt{2}$. Thus the stepped way that PIE derives drop probability p is indeed broadly equivalent to incrementing p' using the core PI function then squaring the result.[2] Using the stability analysis in Appendix B we shall now see that we can make PI^2 more responsive than PIE without risking instability, because K_{PI2} can be greater than K_{PIE}.

Responsiveness without Instability.

In Misra *et al* [26] and Hollot *et al* [19] a fluid model is used to describe the TCP Reno throughput, the queuing process and the PI AQM behaviour, and to perform its stability analysis. Appendix B describes this analysis for TCP Reno over a PI^2 AQM. Based on the derived loop transfer functions (36) and (37), the Bode gain and phase margins are plotted in Figure 7 (the lines labelled 'reno pie' are the PIE auto-tuned margins, and 'reno pi2' the Reno on PI^2 margins).[3]

[1]In the rare cases when this inequality is not valid, it merely means that PI^2 will calculate a higher Δp than PIE would; neither is necessarily more 'correct'.
[2]PIE scales by the old value of p'; PI^2 scales by the new.
[3]The octave scripts that generated these plots and those in Figure 4 are available as auxiliary material with this paper in the ACM Digital Library.

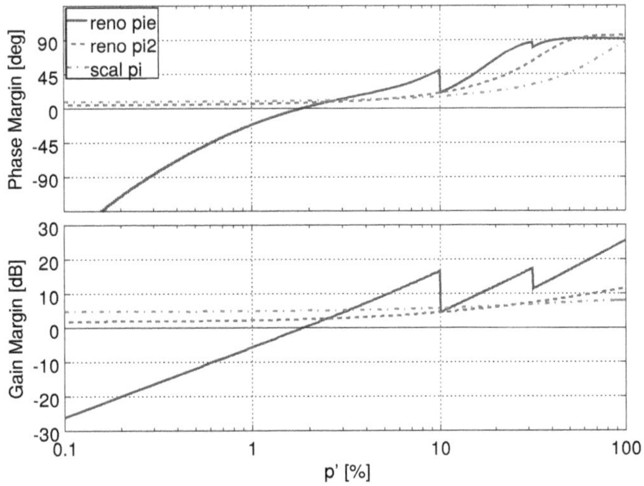

Figure 7: Bode plot margins for R=100ms, α_{PIE}=0.125*tune, β_{PIE}=1.25*tune, α_{PI2}=0.3125, β_{PI2}=3.125, α_{PI}=0.625, β_{PI}=6.25, T=32ms

Applying the squaring outside the PI controller flattens out the otherwise diagonal gain margin and makes it easy to choose values for the gain factors α and β that only depend on the maximum RTT to be supported. Only at high loads, when p' is higher than 60% ($p > 36\%$) is the gain margin of PI^2 slightly above 10dB. Because the gain margin of PI^2 is flatter, it can be made more responsive than PIE by increasing the gain factors by ×2.5 without the gain margin dipping below zero anywhere over the full load range, which could otherwise lead to instability. This makes the gain of PI^2 roughly 3.5 times (or 5.5 dB) greater than that of PIE, because $K_{\text{PI2}}/K_{\text{PIE}} \approx 2.5\sqrt{2} \approx 3.5$.

PI² Design.

In Figure 8 the PI^2 AQM is shown. Compared to PIE, the scaling block is removed and the drop/mark decision block is modified to apply the squared drop probability. The squaring can be implemented either by multiplying p' by itself, or by comparing it with the maximum of 2 random variables during the drop decision. The first is easy to perform in a software implementation, perhaps as an addition to existing PIE hardware. The latter might be preferred for a hardware implementation. As the resolution of p' is half that of its square, the number of random bits used for each of the two random variables only needs to be half that of a PIE decision function.

Coexistence between Congestion Controls.

Additionally the above analysis suggests that control of 'Scalable' controls (see Section 2) such as DCTCP might also exhibit the same stability properties. Equation 11 in Appendix A shows that the window of DCTCP with probabilistic marking is inversely proportional to the drop or marking probability. So it should be possible to apply p' directly to DCTCP packets without the squaring during the drop/mark decision.

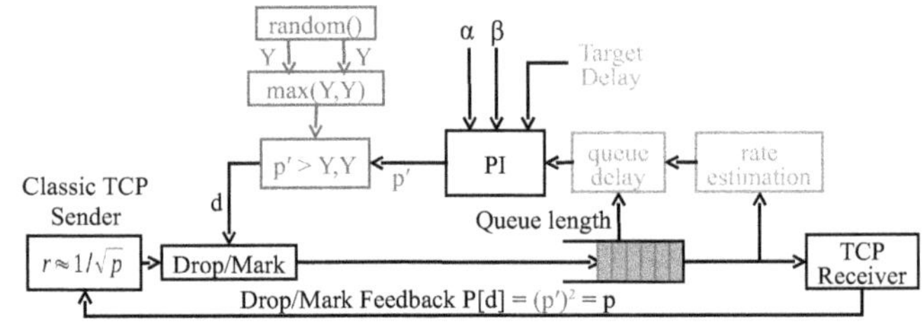

Figure 8: PI^2 for 'Classic' Traffic (PIE changes in blue)

This is confirmed analytically in Appendix B, where stability is analysed for a congestion control that reduces its window by half a packet per mark, which is a good approximation[4] for what DCTCP effectively does when a probabilistic AQM is used. Figure 7 shows its gain margins (lines labelled 'scal pi'). The plots are very similar to the Reno on PI^2 results but there was enough margin to double the α and β parameters (lines labelled 'reno pi2') relative to the Classic α and β parameters.

We have seen that PI^2 can be applied to Classic traffic and PI without the square can be applied to Scalable traffic. When both types of traffic coexist, it should also be possible to apply whichever of the two controls is appropriate, as long as each type of traffic can be distinguished. The drop/mark probability relation between DCTCP and CReno flows for an equal steady state throughput is derived in (14) (see Appendix A): $p_c = (p_s/k)^2$, with p_c the drop or mark probability for CReno flows, p_s the mark probability for Scalable (e.g. DCTCP) flows and k the coupling factor. In (14) a value of 1.19 is derived for k but it is set to 2 in the rest of this paper, having been validated empirically in the following section. Note that $k = 2$ is also the optimal ratio between the Scalable and Classic gain factors for optimal stability. As the gain factors determine the final probability, p_s will also be double $\sqrt{p_c}$, matching k.

5. PI² AQM IMPLEMENTATION

To verify the theoretical predictions, we have modified the PIE Linux AQM to support the PI^2 control method for classic congestion controls (Cubic, Reno, DCCP, SCTP, QUIC, ...), to support control of scalable congestion controls (DCTCP, Relentless, Scalable,...) and to support coexistence between the classic and scalable congestion controls. The Linux qdisc source code used for these experiments is released as open source and can be retrieved at [11]. Figure 9 shows the detailed implementation diagram.

To implement the PI^2 control method, we removed the code in PIE that scales the gain factors dependent on the current probability and instead added code to compare the resulting probability with two random variables.

[4]DCTCP additionally smooths (and consequently delays) the response from the network over a fixed number of RTTs which results in a more sluggish response for bigger RTTs.

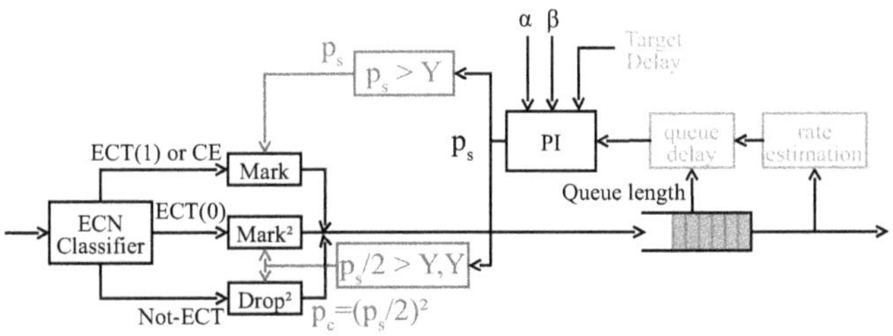

Figure 9: Coupled PI^2 and PI AQMs for Classic and Scalable Traffic in a Single Queue

To support Scalable congestion controls, we also made the squared drop decision conditional on a congestion control family identifier. We used the ECN bits in the IP header to distinguish packets from Scalable and Classic congestion controls.

The more frequent congestion signal induced by a Scalable control makes using drop for congestion signalling intolerable. In contrast, explicit congestion notification provides a congestion signal without also impairing packet delivery. Currently, DCTCP enables the ECN capability by setting the ECT(0) codepoint in the IP header and it expects any AQM in the network to mark congestion using a queue threshold that is both shallow and immediate (not delayed by smoothing).

We modified DCTCP to set the ECT(1) codepoint, which the IETF has recently agreed in principle to make available with a view to using it as the identifier for Scalable traffic [4, 14]. This would allow Classic congestion controls to continue to be able to support 'Classic' ECN by using the ECT(0) codepoint. It is proposed that both Classic and Scalable traffic would have to share the same Congestion Experienced (CE) codepoint to indicate a congestion marking. Then any congestion marking on ECT(0) packets would continue to have the same meaning as a drop. The pros and cons of using different identifiers are outside the scope of this paper, but they are discussed in the above-cited draft.

In the network, all packets use the same FIFO queue, but we classify packets based on their ECN codepoint in order to apply the appropriate drop/mark decision. We emphasize again that this single-queue approach is not intended or recommended for deployment; it is simply an interim step in the research process to avoid changing too many factors at once. To support coexistence we ensure rough throughput equality (a.k.a. TCP-fairness) by applying the $k = 2$ factor to Classic packets before making the drop/mark decision based on the squared probability.

Fewer Heuristics.

For our PI^2 implementation, as well as removing all the scaling heuristics, for PI^2 we additionally disabled the following heuristics that had all been added to the Linux implementation of PIE:

- Burst allowance: In PIE 100ms after the queue was last empty no drop or marking is applied. We disabled this (as also allowed in the PIE specification) so as not to influence DCTCP fairness, which is better when probabilities are constantly coupled (avoiding on-off behaviour).
- In PIE, if the probability is below 20% and the queue delay below half the target, no dropping or marking is applied. This rule was also disabled to avoid on-off behaviour. If this rule were not disabled, the threshold of 20% would have had to be corrected to the square root (around 45%).
- In PIE, if the probability is above 10%, ECN capable packets are dropped instead of marked. This is one possible overload strategy to prevent ECN traffic from overfilling the queue while starving drop based traffic. We disabled this rule and instead placed a maximum limit of 25% on the Classic mark/drop probability and the equivalent limit (100%) on Scalable marking probability. As a result the queue will be allowed to grow over the target if it cannot be controlled with this maximum drop probability. Then, if needed, tail-drop will control non-responsive traffic, whether ECN-capable or not.
- In PIE, if the probability is higher than 10% Δp is limited to 2%. We disabled this for now. Further comparative evaluation is needed to investigate the validity of this rule in the square root domain.
- In PIE, if the queue delay is greater than 250 ms, Δp is set to 2%. We also disabled this for now, again re-evaluation in the square root domain is needed.

So far, the basis on which most of these heuristics were chosen is undocumented and no-one has published an exhaustive assessment of the precise impact on performance of each. Therefore, given we had no sound basis to reconfigure each one to interwork with the restructured PI^2 mechanism, we chose to disable them.

The results for PIE shown in this paper are the ones for the full Linux PIE implementation, with all its heuristics except we reworked the rule that disables ECN marking above 10%, as described above. This avoided a discontinuity in the results for the throughput ratio between Classic and Scalable flows.

We produced an implementation of PIE without the above extra heuristics (called bare-PIE) and repeated all the experiments presented in this paper. We saw no difference in any experiment between bare-PIE and the full PIE. This gives confidence that the results of the PI^2 experiments are only due to the PI^2 improvements, and not due to disabling any of the above heuristics.

6. EVALUATION

Our evaluations of PI^2 consisted of two main sets of experiments: comparing the performance of PI^2 with PIE, and verifying our claims that PI^2 will enable coexistence of Scalable and Classic flows.

Our testbed consists of an AQM, 2 client and 2 server machines, all running Linux (Ubuntu 14.04 LTS with kernel 3.18.9), which contained the implementation of the TCP variants and AQMs.

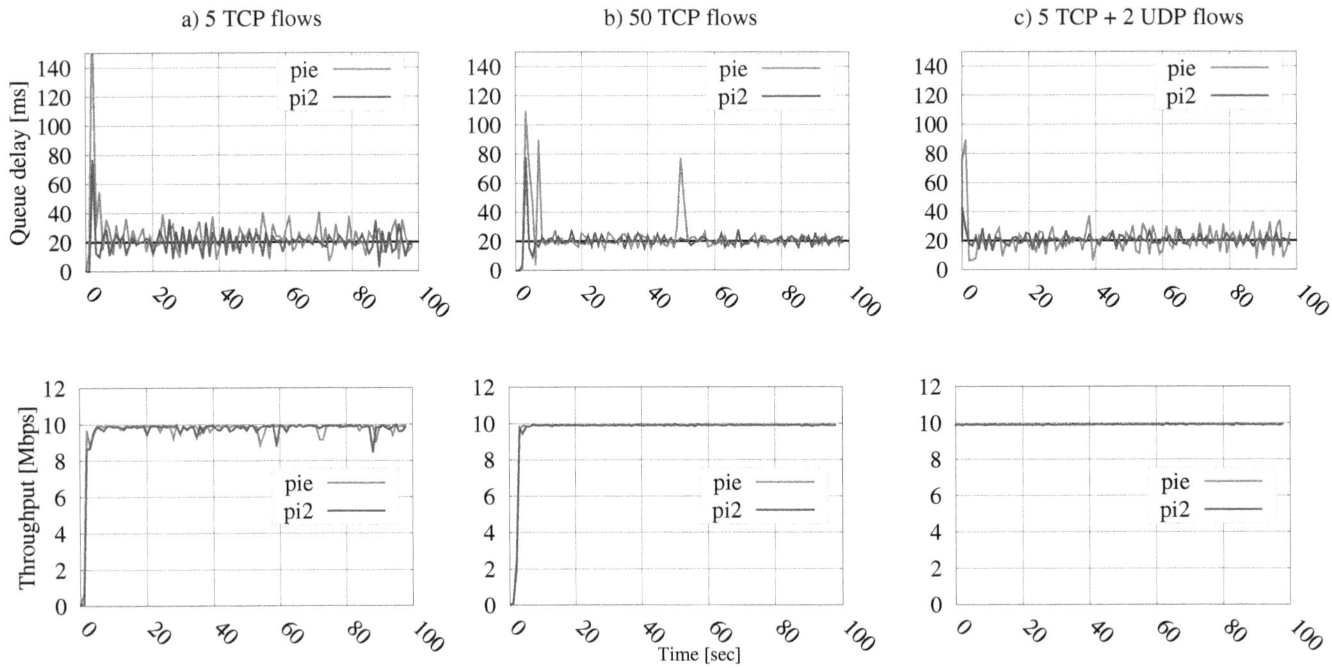

Figure 11: Queuing latency and throughput under various traffic loads: link capacity = 10 Mbps, RTT = 100 ms.

The experiments used unmodified DCTCP and Cubic implementations in their default configurations. For ECN-Cubic, we additionally enabled TCP ECN negotiation on the relevant client and server. The AQM configurations used the options as described in Table 1, unless otherwise stated.

A more detailed overview of how these machines are connected is presented in Figure 10. We used each client-server pair (Client A - Server A, Client B - Server B) for emulating TCP flows of the same congestion control (and UDP flows in addition, if necessary), so that the competition between different congestion control flows could be evaluated. For the experiments where only one congestion control was evaluated, only a single client-server pair was used.

Responsiveness and Stability.

For the first series of stability tests, we repeated the main experiments presented by Pan et al. [28]. We reproduced the PIE results and evaluated PI^2's performance compared to those of PIE. For reference, we will use the same test titles as those used by Pan et al. in their paper (highlighted with italics).

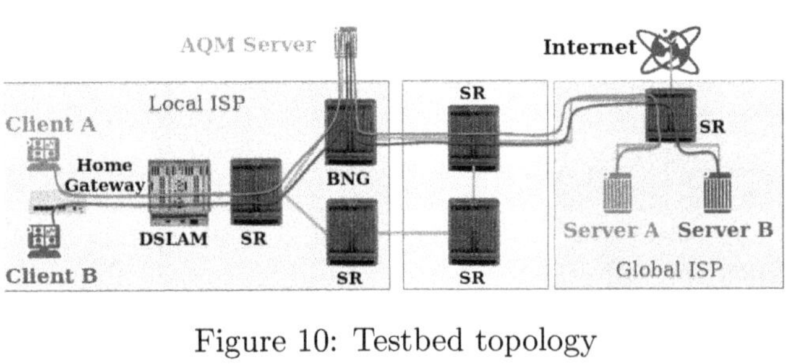

Figure 10: Testbed topology

All	Buffer: 40000 pkt (2.4 s @200 Mb/s), ECN
PI/PIE+Cubic/Reno	Target delay: 20 ms, Burst: 100 ms, α: 2/16, β: 20/16
PI/PI^2+DCTCP	Target delay: 20 ms, α: 10/16, β: 100/16

Table 1: Default parameters for the different AQMs.

We used TCP Reno, on a topology as shown in Figure 10. To reproduce the same environment, the bottleneck link capacity is 10 Mbps (except Figure 12 where we simulate varying link capacity) and the RTT is 100 ms if not specified otherwise. The sampling interval applied in the graphs is 1 s.

Figure 11 shows the queuing delay (upper row), and total throughput for all flows (lower row), where we use the following traffic mixes:

a) *Light TCP traffic*: 5 TCP flows.
b) *Heavy TCP traffic*: 50 TCP flows.
c) *Mixture of TCP and UDP traffic*: 5 TCP flows and 2 UDP flows sending at 6Mbps each

The results show less queue overshoot on start-up for PI^2 and less (damped) oscillations afterwards. This is because the flatter gain margin of PI^2 allowed us to set the responsiveness (gain) 3.5 times higher without risking instability (see section 4).

Figure 12 shows the queuing delay for the test with *Varying Link Capacity* as detailed in the caption. The PI^2 controller again seems to reduce overshoot and also when the link capacity is reduced the queue reduces faster and with less oscillation. The PIE AQM also allows overshoot when flow rates increase to fill the increased capacity at 100 s, while PI^2 shows no visible overshoot. Sampling at 100 ms intervals shows a peak queuing delay at 50 s of 510 ms for PIE and 250 ms for

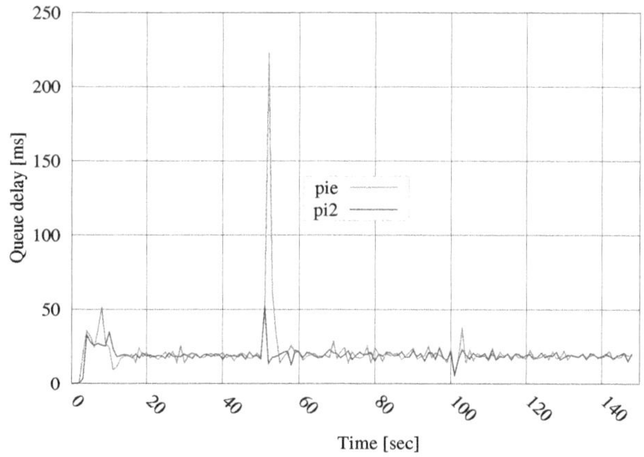

Figure 12: Performance comparison under varying link capacity: 100:20:100 Mb/s over durations 50:50:50 s

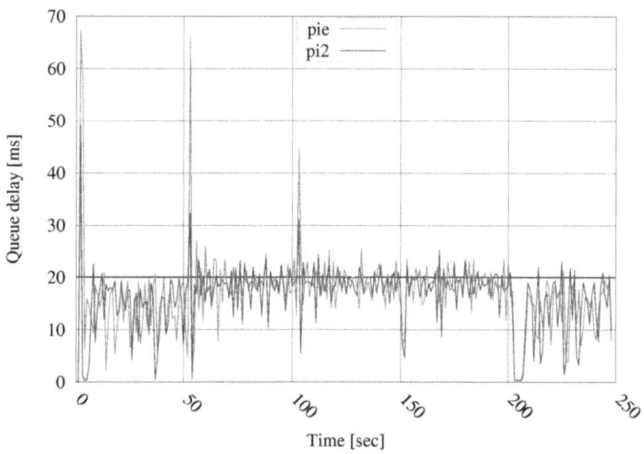

Figure 13: Performance comparison under varying traffic intensity: 10:30:50:30:10 TCP flows over durations 50:50:50:50:50 s, link capacity: 10 Mbps, RTT: 100 ms.

PI^2. PIE has 2 more oscillation peaks above 100 ms immediately afterwards, while PI^2 none at all.

Figure 13 demonstrates queuing delay for the *Varying Traffic Intensity* test as detailed in the caption. Again PI^2 reduces overshoot during load changes and also reduces upward fluctuations during non-transient periods.

Figure 14 shows the CDF of *Queuing Delay Comparison* between PI^2 and PIE, with target delay of 5 ms (upper row) and 20 ms (lower row). For these experiment, we use 20 TCP flows during the first part (a) and 5 TCP + 2 UDP flows during the second part (b). In all situations PI^2 has a similar queue size to PIE.

As we have seen, the improvement in responsiveness and stability of PI^2 is measurable but slight. Our ultimate deployment goal is a dualQ structure [13], in order to significantly reduce latency in the queue for Scalable traffic. The improvement in short flow completion time is evaluated in [12]. Using the single queue arrangement of the present paper, we experimented with mixed flow sizes over an extensive range of link rates and RTTs and, as expected, mixed short flow completion times with PIE, bare PIE and PI^2 under both heavy and light Web-like workloads were essentially the same.

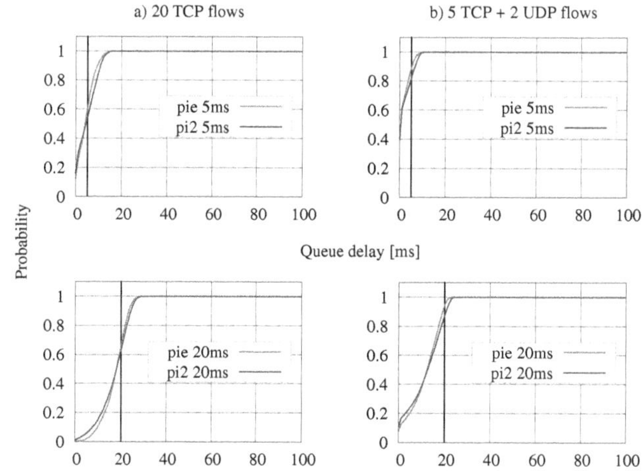

Figure 14: Queuing delay comparison under different traffic loads using 5 ms and 20 ms target delays: link capacity = 10 Mbps, RTT = 100 ms.

Coexistence.

The second series of tests was focused on coexistence between Classic and Scalable congestion controls with different traffic mixes and network conditions, exploring different combinations of link capacity and RTT.

We performed experiments with mixed Cubic and DCTCP flows and measured the ratio of their individual flow throughputs (Figure 15), and the average and 99th percentile of queue delay (Figure 16). We also monitored mark or drop probability (Figure 17) and link utilization (Figure 18) for each experiment.

In a first set of experiments, we used a single long-running flow for each congestion control. Figure 15 demonstrates throughput 'fairness'. As well as the Cubic/DCTCP throughput ratio (blue), we also included Cubic/ECN-Cubic (black) as a control to show the effect of the different congestion control algorithm separately from the addition of ECN. In both cases the ratio is non-ECN-capable to ECN-capable flow rate. As an illustration of the coexistence problem, the Cubic/DCTCP ratio with PIE shows, as expected, that DCTCP effectively starves Cubic, behaving about ten times more aggressively. In contrast, applying PI^2 to Cubic and PI to DCTCP (labelled PI2) works remarkably well over the whole range of link rates and RTTs, keeping the Cubic/DCTCP rate balance close to 1 in all cases, nearly exactly counterbalancing DCTCP's significantly greater aggression. In the control case of Cubic/ECN-Cubic, as expected, we see similar results for both PI^2 and PIE.[5]

As we have emphasized, the ultimate aim is to exploit the low queuing delay of scalable controls using a dualQ.

[5]This experiment uncovered a possible bug in Linux that currently limits the bandwidth-delay product (BDP) to 1 MB. Despite considerable effort, the cause is yet to be ascertained. Unfortunately this caused the anomalous results at the high RTT end of the higher link rates, not only for rate balance, but also for queuing delay, drop/mark probability and utilization.

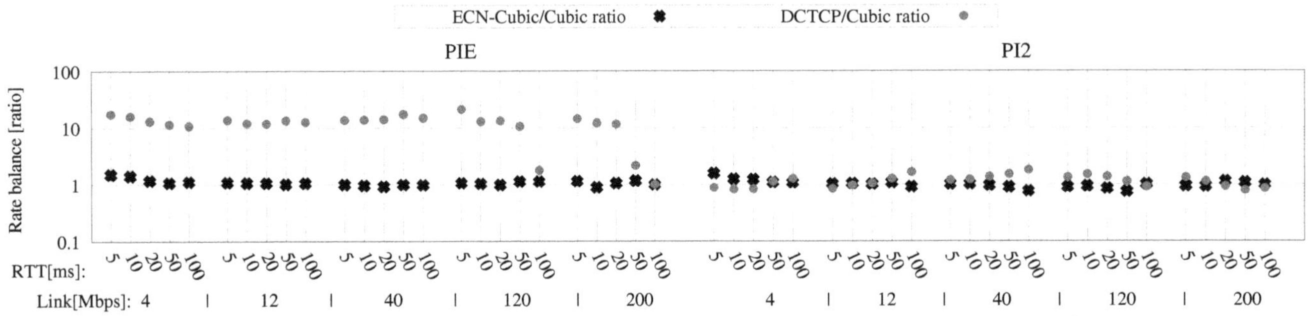

Figure 15: Throughput balance. One flow for each congestion control.[5]

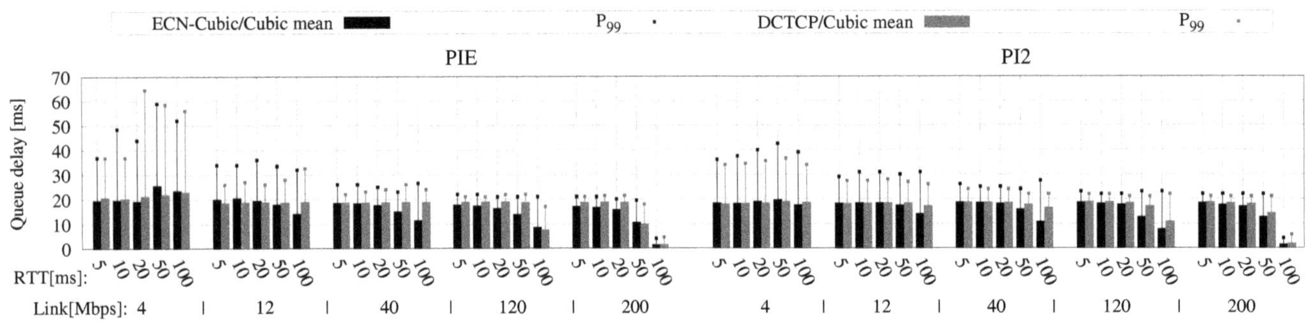

Figure 16: Queuing delay. One flow for each congestion control.[5]

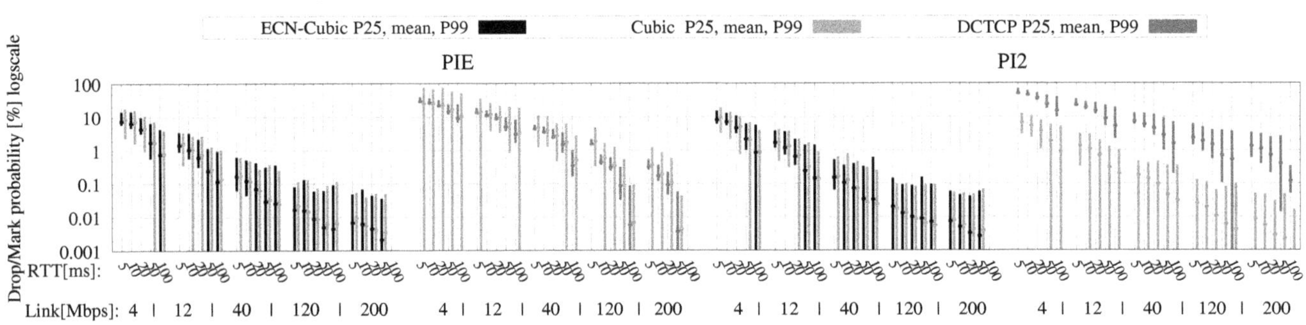

Figure 17: Marking/dropping probability. One flow for each congestion control.[5]

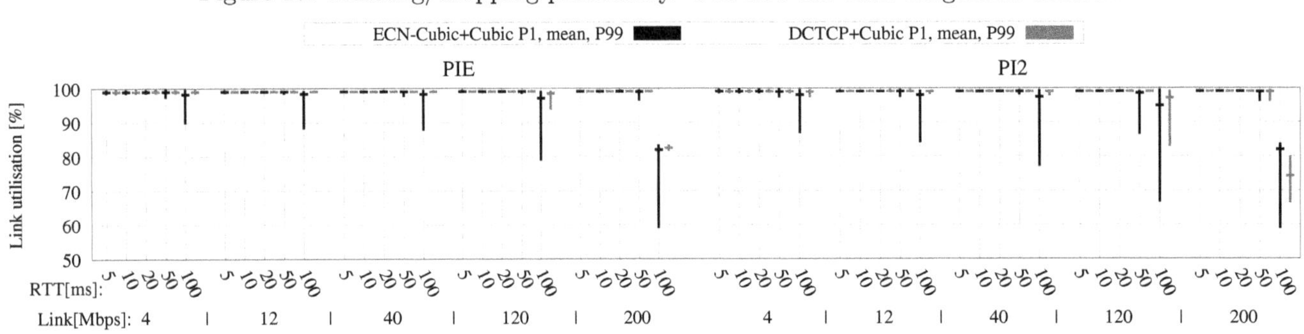

Figure 18: Link utilization. One flow for each congestion control.[5]

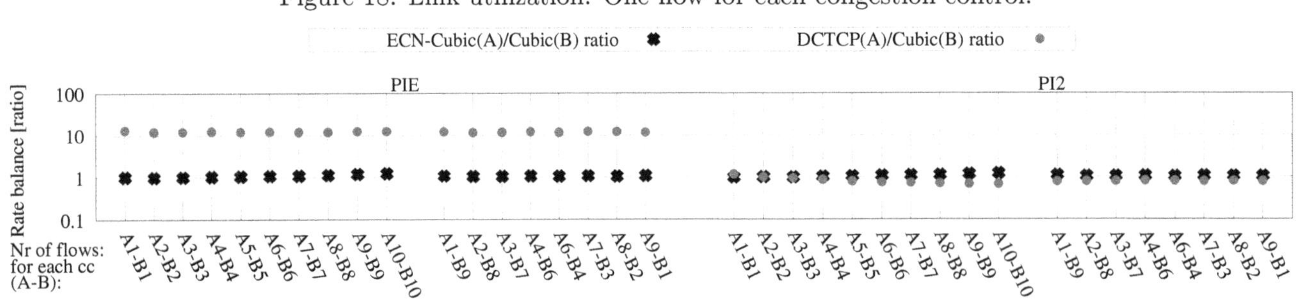

Figure 19: Throughput balance for different combinations of flows, link: 40 Mbps, RTT: 10 ms

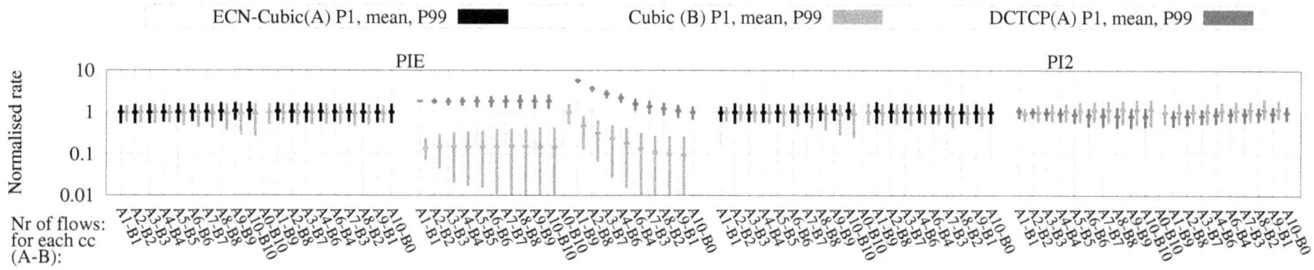

Figure 20: Throughput stability shown as normalized rate per flow (rate per flow divided by 'fair' rate) for different combinations of flows, link: 40 Mbps, RTT: 10 ms

With the single-queue approach studied in this paper, the queuing delay experienced by each type of concurrent flow had to be the same. In Figure 16 we compare the average and 99th %-ile (P_{99}) of queue delay for each packet between the two scenarios: a Cubic flow with an ECN-Cubic or a DCTCP flow. As expected, there is little difference between the scenarios. Nonetheless, the results indicate that PI^2 appears to be no worse than PIE at keeping the queue delay at the target of 20ms. PI^2 even seems to outperform PIE at smaller link rates, which can be seen at the link rate of 4Mbps, where P_{99} is larger for PIE.

To verify whether the throughput ratio is influenced by the number of concurrent flows, we tested it with a range of combinations of flow numbers. Figure 19 shows the per-flow throughput ratio for the combinations of flows displayed on the x-axis, where each combination is represented by two numbers. The first is the number of Cubic flows, while the second is the number of ECN-Cubic or DCTCP flows respectively. The results were similar for different link capacities and RTTs, so we show results for a link capacity of 40 Mbps and 10 ms RTT as an example. Figure 20 visualizes the same experiment, but includes the mean and %-iles by showing normalized rates. The results are very similar to those in Figure 15 showing that PI^2 can maintain equal flow rates irrespective of the number of concurrent flows.

7. CONCLUSIONS

The main conclusions of this work are twofold. Firstly, despite PI^2 being simpler than PIE, it achieves no worse, and in some cases better performance, particularly superior responsiveness during dynamics without risking instability. This has been demonstrated both analytically and through a number of experiments. In other words, the heuristic scaling steps introduced by PIE can be replaced by squaring the output instead, which is less computationally expensive and improves stability in some cases.

Secondly, in contrast to PIE, a combination of PI and PI^2 can support coexistence of Scalable and Classic congestion controls on the public Internet by counterbalancing the more aggressive congestion response of Scalable controls with more aggressive congestion marking. It has been emphasized throughout that the arrangement of both PI and PI^2 in the same queue evaluated in this paper is only a step in the research process, not a recommended deployment. The recommended deployment applies each AQM to separate queues [13] so that Scalable traffic in the PI-controlled queue can maintain extremely low latency while isolated from but coupled to the queue built by Classic traffic controlled by PI^2. A complementary paper explains and evaluates this 'DualQ Coupled' approach [12].

Acknowledgement

The authors' contributions were part-funded by the European Community under its Seventh Framework Programme through the Reducing Internet Transport Latency (RITE) project (ICT-317700). The views expressed here are solely those of the authors.

APPENDIX

A. EQUAL STEADY STATE RATE

Classic TCPs have a throughput equation that is proportional to the square root of the signal probability. For our purposes, it is sufficient to ignore dynamic aspects, and apply the simplified models in (5) and (6) for TCP Reno and Cubic window as in [25] and [16]:

$$W_{reno} = \frac{1.22}{p^{1/2}} \quad (5) \qquad W_{cubic} = \frac{1.17R^{3/4}}{p^{3/4}} \quad (6)$$

where p is drop probabillity and R is the RTT.

As we said, the Cubic implementation in Linux falls back to TCP Reno with a different decrease factor ($B = 0.7$ in Linux), thus the CReno steady state window will deviate from (5) with a slightly higher constant (7).

The implicit switch-over RTT can be derived from (6) and (7). Pure Cubic behaviour (as defined in (6)) will become active when (8) is false.

$$W_{creno} = \frac{1.68}{p^{1/2}} \quad (7) \qquad W * R^{3/2} < 3.5 \quad (8)$$

This shows that the switch-over point does not depend on a single RTT or BDP (bandwidth delay product) value, but a more complex combination of RTT and window (W).

In this paper we focus on fairness between Scalable flows and Cubic flows in their Reno mode (CReno). For the Scalable TCP we use DCTCP with probabilistic (not on-off) marking applied by the AQM. We have derived the steady-state window equation for DCTCP in this case, assuming an idealized uniform deterministic marker, which marks every $1/p$ packets. A DCTCP congestion controller has an incremental window increase per RTT $a = 1$ and a multiplicative decrease factor $b = p/2$ (with p being estimated). So, every RTT, W is increased by $W \leftarrow W + 1$, meaning that under steady state, this must be compensated every RTT by (9). This decrease is steered by ECN marks, as defined in (10).

$$W \leftarrow \left(1 - \frac{1}{W}\right) W \quad (9) \qquad W \leftarrow \left(1 - \frac{p}{2}\right) W \quad (10)$$

From (9) and (10), we see that to preserve this balance, window equation (11) must be true.

$$W_{dc} = \frac{2}{p} \quad (11) \qquad W_{dcth} = \frac{2}{p^2} \quad (12)$$

Note that (12) derived in the DCTCP paper [2] has a different exponent of p compared to (11). The reason is that (12) is defined for a step threshold, which causes an on-off pattern of RTT length marking trains. In contrast, when marking for DCTCP is steered by a PI controller, its random process with a fractional probability will cause an evenly distributed marking pattern, so (11) will be applicable. This explains the same phenomenon found empirically in Irteza *et al* [22], when comparing a step threshold with a RED ramp.

A Scalable congestion controller such as DCTCP achieves low throughput variations by driving the network to give it a more responsive signal with a higher resolution. Therefore, a solution must be found to reduce the congestion signal intensity for Classic congestion controllers (TCP Cubic and Reno), balanced with that for DCTCP.

Knowing the relation between network congestion signal (mark or drop) probability and window, we can adjust feedback from the network to each type of congestion control. For TCP CReno and DCTCP, we substitute (7) and (11) in $W_{creno} = W_{dc}$:

$$\frac{1.68}{p_{creno}^{1/2}} = \frac{2}{p_{dc}} \quad (13) \qquad p_{creno} = \left(\frac{p_{dc}}{1.19}\right)^2 \quad (14)$$

Therefore, if the RTTs are equal, we can arrange the rates to be equal using the simple relation between the probabilities, defined in (14).

Probabilistic mark/drop is typically implemented by comparing the probability p with a pseudo-randomly generated value Y per packet. A signal is applied for a packet when $Y < p$. The advantage of using relation (14) is that p^2 can easily be acquired by comparing p with 2 pseudo-random generated values and signalling only if both random values are smaller than p: $max(Y_1, Y_2) < p$.

The phrase "Think once to mark, think twice to drop" is a useful *aide-mémoire* for this approach, because Scalable controls always uses ECN marking (the marking level is often too high to use drop), while Classic controls typically use drop.

B. FLUID MODEL

In Pan *et al* [29] a PIE controller was designed for TCP Reno. TCP Reno has a throughput that is proportional to $1/\sqrt{p}$. In this analytical section we define first a model for a system that has an adaptor on the output of the controller that squares the signal, so the controller generates a signal $p' = \sqrt{p}$ which is finally applied to the packets as a marking or dropping signal $p = (p')^2$.

Secondly we define a system where the TCP is defined as a so-called scalable congestion control (section 2) with a throughput that is proportional to $1/p'$, so no squaring is needed at the end. We will consistently use p' to indicate a scalable probability and p to indicate a classic probability. One can be derived from the other with the above equation.

We start from the model of the evolution of the window of TCP Reno and the dynamics of the queue from Misra *et al* [26] and [19]:

$$\frac{dW(t)}{dt} = \frac{1}{R(t)} - 0.5\frac{W(t)W(t-R(t))}{R(t-R(t))}p(t-R(t)), \quad (15)$$

$$\frac{dq(t)}{dt} = \frac{W(t)}{R(t)}N(t) - C(t), \quad (16)$$

where $W(t)$ is the window size, $q(t)$ the queue size, R(t) the harmonic mean of the round trip time of the different flows, $N(t)$ is the number of flows, and C(t) is the link capacity, which might also vary over time, but is here assumed independent from all other variables.

The Cubic implementation in Linux provides a fallback to TCP Reno when RTT or rate is small (CReno). For CReno mode the multiplicative reduction factor is 0.7 instead of 0.5, which results in an equation that is just slightly different:

$$\frac{dW(t)}{dt} = \frac{1}{R(t)} - 0.7\frac{W(t)W(t-R(t))}{R(t-R(t))}p(t-R(t)). \quad (17)$$

For TCP Reno that is steered by a squared probability, the following equation is used to derive the transfer function:

$$\frac{dW(t)}{dt} = \frac{1}{R(t)} - 0.5\frac{W(t)W(t-R(t))}{R(t-R(t))}(p'(t-R(t)))^2. \quad (18)$$

Doing the similar linearization exercise for (18) as for (15) in [19], assuming for now $N(t) = N$, $C(t) = C$, $R(t) = R_0$ as constants, we get operating point equations (defined by $dW/dt = 0$, $dq/dt = 0$ and

$(W, q, p') = (W_0, q_0, p'_0))$:

$$W_0^2 p_0'^2 = 2, \quad W_0 = \frac{R_0 C}{N}, \quad R_0 = \frac{q_0}{C} + T_p, \qquad (19)$$

where T_p is the base delay of a specific flow.

The partial derivations are the same as in Appendix I of [19] except:

$$\frac{\partial f}{\partial p'} = -\frac{W_0^2}{2R_0} 2p'_0 = -\frac{\sqrt{2}C}{N},$$

where $f(W, W_R, q, p')$ is defined as the RHS of Equation 18, and $W_R = W(t - R)$. Note that

$$\frac{\partial f}{\partial W} = \frac{\partial f}{\partial W_R} = \frac{-W_0}{2R_0} p_0'^2 = \frac{-W_0}{2R_0} \frac{2}{W_0^2} = \frac{-1}{R_0 W_0} = \frac{-N}{R_0^2 C},$$

$$\frac{\partial f}{\partial q} = -\frac{1}{R_0^2 C} + \frac{W_0^2 p_0'^2}{2R_0^2 C} = -\frac{1}{R_0^2 C} + \frac{2}{2R_0^2 C} = 0,$$

both of which initially have different terms to the analysis in [19], but eventually resolve to the same result as [19]. As a result, the linearized equation for a Reno TCP with a squared p' and its Laplace transform will be:

$$\frac{d(\delta W(t))}{dt} = -\frac{N}{R_0^2 C}(\delta W(t) + \delta W_R) - \frac{\sqrt{2}C}{N} \delta p'(t - R_0); \qquad (20)$$

$$sW(s) = -\frac{N}{R_0^2 C} W(s)(1 + e^{-sR_0}) - \frac{\sqrt{2}C}{N} p'(s) e^{-sR_0}. \qquad (21)$$

Also for a scalable TCP that reduces its current window by half a packet per mark, the following equation can be derived in a similar way:

$$\frac{dW(t)}{dt} = \frac{1}{R(t)} - 0.5 \frac{W(t - R(t))}{R(t - R(t))} p'(t - R(t)). \qquad (22)$$

The difference is that the current window size $W(t)$ is not present as it is not used to determine the window reduction. This makes the reduction term only dependent on the state at time $t - R(t)$.

Re-running the linearization exercise for (22) as in [19], we get operating point equations:

$$W_0 p'_0 = 2, \quad W_0 = \frac{R_0 C}{N}, \quad R_0 = \frac{q_0}{C} + T_p. \qquad (23)$$

The partial derivations are the same as in [19] except for:

$$\frac{\partial f}{\partial W} = 0; \quad \frac{\partial f}{\partial p'} = -\frac{W_0}{2R_0} = -\frac{C}{2N}.$$

Note that

$$\frac{\partial f}{\partial W_R} = -\frac{1}{2R_0} p'_0 = -\frac{1}{2R_0} \frac{2}{W_0} = -\frac{1}{R_0 W_0} = -\frac{N}{R_0^2 C},$$

which initially had different terms to the analysis in [19], but eventually resolves to the same result as [19]. As a result, the linearized equations for a scalable TCP and its Laplace transform will be:

$$\frac{d(\delta W(t))}{dt} = -\frac{N}{R_0^2 C} \delta W(t - R_0) - \frac{C}{2N} \delta p'(t - R_0); \qquad (24)$$

$$sW(s) = -e^{-sR_0} \left(\frac{N}{R_0^2 C} W(s) - \frac{C}{2N} p'(s) \right). \qquad (25)$$

From [26] and [19] we repeat the linearized queue equation, its Laplace transform and Laplace transfer function:

$$\frac{d(\delta q(t))}{dt} = \frac{N}{R_0} \delta W(t) - \frac{1}{R_0} \delta q(t); \qquad (26)$$

$$sq(s) = \frac{N}{R_0} W(s) - \frac{1}{R_0} q(s), \qquad (27)$$

$$P_{queue}(s) = \frac{q(s)}{W(s)} = \frac{\frac{N}{R_0}}{s + \frac{1}{R_0}}. \qquad (28)$$

The PI transfer function in the Laplace domain is:

$$C_{PI}(s) = \frac{\frac{\beta + \alpha/2}{C} s + \frac{\alpha}{TC}}{s}. \qquad (29)$$

The combined PI and queue (=AQM) transfer function in terms of R_0 and W_0 is:

$$A(s) = \frac{(\beta + \frac{\alpha}{2})s + \frac{\alpha}{T}}{s} \frac{\frac{1}{W_0}}{s + \frac{1}{R_0}}, \qquad (30)$$

$$A(s) = \frac{\kappa_A}{W_0} \frac{(s/z_A + 1)}{s(s/s_A + 1)}, \qquad (31)$$

with $\kappa_A = \alpha R_0 / T$, $z_A = \alpha / (T(\beta + \alpha/2))$ and $s_A = 1/R_0$.

The transfer functions of the different TCP and marking combinations in terms of W_0, R_0 and p_0 or p'_0 are:

$$P_{reno_p}(s) = \frac{W(s)}{p(s)} = -\frac{W_0 \kappa_R e^{-sR_0}}{s/s_R + (1 + e^{-sR_0})/2}; \qquad (32)$$

$$P_{reno_{p'2}}(s) = \frac{W(s)}{p'(s)} = -\frac{W_0 \kappa_S e^{-sR_0}}{s/s_R + (1 + e^{-sR_0})/2}; \qquad (33)$$

$$P_{scal_{p'}}(s) = \frac{W(s)}{p'(s)} = -\frac{W_0 \kappa_S e^{-sR_0}}{s/s_S + e^{-sR_0}}, \qquad (34)$$

with $\kappa_S = 1/p'_0$, $s_S = p'_0/(2R_0)$, $\kappa_R = 1/(2p_0) = \kappa_S^2/2$ and $s_R = \sqrt{2}p'_0/R_0 = \sqrt{2p_0}/R_0 = \sqrt{8}s_S$.

The complete loop transfer functions are:

$$L_{reno_p}(s) = \frac{\kappa_R \kappa_A (s/z_A + 1) e^{-sR_0}}{(s/s_R + (1 + e^{-sR_0})/2)(s/s_A + 1)s}; \qquad (35)$$

$$L_{reno_{p'2}}(s) = \frac{\kappa_S \kappa_A (s/z_A + 1) e^{-sR_0}}{(s/s_R + (1 + e^{-sR_0})/2)(s/s_A + 1)s}; \qquad (36)$$

$$L_{scal_{p'}}(s) = \frac{\kappa_S \kappa_A (s/z_A + 1) e^{-sR_0}}{(s/s_S + e^{-sR_0})(s/s_A + 1)s}. \qquad (37)$$

8. REFERENCES

[1] R. Adams. Active Queue Management: A Survey. *IEEE Communications Surveys & Tutorials*, 15(3):1425–1476, 2013.

[2] M. Alizadeh, A. Greenberg, D. A. Maltz, J. Padhye, P. Patel, B. Prabhakar, S. Sengupta, and M. Sridharan. Data Center TCP (DCTCP). *Proc. ACM SIGCOMM'10, Computer Communication Review*, 40(4):63–74, Oct. 2010.

[3] M. Alizadeh, A. Javanmard, and B. Prabhakar. Analysis of DCTCP: Stability, Convergence, and Fairness. In *Proceedings of the ACM SIGMETRICS Joint International Conference on Measurement and Modeling of Computer Systems*, SIGMETRICS '11, pages 73–84, New York, NY, USA, 2011. ACM.

[4] D. Black. Explicit Congestion Notification (ECN) Experimentation. Internet Draft draft-black-tsvwg-ecn-experimentation-00, Internet Engineering Task Force, Sept. 2016. (Work in Progress).

[5] O. Bondarenko, K. De Schepper, I.-J. Tsang, B. Briscoe, A. Petlund, and C. Griwodz. Ultra-Low Delay for All: Live Experience, Live Analysis. In *Proc. ACM Multimedia Systems; Demo Session*, pages 33:1–33:4. ACM, May 2016.

[6] B. Briscoe. Review: Proportional Integral controller Enhanced (PIE) Active Queue Management (AQM). Technical Report TR-TUB8-2015-001, BT, May 2015.

[7] B. Briscoe, A. Brunstrom, A. Petlund, D. Hayes, D. Ros, I.-J. Tsang, S. Gjessing, G. Fairhurst, C. Griwodz, and M. Welzl. Reducing Internet Latency: A Survey of Techniques and their Merits. *IEEE Communications Surveys & Tutorials*, 18(3):2149–2196, 2016.

[8] B. Briscoe (Ed.), K. De Schepper, and M. Bagnulo. Low Latency, Low Loss, Scalable Throughput (L4S) Internet Service: Problem Statement. Internet Draft draft-briscoe-tsvwg-aqm-tcpm-rmcat-l4s-problem-02, Internet Engineering Task Force, July 2016. (Work in Progress).

[9] CableLabs. Data-Over-Cable Service Interface Specifications DOCSIS® 3.1; MAC and Upper Layer Protocols Interface Specification. Specification CM-SP-MULPIv3.1-I01-131029, CableLabs, Oct. 2013.

[10] Y. Choi, J. A. Silvester, and H.-c. Kim. Analyzing and Modeling Workload Characteristics in a Multiservice IP Network. *Internet Computing, IEEE*, 15(2):35–42, March 2011.

[11] K. De Schepper and O. Bondarenko. Linux sch_pi2 qdisc source code available at https://github.com/olgabo/dualpi2, June 2016.

[12] K. De Schepper, O. Bondarenko, I.-J. Tsang, and B. Briscoe. 'Data Centre to the Home': Deployable Ultra-Low Queuing Delay for All. Sept. 2016. (Under Submission).

[13] K. De Schepper, B. Briscoe (Ed.), O. Bondarenko, and I.-J. Tsang. DualQ Coupled AQM for Low Latency, Low Loss and Scalable Throughput. Internet Draft draft-briscoe-aqm-dualq-coupled-01, Internet Engineering Task Force, Mar. 2016. (Work in Progress).

[14] K. De Schepper, B. Briscoe (Ed.), and I.-J. Tsang. Identifying Modified Explicit Congestion Notification (ECN) Semantics for Ultra-Low Queuing Delay. Internet Draft draft-briscoe-tsvwg-ecn-l4s-id-01, Internet Engineering Task Force, Mar. 2016. (Work in Progress).

[15] N. Finn (Ed.). IEEE Standard for Local and Metropolitan Area Networks—Virtual Bridged Local Area Networks - Amendment: 10: Congestion Notification. Standard 802.1Qau, IEEE, Apr. 2010.

[16] S. Ha, I. Rhee, and L. Xu. CUBIC: a new TCP-friendly high-speed TCP variant. *SIGOPS Operating Systems Review*, 42(5):64–74, July 2008.

[17] O. Hohlfeld, E. Pujol, F. Ciucu, A. Feldmann, and P. Barford. A QoE Perspective on Sizing Network Buffers. In *Proc. Internet Measurement Conf (IMC'14)*, pages 333–346. ACM, Nov. 2014.

[18] C. V. Hollot, V. Misra, D. Towsley, and W. Gong. Analysis and design of controllers for AQM routers supporting TCP flows. *IEEE Transactions on Automatic Control*, 47(6):945–959, Jun 2002.

[19] C. V. Hollot, V. Misra, D. F. Towsley, and W. Gong. A Control Theoretic Analysis of RED. In *Proc. INFOCOM 2001. 20th Annual Joint Conf. of the IEEE Computer and Communications Societies.*, volume 3, pages 1510—19, 2001.

[20] Y. Hong and O. W. W. Yang. Self-tuning TCP traffic controller using gain margin specification. *IET Communications*, 1(1):27–33, February 2007.

[21] Y. Hong, O. W. W. Yang, and C. Huang. Self-tuning PI TCP flow controller for AQM routers with interval gain and phase margin assignment. In *Global Telecommunications Conference (Globecom'04)*, volume 3, pages 1324–1328, 2004.

[22] S. Irteza, A. Ahmed, S. Farrukh, B. Memon, and I. Qazi. On the Coexistence of Transport Protocols in Data Centers. In *Proc. IEEE Int'l Conf. on Communications (ICC 2014)*, pages 3203–3208, June 2014.

[23] M. Kühlewind, D. P. Wagner, J. M. R. Espinosa, and B. Briscoe. Using Data Center TCP (DCTCP) in the Internet. In *Proc. Third IEEE Globecom Workshop on Telecommunications*

Standards: From Research to Standards, pages 583–588, Dec. 2014.

[24] M. Kwon and S. Fahmy. A Comparison of Load-based and Queue-based Active Queue Management Algorithms. In *Proc. Int'l Soc. for Optical Engineering (SPIE)*, volume 4866, pages 35–46, 2002.

[25] M. Mathis, J. Semke, J. Mahdavi, and T. Ott. The macroscopic behavior of the TCP Congestion Avoidance algorithm. *Computer Communication Review*, 27(3), July 1997.

[26] V. Misra, W.-B. Gong, and D. Towsley. Fluid-based Analysis of a Network of AQM Routers Supporting TCP Flows with an Application to RED. *SIGCOMM Computer Comms.. Review*, 30(4):151–160, Aug. 2000.

[27] K. Nichols and V. Jacobson. Controlling queue delay. *ACM Queue*, 10(5), May 2012.

[28] R. Pan et al. PIE: A lightweight control scheme to address the bufferbloat problem. In *Proc. IEEE Int'l Conf. on High Performance Switching and Routing (HPSR)*, pages 148–155, 2013.

[29] R. Pan, P. Natarajan, F. Baker, G. White, B. Ver Steeg, M. Prabhu, C. Piglione, and V. Subramanian. PIE: A Lightweight Control Scheme To Address the Bufferbloat Problem. Internet Draft draft-ietf-aqm-pie-10, Internet Engineering Task Force, Sept. 2016. (Work in progress).

[30] K. K. Ramakrishnan, S. Floyd, and D. Black. The Addition of Explicit Congestion Notification (ECN) to IP. Request for Comments RFC 3168, RFC Editor, Sept. 2001.

[31] M. Sågfors, R. Ludwig, M. Meyer, and J. Peisa. Buffer Management for Rate-Varying 3G Wireless Links Supporting TCP Traffic. In *Proc Vehicular Technology Conference*, Apr. 2003.

[32] G. White. Active Queue Management Algorithms for DOCSIS 3.0; A Simulation Study of CoDel, SFQ-CoDel and PIE in DOCSIS 3.0 Networks. Technical report, CableLabs, Apr. 2013.

SMig: Stream Migration Extension For HTTP/2

Xianghang Mi
Indiana University
Bloomington, IN
xmi@iu.edu

Feng Qian
Indiana University
Bloomington, IN
fengqian@indiana.edu

Xiaofeng Wang
Indiana University
Bloomington, IN
xw7@indiana.edu

ABSTRACT

HTTP/2 is quickly replacing HTTP/1.1, the protocol that supports the WWW for the past 17 years. However, HTTP/2's connection management and multiplexing schemes often incur unexpected cross-layer interactions. In this paper, we propose SMig, an HTTP/2 extension that allows a client or server to migrate an on-going HTTP/2 stream from one connection to another. We demonstrate through real implementation that SMig can bring substantial performance improvement under certain common usage scenarios (*e.g.,* up to 99% of download time reduction for small delay-sensitive objects when a concurrent large download is present).

CCS Concepts

•Networks → Application layer protocols;

Keywords

HTTP/2; Stream Migration; Head-of-line Blocking

1. INTRODUCTION

HTTP, the key protocol supporting the World Wide Web, has been evolving. Currently, the most widely deployed HTTP version is HTTP/1.1 [16] standardized 17 years ago. As web pages became rich and complex, HTTP/1.1 started to exhibit performance issues. To address them, several new web protocols have been proposed recently. In particular, HTTP/2 [10], the next version of HTTP, has been standardized in 2015 and is replacing HTTP/1.1 quickly. From July 2015 to June 2016, the fraction of websites using HTTP/2 has increased from 0.3% to 8.1% [8]. Within the Alexa top 100 websites, 31% of them support HTTP/2 [26].

HTTP/2 introduces several new features such as a binary protocol format, header compression, and server push. Among them, a particularly notable feature is *multiplexing*, which consolidates multiple concurrent requests into a single TCP connection. By contrast, HTTP/1.1 only supports serving requests sequentially over a TCP connection[1]. Therefore, HTTP/1.1 needs multiple concurrent connections to support concurrency. Prior studies have shown multiplexing often effectively improves the page load time [28, 27, 24]. However, studies also revealed that multiplexing may incur undesired interaction with other layers, leading to suboptimal performance. Examples include being vulnerable to losses [27], poorly interacting with the cellular radio state machine [15], and under-utilizing the network bandwidth [24]. Note many of these issues also exist in other multiplexing-based web protocols such as QUIC [13].

In this paper, we propose SMig (Stream MIGration extension), an extension that improves the performance and enables new use cases for HTTP/2. In the current HTTP/2 paradigm, (1) objects are usually multiplexed over a single connection; (2) an object transfer including both its request and response must be bound to the same connection. SMig instead allows the delivery of an object to be *migrated* from one connection to another at any time. For example, the request and response can be delivered over different connections; or all bytes except for the first 100KB of an object can be migrated to a different connection. We make the following contributions throughout this paper.

• In §2, we motivate SMig using concrete use cases. (1) When large and small objects are multiplexed together, HTTP/2 suffers from severe sender-side head-of-line (HoL) blocking, toward which no effective solution exists. (2) We found that (explicitly or implicitly) canceling a large file download over HTTP/2 incurs a significantly larger amount of wasted traffic compared to doing so over HTTP/1.1. This can be effectively addressed by SMig. (3) We also describe other new use cases enabled by SMig such as adaptive multipath.

• In §4, we present the design of SMig, which is lightweight, backward compatible, and incrementally deployable. In SMig, a migration can be initiated by either the server or a client, and the migration incurs no additional delay under the common usage scenario. A possible concern of SMig is that it creates additional connections. However, their numbers are still significantly less than those in HTTP/1.1. More

[1] An exception is HTTP Pipelining, which has various limitations and was not widely deployed.

CoNEXT '16, December 12-15, 2016, Irvine, CA, USA
© 2016 ACM. ISBN 978-1-4503-4292-6/16/12... $15.00
DOI: http://dx.doi.org/10.1145/2999572.2999583

importantly, since usually only large objects are migrated, the connection management overhead is amortized by the large transfer carried by a migrated connection.

• We have implemented a prototype of SMig and integrated it with our custom HTTP/2 client and server applications. In §5, we evaluate SMig over wired networks and commercial cellular networks. The results indicate that SMig can bring substantial performance improvement under certain common usage scenarios (*e.g.,* up to 99% of download time reduction for small delay-sensitive objects when a concurrent large download is present, and up to 90% of reduction of wasted traffic when canceling a large object transfer).

2. MOTIVATING EXAMPLES

We first give an overview of the multiplexing mechanism in HTTP/2. HTTP/2 encapsulates HTTP transactions into *streams* each carrying one transaction. A stream is a bidirectional flow of bytes consisting of a series of *frames* carrying the actual data. Each frame also contains a stream ID to allow the receiver to de-multiplex the streams. Next, we describe a few scenarios where applying SMig is beneficial.

2.1 Multiplexing Large and Small Objects

Our prior study [24] identifies an issue of the multiplexing mechanism in SPDY [6], the predecessor of HTTP/2. When a large object download (often delay-tolerant) is multiplexed with small object transfers (usually delay-sensitive), the latter's performance will degrade dramatically. This is attributed to the head-of-line (HoL) blocking at the TCP send buffer that significantly affects HTTP/2 performance. Due to multiplexing, large and small transfers *share* the same send buffer that is inherently FIFO. Therefore, small transfers will be blocked by the large download as long as the TCP send buffer size is not trivially small. Note this is different from another well-known HoL blocking happening at the *receiver* side caused by packet losses or severe out-of-order [27].

Here we further confirm that server-side HoL blocking exists in HTTP/2. We conducted experiments over a wide range of HTTP/2 server implementations (latest versions as of June 2016) including Nghttp2 1.11, LiteSpeed 5.0, Nginx 1.10.1, and H2O 2.0.0. We found all of them, many of which are production-level implementations, are vulnerable to sender-side HoL blocking. It is also worth mentioning that HTTP/2 can be deployed either at a web server or at a proxy. In the former scheme, objects belonging to the same domain are multiplexed together; while in the latter, all traffic from the same client browser is multiplexed, making the sender-side HoL blocking an even more severe issue: a large download will affect the entire browser's performance.

Next, we conduct measurements to reveal that for real websites, it is quite common that large and small objects are hosted under the same domain (so HTTP/2 will use the same connection to deliver them concurrently, causing potential sender-side HoL blocking). The measurement is performed as follows. We study the Alexa top-1500 websites. For each website, we crawl all objects that belong to the first three levels of its *website object tree*, which has its landing page's HTML file as the root node (Level 1). Within the tree, Object Y is a child of Object X if and only if X and Y have the same domain name and X contains the URL of Y (therefore X must be an HTML page and all objects in the tree have the same domain name as the landing HTML page). We first observe that the vast majority of objects are small, with the 25-th, 50-th, and 75-th percentiles measured to be 18KB, 40KB, and 115KB, respectively, across all websites. Prior studies [25] show that for mobile versions of web pages, their object sizes are even smaller. On the other hand, Table 1 lists the number of websites (*i.e.,* their object trees with up to three levels of objects) that contain at least one large object whose size is at least $X \in \{1, 5, 10, 25, 50\}$ MB. As shown, many websites contain large objects that are under the same domain name as the landing page. If such large objects are concurrently fetched with other small objects, sender-side HoL blocking will occur. As will be demonstrated in §5.1, even a mid-sized file of 1MB can cause severe HoL blocking.

Contain Objects with Size...	# Websites
$\geq$ 1MB	209
$\geq$ 5MB	43
$\geq$ 10MB	21
$\geq$ 25MB	10
$\geq$ 50MB	4

Table 1: Websites among the Alexa top-1500 sites that contain large objects in the first three levels of their website object trees.

Scenario	Tail Bytes
1. HTTP/1.1, cancel DL	150 KB
2. HTTP/2, cancel DL	2.5 MB
3. HTTP/2, close browser	150 KB

Table 2: Tail bytes in three scenarios.

2.2 Canceling HTTP/2 Download

We found that compared to HTTP/1.1, after a single HTTP/2 file download is canceled, the client may still receive a large number of bytes. To demonstrate this, we conduct three experiments under the same network condition (emulated 10Mbps link, ~80ms RTT): (1) cancel an on-going large HTTP/1.1 file download in Chrome browser while keeping the browser open, (2) cancel an on-going HTTP/2 download of the same size while keeping the browser open, and (3) cancel an HTTP/2 download by directly closing the browser. The cancellation is done manually as how a normal user would do. We then measure the number of bytes delivered to the client (we call them "tail bytes") after taking the cancellation action. As shown in Table 2, 2.5 MB of tail bytes appear in Scenario (2) while much fewer tail bytes appear in Scenario (1) and (3). The issue of Scenario (2) is also severe in cellular networks (up to a 20x difference compared to Scenario 3) as will be shown in §5.2. This causes bandwidth waste and monetary cost since cellular customers are billed by bytes.

When canceling a file download in HTTP/2, the client sends a `RST_STREAM` control frame to shut down its corresponding stream. However, the stream's underlying connection *cannot* be closed, because a TCP connection in HTTP/2 is persistent and long-lived [10] *i.e.,* it needs to be shared by all streams of the same domain (or all traffic of the entire browser, if a proxy is used). Therefore, although the server application stops delivering data of that closed stream to TCP, all remaining data in the TCP send buffer will still be transferred to the client. In contrast, when canceling a file download in HTTP/1.1 or by closing the browser, the TCP connection (with all data in its send buffer) is immediately torn down, leaving much fewer tail bytes to arrive.

It is important to note that download cancellation occurs frequently in the real world. It is not limited to user explicitly hitting a "cancel" button. Instead, it usually happens *implicitly*, such as user skipping a song in a media player, repositioning a video playback, navigating to another page before the current page finishes loading a large object, pausing background synchronization, *etc.* All above scenarios will incur more tail bytes in HTTP/2 than in HTTP/1.1.

2.3 Download Accelerator Using Multipath

Mobile devices are usually equipped with multiple interfaces. Samsung recently introduced a new feature called Download Booster to its Android devices, for accelerating large HTTP download (> 30MB) using both Wi-Fi and cellular [5]. Download Booster is realized using concurrent HTTP byte range requests: requests for different ranges of a large file are simultaneously sent over two connections, one over Wi-Fi and one over cellular. This approach has two limitations. First, since the byte ranges are pre-calculated, Download Booster usually cannot achieve the optimal download time (*e.g.,* when cellular finishes sooner than Wi-Fi). Second, download booster does not work with files whose sizes are not known beforehand. In §4.1, we discuss how SMig can easily work with existing off-the-shelf multipath solutions to addresses the above limitations.

Summary. Due to multiplexing, connection management in HTTP/2 differs from that in HTTP/1.1 significantly. The HTTP/2 RFC [10] recommends that clients "should[2] not open more than one HTTP/2 connection to a given host and port pair". However, our findings indicate that blindly using the single connection may lead to performance degradation (§2.1), unnecessary network traffic (§2.2), and obstacles to realizing new use cases (§2.3). We describe how SMig can be used in the above scenarios in §4.1.

3. RELATED WORK

Our proposal complements existing work of modeling [28, 27], measuring [13, 26], optimizing [17, 15], and applying [12, 9, 14] emerging protocols such as HTTP/2, SPDY, and QUIC. Next, we further motivate SMig by explaining the limitations of existing solutions to the sender-side HoL blocking problem described in §2.1.

Stream Prioritization. HTTP/2 supports assigning to streams different priorities, which "can be used to select streams for transmitting frames when there is limited capacity for sending" [10]. Stream prioritization however does not help mitigate the sender-side HoL blocking when the shared buffer is at the lower (*e.g.,* transport) layer.

Shrinking TCP Buffer can mitigate the sender-side HoL blocking and reduce the tail bytes. But doing so may cause performance degradation as the TCP send buffer size limits the TCP congestion window that is often highly fluctuating. This makes estimating the right TCP buffer size difficult.

Priority Queue Support for TCP. Nowlan *et al.* proposed uTCP [22], which adds unordered delivery and multi-queue support to TCP. Leveraging uTCP, the server can avoid HoL blocking by directing large and small transfers to different queues. However, uTCP requires changing the OS kernel. More importantly, uTCP is incompatible with TLS cipher suites using chained encryption where a TLS record cannot be decrypted until all prior records are processed.

Packet Late Binding. In our prior work [24], we built TM^3, a multiplexing proxy without sender-side HoL blocking. The basic idea is packet late binding: TM^3 moves the multiplexer deep into the OS kernel so that an outgoing packet is not filled with real data until it exits shared buffers. This essentially "skips" shared buffers and thus eliminates the HoL blocking. However, as a general transport-layer proxy, TM^3 is designed to transparently multiplex concurrent HTTP/1.1 (or any short-lived) TCP connections, and it cannot optimize an HTTP/2 flow that has already been multiplexed at the application layer. Also, the late binding mechanism enforces restrictions on frame size and format. TM^3 also requires OS kernel modification.

Other Protocols. Sender-side HoL blocking may also occur at other shared buffers such as Qdisc and driver buffer. But their sizes are usually much smaller. For example, TCP Small Queues (TSQ [7]) can be applied to limit the per-connection Qdisc buffer size with little performance degradation. Also, HoL blocking occurs in other multiplexing-based web protocols such as SPDY [6] and QUIC [4]. QUIC employs UDP as the transport layer. Because UDP buffers are also FIFO, sender-side HoL blocking still exists [24].

4. SMig DESIGN

The Stream Migration Extension (SMig) is an extension for HTTP/2 allowing *an on-going stream to be migrated from one connection to another.* Either the server or a client can initiate a migration. As an application protocol extension, SMig only adds lightweight logic to HTTP/2 and requires no change to the underlying OS. Note that the HTTP/2 specification indeed permits extending the protocol by adding new frame types or new settings [10].

4.1 Usage Scenarios of SMig

A common usage scenario of SMig is to migrate the response of an HTTP transaction. Consider the issues described in §2.1 and §2.2. Suppose the client sends one or more HTTP/2 requests to the server over a multiplexed

[2]The word "should" in RFC means "there may exist valid reasons in particular circumstances to ignore a particular item" [11].

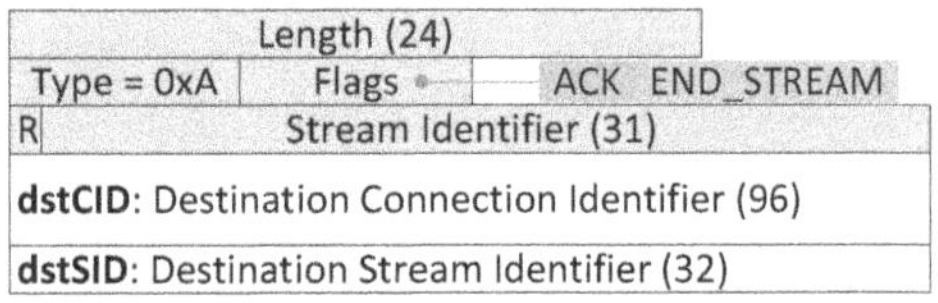

Figure 1: Format of the **MIGRATE** frame. The gray fields belong to the fixed 9-byte header of any HTTP/2 frame.

connection. If any of the requested object(s) are large and there are a non-trivial number of small objects being (or to be) transferred over the same connection, then the server will initiate migrations by moving each large object to a separate connection so that small and large objects are not mixed together. In other words, in this scenario, for a migrated stream, (1) its (usually small) request and large response are delivered over different connections, and (2) its large response uses a dedicated connection. Note the entire migration process is transparent to the upper layer. As a result, (1) as large transfers are migrated to different connections with separate buffers, they will not create HoL blocking for small object transfers; (2) since each large transfer now uses a dedicated connection without being multiplexed, to cancel its download, its underlying connection can be directly torn down, leading to much fewer tail bytes.

A counter-argument toward the above solution is, for large objects, if the client can initiate their requests over separate connections in the first place, then why do we still need SMig? The key reason is that *it is difficult for a client to know the size of an object beforehand*, so the client has to follow the default paradigm by sending all requests over a multiplexed connection. On the other hand, the server usually knows the sizes of their hosted objects (the vast majority of objects have the "Content-Length" field in their response headers). This makes it trivial for the server to make the migration decision based on the object size. Nevertheless, there do exist objects whose precise sizes are not known by server beforehand. We discuss how they can be handled in §4.4.

SMig can also be leveraged to enable new use cases for HTTP/2. For example, to overcome the limitations of Download Booster (§2.3), SMig can be used with MPTCP [3], the *de-facto* multipath solution with off-the-shelf Linux implementation. MPTCP transparently splits the byte stream of a TCP connection into multiple coupled paths (*e.g.*, one over Wi-Fi and one over cellular). However, it is well known that MPTCP provides little benefit for small file download [19]. The server can thus adopt the following strategy to use MPTCP in an adaptive manner. By default, for saving energy, only single path TCP over Wi-Fi is used for file download. If the server finds the file to be large, it can employ SMig to migrate the transfer to an MPTCP connection that reduces the overall download time.

4.2 Stream Migration

We begin with introducing a new type of control-plane frame defined by SMig. A **MIGRATE** frame is used to expresses the intent of a stream migration, or to acknowledge a migration initiated by a peer. As shown in Figure 1, there are two key fields in a **MIGRATE** frame: **dstCID** is the connection identifier (**CID**) of the destination connection that the stream is migrated to; **dstSID** is the stream identifier (**SID**) that the stream will be assigned to after it migrates to **dstCID**. **SID** and its numbering convention are already defined in the HTTP/2 specification. In SMig, **CID** identifies a connection. It is a 96-bit number generated when a connection is established, as to be detailed in §4.3. Note that **SID** is defined within the namespace of **CID** so a stream between two hosts is uniquely identified by (**CID**,**SID**).

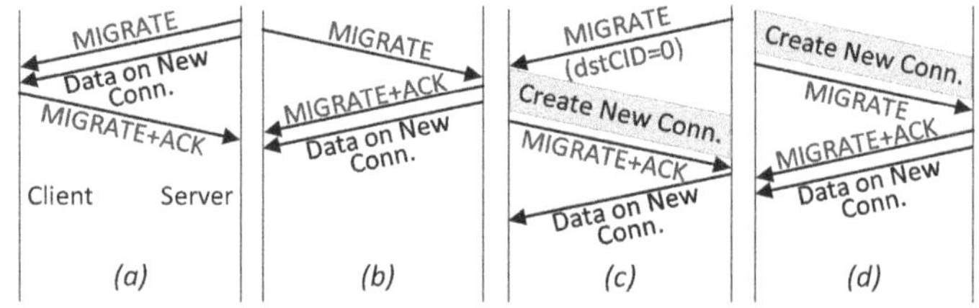

Figure 2: Four stream migration scenarios (only downlink data of the stream after the migration is shown).

C1, S1	C1, S1	C2, S2	C1, S1	C1, S1	C2, S2
Frame 1	Frame 2	Frame 4	Frame 3	MIG-ACK	Frame 5

Figure 3: Frames received by the server during migration.

The gray fields in Figure 1 belong to the fixed 9-byte common header of any HTTP/2 frame. The "Stream Identifier" field is the **SID** of the stream (in its original connection) to be migrated. The "Flag" field defines two types of flags. The **END_STREAM** flag can be set to half-close a stream to be migrated (an HTTP/2 stream is bidirectional; either side can close the one-way data channel to its peer). The usage of the **ACK** flag is explained next.

We now detail the stream migration procedure. Suppose a stream with **SID**=S_1 on connection **CID**=C_1 needs to be migrated. We first assume (1) the migration is initiated by the server (the common case), and (2) there exists an idle connection **dstCID**=C_2 that the stream can be migrated to. Note that neither assumption is mandatory for SMig. We will describe client-initiated migration and the scenario where no idle connection exists soon. The message exchange is shown in Figure 2(a). The server first generates an unused stream ID **dstSID**=S_2 within C_2. It then sends the corresponding **MIGRATE** frame with **ACK**=0 to the client over S_1 on C_1. The main purpose of the **MIGRATE** frame is to inform the peer of the **dstSID** and **dstCID** so that the migrated stream can be seamlessly handled. **MIGRATE** also ensures the cross-connection ordering of frames by marking the last downlink (server to client) frame transferred over the old connection (example shown soon). All subsequent downlink frames must be transferred over the new connection C_2 using the new **SID** S_2. Also as shown, the data over the new connection can be piggybacked with the **MIGRATE** frame.

Upon the reception of the **MIGRATE** frame, the peer (in this case, the client) acknowledges it by sending an identical **MIGRATE** with **ACK**=1. Despite TCP ensures reliable delivery of the original **MIGRATE** frame, this **ACK** is still needed because (similar to the downlink case) as the last uplink frame transferred over (C_1,S_1), this **MIGRATE** with **ACK** ensures the cross-connection ordering of frames. Figure 3 shows a possible sequence of uplink frames received by the server. As shown, Frame 3 and 4 are out of order. The server needs to buffer all frames received on the new connection (Frame 4 in this example) until the reception of **MIGRATE** with **ACK**, without which the server has no way to know when the old stream ends. Note frames do not have sequence numbers; their ordering *within* a connection is guaranteed by TCP.

Despite not a common use case, a migration can also be initiated by a client by following a similar procedure: the client sends a **MIGRATE** and the server acknowledges it with a **MIGRATE** with **ACK**, as shown in Figure 2(b). Note regardless of who initiates the migration, the connection that carries the migrated object is always initiated by the client.

Next we consider scenarios where there does not exist an idle connection. If the client initiates the migration, it first creates the connection before sending **MIGRATE**, as shown in Figure 2(d). If the server initiates the migration, it sends a **MIGRATE** with **dstCID**=0. The client will then create a new connection on behalf of the server before sending a **MIGRATE** with **ACK** and a valid **dstCID**, as shown in Figure 2(c).

Migration Overhead. We analyze the migration overhead for the scenarios in Figure 2. We consider the delay incurred by migration on the downlink data (the uplink cases are symmetric). In plot (a), when the server initiates a migration to an existing connection, the migration takes no additional delay as the data over the new connection can be piggybacked with the **MIGRATE** frame. The same case happens in (b) except that the migration will be delayed by one RTT. If the connection needs to be created, the overhead is higher: in both (c) and (d), it takes the connection establish time (including the SSL/TLS handshake delay) plus one RTT before data appears on the new connection. During this period, data transmission of the stream being migrated is paused. However, note that since usually only large objects are migrated, such delay is dwarfed by the long object transfer time. To eliminate the connection establishment overhead, a client application can always be ready for migration by maintaining one idle connection for certain (host, port) pairs (detailed in §4.3). Note SMig never affects the performance of objects that are *not* migrated.

4.3 Other Design Considerations

CID Generation. When creating a new HTTP/2 connection, an SMig-capable client generates a 96-bit **CID**, and embeds it to a **SETTINGS** frame sent to the server. A **CID** has two parts. The first 64-bit string is called **AppID**, which is used for distinguishing multiple applications (apps) on the same host; the last 32 bits identify a particular connection within an app. When generating a **CID**, a client app thus needs to ensure that (1) the **CID** is unique among all currently established connections to the same (host, port) pair, and (2) all **CID** belonging to the same app session have the same **AppID**. When a stream is migrated from one connection to another, their **CID** must have the same **AppID**. This prevents a stream from being migrated to a connection belonging to a different app running on the same client. The **SETTINGS** frame also ensures backward compatibility: an SMig-capable server must ACK it so both sides know SMig is enabled; otherwise it will be ignored per HTTP/2 specification. The **SETTINGS** frames can be piggybacked with the very first request and response so they do not incur additional delay.

Internal State Migration. When a stream migrates to a new connection, its internal states are migrated together with the stream. They include header compression state [23], flow control state, stream priority *etc.* Note that there is no need to migrate the states at TLS and TCP layers. Optimization can be made though to allow a migrated connection to cache a subset of the old connection's lower-layer states (*e.g.,* certain congestion control parameters) for better performance.

Idle Connection Management. As described in §4.2, a client can optionally "cache" idle connections to reduce the migration overhead. One issue here is to decide the set of domains whose idle connections will be cached. Here the tradeoff is between performance and connection management overhead. Consider two extreme cases. Caching an idle connection for every domain essentially doubles the number of connections, while not performing any caching may slightly delay a migration as illustrated in Figure 2(c)(d). A possible strategy here is to leverage historical information to predict on which domains migrations are more likely to happen. Then the browser will only create additional idle connections for those domains.

Interplay with Server Push. Server push is a new feature introduced in HTTP/2. Using server push, a server can preemptively push (*i.e.,* send) resources to a client without requiring the client to request for the resource. Server push enables early resource discovery and thus can potentially reduce the page load time [18]. To push an object, the server first sends a **PUSH_PROMISE** frame on an existing client-initiated stream. The **PUSH_PROMISE** frame contains a *Promised Stream ID* as well as the header information of the to-be-pushed object. After that, the server initiates the new stream over which the object's data is transferred. SMig works well with server push. The procedure for migrating a pushed object is largely the same as that for migrating a regular object as illustrated in Figure 2. Note if the migration is initiated by the server, the server must send the **MIGRATE** frame after the **PUSH_PROMISE** frame, and set the stream identifier in the **MIGRATE** frame to be the ID of the promised stream, which is the stream to be migrated.

Simultaneous MIGRATE. Consider a corner case where both sides send **MIGRATE** frames simultaneously for the same stream. They can be reconciled if their **dstCID** are the same (or server-side **dstCID** is zero) despite their **dstSID** being different (details omitted). To avoid the case where two simultaneous **MIGRATE** frames contain different **dstCID**, SMig requires that when multiple idle connections are available, the one with the smallest **CID** should be picked as **dstCID**.

Security. To our knowledge, SMig brings no new security vulnerability to HTTP/2. A possible concern is information leak: an adversary can infer a possible migration by observing data being sent over a new connection. It can further infer that, for example, the client is downloading large files. Nevertheless, we believe this is not a big concern because the leaked information is insignificant.

4.4 The Migration Policy

SMig provides the protocol support for stream migration. Applications (*e.g.*, web server) also need migration *policies*, which are expected to be simple, concise, and easy to configure. We next exemplify policies for mitigating sender-side HoL blocking and reducing tail bytes.

The policy executes on the server side. When an HTTP request arrives, the server checks the object size s, and the number of on-going and pending HTTP transactions on the same connection n. A simple policy is to invoke migration if both s and n are larger than pre-defined thresholds. A more adaptive policy is to further consider the network condition: the server measures the network bandwidth b (*e.g.*, using existing methods [20]) and performs migration when both s/b and n are larger than pre-defined thresholds where s/b is the estimated HoL blocking time (an upper bound).

The above policy assumes that the object's size s is known by the server. To handle the less common case where the file size is not known, the server can use robust heuristics to roughly estimate the size. Note even in this case, the server has more knowledge than the client so server-initiated migration is still helpful. An alternative approach is to allow up to t bytes (a pre-defined threshold) of an object with unknown size to be multiplexed into the existing connection. If the object size turns to be larger than t, the remaining part of the object will be migrated. This approach does not need file size estimation but it may incur slight HoL blocking caused by the first t bytes.

5. IMPLEMENTATION AND EVALUATION

We have implemented our custom HTTP/2 client and server, which are user-level applications for Linux/MacOS ($\sim$7.5K C++ LoC). They conform to the HTTP/2 specification except that a small number of advanced features such as server push were left as future work. We then implemented the SMig extension ($\sim$1K LoC) and integrated it with our client and server.

Our evaluation testbed consists of the following. The client is a commodity Macbook with 2.7GHz Intel Core i5 CPU and 8GB memory; the server is a Ubuntu 14.04 machine with 3GHz Intel Core2 Duo E8400 CPU and 4GB Memory. We use default TCP settings unless otherwise mentioned. We conduct experiments over two types of networks: an emulated 10Mbps link with 50ms RTT and a commercial LTE network provided by a large cellular ISP. The cellular connectivity is provided to the laptop by a tethered LTE smartphone. We next use this testbed to evaluate SMig, focusing on addressing the issues described in §2.1 and §2.2 (the use case in §2.3 is more self-explained).

One limitation here is our experiments were not conducted on commercial browsers and servers (integrating them with SMig is our on-going work). Nevertheless, we believe SMig will work with them effectively given that the SMig logic is simple and does not depend on a particular server/browser implementation.

5.1 Mitigating Sender-side HoL Blocking

We first evaluate how well SMig mitigates sender-side HoL blocking under the following setting. The client keeps fetching a 10KB object every 1 sec. During this process, the client also fetches a large file (50 MB) using the four migration schemes: (1) *NoMig*: the large file is still multiplexed with small objects without migration; (2) *MigSW*: the migration is initiated by the server and the whole response is migrated immediately after the request is received by the server; (3) *MigSP*: the migration is initiated by the server and only part of the response (after the first 100KB) is migrated. This corresponds to the scenario where the large file's size is not known so migration is performed in a "lazy" manner; (4) *MigCP*: the migration is initiated by the client and part of the response (after the first 100KB) is migrated.

Figure 4 measures the small object download time over emulated wired network with the default server-side TCP send buffer configuration (min: 4KB, default: 16 KB, max: 1MB). We repeat the experiment for 10 times, each downloading 25 small objects after the large file's request is sent. We report the average download time across all runs (the variation is small). As shown, SMig dramatically reduces the download time for small objects, which are usually delay-sensitive, by up to 90%. Figure 6 repeats the above experiments over cellular network, and qualitatively similar results are observed.

Next, instead of using the default TCP send buffer, we increase it (min: 1MB, default: 4MB, max: 8MB) and do the experiments again, with results shown in Figure 5 and 7 for wired and cellular networks, respectively. Note that it is a common practice of network administrators to increase TCP buffers [2, 1] for improving the network performance. For HTTP/2, however, a key downside is that this exacerbates sender-side HoL blocking. In Figure 5 and 7, SMig reduces the small file download time by up to 93% and 92%, respectively. We observe *MigCP* leads to worse performance than other migration schemes do. This is because when a migration is initiated by the client, the server's send buffer already becomes heavily occupied, making small objects vulnerable to HoL blocking before the buffer drains.

Impact of Object Sizes. The above experiments use 10KB small objects. Figure 8 plots how SMig accelerates small file download with different sizes (wired network, large TCP buffer) when a concurrent large file download (50MB) is present. The Y axis corresponds to the ratio of the download time for *MigSW* to that for *NoMig*. As shown, decreasing the small object size makes SMig more effective *e.g.*, for 1KB small files, SMig reduces their download time by 95%. This is because when the size of small objects decreases, their download time without blocking is reduced while their HoL blocking time largely remains the same. Over cellular network, we observe even more download time reduction – up to 99% brought by SMig (figure not shown).

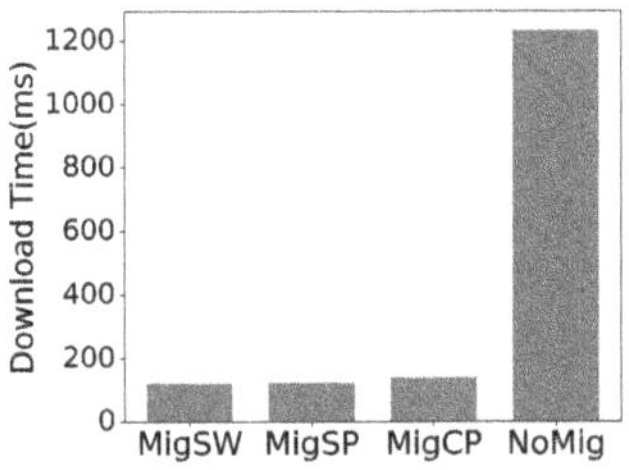

Figure 4: SMig's impact on small file download (default TCP buffer, wired)

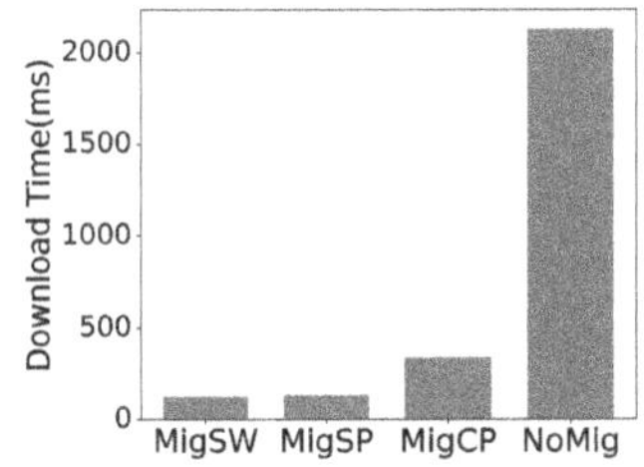

Figure 5: SMig's impact on small file download (large TCP buffer, wired)

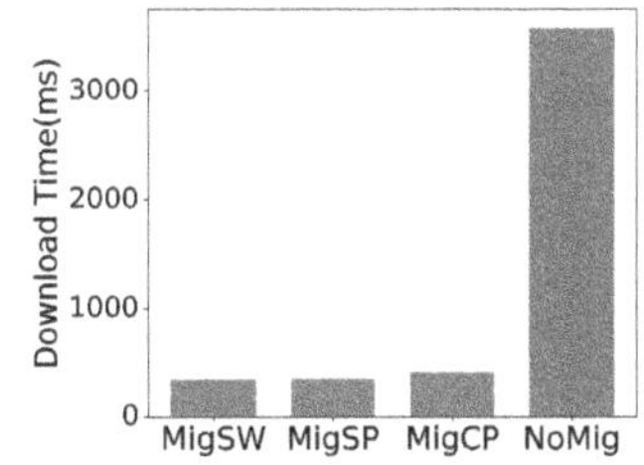

Figure 6: SMig's impact on small file download (default TCP buffer, cellular)

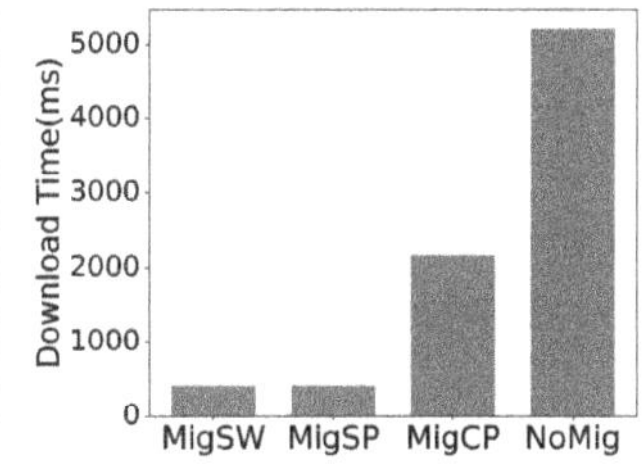

Figure 7: SMig's impact on small file download (large TCP buffer, cellular)

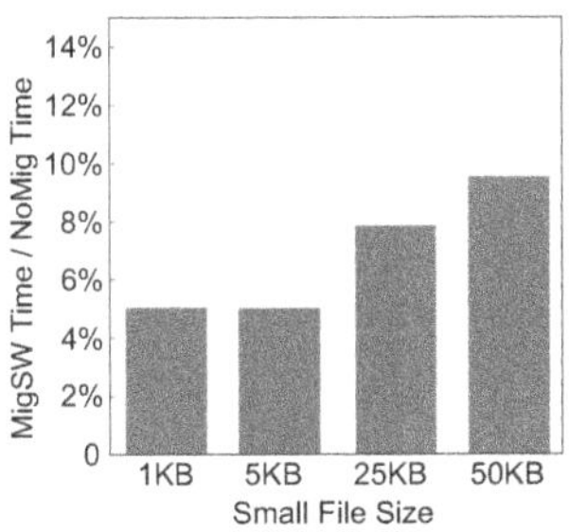

Figure 8: SMig's impact on small file download. Changing small file sizes (large TCP buffer, wired)

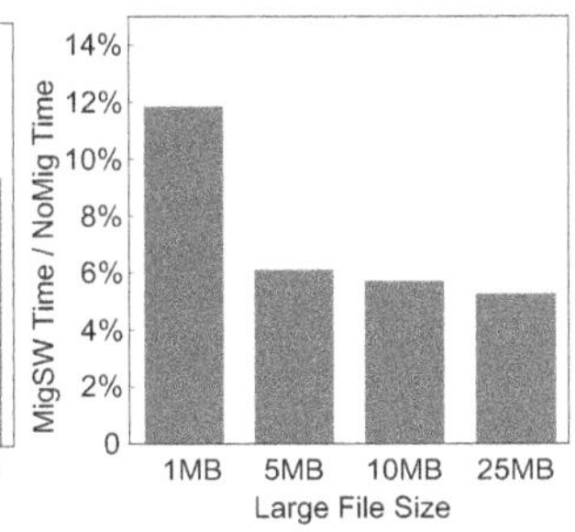

Figure 9: SMig's impact on small file download. Changing large file sizes (large TCP buffer, wired)

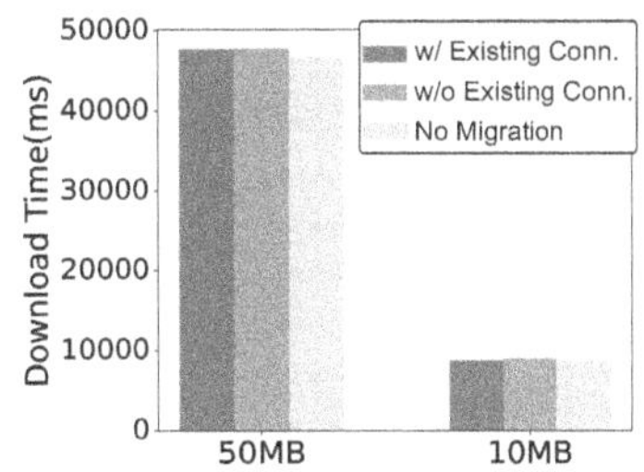

Figure 10: SMig's impact on migrated large file download time (default TCP buffer, wired network)

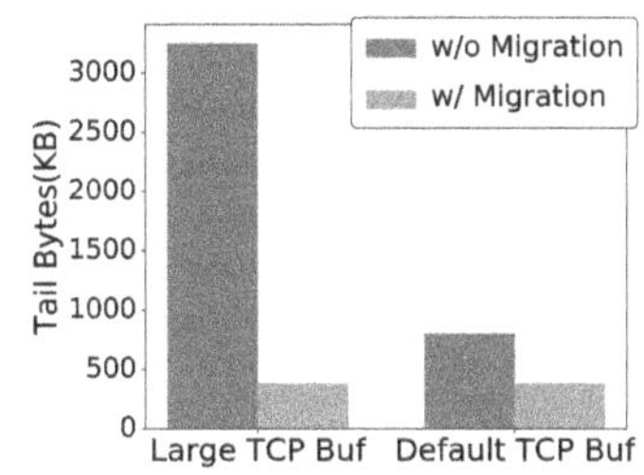

Figure 11: Impact of SMig on incurred tail bytes (cellular network, default/large TCP buffer)

On the other hand, when the large file's size changes, the HoL blocking duration changes accordingly. Figure 9 plots the impact of SMig on 10KB file download time when downloading different large files over wired networks. As shown, even when simultaneously fetching a mid-sized file of 1MB, SMig can effectively reduce the 10KB file download time by 88%. We observe similar results over LTE networks. For example, on LTE, even downloading a 10MB file over HTTP/2 (*e.g.,* an HD video chunk or a podcast audio) can block small objects for more than 5 seconds. This can be effectively mitigated by SMig.

Impact of Large File Download Time. SMig incurs no impact on objects that are not migrated. For migrated (large) objects, the performance impact of SMig on them is small. Figure 10 plots the large object (50MB and 10MB) download time under three scenarios: (1) no migration, (2) migrating the object to an existing idle connection (Figure 2(a)), and (3) creating a new connection and then performing migration (Figure 2(c)). The download time increase in Scenario (2) and (3) is less than 2.5% compared to Scenario (1). The slight increase is due to two reasons. First, in Figure 2(c), the large file download needs to be paused while the new connection is being established. Second, the new connection needs to experience an additional slow start.

5.2 Reducing Tail Bytes

Recall that in the current HTTP/2 paradigm, an HTTP/2 connection is by default long-lived. As a result, even when a large stream is closed, its data in the TCP buffer cannot be removed, leading to many tail bytes. After migrating a large object to a dedicated connection, canceling its download can be done by directly tearing down its connection, resulting in much fewer tail bytes. Figure 11 measures the tail bytes without and with migration for LTE network. When the TCP buffer is large, migration helps cut the tail bytes by 90%. Under the scenario of default TCP buffer, migration still reduces the tail bytes by 53%. The findings are consistent with the measurement over wired networks (Table 2). Note SMig cannot eliminate all tail bytes because they also include all "in-flight" bytes being transmitted in the network when the TCP connection is closed/reset. We also note that even with migration, cellular incurs more tail bytes than the emulated wired network does. Besides the apparent reason of their different bandwidth-delay products, another reason is that there exist buffers *inside* cellular networks causing the tail bytes to inflate [21]. But as shown, the main contributor of tail bytes is still the on-device TCP send buffer whose impact can be eliminated by SMig.

6. CONCLUDING REMARKS

We have designed and implemented SMig, a novel HTTP/2 extension that substantially improves the HTTP/2 performance in certain common usage scenarios. It also enables several new use cases for HTTP/2. SMig is backward compatible, incrementally deployable, and incurs negligible runtime overhead. We are currently working on adding SMig support to the Chrome browser and Nginx HTTP/2 server.

Acknowledgements

We would like to thank our shepherd, Ramesh Sitaraman, and the anonymous reviewers for their valuable comments and suggestions. This research was supported in part by the National Science Foundation under grant CNS-1566331.

7. REFERENCES

[1] How To: Network / TCP / UDP Tuning. https://wwwx.cs.unc.edu/~sparkst/howto/network_tuning.php.

[2] Linux Tune Network Stack (Buffers Size) To Increase Networking Performance. http://www.cyberciti.biz/faq/linux-tcp-tuning/.

[3] MultiPath TCP - Linux Kernel implementation. http://www.multipath-tcp.org/.

[4] QUIC, a multiplexed stream transport over UDP. https://www.chromium.org/quic.

[5] Samsung Download Booster. http://www.samsung.com/uk/support/skp/faq/1061358.

[6] SPDY Protocol Version 3.1. http://www.chromium.org/spdy/spdy-protocol/spdy-protocol-draft3-1.

[7] TCP Small Queues (TSQ). http://lwn.net/Articles/507065/.

[8] Usage of HTTP/2 for Websites. https://w3techs.com/technologies/details/ce-http2/all/all.

[9] V. Agababov, M. Buettner, V. Chudnovsky, M. Cogan, B. Greenstein, S. McDaniel, M. Piatek, C. Scott, M. Welsh, and B. Yin. Flywheel: Google's Data Compression Proxy for the Mobile Web. In *NSDI*, 2015.

[10] M. Belshe, R. Peon, and M. Thomson. Hypertext Transfer Protocol Version 2 (HTTP/2). RFC 7540, 2015.

[11] S. Bradner. Key words for use in RFCs to Indicate Requirement Levels. RFC 2119, 1997.

[12] M. Butkiewicz, D. Wang, Z. Wu, H. V. Madhyastha, and V. Sekar. Klotski: Reprioritizing Web Content to Improve User Experience on Mobile Devices. In *NSDI*, 2015.

[13] G. Carlucci, L. D. Cicco, and S. Mascolo. HTTP over UDP: an Experimental Investigation of QUIC. In *ACM SAC*, 2015.

[14] W. Cherif, Y. Fablet, E. Nassor, J. Taquet, and Y. Fujimori. DASH fast start using HTTP/2. In *NOSSDAV*, 2015.

[15] J. Erman, V. Gopalakrishnan, R. Jana, and K. Ramakrishnan. Towards a SPDY'ier Mobile Web. In *CoNEXT*, 2013.

[16] R. Fielding, J. Gettys, J. Mogul, H. F. L. Masinter, P. Leach, and T. Berners-Lee. Hypertext Transfer Protocol - HTTP/1.1 . RFC 2616, 1999.

[17] B. Han, S. Hao, and F. Qian. MetaPush: Cellular-Friendly Server Push For HTTP/2. In *All Things Cellular Workshop*, 2015.

[18] B. Han, S. Hao, and F. Qian. MetaPush: Cellular-Friendly Server Push For HTTP/2. In *All Things Cellular*, 2015.

[19] B. Han, F. Qian, S. Hao, and L. Ji. An Anatomy of Mobile Web Performance over Multipath TCP. In *CoNEXT*, 2015.

[20] Q. He, C. Dovrolis, and M. Ammar. On the Predictability of Large Transfer TCP Throughput. In *SIGCOMM*, 2005.

[21] H. Jiang, Y. Wang, K. Lee, , and I. Rhee. Tackling Bufferbloat in 3G/4G Networks. In *IMC*, 2012.

[22] M. F. Nowlan, N. Tiwari, J. Iyengar, S. O. Amin, and B. Ford. Fitting Square Pegs Through Round Pipes: Unordered Delivery Wire-Compatible with TCP and TLS. In *NSDI*, 2012.

[23] R. Peon and H. Ruellan. HPACK: Header Compression for HTTP/2. RFC 7541, 2015.

[24] F. Qian, V. Gopalakrishnan, E. Halepovic, S. Sen, and O. Spatscheck. TM3: Flexible Transport-layer Multi-pipe Multiplexing Middlebox Without Head-of-line Blocking. In *CoNEXT*, 2015.

[25] F. Qian, S. Sen, and O. Spatscheck. Characterizing Resource Usage for Mobile Web Browsing. In *MobiSys*, 2014.

[26] M. Varvello, K. Schomp, D. Naylor, J. Blackburn, A. Finamore, and K. Papagiannaki. Is The Web HTTP/2 Yet? In *PAM*, 2016.

[27] X. S. Wang, A. Balasubramanian, A. Krishnamurthy, , and D. Wetherall. How speedy is SPDY? In *NSDI*, 2014.

[28] K. Zarifis, M. Holland, M. Jain, E. Katz-Bassett, and R. Govindan. Modeling HTTP/2 Speed from HTTP/1 Traces. In *PAM*, 2016.

MP-DASH: Adaptive Video Streaming Over Preference-Aware Multipath

Bo Han Feng Qian* Lusheng Ji Vijay Gopalakrishnan

AT&T Labs – Research
Bedminster, NJ
{bohan, lji, gvijay}@research.att.com

*Indiana University
Bloomington, IN
fengqian@indiana.edu

ABSTRACT

Compared with using only a single wireless path such as WiFi, leveraging multipath (*e.g.,* WiFi and cellular) can dramatically improve users' quality of experience (QoE) for mobile video streaming. However, Multipath TCP (MPTCP), the *de-facto* multipath solution, lacks the support to prioritize one path over another. When applied to video streaming, it may cause undesired network usage such as substantial over-utilization of the metered cellular link. In this paper, we propose MP-DASH, a multipath framework for video streaming with the awareness of network interface preferences from users. The basic idea behind MP-DASH is to strategically schedule video chunks' delivery and thus satisfy user preferences. MP-DASH can work with a wide range of off-the-shelf video rate adaptation algorithms with very small changes. Our extensive field studies at 33 locations in three U.S. states suggest that MP-DASH is very effective: it can reduce cellular usage by up to 99% and radio energy consumption by up to 85% with negligible degradation of QoE, compared with off-the-shelf MPTCP.

Keywords

Multipath TCP; DASH; Adaptive Video Streaming; WiFi; Cellular; Preference

1. INTRODUCTION

Video streaming has become one of the most critical applications on mobile devices. A recent study indicates that video accounted for 55% of total mobile traffic in 2015, and this percentage will increase to 75% by 2020 [4]. However, mobile users' quality of experience (QoE) for video streaming is still often far from satisfactory, especially under challenging network conditions such as unstable WiFi connectivity and mobility. Based on our field studies at 33 locations such as restaurants and hotels, we found in about 80% of locations their open WiFi does not provide stable throughput for streaming a 1080p video at its highest quality, while the combined bandwidth of WiFi and cellular almost always does (§2.2). Although LTE may be enough at most locations, users may want to limit their cellular data usage.

The above findings motivate us to consider streaming over *multipath*, a common feature on today's laptops, smartphones, and even wearables. Multipath TCP (MPTCP [15]) is the *de-facto* multipath solution allowing applications to transparently use multiple paths. It can dramatically improve the QoE of video streaming by providing additional network capacity and robust communications (*e.g.,* facilitating smooth handover). However, it is challenging for MPTCP to support the network interface preference required by mobile users (*e.g.,* preferring WiFi over LTE when at home) [20]. As a consequence, when streaming video over MPTCP, it may incur undesired network usage such as substantial over-utilization of the metered cellular link. This will considerably reduce users' incentive of using multipath due to concerns of cellular data limits.

In this paper, we propose MP-DASH, a novel multipath video streaming framework. The overall goal is to *enhance MPTCP to support adaptive video streaming under user-specified interface preferences.* Dynamic Adaptive Streaming over HTTP (DASH) is the state-of-the-art standard of video streaming [35]. Unlike other Internet video protocols such as Adobe HDS [2], Apple HLS [3], and Microsoft Smooth Streaming [6], DASH is agnostic of the video codec and can use any codec including H.264 and H.265. DASH is becoming the dominant video streaming solution, due to the extreme success of HTTP that is easy to deploy, middlebox-friendly, and supported by infrastructures such as CDN [41, 42].

MP-DASH has two major components: the MP-DASH scheduler and the video adapter. The scheduler takes as input the interface preference from users, as well as video chunks' size and delivery deadline from the video player. It then intelligently determines the best fetching strategy of the video chunks over multipath by leveraging their

CoNEXT '16, December 12-15, 2016, Irvine, CA, USA

DOI: http://dx.doi.org/10.1145/2999572.2999606

delay tolerant nature. The key challenge is the scheduling algorithm needs to be online, lightweight, robust, and generalizable to different user preferences.

The MP-DASH video adapter is a lightweight add-on that makes an existing off-the-shelf DASH algorithm multipath-friendly. Lying in the middle between the original DASH algorithm and the MP-DASH scheduler, it handles the interactions between them. This is also challenging because the interactions are not only complex, but also different across different DASH rate adaptation algorithms. These two building blocks (MP-DASH scheduler and video adapter) work in synergy to improve the efficiency of video delivery through preference-aware multipath.

We have instantiated the MP-DASH framework in the context of improving video delivery over WiFi and cellular networks, with the goal of reducing the cellular data usage while maintaining user QoE. Specifically, we made the following contributions in this paper.

- We design the MP-DASH scheduler as an overlay of MPTCP (§4). It serves as a building block for multipath-friendly video streaming. In addition, it can benefit a wide range of other applications with delay-tolerant transfers.
- We investigate how to use the MP-DASH scheduler for improving DASH video delivery. We study two representative categories of DASH rate adaptations (throughput-based and buffer-based) and propose solutions for them to effectively use MP-DASH with only a few lines of code change (§5).
- We implement the MP-DASH scheduler in the Linux kernel and MP-DASH enhanced state-of-the-art DASH algorithms such as FESTIVE [24] and BBA [23] on an open-source video player [5]. We also build a first cross-layer multipath video analysis tool to facilitate our research (§6).
- We conduct extensive in-field experiments to study mobile video performance over multipath in realistic settings, by visiting 33 public places in three states of the U.S. The results show that MP-DASH can reduce cellular usage by up to 99% and radio energy consumption by up to 85% with negligible degradation of QoE (§7).

2. MOTIVATIONS

In this section, we provide the background of MPTCP and motivate MP-DASH through both real-world measurement studies and controlled experiments.

2.1 Multipath TCP (MPTCP)

MPTCP [15] is a standardized multipath solution allowing applications to *transparently* use multiple paths. MPTCP has already been implemented in the Linux kernel [31]. However, it has no ability for users to specify their preference of how to utilize wireless interfaces [20]. Instead, the path utilization is mainly determined by the MPTCP scheduling algorithms. The default scheduler of MPTCP prefers low latency paths: when multiple subflows have spaces in their congestion windows, it selects the subflow with the smallest RTT estimation to transmit the next packet. MPTCP also supports round-robin scheduling.

In this paper, we consider "decoupled" congestion control, *i.e.,* each path runs congestion control independently. This is the typical congestion control configuration for mobile multipath [18]. The reason is that the goal of coupled congestion control [39] is mainly to offer fairness at shared bottlenecks; however, the bottleneck is usually the last mile for wireless networks which is unlikely to be shared by WiFi and cellular networks. We next demonstrate that blindly applying MPTCP scheduling algorithms to DASH video can lead to severe resource inefficiency such as excessive use of cellular data.

2.2 Measurement Study in the Wild

We consider mobile video streaming using WiFi and cellular. To motivate the need for multipath, we first answer the question of whether WiFi alone can provide the best video streaming experience. We measure the throughput and RTT of the WiFi networks at 33 locations in three far-apart U.S. states. The locations cover a wide range of public places including both indoor environments, such as airport, hotel, and restaurant, and outdoor parking lot. They represent three different scenarios: (1) WiFi only is never able to support the highest bitrate of a 1080p video, (2) WiFi can sometimes play the best quality, but not always, and (3) WiFi can almost always stably support the highest bitrate. Among these locations, 64%, 15%, and 21% of them belong to the respective scenarios.

The results imply that in the real world, it is very likely the public WiFi itself cannot provide the best video streaming experience. The poor WiFi performance is usually caused by either bandwidth throttling (*e.g.,* applied by hotels [1]) or limited backhaul connectivity [25]. Thus, upgrading to high throughput WiFi, such as 802.11ac, may not always solve the problem. In contrast, MPTCP can sustain the highest playback bitrate at *all* locations (we consider the HD video case separately in §7.3.5). This indicates that MPTCP is indeed useful for improving the QoE of mobile video streaming in diverse realistic settings.

Although MPTCP is helpful, it causes unnecessary use of cellular data, in particular in scenario (3) where cellular is not needed. For example, the measured WiFi and LTE throughputs at an office building are 12.1 and 14.6 Mbps. If a user plays a 1080p DASH video with the highest bitrate close to 4.0 Mbps, WiFi alone can already sustain the highest rate. However, when streaming the video over MPTCP blindly, more than half of data is still sent over LTE.

2.3 Controlled Experiments

We next employ controlled in-lab experiments to detail the issue of MPTCP overusing cellular data when playing a DASH video. The following observations also exist in real-world experiments (§7) and we use controlled experiments only for easy presentation. Suppose a user wants to play the same video mentioned above with the highest rate which is around 4.0 Mbps. However, the bandwidth of WiFi network is only 3.8 Mbps. To enjoy the best video-watching experience, she can also leverage the LTE dongle on her laptop and play this video over MPTCP. The throughput of LTE network is 3.0 Mbps. Figure 1 plots the throughputs of WiFi and LTE subflows and the entire MPTCP flow in the steady playing state.

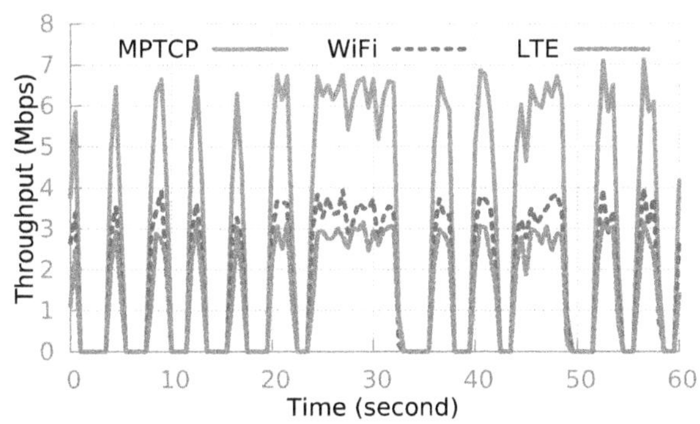

Figure 1: WiFi/LTE throughput when playing a DASH video over MPTCP.

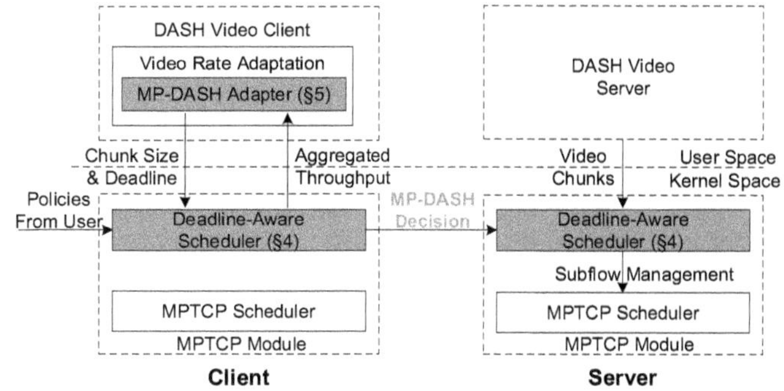

Figure 2: System architecture of MP-DASH.

There are two key observations from Figure 1. First, to download video chunks, the capacity of LTE link is almost fully utilized, as the MPTCP schedulers are not aware of user preferences. Since data limits on LTE networks are common, ideally the user wants to use only 0.2 Mbps of the LTE bandwidth to fill the gap. This is the problem we aim to solve through making the scheduling decision *user-preference-aware*. In §7.3.3, we will also demonstrate through extensive field studies the real-world prevalence of this problem.

We aim to address the above issue by taking advantage of the fact that video chunks are *delay-tolerant*. As shown in Figure 1, when the player's buffer is full, after finishing downloading a chunk, the networks will be idle for a while before fetching the next chunk (*i.e.*, waiting for the player to consume its buffer). Thus, the QoE will not be affected if the chunks arrive a bit late, as long as the playback deadline is met. This offers opportunities of tweaking the MPTCP scheduler to reduce cellular data usage.

3. THE MP-DASH FRAMEWORK

We propose MP-DASH, a network interface preference aware multipath framework for DASH video streaming.

3.1 MP-DASH System Design

There are three major requirements for MP-DASH: First, it should be able to accommodate the interface preferences specified by users and schedule the video delivery based on the preferences. Second, there needs to be a mechanism for video-specific information to be exchanged between a video player and the MP-DASH framework. Third, the overall system needs to be scalable and lightweight.

To satisfy them, our proposed framework consists of two key components: the MP-DASH scheduler and the MP-DASH video adapter, as shown in Figure 2. The scheduler enhances MPTCP in two aspects. First, it is aware of the preference of multiple paths. Second, it is aware of the deadline of each video chunk. By using these pieces of information, the scheduler strategically manages the network paths with the goal of meeting deadlines while satisfying user-specified preference, as to be detailed in §4.

The MP-DASH video adapter is a lightweight add-on that makes existing DASH algorithms multipath-friendly. Lying in the middle between the original DASH algorithm and the MP-DASH scheduler, its main job is to inform the MP-DASH scheduler through a unified interface of each chunk's size and deadline. Also, depending on the specific characteristics of a DASH algorithm category, the MP-DASH adapter may have additional interactions with the DASH algorithm, as to be elaborated in §5.

3.2 Specific Design Decisions

We now detail specific aspects of the MP-DASH framework.

The Interface of the MP-DASH Scheduler. The MP-DASH scheduler exposes a simple and unified interface to video applications, similar to existing approaches [20, 34]. As shown in Figure 2, the interface consists of two parts. First, the scheduler offers a socket option, **MP_DASH_ENABLE**, to convey the data size S and the deadline D from the user space to the kernel. Upon the reception of this information, MP-DASH is activated for the next S bytes of data. MP-DASH is deactivated when any of the following happens: (1) S bytes have been successfully transferred, (2) the deadline has passed, or (3) the application explicitly deactivates MP-DASH using **MP_DASH_DISABLE**, another socket option. The second part of the interface enables a DASH adapter to obtain necessary information (*e.g.*, the aggregated throughput across all paths as shown in Figure 2) for rate adaptation. This interface is needed because a video player does not have the visibility of the network conditions of all paths since MPTCP is oblivious to the player. We demonstrate its usage in §5.

Function Split between Client and Server. The MP-DASH scheduler should ideally run at the video streaming server where it can directly distribute traffic onto different paths. However, a video server does not run the DASH logic and thus the MP-DASH adapter should reside on the client side. We split the scheduler into two parts, the *decision function* on the client and the *enforcement function* on the server. The decision function determines how to manage the paths (*e.g.*, whether the cellular subflow should be enabled) based on the information from the video player, and notifies the enforcement function of the decision using a reserved bit in the MPTCP option. This design makes MP-DASH scalable as the server side becomes stateless.

Interface for the User. As a self-contained framework, MP-DASH allows users to specify the multipath policies such as interface preferences. Our current prototype supports two policies in the context of optimizing video delivery over wireless networks: preferring WiFi over cellular, and preferring cellular over WiFi. Despite the former being the common case, there are situations where a user prefers the latter (*e.g.,* when the user is moving). Given the two policies are symmetric, in the rest of the paper we focus on the first one. We enforce the policy by setting the preferred interface as the primary interface of MPTCP. More sophisticated policies can be plugged in by only changing the scheduler without affecting the DASH adapter (§4).

4. DEADLINE-AWARE MP-DASH SCHEDULER

We design a deadline-aware MP-DASH scheduler that takes both the interface preference and the delay-tolerant nature of video traffic into consideration. The preference can be quantified by cost associated with each path. The cost could be data usage, energy consumption, or a combination of both, configured either statically or dynamically. The goal of the MP-DASH scheduler is to meet the playback deadline of a chunk while minimizing the overall cost. Deadline-awareness has been investigated in various scenarios such as base station scheduling for multimedia traffic [14] and data center TCP [38]. Different from existing works, MP-DASH targets at DASH video delivery over multipath.

General Formulation. We first provide a general formulation of MP-DASH's scheduling algorithm. Let $N \geq 1$ be the number of network paths. Let S be the chunk size and D (in discretized time slots) be its download deadline. The duration of each time slot is d. Let $b(i,j)$ be the available bandwidth of interface i at time slot j ($1 \leq i \leq N$, $0 \leq j < D$), and $c(i,j)$ be the unit-data cost of using interface i at time j. $x(i,j)$ is a binary decision variable where $x(i,j)$=1 iff interface i is used at time j, otherwise $x(i,j)$=0. The goal is to minimize the overall cost

$$C = \sum_{1 \leq i \leq N, 0 \leq j < D} c(i,j) b(i,j) x(i,j) d$$

under the constraint that the deadline is met:

$$\sum_{1 \leq i \leq N, 0 \leq j < D} b(i,j) x(i,j) d \geq S$$

This is a 0-1 min knapsack problem [16]: we have $D * N$ items whose weights and values are $b(i,j)d$ and $c(i,j)b(i,j)d$, respectively. We want to choose items such that the total weight is at least S and the total value is minimized. According to the duality for the Integer Linear Programming, this is equivalent to the traditional 0/1-knapsack problem (proof omitted). We can solve it optimally using dynamic programming with the complexity of $O(N * D * S)$, or approximately by heuristic algorithms.

Practical Online Algorithm. In practice, MP-DASH needs to run in an online fashion where the throughput estimation is continuously updated. Meanwhile, when applied on today's mobile devices, the formulation can be simplified by assuming N=2 (only WiFi and cellular interfaces). In the following we assume WiFi is always preferred over cellular. Thus, we can set $c(\text{WiFi}, j) < c(\text{cell}, j)$ for $\forall j$. A similar greedy algorithm can be devised to handle general numerical costs of multiple paths, as to be described later.

Algorithm 1 Deadline-Aware Scheduling Algorithm

1: Input: S – video chunk size and D – deadline window;
2: $sentBytes = 0$;
3: $cellularEnabled = FALSE$;
4: $timeStart = gettimeofday()$;
5: **while** ($sentBytes < S$) **do**
6:   **if** $S - sentBytes > packetSize$ **then**
7:     $n = packetSize$;
8:   **else**
9:     $n = S - sentBytes$;
10:   **end if**
11:   Get n bytes from the chunk and send them using MPTCP;
12:   $sentBytes += n$;
13:   $timeNow = gettimeofday()$;
14:   $timeSpent = timeNow - timeStart$;
15:   Get the estimated WiFi throughput R_{WiFi};
16:   **if** $(\alpha \times D - timeSpent) \times R_{WiFi} > (S - sentBytes)$ && $cellularEnabled == TRUE$ **then**
17:     Disable the cellular path;
18:   **end if**
19:   **if** $(\alpha \times D - timeSpent) \times R_{WiFi} < (S - sentBytes)$ && $cellularEnabled == FALSE$ **then**
20:     Enable the cellular path;
21:   **end if**
22: **end while**

MP-DASH *leverages the existing MPTCP schedulers to distribute packets over multiple paths and adds the intelligence of how to control the cellular subflow.* Essentially, MP-DASH introduces both deadline-awareness and priority into these schedulers. The online version of MP-DASH is depicted in Algorithm 1. It has two input parameters, the video chunk size S and the length of download time window D (from when a download starts till the deadline). MP-DASH drives the WiFi subflow to its full capacity and turns off the cellular subflow at the beginning. It then monitors the progress of data transfer and turns the cellular subflow on if necessary, *i.e.,* when the WiFi path underperforms and the deadline would be missed if we continue using WiFi alone. The *while* loop is responsible for sending the chunk's data using MPTCP (line 11). R_{WiFi} in line 15 is the current estimation of WiFi throughput. After sending out each packet, MP-DASH checks if WiFi alone is sufficient to transmit the remaining data and disables the cellular subflow when possible (lines 16–18). Since the WiFi throughput may change over time, it also needs to check if the cellular subflow should be enabled again, in case using WiFi alone cannot fully deliver the remaining data before the deadline (lines 19–21). To be conservative, our target finish time could be ahead of the real deadline by setting α in lines

16 and 19 to be less than 1, to compensate for estimation inaccuracy of WiFi throughput. The smaller the value of α is, the less likely we will miss the actual deadline. However, a smaller α also leads to more data over cellular links.

A key design decision we make is, if MP-DASH decides to use cellular, it should utilize the maximum bandwidth by transmitting as quickly as possible. Another naive solution is to throttle the cellular bandwidth just to be what is needed. We will demonstrate its drawbacks in §7.3.1.

Optimality. As a special case (N=2), Algorithm 1 yields the optimal solution (in terms of cellular usage) if we can always accurately estimate the bandwidth till the deadline (proof omitted). Intuitively, assume a solution that uses even fewer cellular bytes exists. This means we either disable cellular too late or enable cellular too early. However, neither can happen if we have the perfect knowledge of the bandwidth in lines 16 and 19.

The online MP-DASH scheduling algorithm can be generalized to multiple interfaces with varying costs. For example, we can first sort the interfaces based on their costs, and then feed data from low-cost to high-cost interfaces, by turning on/off the paths accordingly. This cost-varying version is an approximation algorithm and may not be optimal. Meanwhile, the interface to applications remains the same, which allows the same MP-DASH enhanced DASH algorithm in our framework to work under diverse multipath contexts with different numbers of paths or different cost/preference profiles.

5. MP-DASH VIDEO ADAPTER

We leverage the MP-DASH scheduler as a building block to improve the cellular usage and energy efficiency for DASH video over multipath. It is challenging due to the following two reasons.

- The interaction between the DASH rate adaptation algorithms and the MP-DASH scheduler is complex. In particular, there exists a control loop: MP-DASH's scheduling decision will affect DASH's rate selection, which in turn impacts MP-DASH's scheduling through settings of chunk size and deadline. This is quite different from using the MP-DASH scheduler to download a single file where the application and the scheduler are very loosely coupled.
- There are many DASH rate control algorithms. Ideally, we want to plug the MP-DASH scheduler into them in the same (and simple) manner. However, we found due to their different rate adaptation logics (*e.g.,* throughput vs. buffer-based), DASH algorithms incur different cross-layer interactions with the scheduler. This inevitably requires modifications to DASH algorithms on a category-by-category basis, although we try to minimize the changes.

5.1 The Basic Approach

We first provide the background of rate adaptation algorithms for DASH. In a DASH system, a video is split into multiple chunks of the same play time (usually 1 to 15 seconds) and each video chunk is encoded with multiple discrete bitrate levels. A video player can switch between different bitrate streams at a chunk boundary, as the chunks are time-wise aligned. Thus, it requires an algorithm to select the chunks' bitrates for achieving an optimal QoE. There are largely two categories of DASH rate adaptation algorithms, *throughput-based* and *buffer-based*. The throughput-based adaptation adjusts the encoding rate of chunks based on the estimated throughput, which indicates the future network capacity. For instance, FESTIVE [24] uses the harmonic mean of previous chunks' throughputs to estimate the future throughput, which dictates the rate selection. On the other hand, Buffer Based Adaptation (BBA) [23] chooses the bitrate based on a video player's buffer occupancy level, which implicitly encodes information of the network capacity when the video playing is at the steady state.

We now describe the basic approach of integrating the MP-DASH scheduler with DASH video. Recall in §4 that MP-DASH's scheduling algorithm is invoked at the chunk level, and the video player needs to provide the chunk size and deadline to MP-DASH. Currently the chunk size is not a mandatory field in the DASH manifest file. Despite this, in practice, we can almost always find the chunk size in the "Content-Length" header field of HTTP responses. This issue has also been raised by a recent work [42], which advocates that chunk size is a key requirement for DASH control algorithms and thus should be a mandatory part of the DASH manifest.

We then consider how to set the deadline D. Intuitively, it should be configured in such a way that if we do not receive the chunk at time $t_0 + D$, the playback will stall (t_0 is the current time). It is, however, too risky in that missing the deadline due to inaccurate throughput estimation or temporary wireless blackout will cause significant QoE degradation. In fact, preventing this is exactly the purpose of having playback buffers that act as a cushion for unpredicted network quality changes.

We instead set the deadline by *keeping the buffer occupancy not decrease*. Specifically, we propose two approaches: duration-based and rate-based. For the *duration-based* setting, D is a video chunk's playout duration. For example, the deadline of a 4-second video chunk is simply 4 seconds. For the *rate-based* scheme, D is the chunk size divided by the nominal (*i.e.,* average) video encoding bitrate. For example, for a 1 MB chunk in a quality level of 4.0 Mbps average bitrate, D is set to 1*8/4=2 seconds. The difference between them is, the duration-based scheme aims to maintain the buffer level in the short term: a player consumes D-second buffer to download a D-second chunk which is then supplied to its buffer, thus leading to a stable buffer level. In contrast, the rate-based setting attempts to maintain the buffer level in the long run, since it leverages the *average* bitrate of the entire video.

We further design a mechanism called *deadline extension* that makes MP-DASH even more efficient. The intuition is, it is unlikely for a stall to happen when the buffer occupancy is close to becoming full. In this "safe region", we can relax (*i.e.,* extend) the deadline to give more opportunities for MP-DASH to reduce the cellular usage. Assuming the buffer level threshold for enabling deadline extension is Φ

and the current buffer level is $b > \Phi$, we then extend the deadline by $b - \Phi$ (both b and Φ have the unit of seconds). The threshold Φ incurs a tradeoff between the cellular usage and playback robustness. We discuss its setting for different DASH algorithms in §5.2.1 and §5.2.2.

We extend the deadline when the buffer level is high. Then how to deal with the situation of low buffer level? This happens, for example, during the initial buffering phase or a path temporarily blacks out. Thus, we disable the MP-DASH scheduler for MPTCP when the buffer level is lower than a threshold Ω. The setting of Ω also depends on the DASH algorithms, which we discuss next.

5.2 Handling Different Categories of DASH Rate Adaptation Algorithms

Following the unified high-level framework described in §5.1, we now detail how to seamlessly integrate the MP-DASH scheduler with different categories of DASH rate adaptation algorithms.

5.2.1 *Throughput-based DASH Rate Adaptation*

A throughput-based rate adaptation algorithm uses previous chunks' throughputs to estimate the future throughput, which is then mapped to the quality level of the next chunk using algorithm-specific logics. The throughput-quality mapping logic is transparent to MP-DASH. However, the player is not aware of multipath and may under-estimate the actual MPTCP throughput when the MP-DASH scheduler disables the cellular path. To address this issue, we expose to applications the MPTCP throughput estimation via the interface described in §3, which *overrides* the player's own estimation. In this way, the player has a consistent view of the overall available network resources based on which it makes the rate-selection decision.

For the deadline extension, we empirically set Φ to be 80% of the overall buffer capacity. We set Ω, the low-buffer threshold for disabling the MP-DASH scheduler, as follows. Consider a time window of the next T seconds. Assuming we stay at the lowest bitrate, we estimate the length (in time) of chunks that can be downloaded during this window to be T'. Then the threshold of disabling the MP-DASH scheduler is $\Omega = T - T'$ where T and T' are the buffering time to be consumed and supplied, respectively. A negative Ω is treated as 0. We set T to be twice of the duration of the entire buffer. Changing T to 1x or 3x of the buffer duration does not qualitatively change the results. To be conservative, we set the minimum value of Ω to be 40% of the buffer capacity.

5.2.2 *Buffer-Based DASH Rate Adaptation*

We then shift to the buffer-based rate adaptation, which maps the buffer occupancy to video qualities. The intuition is that the buffer occupancy implicitly encodes the relation between the network capacity and the selected video bitrate.

Based on our experiments in §7, we found the original buffer-based rate adaptation algorithm is very aggressive in utilizing the bandwidth. Assume the MPTCP throughput is stable at around R=3.4 Mbps, whose nearest video encoding bitrates are r_1=2.4 Mbps and r_2=3.9 Mbps. A throughput-based scheme (*e.g.*, FESTIVE) will only fetch chunks of r_1,

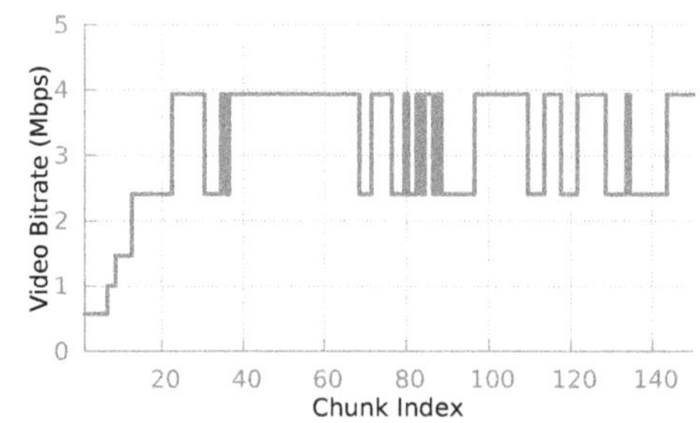

Figure 3: Bitrate oscillation of the original BBA algorithm.

which is the highest bitrate that the network can sustain. On the other hand, a buffer-based scheme starts with rate r_1. Since $r_1 < R$, the buffer occupancy grows, which switches the encoding bitrate to $r_2 > R$. Then the buffer level decreases, eventually switching the encoding bitrate back to r_1. As a result, the selected bitrate keeps oscillating between r_1 and r_2, as shown in Figure 3. This behavior of BBA not only degrades the QoE [37, 42] but also limits the resource-saving capability of MP-DASH. To address this problem, we modified the original buffer-based adaptation algorithm (BBA) by forcing the selected bitrate to be *no higher* than the actual MPTCP throughput. We call the modified scheme BBA-C (Cellular-friendly version of BBA). We evaluate both BBA and BBA-C in §7.

We discuss how to configure Φ and Ω. To keep the buffer not full, we conservatively set Φ (the high-buffer threshold for deadline extension) to be the overall buffer capacity minus one chunk's duration. For Ω (the low-buffer threshold), we cannot use a single buffer occupancy threshold as used in the throughput-based scheme, because in a buffer-based scheme, each encoding bitrate has its own buffer occupancy range. We enable the MP-DASH scheduler only when the player reaches the highest bitrate that the network can sustain. At this point, we need to keep the buffer occupancy higher than the lowest level of the current encoding bitrate, otherwise the bitrate will drop to the next lower level. Therefore, we disable the MP-DASH scheduler whenever the buffer occupancy is getting close to the lowest level of the current encoding bitrate, e_l. We empirically set Ω to be e_l plus one chunk's duration. For example, assume the current video quality maps to a buffer level range from e_l=20 to e_h=40 seconds, and a chunk's duration is 4 seconds. Then we enable the MP-DASH scheduler only when the buffer contains at least 24 seconds' content.

The high-level principle of choosing the proper values of Φ and Ω for both the throughput-based and buffer-based rate adaptations is to be conservative with the purpose of preventing stalls. However, we empirically found the current settings of Φ and Ω yield good resource savings while incurs negligible playback rate degradation in realistic settings (§7). We plan to evaluate how different values of these parameters impact other QoE metrics, such as stalls and video bitrate switches, in our future work.

5.2.3 *Hybrid DASH Rate Adaptation*

We can leverage the MP-DASH scheduler for a wide range of DASH algorithms. We consider one example of

MPC [42], a recent model predictive control algorithm that leverages both throughput estimation and buffer occupancy. At a high level, MPC works as follows. Instead of solving an optimization problem for each chunk, its online version looks up a *pre-generated* table to select the optimal bitrate based on the buffer level, previous bitrate, and throughput estimation. To support MP-DASH, MPC can set a chunk's deadline as the chunk size divided by the minimum throughput required by the optimal bitrate known from the table. Meanwhile, since MPC is a hybrid approach of using both throughput and buffer occupancy for rate adaptation, we can reuse several solutions described in §5.2.1 and §5.2.2. We leave the detailed design and implementation as future work.

6. IMPLEMENTATION

We have implemented the MP-DASH **Scheduler** on Linux platform in the kernel instead of the user space, which is more suitable for complex application-specific schedulers [20]. Given the simplicity of MP-DASH scheduler and since it tightly couples with MPTCP, realizing it in the kernel significantly reduces its communication overhead with the basic functions of MPTCP. Based on the online algorithm, a client uses a reserved bit in the MPTCP DSS (Data Sequence Signal) option [15] to notify a server of its decision about whether the cellular subflow should be enabled. The user-specified interface preference is realized by setting the primary MPTCP interface accordingly. Implementing a general policy framework is still an open problem and we leave it as our future work. To estimate the throughput of a subflow, we employ the non-seasonal Holt-Winters (HW) predictor [19], which is known to be more robust than other approaches such as exponentially weighted moving average (EWMA) for non-stationary processes. The HW predictor is essentially a double exponential smoothing method that takes into account the possible trend in the measurement data. We implement it in MP-DASH using the parameters suggested by He *et al.* [19]. Overall, we add about 300 lines of Linux kernel code as a portable patch of MPTCP. We have also applied this patch to the Linux kernel of Google Nexus 5 with Android 4.4.2.

A key challenge of implementing the MP-DASH scheduler is that we need to manage the secondary subflow (*i.e.*, cellular subflow in our case) in an energy efficient manner. Instead of actually switching on/off the cellular radio, or adding/removing the cellular subflow (which is supported by a recent work [20] at the cost of increased TCP handshake delay), we leverage the existing MPTCP schedulers that select the available subflow for each packet. When we "disable" the cellular subflow, we simply *skip* it in the scheduling function, thus incurring no overhead of handshake message exchange. This design works as a simple overlay with both the default and the round-robin MPTCP schedulers (and presumably others). As a result, MP-DASH can handle diverse network conditions (*e.g.*, the paths have drastically different delay or bandwidth) as the off-the-shelf MPTCP schedulers do. Note that keeping the LTE radio interface always on incurs very small additional energy overhead (only periodical Discontinuous Reception (DRX) spikes [21]). We discuss the implication of our design on radio energy consumption in §7.

Our implementation of the MP-DASH **Video Adapter** is based on the open-source GPAC video player (v0.5.2) [5]. It has a simple throughput-based rate adaptation algorithm, referred to as GPAC, which estimates the throughput by measuring the download time of the last chunk, and selects the highest encoding bitrate lower than the estimated throughput. We have further implemented three other DASH algorithms (FESTIVE [24], BBA [23] and BBA-C) in the GPAC player. FESTIVE is a representative throughput-based DASH algorithm providing better robustness, fairness, and stability. BBA is the original buffer-based adaptation algorithm, and we have implemented its full version (BBA-2). BBA-C is our modified version of BBA-2 with less aggressive bandwidth usage as described in §5.2.2. For all four DASH algorithms, we have implemented their MP-DASH adapters with from around 30 to 100 lines of C code. This confirms the easy integration between the MP-DASH framework and existing off-the-shelf DASH algorithms.

We have also built a **Multipath Video Analysis Tool**, consisting of about 3,000 lines of C++ code. Its purpose is to facilitate our evaluation by analyzing key metrics of video streaming over multipath, such as path utilization, rebuffering, video quality switch, and energy consumption. It takes as input a network packet trace containing the video content, as well as a player's event logs. It then correlates them to perform the analysis. A key strength of this tool is it understands multiple protocol layers including MPTCP, TLS (if encryption is used), HTTP, and DASH. It also visualizes the analysis as illustrated in Figure 8.

7. EVALUATION

We evaluate the MP-DASH scheduler and conduct extensive evaluations of MP-DASH enhanced video streaming through both controlled experiments and real field studies.

7.1 Methodology

We set up an MPTCP testbed using a client laptop and a server machine, both with Linux kernel 3.18.20. They all run the stable version of MPTCP v0.90.0 [31] enhanced with MP-DASH. The client is equipped with an external LTE dongle and a built-in WiFi interface. We use a dedicated 802.11n WiFi access point running on the 5 GHz frequency band, providing $<$1 ms RTT and $>$50 Mbps bandwidth between client and server. We use Dummynet [8] to configure the WiFi latency to be 50 ms, resembling the RTT experienced by typical metropolitan WiFi users [36]. Although Dummynet creates additional buffers, as we use it to control latency explicitly, it will not create severe bufferbloat problems on our testbed. The cellular path is provided by a major U.S. carrier's commercial LTE network with around 50-60 ms RTT. We set up an Apache2-based DASH server for the experiments in §7.3.

Our current MP-DASH scheduler aims at reducing cellular data usage. This also leads to reduced energy

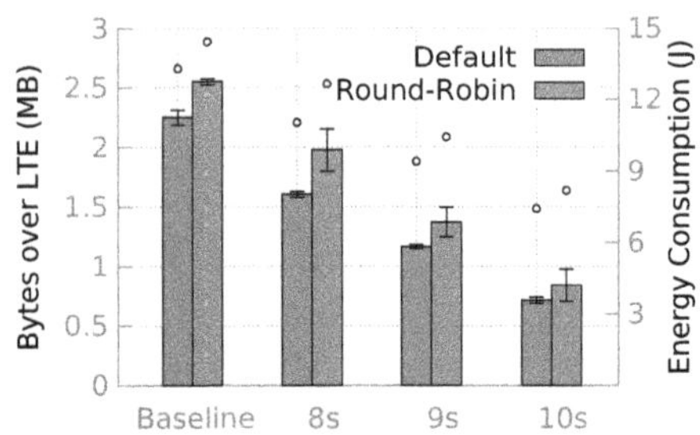

Figure 4: Comparing baseline MPTCP and MP-DASH with different deadlines using the default and round-robin schedulers.

consumption. Despite conducting the experiments on a laptop, we also want to understand the radio energy consumption, which accounts for at least half of the overall device energy consumption for a typical mobile device [30], if MP-DASH is deployed on a smartphone or tablet. The energy impact of MP-DASH on other components such as display is negligible, as it has almost no impact on the video quality. We use a simulation-based approach by feeding the collected network traces to a custom simulator with a recently proposed model [30]. This is the most comprehensive and up-to-date multipath radio energy model that considers both DRX and energy tails [21]. We compute the radio energy using two devices' parameters: Samsung Galaxy Note and Samsung Galaxy S III, both yielding similar results. We therefore report the first one. Note the above energy analysis is feasible because given the same network condition, MP-DASH incurs deterministic traffic pattern, which allows us to "replay" the trace under different power models for different types of devices. In our future work, we plan to directly measure the energy consumption of MP-DASH on smartphones.

7.2 Performance of MP-DASH Scheduler

We begin with evaluating the MP-DASH scheduler individually, using single file download as the workload. This evaluation (in particular, the trace-driven simulation) allows us to compare our online scheduling results with the optimal offline scheduling results.

7.2.1 Experiments over Real WiFi and LTE

We consider again the motivating example in §2.3. The client downloads from server 5MB data. We use Dummynet [8] to throttle the bandwidth of WiFi and cellular links to be 3.8 and 3.0 Mbps, respectively. Under this setup, it takes ~10.5 seconds to download the 5MB data using WiFi alone and ~6 seconds when using MPTCP. As a result, we experiment with three deadlines of 8, 9 and 10 seconds.

We evaluate the impact of the MP-DASH scheduler on both the default and round-robin MPTCP schedulers. We examine three metrics: download time, cellular bytes, and radio energy consumption. We plot the number of bytes over LTE using bars and mark the radio energy consumption as round dots in Figure 4 (averaged over 10 runs). MP-DASH significantly reduces the cellular data and radio energy usage, compared to unmodified MPTCP. The longer the deadline is, the more the saving is. When the deadline is 10 seconds, the saving is 68% for cellular data and 44% for radio energy.

All data transfers finish before the deadline and the average finish time is close to the deadline. However, under the scenarios with high bandwidth prediction errors, the deadline might be missed (after that both interfaces will always be used) and we show in §7.2.2 this is unlikely in practice. Missing a deadline can further be prevented by tuning the α parameter in Algorithm 1. In the above experiments, we set α to be 1. We also experiment with different α values when the deadline is 10 seconds. Even when α is 0.8, the MP-DASH scheduler achieves savings for cellular data and radio energy of 28% and 15%, respectively.

Trace Name	File Size	Avg WiFi Bandwidth	Avg Cell Bandwidth
Synthetic (σ=10%)	5 MB	3.8 Mbps	3.0 Mbps
Synthetic (σ=30%)	5 MB	3.8 Mbps	3.0 Mbps
Fast Food B	20 MB	5.2 Mbps	8.1 Mbps
Coffeehouse D	5 MB	1.4 Mbps	7.6 Mbps
Office	50 MB	28.4 Mbps	19.1 Mbps

Table 1: WiFi/cellular bandwidth and file sizes for simulation.

Trace Name	D/L sec.	Cell % Optimal	Cell % Online	Diff.	Miss?
SYNTH σ=10%	8	24.77%	27.13%	2.36%	No
	9	15.29%	19.17%	3.88%	No
	10	6.16%	11.74%	5.58%	No
SYNTH σ=30%	8	26.32%	30.79%	4.47%	No
	9	16.88%	24.32%	7.44%	No
	10	8.48%	16.66%	8.18%	No
FastFood	15	60.49%	61.82%	1.33%	No
	20	48.52%	52.79%	4.27%	No
	25	38.09%	42.99%	4.90%	No
	30	26.91%	33.13%	6.22%	No
Coffee	5	83.26%	81.22%	-2.04%	10ms
	10	65.03%	67.18%	2.15%	No
	15	47.86%	55.48%	7.62%	No
	20	30.48%	35.52%	5.04%	No
Office	9	27.21%	27.48%	0.57%	No
	12	12.98%	15.46%	2.48%	No
	15	0.00%	3.82%	3.82%	No
	18	0.00%	0.00%	0.00%	No

Table 2: Comparing MP-DASH's online algorithm with the optimal using trace-driven simulation. "SYNTH" stands for Synthetic and "D/L" stands for Deadline.

7.2.2 Trace-Driven Simulation

We also conduct a trace-driven simulation of the MP-DASH scheduler to understand its performance under realistic network conditions with throughput prediction errors, compared with the optimal case where the throughput is perfectly known.

The simulation methodology is as follows. First, we create different bandwidth profiles listed in Table 1. We

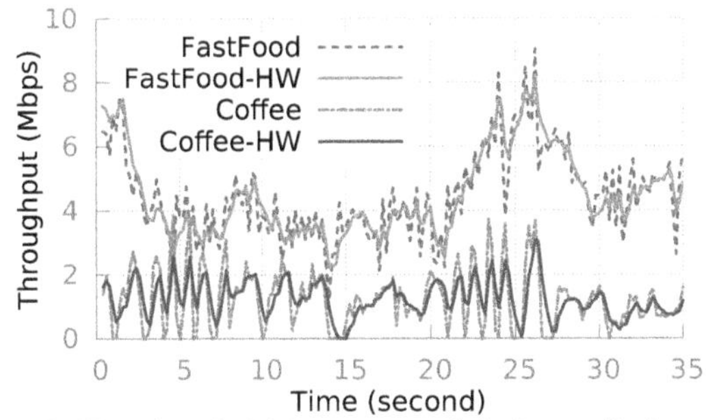

Figure 5: Two bandwidth traces and their prediction results.

Video quality level	1	2	3	4	5
Big Buck Bunny	0.58	1.01	1.47	2.41	3.94
Red Bull Playstreets	0.50	0.89	1.50	2.47	3.99
Tears of Steel	0.50	0.81	1.51	2.42	4.01
Tears of Steel HD	1.51	2.42	4.01	6.03	10.0

Table 3: Average encoding bitrates (in Mbps) for four DASH videos.

generate two synthetic profiles with the average WiFi and cellular bandwidth of 3.8 Mbps and 3.0 Mbps, and the standard deviation of instantaneous throughput being σ=10% and 30% of the average. We also collect real traces from three public locations. Next, we build a simulator that performs discrete-time simulation of Algorithm 1 (with α set to 1) and the Holt-Winter algorithm with the length of each time slot being the round-trip time (we use 50 ms for the synthetic traces). We then run the simulator on all bandwidth profiles with different combinations of deadline and file size, and summarize the results in Table 2. The file size is determined by the average aggregated bandwidth and download deadline. The key metrics are whether the deadline is missed, and the fraction of cellular bytes. The "Cell % (Optimal)", "Cell % (Online)", and "Diff." columns correspond to the solution with the perfect knowledge of bandwidth, our online algorithm, and their difference, respectively. The optimal solution always incurs the minimum cellular usage without missing the deadline.

We discuss our findings. First, the online MP-DASH scheduler tends to be conservative even with α set to 1. For the vast majority of cases, the inaccuracy in bandwidth estimation results in using more cellular data instead of missing the deadline. This is likely attributed to the nature of the bandwidth patterns. Deadlines are missed only when the WiFi throughput drops steeply and continuously; while in reality, WiFi bandwidth tends to be fluctuating, as exemplified in Figure 5. The second observation is the good performance of the online algorithm, whose additional cellular usage is consistently small (less than 10% of the total transfer size, as shown in the "Diff." column).

7.3 Evaluation of the MP-DASH Framework

We now evaluate the overall MP-DASH framework using four videos from a public dataset [26] listed in Table 3. In the rest of this section, unless otherwise mentioned, we show the results of only *Big Buck Bunny* due to space limit (the other two non-HD videos yield qualitatively similar results). We study the HD version of *Tears of Steel* in §7.3.5.

All presented results use chunk duration of 4 seconds. We also experiment with 6 and 10-second video chunks, and obtain similar results. The length of each video is 10 minutes. Thus, for 4-second chunk duration, a full playback consists of 150 chunks each being selected from 5 quality levels. In all experiments, we report various statistics for the last 80% chunks, when the player is in its steady state. The statistics for all chunks show very similar results. We consider four evaluation metrics: number of stalls, playback bitrate, cellular data usage, and radio energy consumption (computed using the way described in §7.2). In our evaluations, no stall occurs. Therefore we focus on the last three metrics. We set α in Algorithm 1 to be 1. As we have shown in §7.2, using a smaller value of α will lead to less savings of cellular data and radio energy.

	Default	700 K	1000 K	MP-DASH
Cell Bytes	96.16	33.41	45.74	18.51
% of Cell Data	43.62	15.94	20.70	8.373
Radio Energy	641.6	855.0	834.6	281.9

Table 4: Cellular throughput-throttling vs MP-DASH. Cellular Bytes are in MB and Radio Energy is in Joule.

7.3.1 Inefficiency of Throughput Throttling

We first examine the alternative solution mentioned in §4: simply throttling the cellular path. We quantitatively compare three approaches using the default GPAC rate adaptation algorithm: the unmodified MPTCP, MPTCP with cellular being throttled, and MPTCP with MP-DASH (rate-based deadline setting). We use the same network setting as that in §7.2 where the WiFi and cellular throughputs are 3.8 and 3.0 Mbps, respectively. We throttle the cellular throughput at 200, 700 and 1000 Kbps. For the first two settings, as the actual MPTCP throughput is usually smaller than the available bandwidth due to, for example, TCP congestion control, a large number of the downloaded chunks (> 22%) are not encoded at the highest bitrate level. In the real-world settings, the throttling approach is further complicated by the fluctuating WiFi throughput, making it difficult to adjust the cellular throttling cap accordingly in real time.

Table 4 summarizes the bytes and percentage of cellular data, as well as the radio energy consumption under four configurations: the default MPTCP, MPTCP with 700 Kbps cellular throttling, 1000 Kbps throttling, and MPTCP with MP-DASH. Although throttling the cellular path reduces the cellular traffic, it pays a significant penalty for high radio energy consumption. In contrast, MP-DASH achieves both the lowest cellular usage and radio energy. Figure 6 visualizes the traffic patterns of three configurations in Table 4: throttling at 700 Kbps (top), MP-DASH (middle), and the default MPTCP (bottom). In the throttling scheme, LTE is slowly "dribbling" data, leading to considerable radio energy waste [33]. The default MPTCP incurs a traffic

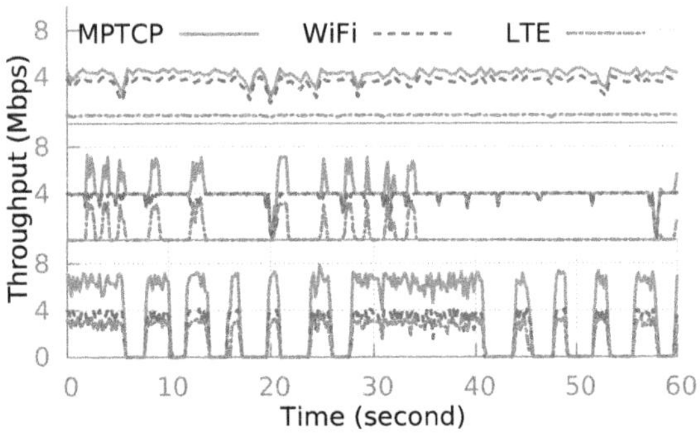

Figure 6: Traffic patterns of MPTCP with 700 Kbps cellular throttling (top), MP-DASH (middle), and default MPTCP (bottom).

pattern similar to that in Figure 1 with heavy cellular usage. For MP-DASH, cellular is not used during most of the time, and is only consumed adaptively when the deadline cannot be met using WiFi alone.

7.3.2 *Controlled Experiments*

We now evaluate MP-DASH enhanced players using controlled experiments under different bandwidth combinations of WiFi and LTE. We consider three network conditions: (1) WiFi 3.8 Mbps, LTE 3.0 Mbps, (2) WiFi 2.8 Mbps, LTE 3.0 Mbps, and (3) WiFi 2.2 Mbps, LTE 1.2 Mbps. For (1) and (2), the MPTCP throughput is higher than the highest video encoding rate (3.94 Mbps); while for (3) the overall network capacity cannot support the highest video quality. Note that using higher LTE throughput will lead to more savings of cellular data brought by MP-DASH.

We investigate four DASH algorithms: FESTIVE, GPAC, BBA, and BBA-C with and without MP-DASH. We observe no stalls in all experiments, and MP-DASH has no impact on the average playback rate. Thus, we focus on the metrics of cellular data usage and radio energy consumption. Next, we describe the results for each DASH algorithm.

FESTIVE AND GPAC. Figure 7a plots the results of FESTIVE. In each group of network conditions, "Baseline", "Duration", and "Rate" correspond to MPTCP without MP-DASH, MP-DASH with duration-based deadline setting, and MP-DASH with rate-based deadline scheme, respectively. The cellular data usage is shown in bars and the energy consumption is marked as round dots. We observe that compared to the default MPTCP, MP-DASH significantly reduces both cellular data and radio energy. When WiFi bandwidth drops from 3.8 to 3.0 Mbps, the savings become less because more cellular data will be required by the player. The savings increase for the worst network condition (W2.2/L1.2) because the chunk quality drops from Level 5 to 4 (Table 3) and the WiFi throughput is close to the average bitrate of Level 4 (2.41 Mbps). For GPAC, which is also a throughput-based DASH algorithm, we observe qualitatively similar results.

Figure 7a shows the rate-based deadline setting outperforms the duration-based one. Recall in §5.1 that in these two settings, the cellular usage is budgeted based on the average video bitrate and a particular chunk's bitrate, respectively. Therefore, for chunks with higher-than-average encoding bitrate, the duration-based setting requires more cellular data than the rate-based one. This is visualized in Figure 8 by our analysis tool (§6). The figure also illustrates that MP-DASH eliminates most of the idle gaps appearing in the default MPTCP case (the top subfigure).

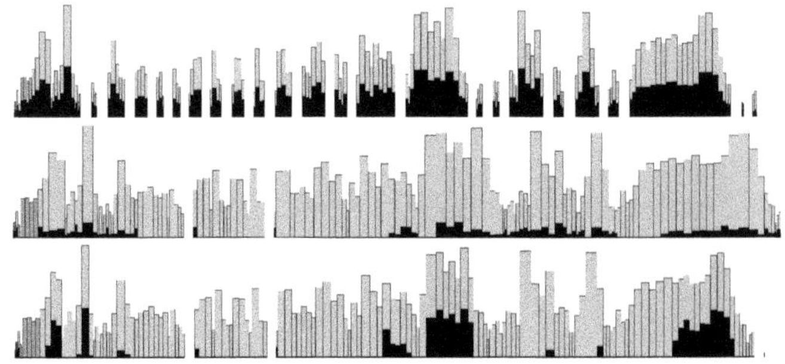

Figure 8: Visualization results produced by our multipath video analysis tool (§6). The X axis is the time. Each bar is a chunk. Its height and width represent its size and download duration, respectively. The color of a chunk is its bitrate level (1 to 5) with light blue being the highest level. The black component of each chunk represents the fraction that is delivered through cellular. The top, middle, and bottom subfigures correspond to the default MPTCP, MP-DASH with rate-based deadline selection, and MP-DASH with duration-based deadline selection, respectively, using FESTIVE.

BBA. Figure 7b shows the results for BBA. For the first two groups of network conditions, MP-DASH brings less savings than it does for FESTIVE, because BBA itself is known to be more aggressive, leaving less saving opportunities for MP-DASH. Note MP-DASH is *adaptive* in that it saves resources on the premise that the application's bandwidth requirement is satisfied. The interesting case is the W2.2/L1.2 scenario, where MP-DASH brings no cellular data saving. The reason, as explained in §5.2.2, is that the original BBA algorithm is even more aggressive when the overall network capacity cannot support the highest encoding bitrate. In this case, the fetched chunk bitrate may oscillate as illustrated in Figure 3, worsening users' watching experience.

BBA-C. We plot the results for BBA-C in Figure 7c. BBA-C is the cellular-friendly version of BBA that forces the selected bitrate to be no higher than the actual network capacity, to prevent the bitrate oscillation. For the first two groups of network conditions, BBA and BBA-C have the same results, because the overall bandwidth is capable of supporting the highest bitrate and thus the bitrate capping feature of BBA-C is not invoked. The difference is the W2.2/L1.2 scenario where BBA-C effectively prevents the bitrate oscillation by locking the highest bitrate to Level 4. This provides room for MP-DASH to save cellular data. By comparing Figure 7b and 7c, we observe that BBA-C with MP-DASH reduces cellular data usage and radio energy consumption by 69% and 50%, respectively, at the cost of reducing the playback bitrate from oscillating between

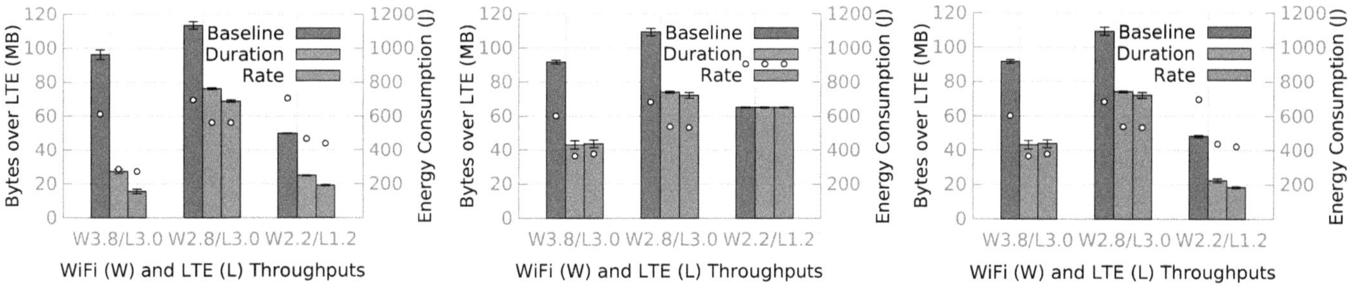

(a) FESTIVE (b) BBA (c) BBA-C

Figure 7: Resource savings of MP-DASH under three network conditions for FESTIVE, BBA, and BBA-C (Baseline is the vanilla MPTCP). Throughput is in Mbps.

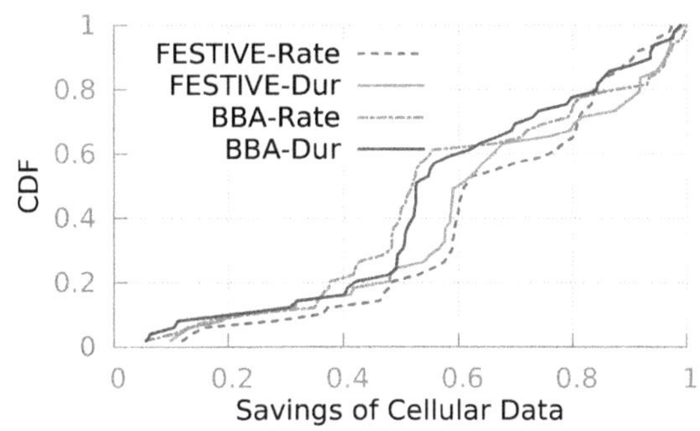

Figure 9: Cellular data savings brought by MP-DASH in all locations.

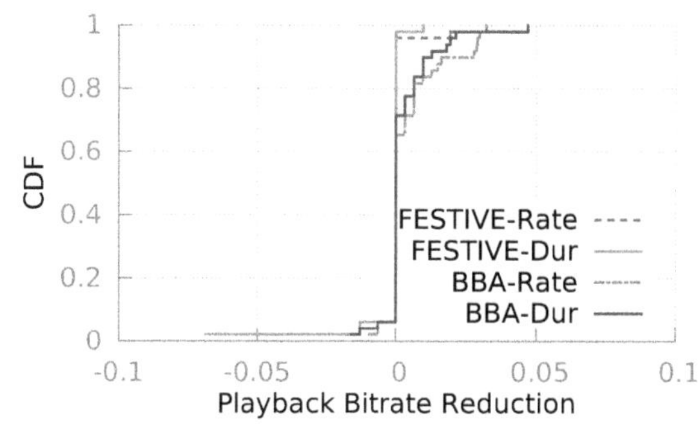

Figure 10: Playback bitrate reduction of experiments in all locations.

Levels 4 and 5 to constantly being at Level 4 (29% reduction of average playback bitrate). We therefore believe BBA-C strikes a good tradeoff among resource usage, playback bitrate, and playback smoothness for mobile video.

7.3.3 *MP-DASH in Real-World Settings*

We now investigate how MP-DASH helps make DASH video over MPTCP user-preference-aware under realistic settings through extensive in-field experiments. We conduct the experiments multiple times at 33 locations in three U.S. states, at different times of a day and during both weekdays and weekends. The locations include airport, hotel, fast food restaurant, shopping mall, retailer store, food market, coffeehouse, electronics store, parking lot, office building, grocery store, public library, *etc.* (described in §2). We use the free public WiFi networks, and the LTE provided by a large commercial carrier in the U.S. During the course of 3 months, we have collected more than 150 GB of data. We focus on two DASH algorithms: FESTIVE and BBA, and experiment with each algorithm under three configurations: vanilla MPTCP and MP-DASH with rate-based and duration-based deadline settings. A group of experiments thus consists of playing the *Big Buck Bunny* video under these six schemes in a random order. BBA-C performs the same as BBA for the experiments in this section, as the MPTCP capacity is higher than the highest video bitrate. We evaluate the performance of BBA-C for HD videos in §7.3.5.

Figure 9 plots the distribution of cellular data savings brought by MP-DASH at the above locations for four streaming schemes. Across all experiments, the 25th, 50th, and 75th percentile of the savings are 48%, 59%, and 82%, respectively. In general, MP-DASH achieves more savings for FESTIVE than it does for BBA. We observe similar results for radio energy consumption savings (figure not shown): the 25th, 50th, and 75th percentiles are 7.7%, 17%, and 53%, respectively. There is no playback bitrate reduction for 82.65% of the experiments, as shown in Figure 10. For the rest experiments, the average reduction is only 2.5%. Note a negative reduction means the increase of bitrate. The results demonstrate MP-DASH can effectively reduce the cellular data usage and radio energy for DASH video streaming over multipath, compared with using the vanilla MPTCP.

To gain more insights of the results, for each of the three categories described in §2.2, we pick several representative results and list them in Table 5 where groups (in the order of scenarios 1, 2, and 3 defined at the beginning of §2.2) are separated by horizontal lines. Thc numbers in the last 8 columns of the table are the savings in % of cellular bytes or radio energy compared to using the vanilla MPTCP without MP-DASH. The overall observation is, MP-DASH provides more savings as the WiFi throughput increases. For scenario 2 (WiFi can sometimes play the best quality), although the average WiFi throughput (based on our measurements before playing a video) is higher than the encoding bitrate of

	WiFi		LTE		FESTIVE/Bytes		FESTIVE/Energy		BBA/Bytes		BBA/Energy	
Location	BW	RTT	BW	RTT	Rate	DUR	Rate	DUR	Rate	DUR	Rate	DUR
Hotel Hi	2.92	14.1	11.0	51.9	52.92	49.43	9.735	29.74	41.74	40.74	23.52	35.74
Hotel Ha	2.96	40.8	14.0	68.6	59.25	57.68	11.68	19.53	49.54	47.84	15.50	13.13
Food Market	3.58	75.4	22.9	53.4	59.95	66.70	7.083	21.56	74.93	55.71	12.32	12.64
Airport	5.97	32.2	12.1	67.3	84.00	65.53	42.53	25.11	37.75	74.00	11.85	27.49
Coffeehouse	6.04	28.9	18.1	69.0	80.05	91.65	44.42	48.73	79.80	78.92	41.49	40.53
Library	17.8	23.3	5.18	64.1	97.44	97.81	77.78	85.19	95.12	97.54	80.29	79.72
Elec. Store	28.4	10.8	18.5	59.4	91.24	99.56	65.43	82.48	86.15	93.58	58.91	68.43

Table 5: Savings of cellular data and radio energy consumption at locations with different network conditions (BW in Mbps, RTT in ms, and savings in %). "DUR" stands for Duration.

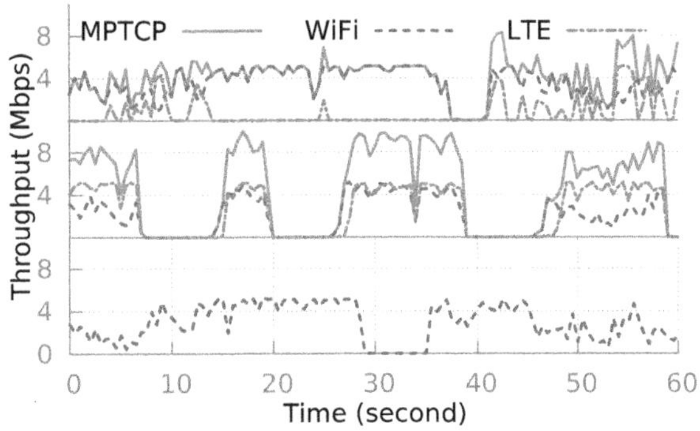

Figure 11: Traffic patterns of mobility experiments with MP-DASH (top), default MPTCP (middle), and single path WiFi (bottom).

the highest quality, using only WiFi cannot always support the highest bitrate, as the throughput of open WiFi networks is not always stable during the 10-minute playback period (figure not shown). Therefore, to ensure smooth playback at the highest quality, MPTCP still needs to use cellular from time to time. For scenario 3 (WiFi can almost always stably support the highest bitrate), one may argue that it is not necessary at all to use MPTCP. This is indeed true. However, it is inconvenient to ask users or video players to switch between single-path and multipath. Instead, MP-DASH provides a general OS support for applications to *transparently* and *adaptively* switch between them.

7.3.4 MP-DASH under Mobility Scenario

To evaluate the performance of MP-DASH under the mobility scenario, we walk around a WiFi AP following the same pre-defined route with the laptop playing the video using the FESTIVE rate adaptation algorithm. The WiFi and cellular bandwidth are both around 5.0 Mbps. Figure 11 plots samples of 60-second throughput for three configurations: MPTCP enhanced by MP-DASH with rate-based deadline setting (top), the default MPTCP (middle), and using only WiFi (bottom). It shows that MP-DASH can adaptively use cellular only when the WiFi throughput drops as the laptop moves far from the AP, whereas the default MPTCP drives the cellular link to almost its full capacity, regardless of the WiFi throughput. As a result, MP-DASH saves cellular data usage and radio energy consumption by 81.43% and 47.30%, respectively, without reducing the video bitrate (all chunks are played at the highest bitrate). Using only WiFi, on the other hand, cannot sustain the highest video bitrate for more than half of the chunks.

	FESTIVE	BBA-C
Playback Bitrate	↑ by 20.92%	↓ by 3.006%
Cellular Data Saving	39.88%	37.47%
Radio Energy Saving	8.624%	10.40%

Table 6: HD video results with the rate-based deadline setting.

7.3.5 High Definition (HD) Video

In all experiments above, the highest video quality is ~4.0 Mbps. We repeat the experiments by using the HD version of the *Tears of Steel* video whose highest bitrate is 10.0 Mbps as listed in Table 3. Note that the emerging 4K videos and 360-degree videos may require an even higher bandwidth [32]. This experiment complements the experiments in §7.3.3 because when playing the HD video, even the aggregated bandwidth of WiFi and LTE cannot sustain the highest bitrate at several locations. In this case, the video is mostly played at bitrate levels 3 & 4, thus allowing us to assess the performance of BBA-C in the wild. Table 6 summarizes the results at one of such locations (a supermarket). MP-DASH still achieves significant savings of cellular bytes (40% for FESTIVE and 37% for BBA-C over the unmodified BBA) and radio energy, compared to the vanilla MPTCP. Counter-intuitively, for FESTIVE, using MP-DASH actually leads to increased playback bitrate. This is likely attributed to the fact that the throughput estimation at the transport layer is more accurate than at the application layer.

8. DISCUSSION

General Applicability of the MP-DASH Scheduler. It is important to note the deadline-aware data transfer provided by MP-DASH is generally applicable to diverse application scenarios besides video streaming. They bear a common characteristic of being delay tolerant: as long as data transfers can finish before their deadline, the user experience will not be impacted. Consider the following examples.

- For music apps using automated recommendation (*e.g.,* Pandora Music), players do not need the next song until the playback of the current song is close to its end.
- For turn-by-turn navigation, a map tile only needs to be fetched before the vehicle is close to the tile's location.

• Mobile data offloading can be enhanced by leveraging many applications' delay-tolerant nature [7, 17, 27].

In the above scenarios, we can use MPTCP to boost the system performance, and use the MP-DASH scheduler to reduce the cellular data usage without sacrificing QoE. Note that even for applications such as turn-by-turn navigation which do not generate a significant amount of data, MP-DASH can help offload cellular traffic to WiFi networks when possible while bringing the benefits of multipath.

Deployment of MP-DASH requires upgrading MPTCP. This can be realized by system updates routinely launched by mobile carriers or device vendors. To use MP-DASH, the video rate control algorithms also need to be upgraded. As described in §6, the modifications to video players are very light. Since almost all of MP-DASH's logic resides on the client side, the change required on the server side is minimal: only its MPTCP stack needs to support MP-DASH. No change to the video server application is required. Also, by using standard TCP splitting proxies with MP-DASH enabled MPTCP, we can make MP-DASH fully transparent to video servers. The proxy is TLS/SSL friendly as it runs at the transport layer and therefore does not need to perform any decryption.

Runtime Overhead. MP-DASH incurs negligible runtime overhead, as both the MP-DASH's scheduling algorithm itself and the Holt-Winters throughput prediction has low complexity. We have measured the CPU utilization with and without MP-DASH and have not noticed any measurable increase of CPU usage.

Limitations. We conduct all experiments on a laptop instead of a smartphone. We expect though the impact of device selection to be small given the low runtime overhead of MP-DASH. Other limitations include using a lab server instead of a production server (*e.g.,* YouTube) for experiments, having not performed tests on other cellular technologies such as 3G/HSPA, and having not evaluated other DASH algorithms such as MPC [42]. We plan to address them in our future work.

9. RELATED WORK

Mobile MPTCP. MPTCP has been recently investigated for mobile devices with multiple network interfaces. Chen *et al.* [10] and Deng *et al.* [13] characterized the performance of MPTCP on WiFi and cellular networks, both focusing on file download. The mobile kibbutz [29] consolidates cellular traffic from multiple users through MPTCP, leading to reduced latency and improved energy efficiency. Croitoru *et al.* [12] leveraged MPTCP to achieve seamless mobility among multiple WiFi APs. eMPTCP [28] combines delayed subflow establishment and power-aware subflow management to make MPTCP energy efficient. In our previous work, we measured the performance of mobile web over MPTCP for both HTTP and SPDY [18]. Differently from the above works, we propose a novel multipath framework for video streaming.

Recently, Corbillon *et al.* [11] proposed a cross-layer MPTCP scheduler to prioritize video packets for non-adaptive video streaming and evaluated its performance through a simulation study. ADMIT [40] is an analytical framework that leverages forward error correction to improve the QoE for non-adaptive video over MPTCP. Instead of improving the quality of video streaming, our goal is to reduce cellular data usage, while not impacting user perceived QoE. Moreover, we investigate the interaction of *adaptive* video streaming and MPTCP though MP-DASH and extensive experiments in the wild.

Adaptive Video Streaming. There is a plethora of work on understanding and improving the QoE for adaptive video streaming. Besides FESTIVE [24] and BBA [23], Tian and Liu [37] proposed rate control algorithms that explore the smoothness and responsiveness trade-off in DASH and use video buffer level at the client side as a feedback signal. Huang *et al.* [22] measured the performance of three popular adaptive video streaming services (Hulu, Netflix, and Vudu) for motivating BBA [23]. Yin *et al.* [42] developed a control-theoretic approach to understand the fundamental trade-offs between various strategies for DASH rate adaptation algorithms. AVIS [9] is a resource management framework that separates adaptive video streams from regular ones through cellular resource virtualization. PBA [43] improves video QoE by leveraging bandwidth predictions and it can be further enhanced through a combination with rate stabilization functions. piStream [41] improves the QoE of adaptive video streaming by taking advantage of the PHY information of LTE networks for accurate bandwidth estimation. Compared to them, we tweak the MPTCP schedulers to save cellular data usage and energy consumption for video streaming on mobile devices.

10. CONCLUSION

We conducted, to the best of our knowledge, a first study of preference-aware multipath for adaptive video streaming. We proposed the MP-DASH framework and instantiated it in the context of optimizing video delivery over WiFi and cellular networks. We also designed MP-DASH adapters for two representative categories of DASH algorithms (throughput-based and buffer-based) by making them multipath-friendly, and we seamlessly integrated the MP-DASH adapters into them. We demonstrated through extensive field studies at 33 public places in three far-apart U.S. states that MP-DASH enhanced video players are robust and adaptive. Compared with players using the off-the-shelf MPTCP, they dramatically reduce the cellular data usage and radio energy consumption without sacrificing users' QoE. We plan to open source our MP-DASH implementation in the near future.

Acknowledgements

We thank Rittwik Jana, Emir Halepovic, and the anonymous reviewers for their valuable comments and suggestions, and in particular Adrian Perrig for shepherding the paper. We thank Yeon-sup Lim, Xiufeng Xie, Xinyu Zhang, and Darijo Raca for their help to implement MP-DASH. Feng Qian's research was supported in part by National Science Foundation Grant CNS-1566331.

11. REFERENCES

[1] About Hotel WiFi Test. https://www.hotelwifitest.com/about/.

[2] Adobe HTTP Dynamic Streaming. http://www.adobe.com/products/hds-dynamic-streaming.html.

[3] Apple HTTP Live Streaming. https://developer.apple.com/streaming/.

[4] Cisco Visual Networking Index: Global Mobile Data Traffic Forecast Update, 2015–2020 White Paper. http://goo.gl/ylTuVx.

[5] GPAC DASH Video Player. https://gpac.wp.mines-telecom.fr/.

[6] Microsoft Smooth Streaming. http://www.iis.net/downloads/microsoft/smooth-streaming.

[7] A. Balasubramanian, R. Mahajan, and A. Venkataramani. Augmenting Mobile 3G Using WiFi. In *MobiSys*, 2010.

[8] M. Carbone and L. Rizzo. Dummynet Revisited. *ACM SIGCOMM Computer Communication Review*, 40(2):12–20, Apr. 2010.

[9] J. Chen, R. Mahindra, M. A. Khojastepour, S. Rangarajan, and M. Chiang. A Scheduling Framework for Adaptive Video Delivery over Cellular Networks. In *MobiCom*, 2013.

[10] Y.-C. Chen, Y.-S. Lim, R. J. Gibbens, E. M. Nahum, R. Khalili, and D. Towsley. A Measurement-based Study of MultiPath TCP Performance over Wireless Networks. In *IMC*, 2013.

[11] X. Corbillon, R. Aparicio-Pardo, N. Kuhn, G. Texier, and G. Simon. Cross-Layer Scheduler for Video Streaming over MPTCP. In *MMSys*, 2016.

[12] A. Croitoru, D. Niculescu, and C. Raiciu. Towards WiFi Mobility without Fast Handover. In *NSDI*, 2015.

[13] S. Deng, R. Netravali, A. Sivaraman, and H. Balakrishnan. WiFi, LTE, or Both? Measuring Multi-homed Wireless Internet Performance. In *IMC*, 2014.

[14] A. Dua, C. W. Chan, N. Bambos, and J. Apostolopoulos. Channel, Deadline, and Distortion (CD^2) Aware Scheduling for Video Streams Over Wireless. *IEEE Transactions on Wireless Communications*, 9(3):1001–1011, Mar. 2010.

[15] A. Ford, C. Raiciu, M. Handley, and O. Bonaventure. TCP Extensions for Multipath Operation with Multiple Addresses. RFC 6824, 2013.

[16] M. R. Garey and D. S. Johnson. *Computers and Intractability: A Guide to the Theory of NP-Completeness*. W. H. Freeman and Company, 1979.

[17] B. Han, P. Hui, V. S. A. Kumar, M. V. Marathe, J. Shao, and A. Srinivasan. Mobile Data Offloading through Opportunistic Communications and Social Participation. *IEEE Transactions on Mobile Computing*, 11(5):821–834, May 2012.

[18] B. Han, F. Qian, S. Hao, and L. Ji. An Anatomy of Mobile Web Performance over Multipath TCP. In *CoNEXT*, 2015.

[19] Q. He, C. Dovrolis, and M. Ammar. On the Predictability of Large Transfer TCP Throughput. In *SIGCOMM*, 2005.

[20] B. Hesmans, G. Detal, S. Barré, R. Bauduin, and O. Bonaventure. SMAPP: Towards Smart Multipath TCP-enabled APPlications. In *CoNEXT*, 2015.

[21] J. Huang, F. Qian, A. Gerber, Z. M. Mao, S. Sen, and O. Spatscheck. A Close Examination of Performance and Power Characteristics of 4G LTE Networks. In *MobiSys*, 2012.

[22] T.-Y. Huang, N. Handigol, B. Heller, N. McKeown, and R. Johari. Confused, Timid, and Unstable: Picking a Video Streaming Rate is Hard. In *IMC*, 2012.

[23] T.-Y. Huang, R. Johari, N. McKeown, M. Trunnell, and M. Watson. A Buffer-Based Approach to Rate Adaptation: Evidence from a Large Video Streaming Service. In *SIGCOMM*, 2014.

[24] J. Jiang, V. Sekar, and H. Zhang. Improving Fairness, Efficiency, and Stability in HTTP-based Adaptive Video Streaming with FESTIVE. In *CoNEXT*, 2012.

[25] S. Kandula, K. C.-J. Lin, T. Badirkhanli, and D. Katabi. FatVAP: Aggregating AP Backhaul Capacity to Maximize Throughput. In *NSDI*, 2008.

[26] S. Lederer, C. Müller, and C. Timmerer. Dynamic Adaptive Streaming over HTTP Dataset. In *MMSys*, 2012.

[27] K. Lee, J. Lee, Y. Yi, I. Rhee, and S. Chong. Mobile Data Offloading: How Much Can WiFi Deliver? In *CoNEXT*, 2010.

[28] Y.-S. Lim, Y.-C. Chen, E. M. Nahum, D. Towsley, R. J. Gibbens, and E. Cecchet. Design, Implementation and Evaluation of Energy-Aware Multi-Path TCP. In *CoNEXT*, 2015.

[29] C. Nicutar, D. Niculescu, and C. Raiciu. Using Cooperation for Low Power Low Latency Cellular Connectivity. In *CoNEXT*, 2014.

[30] A. Nika, Y. Zhu, N. Ding, A. Jindal, Y. C. Hu, X. Zhou, B. Y. Zhao, and H. Zheng. Energy and Performance of Smartphone Radio Bundling in Outdoor Environments. In *WWW*, 2015.

[31] C. Paasch, S. Barré, et al. Multipath TCP in the Linux Kernel. http://www.multipath-tcp.org.

[32] F. Qian, B. Han, L. Ji, and V. Gopalakrishnan. Optimizing 360 Video Delivery Over Cellular Networks. In *All Things Cellular*, 2016.

[33] F. Qian, Z. Wang, A. Gerber, Z. M. Mao, S. Sen, and O. Spatscheck. Profiling Resource Usage for Mobile Applications: a Cross-layer Approach. In *MobiSys*, 2011.

[34] P. S. Schmidt, T. Enghardt, R. Khalili, and A. Feldmann. Socket Intents: Leveraging Application Awareness for Multi-Access Connectivity. In *CoNEXT*, 2013.

[35] I. Sodagar. The MPEG-DASH Standard for

Multimedia Streaming Over the Internet. *IEEE MultiMedia*, 18(4):62–67, Apr. 2011.

[36] J. Sommers and P. Barford. Cell vs. WiFi: On the Performance of Metro Area Mobile Connections. In *IMC*, 2012.

[37] G. Tian and Y. Liu. Towards Agile and Smooth Video Adaptation in Dynamic HTTP Streaming. In *CoNEXT*, 2012.

[38] B. Vamanan, J. Hasan, and T. N. Vijaykumar. Deadline-Aware Datacenter TCP (D^2TCP). In *SIGCOMM*, 2012.

[39] D. Wischik, C. Raiciu, A. Greenhalgh, and M. Handley. Design, Implementation and Evaluation of Congestion Control for Multipath TCP. In *NSDI*, 2011.

[40] J. Wu, C. Yuen, B. Cheng, M. Wang, and J.-L. Chen. Streaming High-Quality Mobile Video with Multipath TCP in Heterogeneous Wireless Networks. *IEEE Transactions on Mobile Computing*, 15(9):2345–2361, Sept. 2016.

[41] X. Xie, X. Zhang, S. Kumar, and L. E. Li. piStream: Physical Layer Informed Adaptive Video Streaming Over LTE. In *MobiCom*, 2015.

[42] X. Yin, A. Jindal, V. Sekar, and B. Sinopoli. A Control-Theoretic Approach for Dynamic Adaptive Video Streaming over HTTP. In *SIGCOMM*, 2015.

[43] X. K. Zou, J. Erman, V. Gopalakrishnan, E. Halepovic, R. Jana, X. Jin, J. Rexford, and R. K. Sinha. Can Accurate Predictions Improve Video Streaming in Cellular Networks? In *HotMobile*, 2015.

ExBox: Experience Management Middlebox for Wireless Networks

Ayon Chakraborty[†], Shruti Sanadhya, Samir R. Das[†], Dongho Kim, Kyu-Han Kim
[†] Stony Brook University, Hewlett Packard Laboratories
[†] {aychakrabort,samir}@cs.stonybrook.edu
{shruti.sanadhya,dongho.kim,kyu-han.kim}@hpe.com

ABSTRACT

Enterprise wireless networks face significant challenges to deliver Quality-of-Experience (QoE) with the variety of mobile applications. One of the fundamental challenges is that the traditional definition of network capacity (often defined as throughput capacity) is not sufficient to reflect applications' requirements in wireless networks. In this paper, we propose to rethink the network capacity of wireless networks to better incorporate QoE. Specifically, we first propose a novel concept of an Experiential Capacity Region (*ExCR*) for wireless networks. *ExCR* is defined as a set of simultaneous application flows whose QoE requirements can be satisfied by the network. Next, we present the infrastructure based ExBox system that measures per-application QoE metrics and determines the *ExCR* for wireless networks to better serve a set of mobile application flows. In its core, ExBox employs light-weight machine learning techniques that are tailored for dynamic wireless environments. Through both large-scale simulations and extensive real-life experiments on WiFi and LTE networks, we show that ExBox delivers QoE in admission control decision with a precision of $\approx 0.8-0.9$, even when clients experience diverse channel quality. Moreover, ExBox quickly adapts to changing network environments without much overhead.

1. INTRODUCTION

Enterprise wireless networks (e.g., building, campus, metros) are moving towards highly mobile environment. At the same time, the diversity of applications as well as network infrastructures is growing. For example, applications range from web downloads to audio/video streaming, speech recognition and desktop sharing. Networks range from various incarnations of WiFi alongside LTE small cells [20]. It is often a challenge for enterprise network administrators to develop a good balance between network capacity and user experience. Blindly over-provisioning access networks to support all possible user demands is clearly prohibitive due to both operational and spectrum costs. There is thus a need for Quality of Experience (QoE) management so that specific demands are directed to right networks (i.e., network selection) according to their respective loads. Moreover, even when only one network is available, admission control policies are needed such that aggregated user experience of existing traffic does not suffer due to newly arriving flows.

There is already a large volume of research in network selection and/or admission control (e.g., [10, 7, 31, 65, 51, 45, 56, 63]) that appears to be addressing these challenges. However, these solutions have three critical limitations:

Focus on single QoS metric or application type: Most approaches focus on modeling Quality-of-Service (QoS) metrics, such as throughput, delay or loss. Often the focus is on using only one such metric, typically throughput [65, 51, 45], either directly or via a utility function-based formulation [55]. However, such metrics do not relate in a straightforward manner to the eventual quality of experience (QoE) of the user, specifically for modern interactive and streaming applications. In particular, there is a growing understanding that *multiple QoS metrics influence user QoE in complex ways* [29, 28]. Commercial admission control solutions focus purely on authentication [10] or use simplistic metrics, such as maximum number of flows [7, 13] or bandwidth [55, 9, 2, 22]. While QoE based capacity has been proposed for VoIP [62] and video flows [59], these models still cannot be applied to real enterprise networks, which often contain a mix of applications [34]. For instance, these models cannot answer, "How does the QoE of existing VoIP flow change when a new streaming video flow enters the network?"

Lack of ability to capture dynamic behavior: Unlike wired networks, wireless networks suffer from multi-path fading, interference and user mobility. Accordingly, the total *capacity* of these networks also changes. Network administrators, thus, need to adapt to these dynamic network scenarios. For example, at some instant one VoIP and one Web flow may be admissible in a WiFi network, but if the VoIP user moves away from the access point, the observed QoE

CoNEXT '16, December 12-15, 2016, Irvine, CA, USA

DOI: http://dx.doi.org/10.1145/2999572.2999597

for VoIP flow may go down. Existing approaches cannot capture such dynamic behavior.

Lack of 'blackbox' solution: Conventional admission control solutions such as [56, 53, 63] depend on a meticulous modeling of packet queuing and traffic behavior. Most network elements today (e.g., APs, middleboxes, switches) are closed devices. This makes it hard to model their performances accurately. For example, commodity WiFi routers with apparently similar specifications can exhibit widely different performances in benchmarking [17]. Thus, a 'blackbox' modeling approach is preferred where a specific network could be modeled via external measurements even when complete internal specifications are unknown.

To address these limitations, we propose ExBox, an Experience MiddleBox, which continuously explores the capacity of a wireless network.[1] ExBox models network capacity in terms of a new notion of *Experiential Capacity Region (ExCR)* that we develop in this work. While *ExCR* is motivated by the general idea of capacity region [65, 51, 45] long been used to model the throughput-based capacity of multi-user wireless networks, it specifically considers experiential capacity helpful to manage QoE of users. Overall, *ExCR* models the set of flows of different application classes that can be accommodated in the network without hurting user experience.

ExBox is capable of modeling diverse set of applications with diverse QoE requirements and is able to capture dynamic environments. It models *ExCR* using a *measurement-driven, online* learning approach that can be applied in a *blackbox* setting, where detailed characteristics of individual network elements are unknown or cannot easily be modeled. ExBox can be deployed as a middlebox in a gateway device in the enterprise setting, as shown in Figure 1. For enterprise networks with different types of access networks, a separate *ExCR* can be learnt for each access point/eNodeB and can be used for implementing network selection.

Roadmap and Contributions: In summary the paper makes the following contributions.

- We motivate the need for a new approach for capacity modeling in wireless networks, based on user experience, and introduce the notion of *Experiential Capacity Region (*ExCR*)* (Section 2).
- We formulate the ExBox approach to learn *ExCR* and layout its different components (Section 3). We discuss the deployment issues for ExBox in real world (Section 4).
- We evaluate ExBox using WiFi and LTE network testbeds involving 10 mobile clients and a single WiFi access point or LTE eNodeB respectively (Section 5). We also perform a scale-up study using the `ns-3` simulator [18] and demonstrate the performance with 50 concurrent client devices (Section 6). Overall, ExBox is able to manage network-wide QoE through admission control decisions with precision and recall rates of $\approx 0.8-0.9$ and $\approx 0.65-0.8$, respectively.

[1]Here, by network we refer to coverage of a single WiFi access point or LTE eNodeB. See more on this in Section 4.4

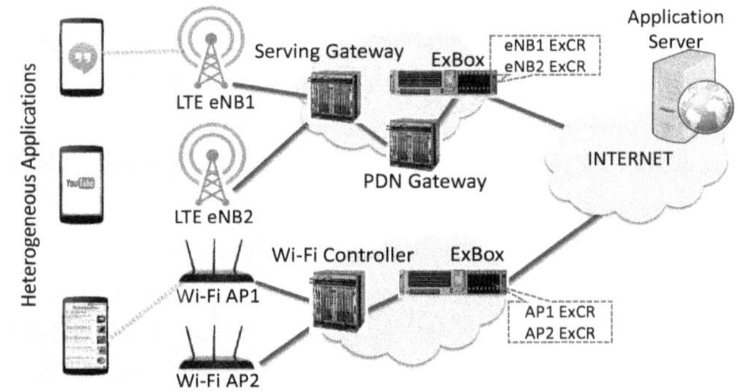

Figure 1: ExBox is implemented as a middlebox collocated with gateway devices.

2. RETHINKING NETWORK CAPACITY

Our broad goal is to model network capacity in terms of QoE across diverse application classes. This goes much beyond the single metric-based network capacity definitions. The general notion of this *experiential capacity* is not entirely new. For example, prior work has developed a similar notion of network capacity for QoE-aware admission control [59], which focuses on increasing the number of simultaneous video flows in 802.11 networks without compromising the QoE. However, studies such as this are unable to model diverse application classes that co-exist in the network [34]. An efficient admission control mechanism needs to capture this mixed traffic.

To further highlight this, we have conducted a simulation study using `ns-3` and packet traces from Skype video conferencing and YouTube high-definition video streaming. The simulation setup is described in Section 6. In a simulated WiFi network, we increase the number of video conferencing and streaming flows simultaneously. For each of these applications, we calculate the per-application median QoE and the average QoE of the network. QoE refers to user-perceived quality of experience. For Skype video conferencing we use PSNR (peak signal-to-noise ratio) of the received video as the QoE metric, while startup delay[2] is used as the QoE metric for the YouTube video streaming. Our simulation does not have a real video conferencing application or a streaming player, we estimate QoE in the following way. QoS is modeled as the ratio of average throughput to delay. We use the IQX model (to be discussed in Section 3.2) to map such QoS values to corresponding QoE values. Figure 2 shows this QoE as a heatmap. The QoE values are normalized for comparison purposes and also to calculate the average QoE of the network which is the mean QoE for all apps in the network (Figure 2c). We observe in Figure 2a that as number of streaming flows increases in the network, the QoE for streaming goes down. However, the increase in number of conferencing flows does not impact streaming QoE significantly. This shows that with ≈ 20 streaming flows, the

[2]Startup delay is the time difference between the events when a video playback is requested and it actually starts playing.

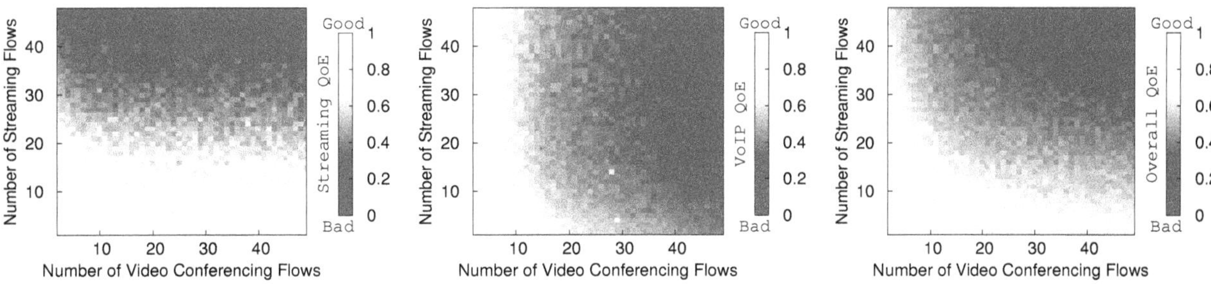

(a) Median QoE for Streaming Flows (b) Median QoE for Video Conferencing Flows (c) Average QoE of the Network

Figure 2: QoE as a function of the number of flows of two applications in the network

network may not be able to accommodate any more streaming flows without hurting QoE, but it may still be able to accommodate ≈ 10 more video conferencing flows. The video conferencing QoE shows a different capacity in Figure 2b. Up to 50 streaming flows can co-exist with ≈ 10 conferencing flows, without hurting the conferencing QoE. When we compute the overall network QoE, i.e. median QoE of all flows, we get the multi-dimensional capacity region seen in Figure 2c. A simple count based admission control [7, 13] will not be able to capture this multi-dimensional capacity as there is no single number to limit all applications. For the capacity region shown in Figure 2c, the maximum count of admissible conferencing flows is ≈ 40, but the maximum count of admissible streaming flows is only ≈ 25.

In addition to application diversity, there is also channel diversity in wireless networks. We conducted testbed experiments to show the impact of wireless channel quality, measured in terms of Signal-to-Noise Ratio (SNR), on the experiential capacity. We use 4 phones connected to the same Wi-Fi AP, where all or some of them have high SNR (placed close to the AP, received signal strength of –30 dBm) and others have low SNR (placed further away from AP, received signal strength of –80 dBm). The phones simultaneously play a YouTube video and record the video startup delay as the QoE metric. Let us assume a desirable value of this QoE metric is 5 seconds. In Figure 3 we see when all phones have high SNR, all 4 video flows satisfy the QoE requirement, however it is not the case when 2 of them have low SNR. The video does not even play in some of the phones when all phones have low SNR. It is interesting to note that the QoE of clients in high SNR location is also impacted when some clients move to a low SNR location. A pure rate-based admission control [51, 9, 2, 22] will not capture this characteristic. It will continue admitting low SNR clients as long as the maximum rate usage allows, without considering the impact on the high SNR clients.

2.1 Experiential Capacity Region

To accommodate these insights, we need a new model of capacity that can handle QoE of multiple wireless users using diverse applications. One way to do this is to rethink the traditional modeling approach of the rate-based capacity in terms of capacity region [51, 65]. Here, the

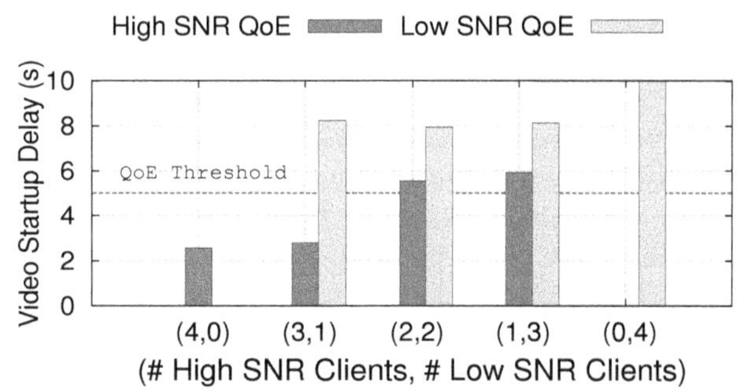

Figure 3: Impact of SNR on Video Streaming QoE.

multi-dimensional region representing the set of all possible achievable rate vectors $< r_1, \ldots, r_n >$ (where r_i is the rate of flow i and n is the number of total flows) models the capacity region. In the following, we extend this notion to develop the *experiential capacity region.*

Assume that there are k application classes and r levels of SNR. SNR levels are formed by simply splitting the range of SNRs possible in r discrete bins. Further, $a_{i,j}$ denotes the number of active flows in the network for class i with SNR of the wireless link in SNR level s_j. For each flow, we assume a 'thresholded' model for QoE, where the QoE metric has been thresholded to *acceptable* or *unacceptable* levels. This thresholding works because QoE often indeed changes sharply from an unacceptable to acceptable level with changes in related QoS parameters. This makes a traffic matrix representing a number of flows of different classes from different users $< a_{1,1}, \ldots, a_{k,r} >$ either achievable or not achievable depending on the whether acceptable levels of QoE for all these flows can be satisfied by the network simultaneously. We call the discrete set of achievable traffic matrices $< a_{1,1}, \ldots, a_{k,r} >$ the *Experiential Capacity Region (ExCR)*. Our goal in this work is to develop empirical methods to derive this region for a given wireless network.

A careful reader will note that this model of *ExCR* bears similarity to the notion of 'call admission region' or 'admissible load region' concepts developed in connection with broadband networks and mobile cellular networks during the 90s and 00s. Many such studies do consider a mix of different types of traffic, e.g., realtime and non-realtime. See, e.g., [56, 53, 63]. But they still use a single QoS metric:

rate. Further, these studies use an analytical modeling approach that requires full knowledge of system components, e.g., queueing network model, service rates, etc. Instead, we are interested in a blackbox approach where the network must be probed to learn its characteristics. We elaborate on the learning process next.

3. THE EXBOX DESIGN

In this section, we present ExBox, an Experience MiddleBox that continuously explores the *experiential capacity region* (*ExCR*) of a wireless network. Following the description in the previous section, ExBox captures the network traffic matrix as $< a_{1,1}, \ldots, a_{k,r} >$, where $a_{i,j}$ denotes the number of flows for application class i with SNR of the wireless link in SNR level s_j. We restrict ourselves to SNR as the wireless channel metric in this work as this directly influences PHY layer bit rate and bit error rate, and thus has a direct correlation with the overall QoS of the link. In our experiments reported in Section 6 only two levels were found to be sufficient (low and high).

Classifying flows into application classes is the first step in ExBox. Traffic classification has been extensively studied for both legacy and mobile applications [41, 58, 69, 47, 42, 67, 54, 32, 33] and we can leverage this work to classify an incoming flow into an application class (more in Section 4.5). For the rest of the discussion, we assume that the class of a flow is determined. ExBox defines the *ExCR* as set of all traffic matrices of the form $< a_{1,1}, \ldots, a_{k,r} >$ that have acceptable QoEs. Exploring this search space in a brute force manner is: (i) *prohibitive* with multiple users, multiple application classes and multiple SNR categories, and (ii) *indeterminable* in scenarios where network characteristics fluctuate. Instead, ExBox tries to *learn* the boundary of the capacity region by using a binary classifier implemented using off-the-shelf machine learning tools. The learning problem in ExBox lends itself easily to SVM-based solution [40]. This is the approach we take here.

SVM is typically used for supervised deterministic binary classification of multi-dimensional data. Intuitively, SVM uses the training data to construct a hyperplane in the $kr + 1$ dimensional space, where k is the number of application classes and r is the number of SNR levels, as above. This hyperplane separates the universe in two separate classes. The hyperplane intuitively defines the boundary of the capacity region. While other supervised classification methods (e.g., decision trees) could be used by ExBox as well, we investigate SVM for its intuitive fit with ExBox. The performance results later will show that it works quite well relative to existing baselines. Regardless, the actual learning technique is not central to the concept of ExBox and can be implemented as a separate module that can be refined as needed.

Overall, ExBox consists of two main components: (i) *Admittance Classifier*: it uses SVM to classify incoming flows as admissible or non-admissible and (ii) *QoE Estimator*: it builds QoE estimates of existing flows on the network-side. We discuss these components next, followed by the software architecture of ExBox.

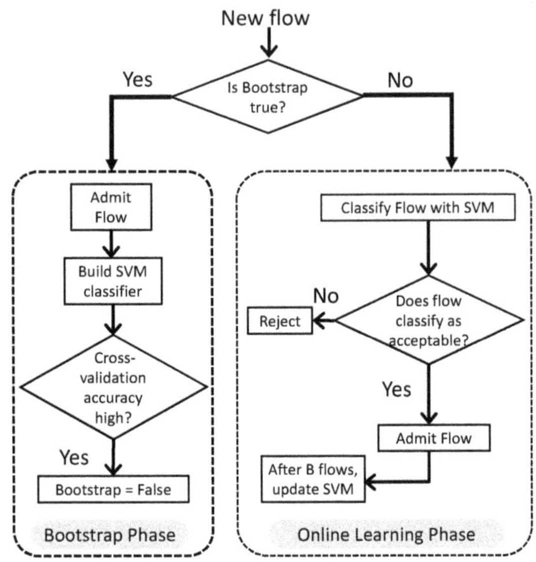

Figure 4: Flowchart for the Admittance Classifier

3.1 Admittance Classifier

One can visualize the boundary of experiential capacity region as a multi-dimensional surface that separates the traffic matrices with *acceptable* QoE from the traffic matrices with *unacceptable* QoE. This forms the basic intuition of the Admittance Classifier, which *classifies* the universe of possible traffic matrices in two regions. Further, in order to adapt to changing network conditions, Admittance Classifier continues to re-learn the capacity region boundary. Our current implementation of the Admittance Classifier uses off-the-shelf Support Vector Machines (SVM) with batch updates for online binary classification. Prior literature [64, 52] has shown suitability of incremental or online learning with SVM. Figure 4 shows the flowchart for Admittance Classifier. The algorithm operates in two phases:

Bootstrap Phase is the phase where ExBox initializes the classifier from zero information. In this phase, ExBox simply *observes* the network. All flows are admitted in the network just as they were in the absence of ExBox. This allows ExBox to learn traffic matrices with both acceptable as well as unacceptable QoEs. It starts with $a_{i,j} = 0, \forall i \in 1, \ldots, k$ and $\forall j \in 1, \ldots, r$. As a new flow m of class c and SNR s_ℓ joins the network, $a_{c,\ell}$ is incremented by 1. Next, the Admittance Classifier estimates the QoE of entire set of active flows (including the new one) as $Y_m \in \{+1, -1\}$ using the IQX hypothesis [44]. This is learnt using the QoE Estimator described in the following subsection. A value of +1 for Y_m denotes that if flow m is admitted then still the new traffic matrix will have an acceptable QoE. Similarly, a value of -1 for Y_m denotes that upon admitting the flow m the QoE of one or more flows will be unacceptable.

Each incoming flow can impact the QoE of all ongoing flows. ExBox defines the tuple $X_m = (< a_{1,1}, \ldots, a_{k,r} >, (c, \ell))$ to indicate a newly arrived flow m of application class c and SNR s_ℓ when the current traffic matrix is $< a_{1,1}, \ldots, a_{k,r} >$. The tuple (X_m, Y_m) describes the influence of such a new flow on the existing traffic matrix, where Y_m classifies this influence in one of two possible classes as described earlier. Over time, Admittance Classifier learns many such (X_m, Y_m) tuples and uses them to train the SVM. Note that in the bootstrapping phase, ExBox does not perform any admission control – all flows are admitted regardless of any impact on QoE of other flows. This phase is needed in order to collect a diverse training set for Admittance Classifier. We show in the evaluation that this phase is typically not too long.

As ExBox builds the Admittance Classifier from the training set, it also performs n-fold cross validation on the training set periodically. This is done by splitting the *training set* into n random subsets, out of which the Admittance Classifier is trained using $n-1$ subsets and is tested with the remaining subset. To test the Admittance Classifier when a flow p arrives, an X_p tuple is created and the $\hat{Y}_p$ label is computed for X_p from the trained SVM model. This estimated $\hat{Y}_p$ is then compared with the Y_p observed in the network to compute accuracy. This process is repeated for all the n subsets. When a predefined accuracy threshold is reached, ExBox stops the bootstrapping phase. The Admittance Classifier becomes operational, enters the Online Learning Phase and starts classifying each incoming flow as $+1$ (admissible) or -1 (inadmissible).

Online Learning Phase executes in rounds and each round is determined by a 'batch' of flows. After a batch-size B number of flows has been admitted, ExBox re-computes the Admittance Classifier with all the (X_m, Y_m) observed so far. Additionally, if the new batch contains a traffic matrix $< a_{1,1}, \ldots, a_{k,r} >$ which has been seen in the past, the observed QoE for that traffic matrix is replaced with the new observed QoE. The Online Learning Phase enables ExBox to adapt to changes in network and client population. For example, if clients move farther from the WiFi AP, the QoE of their new flows may worsen. Additionally, popularity of Self Organizing Network (SON) solutions [1, 11, 21] enables operators to dynamically change network configuration and, in turn, change network capacity. In such cases, the Admittance Classifier may classify new flows incorrectly and needs to re-learn the capacity region. The online phase enables this possibility.

3.2 QoE Estimator

The Admittance Classifier described above assumes knowledge of QoE for each application class. In a real network, obtaining QoE values from the users may not be practical as it involves deploying custom applications [26] or modifying user devices [38]. A solution that requires end-device modifications has a significant barrier for adoption, given the BYOD trends prevalent in enterprise and campus networks today. At the same time, user experience can be most accurately measured at end device as different applications react differently to network characteristics.

Thus, ExBox uses an intermediate modeling-based approach where the QoE is estimated on the 'network-side' but with some help from client devices introduced in the network specifically for model training purposes. Such training needs in ExBox are fairly modest and can be accomplished by the network administrator. Based on this initial training, ExBox can estimate QoE of future flows from passive network measurements on the network-side. Several approaches have been proposed in the past [37, 28, 29, 26, 44] to measure application QoE from network measurements. Among these, the IQX hypothesis [44] proposes a generic relationship between QoE and QoS for multiple applications. This is useful to network administrator, who can measure the network's QoS but may not have knowledge of application level experience. The basic formulation of the IQX hypothesis is as follows:

$$QoE = \alpha + \beta . e^{-\gamma . QoS}, \tag{1}$$

where QoS and QoE are suitable metrics modeling dominant QoS or QoE. The parameter γ regulates the contribution of QoS in QoE. The dominant QoS parameter varies across applications, e.g. latency for web browsing and VoIP, throughput for streaming, etc. The IQX hypothesis estimates different QoE metrics for different applications. For instance, QoE of web browsing is measured in terms of *Page Load Time*, QoE of VoIP applications is measured in terms of *Peak Signal to Noise Ratio (PSNR)*, QoE of video streaming is measured in terms of *Startup Delay*. ExBox uses the IQX hypothesis to estimate per-application QoE. From a training device in the network, controlled experiments can be done to find the best fitting α, β and γ for a given application. ExBox uses pre-defined thresholds [39] to map the QoE of each flow m to $Y_m \in \{+1, -1\}$. Section 5 presents performance evaluation of the IQX model in a real testbed.

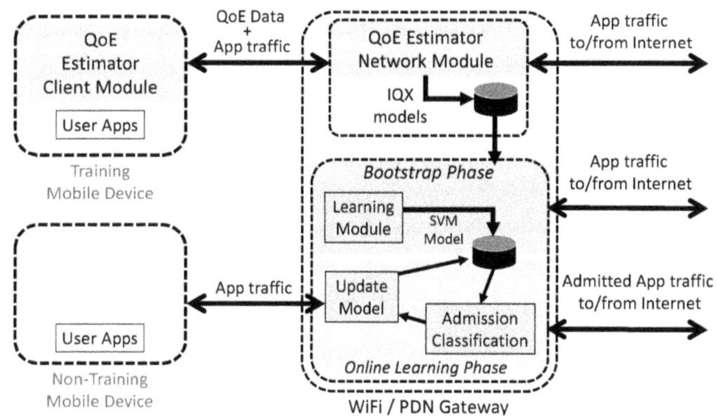

Figure 5: Software Architecture of ExBox

3.3 Software Architecture

Figure 5 shows the software architecture of ExBox. ExBox learns the IQX model [44] for each application class via an initial training with actual measured QoE values on the client device. For this training the application class is identified via established traffic classification methods [41, 58, 69, 47, 42, 67, 54, 32, 33][3].

A single training client device is used to record per application QoE information via direct measurement using instrumented apps, and share the data with the QoE Estima-

[3]Note that the proposed traffic classification solutions work for encrypted traffic as well.

tor module in the network. The QoE Estimator fits an IQX model per application class and stores it for future use by the Admittance Classifier. Finally, once relevant IQX models are built, any regular flow (i.e., from a non-training mobile device) is passed to the Admittance Classifier and steps described in Section 3.1 and Figure 4 are executed. The SNR level of a flow is computed from the SNR reported by the WiFi access point (AP) or Channel Quality Indicator (CQI) collected by the LTE base station (eNodeB).

4. QOE MANAGEMENT WITH EXBOX

We now discuss how ExBox can be used for QoE management and address various practical operational challenges.

4.1 Network Selection

ExBox, as defined in previous section, can be used to explore the experiential capacity region of a given wireless network. In enterprise networks where WiFi and LTE Small Cells may co-exist, ExBox can be used to simultaneously explore the capacity regions of both networks. It can bootstrap and learn two separate Admittance Classifiers. Further, when a new flow comes in, it can be used to decide whether the flow can be admitted in either of the available networks. If the answer is $+1$ from both classifiers, ExBox can select the best suited network based on how much 'inside' the capacity region the new test point is. There is a straightforward mechanism to do this in SVM by evaluating how far away from the separating hyperplane the test point lies. ExBox can operate from within the infrastructure with limited support from a training device in the network. In the case of hybrid WiFi-LTE networks, ExBox can be collocated on the LTE PDN gateway, which can view both WiFi and LTE traffic and perform network selection.

4.2 Admission Control

Before ExBox can make the admission decision for a flow, it needs to know the application class of that flow. Existing traffic classification solutions [41, 58, 69, 47, 42, 67, 54, 32, 33] analyze the first few packets of the flow to decide which category it belongs to. Thus, a flow needs to be *admitted* briefly before any admission control decision is made. Once ExBox makes the admission decision, it can be executed in multiple ways. In a single network scenario, if ExBox determines the flow to be admissible it goes through the network. However, if a flow is determined to be inadmissible, then the flow can be (i) discontinued from the gateway or (ii) admitted in a low priority access category,such as in 802.11e. In case a flow is not admitted the user is notified by a message (e.g., Smart TVs already reject flows because of insufficient bandwidth [3]). In a wide multi-cell deployment, ExBox determines the best network suited for an incoming flow and moves the flow to the accepting network. In multi-cell WiFi networks, flows can be easily migrated from one AP to another through the WiFi controller [6]. In LTE networks, the serving gateway (SGW) can assist mobility across 3GPP entities. In hybrid LTE-WiFi deployments, the 3GPP IP flow mobility standard [14] allows for seamless offload between LTE and WiFi. Note that executing ExBox's decision of rejecting flows may leave some users disconnected or unable to use intended applications. This is governed by the *admittance policy* of the network administrator. They can choose to allow best-effort connectivity to as many flows or maintain their promise of good QoE to certain users at the cost of disappointing other users. ExBox aids them in making a more informed choice.

4.3 Dealing with Network/App Dynamics

While the Admittance Classifier defined in the previous section focuses on admission control, a flow's behavior may change after being admitted. One reason is that the application adapts to changes in the end-to-end network throughput or delay. This may lead to change in QoE of the flow, e.g. YouTube can downgrade the video quality from high-definition to low-definition. Another reason could be user mobility. The wireless link quality between a device and the WiFi AP (or LTE eNodeB) can change depending on the distance of device from AP, multi-path fading, etc. If a flow is admitted in the network when the device is close to the AP, its QoE may deteriorate when the device moves farther from the AP. Additionally, in a contention based system, such as 802.11 WiFi, a low rate device can reduce the rates experienced by others (throughput fairness). In such cases, ExBox needs to revise its decision of admitting such a flow. For this purpose, ExBox periodically polls the network to check if the flow characteristics (throughput, delay, loss) have drastically changed or if the SNR levels of any device have changed. It then constructs a new tuple X_m from the current traffic matrix and computes Y_m from the Admittance Classifier. If the new Y_m is -1, this flow is considered inadmissible and offloaded to another network or discontinued, as governed by the *admittance policy* discussed above.

4.4 Scaling to Large Networks

In this work we modeled only one access device or cell (WiFi AP or LTE eNodeB) to limit the state space to be considered. In a typical enterprise or campus network, multiple WiFi or LTE cells are deployed to cater to the large population. To better serve all users, the network administrator can scale up the ExBox system to simultaneously learn classifiers for multiple cells. Being located on the WiFi controller or PDN gateway enables ExBox to have this wide view of the network. The classifier is a $kr + 1$ dimension vector for k application classes and r SNR classes. One such classifier needs to be periodically learned per cell.

One can argue that the single access device model limits the applicability of ExBox, as it cannot consider interference arising from neighboring cells. However, we expect that in most enterprise deployments the channel/cell planning is done carefully enough that the influence of such interference actually affecting capacity is minimal. On the other hand, this simplification is computationally convenient. In our future work, we plan to perform evaluations on larger networks to determine whether any refinement of the basic ExBox will be necessary.

In ExBox can be deployed widely, it is also possible to

share IQX models over different networks of similar characteristics. This will reduce the training effort substantially and/or will help in more robust model creation, e.g. influence of device heterogeneity on IQX models can be considered. Existing work on QoE estimation [26, 28, 29, 38] does not consider such heterogeneity in their models. This is an interesting direction of future work.

4.5 Flows, Apps and Users

We have used ExBox to do flow-based admission control in this work. However, many modern applications use multiple flows in the same app. For example, YouTube uses separate flows to play the main video and to load video recommendations. Thus, flow-based admission control may not always be appropriate and an app-based admission control may be preferred. ExBox can be extended to handle such cases through an app-based admission control. This can be achieved by leveraging the flow classification tool to identify the dominant flow that determines the app's QoE [60, 38]. For example, in a video streaming app, the flows carrying video data and control are dominant although other flows carrying app-analytics data or advertisements may be present. The admission control now can use a heuristic that admits all flows for that app if the dominant flows are admitted. This is an interesting direction of future work.

In the same note, a single user may use multiple apps concurrently, that are to be considered separately. It is possible that some apps are admissible and others are not for the same user. The inadmissible flow/app may be discontinued from the WiFi controller or PGW, or selectively offloaded to another network. Distributing flows over multiple wireless interfaces or wireless networks has also been studied in prior research [46, 50, 35].

5. EXPERIMENTAL EVALUATION

In this section we evaluate ExBox using QoE traces collected from a mobile testbed. We first explain how we collect the traces and then present results from our trace-based evaluation. We evaluate the Admittance Classifier and the QoE Estimator modules separately over the same testbed. In the next section we evaluate the entire ExBox solution through large-scale `ns-3` simulations.

5.1 Testbed Setup

Mobile clients: We use 10 Samsung Galaxy S6 phones, running Android OS, as clients or user equipments (UEs) to generate different types of flows. The clients either connect to a WiFi access point or to an LTE eNodeB that are deployed as a part of our testbed.

WiFi Network: We host the WiFi access point on a laptop whose WiFi interface can be switched into access point mode and serve as a WiFi hotspot. We use a well provisioned laptop (an HP ZBook with 16 GB memory and quad-core Intel i7 processor). The Linux utility `hostapd` is used to configure it as a WiFi hotspot. This setup enables us to capture network traffic from the UEs connecting to the hotspot at the very first hop. It also allows us to shape traffic parameters (throttle bandwidth, introduce delay, losses) using Linux utilities `tc` and `netem` on the laptop. We use WiFi channel number 5 that is interference free in our lab area. The WiFi testbed setup is shown in Figure 6a. We run capacity tests on the WiFi link and observe 20 Mbps `iperf` UDP throughput and $\approx 30-40$ ms `ping` latency. The low throughput is an artifact of the WiFi driver on the laptop but it does not impact our evaluation as ExBox does not make any assumptions on the maximum bandwidth.

LTE Network: We have an LTE small-cell testbed in our lab. It consists of LTE core network as well as eNodeB. We use ip.access E-40 [15] as our eNodeB. In the core network we use licensed OpenEPC [19] software stack. The core network consists of 3GPP [23] standard-compliant EPC components such as MME, SGW, PGW and HSS. Each component runs in a Linux-based virtual machine. For each UE, we have our own user subscription information (*e.g.* IMSI) programmed on a SIM card. We are able to simultaneously connect 8 UEs to the E-40 eNodeB. This is the maximum bound of the current version of software in ip.access E-40. This is the best we can currently do in a lab-grade EPC deployment[4]. We run the packet capture (`tcpdump`) and traffic shaping tools (`tc`, `netem`) in the virtual machine hosting PGW. The LTE testbed setup is shown in Figure 6b. `iperf` and `ping` tests on the LTE link show more than 30 Mbps capacity and $\approx 30-40$ ms latency.

5.2 Experiment Methodology

Client Apps: For our experiments we developed two Android apps and a UI automation script to generate web, video streaming and video conferencing flows. We chose these three application classes because their respective QoE is influenced by different underlying network attributes. Each app also records the corresponding QoE ground truth. None of the apps require root privilege.

- **Web Browsing App:** The web browsing app embeds a `Webview` client acting as the browser which continually loads a specific sequence of webpages. The app records *page load time* as the QoE metric. For benchmarking we focused on similar sized webpages: we use mobile websites of Amazon, BBC and YouTube. No video is played on YouTube as we just load the homepage. The app clears the browser cache after a page load is over to make sure a fresh copy of the page is fetched every time.
- **Video Streaming App:** The video streaming app embeds a YouTube–video player that repeatedly plays a video. We use a 2–minute video clip from YouTube that is available in HD-format (720p).[5] We use the YouTube Android Player API [25] that captures video playback events like *video loaded*, *video started*, *video buffering*, *video playing* and so on. Every time a video is played the app logs all

[4]Open Air Interface (OAI), another popular EPC implementation, currently supports only a couple of UEs stably.

[5]The median video clip playback length in YouTube is ≈ 2.5 sec [61].

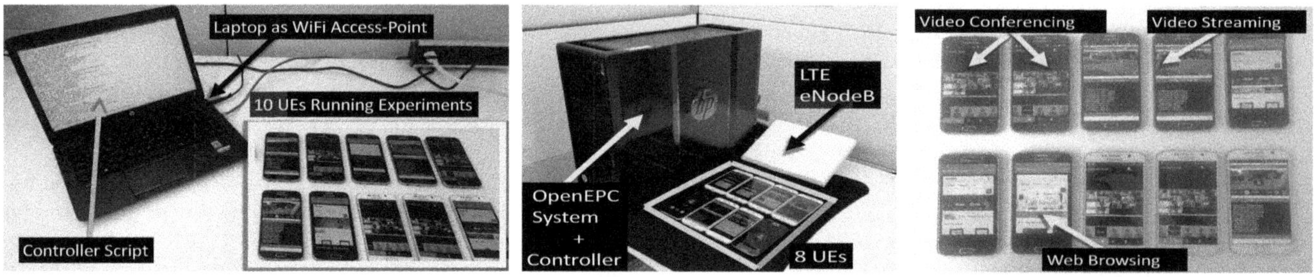

(a) Wi-Fi Testbed with 10 UEs (b) LTE Testbed with 8 UEs (c) Apps running on UEs

Figure 6: WiFi and LTE testbed setup for evaluation of ExBox

such player events with corresponding timestamps. The video *startup delay* is used as the QoE metric. This is measured as the time it takes the video to start playing from the instant the video is requested [68]. We rarely observe additional video stalls as the most of the content is downloaded during the initial start-up delay period. Hence we do not consider buffering ratio or buffering rate or average bit rate as the QoE metric in our setup, however they can be used in principle.

- **Video Conferencing App:** For video conferencing, we use Google Hangouts along with a UI automation script. One peer of the Hangouts call runs in a cloud server and the other peer on the phone initiates a call. For tasks such as choosing the contact, placing a call and ending the call, we use the AndroidViewClient library [5] that can perform UI automation over Android Debug Bridge (`adb`) tool[4]. This allows us to control the Google Hangouts sessions on the phone from the client controller described below. On the cloud peer a prerecorded video file is played through a virtual camera software (e2e Vcam software [12]) and is put as camera input to the Google Hangouts call. The video received on UE is screen recorded. The QoE of video is measured in terms of PSNR (Peak Signal-to-Noise Ratio) in dB [66]. PSNR measures the relative degradation in the frame quality between the sent and received videos.

Client Controller: Figure 6c shows all 10 UEs running a combination of the apps defined above. The apps are scheduled by a central controller that resides in the access-point (laptop), in case of the WiFi network, or PGW, in case of the LTE network. The clocks on UEs and the controller are synchronized with an NTP server. The controller communicates to the UEs, wirelessly, using the `adb` tool. The controller can start or stop any application on any of the UEs, including the Google Hangouts calls. It also periodically runs a `ping` command to the UEs and logs corresponding RTT values. It can also capture network traffic using `tcpdump`. The controller gives a systematic interface to conduct experiments on the mobile testbed. For example, in order to measure the ground truth for experiential capacity we need to run different number of web, streaming and video conferencing flows. The controller takes the traffic matrix (*#web*, *#stream*, *#videoconf*) as input and launches corresponding number of apps in terms of the number of flows belonging to the three different classes on a random subset of the UEs.

Traffic Patterns: We use two schemes to generate these traffic matrices:
(i) Random: This scheme considers completely random flow arrival/departure traffic pattern. Thus (*#web*, *#stream*, *#videoconf*) can change randomly and drastically.
(ii) LiveLab: To create more realistic traffic pattern we mined Rice University's LiveLab dataset [16]. This dataset has 34 users and application usage logs with ≈ 1.4 million entries. Each entry consists of the application name and the time it is triggered. It also contains the length of time the application was used. We filtered the set of application to a few limited ones that specifically indicated web (e.g., Opera, Safari, Chromium etc), video streaming (e.g., YouTube, Netflix etc.) or video conferencing activities (e.g., Google Hangouts, Skype etc.). Using this set of apps and their start and end time, we were able to compute the number of flows of each application class that are active simultaneously. This provided us with the traffic-matrix. We converged to ≈ 1700 traffic matrices of (*#web*, *#stream*, *#videoconf*), which are sorted in chronological order. Several traffic matrices do repeat in this set. In our experiments, we only consider those traffic matrices where total number of flows is less than 8 (LTE Network) or 10 (WiFi Network) due to limitation in our testbed. We assume that all users are present in the same network. We place all devices in high SNR locations. We evaluate diverse SNR scenarios later, using simulations.

5.3 Evaluation Results

We first evaluate the performance of Admittance Classifier. We run all the traffic matrices observed in the traffic schemes defined above, multiple times in each testbed. For every traffic matrix, we record *ground truth* QoE of each application running on each UE. If the QoE falls beneath a certain threshold (e.g., 3 secs page load time in case of web browsing) we deem that particular flow to be inadmissible in that traffic matrix. This gives us a large dataset of traffic matrices consisting of flows with acceptable as well as unacceptable QoE. Thereafter, we use a Python based implementation of Admittance Classifier, which does a trace based learning of *ExCR*. For each traffic pattern, Admittance Classifier trains the SVM with an initial set of traffic matrices (bootstrapping phase). In our experiments we observe that bootstrapping can be done with ≈ 50 samples, providing $0.5-0.6$ precision and recall at the end of bootstrap. Note that each sample in our evaluation represents a traffic matrix. As flows enter and leave the network, a new traffic matrix is recorded and added to the training set. Depending on the activity level in a network 50 samples could be observed over few hours or over a day. In networks with diverse and active users, different traffic matrices can be observed quickly, speeding up the bootstrapping phase in networks where admission control is most effective.

After bootstrapping phase, Admittance Classifier enters the Online Learning Phase, where it takes admission decision for each incoming flow. This is the testing phase. Note that Admittance Classifier also updates its model after a batch of flows has been admitted. We consider a batch size of 20 samples for WiFi experiments and a batch size of 10 samples for LTE experiments. We will present sensitivity results for batch size later in this section.

We also implement two commonly used schemes to serve as baselines in our evaluation.

(i) **RateBased**: This scheme considers a purely rate based admission control. This approach is used exclusively by many vendors (Cisco [9], Rukus [22]) and industry software (Microsoft [2]). It assumes the network capacity as C and rate requirements of each flow f as c_f. A new flow g is admitted in the network only when $C\text{-}\sum c_{\text{ongoing flows}} \geq c_g$. In our experiments we set C as the maximum UDP throughput measured in our WiFi and LTE testbeds.

(ii) **MaxClient**: This scheme admits up to a maximum number of flows and rejects all flows beyond that. In our experiments we set the maximum client limit to 10, as in [7] (Aruba Wireless) or [13] (IBM). This is also the maximum number of clients in our testbed.

Latency benchmarks: We benchmark the latencies incurred by the Admittance Classifiers for our python based implementation of ExBox, RateBased and MaxClient algorithms. The latency is measured as the time interval between the instant a new flow arrives and the admission decision (admit or reject) decision is taken on it. We use a HP ZBook equipped with 16 GB memory and a quad-core i7 processor for our benchmark study. For both RateBased and MaxClient the latencies are negligible (≤ 2 ms median latency). For ExBox, the median latency observed is ≈ 5 ms. Both RateBased and MaxClient do not involve an explicit training phase. However ExBox involves training Admittance Classifier (SVM based) both at the bootstrap phase and during online updates. Training the Admittance Classifier for ExBox with 50 samples takes ≈ 360 ms median latency. The training latency increases to more than 2 seconds when 1000 samples are considered. This is an artifact of our current implementation (e.g., choice of SVM kernel) and platform/libraries. For example, libraries such `libsvm` written in C have more a optimized implementation. A recent work on SVM optimization [36] actually argues that with increasing training size (number of samples) the latency incurred in building the classifier might actually *decrease* with the right implementation. Investigating SVM implementation options is somewhat tangential to our work. But evidently latency of the learning technique is a bottleneck in ExBox.

Macro results: We compare ExBox, RateBased and MaxClient using three well-known performance metrics: viz., *precision*, *recall* and *accuracy*. *Precision* is defined as the ratio of correctly admitted flows to the number of admitted flows, while *recall* is defined as the ratio of correctly admitted flows to the number of flows that could have been admitted. *Accuracy* refers to the overall fraction of correct decisions made (admit or reject). Intuitively, a high value of precision indicates that ExBox makes few mistakes in preserving the network QoE. However, a conservative admission control approach will also preserve QoE quite well (e.g., admit very few flows and reject everything else). The recall metric will catch such overly conservative behavior.

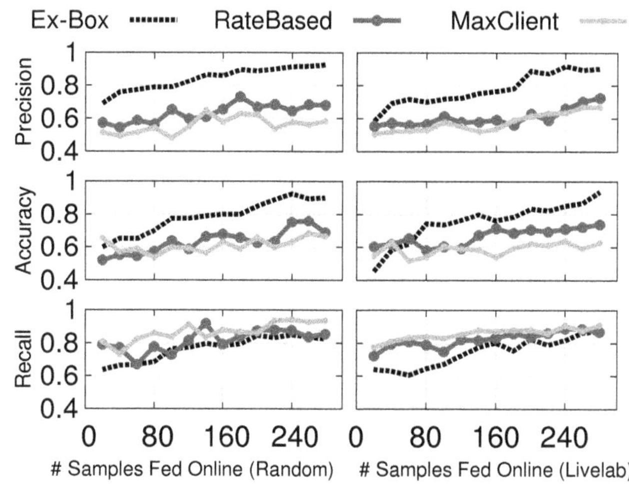

Figure 7: WiFi testbed results for Random Traffic and LiveLab traces, compared with baseline

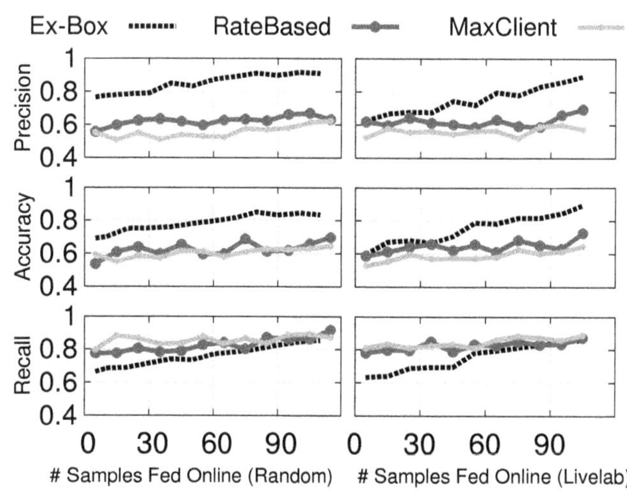

Figure 8: LTE testbed results for Random Traffic and LiveLab traces, compared with baseline

Figure 7 compares ExBox, RateBased and MaxClient with both Random and LiveLab traces on the WiFi testbed.

Compared to RateBased and MaxClient, ExBox always has higher precision ($\geq$ 0.8 mostly) and accuracy ($\geq$ 0.85 mostly), but a lower recall ($\leq$ 0.85 mostly). However, with more training (i.e., number of samples), its recall catches up with other approaches. In the context of admission control, accuracy is an important metric as it captures flows that have been correctly accepted and flows that have been correctly rejected, in order to maintain the QoE of existing users. ExBox has an accuracy of 0.6 with initial bootstrapping and it grows to 0.8 after 160 samples. At the same time, accuracy of RateBased and MaxClient stays less than 0.7. Figure 8 shows similar results for the three approaches on the LTE testbed. Across both networks, the random scheme shows better results than LiveLab traces, as random scheme provides more diverse training.

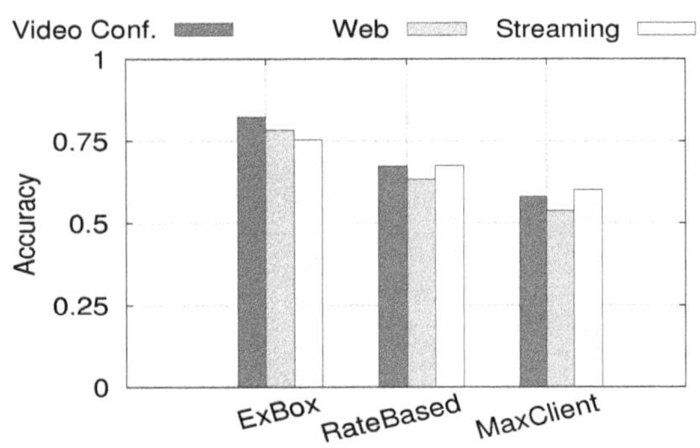

(a) Accuracy in WiFi Network

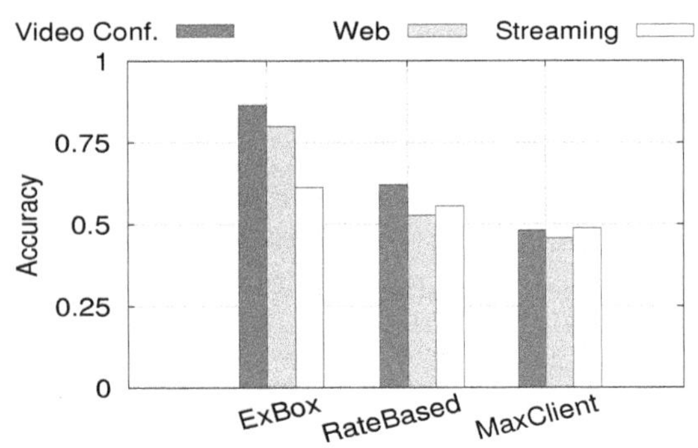

(b) Accuracy in LTE Network

Figure 9: Accuracy per application type

Micro results: We further compare the performance of ExBox, RateBased and MaxClient for each application class. Figure 9 compares the accuracy of video conferencing, web and streaming for Random traffic on both the networks. Here, accuracy is computed as the fraction of flows of each application which were correctly *admitted* or *rejected*. ExBox performs better than other baselines for all applications. Its accuracy for streaming is closer to RateBased as streaming is a rate-sensitive application. But for delay-sensitive applications such as web and video conferencing, ExBox performs significantly better.

Sensitivity to batch size: While the macro-results shown above consider a single batch-size for updating Admittance

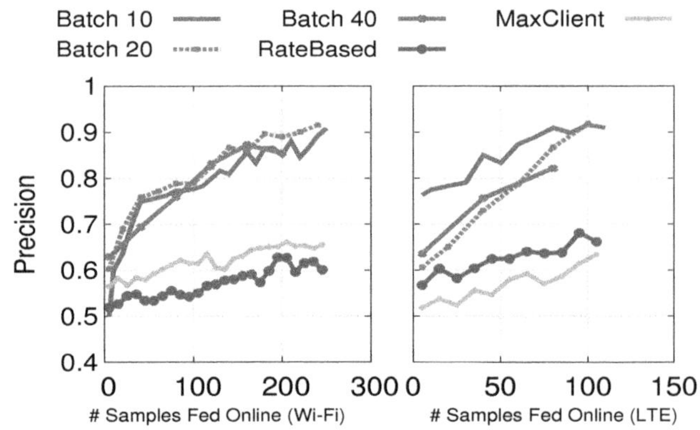

Figure 10: Sensitivity to batch size: WiFi and LTE

Classifier, we also tested Admittance Classifier with varying batch-sizes. Figure 10 shows the precision for batch sizes of 10, 20 and 40. The Admittance Classifier performance is sensitive to the batch size. Size 20 works better for the WiFi network while size 10 works better for the LTE network. The RateBased and MaxClient approaches are not sensitive to batch size as they do not have any online updates. Thus, we only present one plot for each of them. Note that Admittance Classifier has higher precision than others for all batch sizes.

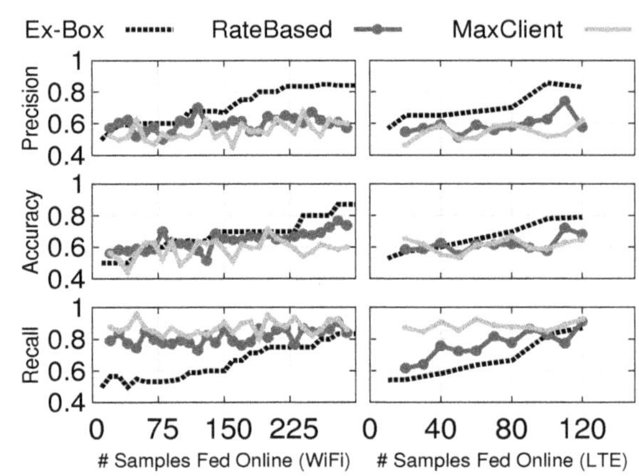

Figure 11: Admittance Classifier performance when network behavior changes in WiFi and LTE testbeds

Adapting to network changes: In the macro results, we make sure that the wireless network does not experience any fluctuations in data rate and latency. Now, we evaluate Admittance Classifier when network behavior fluctuates. We run the traffic matrices from both Random and LiveLab traffic in a throttled WiFi and LTE network (using `tc` utility). In Figure 11, we bootstrap the classifier using 10% data points from the unthrottled network and then start testing the model from a traffic-shaped network with a latency of 200 ms. Note that the initial performance is extremely poor (precision $\approx$ 0.5), however with subsequent batches the model adapts to the network condition. With 200+ data points in WiFi it catches up to precision level of

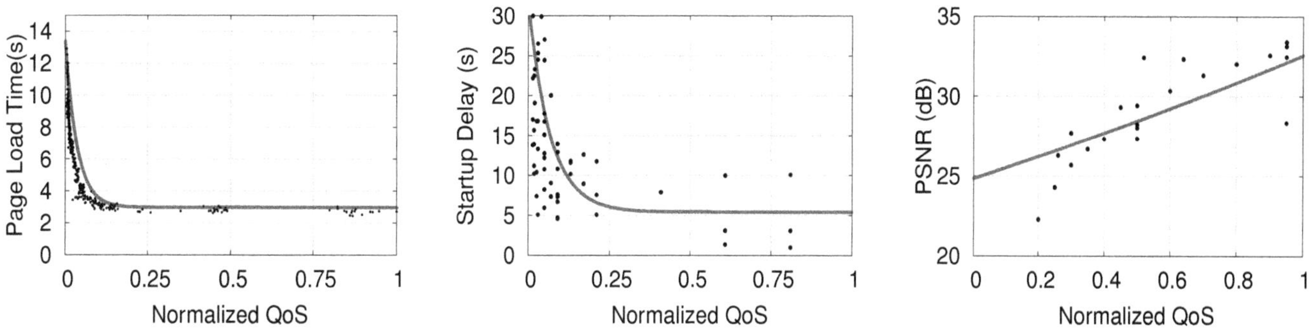

(a) Web QoE IQX (RMSE 1.37s) (b) Video Streaming QoE IQX (RMSE 3.64s) (c) Video conf. QoE IQX (RMSE 4.462dB)

Figure 12: Fitting the IQX Equation for Web, Video Streaming and Video Conferencing flows

≈ 0.8. ExBox over LTE adapts faster. This shows the necessity of the online updates and how ExBox adapts to fluctuating environments [57].

Estimating QoE using IQX: As discussed in Section 3, ExBox uses IQX hypothesis to estimate per-application QoE. We now show empirical evidence of the same. We use `tc` utility to vary the data rate from 100 Kbps to 20 Mbps and latency from 10 ms to 250 ms in our WiFi network setup. For each data rate-latency profile we run each of the three applications defined earlier 10 times on a single client. This is the *training device* shown in Figure 5. In every run we record the relevant QoE metrics on the client and the QoS metrics on the controller. In our experiments, QoS is modeled as the ratio of average throughput to delay.

Figure 12 shows the relationship between QoS and achieved QoE for the Web Browsing app, Video conferencing app (Google Hangouts) and Video Streaming (YouTube) app. For each of these applications, we fit the IQX equation (1) and evaluate the parameters α, β and γ by using the *least squares* approach. The three different fits (web, video streaming and conferencing) show the differing nature of these applications. The IQX relationship learnt here is used by ExBox to estimate QoE purely from the network traces in the simulations in next section. This experiment demonstrates the suitability of the IQX hypothesis. Different applications may have different IQX models that the network administrator needs knowledge of. However this exercise is not prohibitive as the number of popular application classes within a network (say, an enterprise) is limited. A more rigorous study of IQX is part of our future work.

6. SCALE UP STUDY

The E-40 eNodeB in our testbed only supports a maximum of 8 users and the WiFi card on the laptop could not handle more than 10 users. However, real campus and office networks can have up to 50 concurrently active users [8]. To evaluate ExBox in more populous networks, we perform a scaled up study through network simulator `ns-3` [18]. We simulate both WiFi and LTE networks using `ns-3` and feed in real application traces to generate traffic on these networks. As the simulation progresses, we collect QoS information and compute QoE using IQX. The network simulation setup and traffic generation are described below.

6.1 Simulation Setup

WiFi network: We simulate an 802.11n 5GHz Wireless LAN with varying number of clients connected to the Internet through an access point (AP). The AP is connected to three remote servers (Server 1, Server 2 and Server 3) through a 1 Gbps link and 0.3 ms delay. We do not consider wide area network delays in the simulation, as we focus on the WLAN dynamics alone. With the increasing penetration of content delivery networks, last-hop networks are becoming more dominant in application performance. Similar to the testbed study, these simulations also consider three application classes: video conferencing, web browsing and video streaming. So the traffic matrices considered here are in the space $<a_{\text{web}}, a_{\text{streaming}}, a_{\text{conferencing}}>$. For each such traffic matrix, $a_{\text{web}} + a_{\text{streaming}} + a_{\text{conferencing}}$ wireless clients are simulated in the network, each with one flow. One remote server is assigned to each of the three application classes. All clients for one application class connect to the same remote server. Note that we do not split the application classes in different SNR levels as all clients are in high SNR location, unless mentioned otherwise.

LTE network: We simulate an indoor LTE network in `ns-3` with an eNodeB having 23 dBm transmit power, connected to the Internet through a Packet Data Network Gateway (PGW). The PGW connects to three remote servers, each supporting one application class. For each traffic matrix $<a_{\text{web}}, a_{\text{streaming}}, a_{\text{conferencing}}>$, $a_{\text{web}} + a_{\text{streaming}} + a_{\text{conferencing}}$ LTE user equipment (UE) nodes are simulated in the network, each with one flow. All clients for one application class connect to the same remote server. All clients are in high CQI location, unless mentioned otherwise.

6.2 Traffic Generation

In our simulations, all the wireless clients connect to one of three remote servers either over WiFi or LTE network. To simulate a realistic mix of application flows in the network, we need a traffic generator which can accurately simulate diverse application behavior. As `ns-3` does not support sophisticated traffic generators, we leverage real packet traces. In the topologies described above, each of the three simulated remote servers is configured to have a Tap interface [24]. This tap interface connects to the local host through a bridge. We feed in real traffic traces of different application types to these tap interfaces and eventually, into the simulated wireless network. For Video Conferencing, we record a packet trace of an ongoing Skype Video Call and extract 30 seconds of the trace. Similarly, for web browsing and video streaming, we capture the packet trace while loading BBC webpage on Chrome browser and while playing high-definition videos on YouTube, respectively.

For a traffic matrix <a_{web}, $a_{\text{streaming}}$, $a_{\text{conferencing}}$>, the traffic generator creates a_{web} instances of the BBC packet trace, merges them and injects the merged trace to the tap interface of Server 1. Similarly, it also creates $a_{\text{streaming}}$ ($a_{\text{conferencing}}$) instances of the YouTube (Skype) trace, merges them and injects the merged trace to tap interface of Server 2 (Server 3). We use the `tcpreplay` suite to modify the packet headers in the real traces to comply with `ns-3` IP and MAC address space. Note that we only use the downlink flows in our simulation. So for Skype, we only capture one-way video conferencing traffic.

For brevity, we do not present scale up studies for all traffic schemes discussed in previous section on all wireless networks. Instead, we present one scheme and one network for each scale up study. The results are similar in other schemes.

6.3 ExBox in Mixed SNR Scenarios

All the experiments in the testbed have all the phones in high SNR location. Since adding the SNR diversity in the traffic matrices explodes the search space, we perform these tests in simulation. We run the LiveLab traffic trace over the simulated 802.11n WLAN. Additionally, for each new flow, we randomly position the client in a high SNR ($\approx$53 dB) or a low SNR ($\approx$23 dB) location. This generates a large dataset ($\approx$21000 samples) of X_m: <$a_{\text{web,high}}$, $a_{\text{web,low}}$, $a_{\text{streaming,high}}$, $a_{\text{streaming,low}}$, $a_{\text{conferencing,high}}$, $a_{\text{conferencing,low}}$, c, l> for flow m of class c and SNR level s_l. The $Y_m \in \{-1, +1\}$ is computed by using the IQX model. We compare ExBox, RateBased and MaxClient on this large dataset of mixed SNR flows. Figure 13 shows the precision results for all three approaches with varying batch sizes. ExBox gives more than 0.8 precision. This is because we could bootstrap with a larger training set here, which is the case in populous, diverse networks. Also note that the batch sizes in this case are larger than the ones in testbed, implying less frequent updates to the model. The batch updates further improve the precision to 0.95. The precision for RateBased stays around 0.65 throughout.

6.4 ExBox in Populous Networks

We simulate multiple traffic matrices with $a_{\text{web}} \in [0, 50]$, $a_{\text{streaming}} \in [0, 50]$ and $a_{\text{conferencing}} \in [0, 50]$. For each traffic matrix, the simulation runs for 16 seconds and we record the QoS observed by each flow. Similar to the testbed study, each run is captured as the tuple X_m : <a_{web}, $a_{\text{streaming}}$, $a_{\text{conferencing}}$, j> and label Y_m, where $j \in \{1, 2, 3\}$. Here Y_m represents the QoE (calculated from IQX) of flow m of application class j in the given traffic matrix. Note that X_m has fewer dimensions here than previous simulations as all clients are in high SNR locations.

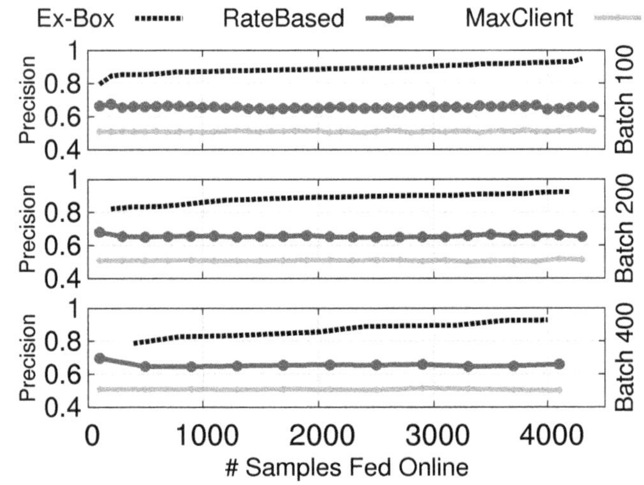

Figure 13: ExBox performance with diverse SNR, compared with baselines

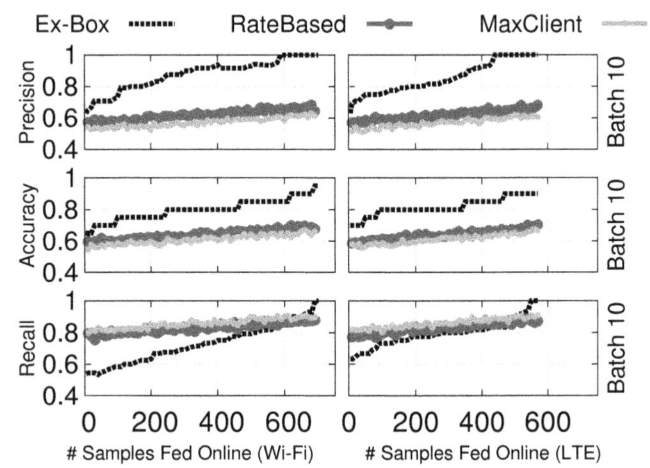

Figure 14: Precision, Accuracy and Recall for admission control in `ns-3` Wi-Fi and LTE simulations

To simulate populous networks we only consider traffic matrices with more than 20 simultaneous flows in WiFi. From these traffic matrices, we generate multiple random sets of 800 (X_m, Y_m) each for our analysis. Figure 14 shows the performance of ExBox with initial training using 10% (80) of the data points. We calculate the *precision*, *accuracy* and *recall* metrics on each batch of data. The model then learns from the flows admitted in that batch, as explained in the previous section. Similar to the testbed results, the performance of ExBox is sensitive to batch size of online updates. The left half of Figure 14 presents results on WiFi network. ExBox has a good precision rate ($\approx$0.9), compared to RateBased and MaxClient, indicating the model did a right job if it admitted a flow. However recall being slightly lower indicates the model behaves conservatively. Note that, like the testbed, a small batch size of 10 is needed for this network as there is no SNR diversity.

The right half of Figure 14 shows the same analysis for LTE network with the LiveLab traces. Here, we do not restrict the total number of flows to be less than 8. Thus, we simulate all unique traffic matrices encountered in the LiveLab traces over LTE network and record 650 different (X_m, Y_m) tuples. With more than 100 samples fed online the classifier's precision reaches to ≈ 0.8 and it improves further on to ≈ 0.9 with 400+ samples fed online. Recall is ≈ 0.75. Similar to our testbed experiments, the Admittance Classifier performs better in LTE than in WiFi.

7. RELATED WORK

There is a huge body of prior work on admission control and network capacity modeling. In this section, we place our work with respect to the current state-of-the-art, which can be broadly categorized as follows:

Flow classification: ExBox assumes a priori knowledge of the application class to which a flow belongs. It thus relies on traffic flow classification techniques. Recent literature has already explored an array of such classification techniques with modest accuracy figures. Some of them handle real-time traffic classification using machine learning techniques [30, 27] while some others focus on classifying encrypted traffic [32, 49].

QoE as a performance metric: The notion of QoE has been around for a long time. Chen *et al.* [37] model Skype QoE in terms of rate, delay and jitter. Balachandran *et al.* leverage Machine Learning to capture cross-layer features that impact web QoE [28] and video QoE [29, 43]. QoE-Doctor [38] extends QoE modeling to mobile applications. However, they require modifications on the device to learn QoE accurately. Authors in [26] propose to model mobile application QoE from passive network measurements, but still require human training to build the model. In this work we leverage the IQX hypothesis [44] that provides a generic relationship between QoE and QoS. The strength of IQX lies in its applicability to different application classes. Our testbed experiments show that it can learn QoE-QoS relationship with minimal human involvement.

Capacity and admission control: In the past decade and half, a significant body of work has been invested in understanding capacity regions of various forms of wireless networks [65, 51, 45]. However, these studies focus on QoS as the predominant performance metric. With recent proliferation of the *app-based* ecosystem we argue QoE as a more suitable metric to measure network capacity. We are not alone in this argument. Song *et al.* [63] proposed a probabilistic admission control parameter for integrated cellular/WLAN networks by modeling QoE, in terms of delay and rate, in these networks. However, they require meticulous modeling of traffic arrival and contention procedure in each network. Similarly, Piamrat *et al.* [59] proposed QoE-aware admission control for simultaneous video calls in 802.11 networks. However, they only consider video calls in their traffic pattern, which is an over-simplification of the traffic mix found in today's networks. In contrast, ExBox aims to define *experiential capacity region* for diverse mix of application flows in dynamic wireless networks. We foresee ExBox to be easily deployed in operational networks.

Experience-oriented architecture: Recently, Jiang *et al.* [48] have proposed an experience-oriented network architecture wherein application providers and network providers collaborate to provide better user experience. Their work is complementary to ours as they try to diminish the administrative boundaries in order to guarantee better QoE to end users.

8. CONCLUSIONS

In this work, we motivate the need to define network capacity in terms of QoE, and not QoS. We define an *experiential capacity region*, which consists of flows of diverse applications and diverse channel quality, all with acceptable QoE. We propose ExBox, a middlebox which can learn the *experiential capacity* of a network, through in-network QoE estimation and machine learning. ExBox also adapts to changing network environments and continues to learn the experiential capacity. Our evaluation in a WiFi testbed and LTE testbed shows that ExBox correctly admits the flows with a precision rate of $\approx 0.8 - 0.9$ and recall rate of $\approx 0.6 - 0.8$. As part of future work, we plan to evaluate ExBox on a large scale testbed with multiple WiFi and LTE cells.

9. ACKNOWLEDGEMENTS

The authors would like to thank Abhinav Parate for helping in the initial problem formulation. and the paper's shepherd Patrick Thiran for guiding the camera-ready version. This work was partially supported by NSF award AST-1443951.

10. REFERENCES

[1] 3GPP Specification: Self Organizing Networks. http://www.3gpp.org/DynaReport/32500.htm.
[2] Admission control in Skype for Business Server, Microsoft. https://technet.microsoft.com/en-us/library/gg398529.aspx.
[3] Amazon instant video forum. http://amzn.to/2df0kdy.
[4] Android Debug Bridge (adb). developer.android.com/tools/help/adb.html.
[5] Android view client. https://github.com/dtmilano/AndroidViewClient/wiki.
[6] Aruba mobility controllers for next-gen networks. www.arubanetworks.com/products/networking/controllers/.
[7] Aruba: Working with QoS for voice and video. http://bit.ly/2eNeGCq.
[8] Benchmark 802.11ac Wave 2 performance. http://blog.mojonetworks.com/benchmark-802.11ac-wave-2-performance.
[9] Cisco admission control solutions. http://bit.ly/261Wx8y.

[10] Cisco network admission control. http://www.cisco.com/c/en/us/solutions/enterprise-networks/network-admission-control/index.html.

[11] Cisco SON architecture. www.cisco.com/c/en/us/solutions/service-provider/son-architecture/index.html.

[12] E2E Virtual Camera Software. http://www.e2esoft.cn/vcam/.

[13] IBM admission control solutions. http://ibm.co/1ZWXBU0.

[14] IP flow mobility and seamless wireless local area network (WLAN) offload. ww.3gpp.org/DynaReport/23261.htm.

[15] ip.access:lte. http://www.ipaccess.com/en/lte.

[16] LiveLab dataset from Rice University. http://livelab.recg.rice.edu/traces.html.

[17] Miercom wireless controller comparative performance. http://bit.ly/2eNdMWu.

[18] ns-3 simulator. www.nsnam.org.

[19] OpenEPC. http://www.openepc.com/.

[20] Qualcomm extends LTE to unlicensed spectrum to enhance mobile experiences. http://bit.ly/1XYoJ8i.

[21] Qualcomm WiFi SON. www.qualcomm.com/videos/qualcomm-wi-fi-son.

[22] Rukus WiFi calling. http://www.ruckussecurity.com/Wi-Fi-Calling.asp.

[23] The Evolved Packet Core - 3GPP. http://www.3gpp.org/technologies/keywords-acronyms/100-the-evolved-packet-core.

[24] Universal tun/tap device driver. https://www.kernel.org/doc/Documentation/networking/tuntap.txt.

[25] YouTube Android Player API. https://developers.google.com/youtube/android/player/.

[26] AGGARWAL, V., HALEPOVIC, E., PANG, J., VENKATARAMAN, S., AND YAN, H. Prometheus: Toward quality-of-experience estimation for mobile apps from passive network measurements. In *Proc. ACM MobiSys 2014.*

[27] ALSHAMMARI, R., AND ZINCIR-HEYWOOD, A. N. Machine learning based encrypted traffic classification: Identifying SSH and Skype. *CISDA 9* (2009).

[28] BALACHANDRAN, A., AGGARWAL, V., HALEPOVIC, E., PANG, J., SESHAN, S., VENKATARAMAN, S., AND YAN, H. Modeling web quality-of-experience on cellular networks. In *Proc. ACM Mobicom 2014.*

[29] BALACHANDRAN, A., SEKAR, V., AKELLA, A., SESHAN, S., STOICA, I., AND ZHANG, H. Developing a predictive model of quality of experience for internet video. In *ACM SIGCOMM Computer Communication Review* (2013), vol. 43, ACM, pp. 339–350.

[30] BAR-YANAI, R., LANGBERG, M., PELEG, D., AND RODITTY, L. Realtime classification for encrypted traffic. In *International Symposium on Experimental Algorithms* (2010), Springer, pp. 373–385.

[31] BARI, F., AND LEUNG, V. Automated network selection in a heterogeneous wireless network environment. *Network, IEEE 21*, 1 (2007), 34–40.

[32] BERNAILLE, L., TEIXEIRA, R., AKODKENOU, I., SOULE, A., AND SALAMATIAN, K. Traffic classification on the fly. *SIGCOMM Computer Communication Review 36*, 2 (2006), 23–26.

[33] BERNAILLE, L., TEIXEIRA, R., AND SALAMATIAN, K. Early application identification. In *Proc. ACM CoNEXT 2006.*

[34] BISWAS, S., BICKET, J., WONG, E., MUSALOIU-E, R., BHARTIA, A., AND AGUAYO, D. Large-scale measurements of wireless network behavior. In *Proc. ACM SIGCOMM 2015.*

[35] CHANDRA, R., AND BAHL, P. Multinet: Connecting to multiple IEEE 802.11 networks using a single wireless card. In *Proc. IEEE INFOCOM 2004.*

[36] CHAPELLE, O. Training a support vector machine in the primal. *Neural computation 19*, 5 (2007), 1155–1178.

[37] CHEN, K.-T., HUANG, C.-Y., HUANG, P., AND LEI, C.-L. Quantifying Skype user satisfaction. In *Proc. ACM SIGCOMM 2006.*

[38] CHEN, Q. A., LUO, H., ROSEN, S., MAO, Z. M., IYER, K., HUI, J., SONTINENI, K., AND LAU, K. QoE doctor: Diagnosing mobile app QoE with automated UI control and cross-layer analysis. In *Proceedings of the 2014 Conference on Internet Measurement Conference* (2014), IMC '14, ACM, pp. 151–164.

[39] CHEN, Y., FARLEY, T., AND YE, N. QoS requirements of network applications on the Internet. *Inf. Knowl. Syst. Manag. 4*, 1 (Jan. 2004), 55–76.

[40] CORTES, C., AND VAPNIK, V. Support-vector networks. *Machine learning 20*, 3 (1995), 273–297.

[41] DAI, S., TONGAONKAR, A., WANG, X., NUCCI, A., AND SONG, D. Networkprofiler: Towards automatic fingerprinting of android apps. In *Proc. IEEE INFOCOM 2013.*

[42] DAINOTTI, A., PESCAPÉ, A., AND SANSONE, C. Early classification of network traffic through multi-classification. In *Proceedings of the Third International Conference on Traffic Monitoring and Analysis* (2011), TMA'11, pp. 122–135.

[43] DOBRIAN, F., SEKAR, V., AWAN, A., STOICA, I., JOSEPH, D., GANJAM, A., ZHAN, J., AND ZHANG, H. Understanding the impact of video quality on user engagement. In *ACM SIGCOMM Computer Communication Review* (2011), vol. 41, ACM, pp. 362–373.

[44] FIEDLER, M., HOSSFELD, T., AND TRAN-GIA, P. A generic quantitative relationship between quality of experience and quality of service. *Network, IEEE 24*, 2 (March 2010), 36–41.

[45] GASTPAR, M., AND VETTERLI, M. On the capacity of wireless networks: The relay case. In *Proc. IEEE INFOCOM 2002.*

[46] HIGGINS, B. D., REDA, A., ALPEROVICH, T., FLINN, J., GIULI, T. J., NOBLE, B., AND WATSON, D. Intentional networking: Opportunistic exploitation of mobile network diversity. In *Proc. ACM Mobicom 2010.*

[47] HUANG, N.-F., JAI, G.-Y., CHAO, H.-C., TZANG, Y.-J., AND CHANG, H.-Y. Application traffic classification at the early stage by characterizing application rounds. *Inf. Sci. 232* (May 2013), 130–142.

[48] JIANG, J., LIU, X., SEKAR, V., STOICA, I., AND ZHANG, H. Eona: Experience-oriented network architecture. In *Proc. ACM HotNets 2014.*

[49] KARAGIANNIS, T., PAPAGIANNAKI, K., AND FALOUTSOS, M. Blinc: multilevel traffic classification in the dark. In *ACM SIGCOMM*

Computer Communication Review (2005), vol. 35, ACM, pp. 229–240.

[50] KIM, K. H., AND SHIN, K. G. Prism: Improving the performance of inverse-multiplexed TCP in wireless networks. *IEEE Transactions on Mobile Computing 6*, 12 (Dec 2007), 1297–1312.

[51] KODIALAM, M., AND NANDAGOPAL, T. Characterizing the capacity region in multi-radio multi-channel wireless mesh networks. In *Proc. ACM Mobicom 2005*.

[52] LASKOV, P., GEHL, C., KRÜGER, S., AND MÜLLER, K.-R. Incremental support vector learning: Analysis, implementation and applications. *Journal of machine learning research 7*, Sep (2006), 1909–1936.

[53] LEONG, C. W., ZHUANG, W., CHENG, Y., AND WANG, L. Call admission control for integrated on/off voice and best-effort data services in mobile cellular communications. *Communications, IEEE Transactions on 52*, 5 (2004), 778–790.

[54] LI, W., AND MOORE, A. W. A machine learning approach for efficient traffic classification. In *2007 15th International Symposium on Modeling, Analysis, and Simulation of Computer and Telecommunication Systems* (Oct 2007), pp. 310–317.

[55] MAHINDRA, R., VISWANATHAN, H., SUNDARESAN, K., ARSLAN, M. Y., AND RANGARAJAN, S. A practical traffic management system for integrated LTE-WiFi networks. In *Proc. ACM Mobicom 2014*.

[56] NAGHSHINEH, M., AND ACAMPORA, A. S. QOS provisioning in micro-cellular networks supporting multimedia traffic. In *Proc. IEEE INFOCOM 1995*.

[57] PEFKIANAKIS, I., LUNDGREN, H., SOULE, A., CHANDRASHEKAR, J., LE GUYADEC, P., DIOT, C., MAY, M., VAN DOORSELAER, K., AND VAN OOST, K. Characterizing home wireless performance: The gateway view. In *Proc. IEEE INFOCOM 2015*.

[58] PENG, L., YANG, B., CHEN, Y., AND CHEN, Z. Effectiveness of statistical features for early stage internet traffic identification. *Int. J. Parallel Program. 44*, 1 (Feb. 2016), 181–197.

[59] PIAMRAT, K., KSENTINI, A., VIHO, C., AND BONNIN, J. QoE-Aware Admission Control for Multimedia Applications in IEEE 802.11 Wireless Networks. In *Vehicular Technology Conference, 2008. VTC 2008-Fall. IEEE 68th* (Sept 2008), pp. 1–5.

[60] QIAN, F., WANG, Z., GERBER, A., MAO, Z., SEN, S., AND SPATSCHECK, O. Profiling resource usage for mobile applications: a cross-layer approach. In *Proc. ACM MobiSys 2011*.

[61] SHAFIQ, M. Z., ERMAN, J., JI, L., LIU, A. X., PANG, J., AND WANG, J. Understanding the impact of network dynamics on mobile video user engagement. In *ACM SIGMETRICS Performance Evaluation Review* (2014), vol. 42, ACM, pp. 367–379.

[62] SHIN, S., AND SCHULZRINNE, H. Experimental measurement of the capacity for voip traffic in IEEE 802.11 wlans. In *Proc. INFOCOM 2007*.

[63] SONG, W., CHENG, Y., AND ZHUANG, W. Improving voice and data services in cellular/wlan integrated networks by admission control. *Wireless Communications, IEEE Transactions on 6*, 11 (2007), 4025–4037.

[64] TAX, D. M., AND LASKOV, P. Online SVM learning: from classification to data description and back. In *Neural Networks for Signal Processing, 2003. NNSP'03. 2003 IEEE 13th Workshop on* (2003), IEEE, pp. 499–508.

[65] TOUMPIS, S., AND GOLDSMITH, A. J. Capacity regions for wireless ad hoc networks. *Wireless Communications, IEEE Transactions on 2*, 4 (2003), 736–748.

[66] VELDHUIZEN, T. Measures of image quality. *CVonline: The Evolving, Distributed, Non-Proprietary, On-Line Compendium of Computer Vision* (2010).

[67] YANG, B., HOU, G., RUAN, L., XUE, Y., AND LI, J. Smiler: Towards practical online traffic classification. In *Architectures for Networking and Communications Systems (ANCS), 2011 Seventh ACM/IEEE Symposium on* (Oct 2011), pp. 178–188.

[68] ZARINNI, F., CHAKRABORTY, A., SEKAR, V., DAS, S. R., AND GILL, P. A first look at performance in mobile virtual network operators. In *Proc. ACM IMC 2014*.

[69] ZHANG, J., CHEN, X., XIANG, Y., ZHOU, W., AND WU, J. Robust network traffic classification. *IEEE/ACM Transactions on Networking 23*, 4 (Aug 2015), 1257–1270.

AmorFi: Amorphous WiFi Networks for High-density Deployments

Ramanujan K Sheshadri[1], Mustafa Y. Arslan[2], Karthikeyan Sundaresan[2],
Sampath Rangarajan[2], and Dimitrios Koutsonikolas[1]
[1]University at Buffalo, SUNY
[2]NEC Laboratories America, Inc.
{ramanuja, dimitrio}@buffalo.edu
{marslan, karthiks, sampath}@nec-labs.com

ABSTRACT

The static capacity provisioning in traditional WiFi networks (WLANs) cannot cope with the high spatiotemporal traffic variations in high-density venues such as conference centers, stadiums etc. To guarantee reliable performance, venue owners are forced to over-provision their WLANs based on worst-case traffic demand estimations, increasing capital and operational expenses. We propose AmorFi, a radically new way of deploying WLANs to handle peak traffic demands with average-case provisioning. Our key idea is to decouple baseband processing from RF transmission (inspired by the cloud-RAN concept in cellular networks) and introduce software programmability to flexibly allocate WiFi capacity in real time based on varying traffic demands. We implement AmorFi using off-the-shelf WiFi APs over a RF-over-fiber cloud-RAN testbed. Our experiments and simulations demonstrate that the software-defined capacity allocation enabled with AmorFi delivers more than $2x$ throughput than traditional WLANs.

CCS Concepts

•**Networks** → **Wireless local area networks;**

Keywords

WLAN; Cloud RAN; Testbeds

1. INTRODUCTION

Despite the large WiFi deployment footprint and technological advances such as beamforming and MIMO, WiFi experience is still far from ideal in high-density venues such as conference/event centers, stadiums, airports etc., where thousands of users demand reliable wireless service at once. The root cause of this problem is the disconnect between fixed WiFi provisioning (where the capacity is allocated a priori) and the high spatiotemporal traffic variation characteristically found in such venues.

State-of-the-art: Current WLANs in high-density venues are planned based on estimated per-user bandwidth requirements. Once an aggregate throughput requirement is determined for a particular area, the next step is to decide on the number of APs to provide the required capacity and assign channels to address inter-AP interference [15, 39]. The traffic demand is then distributed across the APs that serve the given area, using load balancing techniques.

When a traffic surge exceeds the planned capacity allocation, WiFi performance quickly deteriorates since it is virtually impossible to provide additional capacity in a reasonable time. To ensure reliable network-wide performance, venue owners are often forced to over-provision their WLANs based on worst-case traffic estimations, leading to increased equipment and maintenance costs [38]. In short, there is no efficient way for WLANs to adapt to changing traffic patterns other than manually deploying more APs (which is impractical) or worst-case provisioning (which is expensive).

In addition to the lack of adaptive capacity provisioning, today's WLANs also face the challenge of efficiently delivering broadcast traffic at a large scale. With the growing consumer interest in video applications (e.g., watching HD replays in stadiums), venues often feel the pressure to support wireless broadcast but do not have the mechanisms to do so efficiently [24, 27]. Traditional WLANs are known to exhibit many problems associated with broadcast traffic especially when it coexists with unicast applications such as e-mail and social media [10]. In this paper, we thus seek to answer the following question: *Can we satisfy worst-case traffic demands with average-case provisioning by allowing WLANs to change their capacity distribution in real time and support a heterogeneous mix of unicast (e.g., file download) and broadcast (e.g., live TV) applications?* To answer in the affirmative, we draw inspiration from a popular concept in cellular industry - cloud radio access networks or C-RANs.

CoNEXT '16, December 12-15, 2016, Irvine, CA, USA
© 2016 ACM. ISBN 978-1-4503-4292-6/16/12...$15.00
DOI: http://dx.doi.org/10.1145/2999572.2999586

A Potential Solution: The core idea in a C-RAN is to decouple radio frequency transmissions from baseband processing. This allows for multiple light-weight remote radio heads (RRHs) to be deployed for RF transmission, while the baseband processing is handled in a central processing cluster (i.e., a data center). The RRHs and the processing cluster is connected via a low-delay optical fiber network called the C-RAN front-haul (see Figure 1). The front-haul is the critical component that defines how the baseband processing units (BPUs) are mapped to RRHs, thus defining the capacity distribution across the network.

A given RRH supports simultaneous mappings from multiple BPUs. In a C-RAN-based WLAN, this would mean that multiple APs (acting as BPUs) can be mapped to the same RRH albeit on orthogonal channels. Note that since the C-RAN decouples an AP's capacity from its actual physical location, any AP can be mapped to any set of RRHs (not possible in a traditional WLAN). Thus, the C-RAN architecture allows dynamic re-purposing of capacity through appropriate re-configuration of the front-haul, thereby obviating the need for worst-case provisioning.

A Unique Benefit for WiFi: Unlike a cellular network, wherein each base station and user can communicate on multiple channels concurrently (i.e., carrier aggregation), this is not possible in WLANs. Even if latest WiFi clients support channel bonding up to 160 MHz in the 5 GHz band with 802.11ac APs, the legacy ones (11a/b/g/n clients) support 40 MHz bandwidth at most. Thus, legacy clients limit the effective bandwidth of the AP and create a performance bottleneck, warranting the deployment of as many APs as needed to use up all the orthogonal channels in the band (i.e., worst-case provisioning). C-RAN makes it possible to add radio resources (on different channels) to a RRH on the fly, allowing to borrow capacity from under-utilized areas of the network and use it to address the traffic surge where needed (i.e., avoiding over-provisioning and mitigating wastage).

Challenges: While adopting the C-RAN model in WLANs is a welcome step, the key challenge is orchestrating the C-RAN front-haul in real time to track and adapt to the spatiotemporal traffic fluctuations, so as to maximize the supported traffic demand. Further, with the increasing importance of wide-area broadcast applications (e.g., live sports replays [30]), the orchestration should consider unicast as well as broadcast traffic demands. While LTE has built-in support for wide-area broadcast [25], WiFi handles broadcast only at the cell level where each AP independently broadcasts the same content to its clients and contends for medium access (as it would for unicast traffic) [45]. If orchestrated properly, the front-haul has the potential to bring efficient wide-area broadcast support to WLANs. However, it is difficult to optimally satisfy both unicast and broadcast demands since each benefits from different front-haul configurations (detailed later in § 2).

AmorFi: We propose AmorFi ("Amorphous WiFi") – a first-of-its-kind C-RAN-based WLAN that adapts itself to cater to changing traffic demands (both unicast and broadcast). AmorFi realizes this through software-defined access (SDA), wherein it re-programs the C-RAN front-haul, to create different cell configurations in real time. In designing AmorFi , we leverage the full potential of the C-RAN architecture for WiFi and make the following key contributions.

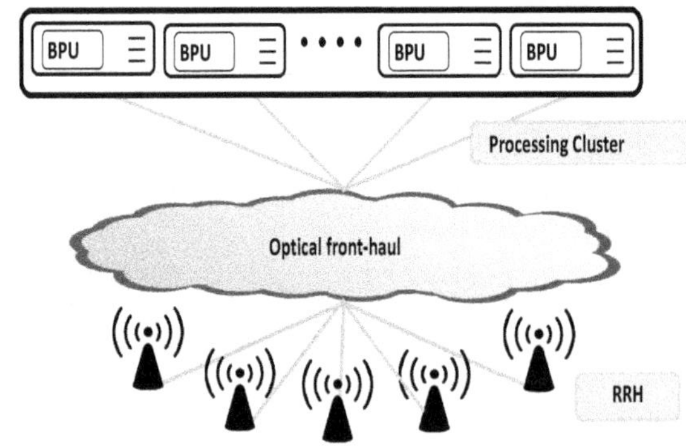

Figure 1: C-RAN architecture.

(1) Designing algorithms to determine the optimal front-haul configurations. Interference across WiFi APs (cells) is managed through CSMA and channel assignment. The latter is a hard problem in itself and requires taking into account interference conflicts between APs. The amorphous notion of cells in AmorFi makes this problem even more challenging. Further, we address an inherent tradeoff between wide-area coverage (useful for broadcast traffic efficiency) and spatial reuse (useful for unicast throughput) in determining the optimal configuration. AmorFi employs efficient algorithms to address this tradeoff and not only maximizes the traffic that can be supported, but also does so in an energy-efficient manner, employing a few BPUs.

(2) Deploying AmorFi in practice. This is challenging due to the lack of SDA support in today's WLANs. SDA requires AmorFi to re-map the signals on the fly from any AP (BPU) to any remote antenna (RRH), with negligible latency. We realize this in the analog domain using RF-over-fiber technology and use an optical switch to apply the desired front-haul configurations in real time. Using a testbed of four APs and four RRHs, we comprehensively evaluate AmorFi for both unicast and broadcast (video) applications. Our results indicate that AmorFi delivers twice the throughput supported by baseline schemes and supports a higher quality broadcast video. We also complement our testbed evaluations with large-scale simulations to demonstrate AmorFi 's performance in larger deployments. A case study with IEEE Globecom 2003 attendance data reveals that AmorFi increases the median user throughput by more than 100%.

2. C-RAN BASED WLAN: AN OVERVIEW

2.1 Background

The C-RAN architecture (see Fig. 1) consists of the following components: **Processing Cluster:** centrally located baseband processing units (BPUs) responsible for signal processing and providing capacity. **Front-haul:** an optical fiber network that supports wavelength multiplexing to deliver the

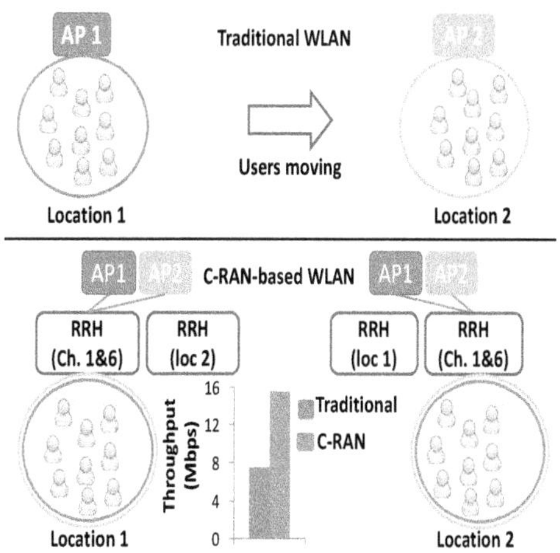

Figure 2: Repurposing capacity in C-RAN-based WLANs.

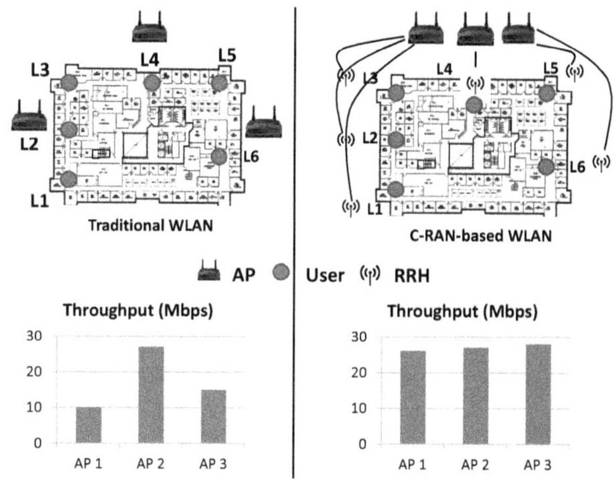

Figure 3: Larger AP coverage in C-RAN-based WLAN.

signals between the BPUs and remote antennas (RRHs), using either (a) CPRI (Common Public Radio Interface) - an interface standard for transmitting digitized IQ samples, or (b) RF-over-fiber, where analog RF is carried over the fiber. **Remote Radio Heads (RRHs):** light-weight antennas that convert optical signals to RF on the downlink (and RF to optical for uplink), providing wireless access to users. The front-haul is perhaps the most critical component that defines how the capacity of the BPUs is distributed across the RRHs. Next, we describe how a software programmable front-haul would help a C-RAN-based WLAN handle various scenarios that are challenging for traditional WLANs.

2.2 Architectural Advantages

We demonstrate the benefits of C-RAN with experiments conducted on our testbed (setup details deferred to § 4)

2.2.1 Repurposing Capacity

With user mobility, the traffic demand shifts across the network, potentially creating overloaded APs as well as leaving some APs under utilized. Past solutions that recommend centralized WLAN [8, 9], and other resource management techniques [47, 48, 5, 7, 34] are mostly intended at efficient load balancing and mitigating resource wastage during under-utilization. In the case of high traffic surge at a single location, even the most optimized algorithm of a traditional WLAN can only handle traffic demands equal to the capacity of the AP deployed at that location. Traffic demands higher than the capacity of the AP is dealt with either admission control (rejecting some users), or by simply providing sub-par performance to all (or few) clients. In contrast, the C-RAN based architecture offers the flexibility to repurpose the capacity of lightly loaded APs in overloaded areas, by converging the capacity of multiple under-utilized APs to a single location that requires additional capacity.To illustrate this with an example, we conduct an experiment (Fig. 2), where a group of 8 users move between two locations (location 1 and location 2) in our testbed. We keep the users close to the AP to avoid poor channel quality. The maximum achievable per-user throughput in either location 1 or location 2 is measured to be around 60 Mbps (channel capacity). In the case of traditional WLANs, when all 8 users congregate at a single location (first in location 1 and then all move to location 2), they are all forced to share a single AP (one channel) - first, the AP at location 1 and then the AP at location 2. This results in a reduced per-user throughput of around 7.4 Mbps. In contrast, a C-RAN based WLAN gives the flexibility to map both the APs to the same RRH (on two different channels), enabling both the APs to serve at both the locations (initially at location 1 and then at location 2), as shown in Fig. 2. This allows the users to be re-distributed over two APs resulting in an increased per-user throughput of $\approx$15 Mbps), proving that software-defined front-haul is essential to gracefully handle the traffic surge.

2.2.2 Adaptable Coverage

In traditional WLANs, an AP is deployed in one physical location and its coverage area gets defined by its transmit power. Some users may be positioned far from an AP and thus have low data rates (e.g., in sparse traffic areas with low AP density). With packet-fair scheduling in WiFi, such low rate users adversely impact other users served by the AP. On the other hand, C-RAN-based WLANs allow mapping the signal of a given AP to more than one RRH simultaneously creating a one (BPU)-to-many (RRH) mapping in the front-haul. Since RRHs are light-weight (in cost and size), they can be deployed densely. With the help of one-to-many front-haul mapping, each user can then be served through its closest RRH with high data rates.

To understand the impact of coverage, we experiment with three APs and six clients. There are six candidate locations (**L1-L6**) to deploy the three APs (see Fig. 3). Once we choose a location for an AP, we let clients associate to their nearest AP and run multiple *iperf* sessions from each AP to its clients. We fix the locations that yield the best throughput for traditional WLAN (**L2**, **L4** and **L6**). For C-RAN-based WLAN, we deploy RRHs at all six locations but use the same three APs to drive them (see Fig 3 for AP-

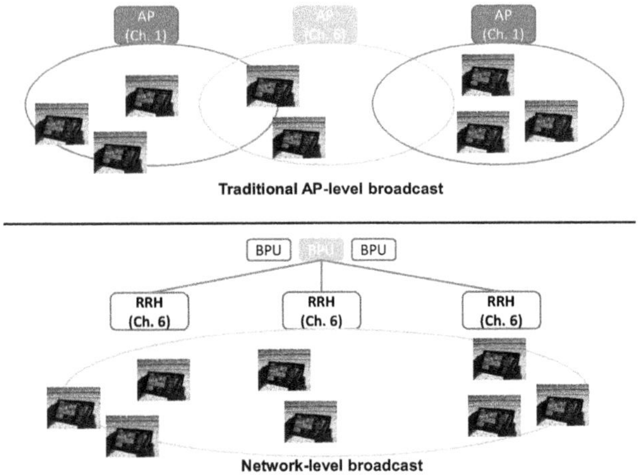

Figure 4: Network-level broadcast in C-RAN based WiFi.

RRH mapping). We see that per-user throughput is higher in C-RAN since each user receives data via its closest RRH (enabled by one-to-many mapping). Note that this is not possible in traditional WLANs due to limited AP transmit power. Even with the same power limit on each RRH, C-RAN-based WLAN allows for larger coverage owing to the decoupling of APs from physical locations and the transmit diversity benefit from synchronous RRH transmissions.

2.2.3 Efficient Network-level Synchronous Broadcast

In addition to unicast applications, supporting broadcast applications (e.g,. live video) is also important in high-density venues [30]. Broadcasting MAC frames is inefficient in traditional WLANs due to the lack of acknowledgments and the use of low bitrates [10]. Even with the advances made by earlier works ([27, 10, 42]) and proposals by the IEEE 802.11aa amendment to 802.11 [1], broadcast transmission remains at the AP-level, requiring each AP to independently broadcast data to its clients (Fig.4). With AP-level broadcast, APs contend for medium access (similar to what they would do for unicast) even though they deliver the same content. On the other hand, one-to-many mapping in the C-RAN front-haul enables what we call *network-level broadcast* where an AP broadcasts content over a wide area (see Fig.4). This leads to better transmission efficiency for broadcast, freeing up the remaining APs to serve other applications. We note here that LTE already has built-in support for network-level broadcast, where base stations use a synchronization protocol to jointly transmit the broadcast content. Thus, the notion of one-to-many front-haul mappings is not as critical in cellular C-RANs as it is for C-RAN-based WLANs, where the latter benefits from synchronization in the optical domain overcoming the lack of an existing protocol.

2.3 Economic Viability

Plethora of studies [17, 20, 18, 19] argue that the C-RAN technology thrives in the form of micro C-RANs for high-density venues, and is economically viable considering the long term operational cost benefits (up to 53%). With increasing number of enterprises gearing towards deploying micro C-RANs for cellular connectivity, there is a strong need for WiFi that can co-exist with and complement the cellular network. To this end, we believe AmorFi to be a perfect fit that can help create a C-RAN eco-system for all wireless connectivity. Since AmorFi can essentially be deployed on existing C-RAN infrastructure, the initial deployment cost can be minimal as well. Compared to traditional WLANs where low deployment costs are often offset by high operational costs [49, 36], a C-RAN based WLAN can indeed be economically beneficial for large enterprises, in the long run.

2.4 Determining Optimal Configurations

The true advantage of the C-RAN architecture in WLANs is SDA – orchestrating the front-haul (in software) to tailor capacity allocations based on prevailing traffic demands in real time. The spatiotemporal traffic variations requires constant tracking of the load and choosing the appropriate configuration. With dynamic front-haul configurations, the interference dependencies between APs change, making network planning a much harder task than it is for statically-deployed WLANs. Thus, even when the WLAN supports unicast traffic alone, it is challenging to come up with the optimal front-haul mapping that supports as much of the demand as possible.

When a WLAN supports a mix of unicast and broadcast applications, the problem becomes even harder since each application type has conflicting requirements on the type of front-haul mapping that needs to be adopted. With one-to-one mapping, each AP gets mapped to one RRH, creating smaller cells. This emphasizes spatial reuse, which increases the network capacity to support unicast applications. In contrast, one-to-many mapping creates larger cells (decreasing spatial reuse), which is important to efficiently deliver the same broadcast content over a wide-area. The problem is exacerbated by the clients not being able to seamlessly access multiple WiFi channels (unlike LTE), thereby requiring both unicast and broadcast applications to be delivered on the same channel (AP).

To summarize, the key challenge in C-RAN-based WLANs is to discover the optimal front-haul configuration that caters to both unicast and broadcast applications and adapt the configuration based on spatiotemporal changes in traffic demand. In doing so, one also has to manage interference conflicts across cells, which becomes harder since the cells themselves keep changing as determined by the front-haul.

Lack of Existing Solutions: To the best of our knowledge, no study in the traditional WLAN space addresses our problem of dynamic capacity provisioning to support unicast and broadcast traffic. There are some cellular C-RAN studies that advocate software-programmable front-haul such as [46], but they are not directly applicable to WiFi because of the following reasons. First, while WiFi channel bonding may aggregate capacity to some extent, it is limited due to the presence of legacy clients and CSMA requiring orthogonal channels between neighboring APs. Thus, it is essential

Table 1: Notations used in our problem

Symbol	Type	Description
$\mathbb{A}$	Input	The set of APs
$\mathbb{R}$	Input	The set of RRHs
$\mathbb{K}$	Input	The set of channels
T_r	Input	Traffic demand of RRH r
P	Input	Channel capacity of an AP (cluster)
$\mathbb{N}$	Output	The set of clusters
X_{ik}	Output	Binary variable denoting the assignment of channel k to cluster $i \in \mathbb{N}$
$Int(i_1, i_2)$	Output	Binary variable denoting that clusters i_1 and i_2 interfere with each other
$S(r)$	Output	The set clusters which include RRH r
$R(i)$	Output	The set of RRHs contained in cluster i

to map multiple APs to the same RRH to increase capacity and carefully assign channels to them to avoid co-channel interference. In contrast, cellular base stations and clients have access to all the channels in the spectrum; a base station can handle the traffic surge by increasing its bandwidth as needed (i.e., not needing channel assignment). Second, the lack of network-wide broadcast support in WiFi makes one-to-many front-haul mapping more critical than it is for cellular. Thus, one has to balance between supporting unicast and broadcast traffic in C-RAN-based WLANs since each requires different front-haul mappings.

3. AMORFI: DESIGN

In our network model, $\mathbb{A}$ and $\mathbb{R}$ denote the set of APs (BPUs) and RRHs, respectively. While RRHs act as transmit/receive points, APs provide the wireless capacity. We envision AmorFi to track traffic fluctuations and adapt its front-haul configurations (AP-RRH mappings) at the granularity of epochs where measurements from previous epochs serve as input to drive the optimization for the current epoch. (The actual value of the epoch can be in minutes and tuned further based on the changing traffic patterns or past knowledge.)Hence, each RRH $r \in \mathbb{R}$ poses (requires) a traffic demand T_r for the current epoch (based on a weighted average from previous epochs), which is an estimate of aggregate throughput requirements for all users accessing the network via RRH r. The function $f : \mathbb{A} \to \mathbb{R}$ maps each AP to zero or more RRHs; the former denotes an idle AP (not serving users), while the latter defines a cluster i of RRHs (where $R(i) \in \mathbb{R}$), sharing the capacity P of the corresponding AP. P is estimated based on the aggregate throughputs delivered by the each of the RRHs in $R(i)$ from the previous epoch. When a cluster i is formed for an AP, it is assigned a channel $k \in \mathbb{K}$, where $\mathbb{K}$ is the set of channels in the WiFi spectrum. $X_{ik} = 1$ captures this assignment (see Table 1).

Remarks: Although we do not explicitly consider external interference in our formulation, it must be noted that, interference estimation can be done using techniques described in [44, 14, 13], and the result can be easily factored in while determining the channel capacity of an AP (P).

3.1 Problem Definition

$$ONC: \underset{\mathbb{C}}{Maximize}\ \lambda$$

such that:

$$(1) \lambda_r = \min\{1, \sum_{i \in S(r)} \sum_{k=1}^{|\mathbb{K}|} \frac{X_{ik} P_i}{\sum_{l \in R(i)} T_l}\} \geq \lambda, \forall r \in \mathbb{R}$$

$$(2) \sum_{i=1}^{|\mathbb{N}|} \sum_{k=1}^{|\mathbb{K}|} X_{ik} \leq |\mathbb{A}|$$

$$(3) \sum_{i \in S(r)} \sum_{k=1}^{|\mathbb{K}|} X_{ik} \geq 1, \forall r \in \mathbb{R}$$

$$(4) X_{i_1 k} + X_{i_2 k} \leq 1, \forall (i_1, i_2) \in S(r), \forall r \in \mathbb{R}, \forall k \in \mathbb{K}, i_1 \neq i_2$$

$$(5) X_{i_1 k} + X_{i_2 k} \leq 1, \forall (i_1, i_2) \in \mathbb{N}\ s.t\ Int(i_1, i_2) = 1, \forall k \in \mathbb{K}$$

For an easier exposition, we describe the problem formulation and our solution for addressing unicast traffic first. Then, we extend them to accommodate broadcast traffic as well in Section 3.3. For a given number of APs (radios) and WiFi channels, AmorFi aims to maximize the amount of traffic demand (unicast) that can be satisfied at each of the RRHs in the current epoch. Towards capturing this objective, we formulate the following optimization problem, (ONC: optimal network configuration), where our goal is to find the network configuration (over the universe $\mathbb{C}$ of all configurations) that maximizes $\lambda \in [0, 1]$. We define λ to be the minimum fraction of traffic demand satisfied across all the RRHs in the network. A network configuration includes the AP-RRH mapping (determining the capacity allocation) and the channel assignment to each of the clusters (APs).

The first constraint indicates that the fraction of traffic demand satisfied at each RRH r (denoted as λ_r; called traffic satisfaction metric taking into account all APs serving it), is greater than λ. This makes λ the minimum such value (that is maximized) across the network. To calculate λ_r, we first determine the channel capacity share that RRH r has (out of the cluster capacity P), when it is included in a cluster together with other RRHs. Here, we assume that P is shared in proportion to the unicast traffic demand of each RRH in the cluster. The second constraint ensures that the number of clusters generated does not exceed the number of APs ($|\mathbb{A}|$). The third constraint ensures that all the RRHs (with users to serve) are covered in a cluster, and every RRH has an AP assigned. The fourth constraint requires that all the clusters sharing a common RRH, will be assigned different channels. The last constraint ensures that clusters that are in the interference range of each other, are not assigned the same channel.

Remark: It is important to map an AP to a *contiguous* set of RRHs, i.e., the clustered RRHs form a connected set, where connectivity captures RRHs that are within range of each other. The lack of such contiguity creates two drawbacks: (i) Mapping an AP to RRHs that are spread across the network, will reduce the spatial reuse for that channel.

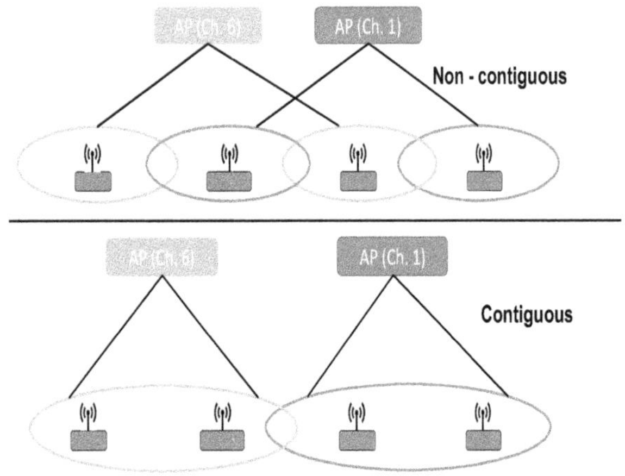

Figure 5: Non-contiguous vs. contiguous clustering.

(ii) As seen in Fig. 5, with non-contiguous clusters, a mobile user experiences frequent handoffs (not desirable for delay-sensitive applications). A contiguous cluster creates a virtual large cell that reduces such disruptions. We thus require that the clusters ($R(i)$) be contiguous.

3.2 Algorithms in AmorFi

3.2.1 Overview of Solution

ONC requires us to solve the problems of contiguous clustering and channel assignment *jointly*. Since each individual problem is NP-hard in itself, solving them jointly is much harder. Hence, we aim to design efficient, yet simple algorithms to solve ONC with the following intuition.

Intuition: Two parameters impact how much traffic can be supported: number of radios (APs) and channels. The number of APs control the maximum capacity that can be offered, and limit the number of RRH clusters that can be formed, while the clustering process itself determines how the available capacity is efficiently used (and not wasted) to satisfy the demand. When the channels are assigned to the clusters, they impact the supported traffic demand by a cluster, based on the sharing of its channel (and hence capacity) with other clusters in its neighborhood. While both clustering and channel assignment impact the net traffic served, their relative contribution to λ is biased, where clustering plays a bigger role. The impact of channel assignment varies with the number of channels. For example, it has little impact in 5 GHz, where many channels (nine) are available, making it easier for a conflict-free assignment, compared to 2.4 GHz (three channels), where it has appreciable impact.

Optimization: Given this biased effect, we see that the additional gains from solving the two problems jointly are not appreciable to justify the high complexity. Hence, AmorFi decouples the clustering process from channel assignment for a two-step approach as follows. It solves the clustering problem first, without accounting for channel assignment (conflicts) between clusters (APs), to maximize λ. Given the clustering solution, it then assigns channels to clusters to resolve as many of the inter-cluster conflicts and retain as much of the λ (traffic satisfaction) from the clustering process ($\hat{\lambda}$, where $\hat{\lambda} \leq \lambda$). While this decoupled approach is less complex, it faces the challenge that the clustering solution that maximizes λ in the first step, may not contribute to a final solution (after channel assignment) with the best traffic satisfaction ($\hat{\lambda}$). In other words, a clustering solution with a smaller λ (after clustering) could potentially incur a less loss during channel assignment to yield a higher $\hat{\lambda}$.

To address this challenge, AmorFi adopts an iterative optimization approach. At the start of each epoch, the controller receives the aggregate traffic demand of each RRH (based on estimates from previous epochs). It then runs the iterative optimization, where it solves a dual of the problem in each iteration to determine the best network-wide configuration.

Step 1 - Initialize: Initialize λ with an upper bound (λ_0) on the traffic demand that can be satisfied at each RRH. This represents a configuration with maximum spatial reuse by mapping each AP to a separate RRH.

Step 2 - Cluster: In each iteration i, translate the λ-maximization problem into its dual; given a λ_i, determine the smallest number of APs (clusters) required to satisfy λ_i of the net traffic demand in each of the clusters. Here, impose a logical connectivity structure on the network of RRHs using breadth-first-search (BFS). The structure determines the smallest number of contiguous clusters of RRHs (m_i) that serve at least λ_i of the traffic demand in each cluster.

Step 3 - Assign Channels: Given the clusters and the available channels, try to find a conflict-free channel assignment. When the same channel has to be assigned to interfering clusters, update traffic satisfaction ($\hat{\lambda}_i$) to reflect the reduction in capacity (due to time sharing).

Step 4 - Iterate: Decrement λ by a small constant δ (say 0.01) for the next iteration ($\lambda_{i+1} = \lambda_i - \delta$) and repeat steps 2 and 3. Terminate when $\lambda = \delta$.

Step 5 - Output Configuration: Determine the network-wide configuration corresponding to the highest $\hat{\lambda}$, namely $\max_i\{\hat{\lambda}_i\}$ such that number of APs employed $m_i \leq |\mathbb{A}|$.

The time complexity of our solution is $O(I(|\mathbb{R}|^2 + |\mathbb{A}|^2)$, where I is the number of iterations, $O(|\mathbb{R}|^2)$ and $O(|\mathbb{A}|^2)$ are the complexities of the clustering and channel assignment components in each iteration, respectively. We now explain these steps in detail.

3.2.2 Initialize λ (Step 1)

At the start of an epoch t, the controller obtains traffic statistics from the previous epoch $t-1$. Specifically, each AP a reports (i) average capacity P_a: the average of all the MCSs (Modulation and Coding Scheme) used for transmissions (from RRHs in its cluster) to all its clients; (ii) aggregate traffic demand $T^a(t-1)$: aggregate of the traffic served to all its users per unit time of the epoch $t-1$; and (iii) number of RRHs $n_a(t-1)$ serving it. For epoch t, the controller combines AP reports to estimate: (i) P as the average of the capacity seen by all the active APs in the last epoch $t-1$; and (ii) aggregate traffic demand per RRH r, $T_r(t)$ as the ex-

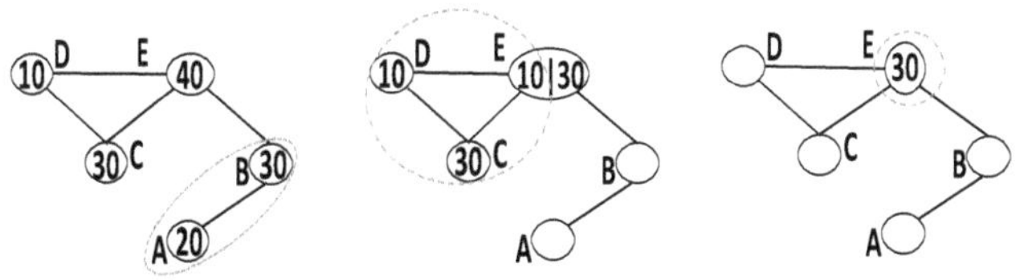

Figure 6: Clustering procedure (cluster capacity = 50 units)

ponentially weighted moving average of traffic demand from prior epochs, i.e. $T_r(t) = \alpha \cdot \sum_{a:r\in R(a)} \frac{T^a(t-1)}{n_a(t-1)} + (1-\alpha)\cdot T_r(t-1)$, where $\alpha = 0.9$ is the filtering coefficient used in our implementation.

AmorFi starts by initializing λ to the theoretical upper-bound, calculated as the ratio of total network capacity to the total traffic demand. The total network capacity is the product of the number of APs ($|\mathbb{A}|$) and the average channel capacity (P), assuming that every AP gets a non-overlapping channel (upper-bound). Thus, $\lambda_0 = (P * |\mathbb{A}|)/(\sum_{r=1}^{|\mathbb{R}|} T_r)$.

3.2.3 *Clustering (Step 2)*

Since the traffic requirement at an RRH r (i.e. $\lambda_i \cdot T_r$, for iteration i) can be split and served by multiple clusters, the contiguous clustering problem to determine the minimum number of APs, can be optimally solved if we can construct a Hamiltonian cycle[1] on a graph where the RRHs are the vertices (edges denote interfering RRHs). Such a cycle would give us the ordering in which the RRHs should be traversed to produce the optimal clustering. However, even determining the existence of a Hamiltonian cycle is NP-complete in general graphs. Hence, AmorFi constructs an alternate ordering by using a breadth-first search (BFS) traversal on the RRH graph, rooted at the RRH with the least degree.

Algorithm: AmorFi clusters (groups) RRHs, level by level as shown in Fig. 6 (numbers in vertices represent unicast traffic demand), starting with the root (vertex A). Note that, a BFS ordering does not ensure that RRHs in the same level are connected (for contiguous clustering purposes). Hence, when AmorFi encounters an RRH that is not connected to the current cluster, it skips the RRH and moves to the next RRH (that is connected) in the ordering, either in the same level if available or next level otherwise. The current cluster terminates when the next vertex's (RRH's) demand uses up the capacity(50 units)– as seen for cluster 1 where it starts with vertex A (20 units) and ends with vertex B (30 units) when 50 units are filled up. When it is not possible to add a vertex to the current cluster and completely cover its demand, AmorFi covers the vertex partially (i.e., satisfying some of its demand). This is shown for cluster 2 where it starts with vertex C (30 units), continues to cover vertex D (10 units) and ends with partially covering vertex E for 10 units (out of 40). Next, a new cluster is started from an un-covered RRH (at the current level) that has the lowest degree. The process continues until all RRHs are completely covered. It is possible for the demand at an RRH to be covered by multiple clusters (APs), e.g., for vertex E. This happens when the demand at the RRH is partially covered by a first cluster; the RRH remains un-covered, with its remaining demand being covered later by other cluster(s). The BFS traversal of the RRH graph has a time complexity of $O(|\mathbb{R}|^2)$.

Sub-optimality: It is possible for a cluster's capacity to be under-utilized at the edges of the RRH graph, when no other connected RRHs can use up the remaining capacity. This could result in more APs (than an optimal scheme) being required to support a given λ. However, by intelligently using BFS and skipping vertices that violate contiguity, as well as initializing a new cluster with a low-degree vertex, AmorFi keeps this sub-optimality low. Further, in a cluster, where there is remaining capacity, we distribute the remaining capacity among its member RRHs to increase the traffic satisfaction of that cluster. Hence, $\lambda_i^r \geq \lambda_i, \forall r$.

3.2.4 *Channel Assignment (Step 3)*

The traffic demand satisfied at each RRH λ_i^r from the clustering process is feasible, only if there exists a conflict-free channel assignment. As the clusters are formed, AmorFi also maintains a cluster graph (i.e., a graph with clusters as vertices) along with its adjacency matrix C_{uv}. $C_{uv} = 1$ if (a) Cluster u and Cluster v cover a common RRH or (b) If one or more RRHs in Cluster u, are in the interference range of one or more of the RRHs from Cluster v. As the vertices are added to the cluster graph (as clusters are formed), AmorFi keeps track of the largest clique[2] in the cluster graph. Note that finding the largest clique in a given graph (i.e., not iteratively tracked) is however a hard problem.

AmorFi employs the DSATUR [6] coloring algorithm for assigning channels on the cluster graph (any other coloring algorithm could be used as well). The general idea is to select the vertex (i.e., cluster) with the highest saturation degree (i.e., number of differently colored neighbors) and assign to it the least admissible color with $O(|\mathbb{A}|^2)$ complexity.

Impact on λ: If the clique number of the cluster graph is greater than the number of colors (channels) – $|\mathbb{A}|$ – one or more adjacent vertices (clusters) will be assigned the same color, decreasing the corresponding clusters' λ_i^r. The number of orthogonal channels in 5 GHz (nine) is larger than typical clique sizes observed in our cluster graphs (two to six). Hence, while AmorFi can eliminate the reduction in λ_r in 5 GHz, this may not be possible in 2.4 GHz, where there are only three channels. In this case, the coloring algorithm will assign the same channel to one or more adjacent clusters (say n) in a clique with size more than three, thereby reducing the per-cluster channel capacity for these clusters by a factor of $\frac{1}{n}$. Correspondingly, the λ_i^r (from the clustering step) of all the RRHs in these adjacent clusters that shared the same channel, will be scaled by $\frac{1}{n}$. The minimum traffic satisfied across all the RRHs at the end of the feasible channel assignment step is given by $\hat{\lambda}_i = \min_r(\lambda_i^r)$.

[1]A path through all the vertices s.t. each vertex is traversed once.

[2]sub-graph where vertices are connected to each other.

3.2.5 Determining Efficient Configurations

As we decrement λ_i in each iteration (in **Step 4**), fewer APs would be required to satisfy it. This is because, with less traffic demand, the size of each cluster would increase as more RRHs can be served by a single AP. Ideally, to maximize λ, it would be sufficient to stop at an iteration, when the number of APs required just equals $|\mathbb{A}|$ (input). However, channel assignment breaks this monotonic trend – while utilizing all APs would support the maximum traffic demand λ_i, it also increases the number of clusters and potentially the clique number, consequently incurring a large reduction to λ_i during channel assignment (resulting in a final lower $\hat{\lambda}_i$). Thus, it is important to search over the entire space of λ (100 iterations with $\delta = 0.01$) to evaluate the relative impact of both the steps (clustering and channel assignment) and identify the best network configuration (**Step 5**).

Remarks: The total execution time of the algorithm depends on various factors like the number of RRHs, number of APs, and the value of δ considered. To get an estimate of the algorithm execution time, we measured the time taken to run our naive python implementation of the algorithm. We selected layouts of 50 popular venues across US [16], and calculated the ideal AP-deployment graph for each of the selected venues using the guidelines in [3]. For each of the AP-deployment graph, we considered the scenario where $|\mathbb{R}| = |\mathbb{A}|$, $\delta = 0.01$, $|\mathbb{K}| = 9$ (No. of non-overlapping channels in 5 Ghz), and a random distribution of the unicast traffic demand. We then measured the total execution time of our program on a desktop computer running Ubuntu 14.04 OS, and equipped with an Intel-Xeon processor [29]. We verified that the total execution time in each case to be in the order of few seconds (average = 6.83 sec), which is significantly less than the epoch considered (in minutes). Furthermore, we would like to point out that a more optimal implementation of the algorithm using techniques like MapReduce [21] can reduce the execution time significantly. Additionally, AmorFi's algorithms can be run in a distributed manner for different subsets of APs, in parallel. This will further enhance the execution efficiency of the algorithm. Thus, we believe that the computational overhead to determine the network conifguration during each epoch is negligible.

3.3 Unifying Unicast and Broadcast traffic

Tradeoff: A characteristic of high-density venues is the co-existence of unicast and broadcast applications. The key challenge in addressing such heterogeneous applications is to account for their contrasting nature. If a user browses the Web (unicast traffic), she would increase the traffic demand at an RRH. However, if she subscribes to an already broadcasting video stream, she would pose no additional demand at the RRH. Optimizing for unicast requires an increase in the capacity at the RRH, favoring configurations with small clusters that enable higher spatial reuse in the network. In contrast, optimizing for broadcast requires expanding the coverage of already available capacity to include multiple RRHs, thereby favoring configurations with large clusters.

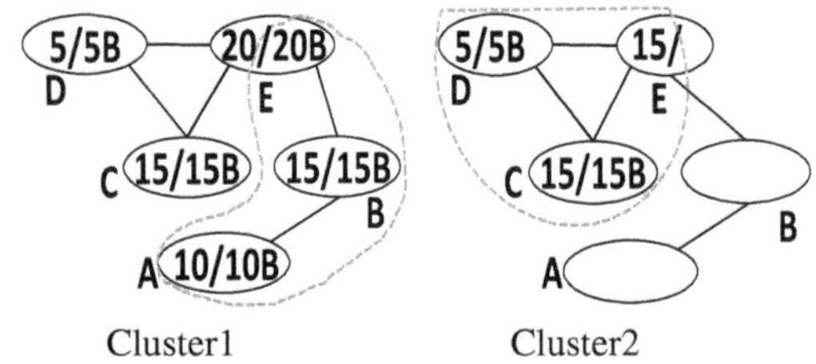

Figure 7: Clustering procedure - 50% of Bcast traffic

One way to address this is to optimize for unicast and broadcast traffic separately, e.g., by treating them as two individual problems. This would yield a solution where the APs would exclusively serve either unicast or broadcast traffic. In practice, a user requesting a broadcast stream while browsing the Web would have to be connected to two different APs (which is impractical), or suffer from poor performance in one of the applications. Thus, the key challenge is to identify a common network configuration that optimizes both the broadcast and unicast traffic jointly.

Problem Formulation: Given a separate traffic demand for unicast ($T_{r,u}$) and broadcast ($T_{r,b}$) traffic at an RRH, the ONC problem formulation remains the same except for the constraint on the unicast traffic satisfaction, which would get replaced by the following two constraints for broadcast and unicast respectively.

$$(1a)\lambda_{r,b} = \min\{1, \sum_{i \in S(r)} \sum_{k=1}^{|\mathbb{K}|} X_{ik}\gamma_i P_i\} \geq \lambda, \forall r \in \mathbb{R}$$

$$(1b)\lambda_{r,u} = \min\{1, \sum_{i \in S(r)} \sum_{k=1}^{|\mathbb{K}|} \frac{X_{ik}(1-\gamma_i)P_i}{\sum_{l \in R(i)} T_l}\} \geq \lambda, \forall r \in \mathbb{R}$$

Here, we desire the same fraction of traffic satisfaction for both broadcast ($\lambda_{r,b}$) and unicast ($\lambda_{r,u}$) traffic at an RRH. γ_i is the output parameter that determines the amount of cluster (AP) capacity that is split between broadcast and unicast demands, and is responsible for the coupling between the heterogeneous demands.

Algorithm: Interestingly, our clustering algorithm is inherently equipped to address unicast and broadcast demand jointly, requiring only a minor tweak. Recall that AmorFi transforms the λ-maximization problem to an iterative minimization of the number of APs required to realize a given λ. Hence, at each iteration, it increases the size (coverage) of the clusters as much as possible, so as to minimize the number of APs employed. This transformation naturally lends itself to optimizing for broadcast traffic. Note that the most efficient use of a cluster's (AP's) capacity (say p) is to leverage the broadcast advantage and serve an equivalent amount (p) of broadcast traffic demand from as many RRHs as possible. Hence, given separate traffic demands for unicast ($T_{r,u}$) and broadcast ($T_{r,b}$) at an RRH and λ_i, AmorFi satisfies the broadcast demand ($\lambda_i T_{r,b}$) first, before satisfying the unicast demand ($\lambda_i T_{r,u}$) at the RRH. This allows AmorFi to leverage the broadcast traffic that is already served by the cluster to also satisfy (completely or partially) the broadcast demand at the new un-clustered RRH being considered, thereby utilizing the cluster's remaining capacity to accommodate additional unicast/broadcast traffic. In other words, whenever a new RRH, $\hat{r}$, is added to a cluster c, only its additional broadcast demand (if positive) not satisfied by the cluster's existing broadcast traffic, i.e., $\lambda_i \cdot (T_{\hat{r},b} - \max_{r \in R(c)}\{T_{r,b}\})$, would eat into the cluster's remaining capacity as new traffic demand. Thus, the broadcast traffic satisfied by the cluster would increase to $\lambda_i T_{\hat{r},b}$. The unicast demand at the RRH is then handled as before.

Fig. 7 illustrates this algorithm where 50% of the total demand at each RRH is broadcast (B). The procedure starts at the root node (A) and cluster capacity is 50 units as before. When adding vertex B to cluster 1, the additional load from broadcast traffic is only 5 units since the cluster already serves 10 units of broadcast from vertex A. With vertices A and B in the cluster, 25 units of the capacity are used for unicast and 15 units for broadcast for a total of 40 units (leaving room for 10 units). Next, the cluster exhausts its capacity by completely covering the broadcast demand of vertex E (for additional $20 - 15 = 5$ units) and partially covering the unicast demand for 5 units. Cluster 2 initiates from vertex C and is formed similarly.

Remarks: AmorFi 's transformed optimization determines efficient network configurations that balance the coverage benefits of large clusters for broadcast and the reuse benefits of small clusters for unicast. If the traffic demand is biased towards a particular traffic type, AmorFi will automatically tailor the configurations to favor the dominant traffic. Further, AmorFi 's approach of delivering a given traffic demand using less radios, also makes it energy-efficient.

4. IMPLEMENTATION

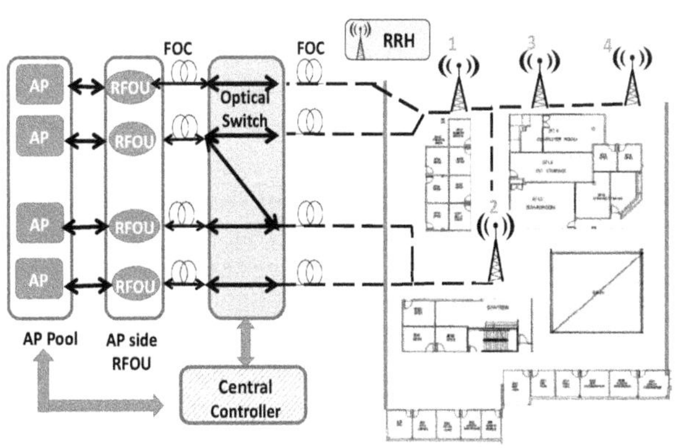

Figure 8: Our system architecture and testbed layout

Our system architecture is shown in Fig. 8. The APs are laptops with dual-band 802.11 a/b/g/n WiFi adapters. The main intelligence of AmorFi resides in the central controller, which is a PC that collects AP reports and executes our algorithms. It then instructs the APs to apply the channel assignment decisions and configures the switching unit to effect the AP-RRH mappings. The mappings are realized in the optical domain where a programmable switching unit (i.e., an optical splitter) maps each AP to zero or more RRHs, allowing a mix of one-to-one and one-to-many configurations [23]. Since the switching is entirely in the optical domain, the switching latency does not incur any excessive overhead. Modern optical switches have switching latencies of a few tens of nanoseconds [35]. We have four APs and four RRHs due to limited number of ports on our optical switch. The RF-to-optical units (RFOUs) are transceivers that convert the RF signal to optical for the downlink, and vice-versa for the uplink [37]. We remove the external antenna of an AP and attach it to the RFOU to provide the RF source at the AP side. On the RRH side, RFOUs transmit/receive RF signals providing wireless access to clients. The RRHs in our testbedhave inbuilt power moderator which provides a constant TX power of $\approx 17dBm$ irrespective of the input optical signal quality.Currently, our RRHs can be fitted with only one RF antenna, restricting us to have SISO experiments. However, we also create a proof-of-concept MIMO deployment as detailed in Section 5. The front-haul is based on Radio-over-fiber (RoF), where an optical signal is modulated based on the input radio signal, and transmitted over Fiber Optic Cable(We used a single mode fiber with 1550 nm wavelength in our testbed) [40].Optical multiplexing helps us carry multiple optical signals (corresponding to multiple RF signals) on the same fiber using different wavelength, allowing RRHs to provide simultaneous service from multiple APs (on different WiFi channels). With fiber latency around 4 μsec/Km, RoF retains the signal synchronization across RRHs, as well as the timing constrains between uplink and downlink signals. The RoF latency when compared to the minimum DIFS duration in 802.11 (34 μsec, and 50 μsec in 5 GHz, and 2.4 GHz band respectively) is almost negligible, allowing APs to carrier sense at the RRHs without any significant delay. Apart from RoF's simplicity, it also has low signal attenuation over long distances when deployed in large venues. Note that a C-RAN-based WLAN can be realized based on technologies other than RoF, e.g., CPRI. AmorFi is compatible with such architectures as well since it does not rely on RoF being available.

5. PERFORMANCE EVALUATION

5.1 Prototype Evaluation

We first evaluate AmorFi with only unicast traffic and later conduct experiments to include broadcast traffic as well. Our RRHs have interference relationships as in Fig. 9, where an edge indicates that the two RRHs overhear each other.

Baselines: We compare AmorFi against two baselines: (a) Traditional WLAN, with no load balancing (Tr_no_LB) - agnostic to AP load, where the clients associate to the AP with the strongest signal and (b) Traditional WLAN with load balancing (Tr_LB) - distributes the clients evenly among all APs that can potentially serve the clients (possibly with weaker signal), to avoid unfair load distribution among APs. We implement these baselines by static one-to-one config-

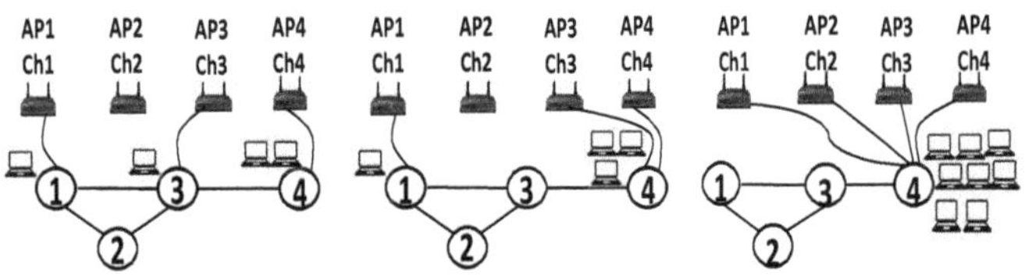

(a) Time: T1 (b) Time: T2 (c) Time: T5

Figure 9: Scenario I : AmorFi 's AP-to-RRH configuration

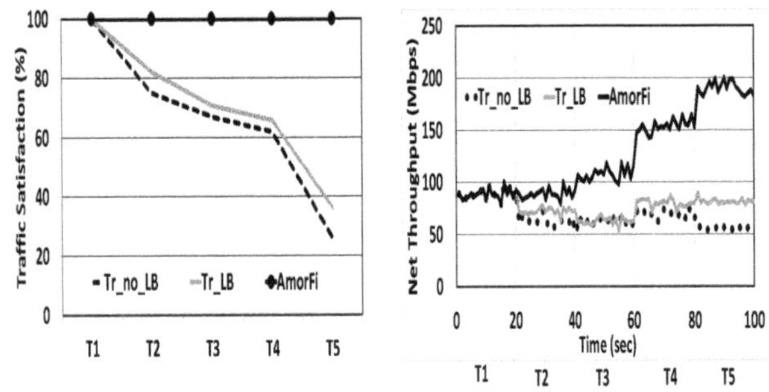

(a) Scenario I: Traffic satisfaction

(b) Scenario I: Throughput

Figure 10: AmorFi Vs. baselines during traffic surge.

uration between the APs and RRHs (AP1 to RRH1, AP2 to RRH2 and so on). We conduct our experiments at night without any external interference in the 5 GHz band. Each AP is assigned an orthogonal 20 MHz channel. We represent these channels as Ch1, Ch2, Ch3 and Ch4.

We used *iperf* to measure the maximum per-AP throughput for UDP and TCP to be ~58 Mbps and ~49 Mbps, respectively with 64-QAM (one spatial stream, 800 ns. guard interval and 65 Mbps bit rate). The total UDP and TCP network capacity with four APs is thus ~232 Mbps and ~198 Mbps, respectively. We used eight Wi-Fi clients and set the traffic demand of each client to $\frac{Network capacity}{8}$, meaning that an AP can only satisfy the traffic demands of two clients.

Scenario I: Handling Traffic Surge: We first test the case when traffic demand gradually increases due to new clients arriving over five time intervals (**T1-T5**), each interval lasting 20 seconds. The initial AmorFi mapping is similar to the baselines where each AP is mapped to a separate RRH. Fig. 9 shows how this configuration evolves to accommodate the increase in load at the end of a subset of the intervals. In Fig. 10, we show the traffic satisfaction metric ($\lambda = 1$ is represented as 100%) and the TCP throughput for the three schemes. UDP results are similar and thus omitted Initially, all schemes satisfy 100% of the demand since each AP serves at most two users. During **T2**, one user moves from RRH3 to RRH4 as in Fig. 9b. Without load balancing, traditional WLAN connects this user to AP4 (mapped to RRH4), overloading the AP since it ends up serving three users. With load balancing, the same user associates to AP3 (via RRH3), avoiding overload at the expense of reduced throughput due to lower SNR. With the ability to map multiple APs to an RRH, AmorFi re-maps AP3 (from RRH3) to

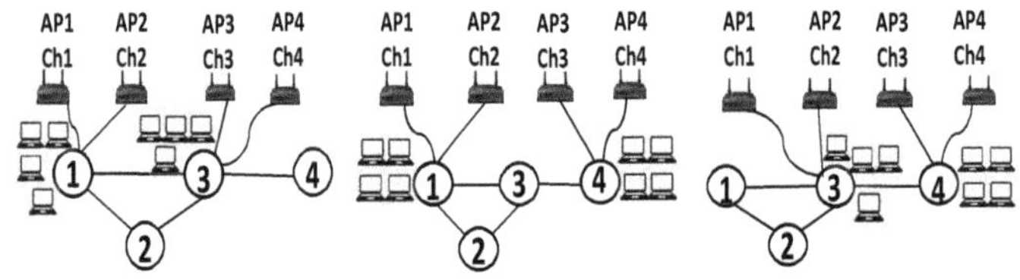

(a) Time: T2 (b) Time: T3 (c) Time: T4

Figure 11: Scenario II : AmorFi 's AP-to-RRH configuration

RRH4 in addition to AP4 (see Fig. 9b). AmorFi also balances the load at RRH4 between AP3 and AP4, avoiding overload without the SNR penalty for the new user. Such ability to re-purpose the capacity of under-utilized APs on the fly is unique to a C-RAN-based deployment and is one of the key features enabled by AmorFi .

In subsequent intervals (**T3, T4**), as new clients join, the baseline schemes have lower traffic satisfaction with load balancing being slightly better (66% vs 61%). The final time interval **T5** shows the case when all eight users congregate at RRH4. AmorFi maps all four APs to RRH4 on different channels (Fig. 9c), distributing the clients evenly and efficiently utilizing the capacity. This helps AmorFi completely satisfy the demand while the baseline schemes satisfy 38% (with load balancing) and 25% (no load balancing) of the demand. The higher traffic satisfaction with AmorFi also reflects on aggregate throughput, where it delivers more than twice the throughput of baseline schemes as seen in Fig. 10b.

Scenario II: Handling Traffic Migration: We now test the case when the traffic demand is constant, but shifts across the network due to user mobility. The configurations of AmorFi and the comparisons with baseline schemes are shown in Figs. 11 and 12. We demonstrate AmorFi 's ability to move capacity end-to-end in a network to address the spatial movement of traffic demand. During **T1,** eight users are concentrated at RRH1 and AmorFi maps all four APs to RRH1. During **T2** through **T4**, users in groups of four move towards RRH4 as seen in Fig. 11, and all users end up at RRH4 during **T5**. While the baseline schemes achieve traffic satisfaction of only 60% and 51% in the best case (**T2-T4**), and only 36% and 25%, respectively in the worst case (**T1 and T5**), AmorFi always maintains 100% traffic satisfaction by distributing the demand evenly between the APs , which also increases the aggregate network throughput (Fig 12b).

Scenario III: Network-level Video Broadcast with Background Unicast traffic: Broadcasting videos over WiFi is becoming increasingly popular in high-density venues. Accommodating such high-bandwidth broadcast applications is challenging since any increase in the unicast traffic demand will invariably affect the quality of the broadcast video. We conduct an experiment where we measure the video quality of broadcast videos while varying the background (unicast) traffic. We use three 8 Mbps video streams as broadcast traffic (delivered by VLC). The total broadcast traffic constitutes about 40% of the channel capacity of an AP. We modified the original WiFi driver to transmit broadcast MAC frames at higher bit rates (the stock driver allows only basic rates).

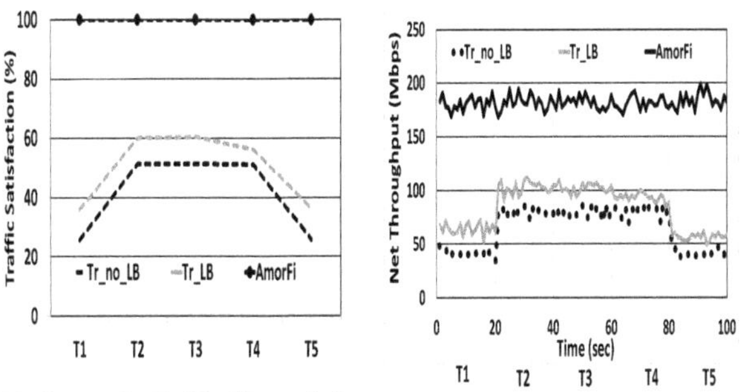

(a) Scenario II: Traffic satisfaction

(b) Scenario II: Throughput

Figure 12: AmorFi Vs. baselines during traffic migration.

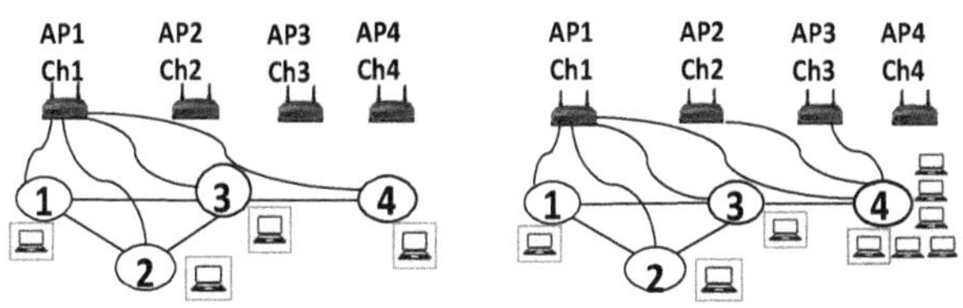

(a) Time: T1

(b) Time: T4

Figure 13: ScenarioIII: AmorFi 's AP-to-RRH configuration

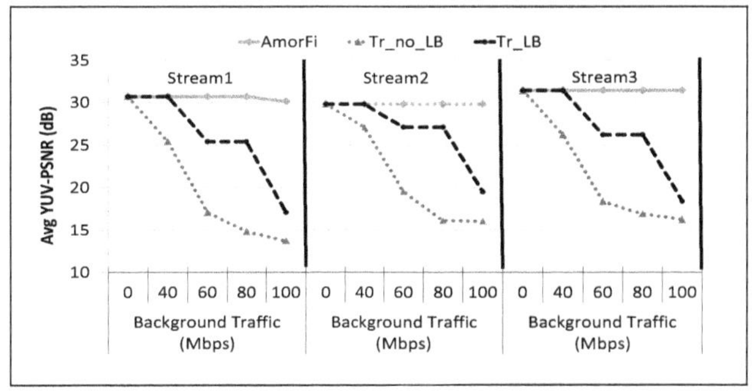

Figure 14: PSNR of received broadcast video

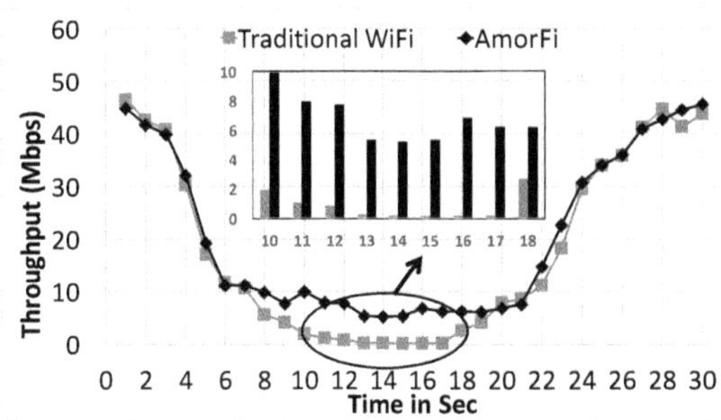

Figure 15: Mobility benefits with AmorFi

We fix the MCS of all the APs to 64-QAM and keep the clients in close proximity to the RRHs.

Experiment: The experiment spans four one minute long time intervals (**T1-T4**). Fig 13 shows the initial user distribution during **T1**. Users subscribing to broadcast traffic at each RRH, are collectively represented by one user with a box around it. To serve the broadcast demand, the baseline schemes require all four APs (and four channels) to broadcast the same videos at cell level. Owing to its network-wide broadcast capability, AmorFi requires only one AP (and one channel) mapped to all four RRHs to deliver broadcast videos to all subscribers (see Fig. 13a). Starting with **T2**, unicast users (each with traffic demand of 20 Mbps) gradually join the network at RRH4. As the unicast traffic demand increases, video quality with baseline schemes suffer significantly as indicated by the drop in PSNR (in Fig. 14) of the videos received by a user at RRH4. On the other hand, AmorFi maps additional APs (on channels 2 and 3) to RRH4 and utilizes them to serve the unicast users. This allows the AP on channel 1 to continue serving the broadcast traffic over four RRHs (Fig. 13b), yielding a much better video than the baseline schemes.

5.2 Mobility Support in AmorFi

Even though we do not explicitly optimize for mobility, one-to-many configurations (large cells) in AmorFi aids in reducing the disruptions due to handoffs for mobile users. We verify this by moving a user between two RRHs connected to the same AP (creating a large virtual cell). We compare the TCP throughput to a traditional WLAN where the two RRHs are mapped to two different APs, requiring the user to handoff from one AP to the other. As seen in Fig. 15, AmorFi results in a much more graceful transition as the user leaves the first RRH and enters the coverage of the second RRH.

5.3 Realizing MIMO in AmorFi

MIMO configurations can be realized just as easily as SISO using RRHs with multiple antennas. We enable 2x2 MIMO in our testbed by placing two RRHs next to each other to emulate a "super RRH" with two antennas. Using the four RRHs, we thus have two super RRHs in two locations. Each antenna port of a MIMO AP (each corresponding to a spatial stream) is split (optically) and fed to one of the RRHs in each super RRH location. This creates a MIMO system with transmit diversity since a spatial stream

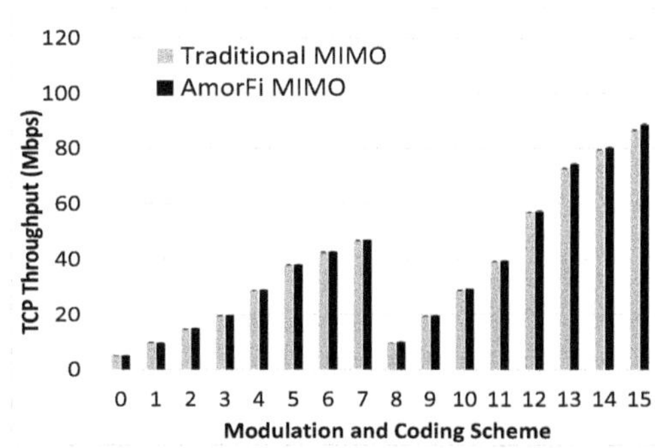

Figure 16: AmorFi MIMO: TCP Throughput

is served by two RRHs at different locations. We place a user in between our super RRHs and compare its TCP throughput to a case where it is placed in close proximity to a MIMO AP (i.e., no C-RAN involved). As seen in Fig.16, the throughputs are highly similar suggesting that our testbed successfully emulates MIMO transmissions in AmorFi.

5.4 Large Scale Simulations

To evaluate AmorFi in larger deployments, we consider the layout of 50 popular venues across the US [16]. Due to lack of any publicly available data (to the best of our knowledge) on the WLANs in these venues, we followed the guidelines in [3] to build the best possible representation of the ideal AP deployment in each venue. For each of the 50 venues, we created WLANs that represent low, medium, and high AP density for a total of 150 deployments.

The peak hour traffic demand is estimated to be equal to the total capacity of a deployment, calculated as the product of the number of APs ($|\mathbb{A}|$), and channel capacity P. We consider three different load distributions: (a) 60-40: 60% of the total traffic demand is randomly distributed across 40% of the RRHs, (b) 70-30 and (c) 80-20. We measure the traffic satisfaction metric (λ), using a custom simulator when (a) number of APs = 25% of RRHs (b) number of APs = 50% of RRHs (c) number of APs = 100% of RRHs. To have a fair comparison, especially for the first two cases when the number of APs are fewer than the number of RRHs, we create a new baseline scheme that also has C-RAN front-haul capability albeit with simpler clustering than AmorFi .

Baseline: The baseline decides on the AP-to-RRH mapping by spatially partitioning adjacent RRHs into clusters, such that the number of clusters formed is equal to the number of APs. The number of RRHs per cluster is given by $\frac{\#of RRHs}{\#of APs}$. When the number of APs are equal to the number of RRHs, it converges to a traditional WLAN, where each AP is mapped to a separate RRH.

5.4.1 Results

In the interest of space, we only discuss the results when the number of APs is 50% of the number of RRHs. However, our observations and conclusions remain the same for other cases.

Fig 17a, 17b, 17c show the CDF of the traffic satisfaction ratio for different load distributions, considering only unicast traffic. AmorFi-2.4 represents AmorFi in 2.4 GHz (three orthogonal channels) and AmorFi-5 represents AmorFi in 5 GHz (nine channels). We see that AmorFi-2.4 and AmorFi-5 increase the median traffic satisfaction (by 33 percentage points and 75 percentage points, respectively) when averaged over the three load distribution cases. AmorFi performs worse in the 2.4 GHz band due to fewer channels than the 5 GHz band. Thus, when our clustering algorithm reveals a cluster graph with a large clique size (e.g., five), the reduction in λ in the channel assignment stage is correspondingly higher (since some neighbor clusters are assigned the same channel). In 2.4 GHz, we observe that the configuration with the maximum λ is usually the one with smaller clique sizes, utilizing a smaller fraction of the available APs compared to the 5 GHz band. 5 GHz band allows more APs to be used in highly-loaded areas (i.e., larger cliques) without significant co-channel assignment penalty.

We also observe that a given scheme performs worse for higher skew in load distribution (e.g., with 80-20 case). With such high skew, few RRHs have very high load requiring many APs mapped to them. However, the number of channels restrict how many APs can be effectively mapped to an RRH making it more difficult to support the demand in highly skewed regimes. Nevertheless, we observe that AmorFi provides 80% median traffic satisfaction even with the 80-20 case owing to its efficient clustering algorithm. Interestingly, we observe that the baseline scheme performs the same in both bands. Upon closer inspection, we find that the spatial division of RRHs into clusters creates a cluster graph for the baseline where the clique size is at most three. Thus, the baseline cannot take advantage of the additional number of channels available in the 5 GHz band.

Finally, Fig. 17d shows traffic satisfaction ratio (for 80-20 load distribution), when broadcast traffic comprises 50% and 80% of the demand at each RRH. We see that the baseline scheme performs similarly in both cases. This is because the static partitioning of RRHs into clusters is agnostic to the traffic distribution within each cluster. Since AmorFi explicitly accounts for broadcast and unicast traffic demands and has the front-haul support for mixed configurations, it provides a traffic satisfaction of more than 90% while the baseline provides only about 25%.

5.5 Case Study: IEEE Globecom

Finally, we test AmorFi using NS3 simulator, based on the attendance data of a real event – IEEE Globecom 2003, which was held at the Marriott hotel in San Francisco with 1447 people attending the event [26, 33]. We consider the conference events on 2nd and 3rd of December, when the conference scheduled multiple technical presentations between 9AM-12PM and 2PM-5PM. There was also a luncheon on 2nd between 12PM-2PM, and a banquet on 3rd between 6PM-9PM. Technical presentations were held in rooms which was 77 sq. meters, and the social events was in a ballroom which was 3681 sq. meters. Based on this data, we deduced the AP interference graph using [3]. To make the results relevant to the present day, we assume all the APs and clients to implement the 802.11n WiFi standard, and thus emulate modern WiFi network.With traditional WLAN, the APs at the ballroom would be under-used during technical presentations, while the APs in the technical presentation rooms would remain idle during the social events. Assuming the attendees to be equally distributed in each event, we calculate the best throughput each user can get using the NS3 simulator based on the AP locations and the seating arrangements [33]. This throughput estimate is then input as traffic demand to AmorFi . Fig 18 plots the CDF of per-user TCP throughput using the traditional WLAN (with load balancing -Tr_LB) and AmorFi, when 50% of attendees accessed the network. We see that AmorFi clearly outperforms traditional WLAN by providing more than $2x$ median through-

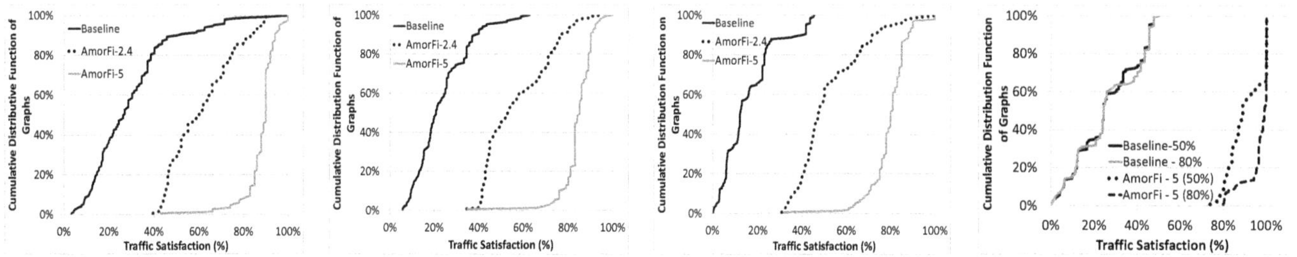

(a) 60-40: Unicast traffic (b) 70-30: Unicast traffic (c) 80-20: Unicast traffic (d) Broadcast -5Ghz

Figure 17: CDF of Traffic satisfaction - No. of APs = 50% RRHs

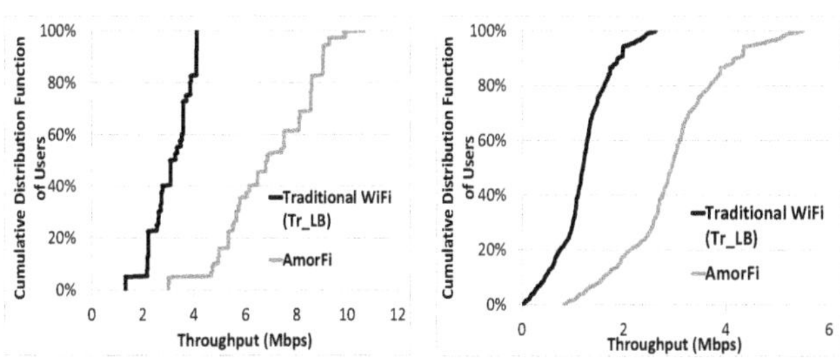

(a) Technical Sessions (b) Social Gathering

Figure 18: Simulated per-user throughput in Globecom 2003

put. Interestingly, the absolute performance is less but the gain (over the baseline) is more for the social events ($2.5x$ vs. $2.2x$) since they have a higher user concentration (similar to the highly skewed load distribution in our simulations).

6. RELATED WORK

Traditional WLANs: Supporting WLAN traffic demand is a problem that has been extensively studied both in academia and industry (e.g., [47, 48, 5, 7, 4, 15, 2, 34]). The proposed solutions mainly incorporate improved channel management and load balancing, which are some of the functionalities that we also implement in AmorFi . However, our objective is not to come up with a better channel assignment or load balancing method (AmorFi can incorporate existing procedures). Instead, AmorFi proposes a novel architecture for WLANs and addresses unique challenges to take full advantage of this architecture. Specifically, real time adaptation of capacity to efficiently support unicast and broadcast traffic, has not been addressed by any of these prior studies.

RoF in WLANs: Although some studies (e.g., [11, 43, 22, 12]) do talk about the feasibility and challenges of delivering WiFi services using RoF, they do not offer any concrete solution to our problem of catering to dynamic unicast and broadcast traffic demands.

SDN in WLANs: Studies such as [41, 50] propose a SDN-based WLAN architecture by decoupling control plane functions (power control, channel allocation, handoff etc.) from the data plane. However, since the decoupling is not at the physical layer, these architectures lack some of the key benefits that come with our C-RAN-based architecture, e.g., the ability to add/remove capacity in real time and the support for network-wide broadcast.

Software-programmable C-RAN in cellular: The idea of employing re-configurable front-haul was first discussed in [31]. Subsequently in [46], the authors leveraged the re-configurable front-haul to conserve resource (BPU) usage in the processing cluster. We feel that this is the work most similar to ours in principle. However, the problem and the eventual solution discussed in [46] is specific to cellular and cannot be directly applied to WLANs due to vast technical differences between the two domains. Further, the particular optimization problem is different and thus is not applicable.

Reconfigurable networks in datacenter: Lastly, the ability to dynamically reconfigure a network, based on the input traffic demand has been explored in [32, 28]. However, these works do not consider 802.11 WLANs.

7. CONCLUSIONS

In this work, we propose AmorFi — a first-of-its-kind system that dynamically provisions WLAN capacity to handle spatiotemporal traffic changes. AmorFi's architecture empowers WLANs with the ability to support network-level broadcast in its truest sense, thereby eliminating AP contention when delivering broadcast content. We evaluate AmorFi on a C-RAN testbed using detailed experimentation and large scale simulations. We show that AmorFi significantly outperforms traditional WLAN schemes owing to its software-defined access capability.

8. ACKNOWLEDGMENTS

We would like to thank our shepherd Samir Das and other anonymous reviewers for their insightful comments and feedback.

9. REFERENCES

[1] 802.11aa-2012 - Amendment to IEEE Std 802.11(TM)-2012. https://standards.ieee.org/findstds/standard/802.11aa-2012.html.

[2] N. Ahmed and S. Keshav. SMARTA: A Self-Managing Architecture for Thin Access Points.

In *ACM CoNEXT*, 2006.

[3] Cisco connected mobile experiences. http://www.cisco.com/c/en/us/td/docs/solutions/Enterprise/Borderless_Networks/Unified_Access/CMX.html.

[4] High density wireless networks. http://community.arubanetworks.com/aruba/.

[5] P. Bahl, M. Hajiaghayi, K. Jain, V. Mirrokni, L. Qiu, and A. Seberi. Cell Breathing in Wireless LANs: Algorithms and Evaluation. In *IEEE Transactions on Mobile Computing*, 2006.

[6] D. Brelaz. New methods to color the vertices of a graph. In *Communications of the ACM*, volume 24(2), 1979.

[7] I. Broustis, K. Papagiannaki, S. V. Krishnamurthy, and M. Faloutsos. MDG: Measurement-driven Guidelines for 802.11 WLAN Design. In *ACM MobiCom*, 2007.

[8] Benefits of Centralization in Wireless LANs. https://www.cisco.com/web/AP/wireless/pdf/Benefits_of_centralizedWLan.pdf.

[9] Centralized Management and RF Security Moves Ariba to Aruba. http://www.arubanetworks.com/pdf/solutions/CS_ariba.pdf.

[10] R. Chandra, S. Karanth, T. Moscibroda, V. Navda, J. Padhye, R. Ramjee, and L. Ravindrananth. DirCast: A Practical and Efficient Wi-Fi Multicast System. In *IEEE ICNP*, 2008.

[11] G. Chang, C. Liu, and L. Zhang. Architecture and Applications of a Versatile SmallCell, Multi-Service Cloud Radio Access Network Using Radio-over-Fiber Technologies. In *IEEE ICC*, 2013.

[12] B. Charbonnier, H. Le Bras, P. Urvoas, Q.T. N'Guyen, M. Huchard, and A. Pizzinat. Upcoming perspectives and future challenges for ROF. In *IEEE report*, 2007.

[13] Yu-Chung Cheng, Mikhail Afanasyev, Patrick Verkaik, Peter Benko, Jennifer Chiang, Alex C. Snoeren, Stefan Savage, and Geoffrey M. Voelker. Automating Cross-Layer Diagnosis of Enterprise Wireless Networks. In *ACM Sigcomm*, 2007.

[14] Yu-Chung Cheng, John Bellardo, Peter Benko, Alex C. Snoeren, Geoffrey M. Voelker, and Stefan Savage. Jigsaw: Solving the Puzzle of Enterprise 802.11 Analysis. In *ACM Sigcomm*, 2006.

[15] Wireless lan design guide for high density client environments in higher education. http://www.cisco.com/c/dam/en_us/solutions/industries/docs/education/cisco_wlan_design_guide.pdf.

[16] Us convention centers. https://en.wikipedia.org/wiki/List_of_convention_centers_in_the_United_States.

[17] Time for Some New Acronyms for CRAN. http://www.lightreading.com/mobile/fronthaul-c-ran/time-for-some-new-acronyms-for-cran/a/d-id/716159.

[18] C-RAN and Future of Small Cells. http://www.techmahindra.com/sites/blogs/C-RAN-and-Future-of-Small-Cells.aspx.

[19] ENABLING CLOUD-RAN WITH MOBILE FRONTHAUL. https://www.infinera.com/wp-content/uploads/2016/02/AN-Enabling-Cloud-RAN-with-Mobile-Fronthaul.pdf.

[20] Benefits of Cloud RAN Virtualization Delayed, but Centralized RAN Saved Millions in 2014 OPEX. http://www.advfn.com/news_Benefits-of-Cloud-RAN-Virtualization-Delayed-but_65246303.html.

[21] Jeffrey Dean and Sanjay Ghemawat. MapReduce: Simplied Data Processing on Large Clusters. In *USENIX OSDI*, 2004.

[22] S. Deronne, V. Moeyaert, and S. Bette. WiFi Transmission in Radio-over-Fiber Systems: Performance of the IEEE 802.11n Aggregation Mechanism. In *ONDM*, 2013.

[23] Dicon Fiberoptics, Inc. http://www.diconfiberoptics.com/products/mems_multicast_optical_switches.php.

[24] Stadiums race to digitize:How sports teams are scrambling to keep Millennials coming to games. http://www.techrepublic.com/article/how-sports-teams-are-scrambling-to-keep-\\-millennials-coming-to-games.

[25] Delivering content with LTE Broadcast. http://www.ericsson.com/res/thecompany/docs/publications/ericsson_review/2013/er-lte-broadcast.pdf.

[26] Globecom2003 attendees. https://www.cs.ucsb.edu/~almeroth/conf/stats/#globecom.

[27] Varun Gupta, Craig Gutterman, Yigal Bejerano, and Gil Zussman. Experimental Evaluation of Large Scale WiFi Multicast Rate Control. In *CoRR*, 2016.

[28] Navid Hamedazimi, Zafar Qazi, Himanshu Gupta, Vyas Sekar, Samir R. Das, Jon P. Longtin, Himanshu Shah, and Ashish Tanwer. FireFly: A Reconfigurable Wireless Data Center Fabric Using Free-Space Optics. In *ACM SIGCOMM*, 2014.

[29] Intel-Processor. http://ark.intel.com/products/91750/Intel-Xeon-Processor-E5-2687W-v4-30M-Cache-3_00-GHz.

[30] Stadium App - Levi's Stadium. http://www.levisstadium.com/stadium-info/stadium-app/.

[31] C. Liu, K. Sundaresan, M. Jiang, S. Rangarajan, and G. Chang. The Case for Re-configurable Backhaul in Cloud-RAN based Small Cell Networks. In *IEEE Infocom*, 2013.

[32] He Liu, Matthew K. Mukerjee, Conglong Li, Nicolas Feltman, George Papen, Stefan Savage, Srinivasan Seshan, Geoffrey M. Voelker, David G. Andersen, Michael Kaminsky, George Porter, and Alex C. Snoeren. Scheduling Techniques for Hybrid Circuit/Packet Networks. In *ACM CoNEXT*, 2015.

[33] Marriott marquis. http://www.marriott.com/hotels/event-planning/business-meeting/sfodt-san-francisco-marriott-marquis/.

[34] R. Murty, J. Padhye, R. Chandra, A. Wolman, and B. Zill. Designing High Performance Enterprise Wi-Fi

Networks. In *Usenix NSDI*, 2008.

[35] Low Latency Switching: The Race to Zero. http://www.netscout.com/uploads/2015/03/NetScout_WP_Low_Latency.pdf.

[36] Comparing costs of wireless LAN options. http://www.computerworld.com/article/2574368/mobile-wireless/comparing-costs-of-wireless-lan-options.html.

[37] Optical Zonu Corporation. http://www.opticalzonu.com/standalone/oz816/.

[38] LTE-U/LAA, MuLTEfire and Wi-Fi; making best use of unlicensed spectrum. https://www.qualcomm.com/media/documents/files/whitepaper-making-the-best-use-of-unlicensed-spectrum.pdf.

[39] Deploying very high density wi-fi: Design and configuration guide for stadiums. http://c541678.r78.cf2.rackcdn.com/appnotes/bpg-highdensity.pdf.

[40] Michael Sauer, Andrey Kobyakov, and Jacob George. Radio Over Fiber for Picocellular Network Architectures. In *Journal of Lightwave Technology,25,3301-3320*, 2007.

[41] J. Schulz-Zander, L. Suresh, N. Sarrar, A. Feldmann, T. Huehn, and R. Merz. Programmatic Orchestration of WiFi Networks. In *USENIX ATC*, 2014.

[42] S. Sen, N. K. Madabhushi, and S. Banerjee. Scalable WiFi Media Delivery through Adaptive Broadcasts. In *Usenix NSDI*, 2010.

[43] X. Shen, K. Xu, X. Sun, J. Wu, and J. Lin. Optimized Indoor Wireless Propagation Model in WiFi-RoF Network Architecture for RSS-Based Localization in the Internet of Things. In *IEEE MWP*, 2011.

[44] Vivek Srivastava, Shravan Rayanchu, Suman Banerjee, and Konstantina Papagiannaki. PIE in the Sky: Online Passive Interference Estimation for Enterprise WLANs. In *Usenix NSDI*, 2011.

[45] Cisco StadiumVision Mobile. http://www.cisco.com/c/en/us/solutions/industries/sports-entertainment/stadiumvision-mobile.html.

[46] K. Sundaresan, M. Y. Arslan, S. Singh, S. Rangarajan, and S. V. Krishnamurthy. FluidNet: A Flexible Cloud-based Radio Access Network for Small Cells. In *ACM Mobicom*, 2013.

[47] A. Vasan, R. Ramjee, and T. Woo. ECHOS - Enhanced Capacity 802.11 Hotspots. In *IEEE Infocom*, 2005.

[48] S. Vasudevan, K. Papagiannaki, C. Diot, J. Kurose, and D. Towsley. Facilitating Access Point Selection in IEEE 802.11 Wireless Networks. In *ACM IMC*, 2005.

[49] Enterprise Network Mobility: A TCO Analysis. http://www.arubanetworks.com/pdf/technology/whitepapers/wp_Lippis-TCO.pdf.

[50] Y. Yiakoumis, M. Bansal, A. Covington, J. van Reijendam, S. Katti, and N. McKeown. BeHop: a testbed for dense WiFi networks. In *ACM WinTECH*, 2014.

SlickFi: A Service Differentiation Scheme for High-Speed WLANs using Dual Radio APs

Kamran Nishat, Farrukh Javed, Saim Salman, Nofel Yaseen, Ans Fida, and Ihsan Ayyub Qazi
Computer Science Department
SBA School of Science and Engineering, LUMS, Pakistan
{mkamran,15100031,17100201,17100046,17100098,ihsan.qazi}@lums.edu.pk

ABSTRACT

Wireless LANs (WLANs) carry a diverse mix of traffic, ranging from delay-sensitive real-time applications to bulk transfers. Using existing QoS mechanisms in high speed WLANs (e.g., 802.11n/ac) presents a tradeoff between maximizing the performance of real-time applications and achieving high throughput. We propose SlickFi, a service differentiation scheme for high-speed WLANs that addresses this tradeoff by leveraging existing dual radio WiFi access points (APs). SlickFi *opportunistically* adapts channel width on a per-frame basis based on application demands and communicates traffic information across radios to control aggregate frame sizes for improving channel efficiency. SlickFi can be readily deployed on commodity devices using only driver-level changes at the AP-side. We implemented SlickFi in the ath9k driver and using real testbed experiments, show that it can improve aggregate throughput by up to 1.8x and 2.2x over 802.11n and 802.11e, respectively and the PSNR of 1080p videos by up to 3.4x and 1.7x over 802.11n and 802.11e, respectively.

1. INTRODUCTION

The last decade has witnessed a tremendous growth of traffic from real-time applications (e.g., NetFlix, YouTube, and iTunes). Cisco predicts that by 2020, 82% of global traffic will be IP video [5]. As a result, it is increasingly common for 802.11 based wireless LANs (WLANs) to carry a mix of real-time traffic and bulk transfers (e.g., file sharing via cloud-based services like Dropbox and Google Drive) [14]. A key challenge in high-speed WLANs is to meet the Quality of Service (QoS) requirements of different applications (e.g., low delay for real-time traffic and high throughput for bulk transfers).

CoNEXT '16, December 12-15, 2016, Irvine, CA, USA
© 2016 ACM. ISBN 978-1-4503-4292-6/16/12...$15.00
DOI: http://dx.doi.org/10.1145/2999572.2999594

As WLAN data rates increase, from hundreds of Mbps in 802.11n [11] to over Gbps in 802.11ac [3], lack of QoS differentiation can lead to either higher loss of throughput or poor QoS for real-time traffic. High data rate WLAN standards (e.g., 802.11n/ac) achieve high throughput efficiency by using *frame aggregation*[1]. While large aggregate frames improve throughput by amortizing the access overhead, senders must wait to collect enough frames, which increases delay and thus can adversely affect real-time traffic. For example, achieving a throughput efficiency of 80% at 300Mbps requires the aggregate frames to be as large as 23KB [40]. On the other hand, small aggregate frames improve delay performance but lead to low throughput. For example, using an aggregate frame size of 1.5KB at 300Mbps reduces the maximum user-level throughput to only 60Mbps [40, 28].

QoS differentiation can be achieved by prioritizing real-time traffic over data traffic by using multiple priority classes, as done in IEEE 802.11e [13], which introduces QoS mechanisms in the 802.11 standards. However, since prioritization based schemes assign higher channel access probability to packets from real-time applications, they can significantly degrade network throughput as they result in small aggregate frame sizes.

Another possible solution can be to leverage widely used dual radio APs [6] to isolate real-time traffic and delay-tolerant traffic into non-overlapping parts of the spectrum by mapping them to different radios. This approach offers two key benefits: (a) it allows parallel transmissions thereby amortizing the access overhead and (b) it allows each radio to be optimized for the type of traffic it carries (e.g., having smaller retry limits for real-time traffic). While this approach can improve the performance of real-time traffic, it results in low throughput on the real-time radio due to low application sending rates and the resulting small aggregate frames. In this work, we ask: *"How can we maximize the performance of real-time applications while maintaining high throughput in high-speed WLANs with dual radio APs?"*.

We propose SlickFi, a QoS differentiation scheme that leverages dual radio APs to maximize the performance of

[1]With frame aggregation, multiple frames (or MPDUs) are packed into a single aggregate frame (called A-MPDU) and sent as a single transmission.

real-time applications as well as achieve high network throughput. SlickFi achieves this by (a) dynamically adapting the channel width on a per-frame basis to make efficient use of the channel bandwidth and (b) communicating traffic information across radios to control aggregate frame sizes. SlickFi can be readily deployed in existing WLANs as it does not require any changes to commodity WiFi hardware and can co-exist with existing 802.11 clients.

The design of a scheme like SlickFi, however, raises several challenges. First, how can we ensure efficient use of the channel when we map different types of traffic on to seperate non-overlapping parts of the spectrum? Second, how can we mitigate the impact of adjacent-channel interference (ACI), which is known to significantly degrade throughput performance when using multiple radios? [36, 24]. Third, since real-time traffic results in smaller aggregate frames than high rate data traffic, we need to limit the aggregate frame sizes of the latter traffic when both radios transmit concurrently (i.e., use a channel width of 20MHz) so that data traffic could be sent over wider channels (e.g., 40MHz) for a longer duration to maximize throughput. This can be achieved by communicating aggregate frame size information between radios. Unfortunately, most off-the-shelf radios (e.g., based on the Atheros chipsets [1]) do not provide precise control over radio parameters (e.g., determining the aggregate frame length), making it challenging to accurately estimate parameter values.

With SlickFi, we address all these challenges. The first challenge is addressed by *opportunistically* using a larger channel width (e.g., 40MHz) for high throughput data traffic (e.g., bulk transfers) in the absence of packets from real-time traffic. This allows bulk transfers to use higher PHY data rates and larger aggregate frame sizes, which in turn, can lead to substantial throughput improvements. To achieve this without requiring changes in hardware, we exploit the 20/40 mixed mode of 802.11n.

We address the second challenge by periodically carrying out spectral scans and adaptively disabling default carrier sense (CS) in the presence of concurrent transmissions on adjacent channels. To address the third challenge, we use the size of the hardware queue to estimate the A-MPDU length and use high priority hardware queues to synchronize the transmission of A-MPDUs from different radios. We do this asynchronously to add minimal overhead.

Figure 1 illustrates the working of SlickFi for the case of three clients that are downloading traffic via the SlickFi access point (AP). One client is receiving saturated data traffic whereas the other two clients are streaming video. Suppose the AP can use a channel width of 20MHz or 40MHz for its transmissions. With SlickFi, when both types of traffic is present, radios use adjacent 20MHz channels for sending traffic. However, when real-time traffic is absent, the other radio starts using 40MHz of channel width to maximize throughput. This allows SlickFi to decouple the channel access overheads of different applications resulting in improved MAC efficiency.

SlickFi provides QoS differentiation without explicitly *prioritizing* one type of traffic over the other. This helps in

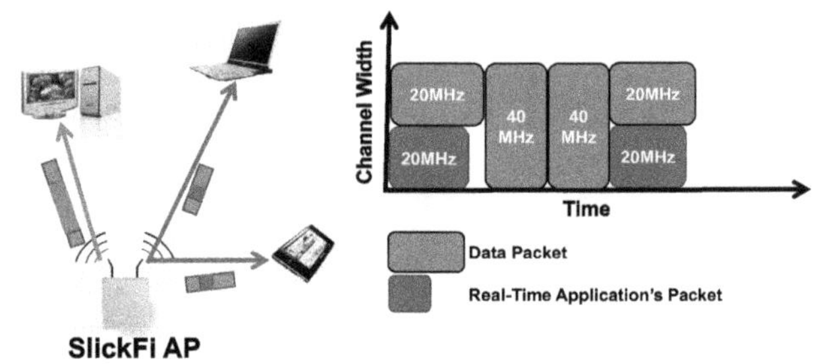

Figure 1: SlickFi Illustration.

aligning incentives for different types of traffic as low priority users no longer have the incentive to use the higher priority class to gain a higher share of resources [29].

There have been earlier works that propose the use of multiple radios in WLANs [12, 15, 19, 20, 34, 33, 37, 38]. However, they focus on addressing issues related to wireless handoffs, energy management, dynamic bandwidth adaptation, and channel management.

TDMA-based schemes have been proposed in the past for service differentiation, however, they are complex to implement [41, 32, 23] and the coordination overhead may be excessive for high-speed WLANs. To the best of our knowledge, this is the first work that uses multiple off-the-shelf (OTS) WiFi radios to provide service differentiation in high-speed WLANs that support frame aggregation. In addition, SlickFi does not require any changes to the hardware or firmware of the WiFi radios.

Altogether, this paper makes the following contributions:

- **Detailed measurement study**: We present a detailed case study over a real 802.11n testbed to quantify the tradeoff between network throughput and the QoS of real-time applications in existing high-speed WLANs.
- **Design and analysis of SlickFi**: We present the design of SlickFi, a service differentiation scheme that maximizes the performance of real-time applications as well as achieves high network throughput without explicitly prioritizing of one type of traffic over the other. SlickFi is readily deployable on commodity devices as it requires only driver-level changes at the APs.
- **In-kernel implementation**: We implement SlickFi in ath9k [1] (an open source driver for Atheros IEEE 802.11n based chipsets) on the AP-side.
- **Extensive real testbed evaluation**: We conduct evaluation of SlickFi across a diverse range of scenarios including varying number of clients, different video qualities, VoIP clients, mobility, upload and download traffic scenarios, with UDP and TCP sources, as well as with mixture of traffic to a single client. Our results show that SlickFi improves aggregate throughput by up to 1.8x and 2.2x over 802.11n and 802.11e, respectively and the peak signal-to-noise ratio (PSNR) of 1080p FHD video by up to 3.4x and 1.7x over 802.11n, and 802.11e, respectively. In addition, SlickFi improves TCP throughput by up to 1.1x

and 2.2x over 802.11n and 802.11e, respectively without degrading video quality.

The rest of this paper is organized as follows. We discuss background and present our measurement study on a real 802.11n testbed in Section 2. SlickFi's design and analysis is presented in Section 3. We present SlickFi's evaluation in Section 4. We discuss related work in Section 5 followed by some discussion in Section 6. We offer concluding remarks in Section 7.

2. BACKGROUND AND MOTIVATION

In this section, we begin by introducing some of the key features supported by high-speed WLAN standards (such as IEEE 802.11n [11] and IEEE 802.11ac [3]) for improving performance over earlier WLAN standards and review the QoS support provided by the IEEE 802.11e standard [13]. We then explore the challenges and tradeoffs in using existing high-speed standards and IEEE 802.11e for supporting different types of traffic. Finally, we summarize our design goals.

2.1 Features in IEEE 802.11n/ac

High-speed WLAN standards introduce several features (e.g., frame aggregation, MIMO) to boost performance and efficiency over earlier standards.

Frame Aggregation: With aggregation, *multiple* MAC Protocol Data Units (MPDUs) can be combined into a single aggregate MPDU frame (or A-MPDU)[2], which is transmitted as a single PHY Protocol Data Unit (PPDU). Thus, frame aggregation improves performance efficiency by amortizing the channel access overhead over multiple packets.

Block Acknowledgements (blockACK): A blockACK allows multiple MPDUs within an A-MPDU to be individually acknowledged in a *single* acknowledgement frame. The blockACK contains a 64-bit bitmap, where each bit indicates the status (success or failure) of an MPDU. This implies that in the 802.11n standard, up to 64 MPDUs can be acknowledged using a single blockACK.

Multiple-Input Multiple-Output (MIMO): MIMO employs multiple transmit and receive antennas to achieve spatial multiplexing and spatial diversity. With spatial multiplexing, each antenna transmits independent and separately encoded spatial stream. With spatial diversity, the same stream is sent over *all* antennas. It enhances signal diversity by leveraging independent fading over multiple antenna links [11].

2.2 IEEE 802.11e EDCA

To provide different QoS for different types of traffic, an extension of IEEE 802.11, known as IEEE 802.11e, was introduced, which defines the Enhanced Distributed Channel Access (EDCA) [13]. EDCA provides (statistical) service differentiation by giving different access priorities to different types of traffic. In particular, different types of traffic are mapped to one of four Access Categories (ACs). Each AC has an independent queue and implements independent DCF. These ACs achieve QoS by using different values of different MAC service differentiation parameters.

[2]In this work, we will use the term *aggregate frame* to refer to an A-MPDU.

PSNR Range	Video Quality (MOS)
> 37	Excellent
$31 - 37$	Good
$25 - 31$	Fair
$20 - 25$	Poor
< 20	Bad

Table 1: Relationship between PSNR and MOS [43].

2.3 Real-time Traffic over WiFi

We now explore the challenges associated with simultaneously supporting different types of traffic in high-speed WLANs through an experimental study over a 802.11n testbed.

When real-time traffic co-exists with high throughput data traffic, congestion from the latter traffic causes queueing that delays traffic from real-time applications, thereby degrading their performance. While 802.11e EDCA, which prioritizes real-time traffic over best effort traffic, improves the performance of real-time traffic, it degrades network throughput.

To quantify this performance tradeoff, we carried our experiments over an indoor 802.11n testbed. For generality of results, the testbed is organized to contain a diverse mix of links including line-of-sight and non-line-of-sight links, links with different distances, and links that experience different fading and shadowing effects. The resulting Received Signal Strength Indicator (RSSI) for different links ranged from -45dBm to -70dBm, which is a common RSSI range in real deployments [26]. Our setup comprises of an AP and variable number of clients. We generate saturated UDP traffic using *iperf* [8] from the AP to one client. In addition, we introduce full high-definition (FHD) video (1080p FHD mode) streaming with varying number of clients (i.e., one download per client). We measure the video quality using PSNR, a widely used metric [43]. PSNR compares the maximum possible signal energy to the error energy. The PSNR of each frame can be mapped to the Mean Opinion Score (MOS), which is a metric of user perception video quality (see Table 1).

Figure 2 shows the aggregate throughput and PSNR for the FHD video clients in case of 802.11n and 802.11e EDCA. With 802.11n DCF, the aggregate throughput decreases by ~25Mbps for every video client we add. This happens because video packets result in small aggregate frame sizes (due to their lower sending rates relative to the PHY data rates), which reduces MAC efficiency and thus degrades throughput. For example, the average aggregate frame size for the iperf client was ~23 whereas for the video clients[3], it was 5.5 as shown in Table 2. As more clients are added, more A-MPDUs with smaller sizes are transmitted, which degrades throughput substantially. In addition, the performance of

[3]Note that lower quality videos (e.g., 720p) result in smaller aggregate frame sizes as shown in Table 2.

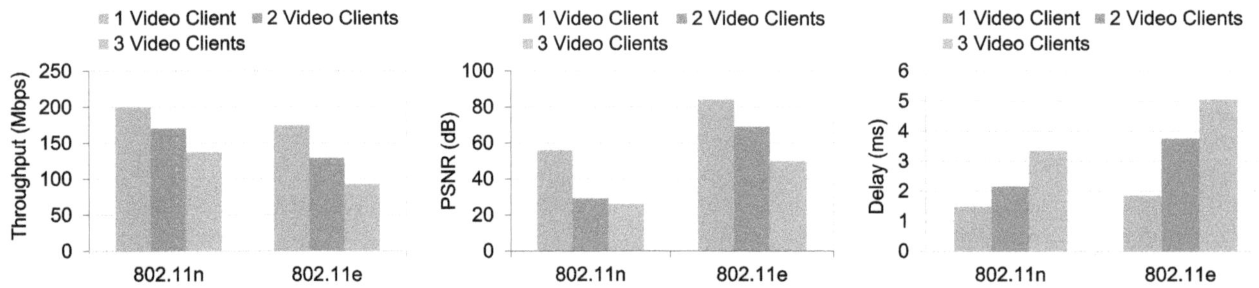

Figure 2: Peformance with 1-3 video clients and one saturated iperf client under 802.11n DCF and 802.11e EDCA. (a) Aggregate throughput, (b) PSNR, and (c) delay between A-MPDUs of the iperf client.

	iperf	Video (1080p)	Video (720p)
A-MPDU Len	22.8	5.5	2.1

Table 2: Aggregate frame length (or A-MPDU length) for the iperf client and the FHD (or full high-definition) video clients for different resolutions.

video traffic also decreases significantly. For example, the PSNR reduces by more than 30dB when the second video client is added. This happens because the iperf traffic and the video traffic share the same queue at the MAC layer, which increases the delay experienced by video packets.

Obervation 1: *With 802.11n, the QoS of real-time traffic degrades in the presence of high throughput traffic. Moreover, increase in real-time traffic degrades network throughput.*

With 802.11e EDCA, iperf traffic is mapped to the best effort class (AC_BE) and video traffic to a higher priority traffic category (AC_VI). Observe that the PSNR of video traffic improves substantially under EDCA. This happens because video packets and iperf packets are mapped to separate queues and the video traffic gets preferential access, which in turn, improves the video quality. However, 802.11e significantly degrades network throughput (which is much lower than under the 802.11n DCF). Moreover, there is a greater loss in throughput ($\sim$30Mbps per new video client). This happens due to the prioritization of video packets, which results in small aggregate frame sizes, thereby making inefficient use of the channel. Figure 2 (c) shows the inter-A-MPDU delay experienced by iperf transmissions. Observe that due to prioritization of video traffic, iperf frames experience much greater delay between transmissions, which results in throughput degradation.

Obervation 2: *802.11e EDCA cannot maintain high network throughput in the presence of real-time traffic.*

These experiments show that prioritization schemes, like 802.11e, are unable to significantly benefit from throughput-enhancing features in 802.11n/ac, such as frame aggregation and channel bonding, when different types of traffic co-exist.

2.4 Design Goals

Motivated by the above problems, we aim to design a QoS differentiation scheme for high-speed WLANs that achieves the following properties:

- **High network throughput:** Our scheme must be able to achieve high throughput in the presence of real-time traffic as long as there is enough demand.
- **High performance for real-time traffic:** Our scheme should be able to maximize the QoS of real-time traffic in the presence of throughput-intensive traffic.
- **Compatible with existing WiFi devices:** We choose to design a scheme that does not require any changes in the WLAN standards and can benefit from the widely available commodity WiFi hardware.
- **Incentive compatible:** Our scheme should be able to provide service differentiation without *prioritizing* one type of traffic over the other. This helps in aligning incentives for different types of traffic as low priority users no longer have the incentive to use the higher priority class to gain a higher share of resources [29].

We show how SlickFi achieves the above design goals in the next section.

3. SLICKFI'S DESIGN

3.1 Design Rationale and Challenges

We now present the design of SlickFi, a system that achieves QoS differentiation in high-speed WLANs while maintaining high network throughput. SlickFi's design is based on two key principles:

1. **Radio-based decoupling of traffic:** To achieve high performance for real-time traffic, it should be shielded from the queueing caused by packets of high throughput data traffic. To realize such traffic isolation, SlickFi maps real-time traffic and data traffic on to separate radios (at the AP-side) that operate in *non-overlapping* parts of the spectrum. While traffic isolation can also be provided by using multiple queues on a single interface, doing so leads to *multiplexing* of traffic, which degrades throughput due to small aggregate frame sizes of real-time traffic.

2. **Opportunistic use of channel bandwidth:** To achieve high network throughput, the radio carrying bulk transfer traffic should be able to *adapt* the channel width on a per-frame basis in order to efficiently utilize the available spectrum whenever possible (i.e., when there is no real-time traffic).

However, realizing the above design features raises several challenges:

- **Adjacent-channel interference (ACI):** ACI is a major challenge in multi-radio WiFi systems like SlickFi because it diminishes concurrent transmission opportunities, thereby degrading throughput. Slick uses spectral scan based adaptive carrier sensing to address this challenge.
- **Efficient channel usage:** Achieving high network throughput requires opportunistic use of the channel as well as accurate estimation and communication of transmission parameters (e.g., aggregate frame sizes) across radios. SlickFi uses the 20/40 mixed mode of 802.11n/ac for per-frame channel width adaptations and leverages hardware queues for estimating aggregate frame sizes.

We now discuss SlickFi's design details.

3.2 Using Multiple Radios Flexibly

In SlickFi, every AP has two interfaces: the real-time interface (RI) and the best-effort interface (BI). Both interfaces operate on adjacent non-overlapping 20MHz channels. While RI carries latency-sensitive real-time traffic, BI carries throughput-sensitive data traffic. The goal of RI is to avoid degrading the quality of real-time traffic by mitigating unnecessary delays whereas the goal of BI is to maximize throughput of data traffic.

Using multiple radios operating in non-overlapping parts of the spectrum ensures that real-time traffic remains insulated from data traffic and thus is not delayed because of queueing delays caused by data traffic. One challenge with this approach is that RI can go substantially underutilized, thereby wasting channel bandwidth. This can happen because real-time applications, such as VoIP and video streaming, generally have much lower sending rates compared to PHY data rates supported by high-speed WLANs. For example, streaming a HD 720p video results in a sending rate of ≈19Mbps whereas PHY rates in 802.11n can be as high as 600Mbps. To avoid wasting channel bandwidth, SlickFi allows BI to opportunistically use a larger channel width on a per-frame basis. In particular, it increases the channel width from 20MHz to 40MHz if RI is idle. However, if there is an ongoing transmission on RI, BI uses 20MHz of channel width for its transmissions.

To allow fast switching of channel width on a per-frame basis using existing commodity WiFi radios, we leverage the 20/40 mixed mode of 802.11n/ac. In this mode, every 802.11n station can opportunistically change its channel width from 20MHz to 40MHz bandwidth on a per-frame basis. A transmission uses 40MHz of channel width only if the primary channel is idle and in addition, the secondary channel is idle for the PIFS ($25\mu s$) duration[4] immediately preceding the expiration of the backoff counter. Otherwise, the frame is transmitted on the primary (20MHz) channel [11]. Therefore, almost no additional time is wasted in channel switching.

We observed that because the sensing duration of the secondary channel is basically part of MAC backoff, 40MHz transmissions get implicitly prioritized [11]. When the load on RI is high, this can add delays to real-time traffic due to 40MHz transmissions (that usually have large aggregate frame sizes) on BI. To overcome this issue, we enforce BI to use 20MHz of channel width when RI gets saturated.

Alternate Approach: One possible way of improving aggregate throughput (as opposed to adapting the channel width) is to spray packets on both interfaces. However, this may lead to packet reordering, which is known to degrade TCP performance [46].

3.3 Dealing with ACI

ACI is a major challenge in multi-radio WiFi systems like SlickFi because it diminishes concurrent transmission opportunities, thereby degrading throughput. One can reduce ACI by adding shielding between radios but that can still result in throughput degradation by up to 10% [36]. Additionally, the use of frame aggregation in 802.11n/ac standards can exacerbate the performance loss due to ACI because large aggregate frame sizes lead to more wasted air time. Moreover, different aggregate frame sizes makes it difficult to align parallel transmissions from multiple interfaces.

We address this issue by using spectral scan based adaptive carrier sensing. With the spectral scan feature (which is available in several commodity WiFi cards), the radio hardware has the ability to report FFT summary information about the received wireless signal [4]. If a radio receives an error frame then its FFT summary is passed by the physical layer to the MAC layer. One of the main parts of this FFT summary information is the absolute magnitude (i.e., $|I| + |Q|$, where I and Q phases are of the wireless signal) for each FFT bin—56 for subcarriers in the 20MHz channel and 114 for the 40MHz channel. Note that this is fundamentally different from the standard Channel State Information (CSI) format [11]. In CSI, each channel matrix entry is a complex number, with signed 8-bit resolution each for the real and imaginary parts [22]. CSI is the channel state information sent by the receiver to a sender whereas spectral scan is the FFT bin information observed by a receiver in case of error. The WiFi card allows obtaining this data for different frequencies through the driver.

In SlickFi, we sense the energy level of each OFDM subcarrier $bin(i)$ (absolute energy level in ith sub-carrier) before sending a frame. If the sum of sub-carrier energy levels on the primary channel is higher than the sum of sub-carrier

[4]The PIFS duration is used only if the station is operating in the 5GHz band. In the 2.4GHz band, the secondary channel is sensed for the DIFS duration just before the backoff counter expires.

energy levels on the secondary channel, then it is a strong indicator of ACI from RI.

$$\Delta = \sum_{i=0}^{Bin_{40}/2} bin(i) - \sum_{j=Bin_{40}/2}^{Bin_{40}} bin(j)$$

where Bin_{40} is the total number of sub-carriers in 40MHz. Thus, when $\Delta > 0$ we switch off physical carrier sensing and transmit the frame on the 20MHz (primary) channel. To understand the effects of ACI on spectral scan we performed experiments with a dual-radio AP and different receivers.

Figure 3 shows the CDF of Δ when there is interference on (a) primary channel, (b) secondary channel (due to the adjacent WiFi radio in the AP), and (c) secondary channel (due to other nodes in the network[5]). We observe that we can use a simple threshold τ to determine the presence of ACI (i.e., when $\Delta > \tau$, SlickFi concludes the presence of ACI) with reasonably high detection accuracy and low false positive rate. This technique is inspired from [24]. However, unlike SlickFi, they use the increase in RSSI values as a signal for the presence of ACI, which is a coarse-grained approach for adapting physical carrier sensing.

3.4 Communication between Radios

In Section 2, we observed that there is usually a significant difference in the size of A-MPDUs from real-time (video) traffic and high throughput data traffic. This difference is substantial even for FHD videos (see Table 2), which are one of the highest resolution streaming videos used nowadays. Transmitting A-MPDUs of different lengths will cause the spectrum to be occupied for 40MHz transmissions until the completion of the longest transmission. If the number of clients using RI is small then considerable transmission time may be wasted. To realize this opportunity for throughput improvement, SlickFi adapts the A-MPDU length on BI using feedback from the RI driver. This feedback is generated when an A-MPDU is about to be pushed in the hardware queue by the MAC layer driver. This feedback is used to set the A-MPDU size for the next transmission by BI. It is possible to have multiple A-MPDUs already waiting for transmission. We use a high priority hardware queue to synchronize this A-MPDU of adapted size. This increases the chances of parallel transmissions of same sizes, which will result in more time available for 40MHz transmissions. We also stop sending this feedback if there is an increase in the number of clients on RI. In such scenarios, most of the transmissions from BI use 20MHz of channel width, thus it is advantageous to send A-MPDU of maximum size.

3.5 Clients Carrying a Mixture of Traffic

SlickFi's design does not require client devices to support multiple radios as single radio WiFi devices are very common today. However, individual clients may generate multiple types of traffic simultaneously, which can potentially de-

[5]We use 3 receivers and choose their locations to create links with line-of-sight, non-line-of-sight, and links that experience different multi-path fading and shadowing effects.

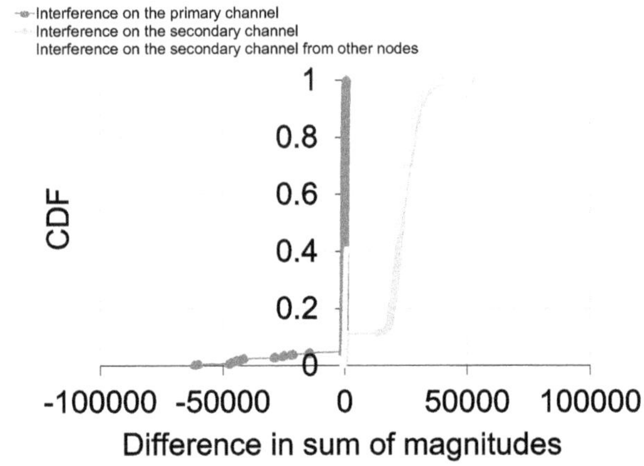

Figure 3: CDF of Δ when there is interference on the (a) primary channel, (b) secondary channel (from the adjacent radio), and (c) secondary channel due to other node in the network. These results show that Δ can be used to detect the presence of ACI.

grade performance. To handle such scenarios, we map both types of traffic to BI for two reasons: (a) it can transmit aggregate frames on a larger 40MHz of channel and (b) packets from different traffic types destined for the same client can be aggregated to create large A-MPDUs, thereby improving throughput performance. Thus, SlickFi performs well in most common scenarios, however, in the rare case when all clients in the WLAN generate both saturated best effort and real-time traffic at the same time, then SlickFi's performance will be reduced to the performance of default 802.11n[6].

3.6 Throughput Analysis

We now present a simple analytical model to determine the maximum achievable throughput with SlickFi (and its variants) and the default 802.11n. We do not model the throughput with 802.11e as it is known to have lower throughput performance compared to the default 802.11n as also observed in the experimental study in Section 2. We consider two variants of dual radio schemes in comparison with SlickFi; one where RI uses a static 20MHz channel but BI dynamically switches between 20MHz and 40MHz channels (we term this variant as Dynamic 20/40) and the other where both RI and BI use static 20MHz channels (we term this variant as Static 20/20). Finally, we analyze SlickFi, which in addition to dynamic switching of the channel width, also adapts the A-MPDU length of BI traffic to decrease the lost transmission opportunities due to mismatch in A-MPDU lengths when BI and RI transmit in parallel (see Figure 4).

We consider a scenario where BI is saturated but RI carries bursty[7] real-time traffic. We assume that after every δ

[6]Note that if both BI and RI received saturated traffic, SlickFi will lead to higher throughput than 802.11n as parallel transmissions are more throughput efficient [40].

[7]Our experimental evaluation revealed that many real-time applications (e.g., video streaming and VoIP) exhibit bursty/ON-OFF traffic characteristics.

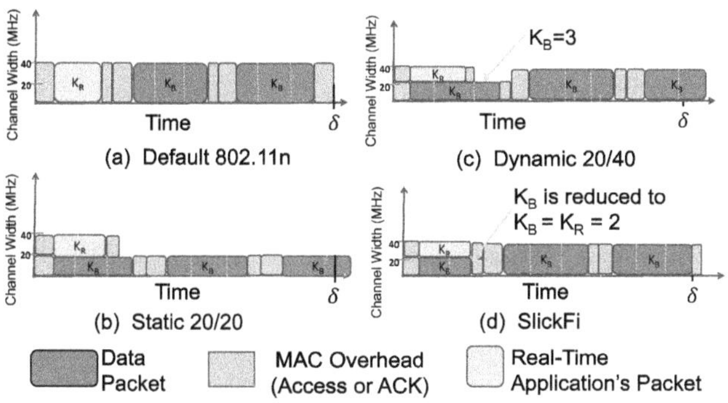

Figure 4: Illustration of schemes consider in the throughput analysis including Default 802.11n, Static 20/20, Dynamic 20/40, and SlickFi. Note that the figure is not drawn to scale.

interval, RI receives a burst of size k_R packets where each individual packet is of size P_R. Each burst is then sent as a single A-MPDU at the MAC layer. Moreover, we assume that BI sends A-MPDUs of size k_B frames, where each frame is of size P_B. We determine the maximum throughput that can be achieved by each scheme every δ interval.

The transmission of a single A-MPDU results in several overheads at the MAC layer. The cumulative overhead t_{ov} is given by:

$$t_{ov} = t_{DIFS} + t_{slot} \cdot W + t_{pr} + t_{SIFS} + t_{ACK}$$

where t_{slot} is the slot duration, t_{DIFS} is the duration of DIFS (Distributed Inter-Frame Space) interval, t_{SIFS} is the duration of the SIFS (Short Inter-Frame Space) interval, t_{pr} is the time used for transmitting per-frame training symbols, t_{ACK} is the transmission time of the acknowledgment (ACK), and W is the expected number of backoff slots. If we assume loss-less transmissions, then since each node chooses a random backoff value from the interval $[0, CW_{min})$, where CW_{min} is the minimum contention window size. Thus, W=$CW/2$ is the average backoff in terms of number of slots[8]

3.6.1 *Default 802.11n*

Assuming a channel width of 40MHz and a single WiFi interface, the default 802.11n transmits one A-MPDU from real-time traffic every δ interval. The remaining time in the interval is used for transmitting A-MPDUs of best-effort traffic as shown in Figure 4(a). Thus, the total number of A-MPDUs sent by default 802.11n during δ is given by

$$\eta_{def} = \frac{\delta - t_{R40}}{t_{B40}} \tag{1}$$

where $t_{R40} > 0$ and $t_{B40} > 0$ are the transmission times of A-MPDUs from real-time and best-effort traffic, respectively, when using 40MHz of channel width and $\delta > t_{R40}$.

[8]Note that these overheads remain the same for 20MHz and 40MHz channels [26].

Then the achievable (lossless) throughput is given by

$$T_{def} = \frac{k_B P_B \eta_{def} + k_R P_R}{\delta}. \tag{2}$$

3.6.2 *Static 20/20*

Under this scheme, *all* A-MPDUs are sent using 20MHz of channel width. Moreover, A-MPDUs from RI and BI are transmitted in parallel (see Figure 4(b)). Thus, the total number of A-MPDUs transmitted during the δ interval is

$$\eta_{static} = \frac{\delta}{t_{B20}}, \tag{3}$$

where t_{B20} is the duration of an A-MPDU from BI sent on a 20MHz channel. Therefore, the throughput is given by

$$T_{static} = \frac{(k_B P_B \eta_{static}) + (k_R P_R)}{\delta}. \tag{4}$$

3.6.3 *Dynamic 20/40*

Under this scheme, every δ interval begins with parallel transmissions from RI and BI at 20MHz. Since k_B is usually greater than k_R (see Table 2), the A-MPDU transmission from RI finishes before the transmission from BI ends. For the remaining time in the δ interval, all transmissions from BI are sent at 40MHz as shown in Figure 4(c). Thus, we can send $\eta_{dynamic}$ A-MPDUs at 40MHz.

$$\eta_{dynamic} = \frac{\delta - t_{B20}}{t_{B40}}. \tag{5}$$

The maximum achievable throughput is then given by:

$$T_{dynamic} = \frac{k_B P_B + k_B P_B \cdot \eta_{dynamic} + k_R P_R}{\delta}. \tag{6}$$

Note that the transmission time of an A-MPDU from BI sent at a data rate R_{20} and a channel width of 20MHz is given by

$$t_{B20} = t_{ov} + \frac{k_B \cdot P_B}{R_{20}} \tag{7}$$

Similarly, t_{B40} is the data transmission time of an A-MPDU on the 40MHz channel. We assume that R_{40}, the data rate at 40MHz, will be at most twice the data rate in case of 20MHz channels (i.e., $R_{40} = 2 \cdot R_{20}$) [11].

3.6.4 *SlickFi*

When both BI and RI transmit in parallel using 20MHz of channel width, RI finishes transmission first due to smaller A-MPDU sizes of real-time traffic. However, BI continues transmitting on the 20MHz channel for an additional $(t_{B20} - t_{R20})$ seconds even though the other channel is idle. This leads to wasted opportunities for improving throughput. This difference between $\eta_{dynamic}$ and η_{def} (which is also the maximum number of A-MPDUs that can be sent on BI at 40MHz during δ) can be reduced by decreasing t_{B20}, which in turn can be achieved by reducing the size of A-MPDUs from BI that are sent at 20MHz of channel width.

By doing so, we can increase the number A-MPDUs that can be sent using 40MHz of channel width. SlickFi uses this approach i.e., when transmitting in parallel it reduces the A-MPDU size of RI traffic to that of the BI traffic so as to maximize transmissions on 40MHz channels (see Figure 4(d)).

To capture the improvement in throughput, we calculate the gain in $\eta_{dynamic}$ by sending one less MPDU from BI at 20MHz as follows:

$$\Delta\eta_{dynamic} = \eta_{dynamic,(k_B-1)} - \eta_{dynamic,k_B},$$

where $\eta_{dynamic,(k_B-1)}$ is η when an A-MPDU of size $(k_B - 1)$ is sent from BI on a 20MHz channel and $\eta_{dynamic,k_B}$ is η when an A-MPDU of size k_B is sent using 20MHz transmissions. Using Equations (5) and (7), we get:

$$\Delta\eta_{dynamic} = \frac{P_B}{t_{B40} \cdot R_{20}} \tag{8}$$

Since $\Delta\eta_{dynamic} > 0$, reducing the A-MPDU size by one will result in an increase in the number of A-MPDUs that can be sent over the 40MHz channel, thereby leading to throughput improvements. Note that this will not hold if we decrease the size of A-MPDU of BI at 20MHz less than size of A-MPDU of RI. We can calculate the difference in throughput using Equation (6) as

$$\Delta T_{dynamic} = \frac{k_B P_B \cdot \Delta\eta_{dynamic} - P_B}{\delta}. \tag{9}$$

The first term in the above expression indicates the increase in throughput resulting from 40MHz transmissions whereas the second (negative) term represents the lost opportunity of not sending an MPDU at 20MHz. We can simplify this expression using equation (5) and by replacing $t_{B40} = t_{ov} + \frac{k_B \cdot P_B}{2 \cdot R_{20}}$

$$\Delta T_{dynamic} = \frac{P_B \cdot (\frac{k_B \cdot P_B}{2} - t_{ov} \cdot R_{20})}{\delta \cdot t_{B40} \cdot R_{20}} \tag{10}$$

Thus, $\Delta T_{dynamic}$ will be positive (i.e. there will be gain in throughput) if

$$\frac{k_B \cdot P_B}{R_{40}} > t_{ov}.$$

The above inequality shows that if the payload duration of A-MPDUs (sent at 40MHz) is greater than the duration of access overheads, then decreasing the size of BI A-MPDUs (sent at 20MHz) will lead to increase in throughput.

Figure 5 shows the throughput under different schemes as a function of the PHY data rates. Observe that SlickFi achieves ~15-20% higher throughput compared to Dynamic 20/40 as it is able to send more transmissions over 40MHz channels while dynamically adapting the A-MPDU size.

Observe that SlickFi and the default 802.11n achieve similar throughput performance. While the performance of real-time traffic suffers in case of 802.11n, SlickFi is able to maximize the performance of both types of traffic.

Our model does not consider channel losses. However, in practice, channel losses are often inevitable [30]. Our experimental evaluation in Section 4 shows that SlickFi outperforms 802.11n in terms of throughput in the presence of channel losses. First, channel losses lead to MAC layer backoffs that delay all transmissions in case of 802.11n as it uses a channel width of 40MHz. With SlickFi, a loss on one 20MHz channel does not necessarily imply a loss on the other 20MHz channel, thereby leading to less wasted time. Second, SlickFi uses 20MHz channels when it transmits both real-time traffic and data traffic at the same time. Using 20MHz channels increases the power/hertz, which reduces the PER for such transmissions, thereby improving throughput compared to 802.11n.

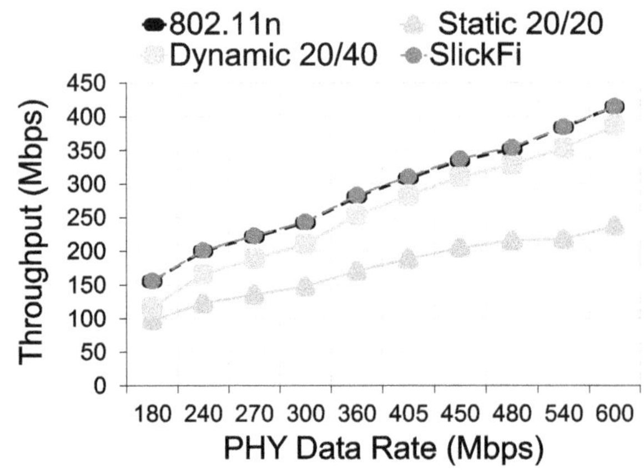

Figure 5: Throughput analysis of SlickFi and other schemes under the scenario of a single video client and a single bulk transfer. The throughput is obtained by using experimentally determined A-MPDU sizes (see Table 2) and parameter values from [40].

4. EVALUATION

We evaluate SlickFi on a real 802.11n testbed across a diverse set of scenarios including varying number of video clients, clients with different video qualities, mobile clients, VoIP clients, combined upload and download traffic scenario, evaluation with UDP and TCP traffic, as well as evaluation with single radio clients. To generate both UDP and TCP data traffic, we use iperf [8]. We use 1080p FHD and 720p HD videos in our evaluation using FFServer and they are streamed using the VLC player on the client-side. In most of our experiments, we use 1080p FHD video as it is generally the highest video quality used in online streaming services. All the experiments are run for 40 seconds and the results are averaged over five runs.

4.0.1 Experimental Platform

We conduct our experiments on an indoor testbed in a campus setting. Our testbed comprises of a diverse mix of links including line-of-sight and non-line-of-sight links, links with varying distances, and links that experience different fading and shadowing effects. In our testbed, the RSSI of links ranged from -45dBm to -70dBm.

While carrying out the experiments, we ensure that no other device operates on the same channel or on any of the

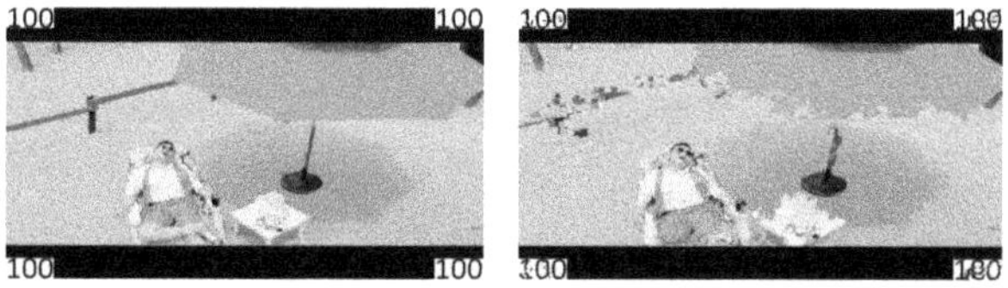

(a) Reference Frame (b) Streamed Frame

Figure 6: Reference frame and streamed video frame for PSNR calculation.

overlapping channels. This ensures that no external interfering source affects our experimental results. We perform all our experiments in the 5GHz band. The SlickFi AP for prototyping comprises of two TP-Link 4300 wireless APs joined together to form a single node. The WiFi chips in the APs are based on Atheros AR9381, which is compatible with the ath9k driver. The APs run OpenWrt barrier breaker 14.07. We patch OpenWrt and the ath9k driver to implement the SlickFi interface. We use `Ministrel_ht` as the rate control algorithm, which is the default rate adaptation scheme in ath9k.

We evaluate SlickFi on a network of 10 nodes. Each node runs Ubuntu 12.04 with kernel 3.13.2 and contains one PCI based Atheros 9380 card connected to a PC. We restrict the maximum data rates to 130Mbps and 300Mbps for 20MHz and 40MHz channels, respectively. This resulted in smaller variations in PERs and reduced the impact of rate control. Frame aggregation and blockACKs are available and have been used in all experiments. Both APs and clients use a 3×3 antenna configuration that supports 3 spatial streams. SlickFi classifies flows into different WiFi radios based on the IP Type of Service (ToS) field[9].

4.0.2 Calculating PSNR

PSNR is an objective quality metric that compares each pixel of the received video with the original video. Bursty packet losses can result in multiple frame losses that can often lead to the comparison of non-corresponding frames in the PSNR calculation. Unfortunately, many existing PSNR-based schemes do not take into account the impact of frame losses [10]. This limitation gets amplified in wireless networks, where high packet loss rates contribute to the inaccuracy in assessing the video streaming quality [17]. In order to address this shortcoming, we devised a new algorithm for calculating PSNR in the presence of frame losses. In particular, we append a unique code to each of the four corners of every frame in the original video, making it less susceptible to distortions due to partial frame loss (see Figure 6). The original frames corresponding to the streamed frames are found by matching this unique code. Finally, the PSNR calculation is carried out frame by frame. The correctly received frames are assigned a PSNR of 100dB as done in [17].

[9]Note that applications using the 802.11e standard are also classified based on the ToS field [42].

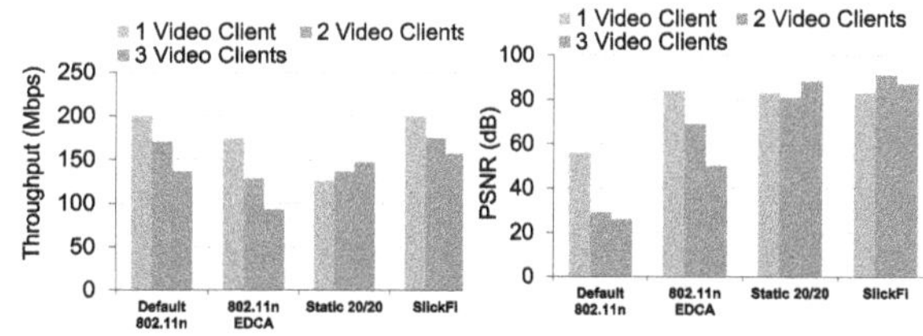

Figure 7: Aggregate throughput and PSNR with 802.11n, 802.11e, Static 20/20, and SlickFi for 1-3 video clients and one saturated iperf client. Links with RSSI between -45dBm to -55dBm.

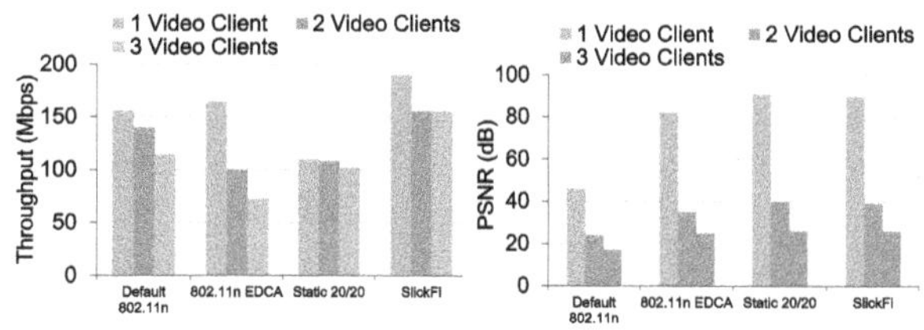

Figure 8: Aggregate throughput and PSNR with 802.11n, 802.11e, Static 20/20, and SlickFi for 1-3 video clients and one saturated iperf client. Links with RSSI between -58dBm to -70dBm.

4.1 Static SlickFi Clients

We now compare the performance of SlickFi with the default 802.11n DCF as well as with 802.11n EDCA (or 802.11e) while considering stationary clients. Our results show that SlickFi with dynamic adaptation consistently outperforms all other schemes both in terms of aggregate throughput as well as video quality under all scenarios.

4.1.1 UDP

For UDP-based best effort traffic, we performed experiments using 1080p FHD video under two settings. One with strong to moderate signal strength (RSSI ranged between -45dBm to -55dBm) and the other with moderate to worse signal strength (RSSI ranged between -58dBm to -70dBm). Figure 7 shows the average PSNR and the aggregate throughput when nodes are placed relatively close to the AP, resulting in a good signal strength. We observed that SlickFi provides up to 21Mbps increase in throughput compared to 802.11n. This happens due to two reasons (a) SlickFi uses the channel more efficiently by enabling parallel transmissions on narrower channels, which amortizes the channel access overhead [40] and (b) 20MHz transmissions result in more robust link conditions due to higher power per hertz as the total total transmission power does not change, which leads to lower packet loss rates and thus improves system throughput. At the same time, SlickFi provides substantial improvement in PSNR. For example, it improves the PSNR by up to 4x when there are three video streaming clients.

Figure 8 shows the PSNR and aggregate throughput when all clients have moderate to worse channel conditions. In such scenarios, SlickFi provides up to ∼1.3x and ∼2x im-

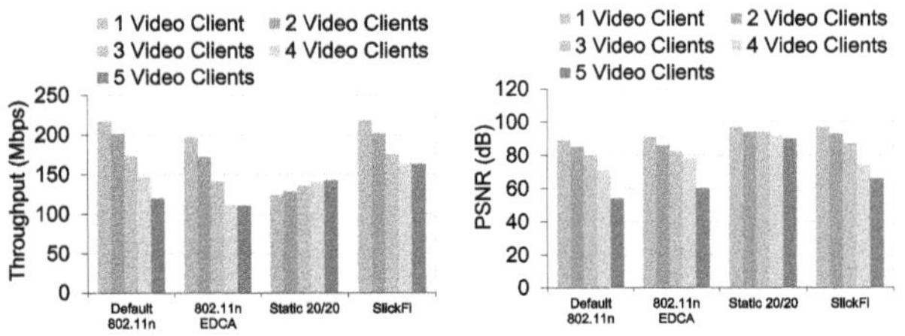

Figure 9: Aggregate throughput and PSNR for 1-5 (720p) video clients and one saturated iperf client.

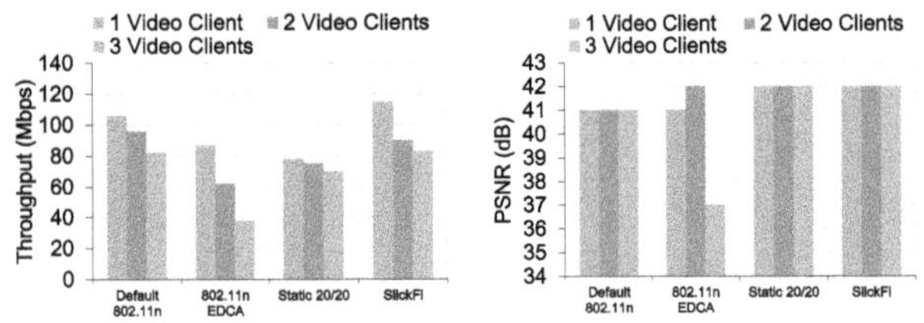

Figure 10: TCP iperf throughput and PSNR for 1-3 video clients and one TCP iperf client.

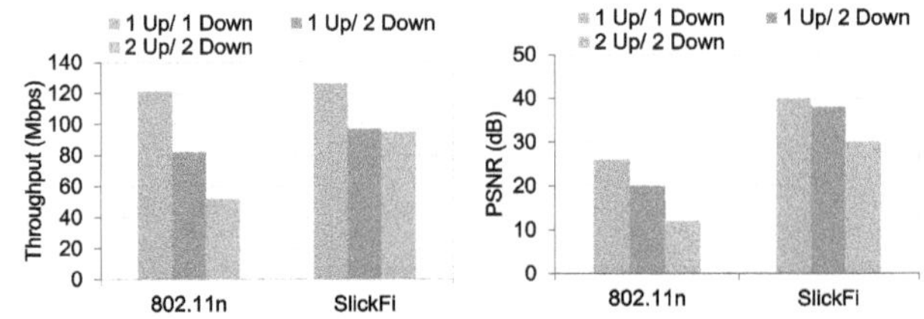

Figure 11: Aggregate throughput and PSNR for a mixture of upload and download video clients and one saturated iperf client.

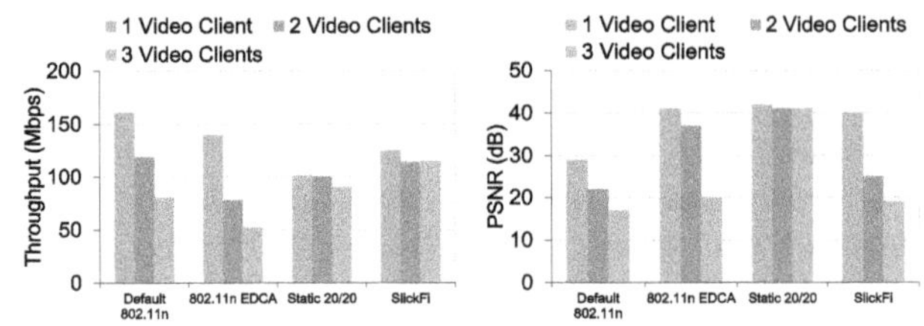

Figure 12: iperf throughput of one static client and the PSNR of one moving video client. Other 0-2 video clients are static.

provement in throughput over 802.11n DCF and 802.11n EDCA, respectively. Observe that SlickFi provides greater improvement in video quality compared to the previous scenario. When there is one video client, SlickFi provides up to 4x improvement in PNSR. This improvement gets diminished as we increase number of clients due to increased channel contention, however, SlickFi still provides acceptable video quality along with high throughput in these cases.

We also carried out experiments with 720p HD video to show the generality of our scheme. Figure 9 shows the aggregate throughput and the average PSNR under this scenario for up to five clients. With this quality of video SlickFi's advantages are less but still evident even with one video client. They got more apparent when we increase number of clients.

Observe that with Static 20/20, the aggregate throughput increases when more video clients are added whereas with SlickFi, the throughput decreases in such cases (e.g., see Figures 7 and 9) even though SlickFi always achieves higher throughput than Static 20/20. This happens because with Static 20/20, the RI channel goes under-utilized when there is one video client. When more clients are added, the channel utilization increases, which translates into throughput improvements. SlickFi, on the other hand, already maximizes throughput by opportunistically sending packets over 40MHz channels. When more clients are added, this opportunity reduces and therefore, its performance converges to the performance of Static 20/20.

4.1.2 TCP

We also evaluated SlickFi with TCP traffic. We found that SlickFi provides up to 10Mbps, 37Mbps, and 44Mbps compared to Default 802.11n, Static 20/20, and 802.11n EDCA, respectively. However, we found that the PSNR of the received video remained largely unchanged with TCP across all schemes. This happens due to TCP's congestion control mechanism, which reduces the sending rate in the presence of congestion (e.g., when packet losses occur). This helps in maintaining a high PSNR for real-time traffic. Observe that SlickFi is still able to achieve higher throughput compared to Static 20/20 and 802.11n EDCA across a range of scenarios.

Note that prior works on service differentiation, such as [41], report a degradation in TCP throughput in the presence of real-time traffic.

4.1.3 Video Uploads and Downloads

We designed this experiment to show the ability of SlickFi to improve performance and QoS in the presence of multiple senders. Figure 11 shows the aggregate throughput and average PSNR when one or more videos are uploaded and downloaded simultaneously. Observe that SlickFi provides up to 2x increase in throughput and 2.5x improvement in PSNR under these scenarios. This improvement comes primarily because of segregation of real-time traffic and data traffic in separate parts of the spectrum. In addition, any lost transmission opportunities in RI are leveraged by BI using 40MHz A-MPDUs.

4.2 Mobile Clients

Mobile video clients are getting increasingly common nowadays. Therefore, we now assess the effectiveness of SlickFi under fast changing channel conditions. We carry a client and walk away from the AP at roughly a constant speed of 1 meter/s. During this walk, the RSSI changed from -30dBm to -65dBm. Figure 12 shows average throughput and PSNR for the moving client. In the single (mobile) video client scenario, SlickFi provides $\sim$1.3x improvement in PSNR with comparable throughput compared to 802.11n. As we increase the number of video clients, we observe up to 1.4x increase in throughput along with at least 3dBm increase in PSNR.

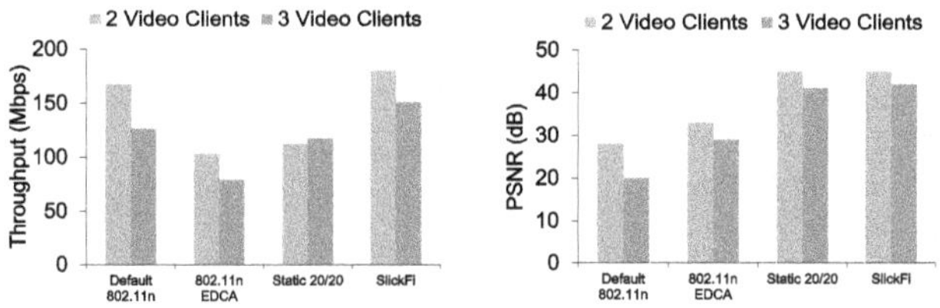

Figure 13: iperf throughput and PSNR for a single radio video client. It competes with 0-2 video clients and one saturated UDP client.

	Throughput (Mbps)	Dropped Calls (%)
802.11n	9.2	10%
SlickFi	16.1	2%

Table 3: Throughput of the UDP iperf client and the percentage of VoIP calls dropped.

4.3 Clients Carrying Mixture of Traffic

In this experiment, we evaluate the performance of SlickFi in the presence of a (single radio) client carrying both types of traffic. In this case, SlickFi maps both of them to BI so that it can opportunistically use 40MHz of channel width.

Figure 13 shows the aggregate throughput and PSNR of the received video at the single client. Observe that SlickFi gives better throughput then default 802.11n and up to 2x better PSNR compared to 802.11e.

4.4 Using VoIP on RI

We perform this experiment with VoIP traffic to study the effectiveness of SlickFi for non-video real-time traffic. We used `SIPp` [9] VoIP call generator to generate 50 calls per client. Duration of each call is 5 seconds. We used six clients for VoIP and one saturated UDP client. To see the effect of very low data rate VoIP clients, we restrict the PHY data rate to 30Mbps.

Table 3 shows that SlickFi provides ~2x improvement in throughput over the default 802.11n. Moreover, it considerably reduces the fraction of dropped calls.

5. RELATED WORK

There are various approaches for providing QoS to different types of traffic. IEEE 802.11 defines the point coordination function (PCF) mode and the hybrid coordination function (HCF) mode in which the AP explicitly arbitrates channel access in a TDMA-like manner. Unfortunately, both these modes are not widely implemented. Moreover, the coordination overhead of these approaches becomes a concern under low loads and at high data rates.

Several TDMA-based approaches have previously been proposed [41, 21, 32, 25, 35]. STDMA focusses on VoIP performance but use TDMA for all traffic. However, STDMA is not backward compatible with 802.11 devices. Overlay MAC Layer (OML) and ARGOS enable time-slots on the order of 20ms, granularities that are too coarse for effectively supporting real-time applications. SoftSpeak [41] combines downlink aggregation[10] with uplink TDMA. All these TDMA based schemes did not consider higher data rates of 802.11n/ac also they focused on packets without frame aggregation. Prioritization based schemes and multi-queue schemes like (e.g., 802.11 EDCA and [44]) improve the performance of real-time applications but degrade network throughput especially in high-speed networks.

In TAR [27], a time-based retry mechanism was proposed video streaming applications. Chan et al. [16] propose a video-aware rate adaptation protocol (see references therein). These works customize the MAC functionality based on application requirements but focus on a single WiFi radio. Also they do not focus on diminishing the throughput degradation in the presence of video traffic.

FICA [40] and WiFi-NC [18] advocate the use of narrow channels for improving MAC efficiency but they do not consider service differentiation and require custom hardware. Glia [24] aims to maximize aggregate throughput between a single sender/receiver pair using an array of WiFi radios while focusing on overcoming the power leakage from orthogonal channels. However, they do not deal with QoS differentiation. Yun et al. [45] propose to adapt the spectrum on a per-frame basis but their scheme requires custom hardware support.

802.11ac supports downlink MU-MIMO, which allows multiple frames to be sent from the AP to multiple receivers *simultaneously* through multiple spatial streams. MU-MIMO schemes need channel state information at the transmitter through null data packets. In addition, they require Block Acknowledgment Request (BAR) to coordinate ACKs from multiple clients. SlickFi does not incur such overheads. In a way, our work is complementary to MU-MIMO. SlickFi's dynamic channel-width adaptation can allow MU-MIMO systems to work well in dense deployments when 802.11n/ac devices are operating on the secondary channels using 20MHz of channel width [31].

6. DISCUSSION AND FUTURE WORK

Supporting multiple types of real-time traffic: SlickFi uses two WiFi interfaces for service differentiation. Therefore, it naturally supports two traffic classes, i.e., delay-sensitive real-time traffic and best effort data traffic. QoS differentiation among more than two traffic types (e.g., voice, video, and data traffic) can be achieved by using 802.11e EDCA on the RI to map voice and video traffic to separate queues [13]. Note that by default, 802.11e EDCA support four traffic classes and prioritizes voice traffic over video traffic by using a smaller average contention window size. Such an approach will ensure that the real-time traffic (i.e., voice and video traffic) will remain shielded from the long A-MPDU transmissions of data traffic.

Cost of radios: One could ask if SlickFi's design is cost-effective as it requires two WiFi radios at the APs. First, many existing WiFi APs are already equipped with at least

[10]With downlink aggregation, an AP encapsulates multiple VoIP packets into a single packet addressed to all VoIP stations associated with the same AP.

two WiFi interfaces [6, 2]. For such APs, SlickFi would incur no additional cost. Second, the cost of a WiFi has decreased substantially in the last decade. Thus, it is not uncommon for a radio to cost under $10 [7].

SlickFi under multi-AP scenarios and legacy clients: In this work, we focussed on a single AP scenario as such scenarios are fairly common (e.g., in offices with coordinated placement of APs to avoid interference). To avoid co-channel interference, APs usually employ algorithms to pick unused channels. However, in several cases interference from other APs may be inevitable due to the availability of only a small number of non-overlapping channels. SlickFi can work well in such scenarios. As SlickFi is compatible with the 802.11 standard, it can seamlessly co-exist with other APs. However, to further optimize performance one can add a centralized controller to perform channel coordination between APs. Prior work has shown that microsecond level coordination is achievable through centralized controllers [39]. Legacy clients can also connect with SlickFi APs, however, they will not be able to obtain the performance improvements offered by SlickFi if they use the RI for data traffic or use the BI for real-time traffic. To avoid degrading performance in such scenarios, we can restrict each interface to use 20MHz channels only.

Adapting channel width of both radios: One could ask if the RI radio could also adapt its channel width. This could be done if RI becomes saturated whereas BI experiences low load, which is a less common scenario [41]. However, we leave evaluation of such a functionality as part of future work.

Power Consumption: The use of two radios will increase the power consumption of devices, thereby impacting battery lifetime. This could be reduced by putting radios in sleep mode when they are not being used.

7. CONCLUSION

In this paper, we proposed SlickFi, a QoS differentiation scheme for high-speed WLANs that achieves high performance for real-time traffic while maintaining high network throughput. SlickFi achieves this performance by (a) isolating real-time traffic and data traffic into non-overlapping parts of the spectrum using two radios in APs, (b) allowing per-frame channel width adaptations to maximize throughput, and (c) effectively managing adjacent-channel interference. SlickFi is readily deployable as it does not require custom hardware or changes in the WiFi protocol. Our real testbed implementation and evaluation shows that SlickFi improves the performance of real-time applications as well as achieves high throughput across a diverse range of WLAN scenarios.

Acknowledgements

We thank our shepherd, Nicolas Christin, the anonymous CoNEXT reviewers, and Fahad Rafique Dogar for their valuable feedback. We also thank Ahmed Mehfooz, Hammad Mazhar, Amna Abid, and Shanzae Nadeem Khan for their help with the initial experiments.

8. REFERENCES

[1] ath9k. http://linuxwireless.org/en/users/Drivers/ath9k/.

[2] Tri-radio AP. http://https://goo.gl/gjU6W3.

[3] 802.11ac: The Fifth Generation of Wi-Fi. Cisco Technical White Paper. http://bit.ly/1MBCljm,.

[4] ath9k spectral scan.

[5] Cisco visual networking index: Forecast and methodology. http://bit.ly/1OdTJgJ.

[6] Dual band access points. http://www.broadbandbuyer.com/store/dual-band-wifi/dual-band-access-points/.

[7] Intel wifi link 5000. www.intel.com/products/wireless/adapters/5000/.

[8] iperf. http://sourceforge.net/projects/iperf/.

[9] Sipp. http://sipp.sourceforge.net/.

[10] VQMT: Video Quality Measurement Tool. http://mmspg.epfl.ch/vqmt.

[11] IEEE Standard for local and metropolitan area networks part 11; amendment 5: Enhancements for higher throughput, 2009. 802.11n.

[12] P. Bahl, A. Adya, J. Padhye, and A. Wolman. Reconsidering wireless systems with multiple radios. In *SIGCOMM CCR 2004*.

[13] G. Bianchi, I. Tinnirello, and L. Scalia. Understanding 802.11e contention-based prioritization mechanisms and their coexistence with legacy 802.11 stations. *Network, IEEE*, 19(4):28–34, July 2005.

[14] S. Biswas, J. Bicket, E. Wong, R. Musaloiu-E, A. Bhartia, and D. Aguayo. Large-scale measurements of wireless network behavior. In *SIGCOMM '15*.

[15] V. Brik, A. Mishra, and S. Banerjee. Eliminating handoff latencies in 802.11 wlans using multiple radios: Applications, experience, and evaluation. In *IMC '05*.

[16] A. Chan, H. Lundgren, and T. Salonidis. Video-aware rate adaptation for mimo wlans. In *ICNP'11*.

[17] A. Chan, K. Zeng, P. Mohapatra, S.-J. Lee, and S. Banerjee. Metrics for evaluating video streaming quality in lossy ieee 802.11 wireless networks. In *INFOCOM'10*.

[18] K. Chintalapudi, B. Radunovic, V. Balan, M. Buettener, S. Yerramalli, V. Navda, and R. Ramjee. Wifi-nc: Wifi over narrow channels. In *NSDI'12*.

[19] P. Deshpande and S. R. Das. Brave: Bit-rate adaptation in vehicular environments. In *VANET '12*.

[20] P. Deshpande, Z. A. Qazi, and S. R. Das. Mrmv: Design and evaluation of a multi-radio multi-vehicle system for metro-wifi access. In *VANET '13*.

[21] F. Guo and T. cker Chiueh. Software tdma for voip applications over ieee802.11 wireless lan. In *INFOCOM'07*.

[22] D. Halperin, W. Hu, A. Sheth, and D. Wetherall. Predictable 802.11 packet delivery from wireless channel measurements.

[23] U. Ismail. Virtual pcf: Improving voip over wlan performance with legacy clients. *Master's thesis, University of Waterloo*, 2009.

[24] S. Kakumanu and R. Sivakumar. Glia: A practical solution for effective high datarate wifi-arrays. In *MobiCom 2009*.

[25] R. R. Kompella, S. Ramabhadran, I. Ramani, and A. C. Snoeren. Cooperative packet scheduling via pipelining in 802.11 wireless networks. In *E-WIND '05*.

[26] E. B. S.-J. L. K. A. Lara Deek, Eduard Garcia-Villegas. The impact of channel bonding on 802.11n network management. In *CoNEXT '11*.

[27] M.-H. Lu, P. Steenkiste, and T. Chen. A time-based adaptive retry strategy for video streaming in 802.11 wlans: Research

articles. *Wirel. Commun. Mob. Comput.*, 7(2):187–203, Feb. 2007.

[28] E. Magistretti, K. K. Chintalapudi, B. Radunovic, and R. Ramjee. Wifi-nano: Reclaiming wifi efficiency through 800 ns slots. In *MobiCom '11*.

[29] S. Nguyen, H. Vu, and L. Andrew. Service differentiation without prioritization in ieee 802.11 wlans. *Mobile Computing, IEEE Transactions on*, 12(10):2076–2090, Oct 2013.

[30] K. Nishat, R. Anwar, M. Ali, Z. Akhtar, H. Niaz, and I. A. Qazi. Loss Differentiation: Moving onto High-Speed Wireless LANs. In *INFOCOM '14*.

[31] M. Park. Ieee 802.11ac: Dynamic bandwidth channel access. In *ICC'11*.

[32] G. S. Paschos, I. Papapanagiotou, S. A. Kotsopoulos, and G. K. Karagiannidis. A new mac protocol with pseudo-tdma behavior for supporting quality of service in 802.11 wireless lans. *EURASIP J. Wirel. Commun. Netw.*, pages 76–84, Mar. 2006.

[33] A. Patro, S. Govindan, and S. Banerjee. Observing home wireless experience through wifi aps. In *MobiCom '13*.

[34] T. Pering, Y. Agarwal, R. Gupta, and R. Want. Coolspots: Reducing the power consumption of wireless mobile devices with multiple radio interfaces. In *MobiSys '06*.

[35] A. Rao and I. Stoica. An overlay mac layer for 802.11 networks. In *MobiSys '05*.

[36] J. Robinson, K. Papagiannaki, C. Diot, X. Guo, and L. Krishnamurthy. Experimenting with a multi-radio mesh networking testbed. In *WiNMee Workshop 2005*.

[37] S. Sen, M. Griepentrog, J. Yoon, and S. Banerjee. Eliminating handoff latencies in 802.11 wlans using multiple radios: Applications, experience, and evaluation. In *IMC '05*.

[38] S. B. R. C. Shravan Rayanchu, Vivek Shrivastava. Fluid: Improving throughputs in entreprise wireless lans through flexible channelization. In *MobiCom '11*.

[39] V. Shrivastava, N. Ahmed, S. Rayanchu, S. Banerjee, S. Keshav, K. Papagiannaki, and A. Mishra. Centaur: Realizing the full potential of centralized wlans through a hybrid data path. In *MobiCom '09*.

[40] K. Tan, J. Fang, Y. Zhang, S. Chen, L. Shi, J. Zhang, and Y. Zhang. Fine-grained channel access in wireless lan. In *SIGCOMM '10*.

[41] P. Verkaik, Y. Agarwal, R. Gupta, and A. C. Snoeren. Softspeak: Making voip play well in existing 802.11 deployments. In *NSDI 2009*.

[42] Z. Yang, J. Zhang, kun tan, Q. Zhang, and Y. Zhang. Enabling tdma for today's wireless lans. In *INFOCOM '15*.

[43] J. Yoon, H. Zhang, S. Banerjee, and S. Rangarajan. Muvi: A multicast video delivery scheme for 4g cellular networks. In *Mobicom '12*.

[44] J. Yu, S. Choi, and J. Lee. Enhancement of volp over ieee 802.11 wlan via dual queue strategy. In *ICC'04*.

[45] S. Yun, D. Kim, and L. Qiu. Fine-grained spectrum adaptation in wifi networks. In *MobiCom 2013*.

[46] M. Zhang, B. Karp, S. Floyd, and L. Peterson. Rr-tcp: A reordering-robust tcp with dsack. In *ICNP '03*.

Enabling ECN over Generic Packet Scheduling

Wei Bai[1] Kai Chen[1] Li Chen[1] Changhoon Kim[2] Haitao Wu[3]

[1]SING Group, Hong Kong University of Science and Technology
[2]Barefoot Networks [3]Microsoft

ABSTRACT

Explicit Congestion Notification (ECN) is crucial for production datacenters, but current queue-length based ECN/RED implementation does not work with generic packet schedulers, leading to either degraded network performance or violated scheduling policies. In this paper, we first dive into this issue and reveal that the invalidity of ECN/RED lies in the difficulty of measuring changing queue capacities under various schedulers and traffic dynamics. Then we present Time-based Congestion Notification (TCN), a simple yet effective ECN solution, by combining two successful ideas: the sojourn time from CoDel [23] and the instantaneous marking from DCTCP [6]. Using packet sojourn-time, as opposed to queue-length, as the congestion signal, TCN eliminates the need of measuring dynamic queue capacities, making it suitable for arbitrary schedulers with traffic dynamics. By performing stateless instantaneous ECN marking rather than complex stateful dropping, TCN is designed to be inexpensive to implement on commodity switching chips. Through extensive testbed experiments and large-scale simulations, we show TCN can strictly preserve scheduling policies while providing desirable network performance. For example, TCN significantly reduces the average and 99th percentile completion times for small flows by up to 82.8% and 95.3% compared to current practice in a testbed experiment with production workload.

1. INTRODUCTION

Datacenters must simultaneously deliver high throughput and low latency to applications they host—some such as web search [6] and distributed memory caches [24] require low latency for short messages, while others like cloud storage and data-parallel computation [15] desire high throughput for large data transfers. To accommodate these two requirements, ECN is adopted by recent datacenter transport designs [6, 8, 22, 32, 35, 37], and they have shown that a well-tuned ECN marking threshold can deliver both high throughput and low latency [6, 35]. For this reason, ECN-based transports, like DCTCP [6] and DCQCN [37], have been widely implemented in various OS kernels [1, 2] and NICs [37] and deployed in production datacenters [19, 28, 37].

CoNEXT '16, December 12-15, 2016, Irvine, CA, USA

DOI: http://dx.doi.org/10.1145/2999572.2999575

Basically, ECN requires both ECN-enabled transport protocols at end hosts and ECN-capable switches in the network. At the switch, ECN is typically combined with an active queue management (AQM) scheme. Current switching chips typically adopt random early detection (RED) to enable ECN [5]. In ECN/RED, an ECN mark on a packet simply indicates that the average or instantaneous buildup of the queue corresponding to the packet exceeds a static ECN marking threshold.

Meanwhile, existing commodity switching chips also support multiple queues (typically 4-8 [9, 10]) per egress port. To improve network performance and provide QoS, the current practice is to use these multiple queues to classify traffic (*e.g.*, interactive applications vs data backup) and enforce various scheduling algorithms (*e.g.*, Weighted Fair Queueing (WFQ) or Strict Priority (SP)) among different queues/classes.

However, current ECN/RED marking scheme does not support generic packet schedulers [11, 21]. The crux is that RED uses queue-length as the congestion signal, and compares it against a pre-configured ECN marking threshold to mark packets. The ideal queue-length marking threshold depends on the queue capacity (the effective instantaneous drain rate of a queue). When multiple queues share a port, the individual queue capacities can vary significantly subject to both scheduling disciplines and traffic dynamics. This entails changing ECN marking thresholds in response to dynamic queue capacities. But today's commodity switches only support static thresholds, leading to either degraded performance or violated scheduling policies (§3.2).

Recently, MQ-ECN [11] makes a first effort to enable dynamic ECN/RED for multi-queue. It leverages special properties of round-robin schedulers to calculate dynamic ECN marking threshold for each queue. While it works for round-based schedulers like Weighted Round Robin (WRR) and Deficit Weighted Round Robin (DWRR), this solution does not generalize to other schedulers such as WFQ and SP that do not possess the concept of "round". Furthermore, with the advent of programmable schedulers such as PIFO [30] and UPS [20], we are faced with more sophisticated packet scheduling algorithms that MQ-ECN does not apply.

In this paper, we move one step further and ask a fundamental question: *can we enable ECN over arbitrary packet schedulers in datacenter networks?*

Towards answering this question, we first revisit ECN/RED (§3). In order to enable ECN/RED for generic packet schedulers, the key is to seek a generic solution to estimate dynamic queue capacities. However, through extensive experiments, we find that it is very hard to accurately measure dynamic queue capacities in practice. The reason is that it is extremely difficult to determine an ideal measurement window for generic packet schedulers with traffic dynamics. A smaller measurement window (*i.e.*, sampling too frequently) degrades accuracy, while a larger one (*i.e.*, sampling insufficiently) fails to timely capture fine-grained queue capacity changes (§3.3).

Based on above observation, we exploit latency experienced by a packet, instead of queue-length, as the congestion signal and present Time-based Congestion Notification (TCN), a simple yet effective sojourn-time based solution (§4). TCN synthesizes two successful ideas: the sojourn time from CoDel [23] and the instantaneous marking from DCTCP [6]:

- By using the sojourn time as the congestion signal, the marking threshold of TCN is *independent* of the changing queue capacities, making it particularly suitable for arbitrary packet schedulers (§4.1).
- With *instantaneous* ECN marking, TCN operates in a stateless fashion. This makes TCN much simpler than CoDel [23] which tracks the minimum sojourn time over a complex varying time window to drop (or mark) packets. Therefore, we expect TCN will be simpler to implement in hardware (§4.2). Moreover, compared to CoDel, TCN achieves faster reaction to bursty datacenter traffic (§6.1).

We have implemented a TCN software prototype as a Linux `qdisc` kernel module which supports a variety of packet scheduling algorithms (§5), and built a small-scale testbed with 9 servers connected to such a server-emulated TCN software switch. We use this testbed to evaluate basic properties of TCN (§6.1). Our experiment results demonstrate that TCN can strictly preserve different scheduling policies while delivering high throughput and low latency simultaneously. For example, in a realistic datacenter web search workload [6], we find that TCN significantly reduces the average and 99th percentile completion times for small flows by up to 82.8% and 95.3% respectively while delivering similar performance for large flows, compared to current operation practice (§6.1.3).

To complement small-scale testbed experiments, we also conduct large-scale ns-2 [4] simulations with 4 realistic datacenter workloads (§6.2). Our simulation results confirm that TCN maintains its superior performance in large-scale multi-hop datacenter topologies, For example, TCN achieves up to 94.3% lower 99th percentile completion time for small flows compared to current practice (§6.2.1). We further use a series of targeted simulations to show that TCN is robust to different network settings, such as the number of queues and transport protocol (§6.2.2).

To make our work easy to reproduce, we make our experiment and simulation code available online at http://sing.cse.ust.hk/projects/TCN.

2. BACKGROUND

2.1 ECN/RED

In current switching chips, ECN is typically combined with RED [16] that uses *average* buffer occupancy[1] as the congestion signal. RED has (at least) 3 parameters to configure: low buffer occupancy threshold K_{min}, high buffer occupancy threshold K_{max}, and maximum probability P_{max}.

In production datacenters, network operators usually make two changes to simplify ECN/RED configuration [6, 35]. First, they use *instantaneous* buffer occupancy rather than average buffer occupancy to faster react to traffic bursts. Second, they set both K_{min} and K_{max} to K. An arriving packet gets ECN marked only when the instantaneous buffer occupancy is larger than K. In this paper, we also adopt such simplified ECN/RED scheme.

Obviously, the choice of marking threshold K greatly affects network performance. Unlike Internet, the number of concurrent large flows is very low in datacenter environments (*e.g.*, 2 in the 75th percentile) [6]. Given such low degree statistical multiplexing, we consider an ideal model where several synchronized long-lived flows with identical round-trip times RTT share a bottleneck link with capacity C. As previous works [6, 11, 35] have shown, to fully utilize link capacity while delivering low latency, the ECN marking threshold K should be set as follows:

$$K = C \times RTT \times \lambda \tag{1}$$

where λ is a parameter determined by congestion control algorithms (*e.g.*, $\lambda = 1$ for ECN* [35][2]). In this paper, we call such $C \times RTT \times \lambda$ as the *standard marking threshold for ECN/RED*.

Prior experience has shown that computing the standard marking threshold in production datacenters is feasible [35]. This is because, unlike Internet, round-trip times in datacenter networks are relatively stable and can be well estimated through large-scale measurements [18, 35]. For example, in a Microsoft production datacenter, the 23%, 74% and 90% percentile inter-rack RTT are around $200us$, $300us$ and $400us$, respectively [35]. Moreover, since operators have full control of end-host network stacks, λ can be easily obtained. Hence, it is fairly easy to compute such a static standard marking threshold in production datacenters.

2.2 Packet Scheduling

Current commodity switches usually provide some fixed-function packet scheduling algorithms (*e.g.*, SP and DWRR) across several queues (*e.g.*, 4-8) per egress port. Packet schedulers are used by operators to improve network performance. Here, we give two examples.

- **Inter-Service Traffic Isolation:** Modern production datacenters host a variety of services (applications) with diverse network requirements. For example, a real-time online service desires ultra-low latency for short messages while a

[1]We use buffer occupancy and queue length interchangeably here.

[2]ECN* is regular ECN-enabled TCP which simply cuts the window by half in the presence of an ECN mark.

data backup service requires high throughput for large flows. Current practice is to use queues to isolate traffic from different services [9, 11] and configure DWRR/WRR among the queues. In this way, we can reserve a minimum guarantee bandwidth for each service and mitigate inter-service network interference to some extent.

- **Traffic Prioritization:** A service may have a small amount of important traffic, such as SDN control traffic, BGP control traffic, RDMA Congestion Notification Packets (CNP) [37], ACK packets [21], latency-sensitive query messages. The completion times of this traffic greatly affect service operation and user-perceived performance. Hence, network operators usually reserve some (typically one) strict higher priority queues to prioritize the delivery of such important traffic [11]. The rest of queues in the lowest priority can still be used for inter-service isolation.

Further, very recently, Sivaraman et al. [30] have proposed a programmable packet scheduler allowing operators to implement custom scheduling algorithms for specific application-level objectives. Mittal et al. [20] have shown that the classical Least Slack Time First (LSTF) scheduling could be used to emulate different scheduling algorithms in practice. Given above efforts in programmable schedulers, we envision that more and more scheduling algorithms will be used in the future.

2.3 Combining ECN & Packet Scheduling

In some production datacenters, ECN and packet scheduling are used simultaneously, and operators usually configure them in a hierarchical style: they employ various packet scheduling algorithms among different queues while leveraging ECN to achieve high throughput and low latency in the same queue. Given that more and more packet scheduling algorithms will be used in the future, it is important to find an ECN marking scheme that can efficiently support any packet scheduler.

3. ECN/RED DEEP DIVE

In this section, we first present the ideal ECN/RED solution for generic packet scheduling. Then, we show that current practice is far from the ideal. Finally, we demonstrate that the ideal ECN/RED for generic schedulers is intrinsically hard to realize, motivating our design of TCN.

3.1 Ideal ECN/RED for Generic Schedulers

We consider a switch egress port with multiple queues. We consider a per-queue ECN/RED marking model where each queue only tracks its own buffer occupancy and performs ECN marking independently to other queues. The ECN/RED marking threshold of queue i is denoted as K_i. Based on Equation 1, K_i should be set as follows:

$$K_i = C_i \times RTT \times \lambda \quad (2)$$

where C_i is the capacity (effective instantaneous drain rate) of queue i, which is determined by traffic demands and the underlying packet scheduler. Thus, given a packet scheduler, the per-queue marking threshold K_i should be dynamically adjusted according to traffic dynamics.

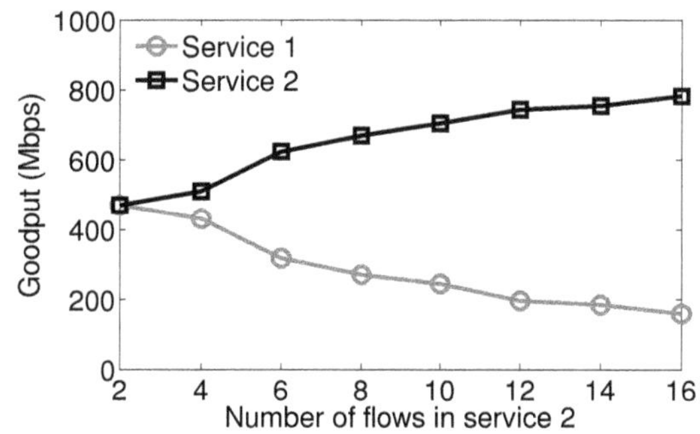

Figure 1: [Testbed] Aggregate goodputs achieved by per-port ECN/RED. Note that service 1 always has 1 flow.

3.2 Current Practice

Today's switching chips provide multiple ECN/RED configuration schemes, such as per-queue, per-port and per-service-pool[3] ECN/RED [11]. The key difference among them is that they use buffer occupancies of different egress entities when making marking decisions. However, all these ECN/RED schemes are essentially *static*: operators can only configure static per-queue/port/service-pool marking thresholds. Hence, compared to the ideal ECN/RED solution that dynamically adjusts the per-queue marking threshold, existing ECN/RED implementation unavoidably introduces some performance impairments. We use the following two examples to illustrate them.

3.2.1 Per-queue ECN/RED

Network operators usually configure per-queue ECN/RED for its ideal isolation among different queues [6, 19]. However, how to set fixed per-queue marking threshold is a challenge. Considering that the queue capacity C_i is always no larger than the link capacity C, in current practice, many operators chose to configure the standard marking threshold $C \times RTT \times \lambda$ for each queue [11]. Such configuration can achieve high throughput while strictly preserving any scheduling algorithm. However, when many queues are busy simultaneously, C_i will be much smaller than C. Under such circumstances, the standard marking threshold $C \times RTT \times \lambda$ will result in excess queue buildups, thus degrading packet latency and burst tolerance.

Remark 1: Per-queue ECN/RED with the standard threshold can seriously degrade packet latency and burst tolerance, especially when many queues are busy simultaneously.

3.2.2 Per-port/service-pool ECN/RED

Though the per-queue capacity C_i is dynamically changing, the aggregate capacity of all the queues belonging to a switch port keeps the same. Hence, the reader may wonder whether per-port ECN/RED can meet our requirements.

By setting the per-port marking threshold to the standard threshold $C \times RTT \times \lambda$, per-port ECN/RED can achieve high throughput and low latency simultaneously. However, it fails to preserve scheduling policies. A packet, which should not be marked according to Equation 2, may get ECN marked due

[3]A service pool is a shared buffer region.

to the buffer occupancies of the other queues belonging to the same port. Such impact will become more serious if we enable per-service-pool ECN/RED because queues from different ports can interfere with each other.

To confirm such impairment, we conduct a simple testbed experiment. We connect 3 servers to a Pica8 P-3295 GbE switch. We enable DCTCP [6] on the servers. At the switch, we configure per-port ECN/RED and DWRR with 2 equal-quantum queues. We set the per-port marking threshold to 30KB as the DCTCP paper recommends [6]. We start several TCP long-lived flows from two senders to the same receiver. We classify flows into two services based on their senders. Both services have their dedicated queues at the switch.

In this experiment, service 2 has a varying number of TCP flows from 2 to 16 while service 1 always has 1 flow. Ideally, based at the switch scheduling policy, two services should always fairly share the link capacity equally. Figure 1 shows the final goodput sharing results. The aggregate goodput of service 2 becomes higher and higher as we increase its number of flows. For example, service 2 can achieve 670Mbps goodput with 8 flows and 782Mbps goodput with 16 flows. This suggests that, under per-port ECN/RED, traffic from service 1 gets excess ECN marked due to the impact of traffic from service 2, thus violating the scheduling policy.

Remark 2: Per-port/service-pool ECN/RED can seriously violate scheduling policies.

3.3 Fundamental Difficulty for Ideal ECN/RED

Given existing ECN/RED configuration schemes do not satisfy our requirements, we need to design a new AQM to enforce the ideal ECN/RED solution (Equation 2). To perform the ideal ECN/RED marking, the key is to find a general solution to estimate the queue capacity C_i for any packet scheduling algorithm under traffic dynamics.

We observe that queue capacity is equal to actual queue departure rate when the queue remains non-empty. Hence, when a queue always has data in the buffer, we can use the queue departure rate as the estimate for queue capacity. MQ-ECN [11] leverages the special properties of round-robin schedulers (*e.g.*, WRR and DWRR) to realize this. In round-robin schedulers, a non-empty queue i can transmit $quantum_i$ worth of bits at most in each round. Therefore, MQ-ECN uses $quantum_i$ over the round time T_{round}[4] to estimate the capacity of queue i. Since MQ-ECN relies on the special properties of round-robin schedulers, it does not generalize to other schedulers such as WFQ and PIFO [30] that do not have the round concept. To this end, we employ the departure rate measurement technique in Algorithm 1. Note that this is the best solution we learned in PIE [25].

Basically, we start a measurement cycle *only* when the queue length is over a threshold, dq_thresh. This ensures there are sufficient data in the buffer. Then, we use dq_count to track the number of bytes departed in this measurement cycle. Once dq_count crosses dq_thresh, we stop the current cycle and obtain a sample dq_rate. Note that this method ensures that the queue buffer is non-empty during the measurement cycle. After that, we exponentially average dq_rate to calculate a smooth departure rate, avg_rate, which is the estimate for the queue capacity. Finally, we use $avg\_rate \times RTT \times \lambda$ (Equation 2) to calculate the ECN marking threshold.

[4] T_{round} is the total time to serve all the queues once.

Parameter	Description
dq_thresh	queue length threshold
$is\_measure$	whether in a measurement cycle
dq_count	number of bytes depart in the measurement
dq_start	start time of measurement cycle
$dq\_pktsize$	size of current dequeue packet
dq_rate	sample departure rate
avg_rate	smoothed departure rate

Table 1: Parameters used in Algorithm 1

Algorithm 1 Departure rate (queue capacity) measurement:

```
Upon packet departure;
1. Decide to be in a measurement cycle:
if qlen ≥ dq_thresh and !is_measure then
    dq_count = 0;
    dq_start = now;
    is_measure = true;
2. During the measurement cycle:
if is_measure then
    dq_count = dq_count + dq_pktsize;
    if dq_count ≥ dq_thresh then
        dq_rate = dq_count/(now − dq_start);
        avg_rate = ε × avg_rate + (1 − ε) × dq_rate;
        is_measure = false;
```

In the algorithm, the parameter dq_thresh is key, which determines the measurement frequency. Conventional wisdom recommends 10KB [25]. However, we find there is an intrinsic tradeoff in the choice of dq_thresh. In datacenter environment with dynamic traffic, it is unlikely to choose a *right* value for generic packet schedulers. A smaller dq_thresh value (results in too frequent measurement) can degrade measurement accuracy; whereas a larger dq_thresh value (leads to insufficient measurement) cannot accurately capture the dynamic changes of queue capacity. We believe this tradeoff applies to any general departure rate estimation.

To demonstrate such a tradeoff, we conduct a simple ns-2 [4] simulation. We simulate a 10Gbps topology with 11 servers connected to a switch. The base RTT is $100us$. We employ ECN* [35] as the transport protocol. Hence, the standard threshold is 125KB ($100us \times 10Gbps$) in our setup. We configure DWRR with two queues at the switch. Both queues have a quantum of 18KB. We evaluate three ECN/RED schemes: the ideal ECN/RED solution with dq_thresh of 40KB and 10KB and MQ-ECN [11], the state-of-the-art dynamic ECN/RED solution for round robin schedulers. We use 0.875 as the averaging parameter. Among 11 servers, 10 act as the senders and the rest one is the receiver. We first start 8 TCP flows from 8 senders, which are mapped to queue 1. At time 0.01s, we start another 2 TCP flows from the rest 2 senders, which are mapped to queue 2. Hence, the capacity of queue 1 should be decreased to 5Gbps after 0.01s.

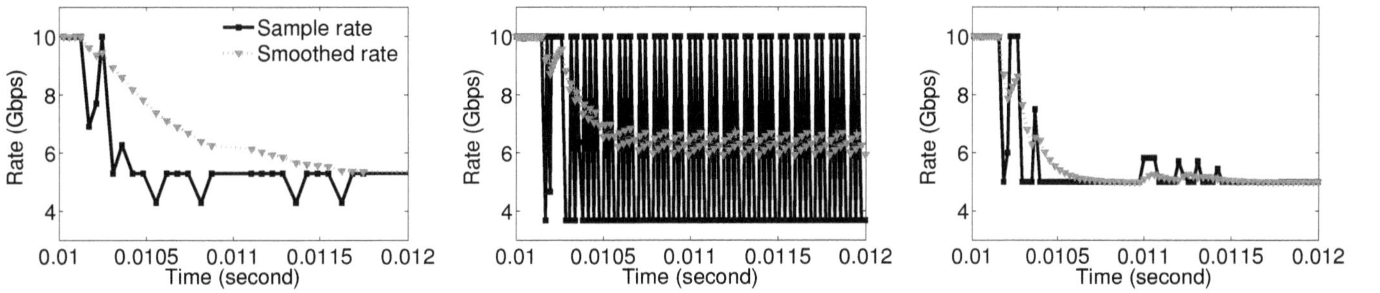

(a) dq_thresh = 40KB (b) dq_thresh = 10KB (c) MQ-ECN

Figure 2: [Simulation] The capacity of queue 1 estimated by different schemes. Note that rates in (a) and (b) are estimated by Algorithm 1 with different dq_thresh values. In (c), MQ-ECN only works for round-robin schedulers, not others.

Figure 2 plots the capacity of queue 1 estimated by different schemes. Note that we use the smoothed rates in the figures to calculate ECN marking thresholds. We make the following three key observations.

- First, with dq_thresh of 40KB, the ideal ECN/RED solution can only obtain 29 sample rates in 2ms period. Consequently, it takes more than 2ms for the smoothed capacity to converge to 5Gbps, which is too long for highly dynamic datacenter workloads. Moreover, a large dq_thresh may increase packet latency as the ECN marking scheme starts to react only when it sees a large queue buildup.
- Second, with dq_thresh of 10KB (recommended by [25]), the sample rates of the ideal ECN/RED solution drastically oscillate between 3.7Gbps and 10Gbps. This is because dq_thresh (10KB) is smaller than the queue quantum (18KB), we obtain either a very high sample rate (10Gbps) if the measurement cycle is inside the same round or a very low sample rate (3.7Gbps) if the measurement cycle spans across several rounds. Such highly oscillated samples not only result in the oscillation of the smoothed rate, but also lead to a wrong queue capacity estimate above 6Gbps, deviating from 5Gbps by over 20%. Thus, using it for ECN marking threshold calculation will introduce excess latency.
- Third, MQ-ECN [11] can obtain a large number of accurate samples by explicitly using the round time, T_{round}, as the measurement window. Within T_{round}, all the queues exactly get served once and queue i can transmit $quantum_i$ worth of bits at most according to the scheduling policy. Hence, using $quantum_i/T_{round}$ as the estimate, MQ-ECN's smoothed rate quickly converges to 5Gbps within $600us$. Despite its good performance, MQ-ECN can only handle round-robin schedulers. In case of WFQ, SP or other advanced programmable schedulers, there is no way to have such a round, and MQ-ECN does not apply.

Due to the above tradeoff, network operators need to cautiously tune a suitable rate measurement frequency. However, this frequency is related to both underlying packet schedulers and network traffic situations, instead of a static universal value. Such effort is a huge burden for network operators, which is almost impossible to achieve in practice, even for a given scheduler, *e.g.*, WFQ, under highly dynamic traffic.

Remark 3: Network operators need to cautiously tune the rate measurement frequency for the ideal ECN/RED solution. This greatly increases their burden and is hard to accomplish.

4. TCN

The goal of TCN is to enable ECN over generic packet schedulers, while maintaining good network performance. The main problem with ECN/RED, as introduced above, is that its use of queue-length as the congestion signal is conflated with the queue capacity, which is very hard to measure in highly dynamic datacenter networks. Motivated by this, TCN exploits packet sojourn-time, instead of queue-length, as the congestion signal. By using the sojourn time as the congestion signal, the marking threshold of TCN is *independent* of the changing queue capacities, making it suitable for arbitrary packet schedulers.

4.1 Mechanism

We use Q_i to denote the length of queue i. According to the ideal ECN/RED solution (Equation 2), the switch should mark arriving packets when Q_i is larger than $C_i \times RTT \times \lambda$. Thus, an arriving packet should get ECN marked when $\frac{Q_i}{C_i}$ is larger than $RTT \times \lambda$.

$\frac{Q_i}{C_i}$ is exactly the sojourn time (the amount of time a packet spends in the switch queue) for packets in queue i. We consider that a packet pkt enqueued to queue i sees Q_i worth of bits behind it. Before pkt is transmitted, queue i keeps non-empty. Hence, C_i is equal to the departure rate during this period. Therefore, pkt spends $\frac{Q_i}{C_i}$ time in queue i.

Inspired by above analysis, TCN employs sojourn time as the congestion signal. Sojourn time can be directly measured in today's switching chips (more details in §4.2). A departing packet gets ECN marked when its sojourn time is larger than the threshold T. Obviously, T can be given as:

$$T = RTT \times \lambda \quad (3)$$

In this paper, we call $RTT \times \lambda$ as the *standard marking threshold for* TCN. Compared to previous ECN/RED solution, TCN mainly has the following three benefits.

Maintain good network performance: TCN starts to notify the sources of congestion when sojourn times of packets exceed $RTT \times \lambda$. The choice of $RTT \times \lambda$ ensures that TCN can fully utilize link capacity while delivering low latency. By contrast, per-queue ECN/RED with standard threshold suffers from poor packet latency and burst tolerance (**Remark 1**).

Support arbitrary schedulers: TCN employs the same sojourn time marking threshold for all the queues. Sojourn time directly reflects congestion states regardless of traffic demands and packet schedulers. Hence, TCN allows any scheduling policy. By contrast, MQ-ECN [11] can only handle round-robin schedulers while per-port ECN/RED can violate scheduling policies (**Remark 2**)

Easy to configure: To enable TCN, network operators only need to configure a static sojourn time threshold: $RTT \times \lambda$. As §2.1 has shown, RTT and λ can be well estimated and easily known in production datacenters. Hence, it is easy for operators to configure TCN. By contrast, it is hard, almost impossible, for operators to choose a proper measurement frequency for the ideal ECN/RED solution for generic schedulers and various traffic patterns (**Remark 3**).

4.2 Hardware Implementation Feasibility

TCN is simple and inexpensive to implement in hardware. In this section, we briefly analyze the feasibility of TCN and present a few observations; we leave a prototype implementation of a TCN-capable hardware as future work. We implement a software TCN prototype in §5, and believe realizing TCN on a switch equipped with programmable data plane technologies [12, 13] is relatively simple and cheap.

Calculating packet sojourn time: To track the packet-level sojourn time, the switching chip simply needs to attach one more metadata to each packet at the enqueue time: enqueue-time timestamp. Because draining a smallest (64B) frame takes around 13ns at 40Gbps or 5ns at 100Gbps, and a typical RTT in a datacenter is at most a few hundred us, a 2B-long timestamp with a resolution of 4 or 8ns would be sufficient ($4ns * 2^{16} \approx 262us, 8ns * 2^{16} \approx 524us$). When the packet is drained from the queue, the scheduler or the egress pipeline logic can simply take the current timestamp (*i.e.*, the dequeue-time timestamp) from the chip-local clock and perform an integer subtraction operation (*e.g.*, an unsigned subtraction with two 17b or 18b operands to cope with the case when a timestamp value wraps). Performing such an operation is trivial in hardware. The overhead of attaching a 2B-long metadata to every buffered packet introduces only a marginal complexity for two reasons. First, 2B is already a tiny fraction of an average packet size. Second, today's switching chips already attach some tens to a lower hundred bytes of metadata to each packet for statistics monitoring, forwarding, hints for scheduling, (*e.g.*, broadcast domain ID, VRF ID). Note that the latest P4 behavior model has already exposed the sojourn time as the metadata [3].

Making marking decision: TCN makes marking decisions in a completely stateless fashion. The switching chip simply needs to compare the sojourn time (a local variable) with a static threshold (a constant) to make the marking decision for a packet. Hence, the chip does not need to keep any state across packets or queues. This is in contrast to CoDel [23], which requires four state variables per queue and modifies these states in a sophisticated fashion (described below §4.3).

Marking, as opposed to dropping: To obtain the sojourn time, TCN needs to be implemented on the dequeue side of a switching chip. Since TCN only marks packets instead of dropping packets, it does not cause any bubble (*i.e.*, idle time) on the output link, which otherwise, can seriously reduce the effective throughput. By contrast, CoDel [23] requires a special speed-up or prefetching logic on the dequeue side to avoid introducing bubbles when it drops packets that are just dequeued. This speed-up logic is particularly complicated and expensive to build in high-speed switching silicon, which must ensure a full line rate (a few Tbps today) under any circumstances, irrespective of dropping dequeued packets or not.

4.3 Deeper Understanding of TCN

TCN vs CoDel [23]: TCN draws inspiration from CoDel [23], an AQM solution to address the bufferbloat problem on Internet. Similar to TCN, CoDel also uses sojourn time as the congestion signal. However, CoDel tracks the *minimum* sojourn time in a varying time window $interval$ to identify persistent packet delay (or bad queues). If the *minimum* sojourn time of recent $interval$ is larger than a threshold, a packet gets dropped (or ECN marked) at dequeue. Despite its potential in theory, CoDel is expensive and complex to implement in hardware as introduced in §4.2 and [25, 29].

Unlike CoDel, TCN marks packets simply based on the *instantaneous* sojourn time of each departing packet. It is important to note that such simplicity of TCN is mainly driven by the homogeneous network environments of datacenters. In datacenters, round-trip times do not change drastically and the statistical multiplexing degree of large flows is known to be very low (§2.1). Further, we have full control of end hosts. Thus, it is feasible to compute a static threshold $RTT \times \lambda$ in datacenters for instantly identifying potential excess delay and marking packets in a completely stateless fashion.

By contrast, on Internet, it is hard to figure out such a $RTT \times \lambda$ due to the significant variations of round-trip times and unknown statistical multiplexing degree. As a result, CoDel needs to conservatively identify the persistent delay by using the minimum sojourn time over a time interval against an empirical threshold.

Compared to CoDel, TCN has following two advantages:

- **Cheaper to implement in hardware:** TCN is stateless as it does not modify state in the data plane. Therefore, we expect TCN is easier to implement in hardware. By contrast, CoDel creates and modifies states in a sophisticated fashion, which increases hardware implementation complexity. For example, Sivaraman et al. [29] found that CoDel could not be implemented on their targets as it required a complex square root operation to update time window. Moreover, due to lack of control of end hosts, CoDel should support dequeue dropping for non-ECT (ECN-Capable Transport) Internet traffic, which is also expensive to implement in hardware [25].
- **Faster reaction to bursty traffic:** TCN delivers faster congestion notification since it makes marking decisions instantly rather than after a time window. So TCN can better handle bursty datacenter traffic (*e.g.*, incast [33, 34]). Our evaluation results (§6.1) confirm this.

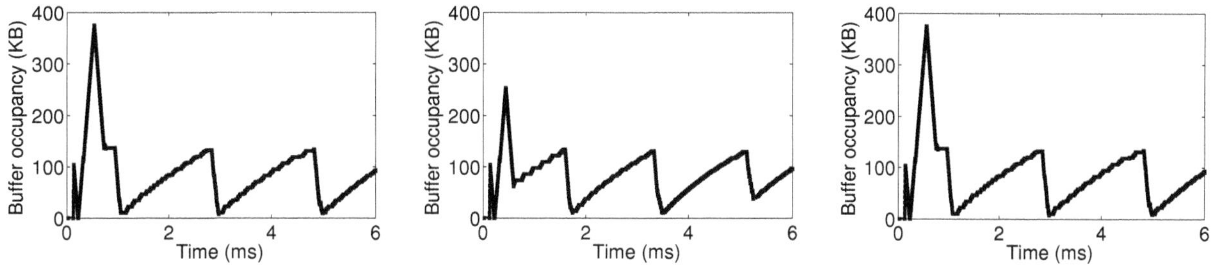

(a) Enqueue ECN/RED (b) Dequeue ECN/RED (c) TCN

Figure 3: [Simulation] Switch buffer occupancies achieved by enqueue ECN/RED, dequeue ECN/RED and TCN.

TCN vs dequeue ECN/RED marking: Wu et al. [35] have proposed dequeue ECN/RED marking. When a packet is dequeued, it compares current queue length against the marking threshold to make the marking decision. Since dequeue ECN/RED is still based on queue length, it has all the drawbacks discussed in §3. However, compared to traditional enqueue ECN/RED marking, dequeue ECN/RED marking can deliver the congestion information earlier when queues are building up, thus providing better burst tolerance.

Similar to dequeue ECN/RED marking, TCN also marks packets at dequeue side as it relies on the sojourn time. Hence, the reader may wonder whether TCN can accelerate the delivery of congestion information like dequeue ECN/RED. Our answer is **no**. This is because TCN leverages congestion states of *current* dequeued packets to make marking decisions, while dequeue ECN/RED indeed uses congestion states of *future* dequeued packets. Hence, when the switch buffer occupancy keeps increasing, dequeue ECN/RED marking reacts earlier than TCN as it predicts that future dequeued packets will experience congestion.

To confirm this, we simulate a 10Gbps network with 9 servers connected to a switch using ns-2 [4]. The base RTT is $100us$. We employ ECN* [35] (regular ECN-enabled TCP) as the transport protocol. We start 8 synchronized long-lived TCP flows from 8 senders to the same receiver. All the flows are classified to the same switch queue. We evaluate three ECN marking schemes: dequeue ECN/RED, enqueue ECN/RED and TCN. The marking thresholds for both ECN/RED schemes are 125KB ($100us \times 10Gbps$) in our setup. The marking threshold for TCN is $100us$.

Figure 3 shows the switch buffer occupancies versus time achieved by the three schemes. At the beginning, there is a peak buffer occupancy. This is because TCP window grows exponentially during the slow start phase before ECN takes effect. The peak value is around 375KB (3× Bandwidth Delay Product (BDP)) for both TCN and enqueue ECN/RED. In theory, enqueue ECN/RED and TCN should make the same marking decisions in this simulation. This is because when the queue capacity is fixed, we can directly convert a buffer occupancy to a corresponding sojourn time. By contrast, dequeue ECN/RED achieves a smaller peak value, which is around 250KB (2× BDP). This is because dequeue ECN/RED reacts earlier than the other two schemes, thus reducing peak buffer occupancy. After getting ECN marked, TCP flows enter congestion avoidance phase. Therefore, all the three marking schemes deliver very similar buffer occupancy variations from 0 to 125KB after the peak.

RED-like, probabilistic TCN marking: Raw ECN/RED has two marking thresholds and a maximum probability to perform a probabilistic marking (§2.1). In the previous analysis, TCN assumes only one marking threshold by using the same value for both thresholds. However, some ECN-based transports, like DCQCN [37], do require RED-like probabilistic marking to alleviate the unfairness problem.

TCN can be easily extended to perform such probabilistic marking. Similar to RED, TCN can also have two sojourn time thresholds T_{min}, T_{max} and a maximum marking probability P_{max}. If the sojourn time is $< T_{min}$, the packet does not get ECN marked. If the sojourn time is $> T_{max}$, the packet gets ECN marked. Otherwise, the packet is marked with a probability in the range of $(0, P_{max})$.

Discussion: We note that delay-based transports [14, 31] have long been studied in Internet. But they are not widely used in datacenters because in-network delays are comparable to sources of noise in the system. Recently, TIMELY [21] leverages special NIC hardware functions (*e.g.*, high-quality timestamping, hardware-generated ACKs, *etc.*) to better measure in-network delays in datacenters and uses delay gradients for congestion control. Compared to TIMELY, TCN is actually a sojourn-time based AQM to enable ECN at each hop. One goal of TCN is to make ECN-based transports, like DCTCP [6] or DCQCN [37] that are already adopted in production datacenters, work under multi-queue scenarios. It would be interesting to compare the performance of TCN-empowered DCQCN with TIMELY under multi-queue scenarios, which is part of our future work.

5. SOFTWARE PROTOTYPE

We use a server with multiple Gigabit Network Interface Cards (NICs) to emulate the switch. As a software prototype, we implement TCN, CoDel, MQ-ECN and per-queue/port ECN/RED and in a Linux queueing discipline (`qdisc`) kernel module running at the server-emulated switch. Consequently, packets are completely processed in kernel space without introducing data copy or context switch overhead between user and kernel space.

In summary, our `qdisc` kernel module has five components: packet classifier, enqueue ECN marking, packet scheduler, rate limiter and dequeue ECN marking (based on packet processing order). We now describe them in detail.

Packet Classifier: The `qdisc` kernel module maintains multiple FIFO transmission queues for each NIC. When the kernel module receives a packet from IP layer, it classifies the packet based on the Differentiated Services Code Point (DSCP) field. Then this packet is enqueued to the corresponding queue.

Enqueue ECN Marking: Upon an arrival packet is enqueued, we start to perform enqueue ECN marking. Per-queue/port ECN/RED directly compare buffer occupancy against the static threshold to make the marking decision. MQ-ECN needs to calculate the dynamic threshold of the corresponding queue and then make the marking decision. By contrast, TCN and CoDel use `tstamp` field of `sk_buff` to record enqueue timestamp here, leaving the marking decision on the dequeue side.

Packet Schedulers: We implement 4 common packet scheduling algorithms: WFQ, DWRR, SP/WFQ, and SP/DWRR.

- **WFQ:** To implement WFQ, we maintain a *virtual time* for the head packet of each queue. The WFQ scheduler chooses the head packet with the smallest virtual time to transmit.
- **DWRR:** The DWRR scheduler maintains a linked list to store all the active queues. When a packet arrives at an empty queue, this queue is inserted into the tail of the linked list. The DWRR scheduler always serves the head queue of the linked list. If a queue just finishes its service but still has packets, it is attached to the tail of the linked list again. Furthermore, to implement MQ-ECN, we maintain a timestamp for each queue to track round time.
- **SP/WFQ and SP/DWRR:** Both schedulers reserve several strict higher priority queues while leaving all the WFQ/DWRR queues on the lowest priority. They schedule packets as follows: they first try to schedule packets from strict higher priority queues based on priorities; only when all the higher priority queues are empty, they start to schedule packets on the lowest priority according to WFQ/DWRR.

Rate Limiter: A packet dequeued by `qdisc` will further go through NIC driver and NIC hardware before it is pushed to the wire. If we dequeue packets from `qdisc` without any rate control, many packets can still get queued on NIC driver TX ring buffer and NIC hardware. Consequently, the buffer occupancy monitored by `qdisc` can be much smaller than the real value of a switch port, thus degrading the accuracy of ECN marking and packet drop decisions. Such issue was also identified by many previous works [11, 36].

To address above issue, we use a Token-Bucket rate limiter to shape outgoing traffic from `qdisc` at 99.5% of the NIC capacity (995Mbps). To minimize traffic burstiness, we use a small bucket size of ~1.67MTU (2.5KB) which can achieve 99% link utilization. In this way, we can minimize undesirable buffering in other places and make the buffer occupancy of `qdisc` better reflect the real buffer occupancy of a switch port.

Dequeue ECN Marking: Eventually, TCN and CoDel mark dequeued packets when they are about to be delivered to NIC driver. Both schemes uses current system time minus the enqueued timestamp to obtain the sojourn time and makes the marking decision. Our CoDel implementation closely tracks the Linux source code.

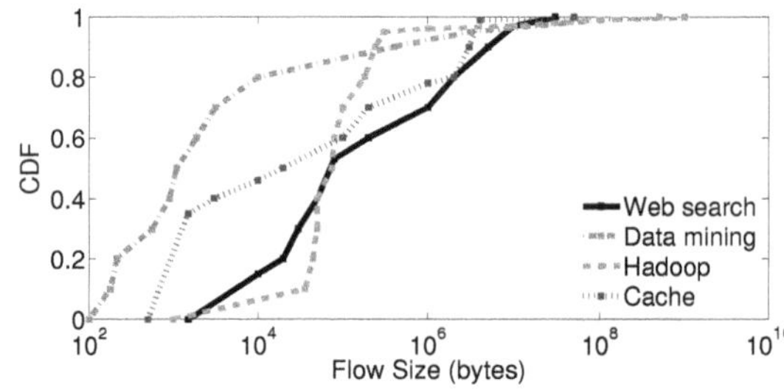

Figure 4: Traffic distributions for evaluation.

6. EVALUATION

In this section, we use a combination of testbed experiments and ns-2 simulations to answer the following three questions:

- **How does TCN perform in practice?** In the static flow experiment (§6.1.1), we find that TCN can achieve high throughput and low latency while strictly preserving the scheduling policies. With realistic workloads (§6.1.2 and §6.1.3), we find that TCN can maintain its good performance with various scheduling policies (including WFQ and SP/WFQ that MQ-ECN cannot support). For example, compared to per-queue ECN with standard threshold, TCN (with SP/DWRR) reduces the average and 99th percentile completion times for small flows by up to 82.8% and 95.3%, respectively. Compared to CoDel, TCN (with SP/WFQ) achieves up to 84% lower 99th percentile completion time for small flows.
- **Does TCN perform well in large datacenters?** In large-scale ns-2 simulations (§6.2.1), we find that TCN generally achieves the best performance in large multi-switch topologies. For example, compared to per-queue ECN with standard threshold, TCN achieves up to 94.3% lower 99th percentile completion time for small flows.
- **How robust is TCN to network settings?** Using a series of targeted simulations, we show that TCN is robust to transport protocol and the number of queues (§6.2.2) .

Schemes compared: We mainly evaluate the performance of four ECN solutions: TCN, CoDel [23], MQ-ECN [11] and per-queue ECN/RED with standard threshold (current practice §3.2). In the simple static flow experiment (§6.1.1), we also consider the ideal ECN/RED solution (Equation 2) by assuming the prior knowledge of queue capacities. We exclude per-port ECN/RED as it can violate scheduling policies.

Among above solutions, MQ-ECN and per-queue ECN/RED with standard threshold are queue-length based solutions. Instead using the static standard threshold, MQ-ECN dynamically adjusts the queue-length threshold based on the estimated queue capacity. For MQ-ECN, we set β to 0.75 and T_{idle} to the transmission time of a MTU as the paper [11] suggests. Note that MQ-ECN can only support pure round-robin schedulers.

CoDel and TCN are sojourn-time based solutions and mark packets on the dequeue side. To achieve a fair comparison, we

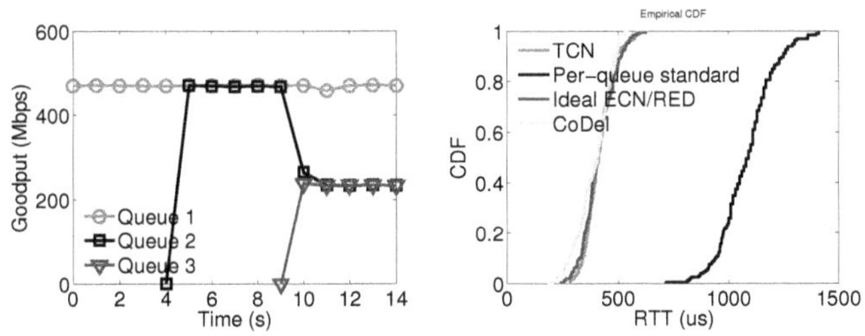

(a) Aggregate goodputs (b) RTT

Figure 5: [Testbed] (a) Aggregate goodputs of three queues achieved by TCN. (b) RTT distributions of queue 3.

configure CoDel to only mark packets (rather than drop) in our evaluation.

Benchmark traffic: We use four traffic distributions based on measurement from production datacenters (Figure 4): a web search workload [6], a data mining workload [17], a Hadoop workload [27] and a cache workload [27]. In general, all the workloads are heavy-tailed. Among them, the web search workload is less skewed: ~60% of its all bytes are from flows smaller than 10MB. Hence, the web search workload is more difficult to handle as it is likely that multiple flows are concurrently active on the same link. Therefore, we focus on the more challenging web search workload in testbed experiments while using all the four in large-scale simulations.

Performance metric: We use flow completion time (FCT) as the performance metric. We consider average FCT across all flows, small flows and large flows. To evaluate tail latency, we also give the 99th percentile FCT of small flows. For clear comparison, we normalize final FCT results to the values achieved by TCN.

6.1 Testbed Experiments

Testbed setup: We built a small-scale testbed that consists of 9 servers connected to a 9-port server-emulated switch. Each server is a Dell PowerEdge R320 with a 4-core Intel E5-1410 2.8GHz CPU, 8G memory, a 500GB hard disk. All the servers run Linux kernel 3.18.11. We enable DCTCP as the transport protocol and set TCP RTOmin to 10ms as many proposals suggest [6, 33]. The server-emulated switch has 10 Broadcom BCM5719 NetXtreme Gigabit NICs in total where one is reserved for control access. To better emulate real switches, we disable NIC offloading techniques at the switch to avoid large segments. Each switch port has a 96KB buffer which is completely shared by all the queues in a first-in-first-serve basis. Given the base RTT is around $250us$, the standard ECN marking threshold is 32KB for ECN/RED and $256us$ for TCN. For Codel, we experimentally determine its best setting ($target = 51.2us, interval = 1024us$) since the recommendation setting ($5ms$ and $100ms$) in [23] is for Internet.

6.1.1 Static Flow Experiment

We begin with a simple experiment to show that TCN can achieve good network performance while preserving the scheduling policies. At the switch, we configure SP/WFQ with three queues: queue 1 has a strict higher priority while queue 2 and 3 have equal weights in the lowest priority. We use three servers as the sender and one as the receiver. We first start a 500Mbps TCP flow from sender 1, then start a TCP flow from sender 2, and finally, start 4 TCP flows from sender 3. The packets from sender 1, 2 and 3 are classified to queue 1, 2 and 3, respectively. Based on the SP/WFQ scheduling policies, the final aggregate throughput of queue 1, 2 and 3 should be 500Mbps, 250Mbps, and 250Mbps, respectively.

Figure 5(a) gives per-queue aggregate goodputs versus time achieved by TCN. During the experiment, queue 1 maintains its ~470Mbps goodput (goodput is slightly smaller than throughput due to the IP/TCP header overhead), matching its strict higher priority at the switch. When queue 3 becomes active, queue 2 and queue 3 fairly share the remaining capacity regardless of the numbers of flows. We also use ns-2 simulation to reproduce above experiment and find that TCN can achieve similar convergence time as per-queue ECN with standard threshold. This suggests that TCN can strictly preserve the scheduling policies (a combination of WFQ and SP) while achieving high throughput.

We also measure RTT of queue 3 using `ping` packets. Figure 5(b) gives RTT distributions achieved by TCN, per-queue ECN with standard threshold, the ideal ECN/RED (equation 2) and CoDel. Note that for the ideal ECN/RED, the marking thresholds of queue 2 and 3 are both 8KB ($250Mbps \div 1000Mbps \times 32KB$). TCN provides similar latency as the ideal ECN/RED and CoDel while significantly outperforming per-queue ECN/RED with standard threshold. Compared to per-queue ECN/RED with standard threshold, TCN achieves 61.7% ($1084us$ to $415us$) and 58.4% ($1400us$ to $582us$) lower RTT in average and the 99th percentile. If we exclude the base RTT ($250us$), TCN indeed achieves more than 4× improvement in queueing delay. This suggests that TCN can also deliver low latency.

6.1.2 Inter-Service Traffic Isolation

In this experiment, we develop a client/server application to generate realistic traffic according to the web search workload (Figure 4) and measure the FCT on the application layer. The client application, running on 1 server, initially opens 5 persistent TCP connections to each of the rest 8 servers. During the experiment, the client application generates requests based on a Poisson process through available connections (or create new connections if no available connection) to the other servers to fetch data. The server applications, running on the rest 8 servers, respond with requested data. Hence, a TCP connection can carry multiple flows (messages). At the switch, we configure DWRR and WFQ with 4 equal weight/quantum (1.5KB) queues. To emulate inter-service traffic isolation, the server application uses `setsockopt` to set DSCP values for outgoing traffic, thus mapping different flows to different queues. Note that a flow is randomly mapped to one of the 4 service queues. We vary the network load from 10% to 90% and run 5000 flows for each setting.

Figure 6 and 7 show the FCT results across all flows (a), small flows (0,100KB] (b,c), and large flows (10MB,∞) (d) respectively. We omit the results for medium flows due to space

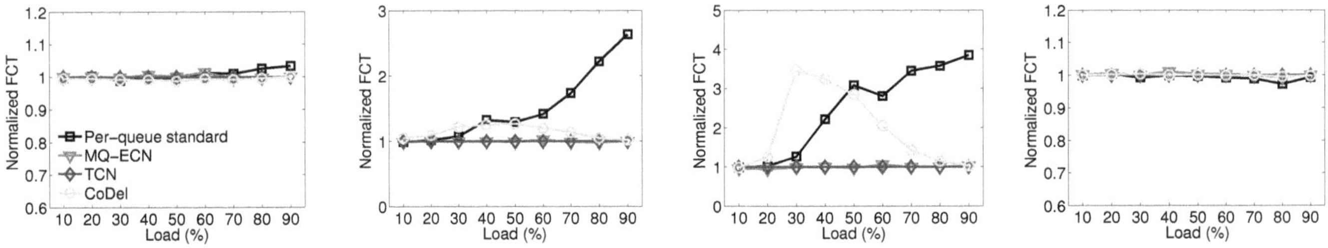

(a) Overall (b) (0,100KB]: Avg (c) (0,100KB]: 99th percentile (d) (10MB,∞): Avg

Figure 6: [Testbed] Inter-service traffic isolation with DWRR (4 queues) and DCTCP: FCT statistics.

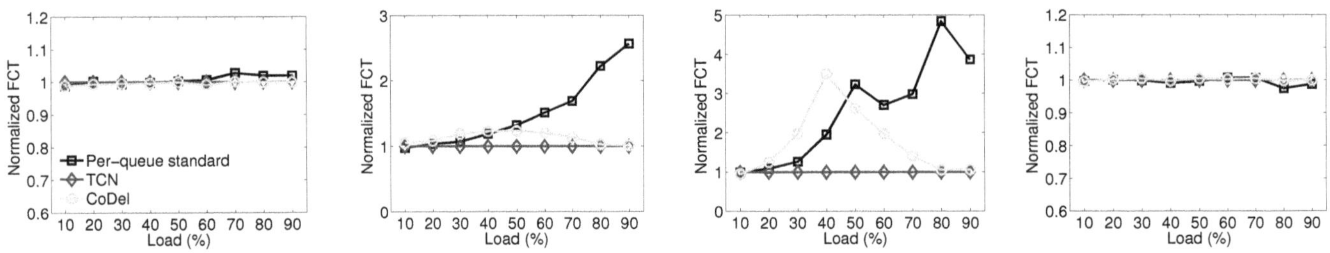

(a) Overall (b) (0,100KB]: Avg (c) (0,100KB]: 99th percentile (d) (10MB,∞): Avg

Figure 7: [Testbed] Inter-service traffic isolation with WFQ (4 queues) and DCTCP: FCT statistics.

limitation. Note that we exclude MQ-ECN from Figure 7 as it does not support WFQ. Based on the results, we make the following three observations:

Overall: Generally, all the schemes achieve similar overall average FCTs. This is expected. In a long-tailed traffic distribution, the majority of bytes are from a small number of throughput-sensitive large flows. Therefore, the overall average FCT is mainly determined by throughput. Since all the schemes can fully the link capacity, they achieve similar overall average FCT results.

Despite this, we observe that TCN, CoDel and MQ-ECN (for DWRR only) slightly outperform per-queue ECN with standard threshold at high loads ($\geq 70\%$). For example, compared to per-queue ECN with standard threshold, TCN reduces the overall average FCT by up to 2.5% and 2.7% for DWRR and WFQ, respectively. This is because, when networks run at high loads, per-queue ECN with standard threshold suffers from frequent packet drops and TCP timeouts as multiple queues are likely to be active simultaneously. By contrast, TCN can still keep low buffer occupancies to minimize such impact.

Small flows: For small flows, TCN performs similarly as MQ-ECN for DWRR while maintaining good performance for WFQ. Compared to per-queue ECN with standard threshold, the average FCT for the small flows with TCN is up to 61.4% ($9679us$ to $3733us$) lower for DWRR and 61.1% ($9529us$ to $3711us$) lower for WFQ. As expected, TCN achieves larger performance improvement at the 99th percentile: up to 73.3% (DWRR) and 79.3% (WFQ) lower 99th percentile FCT compared to per-queue ECN with standard threshold. Compared to CoDel, TCN achieves up to 71.2% ($11370us$ to $3273us$) and 71.4% ($12323us$ to $3525us$) lower 99th percentile FCT for DWRR and WFQ, respectively. The reason is that CoDel introduces many packet drops and TCP timeouts ($\geq$10ms) as it cannot quickly react to bursty traffic. All above suggest that TCN can provide low latency and good burst tolerance, thus minimizing the FCT for small flows.

Large flows: TCN also maintains good performance for large flows. Compared to per-queue ECN with standard threshold, the average FCT for large flows with TCN is within 2.8% for DWRR and 2.6% for WFQ. This shows that TCN can achieve high throughput in highly dynamic workloads by using $RTT \times \lambda$ as the sojourn time marking threshold.

6.1.3 *Traffic Prioritization*

In this experiment, we use the same setting as §6.1.2 except for two changes. First, at the switch, we configure SP/DWRR and SP/WFQ by adding a new strict higher priority queue to prioritize the delivery of latency-sensitive small flows. Second, at end host, we install a Linux `Netfilter` kernel module to perform a two-priority PIAS [10] flow scheduling. For each flow (message), the first 100K bytes are classified into the shared strict higher priority queue while the rest bytes are classified into their dedicated service queues in the low priority[5]. In this way, small flows are prioritized over large flows in general.

Figure 8 and 9 show the FCT results with SP/DWRR and SP/WFQ. Here we exclude MQ-ECN [11] as it does not support SP in general. Again, we breakdown FCT across different flow sizes, and make the following two observations:

Overall and large flows: In general, TCN and CoDel achieve

[5]Our kernel module can identify flow (message) boundaries over a persistent connection by tracking `tcp_sendmsg` called times. When the time gap between two consecutive calls over the same connection is larger than a threshold ($500us$ in our experiments) and TCP send buffer is empty, we regard this as the beginning of a new flow.

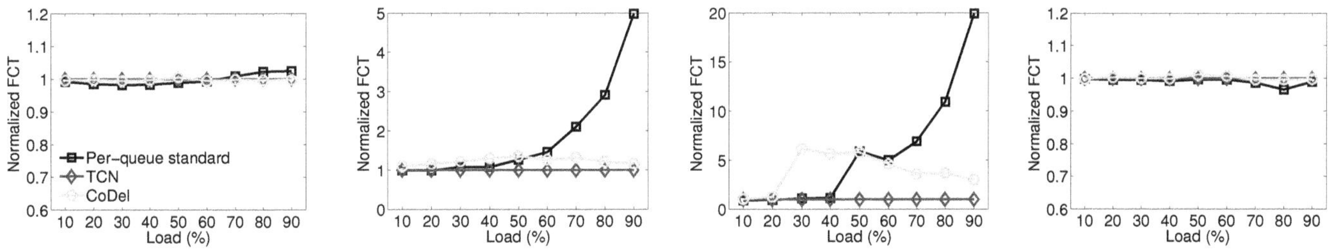

(a) Overall (b) (0,100KB]: Avg (c) (0,100KB]: 99th percentile (d) (10MB,∞): Avg

Figure 8: [Testbed] Traffic prioritization with SP (1 queue) / DWRR (4 queues) and DCTCP: FCT statistics.

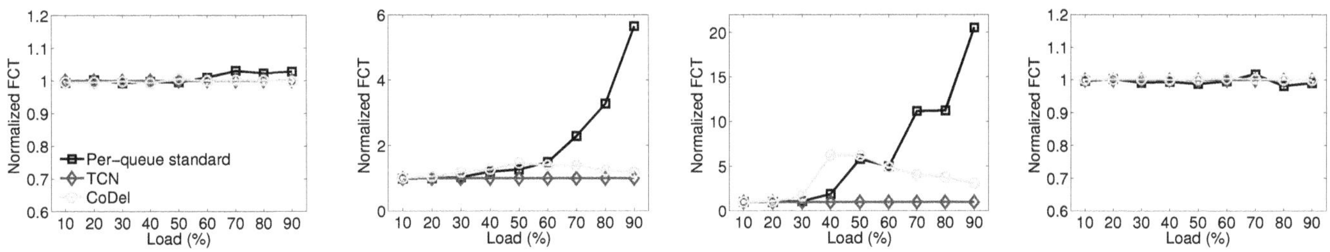

(a) Overall (b) (0,100KB]: Avg (c) (0,100KB]: 99th percentile (d) (10MB,∞): Avg

Figure 9: [Testbed] Traffic prioritization with SP (1 queue) / WFQ (4 queues) and DCTCP: FCT statistics.

similar performance as per-queue ECN with standard threshold while slightly outperforming it at high loads. TCN achieves up to 3.7% and 3% lower overall average FCT, for SP/DWRR and SP/WFQ, respectively. This is mainly because TCN can greatly reduce packet drops and TCP timeouts at high loads by maintaining low buffer occupancies.

TCN also maintains good performance for large flows. Compared to per-queue ECN with standard threshold, TCN's performance is within 2.1% for SP/DWRR and within 1.9% for SP/WFQ. This suggests that TCN can efficiently utilize the link capacity in highly dynamic datacenter workloads.

Small flows: Compared to the previous service isolation experiment (§6.1.2), all ECN marking schemes indeed achieve much lower FCT for small flows since small flows are all finished in the high priority queue[6]. For example, at 90% load, TCN with PIAS (SP/DWRR) achieves 71.3% (3733us to 1073us) lower average FCT for small flows compared to TCN without PIAS.

Even with flow scheduling, TCN still significantly outperforms per-queue ECN with standard threshold and CoDel. For example, TCN (SP/DWRR) reduces the FCT for small flows by up to 82.8% (6222us to 1073us) and 95.3% (82658us to 3860us) in average and the 99th percentile, respectively. Given all small flows are finished in the high priority queue, why can TCN still gain such a large performance improvement? This is because packets in the high priority queue can still get dropped under the buffer pressure from other low priority queues according to shared buffer policy. TCN can greatly mitigate this impact by maintaining low buffer occupancies. By contrast, per-queue ECN with standard threshold causes frequent packet drops and TCP timeouts ($\geq$10ms) at high loads, leading the tail FCT to as high as tens of milliseconds. Compared to CoDel, TCN (SP/WFQ) achieves up to 84% lower 99th percentile FCT for small flows. This further confirms that TCN can quickly react to traffic burstiness with instantaneous marking.

[6]Due to space limitation, we omit raw FCT results here.

6.2 Large-Scale NS-2 Simulations

In this section, we use ns-2 [4] simulator to evaluate the performance of TCN in large-scale multi-hop datacenter networks. Similar to the testbed experiments, we have evaluated both inter-service traffic isolation and traffic prioritization in simulations. In the interest of space, we only show results for the more complex case of traffic prioritization here.

Topology: We simulate a 144-host leaf-spine topology with 12 leaf (ToR) switches and 12 spine (Core) switches. Each leaf switch has 12 10Gbps links to hosts and 12 10Gbps links to spines, forming a non-blocking fabric. We employ ECMP for load balancing. The base RTT across the spine (4 hops) is 85.2us which 80us is spent at end hosts.

Transport: We use DCTCP [6] by default. The initial window is 16 packets. We set both minimum value and the initial value of TCP RTO to 5ms. Note that initial TCP RTO is 3 seconds by default which is too large for datacenter networks.

Switch: Each switch port has a 300KB buffer which is completely shared by 8 queues in a first-in-first-serve basis. The standard marking threshold is 65 packets for ECN/RED and 78us for TCN. We configure SP/WFQ and SP/DWRR where one queue has a strict higher priority over the rest 7 equal weight/quantum (1.5KB) WFQ/DWRR queues.

Workloads: Since we have 144 hosts, there are 144×143 communication pairs in total. We evenly classify these pairs into 7 services. Different services use different traffic distributions in Figure 4. Each service has its own dedicated service queue while sharing the same high priority queue at the switch. Same

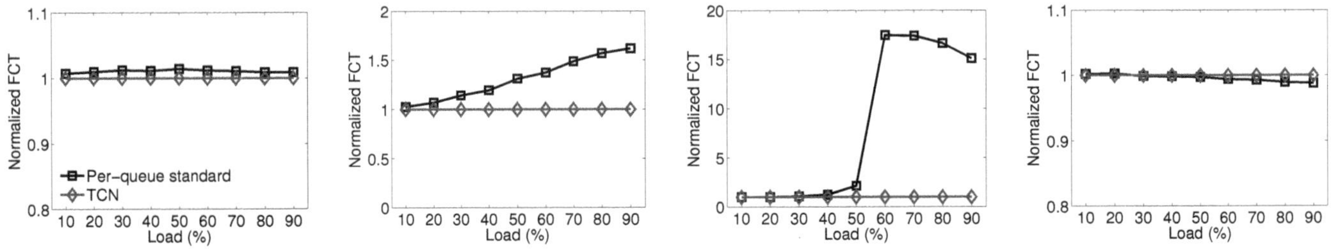

(a) Overall (b) (0,100KB]: Avg (c) (0,100KB]: 99th percentile (d) (10MB,∞): Avg

Figure 10: [Simulation] Traffic prioritization with SP (1 queue) / DWRR (7 queues) and DCTCP: FCT statistics.

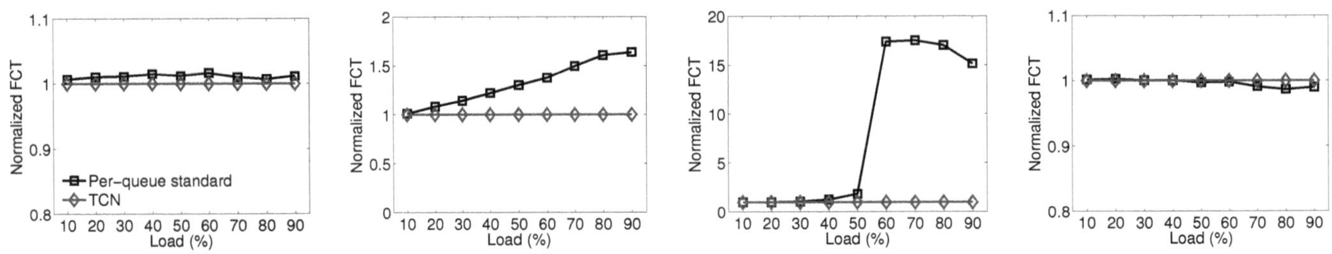

(a) Overall (b) (0,100KB]: Avg (c) (0,100KB]: 99th percentile (d) (10MB,∞): Avg

Figure 11: [Simulation] Traffic prioritization with SP (1 queue) / WFQ (7 queues) and DCTCP: FCT statistics.

as §6.1.3, we perform a two-priority PIAS [10] flow scheduling. The first 100K bytes of a flow are classified to the shared high priority queue while the rest bytes are classified to their dedicated service queues in the low priority. All simulations last for 50000 flows.

6.2.1 *Overall Performance*

Figure 10 and 11 show the FCT results across different flow sizes. We make the following two observations.

Overall and large flows: TCN slightly outperforms per-queue ECN with standard threshold across all flows in all scenarios. It achieves ~0.72-1.38% and ~0.61-1.62% lower overall average FCT for SP/DWRR and SP/WFQ, respectively. TCN also achieves very good performance for large flows. TCN's performance is within 1.2% of per-queue ECN with standard threshold for SP/DWRR and within 1.37% for SP/WFQ. This suggests that TCN can achieve high throughput in large-scale multi-hop datacenter networks.

Small flows: Compared to per-queue ECN with standard threshold, the average FCT for the small flows with TCN is up to 38.2% lower for SP/DWRR and up to 38.8% lower for SP/WFQ. As expected, TCN achieves larger improvements at the 99th percentile: it reduces the 99th percentile FCT by up to 94.3% for both schedulers. With PIAS, the performance for small flows is mainly determined by the burst tolerance of the ECN marking scheme. For example, at 90% load, per-queue ECN with standard threshold (with SP/DWRR) causes 589 TCP timeouts for small flows, resulting in a very large 99th percentile FCT (5390us). This indicates that more than 1% small flows experience at least one TCP timeout. By contrast, TCN only experiences 46 TCP timeouts for small flows in the same scenario, thus achieving a very small 99th percentile FCT (357us).

6.2.2 TCN *Deep Dive*

In this section, we evaluate TCN's robustness to network settings through a series of targeted simulations.

Impact of transport protocol: In addition to DCTCP [6], there are many other ECN-based transport protocols, such as DCQCN [37] and ECN* [35]. Among them, ECN* may be the most challenging one as it simply cuts window by half in the presence of ECN without any smoothing. Consequently, ECN* is more sensitive to premature ECN markings than DCTCP. A lower ECN marking threshold can severely degrade the throughput of ECN*. For example, with zero buffering, DCTCP can still maintain 94% throughput in theory while ECN* can only deliver 75% throughput [7].

We run simulations using ECN* instead of DCTCP. We set the standard ECN marking threshold to 84 packets for ECN/RED and 101us for TCN. Figure 12 gives the FCT with ECN*. We find that, compared to per-queue ECN with standard threshold, TCN achieves similar performance for large flows while showing large improvements for small flows. Even with very challenging ECN*, TCN's performance is still within 1.8% of per-queue ECN with standard threshold for large flows. This indicates that TCN is robust to transport protocol.

Impact of the number of queues: In the future, switching chips may provide more and more queues. To evaluate TCN's robustness to the number of queues, we increase the number of switch queues to 32 which 31 queues with equal quantum run in the low priority. To create more challenges, we still employ ECN* as the transport protocol.

Figure 13 gives the FCT results with 32 queues and ECN*. In general, TCN still outperforms per-queue ECN with standard threshold. By comparing Figure 13 and 12, we observe that TCN shows larger performance improvements over per-queue

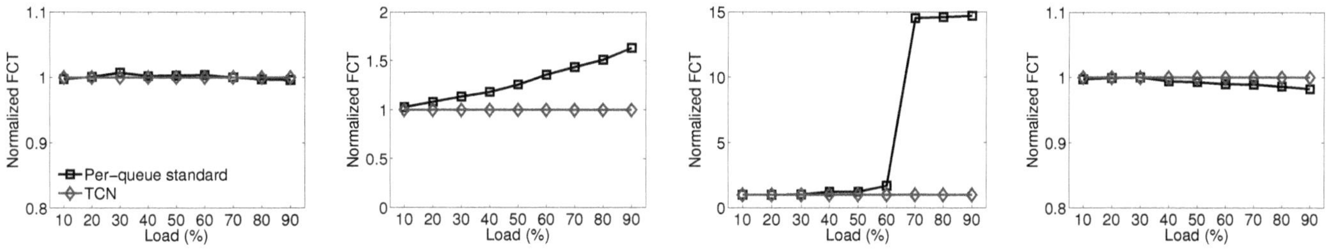

(a) Overall (b) (0,100KB]: Avg (c) (0,100KB]: 99th percentile (d) (10MB,∞): Avg

Figure 12: [Simulation] Traffic prioritization with SP (1 queue) / DWRR (7 queues) and ECN*: FCT statistics.

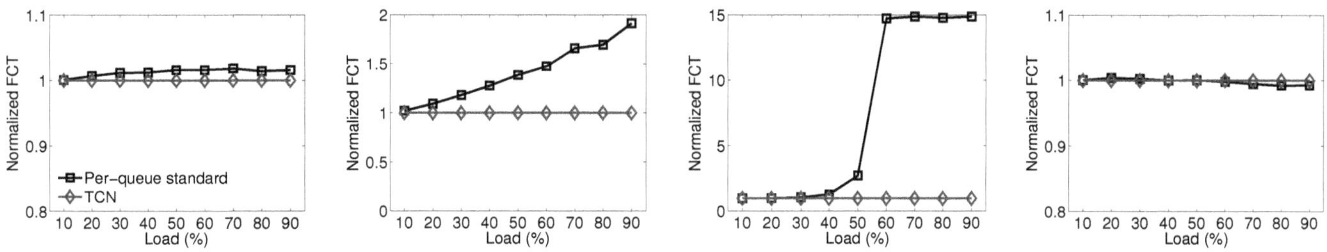

(a) Overall (b) (0,100KB]: Avg (c) (0,100KB]: 99th percentile (d) (10MB,∞): Avg

Figure 13: [Simulation] Traffic prioritization with SP (1 queue) / DWRR (31 queues) and ECN*: FCT statistics.

ECN with standard threshold for small flows with 32 queues. For example, at 90% load, TCN shows 38.7% and 47.8% lower average FCT for small flows with 8 queues and 32 queues, respectively. This is because per-queue ECN with standard threshold causes more packet drops and TCP timeouts with more queues. At 90% load, per-queue ECN with standard threshold causes 2469 and 4478 TCP timeouts with 8 queues and 32 queues, respectively. By contrast, TCN does not have such performance degradation. This suggests that TCN is robust to the number of queues.

7. RELATED WORK

Generally, ECN-related works in datacenters are vast [6, 11, 26, 32, 35, 37]. But the closest related one to TCN is MQ-ECN [11], which also tries to enable ECN for multiple queues. However, MQ-ECN only works for round-robin schedulers, whereas TCN enables ECN for arbitrary packet schedulers. More fundamentally, MQ-ECN is still designed along the line of ECN/RED principle that uses queue-length as congestion signal, thus sharing all the problems we discussed in §3. By contrast, TCN completely dismisses queue-length based ECN/RED after identifying its limitations, and instead uses packet sojourn-time as congestion signal to activate ECN.

CoDel [23] is the state-of-the-art sojourn-time based AQM for Internet. Compared to CoDel, TCN can better handle bursty datacenter workloads and be easier to implement in hardware due to its stateless fashion.

Recently, Mittal et al. [20] have proposed an edge-based AQM solution, in which they use one-way cumulative queuing delay as the congestion signal and only mark ECN at the network edge. In comparison, TCN relies on packet sojourn time at each hop.

8. CONCLUSION

With the goal of supporting ECN over generic packet schedulers, this paper has delivered two points: 1) queue-length based ECN/RED is fundamentally hard to achieve it; 2) sojourn-time based TCN is a simple yet elegant solution to it. We have spent extensive experimental efforts demonstrating not only the validity of TCN, but also the invalidity of ECN/RED.

Acknowledgements

This work is supported in part by the Hong Kong RGC ECS-26200014, GRF-16203715, GRF-613113, CRF-C703615G, and the China 973 Program No.2014CB340303. Wei is also supported by a Microsoft Research Asia PhD Fellowship. We thank our shepherd, Colin Dixon, and the anonymous reviewers for their valuable feedback.

9. REFERENCES

[1] "DCTCP in Linux kernel 3.18," http://kernelnewbies.org/Linux_3.18.

[2] "DCTCP in Windows Server 2012," http://technet.microsoft.com/en-us/library/hh997028.aspx.

[3] "P4 Behavior Model," https://github.com/p4lang/behavioral-model/blob/master/targets/simple_switch/tests/testdata/queueing.p4.

[4] "The Network Simulator NS-2," http://www.isi.edu/nsnam/ns/.

[5] "WRED Explicit Congestion Notification on Cisco switches," http://www.cisco.com/c/en/us/td/docs/ios-xml/ios/qos_conavd/configuration/xe-3s/asr1000/qos-conavd-xe-3s-asr1000-book/qos-conavd-wred-ecn.pdf.

[6] M. Alizadeh, A. Greenberg, D. A. Maltz, J. Padhye, P. Patel, B. Prabhakar, S. Sengupta, and M. Sridharan, "Data center TCP (DCTCP)," in *SIGCOMM 2010*.

[7] M. Alizadeh, A. Javanmard, and B. Prabhakar, "Analysis of DCTCP: stability, convergence, and fairness," in *SIGMETRICS 2011*.

[8] M. Alizadeh, A. Kabbani, T. Edsall, B. Prabhakar, A. Vahdat, and M. Yasuda, "Less is more: trading a little bandwidth for ultra-low latency in the data center," in *NSDI 2012*.

[9] M. Alizadeh, S. Yang, M. Sharif, S. Katti, N. McKeown, B. Prabhakar, and S. Shenker, "pfabric: Minimal near-optimal datacenter transport," in *SIGCOMM 2013*.

[10] W. Bai, L. Chen, K. Chen, D. Han, C. Tian, and H. Wang, "Information-Agnostic Flow Scheduling for Commodity Data Centers," in *NSDI 2015*.

[11] W. Bai, L. Chen, K. Chen, and H. Wu, "Enabling ECN in Multi-Service Multi-Queue Data Centers," in *NSDI 2016*.

[12] P. Bosshart, D. Daly, G. Gibb, M. Izzard, N. McKeown, J. Rexford, C. Schlesinger, D. Talayco, A. Vahdat, G. Varghese, and D. Walker, "P4: Programming Protocol-independent Packet Processors," *SIGCOMM Comput. Commun. Rev.*, 2014.

[13] P. Bosshart, G. Gibb, H.-S. Kim, G. Varghese, N. McKeown, M. Izzard, F. Mujica, and M. Horowitz, "Forwarding Metamorphosis: Fast Programmable Match-action Processing in Hardware for SDN," in *SIGCOMM 2013*.

[14] L. S. Brakmo and L. L. Peterson, "TCP Vegas: end to end congestion avoidance on a global Internet," *IEEE J.Sel. A. Commun.*, pp. 1465–1480.

[15] J. Dean and S. Ghemawat, "MapReduce: simplified data processing on large clusters," *Communications of the ACM*, pp. 107–113, 2008.

[16] S. Floyd and V. Jacobson, "Random early detection gateways for congestion avoidance," *IEEE/ACM Trans. Netw.*, pp. 397–413.

[17] A. Greenberg, J. R. Hamilton, N. Jain, S. Kandula, C. Kim, P. Lahiri, D. A. Maltz, P. Patel, and S. Sengupta, "VL2: a scalable and flexible data center network," in *SIGCOMM 2009*.

[18] C. Guo, L. Yuan, D. Xiang, Y. Dang, R. Huang, D. Maltz, Z. Liu, V. Wang, B. Pang, H. Chen, Z.-W. Lin, and V. Kurien, "Pingmesh: A Large-Scale System for Data Center Network Latency Measurement and Analysis," in *SIGCOMM 2015*.

[19] G. Judd, "Attaining the Promise and Avoiding the Pitfalls of TCP in the Datacenter," in *NSDI 2015*.

[20] R. Mittal, R. Agarwal, S. Ratnasamy, and S. Shenker, "Universal Packet Scheduling," in *NSDI 2016*.

[21] R. Mittal, V. T. Lam, N. Dukkipati, E. Blem, H. Wassel, M. Ghobadi, A. Vahdat, Y. Wang, D. Wetherall, and D. Zats, "TIMELY: RTT-based Congestion Control for the Datacenter," in *SIGCOMM 2015*.

[22] A. Munir, I. A. Qazi, Z. A. Uzmi, A. Mushtaq, S. N. Ismail, M. S. Iqbal, and B. Khan, "Minimizing flow completion times in data centers," in *INFOCOM 2013*.

[23] K. Nichols and V. Jacobson, "Controlling queue delay," *Communications of the ACM*, vol. 55, no. 7, pp. 42–50, 2012.

[24] R. Nishtala, H. Fugal, S. Grimm, M. Kwiatkowski, H. Lee, H. C. Li, R. McElroy, M. Paleczny, D. Peek, P. Saab, D. Stafford, T. Tung, and V. Venkataramani, "Scaling Memcache at Facebook," in *NSDI 2013*.

[25] R. Pan, P. Natarajan, C. Piglione, M. S. Prabhu, V. Subramanian, F. Baker, and B. VerSteeg, "PIE: A lightweight control scheme to address the bufferbloat problem," in *HPSR 2013*.

[26] K. Ramakrishnan, S. Floyd, D. Black *et al.*, "RFC 3168: The addition of explicit congestion notification (ECN) to IP," 2001.

[27] A. Roy, H. Zeng, J. Bagga, G. Porter, and A. C. Snoeren, "Inside the Social Network's (Datacenter) Network," in *SIGCOMM 2015*.

[28] A. Singh, J. Ong, A. Agarwal, G. Anderson, A. Armistead, R. Bannon, S. Boving, G. Desai, B. Felderman, P. Germano *et al.*, "Jupiter Rising: A Decade of Clos Topologies and Centralized Control in Google's Datacenter Network," in *SIGCOMM 2015*.

[29] A. Sivaraman, A. Cheung, M. Budiu, C. Kim, M. Alizadeh, H. Balakrishnan, G. Varghese, N. McKeown, and S. Licking, "Packet Transactions: High-level Programming for Line-Rate Switches," in *SIGCOMM 2016*.

[30] A. Sivaraman, S. Subramanian, A. Agrawal, S. Chole, S.-T. Chuang, T. Edsall, M. Alizadeh, S. Katti, N. McKeown, and H. Balakrishnan, "Programmable Packet Scheduling," in *SIGCOMM 2016*.

[31] K. Tan, J. Song, Q. Zhang, and M. Sridharan, "A compound TCP approach for high-speed and long distance networks," in *INFOCOM 2006*.

[32] B. Vamanan, J. Hasan, and T. Vijaykumar, "Deadline-aware datacenter tcp (d2tcp)," in *SIGCOMM 2012*.

[33] V. Vasudevan *et al.*, "Safe and effective fine-grained TCP retransmissions for datacenter communication," in *SIGCOMM 2009*.

[34] H. Wu, Z. Feng, C. Guo, and Y. Zhang, "ICTCP: Incast Congestion Control for TCP in data center networks," in *CoNEXT 2010*.

[35] H. Wu, J. Ju, G. Lu, C. Guo, Y. Xiong, and Y. Zhang, "Tuning ECN for data center networks," in *CoNEXT 2012*.

[36] D. Zats, A. P. Iyer, G. Ananthanarayanan, R. Agarwal, R. Katz, I. Stoica, and A. Vahdat, "FastLane: Making Short Flows Shorter with Agile Drop Notification," in *SOCC 2015*.

[37] Y. Zhu, H. Eran, D. Firestone, C. Guo, M. Lipshteyn, Y. Liron, J. Padhye, S. Raindel, M. H. Yahia, and M. Zhang, "Congestion Control for Large-Scale RDMA Deployments," in *SIGCOMM 2015*.

Xpander: Towards Optimal-Performance Datacenters

Asaf Valadarsky*
asaf.valadarsky@mail.huji.ac.il

Gal Shahaf†
gal.shahaf@mail.huji.ac.il

Michael Dinitz‡
mdinitz@cs.jhu.edu

Michael Schapira*
schapiram@huji.ac.il

ABSTRACT

Despite extensive efforts to meet ever-growing demands, today's datacenters often exhibit far-from-optimal performance in terms of network utilization, resiliency to failures, cost efficiency, incremental expandability, and more. Consequently, many novel architectures for high performance datacenters have been proposed. We show that the benefits of state-of-the-art proposals are, in fact, derived from the fact that they are (implicitly) utilizing "expander graphs" (aka expanders) as their network topologies, thus unveiling a unifying theme of these proposals. We observe, however, that these proposals are not optimal with respect to performance, do not scale, or suffer from seemingly insurmountable deployment challenges. We leverage these insights to present Xpander, a novel datacenter architecture that achieves near-optimal performance and provides a tangible alternative to existing datacenter designs. Xpander's design turns ideas from the rich graph-theoretic literature on constructing optimal expanders into an operational reality. We evaluate Xpander via theoretical analyses, extensive simulations, experiments with a network emulator, and an implementation on an SDN-capable network testbed. Our results demonstrate that Xpander significantly outperforms both traditional and proposed datacenter designs. We discuss challenges to real-world deployment and explain how these can be resolved.

*School of Computer Science and Engineering, The Hebrew University of Jerusalem, Israel

†Dept. of Mathematics, The Hebrew University, Jerusalem, Israel

‡Department of Computer Science, Johns Hopkins University, USA

CoNEXT '16, December 12-15, 2016, Irvine, CA, USA

© 2016 ACM. ISBN 978-1-4503-4292-6/16/12...$15.00

DOI: http://dx.doi.org/10.1145/2999572.2999580

CCS Concepts

•Networks → Topology analysis and generation; Data center networks;

1. INTRODUCTION

The rapid growth of Internet services is placing tremendous demands on datacenters. Yet, as evidenced by the extensive research on improving datacenter performance [22, 23, 6, 46, 50, 21, 43], today's datacenters often exhibit far-from-optimal performance in terms of network utilization, resiliency to failures, cost efficiency, amenability to incremental growth, and beyond.

1.1 The Secret to High Performance

We show that state-of-the-art proposals for next-generation datacenters, e.g., low-diameter networks such as Slim Fly [8], or random networks like Jellyfish [46], have an *implicit* unifying theme: utilizing an "expander graph" [24] as the network topology and exploiting the diversity of short paths afforded by expanders for efficient delivery of data traffic. Thus, our first contribution is shedding light on the underlying reason for the empirically good performance of previously proposed datacenter architectures, by showing that these proposals are specific points in a much larger design space of "expander datacenters". We observe, however, that these points are either not sufficiently close to optimal performance-wise, are inherently not scalable, or face significant deployment and maintenance challenges (e.g., in terms of unpredictability and wiring complexity).

We argue that the quest for high-performance datacenter designs is inextricably intertwined with the rich body of research in mathematics and computer science on building good expanders. We seek a point in this design space that offers *near-optimal performance* guarantees while providing a *practical* alternative for today's datacenters (in terms of cabling, physical layout, backwards compatibility with today's protocols, and more). We present Xpander, a novel expander-datacenter architecture carefully engineered to achieve both these desiderata.

Importantly, utilizing expanders as network topologies has been proposed in a large variety of contexts, ranging from parallel computing and high-performance computing [47, 14, 13, 8] to optical networks [39] and peer-to-peer networks [38, 37]. Our main contributions are examining the performance and operational implications of utilizing expanders in the *datacenter networking context*, and seeking optimal design points in this specific domain (namely, Xpander). Indeed, despite the large body of research on expanders, many aspects of using expanders as datacenter networks (e.g., throughput-related performance measures, specific routing and congestion control protocols, deployment costs, incremental growth, etc.) remain little understood. We next elaborate on expanders, expander datacenters, and Xpander.

1.2 Why Expanders?

Intuitively, in an expander graph the total capacity from any set of nodes S to the rest of the network is large with respect to the size of S. We present a formal definition of expanders in Section 2. Since this implies that in an expander every cut in the network is traversed by many links, traffic between nodes is (intuitively) never bottlenecked at a small set of links, leading to good throughput guarantees. Similarly, as every cut is large, every two nodes are (intuitively) connected by many edge-disjoint paths, leading to high resiliency to failures. We validate these intuitions in the datacenter context.

Constructing expanders is a prominent research thread in both mathematics and computer science. In particular, building well-structured, deterministic expanders has been the subject of extensive study (see, e.g., [32, 30, 41]).

1.3 Why Expander Datacenters?

We refer to datacenter architectures that employ an expander network topology as "expander datacenters". We evaluate the performance of various expander datacenters through a combination of formal analyses, extensive flow-level and packet-level simulations, experiments with the mininet network emulator, and implementation on an SDN-capable network testbed (OCEAN [3]).

Our results reveal that expander datacenters achieve near-optimal network throughput, significantly outperforming traditional datacenters (fat trees [6]). We show, in fact, that expander datacenters can match the performance of today's datacenters with roughly $80 - 85\%$ of the switches. Beyond the above improvements in performance, our results establish that expander datacenters are significantly more robust to network changes than today's datacenters.

Studies of datacenter traffic patterns reveal tremendous variation in traffic over time [7]. Unfortunately, a network topology that fares well in one traffic scenario might fail miserably in other scenarios. We show that expander datacenters are robust to variations in traffic. Specifically, an expander datacenter provides close-to-optimal performance guarantees with respect to *any* (even adversarially chosen!) traffic pattern. We show, moreover, that *no* other network topology can do better. The performance of expander datacenters also degrades much more gracefully than fat trees in the presence of network failures.

Alongside the above merits, expander datacenters, unlike today's rigid datacenter networks, can be incrementally expanded to any size while preserving high performance, thus meeting the need to constantly grow existing datacenters.

1.4 Why Xpander?

While our results indicate that expander datacenters universally achieve high performance, different expander datacenters can differ greatly both in terms of the exact level of performance attained, and in terms of their deployability. We thus seek a point in the space of expander datacenters that achieves near-optimal performance while presenting a practical alternative for today's datacenters. We present Xpander, which we regard as a good candidate for such a point. We evaluate Xpander's performance guarantees, showing that it achieves the same level of performance as random networks, the current state-of-the-art with respect to performance [46, 45, 25] (but which suffer from severe impediments to deployment, as discussed later), and that it outperforms low-diameter datacenter designs (namely, Slim-Fly [8]).

We analyze the challenges facing the deployment of Xpander in practice through detailed investigations of various scenarios, from "container datacenters" to large-scale datacenters. Our analyses provide evidence that Xpander is realizable with monetary and power consumption costs that are comparable or lower than those of today's prevalent datacenter architectures and, moreover, that its inherent well-structuredness and order make wiring Xpanders manageable (avoiding, e.g., the inherent unstructuredness and complexity of random network designs a la Jellyfish [46]).

1.5 Organization

We provide a formal exposition of expanders and expander datacenters in Section 2, and of Xpander in Section 3. We show that expander datacenters such as Xpander indeed attain near-optimal performance in Section 4, matching the performance of randomly networked datacenters. We compare Xpander to fat trees [6] and Slim Fly [8] in Sections 5 and 6, respectively. We discuss deployment challenges and solutions in Section 7, and related work in Section 8. We conclude in Section 9. Due to space constraints, our proofs and some additional materials appear in the Xpander project webpage [5].

2. EXPANDER DATACENTERS

We provide below a formal exposition of expanders. We discuss past proposals for high-performance datacenters and explain why these are, in fact, "expander datacenters".

Consider an (undirected) graph $G = (V, E)$, where V and E are the vertex set and edge set, respectively. For any subset of vertices S, let $|S|$ denote the size of S, let $\partial(S)$ denote the set of edges leaving S, and let $|\partial(S)|$ denote the size of $\partial(S)$. Let n denote the number of vertices in V (that is, $|V|$). The *edge expansion* $EE(G)$ of a graph G on n vertices is $EE(G) = \min_{|S| \leq \frac{n}{2}} \frac{|\partial(S)|}{|S|}$. We say that a graph G is *d-regular* if the degree of each vertex is exactly d. We call a d-regular graph G an *expander* if $EE(G) = c \cdot d$ for some constant $c > 0$. We note that the edge expansion of a d-regular graph cannot exceed $\frac{d}{2}$.[1] Constructions of expanders

[1]This is what is achieved by a random bisection and thus the worst bisection is no better.

whose edge expansion (asymptotically) matches this upper bound exist (see more below).

We refer to datacenters that rely on an expander graph as their network topology as "expander datacenters". We consider two recent approaches to datacenter design that have been shown to yield significantly better performance than both today's datacenters and many other proposals: low-diameter networks, e.g., Slim Fly [8], and randomly networked datacenters, e.g., Jellyfish [46]. We observe that these two designs are, in fact, expander datacenters. We show in the subsequent sections that this is indeed what accounts for their good performance.

Randomly networked datacenters. Recent studies [46, 45] show that randomly networked datacenters achieve close-to-optimal performance guarantees. Indeed, to date, randomly networked datacenters remain the state-of-the-art (performance-wise) in terms of network throughput, resiliency to failures, incremental expandability, and more. Our results for expander datacenters suggest that these merits of randomly-wired, d-regular, datacenters are derived from the fact that they achieve near-optimal edge expansion (close to $\frac{d}{2}$), as established by classical results in random graph theory [10, 18].

Unfortunately, the inherent unstructuredness of random graphs makes them hard to reason about (diagnose and troubleshoot problems, etc.) and build (e.g., cable), and thus poses serious, arguably insurmountable, obstacles to their adoption. Worse yet, as with any probabilistic construct, the good traits of random graphs are guaranteed only with *some* probability. Hence, while utilizing random network topologies in datacenters is an important thought experiment, the question arises: Can a *well-structured* and *deterministic* construction achieve the same benefits *always* (and not probabilistically)? We show later that Xpander indeed accomplishes this.

Low-diameter datacenters. Slim Fly [8] (SF) leverages a graph-theoretic construction of low-diameter graphs [33] (of diameter 2 or 3). Intuitively, by decreasing the diameter, less capacity is wasted when sending data, and hence overall performance is higher. As shown in [8], SF outperforms both existing and proposed datacenter architectures, but performs worse than random network topologies. We present the following new theoretical result for SF, showing that SF is a good expander. The proof appears in [5].

THEOREM 2.1. *A Slim-Fly network of degree* d *and diameter* 2 *has edge expansion at least* $\frac{d}{3} - 1$.

This result suggests that SF's good edge expansion may, in fact, be the explanation for its good performance, and *not* its low diameter. Indeed, our findings (see Section 6) suggest that by optimizing the diameter-size tradeoff, Slim Fly sacrifices a small amount of expansion, which leads to worse performance than random networks (and Xpander) as the network gets larger. Worse yet, the low diameter of SF imposes an extremely strict condition on its size (as a function of port count of each switch), imposing, in turn, a strict limit on the scalability of Slim Fly. Xpander, in contrast, can

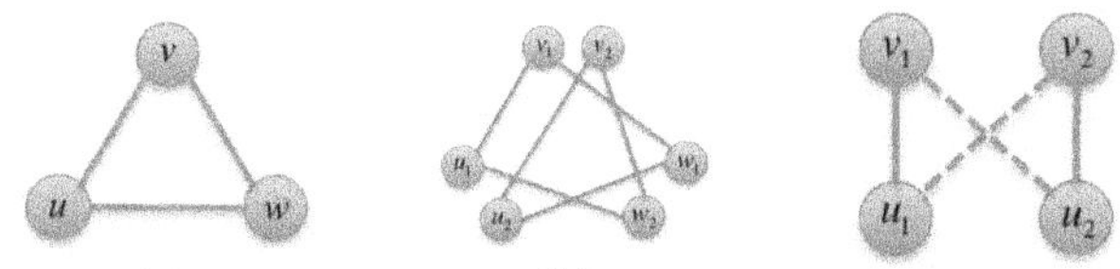

(a) (b) (c)

Figure 1: Illustration of 2-Lift

be constructed for virtually any given switch port-count and network size, as discussed in Section 6.

Other expander datacenters. A rich body of literature in mathematics and computer science deals with constructions of expanders, e.g., Margulis's construction [32], algebraic constructions [30], and constructions that utilize the so-called "zig-zag product" [41]. Such constructions can be leveraged as network topologies in the design of expander datacenters. For example, our construction of the Xpander datacenter topology utilizes the notion of 2-lifting a graph, introduced by Bilu and Linial [9, 31] (see Section 3). However, as evidenced by the above discussion, different choices of expanders can yield different performance benefits and greatly differ in terms of deployability. We next discuss the Xpander architecture, designed to achieve near-optimal performance *and* deployability.

3. XPANDER: OVERVIEW AND DESIGN

In light of the limitations of past proposals, our goal is to identify a datacenter architecture that achieves near-optimal performance yet overcomes deployment challenges. We next present the Xpander datacenter design, and show that it indeed accomplishes these desiderata.

3.1 Network Topology

Lifting a graph. Consider the graph G depicted in Figure 1(a). Our construction of Xpander leverages the idea of "lifting" a graph [9, 14]. We start by explaining *2-lifts*. A 2-lift of G is a graph obtained from G by (1) creating two vertices v_1 and v_2 for every vertex v in G; and (2) for every edge $e = \{u, v\}$ in G, inserting two edges (a matching) between the two copies of u (namely, u_1 and u_2) and the two copies of v (namely, v_1 and v_2). Figure 1(b) is an example of a 2-lift of G. Observe that the pair of vertices v_1 and v_2 can be connected to the pair u_1 and u_2 in two possible ways, described by the solid and dashed lines in Figure 1(c). When the original graph G is an expander, the 2-lift of G obtained by choosing between every two such options at random is also an expander with high probability [9]. Also, these simple random choices can be *derandomized*, i.e., the same guarantee can be derived in a deterministic manner [9].

2-lifting can be generalized to k-lifting for arbitrary values of k in a straightforward manner: create, for every vertex v in G, k vertices, and for every edge $e = \{u, v\}$ in G, insert a matching between the k copies of u and the k copies of v. As with 2-lifting, k-lifting an expander graph via random matchings results in a good expander [14, 17]. We are

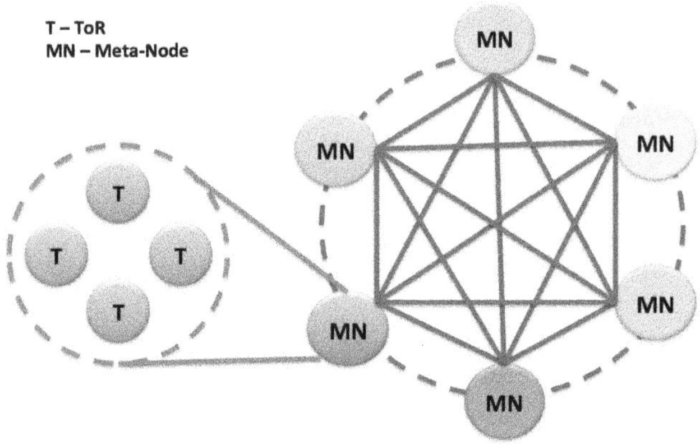

Figure 2: An Xpander topology sketch

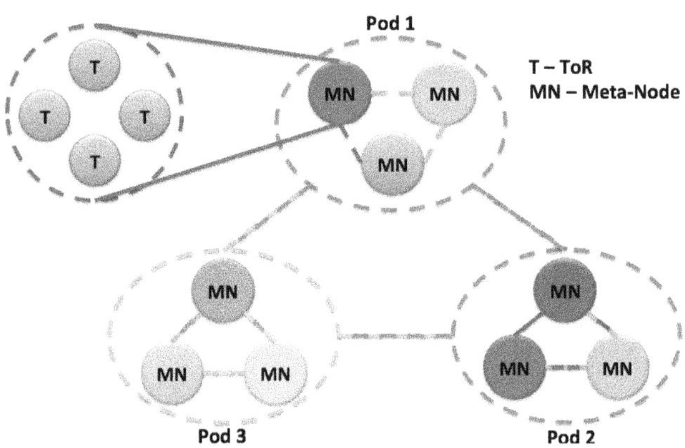

Figure 3: Division of an Xpander into Xpander-pods.

unaware of schemes for de-randomizing k-lifts for $k > 2$. However, we show empirically that k-lifts for $k > 2$ can also be derandomized (see [5]).

Xpander's network topology. To construct a d-regular Xpander network, where each node (vertex) represents a top-of-rack (ToR) switch, and d represents the number of ports per switch used to connect to other switches (all other ports are connected to servers within the rack), we do the following: start with the complete d-regular graph on $d+1$ vertices and repeatedly lift this graph in a manner that preserves expansion.

Although lifting a graph (at least) doubles the number of nodes, we show in Section 4.3 how Xpander topologies can be incrementally grown (a single node at a time) to any desired number of nodes while retaining good expansion.

Selecting the "right" Xpander. Today's rigid datacenter network topologies (e.g., fat trees) are only defined for very specific combinations of number of nodes (switches) n and per-node degree (port count) d. An Xpander, in contrast, can be generated for virtually any combination of n and d by varying the number of ports used for inter-switch connections (and, consequently, for switch-to-server connections), or through the execution of different sequences of k-lifts. The choice of specific Xpander depends on the objectives of the datacenter designer, e.g., minimizing network equipment (switches/links) while maintaining a certain level of performance. See Section 5 for a few more details. To select the "right" Xpander, the datacenter architect can play with Xpander's construction parameters to generate several Xpander networks of the desired size, number of servers supported, etc., and then measure their performance, in terms of expansion[2] and throughput, to identify the best candidate.

3.2 Xpander's Logical Organization

Observe that, as described in Figure 2, an Xpander network can be regarded as composed of multiple "meta-nodes" such that (1) each meta-node consists of the same number of ToRs, (2) every two meta-nodes are connected via the same number of links, and (3) no two ToRs within the same meta-node are directly connected. Each meta-node is, essentially, the group of nodes which correspond to one of the original $d+1$ nodes. Also, an Xpander can naturally be divided into smaller Xpanders ("Xpander-pods"), each of the form depicted in Figure 2, such that each pod is simply a collection of meta-nodes. See Figure 3 for an illustration of an Xpander with 9 meta-nodes (i.e., $d = 8$), divided into 3 equal-sized pods. Observe that division of an Xpander into Xpander-pods need not be into pods of the same size.

We show in Section 7 how this "clean" structure can be leveraged to tame cabling complexity.

3.3 Routing and Congestion Control

To exploit Xpander's rich path diversity, traditional routing with ECMP and TCP congestion control are insufficient [5]. Xpander thus, similarly to [46], employs multipath routing via K-shortest paths [51, 16] and MPTCP congestion control [49]. K-shortest paths can be implemented in several ways, including OpenFlow rule matching [34], SPAIN [35], and MPLS tunneling [42].

4. NEAR-OPTIMAL PERFORMANCE

We show that Xpander achieves near-optimal performance in terms of throughput and bisection bandwidth guarantees, robustness to traffic variations, resiliency to failures, incremental expandability, and path lengths. Both our simulations and theoretical results benchmark Xpander against a (possibly unattainable) theoretical upper bound on performance for *any* datacenter network. To benchmark also against the state-of-the-art, we show that Xpander matches the near-optimal performance of random datacenter architectures, demonstrated in [46, 45]. We will later explain how Xpander's design mitigates the deployment challenges facing randomly networked datacenters (Section 7).

We note that Xpander's near-optimal performance benefits are derived from utilizing a nearly optimal expander network topology [9]. Indeed, our results for Xpander's performance extend to all expander datacenters whose d-regular network topology exhibits near-optimal edge expansion (i.e.,

[2]Importantly, computing edge expansion is, in general, computationally hard [28], yet edge expansion can be approximated via the tractable notion of spectral gap [24].

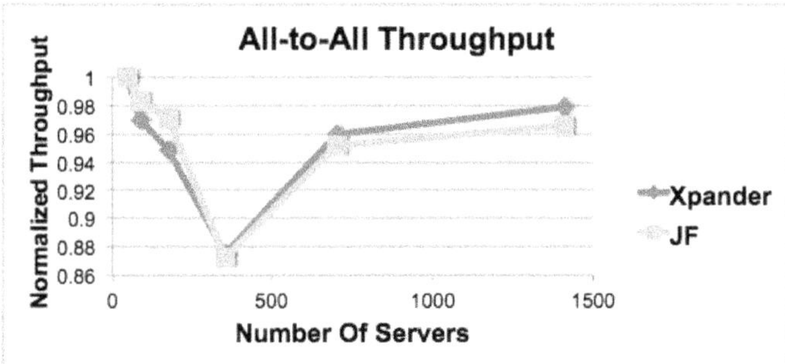

(a) $k = 14$. There are 4 servers placed under each switch

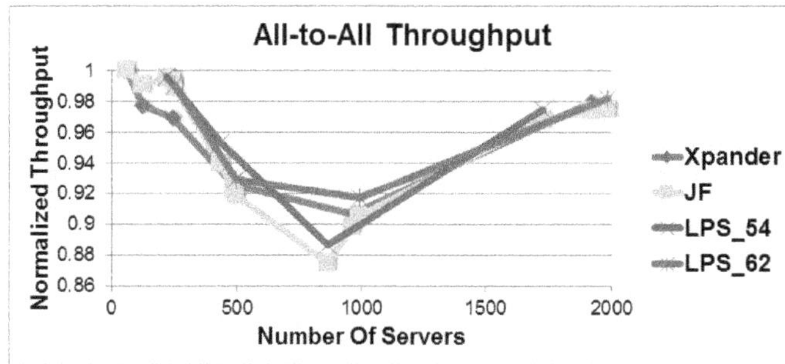

(b) $k = 18$. There are 4 servers placed under each switch.

Figure 4: Results for all-to-all throughput

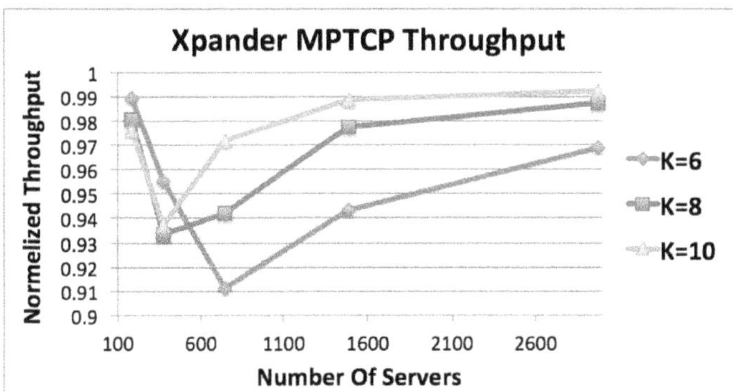

(a) Xpander

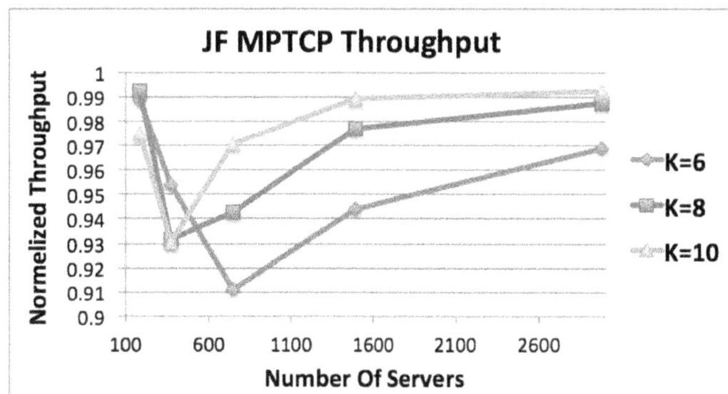

(b) Jellyfish

Figure 5: Results for K-Shortest & MPTCP with $K = \#Subflows$. 6 servers placed under each 36-port switch.

edge expansion close to $\frac{d}{2}$), such as random networks and algebraic constructions of expanders [30]. To simplify exposition, our discussion below focuses on Xpander and Jellyfish [46]. We refer the reader to [5, 48] for more results for other expander datacenters.

4.1 Near-Optimal Throughput

4.1.1 Simulation Results

Simulation framework. We ran simulations on Xpander networks for many choices of number of nodes n and node-degree d. The node degree d in our simulations refers only to the number of ports of a switch used to connect to other switches and not to switch-to-server ports. We henceforth use k to refer to the total number of ports at each switch (used to connect to either other switches or servers). We tested every even degree in the range 6-30 and up to 600 switches (and so thousands of servers) using a flow-level simulator described below. As our simulations show the exact same trends for all choices of parameters, we display figures for selected choices of n and d. To validate that Xpanders indeed achieve near-optimal performance, we benchmarked Xpanders also against Jellyfish's performance (averaged over 10 runs). We also simulate large Xpander networks, the largest supporting 27K servers, using the MPTCP packet simulator [2].

We compute the following values for every network topology considered: (1) the maximum all-to-all throughput, that is, the maximum amount of flow-level traffic α that can be concurrently routed between every two switches in the network without exceeding link capacities (see formal definition in Section 4.1.2); (2) the flow-level throughput under skewed traffic matrices (elephants and mice); and (3) the throughput under K-shortest paths [51] combined with MPTCP. Intuitively, (1)+(2) capture the maximum flow achievable when the full path diversity of Xpanders and Jellyfish can be exploited, whereas (3) captures the packet-level performance under Xpander's routing and congestion control. Thus, our simulations quantify both the best (flow-level) throughput achievable *and* how closely Xpander's routing and congestion control protocols approach this optimum.

To compute (1)+(2), our simulations ran the CPLEX optimizer [1] on a 64GB, 16-core server. Our simulation framework is highly-optimized, allowing us to investigate datacenter topologies with significantly higher parameter values (numbers of switches n, servers, and per switch port counts d) than past studies. To compute the throughput under K-shortest paths and MPTCP we use the MPTCP packet-level simulator [2]. We later validate these results using the mininet network emulator [27] (Section 5.3).

Results. Figure 4 describes our representative results for all-to-all throughput (the y-axis) as a function of the number of servers in the network (the x-axis) when the switch's inter-switch degree (ports used to connect to other switches) is $d = 10$ (left) and $d = 14$ (right). The results are normalized by the theoretical upper bound on the throughput of *any* network [45]. To show that our results are not specific to Xpander of Jellyfish, but extend to all network topologies with comparable edge expansion, Figure 4 also plots the performance of 2-lifts of the algebraic construction of expanders due to Lubotzky et al. [30], called "LPS". To evaluate LPS-based expanders of varying sizes, we generated an LPS expander and then repeatedly 2-lifted it to generate larger expanders (the subscript in the figure specifies the number of nodes in the initial LPS expander, before 2-lifting). More results for other expander datacenters can be found in [5].

Clearly, the achieved performance for all evaluated expander datacenters is essentially identical and is close to the (possibly unattainable) theoretical optimum. Note that there is a dip in the performance, but as explained in [45], this is a function of how the upper bound, which at this point becomes unattainable, is calculated. Even here, however, both Xpander and Jellyfish remain fairly close to the (unattainable) upper bound. We show in the subsequent sections that this level of performance is above that of both today's datacenters and Slim Fly [8].

We also measured, using the MPTCP packet-level simulator [2], the average per-server throughput (as a percentage of the servers' NIC rate) for different choices of parameter K in K-shortest paths. Specifically, we measured (1) the throughput when the number of MPTCP subflows is 8 (the recommended value [46, 49]), and (2) the throughput when the number of subflows equals K. We present our representative results in Figure 5, where we use $d = 30$ and up to 496 switches (or nearly 3K servers). The results for other choices of d and n exhibit the same trends. Our results show that when $K \geq 6$ and the number of MPTCP subflows equals K, the server average throughput is very close to its maximum outgoing capacity.

We also evaluated the throughput of Xpander for skewed traffic matrices, where each of T randomly-chosen pairs of nodes wishes to transmit a large amount of traffic, namely β units of flow, and all other pairs only wish to exchange a single unit of flow (as in the all-to-all scenario). We simulated this scenario for network size $n = 250$, every even $d = 2, 4, \ldots, 24$, and all combinations of $T \in \{1, 6, 11, \ldots, 46\}$ and $\beta \in \{4, 40, 400\}$.

For each choice of parameters, we computed the network throughput α, that is, the maximum fraction of each traffic demand that can be sent through the network concurrently without exceeding link capacities. The results are again normalized by a simple theoretical (and unattainable) upper bound on *any* network's throughput for these traffic demands (calculation omitted). Our simulation results for skewed traffic matrices show that the throughput achieved by Xpander is almost always (over 96% of results) within 15% of the optimum throughput, and typically within 5 – 10% from the theoretical optimum. See Table 1 for a breakdown of the results. We use the MPTCP simulator to compare Xpander to fat trees in Section 5, showing that Xpander provides the same level of performance with much fewer switches.

Distance from Optimum	Xpander	JellyFish
throughput<80%	<1%	<1%
80% ≤ throughput <85%	2.3%	2.3%
85% ≤ throughput <90%	16.14%	16.14%
90% ≤ throughput <95%	44.48%	48.03%
95% ≤ throughput	36.61%	32.67%

Table 1: Distance of throughput from the (unattainable) optimum for various combinations of β, T, d.

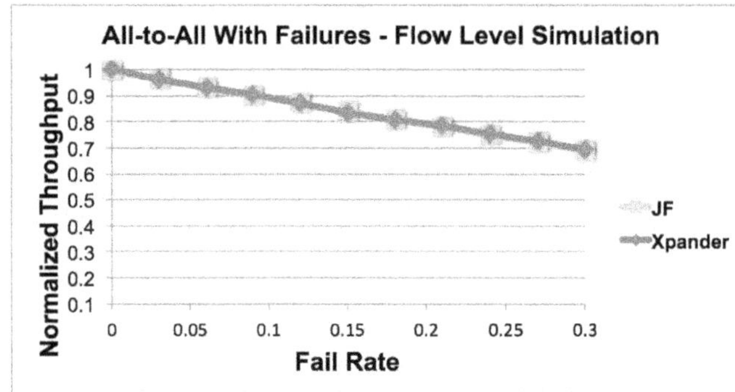

Figure 6: Throughput under link failures.

4.1.2 Theoretical Results

Near-optimal bisection bandwidth. Recall that bisection bandwidth is the minimum number of edges (total capacity) traversing a cut whose sides are of *equal* size [52], or formally $\min_{S:|S|=\frac{n}{2}} |\partial(S)|$ using the notation from Section 2. Since in an expander intuitively *all* cuts are large, not surprisingly Xpander indeed achieves near-optimal bisection bandwidth. Note that the bisection bandwidth of any d-regular graph is at most $\frac{n}{2} \cdot \frac{d}{2} = \frac{nd}{4}$.[3]

THEOREM 4.1. *An Xpander graph on n vertices has bisection bandwidth at least $\frac{n}{2}\left(\frac{d}{2} - O(d^{3/4})\right)$.*

Moreover, the definition of edge expansion of a graph G, $EE(G)$, immediately implies the bisection bandwidth of an arbitrary d-regular graph is at least $\frac{n}{2} \cdot EE(G)$, and so even in an arbitrary d-regular expander the bisection bandwidth must be quite high.

Near-optimal throughput. We consider the following simple fluid-flow model of network throughput [25]: A network is represented as a capacitated graph $G = (V, E)$, where vertex set V represents (top-of-rack) switches and edge set E represents switch-to-switch links. All edges have a capacity of 1. A *traffic matrix* T specifies, for every two vertices (switches) $u, v \in V$, the total amount of requested flow $T_{u,v}$

[3]This is what is achieved by a random bisection and thus the worst bisection is no better.

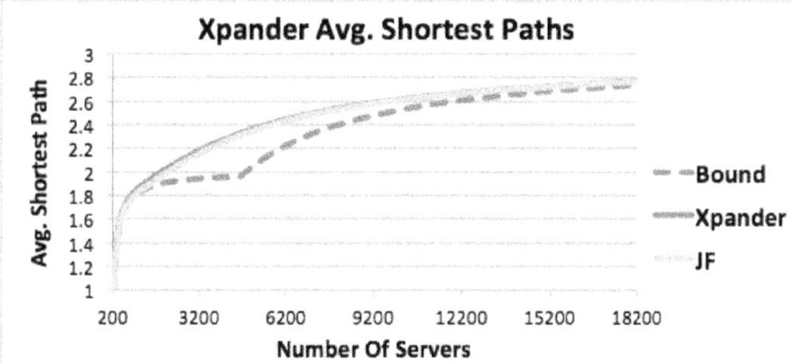

(a) $k = 32$. There are 8 servers placed under each switch.

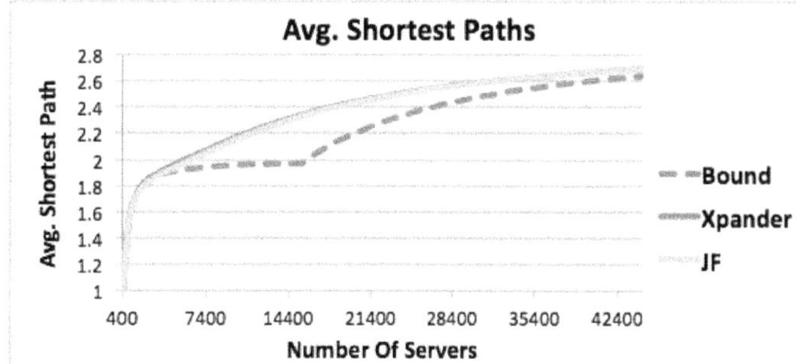

(b) $k = 48$. There are 12 servers placed under each switch.

Figure 7: Results for avg. path length

from servers connected to u to servers connected to v. The *network throughput* under traffic matrix T is defined as the maximum value α such that $\alpha \cdot T_{u,v}$ flow can be routed *concurrently* from each vertex u to each vertex v without exceeding the link capacities. For a graph G and traffic matrix T, let $\alpha(G,T)$ denote the throughput of G under T. We refer to the scenario in which $T_{u,v} = 1$ for every $u, v \in V$ (i.e. every node aims to send 1 unit of flow to every other node) as the "*all-to-all setting*". We will slightly abuse notation and let $\alpha(G)$ denote the throughput of G in the all-to-all setting.

We present several simple-to-prove results on the throughput guarantees of expander datacenters. Beyond accounting for Xpander's good performance, these results also account for the good performance of other expander datacenters, e.g., Jellyfish and Slim Fly. While possibly folklore, to the best of our knowledge, these results do not appear to have been stated or proven previously. We thus include them here for completeness.

THEOREM 4.2. *In the all-to-all setting, the throughput of a d-regular expander G on n vertices is within a factor of $O(\log d)$ of that of the throughput-optimal d-regular graph on n vertices.*

The next two results, when put together, show that expanders (and so also Xpander) are, in a sense, the network topology most resilient to adversarial traffic scenarios.

THEOREM 4.3. *For any traffic matrix T and d-regular expander G on n vertices, $\alpha(G,T)$ is within a factor of $O(\log n)$ of that of the throughput optimal d-regular graph on n vertices with respect to T.*

THEOREM 4.4. *For any d-regular graph G on n vertices, there exists a traffic matrix T and a d-regular graph G^* on n vertices such that $\alpha(G^*, T) \geq \Omega(\log_d n) \cdot \alpha(G,T)$.*

4.2 Near-Optimal Resiliency to Failures

It is easy to prove that in any d-regular expander datacenter, the number of edge-disjoint paths between any two vertices is exactly d [5]. Since this is the maximum possible number of such paths in a d-regular graph, Xpander's network topology provides optimal connectivity between any

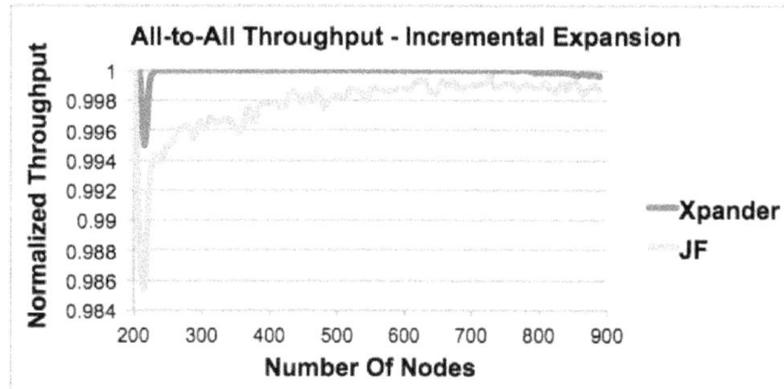

Figure 8: Throughput under incremental expansion for $k = 32$, incrementally adding 1 switch and 8 servers at each step.

two communicating end-points and can thus withstand the maximum number of link-failures (specifically, $d - 1$) without disconnecting two switches.

We compute the all-to-all server-to-server throughput in Xpander and Jellyfish after failing X links uniformly at random, where X ranges from 0% to 30% in increments of 3%. We repeated this for Xpander networks of many sizes and node-degrees. Figure 6 shows our (representative) results for Xpander and Jellyfish of 708 servers and 236 14-ports switches (with one switch port left unused). As shown in the figure, the throughput of Xpander degrades linearly with the failure rate. We show in Section 5 through both flow-level and packet-level simulations that the throughput of Xpanders indeed dominates that of fat trees (both with and without failures).

Intuitively, this linear dependence on the failure rate is natural. If the probability of link failure is p, then after failures the graph is similar to a $((1-p)d)$-regular Xpander. This is because for each cut S the number of edges across it ($|\partial(S)|$) before failure was large, owing to G being an expander, and so after failure the number of edges across the cut is tightly concentrated around its expectation, which is $(1-p)|\partial(S)|$.

4.3 Incremental Expandability

Companies such as Google, Facebook and Amazon constantly expand existing datacenters to meet ever-growing demands. A significant advantage of random graphs (i.e., Jellyfish [46]) over traditional datacenter topologies (e.g., fat trees) is the ability to incrementally expand the network without having to leave many ports unused etc.

We present a deterministic heuristic for incrementally expanding a d-regular expander datacenter with few wiring changes when adding a new node (ToR): To add a new node to the datacenter, disconnect $\frac{d}{2}$ existing links and connect the d incident nodes (ToRs) to the newly added node (recall that d is the number of ports used to connect to other switches). Observe that this is indeed the minimal rewiring needed as at least $\frac{d}{2}$ links must be removed to "make room" for the new switch. The key challenge is selecting the links to remove. Intuitively, our heuristic goes over all links and quantifies the loss in edge expansion from removing each link, and then removes the $\frac{d}{2}$ links whose removal is the least harmful in this regard. Importantly, since computing edge expansion is, in general, computationally hard [28], our heuristic relies on the tractable notion of spectral gap [24], which approximates the edge expansion. We refer the reader to [5] for a technical exposition of this heuristic.

We compute the all-to-all throughput of topologies that are gradually expanded from the complete d-regular graph using our deterministic incremental growth algorithm, and compare them to the theoretical upper bound on the throughput of *any* d-regular datacenter network.

Figure 8 shows the all-to-all throughput results for an Xpander with 32-port switches. At each size-increment-step, one switch (and 8 servers) is added, thus gradually growing the datacenter network from 200 servers to 900 servers. As shown in Figure 8, all Xpander datacenter networks obtained in this manner achieve near-optimal throughput. We compare Xpander against the incremental growth of Jellyfish, as presented in [46].

4.4 Short Path-Lengths and Diameter

As shown in Figure 7, all evaluated Xpander (and Jellyfish) networks exhibit the same average shortest path lengths and are, in fact, usually within 5% of the lower bound on average path length in [12]. (Results for many other choices of n and d lead to the same conclusion.) Thus, Xpander effectively minimizes the average path length between switches.

A straightforward argument (omitted) shows that $\lceil \log_d n \rceil$ is a lower bound on the diameter of a d-regular graph. All Xpanders evaluated are within just 1 hop from this theoretical lower bound. See [5] for an exposition of our results for network diameter.

5. XPANDER *VS.* FAT TREE

We next detail the significant performance benefits of Xpander datacenters over fat trees. We show that Xpander can support the same number of servers as a fat tree at the same (or better) level of performance with only about $80-85\%$ of the switches. We also show that Xpander is more resilient to failures.

fat tree Degree	#Switches	#Servers	Throughput
8	80%	100%	121%
10	100%	100%	157%
12	80.5%	100%	103%
14	96%	103%	122%
16	80%	100%	120%
18	90%	100%	137%
20	80%	100%	118%
22	89%	102%	121%
24	80%	100%	111%

Table 2: Xpanders vs. fat trees (FT), flow-level simulations. Percentages are Xpander/FT.

5.1 Better Performance, Less Equipment

We examine uniform fat tree topologies for every even degree (number of ports per switch) between 8 and 24. Unlike a fat tree, which is uniquely defined for a given switch port-count, Xpander gives the datacenter designer much greater flexibility (see discussion in Section 3.1). We identify, for each fat tree in the above range, an Xpander with much fewer (roughly 80-85%) switches that supports the same number of servers with at least the same level of server-to-server throughput.[4] See details in Table 2.

5.2 Simulation Results

Throughput. We evaluate the all-to-all throughput of Xpander and fat trees. We show in Table 2 the all-to-all server-to-server throughput in fat trees and Xpanders without any link failures. As can be seen in Table 2, Xpander is able to achieve comparable, if not better, server-to-server throughput than fat trees *even* with as few as 80% of the switches. Table 3 shows the results of extensive packet based-simulations using the MPTCP network simulator for Xpander and fat trees with $k = 32$ and $k = 48$, containing 8K and 27K servers, respectively. Again, Xpander networks achieve similar or better performance to that of fat trees, with significantly fewer switches.

To explore how Xpander and fat trees compare for other traffic patterns, we also simulate a fat tree of 8K servers (i.e., $k = 32$) and its matching Xpander under the following "Many-to-One" scenario using the MPTCP packet level simulator. We randomly select 10% of the servers as our destinations and for each such server we select at random x% of the servers to generate traffic destined for that server, where x=1%, 1.5%, 2%, 2.5% and 3% (1% is roughly 80 servers). Table 5 presents the averaged results of 4 such simulations. We conclude that, once again, Xpander provides the same level of performance with less network equipment.

Robustness to failures. We compute the all-to-all server-to-server throughput in fat trees and Xpanders after failing X links uniformly at random, where X ranges 0% to 30% in

[4] We now consider server-to-server all-to-all throughput and not switch-to-switch all-to-all throughput, since in a fat tree not all switches originate traffic.

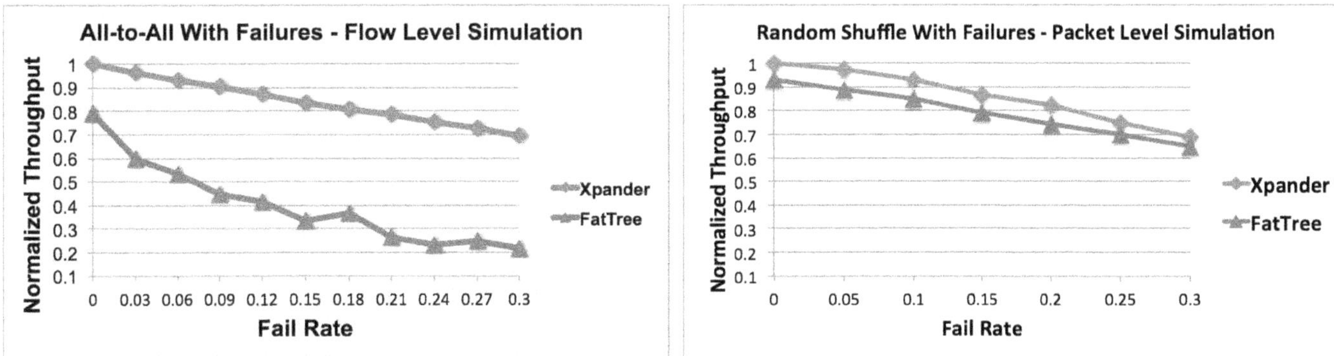

(a) d=14

(b) d=32

Figure 9: Server-to-server throughput degradation with failures. All-to-All flow level (on the left) and Random-Shuffle packet level (on the right

Tested Topology	Random Shuffle		One-to-Many		Many-to-One		Big-and-Small	
	Avg	Max	Avg	Max	Avg	Max	Avg	Max
Xpander	19.66	58.86	79.52	104.03	70.09	90.88	28.66	120.21
FatTree (TCP+ECMP)	26.7	102.86	80.72	89.94	80.79	91.51	42.72	220.1
FatTree (MPTCP+ECMP)	17.94	105.71	78.18	138.5	69.56	91.31	31.75	180.64

Table 4: Xpander and fat trees under various traffic matrices. Values are given in seconds and indicate the average finishing time for transmission.

Fat Tree Degree	#Switches	#Servers	Packet Simulation Throughput
32	90%	98.5%	110%
48	88%	100%	102%

Table 3: Xpanders vs. fat trees, packet-level simulation results. Percentages are Xpander/FT.

Percentage Of Servers Routing To Each Destination	Packet Simulation Throughput
1%	99.6%
1.5%	99.3%
2%	101%
2.5%	103%
3%	103%

Table 5: Xpanders vs. fat trees, 10% of the servers are selected as destinations. Percentages for throughput are Xpander/FT.

increments of 3%. We repeated this for fat trees of all even degrees in the range 8-24 and the corresponding Xpander networks from Table 2. Figure 9(a) describes our (representative) results for fat trees of degree $k = 14$ (vs. Xpander). We further simulate a fat tree with $k = 32$, containing 1280 switches and 8192 servers, against an Xpander containing 90% of the switches and 98.5% of the servers, under a random-shuffle permutation matrix after failing S links uniformally at random, where S ranges from 0% to 30% in increments of 5%. The results of this simulation are described in Figure 9(b). Both results (flow-level and packet-level alike) show that Xpander indeed exhibits better resiliency to failures than fat tree. We note that the smaller gap between Xpander and fat tree in the MPTCP simulations can be explained by the fact that the per switch degree is higher and so naturally routing is less affected by failures.

5.3 Xpander Emulation

To show that an Xpander with significantly less switches can achieve comparable performance to fat trees, we used mininet [27] and the RipL-POX [4] controller to simulate fat tree [6] networks under various workloads, and for two routing & congestion control schemes: (1) ECMP with TCP and (2) K-shortest-paths with $K = 8$ and MPTCP with 8 subflows. We also simulated Xpanders for the same workloads under K-shortest-paths with $K = 8$ and MPTCP with 8 subflows. These simulations were performed on a VM running Ubuntu 14.04 with MPTCP kernel version 3.5.0-89 [11]. We chose, for compute and scalability constraints, to evaluate a fat tree network of degree 8, which contains 80 switches and 128 servers. We tested against this fat tree topology the corresponding Xpander datacenter from Table 2, which contains only 64 switches and the same number of servers. All links between switches in both networks are of capacity 1Mbps.

The workloads considered are: (1) Random Shuffle, where the 128 servers are divided into two halves, and each member of the first half sends a 1Mb file to a (unique) randomly chosen member of the other half; (2) One-to-Many, where 4 servers are randomly selected and these servers send a

#Ports per Switch (Sw2Sw / Total)	#Switches (XPNDR / SF)	#Servers (XPNDR / SF)	Bisection Bandwidth	Cost per node	Power per node	Expansion
5 / 8	18 / 18 (100%)	54 / 54 (100%)	86%	123%	114%	77%
7 / 11	48 / 50 (96%)	192 / 200 (96%)	67%	79%	81%	72%
11 / 17	96 / 98 (98%)	576 / 588 (98%)	98%	106%	104%	84%
17 / 26	234 / 242 (96%)	2,106 / 2,178 (96%)	102%	102%	100%	92%
19 / 29	340 / 338 (104%)	3,400 / 3,380 (104%)	103%	95%	94%	96%
25 / 38	572 / 578 (99%)	7,436 / 7,541 (98%)	109%	95%	94%	102%
29 / 44	720 / 722 (99%)	10,800 / 10,830 (99%)	118%	104%	102%	103%
35 / 51	1080 / 1058 (102%)	17,280 / 16,928 (102%)	119%	102%	100%	101%
43 / 65	1672 / 1682 (99%)	36,784 / 37,004 (99%)	117%	99%	96%	107%
47 / 71	1920 / 1922 (99%)	46,080 / 46,128 (99%)	122%	103%	101%	108%
55 / 83	2688 / 2738 (96%)	75,264 / 76,664 (98%)	119%	91%	88%	112%

Table 6: Xpander vs. Slim-Fly. The first column specifies the number of ports per switch used for switch-to-switch and the total port count (for both Xpander and SF). Percentages are Xpander/SF.

Scenario	Min	Max	Average
Random Shuffle	234%	83%	135%
One-to-Many	94%	138%	123%
Many-to-One	115%	86%	92%

Table 7: Results for the physical simulations, all values are the averaged value of Xpander/FatTree.

1Mb file to 10 other randomly chosen (unique) hosts; (3) Many-to-One, where 40 different servers send 1Mb file each to 4 servers (10 sending servers per each receiving server); and (4) Big-And-Small, which is similar to Random Shuffle, only in addition each of 8 randomly chosen servers sends a 10Mb file to a unique other server. Our results are summarized in Table 4. Observe that even with 80% of the switches, Xpander provides comparable or better performance.

5.4 Implementation on a Network Testbed

To validate the above findings, we use OCEAN [3], an SDN-capable network testbed composed of 13 Pica8 Pronto 3290 switches with 48 ports eac. We used the OCEAN platform to experimentally evaluate two datacenter networks: (1) a fat tree composed of 20 4-port switches, of which 8 are top-of-rack switches, each connected to 2 servers (16 servers overall), and (2) an Xpander consisting of 16 4-port switches, each connected to a single server (again, 16 servers overall). Observe that while both networks support the same number of servers, the number of switches in the Xpander is 80% of the number of switches in the fat tree (16 vs. 20). Similarly, the number of links connecting switches to other switches in the Xpander is 75% that of the fat tree (24 vs. 32). Note, however, that the network capacity *per server* in Xpander is much higher as the number of ToRs is higher (16 vs. 8), and each ToR is connected to less servers (1 vs. 2) and to more other switches (3 vs. 1). Thus, intuitively, the Xpander can provide comparable or better performance with less network equipment. Our experiments on OCEAN confirm this intuition.

ECMP routing and TCP are used to flow traffic in the fat tree, whereas for the Xpander we use K-Shortest Paths, with $k = 3$, and MPTCP with 3 subflows (and so on each of the 3 distinct paths between a source and a destination there is a separate MPTCP subflow). We evaluate the min, max, and average throughput under three different traffic scenarios: (1) random shuffle, in which every server routes to a single random destination, (2) many-to-one, in which a randomly chosen server receives traffic from the other 15 servers, and (3) one-to-many, in which a randomly chosen server sends traffic to all other servers. To compute the throughput for two communicating servers, an "endless" flow between these servers is generated using of an iperf client and server and the averaged throughput is computed after 10 minutes. Our results for each simulation setting are averaged over 5 independent runs.

Table 7 shows our results for the above three traffic scenarios (the rows) and for min, max, and average throughput (the columns), where % are Xpander/FT. Xpander achieves comparable or better results in each of the evaluated scenarios (again, using only 80% of the network equipment).

6. XPANDER *VS.* SLIM FLY

We also contrast Xpander with Slim Fly, a recent proposal from the world of high-performance computing (HPC). SF leverages a graph-theoretic construction of low-diameter graphs [33] (either diameter of 2, the situation most explored in [8], or diameter of 3).

Intuitively, by decreasing the diameter, less capacity is wasted when sending data, and hence overall performance is higher. Indeed, [8] shows that SF outperforms existing and proposed datacenter architectures, but performs worse than random topologies, e.g., in terms of bisection bandwidth and resiliency to failures.

When comparing SF to Xpander, we first note that the low diameter of SF imposes an extremely strict condition on the relationship between the per node degree d and the number of nodes n: by requiring diameter 2, SF requires

$d \geq \Omega(\sqrt{n})$. (Importantly, d here represents only the ports used to connect a switch to other switches, and so, to support servers, the actual port count must be even higher.) This imposes a strict limit on the scalability of Slim Fly. Xpander topologies, on the other hand, exist for essentially any combination of n and d and, in particular, can be used for arbitrarily large datacenters even with a fixed per-switch degree d.

Not only is Xpander more flexible than SF in supporting more nodes with smaller degrees, but it exhibits better performance than SF as the network grows, even in the degree/node regimes in which SF is well-defined. We used the simulation framework published in [8] to compare SF to Xpander in terms of performance and costs. The METIS partitioner [26] was used for approximating bisection bandwidth (as in [8]) and the code from [8] for cost and power consumption analysis (using the switch/cable values in [8]). We also computed the expansion for both categories of graphs using spectral gap computation, which approximates edge expansion. See our results for Xpanders in Table 6 and for Jellyfish in [5].

Our findings suggest that, in fact, the good performance of SF can be attributed to the fact that it is an expander datacenter. We back these empirical results with the new theoretical result presented in Section 2, which shows that a Slim-Fly network of degree d and diameter 2 has edge expansion at least $\frac{d}{3} - 1$, and is thus not too far from the best achievalbe edge expansion of $\frac{d}{2}$.

We argue, however, that by optimizing the diameter-size tradeoff, Slim Fly sacrifices a small amount of expansion leading to worse performance than random networks and Xpander as the network gets larger. Our results reveal that for networks with less than 100 switches, SF is a better expander than both Xpander and Jellyfish and exhibits better bisection bandwidth. This advantage is reversed as the network size increases and in turn Xpander and Jellyfish become better expanders. Our results thus both validate and shed light on the results in [8], showing why random graphs (and Xpander) outperform SF for large networks.

We also show (Table 6) that Xpander's cost and power consumption are comparable to those of SF.

7. DEPLOYMENT

We grapple with important aspects of building Xpander datacenters: (1) equipment and cabling costs; (2) power consumption; and (3) physical layout and cabling complexity. We first present a few high-level points and then the results of a detailed analysis of Xpander deployment in the context of both small-scale (container-sized) datacenters and large-scale datcenters. We stress that our analyses are straightforward and, naturally, do not capture all the intricacies of building an actual datacenter. Our aim is to illustrate our main insights regarding the deployability of Xpanders, demonstrating, for instance, its significant deployability advantages over random datacenter networks like Jellyfish.

Physical layout and cabling complexity. As illustrated in Figures 2 and 3, an Xpander consists of several meta-nodes, each containing *the same* number of ToRs and connected to each other meta-node via *the same* number of cables. No two ToRs within the same meta-node are connected. This "clean" structure of Xpanders has important implications: First, placing all ToRs in a meta-node in close proximity (the same rack / row(s)) enables bundling cables between every two meta-nodes. Second, a simple way to reason about and debug cabling is to color the rack(s) housing each meta-node in a unique color and color the bundle of cables interconnecting two meta-nodes in the respective two-color stripes. See the illustration in Figure 2.

Thus, similarly to today's large-scale datacenters [44], Xpander's inherent symmetry allows for the taming of cabling complexity via the bundling of cables. Unlike Xpander networks, whose construction naturally induces the above cabling scheme, other expander datacenters (e.g., Jellyfish [46]) do not naturally lend themselves to such homogeneous bundling of cables. Our strong suspicion, backed by some experimental evidence, is that Jellyfish does not (in general) allow for a clean division of ToRs into equal-sized meta-nodes where every two meta-nodes are connected by the same number of cables (forming a matching), as Xpander does. Unfortunately, proving this seems highly nontrivial. Identifying practical cabling schemes for other expander datacenters is an important direction for further research.

Equipment, cabling costs, and power consumption. As shown in Table 2 and validated in Sections 5.3 and 5.4, Xpanders can support the same number of servers at the same (or better) level of performance as traditional fat tree networks with as few as 80% of the switches. This has important implications for equipment (switch/serve) costs and power consumption. We show, through analyzing cable numbers and lengths, that the reduced number of inter-ToR cables in Xpanders, compared to Clos networks/fat trees, translates to comparable or lower costs. In addition, beyond the positive implications for cabling complexity, the bundling of cables afforded by Xpander also has implications for capex and opex costs. As discussed in [44], manufacturing fiber in bundles can reduce fiber costs considerably (by nearly 40%) and expedite deployment of datacenter fabric by multiple weeks.

Analyzing deployment scenarios. We analyze below two case studies: (1) small clusters ("container datacenters"), and (2) large-scale datacenters.

7.1 Scenario I: Container Datacenters

As several ToR switches can sometimes be placed in the same physical rack along with the associated servers, we distinguish between a Virtual Rack (VR), i.e., a ToR switch and the servers connected to it, and a Physical Rack (PR), which can contain several VRs. Our analyses assume that all racks are 52U (this choice is explained later) and are of standard dimensions, switches are interconnected via Active-Optical Cables (AOC), and servers are connected to ToR switches via standard copper cables.

We inspect 2-layered folded-clos network (FCN) of degrees 32 and 48 (see [5]). We select, for each of these two

	#Switches	#Servers	#Physical Racks	#Cables	Cable Length	All-to-All Server to Server Throughput
k=32	42 vs. 48 (87.5%)	504 vs. 512 (98.44%)	11 vs. 11 (100%)	420 vs. 512 (82%)	4.2km vs. 5.12km (82%)	109%
k=48	66 vs. 72 (91.76%)	1,056 vs. 1,152 (91.67%)	22 vs. 25 (88%)	1056 vs. 1152 (91.6%)	10.56km vs. 11.52km (91.6%)	142%

Table 8: Xpander vs. 2-FCN. Percentages are Xpander/2-FCN

Switch Degree	#Switches	#Servers	#Physical Racks	#Cables	Cable Length (m)	Ttl. Space (ft^2)
30 vs. 32 (93.75%)	1,152 vs. 1,280 (90%)	8,064 vs. 8,192 (98.44%)	192 vs. 221 (86.87%)	13,248 vs. 16,348 (80.85%)	220.8k vs. 174k (127%)	3.24k vs. 4k (81%)

Table 9: Xpander vs. fat tree. Percentages are Xpander/fat tree

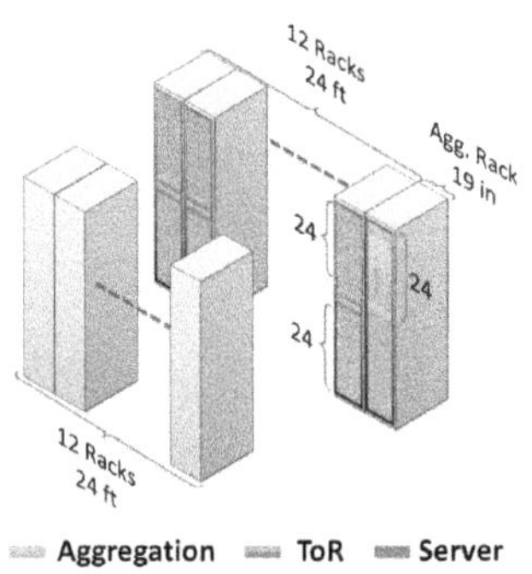

(a) 2FCN

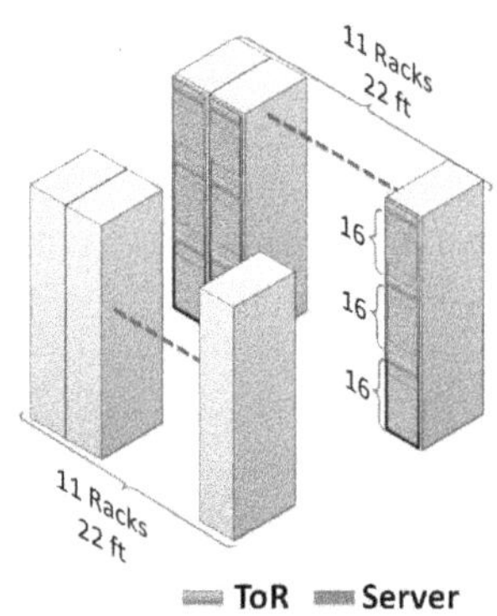

(b) Xpander

Figure 10: A $k = 48$ 2FCN network topology and the matching Xpander

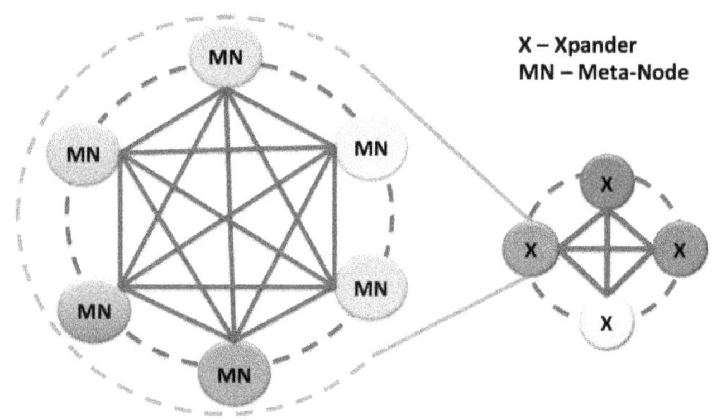

Figure 11: A sketch of an Xpander of Xpander graphs

topologies, a matching Xpander with better performance. We consider 52U racks as these provide the best packing of VRs into PRs for Clos networks. Specifically, 3 VRs fit inside each physical rack for the $k = 32$ Clos network and 2 VRs fit into a PR for $k = 48$ Clos network. The two matching Xpanders are created via a single 2-lift. As each VR in an Xpander contains less servers than that of the comparable 2-FCN network, more VRs can reside in each physical rack (for both degrees). We present the physical layouts of both the 2-FCNs and Xpander networks in Figure 10 and [5], and our analysis in Table 8.

Clearly, the use of less switches in Xpanders immediately translates to a reduction in costs. An Xpander network of switch-to-switch degree d, where each meta-node contains x ToRs, requires $x \cdot \frac{d \cdot (d+1)}{2}$ AOC cables, whereas for a 2-FCN of switch degree (total port count) k there are $\frac{k^2}{2}$ cables. The lower number of AOC cables in Xpanders, assuming 10m-long AOC cables, yields the cable lengths in Table 8. Importantly, the marginal cost of AOC cables greatly decreases with length and so the reduction in number of cables translates to potentially greater savings in costs.

A detailed analysis appears in [5].

7.2 Scenario II: Large-Scale Datacenters

We now turn our attention to large-scale datacenters. Specifically, we analyze the cost of building a uniform-degree fat tree with port-count $k = 32$ per switch (and so of size 1280 switches and 8192 servers) vs. a matching Xpander. We first present, for the purpose of illustration, the physical layout of each network in a single floor. We point out, however, that while deploying a fat tree (or the matching Xpander) of that scale in a single room might be physically possible, this might be avoided in the interest of power consumption and cooling considerations. We hence also discuss large-scale datacenters that are dispersed across multiple rooms/floors.

7.2.1 Single Floor Plan

A fat tree with total port count $k = 32$ per node contains 32 pods and $\frac{d^2}{4} = 256$ core switches, where each pod contains 16 ToRs, 512 servers and 16 aggregation switches, totaling in 8192 servers, 512 ToRs, and 512 aggregation switches. We present a straightfoward, hypothetical floor plan for deploying such a fat tree in [5]. Again, we assume 52U physical racks as this is the most suitable for packing VRs in the fat tree, allowing us to fit 3 VRs in each PR and consequently an entire pod (including the aggregation switches) in a row of 6 PRs. We can place 2 such pods (rows) inside a hot/cold-aisle containment enclosure, resulting in 16 such enclosures for the entire datacenter. We end up with 12 rows, each containing exactly 18 physical racks (which, in turn, can house 3 pods), and core switches placed in 5 additional physical racks. We assume that, within a pod, 5m AOC cables are used to connect each ToR to its aggregation layer switches. Each of the 2-pod enclosures can be connected to the row of core switches using combination of 10m/15m/20m/25m AOC cables, depending of their proximity.

We compare this fat tree network with an Xpander network of degree 23 ($k = 30$-port switches instead of $k = 32$), constructed using four 2-lifts and another 3-lift. See the side by side comparison of the two networks in Table 9. This specific Xpander houses 8064 servers under 1152 ToRs and consists of 24 meta-nodes, each containing 48 VRs with 7 servers per VR. We present a possible floor plan for deploying this Xpander in [5]. Using 52U racks, 6 VRs can be packed into a physical rack, resulting in a total of 8 racks per meta node. Again, each hot/cold-aisle containment enclosure houses 2 rows, resulting in 16 52U racks (8 in each row). We present the physical layout analysis for both networks in Table 9. See a more detailed analysis in [5].

7.2.2 *Xpander of Xpanders*

So far, our analysis of large-scale Xpanders assumed that the whole datacenter network fits in a single floor. This might not be feasible due to power supply and cooling constraints. To this end, the Xpander must be "broken" into several, dispersed, components. One approach to do so is to place a single Xpander-pod, or several such pods, in a separate floor. Another possible approach is constructing an Xpander network interconnecting smaller Xpander networks, as illustrated in Figure 11: (1) each smaller Xpander will be housed in a single container/room/floor and be constructed as illustrated above; (2) several (higher-degree) switches in each of these Xpanders will be designated as "core switches"; (3) these core switches will then be interconnected through an Xpander overlay network. Since, as evidenced by our results, an Xpander provides near-optimal performance guarantees (throughput, failure resiliency, average path length, etc.), this construction can yield good peformance both within each smaller Xpander and between the Xpander networks.

8. RELATED WORK

Datacenter networks. Datacenters have been extensively researched from many different angles, e.g., throughput optimization [45, 40, 25], failure resiliency [29, 20, 19], and expandability [46, 15]. In particular, many datacenter topologies have been proposed, including Clos networks [6, 21, 36], hypercubes [22, 50], small-world graphs [43], and random graphs [46, 45].

Expanders. Expanders play a key role in a host of applications, ranging from networking to complexity theory and coding. See the survey of Hoory, Linial, and Wigderson [24]. A rich body of literature in mathematics and computer science deals with constructions of expanders, e.g., Margulis's construction [32], algebraic constructions [30], and constructions that utilize the so-called "zig-zag product" [41]. Our construction of the Xpander datacenter topology utilizes the notion of 2-lifting a graph, introduced by Bilu and Linial [9, 31]. Utilizing expanders as network topologies has been proposed in the context of parallel computing and high-performance computing [47, 14, 13, 8], optical networks [39] and also for peer-to-peer networks and distributed computing [38, 37]. Our focus, in contrast, is on datacenter networking and on tackling the challenges that arise in this context (e.g., specific, throughput-related performance measures, specific routing and congestion control protocols, costs, incremental growth, etc.).

Relation to [48]. Our preliminary results on Xpander appeared at HotNets 2015 [48]. Here, we provide a deeper and much more detailed evaluation of the merits of expander datacenters in general, and of Xpander in particular, including (1) implementation and evaluation on the OCEAN SDN testbed [3], (2) comparison of Xpander to Slim-Fly including theoretical results and simulations, (3) many additional simulation results with the MPTCP simulator for Xpander and fat tree, (4) results for path-lengths, diameter and and incremental growth, (5) results for bisection bandwidth of Xpander, and (6) a detailed discussion of Xpander's deployment scenarios.

9. SUMMARY

We showed that expander datacenters offer many valuable advantages over traditional datacenter designs and that this class of datacenters encompasses state-of-the-art proposals for high-performance datacenter design. We suggested practical approaches for building such datacenters, namely, the Xpander datacenter architecture. We view Xpander as an appealing and practical alternative to traditional datacenter designs.

Acknowledgements

We thank Nati Linial for many insightful conversations about expander constructions and Daniel Bienstock for his help in optimizing linear programs for throughput computation. We thank Brighten Godfrey and Ankit Singla for sharing the Jellyfish code with us and for helpful discussions. We thank Soudeh Ghorbani for helping with running experiments on the OCEAN platform. We thank Noga Alon, Alex Lubotzky, and Robert Krauthgamer for useful discussions about expanders. We also thank Jonathan Perry for suggesting Xpander's color coding, presented in Section 7. Finally, we thank our shepherd, Siddhartha Sen, and the anonymous CoNEXT reviewers, for their valuable feedback. The 1st author is supperted by a Microsoft Research Ph.D. Scholarship. The 2nd and 4th authors are supported by the Israeli Center for Research Excellence (I-CORE) in Algorithms. The 1st and 4th authors are supported by the PetaCloud industry-academia consortium. The third author is supported in part by NSF awards 1464239 and 1535887.

10. REFERENCES

[1] IBM ILOG CPLEX Optimizer. http://www-01.ibm.com/software/commerce/optimization/cplex-optimizer/index.html.

[2] MPTCP Simulator v0.2. http://nets.cs.pub.ro/~costin/code.html.

[3] Ocean cluster for experimental architectures in networks (ocean). http://ocean.cs.illinois.edu/.

[4] RipL-POX, simple datacenter controller build on RipL. https://github.com/brandonheller/riplpox.

[5] Xpander Project Page. http://husant.github.io/Xpander.

[6] AL-FARES, M., LOUKISSAS, A., AND VAHDAT, A. A scalable, commodity data center network architecture. In *SIGCOMM* (2008).

[7] AL-FARES, M., RADHAKRISHNAN, S., RAGHAVAN, B., HUANG, N., AND VAHDAT, A. Hedera: Dynamic flow scheduling for data center networks. In *NSDI* (2010).

[8] BESTA, M., AND HOEFLER, T. Slim Fly: A cost effective low-diameter network topology. In *SC14* (2014).

[9] BILU, Y., AND LINIAL, N. Lifts, discrepancy and nearly optimal spectral gap. *Combinatorica* (2006).

[10] BOLLOBÁS, B. The isoperimetric number of random regular graphs. *Eur. J. Comb.* (1988).

[11] C. PAASCH, S. BARRE, ET AL. Multipath TCP in the Linux Kernel. http://www.multipath-tcp.org.

[12] CERF, V. G., COWAN, D. D., MULLIN, R. C., AND STANTON, R. G. A lower bound on the average shortest path length in regular graphs. *Networks* (1974).

[13] CHONG, F. T., BREWER, E. A., LEIGHTON, F. T., AND KNIGHT, T. F., J. Building a better butterfly: the multiplexed metabutterfly. In *ISPAN* (1994).

[14] CHONG, F. T., BREWER, E. A., LEIGHTON, F. T., AND KNIGHT, T. F., J. Scalable expanders: Exploiting hierarchical random wiring. In *Parallel Computer Routing and Communication*. 1994.

[15] CURTIS, A. R., KESHAV, S., AND LÓPEZ-ORTIZ, A. Legup: using heterogeneity to reduce the cost of data center network upgrades. In *CoNEXT* (2010).

[16] DE QUEIRÓS VIEIRA MARTINS, E., AND PASCOAL, M. M. B. A new implementation of yen's ranking loopless paths algorithm. *4OR* (2003).

[17] FRIEDMAN, J. Relative expanders or weakly relatively ramanujan graphs. *Duke Math. J. 118*, 1 (05 2003), 19–35.

[18] FRIEDMAN, J. *A Proof of Alon's Second Eigenvalue Conjecture and Related Problems*. Memoirs of the American Mathematical Society. American Mathematical Soc., 2008.

[19] GEORGE B. ADAMS, I., AND SIEGEL, H. J. The extra stage cube: A fault-tolerant interconnection network for supersystems. *IEEE Trans. Computers* (1982).

[20] GILL, P., JAIN, N., AND NAGAPPAN, N. Understanding network failures in data centers: measurement, analysis, and implications. In *SIGCOMM* (2011).

[21] GREENBERG, A. G., HAMILTON, J. R., JAIN, N., KANDULA, S., KIM, C., LAHIRI, P., MALTZ, D. A., PATEL, P., AND SENGUPTA, S. Vl2: a scalable and flexible data center network. In *SIGCOMM* (2009).

[22] GUO, C., LU, G., LI, D., WU, H., ZHANG, X., SHI, Y., TIAN, C., ZHANG, Y., AND LU, S. Bcube: a high performance, server-centric network architecture for modular data centers. In *SIGCOMM* (2009).

[23] GUO, C., WU, H., TAN, K., SHI, L., ZHANG, Y., AND LU, S. Dcell: a scalable and fault-tolerant network structure for data centers. In *SIGCOMM* (2008).

[24] HOORY, S., LINIAL, N., AND WIGDERSON, A. Expander graphs and their applications. *Bull. Amer. Math. Soc.* (2006).

[25] JYOTHI, S. A., SINGLA, A., GODFREY, P. B., AND KOLLA, A. Measuring throughput of data center network topologies. In *SIGMETRICS* (2014).

[26] KARYPIS, G., AND KUMAR, V. A fast and high quality multilevel scheme for partitioning irregular graphs. *SIAM J. Sci. Comput.* (1998).

[27] LANTZ, B., HELLER, B., AND MCKEOWN, N. A network in a laptop: Rapid prototyping for software-defined networks. In *HOTNETS* (2010).

[28] LINIAL, N., LONDON, E., AND RABINOVICH, Y. The geometry of graphs and some of its algorithmic applications. *Combinatorica* (1995).

[29] LIU, V., HALPERIN, D., KRISHNAMURTHY, A., AND ANDERSON, T. F10: A fault-tolerant engineered network. In *NSDI* (2013).

[30] LUBOTZKY, A., PHILLIPS, R., AND SARNAK, P. Ramanujan graphs. *Combinatorica* (1988).

[31] MARCUS, A., SPIELMAN, D. A., AND SRIVASTAVA, N. Interlacing families I: Bipartite ramanujan graphs of all degrees. In *FOCS* (2013).

[32] MARGULIS, G. A. Explicit constructions of expanders. *Problemy Peredači Informacii* (1973).

[33] MCKAY, B. D., MILLER, M., AND ÃĚÂĂIRÃČÂĄÃĚÂĹ, J. A note on large graphs of diameter two and given maximum degree. *Journal of Combinatorial Theory, Series B* (1998).

[34] MCKEOWN, N., ANDERSON, T., BALAKRISHNAN, H., PARULKAR, G., PETERSON, L., REXFORD, J., SHENKER, S., AND TURNER, J. Openflow: Enabling innovation in campus networks. In *SIGCOMM* (2008).

[35] MUDIGONDA, J., YALAGANDULA, P., AL-FARES, M., AND MOGUL, J. C. Spain: Cots data-center ethernet for multipathing over arbitrary topologies. In *NSDI* (2010).

[36] MYSORE, R. N., PAMBORIS, A., FARRINGTON, N., HUANG, N., MIRI, P., RADHAKRISHNAN, S., SUBRAMANYA, V., AND VAHDAT, A. Portland: a

scalable fault-tolerant layer 2 data center network fabric. In *SIGCOMM* (2009).

[37] NAOR, M., AND WIEDER, U. Novel architectures for p2p applications: The continuous-discrete approach. In *SPAA* (2007).

[38] PANDURANGAN, G., ROBINSON, P., AND TREHAN, A. DEX: Self healing expanders. In *SPAA* (2014).

[39] PATURI, R., LU, D.-T., FORD, J. E., ESENER, S. C., AND LEE, S. H. Parallel algorithms based on expander graphs for optical computing. *Appl. Opt.* (1991).

[40] POPA, L., RATNASAMY, S., IANNACCONE, G., KRISHNAMURTHY, A., AND STOICA, I. A cost comparison of datacenter network architectures. In *CoNEXT* (2010).

[41] REINGOLD, O., VADHAN, S., AND WIGDERSON, A. Entropy waves, the zig-zag graph product, and new constant-degree expanders and extractors. In *FOCS* (2000).

[42] ROSEN, E., VISWANATHAN, A., AND CALLON, R. Multiprotocol Label Switching Architecture. RFC 3031, 2001.

[43] SHIN, J.-Y., WONG, B., AND SIRER, E. G. Small-world datacenters. In *SoCC* (2011).

[44] SINGH, A., ONG, J., AGARWAL, A., ANDERSON, G., ARMISTEAD, A., BANNON, R., BOVING, S., DESAI, G., FELDERMAN, B., GERMANO, P., KANAGALA, A., PROVOST, J., SIMMONS, J., TANDA, E., WANDERER, J., HÖLZLE, U., STUART, S., AND VAHDAT, A. Jupiter rising: A decade of clos topologies and centralized control in google's datacenter network. In *Proceedings of the 2015 ACM Conference on Special Interest Group on Data Communication* (2015), SIGCOMM '15, ACM.

[45] SINGLA, A., GODFREY, P. B., AND KOLLA, A. High throughput data center topology design. In *NSDI* (2014).

[46] SINGLA, A., HONG, C.-Y., POPA, L., AND GODFREY, P. B. Jellyfish: Networking data centers randomly. In *NSDI* (2012).

[47] UPFAL, E. An o(log n) deterministic packet-routing scheme. *J. ACM* (1992).

[48] VALADARSKY, A., DINITZ, M., AND SCHAPIRA, M. Xpander: Unveiling the Secrets of High-Performance Datacenters. In *HOTNETS* (2015).

[49] WISCHIK, D., RAICIU, C., GREENHALGH, A., AND HANDLEY, M. Design, implementation and evaluation of congestion control for multipath TCP. In *NSDI* (2011).

[50] WU, H., LU, G., LI, D., GUO, C., AND ZHANG, Y. Mdcube: a high performance network structure for modular data center interconnection. In *CoNEXT* (2009).

[51] YEN, J. Y. Finding the k shortest loopless paths in a network. *Management Science* (1971).

[52] ZOLA, J., AND ALURU, S. *Encyclopedia of Parallel Computing*. Springer.

Network Scheduling Aware Task Placement in Datacenters

Ali Munir[1], Ting He[2], Ramya Raghavendra[2], Franck Le[2], Alex X. Liu[1]
[1]Michigan State University, [2]IBM Research

ABSTRACT

To improve the performance of data-intensive applications, existing datacenter schedulers optimize either the placement of tasks or the scheduling of network flows. The task scheduler strives to place tasks close to their input data (i.e., maximize data locality) to minimize network traffic, while assuming fair sharing of the network. The network scheduler strives to finish flows as quickly as possible based on their sources and destinations determined by the task scheduler, while the scheduling is based on flow properties (e.g., size, deadline, and correlation) and not bound to fair sharing. Inconsistent assumptions of the two schedulers can compromise the overall application performance. In this paper, we propose NEAT, a task scheduling framework that leverages information from the underlying network scheduler to make task placement decisions. The core of NEAT is a task completion time predictor that estimates the completion time of a task under given network condition and a given network scheduling policy. NEAT leverages the predicted task completion times to minimize the average completion time of active tasks. Evaluation using ns2 simulations and real-testbed shows that NEAT improves application performance by up to 3.7x for the suboptimal network scheduling policies and up to 30% for the optimal network scheduling policy.

Keywords

Cluster schedulers; Network schedulers; Compute placement; Cross-layer optimization

1. INTRODUCTION

Data transfer time has a significant impact on task completion times within a datacenter because most datacenter applications (such as MapReduce [1], Pregel [2], MPI [3], Dryad [4]) are data-intensive and they need to access data that are distributed throughout the network. For example, for MapReduce, 30% task completion time is spent on transferring data across the network [5]. For large commercial datacenters, the transfer of shuffle data is the dominant source of network traffic [6]. In Facebook [5] MapReduce clusters, 20% jobs are shuffle-heavy (i.e., generate a large amount of shuffle data), and in Yahoo! clusters [7] this goes up to 60%. The network congestion caused by shuffle data is a key factor that degrades the performance of MapReduce jobs [8]. Therefore, data transfer time in datacenter is critical for improving application performance.

Prior work on minimizing data transfer time falls into two categories: task placement ([5, 6, 9, 10, 11, 12]) and network scheduling ([13, 14, 15, 16, 17, 18, 19, 20, 21, 22, 23]). The idea of task placement is to place compute tasks close to input data so that data locality is maximized and network traffic is minimized [5, 9, 10]. The idea of network scheduling is to schedule the flows or groups of flows (i.e., coflows) generated by tasks, at shared links, based on given flow properties (such as size, deadline, and correlation among flows) and given task placement to minimize flow completion times[13, 15, 16, 17, 21]. The limitation of prior task placement policies is that they design traffic matrix assuming fair sharing of network bandwidth and ignore the priorities assigned to different flows by the network scheduler; meanwhile, network schedulers schedule flows based on flow priorities (such as size or deadline) and the flow completion time of a low priority flow can increase if placed on a path sharing links with high priority flows. The limitation of network schedulers is that the source/destination of each flow is independently decided by the task schedulers and not necessarily optimal.

In this paper, we propose NEAT, a **N**etwork-sch**E**duling-**A**ware **T**ask placement framework that leverages *network scheduling policy* and *network state* in making task placement decisions for data-intensive applications. The placement by NEAT coupled with a properly selected network scheduling policy ensures that tasks are finished as quickly as possible. The intuition behind NEAT is that a good placement of data-intensive tasks should spread the flows to minimize the sharing of network links. When sharing is inevitable, however, the preferred placement strategy depends on how the network schedules flows, as illustrated by the following example.

CoNEXT '16, December 12-15, 2016, Irvine, CA, USA

DOI: http://dx.doi.org/10.1145/2999572.2999588

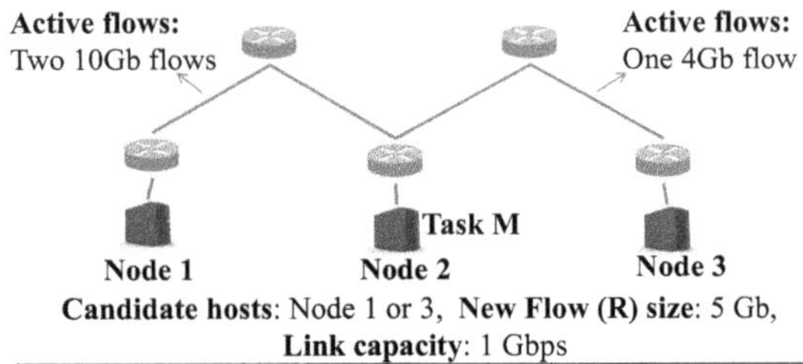

Network Scheduling Policy	Placement of R	Completion time of R (s)	Increase in Total Completion time (s)
FCFS	Node 1	25	25
	Node 3	**9**	**9**
Fair	Node 1	15	25
	Node 3	**9**	**13**
SRPT	**Node 1**	**5**	**15**
	Node 3	9	9

Figure 1: Network scheduling aware placement

Motivating Example: Let us consider a simple scenario in Figure 1, where we want to place a task R that needs to read data from task M running on node 2 onto candidate hosts node 1 or node 3. At the current time, the network has one flow with remaining size of 4 Gb on path $2 \rightarrow 3$ and requires four more seconds (on 1 Gbps link) to finish if running alone. There are two other flows on path $2 \rightarrow 1$, each of remaining size 10 Gb, thus requiring ten more seconds if running alone. Suppose that the input data of candidate task R is of size 5 Gb and our goal is to finish the task as quickly as possible. Assuming First Come First Serve scheduling (FCFS) in the network, we will place task R on node 3, as it provides the smaller completion time of 9 seconds as compared to 25 seconds when placed on node 1, because flow R will not be scheduled until the existing flows finish data transfer. Assuming fair scheduling (Fair) in the network, we will place task R on node 3, as it requires 9 seconds to complete flow R on node 3 compared to 15 seconds on node 1. Assuming the network uses shortest remaining processing time (SRPT) scheduling, we will place task R on node 1, as it can finish in 5 seconds on node 1 by preempting both the existing flows. We assume flows with the same priority share the network fairly as in existing solutions [16, 17]. However, if the goal is to minimize the increase in total (i.e., sum) flow completion time of all the active flows in the network, then under SRPT, the scheduler will choose node 3 to minimize the increase in completion time of flows in the network (i.e., completion time of new flow plus increased completion times of existing flows). We see that the optimal task placement in a network can vary depending on the network scheduling policy and the network performance metric.

NEAT Overview: NEAT leverages these insights in its design and provides a task placement framework to minimize the average flow completion time (AFCT) in the network. NEAT employs a task performance predictor that predicts the completion time of a given task under an arbitrary network scheduling policy. NEAT is quite pluggable in terms of better resource or application models and predictors. NEAT makes task placement decision in two steps: first, it predicts task performance by hypothetically placing

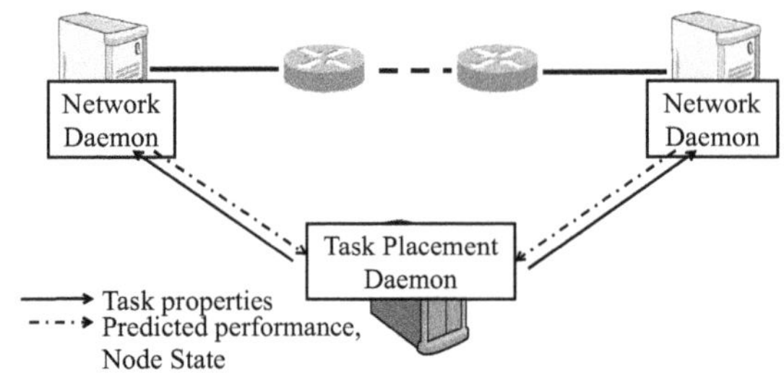

Figure 2: NEAT Architecture

a task on each candidate node and analyzing its performance based on the network scheduling policy and the network state. Next, it selects a node for the task based on the predicted task completion time and a node state, that characterizes the sizes of existing flows. The proposed task placement mechanism focuses on network performance in task placement decisions and only uses node properties (e.g., CPU, memory) to determine whether a node is a candidate host. We leave joint placement to future work. To realize this idea, NEAT addresses two challenges:

The first technical challenge in designing NEAT is to *accurately predict the performance of a task for a given network state and scheduling policy.* We use the completion time of data transfer, i.e., the *flow completion time (FCT)* or the *coflow completion time (CCT)*, to measure the overall task performance. Compared to network-centric performance metrics such as delay, jitter, and available bandwidth, completion time is task-centric and better models network conditions in terms of their impact on task performance (§6).

The second technical challenge is to *efficiently collect network state information and make placement decisions.* As illustrated in Figure 2, NEAT uses a distributed control framework with two components: a local controller (network daemon) that maintains a *compressed* state of all active flows (or coflows) on each node to predict task completion times, and a global controller (task placement daemon) that gathers the predicted task completion times from local controllers to make task placement decisions. Here, a "node" refers to an endhost (e.g., server) capable of running tasks. Using the flow state information, the local controllers predict the FCT/CCT on edge links (i.e., links directly connected to nodes), based on which the global controller uses a greedy algorithm to pick the node whose edge link has the smallest FCT/CCT. To reduce communications with the local controllers, the global controller also maintains a *state* for each node, defined as the remaining size of the smallest active flow on that node, such that only nodes with preferred states (no less than the size of the current flow) are contacted.

NEAT does not require any changes to the network. However, it requires task information (e.g., size) from applications, similar to prior works [16, 17, 19], to accurately predict task completion time. For recurrent workloads, this information can be inferred by monitoring task execution [12].

NEAT's performance is upper-bounded by the underlying network (flow/coflow) scheduling policy. When the network scheduling policy is suboptimal (e.g., Fair, LAS), when our goal is FCT, there is plenty of room for improvement and NEAT is able to significantly improve the task performance;

when the network scheduling policy is near optimal (SRPT), the room for improvement is reduced, NEAT still achieves notable improvement for such scenarios.

NEAT Evaluation: We evaluate NEAT using both a trace-driven simulator and a 10-machine testbed based on a variety of production workloads [1, 16] and network scheduling policies such as DCTCP [24], L^2DCT [15], PASE [17], and Varys [21]. We evaluate two other state-of-art task placement policies: *minLoad* that always selects a node with the minimum load, measured by the total size of flows scheduled on that node, and *minDist* that always selects a node closest to the input data. NEAT performs 3.7x better than alternative strategies when the underlying network scheduling policy is Fair (DCTCP [24]), 3x better when the policy is least attained service (LAS) (L^2DCT [15]), and 30% better when the policy is SRPT (PASE [17]). In both cases, NEAT improves performance by being aware of the network scheduling policy. In particular, since Fair is the underlying policy in most commercial datacenters, NEAT can significantly improve the performance of data-intensive applications in majority of cases.

Summary of Contributions:

- We propose a unified task completion time prediction model, that can accurately predict task performance for a given network scheduling policy.
- We propose a distributed framework, NEAT, to gather network state and make task placement decisions in an online fashion.
- We evaluate NEAT across a range of network scheduling policies and network conditions using simulations and real testbed experiment.

2. LIMITATIONS OF PRIOR ART

The overall performance of data-intensive workloads depends on both (1) scheduling of compute tasks, and (2) scheduling of the resulting network flows. However, existing solutions address either the task placement problem or the network scheduling problem in isolation, leaving significant room for further improvement. Below, we first summarize related work and then provide a comparative study to highlight limitations of existing schemes.

2.1 Related Work

The related work can be divided in two categories: Task placement (or scheduling) and network scheduling.

Task Scheduling: State-of-art task schedulers follow the principle of "maximizing data locality" to minimize data transfer over the network. For the first stage of jobs (e.g., Map), techniques such as delay scheduling [5] and flow-based scheduling [9] try to place tasks on the machines or racks where most of their input data are located. Mantri instead optimizes the data locality while placing reducers [10]. However, when the data is spread throughout the cluster (e.g., in distributed file systems like HDFS [25]), the subsequent job stages (e.g., shuffle phase) have to read data using cross-rack links, and often suffer from heavy network congestion [26]. To alleviate the problem, techniques like ShuffleWatcher [6] attempt to localize the Map tasks of a job to one or a few racks, and thus reduce cross-rack shuffling. However, such techniques end up increasing the cross-rack transfer of the input data. A similar idea was exploited in Sinbad [26] to place the endpoints of flows to avoid congested links, but Sinbad is for a special type of flows (replicated file system writes) and is agnostic to the underlying network scheduling policy. When the input data of a job is known beforehand, techniques like Corral [12] can be used to pack the input data to a few racks such that all computation can be performed on local data. Similarly, many fairness based cluster scheduling frameworks [27, 28, 29, 30, 31] or straggler mitigation techniques [32, 10, 33, 34] have been proposed. However, these works assume fair sharing in the network and does not consider effect of underlying network scheduling policies. Another category of works [35, 36] does joint network and task execution scheduling, however these works assume that they have knowledge about task arrival times and make offline task scheduling decisions.

Network Scheduling: Generally, data-intensive jobs spend a substantial fraction of their execution time on data transfer [5], and consequently, their performance critically depends on the performance of network scheduling. In recent years, a variety of network scheduling systems such as DCTCP [24], L^2DCT [15], PASE [17], Varys [21], and Baraat [20] have been proposed. Many of these protocols provide near-optimal data transfer time, but the improvement to the overall task performance is limited as they do not optimize the placement of sources/destinations of the flows.

NEAT addresses these limitations in two ways: it places the destinations of flows (via task placement) while taking into account the underlying network scheduling policy to minimize the overall data transfer time, and it uses a performance predictor that captures network state and essence of the network scheduling policies.

2.2 Comparative Study

Task placement policies perform differently when used with different network scheduling policies. To illustrate this, we compare the performance of two task scheduling policies under two different network scheduling policies. For task scheduling policies, we consider: minimum-distance placement (minDist), which places each task to minimize its distance to the input data, and minimum-load placement (minLoad), which places each task on the server with the minimum traffic load. For network scheduling policy, we consider: DCTCP [24], which approximates the Fair sharing policy, and PASE [17], which approximates the shortest remaining processing time (SRPT) policy in the network.

We simulate a topology of 160 machines, connected using a folded CLOS topology as in [17]. We configure the links to have 200μsec RTT and 1 Gbps (edge) or 10 Gbps (core) bandwidth. We evaluate each combination of the above task/network scheduling policies under flow demands generated according to the data-mining workload [16]. Figure 3(a) and Figure 3(b) show the ratio between the FCT of minDist and the FCT of minLoad for various flow sizes under the

Fair, and SRPT network scheduling policy, respectively. A bar with coordinates (x, y) indicates that flows of sizes x have an FCT ratio of y, where y<1 indicates that minDist outperforms minLoad and y>1 indicates the opposite.

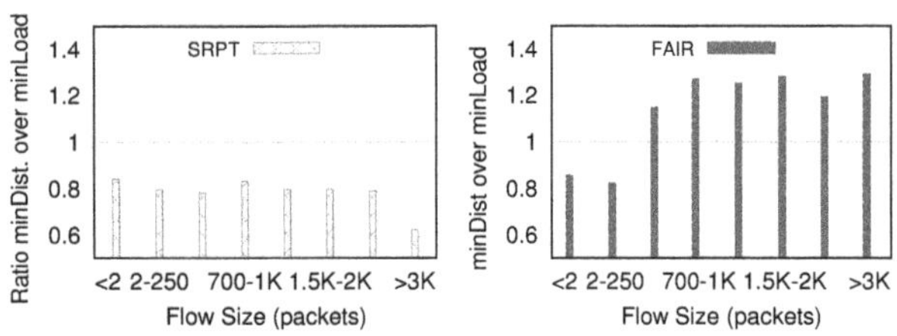

(a) SRPT (PASE) (b) Fair (DCTCP)

Figure 3: Comparison of minDist and minLoad placement under SRPT and Fair network scheduling policy

The results show that when the network follows SRPT policy (Figure 3(a)), minDist placement works better (ratio less than 1). In contrast, when the network follows a Fair policy (Figure 3(b)), minLoad placement works better for the majority of the flow sizes. The results can be explained by the following observations: when the network follows SRPT policy (Figure 3(a)), short flows preempt long flows, and receive full link bandwidth. Short flows therefore achieve near-optimal completion time. We verified it in the FCT logs but omit the details because of page limitations. After the short flows complete, more bandwidth becomes available to the long flows, allowing them to finish quickly. The minDist placement outperforms minLoad placement because it minimizes the total network load, defined as sum of the product of the size and the hop count for each flow. In contrast, when the network follows the Fair policy (Figure 3(b)), short flows no longer preempt long flows. The minLoad placement works better – especially for long flows – because it ensures that long flows avoid being placed on nodes with existing long flows. However, Figure 3(b) shows that short flows may suffer longer FCTs under the minLoad placement compared to the minDist placement. This usually happens when newly arriving long flows are placed on nodes with ongoing short flows, thus increasing the FCTs of short flows. In conclusion, this experiment demonstrates that the performance of task placement depends on the underlying network scheduling policy. Therefore, it is important to design a task placement framework that takes into account the underlying network scheduling policy.

3. SYSTEM OVERVIEW

NEAT, is a **N**etwork-sch**E**duling-**A**ware **T**ask placement framework that considers the *network scheduling policy* and the *network state* while making task placement decisions. NEAT considers placing both flows and coflows in the network via placing the tasks on the nodes that act as destinations of these flows (coflows). The placement framework, coupled with the underlying network scheduling policy (e.g., Fair, FCFS, LAS, SRPT), ensures that network resources are properly allocated among tasks to minimize their average completion time.

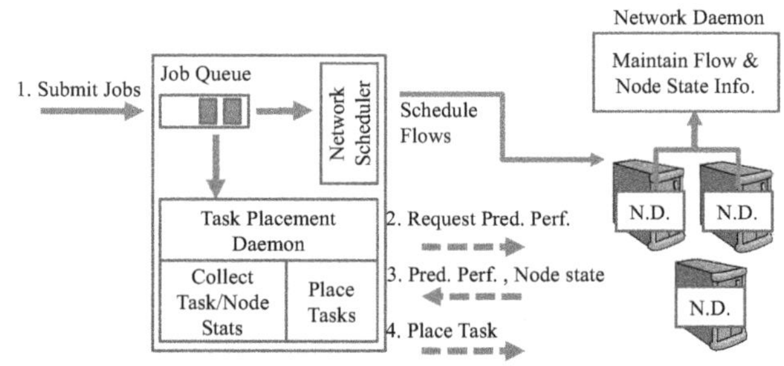

Figure 4: NEAT components

NEAT uses a distributed architecture to make task placement decisions, as shown in Figure 4. It leverages the master-slave architecture of existing task scheduling systems [28, 31] to achieve its functionality in a distributed fashion. NEAT has two components, i) a global task placement daemon and ii) a per-node network daemon. The two components exchange information to perform network-aware task scheduling.

Network Daemon: NEAT network daemon (similar to node manager in Hadoop) runs on all the nodes (i.e., end-hosts) in the network and uses the completion time of data transfer (FCT for flow, CCT for coflow) as a metric for predicting task performance. The prediction is based on the network state, e.g., (residual) sizes of all active flows, and the network scheduling policy. Therefore, network daemon performs two functions: (i) maintaining network information of all the active tasks on the node (such as the number of flows and their residual sizes), and ii) predicting the performance of a new task when requested by the task placement daemon, based on the analysis in section 4. NEAT considers only the edge links for task performance prediction. Therefore, the task performance prediction is based on the assumption that only the edge links are bottleneck in the network and core is congestion free. As a result NEAT needs to maintain flow information at the end-hosts only and does not require any feedback from the network.

Task Placement Daemon: NEAT task placement daemon makes placement decisions in two steps: First, it queries the network daemons on nodes that are valid hosts (determined by node state, CPU and memory) of a given task for their predicted task performance. Next, it chooses the best node or subset of nodes for placing the task using the predicted task completion times and node states (i.e., the smallest residual flow size of active tasks on each node). It also caches the node states locally to facilitate future placement decisions, as discussed below. The node states cache is updated whenever a new task is placed on the node or an existing task is completed.

NEAT Workflow: As illustrated in Figure 4, when the task placement daemon receives a request to place a new task (step 1), it identifies a set of preferred hosts based on local copies of node states and contacts the respective network daemons to get predicted performance of the new task (step 2). Each network daemon maintains the local network state (such as the number and the sizes of flows starting/ending at the node) and uses this state together with knowledge of the network scheduling policy to predict the performance of the new task. The task placement daemon then gathers this information (step 3) and places the task on the best of the preferred hosts based on the predicted performance (step 4).

Discussions: It is worthwhile to clarify a few points. First of all, NEAT is a task placement framework and as such, it does not impose any changes in the network switches or network scheduling mechanism. The network congestion is managed by the underlying network scheduling policy. However, NEAT helps to mitigate the network congestion by properly distributing traffic loads across the network. Moreover, in the current design, NEAT abstracts network as a single-switch topology, as assumed in earlier works [12, 16]. The single-switch assumption means that only edge links are the bottleneck and thus for task completion time (FCT/CCT) prediction, it only considers edge links. However, such restriction is not fundamental to NEAT, and we discuss in Section 7 how it can be extended to other topologies.

In the next two sections, we discuss task performance prediction and NEAT design in more detail.

4. TASK PERFORMANCE PREDICTOR

NEAT has a pluggable task performance predictor that can predict the completion time of a given task under an arbitrary network scheduling policy. An interesting insight of our analysis is that: for flow-based scheduling, it suffices to predict FCT according to the Fair policy under mild conditions even if the underlying policy is not Fair; for coflow-based scheduling, however, this is generally not true.

From a networking perspective, placing a task onto a server is equivalent to placing a flow onto a path (or a coflow onto a set of paths). We now define the objective function for flow placement; the objective function for coflow placement is analogous. For flow placement, our goal is to place each flow onto the path that minimizes the sum (and hence average) FCT over all active flows. Consider a flow f placed on path p_f with size s_f (bits). Let $\mathrm{FCT}(f, l)$ denote the completion time of flow f on link $l \in p_f$ (i.e., time taken for the flow to finish transmission over link l). Now consider placing a new flow f_0 onto path p_{f_0}. Let $\Delta\mathrm{FCT}(f, l)$ denote the increase in the completion time of f on link l due to the scheduling of f_0. Let F be the set of cross-flows in the network (i.e., flows that share at least one link with f_0). Then the increase in the sum FCT over all active flows due to the placement of f_0 equals

$$\max_{l \in p_{f_0}} \mathrm{FCT}(f_0, l) + \sum_{f \in F} \Big(\max_{l \in p_f} (\mathrm{FCT}(f, l) + \Delta\mathrm{FCT}(f, l)) - \max_{l \in p_f} \mathrm{FCT}(f, l) \Big), \quad (1)$$

and the optimal online placement is to place f_0 such that (1) is minimized (note that (1) depends on p_{f_0}).

The original objective (1) requires calculation of the FCT before and after placing f_0 for every flow $f \in F$ and every hop l traversed by f. To simplify computation, we exchange the order of summation and maximization to obtain an alternative objective function

$$\max_{l \in p_{f_0}} \mathrm{FCT}(f_0, l) + \max_{l \in p_{f_0}} \sum_{f \in F_l} \Delta\mathrm{FCT}(f, l) \geq \max_{l \in p_{f_0}} \left(\mathrm{FCT}(f_0, l) + \sum_{f \in F_l} \Delta\mathrm{FCT}(f, l) \right), \quad (2)$$

where F_l is the set of flows traversing link l. Note that (2) is only an approximation of (1) and thus minimizing (2) is not guaranteed to minimize the sum FCT. However, as we show later, the alternative objective (2) has a nice property that it is invariant, up to a constant scaling, to the network scheduling policy under certain conditions (see Propositions 4.1 and 4.2), and the placement that minimizes (2) achieves superior performance in minimizing the FCT for a variety of flows and network scheduling policies.

For simplicity of analysis, we do not consider the impact of future task arrivals or task completion on the prediction. We choose this design in favor of applicability (not requiring prediction capability) and stability (not moving existing flows) of NEAT design (see remark § 5.1.1).

4.1 FCT Prediction for Flow Scheduling

Given a placement of flow f_0 and its cross-flows, the FCT of f_0 is determined by the scheduling policy employed by the network. We therefore study FCT prediction under several widely-adopted scheduling policies, including FCFS, Fair, LAS, and SFF. For ease of presentation, we fix a (candidate) placement and consider the prediction for a given link l with bandwidth B_l. The key idea of NEAT predictor is to compute the total number of bytes that will be transmitted across the bottleneck link by the time the current flow finishes transmission, which is then divided by the link bandwidth to predict the completion time of the current flow. For example, to predict the completion time of a flow f when placed onto a path p, we compute for each link l on p the total traffic volume V_l from f and coexisting flows that will cross l upon the completion of f, and then the maximum of V_l/B_l (B_l is the bandwidth of l) over all the links $l \in p$ gives the predicted completion time of f. This approach applies to any work-conserving scheduling policy (i.e., a link is never idle when there is pending traffic on that link), while different policies differ in the computation of V_l.

4.1.1 *FCT under FCFS Scheduling*

Under FCFS scheduling, flows are served in the order they arrive, and FCT of the new flow can be predicted as:

$$\mathrm{FCT}^{\mathrm{FCFS}}(f_0, l) = \frac{1}{B_l}(s_{f_0} + \sum_{f \in F_l} s_f), \quad (3)$$

and $\Delta\mathrm{FCT}^{\mathrm{FCFS}}(f, l) \equiv 0$ for all $f \in F_l$ since the new flow does not affect the completion of existing flows. Hence, the two objectives in (1) and (2) coincide in this case, both equal to $\max_{l \in p_{f_0}} \mathrm{FCT}^{\mathrm{FCFS}}(f_0, l)$.

4.1.2 FCT under Fair or LAS Scheduling

Under a scheduling policy that performs fair sharing, all flows will receive equal service until completion, i.e., by the time flow f_0 completes transmission over link l, each existing flow $f \in F_l$ will have transmitted $\min(s_f,\ s_{f_0})$ bytes over l. The FCT of f_0 can thus be predicted as:

$$\text{FCT}^{\text{FAIR}}(f_0, l) = \frac{1}{B_l}\left(s_{f_0} + \sum_{f \in F_l} \min(s_f,\ s_{f_0})\right). \quad (4)$$

Meanwhile, the fair sharing rule implies that for each flow $f \in F_l$ of size $s_f < s_{f_0}$, scheduling f_0 increases its FCT by imposing an additional traffic load of s_f on link l (during the lifetime of f); for each flow $f \in F_l$ of size $s_f \geq s_{f_0}$, f_0 will finish earlier, causing an additional load of s_{f_0}. Thus, the change in FCT of existing flows is:

$$\Delta\text{FCT}^{\text{FAIR}}(f, l) = \frac{\min(s_f,\ s_{f_0})}{B_l}. \quad (5)$$

Substituting (4) and (5) into (1) gives the overall increase in the sum FCT.

The alternative objective (2) accepts a more compact form in this case. Specifically, for given l,

$$\text{FCT}^{\text{FAIR}}(f_0, l) + \sum_{f \in F_l} \Delta\text{FCT}^{\text{FAIR}}(f, l)$$
$$= \frac{s_{f_0}}{B_l} + \frac{2}{B_l}\sum_{f \in F_l} \min(s_f,\ s_{f_0}) \approx 2\text{FCT}^{\text{FAIR}}(f_0, l), \quad (6)$$

where the approximation is accurate when s_{f_0} is small relative to $\sum_{f \in F_l} \min(s_f,\ s_{f_0})$.

Remark: Since LAS scheduling (with preemption) is equivalent to fair sharing, the above result also applies to LAS scheduling.

4.1.3 FCT under SRPT Scheduling

If the network employs SRPT scheduling, then only flows of remaining sizes smaller than or equal to the current flow will be served before the current flow finishes (assuming FCFS rule is applied to break ties among flow sizes), and larger flows will be preempted. Hence, the FCT of the new flow f_0 under SRPT can be predicted as:

$$\text{FCT}^{\text{SRPT}}(f_0, l) = \frac{1}{B_l}\left(s_{f_0} + \sum_{f \in F_l : s_f \leq s_{f_0}} s_f\right). \quad (7)$$

Meanwhile, each flow of size $s_f > s_{f_0}$ will be delayed by s_{f_0}/B_l due to the placement of f_0, while flows of size $s_f \leq s_{f_0}$ will not be affected, implying:

$$\Delta\text{FCT}^{\text{SRPT}}(f, l) = \frac{s_{f_0}}{B_l}\mathbb{1}_{s_f > s_{f_0}}, \quad (8)$$

where $\mathbb{1}.$ is the indicator function. Applying (7) and (8) to (1) gives the first objective. For second objective, we have

$$\text{FCT}^{\text{SRPT}}(f_0, l) + \sum_{f \in F_l} \Delta\text{FCT}^{\text{SRPT}}(f, l)$$
$$= \frac{1}{B_l}\left(s_{f_0} + \sum_{f \in F_l} \min(s_f,\ s_{f_0})\right) = \text{FCT}^{\text{FAIR}}(f_0, l). \quad (9)$$

4.1.4 Invariance Condition

Although the predicted FCT varies for different network scheduling policies, we show that the optimal placement can be invariant under certain conditions. Specifically, we have shown that under SRPT scheduling, the alternative objective (2) reduces to the fair-sharing FCT of the newly arrived flow (see (9)), and under Fair/LAS scheduling, this objective is approximately twice of the fair-sharing FCT (see (6)). Since constant-factor scaling does not affect the selection of placement, these results imply that we can use the same objective function to place flows no matter whether the network performs Fair, LAS, or SRPT scheduling.

PROPOSITION 4.1. *If the network performs Fair, LAS, or SRPT flow scheduling and each flow is small relative to the total load on each link, then the optimal placement that minimizes (2) is always the one that minimizes bottleneck fair-sharing FCT of the newly arrived flow as predicted by (4).*

Remark: Surprisingly, we have shown that when the network schedules flows by LAS or SRPT, we should place flows to minimize their predicted FCTs under Fair scheduling in order to optimize the objective (2).

4.2 CCT Prediction for Coflow Scheduling

We now revise the above formulas for the case that the network schedules traffic at the level of coflow. We study the following policies applied to coflow scheduling, including FCFS [20], Fair, LAS [23], and an extension of SRPT called *permutation scheduling* [21]. For a coflow c, let s_c denote its total size (in number of bytes), and $s_{c,l}$ denote the sum size of the individual flows in c that traverse link l. We show that the idea of computing FCT can be generalized to predict the performance of coflows.

We make the following assumptions: (i) all flows of a coflow have the same priority, and (ii) all flows of a coflow complete simultaneously. The first assumption is based on a principle adopted by state-of-art coflow schedulers [20, 21] that flows within a coflow should progress together; the second assumption is based on a state-of-art coflow rate adaptation mechanism [21], which slows down all but the slowest flows in a coflow to match the completion time of the slowest flow so as to conserve bandwidth without increasing the CCT. In particular, assumption (ii) allows us to apply the same objective functions (1, 2) in placing coflows, with f (f_0) replaced by c (c_0), FCT replaced by CCT, and p_f replaced by p_c (denoting the set of links traversed by any flow of a coflow c). The computation of $\text{CCT}(c, l)$ and $\Delta\text{CCT}(c, l)$ is, however, different from their single-flow counterparts, and will be detailed below. We redefine F_l to be the set of coflows with at least one constituent flow traversing link l.

4.2.1 CCT under FCFS Scheduling

Under FCFS scheduling, each link will serve traffic from existing coflows before serving the newly arrived coflow, thus

$$\mathrm{CCT}^{\mathrm{FCFS}}(c_0, l) = \frac{1}{B_l}(s_{c_0,l} + \sum_{c \in F_l} s_{c,l}), \tag{10}$$

and $\Delta\mathrm{CCT}^{\mathrm{FCFS}}(c, l) \equiv 0$ for all $c \in F_l$.

4.2.2 CCT under Fair or LAS Scheduling

Under fair sharing or LAS scheduling, all coflows of size smaller than c_0 will have finished and all coflows of size larger than c_0 will have transmitted s_{c_0} bytes when coflow c_0 completes. Under assumption (ii), flows within a coflow make progress proportionally to their sizes, and thus when a coflow traversing link l finishes b bytes over all its constituent flows, $bs_{c,l}/s_c$ bytes must be transmitted over link l. Therefore, each coflow $c \in F_l$ introduces a load of $\min(s_c,\ s_{c_0})s_{c,l}/s_c$ on link l during the lifetime of coflow c_0 and vice versa. The above arguments imply that

$$\mathrm{CCT}^{\mathrm{FAIR}}(c_0, l) = \frac{1}{B_l}\left(s_{c_0,l} + \sum_{\substack{c \in F_l \\ s_c \leq s_{c_0}}} s_{c,l} + \sum_{\substack{c \in F_l \\ s_c > s_{c_0}}} \frac{s_{c_0} s_{c,l}}{s_c}\right) \tag{11}$$

for the newly arrived coflow c_0, and

$$\Delta\mathrm{CCT}^{\mathrm{FAIR}}(c, l) = \frac{s_{c_0,l}}{B_l s_{c_0}} \min(s_c,\ s_{c_0}) \tag{12}$$

for each existing coflow $c \in F_l$. From the above, we see that

$$\sum_{c \in F_l} \Delta\mathrm{CCT}^{\mathrm{FAIR}}(c, l) = \frac{1}{B_l}\left(\sum_{\substack{c \in F_l \\ s_c \leq s_{c_0}}} \frac{s_c s_{c_0,l}}{s_{c_0}} + \sum_{\substack{c \in F_l \\ s_c > s_{c_0}}} s_{c_0,l}\right), \tag{13}$$

which is different from (11) unless $s_{c,l}/s_c = s_{c_0,l}/s_{c_0}$ for all $c \in F_l$. It means that compared to the single-flow Fair/LAS scheduling, where minimizing the objective (2) reduces to minimizing the FCT of the newly arrived flow, we have to explicitly consider the impact on existing coflows through (13) (in addition to (11)) under coflow Fair/LAS scheduling.

4.2.3 CCT under Permutation Scheduling

Permutation scheduling [21] serves the coflows sequentially and includes many scheduling policies as special cases (e.g., FCFS and all variations of SRPT). Given a permutation $\pi = (\pi_c)_{c \in F_l \cup \{c_0\}}$ of all the coflows sharing link l, where π_c is the order of scheduling coflow c, the CCT of the newly arrived coflow c_0 equals

$$\mathrm{CCT}^{\pi}(c_0, l) = \frac{1}{B_l} \sum_{\pi_c \leq \pi_{c_0}} s_{c,l}, \tag{14}$$

and the increase in CCT for each existing coflow $c \in F_l$ equals

$$\Delta\mathrm{CCT}^{\pi}(c, l) = \frac{s_{c_0,l}}{B_l}\ {}_{\pi_c > \pi_{c_0}}, \tag{15}$$

which can be used to evaluate the first objective (1).

For the second objective (2), we have

$$\mathrm{CCT}^{\pi}(c_0, l) + \sum_{c \in F_l} \Delta\mathrm{CCT}^{\pi}(c, l)$$
$$= \frac{1}{B_l}\left(\sum_{\pi_c \leq \pi_{c_0}} s_{c,l} + s_{c_0,l}|\{c \in F_l : \pi_c > \pi_{c_0}\}|\right). \tag{16}$$

In particular, for a counterpart of SRPT called *smallesT-Coflow-First (TCF)* [21], (16) becomes

$$\mathrm{CCT}^{\mathrm{TCF}}(c_0, l) + \sum_{c \in F_l} \Delta\mathrm{CCT}^{\mathrm{TCF}}(c, l)$$
$$= \frac{1}{B_l}\left(s_{c_0,l} + \sum_{\substack{c \in F_l \\ s_c \leq s_{c_0}}} s_{c,l} + \sum_{\substack{c \in F_l \\ s_c > s_{c_0}}} s_{c_0,l}\right), \tag{17}$$

which is similar to the CCT under fair sharing (11) if $s_{c,l}/s_c = s_{c_0,l}/s_{c_0}$ for all $c \in F_l$, $s_c > s_{c_0}$.

4.2.4 Invariance Condition

The above analysis shows that in the special case of $s_{c,l}/s_c = s_{c_0,l}/s_{c_0}$ for all $c \in F_l$, i.e., all coflows split traffic among traversed links in the same way, the objective (2) satisfies $\mathrm{CCT}^{\mathrm{FAIR}}(c_0, l) + \sum_{c \in F_l} \Delta\mathrm{CCT}^{\mathrm{FAIR}}(c, l) \approx 2\mathrm{CCT}^{\mathrm{FAIR}}(c_0, l)$ under Fair/LAS scheduling (assuming $s_{c_0,l} \ll \sum_{c \in F_l s_c \leq s_{c_0}} s_{c,l} + \sum_{c \in F_l s_c > s_{c_0}} s_{c_0,l}$), and $\mathrm{CCT}^{\mathrm{TCF}}(c_0, l) + \sum_{c \in F_l} \Delta\mathrm{CCT}^{\mathrm{TCF}}(c, l) = \mathrm{CCT}^{\mathrm{FAIR}}(c_0, l)$ under TCF scheduling. By arguments similar to Proposition 4.1, we have the following statement.

PROPOSITION 4.2. *If the network performs Fair, LAS, or TCF coflow scheduling, each coflow imposes a small load on each link (relative to its total load), and $s_{c,l}/s_c$ are identical among all coflows $c \in F_l$ for each link l, then the optimal placement that minimizes (2) is always the one that minimizes the bottleneck fair-sharing CCT of the newly arrived coflow as predicted by (11).*

Remark: We note that compared to the case of flow scheduling (Proposition 4.1), the invariance property for coflow scheduling only holds in very special cases when all the coflows split traffic in the same way. It means that in contrast to flow placement, there is rarely a uniformly optimal placement for coflows under different coflow scheduling policies, and it is crucial to customize coflow placement according to the underlying coflow scheduling policy in the network.

Algorithm 1: Task Placement Algorithm

```
  Input: < predFCTNode, nodeState >
  Output: < assignNode >
1 /*predFCTNode = predicted task completion time of the node.
  nodeState = minSize of flows scheduled on a node */
2 Initialize: assignNode = 1, found = 0.;
3 for node := 1 to M do
4     /* identify candidate hosts */;
5     /* if node is empty or the nodeState is larger than task size*/;
6     if (predFCTNode == null) || (nodeState >= taskSize )
      then
7         NodeSet + = node;
8         found == 1;
9 /* If no host available, choose the hosts one-hop away */;
10 if (found! = 1) then
11     /* Among the hosts, 1-hop away */;
12     NodeSet + = node;
13 /* Select the best host that gives minimum FCT */;
14 for nodes := 1 to NodeSet do
15     if predFCTNode <= minFCT then
16         assignNode = node;
17 return assignNode;
```

5. NEAT DESIGN

NEAT targets data-intensive applications such as MapReduce or directed acyclic graph DAG-based systems (such as Spark, Tez etc.). Such applications run in multiple stages and NEAT aims at placing tasks in each stage with the goal of minimizing the average completion time of all the active tasks in the system. For example, a MapReduce job has two stages, Map (where input data is processed) and Reduce (where results of Map stage are summarized) and each stage may have a data shuffle part and a data processing part. Both data shuffle and data processing contribute to the total completion time of a job. Similarly, DAG-based applications can be considered an extension of MapReduce applications, which can have multiple Map/Reduce phases [12]. Therefore, in this work for simplicity, we use MapReduce as the base model and then extend it to DAG for multi-stage jobs.

5.1 NEAT Task Placement

In this section, we discuss how a new task is placed in NEAT framework and it's applications to MapReduce and DAG-based applications.

5.1.1 Flow Placement

NEAT places a new task in two steps: First, it identifies a set of candidate hosts for task placement (see algo 1 lines 4-14) and next, it selects a best host among these for task execution (see algo 1 lines 15-18).

1) *Identification of preferred hosts:* For a given task, NEAT divides nodes into *preferred* hosts and *non-preferred* hosts based on the the size of the current task and the node state (defined as the smallest remaining flow size on each node). If the task generates a flow of size s, then a node is a preferred host if it is idle or all the flows currently scheduled on this node are no smaller than s. Using preferred hosts provides various benefits. First, it reduces the communication overhead among the network daemons and task placement daemons. For each new task, the task daemon contacts only a subset of hosts to get predicted task completion times. Thus, it improves the time taken to search the right candidate such that the selection time is linear in the number of candidate hosts. Secondly, using preferred hosts compliments the benefits of different network scheduling policies. For example, under the Fair or LAS policy, it ensures that long flows are not placed with existing short flows (although short flows can be placed with existing long flows under LAS scheduling), thus improving separation between short and long flows and reducing the switch queuing delays experienced by the short flows. Similarly, under the SRPT policy, it makes sure that the new task can start data transfer immediately. The preferred hosts are further compared in the next step. If there is no preferred host, such that every node has at least one flow smaller than the flow of the current task, then this preference is ignored, i.e., all the nodes are considered preferred hosts. NEAT, in case of large set of preferred hosts, can also consider input data placement to limit the number of preferred hosts for each task.

2) *Selection of a best host:* Given a set of preferred hosts, the next step is to select a host that achieves the minimum task completion time. The *completion time* of a task depends on: i) the time required to transfer input data, and ii) the time required to process the data. The data transfer time is captured by the predicted FCT/CCT, which is obtained from the network daemon (see Section 3). The data processing time depends on the available node resources (e.g., CPU and memory), which can be obtained from an existing per-node resource manager (e.g., Hadoop node manager). In the current design, NEAT compares the available node resources of each preferred host with requirements imposed by the application (e.g., minimum CPU and memory) to identify candidate hosts, and then selects the one that gives the minimum data transfer time (see algo 1 lines 15-18). However, this design can be easily extended with a processing time predictor to minimize the total task completion time; we leave the details to future work.

Remark: NEAT is an online scheduler that greedily optimizes the performance of each new task. We choose this design because: (i) it significantly simplifies the computation per placement, and (ii) it approximates the optimal placement under certain conditions as specified in Proposition 4.1 and 4.2. Note that NEAT only places each task once at the beginning of its lifetime, and does not move any task during its execution.

5.1.2 Coflow Placement

Compared to flow placement, coflow placement poses additional challenges. Ideally, we want to jointly place all the flows in a coflow to minimize the completion time of the slowest flow. However, in the case of one-to-many or many-to-many coflows, joint placement of all the flows in a coflow has exponential complexity due to the exponentially many possible solutions. To solve this problem, we use a sequential heuristic, where we first place the largest flow within the coflow using the flow placement algorithm, and then place the second largest flow using the same algorithm based on the updated network state, and so on. This sequential heuristic used for coflow placement should have quadratic complexity. The reason for placing flows in descending order of their sizes is that larger flows are more likely to be the critical flows determining the completion time of the coflow and hence should be placed on nodes that have more available resources. We leave evaluation of other coflow placement algorithms as a future work. Note that many-to-one coflows do not have the complexity problem and thus can be placed optimally.

5.1.3 Application to MapReduce Scheduling

NEAT considers each MapReduce job as a concatenation of two tasks, one for the Map stage and one for the Reduce stage. Since there are generally multiple Map "tasks" in a job[1], this requires NEAT to place two coflows, one many-to-many coflow for reading input data into Map tasks and one many-to-one coflow for shuffling intermediate results to Reduce task (or many-to-many if there are multiple Reduce tasks). In both the cases, NEAT strives to achieve data locality if possible (as a node with the input data will have zero FCT/CCT), and minimizes data transfer time otherwise. For example, for placing Map tasks, it can leverage the data placement policy of the cluster filesystem (such as HDFS in Apache Yarn). In HDFS, data is usually placed on multiple locations for fault tolerance and to provide better data locality. During Map task placement, NEAT can either place task on the nodes that has the input data available or choose the nodes using it's placement heuristic.

5.1.4 Application to DAG Scheduling

DAG-style applications can be modelled as an extension of MapReduce applications, except that a DAG may have multiple shuffle stages. NEAT considers each stage of a DAG job as a separate task and places flows (coflows) within a task using the procedure discussed in sections 5.1.1 and 5.1.2. The placement algorithm used by NEAT encourages placing tasks of same job on nodes close to the input data.

5.2 NEAT Optimizations

NEAT needs the state of all the active flows in the network to make optimal task placement decisions, which can incur significant overhead at both the network daemons and the task placement daemon. To reduce the overhead, NEAT introduces two optimizations: (i) instead of keeping individual states of all the active flows, each network daemon only maintains a compressed state with a constant size, (ii) instead of contacting all the network daemons, the task placement daemon determines a subset of nodes as candidate hosts based on local information and only contacts the network daemons at the candidate hosts.

Compressed Flow State: Keeping the original flow state requires space that grows linearly with the number of active flows, which limits scalability of the network daemon (with respect to network load). NEAT addresses this issue by approximating the FCT/CCT prediction using a compressed flow state. Each network daemon compresses information of its local flows (coflows) by quantizing the flow sizes into a fixed number of bins and maintaining summary statistics (e.g., total size and number of flows) in each bin. Compared with the original flow state that keeps track of individual flows, this compressed state has a size that is determined by the number of bins, regardless of the number of flows in the network.

We refer to the set of active flows F_l on link l as the *flow state* of link l. The flow states of all the links form the overall flow state F of the network. Note that under FCFS, we can easily compress F_l by storing only the total load ($\sum_{c\in F_l} s_f$ for flow scheduling and $\sum_{c\in F_l} s_{c,l}$ for coflow scheduling), which suffices for FCT/CCT prediction. We thus focus on the other scheduling policies in the sequel.

For FCT prediction, our idea is to divide flows on each link into a finite number of bins $n = 1, \ldots, N$, where we keep the following parameters for each bin: the minimum and maximum flow size ($s^{(1)}_{l,n}$, $s^{(2)}_{l,n}$), the total flow size (in number of bytes) $b_{l,n}$, and the number of flows $c_{l,n}$. In essence, we compress a set of flow sizes into a histogram of flow sizes with flexible bin boundaries ($s^{(1)}_{l,n}$, $s^{(2)}_{l,n}$). Using the compressed flow state, we can approximate (4) by:

$$\mathrm{FCT}^{\mathrm{FAIR}}(f_0, l) \approx \frac{1}{B_l}\left(s_{f_0} + \sum_{n=1}^{p} b_{l,n} + s_{f_0}\sum_{n=p+1}^{N} c_{l,n}\right), \tag{18}$$

where $p = m_l(s_{f_0})$ and $m_l(s) \in \{1, \ldots, N\}$ is the index of the bin containing flow size s (i.e., $s^{(1)}_{l,m_l(s)} \le s < s^{(2)}_{l,m_l(s)}$). Other predictions in § 4.1 can be approximated similarly, although we only need to approximate (4) if the invariance condition in Proposition 4.1 is satisfied. Note that storing $b_{l,n}$ is optional as it can be approximated by $c_{l,n}s$ for some $s \in [s^{(1)}_{l,n}, s^{(2)}_{l,n})$.

For CCT prediction, the compressed flow state in each bin has two additional attributes: $d_{l,n}$, denoting the total load on link l (i.e., sum of $s_{c,l}$ over coflows in this bin), and $e_{l,n}$, denoting the total normalized load on link l (i.e., sum of $s_{c,l}/s_c$ over coflows in the bin). Assuming $q = m_l(s_{c_0})$, for Fair/LAS scheduling, we can approximate (11) by

$$\mathrm{CCT}^{\mathrm{FAIR}}(c_0, l) \approx \frac{1}{B_l}\left(s_{c_0,l} + \sum_{n=1}^{q} d_{l,n} + s_{c_0}\sum_{n=q+1}^{N} e_{l,n}\right), \tag{19}$$

and (13) by

$$\sum_{c\in F_l} \Delta\mathrm{CCT}^{\mathrm{FAIR}}(c, l) \approx \frac{s_{c_0,l}}{B_l s_{c_0}}\left(\sum_{n=1}^{q} b_{l,n} + s_{c_0}\sum_{n=q+1}^{N} c_{l,n}\right). \tag{20}$$

[1] Note that NEAT defines "task" differently from the MapReduce framework.

Under TCF scheduling, we can approximate the righthand side of (17) by

$$\frac{1}{B_l}\left(s_{c_0,l}+\sum_{n=1}^{q}d_{l,n}+s_{c_0,l}\sum_{n=q+1}^{N}c_{l,n}\right). \quad (21)$$

Here storing $e_{l,n}$ is also optional as it can be approximated by $d_{l,n}/s$ for some $s \in [s_{l,n}^{(1)}, s_{l,n}^{(2)})$.

Remark: The compressed flow state has a size that is linear in the number of bins (which is a design parameter), regardless of the number of flows in the network. The cost of this compression is the loss of accuracy in the FCT/CCT prediction, caused by uncertainty in the sizes of flows (coflows) that are in the same bin as the newly arrived flow (coflow). The bin sizes can be set based on the datacenter traffic distribution. For example, for heavy tailed traffic [24], one can use exponentially growing bin sizes to have smaller bin sizes for short flows and large bin sizes for long flows.

Reduced Communication Overhead: NEAT uses distributed components (network daemons) spread across the network to maintain the flow states (see Figure 2). To minimize the communication overhead between the task placement daemon and the network daemons, the network daemons do not always report their updated flow states; instead, the task placement daemon pings the network daemons to get the predicted task performance when it needs to place a new task.

In a large cluster, the task placement daemon has to contact a large number of network daemons to place a task. To further reduce the overhead, the task placement daemon uses local information to reduce the number of network daemons it needs to contact. Specifically, it only contacts a network daemon if (i) the node it resides on is sufficiently close to the input data (e.g., in the same rack or a rack one-hop away from the input data), and (ii) if the node state (i.e., the smallest residual size of flows currently scheduled on this node) is no smaller than the size of the current task. Note that without contacting the network daemon, the task placement daemon does not know the current node state. In our design, the task placement daemon caches the node states previously reported by the network daemons and uses the cached values as estimates.

6. EVALUATION

We evaluate NEAT using trace-driven simulations based on ns2 [37] as well as experiments on a small-scale testbed.

6.1 Simulation Settings

Datacenter Topology: We use a 160 node, 3-tier multi-rooted topology for our evaluation comprising layers of ToR (Top-of-Rack) switches, aggregation switches and core switches, similar to [38, 39, 40]. Each host-ToR link has a capacity of 1 Gbps whereas all other links are of 10 Gbps. The end-to-end round-trip propagation delay (in the absence of queuing) between hosts via the core switch is 300μs.

Traffic Workloads: We consider traffic workloads that are derived from patterns observed in production datacenters.

Scheme	Parameters
DCTCP	qSize = 250 pkts markingThresh = 65
L^2DCT	minRTO = 10 msec
PASE	qSize = 250 pkts minRTO (flows in top queue) = 10 msec minRTO (flows in other queues) = 200 msec numQue = 8

Table 1: Default parameter settings used in simulation.

We evaluate NEAT using the benchmark Hadoop (map-reduce)[1] and web-search [16] workloads. These workloads contain a diverse mix of short and long flows with a heavy-tailed flow size distribution. In the web-search workload, more than 75% of all bytes are from 50% of the flows with sizes in the range [1,20MB]. The hadoop workload is less skewed: ~50% of the flows are less than 100MB in size and 4% flows are larger than 80GB. Note that we always use these settings unless specified otherwise.

Protocols Compared: We compare NEAT with two task scheduling strategies: load aware placement (minLoad) and locality aware placement (minDist). We consider several state-of-art datacenter network scheduling strategies including DCTCP (that implements Fair) [24], L^2DCT (that implements LAS) [15], and PASE (that implements SRPT) [17] for flow scheduling and Varys [21] for coflow scheduling. minLoad places each task on the node with the minimum network load, defined as the utilization ratio of its link to ToR. minDist places each task as close as possible to its input data, as proposed by earlier schemes [12]. We also test coflow performance using smallest coflow first (SCF) heuristic. We implemented DCTCP, L^2DCT, PASE, and Varys using the source code provided by the authors to evaluate their scheme. The parameters of these protocols are set according to the recommendations provided by the authors, or reflect the best settings, which we determined experimentally (see Table 1). For FCT prediction, we use Fair sharing based prediction model unless stated otherwise and for CCT prediction, we use the prediction models corresponding to each evaluated coflow scheduling scheme.

Performance Metrics: We consider the average flow completion time (AFCT) for the flow-based scheduling and coflow completion time (CCT) for coflow-based scheduling schemes. We use *gap from optimal* as the performance metric. For example, for FCT based schemes, the gap from optimal is calculated as $(FCT - FCT^{opt})/FCT^{opt}$, where FCT^{opt} is the optimal FCT defined as the time it takes to complete the data transfer when that is the only flow (coflow) in the network. Note that the gap from optimal equals slowdown (a.k.a. stretch) minus one. The gap from optimal tells us the margin for performance improvement for different kind of network scheduling policies. For example, we observe in our evaluation that the room for improvement is more for suboptimal scheduling policies, in terms of FCT, (such as FAIR, LAS) and less for near-optimal network scheduling policies (such as SRPT).

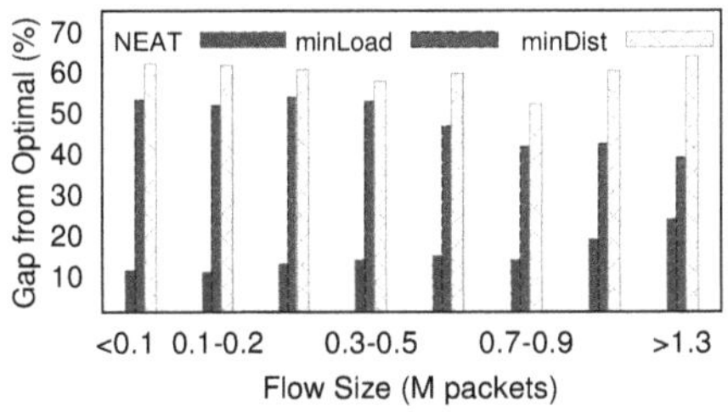

(a) Hadoop

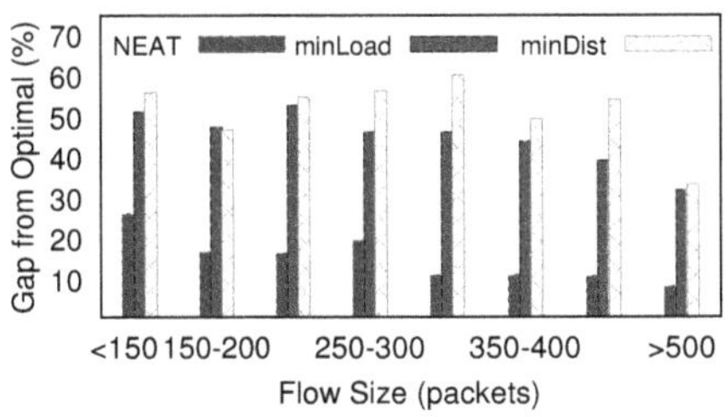

(b) Websearch

Figure 5: Flow placement under DCTCP

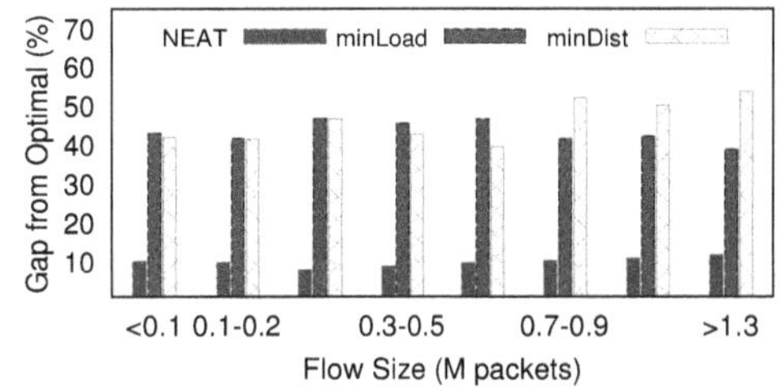

(a) LAS (L^2DCT)

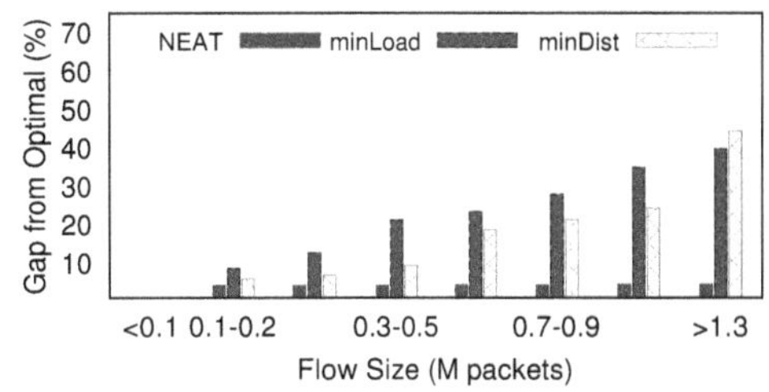

(b) SRPT (PASE)

Figure 6: Flow placement under Hadoop workload

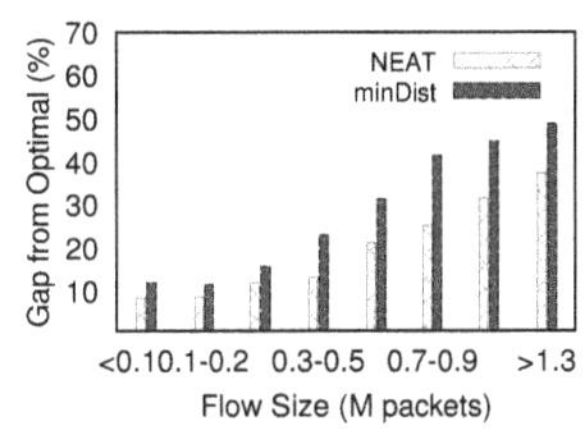

(a) Varys

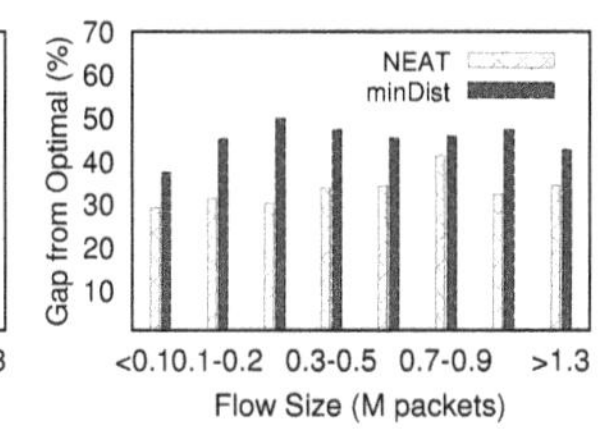

(b) SCF

Figure 7: CoFlow placement for Hadoop workload

6.2 Macrobenchmarks

NEAT improves application performance upto 3.7x, compared to the existing task placement algorithms that only consider data and compute, by incorporating network state and network scheduling policies into task placement decisions. Below, we first discuss NEAT performance in placing flows and then its performance in placing coflows.

Flow placement performance under Fair sharing: Figure 5 shows that NEAT outperforms minLoad and minDist by up to 3.6x for web-search workload and up to 3.7x for Hadoop workloads when the network employs Fair sharing scheduling policy. This is because NEAT chooses the node with minFCT to finish flows faster and uses node state NEAT to avoid placing short flows on same links with long flows. Note that many of the existing policies deployed in the datacenter employ Fair sharing discipline. This shows that even if datacenter does not implement any optimized network scheduling mechanism, NEAT can improve application performance significantly by being aware of network state.

Flow placement performance under different network scheduling policies: Figure 6 shows NEAT performance for Hadoop workload when the network uses L^2DCT (LAS) and PASE (SRPT) as network scheduling policies. NEAT improves the performance by 2.7x compared to minLoad and by upto 3.2x compared to minDist when used with L^2DCT. NEAT also improves the performance by 30% compared to minLoad and by upto 20% compared to minDist when used with PASE. Note that PASE is a near-optimal algorithm and there is very little performance improvement margin for NEAT. Also, observe that minDist and minLoad perform differently under different scheduling policies, whereas, NEAT consistently performs better than both for all the evaluated network scheduling policies. We observe similar performance trends with websearch workloads.

CoFlow placement performance under different network scheduling policies: NEAT improves the CCT performance for Hadoop workloads by upto 25% for two coflow scheduling policies, 1) Varys (Figure 7(a)) and 2) Smallest Coflow First (SCF) (Figure 7(b)). Coflow placement requires a group of flows to be placed in a batch. For coflow placement, NEAT works as described in Section 5.1, while minLoad and minDist are modified as follows - For minLoad, we place each flow of the coflow separately, in the decreasing order of flow sizes, on a node that has the minimum network load. For minDist, our goal is to place flows of the same coflow within the same rack and close to input data and we start by placing the largest flow of a coflow first. NEAT performs better under both coflow scheduling policies, however its gains are limited by the performance of underlying coflow scheduling policy. For example, minDist with Varys scheduling performs better than NEAT with SCF scheduling. The reason for this is that Varys, which adjusts the flow rates based on the smallest bottleneck heuristic, is a much better heuristic than SCF. However, we observe that the gap from optimal is substantial (30% to 50%), for these strategies, for large flow sizes with Varys and nearly for all flow sizes with SCF. The reason for this gap is that the optimal completion time is not always achievable, even under the optimal scheduling, as our definition of optimal ignores resource competition from other flows/coflows. Also, many of these protocols implement certain approximations, instead of the actual optimal scheduling algorithm, to be more deployment friendly.

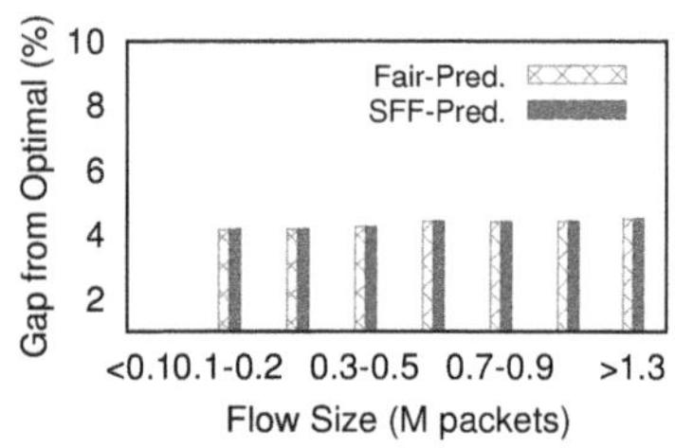

Figure 8: Fair prediction vs SRPT prediction

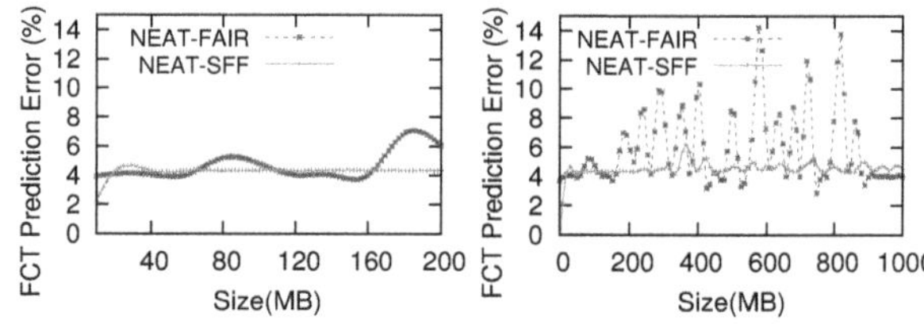

(a) Short flows (b) Long flows

Figure 10: Completion time prediction error

6.3 Microbenchmarks

In this section, we discuss various aspects of NEAT design, with the help of several micro-benchmarks. We analyze NEAT dynamics using Hadoop workload under SRPT (PASE) network scheduling policy, unless stated otherwise. Our evaluation shows that NEAT optimizations (such as prediction assuming FAIR policy only, preferred hosts) improve the application performance and it can predict task completion times quite accurately.

Benefits of using Fair predictor: Figure 8 shows the NEAT performance when task completion time is predicted using the Fair-sharing model (Eq. 4) or the SRPT-sharing model (Eq. 7) when the underlying network scheduling mechanism is SRPT. Both predictors achieve similar performance, therefore, even though the network performs SRPT flow scheduling, NEAT can perform FCT prediction by assuming the fair-sharing principle. This validates our proposition, in §4.1.4, which states that for flow based network scheduling mechanisms, task placement using minimum predicted task completion time, assuming FAIR predictor, can provide better performance for any flow based network scheduling policy.

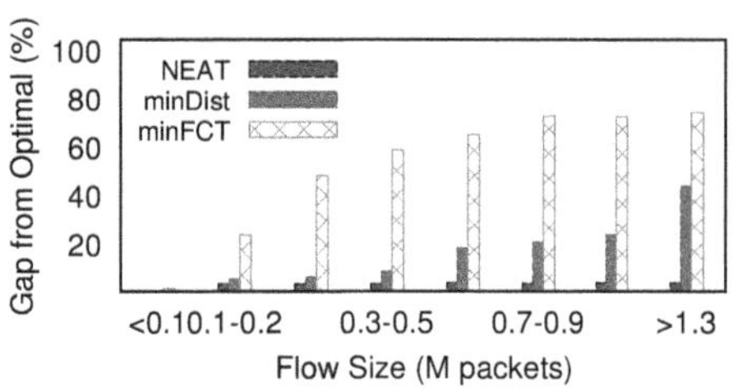

Figure 9: Benefits of using preferred hosts placement

Benefits of using preferred hosts aware placement: Figure 9 shows the benefits of using preferred hosts for making task placement decisions. To evaluate the impact on performance, we compare NEAT performance to minFCT. minFCT strategy makes task placement decision based on the predicted task completion times alone and ignores the node states i.e., it places each task on to a node with the smallest predicted FCT and does not consider the priority of the tasks already scheduled on that node. Figure 9 shows that minFCT placement degrades application performance by up to 50%, and performs even worse than minDist placement. NEAT on the other hand achieves better performance by being aware of node states. Intuitively, minFCT hurts performance in two ways: i) it groups short flows together, thus increasing fair sharing among short flows. ii) for long flows it selects nodes with many short flows, thus long flows experience more preemption by the currently scheduled and newly arriving short flows. We note that the comparison between minFCT and minDist is workload-dependent, e.g., for the workloads, where short and long flows have proportional number of bytes, minFCT performs similar to or better than minDist placement. Thus, using preferred hosts based task placement not only minimizes communication overhead, but it also improves application performance.

Flow completion time prediction accuracy: NEAT can predict flow completion times with reasonable accuracy as shown in Figure 10. NEAT performance depends on accurately predicting completion times. It is important to keep the prediction error small because NEAT only considers currently active tasks while predicting FCTs and future task arrivals may make current placement decisions sub-optimal. Figure 10 reports the prediction accuracy, which is calculated as $(FCT^{flow} - FCT^{pred})/FCT^{pred}$, where FCT^{flow} is the actual FCT and FCT^{pred} is the FCT predicted by NEAT. Figure 10 shows the prediction accuracy for short flows (Figure 10(a)), and long flows (Figure 10(b)) and we observe that the prediction error increases with the flow size. This is because, with the increase in flow size, the flow spends more time in the network and is affected more by the tasks arriving later in time. In many practical datacenter applications, most tasks generate short flows, for which NEAT can predict the FCT within 5% error. This experiment shows that NEAT is not very sensitive to mis-prediction in task completion time estimate and it is able to achieve good performance even in the presence of small inaccuracies in task completion time estimates.

6.4 Testbed Evaluation

We discuss testbed implementation and evaluation results.

Implementation: NEAT follows a master/slave architecture similar to Hadoop-Yarn [41], and we implement NEAT in Scala using support from Akka for messaging between task placement daemon (TD) and network daemons (ND). We currently implement NEAT as an application layer program by extending Varys implementation [21] and leave the integration with Hadoop-Yarn as a future work. Similar to Yarn, the TD acts as the resource manager (RM) and makes task placement decisions, and NDs act as node managers, which maintain flow state of the active jobs and share the network state upon receiving requests from the task placement daemon. The TD accepts a user job similar to RM and invokes network daemon APIs at the nodes (endhosts). Cluster framework (e.g., Spark or Hadoop) drivers can submit a job using the `register()` API to interact with NEAT. Upon receiving a request from the TD, NDs update their local states and reply with predicted task performance and node state. The TD then runs our placement algorithm

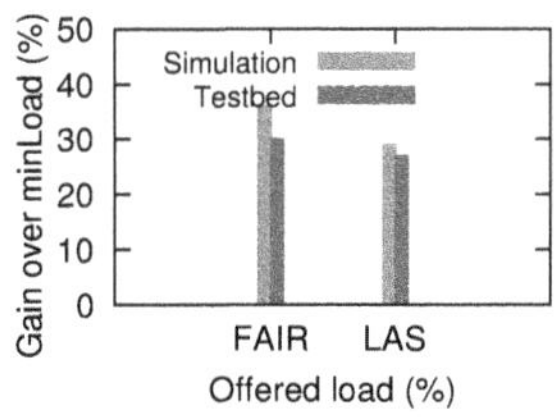

Figure 11: Testbed: minLoad vs NEAT

to schedule flows on selected nodes. To support multiple network scheduling policies, we reuse Varys' `put()` and `get()` method to send and receive data between different nodes. Cluster frameworks can use NEAT `InputStream` and `OutputStream` to leverage various network scheduling policies. The desired network scheduling policy can be specified during network configuration phase.

Evaluation Results: We evaluate NEAT using a 10-node single-rack cluster consisting of DELL servers (with 1G NICs) and PICA-8 Gigabit switch with ECN support enabled. We consider scenario with all-to-all traffic based on Hadoop workload [1] and generate traffic such that the average network load is 50%. We first generate the traffic using ns2 and replay the same traffic in the testbed. The hadoop workload generates many long flows as ~50% of the flows are less than 100MB in size and 4% flows are larger than 80GB. We compare NEAT to minLoad task placement under Fair (implemented by DCTCP) and LAS (implemented by L^2DCT) network scheduling policies. Because of the small scale of the testbed, we do not compare with minDist (since all node pairs have the same distance), and only evaluate using flow-based network scheduling policies.

Our evaluation shows that, compared to minLoad, NEAT can improve application performance by upto 30% under Fair scheduling and upto 27% under LAS scheduling policy, see Figure 11. The gain in testbed scenario is much less than the large scale simulations, and the reason for small gain is the small scale of the testbed. In our evaluation, we observe that a lot of long flows are generated that run simultaneously in the network and share links with short flows. Both the placement algorithms spread large flows across all the nodes in the network, over the time, and therefore increase the completion time of short flows because they share the network links and switch buffers, most of which are occupied by long flows. This effect is not observed in large scale networks where a flow can mostly have many available nodes to chose from. Although, the size of the testbed limits the amount of improvement, NEAT is able to improve the performance under both the network scheduling policies by making better placement decisions. We also compare testbed results to ns2 simulations using same settings as testbed setup and observe similar performance gains.

7. DISCUSSION

Input Data Placement: NEAT can leverage the knowledge of input data locations to improve scalability and make more accurate placement decisions. However, input data may not be optimally placed, which limits the performance of NEAT. In such cases, NEAT can be combined with strategies like corral [12] to make input data and task placement decisions based on the task execution history.

Flow Size Information: NEAT requires flow size information to predict task performance, however, flow size may not always be available. For example, the motivation behind using LAS-based network scheduling is to address this challenge [15]. In such scenarios, NEAT can use approximate flow sizes based on the task execution history for performance prediction, as we have shown that NEAT minimizes task completion time even with some inaccuracy in predicted task completion times (§6.3). We leave evaluation of such scenarios for future work.

Generalization of Network Topologies: Currently, NEAT assumes a single-switch topology and predicts task performance based on the edge links only, however, any link in the network can be bottleneck in other topologies. To make better placement decisions, one can use a distributed state maintenance mechanism similar to PASE [17] where a dedicated arbitrator maintains flow state for each link in the network. NEAT can choose the destination that gives the minimum completion time along the path from source to destination. Nevertheless, our evaluation shows that the single-switch abstraction already provides substantial performance improvement over existing solutions (section 6).

NEAT Scalability: NEAT introduces several optimizations to make system more scalable. For example, to mitigate the communication overhead among daemons, it uses node states while contacting nodes for performance prediction estimate. This reduces the amount of overhead messages sent over the network for communication among network and task placement daemons. Also, to reduce the overhead of task state maintenance by the network daemons, NEAT uses compressed flow state while predicting the task performance. As shown in §6.3, these optimizations help improve NEAT performance, however, we leave large scale scalability analysis of these optimizations as a future work.

8. CONCLUSION

This work proposes a task placement framework that takes into account the network scheduling policy and shows that significant performance gains can be obtained over task schedulers oblivious to network scheduling. NEAT task scheduler makes task placement decisions by using a pluggable task performance predictor that predicts the data transfer time of a given task under given network conditions and network scheduling policy. Despite several simplifying assumptions, NEAT achieves promising performance improvement under several commonly used network scheduling policies. Its pluggable architecture allows easy incorporation of sophisticated resource and application models.

Acknowledgement

This work is partially supported by the National Science Foundation under Grant Numbers CNS-1318563, CNS-1524698, and CNS-1421407, and the National Natural Science Foundation of China under Grant Numbers 61472184 and 61321491, and the Jiangsu High-level Innovation and Entrepreneurship (Shuangchuang) Program. Part of the work was done while Ali Munir was at IBM Research Watson. The authors would like to thank anonymous reviewers and shepherd Mosharaf Chowdhury for their useful feedback.

9. REFERENCES

[1] Jeffrey Dean and Sanjay Ghemawat. Mapreduce: simplified data processing on large clusters. *Communications of the ACM*, 51(1):107–113, 2008.

[2] Grzegorz Malewicz, Matthew H Austern, Aart JC Bik, James C Dehnert, Ilan Horn, Naty Leiser, and Grzegorz Czajkowski. Pregel: a system for large-scale graph processing. In *ACM SIGMOD 2010*, pages 135–146.

[3] William Gropp, S Huss-Lederman, A Lumsdaine, E Lusk, B Nitzberg, W Saphir, and M Snir. Mpi. *The Complete Reference. The MPI-2 Extensions*, 2, 1998.

[4] Michael Isard, Mihai Budiu, Yuan Yu, Andrew Birrell, and Dennis Fetterly. Dryad: distributed data-parallel programs from sequential building blocks. In *ACM SIGOPS Operating Systems Review*, volume 41, pages 59–72. ACM, 2007.

[5] Matei Zaharia, Dhruba Borthakur, Joydeep Sen Sarma, Khaled Elmeleegy, Scott Shenker, and Ion Stoica. Delay scheduling: a simple technique for achieving locality and fairness in cluster scheduling. In *Proceedings of the 5th European conference on Computer systems*, pages 265–278. ACM, 2010.

[6] Faraz Ahmad, Srimat T Chakradhar, Anand Raghunathan, and TN Vijaykumar. Shufflewatcher: Shuffle-aware scheduling in multi-tenant mapreduce clusters. In *Proceedings of the USENIX Annual Technical Conference*, pages 1–12. USENIX Association, 2014.

[7] Yanpei Chen, Archana Ganapathi, Rean Griffith, and Randy Katz. The case for evaluating mapreduce performance using workload suites. In *Modeling, Analysis & Simulation of Computer and Telecommunication Systems (MASCOTS)*, pages 390–399. IEEE, 2011.

[8] Paolo Costa, Austin Donnelly, Antony Rowstron, and Greg O'Shea. Camdoop: exploiting in-network aggregation for big data applications. In *Proceedings of the 9th USENIX conference on Networked Systems Design and Implementation*, pages 3–3. USENIX Association, 2012.

[9] Michael Isard, Vijayan Prabhakaran, Jon Currey, Udi Wieder, Kunal Talwar, and Andrew Goldberg. Quincy: fair scheduling for distributed computing clusters. In *Proceedings of the ACM SIGOPS 22nd symposium on Operating systems principles*, pages 261–276. ACM, 2009.

[10] Ganesh Ananthanarayanan, Srikanth Kandula, Albert G Greenberg, Ion Stoica, Yi Lu, Bikas Saha, and Edward Harris. Reining in the outliers in map-reduce clusters using mantri. In *OSDI*, volume 10, page 24, 2010.

[11] Jian Tan, Alicia Chin, Zane Zhenhua Hu, Yonggang Hu, Shicong Meng, Xiaoqiao Meng, and Li Zhang. Dynmr: Dynamic mapreduce with reduce task interleaving and maptask backfilling. In *ACM EuroSys*, page 2. ACM, 2014.

[12] Virajith Jalaparti, Peter Bodik, Ishai Menache, Sriram Rao, Konstantin Makarychev, and Matthew Caesar. Network-aware scheduling for data-parallel jobs: Plan when you can. In *Proceedings of the ACM Conference on Special Interest Group on Data Communication*, pages 407–420. ACM, 2015.

[13] Chi-Yao Hong, Matthew Caesar, and P Godfrey. Finishing flows quickly with preemptive scheduling. *ACM SIGCOMM Computer Communication Review*, 42(4):127–138, 2012.

[14] David Zats, Tathagata Das, Prashanth Mohan, Dhruba Borthakur, and Randy Katz. Detail: reducing the flow completion time tail in datacenter networks. *ACM SIGCOMM Computer Communication Review*, 42(4):139–150, 2012.

[15] Ali Munir, Ihsan Ayyub Qazi, Zartash Afzal Uzmi, Aisha Mushtaq, Saad N Ismail, M Safdar Iqbal, and Basma Khan. Minimizing flow completion times in data centers. In *INFOCOM, 2013 Proceedings IEEE*, pages 2157–2165. IEEE, 2013.

[16] Mohammad Alizadeh, Shuang Yang, Milad Sharif, Sachin Katti, Nick McKeown, Balaji Prabhakar, and Scott Shenker. pfabric: Minimal near-optimal datacenter transport. *ACM SIGCOMM Computer Communication Review*, 43(4):435–446, 2013.

[17] Ali Munir, Ghufran Baig, Syed M Irteza, Ihsan A Qazi, Alex X Liu, and Fahad R Dogar. Friends, not foes: synthesizing existing transport strategies for data center networks. In *Proceedings of the ACM conference on SIGCOMM*, pages 491–502. ACM, 2014.

[18] Wei Bai, Li Chen, Kai Chen, Dongsu Han, Chen Tian, and Hao Wang. Information-agnostic flow scheduling for commodity data centers. In *12th USENIX Symposium on Networked Systems Design and Implementation (NSDI 15)*. USENIX Association, 2015.

[19] Mosharaf Chowdhury and Ion Stoica. Coflow: a networking abstraction for cluster applications. In *ACM Hotnets*, pages 31–36. ACM, 2012.

[20] Fahad R Dogar, Thomas Karagiannis, Hitesh Ballani, and Antony Rowstron. Decentralized task-aware scheduling for data center networks. In *Proceedings of the 2014 ACM conference on SIGCOMM*, pages 431–442. ACM, 2014.

[21] Mosharaf Chowdhury, Yuan Zhong, and Ion Stoica. Efficient coflow scheduling with varys. In *Proceedings of the 2014 ACM conference on SIGCOMM*, pages 443–454. ACM, 2014.

[22] Yangming Zhao, Kai Chen, Wei Bai, Chen Tian, Yanhui Geng, Yiming Zhang, Dan Li, and Sheng Wang. Rapier: Integrating routing and scheduling for coflow-aware data center networks. In *Proc. IEEE INFOCOM*, 2015.

[23] Mosharaf Chowdhury and Ion Stoica. Efficient coflow scheduling without prior knowledge. In *Proceedings*

of the ACM Conference on Special Interest Group on Data Communication, pages 393–406. ACM, 2015.

[24] Mohammad Alizadeh, Albert Greenberg, David A Maltz, Jitendra Padhye, Parveen Patel, Balaji Prabhakar, Sudipta Sengupta, and Murari Sridharan. Data center tcp (dctcp). *ACM SIGCOMM computer communication review*, 41(4):63–74, 2011.

[25] Dhruba Borthakur. The hadoop distributed file system: Architecture and design. *Hadoop Project Website*, 11(2007):21, 2007.

[26] Mosharaf Chowdhury, Srikanth Kandula, and Ion Stoica. Leveraging endpoint flexibility in data-intensive clusters. In *ACM SIGCOMM Computer Communication Review*, volume 43, pages 231–242. ACM, 2013.

[27] Ali Ghodsi, Matei Zaharia, Benjamin Hindman, Andy Konwinski, Scott Shenker, and Ion Stoica. Dominant resource fairness: Fair allocation of multiple resource types. In *NSDI*, volume 11, pages 24–24. USENIX, 2011.

[28] Benjamin Hindman, Andy Konwinski, Matei Zaharia, Ali Ghodsi, Anthony D Joseph, Randy H Katz, Scott Shenker, and Ion Stoica. Mesos: A platform for fine-grained resource sharing in the data center. In *NSDI*, volume 11, pages 22–22. USENIX, 2011.

[29] Ali Ghodsi, Vyas Sekar, Matei Zaharia, and Ion Stoica. Multi-resource fair queueing for packet processing. In *ACM SIGCOMM*, volume 42, pages 1–12. ACM, 2012.

[30] Ali Ghodsi, Matei Zaharia, Scott Shenker, and Ion Stoica. Choosy: Max-min fair sharing for datacenter jobs with constraints. In *ACM EuroSys*, pages 365–378. ACM, 2013.

[31] Vinod Kumar Vavilapalli, Arun C Murthy, Chris Douglas, Sharad Agarwal, Mahadev Konar, Robert Evans, Thomas Graves, Jason Lowe, Hitesh Shah, Siddharth Seth, et al. Apache hadoop yarn: Yet another resource negotiator. In *ACM SoCC*, page 5. ACM, 2013.

[32] Matei Zaharia, Andy Konwinski, Anthony D Joseph, Randy H Katz, and Ion Stoica. Improving mapreduce performance in heterogeneous environments. In *OSDI*, volume 8, page 7, 2008.

[33] Ganesh Ananthanarayanan, Ali Ghodsi, Scott Shenker, and Ion Stoica. Effective straggler mitigation: Attack of the clones. In *NSDI*, volume 13, pages 185–198. USENIX, 2013.

[34] Xiaoqi Ren, Ganesh Ananthanarayanan, Adam Wierman, and Minlan Yu. Hopper: Decentralized speculation-aware cluster scheduling at scale. In *ACM SIGCOMM*, pages 379–392. ACM, 2015.

[35] Hyunseok Chang, Murali Kodialam, Ramana Rao Kompella, TV Lakshman, Myungjin Lee, and Sarit Mukherjee. Scheduling in mapreduce-like systems for fast completion time. In *INFOCOM, 2011 Proceedings IEEE*, pages 3074–3082. IEEE, 2011.

[36] Fangfei Chen, Murali Kodialam, and TV Lakshman. Joint scheduling of processing and shuffle phases in mapreduce systems. In *INFOCOM, 2012 Proceedings IEEE*, pages 1143–1151. IEEE, 2012.

[37] The network simulator - ns-2. http://www.isi.edu/nsnam/ns/.

[38] Mohammad Al-Fares, Alexander Loukissas, and Amin Vahdat. A scalable, commodity data center network architecture. In *ACM SIGCOMM Computer Communication Review*, volume 38, pages 63–74. ACM, 2008.

[39] Balajee Vamanan, Jahangir Hasan, and TN Vijaykumar. Deadline-aware datacenter tcp (d2tcp). *ACM SIGCOMM Computer Communication Review*, pages 115–126, 2012.

[40] Christo Wilson, Hitesh Ballani, Thomas Karagiannis, and Ant Rowtron. Better never than late: Meeting deadlines in datacenter networks. In *ACM SIGCOMM Computer Communication Review*, pages 50–61. ACM, 2011.

[41] Apache hadoop yarn. https://goo.gl/qEdpo5.

Low Bandwidth Offload for Mobile AR

Puneet Jain
Hewlett Packard Labs
Palo Alto, CA
puneet.jain@hpe.com

Justin Manweiler
IBM Research
Yorktown Heights, NY
jmanweiler@us.ibm.com

Romit Roy Choudhury
University of Illinois
Urbana-Champaign, IL
croy@illinois.edu

ABSTRACT

Environmental fingerprinting has been proposed as a key enabler to immersive, highly contextualized mobile computing applications, especially augmented reality. While fingerprints can be constructed in many domains (e.g., wireless RF, magnetic field, and motion patterns), visual fingerprinting is especially appealing due to the inherent heterogeneity in many indoor spaces. This visual diversity, however, is also its Achilles' heel – matching a unique visual signature against a database of millions requires either impractical computation for a mobile device, or to upload large quantities of visual data for cloud offload. Further, most visual "features" tend to be low entropy – e.g., homogeneous repetitions of floor and ceiling tiles. Our system VisualPrint, proposes a means to offload only the *most distinctive* visual data, that is, only those visual signatures which stand a good chance to yield a unique match. VisualPrint enables cloud-offloaded visual fingerprinting with efficacy comparable to using whole images, but with an order reduction in network transfer.

Categories and Subject Descriptors

H.3.4 [**Information Storage and Retrieval**]: Systems and Software

Keywords

Augmented Reality, Offloading, Bandwidth, Latency

1. INTRODUCTION

Real-time augmented reality (AR) has remained an open problem in mobile computing. The problem is challenging because one's camera preview needs to be matched against a pre-existing image database in real-time. This operation is computationally intensive and our smartphones are resource constrained. Therefore, cloud-offloading is considered as an obvious alternative. Not surprising that most research focus toward reducing computation latency. Several designs of faster server-side pipeline [16, 31, 41], light-weight vision algorithms [36], and reducing visual search space [22] have been proposed. Despite many attempts, substantial drawbacks remain: in deployment practicality, in efficacy, or in robustness. Unpredictable end-to-end network latency is one such drawback. Several factors including the distance between the device and cloud, network bandwidth and channel, and sheer data quantity contribute to it. While edge computing [39], data compression [42], and better wireless deployment [35] can alleviate this issue to some extent, due to large volume, have not proven sufficient. This paper identifies a unique fingerprinting opportunity to substantially reduce the visual data transfer, therefore fixing the network latency issue for mobile vision applications.

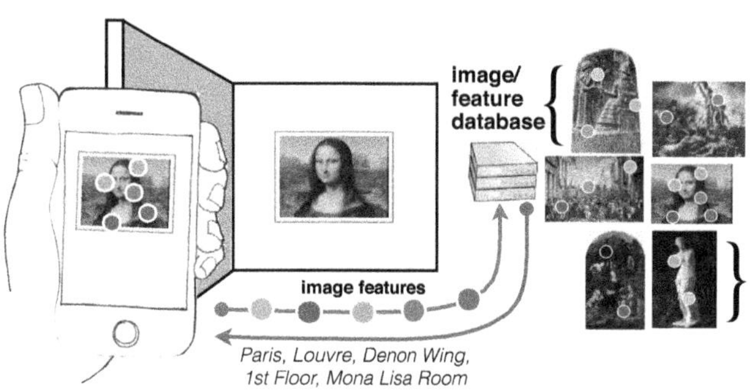

Figure 1: User views scene of interest on smartphone display, image or features shipped to cloud server, cloud returns with 3D AR location context.

Our solution to network latency lies in the observation that indoor spaces naturally lend themselves to high visual diversity. Patterns of color in paintings and photographs on walls, stylized light fixtures, corners on furniture, and even minuscule imperfections in drywall

CoNEXT '16, December 12-15, 2016, Irvine, CA, USA
© 2016 ACM. ISBN 978-1-4503-4292-6/16/12...$15.00
DOI: http://dx.doi.org/10.1145/2999572.2999587

and baseboards collectively create a unique visual "signature" or "fingerprint" of a particular space. Due to the combinatorics, it is highly unlikely that any two places would have a very similar pattern of visual features. Our goal is to create a lightweight mechanism to extract these visual fingerprints at scale. As shown in Figure 1, we want to build a lookup service by which it is possible to instantly map a photo to a unique point in the space; all by using only the essence of the scene – the visual fingerprint. Importantly, the mechanism must be such that the fingerprint size is substantially less than the corresponding visual data.

Practical Challenges of Cloud Offload

While existing approaches for mobile AR might be sufficient for identifying a user's location from a photograph, they would quickly become impractical for continuous, real-time use. A stream of images or video implies a high sustained bandwidth, especially if we take full advantage of modern high-resolution smartphone cameras. As shown in Figure 2, at these resolutions, even 10 frames per second (FPS) requires 2 Mbps using state-of-the-art H264 compression. Worse, such levels of compression result in an almost unusable reduction in the quantity of extractable keypoints (Figure 3). Thus, we would really need lossless compressed frames, such as PNG – at much higher bitrates. On a cellular data connection, even LTE, such a stream is at worst infeasible, or at best, wasteful of the user's data quota and battery life, not to mention finite cellular bandwidth.

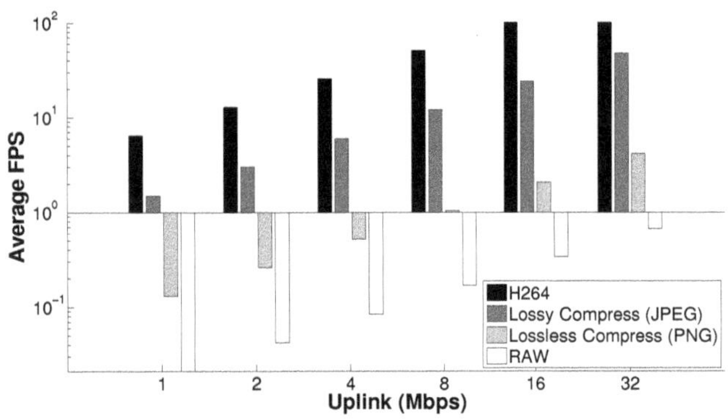

Figure 2: Uplink bandwidth versus sustainable frames per second (FPS), by encoding. Note: log-log scale plot.

It is natural to ask why do mobile AR systems need to process at high frame-rates and why subsampling frames to reduce bandwidth is not sufficient. One may argue that people do not move too fast physically, therefore subsampling should work. However, in mobile AR physical movement is not necessary – one may scan the environment by simply moving hands at fast speed. Moreover, subsampling is related to motion blur. [22] in real-world experiments found majority of frames to be blurred due to motion and shake. Since blurred frames lack ample visual features, they do not result match on the server. Therefore, subsampling can delay upload of a crisp frame for arbitrarily long time and result in perceivable latency on the screen. We discard subsampling to make system more responsive. This also avoids making assumption on the way users use an AR system. Finally, we do not infer whether a frame is blurred or not, because it is non-trivial and adds additional processing latency on the critical path.

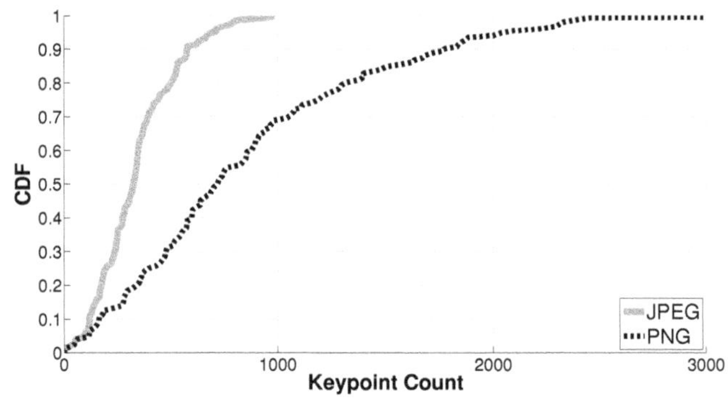

Figure 3: CDF of number of SIFT keypoints, PNG versus JPEG compression (same compression ratio as Figure 2). Under compression, SIFT feature extraction efficacy drops substantially. Peak performance is achieved using lossless compression, such as PNG.

Figure 4: Visualization of SIFT keypoints. For each keypoint, center of circle represents location, radius represents detection scale, and line segment represents direction of orientation.

An alternate approach to solve bandwidth issue could be to just send the visual features. In computer vision, interesting points such as corners are often referred as keypoint. A keypoint is typically represented using

2D pixel coordinate and a multi-dimensional feature description vector. These keypoints can then be used to identify similarity between the two visual scenes. SIFT [32] is a widely popular algorithm used to detect and describe keypoints. Figure 4 shows a visualization of SIFT keypoints. However in our case, sending SIFT keypoints only is also not practical: extracted keypoints typically require *at least* as much space as the image itself. Even after heavy GZIP compression, keypoints require comparable space for most images, and five times more uncompressed (Figure 5). We envision an alternative. What if, instead of shipping the entire image data (or all image keypoints), we ship only those parts which define a unique fingerprint?

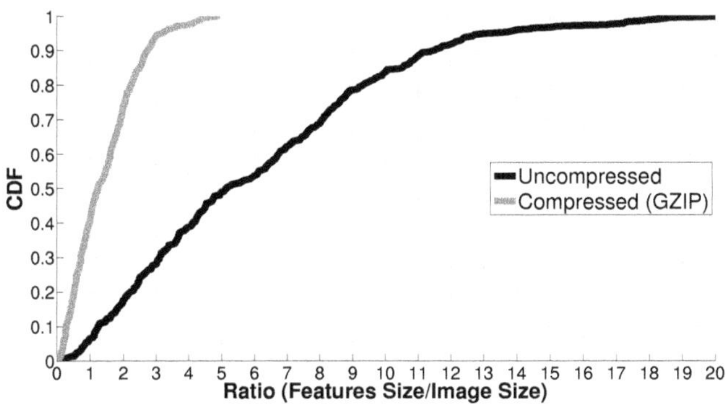

Figure 5: CDF of SIFT feature size (in bytes) ratio to image size. Even after heavy compression, features require comparable space to the original image.

VisualPrint: A Uniqueness "Oracle"

Imagine waking up in a maze of blank, white walls. It is hard to find your way through, given that each area looks the same as the one preceding it. Now imagine you have a marker. By drawing a unique symbol on each wall – equivalent to a few bits of information – you could quickly create a signature to identify where you are at any time. This paper is about finding those few bits of information that naturally occur in real-life environments.

To construct a visual fingerprint, not all parts of an image are equally useful. To reduce cloud-offload bandwidth, we need to distill to only those high-entropy bits. This is analogous to delta (difference) encoding for video compression: all data is thrown away, except the information gain. The challenge here is that the *entropy of any pixel cannot be deduced from strictly local information*. For example, imagine an art gallery. The one-of-a-kind paintings are likely to contain good candidate, highly-unique keypoints. The corners of a checkerboard floor or the regular pattern of ceiling tiles are less so. Many keypoints could be quickly discarded – for example, if two very similar keypoints appear in the same image. However, some might be unique in a particular image, yet common across several. For example, a door knob or light switch might be unique in a room, but repeated in every room of a building. To recognize this global repetition, we need something of a uniqueness "oracle."

We want to create a visual lookup mechanism whereby a smartphone app can capture a photograph or stream of video and quickly identify a handful of keypoints that are highly unique, to define a short fingerprint description. Instead of 2,000 keypoints from a single photograph (not an unusual result from a high-resolution photo using SIFT), we wish to capture the same essence in only 200 – an order of magnitude fewer. The app can then upload this short description ($\approx$ 30KB) of the scene to a cloud service. On that service, we can apply existing techniques of image-based content retrieval (like Google Reverse Image Search or TinEye.com). Instead of similar images, the service replies with metadata, an estimate of location and camera pose.

We call our approach *VisualPrint*. VisualPrint uses only local information (on the smartphone) to leverage a global awareness of which visual data is worthwhile (curated on the server and downloaded to the client in advance). Since this table can be aggressively probabilistic – false positives create a minimal performance penalty – the representation can be extremely compact. Our design ensures that lookups are cheap – constant time per image keypoint – so we can filter all captured image data to only the most essential (the "compact" fingerprint).

In Figure 6, we present our intuition for the opportunity. Most of the 128 dimensions of a SIFT descriptor contain minimal information to differentiate it from all others. Generally, only a few dimensions are required to isolate a descriptor from its closest neighbor. Locality-sensitive hashing (LSH) is a natural choice to re-project a minority of valuable dimensions into a more manageable low-dimensional space – enabling efficient high-dimensional nearest neighbor search.

With feature descriptors distilled using LSH, our key technique applies counting Bloom filters to build small, probabilistic lookup tables. These tables (10s of MBs) are downloaded to a user's device in advance to summarize vast quantities of visual data (1000s of MBs). An image keypoint can be quickly tested against these tables to quantify its uniqueness – how often it appears in other images, globally. Quickly, thousands of keypoints can be sorted according to these uniqueness. The several (200) most unique are then chosen for matching on the cloud – others immediately discarded.

Beyond the core intuition, our end-to-end implemented VisualPrint prototype consists of three major system components: (1) a wardriving app based on Google Project Tango [6] using Simultaneous Localization and Mapping (SLAM) techniques to quickly construct a 3D database of visual features, applicable to indoor environments; (2) a cloud storage and compute service

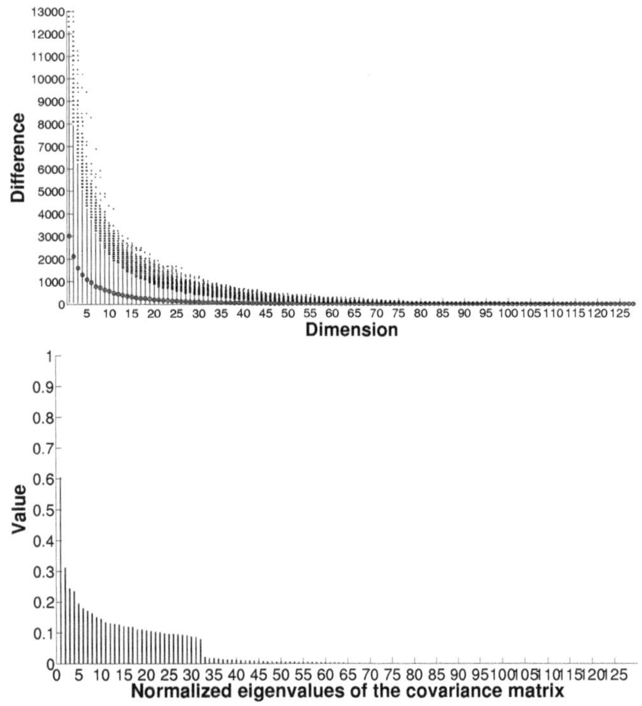

Figure 6: (a) For 500 images, each feature descriptor $\vec{A}$ matched to nearest neighbor in the database $\vec{B}$. Boxplots show `sort_reversed`$[(\vec{A} - \vec{B})^2]$**. Few dimensions provide most of the Euclidean distance between $\vec{A}$ and $\vec{B}$. (b) Principal component analysis (PCA) confirms this intuition, as only a few PCA dimensions (far less than 128) are enough to account for the majority of covariance.**

to curate this database, by identifying the most unique visual features, and respond to fingerprint queries with a location estimate; and (3) a smartphone app to capture photographs and extract visual features, subselect features by estimated uniqueness to a concise "fingerprint," and perform location lookups on the cloud service.

VisualPrint makes the following contribution:

VisualPrint enables mobile devices to filter visual data by global uniqueness — allowing only the most important bits to be used in a query — and reducing network offload by an order of magnitude.

2. RELATED WORK

VisualPrint builds upon a large body of prior art, especially in the areas of image-based content retrieval, cloud offload support for mobile systems, visual approaches for localization and mapping, and multi-sensory indoor localization. Additionally, the VisualPrint approach can enhance several emerging mobile applications beyond localization.

Image-based Retrieval: Image-based content retrieval has been extensively studied, including consideration for resource constraints applicable to mobile devices. [45] proposes a method to match two uncalibrated stereo images robustly. [13, 32] identify robust features in an image to achieve high accuracy. [9, 37] are binary variants of image features which can be used to perform faster image matching based on Hamming distances. While better feature design improves matching latency between a pair of images – this is insufficient to scale to a database of a large size. Approximate matching schemes such as [15, 41] address this issue to some extent, but memory and computation overheads of indexing hinder their applicability to resource-constrained smartphones. Similarly, running matching algorithms on GPUs [17] is feasible on a server but not readily on smartphones. [20, 25] design locality-sensitive Bloom-filters to address memory limitations of approximate high-dimensional matching. We extend these approaches for VisualPrint, but in a novel application to identify unique image features.

Cloud Offloading for Mobile Applications: Computation offloading to a remote server has been used to overcome computational, memory, and energy limitations of a smartphone [14, 24, 30]. However, real-time offloaded image processing remains challenging for several reasons: upload throughput between the phone and the cloud is often limited (especially over cellular, even LTE uplinks); wireless network latencies between the phone and cloud are unpredictable and can not guarantee a consistent user experience [27]; and high power consumption in continuous uploading defeats a primary incentive for offloading [22, 26]. Hybrid architectures leveraging the phone to do some local computation to (e.g., to pick frames to be uploaded on the cloud) partially address this issue [19]. [39] proposes an alternate architecture of bringing computation power in the proximity of the mobile device.

Visual Simultaneous Localization and Mapping (VSLAM): VSLAM refers to the problem of simultaneously constructing/updating a map while tracking the location of a device, using a camera and other onboard sensors [23]. The Project Tango hardware, used in VisualPrint, is essentially VSLAM put into practice. VSLAM heavily relies on statistical techniques such as Kalman or particles filter to smooth and correct dead reckoning errors of noisy sensor data. Bundle adjustment [43] is used to generate a 3D model of the scene, while simultaneously estimating and correcting optical parameters of the camera. Later, image registration [33] and inertial tracking is used to find an instantaneous localization of the device [38]. VSLAM is implicitly applied in VisualPrint, through our reliance on Google Tango during the initial 3D wardriving phase.

Indoor Localization in Other Domains: WiFi and inertial sensing have been applied for indoor localization [11, 44]. Our approach to visual fingerprinting is complementary to, and can be further enhanced by, these works: location context can be used to reduce image search on the server. However, this context is not ubiquitously available. Thus, we do not assume such a location service, to the benefit of generalizability.

Applications: Crowdsourced video is rising in importance, as evident in the popularity of Youtube, Periscope [8], and Meerkat [7]. Several applications built atop demand real-time understanding of location context in the video streams [2], as can be provided by VisualPrint. Image-derived location context can also immediately benefit applications for augmented reality [3, 5], mobile object recognition [1], movable-camera surveillance [4], life-logging [18], sports video analytics [21], mood-sensing [29], and reaction sensing [12]. We believe that VisualPrint can be productively applied to each of these domains.

3. SYSTEM DESIGN

Figure 7 illustrates VisualPrint's simplified system architecture, consisting of three major components: (1) a client app for commodity off-the-shelf Android smartphones, providing visual fingerprinting and localization; (2) a cloud server module, providing visual fingerprint pre-processing and fingerprint-to-location lookup services; and (3) a wardriving app for Google Tango app, to populate the server with visual fingerprint data, each time a new building is added to the database.

The smartphone client "app" is really a proof of concept. It exists only to demonstrate and test the VisualPrint client library, which could be easily incorporated into any Android app requiring fingerprinting and/or localization services. Or, it might be plausibly incorporated as a cross-app system-level service – enabling camera-based localization applicable indoors when GPS is untenable.

When the library loads the first time, it contacts the VisualPrint cloud service to download up-to-date feature-uniqueness tables (to be refreshed periodically). These are structured as a set of counting Bloom filters, indexed using locality-sensitive hashing. In the next subsection, we describe this in details.

Uniqueness "Oracle" Construction

Primer – Bloom Filters: A Bloom filter is a probabilistic data structure, designed for efficient (constant time and memory) set membership queries. That is, one can look for the presence of a particular (exact) element: range or nearest-neighbor queries are not supported. There is some uncertainty to a lookup, hence considered probabilistic. The filter can determine that an element is either *definitely not* in the set or *may be* in the set. Bloom filters are typically implemented using a fixed-size bit vector. To insert, an element is hashed multiple times using a non-cryptographic hash (typically, a hash is selected for execution speed over cryptographic guarantees, such as Murmur-3). The hash output is taken modulo the size of the bit vector as an index – setting these positions to true. To test set membership, the query element is simply hashed again and the corresponding bits are checked. If all the hashed bits set to true, the element is probabilistically assumed to be present. If a single hashed bit is set to false, the element is definitely not present.

A *counting* Bloom filter is a variant that maintains counters (rather than binary bit flips), enabling accumulation for multiple occurrences of an element. VisualPrint leverages counting Bloom filter with a low saturation point (beyond which additional insertions of the same value have no effect). Once saturated for a particular feature, we can be confident that the corresponding keypoint is fairly common, not useful to our purpose.

Primer – Locality Sensitive Hashing (LSH): LSH techniques widely apply to efficient searching in a high dimensional dataset. The intuition is to reduce dimensions of the data in such a way that similar items map to similar or nearby buckets with high-probability. Assuming the number of buckets is much smaller compared to the original data, an efficient nearest-neighbor lookup can be performed. For VisualPrint, we wish to enable an efficient lookup mechanism of image descriptors. The closeness of two descriptors is measured by the Euclidean distance between them. Due to this requirement, from a variety of LSH variants, E^2LSH [10] is most natural for VisualPrint.

E^2LSH belongs to a family of random projection-based LSH schemes. Specifically, a point to be indexed is projected randomly on several hyperplanes. The expectation is that for two nearby points, most projections will also yield nearby scalar values for each. Therefore, once discretized, most nearby points will be indexed to the same LSH "bucket." What distinguishes E^2LSH from related schemes is in how it selects coefficients to each of the random projection hyperplanes. Critically, it has been shown that when one constructs hyperplanes with coefficients drawn as random samples of a p-stable distribution [15], the projection values preserve the L_p norm. Thus, under a 2-stable distribution, the L_2 norm – the metric of Euclidean distances – is preserved. The Gaussian distribution is 2-stable, and thus an appropriate choice. Hence, E^2LSH (under Gaussian coefficient selection) supports nearest neighbor lookup by Euclidean distance, appropriate for SIFT keypoints.

Locality-Sensitive Bloom Filters

VisualPrint blends the advantages of LSH and Bloom filters. LSH enables imprecise queries based on Euclidean distances; Bloom filters provide a compact representa-

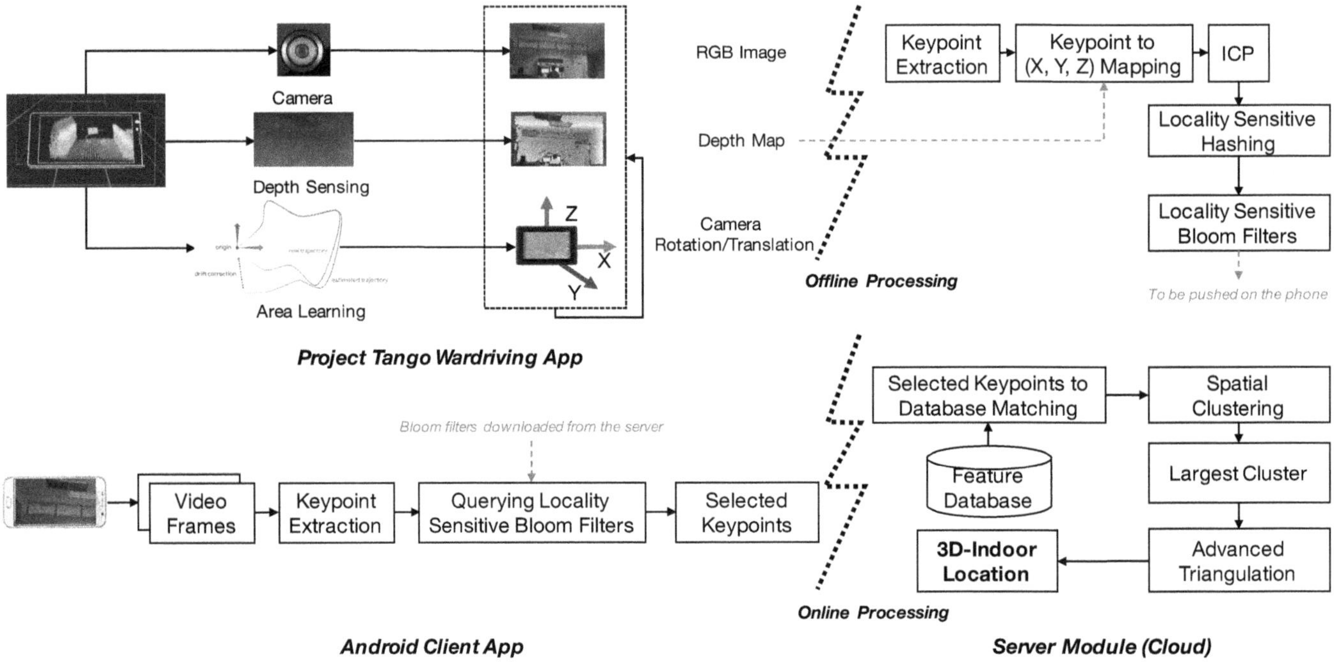

Figure 7: System overview. Top left: wardriving-app based on Google Tango. The output of wardriving app consists of 2D image keypoints with corresponding 3D metadata. Top right: server processes wardriven image 2D/3D data and constructs concise representation in the form of locality-sensitive bloom filters. Bottom left: phone (client) app captures video frames, extracts keypoints, identifies a subset of highly-unique keypoints, and queries to server. Bottom right: server processes and infers 3D location from a client query (2D, comprised of several highly-unique keypoints).

tion. Figure 8 illustrates our locality-sensitive Bloom filter construction. From top to bottom, we begin with a single keypoint descriptor. A SIFT descriptor exists in 128-dimensional space (each dimension being a one-byte integer value). The first step is to take M random projections of the 128-dimension descriptor. Each singular projection yields a single scalar value, with M projections yielding a M-dimensional vector. Each projection is quantized into a discrete space based on width parameter W. We construct L such M-dimensional vectors to create L LSH "buckets." Each of the $M \times L$ randomly-chosen projections is held constant for the life of the data structure. For each of the L buckets, we apply one of L cryptographic hash functions g_i from the same family (Murmur-3) on the M-dimensional vector. The hash output provides K indices into a counting Bloom filter (K for each of the L LSH buckets). For each index, we increase the corresponding count by one. Each bit index counter is represented in 10 bits, for a count saturation (maximum count that can be represented) of 1024. Beyond 1024, we treat a keypoint as not unique enough for consideration. We empirically optimize the various parameters to LSH and Bloom filters from a generic image keypoint dataset: $L = 10$, $M = 7$, $W = 500$, and $K = 8$.

Challenge, False Positives: Three sources of false positives exist in our scheme: (1) Bloom filters, (2) LSH, and (3) the interplay of Bloom filters and LSH. The probability of Bloom filter false positive is tunable – trading off memory consumption. We tune Bloom filters to support up to 2.5M unique feature vectors with less than 1% false positives. LSH false positives are mitigated through empirical tuning of L, M, and W. After tuning, we observe few false positives from LSH alone. However, the interplay of LSH and Bloom is more problematic. The primary cause is due to the quantization of features (as tuned using LSH parameter W). Quantization must be coarse enough to capture similarity of two nearby feature descriptors. However, when W is selected to be more coarse, there are fewer unique "bins." Thus, the Bloom filter is used less uniformly – bits are only flipped to represent this smaller number of bins. After many insertions, "hotspots" in the Bloom filter may result. We address these in two ways. First, we choose a relatively higher saturation point for counting Bloom filters: we use 10 bits per Bloom filter index, for saturation at 1024, when fewer would otherwise be required. Secondly, we leverage an established technique from prior art – a *verification* Bloom filter. For each insertion to a primary Bloom filter, a second insertion is performed into the verification Bloom filter. However, instead of hashing the original data, we hash the bit positions of the insertions to the primary Bloom filter. During the query, a positive result is returned if and

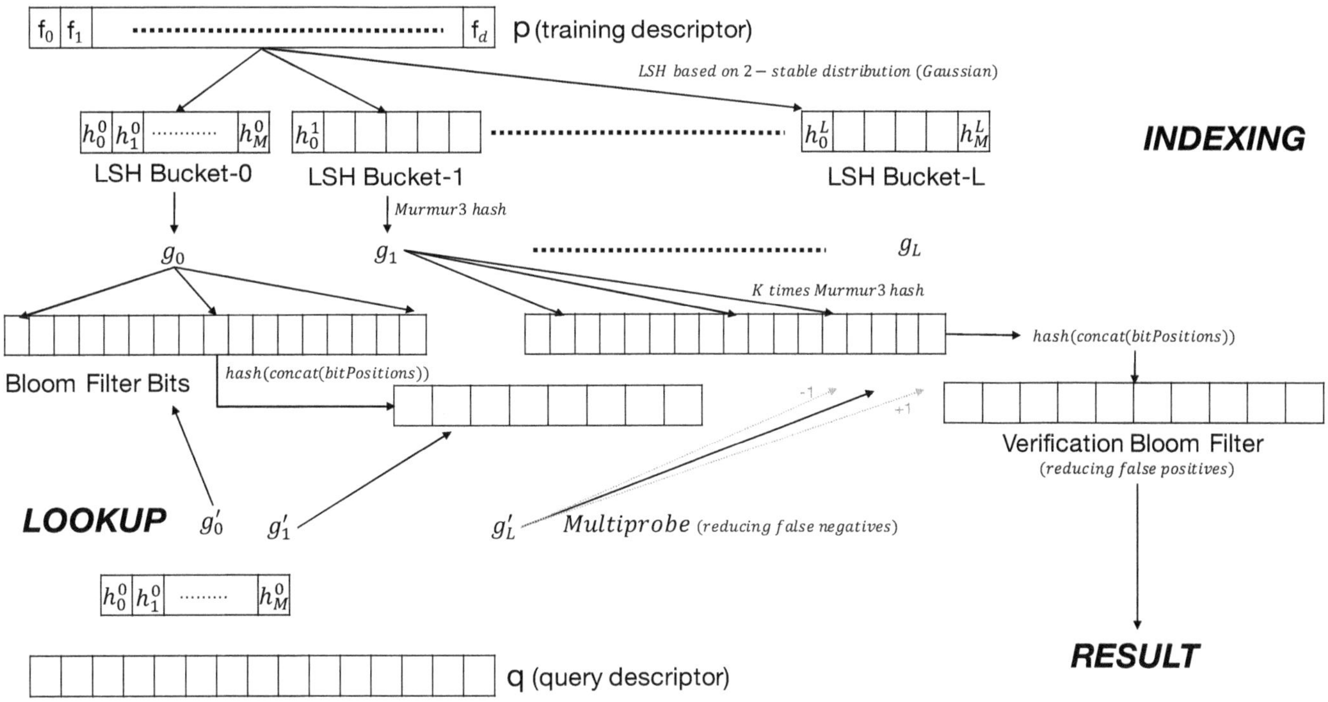

Figure 8: Locality-sensitive Bloom filter "oracle" construction. From top (indexing): image keypoint descriptor passes first through a locality-sensitive, then secondly, a cryptographic hash, yielding several bit indices into counting Bloom filters (middle). From bottom left (lookup): keypoint descriptor checked against Bloom filters. "Multiprobe" protects against off-by-one false negatives. Non-counting verification Bloom filter (far right) protects against false positives.

only if a positive match is found in both the primary and verification Bloom filters.

Challenge, False Negatives: False negatives may occur in LSH, due to the quantization boundaries. Irrespective of the choice of quantization parameter W, it is possible that two nearby feature descriptors would be mapped to different quantization buckets (if the quantization boundary happens to fall in between). Fortunately, the error can be at most a single quantization bucket. Borrowing a technique from [34], we perform "multi-probe" checks into adjacent quantization buckets to reduce these cases. During retrieval, we consider off-by-one partial matches in the Bloom filter – those with $K-1$ of K bits matching. This requires a total of $2K+1$ Bloom filter checks – easily accommodated, as each Bloom filter test is extremely fast. If such a partial match is found, we declare this as a *potential* false negative case – accepting it a "pass" of the primary Bloom filter. The verification Bloom filter provides the final check. Given that multi-probes increase the probability of false positives, the verification Bloom filter becomes all the more crucial to our scheme.

Keypoint-to-3D Position Wardriving

The core data structure of the VisualPrint cloud service is a large-scale lookup table – mapping image features to their corresponding 3D positions. Before VisualPrint can be used to *retrieve* visual fingerprints in an indoor space, the environment must be wardriven – populating this table. We build a visual-wardriving app for Google Tango [6] hardware. While the user walks around a building, the app captures photographs (from a traditional RGB sensor), a depth map (from an integrated IR depth sensor), and the location of the user (relative to the start position, tracked through VSLAM).

During the wardriving phase, the VisualPrint app for Tango is used to collect a series of snapshots with corresponding metadata: the six degree of freedom (6-DoF) pose of the device, an RGB image (from which keypoints will be extracted), and a lower resolution depth map of the corresponding view (from an embedded IR-based depth sensor). The 6-DoF pose is relative to the initial position (where the app was initialized). It includes three dimensions of translation in (x, y, z) and three dimensions of device rotation/orientation (yaw, pitch, roll). To wardrive a venue, a user needs to walk throughout the indoor space to be captured. This process is manual (the user must physically walk), but could be automated using area-covering robots like Roomba. During collection, the Tango app pushes images, depth context, and positioning metadata to the VisualPrint cloud service. As described in the next subsection, the VisualPrint cloud service pre-processes this data to establish mappings between unique image keypoints and their corresponding 3D locations. The number of such mappings in a building can be exceedingly large from hundreds of thousands to millions.

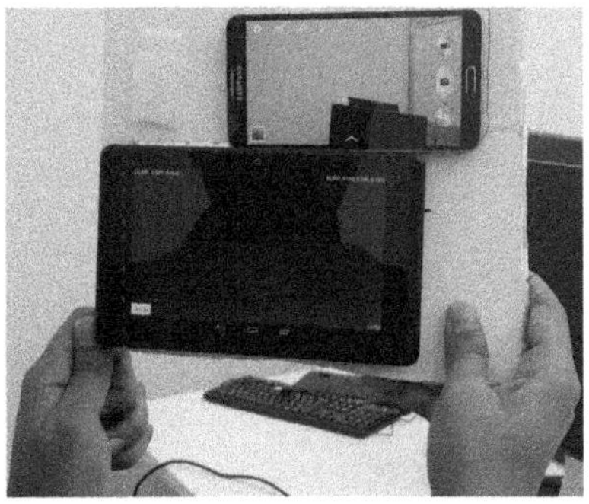

Figure 9: Tango connected with phone using double-backed tape and foam board.

The Tango prototype does not immediately provide all of the required data for VisualPrint. Practical limitations, due to Tango's unpolished beta status, complicate our implementation. Principally, when leveraging Tango visual-SLAM and depth mapping functionality, all visual sensing hardware is locked, and cannot be otherwise accessed by third party Tango (a form of Android) apps. We leverage area learning and depth perception to achieve an understanding of where a depth map exists in relation to others in the same indoor space. Unfortunately, Tango blocks access to the RGB camera when using these services. So, it is less straightforward to map a 3D depth estimate, projected into a shared indoor space via area learning, to a portion of an RGB image frame. Note that much of Tango exists in closed source, so we were not able to circumvent the hardware protections. While it is possible to grab the RGB screen buffer, this is too low resolution for our needs. Instead, we used a low-tech workaround: we taped a second Android device to the back of our Tango and created a simple network API to synchronously grab image frames in concert with Tango-recorded depth maps (see Figure 9). Of course, limited RGB access is not fundamental, and we expect this shortcoming to be addressed in the future. Figure 10 shows how we merge Tango-acquired depth data into RGB.

Challenge, Positioning Error and Uniqueness: Unfortunately, but unsurprisingly, there are inaccuracies in Tango's visual-SLAM positioning. As the user walks around, location estimates naturally reflect some amount of drift from true positions. While small amounts of positioning error might not cause undue harm to many potential Tango applications, for VisualPrint, this can be problematic. If two photographs appear to be of different objects (due to erroneous location estimates), truly-unique keypoints may appear to be repeated – a false negative for our uniqueness tracking. We resolve this issue by post-processing Tango's depth map output – a 3D *point cloud*. We apply iterative closest point (ICP) heuristics to merge Tango 3D depth maps (from separate snapshots) into a single coherent point cloud for the entire indoor space. Only from this converged, comprehensive depth map we can be sure that two keypoints reflect truly independent locations. This post processing also has a secondary advantage of reducing some error in our location estimates.

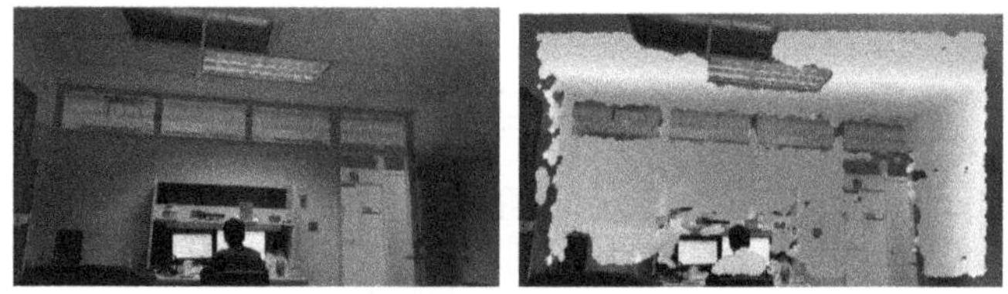

Figure 10: Tango RGB+depth: (a) original RGB image; (b) heat map of depth from observer, red is farther away.

Cloud Processing and 3D Positioning

VisualPrint cloud service accepts keypoint-to-3D position mappings from the Tango wardriving app. As they are received, the service updates two data structures: (1) the keypoint-to-3D position lookup tables and (2) LSH-indexed Boom filters for keypoint uniqueness.

The lookup table is really a large-scale image-based content retrieval table, as one might apply for reverse image search. For our prototype, we apply standard LSH. Rather than a reference to an image or other content, the LSH table stores the 3D position of the keypoint. The service accepts queries to this table in the form of keypoint-plus-2D coordinate pairs (the x, y coordinate of the keypoint in the camera frame). The service performs an LSH lookup on each keypoint to retrieve its 3D position. It then applies a localization step, described next, and returns the estimated client location and pose.

The second data structure, the LSH-indexed Bloom filter, is the same exact data structure downloaded by VisualPrint clients as the uniqueness oracle. As new keypoint-to-3D mapping arrives at the VisualPrint cloud service, we simply perform an LSH lookup followed by insertion to the primary and verification Bloom filters. With this simple design, new keypoint-to-location mappings can be incorporated continuously, in constant time and memory.

VisualPrint Application: Localization

For each client localization query, the cloud service retrieves the 3D position associated with each image keypoint. This is a straightforward query to a standard LSH-indexed lookup table. However, the retrieved 3D positions are only the first step towards localizing the client user. When combined with the 2D data of how the 3D position is perceived by the client device, it is possible to infer the clients 6-DoF camera pose, including translation (x, y, z) and orientation (yaw, pitch, roll). In the final effect, we achieve a similar positioning fidelity as Google Tango, but *with only a standard, 2D, RGB camera*. Unlike several approaches in prior art [28, 40, 44], VisualPrint achieves instantaneous localization – continuous tracking not required.

From a single image I, a client queries VisualPrint with a set of keypoints K. From the LSH-indexed lookup table, VisualPrint finds $|K| \cdot n$ nearest-neighbor matches (since there is uncertainty in the match), and accordingly $|K| \cdot n$ 3D points. On these points, VisualPrint applies spatial clustering to filter down to only those 3D points in the largest cluster P, discarding others. $K' \subseteq K$ keypoints remain, for $|P|$ 3D points, where $|K'| \leq |P| \leq |K'| \cdot n$. For each 3D point $p \in P$, there is a single corresponding keypoint $k^p \in K'$. We also know that k has a corresponding 2D pixel coordinate (x_p, y_p) in the original client query image I.

Figure 11 illustrates the spatial relationship between a VisualPrint client camera capturing an image I and the known 3D points corresponding to keypoints found in I. Assume the client's camera exists in 3D space at point A. B is at the center-right (along the edge) and C is at the center of the image. Therefore, $\angle CAB$ is half of the horizontal field-of-view of the camera. The diagram shows how one can calculate angles from A, w.r.t to the center C. Let (p_x, p_y) be the pixel coordinates of a keypoint P and γ_x be the angle $\angle CAP$ (P's projection on the x-axis). Using known 2D pixel coordinates $B = (width, height/2)$ and $C = (width/2, height/2)$, and the camera's field of view (FoV_h, FoV_v), we may estimate γ_x and γ_y.

Similarly, for a pair of keypoints P_0 and P_1, we may compute x-axis angles $\gamma_x(P_0)$, $\gamma_x(P_1)$, and y-axis angles $\gamma_y(P_0)$, $\gamma_y(P_1)$. Now, the x-axis angle between P_0 and P_1 is $\gamma_x(P_0) + \gamma_x(P_1)$, if P_0 and P_1 fall on opposite sides of C, or $|\gamma_x(P_0) - \gamma_x(P_1)|$ if they are on the same side. The same method applies for the y-axis angle.

From several such point pairs (in the same image), VisualPrint estimates the client's location in 3D. VisualPrint models this geometry as a nonlinear optimization. Figure 12 presents the objective function, constraints, variables, and parameters of the optimization.

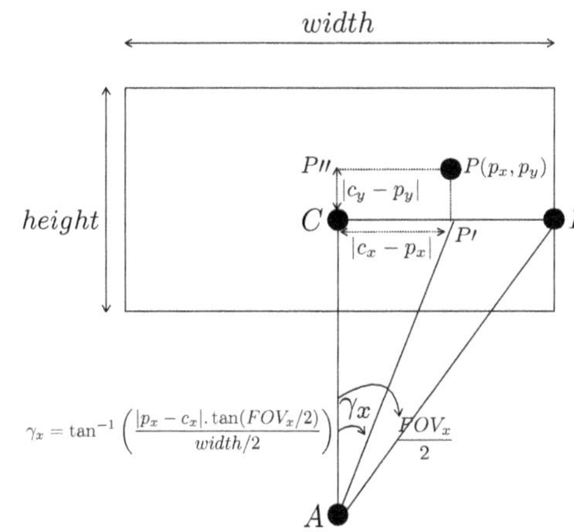

Figure 11: Geometry of angular separation from a keypoint P and the center of the screen C, respective to the 3D location of the client's camera at A. The angle $\angle CAP$ (called γ_x) is of interest – the angle from center to a projection of P along the x-axis. All expressions treat the distance of line segments $\overline{AC}$, $\overline{AP}$, and $\overline{AB}$ as unknown.

Client Android App

The client app serves as a proof of concept for our client library, intended to bring visual fingerprint matching to any application. The app demonstrates systems capabilities for realtime localization, based on visual features.

When launched for the first time, the app retrieves the current state of the uniqueness LSH Bloom filter ("oracle") from the cloud server. In our testing, this download is approximately 10MB, but may be more or less, varying with the number of unique keypoints on the server. Although the Bloom filters are of fixed size, we compress them with GZIP for efficient retrieval, and compressibility reduces as the Bloom filter becomes more saturated. The app periodically refreshes its copy of the Bloom filter to stay current with the server. We could reduce data transfer by sending only a compressed bitmask representing the diff between versions (not yet implemented).

Once ready, the app activates the smartphone camera. The app continuously extracts video frames. It performs a quick check on each frame to detect blur (often due to quick motion), discarding such frames. It also rejects frames when processing falls behind the realtime stream. That is, the app only processes extremely recent frames. For each frame passing all checks, the app extracts SIFT keypoints – up to several thousand per frame, depending on image content. The app then queries the uniqueness LSH Bloom filter for each keypoint. Recall that the primary Bloom filter is of the counting variety. Thus, uniqueness counts (up to the saturation point of 1024) yield a partial ordering, ranking keypoints from highly unique to common. The app then uploads several of the most unique keypoint de-

$$\begin{aligned}
\textbf{Minimize} \quad & \sum_{\forall i<j\in 1\ldots K} E^x_{ij} + E^y_{ij} \\
\textbf{Subject to} \quad & \\
\gamma^x_{ij} &= \gamma(p^x_i, C_x, F_h, W) - \gamma(p^x_j, C_x, F_h, W) \\
\gamma^y_{ij} &= \gamma(p^y_i, C_y, F_v, H) - \gamma(p^y_j, C_y, F_v, H) \\
\cos(\gamma^x_{ij} + E^x_{ij}) &= \frac{d(x,z,x_i,z_i) + d(x,z,x_j,z_j) - d(x_i,z_i,x_j,z_j)}{2\sqrt{d(x,z,x_i,z_i)}\sqrt{d(x,z,x_j,z_j)}} \\
\cos(\gamma^y_{ij} + E^y_{ij}) &= \frac{d(y,z,y_i,z_i) + d(y,z,y_j,z_j) - d(y_i,z_i,y_j,z_j)}{2\sqrt{d(y,z,y_i,z_i)}\sqrt{d((y,z,y_j,z_j)}} \\
\gamma(p,C,F,S) &= \tan^{-1}\left(\frac{|p-C|.\tan(F/2)}{S/2}\right) \\
d(x_1,y_1,x_2,y_2) &= (x_1-x_2)^2 + (y_1-y_2)^2 \\
\textbf{Solving for} \quad & \\
\forall i<j\in 1\ldots K \quad &: \quad x, y, z, E^x_{ij}, E^y_{ij} \\
\textbf{With parameters} \quad & \\
\forall i<j\in 1\ldots K \quad &: \quad p^x_i, p^y_i, p^x_j, p^y_j, x_i, y_i, z_i, x_j, y_j, z_j
\end{aligned}$$

Left Side	Interpretation
i, j	Keypoint indices, $i < j$.
γ^x_{ij}	Angle from keypoint i to j, projected on the x-axis.
$\cos(\gamma^x_{ij} + E^x_{ij})$	Geometric constraint derived from law of cosines.
$\gamma(p, C, F, S)$	Angle from client at A to keypoint, as a function of pixel location, image center, field of view, and side length (width or height).
$d(x_1, y_1, x_2, y_2)$	Square of Euclidean distance $(x_1, y_1) \leftrightarrow (x_2, y_2)$.
(x, y, z)	Optimized 3D coordinate of client (position A).
$E^x_{ij} + E^y_{ij}$	Minimized angular error between keypoints i, j.
(x_i, y_i, z_i)	Known 3D position of i.
(p^x_i, p^y_i)	Viewed 2D position of i.

Figure 12: Nonlinear optimization to estimate client camera position (x, y, z), as labeled "A" in the geometry shown by Figure 11. The optimization objective finds x, y, z where perceived angles $\gamma^x_{i,j}$ (on the X/Z plane) and $\gamma^y_{i,j}$ (Y/Z plane) between any keypoint pair i, j are most consistent with their corresponding known 3D locations at $x_i, y_i, z_i, x_j, y_j, z_j$. The objective minimizes summed residual error for all keypoint pairs.

scriptors (experiments with 200 and 500 are presented in the next section).

Upon receiving these unique keypoint descriptors, the cloud service performs the keypoint-to-3D client localization, returning the 3D camera pose estimate to the client. The app then displays the estimate on screen.

4. EVALUATION

Our evaluation considers these research questions:

1. *How does VisualPrint's accuracy compare with other image/keypoint matching schemes?* In particular, we compare VisualPrint to a BruteForce Euclidean distance match (implemented on GPU), a traditional LSH implementation (as would be typical of a large-scale reverse image search), and Random where we uniformly subsample image keypoints.
2. *Are client-side overheads acceptable?* How does VisualPrint reduce data upload compared to conventional cloud offload? Memory? Computation? and Energy?
3. *How effective is VisualPrint in enabling our example application: client localization?*

Matching Accuracy

We photographed 100 non-overlapping scenes across the three floors of our research facility, the Coordinated Science Lab (CSL). Each CSL floor is 50m × 10m in dimension. We captured each scene with a single image. We also capture 400 additional distractor images. These images consist of ceiling, floor, name-plates, furniture, etc. in the building. Since these images naturally contain repeated patterns, they are likely to have repeated visual features as well. For each of the 500 images, we use OpenCV's default SIFT implementation to extract features. Across these 500 images, the database contains a total of ≈2.5M feature descriptors (each descriptor is 128 bytes).

The query database consists of five additional photographs of each scene in the database. We systematically captured these five photograph from substantially different angles. As SIFT matching efficacy degrades substantially with angular separation, these diverse angles are intended to challenge all matching schemes.

The average number of features per query image was 3,500. From these keypoints, we evaluate VisualPrint across five different system regimes. Random picks 500 random keypoints from the query image and uploads them to the server for matching. Random can be understood as lower-bound on VisualPrint's performance (one with no intelligence in feature subselection). For VisualPrint-200 and VisualPrint-500, our complete system selects the 200 and 500 most unique keypoints. LSH applies the reference E^2LSH locality-sensitive hashing implementation for nearest-neighbor search. BruteForce finds the "optimal" nearest neighbor match. Note that unlike Random and VisualPrint-200/500, LSH and BruteForce use all image keypoints. Note that while it may be tempting to consider BruteForce an upper bound on accuracy, it can be misled by homogeneous keypoints across images.

Metrics: Let Y be the set of all processed query frames. Let $V \subset Y$ be the set of frames containing scene k. Let $P \subset Y$ be the set of frames identified by our system as capturing k. Then, $V \setminus P$ denotes our system's false negative predictions, $P \setminus V$ denotes false positive predictions, and $Y \setminus V$ denotes the set of frames which do not contain scene k. *We evaluate VisualPrint's prediction efficacy by the following metrics of information retrieval:*

Precision$_k$ $= |V \cap P|/|P|$
i.e., among all frames that VisualPrint identifies as capturing scene k, what fraction truly captures k.

Recall$_k$ $|V \cap P|/|V|$
i.e., among all frames that truly have capture scene k, what fraction was identified by VisualPrint.

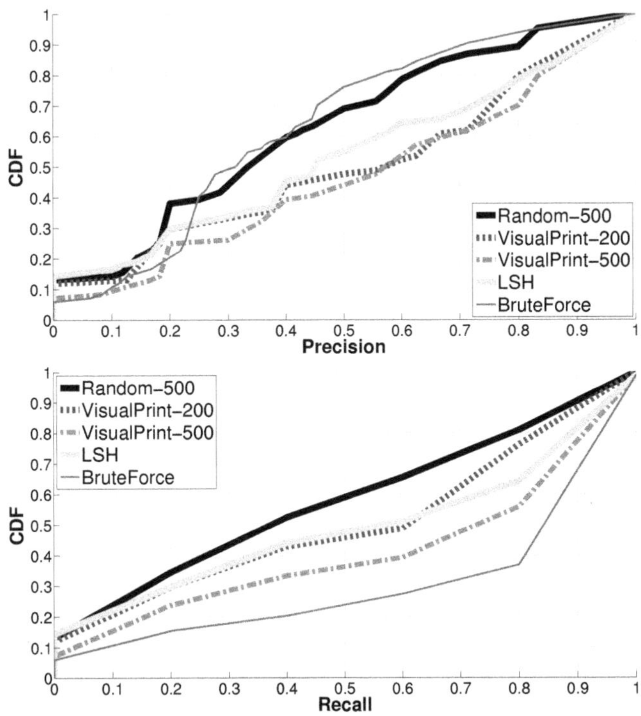

Figure 13: For precision/recall, our goal was for VisualPrint to be roughly comparable with a BruteForce approach — *true gains are measured in substantial network transfer savings*. Incidentally, VisualPrint's precision improves slightly over LSH and BruteForce, as VisualPrint automatically eliminates useless, distracting non-unique keypoints (homogeneous repetitions can lead to false positive matches). Recall suffers slightly against BruteForce (some additional false negatives due to some discarded-but-useful keypoints), but still surpasses LSH (the most realistic server-side comparison) and random keypoint subselection (strawman baseline).

Figure 13 presents CDF of (a) precision and (b) recall results. The precision and recall values are calculated per scene using the above definition. For example, 50% of the test scenes achieve precision > 58% and recall > 61% incase of VisualPrint-200. Unsurprisingly, Random performs poorly in both precision and recall. The results for BruteForce are more nuanced. BruteForce precision is poor, likely due to confusion among homogeneous keypoints. BruteForce recall is most favorable, likely some valuable keypoints are missed by VisualPrint, or it is able to differentiate even among homogeneous keypoints based on their relative quantities (the entire distribution is scored in the BruteForce heuristic). LSH performs comparably to VisualPrint-200, but is inferior to VisualPrint-500 – likely due to the same confusion-under-homogeneity afflicting BruteForce. Note that sole purpose of the precision and recall results is to make sure that VisualPrint does not compromise accuracy to gain bandwidth savings.

Client Overheads

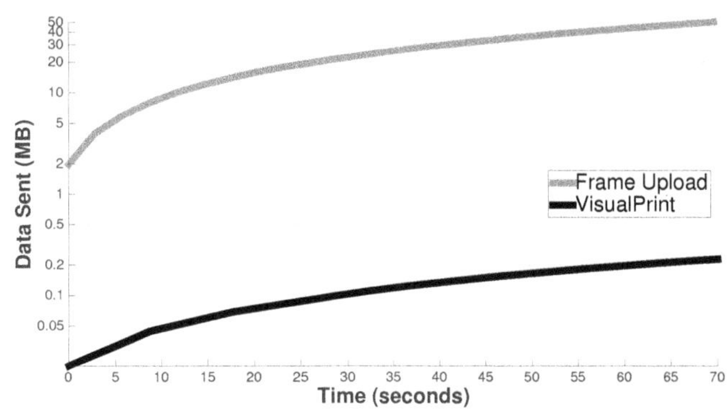

Figure 14: Cumulative data upload by execution time. VisualPrint reduces data consumption by at least one order of magnitude compared to raw frames (sending all raw keypoints would be more than frames, as shown in Figure 5).

Data Upload Savings: Figure 14 compares upload data for VisualPrint versus whole frame upload. Note that, as shown in Figure 5, uploading keypoints (even compressed) does not save any upload bandwidth since their size is comparable (often more) to that of the original frame.

Client Storage and Memory Overhead: Figure 15 compares the client-side storage/memory footprints of Random, VisualPrint, LSH, and BruteForce. Random requires effectively no memory (there is no index). VisualPrint has a substantial memory footprint, due to the Bloom filters. LSH has an extremely large memory footprint, much larger than the input data, due to multiple replications supporting multiple projections. BruteForce has a memory footprint comparable to the database size – here this is implemented on GPU as a SIMD matching

(CPU matching would be nonsensical due to extreme latency). It would be possible to reduce BruteForce memory footprint by loading the database in parts, but with a trade-off of excessive loading latency, rather than a one-time cost.

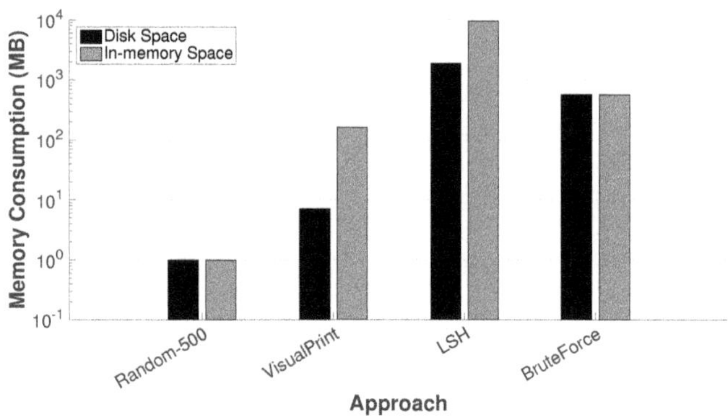

Figure 15: Client disk/memory consumption. VisualPrint uses substantially less memory than conventional LSH, which caches the entire image database. VisualPrint requires somewhat more memory than random keypoint subselection to maintain Bloom filters in memory. BruteForce memory consumption reflects loading all database keypoints into memory for a GPU SIMD parallel execution.

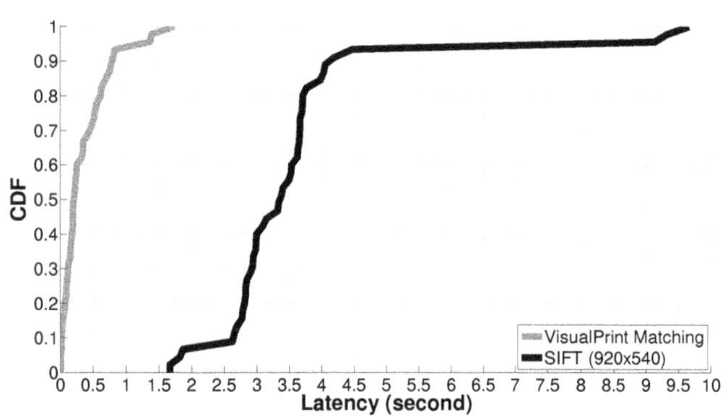

Figure 16: Computational overheads on Galaxy S6. VisualPrint requires an order of magnitude less computation than SIFT feature extraction. Ample room for end-to-end improvement by running SIFT on GPU or a coprocessor.

Client Computational Latency: Figure 16 presents a CDF of VisualPrint computational latency, as compared to SIFT feature extraction. Principally, VisualPrint latency is due to the LSH Bloom filter lookups for each keypoint descriptor, plus sorting. SIFT delay dominates over VisualPrint computation overhead.

Energy: All non-energy experiments were performed on the latest-generation Samsung Galaxy S6 phone. However, as the battery compartment of the S6 is not removable, we revert to the prior generation S5 phone for energy measurements (only). The measurement setup is shown in Figure 17. We use a Monsoon power monitor to measure the average power consumption of the phone. No additional applications apart from VisualPrint and required background services were running during the experiment. The phone was put on airplane mode to avoid cellular communications and WiFi was turned on for VisualPrint tests (only). As energy consumption is impacted by the number of extracted keypoints, lighting conditions and scene were kept same across all schemes. See Figure 18.

Figure 17: Experimental setup for energy measurement. Monsoon power meter provides current to Galaxy S5 phone in place of battery. Measurement at 5,000 Hz.

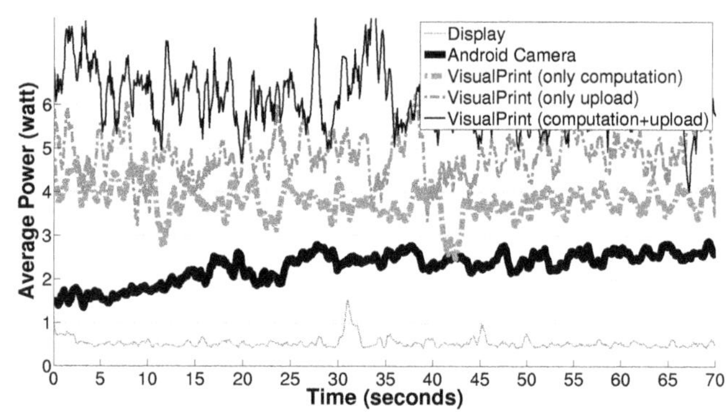

Figure 18: Energy. Including display and camera, complete VisualPrint ≈ 6.5 W. Not shown: whole-frame cloud offload ≈ 4.9 W. Energy consumption of our current prototype is unacceptable but avenues for substantial improvement exist. SIFT and Bloom filter operations can be highly-parallelized using GPU. When using GPU, the processor is occupied for short time, can lead to significant energy savings [36].

Localization

We test VisualPrint's localization performance in three indoor environments: an office space, employee cafeteria, and grocery store. The office environment consisted of similar looking cubicles, a kitchen area, and lounge. In the office, we wardrive a rectangular space of approximate dimensions 50m × 20m. The cafeteria consists of many identical chairs and tables, food menu boards, foodservice and checkout counters, and registers in a 50m × 15m room. The grocery store (80m × 50m) had standard aisle based layout, filled with household items.

During wardriving, the Tango was mounted with a phone (Galaxy Note 3) as shown in Figure 9. During query phase, a different phone (Galaxy S6) was used to take photographs, in arbitrary orientations. We use Tango to collect a "ground-truth" reference to compare query results. Wardriving and query data were collected along similar routes.

Figure 19 shows cumulative localization errors. Figure 20 isolates those errors to X, Y, and, Z directions. While localization is generally quite accurate, some failure cases do occur. We believe that most cases of substandard performance may be attributed to suboptimality at local minima (we solve the localization optimization using a time-bounded differential evolution).

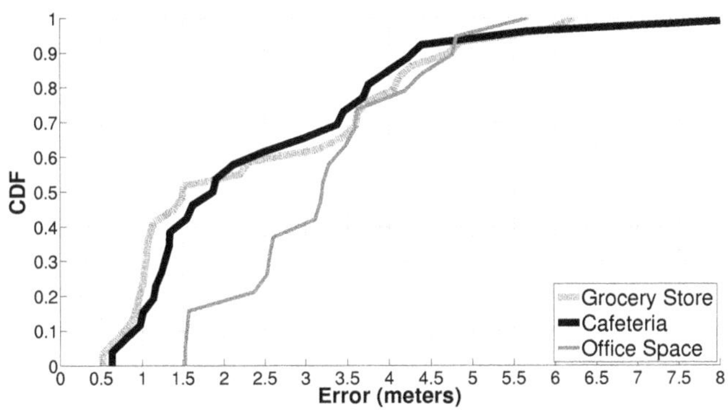

Figure 19: CDF of 3D localization error. Graph shows 3D distance from "ground truth" (as estimated from Google Tango), to VisualPrint's estimate on Galaxy S6.

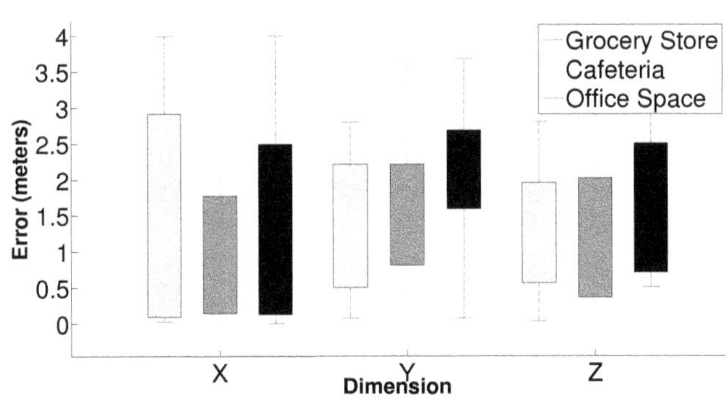

Figure 20: Localization accuracy by dimension. Localization on the horizontal X/Y plane (parallel to floor and ceiling) is more accurate than vertically (changes in elevation). This is expected, as the wardriving motion is also along the X/Y plane.

Evaluation Takeaways

The key findings of our evaluation are as follows:

1. VisualPrint precision and recall are roughly comparable to LSH, the parent scheme on which it is based (Figure 13).
2. VisualPrint requires $1/10^{th}$ bandwidth of whole frame uploads, only 51.2 KB oppose to 523 KB (Figure 14).
3. Based on our 2.5M descriptor database, the VisualPrint client uses 10.5 MB disk space for Bloom filters, stored compressed – $1/124^{th}$ of the server side LSH indices compressed (1.3 GB).
4. Based on our 2.5M descriptor database, the VisualPrint client requires 162 MB in RAM uncompressed – $1/58^{th}$ of the LSH indices uncompressed (9.4 GB), cached in RAM by the server.
5. Client compute latency consists of SIFT extraction (3300 ms at median) and Bloom filter lookups (217 ms at median) for a total median compute latency of 3547 ms, dominated by SIFT (Figure 16). However, using [36], upto 7x latency reduction is possible by running SIFT extraction on a mobile GPU or a coprocessor.
6. Client energy consumption is substantial (6.5 W), principally due to camera and local computation, especially SIFT feature extraction (Figure 18). Again, using [36], upto 87% of the SIFT computation energy can be saved.
7. Results show VisualPrint has a median 3D localization error of 2.5 m (Figure 19).

5. LIMITATIONS AND DISCUSSION

Several practical limitations are apparent from our evaluation of VisualPrint. Principally, SIFT keypoint extraction incurs substantial compute overhead, yielding a large energy impact. Secondly, any visual fingerprinting scheme will incur a large energy cost, simply from turning on the camera. Fundamentally, VisualPrint could never be energy-competitive with lighter-weight sensory approaches.

VisualPrint should also not be taken as a replacement for traditional localization schemes. Rather it is an attempt to leverage visual data when it is anyways available (i.e., the camera is already turned on). Due to its visual nature, VisualPrint cannot always return precise user location. It can fail due to: (1) a lack of ample features in the query image, such as hallway with white walls; (2) insufficient wardriving – the environment at a location may not be well fingerprinted, causing image matching to fail; (3) false positives in keypoint matching – some environmental repetition might not be captured during wardriving; and (4) dead reckoning errors during wardriving – Tango uses IR depth sensing and IMU to track user location, which are prone to errors (especially, in environments with natural sunlight or electromagnetic machinery).

From a cursory look, VisualPrint appears to be SIFT specific; mostly due to the techniques based on LSH and Bloom filter. However, this is not a fundamental systems limitation. Keypoint detection and description are two separate stages in computer vision. One can use any keypoint detection algorithm (e.g., SURF [13]) with another integer keypoint description algorithm without modification in the system pipeline. In the cases where floating point descriptors are desired, one can scale floating point descriptor elements to the integers by multiplying with an order of required decimal precision.

6. CONCLUSION

Environmental fingerprint is a powerful primitive for mobile vision and augmented reality applications. However, the identification of visual fingerprints is challenging from a perspective of data storage, indexing, and retrieval. Cloud offload presents an obvious-if-challenging solution. VisualPrint enables selective cloud offload of only those visual fingerprints that carry the greatest global entropy – those that are highly unique, particular to the user's true location. Beyond visual fingerprints, we believe that the VisualPrint approach can be productively reapplied in other high-dimensional sensory domains, such as wireless RF, auditory, and hyperspectral signatures. We consider these in our ongoing research.

7. ACKNOWLEDGMENTS

We sincerely thank our many volunteers, Dr. Ganesh Ananthanarayanan our shepherd, as well the anonymous reviewers for their invaluable feedback. We are also grateful to Intel, Google, and NSF for partially funding this research through the grant NSF 1430064.

8. REFERENCES

[1] Amazon fire phone. https://developer.amazon.com/public/solutions/devices/fire-phone.

[2] Dextro stream. https://www.dextro.co/.

[3] Microsoft hololens. https://www.microsoft.com/microsoft-hololens/en-us.

[4] Nest cam. https://nest.com/camera/meet-nest-cam/.

[5] Oculus vr. https://www.oculus.com/en-us/.

[6] Project tango. https://www.google.com/atap/projecttango/.

[7] Meerkat: Live stream video. http://meerkatapp.co/.

[8] Periscope: Explore the world through someone else's eyes. https://www.periscope.tv/.

[9] P. F. Alcantarilla, A. Bartoli, and A. J. Davison. Kaze features. In *ECCV*. Springer, 2012.

[10] A. Andoni and P. Indyk. E2lsh: Exact euclidean locality-sensitive hashing, 2004.

[11] P. Bahl and V. N. Padmanabhan. Radar: An in-building rf-based user location and tracking system. In *INFOCOM*. IEEE, 2000.

[12] X. Bao, S. Fan, A. Varshavsky, K. Li, and R. Roy Choudhury. Your reactions suggest you liked the movie: Automatic content rating via reaction sensing. In *UbiComp*. ACM, 2013.

[13] H. Bay, A. Ess, T. Tuytelaars, and L. Van Gool. Speeded-up robust features (surf). *Computer vision and image understanding*, 110(3):346–359, 2008.

[14] E. Cuervo, A. Balasubramanian, D.-k. Cho, A. Wolman, S. Saroiu, R. Chandra, and P. Bahl. Maui: making smartphones last longer with code offload. In *MobiSys*. ACM, 2010.

[15] M. Datar, N. Immorlica, P. Indyk, and V. S. Mirrokni. Locality-sensitive hashing scheme based on p-stable distributions. In *Proceedings of the twentieth annual symposium on Computational geometry*. ACM, 2004.

[16] J. Fung and S. Mann. Openvidia: parallel gpu computer vision. In *MM*. ACM, 2005.

[17] M. Gong and Y.-H. Yang. Near real-time reliable stereo matching using programmable graphics hardware. In *CVPR*. IEEE, 2005.

[18] S. Hodges, L. Williams, E. Berry, S. Izadi, J. Srinivasan, A. Butler, G. Smyth, N. Kapur, and K. Wood. Sensecam: A retrospective memory aid. In *UbiComp*. Springer, 2006.

[19] W. Hu, B. Amos, Z. Chen, K. Ha, W. Richter, P. Pillai, B. Gilbert, J. Harkes, and M. Satyanarayanan. The case for offload shaping. In *HotMobile*. ACM, 2015.

[20] Y. Hua, B. Xiao, B. Veeravalli, and D. Feng. Locality-sensitive bloom filter for approximate membership query. *Computers, IEEE Transactions on*, 61(6):817–830, 2012.

[21] P. Jain, J. Manweiler, A. Acharya, and K. Beaty. Focus: clustering crowdsourced videos by line-of-sight. In *SenSys*, page 8. ACM, 2013.

[22] P. Jain, J. Manweiler, and R. Roy Choudhury. Overlay: Practical mobile augmented reality. In *MobiSys*. ACM, 2015.

[23] N. Karlsson, E. Di Bernardo, J. Ostrowski, L. Goncalves, P. Pirjanian, and M. E. Munich. The vslam algorithm for robust localization and mapping. In *ICRA*. IEEE, 2005.

[24] R. Kemp, N. Palmer, T. Kielmann, and H. Bal. Cuckoo: a computation offloading framework for smartphones. In *Mobile Computing, Applications, and Services*. Springer, 2012.

[25] A. Kirsch and M. Mitzenmacher. Distance-sensitive bloom filters. In *ALENEX*, volume 6. SIAM, 2006.

[26] K. Kumar and Y.-H. Lu. Cloud computing for mobile users: Can offloading computation save energy? *Computer*, (4):51–56, 2010.

[27] K. Lee, J. Lee, Y. Yi, I. Rhee, and S. Chong. Mobile data offloading: how much can wifi deliver? In *CoNext*, page 26. ACM, 2010.

[28] L. Li, P. Hu, C. Peng, G. Shen, and F. Zhao. Epsilon: A visible light based positioning system. In *NSDI*. USENIX Association, 2014.

[29] R. LiKamWa, Y. Liu, N. D. Lane, and L. Zhong. Moodscope: Building a mood sensor from smartphone usage patterns. In *MobiSys*. ACM, 2013.

[30] R. LiKamWa, B. Priyantha, M. Philipose, L. Zhong, and P. Bahl. Energy characterization and optimization of image sensing toward continuous mobile vision. In *MobiSys*. ACM, 2013.

[31] Y. Lin, F. Lv, S. Zhu, M. Yang, T. Cour, K. Yu, L. Cao, and T. Huang. Large-scale image classification: fast feature extraction and svm training. In *CVPR*. IEEE, 2011.

[32] D. G. Lowe. Object recognition from local scale-invariant features. In *ICCV*, volume 2. Ieee, 1999.

[33] B. D. Lucas, T. Kanade, et al. An iterative image registration technique with an application to stereo vision. In *IJCAI*, volume 81, 1981.

[34] Q. Lv, W. Josephson, Z. Wang, M. Charikar, and K. Li. Multi-probe lsh: efficient indexing for high-dimensional similarity search. In *VLDB*. VLDB Endowment, 2007.

[35] G. Papagiannakis, G. Singh, and N. Magnenat-Thalmann. A survey of mobile and wireless technologies for augmented reality systems. *Computer Animation and Virtual Worlds*, 2008.

[36] B. Rister, G. Wang, M. Wu, and J. R. Cavallaro. A fast and efficient sift detector using the mobile gpu. In *ICASSP*. IEEE, 2013.

[37] E. Rublee, V. Rabaud, K. Konolige, and G. Bradski. Orb: an efficient alternative to sift or surf. In *ICCV*. IEEE, 2011.

[38] T. Sattler, B. Leibe, and L. Kobbelt. Fast image-based localization using direct 2d-to-3d matching. In *ICCV*. IEEE, 2011.

[39] M. Satyanarayanan, P. Bahl, R. Caceres, and N. Davies. The case for vm-based cloudlets in mobile computing. *Pervasive Computing, IEEE*, 8(4):14–23, 2009.

[40] S. Sen, J. Lee, K.-H. Kim, and P. Congdon. Avoiding multipath to revive inbuilding wifi localization. In *MobiSys*. ACM, 2013.

[41] C. Silpa-Anan and R. Hartley. Optimised kd-trees for fast image descriptor matching. In *CVPR*. IEEE, 2008.

[42] G. Takacs, V. Chandrasekhar, N. Gelfand, Y. Xiong, W.-C. Chen, T. Bismpigiannis, R. Grzeszczuk, K. Pulli, and B. Girod. Outdoors augmented reality on mobile phone using loxel-based visual feature organization. In *ICMR*. ACM, 2008.

[43] B. Triggs, P. F. McLauchlan, R. I. Hartley, and A. W. Fitzgibbon. Bundle adjustment a modern synthesis. In *Vision algorithms: theory and practice*. Springer, 2000.

[44] H. Wang, S. Sen, A. Elgohary, M. Farid, M. Youssef, and R. R. Choudhury. No need to war-drive: unsupervised indoor localization. In *MobiSys*. ACM, 2012.

[45] Z. Zhang, R. Deriche, O. Faugeras, and Q.-T. Luong. A robust technique for matching two uncalibrated images through the recovery of the unknown epipolar geometry. *Artificial intelligence*, 78(1):87–119, 1995.

D-Watch: Embracing "bad" Multipaths for Device-Free Localization with COTS RFID Devices

Ju Wang[†], Jie Xiong[♯], Hongbo Jiang[‡], Xiaojiang Chen[†], Dingyi Fang[†]
[†]Northwest University; [♯]Singapore Management University;
[‡]Huazhong University of Science and Technology
[†]{wangju,xjchen,dyf}@nwu.edu.cn, [♯]jxiong@smu.edu.sg,[‡]hongbojiang2004@gmail.com

ABSTRACT

Device-free localization, which does not require any device attached to the target is playing a critical role in many applications such as intrusion detection, elderly monitoring, etc. This paper introduces D-Watch, a device-free system built on top of low cost commodity-off-the-shelf (COTS) RFID hardware. Unlike previous works which consider multipaths detrimental, D-Watch leverages the "bad" multipaths to provide a decimeter-level localization accuracy without offline training. D-Watch harnesses the angle-of-arrival (AoA) information from the RFID tags' backscatter signals. The key intuition is that whenever a target blocks a signal's propagation path, the signal power experiences a drop which can be accurately captured by the proposed novel P-MUSIC algorithm. The wireless phase calibration scheme proposed does not interrupt the ongoing communication. Real-world experiments demonstrate the effectiveness of D-Watch. In a rich-multipath library environment, D-Watch can localize a human target at a median accuracy of 16.5 cm. In a table area of 2 m×2 m, D-Watch can track a user's fist at a median accuracy of 5.8 cm. D-Watch is capable of localizing multiple targets which is well known to be challenging in passive localization.

Categories and Subject Descriptors

C.2.1 [**Computer-Communication Networks**]: Network Architecture and Design– *Wireless communication*

Keywords

Device-Free Localization; AoA; MUSIC; Multipath

CoNEXT'16, December 12-15, 2016, Irvine, CA, USA

© 2016 ACM. ISBN 978-1-4503-4292-6/16/12...$15.00

DOI: http://dx.doi.org/10.1145/2999572.2999589

1. INTRODUCTION

While GPS localization has gained a huge success in outdoor environment, we witnessed an ever-increasing roll-out of indoor location-based applications such as shop navigation [31, 38], augmented reality [58, 20] and room occupancy detection [40] in recent years. Diverse technologies have been explored for localization purposes including infrared [21, 19], camera [28, 30], acoustic [14, 56], visible light [25, 26], Wi-Fi [53, 22, 23, 49], RFID [45, 45, 46, 55, 18], etc. Among all the technologies, radio frequency (RF)-based localization is considered most promising due to its ubiquitousness and low cost. In particular, RFID is evolving as a major candidate for identifying and tracking objects in indoor environment [13]. It is no exaggeration to say that we are almost surrounded by RFID tags in our daily lives. These tags are widely used in the bus cards, car keys, clothing security tags, etc. One main reason for this widespread deployment is the simplicity of the tags and the extremely low cost (each tag costs 5–10 cents USD).

The RF-based localization schemes can be further categorized into device-based [53, 22, 23, 45, 46, 52, 50] and device-free [47, 7, 8, 55, 49, 27]. The device-based schemes require the target to be equipped with a device or attached with a tag capable of emitting or reflecting RF signals. However, device-based localization is not applicable in some scenarios. In intruder detection, the targets will deliberately discard any device that can be tracked. In elderly care, old people are usually reluctant [55] to hold mobile devices, wear wearables or be attached with RFID tags. These real-life scenarios motive the needs of device-free localization which does not require any device to be attached to the target. On the other hand, device-free localization is usually more challenging as the weak reflected signals are employed for localization. For example, RFID adopts backscattering strategy for communication and the signal backscattered from the RFID tag is relatively weak. If the backscattered signal gets reflected again from the human target, it becomes extremely weak and it is difficult to retrieve this subtle signal for localization. Also multi-target tracking is not a problem for device-based

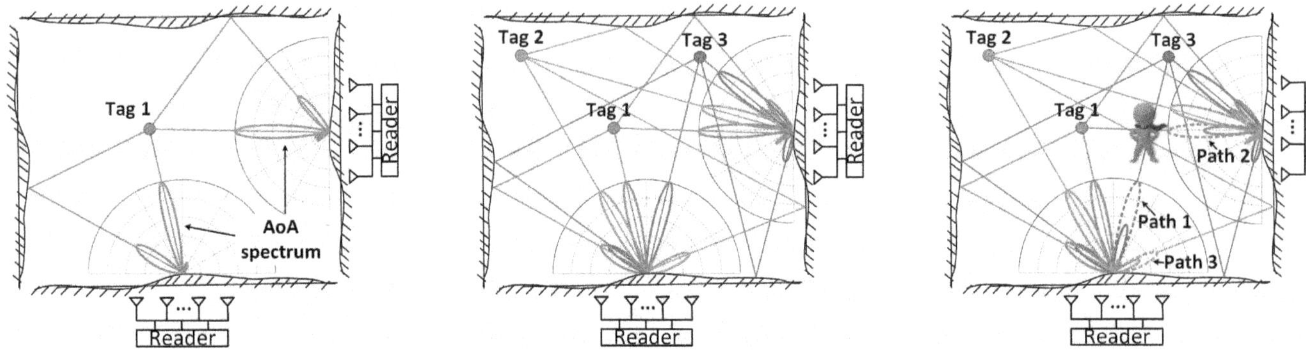

(a) One tag deployed. (b) Three tags deployed. (c) 3 paths are blocked by a target.

Figure 1: Illustration of the basic idea of D-Watch.

localization but becomes challenging for device-free systems as the reflected signals from multiple targets are all mixed together.

Most RF-based device-free systems [18, 10, 57, 49] employ the received signal strength indicator (RSSI) or channel state information (CSI) for localization which are coarse in accuracy and require labour intensive offline training to obtain the fingerprint database. The fingerprints also need to be updated if there are changes in the environment such as furniture movements, making these systems less realistic for real-life deployment. RSSI/CSI model-based schemes [33, 48, 54, 44] are proposed later to mitigate the fingerprint collection load but suffer from low accuracy in rich-multipath environments. In recent years, motivated by the radar array system [40, 53, 17], AoA-based schemes [8, 55, 47, 58] become popular with the opportunity of multiple antennas attached to a single Wi-Fi access point (AP) or an RFID reader. Wi-Fi APs nowadays are usually equipped with an antenna array due to the adoption of MIMO technology [24] in the latest 802.11n and 802.11ac standards. In order to increase the transmission range and accordingly the coverage area, the commodity RFID readers also have multiple antenna ports [46, 5]. The AoA-based schemes are able to achieve a high accuracy without labour intensive offline training. However, one major challenge for the success of AoA-based schemes is the identification of the LoS direct path. This is critical as there are usually rich multipaths indoors and only the direct path signal bouncing off the target contains the true angle information of the target. The multipaths are considered detrimental and several works [7, 8, 55] have been proposed to identify or remove these "bad" multipaths.

This paper introduces D-Watch, the first RFID-based device-free localization system that efficiently leverages the "bad" multipath signals to provide decimeter level accuracy. D-Watch is built on the COTS RFID hardware. To locate the target, D-Watch employs the AoA spectrum as shown in Fig. 1(a) and monitors the AoA peak changes to detect the angle information of the target. Specifically, if a target blocks a signal propagation path between the reader and the tag, the corresponding AoA peak will experience a drop. By monitoring the peak amplitude changes on the AoA spectrum, D-Watch can identify the target's angle information without any tag attached to the target, like a "direction-watcher (D-Watch)". We then combine the angle information from at least two non-collinear readers to localize the target by the triangulation method.

To further illustrate D-Watch's basic idea, Fig. 1 shows a toy example with two readers and three tags. We can see in Fig. 1(b) that the number of signal paths increases rapidly with two more tags added. When there is a human target in the area, D-Watch localizes the target as illustrated in Fig. 1(c). Specifically, multiple corresponding peaks on the AoA spectra are decreased when the target blocks path 1, path 2 and path 3. By rejecting the wrong angle from path 3 as we will discuss in Section 4.3, D-watch is able to localize the target with the other two paths.

D-Watch efficiently utilizes both the direct path and the reflection paths to identify the angle information of the target. With rich multipaths in indoor environment, D-Watch increases the coverage area significantly, so the deployment density can be well reduced. Further, D-Watch does not need to know the RFID tags' locations so the tags can be randomly placed with a high degree of flexibility. D-Watch only requires baseline AoA measurements between tags and readers, which take a few seconds compared with hours measuring and updating the RSS/CSI signatures at all possible locations in existing fingerprint-based location systems.

Though the basic idea sounds straightforward, it is non-trivial to realize D-Watch in practice due to the following challenges:

- **Phase calibration:** accurate AoA estimation is highly dependent on the signal's phase value measured at each antenna. However, each radio front end has a random phase offset introduced by the internal oscillator. This random phase offset needs to be carefully addressed before correct AoA information can be obtained. ArrayTrack [51] proposed a wired calibration method by injecting the same signals to the RF front ends with the help of a splitter. However, the wired calibration scheme requires human intervention to plug/unplug the antennas which is time consuming and interrupts the ongoing communication.

- **Signal power estimation of each path:** the signal power of a certain path can not be estimated accurately with the well-known MUSIC algorithm [34] widely used for AoA estimation. The peak amplitude on an AoA spectrum estimated by MUSIC is a probability function [34] and does not have a clear linear relationship with the signal power. When one path is blocked, more than one peak on the MUSIC spectrum may get changed, resulting in a false positive detection. When multiple paths are blocked, MUSIC may only detect one path and miss the other blocked paths.

To deal with the above challenges, we propose a new wireless phase calibration scheme. Compared to the existing methods [51, 37], the proposed scheme does not interrupt the ongoing data communication and runs automatically without the requirement of human intervention. The basic idea is that the estimated AoA angle will match the true angle if the random phase offsets are removed correctly. By deploying tags with known direct path angles and treating the random phase offsets as unknowns, we can compose enough constraint equations to determine the random phase offsets.

We further propose a novel power MUSIC (P-MUSIC) algorithm, which reserves the AoA estimation capability of the traditional MUSIC and incorporates the signal power estimation capability so both the path angle and path signal power can be obtained at the same time. The key intuition behind P-MUSIC's power estimation is that it applies different weights to the signals received at each antenna so the desired signals at a specific direction add constructively, whereas the signals along other directions add randomly. This alignment boosts the power at the desired direction and averages out the signals along other directions to a small value so the signal power at a specific direction can then be estimated.

We build a prototype of D-Watch using four Impinj readers [5] and 21 Alien tags [1]. We evaluate the localization performance in three typical indoor environments: a library, a laboratory and an empty hall corresponding to high, medium and low multipath environment, respectively. D-Watch is able to achieve a median localization accuracy of 16.5 cm for a human target in the rich-multipath library environment. For a smaller scale deployment, D-Watch is able to perform fine-grained tracking of a user's fist passively at a median accuracy of 5.8 cm. D-Watch also moves one step further to localize multiple targets simultaneously which is well known to be challenging for passive localization. D-Watch is able to localize three glass bottles at the same time at a maximum error of 17.2 cm as long as they are separated by at least 20 cm from each other.

Contributions: The main contributions of this paper are summarized as follows:

- D-Watch is the first device-free RFID system that efficiently utilizes the "bad" multipaths for localization. D-Watch does not require labour intensive offline training nor needs to know the RFID tags' locations, making D-Watch a promising candidate for real life large scale deployments.
- The proposed wireless phase calibration scheme operates without reliance on human intervention. It outperforms the state-of-the-art wireless calibration method and does not interrupt the ongoing communication.
- We propose a novel P-MUSIC algorithm, which does not only capture the angle information as the traditional MUSIC algorithm does but also obtains the signal power information of each path.
- D-Watch is implemented on COTS RFID hardware and comprehensive experiments demonstrate the effectiveness of the system. D-Watch can be easily extended to Wi-Fi and other RF-based systems for localization and tracking purposes.

Paper outline: We introduce the background and challenges in Section 2 and Section 3. We detail D-Watch's design in Section 4. The implementation is described in Section 5 followed by the evaluation in Section 6. The related work is in Section 7. We discuss some related issues in Section 8 and conclude our work in Section 9.

2. BACKGROUND

In this section, we introduce the technical background of RFID and MUSIC algorithm.

2.1 RFID System

An RFID system usually consists of a reader and multiple tags. Tags have no internal battery, so they harvest energy purely from the reader's signal and reply to the reader with a modulated backscatter signal. Typically, a COTS reader is connected to multiple antennas to increase the coverage range. For example, the Impinj xArray reader [5] has 52 antennas and covers more than 139 m^2 space with a price of 2000 USD.

Two points about RFID system are particularly relevant to the device-free localization. First, an RFID tag is extremely cheap at a cost of 5–10 cents USD. RFID reader is relatively expensive (the price [2] of the ThingMagic reader is around 450 USD and the general purpose Impinj R420 reader is around 1200 USD). R420 is relatively expensive because of the HTTP/TCP server function which is not used in our localization system. One R420 reader has four RF port and is capable of being connected to multiple antennas serving many RFID tags so the price is well amortized. RFID-based localization system is thus a promising candidate for large-scale deployments in cargo transportation, retailing and warehouse. Second, the communication range of RFID today is significantly increased to more than 10 meters [5, 45]. Major RFID manufacturers are competing to increase the range [46] and we expect the range

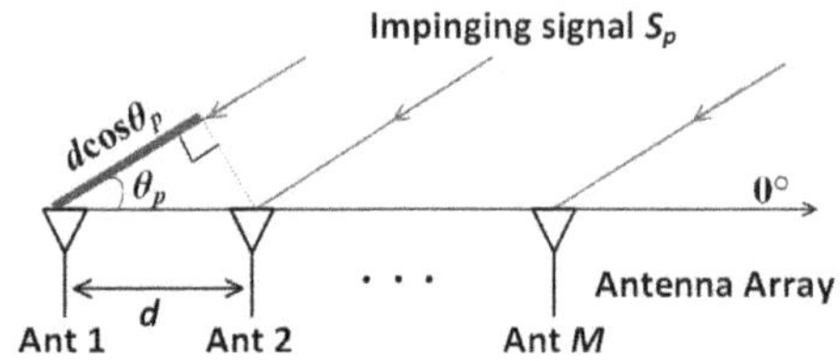

Figure 2: Phase changes are different when a signal arrives at different antennas of a linear array.

to continue growing in the next few years.

2.2 AoA and MUSIC

AoA information. When an RF signal propagates in the air, the phase keeps rotating and one wavelength of distance corresponds to a 2π phase rotation. The basic idea of AoA estimation is to measure the signal phase difference at antennas [32] due to different propagation distances. For example in Fig. 2, the adjacent antennas are placed with a space of $d = \lambda/2$ in between, where λ is wavelength. A signal arrives at the antennas along direction θ_p. If the phase measurements at the first two antennas are ϕ_1 and ϕ_2, we can then estimate the AoA θ_p as:

$$\theta_p = \arccos(\frac{\lambda \cdot |\phi_1 - \phi_2|}{2\pi \cdot d}) = \arccos(\frac{|\phi_1 - \phi_2|}{\pi}). \quad (1)$$

AoA estimation by MUSIC. In reality, Equation (1) does not work because of the multipath signals. MUSIC [34] algorithm is employed for multipath signal AoA estimation. Consider a uniform linear array with M antennas where the first antenna is taken as the reference antenna as shown in Fig. 2. P signals $S = [s_1, s_2, \cdots, s_P]^T$ arrive at the array at directions of $\Theta = [\theta_1, \theta_2, \cdots, \theta_P]$. Since the signals are all mixed, the measured signal x_m at "antenna m" can be expressed as:

$$x_m = \sum_{p=1}^{P} s_p \cdot e^{-j \cdot \omega(m, \theta_p)}, \quad (2)$$

where $\omega(m, \theta_p) = (m-1)\frac{2\pi d}{\lambda} cos(\theta_p)$. The measured signal vector $\mathbf{X} = [x_1, x_2, \cdots, x_M]^T$ at the array is:

$$\mathbf{X} = \mathbf{AS} + \mathbf{n}, \quad (3)$$

where $\mathbf{n}$ is noise, $\mathbf{A} = [\mathbf{a}(\theta_1), \cdots, \mathbf{a}(\theta_p), \cdots, \mathbf{a}(\theta_P)]$ is the steering matrix and $\mathbf{a}(\theta_p)$ is an $M \times 1$ steering vector:

$$\mathbf{a}(\theta_p) = [1, e^{-j \cdot \omega(2, \theta_p)}, \cdots, e^{-j \cdot \omega(M, \theta_p)}]^T, \quad (4)$$

where $(\cdot)^T$ denotes the transpose operation.

MUSIC is based on eigenstructure analysis of the signal vector's correlation matrix $\mathbf{R}$. Based on (3), the correlation matrix $\mathbf{R}$ can be expressed as:

$$\mathbf{R} = \mathbb{E}[\mathbf{X}\mathbf{X}^H] = \mathbf{A}\mathbb{E}[\mathbf{S}\mathbf{S}^H]\mathbf{A}^H + \sigma^2\mathbf{I}, \quad (5)$$

where $(\cdot)^H$ denotes the Hermitian transpose operation, $\mathbb{E}[\mathbf{S}\mathbf{S}^H]$ is the source correlation matrix. The array correlation matrix $\mathbf{R}$ has M eigenvalues $\lambda_1, \cdots, \lambda_M$ associated with M eigenvectors $\mathbf{U} = [\mathbf{u}_1, \cdots, \mathbf{u}_M]$. The largest P eigenvalues correspond to the P incoming signals while the rest $Q = M - P$ correspond to the noise. We choose P value based on how many eigenvalues are larger than a threshold and considered signals. Based on this process, the corresponding eigenvectors in $\mathbf{U}$ can be classified as signal and noise parts:

$$\mathbf{U} = [\mathbf{U}_S, \mathbf{U}_N] = [\underbrace{\mathbf{u}_1, \cdots, \mathbf{u}_P}_{\mathbf{U}_S}, \underbrace{\mathbf{u}_{P+1}, \cdots, \mathbf{u}_M}_{\mathbf{U}_N}]. \quad (6)$$

We refer to $\mathbf{U}_S$ as the *signal subspace* and $\mathbf{U}_N$ as the *noise subspace*. Due to the orthogonality between the signal steering vector and noise subspace [34], we have:

$$\mathbf{a}(\theta)^H \mathbf{U}_N = \mathbf{0}, \quad (7)$$

when $\theta = \theta_1, \cdots, \theta_P$. Accordingly, the AoA spectrum of MUSIC is given as:

$$B(\theta_p) = \frac{1}{\mathbf{a}^H(\theta_p)\mathbf{U}_N\mathbf{U}_N^H\mathbf{a}(\theta_p)}, \quad (8)$$

which yields sharp peaks at the each signal's AoA.

3. CHALLENGE AND VERIFICATION

We discuss the challenges in detail and employ benchmark experiments to validate our claims in this section.

3.1 Phase Calibration

Accurate AoA estimations are the key part of our localization system. The AoA estimations are highly dependent on the accurate phase measurements. However, a reader's RF front ends introduce random phase offsets into the phase measurements. To examine the amount of phase offsets introduced, we conduct an empirical study over the 16 RF ports on four Impinj R420 readers, with 4 RF ports on each reader. We deploy one tag and one antenna with clear LoS path. The antenna is connected to the 16 RF ports via a same RF cable one by one and the phase measurements are recorded. We select the first RF port as the reference and calculate the phase offsets for the other 15 RF ports. Fig. 3 shows the measured phase offsets ranging from $-85.9°$ to $176°$. These offsets are very random and need to be removed in order to achieve reliable AoA estimates. Traditional calibration methods, such as ArrayTrack [51], Argos [37] and Phaser [17], though being able to obtain the phase offsets, require human intervention and take minutes to complete. What is worse, these methods interrupt the ongoing data communication.

3.2 Limitation of Power Estimation

D-Watch detects the target's direction by observing an obvious signal power reduction when the target blocks the signal path. Thus, an accurate path power change detection is critical for D-Watch's localization. However, the signal power of each path can not be estimated accurately with the well-known MUSIC algorithm [35]. The AoA spectrum estimated by MUSIC is a probability function [34] and the peak amplitude does not

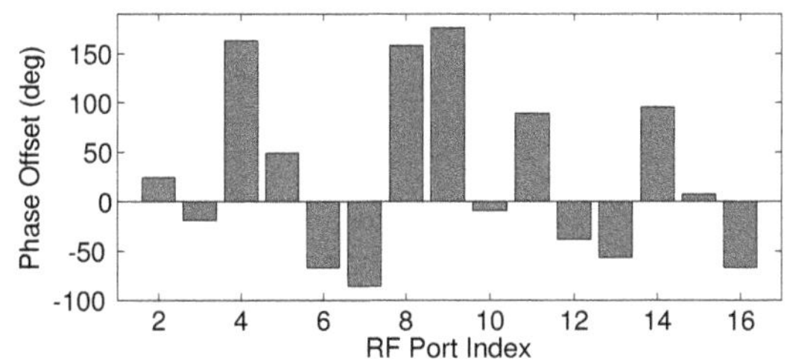

Figure 3: Random phase offsets at different RF ports.

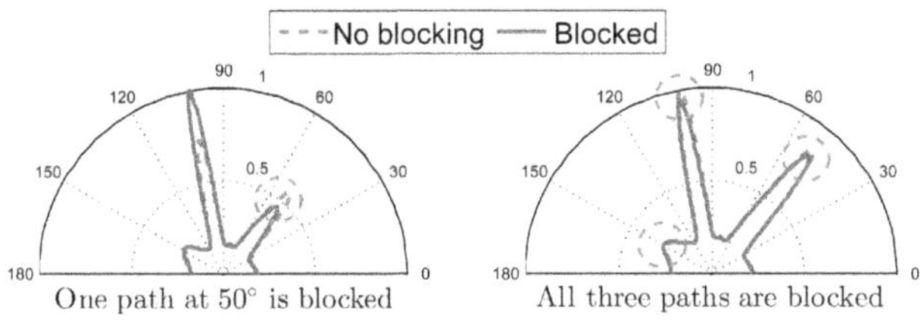

Figure 4: AoA spectrum change estimated by MUSIC.

represent the signal power level. We run a benchmark experiment to verify this observation and show the results in Fig. 4. When one path at 50° is blocked, not just the peak of the blocked path is decreased, the peak amplitudes of other paths may also get changed. That is to say, the power information provided by traditional MUSIC is not reliable for target detection. What is worse, when all three paths are blocked, the amplitudes for all peaks do not change much on the spectrum as shown in Fig. 4. MUSIC will then miss some of the blocked paths and the targets may not even be detected.

4. SYSTEM DESIGN

We present the key components of D-Watch followed by a summary of the system workflow.

4.1 Wireless Phase Calibration

We propose a subspace based wireless calibration method to estimate the phase offsets without interrupting the ongoing communication. The main challenge faced by wireless calibration is the multipath effect. With different propagation paths, the signals combine constructively at some antennas while combine destructively at other antennas. A naive approach is to remove the multipath signals so that we get the phase measurements only caused by the direct path signal and the RF port phase offsets. We can then obtain the phase offsets because the phase difference introduced by the direct path signal can be calculated. However, in a typical indoor environment, multipaths exist and it's difficult to remove the multipath signals from the received mixed signal and only keep the direct path signal.

In contrast, we propose a novel method which is able to work in the presence of multipath signals. The key intuition is the orthogonality property between the signal subspace and noise subspace, if we carry out eigenvalue analysis on the signal correlation matrix [34] as we described in Section 2.2. Based on this orthogonality property, the product of the noise subspace and signal subspace approaches zero at the LoS angle when the phase offsets are correctly removed. This observation motivates us to find the phase offsets by minimizing the product of noise and signal subspace at the known LoS angle[1]. With phase offsets, we revise the array signal model described by (2) as:

$$\mathbf{X} = \Gamma \mathbf{A} \mathbf{S} + \mathbf{n}, \tag{9}$$

where $\mathbf{X}$, $\mathbf{A}$, $\mathbf{S}$ and $\mathbf{n}$ are the array signal vector, steering matrix, source signal and noise. $\Gamma = \text{diag}\left\{1, e^{j\cdot\Delta\beta_{2,1}}, \cdots, e^{j\cdot\Delta\beta_{M,1}}\right\}$ is the phase offset diagonal matrix. $\Delta\beta_{m,1} = \beta_m - \beta_1$ refers to the phase offset between "antenna m" and the reference "antenna 1". From Equation (7), we have $\mathbf{a}(\theta)^H \Gamma^H \mathbf{U}_N = \mathbf{0}$ at $\theta = \theta_1, \cdots, \theta_P$. We then estimate the unknown hardware phase offset matrix $\hat{\Gamma}$ by solving the equation $||\mathbf{a}(\theta)^H \Gamma^H \mathbf{U}_N||_{l_2}^2 = 0$ with the angle θ and the noise eigenvector $\mathbf{U}_N$ known. The direct path angle $\theta_{LoS}^{(k)}$ of the kth tag can be easily measured when the locations of the tags and antennas are known[2]. The estimation accuracy of $\hat{\Gamma}$ can be further improved with larger number of tags. Thus, a more general equation can be given as:

$$\sum_{k=1}^{K} \left\| \mathbf{a}(\theta_{LoS}^{(k)})^H \Gamma^H \mathbf{U}_N^{(k)} \right\|_{l_2}^2 = 0, \tag{10}$$

where K is the total number of tags. Note that the dimensions of $\mathbf{a}(\cdot)$, Γ and $\mathbf{U}_N$ are $1 \times M$, $M \times M$ and $M \times (M-P)$, respectively. By expanding Equation (10), we acquire a number of $K \times (M-P)$ sub-equations. In practice, the number of dominant paths P for indoor environments is no larger than five [51]. Thus, we have more than $K(M-5)$ equations. While $K(M-5)$ grows in a quadratic fashion, the number of unknown phase offsets $M-1$ grows linearly. This suggests that given enough number of tags, there are enough ($K(M-5) \geq M-1$) equations to determine the unknown $\hat{\Gamma}$.

There are several approaches to solve a set of overdetermined equations such as inverting the equations directly or applying the least squares method. However, these approaches are not efficient in solving our problem due to a large amount of non-linear exponential terms in the equations. In this paper, we formulate an optimization problem to find $\hat{\Gamma}$ that minimizing:

$$\hat{\Gamma} = \underset{\Gamma}{\text{argmin}} \sum_{k=1}^{K} \left\| \mathbf{a}(\theta_{LOS}^{(k)})^H \Gamma^H \mathbf{U}_N^{(k)} \right\|_{l_2}^2. \tag{11}$$

The above optimization problem can be solved effectively applying a hybrid method of genetic algorithm (GA) [29] and gradient descent (GD) [9]. Specifically, in each iteration, GA starts initiating all the unknowns

[1]To make sure the LoS path dominates, we place the receiver close to the transmitter with clear LoS path.

[2]The tags' locations are only required for phase calibration. We do not need the tags' locations in localization.

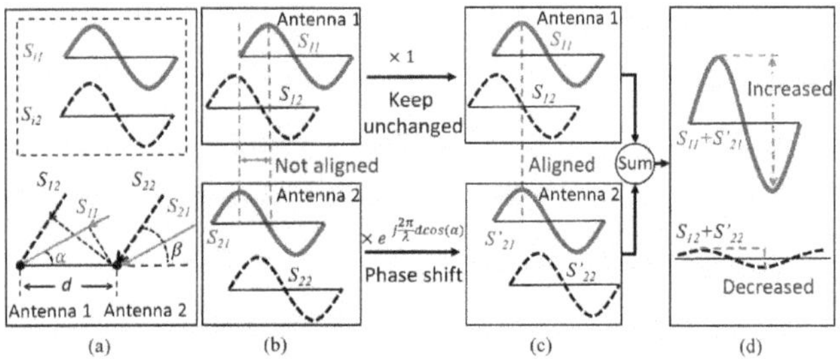

Figure 5: Illustration of obtaining the desired signal at one particular direction with alignment and summation.

and then refines the solution with the GD algorithm to find the closest local minimum.

4.2 Power MUSIC

We introduce a power MUSIC (P-MUSIC) algorithm to address the issue of missing power information in traditional MUSIC algorithm. The key observations are:

- The mixed signal received at one antenna is different from that received at another antenna due to the propagation path difference of signals.
- For a signal at one direction, the phase difference at any two adjacent antennas is the same and can be easily calculated.
- Different phase weights can be applied to the measured signals at different antennas so the signals at a designed direction add constructively, whereas the signals along other directions randomly add. This alignment boosts the power at the desired direction and averages out the signals at other directions to a small value, so the signal power at the designed direction can be obtained.

Fig. 5 (a) shows a toy example with two antennas spaced at a distance of d. Two signals arrive at two different angles α and β. We donate the two signals as S_{i1} and S_{i2} when they reach "antenna i". The two signals are mixed together at each antenna. To obtain the signal power at angle α, we apply two carefully chosen weights $[1, e^{j\frac{2\pi}{\lambda}d\cos(\alpha)}]$ to the measured signals and then sum them up. S_{11} and S'_{21} then add up constructively, while the other signals add up destructively, as shown in Fig. 5 (d). With the alignment and summation, we successfully reduce the power in other angles and obtain the power at angle α. Note that with just two antennas, the other signals may still have a chance of adding up constructively. However, with more antennas, other signals add up with random phase shifts, which will average out to a small value.

Without loss of generality, assume we want to identify the signal power s_1 along direction θ_1. The measured signal at "antenna m" is x_m. Then the sum of the weighted versions of x_m at direction θ_1 is given as:

$$\begin{aligned}&\sum_{m=1}^{M} x_m \cdot e^{j\cdot\omega(m,\theta_1)}\\&= \left(s_1 + \sum_{p=2}^{P} s_p\right) + \left(s_1 + \sum_{p=2}^{P} s_p \cdot e^{-j\cdot[\omega(2,\theta_p)-\omega(2,\theta_1)]}\right)\\&+\cdots+\left(s_1 + \sum_{p=2}^{P} s_p \cdot e^{-j\cdot[\omega(M,\theta_p)-\omega(M,\theta_1)]}\right)\\&= M\cdot s_1 + \sum_{p=2}^{P}\left[s_p\left(\sum_{m=1}^{M} e^{-j\frac{2\pi(m-1)d}{\lambda}[\cos(\theta_p)-\cos(\theta_1)]}\right)\right]\end{aligned} \tag{12}$$

As shown in the above equation, the signal s_1 adds constructively and the amplitude gets increased roughly M times while other signals average out when adding up with random phase shifts of $\frac{2\pi(m-1)d}{\lambda}\cos(\theta_p)$. For any interested signal s_p, with the alignment and summation, the power of the designed signal along direction θ_p will be much higher than the power along other directions with a relatively large M. The signal power along the direction θ_p with the received signals at the M antennas is then given as:

$$P_B(\theta_p) = \|s_p\|^2 \approx \frac{\left\|\sum_{m=1}^{M} x_m \cdot e^{j\cdot\omega(m,\theta_p)}\right\|^2}{M^2}. \tag{13}$$

We then integrate this power information into the traditional MUSIC to acquire both AoA and power estimations. Intuitively, we can simply dot-multiply the power estimation $P_B(\theta_p)$ and the MUSIC AoA spectrum $B(\theta_p)$. However, the MUSIC peak amplitude is a probability value, which distorts the estimated signal power. We solve this problem by designing a normalization function $Nor(B(\theta_p))$ to normalize all the peak amplitudes to "1". We thus remove the peak amplitudes from MUSIC and only keep the angle information of the peaks. Our P-MUSIC function is then given as below:

$$\begin{aligned}\Omega(\theta_p) &= P_B(\theta_p)\cdot Nor(B(\theta_p))\\&= \frac{\left\|\sum_{m=1}^{M} x_m\cdot e^{j\cdot\omega(m,\theta_p)}\right\|^2}{M^2\cdot Nor(\mathbf{a}^H(\theta_p)\mathbf{U}_N\mathbf{U}_N^H\mathbf{a}(\theta_p))},\end{aligned} \tag{14}$$

where M is the number of antennas, $\mathbf{a}(\theta_p)$ and $\mathbf{U}_N$ are the steering vector and the noise subspace eigenvector defined in Section 2.2.

Note that P-MUSIC does not need to know the value of θ_p. By searching θ_p from 0 to π like the traditional MUSIC, P-MUSIC is able to estimate the signal power along each direction of the signal path. The coherence between signals affects the performance of P-MUSIC and we adopt the spatial smoothing method [36] to remove the coherence among received signals.

4.3 Target Localization

D-Watch combines the identified target angles from several readers to determine the target's location. Suppose ξ readers identify a set of AoA spectra changes $\Delta\Omega_1(\theta), \cdots, \Delta\Omega_\xi(\theta)$. To localize a target, we compute the likelihood function $L(O)$ of the target be located

(a) Laboratory environment. (b) Library environment. (c) Hall environment.

Figure 6: Three typical indoor environments corresponding to medium, high and low multipath environment.

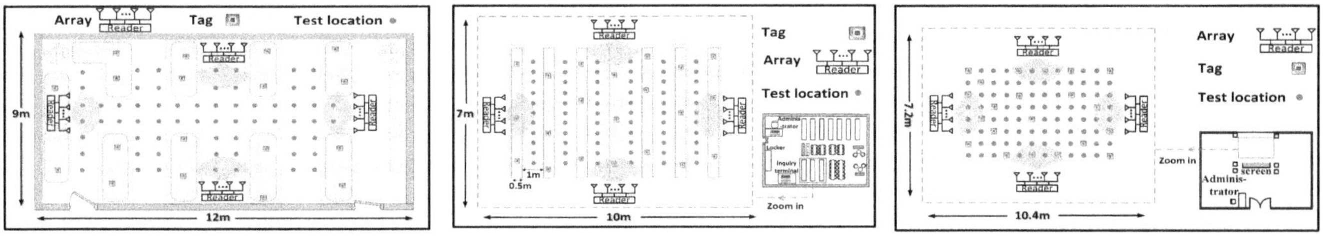

(a) Laboratory deployment layout. (b) Library deployment layout. (c) Hall deployment layout.

Figure 7: Deployment layouts with the positions of arrays, tags and test locations marked.

at a position O, and take the location estimate with a maximum likelihood as the target location. To compute the likelihood, the basic idea is that a larger AoA peak change indicates a higher probability that the target is at this angle. The likelihood $L(O)$ is given as:

$$L(O) = \prod_{i=1}^{\xi} \Delta\Omega_i(\theta). \tag{15}$$

We then divide the monitoring area into grids[3] and search for the grid with the highest $L(O)$. The hill climbing scheme is employed to quickly find the most likely target location estimate.

Note that we may retrieve wrong angle information if the target blocks a reflection path before the signal reaches the reflector. In Fig. 1(b), Path 3 is blocked but the angle information detected is not correct. In reality, this wrong angle information can be identified if there is only one target. Because a target cannot block two paths at the same reader at the same time. Whenever we detect multiple blocked paths at one reader, we know only one of the detected angles is pointing to the true location of the target. We further discover that the locations estimated from the wrong angles are distributed at random positions and even far outside of the monitoring area. On the other hand, the correct angles will localize the target to close-by positions. We can then apply outlier rejection to identify the wrong angle.

4.4 Putting Things Together

Now we put all the pieces together and sketch the workflow of D-Watch.

[3]Smaller grid size leads to more accurate results but takes more time to search. We balance this tradeoff and set the grid size as 5 cm×5 cm for the three indoor environments and 2 cm×2 cm for the smaller table area.

Step 1: Data collection. D-Watch collects a set of baseline AoA data between the tags and the reader when no target is present. Note that this process is very different from the traditional fingerprint database collection which takes hours. This process for D-Watch is just several transmissions between the readers and tags which can be well completed within seconds. D-Watch then acquires another set of measurements when the target moves into the monitoring area.

Step 2: Data pre-processing. D-Watch first employs the proposed wireless phase calibration method to remove the phase offsets that exist in the collected data. Note that the calibration process is a one-time effort for one power on-off cycle so D-Watch does not need to carry out phase calibration frequently.

Step 3: Target angle estimation. With proposed P-MUSIC algorithm, D-Watch generates two sets of AoA spectra based on the online data and the baseline data. By comparing the amplitude changes of the AoA peaks, D-Watch can accurately identify the target's angle information at each reader.

Step 4: Target localization. By combining the identified angle information from multiple readers, D-Watch is able to obtain the target's location estimate with triangulation scheme.

5. IMPLEMENTATION

Experimental environments: we conduct experiments in three typical indoor environments: a library, a laboratory and an empty hall corresponding to high, medium and low multipath environment. The laboratory with a size of 9 m×12 m has many small objects such as test chambers, displays, etc., as shown in Fig. 6(a). Part of the library area with a size of 7 m×10 m has many book shelves full of books, as shown in Fig. 6(b). The shelf has a height of 2.5 m

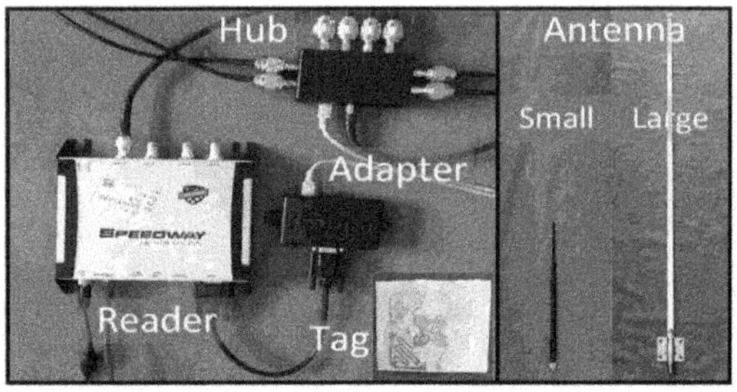

Figure 8: RFID hardware and antennas employed.

and is made of metal and wood, resulting in rich multipaths and strong NLoS. Part of the empty hall with a size of 7.2 m×10.4 m is shown in Fig. 6(c).

Human target and object target: We ask the students to act as the human target in the experiments. To demonstrate the high accuracy of D-Watch in a small scale deployment, we employ three glass bottles full of water as our object targets. The bottle has a bottom diameter of 7.8 cm and a height of 22 cm.

Implementation: (i) *Readers and tags.* We employ four Impinj Speedway R420 readers [5] for our experiments without any hardware or firmware modification. Each reader has four RF ports and is equipped with one Impinj GPIO Adapter [5]. An Impinj antenna hub is connected to one of the reader's four RF ports as shown in Fig. 8. Usually, we need 8 antennas for high accuracy AoA estimation [51]. However, the Impinj Speedway R420 reader only has four antenna ports, thus we use the antenna hub provided by Impinj to support more antennas. The readers are compatible with EPC Gen2 standard [4] and the antennas work in a time division multiplexing mode. The time slot for each antenna is about 200 us [5]. The reader operates in frequency range of 920.5–924.5 MHz, which is the legal UHF band in China. We use 21 cheap Alien ALN-9634 tags [32] as shown in Fig. 8, which cost 1.5 USD in total.

(ii) *Antenna and array.* We employ two different types of antennas for our experiments as shown in Fig. 8. The small one is ANS-900 omni-directional antenna [3] and the large one is Q900F-900 omni-directional antenna [6]. Since RFID devices communicate by backscattering the signal which is usually weak, the small antenna [3] provides a relatively small communication range of 3 m. The large antenna provides a communication range of 12 m. Each linear array is consisted of 8 antennas with a half wavelength space of 16.25 cm between adjacent antennas. The antennas and the RF front ends have been calibrated using the wireless phase calibration method introduced in Section 4.1.

(iii) *Server and algorithm implementation*: The proposed schemes and algorithms are implemented in C# and Matlab. The server is a desktop with 3.6 GHz CPU (Intel i7-4790) and 8 GB memory. The server communicates with the RFID readers using low level reader protocol (LLRP) [15]. All the tags' backscatter packets received at the readers are forwarded to the server through Ethernet cables. The size of a RFID backscatter packet is small since the packet only contains the tag's ID which is 12 bytes at most [5]. The reader does not need to emit signals all the time and a 0.1 s transmission interval is good enough for our localization and does not increase the transmission overheads.

Default deployment setup: The deployment layouts of the three environments are shown in Fig. 7. In each environment, we deploy four[4] readers and 21 tags. The locations of the readers are known while the tags are randomly placed without a need to know their locations. We choose 63, 66 and 75 test locations in the laboratory, library and hall, respectively. The test locations are uniformly distributed with a 0.5 m distance in between. The objects attached with tags are usually placed on the table or held in the hand so their heights are between 1 to 1.5 m above the ground. We place the antenna array at a height of 1.25 m. When we evaluate the impact of number of tags and tag-array height difference, we employ more tags and change the default setup. Unless specifically mentioned, we use the default setup for performance evaluation.

Experimental methodology: When a target moves into the monitoring area, the readers receive 10 backscatter packets from each tag and forward them to the server. At the server side, D-Watch identifies the angle information of the target at each reader and combines the information from several readers to obtain the target's location estimate. We repeat the experiments 40 times at each test location.

6. PERFORMANCE EVALUATION

6.1 Microbenchmark

We start with two benchmark experiments to validate the effectiveness of the proposed wireless calibration method and P-MUSIC algorithm.

6.1.1 *Verification of phase calibration method*

We measure the random phase offsets caused by the reader's radio front ends and compare our method with the state-of-the-art wireless calibration method proposed in Phaser [17]. We take the phase offsets obtained from the wired calibration method proposed in ArrayTrack [51] as the ground truth. In the laboratory environment, tags are randomly attached to objects located 1–8 m away from the array. We vary the number of tags to estimate the phase offset matrix $\hat{\Gamma}$. The phase offset estimation errors are shown in Fig. 9. The proposed method is able to achieve phase error less than 0.05 radians when more than four tags are employed. It suggests that the proposed method achieves a high calibration accuracy even with a relatively small number of tags. Note that a phase calibration error of 0.05 radians will cause an even smaller AoA error since there

[4]Note that the number of readers can be reduced to one if we employ coaxial cables to connect four antenna arrays to one reader.

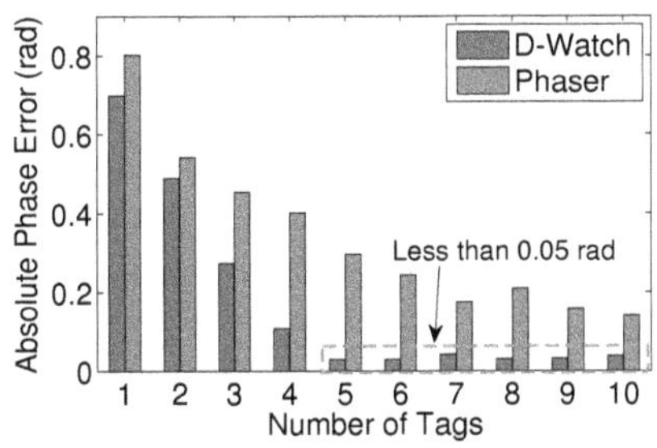

Figure 9: The proposed phase calibration method is much more accurate.

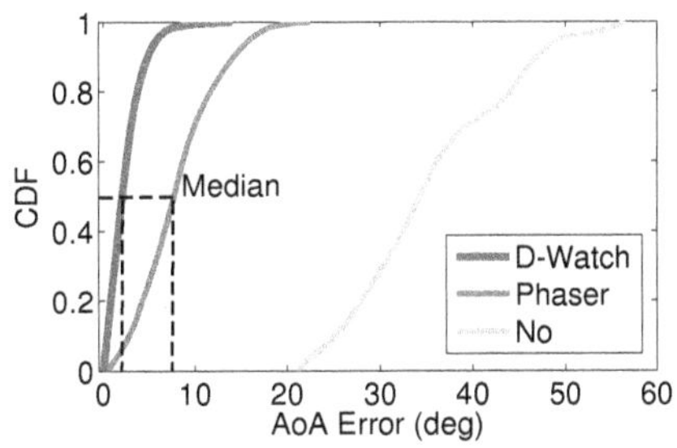

Figure 10: LoS AoA estimation with proposed calibration method.

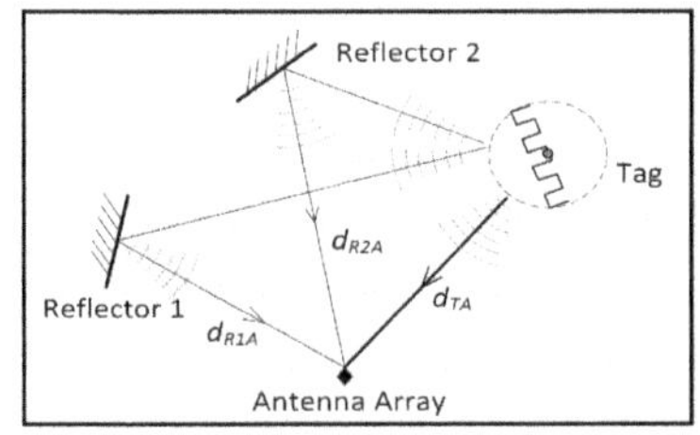

Figure 11: Deployment layout for Power MUSIC verification.

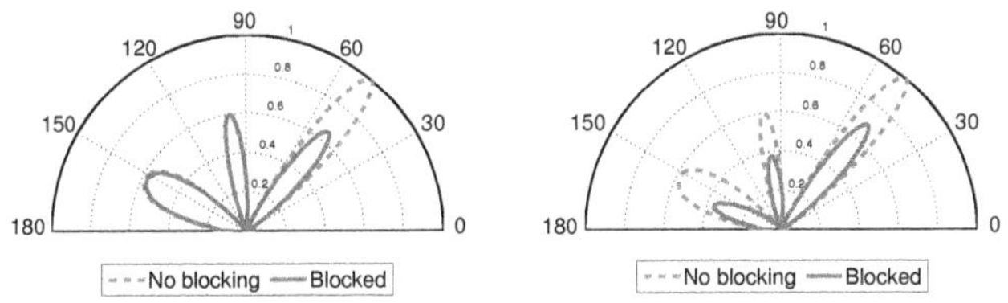

(a) One path is blocked. (b) Three paths are blocked.

Figure 12: AoA spectrum changes estimated by P-MUSIC when one or more paths are blocked.

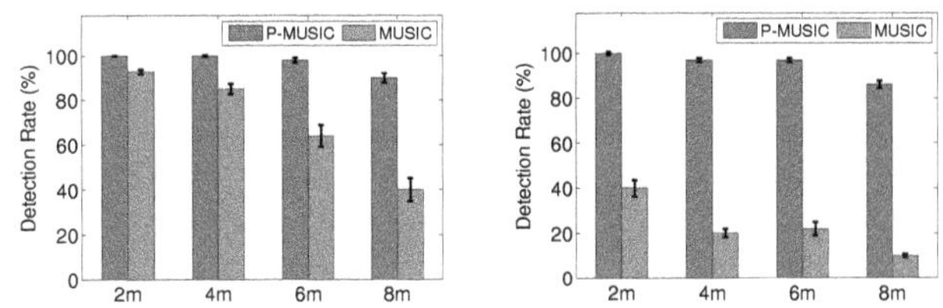

(a) One path is blocked. (b) All paths are blocked.

Figure 13: Target detection rate comparison between MUSIC and P-MUSIC.

are multiple antennas and the calibration errors have positive and negative values which may cancel out each other. We then compare the direct path AoA estimation errors when employing different calibration methods. The results in Fig. 10 show that our calibration method achieves a high AoA estimation accuracy, i.e., a median error of 2°, outperforming the Phaser system.

6.1.2 *Verification of power MUSIC*

To minimize the influence of multipath, we conduct this experiment in the empty hall environment. We place two laptops with metal shells as reflectors to obtain two controlled reflection signals. The deployment layout is shown in Fig. 11. Three human targets walk around to block the direct path and reflection paths. We increase the distance d_{TA} between the tag and the array from 2 m to 9 m, while keep the distances (i.e., d_{R_1A}=2 m and d_{R_2A}=2.6 m) from the two reflectors to the array unchanged. For the same distance, we also change the locations of the tag and the reflectors to have multiple measurements. To detect the presence of targets, we compare the changes of AoA peaks when there is no target and when targets are present.

Fig. 12 illustrates the changes of AoA spectra when we apply P-MUSIC. Compared with traditional MUSIC shown in Fig. 4, the changes of the AoA peaks estimated by P-MUSIC match our expectations, i.e., the blocked path peak experiences a clear drop and the unblocked peaks remain unchanged. The detection rate of P-MUSIC is close to 100% as shown in Fig. 13. On the other hand, the detection performance of traditional MUSIC is poor even when the signal strength is strong. Traditional MUSIC fails when multiple targets are present and block more than one paths at the same time. The proposed P-MUSIC is able to capture the power changes of each path much more accurately than the traditional MUSIC.

6.2 Overall Localization Performance

In reality, human target is too big to be treated as a point. As the human targets have a width of 32 cm to 40 cm, we consider there is no localization error as long as the estimation is within the 36 cm range. Otherwise, we calculate the error as the minimum difference between the estimated location and this 36 cm range.

We show the localization performance for the human target in three different environments in Fig. 14. The results in Fig. 14 (a) show that D-Watch achieves the best performance in the library environment with a median and 90% error as small as 16.5 cm and 28.9 cm, respectively. D-Watch's median accuracy slightly decreases in laboratory and hall environments to 25.3 cm and 32.1 cm. The mean errors are shown in Fig. 14 (b). The results are interesting as indoor localization systems usually achieve worse performance in richer multipath environments. In contrast, D-Watch performs even better, implying that "bad" multipaths are efficiently utilized to improve the localization performance.

6.3 Impact of Number of Antennas

We show the performance of D-Watch with varying number of antennas at the reader. In general, with more antennas at each reader, D-Watch is able to achieve a finer resolution in AoA estimation and capture more

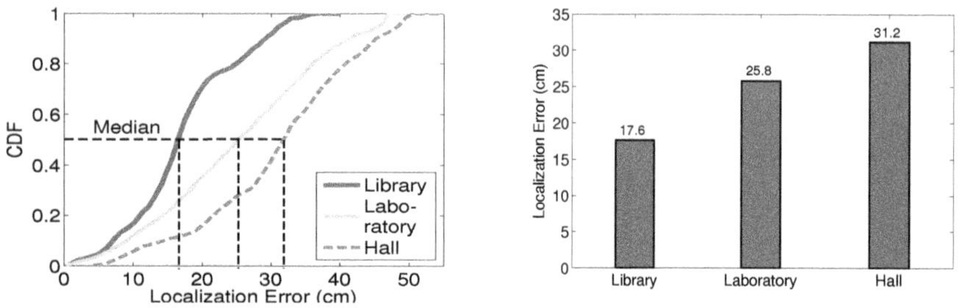

(a) CDF plot localization error. (b) Mean localization error.

Figure 14: Localization performance in different environments.

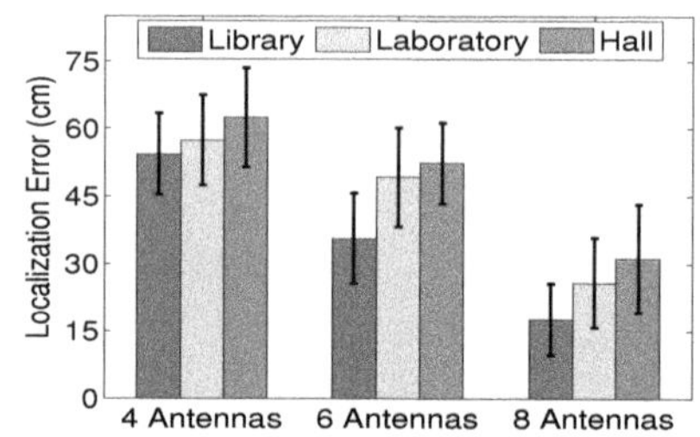

Figure 15: Localization errors with varying number of antennas.

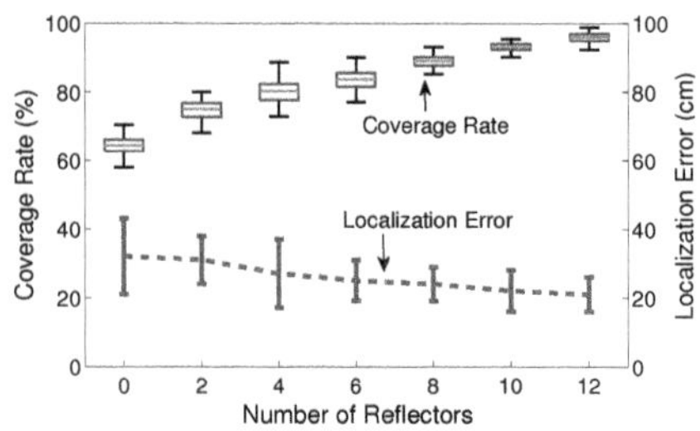

Figure 16: Localization errors with varying number of reflectors.

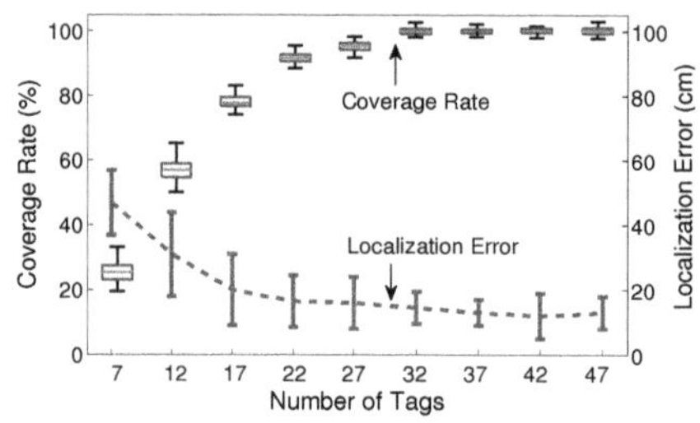

Figure 17: Localization errors with varying number of tags.

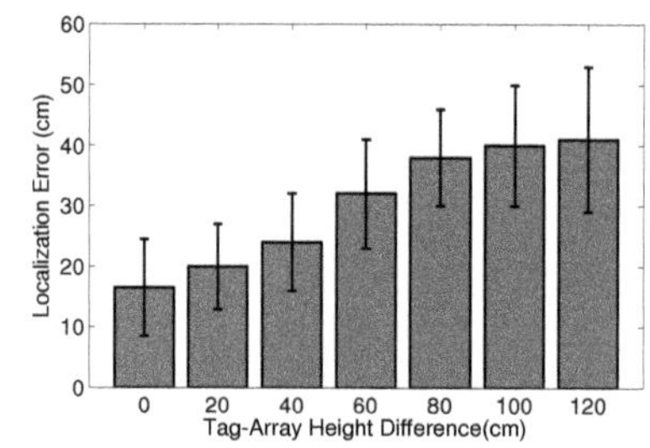

Figure 18: Localization errors with varying tag-array height differences.

paths, which accordingly increases the localization accuracy as shown in Figure 15. In the library environment, the mean localization error is 54.3 cm for four antennas, 35.6 cm for six antennas and 17.6 cm for eight antennas.

6.4 Impact of Number of Multipaths

Besides the direct path, D-Watch utilizes the multipaths to localize a target. With more multipaths, D-Watch achieves a higher coverage rate[5] and improves the localization accuracy. To demonstrate this, we place up to 12 reflectors such as laptops and metal reflectors to create more multipaths in the hall environment. Fig. 16 shows that the coverage rate gets increased significantly since more propagation paths exist in the monitoring area. It also shows a mean error decrease from 31.2 cm to 20.8 cm as more paths are now restricting the target's location estimate.

6.5 Impact of Number of Tags

With more tags, more signals will be reflected creating more paths to cover the monitoring area and constraint the target's location. In the library environment, we vary the number of tags from 7 to 47 with a step size of 5. The experimental results match our expectations as shown in Fig. 17. So both the number of tags and reflectors can actually increase the multipaths in the environment. Thus, in an indoor environment with more reflectors, the density of the tags can then be reduced.

Note that, more tags are helpful for improving the localization accuracy. However, the localization accuracy of D-Watch is mainly related to the AoA estimation accuracy so the number of antennas at the reader side is the main factor deciding the localization accuracy.

[5]Coverage rate is defined as the number of locations can be localized divided by total number of test locations.

6.6 Impact of Tag-Array Height Difference

In reality, tags attached on books or laptops are placed on the table or held in the hand with a height of 1–1.5 m above the ground. If the tags and the arrays are not at the same height, we would like to study whether such a height difference will cause significant localization errors. Fig. 18 shows that D-Watch can still achieve a mean localization error of 40 cm even when the height difference is as large as 120 cm. When the height difference is 40 cm, the mean error is 24 cm which is only slightly higher.

6.7 Multi-Target Localization

The high spatial resolution of D-Watch's AoA spectrum enables a fine-grained multi-target localization. The intuition is that a target is not able to block all the paths simultaneously. When multiple targets are located sparsely, each target will block a disjoint subset of paths and thus can be separated and individually located. However, when many targets exist or two targets are too close to each other, it's still challenging to accurately localize each of them.

We study the performance of D-Watch for multi-target localization. To evaluate the granularity of multi-target localization, we employ three glass bottles placed on a 2 m×2 m table as shown in Fig. 20. The bottles are filled with water. We place two small-antenna arrays at the midpoint of the bottom and right of the table. 26 tags are placed at the other two sides. Fig. 19 (a)∼(c) shows three snapshot localization results when the three targets are separated roughly by 130 cm, 50 cm and

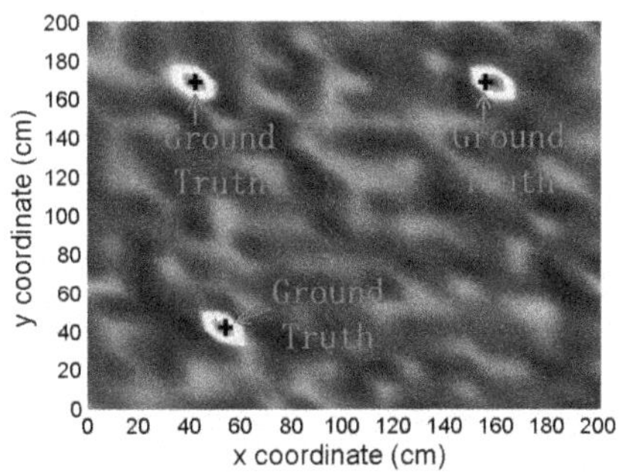

(a) Targets are 130cm apart.

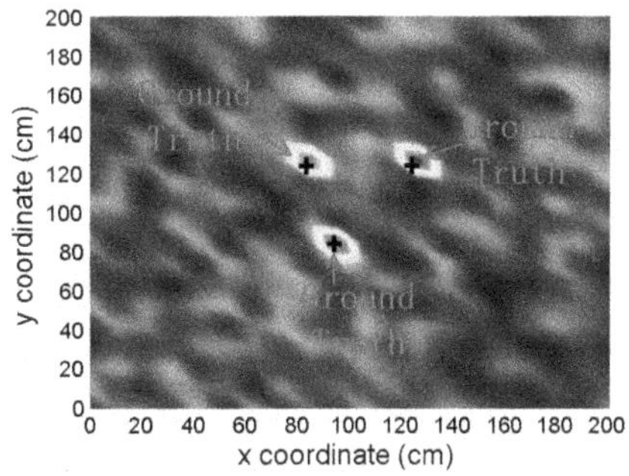

(b) Targets are 50cm apart.

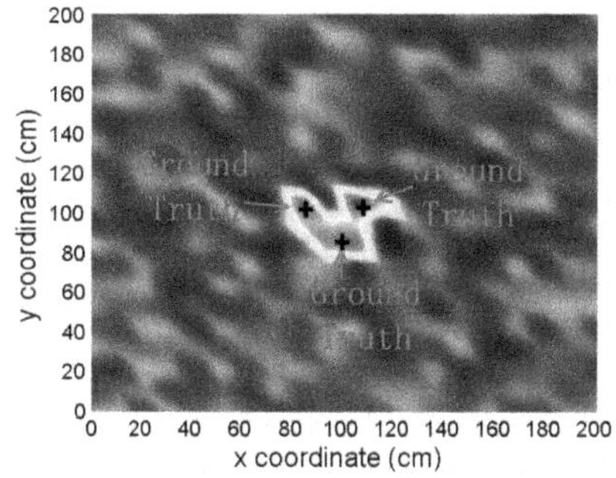

(c) Targets are 20cm apart.

Figure 19: Performance of multi-target localization. (a)-(c) show the heatmaps of three snapshot localization results.

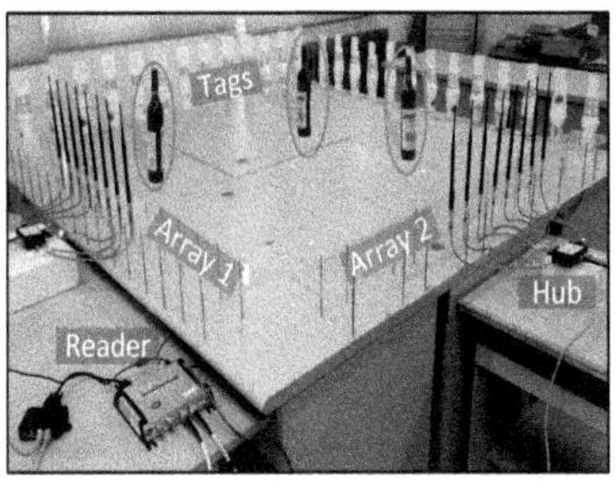

Figure 20: A 2 m × 2 m table area with three glass bottle targets.

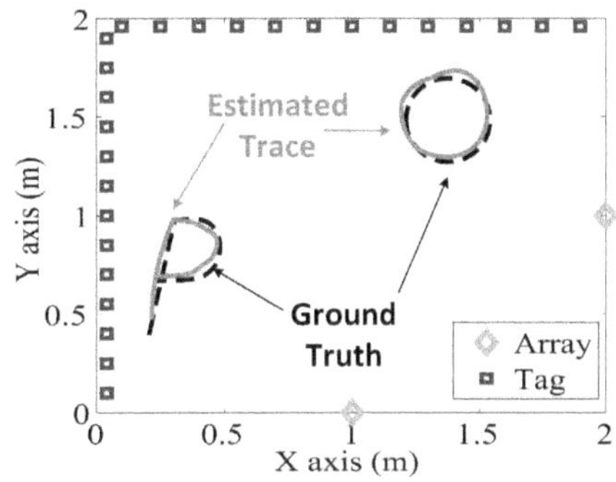

Figure 21: Passively track the fist's writing in the air.

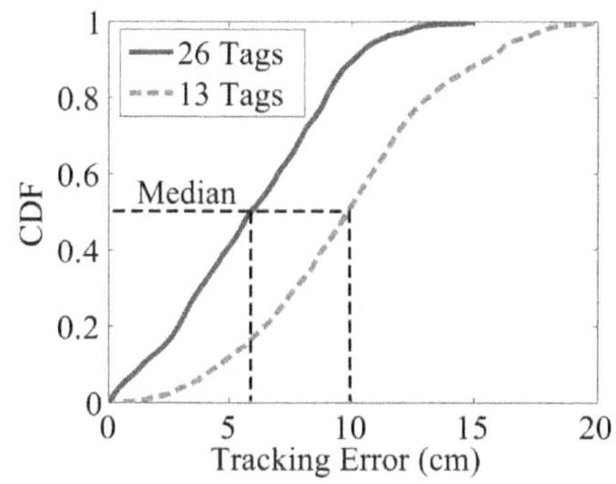

Figure 22: Fist tracking accuracy of D-Watch.

20 cm respectively. For each snapshot, we collect 30 data samples and the localization results are mapped into the heatmap, where the red dot represents the location estimate and the black cross indicates the ground truth. D-Watch localizes the three targets accurately with a maximum error of 17.2 cm when they are located sparsely, such as 130 cm and 50 cm apart. When the three targets are close to each other within 20 cm, the three targets have a tendency to merge into one on the heatmap and D-Watch can not localize each individual of them accurately. We believe with more number of antennas such as 16 and 64, finer AoA resolution can be achieved and we can further increase the accuracy and separability for multi-target localization.

6.8 Application Example: Tracking Fist in the Air for Virtual Screen Touch

One popular application in the research community recently is drawing in the air [39] or tracking the human's fine-grained gestures [12]. We briefly investigate the capability of D-Watch on these applications. We let a human user write the characters "P" and "O" along a pre-marked trajectory using his fist in the 2 m×2 m table area as shown in Fig. 21. The user moves his hand at a natural writing speed, i.e., about 0.5 m/s. Fig. 21 shows that the trajectory of the user's fist measured by D-Watch matches the ground truth quite well. To understand the tracking accuracy of D-Watch, we mark a set of continuous test points on the table. Fig. 22 shows that the median tracking error can be as small as 5.8 cm and 9.7 cm when 26 tags and 13 tags are employed respectively.

7. RELATED WORK

Device-free Localization. Early device-free localization works rely on visible light camera [28, 30] and infrared sensor [21, 19]. Camera-based methods heavily reply on lighting conditions and have severe privacy issue. Infrared-based methods have difficulties to penetrate the walls. On the other hand, low frequency RF waves can penetrate walls easily [7, 8, 55, 16] and RF infrastructures are widely available. Thus, there are growing interests in exploring RF signals for device-free localization. Among RF-based methods, most device-free localization systems are RSSI/CSI fingerprint-based [41, 42, 10, 11, 49, 43]. They translate the localization problem to a fingerprint matching problem while each location is associated with a unique RSSI or CSI fingerprint [49]. The feasibility has been demonstrated for different technologies including RFID [55, 18], Wi-Fi [33, 49] and ZigBee [57, 10]. However, fingerprint-based methods need a large amount of human efforts to acquire and update the fingerprint database. Changes in the environment, such as the movements of furniture, will change the fingerprints [51], causing mismatches between the database and the new measurements. D-Watch on the other hand, does not need any labor-intensive training efforts, and only requires several baseline AoA measurements which can be carried out automatically without human interventions within seconds.

Recently, a lot of RSSI model-based device-free localization systems were proposed in order to reduce or even avoid the offline training efforts, such as RFID-based Tadar [55] and Twins [18] systems, Wi-Fi-based LiFS [44] and ACE [33] systems, ZigBee-based RTI [48] and RASS [57] systems, etc. The basic idea of these approaches is to model the wireless propagation channels mathematically and then estimate the target location from the distorted wireless signal. However, due to the complicated multipath situation in indoor environment, mathematical models do not fit well and the location accuracy is hence coarse. Also as the models focus on the LoS path, a dense transceiver deployment is usually needed to cover the area. Moreover, they require the prior knowledge of the locations of the transceivers, which are sometimes impractical. In contrast, D-Watch utilizes both the LoS path and the reflection paths for localization purpose, which significantly increases the coverage area and accuracy. The deployment density can thus be reduced, making it a promising candidate for large scale deployment. Further, D-Watch does not need to know the locations of the signal sources (such as the RFID tags or mobile devices) so the proposed system has a high flexibility for real life deployment.

Researchers also proposed some fine-grained device-free localization systems, such as Wi-Vi [8], Witrack [7], mtrack [47], etc. These systems though being able to achieve a high accuracy, require either dedicated signal (frequency modulated carrier wave, FMCW), specialized hardware (USRPs, WARP) or a very large bandwidth (60 GHz). Unlike these approaches, D-Watch is built on top of low cost COTS RFID devices and efficiently utilizes the "detrimental" multipaths to improve the coverage rate and localization accuracy.

Phase Calibration. Besides the wired phase calibration method introduced in ArrayTrack [51], some wireless phase calibration methods have also been proposed in Argos [37] and Phaser [17]. The method proposed in Argos can not be applied directly to our case as the RFID reader does not support transmission from one antenna on the reader to the other antennas. Also Argos requires all the transceivers to cooperate with each other for calibration, which interrupts the ongoing data transmissions. To overcome this limitation, Phaser is proposed and can carry out auto-calibration without interrupting the ongoing transmission. However, the calibration accuracy of Phaser is coarse. Our proposed calibration method not only achieves a much higher accuracy but also does not interrupt the ongoing data communication.

8. DISCUSSION

Deadzone problem: When a target does not block any path, it is in a "deadone" where the target can not be detected. In this case, D-Watch can utilize the mobility of a target to mitigate this problem. A human target moves continuously in space and the target can still be localized before and after entering into the "deadzone". These location information can then be utilized to estimate the target's current location when target is in the "deadzone". Moreover, there are rich multipaths in a typical indoor environment and the tags are very cheap so we can increase the number of tags to reduce the amount of deadzones. Thus, the probability of this extreme case is quite low in reality.

Mobility: Since the human target moves continuously, we can track the target by snapshots. In the indoor environment, the walking speed of a human is around 1–2 m/s. Note that the transmission interval of D-Watch is 0.1 s so the target moves only 10–20 cm in this short period which does not affect D-Watch's performance much. Also Doppler shift can be applied to estimate the target's walking speed to further improve the location accuracy.

Latency of D-Watch: The system latency includes the time to collect packets and the time to calculate the target location. We run our localization algorithm many times and the average processing time is 57 ms. 2–3 packets are employed for localization in D-Watch. The time taken to collect data packets depends on how frequently the packets are sent out. If the packet is sent out every 100 ms, the end-to-end system latency of our system is still well below 0.5 s.

9. CONCLUSION

D-Watch is the first device-free localization system that utilizes both the direct path and multipaths to provide decimeter-level localization accuracy without offline training. We propose a wireless phase calibration scheme to remove the random phase offsets at the radio front ends and a novel power MUSIC algorithm to accurately detect the angle information of the target. Comprehensive real-world experiments in different environments demonstrate the effectiveness of D-Watch. D-Watch can further localize multiple targets accurately which is a well known challenging problem in passive tracking. D-Watch outperforms the state-of-the-art systems and can be extended to work with other RF technologies and support other applications.

Acknowledgment

This work is supported by National Natural Science Foundation of China (61272461, 61572219, 61502192, 61572402, 61672428), Fundamental Research Funds for the Central Universities under Grant 2016JCTD118, and the Google fund to Jie Xiong at Singapore Management University. We also would like to thank the shepherd Swarun Kumar as well as the anonymous reviewers for their valuable feedback on this paper. Hongbo Jiang and Dingyi Fang are the corresponding authors.

10. REFERENCES

[1] Alien tags. www.alientechnology.com/tags/.

[2] Amazon, Inc. https://www.amazon.com/.

[3] Ans-900 rfid antenna. rf-links.com/newsite/pdf/ans-900.pdf.

[4] Epc gen2, epcglobal. www.gs1.org/epcglobal.

[5] Impinj, Inc. www.impinj.com/products/readers/speedway-revolution/.

[6] Q900f-900 rfid antenna. www.hrtantenna.com/en/products.

[7] F. Adib, Z. Kabelac, and D. Katabi. Multi-person localization via rf body reflections. In *Proc. Usenix NSDI*, pages 279–292, 2015.

[8] F. Adib and D. Katabi. See through walls with wifi! In *Proc. ACM SIGCOMM*, volume 43, pages 75–86, 2013.

[9] M. S. Bazaraa, H. D. Sherali, and C. M. Shetty. *Nonlinear programming: theory and algorithms*. John Wiley & Sons.

[10] L. Chang, X. Chen, D. Fang, J. Wang, T. Xing, C. Liu, and Z. Tang. Fale: Fine-grained device free localization that can adaptively work in different areas with little effort. *Acm Sigcomm Computer Communication Review*, 45(5):601–602, 2015.

[11] L. Chang, X. Chen, Y. Wang, D. Fang, J. Wang, T. Xing, and Z. Tang. Fitloc: Fine-grained and low-cost device-free localization for multiple targets over various areas. In *Proc. IEEE INFOCOM*, pages 151–159, 2016.

[12] B. Chen, V. Yenamandra, and K. Srinivasan. Tracking keystrokes using wireless signals. In *Proc. ACM Mobisys*, pages 31–44, 2015.

[13] B. Chen, Z. Zhou, and H. Yu. Understanding rfid counting protocols. *IEEE/ACM Trans. on Networking*, 24(1):312–327, 2016.

[14] R. Diamant, H. P. Tan, and L. Lampe. Los and nlos classification for underwater acoustic localization. *IEEE Trans. on Mobile Computing*, 13(2):311–323, 2014.

[15] A. EPCglobal Inc. Low level reader protocol, version 1.0. 1. 2007.

[16] M. Flores, U. Klarman, and A. Kuzmanovic. Wi-fm: Resolving neighborhood wireless network affairs by listening to music. In *Proc. IEEE ICNP*.

[17] J. Gjengset, J. Xiong, G. McPhillips, and K. Jamieson. Phaser: enabling phased array signal processing on commodity wifi access points. In *Proc. ACM MobiCom*, pages 153–164, 2014.

[18] J. Han, C. Qian, X. Wang, D. Ma, J. Zhao, P. Zhang, W. Xi, and Z. Jiang. Twins: Device-free object tracking using passive tags. In *Proc. IEEE INFOCOM*, pages 469–476, 2014.

[19] D. Hauschildt and N. Kirchhof. Advances in thermal infrared localization: Challenges and solutions. In *International Conference on Indoor Positioning and Indoor Navigation (IPIN)*, pages 1–8, 2010.

[20] P. Jain, J. Manweiler, and R. Roy Choudhury. Overlay: Practical mobile augmented reality. In *Proc. ACM Mobisys*, pages 331–344, 2015.

[21] J. Kemper and D. Hauschildt. Passive infrared localization with a probability hypothesis density filter. In *Proc. IEEE workshop on Positioning Navigation and Communication (WPNC)*, pages 68–76, 2010.

[22] M. Kotaru, K. Joshi, D. Bharadia, and S. Katti. Spotfi: Decimeter level localization using wifi. In *Proc. ACM SIGCOMM*, pages 269–282, 2015.

[23] S. Kumar, S. Gil, D. Katabi, and D. Rus. Accurate indoor localization with zero start-up cost. In *Proc. ACM MobiCom*, pages 483–494, 2014.

[24] T.-W. Kuo, K.-C. Lee, K. C.-J. Lin, and M.-J. Tsai. Leader-contention-based user matching for 802.11 multiuser mimo networks. *IEEE Trans. on Wireless Communications*, 13(8):4389–4400, 2014.

[25] L. Li, P. Hu, C. Peng, G. Shen, and F. Zhao. Epsilon: A visible light based positioning system. In *Proc. Usenix NSDI*, pages 331–343, 2014.

[26] T. Li, C. An, Z. Tian, A. T. Campbell, and X. Zhou. Human sensing using visible light communication. In *Proc. ACM MobiCom*, pages 331–344, 2015.

[27] X. Li, S. Li, D. Zhang, J. Xiong, Y. Wang, and H. Mei. Dynamic-music: accurate device-free indoor localization. In *Proc. ACM UbiComp*, pages 196–207, 2016.

[28] H. Ma, C. Zeng, and C. X. Ling. A reliable people counting system via multiple cameras. *ACM Trans. on Intelligent Systems and Technology*, 3(2):67–83, 2012.

[29] T. Mcconaghy, E. Vladislavleva, and R. Riolo. Genetic programming theory and practice 2010: An introduction. *Gecco Companion Publication Proceedings of Annual Genetic & Evolutionary Computation Conference*, 78(1):3015–3056, 2010.

[30] R. Mohedano, A. Cavallaro, and N. GarcÍla. Camera localization using trajectories and maps. *IEEE Trans. on Pattern Analysis & Machine Intelligence*, 36(4):684–697, 2014.

[31] F. M. Naini, J. Unnikrishnan, P. Thiran, and M. Vetterli. Where you are is who you are: User identification by matching statistics. *IEEE Trans. on Information Forensics & Security*, 11(2):358–372, 2016.

[32] S. J. Orfanidis. *Electromagnetic waves and antennas*. Rutgers University New Brunswick, NJ, 2002.

[33] I. Sabek, M. Youssef, and A. V. Vasilakos. Ace: An accurate and efficient multi-entity device-free wlan localization system. *IEEE Trans. on Mobile*

Computing, 14(2):261–273, 2015.

[34] R. O. Schmidt. Multiple emitter location and signal parameter estimation. *IEEE Trans. on Antennas and Propagation*, 34(3):276–280, 1986.

[35] R. O. Schmidt. Multiple emitter location and signal parameter estimation. *IEEE Trans. on Antennas and Propagation*, 34(3):276–280, 1986.

[36] T.-J. Shan, M. Wax, and T. Kailath. On spatial smoothing for direction-of-arrival estimation of coherent signals. *IEEE Trans. on Acoustics, Speech, and Signal Processing*, 33(4):806–811, 1985.

[37] C. Shepard, H. Yu, N. Anand, E. Li, T. Marzetta, R. Yang, and L. Zhong. Argos: Practical many-antenna base stations. In *Proc. ACM MobiCom*, pages 53–64, 2012.

[38] Y. Shu, K. G. Shin, T. He, and J. Chen. Last-mile navigation using smartphones. In *Proc. ACM MobiCom*, pages 512–524, 2015.

[39] L. Sun, S. Sen, D. Koutsonikolas, and K.-H. Kim. Widraw: Enabling hands-free drawing in the air on commodity wifi devices. In *Proc. ACM MobiCom*, pages 77–89, 2015.

[40] D. Vasisht, S. Kumar, and D. Katabi. Decimeter-level localization with a single wifi access point. In *Proc. Usenix NSDI*, pages 165–178, 2016.

[41] J. Wang, X. Chen, D. Fang, C. Q. Wu, Z. Yang, and T. Xing. Transferring compressive sensing based device-free localization across target diversity. *IEEE Trans. on Industrial Electronics*, 62(4):2397–2409, 2015.

[42] J. Wang, D. Fang, X. Chen, Z. Yang, T. Xing, and L. Cai. Lcs: Compressive sensing based device-free localization for multiple targets in sensor networks. In *Proc. IEEE INFOCOM*, pages 145–149, 2013.

[43] J. Wang, D. Fang, Z. Yang, H. Jiang, X. Chen, T. Xing, and L. Cai. E-hipa: An energy-efficient framework for high-precision multi-target adaptive device-free localization. *IEEE Trans. on Mobile Computing*, 12(5):1–12, 2016.

[44] J. Wang, H. Jiang, J. Xiong, K. Jamieson, X. Chen, D. Fang, and B. Xie. Lifs: Low human-effort, device-free localization with fine-grained subcarrier information. In *Proc. ACM MobiCom*, pages 243–256, 2016.

[45] J. Wang and D. Katabi. Dude, where's my card? rfid positioning that works with multipath and non-line of sight. In *Proc. ACM SIGCOMM*, volume 43, pages 51–62, 2013.

[46] J. Wang, D. Vasisht, and D. Katabi. Rf-idraw: virtual touch screen in the air using rf signals. In *Proc. ACM SIGCOMM*, volume 44, pages 235–246, 2014.

[47] T. Wei and X. Zhang. mtrack: High-precision passive tracking using millimeter wave radios. In *Proc. ACM MobiCom*, pages 117–129, 2015.

[48] J. Wilson and N. Patwari. See-through walls: Motion tracking using variance-based radio tomography networks. *IEEE Trans. on Mobile Computing*, 10(5):612–621, 2011.

[49] J. Xiao, K. Wu, Y. Yi, L. Wang, and L. M. Ni. Pilot: Passive device-free indoor localization using channel state information. In *Proc. IEEE international conference on Distributed computing systems (ICDCS)*, pages 236–245, 2013.

[50] J. Xiong and K. Jamieson. Towards fine-grained radio-based indoor location. In *Proc. ACM Workshop on Mobile Computing Systems & Applications*, pages 13–18, 2012.

[51] J. Xiong and K. Jamieson. Arraytrack: a fine-grained indoor location system. In *Proc. Usenix NSDI*, pages 71–84, 2013.

[52] J. Xiong, K. Jamieson, and K. Sundaresan. Synchronicity: pushing the envelope of fine-grained localization with distributed mimo. In *Proc. ACM Workshop on Hot Topics in Wireless*, pages 43–48, 2014.

[53] J. Xiong, K. Sundaresan, and K. Jamieson. Tonetrack: Leveraging frequency-agile radios for time-based indoor wireless localization. In *Proc. ACM MobiCom*, pages 537–549, 2015.

[54] C. Xu, B. Firner, R. S. Moore, Y. Zhang, W. Trappe, R. Howard, F. Zhang, and N. An. Scpl: indoor device-free multi-subject counting and localization using radio signal strength. In *Proc. ACM/IEEE IPSN*, pages 79–90, 2013.

[55] L. Yang, Q. Lin, X. Li, T. Liu, and Y. Liu. See through walls with cots rfid system! In *Proc. ACM MobiCom*, pages 1–12, 2015.

[56] S. Yun, Y.-C. Chen, and L. Qiu. Turning a mobile device into a mouse in the air. In *Proc. ACM Mobisys*, pages 15–29, 2015.

[57] D. Zhang, Y. Liu, X. Guo, and L. M. Ni. Rass: A real-time, accurate, and scalable system for tracking transceiver-free objects. *IEEE Trans. on Parallel and Distributed Systems*, 24(5):996–1008, 2013.

[58] Y. Zhu, Y. Zhu, B. Y. Zhao, and H. Zheng. Reusing 60ghz radios for mobile radar imaging. In *Proc. ACM MobiCom*, pages 103–116, 2015.

RT-OPEX: Flexible Scheduling for Cloud-RAN Processing

Krishna C. Garikipati Kassem Fawaz Kang G. Shin
University of Michigan

ABSTRACT

It is cost-effective to process wireless frames on general-purpose processors (GPPs) in place of dedicated hardware. Wireless operators are decoupling signal processing from basestations and implementing it in a cloud of compute resources, also known as a *cloud-RAN* (C-RAN). A C-RAN must meet the deadlines of processing wireless frames; for example, $3ms$ to transport, decode and respond to an LTE uplink frame. The design of baseband processing on these platforms is thus a major challenge for which various processing and real-time scheduling techniques have been proposed.

In this paper, we implement a medium-scale C-RAN-type platform and conduct an in-depth analysis of its real-time performance. We find that the commonly used (e.g., partitioned) scheduling techniques for wireless frame processing are inefficient as they either over-provision resources or suffer from deadline misses. This inefficiency stems from the large variations in processing times due to fluctuations in wireless traffic. We present a new framework called RT-OPEX, that leverages these variations and proposes a flexible approach for scheduling. RT-OPEX dynamically migrates parallelizable tasks to idle compute resources at runtime, reducing processing times and hence deadline misses at no additional cost. We implement and evaluate RT-OPEX on a commodity GPP platform using realistic cellular workload traces. Our results show that RT-OPEX achieves an order-of-magnitude improvement over existing C-RAN schedulers in meeting frame processing deadlines.

Keywords

Cellular networks; Cloud-RAN; Real-time scheduling

CoNEXT '16, December 12-15, 2016, Irvine, CA, USA
 ISBN 978-1-4503-4292-6/16/12... $15.00
DOI: http://dx.doi.org/10.1145/2999572.2999591

1. INTRODUCTION

The baseband architecture of today's wireless networks is highly inefficient. Basestations use hardware that is usually proprietary, expensive, and difficult to upgrade. More importantly, the hardware resources (such as CPUs, DSPs, etc.) at each basestation are provisioned for their peak usage. This often results in severe resource-underutilization, as wireless traffic is known to exhibit significant spatial and temporal fluctuations within a network [19]. Moreover, as network density increases with deployment of small cells, the operating costs for the maintenance of the hardware (cooling, site visits, etc.) increases rapidly. Consequently, wireless operators are decoupling baseband processing from basestations and implementing it in a centralized pool of compute resources. The idea is to perform radio access network (RAN) functions in a cloud or a datacenter, where resources can be managed more efficiently. This approach, also known as *Cloud-RAN* (C-RAN), has received considerable attention from the industry as a way to reduce network costs [2, 19].

C-RAN attributes most of its advantages to resource pooling in which the aggregate workload of a group of basestations is processed collectively. Resource pooling has been shown to achieve 22% reduction in compute resources [15]. However, the biggest challenge in a C-RAN comes from the timing constraints of frame processing. For example, in LTE, a basestation must process a received subframe within a hard deadline of $3ms$ before sending an acknowledgment.

Meeting deadlines is inherently tied to the design of the wireless frame processing, particularly the scheduling of frames on available processors and the degree of parallel processing. A scheduler must handle wireless frames that arrive periodically at a fixed rate (every $1ms$ in LTE) by assigning each frame to a computing resource, where each frame has a hard processing deadline. On the other hand, parallelism is another design dimension that enables real-time frame processing. A typical baseband chain consists of signal processing blocks, such as FFT, equalizer, and decoder; each of these blocks can be broken down into independent (sub)tasks that can execute concurrently. For instance, FFT operations can run in parallel across different antennas or symbols while well-known parallel algorithms can be applied to Turbo decoding [24].

State-of-the-Art. Existing solutions utilize different scheduling schemes to meet the C-RAN's timing constraints; these fall under *partitioned* scheduling [15, 31, 36]. Partitioned schedulers employ an upper bound on the frames' processing time (a.k.a. the worst-case execution time (WCET)) as the fixed processing time, which enables the design of optimal scheduling of basestations on multiple processors — a problem known to be NP-complete [11–13, 18, 22, 26, 28].

On the other hand, one could also use a *global* scheduler which maintains a shared queue and assigns each incoming frame to the next available processor according to a priority mechanism, such as first-in-first-out (FIFO) or earliest-deadline-first (EDF). Global schedulers are flexible in that they adapt to the available number of cores and the processing time variations [11, 22, 28].

Other existing systems [32,35] exploit parallelism by splitting the baseband processing into parallel subtasks that can be executed on a large number of CPU cores. By achieving fined-grained parallelism and thus reduced processing times, scheduling incoming frames becomes straightforward as an incoming frame can finish processing before the next frame arrives.

Shortcomings. The assumption of fixed processing time, albeit being simple, does not hold in practice. Both basestation traffic and wireless channel state exhibit significant temporal and spatial variations that result in varying subframe processing times. For example, Fig. 1 shows the workload variations of Band-13 and Band-17 LTE basestations (in downlink) measured over a $50ms$ interval in a metropolitan region. As shown in the figure, the workload varies considerably between two consecutive subframes of a basestation, that are transmitted every $1ms$, in addition to variations across the two basestations. Therefore, a partitioned scheduler that relies on WCET (corresponding to peak load), will over-provision compute resources [27]. A global scheduler avoids the pitfalls of the partitioned scheduler by adapting to the variable processing time and available compute resources. Nevertheless, such schedulers are known to suffer from high runtime overhead (due to cache thrashing) [14].

Problem Statement. The compute resources in a typical C-RAN are made up of interconnected physical or virtual machines running on general-purpose processors (GPPs) and optionally, dedicated hardware accelerators. Similar to existing studies on C-RAN scheduling [15], we adopt the separation principle and decouple the problem of assigning basestations to computing nodes of a C-RAN from the problem of scheduling a subset of basestations on a single computing node. In this paper, we focus on the latter problem of scheduling tasks on a multiprocessor host, where each task represents a subframe decoding process of a basestation. In a C-RAN, the deadline misses result from the compute node not being able to decode a subframe within a deadline. In particular, we address the problem of reducing deadline misses at the node level by improving the performance of C-RAN schedulers.

Proposed Approach. To address the shortcomings of existing schedulers, we propose RT-OPEX (*Real-Time OPportunistic EXecution*), a new framework that combines offline scheduling with runtime parallelism. It minimizes deadline-misses of wireless frame processing by utilizing free CPU

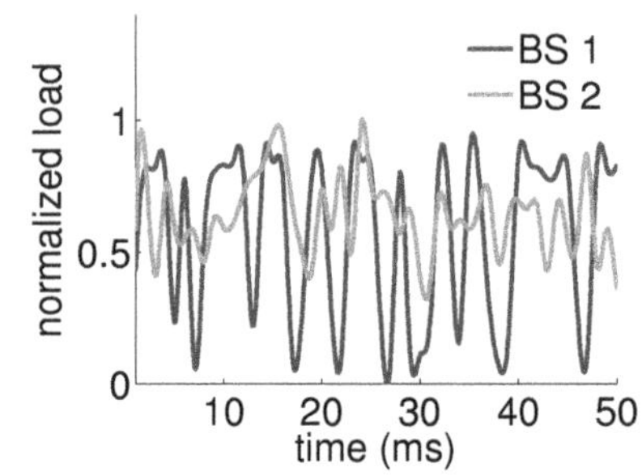

Fig. 1: Variations in cellular load traces.

cycles at runtime to migrate parallelizable tasks to idle cores. The design of RT-OPEX is based on the premise that partitioned scheduling is unable to exploit free CPU cycles, while designing an offline scheduling algorithm with parallel processing is highly intractable. RT-OPEX treads the middle path and adapts offline partitioned scheduling at runtime to utilize the idle CPU cycles.

RT-OPEX vs. Resource Pooling. Existing C-RAN literature [15, 19] has suggested resource pooling in which the statistical information of basestation loads is utilized to aggregate processing. We highlight that RT-OPEX is another variant of resource pooling, except that it consolidates processing at much finer time scales. Specifically, it utilizes the load variations of the order of subframes ($1ms$) to migrate processing on the compute platform. As a result, it maximizes the utilization of the available resources. However, unlike resource pooling, it has the advantage of making no assumptions about the prior knowledge of the load and traffic variations.

We evaluate the performance of RT-OPEX with other well-known schedulers: partitioned and global. For accurate evaluation, we implement a medium-scale testbed comprising 16 radios (frontends), off-the-shelf GPP platform, and Ethernet infrastructure. We profile our implementation to develop an end-to-end (e2e) model for processing that includes transport and processing latency of a wireless frame. Further, we evaluate the merits and demerits of each scheduling scheme under different system configurations, traffic loads, and channel conditions. Our implementation is available as an open-source package [9] that allows comparison of the performance of different C-RAN schedulers. Our results show that RT-OPEX, compared to existing partitioned and global scheduling schemes, reduces the deadline-miss rate by more than orders-of-magnitude.

Contributions. This paper makes the following contributions:

- development of an e2e model for characterizing the wireless frame processing times and the deadline-miss event;
- design, implementation, and evaluation of a flexible scheduling algorithm, RT-OPEX, which reduces deadline misses; and
- comparison of RT-OPEX with different schedulers for a medium-scale testbed under realistic workloads and scenarios.

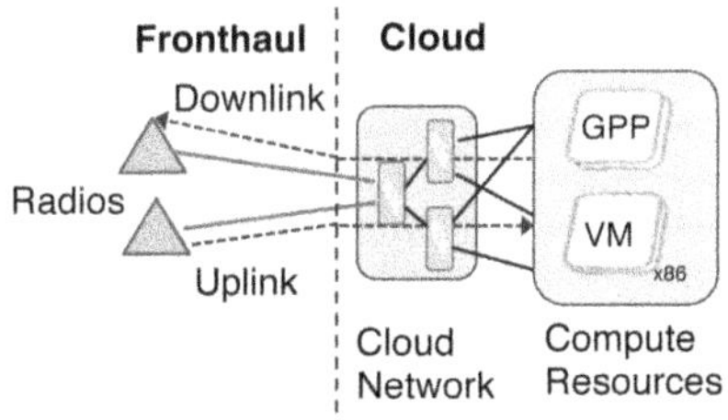

Fig. 2: C-RAN model for processing.

Organization of the paper. The rest of the paper is organized as follows. We present an end-to-end model of C-RAN, including frame processing and transport in Section 2. Section 3 describes the design and implementation of possible schedulers including our proposed RT-OPEX scheduler. Section 4 presents the evaluation results of our implementation. Section 5 discusses the features of the implemented schedulers. Finally, we discuss the related work in Section 6 and conclude the paper in Section 7.

2. END-TO-END MODEL

We assume a pure software-based C-RAN where the entire baseband processing (or L1) is carried out on general-purpose processors (GPPs) or virtual machines (VMs). Fig. 2 shows the main elements in a C-RAN deployment where baseband (or IQ) samples from the radios are transported back and forth over a fronthaul network. We first present a model to calculate the uplink processing time that allows us to characterize the deadline-miss event from an end-to-end perspective. This model is then used to develop C-RAN scheduling algorithms. We restrict our attention to uplink processing as it is significantly more time-consuming and varying than downlink [15,25].

2.1 Uplink processing

A basestation, in the uplink, processes wireless signals from multiple antennas to decode user information. The basic unit of processing in LTE is a subframe ($1ms$ long). Each subframe can be viewed as a precoded sequence of 14 OFDM (Orthogonal Frequency-Division Multiplexing) symbols, which is divided into multiple physical resource blocks (PRBs). The PRBs are then assigned to one or more users; each user encodes information using a modulation and coding scheme (MCS) and transmits it in the allocated PRBs.

The computational load, and therefore, the time to process a subframe, is determined by the number of users, number of antennas, allocation of PRBs to users, MCS assignment, and the number of decoder iterations required to decode user information. To capture this relationship, we present a linear model that accurately approximates the processing time. We first establish the mapping between the MCS and the number of data bits.

Let us consider the transmission of a single user and let the subcarrier load, D, denote the ratio of the number of data bits (packet size) in a subframe to the number of resource elements (REs) available in a subframe, where RE is the basic data carrier unit in an LTE subframe. The packet size as a function of number of PRBs and MCS is determined by a lookup table specified in the LTE standard [7]. For 10MHz bandwidth, which has 8400 REs, D varies from 0.16 to 3.7 bits per RE (for 50 PRBs), corresponding to MCS 0 and MCS 27, respectively. The theoretical subcarrier load is 6 bits per RE when using 64-QAM modulation, but the realized load is much lower due to the overhead of coding, pilots and CRC bits.

LTE's uplink chain consists of commonly used signal processing blocks. To calculate the total processing time, one must model the dependence of each block on the number of antennas, subcarriers, and other block-specific parameters. In general, this can be daunting as the uplink chain contains numerous blocks: FFT/IFFT, channel estimator, equalizer, demapper, descrambler, rate dematcher, and Turbo decoder. However, we can construct a simple yet accurate model by making the following observations: (i) processing time of blocks that operate on the OFDM symbol level (e.g., FFT, equalization), including the memory copy, varies linearly[1] with the number, N, of antennas; (ii) the processing time of blocks using the constellation symbols (e.g., demapper, dematcher) is a function of the modulation order; (iii) the processing time of decoder is determined by the number of iterations (denoted by L), the subcarrier load D, and the observation that the decoder processes D bits per subcarrier in each iteration.

Thus, the total processing time can be written as:

$$T_{rxproc} = w_0 + w_1 \cdot N + w_2 \cdot K + w_3 \cdot D \cdot L + E, \quad (1)$$

where w_0, w_1 and w_2 are constants; E is the error term that includes modeling error and the variability of the execution environment, and K is the modulation order of the MCS. The constants in Eq. (1) are largely implementation- and platform-specific, as they depend on type of optimizations (e.g., vectorization) as well as the architecture.

The processing time depends indirectly on the wireless channel condition through the number of iterations, L, that are required to decode a packet, i.e., pass the CRC checksum. To avoid excessive delay, receivers typically limit decoding to at most L_m iterations. Therefore, irrespective of the channel condition, we obtain an WCET bound on processing time by substituting L with L_m in Eq. (1). Note that the number, L, of iterations is in general non-deterministic (even for fixed SNR) and may take any value in $[1, L_m]$.

To validate our linear model, we collect data (see §4.2) on the total uplink processing time of a 10MHz LTE system (50 PRBs) for different MCS (0–27), SNR values (0–30dB), and different number of antennas. The maximum number, L_m, of Turbo iterations is set to 4. For each measurement, we note the load, D, and the iteration count, L, and then apply a linear regression to determine the model parameters.

Table 1 shows the model parameter estimates obtained from 4×10^6 measurements on a GPP platform. We also show the goodness-of-fit metric, r^2, in each scenario. The fitness metric is observed to be close to 0.99, indicating the

[1]Assuming maximum-ratio combining, the equalization complexity with spatial multiplexing is N^2 [32].

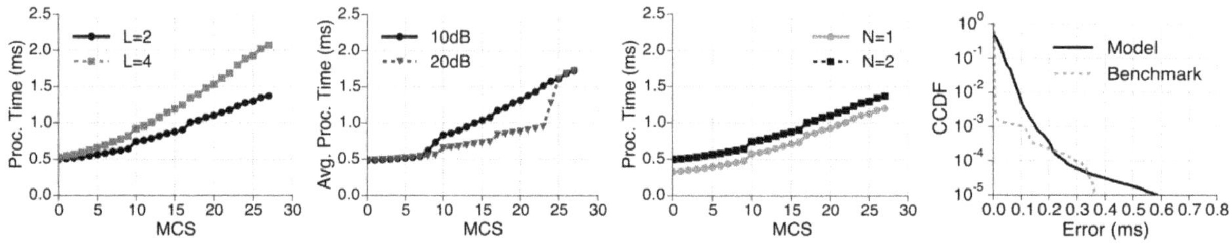

(a) vs. Iterations ($N = 2$) (b) vs. SNR ($N = 2$) (c) vs. Antennas (d) Error (E) distribution

Fig. 3: Plots showing the variations in processing time.

	w_0	w_1	w_2	w_3	r^2
GPP	31.4	169.1	49.7	93.0	0.992

Table 1: Model parameter estimates (in μs).

high accuracy of our model. Based on the model parameter estimates, we can observe, for instance, that each additional antenna adds 169μs while each Turbo iteration at MCS 27 adds 345μs.

Fig. 3 shows the total processing time as we vary the number of iterations, SNR, and the number of antennas. From the plots, it is evident that the processing time exhibits high variability. For instance, it increases by a factor of 2.8 (from $0.5ms$ to $1.4ms$) as MCS changes from 0 to 27 (Fig. 3(a)). Further, the total time with four Turbo iterations compared to two iterations increases the total processing time by more than $0.5ms$, which is consistent with observations made in previous studies [25, 35]. Note that in Fig. 3(b), decreasing the SNR from 20dB to 10dB increases the processing time by more than 50% between MCS 13 and 25. Similarly, for a fixed post-processing SNR, increasing the number of antennas to 2 adds nearly 200μs to processing time.

In summary, we find that wireless processing is a dynamic workload that varies with data rates, channel conditions and the number of antennas used.

Platform Error. Fig. 3(d) shows the distribution of the error between the model and the actual processing time. In 99.9% of observations, the error is less than $0.15ms$. However, for a few measurements, the error can be as high as $0.7ms$. Since the processing runs on a soft real-time system, the processing could be disrupted due to kernel tasks such as interrupt handling. The error term could thus be significant for some observations. Nevertheless, this could also be attributed to a large model error. To confirm otherwise, we perform a separate stress test on the processing platform. We ran the cyclictest [5] latency measurement tool alongside a benchmark load generated using hackbench [6]. The cyclictest was run with the highest system priority and was expected to show a near-constant latency. Fig. 3(d) shows the latency distribution from the benchmark. The mean latency is $0.2ms$, but some of the measurements have a latency above $0.4ms$. We also observe that the *order statistics* of the modeling error is roughly similar to the benchmark latency. For example, 1 in 10^5 measurements had a latency of more than few hundred microseconds. This confirms that the distribution of error term in Eq. (1) is mostly influenced by the platform and not by the model error.

2.2 Parallelism

While our model provides the total processing time, it does not show the processing times of individual blocks. For simplicity, we assume the processing chain comprises of three sequential tasks: FFT, *demod*, and *decode*, where the demod task comprises channel estimation, channel equalizer and constellation-demapper; and decode task includes rate-dematcher, de-scrambler, and Turbo decoder. Similar to Eq. (1), one can obtain a model for the processing time of each block.

Thus far, we have modeled processing time for a single thread running on a single core. However, it is possible to exploit different levels of parallelism, e.g., antenna-level, symbol-level and subcarrier-level parallelism, by making use of multiple CPU cores [35]. The FFT task that runs on each of the 14 OFDM symbols of each antenna is easy to parallelize. Similarly, channel equalization that runs on each OFDM symbol can be parallelized. Turbo decoding which is the most time-consuming operation can be parallelized over code-blocks, where decoding and CRC check can be done independently on each code-block [7]. For instance, at MCS 27, LTE utilizes 6 code-blocks all of which can be decoded concurrently.

Fig. 4 shows the processing times of FFT and decode tasks when it is parallelized over two cores. We can run FFT on 7 OFDM symbols on each core, and nearly halve the processing time (note the maximum overhead of 6μs). In the decode block, as seen in Fig. 4(b), parallelizing the Turbo decoding reduces the processing time by almost 310μs, from 980μs to 670μs.

Based on these observations, Fig. 5 shows a general breakdown of the processing of a subframe into tasks, and further into subtasks. For clarity, each task is shown to be completely parallelizable. For example, the FFT task can be parallelized by executing the FFT operation of each antenna's samples (an FFT subtask) on a different core. Another example is the equalization task, which can be performed independently (thus parallelized) for each group of subcarriers (an equalization subtask). Although a certain task might be parallelized, all of its subtasks must complete execution before moving on to the next stage. This establishes a de-

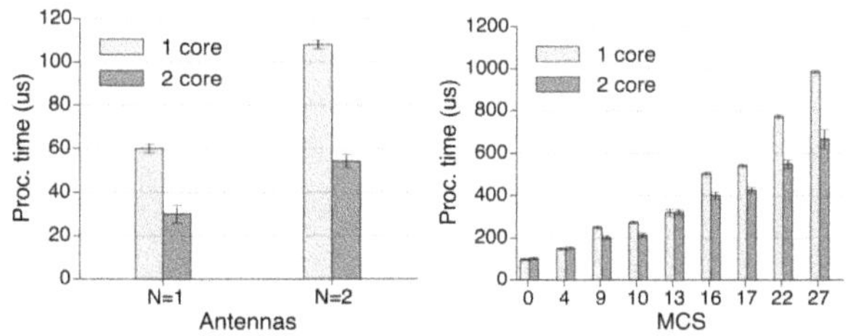

(a) FFT (b) Decode

Fig. 4: Task execution times on multiple cores.

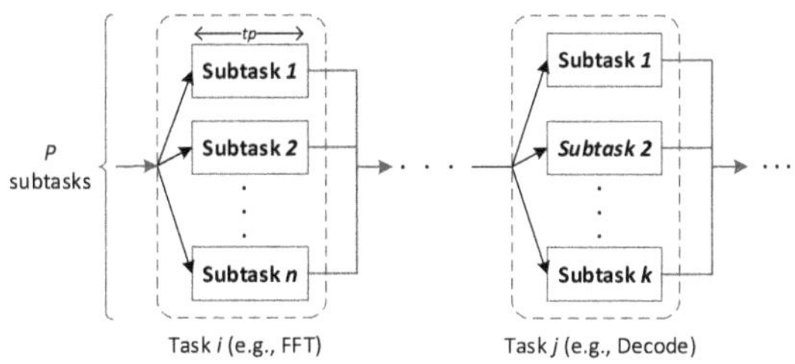

Fig. 5: Breakdown of subframe processing into tasks and subtasks.

pendency/precedence constraint between the different tasks involved in the subframe decoding. So, tasks have to execute in order to ensure correct decoding results. For the rest of the paper, we assume that the execution time of tasks (subtasks), except for the decoder, is deterministic.

2.3 Transport Latency

The transport of IQ samples from the radio front-ends to the cloud involves two separate networks as shown in Fig. 2. The fronthaul network, deployed using an optical fiber network, connects the radios to an optical switch located in the cloud. Various standards such as CPRI [4] have been proposed for transport over fronthaul networks. Also, a cloud network connects the optical switch to the pool of GPPs and VMs. The architecture of the cloud network is similar to a datacenter network (e.g., fat-tree topology) and includes aggregation and top-of-rack switches [19].

A wireless subframe incurs both fronthaul and cloud latencies. The fronthaul latency is a function of the length of the fiber (propagation time of light in fiber is approximately 5μs/Km) and the overhead of optical switching. While the exact fronthaul specifications are still under consideration, it is expected that the distance between remote radios and the cloud can be up to 20–40Km [2], resulting in a one-way propagation delay of 0.1–$0.2ms$ excluding the overheads of (de)-packetization and cloud transport delay. While the fronthaul network has a fixed delay and almost negligible jitter [19], the cloud transport latency is less deterministic as it involves a mix of hardware, software and virtualized interfaces. To see the impact of the cloud network, we measure the one-way latency (measured from the round-trip time) between an external host and cloud resource. The host and the cloud resource are connected over 1/10 GbE Ethernet through a switch. We obtain the measurements by sending 1000 packets per second (LTE processes 1000 subframes per second) between the host and the cloud resource.

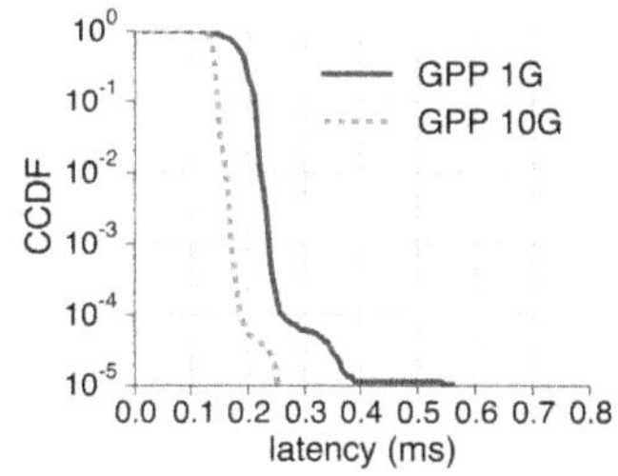

Fig. 6: Distribution of cloud network delay.

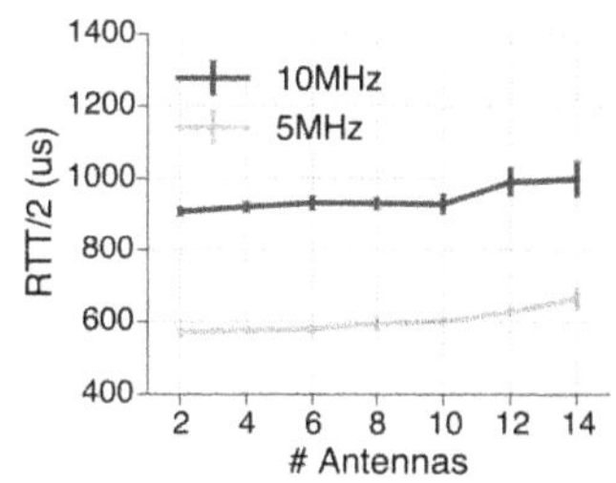

Fig. 7: One-way transport latency for GPP vs. number of antennas for 10GbE.

Fig. 6 shows the distribution of one-way cloud latency for GPP platform with 1 and 10Gbps Ethernet network, respectively. The mean transport latency is around 0.15ms. However, this latency has a long tail distribution where around one in 10^4 packets, for both 1GbE and 10GbE connections, has a latency more than 0.25ms. These observations imply that using the mean statistic of the transport latency is not good enough to provide latency guarantees.

To emulate C-RAN's transport network, we build a medium-size testbed of 16 WARPv3 radios that are connected using Ethernet to an off-the-shelf GPP. The radios are connected via 1 GbE port and then aggregated using a 1/10 GbE switch into GPP's 10GbE port. We use the CWARP transport library [20] to implement the read and write operations. Fig. 7 shows the one-way transport latency as we vary the number of antennas/radios and the bandwidth. In the 5 MHz case, we observe that the maximum latency is 620μs while it exceeds 1000μs (or 1ms) for 10MHz bandwidth. Since LTE frames arrive every 1ms, to prevent queuing delay, at most 8 antennas at 10 MHz can be supported on the GPP.

2.4 Deadline-miss

Once an uplink subframe is received at the radio frontends, an ACK or NACK response must be included in the downlink subframe that is transmitted exactly $3ms$ later. However, as illustrated in Fig. 8, not all of $3ms$is available for Rx processing. For example, subframe N received by the basestation (after acquisition) in the uplink needs to acknowledged by subframe $N+4$ in the downlink. The Tx processing that encodes the response subframe cannot wait indefinitely for the Rx to finish. We assume the Tx processing starts 1ms be-

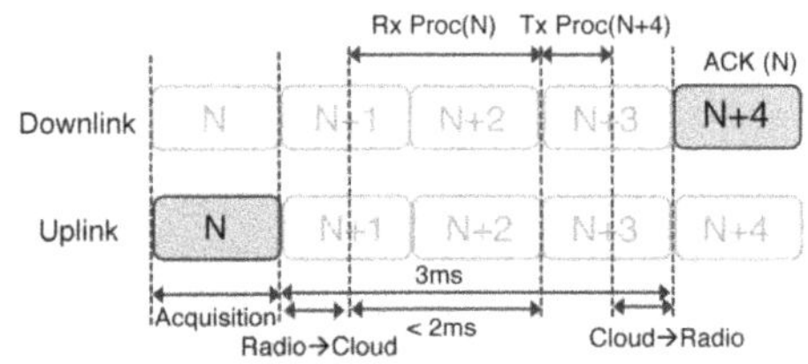

Fig. 8: Example sequence of subframes in LTE showing the Rx and Tx processing timelines.

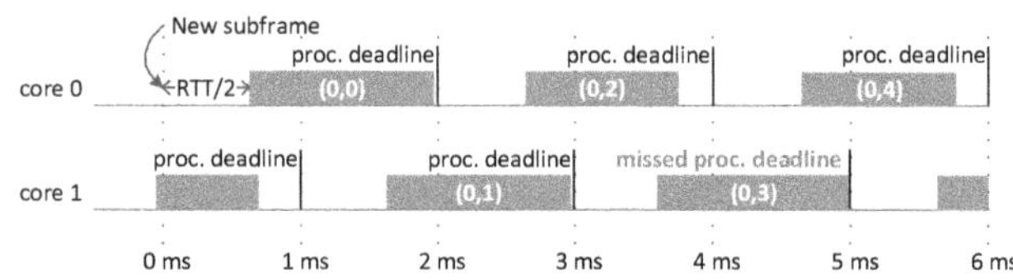

Fig. 9: An example of a partitioned schedule on two cores. Notation (i,j) refer to processing the jth subframe of the ith basestation.

fore the actual over-the-air transmission of downlink frame[2]. As a result, only $2ms$ is effectively available for Rx processing, which includes the transport delay from radios to the cloud.

Formally, we can express the end-to-end timing requirements as:

$$T_{rxproc} + \overbrace{T_{fronthaul} + T_{cloud}}^{\text{RTT/2}} \leq 2ms \tag{2}$$

where $T_{fronthaul}$ is the fixed fronthaul latency and T_{cloud} is the cloud network latency. For ease of notation, the combined transport latency is denoted by RTT/2. One can rewrite Eq. (2) using the model given in Eq. (1). Furthermore, we can use the resulting equation to calculate the probability of a deadline-miss event. Assuming the fronthaul latency is fixed, the calculation requires the underlying distribution of the network latency and platform error. Since the exact distribution is difficult to model, we can use the empirical distribution obtained from separate network and stress tests.

3. C-RAN SCHEDULING

In what follows, we discuss the different approaches to scheduling subframes in C-RAN. We also present the design and implementation of RT-OPEX, a novel scheduling approach that reduces the deadline-miss rate in wireless frame processing.

A typical C-RAN compute resource consists of two main components: transport and processing. The transport component makes an LTE subframe available every $1ms$ for processing. The processing component, on the other hand, receives these subframes and attempts to decode each of them within the available processing time budget. Specifically, the processing time of each subframe, T_{rxproc}, should be less than the processing budget T_{max}, such that

$$T_{rxproc} \leq T_{max} := 2ms - (RTT/2). \tag{3}$$

The compute resource in a C-RAN can be viewed as a multiprocessor host executing a set of processing threads, with each thread continuously running on a single core. The role of a scheduler is then to assign tasks for each processing thread, where a task represents a subframe processing event. Its design takes as inputs the number of available processing cores along with the number of assigned basestations.

[2]Consistent with OpenAirInterface [8] implementation

3.1 Conventional Scheduling Approaches

There are two types of schedulers: *partitioned* and *global*. Described below are their design and implementation.

3.1.1 Partitioned Scheduler

Partitioned schedules are usually determined offline; each incoming subframe is assigned to a core based on a predetermined schedule. Such schedules have the advantages of providing statistical real-time processing guarantees and generating deterministic schedules.

To design the partitioned schedule, we utilize the processing budget T_{max} (note that $T_{max} < 2ms$) as the execution time of each subtask. If the actual execution time exceeds T_{max}, then a deadline-miss will occur. The scheduler assigns $\lceil T_{max} \rceil$ cores for each basestation. Assuming there are M basestations to schedule the processing of subframes, for a basestation of id i ($0 \leq i \leq M-1$), it maps the subframe of index j to core $i * \lceil T_{max} \rceil + j \; mod \lceil T_{max} \rceil$.

As a basestation receives a new subframe each $1ms$, the partitioned scheduler schedules two subframes on the same core each $\lceil T_{max} \rceil \; ms$. This guarantees each subframe to have $\lceil T_{max} \rceil \; ms$ of available processing time on the core it is assigned to, which is larger than its upper bound of T_{max} ms. Fig. 9 shows an example partitioned schedule on a 2-core host (the deadline-miss event in the figure will be discussed in Section 3.2). In this example, $\lceil T_{max} \rceil = 2$, so the partitioned scheduler assigns the subframes in a round-robin fashion on the two cores each $1ms$.

3.1.2 Global Scheduler

We utilize a single queue shared across basestations to implement the global scheduling of subframes on a single computing node. The queue is realized with a fixed-size ring-buffer that holds the incoming subframes from the basestations. A scheduling thread runs on a separate core and dispatches subframes from the queue to the available cores (each running a processing thread) for processing according to EDF schedule. Note that EDF is equivalent to FIFO scheduling when all basestations have the same transport delay, since all subframes have the same deadline T_{max}.

Each core will process at most one subframe at a time. If the processing does not end before the deadline, the processing thread terminates the ongoing task and goes to an idle state. It then waits for the next dispatched subframe. Fig. 10 shows an example global schedule of 2 basestations on a 2-core host. In this example, when the processing finishes

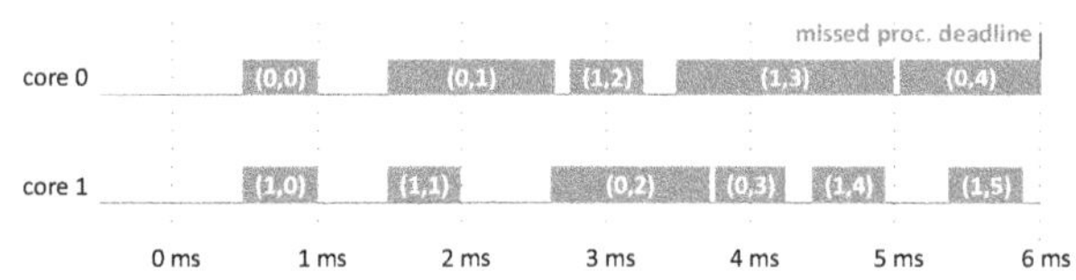

Fig. 10: An example of a global schedule of two basestations on two cores.

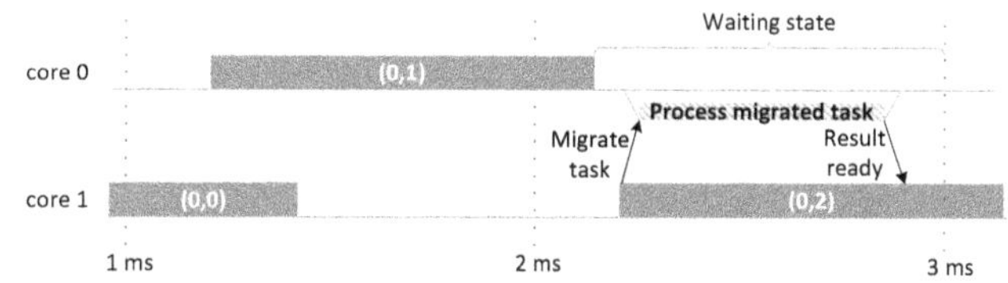

Fig. 11: An example scenario of RT-OPEX showing migration between two cores.

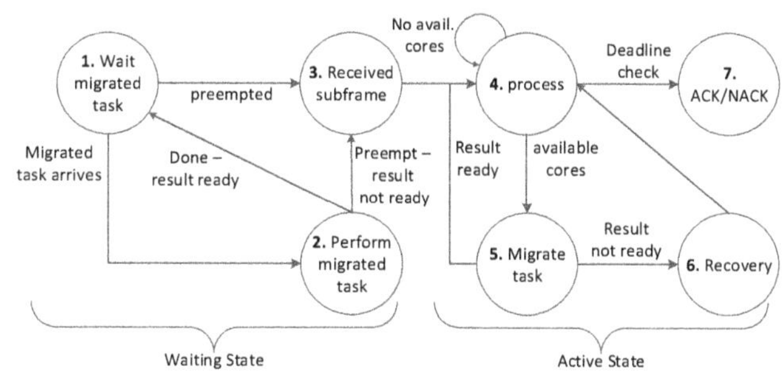

Fig. 12: The state diagram of the processing thread in RT-OPEX.

before the next subframe arrives, no queuing takes place, as seen at $t = 1ms$. On the other hand, at $t = 4ms$, the 4th subframe of basestation 0, is queued and only dispatched at $t = 5ms$, so that it misses its processing deadline (at $6ms$).

Next, we present RT-OPEX, which builds on top of a partitioned scheduler and utilizes idle processor cycles to reduce deadline-misses.

3.2 RT-OPEX

Three characteristics define the subframe processing tasks — they are *periodic*, have *non-deterministic execution times*, and require *real-time constraints* to be met. Due to the non-deterministic nature of wireless frame processing, a partitioned scheduler cannot account for deadline-misses or idle times of the cores at design time. Moreover, subtasks comprising a task (e.g., Turbo decoding) exhibit highly dynamic execution times. A partitioned scheduler considering each subtask as an independent execution unit still suffers from the same issues of potentially missing deadline and idle cores (in addition to the complex scheduler design from precedence constraints).

For example, as shown in Fig. 9, the processing time, T_{rxproc}, of a frame might take time less than $\lceil T_{max} \rceil$, so that the core will be idle for the amount of time equal to $\lceil T_{max} \rceil - T_{rxproc}$. On the other hand, in extreme cases, T_{rxproc} will be larger than T_{max}. This event will force a scheduler to drop the subframe to ensure the schedulability of incoming subframes, causing a deadline-miss. Thus, the processing thread (running at each core) alternates between two states: *active* and *waiting*. The active state corresponds to the case when it is processing a subframe (darkened portions of Fig. 9). The waiting state, on the other hand, corresponds to the case when it is not performing any active processing (empty portions of Fig. 9).

3.2.1 *RT-OPEX Design*

The design of RT-OPEX is inspired by an intuitive observation: if the processing thread of core 1 in Fig. 9 were able to utilize the idle cycles of core 0, then it would not have missed its deadline.

RT-OPEX **opp**ortunistically **ex**ecutes a portion of a processing task on another idle core, which we refer to in the rest of this paper as "migration". RT-OPEX is independent of any partitioned scheduler employed underneath. As long as multiple processing threads are running on different cores, there will be time intervals during which the active and waiting states of these threads will overlap. RT-OPEX exploits this phenomenon to decrease processing time, reduce the deadline-miss probability, and improve performance.

A. High-Level Description: At a high level, RT-OPEX *migrates* a subtask from a processing thread in its active state to another processing thread (running on a different core) in the waiting state. In the rest of this paper, we refer to the subframe processing task assigned to a processing thread by the scheduler as the *processing task*, and the subtask (part of the processing task) migrated by RT-OPEX to another core as the *migrated subtask*.

Fig. 11 shows an example of migration. At $2.3ms$, RT-OPEX finds that the processing thread on core 0 is in its waiting state. So, it migrates a subtask from the processing task of core 1 to run on core 0. At that point of time, the processing task will be executing in parallel on both cores (with independent subtasks executing on both cores). After the migrated subtask finishes execution, it makes its result ready for the processing thread to consume it. The processing task then completes execution on core 1 and the processing thread on core 0 returns to its waiting state.

B. Migration Mechanism: Fig. 12 shows the state diagram of RT-OPEX. A processing thread alternates between two states, active and waiting. In its active state, it executes the processing task, and might execute migrated subtask(s) in its waiting state.

1. Waiting State: When the processing thread is in its waiting state, it waits for a migrated subtask for execution (from another processing thread — state 1). When such a subtask arrives, the processing thread starts executing the migrated subtask immediately (state 2), where two of the following events might happen.

1. The migrated task completes before a new processing task is available, i.e., before it gets preempted. RT-

Algorithm 1 The Migration Algorithm in RT-OPEX.

```
1: Input: P subtasks, each subtask has t_p proc. time.
2: Input: R cores, each core has fc_k > 0 of free time.
3: Input: δ, cost of migrating a subtask to another core.
4: S ← P                    ▷ S is # of left subtasks (not migrated)
5: max_off ← 0              ▷ max # of migrated subtasks per core
6: while S > 1 and k ≤ R do
7:     lim_off = ⌊fc_k / (t_p + δ)⌋   ▷ # of subtasks can be migrated
8:     n_off ← min(S − max_off, lim_off, ⌊S/2⌋)
9:     max_off ← max(n_off, max_off)
10:    Migrate n_off subtasks to k^th core
11:    S ← S − n_off
12:    k ← k + 1
13: end while
```

OPEX sets a *result ready* flag for the "remote" processing thread (the one migrating a subtask) to consume the result. The thread then returns to waiting for a migrated subtask (state 2 → state 1).

2. The migrated subtask is preempted at the deadline before it is completed. This indicates that a new processing task is available for the processing thread. RT-OPEX sets a *result not ready* flag and switches the processing thread to the active state (state 2 → state 3).

While waiting for a migrated subtask (at state 1), the transport component can preempt the processing thread to indicate that a new processing task is available (state 1 → state 3).

2. Active State: When the processing thread receives a new processing task, it switches to the active state, and starts processing the subframe (state 4).

The processing thread starts processing the subframe until it reaches a parallelizable task which offers an opportunity for migration to idle cores (such as FFT or decoder). As the arrival of subframes is deterministic, the underlying scheduler should be able to inform when each idle core will be preempted and switched to active processing. As such, the scheduler can compute the potentially available time budget for migration on each idle core.

RT-OPEX uses this knowledge along with the model of the subtask execution time to decide how many subtasks to migrate to each core (state 4 → state 5) by applying Alg. 1. RT-OPEX follows a greedy approach; it tries to migrate subtasks as much as possible with one caveat. The time to execute local subtasks (i.e., those that are not migrated) should be larger than the maximum time of executing migrated subtasks at each idle core (including the migration overhead). This serves to satisfy one important requirement of RT-OPEX. The performance of RT-OPEX must be equal to or strictly better than the case without use of migration. By the time the processing thread finishes executing the local subtasks, all the migrated subtasks must have finished execution so that it can combine their results without any delay. It is worth noting that, in our model, we associate each subtask (comprising a parallelizable task) with a fixed and deterministic execution time. So, we can treat each subtask as a single execution unit. In particular, the number of migrated subtasks to a core k, n_{off}, should satisfy the following requirements.

R1. It must be less than the maximum number, k. of subtasks core can accommodate (given in line 7 as lim_{off}), such that $n_{off} \leq lim_{off}$. lim_{off} includes the subtask execution time as well as the subtask migration cost: δ, such that: $n_{off} \leq \lfloor \frac{fc_k}{t_p+\delta} \rfloor$, where fc_k is the available time budget at core k, and t_p is the subtask execution time (computed from our model). δ includes costs incurred during subtask migration such as cache thrashing and accessing the CPU states.

R2. The number of subtasks left after migrating $S - n_{off}$ should be larger than the maximum number of subtasks already allocated to any other core such that $S - n_{off} \geq max_{off}$. It follows that $n_{off} \leq S - max_{off}$.

R3. The number of un-migrated subtasks, $S - n_{off}$, should be larger than the number of subtasks migrated to core k. We need this condition as the previous step doesn't count in the subtasks to be migrated to core k. We then have $S - n_{off} \geq n_{off}$ so that $n_{off} \leq S/2$.

In line 8, Alg. 1 combines the three requirements so that $n_{off} = min(S - max_{off}, lim_{off}, \lfloor \frac{S}{2} \rfloor)$. After calculating n_{off}, RT-OPEX migrates n_{off} subtasks to core k. It repeats the same process until either the number of subtasks for migration or the number of cores is exhausted.

Thanks to Alg. 1, the processing thread does not wait for any migrated subtask for completion. By the time the processing thread finishes the local subtasks, all migrated subtasks are completed in the ideal case. Each migrated subtask is associated with a flag that indicates its completion status (*result ready* vs. *result not ready*). The processing thread checks this value to decide whether to engage the recovery procedure or not. If all migrated subtasks have completed execution, the processing thread can use their results and move on with the execution (state 5 → state 4). On the other hand, if the local processing is complete and at least one migrated subtask is not completed (has its flag set to *result not ready*), the processing thread goes to recovery state (state 5 → state 6).

Execution of the migrated subtask can be incomplete because its execution can take longer than anticipated due to background and other kernel processes. The recovery state handles the case of such inaccurate migration decisions by RT-OPEX. It involves computing the results for those incomplete migrated subtasks. This ensures that the performance of RT-OPEX will be no worse than the baseline case. In the baseline case, all subtasks are executed serially which corresponds to the worst-case scenario of RT-OPEX (no migrated subtask completed execution).

After all subtasks corresponding to a single processing task are completed, the processing thread continues executing the rest of the decoding tasks. It repeats the same procedure for any task that can be parallelized. RT-OPEX always monitors whether the processing thread violated the task's processing deadline ($T_{rxproc} > T_{max}$). Depending on the deadline check status, the processing might result in either an "ACK" or "NACK" message to the radio (state 7) after execution has completed. RT-OPEX then switches the processing thread back to the waiting state.

4. IMPLEMENTATION AND EVALUATION

We implement RT-OPEX and rest of the schedulers on a testbed of software radios, Ethernet, and commodity server hardware. In this section, we give the details of the implementation, the evaluation platform, and performance evaluation of the schedulers.

4.1 Implementation

We have built a multiprocessor scheduler for a single computing resource of a C-RAN from the ground up. Our scheduler utilizes the low-level `pthread` library to implement the processing and transport components. Each thread is mapped to a single kernel-level thread (1:1 mapping), and is bound to a single processing core (overrides OS thread-scheduling). The transport threads run on a dedicated set of cores that are separate from processing cores. The transport and the processing threads are synchronized using semaphores. As the transport threads are critical to maintaining synchronization between the radios and the GPP (triggered every $1ms$), we use a *one-way locking* mechanism where processing threads wait for the transport threads (not the other way around). The processing threads are signaled on two occasions: (1) when the transport threads finish writing to the sample IQ buffer indicating the arrival of a new subframe, and/or (2) when a migrated subtask is available from another processing thread. We implement a common watchdog timer that maintains a global reference time that allows detecting deadline-misses across the cores. We also implement a shared data structure, indexed by each core ID, to maintain the CPU states (active, idle — with remaining time) that each processing thread (of each core) updates and polls.

Our scheduler integrates with the OpenAirInterface (OAI) PHY library [8]. OAI is an open-source software implementation of LTE that includes both RAN and Evolved Packet Core, and implements all the PHY-layer functions of LTE Rel 10. OAI implements its out-of-the-box partitioned scheduler for uplink and downlink processing, but it is not amenable to PHY-layer migration. Therefore, we modularize the OAI processing and write an abstraction layer that abstracts the PHY functions at task level, labeled as `taskX`, and subtask level, labeled as `subtaskX`, where $\mathtt{X} \in \{$FFT, demod, decode$\}$. Each of the subtasks can be executed independently, and thus, provides the basis for parallelism. Since OAI implements a complete baseband chain, our abstraction code is tested using traces from OAI simulators to make sure that the processing is reproducible. This step was essential to ensure the correct functioning of the scheduler when the OAI data structures are duplicated for multiple basestations.

Using our system design, partitioned scheduling is realized by fixing the threads on which basestation's subframes are processed, i.e., when a particular subframe is received from the transport, only the corresponding processing thread is notified. In case of global scheduling, there is no binding of a basestation to threads, and any idle processing thread can process an arriving subframe. In RT-OPEX, the migration of subtasks implies that the some of the `subtaskX` routines from the current processing thread are migrated to a different processing thread. As the global OAI variables and the baseband samples are held in a shared memory (L3 or main), migration of data is realized by passing the references to the memory contents.

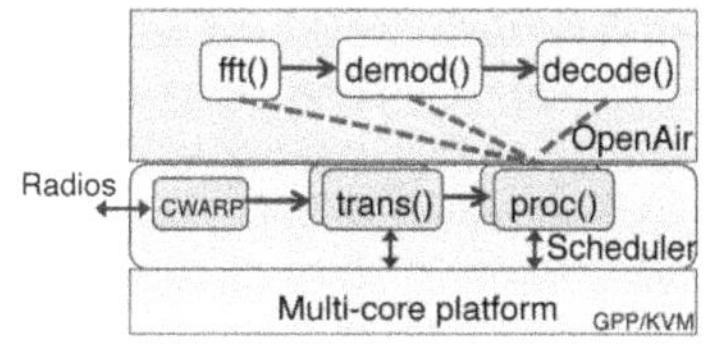

Fig. 13: Implementation framework for RT-OPEX.

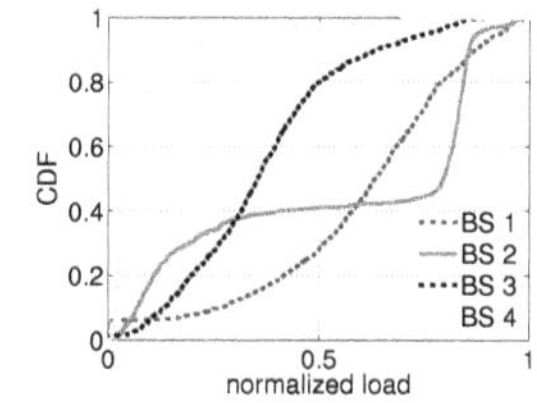

Fig. 14: Basestation load distribution.

Enforcing deadlines. For correct operation of a real-time system, we must ensure that a frame processing task must be completed before, or terminated at its deadline. Implementing this in our system is challenging since we abstract away the low-level PHY routines. One possible solution is to pass a timer to each OAI function, and constantly check on the timer. This approach, however, is not practical. Instead, we check on the slack time (defined as the available time before the task's deadline) before we execute each task; using our task model, we check if the execution time is less than the slack time, else we drop the task and the subframe. The resulting gaps are, however, not used for migration.

Our implementation code is packaged as an open-source tool that evaluates the performance of different schedulers. Fig. 13 depicts the implementation framework used in our evaluation. The tool enables evaluations on different operating systems, including thread scheduling models (e.g., Round-Robin and FIFO), real-time kernel, virtualization, etc. Ultimately, the tool can be used to profile the system performance (deadline-miss rate, load, memory usage) which can, in turn, help operators design and provision compute resources for C-RAN.

4.2 Evaluation Platform

We use different state-of-the-art computing and networking platforms in our evaluations. For computing, we use a general commodity server (i.e.,GPP), a 32-core (hyper-threading enabled) machine with Intel Xeon E5-2660 2.2 GHz x86 CPUs (SandyBridge architecture), 128GB RAM, 15MB L3 cache, and 1/10 GbE Ethernet ports. The evaluation with virtualization platforms such as containers is left to future work. To closely match the performance of data-center networks, we consider 1 GbE and 10 GbE Ethernet links that are connected to the GPP through an HP 6600 series Ethernet switch using standard Intel network drivers.

Optimizations. Several optimizations are applied to get the best computing performance. The OAI workload runs on an Ubuntu 14.04 low-latency kernel. Considered as a soft real-time system, the low-latency version is a stable kernel compared to other hard real-time kernels like RTLinux [10] which require custom patches. Various optimization features, such as SSE3/SSE4 instruction set, O3 flags, etc., are enabled. Further, the power-saving features and sleep states available on Intel processors are disabled. This ensures the CPU cores run at a constant maximum frequency. To minimize disruptions from interrupts, the processing threads are pinned to dedicated cores and use FIFO scheduling. We use the OAI timestamps to calculate the processing time.

Data collection. Since publicly available basestation traces are difficult to obtain, we devise a measurement setup to get the variations of cellular traffic. We use USRP software radios and log RF samples off the air on Band-13 and Band-17 LTE downlink channels in a city environment. Specifically, we log the signal of 4 cellular towers and estimate the load by correlating with the average signal energy every $1ms$. Fig. 14 shows the distribution of the load variations for the 4 basestations. We then ran the scheduler with IQ traces from OAI, where the MCS of each subframe is determined by our basestation load trace. For each experimental setting, we use an AWGN channel model with a fixed SNR of 30dB (and varying MCS according to load) and collect the processing logs of 30000 LTE subframes from each basestation.

Experimental setup. We consider a 4-basestation setup, each with two antennas ($N = 2$), running on a GPP platform. We specify the OAI LTE bandwidth to 10MHz, which corresponds to a sampling rate of 15.36MHz, i.e., each subframe contains 15360 samples. We consider a single user uplink transmission and assume 100% PRB utilization. It is worth noting that 100% PRB utilization constitutes a conservative scenario of a single user for all subframes. This reduces, on average, the opportunities of migrations (resulting in lower performance gains) as compared to a realistic scenario with multiple users and varying PRB utilization. As we were not able to locate decodable real-world BS traces for multiple users, we opted to emulate the BS uplink traffic load through MCS variations and assumed a single user generates that load. Under this configuration, the nominal PHY throughput can vary from 1.3 to 31.7Mbps, depending on the MCS used. Further, we choose $\lceil T_{max} \rceil = 2$, i.e., each basestation is assigned 2 CPU cores under partitioned scheduling.

We first run the processing with our C-RAN testbed with radios and the Ethernet transport. As mentioned earlier, the radios in our testbed are WARPv3 SDR boards. From Fig. 7(a), observe that the one-way latency from radios to the GPP at 10MHz bandwidth is as high as $0.9ms$. This effectively leaves $1.1ms$ to process each subframe (which is much less than the processing time of nearly $1.5ms$ at MCS 27), resulting in a very high deadline-miss rate. Therefore, to accurately emulate real C-RAN deployments, we replace the WARP transport with a fixed transport delay (RTT/2) value ranging from $0.4ms$ to $0.7ms$, that represents various off- and on-site deployment scenarios. In what follows, we describe the C-RAN performance of a GPP platform made up of a single physical machine.

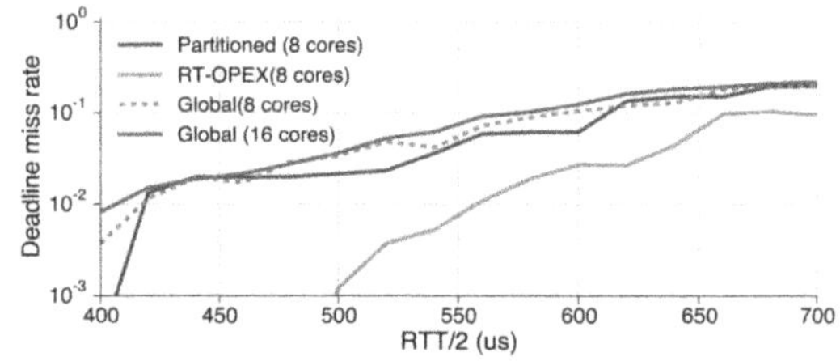

Fig. 15: Deadline-miss comparison of schedulers.

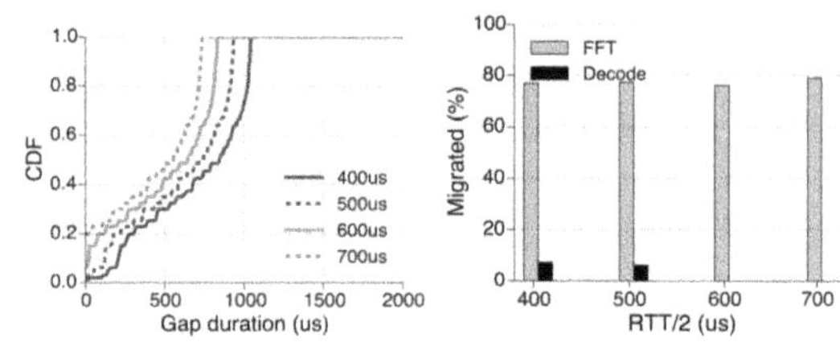

Fig. 16: Gaps and migrations in RT-OPEX.

4.3 Performance comparison

For each transport delay setting, we evaluate the deadline-miss rate for the four basestations and for each scheduler. Fig. 15 shows the deadline-miss performance of the different schedulers. The main takeaways from the figure are as follows.

RT-OPEX **Performance:** RT-OPEX exhibits virtually zero deadline-miss rate when latency is less than $500\mu s$. To understand this further, let's look at Fig. 16. For RTT/2 less than $500\mu s$, the partitioned scheduler has gaps (only due to processing time variation) larger than $500\mu s$ for 60% of the processed subframes. RT-OPEX utilizes these gaps to migrate FFT and decoding subtasks as evident from the right plot of Fig. 16, where 20% of the decode subtasks are migrated. These migrated decode subtasks belong to subframes with high MCS that are responsible for the deadline misses in the original partitioned scheduler. By migrating these tasks, the processing time drops well below $1500\mu s$, which is less than the processing budget.

As latency increases beyond $500\mu s$, the gaps get narrower, thus reducing the chances for migrating the decode subtasks. Nevertheless, RT-OPEX keeps on migrating the smaller size FFT subtasks, resulting in the deadline-miss rate significantly lower than that of the partitioned and global schedulers. As evident from Fig. 15, the deadline-miss rate of RT-OPEX is one order-of-magnitude better ($10^{-2} \rightarrow 10^{-3}$) than that of both partitioned and global schedulers.

Partitioned Scheduler: Unlike RT-OPEX, a partitioned scheduler can't exploit gaps available because of the processing time variations. This is evident from the sudden rise of the deadline-miss rate when RTT/2 exceeds $400\mu s$. The available time budget of processing falls below $1600\mu s$. Referring to Fig. 3(a), the processing time can exceed $1.5ms$ for higher MCS values.

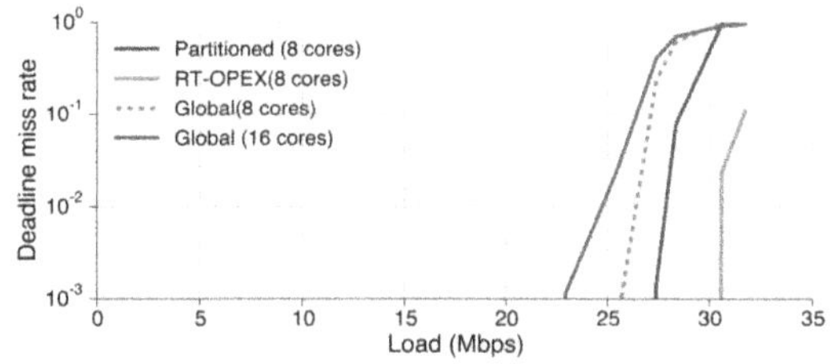

Fig. 17: Deadline-misses vs. load (RTT/2=500μs).

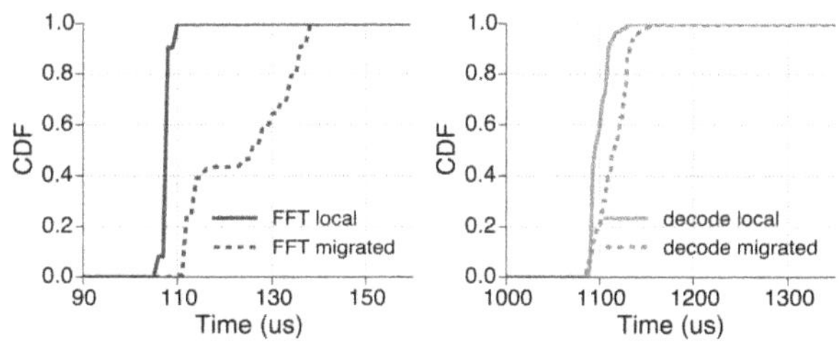

Fig. 18: Comparison of processing times of local and migrated tasks.

As a result, most subframes with MCS larger than 20 will miss their processing deadlines. As RTT further increases above $400\mu s$, the deadline-miss rate increases, albeit at a slower rate. Subframes with lower MCS values can be successfully decoded within $1.3ms$ (corresponding to RTT/2 = $700\mu s$).

Global Scheduler: The global scheduler exhibits the most surprising behavior. We evaluate two global schedulers, one running with 8 cores while the other utilizes 16 cores. Theoretically, this scheduler should perform as good as a partitioned scheduler. Both schedulers provide a subframe with all the time needed to finish decoding before its deadline.

Nevertheless, as evident from Fig. 15, the global scheduler (1) performs slightly worse than the partitioned scheduler, (2) does not improve when the number of cores doubles from 8 to 16, and (3) does not exhibit a zero deadline-miss rate even at the lowest RTT value. As explained later, several factors related to the design and execution of the global scheduler contribute to this surprising phenomenon.

In Fig. 17, we set RTT/2 to 500μs and show the deadline-miss performance for different subframe loads (corresponding to different MCS values). RT-OPEX's gains are shown to be prominent at higher loads (30Mbps and above) where rest of the schedulers miss deadlines for 100% of the frames. Therefore, assuming a deadline-miss threshold of 10^{-2} that is typical of real-time systems, RT-OPEX can support 15% higher load (31Mbps compared to 27Mbps) than a default partitioned scheduler.

4.4 Migration Overhead

The major overhead in migration comes from the transfer of contents from shared memory. The additional overhead of maintaining CPU states via a shared data structure is negligible. Given the complex memory hierarchy of modern processors, providing a detailed cache analysis is outside of the scope of this paper. However, we use our abstraction to calculate the overhead of task migration by simply measuring the time it takes to process a local and a migrated task. Fig. 18 compares the processing times of the tasks that are performed locally and that are migrated to and executed on a different core at runtime. Observe that there is always a non-zero overhead to migrate a task. For example, for FFT, the median processing time increases from 108μs to 126μs when it is migrated, i.e., an 18μs increase. For the decode task, the overhead is nearly the same at 20μs. Thus, the cost of migration is a fixed across the subtasks, which corresponds to the fetching of global OAI variables from shared memory to on-chip/local memory. Note that the subframe buffer and transport block buffer are both referred within the OAI eNB data-structure, and therefore, both FFT and decode migration (including subtask) involve the same amount of memory transfer.

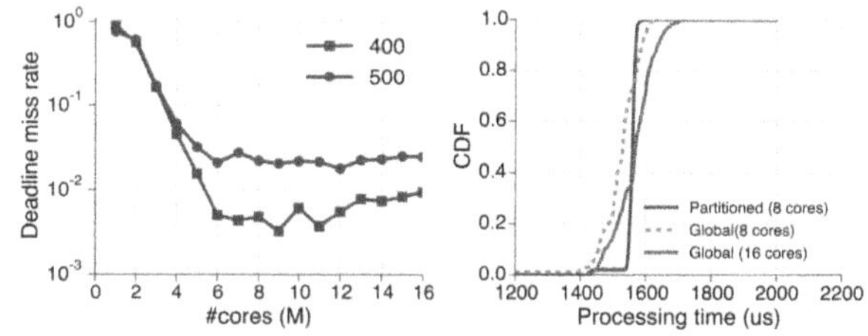

Fig. 19: Global scheduler as cores are varied.

Global scheduling, while offering increased flexibility, suffers from high overheads. More interestingly, increasing the number of cores does not mitigate this (and even decreases performance). To see this, consider Fig. 19, where deadline-miss performance saturates and even worsens beyond eight cores. This is attributed to increased cache thrashing. Each core in global scheduling processes different basestations every few subframes, which leads to frequent flushing of its memory cache and adds to the processing times, as evident from the right plot in Fig. 19, which shows the processing time distribution for MCS 27. From the plot, we observe that global with 16 cores has a considerably larger processing time (80μs) for more than 10% of the subframes.

5. DISCUSSION

Based on our evaluation of the different scheduling approaches, we now discuss them in the context of operator deployments.

A. Overhead: The additional scheduling overhead of a partitioned schedule is minimal; each subframe is assigned to a predetermined core without the need of locking or migration across cores. On the other hand, a global scheduler incurs higher overhead because of frequent cache trashing. RT-OPEX incurs the overhead of subtask migration, which we estimated to be in the order of $20\mu s$ for both FFT and decode subtasks. RT-OPEX takes this overhead into account while migrating so as to guarantee feasible migration. Even with the overhead, we show in §4.3 that RT-OPEX achieves a significant improvement in deadline-miss performance.

Table 2: Qualitative comparison of related scheduling approaches in C-RAN.

	Migration	Compute Resources	Granularity
PRAN [31]	Yes	Dynamic	Subtask
CloudIQ [15]	No	Fixed	Task
WiBench [34]	No	Fixed	Subtask
BigStation [32]	No	Fixed	Subtask
RT-OPEX	Yes	Fixed/Dynamic	Subtask

B. Flexibility to resources: Available resources in C-RAN might change over time as storage, memory, and processor failures are common in a datacenter running on commodity hardware [30]. As a partitioned schedule is provisioned to a set of fixed resources, any change in the available resources results in a significant performance degradation [16]. Alternatively, a global schedule, by virtue of its design, adapts to the underlying resources without the need to design a new schedule (Fig. 19). RT-OPEX suffers from the same limitation of a partitioned schedule, but can automatically exploit any added resources to migrate subtasks.

C. Flexibility to load: From our measurements, we observe that processing times exhibit millisecond-level variations due to varying traffic loads and channel conditions (Fig. 1). However, the partitioned schedule fails to adapt to varying processing times. When the processing time of a subframe exceeds the deadline, partitioned schedules drop the subframe resulting in a deadline miss. This occurs even though processing on another resource might introduce a gap. RT-OPEX fills the scheduling gaps by migrating subtasks to the available cores. It, therefore, adapts to the variations in the load. By design, the global scheduler is inherently flexible to the varying processing time.

D. Generality: The applicability of RT-OPEX is more significant for resource pooling in C-RAN where multiple basestations are processed together on a common platform. Particularly, for a heterogeneous set of basestations and standards (e.g., cellular-IoT [3]) where the traffic and channel conditions vary widely across the basestations, RT-OPEX can easily leverage idle cycles to improve performance.

6. RELATED WORK

Real-time wireless frame processing using software radios has been an active area of research over the past decade [25, 29]. Today, there are commercial software implementations of a fully functional LTE basestation [1]. However, their performance is nowhere close to dedicated hardware platforms. With the introduction of C-RAN [2], a slightly different variant — cloud-based processing — has received considerable attention. Some of the recent work in C-RAN has focused on its real-time implementation and scheduling. In Table 2 we summarize the properties of such approaches and show how RT-OPEX compares to them.

CloudIQ [15] provides a statistical framework to schedule multiple basestations on a multi-core platform in order to meet their processing requirements. However, it assumes fixed processing time (equal to the WCET) for each LTE subframe and does not take into account the idle compute cycles generated at smaller timescales. Moreover, CloudIQ treats each subframe processing task as an atomic execution unit, generates schedules for a fixed set of resources and provides no provisions for task migration. PRAN [31], a more flexible approach to resource management, proposes a pool of shared compute resources based on the dynamics of the load. PRAN further breaks each processing task into a set of subtasks, and allows for subtask migration across CPU cores. Nevertheless, PRAN's scheduling decisions are made before wireless frames are received, and thus cannot account for processing time variations due to channel conditions.

WiBench [34] is an open source framework that allows benchmarking of the wireless processing tasks. The authors analyzed the performance of LTE uplink processing to conclude that hardware acceleration is required for subtasks such as Turbo decoding. In a follow-up work [35], the authors present a system utilizing four GPUs to achieve real-time LTE subframe processing. The WiBench framework assumes fixed compute resources and does not support task migration. Finally, BigStation [32] provides an architecture for processing MU-MIMO frames in real time. It is based on parallelizing the processing subtasks of MU-MIMO and running them on a compute cluster made of commodity hardware. BigStation, similar to WiBench, assumes a fixed number of resources at runtime and provides no task migration.

RT-OPEX is different from the above solutions in that it supports migration at the subtask level. As the scheduling takes place at runtime, it works with both, fixed and dynamic nature of compute resources. It can be viewed as a specific application of work-stealing [17], which is a well-studied dynamic load-balancing technique for scheduling of parallel tasks.

The role of virtualization in RAN was described in [23, 25, 33]. A container approach to virtualization was shown to have a slightly better performance than a hypervisor approach. In [21], the authors adopt a two-tier model to manage a RAN where part of the control that requires less frequent changes goes to a central controller. The design of a remote radio head and its synchronization with the processing units was described in [36]. Finally, [19] and the references therein provide a comprehensive background on the state of the current C-RAN technology.

7. CONCLUSION

C-RAN is a promising solution to the problem of economically managing the scale of wireless processing in cellular networks. However, meeting frame processing deadlines without over-provisioning resources remains a major challenge. We proposed to meet this challenge with a new scheduling framework that builds on top of partitioned scheduling and opportunistically exploits the idle processing cycles for parallel processing of frames. Our evaluation results have demonstrated its potential in reducing deadline-misses at no additional cost.

Acknowledgments

The authors would like to thank the anonymous reviewers for their constructive comments. The work reported in this paper was supported in part by the NSF under Grants CNS-1160775 and CNS-1317411.

8. REFERENCES

[1] Amarisoft. http://amarisoft.com/. [Online; accessed 29-Jan-2016].

[2] C-RAN: The road towards green RAN. http://labs.chinamobile.com/cran/wp-content/uploads/2014/06/20140613-C-RAN-WP-3.0.pdf. [Online; accessed 29-Nov-2015].

[3] Cellular networks for massive IoT. http://www.ericsson.com/res/docs/whitepapers/wp_iot.pdf. [Online; accessed 10-Oct-2016].

[4] CPRI Specification V6.1. http://www.cpri.info/downloads/CPRI_v_6_1_2014-07-01.pdf. [Online; accessed 29-Nov-2015].

[5] Cyclictest. https://rt.wiki.kernel.org/index.php/Cyclictest. [Online; accessed 29-Nov-2015].

[6] Hackbench. http://manpages.ubuntu.com/manpages/trusty/man8/hackbench.8.html. [Online; accessed 29-Nov-2015].

[7] LTE Physical Layer Procedures. http://www.etsi.org/deliver/etsi_ts/136200_136299/136213/08.08.00_60/ts_136213v080800p.pdf. [Online; accessed 29-Nov-2015].

[8] Open Air Interface. http://www.openairinterface.org/. [Online; accessed 29-Nov-2015].

[9] RT-OPEX. https://github.com/gkchai/RT-OPEX. [Online; accessed 10-Oct-2016].

[10] RTLinux. http://rt.wiki.kernel.org/. [Online; accessed 29-Jan-2016].

[11] B. Andersson, S. Baruah, and J. Jonsson. Static-priority scheduling on multiprocessor. In *Proceedings of IEEE Real-Time Systems Symposium*, rtss, pages 193–202, 2001.

[12] T. Baker and S. Baruah. Schedulability analysis of multiprocessor sporadic task systems. In S. H. Son, I. Lee, and J. Y.-T. Leung, editors, *Handbook of Real-Time and Embedded Systems*. Chapman Hall/CRC Press, 2007.

[13] J. Baro, F. Boniol, M. Cordovilla, E. Noulard, and C. Pagetti. Off-line (optimal) multiprocessor scheduling of dependent periodic tasks. In *Proceedings of the 27th Annual ACM Symposium on Applied Computing*, SAC '12, pages 1815–1820, 2012.

[14] A. Bastoni, B. Brandenburg, and J. Anderson. Is semi-partitioned scheduling practical? In *Real-Time Systems (ECRTS), Euromicro Conference on*, pages 125–135, 2011.

[15] S. Bhaumik, S. P. Chandrabose, M. K. Jataprolu, G. Kumar, A. Muralidhar, P. Polakos, V. Srinivasan, and T. Woo. Cloudiq: A framework for processing base stations in a data center. In *Mobicom*, 2012.

[16] S. R. Biyabani, J. A. Stankovic, and K. Ramamritham. The integration of deadline and criticalness in hard real-time scheduling. In *Real-Time Systems Symposium, 1988., Proceedings.*, pages 152–160, Dec 1988.

[17] R. D. Blumofe and C. E. Leiserson. Scheduling multithreaded computations by work stealing. *Journal of ACM*, 46(5):720–748, 1999.

[18] J. Carpenter, S. Funk, P. Holman, A. Srinivasan, J. Anderson, and S. Baruah. A categorization of real-time multiprocessor scheduling problems and algorithms. In J. Y.-T. Leung, editor, *Handbook of Scheduling: Algorithms, Models, and Performance Analysis*. CRC Press LLC, 2004.

[19] A. Checko, H. Christiansen, Y. Yan, L. Scolari, G. Kardaras, M. Berger, and L. Dittmann. Cloud ran for mobile networks – a technology overview. *Communications Surveys Tutorials, IEEE*, 17(1):405–426, 2015.

[20] K. C. Garikipati and K. G. Shin. Improving transport design for warp sdr deployments. In *Proceedings of the 2014 ACM Workshop on Software Radio Implementation Forum*, SRIF '14, 2014.

[21] A. Gudipati, D. Perry, L. E. Li, and S. Katti. Softran: Software defined radio access network. In *Proceedings of the Second ACM SIGCOMM Workshop on Hot Topics in Software Defined Networking*, HotSDN '13, 2013.

[22] J. Y.-T. Leung and J. Whitehead. On the complexity of fixed-priority scheduling of periodic, real-time tasks. *Performance Evaluation*, 2(4):237 – 250, 1982.

[23] C. Liang and F. Yu. Wireless network virtualization: A survey, some research issues and challenges. *Communications Surveys Tutorials, IEEE*, 17(1):358–380, Firstquarter 2015.

[24] R. G. Maunder. A fully-parallel turbo decoding algorithm. *IEEE Transactions on Communications*, 63(8):2762–2775, Aug 2015.

[25] N. Nikaein. Processing radio access network functions in the cloud: Critical issues and modeling. In *Proceedings of the 6th International Workshop on Mobile Cloud Computing and Services*, 2015.

[26] Y. Oh and S. H. Son. Allocating fixed-priority periodic tasks on multiprocessor systems. *Real-Time Systems*, 9(3):207–239, 1995.

[27] Z. Shi, E. Jeannot, and J. J. Dongarra. Robust task scheduling in non-deterministic heterogeneous computing systems. In *Cluster Computing, 2006 IEEE International Conference on*, pages 1–10, Sept 2006.

[28] A. Srinivansan and S. K. Baruah. Deadline-based scheduling of periodic task systems on multiprocessors. *Information Processing Letters*, 84:93–98, 2002.

[29] K. Tan, J. Zhang, J. Fang, H. Liu, Y. Ye, S. Wang, Y. Zhang, H. Wu, W. Wang, and G. M. Voelker. Sora:

High performance software radio using general purpose multi-core processors. In *Proceedings of the 6th USENIX Symposium on Networked Systems Design and Implementation*, pages 75–90, 2009.

[30] K. V. Vishwanath and N. Nagappan. Characterizing cloud computing hardware reliability. In *Proceedings of the 1st ACM Symposium on Cloud Computing*, SoCC '10, pages 193–204, 2010.

[31] W. Wu, L. E. Li, A. Panda, and S. Shenker. PRAN: Programmable radio access networks. In *Proceedings of the 13th ACM Workshop on Hot Topics in Networks*, HotNets-XIII, pages 6:1–6:7, 2014.

[32] Q. Yang, X. Li, H. Yao, J. Fang, K. Tan, W. Hu, J. Zhang, and Y. Zhang. Bigstation: Enabling scalable real-time signal processingin large mu-mimo systems. In *SIGCOMM*, 2013.

[33] L. Zhao, M. Li, Y. Zaki, A. Timm-Giel, and C. Gorg. Lte virtualization: From theoretical gain to practical solution. In *Proc 23rd ITC*, 2011.

[34] Q. Zheng, Y. Chen, R. Dreslinski, C. Chakrabarti, A. Anastasopoulos, S. Mahlke, and T. Mudge. Wibench: An open source kernel suite for benchmarking wireless systems. In *2013 IEEE International Symposium on Workload Characterization (IISWC)*, pages 123–132, Sept 2013.

[35] Q. Zheng, Y. Chen, H. Lee, R. Dreslinski, C. Chakrabarti, A. Anastasopoulos, S. Mahlke, and T. Mudge. Using graphics processing units in an lte base station. *Journal of Signal Processing Systems*, 78(1):35–47, 2015.

[36] Z. Zhu, P. Gupta, Q. Wang, S. Kalyanaraman, Y. Lin, H. Franke, and S. Sarangi. Virtual base station pool: Towards a wireless network cloud for radio access networks. In *Proceedings of the 8th ACM International Conference on Computing Frontiers*, 2011.

Enabling Automatic Protocol Behavior Analysis for Android Applications

Jeongmin Kim* Hyunwoo Choi* Hun Namkung Woohyun Choi
Byungkwon Choi Hyunwook Hong Yongdae Kim Jonghyup Lee† Dongsu Han
KAIST †Gachon University

ABSTRACT

Understanding app-specific behavior is important for network operation and management. However, it is often difficult because it requires an in-depth application-layer protocol analysis due to the common use of HTTP(S) and standard data representations (e.g., JSON). This paper presents Extractocol, the first system to offer an automatic and comprehensive analysis of application protocol behaviors for Android applications. Extractocol only uses Android application binary as input and accurately reconstructs HTTP transactions (request-response pairs) and identifies their message formats and relationships using binary analysis. Our evaluation and in-depth case studies on closed-source and open-source apps demonstrate that Extractocol accurately reconstructs network message formats and characterizes network-related application behaviors.

1 Introduction

Android app is an important class of today's Internet applications that generate roughly 40-50% of mobile Web and app traffic [21]. More than 1.4 million Android apps are offered through Google's open market [18], and tens of thousands of new apps are added every month. However, very little information is known about Android application protocol behaviors because they predominantly use proprietary protocols on top of HTTP(S) [41, 48, 64, 77]. The problem is further exacerbated by the popular use of common data representation, such as JSON and XML. As a result, analyzing application protocol behaviors for Android applications requires an in-depth characterization of application-level payload for each individual application.

Understanding the application behavior within the network is invaluable in providing value-added services, such as application acceleration [4, 35] and dynamic caching [11]. It has been a significant interest for a number of applications, including testing protocol implementations [70], analyzing malware [75], and replaying application dialogs [31, 39, 68].

However, protocol behavior analysis is painstakingly manual, requiring tremendous amount of human effort [32, 38] in reverse engineering. On Android, the popular use of and default support for code obfuscation tools, such as ProGuard, make this even more difficult [24, 47].

This paper presents the first comprehensive protocol analysis framework that automatically extracts protocol behaviors, formats, and message signatures. Providing automatic analysis for Android apps, however, introduces two unique challenges. First, while application binary is readily available through the open market, only the client program is available. Typically the server binary, protocol documentation, and the source code are unavailable. Therefore, we must solely rely on the client program, unlike other approaches that use both the server and client binary [32, 68] or even the source code [70]. Second, it must provide high coverage and accurately infer the message format and track dependency relationships between messages—e.g., an authentication token to be used for subsequent requests may be embedded in a prior login response, or a URI of an object may be embedded in a prior response.

To ensure high coverage and accuracy, we apply static binary analysis, using the Android application binary as input. Our insight is to track the code that generates or processes network messages. Our system, Extractocol, infers dependency relationships of objects that flow in from and flow out to the network buffer using static binary analysis. In particular, it extracts parts of application code (i.e., program slices) that either generate requests or parse response messages. It then internally reconstructs the dependencies between these objects. Finally, it applies a careful semantic analysis to extract message formats and signatures from the target program.

Extractocol outputs signatures for each request/response (including URI, query string, request method, header, and body). By pairing a request with its corresponding response, it accurately reconstructs HTTP transactions. We primarily use regular expression to represent the signatures. However, Extractocol internally maintains a tree representation of a signature, allowing us to represent signature in other forms, such as Document Type Definition (DTD) for XML

*The first two authors contributed equally to this work.

CoNEXT '16, December 12 - 15, 2016, Irvine, CA, USA

 ISBN 978-1-4503-4292-6/16/12...$15.00

DOI: http://dx.doi.org/10.1145/2999572.2999596

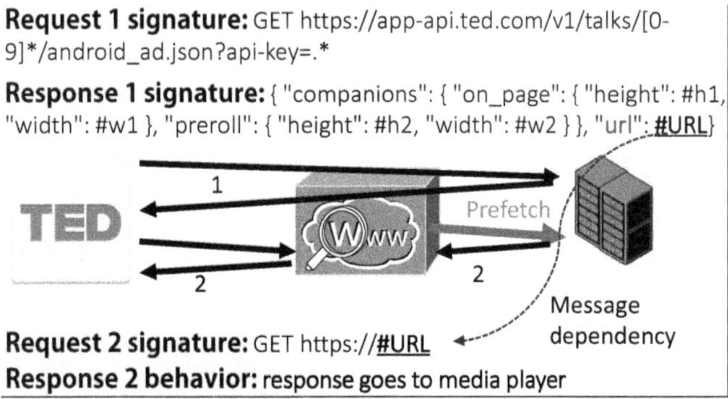

Figure 1: Application acceleration example

and JSON schema for JSON bodies. Extractocol also infers dependencies between transactions by tracking which fields in a request message (e.g., an authentication token) come from an earlier response. Finally, it is able to track how the network originated data is consumed within the Android app (e.g., network data is fed into a video player).

In summary, this paper makes three key contributions:

- **Automatic protocol analysis:** We present the first comprehensive protocol analysis framework for Android applications that is capable of extracting protocol behaviors, formats, and signatures.
- **Novel application of static taint analysis for inferring protocol messages and their relationships:** Extractocol reconstructs request/response pairs, infers fine-grained dependencies between protocol messages, and obtains accurate protocol message formats.
- **System prototype and evaluation:** Our in-depth analysis on open-source and closed-source apps shows that it provides a rich and comprehensive characterization.

2 Motivation and Approach

Applications of protocol analysis: Understanding the app behavior has significant implications in networking. Apart from its *intrinsic* value, it enables the network to provide new application-aware services, often in conjunction with other networking technologies. We provide a few examples of how our protocol analysis can potentially be applied to enable new services.

First, it enables application-aware treatment in the network. Using the request signatures and fine-gained message dependencies, one can intelligently prefetch content, which is one of the key building blocks for application acceleration [4, 7, 11]. Figure 1 shows part of the analysis result of Extractocol for TED Android app. When a talk is requested (request 1), its response contains the URL of an advertisement video. The URL is then requested and the response goes to the video player. Because Extractocol automatically identifies this, one can generate a prefetcher that prefetches advertisements. Also, with the identification of protocol fields and message formats, app-specific dynamic caching can also be automated to accelerate particular applications [11, 16]. Today, the development of dynamic caching proxies is done manually on a per-app basis [16] because it requires the knowledge of application semantics (e.g., which request parameter is dynamically generated) to determine which content is cacheable [11]. A preliminary study has demonstrated the effectiveness of this approach [35] by using the information from tool, Extractocol. The practice is referred to as dynamic site acceleration. For example, Akamai offers a dynamic site acceleration solution [5] where Web applications are accelerated using proxies near the end user, obtains TLS certificate and private key for the service, and serve prefetched dynamic content from the proxy. We believe developing application proxies [35] can be automated and Extractocol is the first step towards this.

In addition, our framework tracks how network data is consumed (e.g., media player) and where the network bound data is originated from (e.g., microphone). This information can be valuable to the network in enhancing the quality of user experience. For example, if the network knows that the response message is streamed into a media player, rather than to a file, it can treat the traffic as such. Similarly, if the app streams data from the microphone or camera, we might infer that the traffic is of high priority or latency-sensitive. Currently, QoS configuration (e.g., preferential traffic treatment) is largely done manually and coarse grained (e.g., on a per-port or per-flow basis). We believe that the understanding of application behavior combined with advances in software-defined networking [44, 71, 88] and visibility of encrypted traffic [6, 13, 14, 67] can enable new dimensions of application-aware networking.

Second, the knowledge on protocol behavior can be used to automate protocol testing. Testing the protocol behavior is often cumbersome and tedious because it requires generating protocol messages exhaustively and also protocol messages often have orderings due to their dependencies. Application protocol analysis can potentially automate this process by generating messages exhaustively while following the dependency between message exchanges.

Third, it can provide useful information for detecting security and privacy issues. For example, taint analysis has long been used for detecting sensitive information leakage [46, 52, 86]. In addition, our tool can be used to finger-print the protocol behaivor of apps, which may be helpful in detecting malicious app behaviors or app repackaging. For example, one approach to malware detection is to match signatures represented as binary patterns or plain strings. However, malwares can easily evade the mechanism by reordering their instructions or functions [10]. In contrast, Extractocol extracts network behavior including network signatures and dependencies between HTTP transactions. This can help detect malware variants in a more robust fashion (unless malwares change their network behaviors significantly).

Goal: Our goal is to provide a comprehensive analysis of each individual application, rather than a large-scale analysis. Note, for the applications above, providing accurate and in-depth analysis with wide coverage is critical. Our system primarily focuses on extracting the application layer interaction that happens over HTTP(S) because most Android apps use HTTP as their primary protocol. Extractocol strives to provide a comprehensive characterization in many regards: it 1) captures all HTTP interactions and reconstructs each transaction; 2) infers relationships and fine-grained dependencies

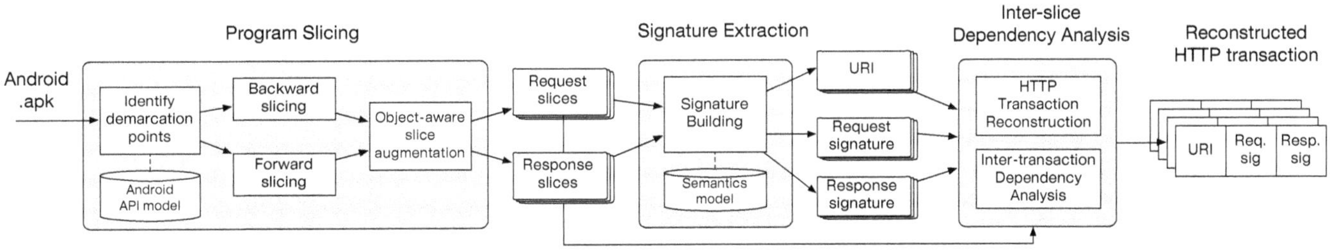

Figure 2: Design overview of Extractocol

between messages; and 3) enables analysis even when apps use HTTPS, which is especially useful for enterprise security applications that decrypt SSL/TLS traffic for enhanced visibility [13, 14, 67].

An HTTP transaction consists of URI, request data (header, mime-type and body), request method, and response data. Our system outputs URI, text, and body signatures using regular expressions.

Approach: Our key insight in protocol analysis is to track all objects that eventually go out to or flow in from the network buffers. To this end, Extractocol identifies and analyzes the program slices that generate/process protocol messages using data dependency analysis. In the process, we solve a number of core challenges for reconstructing program semantics and protocol-related data flows.

The primary contribution is that it is the first system that comprehensively extracts protocol messages and behaviors from Android applications. Our secondary contribution is its novel application of static taint analysis. In particular, we apply taint analysis in three different ways to obtain data dependencies that result from protocol processing. [1] For tracking protocol-related data flow, we extend FlowDroid [27] that provides flow-, context-sensitive, and inter-procedural data flow analysis on Android apps.

3 Extractocol Design

To achieve the end goal, Extractocol performs three tasks: it 1) creates program slices that capture network interaction; 2) incorporates semantics analysis with data dependency analysis to reconstruct message formats and signatures; and 3) identifies fine-grained dependencies between protocol messages by discovering inter-slice dependencies. Figure 2 illustrates the three components.

Network-aware program slicing: A typical program contains many instructions other than protocol processing. Thus, Extractocol pre-processes the APK to extract program slices only related to protocol processing. The goal of this step is to output program slices that generate HTTP requests and process responses. Extractocol extracts all program slices that encompass the objects that either go out to or flow in from the network. We name the out-bound data flow as *request slice* because it captures the code and objects for constructing a request, and the in-bound flow as *response slice* because it captures the code and objects used for processing a response. To obtain these slices, Extractocol employs novel bidirectional taint analysis (§3.1).

Signature extraction: The second phase takes the request/response slices as input and generates message signatures. Since the program slice captures all objects and operations that generate a request or process a response, it encodes all necessary information to extract their signatures. For signature extraction, Extractocol utilizes semantic models for commonly used Android and Java APIs for HTTP processing. It then outputs the request method and signatures for request URIs and request/response headers and bodies (§3.2).

Message dependency analysis: Finally, Extractocol reconstructs a complete transaction by pairing a request URI with its corresponding response. It also infers the relationship between HTTP transactions. In particular, it infers which part of request URI or body is potentially derived from prior responses. The key idea is to identify inter-slice relationships between the request and response slices. For this, Extractocol performs novel inter-slice data flow analysis and addresses a number of issues in handling subtle, but complex inter-slice dependencies that arise due to code reuse (§3.3).

3.1 Network-aware Program Slicing

Extracting program slices that process protocol messages requires keeping track of all operations on data objects that are network I/O bound.[2] Extractocol applies static taint analysis to track network-bound information flow. Unlike static taint analysis whose primary goal is to determine the existence of data flow from taint sources to sinks, Extractocol must track *all operations* on network-bound objects for reconstructing message signatures. Omitting even a single statement that operates on these objects would result in an inaccurate signature. We explain how Extractocol achieves this efficiency.

Demarcation points and bi-directional slicing: Because any object can turn out to be network I/O bound, a naive use of taint analysis would require keeping track of *every* object and its data flow, which is computationally too expensive. Another strawman approach is to carefully select the taint source and sink objects. For example, taint sink can be network access objects (e.g., `org.apache.http`), and source can be JSON, XML, and URI objects. However, this approach is not general enough because generic objects (e.g., array) can turn out to be network bound.

Instead, our main idea is to start from network access methods and taint network buffers. For example, if we taint

[1] Taint analysis is used for bi-directional slicing, inter-slice dependency analysis, and handling asynchronous events as we describe in §3.

[2] We refer to objects as network I/O bound if they either originate from network messages or eventually go out to the network.

Figure 3: Reddit Client (Diode)'s Request & Response slice example

socket buffers, such as `socket.getOutputStream()` and `socket.getInputStream()`, and perform taint propagation, we would be able to track all objects that read from input or write to output socket buffers. Extractocol applies this idea to HTTP processing. We taint HTTP request/response objects used for HTTP interactions, such as `HttpRequest` and `HttpResponse`, as input and output buffers.

Figure 3 shows a code snippet from a reddit client. HTTP access functions, such as `HttpClient.execute()`, take in a `HttpRequest` object and return a `HttpResponse` object. From these statements, Extractocol performs bi-directional (backward and forward) taint propagation, using method's host object, parameters, and return object as the initial tainted objects. The intuition is that forward taint propagation from these functions would track objects that originate from the network (e.g., derived from `HttpResponse`) and backward tainting would track objects that write to the output buffer, such as `HttpRequest`. We refer to such HTTP access functions as *demarcation points (DPs)* because they separate the forward and backward program slices.

As shown in Figure 3, forward taint propagation reveals the data dependency for objects related to response message processing, and backward tainting relates objects that make up the URI, request method, and body. Note, the problem is now reduced to selecting DPs from well-defined Android and Java APIs, which is much more tractable than tracking all objects and much more accurate than heuristically selecting network-bound objects. For this, our semantic model contains information on commonly used HTTP libraries. To help program analysis, the semantic model encodes the semantics of commonly used Android libraries for HTTP processing.

Bi-directional propagation: For high accuracy, the program slices must contain *all operations* related to network-bound objects. To construct such a slice, Extractocol performs open-ended taint propagation to add all statements that include tainted objects into the program slice. Forward taint propagation is handled by FlowDroid's default tainting rules. For backward propagation, however, we flip the edge direction of the control flow graph to inspect the statements in the reverse order. We then apply inverted taint propagation rules—we swap the premise and conclusion of the rules for intra-procedural flows and reverse the taint rules for call and return flows to follow the inter-procedure graph in a reverse order. Namely, a tainted LHS (left-hand side) taints RHS (right-hand side) in an assignment statement, and the taint information of callee's arguments is propagated to caller's arguments. We trace the tainted objects until it has no more objects to propagate. In backward taint propagation, an object is untainted at its definition. In forward taint propagation, objects destructed at the end of procedures are untainted.

Object-aware augmentation: Although, the resulting forward slice reveals data flow for response processing, one limitation is that it may not be self-contained. For example, if an object used in a forward slice is initialized before the demarcation point (DP), the slice does not contain the initialization parameters.

Extractocol augments forward slices with the complete context of objects contained within. It identifies all objects within each forward (response) slice and inspects all backward slices that share the same DP. For each statement in the backward (request) slice, Extractocol checks whether it has direct dependency with objects in the forward slice. If so, we include the statement. We repeat the process until no statements are added. Also, we handle references to resource objects, such as Android.R, whose values are stored user-defined files in the APK (e.g., `res/values/strings.xml`).

3.2 Signature Extraction

This phase takes each request/response slice as input and extracts their formats and signatures and compiles them into regular expressions. It is logically divided into two steps: 1) Extractocol identifies the objects corresponding to URI, request body, and response body through a semantic analysis; for each of the three main objects, it obtains a sub-slice that encompasses statements from the initialization of objects that influence the main object up to their final use. 2) Extractocol actually builds a signature for the sub-slice using semantic models of commonly used Android and Java APIs.

Semantic model: Both steps require program semantic analysis. For this, Extractocol uses semantic models for a set of Android and Java APIs that are commonly used for HTTP protocol processing. The model captures the semantics of each API's operations and its parameters. We model methods and interfaces commonly used for network/HTTP message processing. In particular, we model high-level Java and Android APIs, such as `org.apache.http`, `android.net.http`, `com.android.volley`, `google-http-java-client`, and `java.net`, and popular third-party HTTP libraries [17, 65], such as `OkHttp`, `Retrofit`, `Beefframework` and `rx.android`, for identifying HTTP-related objects, eight commonly used JSON and XML libraries [1], basic containers, such as Array and List, basic Java/Android methods often used for protocol processing, and string/byte manipulation APIs. We also support reflection-based JSON libraries such as Jackson, gson, and retrofit. We find that our model is sufficient for modeling many real-world applications (see §5). To be extensible, we also provide an easy plugin for adding new API semantics. While we currently employ manually derived API models, we believe that Extractocol can be extended to automatically infer the semantics of high-level APIs, as their implementations commonly rely on low-level string manipulations or socket API calls.

1) Semantics-aware object identification: Using the semantic models, Extractocol identifies the URI object, request and response body, and the request method. Extractocol then logically separates the slices by creating a dependency graph for each of the three objects (URI, request, and response body), using the information obtained from program slicing. This process refines the slices for signature building and logically separates the request slice into two sub-slices: one for request body and the other for URI generation. Note the URI slice contains not only the URI, but also the request method and additional HTTP headers that application uses.

sig_pat	::=	*term* | `concat`(*term*, *term*) | `rep`{*term*} | *term* ∨ *term*
term	::=	*constant* | *struct_str* | `unknown`
struct_str	::=	`json` (*obj*) | `xml` (*obj*)
obj	::=	*key_value**
key_value	::=	(*key*, *value*)
key	::=	*constant*
value	::=	*constant* | *obj* | *array*
constant	::=	`num` integer | `str` string
array	::=	*value**

Figure 4: An intermediate language for signature

2) Signature building: Extractocol inspects the three sub-slices to construct their signatures, using the same semantic model. It processes each statement in order and maintains data structures to reconstruct data operations encoded in the slice. For string objects, such as request URIs, query strings, and text bodies, Extractocol maintains a simple data structure that keeps track of the string literals and objects being written to the string object and their relative offsets. For JSON and XML objects, Extractocol maintains a tree data structure.

For each tainted object, it maintains a signature in the signature database. When it encounters a statement that updates tainted objects, it keeps track of the string literals and objects being written to the tainted object and updates their signatures according to the semantics (e.g., string append or JSON put). To aid this process, we use an intermediate language to represent the signature whose simplified form is summarized in Figure 4. The language encodes objects and operations, such as string literals, structured strings, concatenation, repetition, disjunctions, and array. Next, we describe the signature building algorithm in more detail.

Given the program slices, Extractocol inspects each procedure following the inter-procedural data flow encoded in the program slice. *Within* a procedure, it performs flow-sensitive analysis to accurately capture the signatures from all program flows as it may contain branches. For this, we design a new algorithm that efficiently traverses the intra-procedural control flow. Traditional data-flow analysis, such as the worklist algorithm, uses iterative methods to obtain a fixed-point solution. For every change, it revisits the statements in the basic blocks that may be influenced by the change. However, it is known to be very slow and has scalability issues. To be more scalable, we leverage the fact that our objective is to extract signatures for protocol messages and the signatures can be conservatively expressed in our language. We process the statements in basic blocks in topological order of the intra-procedural control flow graph and build the signature database that maps a variable to its signature for each basic block. At confluence points, we merge the signature database from each flow, in the following way. If all the instances of a variable are well-defined (not `unknown`) and the confluence point is not a loop header or latch, Extractocol merges signatures for the variable with logical disjunction (∨). If the confluence point is a loop header or latch, Extractocol

identifies the loop variant part of string objects and den
uses `rep` to mark the part can be repeated in the signa

Finally, Extractocol converts the signature for URI, re
and response objects into regular expressions. The
format of a variable object is derived from its type (e.g.,
for integer variables and .* for string variables). Repe
(`rep`) and disjunctions (∨) are respectively converte
the Kleene star (*) and | in regular expressions. For
and XML objects, the result are of tree structure whose
are string literals or numbers.

Example: Figure 3 shows an example code for Di
popular open-source browser for Reddit, on Google
Extractocol's network-aware program slicing effectivel
tifies the request/response slices. The resulting slice
contain 6.3% of all code, making the signature buildin
cess very efficient.

Extractocol then builds signatures on the slices.
`HttpClient.execute()` (demarcation point in Fi
it identifies a request object, '*request*.' It also recogniz
request method, `GET`, from the object's initialization (i
quest is an *HttpGet* object). Traversing basic blocks, E
tocol inspects each statement of the request slice and e
nine URIs. It employs API semantic model for `St
Builder`, `org.apache.http.message`, and `Li`
generate signatures for the URIs. Finally, our flow-se
signature building process outputs a regular expressio
combines all nine request URI patterns in Figure 3,
which is `http://www.reddit.com/search/.
?q=(.*)&sort=(.*)`.

3.3 Message Dependency Analysis

Extractocol infers the relationships between messages by identifying inter-slice dependencies.

Request-response pairing: We now pair the HTTP request and response messages derived from Extractocol. We use information flow analysis to identify the response that depends on a given request. For this, Extractocol uses URI slices as taint source and response slice as sink and performs taint propagation described in §3.1. However, it is not trivial because of code reuse. When multiple requests and responses share a *common* demarcation point, standard information flow analysis results in a failure; it identifies multiple responses for a single request URI. Figure 5 illustrates such an example.

Two requests and two response slices exist for transactions A and B. Starting from a common method, their paths diverge into `requestA()` and `requestB()`, but soon reconverge to share a common demarcation point in `common2()`. Each box represents a method, and notable code segments are labeled with numbers from 1 to 6. Code segments [1] and [6] respectively mark the beginning of a request and end of response processing for both A and B. As shown in the figure, using request slices (which includes [1]) as the taint source and response slices (which includes [6]) as sink does not identify a one-to-one relationship. Information flow analysis

[3]Although Extractocol analyzes Dalvik bytecode in an intermediate language, we show its source code for illustration purpose.

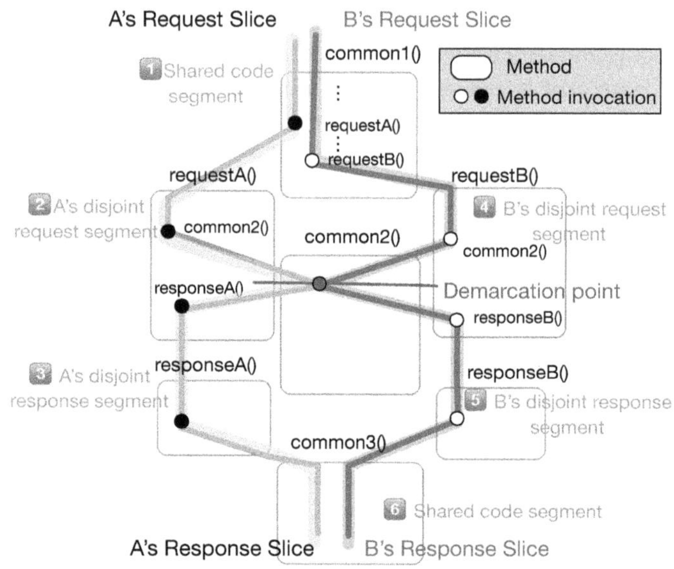

Figure 5: Extractocol locates disjoint code segments, between which only a single path exists.

would discover paths to both A's and B's responses from A's request (i.e., two paths exist from [1] to [6]). Extractocol addresses this problem using a simple intuition: If all request/response slices are disjoint, one-to-one relationship would hold between them. Motivated by this, Extractocol uses disjoint sub-slices (e.g., segments [2],[3],[4], and [5]) as input by preprocessing the slices. The information flow analysis then discovers a path from [2] to [3] and another from [4] to [5]. Thus, we can pair A's request with A's response slice and not with B's response slice. However, pairing may not always be one-to-one in general as there might be a common response handler for multiple requests.

Inter-transactional dependency: Extractocol also identifies fine-grained dependencies by inferring whether objects that are derived from a response is used to construct another request. For this, we identify all objects modified/set as a result of response processing (i.e., response-originated objects) during signature extraction. We also track all objects that make up a request (i.e., request-originating objects). Extractocol infers potential dependency by checking whether the set of response-originated objects overlap with the set of request-originating objects. If they do, we conclude the two transactions have potential dependencies. To ensure object and field sensitivity, we perform object alias analysis by locating common initialization points between the two objects that might overlap. We also track dependencies in field granularity. Extractocol finally outputs which request fields originate from which response fields, which is useful for inferring the protocol common usage and future requests.

3.4 Handling Practical Issues and Challenges

To ensure accurate analysis for real-world apps, Extractocol solves practical challenges in Android program analysis.

Asynchronous events: Asynchronous event handling is very common in Android programming. For example, in our dataset, a weather notification app sets its location inside a callback invoked by a location service. It constructs a part of query string that contains city names and GPS locations into a heap object. Later, another event, such as a user click, actually reads the object to generate an HTTP request. In another example, a server message sets a sub-URI and a timer event triggers a request to that URI. Although, this creates an implicit data flow, it is difficult to infer the ordering between two asynchronous events using static analysis [27]. FlowDroid, in particular, assumes an arbitrarily ordering of these events. This results in a failure to identify the dependencies across these events. In the example above, the dependency between the first (location service) and second event (user click) is lost. Thus, the part of query string created by the location service cannot be identified. Note, dynamic analysis does not solve the problem either because it is difficult to generate all asynchronous events (e.g., server push and timers).

To address the problem, Extractocol tracks all objects that make up a request. For each such object, we identify statements and methods that modify the object (e.g., setter for the object). We then perform backward taint propagation (§3.1) from these statements. This identifies the callers of these functions and the statements that are used to construct the objects in the first place; e.g., it identifies the callback function for location service that constructs part of the URI in the weather app example. In this fashion, we effectively identify implicit data flows that potentially impact the request. Our experience shows that, for closed-source apps with rich UI, this dramatically improves the signature accuracy.

Implicit call flow: Network programming in Android often involves using thread libraries such as `AsyncTask` [3], which introduce implicit call flows. However, existing static taint analysis tools often do not cover them. A recent study, EDGEMINER [33], identified 19,647 callbacks, many of which FlowDroid does not handle. In fact, discovering all implicit callbacks in Android is an active area of research, and a number of studies [33, 69] are devoted to addressing the issue. To enhance the coverage of Extractocol, we add support for many popular implicit callbacks commonly observed in network operation and HTTP libraries [3, 17, 65], such as `AsyncTask`, `volley`, and `retrofit`.

Handling obfuscated libraries: Obfuscation is commonly observed in popular real-world apps. A recent study has shown that 15% of apps are obfuscated [79]. Many tools, including Proguard, rename identifiers with semantically obscure names to make reverse engineering more difficult. Extractocol handles obfuscated application code without any modifications because identifier renaming does not affect its operation. However, when library code included in our semantic model is obfuscated, it becomes more challenging because it requires de-obfuscation. To handle this case, we pre-process the code to generate a map between the obfuscated identifier and the original one. For this, we compare the signatures of the method contained in our semantic model to identify the class and method that has the most similar signature patterns. When there are multiple methods with the same signature, we look at the decompiled code and look for similarity. We find that many real-world apps do not obfuscate library codes, even when their own code is obfuscated. Note, similar techniques have been used in other studies for identifying obfuscated ad libraries in Android apps [62]. Alternatively, one can also use advanced de-obfuscation tools [9, 12] that also handle encrypted strings.

4 Implementation

Our implementation consists of two modules: the data flow analysis module and the signature generation module. The data flow analysis module consists of 2,953 lines of Java code for program slicing and identifying inter-slice dependencies. For this, we extend FlowDroid, a static taint analysis framework, that identifies whether a path exists from a source of sensitive information to a taint sink. It builds upon many existing frameworks such as: Soot, a static analysis framework that provides the Jimple intermediate representation for Java and a call graph analysis framework [60]; Dexpler [28] that converts Dalvik bytecode to Jimple; and IFDS [73] that provides inter-procedural data flow analysis. We modify FlowDroid to find demarcation points and perform bi-directional tainting when necessary. The current implementation of Extractocol uses 39 demarcation points from 16 classes and popular http libraries [17, 65], including `org.apache.http`, `android.net.http`, `android.volley`, `java.net`, `android.media`, `retrofit`, `BeeFramework`, and `ok http`. We also support dependencies that occur between implicit call flows of thread libraries, such as `AsyncTask`, `Volley`, `rx.android`, `Fu tureTask`, and `Beeframew ork`.

The semantic analysis module consists of 8935 lines of Java code. It takes as input an abstract syntax tree of program slices, represented by modified Soot classes. Extractocol operates at Jimple/Shimple code level, instead of the Dalvik bytecode.[4] For the API semantic model, we build-in a number of low-level string APIs and generic data types, including `List`, `Array`, and `HashMap`. Our model also supports the HTTP(S)-related libraries and eight XML and JSON APIs, including `org.json`, `com.google.gson`, `org.xml`, and `com.fasterxml.jackson`, and supports reflection-based nested json serialization.

Discussions and limitations: Extractocol addresses many first-order issues in analyzing HTTP-based application protocols on Android. However, it currently does not handle direct use of `java.net.socket`, automatic modeling of high-level API semantics, binary protocols over HTTP, Android intents, and native binary. Some of them are implemention issues, and Extractocol can be extended to support most of them. Direct use of socket can be handled by modeling socket APIs because Extractocol already parses text-based protocols. API semantics can be automatically inferred by inspecting its code, similar to how we reconstruct signatures from a model of low-level string APIs. Parsing binary protocol requires modeling byte operations. Intents can be also handled by modeling the implicit control flow it introduces, similar to how we handle threads. Supporting native code and JNI is out-of-scope, but more challenging because static analysis

[4]Jimple is a popular intermediate language based on three address code (3AC) often used for bytecode optimization. Shimple only uses the static single assignment (SSA) form.

App	Protocol	Request URI				Request Body/	Response		#Pair
		GET	POST	PUT	DELETE	Query string	JSON	XML	
		(**Extractocol** / Man. UI fuzzing / Source Code)							
Adblock Plus	HTTPS	**2** / 2 / 2	**1** / 1 / 1	-	-	**1** / 1 / 1	-	**1** / 1 / 1	1
AnarXiv	HTTP	**2** / 2 / 2	-	-	-	-	-	**2** / 2 / 2	2
blippex	HTTPS	**1** / 1 / 1	-	-	-	-	**1** / 1 / 1	-	1
Diaspora WebClient	HTTP	**1** / 1 / 1	-	-	-	-	**1** / 1 / 1	-	1
Diode	HTTP(S)	**24** / 24 / 24	-	-	-	-	**2** / 2 / 2	-	5
iFixIt	HTTP	**15** / 15 / 15	**7** / 7 / 7	-	-	**3** / 3 / 3	**14** / 14 / 14	-	14
Lightning	HTTP(S)	**2** / 2 / 2	-	-	-	-	-	**1** / 1 / 1	1
qBittorrent	HTTP	**3** / 3 / 2	**13** / 13 / 2	-	-	**13** / 13 / 13	**3** / 3 / 3	-	3
radio reddit	HTTP(S)	**3** / 3 / 3	**3** / 3 / 3	-	-	**3** / 3 / 3	**4** / 4 / 4	-	4
Reddinator	HTTP(S)	**3** / 3 / 3	**3** / 3 / 3	-	-	-	**6** / 6 / 6	-	6
Twister	HTTP	-	**11** / 11 / 11	-	-	**11** / 11 / 11	**8** / 8 / 8	-	8
TZM	HTTPS	**2** / 2 / 2	-	-	-	-	**1** / 1 / 1	-	1
Wallabag	HTTP	**1** / 1 / 1	-	-	-	-	-	**1** / 1 / 1	1
Weather Notification	HTTP	**2** / 2 / 2	-	-	-	-	-	**2** / 2 / 2	2
		(**Extractocol** / Man. UI fuzzing / Auto UI fuzzing)							
5miles	HTTPS	**24** / 25 / 0	**51** / 12 / 0	-	-	**16** / 6 / 0	**16** / 8 / 0	-	71
AC App for Android	HTTP(S)	**9** / 9 / 7	**15** / 15 / 5	-	-	**15** / 15 / 15	**23** / 23 / 23	-	23
AOL: Mail, News & Video	HTTP	**9** / 9 / 6	-	-	-	-	**9** / 9 / 9	-	9
AccuWeather	HTTP	**15** / 15 / 0	**3** / 3 / 0	-	-	**3** / 3 / 3	**16** / 16 / 16	-	16
Buzzfeed	HTTP(S)	**16** / 5 / 5	**12** / 5 / 1	-	-	**28** / 5 / 5	**6** / 5 / 5	-	27
Flipboard	HTTPS	**23** / 24 / 0	**41** / 13 / 0	-	-	**28** / 13 / 0	**8** / 7 / 0	-	63
GEEK	HTTPS	**0** / 1 / 0	**97** / 48 / 18	-	-	**41** / 48 / 18	**11** / 27 / 18	-	97
KAYAK	HTTPS	**39** / 39 / 15	**7** / 7 / 5	-	-	**7** / 7 / 7	**6** / 6 / 6	-	6
Letgo	HTTPS	**38** / 32 / 10	**10** / 14 / 2	**2** / 2 / 0	**3** / 0 / 0	**20** / 14 / 3	**18** / 13 / 6	-	40
LinkedIn	HTTPS	**38** / 42 / 16	**49** / 17 / 8	**0** / 3 / 0	-	**46** / 17 / 14	**47** / 21 / 14	-	85
Lucktastic	HTTPS	**16** / 2 / 0	**9** / 15 / 0	**2** / 0 / 0	**4** / 0 / 0	**5** / 15 / 0	**19** / 14 / 0	-	31
MusicDownloader	HTTPS	**3** / 10 / 0	**0** / 1 / 0	-	-	**0** / 1 / 0	**4** / 7 / 0	-	2
Offerup	HTTPS	**33** / 20 / 0	**23** / 21 / 0	**8** / 1 / 0	**3** / 0 / 0	**12** / 21 / 0	**25** / 16 / 0	-	63
Pandora Radio	HTTP(S)	**7** / 0 / 0	**53** / 20 / 2	-	-	**53** / 20 / 2	**26** / 16 / 2	-	60
Pinterest	HTTPS	**60** / 62 / 26	**36** / 19 / 16	**32** / 8 / 3	**20** / 10 / 2	**88** / 19 /36	**236** / 58 / 46	-	148
TED	HTTP(S)	**16** / 16 / 10	**2** / 2 / 1	-	-	**2** / 2 / 2	**10** / 10 / 10	-	10
Tophatter	HTTPS	**33** / 24 / 0	**32** / 14 / 0	**1** / 0 / 0	**4** / 1 / 0	**18** / 14 / 0	**32** / 11 / 0	-	62
Tumblr	HTTPS	**12** / 13 / 15	**8** / 5 / 5	-	**1** / 1 / 0	**5** / 5 / 15	**14** / 2 / 14	-	20
WatchESPN	HTTP	**33** / 33 / 17	-	-	-	-	**32** / 32 / 32	-	32
Wish Local	HTTPS	**0** / 1 / 0	**106** / 48 / 21	-	-	**15** / 15 / 21	**28** / 13 / 21	-	106

Table 1: Signatures identified for open-source and closed-source apps (gray box)

on native code is not mature enough for extracting protocols from realistic native binary [82]. One approach is to use dynamic analysis on native code [2, 72] to reconstruct the semantics of JNI.

Finally, our current implementation does not track dependencies across multiple chains of asynchronous events, but only detects dependencies across on hop. One can perform multiple iterations until it does not discover new dependencies for better accuracy and wider coverage.

5 Evaluation

Our goal is to provide a comprehensive analysis of individual applications, rather than a large-scale analysis. Using in-depth case studies of 14 open-source and 20 closed-source apps, we demonstrate that the direct output of Extractocol offers an in-depth analysis of Android applications.

The open source apps were obtained from the open source app repository (F-Droid) [8] (twelve of them are also available on Google Play). We select very popular closed-source apps with 1 million+ downloads that primarily use HTTP and JSON/XML. We exclude apps that primarily use binary protocol or use intent based communication to generate protocol messages because Extractocol currently does not support them (§5.3). Most of them are within top 100 in the Google Play applications category [15].

Our evaluation answers three key questions:

1. *Does it provide accurate signatures with wide coverage for each application?* (§5.1)
2. *Does it effectively characterize app behaviors?* (§5.2)
3. *Can it reverse-engineer (private) REST APIs?* (§5.3)

5.1 Validation of Protocol Analysis

For open source apps, we disable the heuristics for handling asynchronous events, but enable it for closed-source apps. Note, many closed-source apps are obfuscated. For open source apps, we obfuscate their APKs using ProGuard [24] and verify that the same results hold as non-obfuscated APKs. Extractocol takes 4 minutes to analyze an open source app on average. For closed-source apps, the time varies widely from 11 minutes (for a small app) up to 3 hours (for a large app).

Criteria: A protocol analysis must provide high *coverage* by identifying as many HTTP request/response messages as

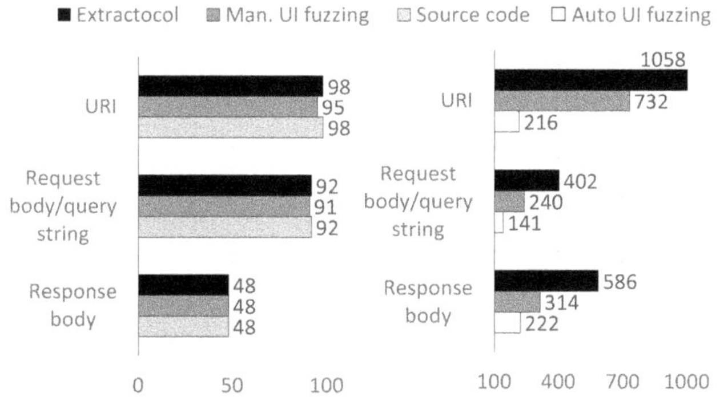

Figure 6: Open source (left) / closed-source (right) apps # signatures

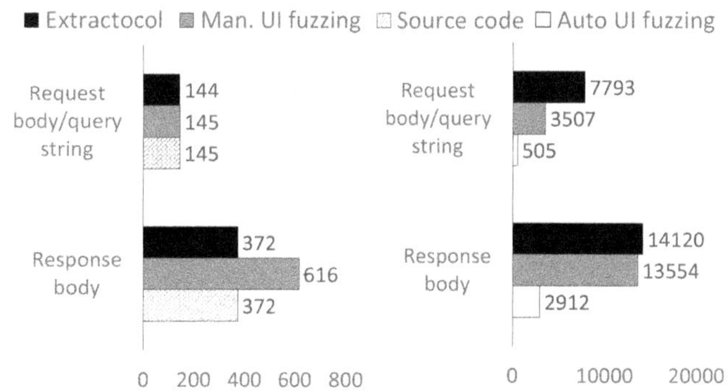

Figure 7: Open source (left) / closed-source (right) apps # keywords

possible. At the same time, its signatures must be *logically equivalent* to the operations encoded in the target program and generate a *valid* match on actual network traces. We verify these criteria as well as *signature quality*.

Coverage: We compare the result of Extractocol with that of manual fuzzing and automatic fuzzing for closed-source apps. For open source apps, instead of automatic fuzzing, we obtain the ground truth by carefully inspecting the *source code*. For all apps, we collect traffic traces of all HTTP(S) transactions using manual UI-fuzzing. Note this often requires manual interventions, such as signing up and logging in for services. For automatic fuzzing, we use PUMA, a UI-automation tool developed for efficient fuzzing.[5] We use man-in-the-middle proxies [19, 23] to capture and decrypt HTTPS messages. We then match the traffic traces with our regex signatures.

Table 1 shows the number of unique HTTP request/response for all apps (e.g., Adblock Plus has two GET and one POST request, out of which one generates an XML response body). For open source apps, the three numbers in each cell respectively show the results for Extractocol, manual UI fuzzing, source code analysis. For closed-source apps (gray), they show results for Extractocol, manual UI fuzzing, automatic UI fuzzing, respectively. Figure 6 shows the total number of unique URIs, request body/query strings, and response bodies identified by each methods.

Extractocol generates much more unique message signatures than manual and automatic fuzzing with PUMA. PUMA fails to recognize custom UI for a number of apps (Table 1) and stops to explore further. One can add PUMA scripts to handle custom UIs for each app. However, UI-fuzzing, including manual fuzzing, fundamentally falls short in providing wide coverage for two reasons. First, some messages are not triggered by human-generated events. For example, we find that some apps trigger APK update requests using timers. Second, some messages are only triggered by actual "actions" with side-effects, such as purchasing products or applying jobs to a company (e.g., LinkedIn). This makes it difficult to explore all cases without a fake server that acts just like the original. In fact, many of the top apps (e.g., 5miles, Letgo, Tophatter, Offerup, Wish Local) are e-commerce/shopping apps where actions, such as payment, delivery, selling and purchasing products, generate HTTP interactions. Upon inspecting the signatures that we did not have traffic traces for, we find that they are related to processing payments, registering new products for sale, viewing products the user has sold/purchased, rating products one purchased, and tracking deliveries.

However, for some apps, Extractocol misses some messages. This is due to two limitations discussed in §4: 1) some messages are triggered by intents; and 2) some apps have multiple chains of dependencies across asynchronous events. We identified that some ad and analytics libraries extensively use multiple asynchronous events and intent. Most of the missed messages stem from the libraries. For example, Luctastic uses various ad and analytics libraries such as chartboost, tapjoy, tap-nexus.appspot, vungle, amplitude and adjust.

Finally, Extractocol pairs responses that have bodies processed by the apps, and it identified 971 HTTP (request URI-response body) pairs. We successfully verified that the signatures and the request-response pairs successfully match with the traffic traces obtained from fuzzing (if present).

Signature validity: For all signatures that have corresponding traffic traces from manual fuzzing, we match them using a regex matcher. All such signatures generated a valid match with the actual traffic trace. In sum, Extractocol provides wide coverage and generates correct signatures.

Logical equivalence: For open-source apps, we verify whether our regex signature and pairings are logically equivalent to the source code. We manually inspect the source code of all 14 open source apps and identify the slices that generate URI, request query and body and that parse the response. We then carefully inspect if the signature and pairing is logically equivalent to the program slice. For example, for request URI, we manually verify if our URI signature accurately represents the URI created by the program slice without unneccessary strings. For a JSON response, we inspect if our signature accurately represents the JSON tree that the response slice is trying to parse. We found all signatures were logically equivalent to the source code.

Signature quality: Note, all regexes that have a corresponding traffic trace generates valid a match with the traffic trace. Here, we attempt to quantify how many constant keywords are present in our regex signature of request/response bod-

[5]Currently, PUMA is the most advanced UI automation tools for Android apps that are publicly available.

	Request Body/ Query String	Response Body (R_k, R_v, R_n)
Open-source apps	47/52/1%	7/48/45%
closed-source apps	48/31/21%	16/35/49%

Table 2: Matched byte count % on actual traffic

ies. For this, we compare the number of constant keywords found in our signature with that in the packet trace obtained by manual fuzzing. We count the keys in key-value pairs of query string, JSON bodies, the tags, and attributes in XML bodies that appear in the traffic trace. For open source apps, we also obtain the ground truth by counting the number of constant keywords appeared in the source code.

Figure 7 shows the number of constant keywords identified. In the request bodies of open-source apps, a total of 145 keywords are identified through manual source code analysis and manual UI-fuzzing. Extractocol identifies all but one. In RRD, a JSON key-value pair string is generated from an user input and stored in a heap object. At a later time, another event triggers an HTTP request. Because we did not use the heuristics for open source apps in §3.4, Extractocol cannot identify implicit dependencies by tracking across multiple asynchronous events. However, Extractocol successfully covers this case when the option enabled. For closed-source apps, the traffic traces from manual fuzzing only contained 3,507 keywords while Extractocol identified 7,793.

We verify the response body signatures in the same way. For closed-source apps, Extractocol identifies 14K JSON keys, while traffic contains 13K. But the gap has decreased from the signature count in Figure 6. This is because response bodies contain JSON keys that are often dynamically generated. For example, a JSON object can contain a list of products as JSON arrays with key being the product ID and value being the product name. For open source apps, responses from the packet traces contain 616 keywords. Extractocol and manual source code analysis identify 60% of them. Upon inspecting the source code, we find that some apps do not inspect all keywords contained in JSON (§3). Despite this, for open source apps with ground truth, all response body signatures were equivalent to the source code.

To further quantify the signature quality, we count the number of bytes that matches with the constant and wildcard of our regex in request body/query string a nd response bodies. R_k and R_v respectively denote the fraction of matched byte count on the constant keywords and the corresponding value parts of our signature (often wildcards). R_n is the fraction of byte count that whose key and values are both wild cards. Table 2 shows the overall fraction of byte count. For open-source apps, 70% bytes of request URIs match with the constant part of our signature (indicated by R_k), and 65% bytes match in closed-source apps. For query strings and request bodies, 100% (R_k + R_v) of all bytes for open-source apps and 91% for closed-source apps match with key-value pairs identified by Extractocol. The rest of 9% (R_n) is covered by the wildcard part of our regex signature. For response body in open-source and closed-source apps, 55% and 51% of bytes match with them respectively, and the rest is covered by wildcards in our regex.

5.2 Characterization of App Behavior

To demonstrate Extractocol's effectiveness in characterizing app's protocol behavior, we present analysis result in greater detail for TED and radio reddit [20] that perform media streaming.

TED is one of the "Best Apps of 2014" on Google Play. We choose this app because it provides rich UI, contains dynamically generated pages including advertisements, and uses third-party libraries, such as the Facebook API.

Extractocol identifies 18 HTTP(S) request and 10 response body signatures (8 responses have no bodies that are processed by the app). Table 4 summarizes notable transactions and their relationships with dependency graph identified by Extractocol. Requests for transaction #1, #3 and #6 use constant string with an *api-key*, which is stored in `android.content.res.Resourcesclass`. It processes their JSON responses and then inserts (or updates if exists) them into a database (`android.database.sqlite.SQLiteDatabase`).

Transaction #1 and #6 show their update operations, and these updated values are later processed in transaction #7 and #8 for their requests, respectively (*Thumbnail URI* and *Audio/video URI* columns of the database). Meanwhile, after parsing JSON responses from transaction #3, transaction #4 retrieves an advertisement URI string, which is then processed for transaction #4's request without database updates. In the same manner, transaction #5 obtains advertisement video URLs for requesting advertisement video streams. Since Extractocol provides Android resource and database semantics, if a data dependency exists between transactions and semantic models such as resources and databases, we are able to identify these transactional relationships. To verify the result with real network traces, we execute TED using PUMA [54], a state-of-the-art automated UI testing tool. Note our system and PUMA have different goals. PUMA merely iterates through all "clickable" elements in the UI to generate all protocol messages, but does *not* identify the relationship between protocol messages unlike ours. PUMA generated a total of 158 HTTP(S) requests. PUMA took 10.3 minutes and Extractocol took 132.5 minutes to complete.

For easy comparison, first we manually group the request URIs into unique patterns. We identify 65 unique URI patterns; URIs in each pattern shared either prefix or postfix. Next, since multiple dynamic traces can map to a single signature, we manually classify each trace into static or dynamic. If all of the URI string are found in a prior response, we classify the request as dynamic. If any part of the URI (delimited by slash) matches with strings in the decompiled APK, we classify it as static. For dynamic requests, we identify their origin (i.e., sources of their dynamic URI).

Using the dataset, we test whether the request URIs and responses obtained from PUMA matches with our signatures, and our transactional relationships match network traffics generated by PUMA. All signatures match with their corresponding traffic traces, and all transactional relationships

```
HTTP Response URI
GET http://www.radioreddit.com/api/hiphop/status.json

HTTP Response Body
[{ "all_listeners":"99999", "listeners":"13586", "online":"TRUE",
  "playlist":"hiphop",
  "relay":"http://cdn.audiopump.co/radioreddit/hiphop_mp3_128k",
  "songs":{ "song":[{
    "album": "", "artist": "stirus", "download_url": …(omitted),
    "genre": "Hip-Hop", "id": "837", "preview_url": …(omitted),
    "reddit_title": "stirus(\/u\/sonus) - Surviving Minds",
    "reddit_url": …(omitted), "redditor": "sonus",
    "score": "6", "title": "Surviving Minds" }]}
}]
```

Figure 8: Traffic trace for RRD transaction #2

also match with their corresponding network traffic traces. Surprisingly, Extractocol identified more than 4 transactions than PUMA did. For example, PUMA did not identify a request triggered in response to content updates, triggered by the server. Such externally triggered events are hard to reproduce using dynamic analysis.

Radio reddit (RR) is an online music streaming client that allows users to choose radio stations and vote on or save songs using their reddit accounts. Table 3 shows the result for RR with six transactions; five of them use HTTP, while login request uses HTTPS. It also shows a dependency graph identified by Extractocol. Extractocol identifies that login request (#3) includes three fields, and its response is a JSON object including "modhash" and "cookie" as keys. The two fields in login response (#3) are used in #4's and #5's requests. They use the "modhash" value in the "uh" field, and add the "cookie" value to their request headers. We verify that the identified information accurately corresponds to reddit's API documentation Extractocol identified the exact API subset that is actually used by the app. It even identified a hidden API *not* discussed in the official document [66].

Figure 8 shows the actual traffic trace of transaction #2 with constant keywords highlighted from our regex representing the JSON's tree structure. The URI signature contains all strings in the URI except "api/hiphop" which is obtained via user input. The response regex signature contains 16 keywords out of 18 in the response; two keywords ("album" and "score") are not processed by the app. The app then passes the station's "relay" URI (Figure 8) to Android's `MediaPlayer`, which generates transaction #6.

5.3 Reverse-Engineering

Manual reverse-engineering attempts use packet traces to analyze popular REST APIs [22, 25, 42, 43, 74, 83]. We use Kayak to demonstrate Extractocol's practical usefulness in reverse-engineering the API syntax. Kayak API is a private REST API used by Kayak.com, a popular fare comparison web site. Its API used to be public, but its service was recently discontinued [22], and a repurposed private API was introduced. We compare our analysis results with a manual analysis result in [22], which lists three APIs related to flight fare comparison.

We only scope the analysis to `com.kayak` classes excluding the external libraries to focus on its API. Extractocol identifies a total of 46 HTTP(S) transactions, including 39 GET and 7 POST requests, 6 JSON responses, and other responses (e.g., text and images). It identifies all three APIs from prior manual analysis [22]. Additionally, Extractocol reveals 14 times more APIs in just 31 minutes. It also identifies the use of app-specific HTTP header, "User-Agent : kayakandroid-phone/8.1". Table 5 shows a summary of requests grouped into eight categories by their URI prefix. Table 6 shows three selected APIs from the results, demonstrating that Extractocol identifies URIs and query strings used by the app.

To verify the results, we implement a simple Python script code (73 LOC) that generates HTTPS requests for flight fare comparison (Table 6) based on our signatures. It first sends a '/k/authajax' request to start a new session using the app-specific 'User-Agent' field. It then sends '/flight/start' and '/flight/poll' requests. We verify that it successfully retrieves flight fare information. We find that the APIs are slightly different from [22] due to the difference in platform (e.g., 'action=registerandroid' for '/k/authajax'). We also find that the 'User-Agent' header that we identified is important because Kayak performs access control using the header to prevent unauthorized access from other platforms.

Summary: Extractocol presents the first automatic and comprehensive protocol analysis for Android apps. It provides higher coverage than dynamic fuzzing and even manual fuzzing. We demonstrate the combination of signature extraction, pairing, and dependency analysis produces a rich characterization. We believe the rich information it provides is valuable to a number of potential applications, including understanding apps, app testing, and reverse-engineering. In fact, Extractocol has been already used to build application acceleration proxies for mobile apps [35].

Discussions: Our evaluation provides a comprehensive analysis of a small number of applications, rather than a large-scale analysis. Although Extractocol provides automatic analysis, large-scale evaluation is still challenging because verifying the result requires manual analysis of signatures and their dependencies takes a long time since most apps are obfuscated. Note, even generating all protocol messages requires manual intervention due to limitations in UI-automation (§5.1). Second, Extractocol does not support binary protocols and its support for implicit callbacks is not complete (§3.4). Finally, to handle obfuscated 3rd party libraries, Extractocol preprocesses the code to generate a map between the obfuscated identifier using heuristics (§3.4). However, if the mapping is inaccurate, Extractocol may not be able to identify the correct semantics and may generate wild card ("*") signatures instead of accurate ones. We expect that the limitations can be overcome by incorporating it with techniques [9, 12, 33, 62] discussed in §3.4.

6 Related Work

This work builds on a large body of work that performs automated program analysis for Android applications. An earlier poster version of this work can be found in [36].

Android program analysis: Prior work on Android program analysis focuses on discovering privacy-sensitive information leakage [27, 34, 46, 51, 53, 57, 63, 69, 81, 86, 87], identifying

#	Request URI	Reque
1	GET (http://www.reddit.com/api/info.json?)	-
2	GET (http://www.radioreddit.com/)(status.json)	-
3	POST (https://ssl.reddit.com/api/login)	(user=).*(&passwd=)(&api_type=json)
4	POST (http://www.reddit.com/api/)(unsave | save)	(id=).*(&uh=)(.*)
5	POST (http://www.reddit.com/api/vote)	(id=).*(&dir=).*(&uh=)(.*)
6	GET (.*)	(.*)

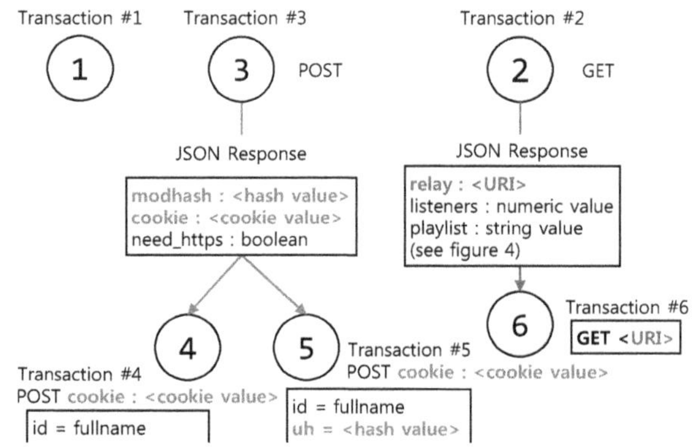

Table 3: Reconstructed HTTP tra

#	**Request** (Static/**D**ynamically-derived URI)	**Response**
1	Speaker's info (S)	JSON name/description inserted to DB
2	Facebook sharing (S)	String
3	Advertisement query (S)	JSON Ad query URI
4	GET (.*): Ad query URI from #3 (D)	XML Ad resource URIs
5	GET (.*): Ad video URI from #4 (D)	Binary
6	Talk info (S)	JSON thumbnail/video URIs inserted to DB
7	GET (.*): Thumbnail URI from DB (D)	Binary
8	GET (.*): Audio/video URI from DB (D)	Binary

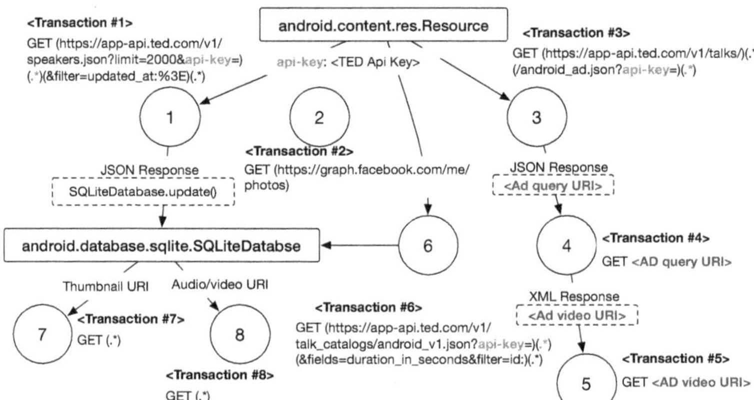

Table 4: Selected HTTP transactions and its dependency graph for TED

application misbehaviors [45, 55, 76], or providing privilege separation for apps [50].

Taint analysis tracks information flows to reveal unintended information leakage. TaintDroid [46] performs real-time dynamic taint analysis to detect privacy-sensitive information leakage on Android. While it is more accurate (i.e., low false positives) than static program analysis, achieving high coverage for ahead-of-time analysis is an important challenge. To overcome this, many studies employ static analysis [27, 51, 86]. These studies commonly reconstruct the inter-procedural control flow graph (ICFG) by modeling Android app's life-cycle. By analyzing the ICFG and data dependencies, they identify whether a path exists from a source of sensitive information to a taint sink (usually a network interface). In this work, we leverage FlowDroid [27] to reconstruct the ICGF and use data dependencies in three different ways for protocol analysis. Finally, CryptoLint [45] detects the misuse of cryptographic libraries using static program slicing. SMV-Hunter [76] identifies Android applications that fail to properly validate SSL certificates. Fratantonio et al. [50] use symbolic execution to enable finer-grained access controls in Android applications.

Finger-printing Android app traffic: FLOWR [84, 85] tries to classify mobile app traffic by extracting key-value pairs from HTTP sessions. NetworkProfiler [41] uses UI-based fuzzing on Android apps to build a comprehensive network trace. The main focus is to generate network traffic and extract unique finger-prints, rather than protocol analysis.

A large body of work addresses protocol analysis for conventional, non-mobile applications. We describe them below.

Protocol analysis using network traces: Many studies [26, 29, 38, 39, 49, 58, 59, 78, 80, 84] use traffic traces as input to derive application protocol information, such as protocol syntax and state machine. Discoverer [38] infers message format to derive application protocol syntax, and ASAP [58] uses machine learning to extract typical communication signatures and their semantics. RolePlayer [39] and ScripGen [59] support automatic protocol replay by reconstructing one side of an application session in different contexts by adjusting protocol fields, such as ports, cookies, and sequence numbers. However, this approach inherently relies on pattern inference which is less accurate [30] than program semantic analysis and cannot handle encrypted messages. Also, a common limitation of the approach is that obtaining a sufficient size

Cat.	Method	URI Prefix	# APIs	Example Sub URI	Response
Travel Planner	GET	https://www.kayak.com/trips/v2	11	/edit/trip/	-
Authentication	POST	https://www.kayak.com/k/authajax	4	-	-
Facebook Auth	POST	https://www.kayak.com/k/run/fbauth	2	/login	-
Flight	GET	https://www.kayak.com/api/search/V8/	6	/flight/start	JSON
Hotel	GET	https://www.kayak.com/api/search/V8/	2	/hotel/detail	JSON
Car	GET	https://www.kayak.com/api/search/V8/	1	/car/poll	JSON
Mobile Specific	GET	https://www.kayak.com/h/mobileapis	12	/currency/allRates	JSON
Advertising	GET	https://www.kayak.com/s/mobileads	1	-	JSON
Etc.	POST	https://www.kayak.com/k	4	/cookie	-

Table 5: A summary of Kayak API analysis results

Sub URIs	Query String
/k/authajax	action=registerandroid&uuid=.*&hash=.*&model=.* &platform=android&os=.*&locale=.*&tz=.*
/api/search /V8/flight/start	cabin=.*&travelers=.*&origin=.*&nearbyO.*=.* &destination.*=.* &nearbyD.*=.*&depart_date.*=.* &depart_time.*=.*&depart_date_flex.*=.* &_sid_=.*
/api/search /V8/flight/poll	searchid=.*&nc=.*&c=.*&s=.*&d=up&currency=.* &includeopaques=true &includeSplit=false

Table 6: Selected Request Signatures for Kayak

of input that exhaustively contains protocol messages is hard especially due to highly skewed message popularity [38].

Protocol analysis using program analysis: Many studies identify application network protocol using program analysis [30–32, 37, 40, 56, 61, 82]. The majority of program analysis techniques [30–32, 37, 40, 61, 82] use dynamic analysis as primary means to extract protocol information with different goals. Dispatcher [30] reverse engineers a botnet's command-and-control (C&C) protocol to actively rewrite C&C messages. Replayer [68] and Rosetta [31] focus on replaying application dialogs, while others [32, 37, 40, 61] aim for identifying protocol fields within a message. Prospex [37] extracts full protocol specification including the state machine. These approaches take protocol messages as input to generate execution traces, use heuristics to decide the field boundary within the message by inspecting the execution traces, and generalize the observation using various inference techniques to infer a generic message format and protocol state. The limitations of dynamic approaches are that 1) they only identify limited information, such as the field or delimiters (i.e., the goal is output fields similar to that used in Wireshark); 2) can only analyze one-side of communication (i.e., can only infer the format of received message) [6]; 3) require the input messages to exhaustively cover all message types; 4) require multiple messages instances per type for inferring general protocol format [37, 40, 61, 82]; and 5) rely on pattern inference for reconstructing client protocol state machine. In contrast, Extractocol provides richer behavioral information. To our best knowledge, it is the first to provide such in-depth behavior analysis. Finally, StateAlyzr [56] applies static analysis techniques to automatically identify states that need to be transferred when replicating middlebox states across virtualized network function instances. It takes middlebox application code to identify all state that must be migrated/cloned to ensure consistent middlebox output in the face of redistribution/cloning. It also uses program-slicing technique to derive the dependencies between state objects and packet processing logic in the source code of middlebox applications. In terms of techniques used, the two main differences between StateAlyzr and Extractocol are: (1) our framework operates on binary whereas StateAlyzr takes source code as input, and (2) Extractocol not only extracts slices but it extracts their semantics to reconstruct protocol messages.

[6]Analyzing both sides requires combining server and client analysis. However, existing work falls short in analyzing two-way communication. For Android apps, the server binary is often unavailable.

7 Conclusions

This work presents the first system for automatic analysis of HTTP(S)-based application protocol behaviors for Android apps. Extractocol uses the application binary as input to reconstruct application-specific HTTP-based interactions using static program analysis. It combines network-aware static taint analysis and semantic analysis to provide a comprehensive characterization of application protocol behaviors. Extractocol provides a rich analysis of app behaviors, including message signatures, request-response pairs, and inter-transactional dependencies. We expect that this provides valuable information for many applications [35]. Our in-depth evaluation on open-source and closed-source apps demonstrate that 1) it provides high coverage and accuracy in identifying protocol messages; 2) it provides rich characterization of app behavior; 3) it is capable of reverse-engineering REST APIs; and 4) it can automatically analyze many applications. Finally, we believe Extractocol and its approach can serve as a basis for generic protocol analysis (other than HTTP) for Android applications.

Acknowledgement

We would like to thank our shepherd Alessandro Finamore and anonymous reviewers for their feedback and suggestions. This work is in part supported by IITP funded by the Korea government (MSIP) under B0126-16-1078 and under IITP-2016-R0992-16-1006.

8 References

[1] Android library statistics - appbrain. http://www.appbrain.com/stats/libraries. Accessed Sep. 2015.

[2] Bitblaze: Binary analysis for computer security. http://bitblaze.cs.berkeley.edu/. Accessed Jun, 2016.

[3] Connecting to the network. https://developer.android.com/training/basics/network-ops/connecting.html. Accessed Jun. 2016.

[4] Dynamic Site Acceleration explained. https://aiscaler.com/dsa-explained#prefetching. Accessed Sep. 2015.

[5] Dynamic site accelerator. https://www.akamai.com/kr/ko/multimedia/documents/product-brief/dynamic-site-accelerator-product-brief.pdf. Accessed Oct. 2016.

[6] Eliminate Blind Spots in SSL Encrypted Traffic. https://www.venafi.com/assets/pdf/sb/SSL_Visibility_Solution_Brief.pdf.

[7] Extending prefetching to json and other objects. https://community.akamai.com/community/web-performance/blog/2015/02/19/extending-prefetching-to-json. Accessed Sep. 2015.

[8] Free and open source android app repository. https://f-droid.org.

[9] Generic android deobfuscator. https://github.com/CalebFenton/simplify. Accessed Jun. 2016.

[10] How antivirus software works: Virus detection techniques. http://searchsecurity.techtarget.com/tip/How-antivirus-software-works-Virus-detection-techniques. Accessed Oct. 2016.

[11] How dynamic site acceleration works: What at&t and akamai offer. http://blog.streamingmedia.com/2010/10/how-dynamic-site-acceleration-works-what-akamai-and-cotendo-offer.html. Accessed Sep. 2015.

[12] A pattern based dalvik deobfuscator which uses limited execution to improve semantic analysis. https://github.com/CalebFenton/dex-oracle. Accessed Jun. 2016.

[13] SSL Decryption. https://www.gigamon.com/products/technology/ssl-decryption. Accessed Oct. 2016.

[14] SSL Encrypted Traffic Visibility and Management. https://www.bluecoat.com/products/ssl-encrypted-traffic-visibility-and-management. Accessed Oct. 2016.

[15] Top applications on google play. https://www.appannie.com/apps/google-play/top-chart/united-states/application/. Accessed Sep. 2015.

[16] An accuweather cloudlet answers a hail of data requests. https://www.yumpu.com/en/document/view/23074646/an-accuweather-cloudlet-answers-a-hail-of-data-requests, 2011.

[17] Android async http clients: Volley vs retrofit. http://instructure.github.io/blog/2013/12/09/volley-vs-retrofit/, 2013.

[18] Number of available android applications. http://www.appbrain.com/stats/number-of-android-apps, 2014.

[19] Proxydroid - android apps on google play. https://play.google.com/store/apps/details?id=org.proxydroid&hl=en, Dec. 2014.

[20] radio reddit v0.7. https://f-droid.org/repository/browse/?fdfilter=radio+reddit&fdid=com.radioreddit.android, 2014. An open-source radio reddit app.

[21] Report: Apple iphone drives half of all mobile internet traffic. http://marketingland.com/report-apple-iphone-drives-half-mobile-internet-traffic-111129, 2014.

[22] Reverse-engineering the kayak app with mitmproxy. http://www.shubhro.com/2014/12/18/reverse-engineering-kayak-mitmproxy/, Dec. 2014.

[23] mitmproxy. https://mitmproxy.org/, 2015.

[24] Proguard, android developers. http://developer.android.com/tools/help/proguard.html, 2015.

[25] M. Amps. Reverse engineering shopify private apis. http://ma.rtin.so/reverse-engineering-shopify-private-apis, 2013.

[26] J. Antunes and N. Neves. Automatically complementing protocol specifications from network traces. In *European Workshop on Dependable Computing*, 2011.

[27] S. Arzt, S. Rasthofer, C. Fritz, E. Bodden, A. Bartel, J. Klein, Y. Le Traon, D. Octeau, and P. McDaniel. Flowdroid: Precise context, flow, field, object-sensitive and lifecycle-aware taint analysis for android apps. In *ACM SIGPLAN PLDI*, 2014.

[28] A. Bartel, J. Klein, Y. Le Traon, and M. Monperrus. Dexpler: Converting android dalvik bytecode to jimple for static analysis with soot. In *ACM SIGPLAN International Workshop on State of the Art in Java Program analysis*, 2012.

[29] M. A. Beddoe. Network protocol analysis using bioinformatics algorithms. http://www.4tphi.net/~awalters/PI/PI.html, 2004.

[30] J. Caballero, P. Poosankam, C. Kreibich, and D. Song. Dispatcher: Enabling active botnet infiltration using automatic protocol reverse-engineering. In *ACM CCS*, 2009.

[31] J. Caballero and D. Song. Rosetta: Extracting protocol semantics using binary analysis with applications to protocol replay and nat rewriting, 2007. Technical Report, UC Berkeley.

[32] J. Caballero, H. Yin, Z. Liang, and D. Song. Polyglot: Automatic extraction of protocol message format using dynamic binary analysis. In *ACM CCS*, 2007.

[33] Y. Cao, Y. Fratantonio, A. Bianchi, M. Egele, C. Kruegel, G. Vigna, and Y. Chen. Edgeminer: Automatically detecting implicit control flow transitions through the android framework. In *NDSS*, 2015.

[34] E. Chin, A. P. Felt, K. Greenwood, and D. Wagner. Analyzing inter-application communication in Android. In *ACM MobiSys*, 2011.

[35] B. Choi, J. Kim, and D. Han. Application-specific Acceleration Framework for Mobile Applications. In *ACM SIGCOMM (poster session)*, 2016.

[36] H. Choi, J. Kim, H. Hong, Y. Kim, J. Lee, and D. Han. Extractocol: Automatic extraction of application-level protocol behaviors for android applications. In *ACM SIGCOMM (poster)*, pages 593–594. ACM, 2015.

[37] P. M. Comparetti, G. Wondracek, C. Kruegel, and E. Kirda. Prospex: Protocol specification extraction. In *IEEE Symposium Security and Privacy*, 2009.

[38] W. Cui, J. Kannan, and H. J. Wang. Discoverer: Automatic protocol reverse engineering from network traces. In *USENIX Security*, 2007.

[39] W. Cui, V. Paxson, N. C. Weaver, and R. H. Katz. Protocol-independent adaptive replay of application dialog. In *NDSS*, 2006.

[40] W. Cui, M. Peinado, K. Chen, H. J. Wang, and L. Irun-Briz. Tupni: Automatic reverse engineering of input formats. In *ACM CCS*, 2008.

[41] S. Dai, A. Tongaonkar, X. Wang, A. Nucci, and D. Song. Networkprofiler: Towards automatic fingerprinting of android apps. In *IEEE INFOCOM*, 2013.

[42] N. Derkach. Reverse engineering the private api: Hacking your couch. http://www.toptal.com/back-end/reverse-engineering-the-private-api-hacking-your-couch, 2014.

[43] T. Dorr. Unofficial documentation of the Tesla Model S JSON API. http://docs.timdorr.apiary.io/, 2013.

[44] P. Edholm. Reverse-engineering the kayak app with mitmproxy. http://www.nojitter.com/post/240153039/hp-and-microsoft-demo-openflowlync-applicationsoptimized-network. Apr. 2013.

[45] M. Egele, D. Brumley, Y. Fratantonio, and C. Kruegel. An empirical study of cryptographic misuse in android applications. In *ACM CCS*, 2013.

[46] W. Enck, P. Gilbert, B.-G. Chun, L. P. Cox, J. Jung, P. McDaniel, and A. N. Sheth. Taintdroid: An

information-flow tracking system for realtime privacy monitoring on smartphones. In *USENIX OSDI*, 2010.

[47] W. Enck, D. Octeau, P. McDaniel, and S. Chaudhuri. A study of android application security. In *USENIX Security*, 2011.

[48] H. Falaki, D. Lymberopoulos, R. Mahajan, S. Kandula, and D. Estrin. A First Look at Traffic on Smartphones. In *ACM Internet Measurement Conference*, 2010.

[49] J. François, H. Abdelnur, R. State, and O. Festor. Automated behavioral fingerprinting. In *International Symposium on Recent Advances in Intrusion Detection*, 2009.

[50] Y. Fratantonio, A. Bianchi, W. Robertson, M. Egele, C. Kruegel, E. Kirda, and G. Vigna. On the Security and Engineering Implications of Finer-Grained Access Controls for Android Developers and Users. In *International Conference on Detection of Intrusions and Malware, and Vulnerability Assessment*, 2015.

[51] C. Gibler, J. Crussell, J. Erickson, and H. Chen. Androidleaks: Automatically detecting potential privacy leaks in android applications on a large scale. In *International conference on Trust and Trustworthy Computing*, 2012.

[52] M. I. Gordon, D. Kim, J. Perkins, L. Gilham, N. Nguyen, and M. Rinard. Information-Flow Analysis of Android Applications in DroidSafe. In *NDSS*, 2015.

[53] M. Grace, Y. Zhou, Z. Wang, and X. Jiang. Systematic Detection of Capability Leaks in Stock Android Smartphones. In *NDSS*, 2012.

[54] S. Hao, B. Liu, S. Nath, W. G. Halfond, and R. Govindan. Puma: Programmable ui-automation for large-scale dynamic analysis of mobile apps. In *ACM Mobisys*, 2014.

[55] J. Huang, X. Zhang, L. Tan, P. Wang, and B. Liang. AsDroid: detecting stealthy behaviors in Android applications by user interface and program behavior contradiction. In *International Conference on Software Engineering*, 2014.

[56] J. Khalid, A. Gember-Jacobson, R. Michael, A. Abhashkumar, and A. Akella. Paving the Way for NFV: Simplifying Middlebox Modifications using StateAlyzr. In *USENIX NSDI*, 2016.

[57] J. Kim, Y. Yoon, K. Yi, J. Shin, and S Center. ScanDal: Static analyzer for detecting privacy leaks in android applications. In *Mobile Security Technologies*, 2012.

[58] T. Krueger, N. Krämer, and K. Rieck. Asap: Automatic semantics-aware analysis of network payloads. In *International Workshop on Privacy and Security Issues in Data Mining and Machine Learning*, 2011.

[59] C. Leita, K. Mermoud, and M. Dacier. Scriptgen: An automated script generation tool for honeyd. In *Annual Computer Security Applications Conference*, 2005.

[60] O. Lhoták and L. Hendren. Scaling Java Points-to Analysis Using SPARK. In *International Conference on Compiler Construction*, 2003.

[61] Z. Lin, X. Jiang, D. Xu, and X. Zhang. Automatic protocol format reverse engineering through context-aware monitored execution. In *NDSS*, 2008.

[62] B. Liu, B. Liu, H. Jin, and R. Govindan. Efficient Privilege De-Escalation for Ad Libraries in Mobile Apps. In *ACM MobiSys*, 2015.

[63] L. Lu, Z. Li, Z. Wu, W. Lee, and G. Jiang. CHEX: statically vetting Android apps for component hijacking vulnerabilities. In *ACM CCS*, 2012.

[64] G. Maier, F. Schneider, and A. Feldmann. A First Look at Mobile Hand-held Device Traffic. In *International Conference on Passive and Active Measurement*, 2010.

[65] mttkay. https://mttkay.github.io/blog/2013/08/25/functional-reactive-programming-on-android-with-rxjava/, 2013.

[66] J. Musser. Reddit's secret api. http://www.programmableweb.com/news/reddits-secret-api/2008/11/25, 2008.

[67] D. naylor, K. Schomp, M. Varvello, I. Leontiadis, D. L. Jeremy Balckburn, P. R. R. Konstantina Papaginnaki, and P. Steenkiste. Multi-Context TLS (mcTLS): Enabling Secure In-Network Functionality in TLS. In *ACM SIGCOMM*, 2015.

[68] J. Newsome, D. Brumley, J. Franklin, and D. Song. Replayer: Automatic protocol replay by binary analysis. In *ACM CCS*, 2006.

[69] D. Octeau, P. McDaniel, S. Jha, A. Bartel, E. Bodden, J. Klein, and Y. Le Traon. Effective inter-component communication mapping in Android with Epicc: an essential step towards holistic security analysis. In *USENIX Security*, 2013.

[70] L. Pedrosa, A. Fogel, N. Kothari, R. Govindan, R. Mahajan, and T. Millstein. Analyzing protocol implementations for interoperability. In *USENIX NSDI*, 2015.

[71] Z. A. Qazi, J. Lee, T. Jin, G. Bellala, M. Arndt, and G. Noubir. Application-awareness in SDN. In *ACM SIGCOMM*, 2013.

[72] C. Qian, X. Luo, Y. Shao, and A. T. S. Chan. On Tracking Information Flows Through JNI in Android Applications. In *IEEE/IFIP International Conference on Dependable Systems and Networks*, 2014.

[73] T. Reps, S. Horwitz, and M. Sagiv. Precise interprocedural dataflow analysis via graph reachability. In *ACM SIGPLAN-SIGACT symposium on Principles of programming languages*, 1995.

[74] S. Saffron. How to reverse engineer the discourse api. https://meta.discourse.org/t/how-to-reverse-engineer-the-discourse-api/20576, 2014.

[75] S. Singh, C. Estan, G. Varghese, and S. Savage. Automated worm fingerprinting. In *USENIX OSDI*, 2004.

[76] D. Sounthiraraj, J. Sahs, G. Greenwood, Z. Lin, and L. Khan. SMV-HUNTER: Large Scale, Automated Detection of SSL/TLS Man-in-the-Middle Vulnerabilities in Android Apps. In *NDSS*, 2014.

[77] A. Tongaonkar, R. Keralapura, and A. Nucci. Challenges in network application identification. In *LEET*, 2012.

[78] A. Trifilò, S. Burschka, and E. Biersack. Traffic to protocol reverse engineering. In *IEEE Symposium on Computational Intelligence for Security and Defense Applications*, 2009.

[79] N. Viennot, E. Garcia, and J. Nieh. A Measurement Study of Google Play. In *ACM SIGMETRICS*, 2014.

[80] Y. Wang, Z. Zhang, D. D. Yao, B. Qu, and L. Guo. Inferring protocol state machine from network traces: A probabilistic approach. In *International Conference on Applied Cryptography and Network Security*, 2011.

[81] F. Wei, S. Roy, X. Ou, and Robby. Amandroid: A Precise and General Inter-component Data Flow Analysis Framework for Security Vetting of Android Apps. In *ACM CCS*, 2014.

[82] G. Wondracek, P. M. Comparetti, C. Kruegel, and E. Kirda. Automatic network protocol analysis. In *NDSS*, 2008.

[83] J. Wright. Reverse Engineering the We Heart It API. http://jordan-wright.github.io/blog/2014/10/12/reverse-engineering-the-we-heart-it-api/, 2014.

[84] Q. Xu, T. Andrews, Y. Liao, S. Miskovic, Z. M. Mao, M. Baldi, and A. Nucci. Flowr: A self-learning system for classifying mobile application traffic. In *ACM SIGMETRICS*, 2014.

[85] Q. Xu, Y. Liao, S. Miskovic, Z. M. Mao, M. Baldi, A. Nucci, and T. Andrews. Automatic generation of mobile app signatures from traffic observations. In *IEEE INFOCOM*, 2015.

[86] Z. Yang and M. Yang. LeakMiner: Detect information leakage on Android with static taint analysis. In *World Congress on Software Engineering*, 2012.

[87] M. Zhang and H. Yin. AppSealer: Automatic Generation of Vulnerability-Specific Patches for Preventing Component Hijacking Attacks in Android Applications. In *NDSS*, 2014.

[88] T. Zinner, M. Jarschel, A. Blenk, F. Wamser, and W. Kellerer. Dynamic application-aware resource management using Software-Defined Networking: Implementation prospects and challenges. In *IEEE/IFIP Network Operations and Management Symposium*, 2014.

Sunflow: Efficient Optical Circuit Scheduling for Coflows

Xin Sunny Huang Xiaoye Steven Sun T. S. Eugene Ng

Rice University

ABSTRACT

Optical Circuit Switches (OCS) are increasingly used in cluster networks due to their data rate, energy and longevity advantages over electrical packet switches. Concurrently, an emerging crucial requirement for modern data-parallel clusters is to achieve high application-level communication efficiency when servicing structured traffic flows (a.k.a. Coflows) from distributed data processing applications. This paper presents the first OCS scheduling algorithm called Sunflow that addresses this requirement.

Preemption decisions are the key to any OCS scheduling algorithm. Sunflow makes preemption decisions at two levels. First, at the intra-Coflow level, Sunflow does not allow subflows within a Coflow to preempt each other. We prove that the performance of this strategy is within a factor-of-two to the optimal. We further demonstrate that under realistic traffic, performance of Sunflow is on average within 1.03× to optimal. Second, at the inter-Coflow level, Sunflow provides a framework for flexible preemption policies to support diverse usage scenarios. In the specific case of the shortest-Coflow-first policy, we find that Coflows on average finish just as fast in a Sunflow-scheduled optical circuit switched network as in a comparable packet switched network employing the state-of-the-art Coflow scheduler.

CCS Concepts

•Networks → Network control algorithms; Network resources allocation; Data center networks;

CoNEXT '16, December 12 - 15, 2016, Irvine, CA, USA

DOI: http://dx.doi.org/10.1145/2999572.2999592

Keywords

Circuit scheduling algorithm; Optical circuit switching; Structured traffic flow; Cluster network; Data center;

1. INTRODUCTION

Optical Circuit Switches (OCS) are increasingly used in cluster networks [35, 16, 36, 15, 30, 25, 34, 26] due to several compelling advantages over electrical packet switches. First, the OCS is future data-rate proof. Because it simply transmits optical signal at the physical layer and does not process packets, it is agnostic to data rate. Thus, an OCS needs no upgrade as link speed increases. Second, OCS, a passive physical layer device, consumes an order of magnitude less power than an electrical packet switch. An OCS consumes as little as 150 mW per port while an electrical packet switch consumes 4 W per port. Third, OCS also have very large mean time to failure (up to 30 years for a commercial 3D-MEMS switch [17, 9]), and its benefits can be enjoyed for years to come. Concurrently, structured traffic flows called Coflows [10] from distributed data processing applications are becoming an increasingly dominant workload in data-parallel clusters; thus, an emerging crucial requirement for data-parallel cluster networks is to achieve high application-level communication efficiency when servicing Coflows [12, 11, 39, 38].

In this paper, we set out to explore the question: how to best service Coflows from distributed data processing jobs in an optical circuit switched network? Previous work has observed that OCS is well suited when the traffic is sparse [35]. However, many Coflows are dense with heavy many-to-many subflows. Therefore, how well circuit switching can serve Coflow traffic remains an open question.

Preemption decisions are the key to any OCS scheduling algorithm: good decisions lead to high circuit utilization, while poor decisions lead to performance problems like head-of-line blocking. We start by exploring how well state-of-the-art circuit scheduling algorithms in the data center context [35, 16, 30, 34, 26] can serve Coflow. Unfortunately, we find their performance disappointing for several reasons. First, they require excessive circuit preemptions, resulting in large latency for Coflow due to heavy switching overhead. Second, they lack the ability to explicitly handle multiple Coflows or meet individual Coflow's performance requirement.

We observe that these algorithms stem from the *all-stop* circuit switch model (§ 2.1), a conventional model commonly used from [21, 7, 28, 33] to [16, 30, 34, 26], spanning decades. In general, an *all-stop* switch requires more preemptions to reduce circuit idleness (§ 3.1.2). However, the modern optical switch is in fact less stringent than required by the *all-stop* model. Under a more accurate, yet less constrained switch model, i.e. the *not-all-stop* switch model (§ 2.1), circuits can be better utilized with fewer preemptions.

Based on these observations, we design Sunflow, the first circuit scheduling algorithm that is efficient for scheduling Coflows. Sunflow makes preemption decisions at two levels. First, at the intra-Coflow level, Sunflow does not allow subflows within a Coflow to preempt each other. This non-preemptive strategy is starvation-free because subflows within a Coflow share the same performance objective. We prove that the performance of this strategy is within a factor-of-two to the optimal, while the other circuit scheduling algorithms have no known performance guarantee. We further demonstrate that under realistic traffic, performance of Sunflow is on average within 1.03× to optimal. Second, at the inter-Coflow level, Sunflow provides a framework for flexible preemption policies to support diverse usage scenarios (e.g. policies that govern how production vs. non-production traffic is handled). In the specific case of the shortest-Coflow-first policy, we find that Coflows on average finish just as fast in a Sunflow-scheduled optical circuit switched network as in a comparable packet switched network employing Varys [12] and Aalo [11], the state-of-the-art Coflow schedulers. With Sunflow's ability to achieve Coflow performance in a circuit switched network approaching that of a packet switched network, an OCS becomes a viable component in a modern data-parallel cluster network especially when the data rate, energy, and longevity advantages of the OCS are simultaneously considered.

2. PROBLEM FORMULATION

2.1 Network Model

We start by describing the conceptual model used to study the scheduling problem. In our network model, the network fabric is abstracted as one non-blocking N-port switch with link bandwidth B. This model is attractive because of its simplicity, yet it is practical because topology designs such as Fat-tree or Clos [5, 20] enable building a network with full bisection bandwidth. We assume the switch ports are connected to Top-of-Rack (ToR) switches, and each ToR switch is connected to a group of machines.

Within this network model, we will investigate two types of switches to study the performance of circuit switched networks and packet switched networks.

Optical Circuit Switch: In the circuit switched network, the switch is an optical circuit switch. An optical switch has *port constraint*: an input (output) port can set up at most one circuit to an output (input) port at a time. In other words, no input (output) port may connect to multiple output (input) ports. Each circuit can be reconfigured with the cost of a fixed time delay δ. This means during a period of δ to set up one circuit, communication stops on the input (output) ports affected, including ports on circuits to be set up, as well as ports on circuits to be torn down. However, circuits unchanged are not impacted and may keep serving traffic. This circuit switch model, referred to as the *not-all-stop* model hereafter, is *a more accurate, yet less constrained model for the optical switch* (off-the-shelf product examples include [17, 9, 29]). However, its counterpart, i.e. the *all-stop* model, would unnecessarily assume communication stops on *all* optical circuits during reconfiguration, but it is commonly used in previous studies [15, 30, 25, 34, 26].

Flows are buffered at the sender machines. Each input port of the switch is to serve flows from sender machines to various output ports. The flows are aggregated and organized into logical virtual output queues (VOQs) associated with each input port. At any time for an input port, at most one VOQ is served, and it is served with the full link bandwidth B. The ordering of flows in a VOQ is to be determined.

Electrical Packet Switch: In the packet switched network, the switch is an electrical packet switch. Denote $b_{i,j}$ as the bandwidth allocated for the link from input port $in.i$ to output port $out.j$. At any time, multiple VOQs may be served simultaneously, but the bandwidth constraints must be satisfied with $\forall j : \sum_{i=1}^{N} b_{i,j} \leq B$ and $\forall i : \sum_{j=1}^{N} b_{i,j} \leq B$.

We focus on the pure circuit (packet) switch models, which is the foundation to different scheduling problem variants, such as scheduling on hybrid circuit/packet networks, where traffic can be filtered and offloaded to different parallel networks [35, 16, 26].

2.2 Traffic Model

In this paper, we focus on a traffic model called Coflow [10], which represents a collection of independent flows that share a common performance goal. A Coflow is defined by the endpoints and size in byte of each flow within the Coflow. A Coflow can represent any communication pattern, such as many-to-many, one-to-many, many-to-one and one-to-one, etc. The traffic demand of a Coflow can be expressed in a demand matrix D, where each element $d_{i,j} \in D$ indicates flow $f_{i,j}$ transfers $d_{i,j}$ amount of data from input

Symbol	Definition
B	link bandwidth
N	switch port count
δ	circuit switching delay
$in.i$, $out.j$	i-th input port, j-th output port
$[in.i, out.j]$	a circuit from $in.i$ to $out.j$
$\|C\|$	Number of subflows in a Coflow C
$p_{i,j}$	data processing time on $[in.i,\ out.j]$ in a Coflow ($p^k_{i,j}$ for k-th Coflow)
T^c_L, T^p_L	CCT lower bound in circuit or packet switching network, respectively.

Table 1: Notations

port $in.i$ to output port $out.j$. Denote $|C|$ as the number of subflows in a Coflow C, and thus $|C|$ is the number of non-zero entries in D. The network scheduler is to decide how individual flows of Coflows are serviced.

2.3 Scheduling Objective

At the intra-Coflow level, the objective is to minimize the Coflow Completion Time (CCT), which is the duration to finish all flows in a Coflow, so as to speed up application level performance. For a Coflow C, denote its arrival time as t^{Arr}, and the finish time of the flow $f_{i,j} \in C$ as $t^F_{i,j}$. Hence CCT is defined as $\max_{f_{i,j} \in C} (t^F_{i,j} - t^{\text{Arr}})$. This objective is also used by all previous work on Coflow scheduling.

In a circuit switched network, the circuit scheduling algorithm must decide *when* to set up *which circuit* to serve the Coflow traffic. Generally, a circuit may be preempted before the demand on the circuit is finished, but preemption has a penalty of δ to reestablish the circuit for the remaining demand. When the preemption penalty is zero, i.e. $\delta = 0$, the problem can be solved optimally with the classic BvN algorithm [31]. When preemption penalty $= \infty$, the problem reduces to the non-preemptive open-shop problem to minimize work span [18], where each job (input port $in.i$) requires processing time ($d_{i,j}/B$) on a specific machine (output port $out.j$). The open-shop problem is *non-preemptive*, which means a machine (output port) would always finish processing a job (flow from one input port) before moving to another job (flow from another input port). The open-shop problem is NP-hard [18].

At the inter-Coflow level, the objective will depend on the resource management policy employed by the system. Coflows may come from different applications that have different importance to the users. If the resource management policy is to give priority service to more important Coflows, then the scheduling objective is to minimize the time when more important Coflows are blocked by less important ones. On the other hand, if the resource management policy is to prioritize smaller Coflows over larger ones, then the objective is to minimize the average CCT.

2.4 CCT Lower Bounds

No efficient optimal algorithm is known for intra-Coflow circuit scheduling in the general case where $0 < \delta < \infty$. Moreover, the optimal CCT may also depend on δ. As a result, we derive CCT lower bounds for the general case.

Note that our CCT lower bound in the circuit switched network, T^c_L (Equation (4)), is more accurate for the optical switch compared with the one in a previous work [26], because their bound is based on the *all-stop* switch model, while our bound is based on the *not-all-stop* switch model.

To derive the CCT lower bounds, we begin by translating a Coflow traffic demand D from size to *data processing time* with

$$p_{i,j} = \frac{d_{i,j}}{B}, \tag{1}$$

where $p_{i,j}$ is the processing time required on the circuit $[in.i,\ out.j]$ incurred by the flow $f_{i,j}$ within the Coflow.

Packet-Switched Lower Bound: In the packet switched network, the CCT lower bound is the maximum time required to finish data transfer on all ports, and it is given by

$$T^p_L = \max\left(\max_i \sum_{j=1}^{N} p_{i,j}, \max_j \sum_{i=1}^{N} p_{i,j}\right) \tag{2}$$

Circuit-Switched Lower Bound: In the circuit switched network, each port must spend time to set up circuits and transfer data. Each flow incurs at least one circuit reconfiguration delay δ. Thus the *minimum* time required to transfer flow $f_{i,j}$ with data processing time $p_{i,j}$ from $in.i$ to $out.j$ is

$$t_{i,j} = \begin{cases} 0, & \text{if } p_{i,j} = 0 \\ p_{i,j} + \delta, & \text{if } p_{i,j} > 0 \end{cases} \tag{3}$$

Hence the CCT lower bound in the circuit switched network is

$$T^c_L = \max\left(\max_i \sum_{j=1}^{N} t_{i,j}, \max_j \sum_{i=1}^{N} t_{i,j}\right) \tag{4}$$

Note that T^p_L and T^c_L are the theoretical lower bounds for CCT. Thus both of them are independent of the scheduling policy. The optimal achievable CCT may be much larger than the lower bound. Nevertheless, we will compare algorithms' performance against these stringent lower bounds.

3. RELATED WORK

3.1 Intra-Coflow Scheduling

In a packet switched network, intra-Coflow scheduling for one Coflow demand can be optimally solved [31]. However, how to best schedule circuits for one Coflow demand remains an open problem.

Coflow	Circuit Switched		Packet Switched
Intra-	Preemptive	§ 3.1.1	§ 3.1
	Non-preemptive	§ 3.1.2	
Inter-	§ 3.2		§ 3.2

Table 2: Taxonomy of related work

3.1.1 *Preemptive Circuit Scheduling*

Researchers have seized the compelling benefits of OCS with a range of infrastructure designs in recent work [35, 16, 36, 15, 30, 25, 34]. These designs involving OCS all rely on the circuit scheduler to compute a series of circuit configurations, and their scheduling algorithms follow a common approach: 1) group requested traffic demand into *one* demand matrix, which amounts to one Coflow demand, and 2) based on the demand matrix, produce a sequence of *circuit assignments* $\{A_1, ..., A_m, ...\}$, each associated with a *duration* of time $\{t_{A_1}, ..., t_{A_m}, ...\}$. Each A_i encodes a set of circuits. To respect the port constraints in the circuit switch, each A_i is a one-to-one matching between the input ports and output ports. The assignments are scheduled one by one so that A_m is active for t_{A_m}. These algorithms are *preemptive* in the sense that circuits in A_m can be *preempted* to allow for the next $A_{(m+1)}$. In many cases, most of the circuits in A_m are preempted, while in rare cases, circuits remain unchanged in two consecutive assignments. Further discussions on three representative algorithms using this approach are provided next. Later in this paper, we will show that Sunflow does not suffer from the problems associated with this approach.

Edmond used in [35, 16, 34] applies the maximum weighted matching algorithm [14] on the demand matrix and makes up *one* assignment from the matching, with the duration determined externally of the algorithm, which is typically fixed and on the order of hundreds of milliseconds. Edmond causes large delay for Coflow, as each assignment scheduled usually does not cover all requested demand of any specific Coflow.

TMS used in [15, 30] applies the classic BvN matrix decomposition algorithm [8]. To use BvN, TMS would 1) *pre-process* the demand matrix to the meet the input assumption of BvN and 2) *decompose* the pre-processed matrix into assignments and weights for each assignment, with durations determined proportionally by the weights. TMS also causes large delay for Coflow because the pre-processing step may heavily modify the original demand matrix, such that the scheduled circuits may poorly serve the original requested demand.

Solstice in [26] is similar to TMS, but has a better pre-processing and decomposition design, as well as a scheduling objective to cover all original requested demand within the minimum time. Particularly, Solstice may add dummy demand to the demand matrix in its pre-processing step. Solstice is shown to be more effective among the preemptive algorithms, but the number of reconfigurations is still a major cause of inefficiency.

These algorithms can be traced back to the classic crossbar switch scheduling problem, or the so-called Time Slot Assignment (TSA) problem. TSA is based on the *all-stop* switch model. Such an *all-stop* switch model has been commonly used in classic papers [21, 7, 28, 33] as well as recent papers [30, 34, 26]. They rely heavily on the techniques of matrix decomposition and schedule circuits in one assignment after another. Note that our problem differs from TSA because our problem is based on a different switch model, i.e. the *not-all-stop* model.

3.1.2 *Non-preemptive Circuit Scheduling*

Under the *all-stop* switch model, while many of the scheduling algorithms are preemptive, there are non-preemptive TSA designs [19, 23]. However, these designs are less favorable in general due to circuit idleness: *all* idle circuits have to wait for *any* transmitting circuits in the same assignment. Moreover, non-preemptive TSA designs are not efficient for the *not-all-stop* switch model, because non-preemptive TSA forces idle circuits to wait and occupy the ports needed to serve demand on other circuits.

Circuit scheduling for one Coflow demand is NP-hard when preemption penalty $= \infty$ (§ 2.3). In a general case where $0 < \delta < \infty$, the problem is already NP-hard [6] in a simplified two-machine case, and such simplification corresponds to a limitation in our problem that the network can only have two ports. A related problem for arbitrary δ under multiple machines is studied in the context of wavelength-division multiplexed (WDM) network [32, 13, 24], but the heuristics depend on rigid conditions (e.g. linear constraints, uniformity) on the input demand, which places impractical limitations on the Coflow demand in our problem.

Later in this paper, we will show that Sunflow provides performance guarantee in the general case with no constraints on δ, Coflow demand or number of ports.

3.2 Inter-Coflow Scheduling

To the best of our knowledge, there is no circuit scheduling algorithm designed for inter-Coflow scheduling. Existing circuit scheduling algorithms can only function on a single demand matrix. These algorithms would need to aggregate the demand from multiple Coflows as one generic demand and schedule without considering the structure of multiple Coflows. To the best of our knowledge, Sunflow is the first circuit scheduling algorithm that supports inter-Coflow scheduling.

In a packet switched network, inter-Coflow scheduling remains an open problem under discussion [12, 11, 31, 39, 27, 38]. Note that inter-Coflow scheduling in a circuit switched network where $\delta > 0$, is different from scheduling in a packet switched network that amounts to $\delta = 0$ in previous works. Particularly, *Varys* [12] and *Aalo* [11] are state-of-the-art packet-switched Coflow schedulers designed to minimize average CCT. Varys assumes all information of a Coflow (endpoints and sizes for all subflows) is known when the Coflow arrives, while

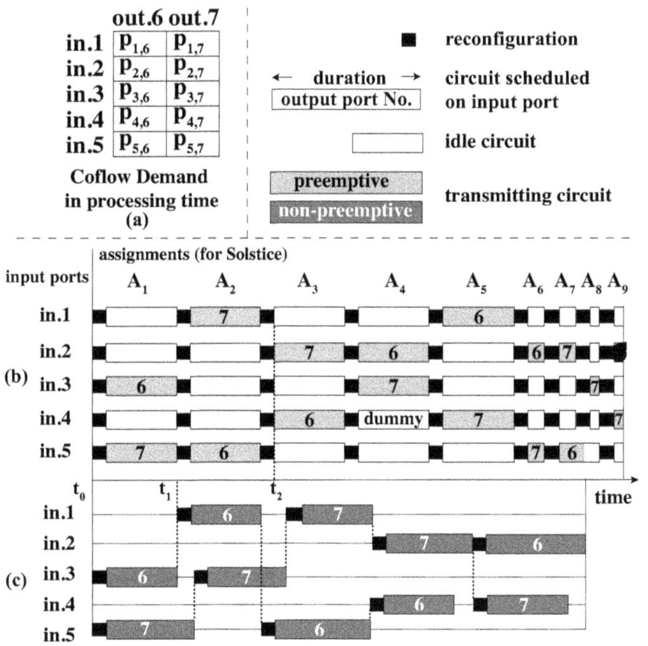

Figure 1: Intra-Coflow Circuit scheduling. (a) Coflow demand with input ports as rows, output ports as columns, and values as data processing time. (b) Preemptive scheduling by Solstice. (c) Non-preemptive scheduling by Sunflow. Circuits for input ports are laid horizontally on the time line. Circuit durations in (b) and (c) are proportional to $p_{i,j}$ in (a).

Aalo assumes known endpoints and *unknown* traffic sizes. In many cases, the Coflow information can be obtained from the application (e.g. the task scheduler can provide information for the shuffle traffic during a map-reduce job). We evaluate Sunflow with the same traffic assumption as Varys because accurate Coflow information removes the effects of traffic uncertainty. Other Coflow related operational issues, such as routing [39] and predicting Coflow volume [11] or structure [38] are out of the scope of this study.

4. SUNFLOW

4.1 Intra-Coflow Scheduling Design

Figure 1 illustrates the key difference between Sunflow and the most viable alternative scheduling algorithm, Solstice, at the intra-Coflow level. The scheduled circuits for different input ports are laid horizontally on the time line. For example, in Figure 1b, two circuits are set up at time t_2, and they are [$in.2$, $out.7$] and [$in.4$, $out.6$]. The circuit schedule should satisfy the Coflow demand in Figure 1a, which means for any input port $in.i$, the sum of the circuit durations for any output port $out.j$ should be no less than $p_{i,j}$.

Solstice produces the schedule in Figure 1b. Like many of the existing circuit scheduling algorithms, Solstice schedules circuits with assignments, and in this example, it produces $\{A_1, ..., A_9\}$.

A new assignment may be scheduled when a circuit becomes idle. For example, in Figure 1b, A_1 finishes $p_{3,6}$ and [$in.3$, $out.6$] turns idle, so A_2 is scheduled, which preempts [$in.5$, $out.7$]. Note that Solstice schedules A_5, because one of the circuits in A_4 is actually created for a dummy demand added in the pre-processing step of Solstice (§ 3.1.1). Consequently, when Solstice considers the dummy demand is "finished" and certain circuit becomes "idle", Solstice schedules a new assignment A_5.

Preempted circuits with unfinished demand incur extra reconfiguration overhead to be re-established. For example, in Figure 1b, [$in.5$, $out.7$] is preempted by A_2, which incurs an extra δ to set up in A_6. Circuits unchanged in two consecutive assignments (such as [$in.5$, $out.6$] in A_7 and A_8) may stay active continuously. Unfortunately, in many cases, few circuits overlap in two consecutive assignments. Consequently, a circuit may need to pay *multiple* reconfiguration penalties to finish a Coflow demand.

In contrast, Sunflow produces a much simpler circuit schedule as shown in Figure 1c. Given a Coflow demand, reconfiguration is minimized for each circuit: a circuit with non-zero demand is set up only once and stays active until the demand is finished. Besides, circuits are interleaving with each other over time with no synchronized setup/teardown times. As shown, Sunflow achieves a smaller CCT than Solstice in the example.

Thus, a key property of Sunflow is that it is non-preemptive at the intra-Coflow level. This approach is supported by the following observations.

A Coflow's traffic volume is not suitable for preemptive intra-Coflow scheduling. The inefficiency of preemptions is less prominent when the data processing time $p_{i,j}$ is very large compared to the preemption overhead δ. However, a Coflow's traffic volume is generally smaller than previous work assumed of the demand volume because a Coflow is an application-level traffic unit, and it is not heavily aggregated. As a result, overhead associated with preemption becomes a significant factor.

Starvation is not a concern. Non-preemption at the intra-Coflow level is starvation-free, because all subflows in a Coflow share the same performance objective.

The optical switch is not all-stop. Under the *all-stop* switch model, non-preemption would be less favorable due to circuit idleness (see discussion in § 3.1.2). However, the optical switch [17, 9, 29] is not all-stop, circuits may be reconfigured individually, and therefore the side effect of non-preemption is small: while one circuit stays non-preempted and transmitting, other circuits are free to be reconfigured, so long as the port constraints are satisfied (§ 2.1). For example, in Figure 1c, the time-overlapping circuits [$in.1$, $out.6$] and [$in.5$, $out.7$] are not allowed in the *all-stop* switch model, because the reconfiguration of [$in.1$, $out.6$] will stop the transmission of [$in.5$, $out.7$]. As a result, the conven-

Algorithm 1 Sunflow

```
1: Global PRT[.]
2: procedure IntraCoflow(Coflow C)
3:     P = all (i, j, p_{i,j}) in C               ▷ Shuffle P if desired
4:     time t = 0
5:     while P not empty do
6:         for all (i, j, p_{i,j}) in P do
7:             p_{i,j} = MakeReservation(i, j, t, p_{i,j})
8:         end for
9:         Remove entries in P where p_{i,j} = 0
10:        Advance t to next circuit release time in PRT[.]
11:    end while
12: end procedure

13: procedure MakeReservation(int i, j, double t, p_{i,j})
14:    reservation length l = 0
15:    if both in.i and out.j are free at t then
16:        t_m = earliest next-reserv-time of in.i, out.j
               ▷ Needed by inter-Coflow scheduling (§ 4.2)
17:        max length l_m = t_m − t
18:        desired length l_d = δ + p_{i,j}
19:        actual length l = l_m < δ ? 0 : min(l_m, l_d)
20:        Reserve in.i, out.j during (t, t + l) in PRT[.]
21:    end if
22:    return l > 0 ? (l_d − l) : p_{i,j}   ▷ Remaining demand
23: end procedure

24: procedure InterCoflow(Coflows C)          ▷ Sorted C
25:    PRT[.] = ∅
26:    for all C in C do
27:        IntraCoflow(C)
28:    end for
29: end procedure
```

tional algorithms based on the *all-stop* model discard many optimization opportunities in an optical switch. In contrast, Sunflow exploits the additional flexibility in the optical switch and achieves higher efficiency.

4.1.1 Algorithm Details

Refer again to the example in Figure 1c. Initially, Sunflow starts at t_0 and begins considering each demand in the Coflow. Within the same Coflow, the ordering of demand to be considered can be arbitrary (Lemma 1). Without loss of generality, we assume Sunflow starts reserving circuits for $p_{3,6}$ and $p_{5,7}$. Then Sunflow advances to the first circuit release time (t_1 in Figure 1c), and makes another reservation for $p_{1,6}$. After each reservation, Sunflow updates the remaining Coflow demand. Then Sunflow advances to the next circuit release time, and continues to schedule new circuits for the remaining demand, until all demand is drained.

Sunflow uses a Port Reservation Table (PRT) data structure to record ports taken by each circuit. The PRT contains entries for all input and output ports, and circuits are scheduled with reservations associated with each port. Each reservation tells when a port is taken and released, as well as the peer port for a circuit. Scheduling a circuit implies making reservations on both the input and output port of the circuit. Figure 1c illustrates the entries for input ports in a PRT.

Algorithm 1 shows the pseudocode of Sunflow. Sunflow starts at t_0 on PRT, considers each flow demand (Line 6), and reserves circuits for the flow(s) if the port constraints are satisfied (Line 15). Note that the ordering of flows to be considered can be arbitrary, since Sunflow's optimality analysis holds for any ordering of scheduled circuits (Lemma 1). The length of a reservation accounts for both the circuit reconfiguration overhead δ and the data processing time for the flow (Line 18) to transmit at link rate B. Sunflow updates the PRT with new reservation(s), which correspondingly adds constraints on ports in the PRT. After each reservation, Sunflow updates the remaining Coflow demand by subtracting the amount of demand fulfilled by the reservation (Line 22).

Note that a flow transmits at the full link bandwidth B when its reserved circuit is set up. This is because in the circuit switched network, servicing a flow would block other flows that compete for the same input or output port. Therefore, by transmitting at B, one subflow may complete as soon as possible to allow other blocked subflows to proceed as soon as possible.

Sunflow always observes port constraints on PRT when scheduling new circuits so that existing circuit reservations on PRT are not preempted. As a result, Sunflow continues by advancing to the most recent time when a circuit is released (Line 10). At this time, the released circuit(s) remove constraints on at least one input port and at least one output port, so that Sunflow may reserve more circuits. Then Sunflow identifies potential reservations by considering the remaining demand. Sunflow keeps reserving circuits until all the demand in the Coflow is satisfied.

4.1.2 Optimality Analysis

Recall that non-preemptive intra-Coflow circuit scheduling is NP-hard (§ 3.1.2). The following lemma establishes that Sunflow achieves a CCT within a factor of 2 to the optimal CCT in a circuit switched network.

LEMMA 1. *Denote T_S as Sunflow CCT, T_O^c as the optimal CCT, both in a circuit switched network, then $T_S \leq 2T_L^c$ and $T_S \leq 2T_O^c$, for any B, any δ, any Coflow, and any ordering of scheduled circuits.*

PROOF. See Appendix. □

The following lemma bounds the gap between Sunflow's CCT and the optimal CCT in a packet switched network.

LEMMA 2. *Denote T_S as Sunflow CCT in a circuit switched network, T_O^p as the optimal CCT in a packet switched network, then $T_S \leq 2(1+\alpha)T_L^p$ and $T_S \leq 2(1+\alpha)T_O^p$, where $\alpha = \frac{\delta}{\min_{f_{i,j} \in C}(d_{i,j}/B)}$ for Coflow C.*

PROOF. See Appendix. □

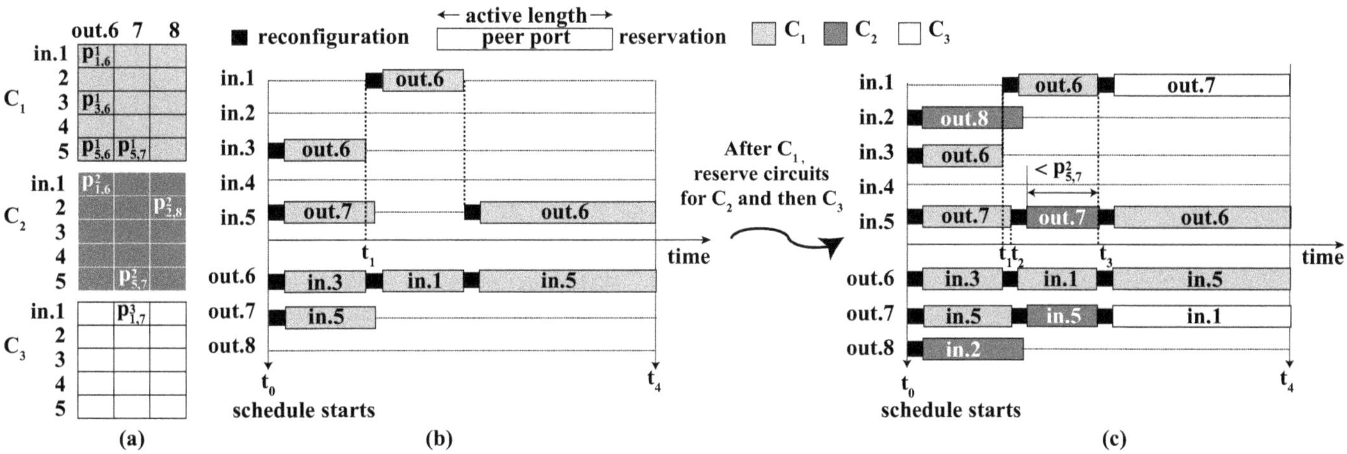

Figure 2: Inter-Coflow Circuit Scheduling. (a) Coflow demand with input ports as rows, output ports as columns, and values as data processing time. The desired order is C_1, C_2, C_3. (b) C_1 reservations. (c) Reservations for C_2 and C_3. Reservations are laid horizontally on the time line for each port. In (c), C_2 on $[in.5, out.7]$ should not block C_1 on $[in.5, out.6]$.

Edmond	TMS	Solstice	Sunflow
$O(N^3)$	$O(N^{4.5})$	$O(N^3 \log^2 N)$	$O(\lvert C\rvert^2)$

Table 3: Time complexity comparison

4.1.3 *Time Complexity*

For a single Coflow with $|C|$ subflows, Sunflow's time complexity is $O(|C|^2)$. In an extreme case where a Coflow covers all input and output ports, $|C| = N^2$. In contrast, the time complexity of other circuit schedulers solely depend on N, so that their running time could be very long even for a small Coflow. Besides, unlike these other algorithms which have no known performance bounds with respect to the optimal, Sunflow has a proven performance bound. Detailed analysis on time complexity is in the Appendix.

4.2 Inter-Coflow Scheduling Design

For inter-Coflow scheduling, when multiple Coflows compete for network resources, an important goal is to accommodate a variety of resource management policies employed by the system operator.

Flexible Management Policies. Different policies may naturally arise from different usage scenarios in data-parallel clusters. As a first example, a usage scenario may consist of privileged and regular users. The policy may require that Coflows requested by privileged users are preferred by the network over Coflows requested by regular users. As a second example, Coflows may be categorized into different classes to match the complex hierarchy for various jobs that generate Coflows. Coflows can be further subdivided into latency-sensitive versus latency-tolerant, and the network should serve them differently. As a third example, when Coflow-dependencies are introduced by multi-stage jobs [22, 37, 2, 1], the policy may require that later-staged Coflows yield to earlier-staged Coflows to avoid the potential creation of stragglers that unnecessarily prolong job runtime [11]. These example scenarios can potentially be mixed as well.

To leave as much flexibility as possible to the network operator, Sunflow provides a very simple framework that only requires the operator to translate the high-level policy into a priority ordering of Coflows. Sunflow then schedules Coflows to minimize the time when more prioritized Coflows are blocked by less prioritized ones. Sunflow also allows multiple Coflows to have the same priority, in which case these Coflows can be further sorted on arrival time and served individually, *or* these Coflows can be combined as one Coflow so that each constituent Coflow may have equal chance to be serviced. This should be a design choice made by the user. However, combining Coflows may come at the cost of a larger average CCT for the Coflows involved. In the simple case where the management policy is to serve shortest-Coflow-first, the Coflows may be ordered by their T_L^p.

To schedule circuits for Coflows, we use the intra-Coflow scheduling algorithm (IntraCoflow in Line 2 of Algorithm 1) as the building block. We apply IntraCoflow to each Coflow in the desired order (Line 26), so more prioritized Coflows complete faster without being blocked by the less prioritized ones. For example in Figure 2, reservation of $[in.5, out.7]$ for C_2 is shorter than desired so as *not* to block C_1 on $[in.5, out.6]$.

Avoiding Starvation Allowing Coflows to block the less prioritized ones may lead to starvation especially if a malicious attacker is involved. To avoid starvation, we introduce a simple and lightweight solution as follows.

We adopt a list of N fixed circuit assignments $\Phi = \{A_1, A_2, ..., A_N\}$, so that all N^2 circuits are covered in the N assignments. Given two tunable parameters

T and τ ($T \gg \tau > \delta$), we schedule circuits with reoccurring intervals of length $(T + \tau)$ over time. Each $(T + \tau)$-interval is divided into two smaller intervals of length T and τ, respectively. For the time T-interval, we apply INTERCOFLOW to ensure the prioritized Coflows are not blocked by the less prioritized ones. For the time τ-interval, we schedule circuits in the assignment $A_k \in \Phi$. A_k is chosen in a round-robin manner so that A_k is scheduled if $A_{(k-1)}$ was scheduled in the last $(T+\tau)$-interval (k wraps around from N to 1). During the τ-interval, when a circuit is set up, subflows from all Coflows share the link bandwidth B on the circuit.

This solution ensures all Coflows receive non-zero service in every $N(T + \tau)$ interval. This is similar to the starvation-prevention design in previous work [12]. Avoiding starvation comes at the cost of reduced circuit utilization because some of the N circuits in one assignment may not have Coflow demand during τ. However, this approach is lightweight and incurs the minimal circuit switching overhead during τ.

5. EVALUATION

5.1 Settings

Workload: We use a realistic workload based on a one-hour Hive/MapReduce trace collected from a Facebook production cluster [4]. The trace contains more than 500 Coflows observed in a 150-port fabric with exact inter-arrival times. The traffic size in the original trace has been rounded to the nearest MB, as a result, many subflows in a Coflow have exactly the same size. We add ±5% perturbation of flow sizes to each flow to account for unequal flow sizes in real MapReduce jobs. The flow sizes are lower bounded at 1 MB (the smallest flow size in the trace) after perturbation, so that we have a factor of 4.5 upper bound of Sunflow's CCT/T_L^p ($\alpha = 1.25$, in Lemma 2) for all Coflows in the trace.

Simulator: We implement a trace-driven flow-level discrete-event simulator with various scheduling algorithms.[1] To evaluate the two levels of scheduling, we reproduce traffic from the trace in two ways. In intra-Coflow evaluation, a Coflow arrives only after the previous one is finished, so that only one Coflow is scheduled at any time and the Coflow arrival time in the original trace is ignored. In inter-Coflow evaluation, we perform detailed trace replay including arrival time.

Within each level of Coflow scheduling, we have evaluations for different settings. We evaluate B from 1 Gbps to 100 Gbps. For the circuit switched network, we evaluate δ from 100 ms to 10 μs. The default value of δ is 10 ms, which is typical of a 3D-MEMS optical switch that can scale to thousands of ports [3].

5.2 Baselines for Comparison

Lower bounds: We compare algorithm performance against the theoretical CCT lower bounds T_L^c and T_L^p.

[1]https://github.com/sunnyxhuang/sunflow

Category	O2O	O2M	M2O	M2M
Coflow%	23.4	9.9	40.1	26.6
Bytes%	0.005	0.024	0.028	99.943

Table 4: Coflow classified by sender-to-receiver ratio: One-to-One (O2O), One-to-Many (O2M), Many-to-One (M2O), and Many-to-Many (M2M).

Solstice: In the intra-Coflow evaluation, we also compare against the existing state-of-the-art circuit scheduling algorithm Solstice [26], whose performance is significantly better than TMS and Edmond for intra-Coflow scheduling. Specifically, in our experience, on average, Solstice services a Coflow more than 2× faster than TMS and more than 6× faster than Edmond.

Varys and Aalo: In the inter-Coflow evaluation, we compare against Varys and Aalo [12, 11], the state-of-the-art Coflow schedulers designed for packet switched networks. Both Varys and Aalo are designed with the objective of minimizing average CCT for a set of Coflows to mitigate the head-of-line blocking problem. We assume Sunflow uses the same Coflow priority policy as in Varys and Aalo, i.e. the shortest-Coflow-first policy.

5.3 Intra-Coflow Scheduling

5.3.1 *Comparison with Circuit Switching Lower Bound*

We begin our evaluation by comparing Sunflow's intra-Coflow performance against the theoretical lower bound T_L^c and Solstice. We observe the primary influence on optimality is the sender-to-receiver ratio in a Coflow, based on which we classify the Coflows as in Table 4, where 1) *One-to-One* Coflow is uni-cast with one sender, one receiver and one flow, 2) *One-to-Many* Coflow is with one sender and more than one receiver, 3) *Many-to-One* Coflow is in-cast with more than one sender and one receiver, and 4) *Many-to-Many* Coflow has more than one sender and more than one receiver.

How close is Sunflow to the optimal? Figure 3 highlights that Sunflow achieves near-optimal circuit scheduling. When B = 1 *Gbps*, the original setting of the Coflow trace (Figure 3a), and δ is 10 ms (typical of a 3D-MEMS optical switch), Sunflow CCT is 1.03× on average and 1.18× at the 95th percentile of the lower bound T_L^c. Note that Sunflow CCT/$T_L^c < 2$ always holds true. On the other hand, Solstice CCT/T_L^c performs much worse with 1.48× on average and 4.74× at the 95th percentile. Furthermore, we observe Solstice CCT can reach up to 10.63× of T_L^c.

Figure 3 also shows that, keeping δ constant, Solstice's performance is worse when B scales up, because the data processing time p becomes smaller compared with δ. The excessive preemptions scheduled by Solstice incurs heavy reconfiguration delays that significantly increase the CCT. From 10 Gbps to 100 Gbps, Solstice's

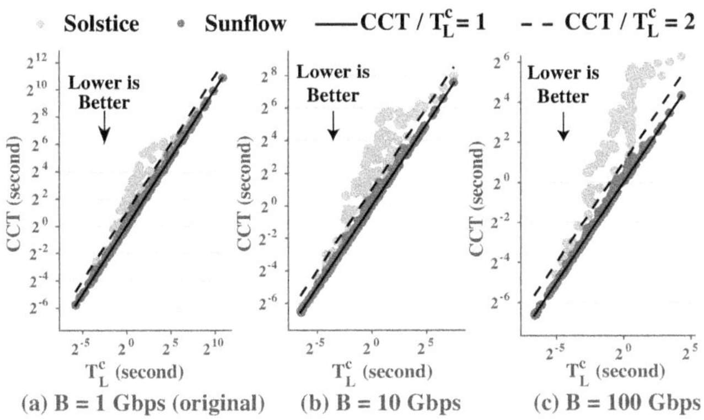

Figure 3: Sunflow and Solstice on different link rate B. Each subfigure shows CCT distribution w.r.t. T_L^c. Both axes are in logarithmic scale.

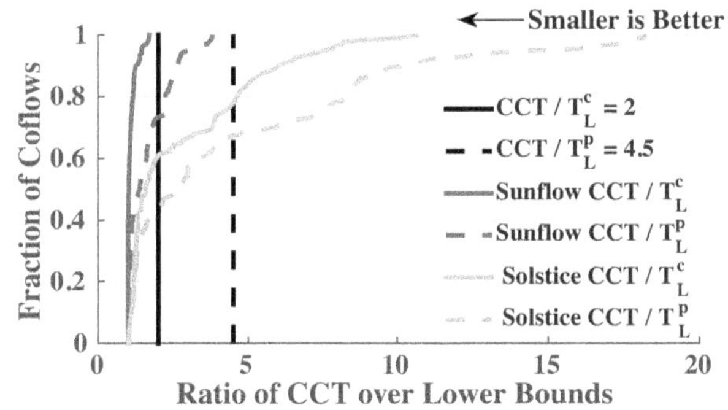

Figure 4: Distribution of CCT/T_L^c and CCT/T_L^p on many-to-many Coflows for Sunflow and Solstice.

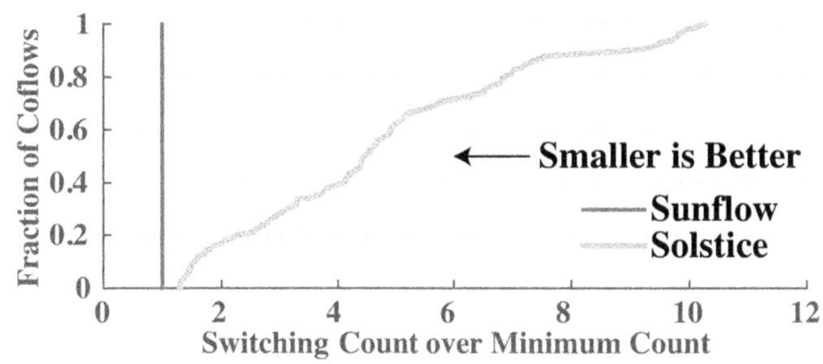

Figure 5: Distribution of switching count for many-to-many Coflows. Normalized over the minimum count for each Coflow.

average (95th percentile) CCT/T_L^c increases from 2.30 (10.06) to 3.17 (13.83), while Sunflow's average (95th percentile) CCT/T_L^c stays at 1.03 (1.24) and 1.04 (1.27).

Sunflow achieves optimal CCT of T_L^c for one-to-one, one-to-many and many-to-one Coflows. In one-to-one, one-to-many and many-to-one Coflows, all flows within a Coflow compete for the same port (visually the flows occupy a single row or column in the demand matrix). Simply scheduling circuits one by one for each flow would yield the optimal CCT in a circuit switching network, i.e. Sunflow CCT equals T_L^c for these Coflows. For these Coflows, Solstice also achieves optimal CCT because these specific Coflow structures happen to be handled by Solstice in a one flow per assignment manner.

Sunflow achieves near-optimal CCT for many-to-many Coflows (which account for over 99% of the bytes). Figure 4 shows the distribution of the ratio between CCT and lower bounds for these Coflows. Note that for Sunflow, CCT is bounded with $\text{CCT}/T_L^c < 2$. We find Sunflow's CCT/T_L^c is 1.10 on average and 1.46 at the 95th percentile. Again Solstice performs much worse with CCT/T_L^c of 2.81 on average and 7.70 at the 95th percentile.

Achieving good performance for many-to-many Coflows is paramount because they account for the vast majority of the Coflow traffic volume. Sunflow's approach excels in this many-to-many case. Figure 5 shows the number of circuit switching events, normalized by the minimum number of necessary switching, in these experiments. The minimum number of necessary switching for a Coflow is given by the number of subflows in the Coflow. Fewer switching events means less time wasted. As can be seen, Sunflow's switching count is optimal, while Solstice incurs numerous switchings for each subflow.

It is interesting to note that the switching count for Sunflow is always optimal regardless of the number of subflows, but for Solstice, the normalized switching count usually grows larger as the number of subflows increases. The linear correlation coefficient between Solstice's normalized switching count and the number of subflows is 0.84 for many-to-many Coflows. In other words, when more subflows are to be scheduled, Solstice would schedule more switchings per circuit.

Sensitivity to δ. We experiment with a range of δ from 100 ms to 10 μs, and the results are in Figure 6, where each CCT is normalized by the CCT when $\delta =$ 10 ms. We find that when δ is one order of magnitude slower than that of 3D-MEMS optical switch (i.e. δ = 100 ms), CCT is significantly worse. On the other hand, CCT can be somewhat improved with an optical switch that is one order of magnitude faster (i.e. $\delta =$ 1 ms). However, the marginal benefit from an even faster switch ($\leq$ 100 μs) is very small. The intuition is that at the intra-Coflow level, CCT is made up of the data transmission time and the switching delays. When δ gets smaller, CCT is dominated by the data transmission time, and δ becomes less relevant. For this reason, it should be expected that, as δ decreases, the inefficiency of Solstice linked to circuit switching overhead diminishes. For $B = 1$ *Gbps*, when δ drops below $O(100\mu s)$, Solstice's CCT performance is slightly better than Sunflow's because more circuit preemptions help Solstice handles skewed traffic slightly more efficiently.

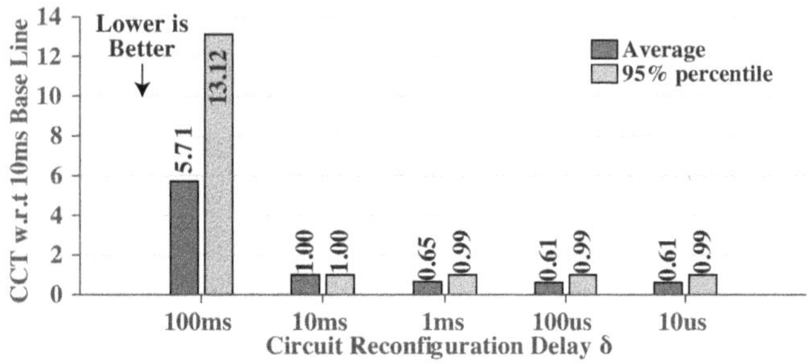

Figure 6: Sensitivity of intra-Coflow scheduling to δ. Normalized over CCT on $\delta = 10$ ms for each Coflow.

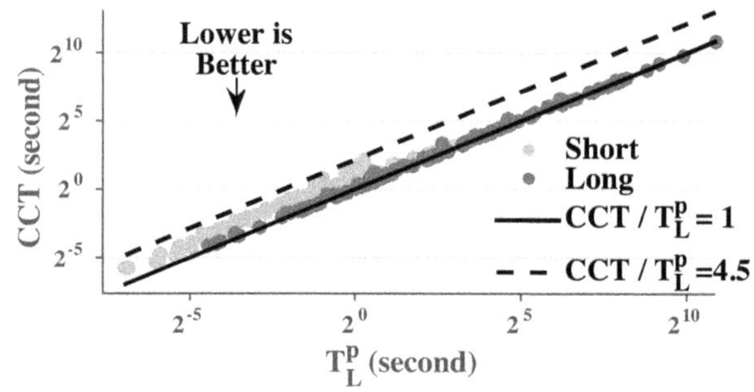

Figure 7: Sunflow CCT and T_L^p. Both axes are in logarithmic scale.

When δ=1 μs, Solstice's 95th-percentile CCT is equal to Sunflow's, and Solstice's average CCT is 0.98× of Sunflow's. Even so, Sunflow's non-preemptive strategy is still extremely critical for good performance since a preemptive algorithm like Solstice can incur more than 10× the switching overhead as shown in Figure 5.

Note that increasing B has the effect of making the circuit switch less efficient at a given δ. For example, if $B = 100$ *Gbps* and flow size does not increase, the Coflow transmission time will be reduced by approximately 100×. In that case, reducing δ by 100× from 10 ms to 100 μs does have benefits – CCTs are reduced to 0.49× at the 95th percentile, but going below 10 μs has marginal benefit.

Interestingly, these results suggest that if the typical data transmission time remains steady (i.e. flow size scales roughly 1:1 with link speed), it may be most fruitful to optimize switching technologies for $\delta = 1ms$, because the cost to develop faster switching technologies may outweigh the actual benefit.

Sensitivity to reservation ordering. To understand whether Sunflow's performance depends on reservation ordering, we conduct a sensitivity test. We change the order of reservations by ordering the demand in a Coflow in the following ways: (1) by sorting on the port label (called *OrderedPort*, used as the default in previous experiments), (2) by random (called *Random*), and (3) by sorting on the demand size (called *SortedDemand*). The average (95th percentile) CCT of *Random* is 0.94× (1.01×) the CCT of *OrderedPort*, while the average (95th percentile) CCT of *SortedDemand* is 0.95× (1.01×) the CCT of *OrderedPort*. These results show that Sunflow's performance is insensitive to reservation ordering.

5.3.2 Comparison with Packet Switching Lower Bound

Figure 7 compares Sunflow's CCT to the Coflow packet switching lower bound T_L^p and shows results for long Coflows separately. We consider a Coflow to be long if its average data processing time is larger than $40\times\delta$ (which corresponds to an average subflow size of ≥ 5 MB in the experiment). Specifically, the average data processing time for a Coflow C is $p_{\text{avg}} = \frac{\sum p_{i,j} \in C}{|C|}$, where $|C|$ is number of subflows in Coflow. Long Coflows account for 25.2% of Coflows and 98.8% of bytes in the trace.

Long Coflows have performance very close to the packet switching lower bound: CCT/T_L^p is 1.09 on average and 1.25 at the 95th percentile. For small Coflows, CCT/T_L^p is larger, but in absolute terms the extra time incurred by Sunflow is also small. Overall, CCT/T_L^p is 1.86 on average and 2.31 at the 95th percentile. Note that all Sunflow CCTs are within the theoretical bound of CCT/$T_L^p = 4.5$.

It is interesting to note that as p_{avg} increases, Sunflow's CCT gets closer to T_L^p. The rank correlation coefficient between p_{avg} and CCT/T_L^p is -0.96. For a Coflow with larger p_{avg}, circuits remain active longer after setup, circuit duty cycle is larger, and CCT/$T_L^p \to 1$.

Even though Sunflow's CCT can never be as low as packet switching due to the delay inherent to circuit switching, by providing CCT performance that is near that of packet switching, Sunflow enables networks to sacrifice some performance for the important data rate, energy, and longevity benefits of OCS (see § 1).

5.4 Inter-Coflow Scheduling

We now extend our evaluation from the intra-Coflow level to the inter-Coflow level. We begin our evaluation by comparing Sunflow against Varys and Aalo under the default settings. Note that Sunflow is based on optical circuit switching with $\delta > 0$, while Varys and Aalo are based on packet switching that amounts to $\delta = 0$. We first adopt the metric used in previous Coflow scheduling studies [12, 11, 38], which is the CCT ratio between competing schemes. Thus, we compute the ratios between Sunflow's CCT over Varys' and Aalo's CCT.

We find that Sunflow is 1.87× (2.52×) of Varys, and 1.69× (2.37×) of Aalo on average (at the 95th percentile). Note that Varys is slightly better than Aalo under the CCT ratio metric, which is consistent with the results in [11].

At first glance, these results are discouraging for Sunflow. However, it is also not hard to see why the average CCT ratio metric does not favor Sunflow. The circuit

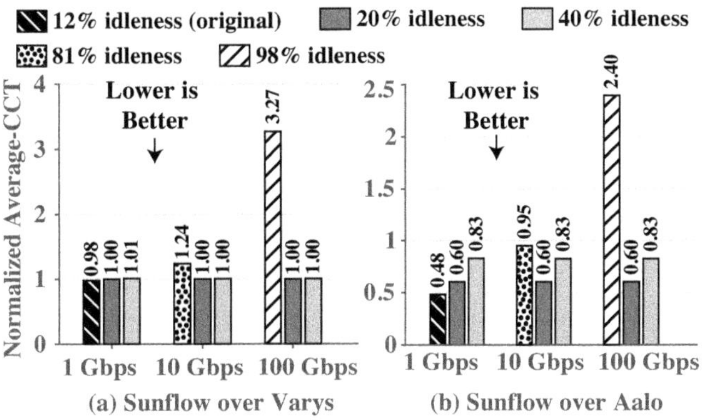

Figure 8: Sunflow average-CCT w.r.t. network idleness. Normalized over the average-CCT of (a) Varys and (b) Aalo under the same idleness.

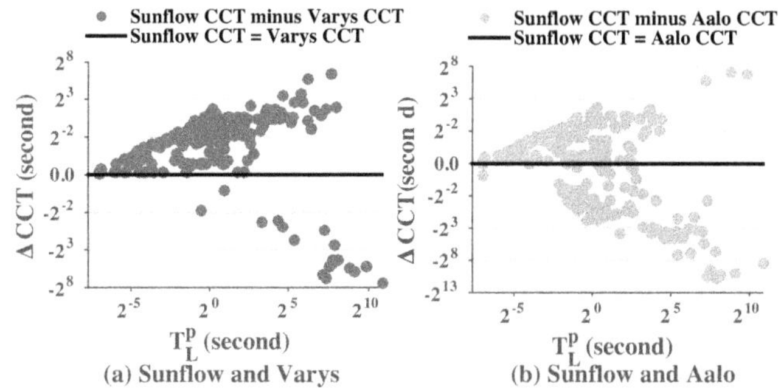

Figure 9: CCT difference between Sunflow (circuit switched) and Varys or Aalo (both packet switched). Coflows are spread out on the X-axis based on their T_L^p. Sunflow CCT is shorter with negative values. Both axes are in logarithmic scale.

switching overhead in Sunflow is significant for short Coflows, leading to large CCT ratios even though the absolute difference in CCT could be small. Specifically, for short Coflows, Sunflow is on average 2.16× to Varys, and 1.96× to Aalo. However, for long Coflows where the most data bytes come from, Sunflow CCT is comparable to Varys and Aalo: Sunflow is on average 1.07× to Varys, and 0.90× to Aalo. Since there are many more short Coflows than long Coflows, the average CCT ratio metric does not favor Sunflow.

Sunflow achieves comparable average CCT as Varys and Aalo. If we do not focus on pairwise CCT comparison, but instead focus on overall network efficiency and use the average CCT achieved by different schemes as the metric, the story becomes quite different.

Before we present the results, to further consider performance under various traffic load, we derive a metric that measures the network *idleness* for a specific set of Coflow traffic on a specific B. We consider a Coflow C to be active from its arrival time t^{Arr} to $t^{\text{Arr}}+T_L^p$, where T_L^p is CCT packet-switched lower bound given bandwidth B. At any time, we define network idleness as the portion of time when there is no active Coflow. This idleness metric considers Coflow characteristics and arrival rate, as well as the network bandwidth. Note that the metric is independent of the scheduling policy, and it is the upper bound on network idle time, because Coflows may stay longer than T_L^p in the network due to waiting for other Coflows. The network idleness in the original trace is 12%. When B is scaled from 1 Gbps to 10 Gbps and 100 Gbps, the idleness increases significantly from 12% to 81% and 98%. To evaluate under reasonable idleness, we scale the byte sizes of Coflows to attain 20% and 40% idleness for various B while preserving Coflows' structural characteristics.

In Figure 8, we compare the network efficiency by average CCT under various network idleness. By comparing across different network idleness from original 12% to 81% and 98%, we observe that Sunflow compares favorably to Varys and Aalo in modest or higher traffic load. When idleness is 81% or 98%, in many cases a Coflow finishes before the next one arrives. Under these underutilized settings, CCT for each Coflow is small, while Sunflow pays a relatively large circuit switching penalty. However, in a network with high or moderate traffic load, Sunflow achieves similarly high network efficiency as Varys and Aalo. This is because with more traffic, Coflows generally have longer waiting time that increases CCT, and thus the effect of δ on CCT is reduced. For 12%, 20% and 40% idleness, Sunflow's average CCT is within 1.01× of Varys and 0.83× of Aalo.

To compare the three algorithms more closely, we examine the individual CCTs under the 12% idleness setting, as shown in Figure 9.

On one hand, Coflows with small T_L^p may finish slower in Sunflow due to circuit switching delay. When multiple Coflows are involved in scheduling, a CCT is impacted by both the transmission time for the Coflow and the waiting time between Coflows that compete for bandwidth resources. In all schedulers, Coflows with smaller T_L^p are prioritized and do not have much waiting. Therefore, their CCT mainly consist of a small transmission time, with Sunflow paying a relatively large penalty due to the circuit reconfiguration overhead.

On the other hand, Coflows with large T_L^p may finish quicker in Sunflow than in Varys because Varys may leave bandwidth underutilized and prolong the CCT of large Coflows. Specifically, in Varys, subflows within the same Coflow may finish at different time because Varys opportunistically allocates different amounts of additional bandwidth to subflows when residual bandwidth is available. However, when a subflow finishes early, the associated bandwidth is left unused until the next rescheduling decision is made, which happens only on Coflow arrivals and completions [12]. Compared with Varys and Sunflow, Aalo introduces an extra inefficiency at the intra-Coflow level. Without known flow sizes, Aalo may allocate more bandwidth to small sub-

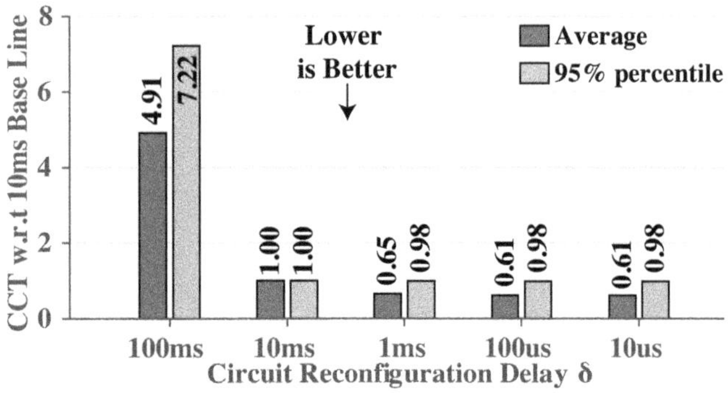

Figure 10: Sensitivity of inter-Coflow scheduling to δ. Normalized over CCT on $\delta = 10$ ms for each Coflow.

flows at the cost of delaying the long subflows, thus prolonging the overall CCT. This effect is more obvious for large Coflows.

When these two observations are combined, the average CCT of Sunflow, Varys, and Aalo become comparable. Thus, Sunflow enables networks to exploit the important data rate, energy, and longevity benefits of OCS (see § 1) while achieving good performance.

Sensitivity to δ. Our observations on Sunflow's sensitivity to δ under intra-Coflow scheduling (§ 5.3.1) generally also applies to inter-Coflow scheduling. Figure 10 shows the sensitivity analysis results. As before, compared to the 10 ms baseline, CCT can be somewhat improved with an optical switch with $\delta = 1$ ms. However, the marginal benefit from an even faster switch (≤ 100 μs) is very small. Thus, it is also the case for inter-Coflow scheduling, if the typical data transmission time remains steady (i.e. flow size scales roughly 1:1 with link speed), it may be most fruitful to optimize switching technologies for $\delta = 1ms$.

6. DISCUSSION

While this work focuses on the algorithmic aspects of circuit scheduling for Coflows, it is useful to discuss how Sunflow can be deployed. Fortunately, the facilities required to deploy Sunflow have been investigated in previous works [12, 25, 30]. Particularly, the OCS architecture for a compute cluster, the synchronization mechanism between host transmission and optical circuit setup, and the system for collecting Coflow requests as well as managing the flow transmissions have been proposed and implemented in previous works.

Centralized OCS control. A single controller can successfully schedule an OCS as shown in the Mordia design [30], which is based on a preemptive scheduling algorithm. Sunflow would require much less frequent circuit reconfigurations due to its non-preemptive nature, thus it would actually be easier to scale Sunflow up for a larger system. Sunflow is meant for controlling a single optical circuit switch. Adapting Sunflow for controlling a network of circuit switches is a subject of our future work.

Coordinating circuits and machines with ToR. As a ToR switch, REACToR [25] is capable of 1) synchronizing machines' transmission with circuit setup with explicit signals, 2) multiplexing between a packet switched network and a circuit switched network. Sunflow could use REACToR to achieve an efficient use of optical circuits. In addition, REACToR's hybrid architecture capable design allows a small-bandwidth packet switched network to help accommodate the little leftover traffic from the circuit switched network due to retransmissions or synchronization glitches.

Centralized Coflow scheduling. Centralized Coflow scheduling with Varys has been demonstrated in [12]. Similar to Varys, Sunflow reschedules only upon Coflow arrivals and completions, which makes centralized Coflow scheduling feasible. In Varys, a daemon agent runs on each machine to manage the flow sending rate, and collect the Coflow requests from the application running on the host. Sunflow asks for a small modification in the Varys agent: Rather than implementing per-flow rate control as instructed by the scheduler in Varys, for Sunflow scheduling, the agent on a sending machine would receive a row in the PRT corresponding to its port, count the circuit setup signals from REACToR, and when a circuit for its flow becomes active, the agent sends the flow at line rate.

Scheduler latency. With our untuned implementation in C++ when running on an Intel 3.5GHz processor, Sunflow's computation time is less than 1 sec for Coflows with up to 3,000 subflows. The performance can be further optimized with the use of more efficient data structures. Besides, unlike other schedulers that schedule circuits in a batch with *assignments* (§ 3.1.1), Sunflow may schedule each computed circuit individually, thus hiding the scheduling latency by overlapping circuit setup with data transmissions. To further reduce computation time, it is possible to leverage approximation schemes (e.g. by rounding subflow sizes up to thresholds to prune the loops of circuit release events in Algorithm 1 Line 10), or to leverage parallelism (e.g. by computing circuit schedules on partitioned demands in parallel). However, approximation and parallelization could reduce the optimality of the resulting schedules.

7. CONCLUSION

We have presented Sunflow, the first circuit scheduling algorithm for Coflow that is provably within a factor-of-two to the optimal, and we have shown that in practice the gap is much smaller. Sunflow handles different kinds of Coflows (e.g. one-to-many, many-to-one, many-to-many) equally well, and its performance is good even with the circuit switching delay typical of today's 3D-MEMS switches. As a Coflow's size increases, Sunflow's CCT performance approaches the packet switching lower bound. Under modest to heavy traffic load,

Sunflow achieves comparable average CCT to a packet switched network employing the state-of-the-art Coflow schedulers. In conclusion, with Sunflow's scheduling benefits, an OCS can be a viable component in a modern data-parallel cluster network.

Acknowledgements

We thank Simbarashe Dzinamarira, Dingming Wu, Yiting Xia, our shepherd Paolo Costa, and the anonymous reviewers for useful feedback. We also thank Mosharaf Chowdhury for sharing the Coflow traffic trace. This research is sponsored by the NSF under CNS-1422925, CNS-1305379 and CNS-1162270.

Appendix

This section contains the theoretical proofs and analysis for results presented in § 4.1.2 and § 4.1.3.

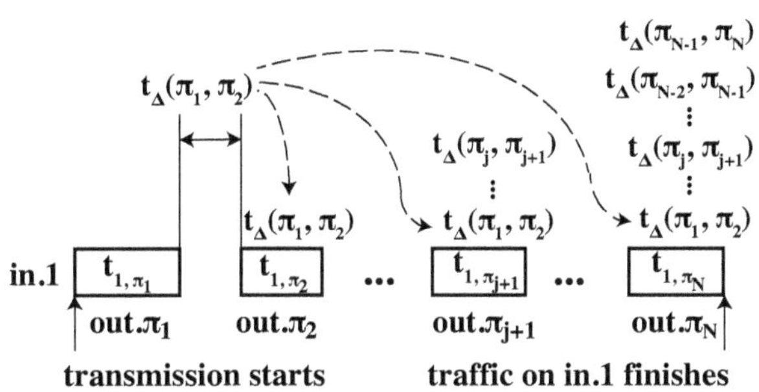

Figure 11: Sunflow scheduling circuits on $in.1$

Proof of Lemma 1. We begin by proving the following proposition: *Under Sunflow scheduling, any input and output port will finish traffic within* $2T_L^c$ *after transmission starts.*

Without loss of generality, consider an input port denoted as $in.1$. In Sunflow, the time spent on each flow is given by Equation (3). There exists a permutation of $\{1, ..., N\}$, denoted as $\{\pi_{(in.1,1)}, ..., \pi_{(in.1,N)}\}$ for $in.1$, so that Sunflow setup circuit $[in.1,\ out.\pi_{(in.1,j)}]$ no later than $[in.1,\ out.\pi_{(in.1,j+1)}]$. Note that the permutation may differ for different ports. For notation simplicity, we refer to $\pi_{(in.1,j)}$ as π_j of $in.1$ in the following proof. Hence the ordering of output ports to be served for $in.1$ is $out.\pi_1$, ..., $out.\pi_j$, $out.\pi_{j+1}$, ..., $out.\pi_N$ (Figure 11). Note that t_{1,π_1} starts as soon as transmission starts, since $in.1$ can always match with an output port.

Denote $t_\Delta(\pi_j, \pi_{j+1})$ as the gap in time between demand t_{1,π_j} finishes and $t_{1,\pi_{j+1}}$ starts. During $t_\Delta(\pi_j, \pi_{j+1})$, $in.1$ is idle. Since Sunflow fails to find an output port to match $in.1$, *all* output ports of $out.\pi_{j+1}, out.\pi_{j+2}, ...,$ $out.\pi_N$ must be transmitting. Thus, during $t_\Delta(\pi_j, \pi_{j+1})$, the demand on output ports $out.\pi_{j+1}$, ..., $out.\pi_N$ is decreased by $t_\Delta(\pi_j, \pi_{j+1})$, as shown by output port $out.\pi_{j+1}$ in Figure 11. Note that the demand served for any output port during $t_\Delta(\pi_j, \pi_{j+1})$ can be demand from any input port *other than* $in.1$.

Consider the output port $out.\pi_N$. t_{1,π_N} is the last to be served among $t_{1,\pi_1}, ..., t_{1,\pi_N}$. The demand on output port $out.\pi_N$ satisfies

$$\sum_{j=1}^{N-1} t_\Delta(\pi_j, \pi_{j+1}) \le \sum_i t_{i,\pi_N} \le T_L^c \tag{5}$$

Thus the total time that $in.1$ stays idle during transmission is at most T_L^c, so $in.1$ will finish its traffic in

$$\begin{aligned} T &= t_{1,\pi_1} + t_\Delta(\pi_1, \pi_2) + ... + t_\Delta(\pi_{N-1}, \pi_N) + t_{1,\pi_N} \\ &= \sum_{j=1}^{N-1} t_\Delta(\pi_j, \pi_{j+1}) + \sum_{j=1}^{N} t_{1,\pi_j} \\ &\le T_L^c + T_L^c = 2T_L^c \end{aligned} \tag{6}$$

Equation (6) holds for all input and output ports, which proves our proposition.

According to our proposition, Sunflow would finish transmission for all input and output ports within $2T_L^c$, thus Sunflow CCT satisfies

$$T_S \le 2T_L^c \tag{7}$$

The CCT under optimal scheduling in a circuit switched network must be at least T_L^c, i.e. $T_O^c \ge T_L^c$. Thus Sunflow's CCT is bounded by

$$T_S \le 2T_L^c \le 2T_O^c \tag{8}$$

Our proof holds for any ordering of the circuits to be scheduled. □

Proof of Lemma 2. For any flow in a Coflow, the relationship between $t_{i,j}$ (Equation (3)) and $d_{i,j}/B = p_{i,j}$ (Equation (1)) is given by

$$t_{i,j} \le p_{i,j} + \delta \le (1+\alpha)p_{i,j} \tag{9}$$

Equation (2), Equation (4), and Equation (9) give

$$T_L^c \le (1+\alpha)T_L^p \tag{10}$$

Note that the port that gives T_L^c may be different from the port that gives T_L^p, but Equation (10) holds true regardless of whether such two ports are identical or not. Therefore we have

$$T_S \le 2T_L^c \le 2(1+\alpha)T_L^p \le 2(1+\alpha)T_O^p, \tag{11}$$

which leads to the conclusion of Lemma 2 □

Time Complexity Analysis. Sunflow stops at each circuit release time in the PRT and tries to schedule circuits (Algorithm 1 Line 10). For a Coflow C, the number of circuit release events is less than $|C|$, where $|C|$ denotes the number of subflows in C. At each circuit release time, Sunflow scans through the Coflow demand to reserve circuits (Algorithm 1 Line 6). The number of entries in the Coflow demand is less than $|C|$. Hence the complexity for a single Coflow is $O(|C|^2)$. In the worst case, a Coflow may cover all input and output ports, resulting in $|C| = N^2$.

8. REFERENCES

[1] Apache Hive. http://hive.apache.org.

[2] Apache Tez. http://tez.apache.org.

[3] Based on private communications with Glimmerglass Networks Inc., an optical switch manufacturer.

[4] Coflow benchmark based on Facebook traces. https://github.com/coflow/coflow-benchmark.

[5] AL-FARES, M., LOUKISSAS, A., AND VAHDAT, A. A scalable, commodity data center network architecture. In *ACM SIGCOMM* (2008).

[6] ALLAHVERDI, A., NG, C., CHENG, T. E., AND KOVALYOV, M. Y. A survey of scheduling problems with setup times or costs. *European Journal of Operational Research 187*, 3 (2008), 985–1032.

[7] BALAS, E., AND LANDWEER, P. R. Traffic assignment in communication satellites. *Operations Research Letters 2*, 4 (1983), 141–147.

[8] BIRKHOFF, G. Tres observaciones sobre el algebra lineal. *Univ. Nac. Tucumán Rev. Ser. A 5* (1946), 147–151.

[9] CALIENT. S series optical circuit switch. http://www.calient.net.

[10] CHOWDHURY, M., AND STOICA, I. Coflow: A networking abstraction for cluster applications. In *ACM Hotnets* (2012).

[11] CHOWDHURY, M., AND STOICA, I. Efficient coflow scheduling without prior knowledge. In *ACM SIGCOMM* (2015).

[12] CHOWDHURY, M., ZHONG, Y., AND STOICA, I. Efficient coflow scheduling with Varys. In *ACM SIGCOMM* (2014).

[13] DASYLVA, A., AND SRIKANT, R. Optimal WDM schedules for optical star networks. *IEEE Transactions on Networking (TON) 7*, 3 (1999), 446–456.

[14] EDMONDS, J. Paths, trees, and flowers. *Canadian Journal of Mathematics 17* (1965), 449–467.

[15] FARRINGTON, N., PORTER, G., FAINMAN, Y., PAPEN, G., AND VAHDAT, A. Hunting mice with microsecond circuit switches. In *ACM HotNets* (2012).

[16] FARRINGTON, N., PORTER, G., RADHAKRISHNAN, S., BAZZAZ, H. H., SUBRAMANYA, V., FAINMAN, Y., PAPEN, G., AND VAHDAT, A. Helios: A hybrid electrical/optical switch architecture for modular data centers. In *ACM SIGCOMM* (2010).

[17] GLIMMERGLASS. Intelligent optical system. http://www.glimmerglass.com.

[18] GONZALEZ, T., AND SAHNI, S. Open shop scheduling to minimize finish time. *Journal of the ACM (JACM) 23*, 4 (1976), 665–679.

[19] GOPAL, I. S., AND WONG, C. K. Minimizing the number of switchings in an SS/TDMA system. *IEEE Transactions on Communications 33*, 6 (1985), 497–501.

[20] GREENBERG, A., HAMILTON, J. R., JAIN, N., KANDULA, S., KIM, C., LAHIRI, P., MALTZ, D. A., PATEL, P., AND SENGUPTA, S. VL2: A scalable and flexible data center network. In *ACM SIGCOMM* (2009).

[21] INUKAI, T. An efficient SS/TDMA time slot assignment algorithm. *IEEE Transactions on Communications 27*, 10 (1979), 1449–1455.

[22] ISARD, M., BUDIU, M., YU, Y., BIRRELL, A., AND FETTERLY, D. Dryad: Distributed data-parallel programs from sequential building blocks. In *ACM EuroSys* (2007).

[23] KESSELMAN, A., AND KOGAN, K. Nonpreemptive scheduling of optical switches. *IEEE Transactions on Communications 55*, 6 (2007), 1212–1219.

[24] LIN, H.-C., AND WANG, C.-H. A hybrid multicast scheduling algorithm for single-hop WDM networks. In *IEEE INFOCOM* (2001).

[25] LIU, H., LU, F., FORENCICH, A., KAPOOR, R., TEWARI, M., VOELKER, G. M., PAPEN, G., SNOEREN, A. C., AND PORTER, G. Circuit switching under the radar with REACToR. In *USENIX NSDI* (2014).

[26] LIU, H., MUKERJEE, M. K., LI, C., FELTMAN, N., PAPEN, G., SAVAGE, S., SESHAN, S., VOELKER, G. M., ANDERSEN, D. G., KAMINSKY, M., ET AL. Scheduling techniques for hybrid circuit/packet networks. In *ACM CoNEXT* (2015).

[27] LUO, S., YU, H., ZHAO, Y., WANG, S., YU, S., AND LI, L. Towards practical and near-optimal coflow scheduling for data center networks.

[28] MCKEOWN, N. The iSLIP scheduling algorithm for input-queued switches. *IEEE Transactions on Networking 7*, 2 (1999), 188–201.

[29] POLATIS. Series 7000 software defined optical switch. http://www.polatis.com.

[30] PORTER, G., STRONG, R., FARRINGTON, N., FORENCICH, A., CHEN-SUN, P., ROSING, T., FAINMAN, Y., PAPEN, G., AND VAHDAT, A. Integrating microsecond circuit switching into the data center. In *ACM SIGCOMM* (2013).

[31] QIU, Z., STEIN, C., AND ZHONG, Y. Minimizing the total weighted completion time of coflows in datacenter networks. In *ACM Symposium on Parallelism in Algorithms and Architectures (SPAA)* (2015).

[32] ROUSKAS, G. N., AND SIVARAMAN, V. Packet scheduling in broadcast WDM networks with arbitrary transceiver tuning latencies. *IEEE Transactions on Networking (TON) 5*, 3 (1997), 359–370.

[33] TOWLES, B., AND DALLY, W. J. Guaranteed

scheduling for switches with configuration overhead. *IEEE Transactions on Networking 11*, 5 (2003), 835–847.

[34] Wang, C.-H., Javidi, T., and Porter, G. End-to-end scheduling for all-optical data centers. In *IEEE INFOCOM* (2015).

[35] Wang, G., Andersen, D. G., Kaminsky, M., Papagiannaki, K., Ng, T. S. E., Kozuch, M., and Ryan, M. c-Through: Part-time optics in data centers. In *ACM SIGCOMM* (2010).

[36] Wang, G., Ng, T. S. E., and Shaikh, A. Programming your network at run-time for big data applications. In *ACM HotSDN* (2012).

[37] Zaharia, M., Chowdhury, M., Das, T., Dave, A., Ma, J., McCauley, M., Franklin, M. J., Shenker, S., and Stoica, I. Resilient distributed datasets: A fault-tolerant abstraction for in-memory cluster computing. In *USENIX NSDI* (2012).

[38] Zhang, H., Chen, L., Yi, B., Chen, K., Chowdhury, M., and Geng, Y. CODA: Toward automatically identifying and scheduling coflows in the dark. In *ACM SIGCOMM* (2016).

[39] Zhao, Y., Chen, K., Bai, W., Yu, M., Tian, C., Geng, Y., Zhang, Y., Li, D., and Wang, S. RAPIER: Integrating routing and scheduling for coflow-aware data center networks. In *IEEE INFOCOM* (2015).

ECN or Delay: Lessons Learnt from Analysis of DCQCN and TIMELY

Yibo Zhu[1], Monia Ghobadi[1], Vishal Misra[2], Jitendra Padhye[1]
[1]Microsoft [2]Columbia University

ABSTRACT

Data center networks, and especially drop-free RoCEv2 networks require efficient congestion control protocols. DCQCN (ECN-based) and TIMELY (delay-based) are two recent proposals for this purpose. In this paper, we analyze DCQCN and TIMELY using fluid models and simulations, for stability, convergence, fairness and flow completion time. We uncover several surprising behaviors of these protocols. For example, we show that DCQCN exhibits non-monotonic stability behavior, and that TIMELY can converge to stable regime with arbitrary unfairness. We propose simple fixes and tuning for ensuring that both protocols converge to and are stable at the fair share point. Finally, using lessons learnt from the analysis, we address the broader question: are there fundamental reasons to prefer either ECN or delay for end-to-end congestion control in data center networks? We argue that ECN is a better congestion signal, due to the way modern switches mark packets, and due to a fundamental limitation of end-to-end delay-based protocols, that we derive.

Keywords

Data center transport; RDMA; ECN; delay-based; congestion control

1. INTRODUCTION

Large cloud service providers are turning to Remote DMA (RDMA) technology to support their most demanding applications [21, 28, 31]. RDMA offers significantly higher bandwidth and lower latency than the traditional TCP/IP stack, while minimizing CPU overhead [7, 21, 31].

Today, RDMA is deployed using the RoCEv2 standard [18]. To ensure efficient operation, RoCEv2 uses Priority Flow Control (PFC) [17] to prevent packet drops due to buffer overflow. Since there are no packet drops, any end-to-end congestion control protocol for RoCEv2 networks must use either ECN markings, or delay as the congestion signal.

Last year, two protocols were proposed for this purpose, namely DCQCN [31] and TIMELY [21]. Though they are designed for enabling RoCEv2 in large data centers, their key assumptions are not RDMA-specific: data centers based on commodity Ethernet hardware, and no packet drops due to congestion. The difference is that DCQCN uses ECN marking as a congestion signal, while TIMELY measures changes to end-to-end delay.

In this paper, we analyze DCQCN and TIMELY for stability, convergence, fairness and flow completion time.

We have two motivations for this work. First, we want to understand the performance of DCQCN and TIMELY in detail. Given their potential for widespread deployment, we want to understand the tradeoffs made by the two protocols in detail, as well as offer guidance for parameter tuning. Second, using insights drawn from the analysis, we want to answer a broader question: are there fundamental reasons to prefer either ECN or delay as the congestion signal in data center networks?

To this end, we analyze DCQCN and TIMELY using fluid models and NS3 [32] simulations. Fluid models are useful for analyzing properties such as stability, and for rapid exploration of parameter space. However, fluid models cannot tractably model all features of complex protocols like DCQCN and TIMELY. Nor can fluid models compute measures like flow completion times. Thus, we also study the protocols using detailed, packet-level simulations using NS3. Our simulations in NS3 implement all known features of the protocols. We have released our NS3 source code at [1].

Before we proceed, we want to stress two things. First, we limit our discussion to ECN and delay as congestion signals and end-host rate-based control, since they are supported by commodity Ethernet switch and NIC hardware [21, 31]. Protocols that require hardware to do more [5, 8, 19] or use a central controller [24, 30] are outside the scope of this paper. We also do not consider designing a new protocol that would use both ECN and delay as congestion signals.

Second, it is not our goal to do a direct comparison of performance of DCQCN and TIMELY. Such comparison makes little sense, since both protocols offer several tuning knobs, and given a specific scenario, either protocol can be made to perform as well as the other. Instead, we focus on the core

CoNEXT '16, December 12-15, 2016, Irvine, CA, USA
© 2016 ACM. ISBN 978-1-4503-4292-6/16/12...$15.00
DOI: http://dx.doi.org/10.1145/2999572.2999593

behavior the two protocols to obtain broader insights. Our key contributions, and findings are summarized as follows.

DCQCN: (i) We extend the fluid model proposed in [31], to show that DCQCN has a unique fixed point, where flows converge to their fair share. Using a discrete model, we also derive that the convergence speed is exponential. (ii) We show that DCQCN is stable around this fixed point, as long as the feedback latency is low. The relationship between stability and the number of competing flows is, strangely, non-monotonic, which is very different from TCP's behavior [15]. DCQCN is stable for both very small, and very large number of flows, and tends to be unstable in between; especially if the feedback latency is high.

TIMELY: (i) We develop a fluid model for TIMELY, and validate it using simulations. The model reveals that TIMELY can have infinite fixed points, resulting in arbitrary unfairness. (ii) We propose a simple remedy, called Patched TIMELY, and show that the modified version is stable and exponentially converges to a unique fixed point.

ECN or Delay: (i) We compare the flow completion time of TIMELY and DCQCN running the same traffic traces. DCQCN outperforms TIMELY due to better fairness, stability and fundamentally it is able to control the queue length better than TIMELY. Patched TIMELY closes the gap, but still cannot match DCQCN performance. We sweep the values of all DCQCN and TIMELY parameters and present the best combinations. Therefore, the performance difference is less about parameter tuning, but more likely due to the fundamental signal they use.

(ii) Based on lessons learnt from analysis of DCQCN and TIMELY, we explain why ECN is a better signal for conveying congestion information. One reason for this is that modern shared buffer switches mark packets with ECN *at egress*, effectively decoupling the queuing delay from feedback delay. This improves system stability. Second, we present a *fundamental* result: for a distributed protocol that uses only delay as the feedback signal, you can achieve either fairness or a guaranteed steady-state delay, but not both simultaneously. For an ECN-based protocol you can achieve both by using a PI [14]-like marking scheme. This is not possible with delay-based congestion control. Finally, ECN signal is more resilient to jitter on the backward path as it only introduces delay in the feedback, whereas for delay based protocols jitter introduces delay *and* noise in the feedback signal.

2. BACKGROUND

The Remote Direct Memory Access (RDMA) technology offers high throughput (40Gbps or more), low latency (few μs), and low CPU overhead (1-2%), by bypassing the end-host kernels during data transfer. Instead, network interface cards (NICs) transfer data in and out of pre-registered memory buffers at the two end hosts.

Modern data center networks deploy RDMA using the RDMA over Converged Ethernet V2 (RoCEv2) [18] standard. RoCEv2 requires a lossless (or, more accurately, drop-free) L2 layer. Ethernet can be made drop-free using Priority Flow Control (PFC) [17]. PFC prevents buffer overflow on Ethernet switches and NICs. The switches and NICs track ingress queues. When the queue exceeds a certain threshold, a PAUSE message is sent to the upstream entity. The uplink entity then stops sending on that link till it gets an RESUME message. PFC is a blunt mechanism, since it does not operate on a per-flow basis. This leads to several well-known problems such as head-of-the-line blocking [31, 28].

PFC's problems can be mitigated using per-flow congestion control. Since PFC eliminates packet drops due to buffer overflow, either ECN or increase in RTT are the only two available "end-to-end" congestion signals. DCQCN relies on ECN, while TIMELY relies on RTT changes.

DCQCN and TIMELY are not RDMA-specific, so our analysis makes no reference to RoCEv2 or RDMA. DCQCN and TIMELY are not designed for wide area traffic, so our analysis focuses on intra-DC networks.

3. DCQCN

DCQCN is an end-to-end, rate-based congestion control protocol that relies on ECN [25]. It combines elements of DCTCP [2] and QCN [16]. DCQCN algorithm specifies behavior of three entities: the sender (called the reaction point (RP)), the switch, (called the congestion point (CP)), and the receiver (called the notification point (NP)). We now briefly describe the protocol; see [31] for more details.

CP behavior: At every egress queue, the arriving packet is ECN-marked [25] if the queue exceeds a threshold, using a RED [10]-like algorithm.

NP behavior: The NP receives ECN-marked packets and notifies the RP about it using Congestion Notification Packets (CNP) [18] Specifically, if a marked packet arrives for a flow, and no CNP has been sent for this flow in last τ microseconds, a CNP is generated immediately.

RP behavior: The RP adjusts its sending rate based on whether it receives a CNP within a period of time.

Upon getting a CNP, the RP reduces its current rate (R_C) and updates the value of the rate reduction factor, α, like DCTCP, and remembers current rate as target rate (R_T) for later recovery, as follows:

$$\begin{aligned} R_T &= R_C, \\ R_C &= R_C(1-\alpha/2), \\ \alpha &= (1-g)\alpha + g, \end{aligned} \tag{1}$$

If RP gets no feedback for τ', α is updated as:

$$\alpha = (1-g)\alpha, \tag{2}$$

Note that τ' must be larger than the CNP generation timer.

RP increases its sending rate using a timer and a byte counter, in a manner identical to QCN [16]. The rate increases has two phases, five stages of so-called "fast recovery", where R_c rapidly approaches R_t, and then a gradual additive increase. DCQCN does not have slow start. Senders start at line rate, in order to optimize the common case of no congestion. DCQCN relies on hardware rate limiters for per-packet rate limiting.

$$
p(t) = \begin{cases} 0, & q(t) \le K_{\min} \\ \frac{q(t)-K_{\min}}{K_{\max}-K_{\min}} p_{\max}, & K_{\min} < q(t) \le K_{\max} \\ 1, & q(t) > K_{\max} \end{cases} \tag{3}
$$

$$
\frac{dq}{dt} = \sum_{i=1}^{N} R_C^{(i)}(t) - C \tag{4}
$$

$$
\frac{d\alpha^{(i)}}{dt} = \frac{g}{\tau'} \left(\left(1 - (1 - p(t-\tau*))^{\tau' R_C(t-\tau*)}\right) - \alpha^{(i)}(t) \right) \tag{5}
$$

$$
\begin{aligned}
\frac{dR_T^{(i)}}{dt} = & - \frac{R_T^{(i)}(t) - R_C^{(i)}(t)}{\tau} \left(1 - (1 - p(t-\tau*))^{\tau R_C^{(i)}(t-\tau*)}\right) \\
& + R_{AI} R_C^{(i)}(t-\tau*) \frac{(1-p(t-\tau*))^{FB} p(t-\tau*)}{(1-p(t-\tau*))^{-B} - 1} \\
& + R_{AI} R_C^{(i)}(t-\tau*) \frac{(1-p(t-\tau*))^{FTR_C^{(i)}(t-\tau*)} p(t-\tau*)}{(1-p(t-\tau*))^{-TR_C^{(i)}(t-\tau*)} - 1}
\end{aligned} \tag{6}
$$

$$
\begin{aligned}
\frac{dR_C^{(i)}}{dt} = & - \frac{R_C^{(i)}(t)\alpha^{(i)}(t)}{2\tau} \left(1 - (1 - p(t-\tau*))^{\tau R_C^{(i)}(t-\tau*)}\right) \\
& + \frac{R_T^{(i)}(t) - R_C^{(i)}(t)}{2} \frac{R_C^{(i)}(t-\tau*) p(t-\tau*)}{(1-p(t-\tau*))^{-B} - 1} \\
& + \frac{R_T^{(i)}(t) - R_C^{(i)}(t)}{2} \frac{R_C^{(i)}(t-\tau*) p(t-\tau*)}{(1-p(t-\tau*))^{-TR_C^{(i)}(t-\tau*)} - 1}
\end{aligned} \tag{7}
$$

Figure 1: DCQCN fluid model

3.1 Model

A fluid model of DCQCN was described in [31]. The original model considers N flows with exactly same rates and states, traversing a single bottleneck link. In this paper, we extend it slightly to account for flows with different rates and states. Instead of having variables that are shared by all flows, we model each flow individually. The model is shown in Figure 1 and Table 1.

We assume that ECN marking is triggered before PFC [31] and does not delay due to PFC at current congestion point (see Section 5, ECN is marked on egress). Hence, we ignore the impact of PFC. Equation 3 calculates the probability of a packet getting marked. Equation 4 describes the queue behavior. Equation 5 captures the evolution of alpha. Equations 6 and 7 describe the calculation of target and sending rate, respectively.

Model Validation: In [31] it was shown that the fluid model matches actual hardware implementation. Here we only show that our NS3 packet-level simulations are in agreement with the model. To do so, we simulate and model a simple topology, in which N senders, connected to a switch, send to a single receiver, also connected to that switch. DCQCN parameters are set to the values proposed in [31]. Note that as per DCQCN specification, all flows start at line rate. Figure 2 shows that the fluid model and the simulator are in good agreement.

Variables	
R_c	Current Rate
R_t	Target Rate
α	See Equation (1)
q	Queue Size
t	Time
Parameters	
$K_{min}, K_{max}, P_{max}$	RED marking parameters.
g	See Equation (1)
N	Number of flows at bottleneck
C	Bandwidth of bottleneck link
F	Fast recovery steps (fixed at 5)
B	Byte counter for rate increase
T	Timer for rate increase
R_{AI}	Rate increase step (fixed at 40Mbps)
τ	CNP generation timer
$\tau*$	Control loop delay
τ'	Interval of Equation (2)

Table 1: DCQCN Fluid model variables and parameters

3.2 Stability

We first obtain the fixed point of the system, and linearize the model around the fixed point. We analyze the linearized model for stability using standard frequency domain techniques [13].

THEOREM 1 (DCQCN'S UNIQUE FIXED POINT). *DCQCN has a unique fixed point of queue length and flow rates.*

PROOF. By setting the left-hand side of Equation 4 to 0, we see that any fixed points of the DCQCN (if they exist) must satisfy:

$$
\sum_{i=1}^{N} R_C^{(i)}(t) = C \tag{8}
$$

At any of the fixed points, we assume the value of p is p^*, which is shared by all flows. The queue length and per-flow $\alpha^{(i)}$ at the fixed points are determined by Equation 3 and 5:

$$
q^* = \frac{p^*}{p_{max}} (K_{max} - K_{min}) + K_{min} \tag{9}
$$

$$
\alpha^{(i)*} = 1 - (1-p^*)^{\tau' R_C^{(i)*}} \tag{10}
$$

Next, we show that p^* exists and is uniquely determined by $R_C^{(i)*}$ in the DCQCN model. Combining Equation 6 and 7, we eliminate the variable $R_T^{(i)*}$. After simplification, we see that the value of p^* is determined by:

$$
\frac{a^2 \alpha^{(i)*}}{(b+d)(c+e)} = \tau^2 R_{AI} R_C^{(i)*} \tag{11}
$$

Where we denote a, b, c, d, e as follows:

$$
\begin{aligned}
& a = 1 - (1-p^*)^{\tau R_C^{(i)*}}, b = \frac{p^*}{(1-p^*)^{-B}-1}, c = \frac{(1-p^*)^{FB} p^*}{(1-p^*)^{-B}-1}, \\
& d = \frac{p^*}{(1-p^*)^{-TR_C^{(i)*}}-1}, e = \frac{(1-p^*)^{FTR_C^{(i)*}} p^*}{(1-p^*)^{-TR_C^{(i)*}}-1}
\end{aligned} \tag{12}
$$

The LHS of Equation (11) is a monotonic function of p when $p \in [0, 1]$. Furthermore, when $p = 0$, the LHS is smaller

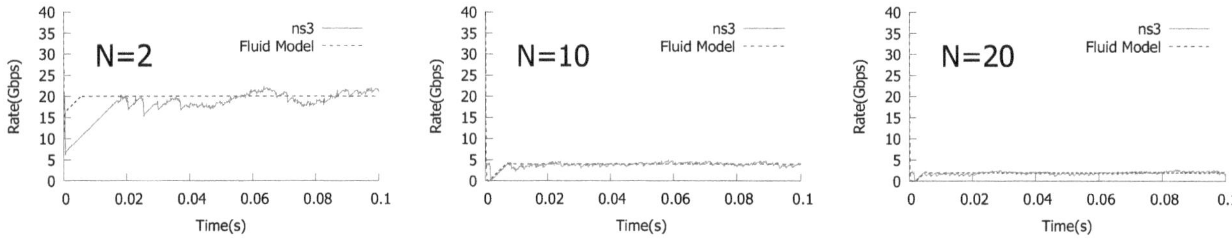

Figure 2: Comparison of DCQCN fluid model and NS3 simulations

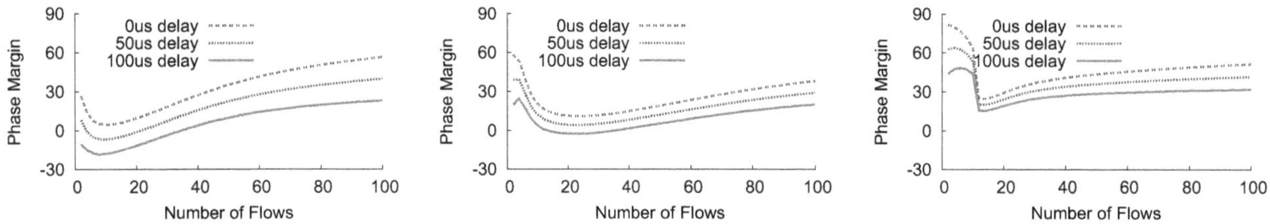

(a) Default parameters (R_{AI} = $40Mbps$, $K_{max} = 200KB$).

(b) $R_{AI} = 10Mbps$.

(c) R_{AI} = $10Mbps$, K_{max} = $1000KB$.

Figure 3: DCQCN stability

than RHS, and vice versa when $p = 1$. Thus DCQCN has a unique fixed point of marking probability p^*, leading to a unique fixed point of queue length q^*.

In § 3.3, we prove that flow rates do not reach a steady state until they converge to the same rate, *i.e.,*

$$R_C^{(1)*} = R_C^{(2)*} = ... = R_C^{(N)*} \tag{13}$$

The fixed point, where by definition the flow rates are steady, must satisfy this equation. Therefore, at the fixed point, $R_C^{(i)*} = \frac{C}{N}, i = 1, 2, ..., N$. □

Next we approximate the value of p^*. Numerical analysis shows that p^* is typically very close to 0. Therefore, we approximate the LHS of Equation 11 using Taylor series around $p = 0$. After omitting the $O(p^4)$ term, we have:

$$p^* \approx \sqrt[3]{\frac{R_{AI}N^2}{\tau' C^2}\left(\frac{1}{B} + \frac{N}{TC}\right)^2} \tag{14}$$

Therefore, the queue length q^* is determined by p^* (Equation 9), which depends on the number of flows N. A potential improvement is to make q^* independent of N. With ECN as the signal, we may achieve this by using a PI-like control mechanism. See more discussion in Section 5.

Stability analysis. We test the system against *Bode Stability Criteria* [13]. The degree of stability is shown as *Phase Margin*. A stable system must have negative *Gain* (in dB) when there is a small oscillation aruond the fixed point, so that it converges back to the fixed point. *Phase Margin* is defined as how far the system is from the 0dB *Gain* state. The system is stable when its *Phase Margin* is larger than 0, and the larger *Phase Margin* means the system is more stable. *Phase Margin* is computed from the characteristic equation of a system. See Appendix A for details of the derivation of the characteristic equation for R_C. The numerical results are shown in Figure 3.

We analyze DCQCN stability in different conditions, particularly with different control signal delays $\tau*$, and different number of flows. An ideal protocol should be tolerant with control signal delays and scalable to any number of flows. In practice, $\tau*$ is dominated by propagation delay since ECN marking is not affected by the queuing delay at the congestion point (see Section 5). In data center environment, propagation delay is usually well below $100\mu s$. There could be tens of flows competing for a single bottleneck. As Figure 3 shows, DCQCN, with default parameters, is mostly stable in such environment.

However, unlike TCP [20], the relationship between number of flows and the phase margin is non-monotonic. When the delay is large, *e.g., 100μs*, the phase margin dips below zero for certain number of flows, before rising again. For the set of parameters we have chosen, the system can be unstable with 10 flows at high feedback delays. DCQCN is increasingly stable with larger number of flows, which means good scalability. This point is further illustrated in the fluid model results shown Figure 4. When the feedback delay is small (4 μs), DCQCN is stable - flow rates, and queue length quickly[1] stabilizes regardless of the number of flows. However, when the delay is large (85μs), the protocol is unstable for 10 flows. It is, however, stable for 2 and 64 flows. Figure 5 shows the instability with packet-level simulations.

While this problem may not be particularly serious in practice, it can be easily fixed by tuning the values of R_{AI} and K_{max}. Smaller R_{AI} means flows increase their rate more gently, and stabilizes the system. Similarly, larger $K_{max} - K_{min}$ makes rate decreasing more fine grained, because the perturbation of queue length leads to smaller perturbation in marking probability. We show these trends in Figures 3(b) and 3(c). With small R_{AI} and large K_{max}, DCQCN can be always stable even when the control signal delay reaches $100\mu s$, which equals to the propagation delay of a $30KM$

[1]Remember that DCQCN flows always start at line rate.

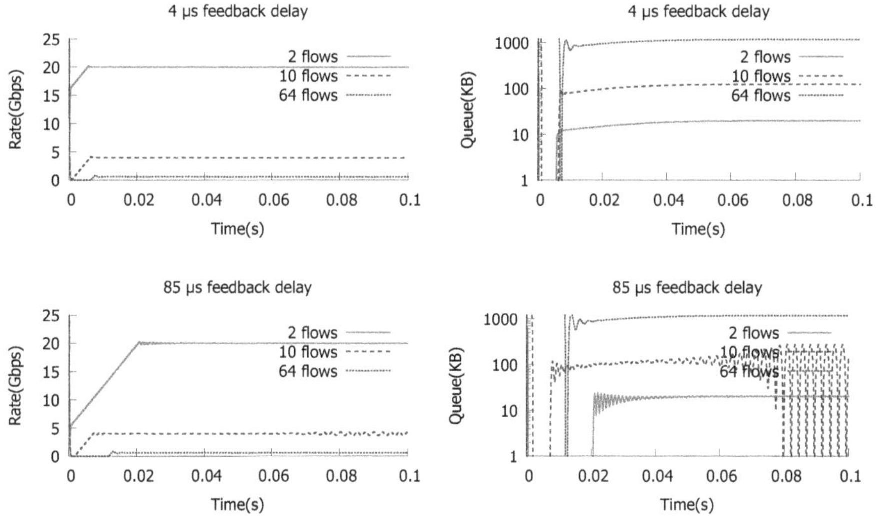

Figure 4: Impact of delay and number of flows on DCQCN stability

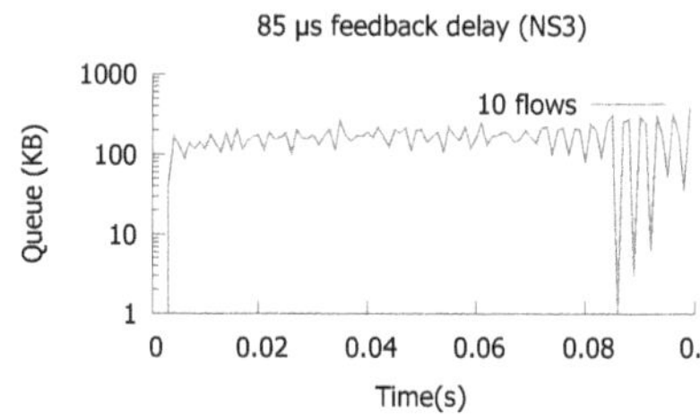

Figure 5: NS simulations confirm lack of stability

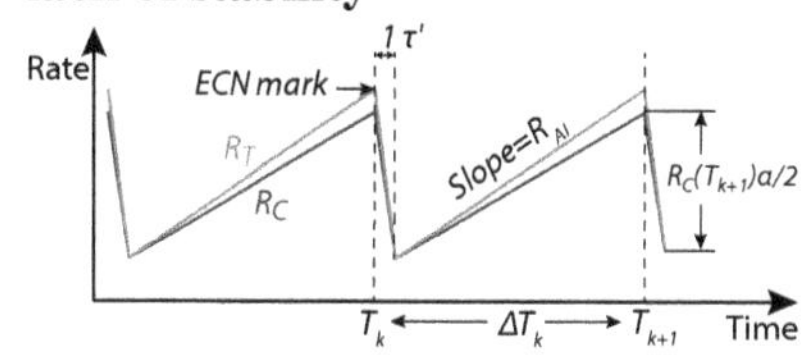

Figure 6: DCQCN's AIMD-style updates of flow rate.

cable, or $500KB$ queuing delay. Such large delays are rare in modern data center networks.

Note that tuning R_{AI} and K_{max} is a trade-off between stability and latency. Smaller R_{AI} leads to slower ramp-up, while larger K_{max} leads to larger queue length. In most cases, the default parameters strike a good enough balance between stability and latency.

3.3 Convergence

In Section 3.2, we showed that for reasonable parameter settings, DCQCN is stable *after* flows converge to the unique fixed point. We also showed that at the fixed point, the flows share the bandwidth equally. However, two questions remain unanswered: (i) do flows the always converge to this fixed point, and (ii) how fast do flows converge?

We cannot answer these questions using the fluid model, so like [3], we construct and analyze a discrete model of the rate adjustment at the RP. The default parameter settings given in [31] set both the Timer T and α update interval τ' equal to $55\mu s$. Thus, we use τ' as the unit of time. The process of DCQCN rate update is similar to TCP AIMD, as shown in Figure 6[2]. The flows get the peak rates at T_k. For simplicity, we assume all flows are synchronized, and peak at the same time. This is a common assumption, for data center environments [3], especially for workloads like distributed storage system and MapReduce-like frameworks.

THEOREM 2 (DCQCN CONVERGENCE). *Under the control of DCQCN, the rate difference of any two flows decrease exponentially over time.*

PROOF. Here we provide a brief proof whereas more details can be found in Appendix B. Whenever a flow gets ECN marks at T_k, it reduces its rate in one unit of time, then starts $\Delta T_k - 1$ consecutive additive rate increases on $R_T^{(i)}$.[3] Here $\Delta T_k \triangleq T_{k+1} - T_k$. According to DCQCN's definition:

$$R_T^{(i)}(T_{k+1}) = \left(1 - \frac{\alpha^{(i)}(T_k)}{2}\right) R_C^{(i)}(T_k) + (\Delta T_k - 1) R_{AI} \tag{15}$$

$$\alpha^{(i)}(T_{k+1}) = (1-g)^{\Delta T_k - 1}\left((1-g)\alpha^{(i)}(T_k) + g\right) \tag{16}$$

For another flow, *e.g.,* the jth flow, we can simply rewrite Equation 16 by replacing (i) with (j). We subtract the equation of jth flow from the equation of ith flow:

$$\begin{aligned}\alpha^{(i)}(T_{k+1}) - \alpha^{(j)}(T_{k+1}) &= (1-g)^{\Delta T_k}\left(\alpha^{(i)}(T_k) - \alpha^{(j)}(T_k)\right)\\ = \dots &= (1-g)^{\sum_{l=0}^{k}\Delta T_l}\left(\alpha^{(i)}(T_0) - \alpha^{(j)}(T_0)\right)\end{aligned} \tag{17}$$

This tells us the difference of $\alpha^{(i)}$ of *any* two flows will decrease exponentially. So $\alpha^{(i)}$ of different flows will converge to the same value. Once the α converged at some $T_{k'}$, we can show the rates R_C converge afterwards. We rewrite the jth flow's Equation 15, and subtract it from Equation 15. Combining the analysis of R_T in Appendix B, we get:

$$\begin{aligned}R_C^{(i)}(T_{k+1}) - R_C^{(j)}(T_{k+1}) &= \left(1 - \tfrac{\alpha(T_k)}{2}\right)\left(R_C^{(i)}(T_k) - R_C^{(j)}(T_k)\right)\\ = \dots &= \prod_{l=k'}^{k}\left(1 - \tfrac{\alpha(T_l)}{2}\right)\left(R_C^{(i)}(T_{k'}) - R_C^{(j)}(T_{k'})\right)\end{aligned} \tag{18}$$

As long as $\alpha(T_k)$ has a lower bound that is greater than 0, the rates R_C of different flows converge exponentially. In Appendix B, we prove that:

$$\alpha(T_0) > \dots > \alpha(T_k) > \alpha(T_{k+1}) > \dots > \alpha^* > 0 \tag{19}$$

where α^* is the fixed point of the Equation 16. Equation 19 concludes our proof. □

From Equation 18, we see that R_C converges at the rate of at least $(1 - \frac{\alpha^*}{2})^k$, where k is the number of AIMD cycles.

[2]Fast recovery does not change the nature of AIMD, since it can be combined with corresponding rate decrease as a multiplicative decrease event. As a common practice, like [4] does, we omit it in the following analysis.

[3]For simplicity, we omit hyper-increase and set $R_T = R_C$ upon rate decrease. This is a slightly simplified version of DCQCN.

Algorithm 1 TIMELY rate calculation

```
newRTTDiff ← newRTT − prevRTT
prevRTT ← newRTT
rttDiff ← (1 − α) · rttDiff + α · newRTTDiff
rttGradient = rttDiff/D_minRTT
if newRTT < T_low then
    rate ← rate + δ
else if newRTT > T_high then
    rate ← rate · (1 − β · (1 − T_high/newRTT))
else if rttGradiant ≤ 0 then
    rate ← rate + δ
else
    rate ← rate · (1 − β · rttGradient)
```

3.4 Summary

We have shown that DCQCN has a unique fixed point, where all flows get a fair share of the bottleneck bandwidth. For typical parameter values flows converge to this fixed point exponentially. DCQCN is generally stable around this fixed point, and R_{AI} and K_{max} can be tuned if needed. However, a PI-controller based approach may be the more principled way to ensure stability and fixed queue length.

4. TIMELY

TIMELY [21] is an end-to-end, rate-based congestion control algorithm that uses changes in RTT as a congestion signal. It relies on NIC hardware to obtain fine-grained RTT measurements. RTT is estimated once per completion event [18], which signals the successful transmission of a chunk (16-64KB) of packets. Upon receiving a new RTT sample, TIMELY computes new rate for the flow, as shown in Algorithm 1. If the new RTT sample is less than (T_{low}), TIMELY increases sending rate additively by δ. If the new sample is more than (T_{high}), rate is decreased multiplicatively by β. If the new sample is between T_{low} and T_{high}, the rate change depends on the RTT gradient. The gradient is defined as the normalized change between two successive RTT samples. If the gradient is positive (i.e. RTT is increasing), sending rate is reduced multiplicatively, in proportion to the RTT gradient. Otherwise, it is increased additively by δ.

TIMELY flows do not start at line rate. If there are N active flows at a sender, a new flow starts at rate C/(N+1), where C is the interface link bandwidth [21].

4.1 Model

Our fluid model of TIMELY is shown in Table 2 and Figure 7. As before, (i) we model N flows, traversing a single bottleneck link, and (ii) and ignore the impact of PFC.

Equation 20 describes the queue behavior. Equation 21 describes rate computation. For simplicity, we ignore the hyperactive increase phase. When RTT is betweenT_{low} and T_{high}, the rate computation depends on RTT gradient, which evolves according to Equation 22. The equation captures the EWMA filter, as well as normalization. Since the gradient is the difference between the current and the previous RTT sample, it depends on two queue lengths in past: one at time $t - \tau'$, and one at time $t - \tau' - \tau$. The value of τ' and $\tau*$ depend on past transmission rates, but to simplify the model,

Variables

R	Rate
g	RTT gradient
q	Queue Size
t	Time
$\tau*$	Rate update interval
τ'	Feedback delay

Parameters

N	Number of flows at bottleneck
C	Bandwidth of bottleneck link
α	EWMA smoothing factor
δ	Additive increase step
β	Multiplicative decrease factor
T_{low}	Low threshold
T_{high}	High threshold
D_{minRTT}	Minimum RTT for normalization
D_{prop}	Propagation delay
Seg	Burst size

Table 2: TIMELY fluid model variables and parameters

we approximate their calculation as shown in Equations 23 and 24. Equation 23 captures the fact that the TIMELY implementation gets RTT feedback once per burst, and rate updates are scaled by D_{minRTT} to ensure that rate update frequency is limited (See Section 5 of [21]).

The fluid model (by its very nature) essentially assumes smooth and continuous transmission of data. The TIMELY implementation is more bursty, since rate is adjusted by modulating gaps between transmission of 16 or 64KB chunks; while the chunks themselves are sent at near-line rate [21]. TIMELY designers made this decision for engineering reasons - they wanted to avoid taking dependence on hardware rate limiters. We will return to this point later.

$$\frac{dq}{dt} = \sum_i R_i(t) - C \tag{20}$$

$$\frac{dR_i}{dt} = \begin{cases} \frac{\delta}{\tau_i^*}, & q(t-\tau') < C * T_{low} \\ \frac{\delta}{\tau_i^*}, & g_i \leq 0 \\ -\frac{g_i \beta}{\tau_i^*} R_i(t), & g_i > 0 \\ -\frac{\beta}{\tau_i^*}(1 - \frac{C*T_{high}}{q(t-\tau')}) R_i(t), & q(t-\tau') > C * T_{high} \end{cases} \tag{21}$$

$$\frac{dg_i}{dt} = \frac{\alpha}{\tau_i^*}(-g_i(t) + \frac{q(t-\tau') - q(t-\tau'-\tau_i^*)}{C * D_{\min RTT}}) \tag{22}$$

$$\tau_i^* = \max\{\frac{Seg}{R_i}, D_{\min RTT}\} \tag{23}$$

$$\tau' = \frac{q}{C} + \frac{MTU}{C} + D_{prop} \tag{24}$$

Figure 7: TIMELY fluid model

Model Validation: Since we do not have access to TIMELY implementation, Figure 8 compares the TIMELY fluid model with the NS3 packet-level simulations, using parameter values recommended[4] in [21]. The simulator can model both per-packet pacing, as well as the bursty behavior of TIMELY

[4] $C = 10Gbps$, $\beta = 0.8$, $\alpha = 0.875$, $T_{low} = 50\mu$s, $T_{high} = 500\mu$s, $D_{minRTT} = 20\mu$s.

implementation; here we use per-packet pacing. As before, we model N senders connected to a switch, sending to a single receiver connected to the same switch. The starting rate for each flow is set to be 1/N of the link bandwidth. We see the fluid model and the simulator are in good agreement.

4.2 Analysis

We now show that TIMELY, as described in Algorithm 1 has *no fixed point.* The implication is that the queue length never converges, nor do the sending rates of the flows. The system operates in limit cycles, always oscillating. Moreover, while the system is oscillating, there are *infinite* solutions for the sending rates of the flows that satisfy the fluid equations at any point. So, even if we can limit the magnitude of the limit cycles by choosing parameters carefully, we can make no claims on the fairness of the protocol since the system could be operating at any of those infinite solutions.

THEOREM 3 (NO FIXED POINT FOR TIMELY). *The system described in Figure (7), has no fixed points.*

PROOF. We prove the result by contradiction. At the fixed point, all differential equations converge to 0. Thus:

$$dq/dt = 0 \text{ and } \sum_i R_i(t) = C \tag{25}$$

Now, either $g_i > 0$ or $g_i \leq 0$. If $g_i \neq 0$, then:

$$\frac{dg_i}{dt} = \frac{\alpha}{\tau_i^*}(-g_i(t) + \frac{q(t-\tau') - q(t-\tau'-\tau_i^*)}{C * D_{\min RTT}}) = -\frac{\alpha}{\tau_i^*} g_i(t) \neq 0 \tag{26}$$

Thus, g_i is zero for dg_i/dt to be zero. But then:

$$dR_i/dt = \delta/\tau_i^* \neq 0 \tag{27}$$

Thus, all derivatives cannot be simultaneously 0 and thus the system has no fixed point. □

If we modify the fluid model very slightly, by moving the equality condition to the term involving g_i, we get:

$$\frac{dR_i}{dt} = \begin{cases} \frac{\delta}{\tau_i^*}, & q(t-\tau') < C * T_{low} \\ \frac{\delta}{\tau_i^*}, & g_i < 0 \\ -\frac{g_i \beta}{\tau_i^*} R(t), & g_i \geq 0 \\ -\frac{\beta}{\tau_i^*}(1 - \frac{C * T_{high}}{q(t-\tau')}) R(t), & q(t-\tau') > C * T_{high} \end{cases} \tag{28}$$

This is equivalent to changing the $\leq$ sign on line 9 of Algorithm 1 to <. This makes little difference in practice, since floating point computations for g_i rarely yield an exact zero value – we have verified this via simulations. With this modification, we can obtain the condition that with $g_i = 0$, $\frac{dq}{dt} = 0$, $\frac{dg_i}{dt} = 0$ and $C * T_{low} < q < C * T_{high}$. However, now we run into the issue that TIMELY moves from zero fixed points to *infinite* fixed points!

THEOREM 4 (INFINITE FIXED POINTS). *The system described by Figure (7), with modification introduced in Equation 28 has infinite fixed points*

PROOF. To obtain $dg_i/dt = 0$, we need $g_i = 0$ and $dq/dt = 0$. Note that q cannot converge to a value outside of the thresholds $C * T_{low}$ and $C * T_{high}$ as that would imply $dR_i/dt \neq 0$.

Any value of q such that $C * T_{low} < q < C * T_{high}$ makes $dR_i/dt = 0$ for any value of R_i as long as $\sum_i R_i(t) = C$ and hence q and R_i have infinitely many fixed points. □

There is no requirement that at the fixed point $R_i = C/N$. In fact, $R_i/R_j, i \neq j$ is not even bounded, so we cannot make any claims on the fairness of TIMELY. Thus the fixed point of TIMELY is entirely unpredictable. This is borne out by the simulation results shown in Figure 9, where we only change the start time and initial rates of two flows, keeping everything else constant, and we end up in completely different operating regimes.

Impact of per-burst pacing: This analysis begs the question – why does TIMELY work well in practice, as reported in [21]? The answer appears to lie in the fact that the TIMELY implementation does not use hardware rate limiters. Instead, the TIMELY implementation controls rate by adjusting delay between successive transmissions of chunks that can be as large as 64KB. Each chunk is sent out at or near line rate.

The results shown in Figure 9 were obtained with per-packet pacing. If, instead we user per-burst pacing, TIMELY appears to converge, as shown in Figure 10(a). The bursts introduce enough "noise" to de-correlate the flows, and this appears to lead the system to a relatively stable fixed point. We attempted to mathematically prove that per-burst pacing would lead to a unique fixed point, but were unable to do so.

In any case, per-burst pacing is not ideal, since it can lead to large oscillations in queue length, leading to poor utilization. This is apparent in Figure 10(b), where we use 64KB chunks. The initial chunks sent by the two senders arrive at the switch near-simultaneously (i.e. "incast"), and both flows receive a very large RTT sample. This causes TIMELY to reduce its rate drastically (line 8 in the TIMELY algorithm). Since the subsequent rate increase occurs in small steps ($\delta = 10Mbps$, see line 6.)[5], it takes a long time for the flow rates to climb back to their fair share.

These problems can be mitigated to some extent by sending bursts at less than line rate[6], by adjusting the burst size, or by adjusting the T_{min} threshold. However, such tuning is fragile, since the right values of these parameters depend not just on the link speed, but also on the number of competing flows, which is unknown at the time of configuration.

In summary, while burst pacing can lead to a fixed point by introducing noise, it can lead to other problems. The fact that TIMELY cannot maintain a stable queue length has a detrimental impact on the flow level performance (*e.g.,* flow completion times), especially at higher percentiles. We illustrate this in Section 5.1.

Rather than rely on "noise" to ensure convergence and stability, we propose a simple fix to the TIMELY algorithm.

---

[5]HAI kicks in only after $RTT > T_{low}$. See Algorithm 1 in [21]

[6]Indeed, the TIMELY does this, see § 5 in [21].

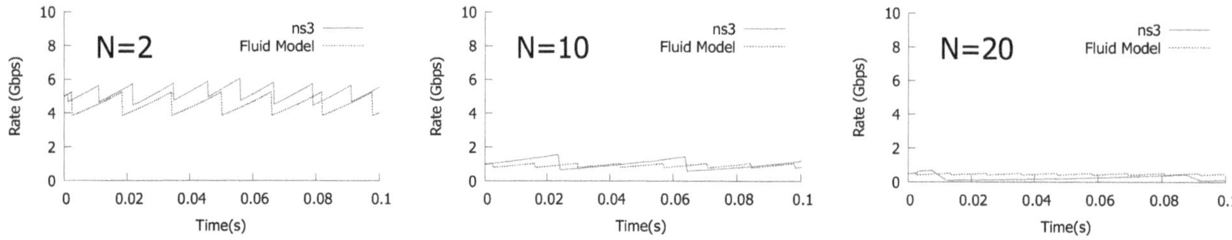

Figure 8: Comparison of TIMELY fluid model and simulations

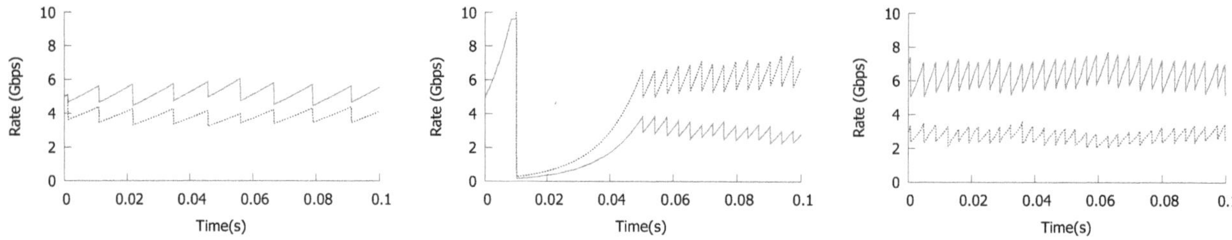

(a) Both flows start at time 0 at 5Gbps (b) Both start at 5Gbps, one starts 10ms late (c) One starts at 7Gbps, the other at 3Gbps

Figure 9: Performance of two TIMELY flows under different starting conditions

Algorithm 2 Patched TIMELY rate calculation

$newRTTDiff \leftarrow newRTT - prevRTT$
$prevRTT \leftarrow newRTT$
$rttDiff \leftarrow (1-\alpha) \cdot rttDiff + \alpha \cdot newRTTDiff$
$rttGradient = rttDiff / D_{minRTT}$
if $newRTT < T_{low}$ **then**
  $rate \leftarrow rate + \delta$
else if $newRTT > T_{high}$ **then**
  $rate \leftarrow rate \cdot (1 - \beta \cdot (1 - T_{high}/newRTT))$
else
  $weight \leftarrow w(rttGradient)$
  $error \leftarrow \frac{newRTT - RTT_{ref}}{RTT_{ref}}$
  $rate \leftarrow \delta(1-weight) + rate \cdot (1 - \beta \cdot weight \cdot error)$

4.3 Patched TIMELY

In order to ensure there is a unique fixed point, and all flows get fair share and are stable at the fixed point, we make two minor modifications over TIMELY, as shown in Algorithm 2. We only modify the last four lines of Algorithm 1.

First, we make the step of rate decrease rely on absolute RTT, instead of the gradient of RTT. In effect, this means that all flows have the knowledge of the bottleneck queue length. This ensures two things. First, the system can have a unique fixed point, determined by the RTT[7]. Second, all flow can converge to the same rate, since they share the knowledge of the bottleneck RTT. The side effect, of course, is that, with different number of flows, the fixed point of queue can be different. We will address this in §5.

Second, we use a continuous weighting function $w(g)$ to make the transition between rate increase and rate decrease smooth. This avoids the on-off behavior that causes oscillation. This is similar to the fact that probabilistic ECN marking stabilizes TCP [20], DCTCP [3], QCN [4] and DCQCN. With $w(g)$, we combine the two conditions of $g \leq 0$ and $g > 0$ in the $dR(t)/dt$ equation:

$$\frac{dR_i}{dt} = \begin{cases} \frac{\delta}{\tau *}, & q(t-\tau') < C * T_{low} \\ \frac{(1-w_i)\delta}{\tau *} - \frac{w_i \beta R_i(t)}{\tau *} \frac{q(t-\tau')-q'}{q'}, & Otherwise \\ -\frac{\beta}{\tau *}(1 - \frac{C * T_{high}}{q(t-\tau')}) R_i(t), & q(t-\tau') > C * T_{high} \end{cases} \tag{29}$$

where w_i, the weight of rate decreasing, is a function of g_i, and must satisfy $0 \leq w_i(g_i) \leq 1$ for any g_i. Intuitively, $w_i(g_i)$ is monotonically increasing with g_i, because larger RTT gradient should lead to larger rate decrease. In original TIMELY protocol, $w_i(g_i)$ is an indicator function of g_i, *i.e.*, $w_i(g_i) = 1$ when $g_i \geq 0$, and $w_i(g_i) = 0$ when $g_i < 0$. Here we simply use a linear function of g_i for w_i:

$$w_i = \begin{cases} 0, & g_i \leq -\frac{1}{4} \\ 2g_i + \frac{1}{2}, & -\frac{1}{4} < g_i < \frac{1}{4} \\ 1, & g_i \geq \frac{1}{4} \end{cases} \tag{30}$$

In Equation 29, q' is a reference queue length. We simply set it as $C * T_{low}$, so that we decrease the rate faster if the queue length exceeds $C * T_{low}$. All other TIMELY parameters remain the same except we set $\beta = 0.008$ and $Seg = 16KB$. We prove that this patched TIMELY protocol has desirable stability and convergence properties that original TIMELY does not guarantee:

THEOREM 5 (PATCHED TIMELY'S FIXED POINT.). *The system described in Equation 29 has a unique fixed point. All flows have the same rate at this fixed point, and the queue length is:*

$$q^* = \frac{N\delta q'}{\beta C} + q' \tag{31}$$

The system described in Equation 29 always exponentially converges to the unique fixed point.

The detailed proof is similar to the proof of Theorem 2 and omitted due to the lack of space.

[7]Recall that the issue with original TIMELY was that RTT gradient could be the same, but absolute RTTs could be different.

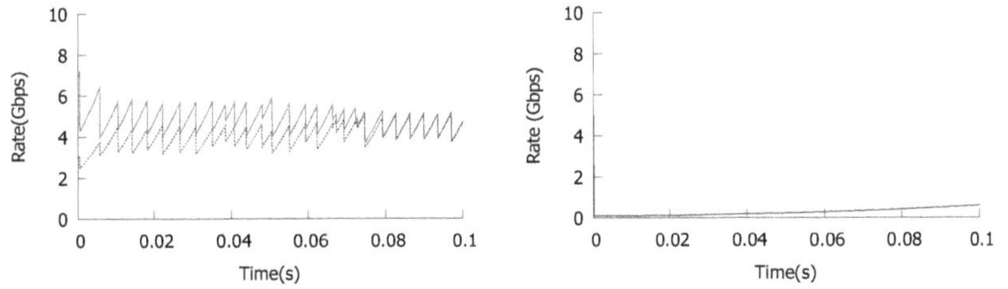

(a) Two flows starting at 7 and 3Gbps, 16KB burst
(b) Two flows starting at 5Gbps, 64KB burst

Figure 10: TIMELY with bursts

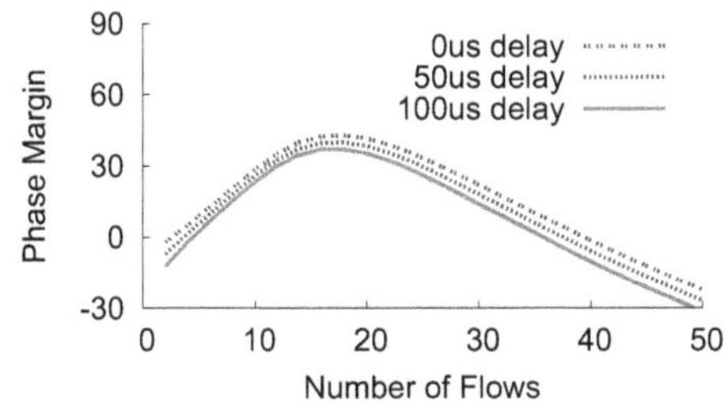

Figure 11: Patched TIMELY stability

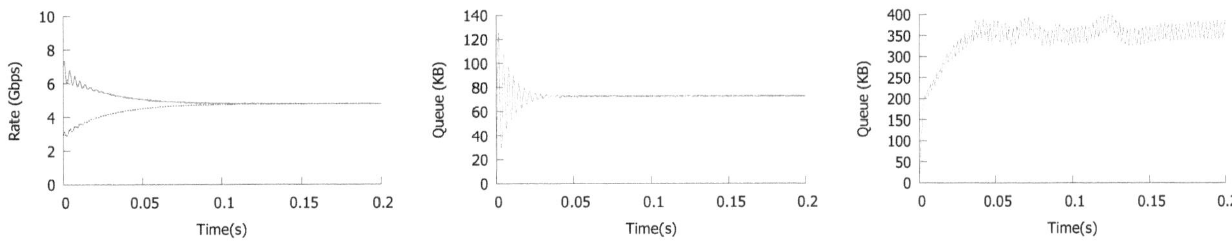

(a) Two flows, 7Gbps and 3Gbps
(b) Two flows, 7Gbps and 3Gbps
(c) 40 flows, starting at 0.25Gbps

Figure 12: Performance of patched TIMELY

We further verify patched TIMELY convergence and stability using simulations. Figure 12(a) and 12(b), shows that flows with different initial rates converge to the fixed point and are stable without oscillation, opposed to Figure 9(c). Results for the case depicted in Figure 9(b) are similar.

Stability. We proceed as we did for DCQCN – linearize the equations, Laplace transform and compute the phase margin of its characteristic equation. The phase margin result shows this system is stable until the number of flows is greater than 40 (Figure 11). This is again confirmed by NS-3 simulation (Figure 12(b) and 12(c)). After 40 flows, the phase margin falls below 0 rapidly because more flows lead to larger queue size (see Equation 31), thus leading to larger feedback delay (see Equation 24). This leads to system instability. In general, with some minor tuning, TIMELY can be stable within a range of number of flows.

4.4 Summary

We showed that the TIMELY protocol, as proposed in [21] can have infinite fixed points. We proposed a small fix to address the problem, and showed that the resulting protocol converges to a fixed point, where all flows share the bottleneck bandwidth equally. The protocol is stable around this fixed point, as long as the number of flows is not too high.

5. ECN VERSUS DELAY

We have now seen that both DCQCN and TIMELY (with a small modification) can achieve desirable properties like fairness, stability and exponential convergence, if properly tuned for a given scenario. Can we thus conclude that ECN and delay are both "equivalent" signals, when it comes to congestion control?

We believe that the answer is no. As an example, we compare the performance of DCQCN (ECN-based) and TIMELY (delay-based), and find that DCQCN outperforms TIMELY. We then discuss the fundamental reasons why ECN-based protocols are better than delay-based protocols.

5.1 Case study: DCQCN versus TIMELY on flow completion time

While we show that both ECN-based DCQCN and delay-based TIMELY can be stable and fair if properly tuned (see Section 3 and Section 4), they may differ on other important performance metrics. For example, the end users often care about flow completion times, especially for short flows [8]. We compare the flow completion times of DCQCN and TIMELY with a simple simulation, using the classic dumbbell topology shown in Figure 13. The topology consists of 20 nodes – 10 senders and 10 receivers. All traffic flows across the bottleneck link between the two switches, SW1 and SW2. All links are 10Gbps with $1\mu s$ latency.

The traffic consists of long and short-lived flows, between pairs of randomly selected sender and receiver nodes. The flow size distribution is derived from the traffic distribution reported in [2]. The interarrival time of flows is picked from am exponential distribution. The load on the bottleneck link is varied by changing the mean of the distribution. This traffic generation model was also used in several recent studies, including pFabric [5] and ProjecToR [12].

Both DCQCN and TIMELY used the default parameter settings recommended in [31] and [21], respectively. The metric of interest is the flow completion time of small flows. Following pFabric [5], we define small flows as flows that send fewer than 100KB. We also tune and test different protocol parameter and small flow threshold settings. The results are similar.

Figure 14 shows the median and 90th percentile of FCT and DCQCN, TIMELY original and patched TIMELY as the load is varied. Patched TIMELY is our modification to TIMELY's protocol to ensure a unique fixed point (§4.3).

The X axis shows relative load: load factor of 1 corresponds to an average of 8Gbps of traffic on the bottleneck link. The scaling is linear. We see that at higher loads, FCT for both TIMELY and patched TIMELY is high, and highly variable. This illustrated in detail in Figure 15, which shows the CDF of the flow completion time for load factor of 0.8.

The reason for TIMELY's poor performance is evident from Figure 16, which shows the queue length at the link between SW1 and SW2 for a load factor of 0.8. As shown, the queue length under TIMELY can grow to a very high value, and is highly variable. In contrast the DCQCN queue has a fixed point between the RED thresholds and even in the transient state the queue stays within the bounds. Note that patched TIMELY is operating in between the original TIMELY protocol and DCQCN. This is because our fix is ensuring a unique fixed point (and thus fairness), without changing the dynamics of TIMELY's queue build up.

We note that in all cases, the link utilization is roughly the same for DCQCN and TIMELY, indicating that the long flows performed similarly with both schemes.

5.2 ECN advantages

As shown above, despite that both protocols are fair and stable, TIMELY has larger queue dynamics than DCQCN, which leads to worse short flow completion time. We believe this is due to the following reasons.

ECN marking is done on packet egress, thus has faster response: Modern shared-buffer switches, especially those that use Broadcom's merchant silicon, do ECN marking on *packet egress*. When a packet is ready to depart, the controller checks the egress queue for that port *at that instant*, and marks the packet according to the specified algorithm (e.g. Equation 3). Thus, the mark always conveys information about the state of the queue at the time of packet *departure*, even if the egress queue is long.

RTT measurements are different: If the egress queue discipline is FIFO within a priority class (which it typically is), the delay experienced by a packet reflects the state of the queue at the time the packet *arrives* at the queue. This means that the control signal carried by the ECN mark is delayed only by the propagation delay, but the control signal carried by the RTT signal is delayed both by the queuing delay as well as the propagation delay.

This is a subtle difference: the claim is not that ECN carries more information; it that the delay of the control loop is decoupled from the queuing delay.

This is why the DCQCN fluid model (Figure 1) assumes that the control loop delay is constant. DCTCP fluid model makes the same assumption [3]. We cannot make the same assumption for TIMELY, and thus we incorporate τ' and Equation 24 in the TIMELY fluid model (Figure 7).

This means that as the queue length increases (e.g. when there are more flows), congestion control algorithms that rely on RTT suffer from increasing *lag* in their control loop, making them more difficult to control. We see this happening for TIMELY (Figure 11). DCQCN is affected less by this effect (Figure 3(a)). To further confirm that ECN marking on egress is important for stability, we run DCQCN with ECN marking on ingress for comparison. Figure 17 shows that marking on ingress leads to queue length fluctuation.

Researchers have observed similar "bufferbloat" [11] problems in the wide area networks solutions such as LEDBAT [26] have been proposed. Similarly, in modern data center networks, queuing delays can easily dominate switching and propagation delays. For example, an Arista 7050QX32 has 40Gbps ports, and a total shared buffer of switch has 12MB. Even if just 1MB worth of queue builds up at an egress port,[8] it takes 200 μs to drain it. In contrast, the one-hop propagation delay, with cut-through forwarding, is around 1-2 μs. Typical DC network diameter is 6 hops, so overall propagation delay is under $25\mu s$.

The reader may argue that it is easy to fix this issue – all we have to do is to build a delay-based protocol that strives to keep the bottleneck queue (more-or-less) constant. Then, the control signal delay experienced by the RTT feedback signal is also fixed, albeit a little higher (propagation delay, plus fixed queuing delay).

However, a delay based congestion control protocol that maintains a fixed queue, cannot ensure fairness.

For delay-based control, fixed queue comes at the cost of fairness: One way to build protocols that guarantee delay to a fixed quantity is to use a controller with *integral* control [14, 6]. The idea behind integral control is to look at an error signal, *e.g.,* the difference between the actual queue length and a desired or reference queue length, and adjust the feedback until the error signal goes to 0. A stable PI controller is guaranteed to achieve this. In a continuous system, the feedback signal $p(t)$ evolves in the following way with a PI controller:

$$\frac{dp}{dt} = K_1 \frac{de}{dt} + K_2 e(t) \tag{32}$$

When the feedback signal converges, both the error signal $e(t)$ as well as the derivative of the error signal, de/dt must converge to 0. The derivative of the error signal, (the derivative of the queue length), goes to 0 when the sum of the rates R_i match the link capacity C. The error signal itself goes to 0 when the queue length matches the reference value. Thus the integral controller implements the "match rate, clear buffer" scheme presented in [6].

For DCQCN we can implement the PI controller to mark the packets at the switch instead of RED (which is a proportional controller without the integral action) and use that p in the usual way to perform the multiplicative decrease.

For (patched) TIMELY, we can measure the delay at the end hosts and implement a PI controller by generating an internal variable "p", using the error signal "$e(t)$" as the difference between the measured delay and some desired delay. This internal variable p can then replace the $\frac{q(t-\tau')-q'}{q'}$ term in Equation (29) as the feedback to control the rates.

We implemented the PI controller for both the DCQCN and patched TIMELY fluid models and performed simulations. As we see in Figure 18 for DCQCN, all the flows

[8]This requires enabling dynamic thresholding, but it is almost always enabled in real deployments.

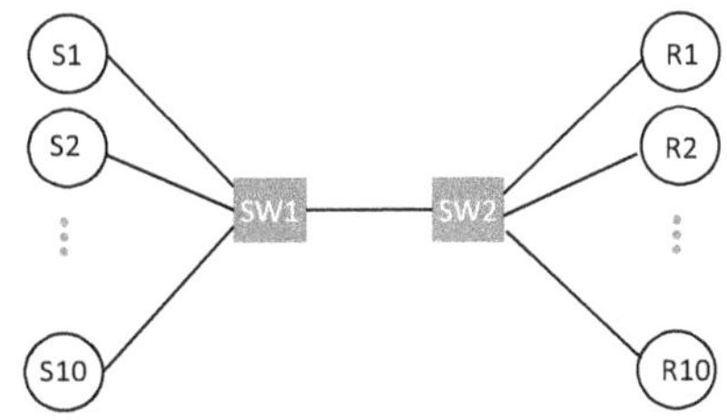

Figure 13: The dumbbell topology. All links are 10Gbps with $1\mu s$ latency.

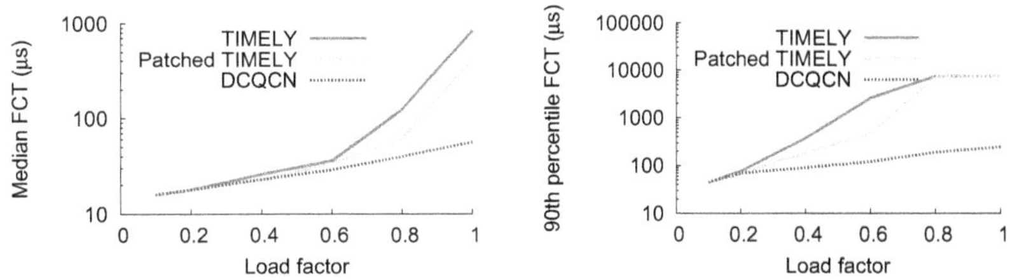

Figure 14: Median and 90th percentile of FCT of small flows. Note log scale on Y axis.

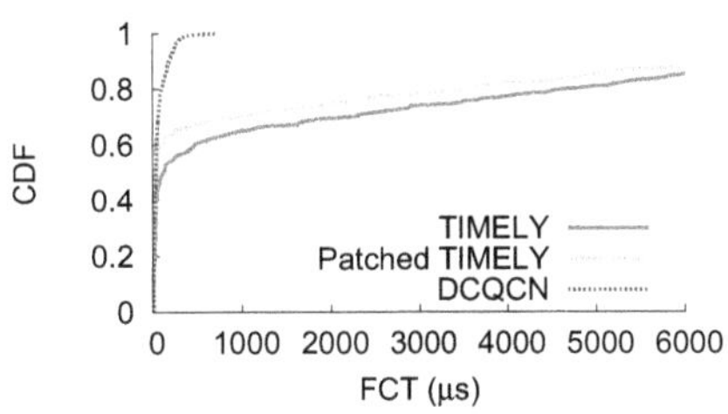

Figure 15: CDF of FCT for load=0.8

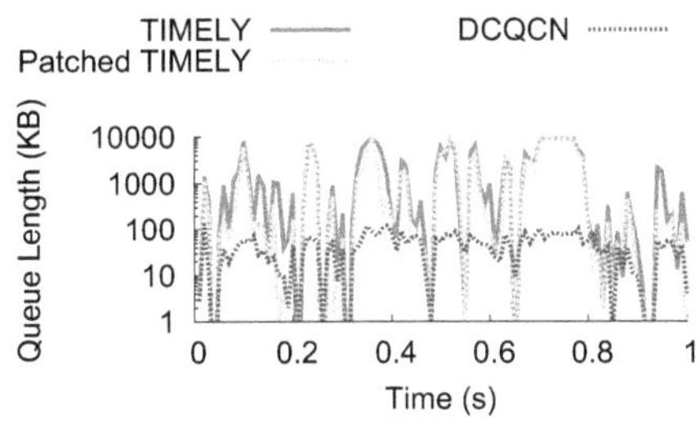

Figure 16: Bottleneck Queue for load=0.8. Note log scale on Y axis.

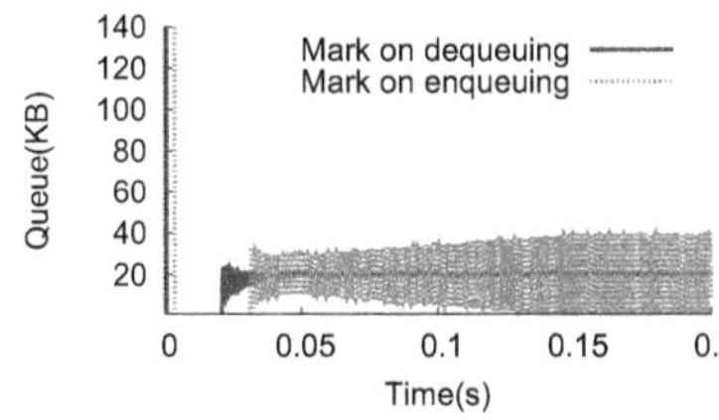

Figure 17: DCQCN stability when two flows compete for a bottleneck with $85\mu s$ feedback delay.

converge to the same (fair) rate and the queue length is stabilized to a preconfigured value, regardless of the number of flows (as well as regardless of propagation delay). This is important not only for stability, but also for performance reasons in a data center networks, where is important to ensure that completion times for short flows do not suffer from excessive queuing delays [2].

In contrast, when we use a PI controller at the end hosts with patched TIMELY, we see that although we can control the queue to a specified value (300 KB), we cannot achieve fairness (Figure 19). Thus, while patched TIMELY was able to achieve fairness without guaranteeing delay, with PI it is able to guarantee delay without achieving fairness.

We next prove a result that formalizes this fundamental tradeoff between fairness and guaranteed steady-state delay for protocols that rely on delay measurements at the end points to implement congestion control. We first assume that the steady state throughput achieved by a congestion control transport protocol is a function of the observed delay d and some feedback value p. The value of p can be the loss probability or the ECN marking probability or some internal variable p computed by the patched TIMELY+PI mechanism we described above. Thus, $R = f(d,p)$ for steady state throughput R and some function $f(d,p)$. Then the following theorem formalizes the fairness/delay tradeoff in such systems.

THEOREM 6 (FAIRNESS/DELAY TRADEOFF). *For congestion control mechanisms that have steady state throughput of the kind $R = f(d,p)$, for some function f, delay d and feedback p, if the feedback is based on purely end to end delay measurements, you can either have fairness or a fixed delay, but not both simultaneously.*

PROOF. To guarantee fairness, the system must have a unique fixed point. Consider N flows sharing a link of capacity C. Then, for each flow, we have $R_i = f(d,p_i), i = 1,\ldots,N$. There is an additional equation constraining the throughput at the link, $\sum R_i = C$. Hence we have $N+1$ equations and $2N$ unknowns – $\{R_i, p_i\}, i = 1\ldots,N$. This is an underdetermined system with infinite (or no) solutions. To make this system consistent, we need a common p_i, reducing the number of variables to $N+1$. That can be achieved either by marking at the switch (violating the assumption of delay being the only feedback), or by making this p_i a function of the (common) queue length. However if we control the delay to a fixed quantity, it becomes agnostic of the number of flows which will make the system of equations inconsistent, since the constraint $\sum_i R_i = C$ implies the steady state throughput of a flow depends on the number of flows contending. Thus, to make the system consistent p_i has to be a function of the common queue length which depends on the number of flows and hence we cannot control the delay to a fixed quantity. □

Remarks: The results of this theorem are generic to congestion control protocols that use delay or ECN as feedback and are not RDMA or TIMELY/DCQCN specific. Note that a **RED** style AQM scheme can guarantee a unique fixed point that depends on the number of flows. However, given the low delay requirements in a data center environment, that would require the RED marking profile to have a steep slope (marking probability that goes from 0 to 1 over a small buffer space). As shown in [15], a steep slope leads to an unstable controller leading to oscillations in the flow rates, increased jitter and loss of utilization. Also, the preceding result does not apply to systems with limit cycles,[9] with which rate-based protocols do not have steady state throughput.

[9] Some window-based protocols have limit cycles [3].

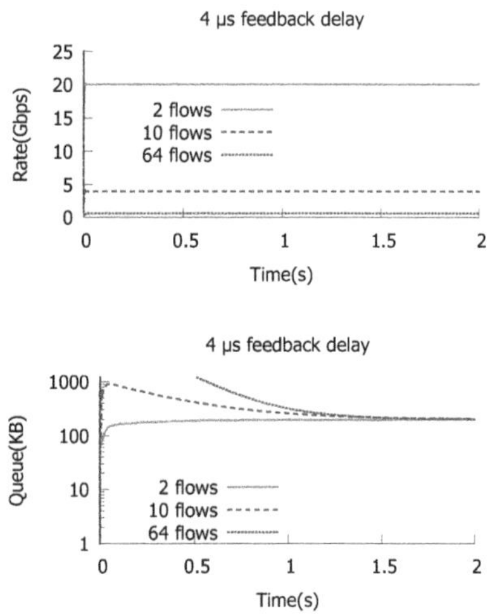

Figure 18: DCQCN with PI controller

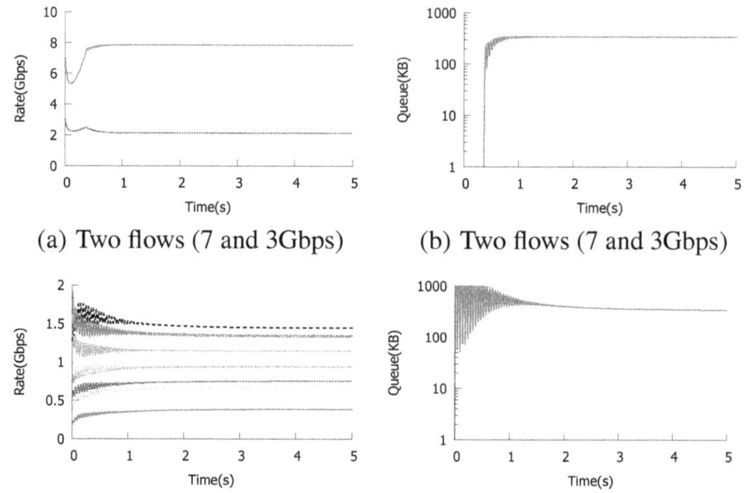

(a) Two flows (7 and 3Gbps) (b) Two flows (7 and 3Gbps)

(c) Ten flows (d) Ten flows

Figure 19: PI controller to stabilize TIMELY

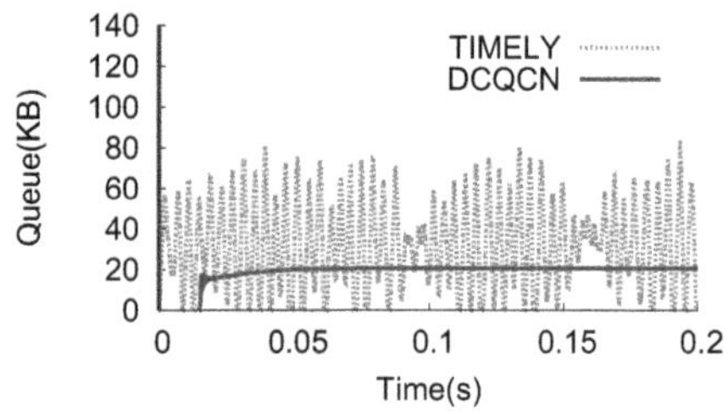

Figure 20: Protocol stability with random feedback delay up to 100 microseconds. DCQCN is more resilient to jitter than TIMELY.

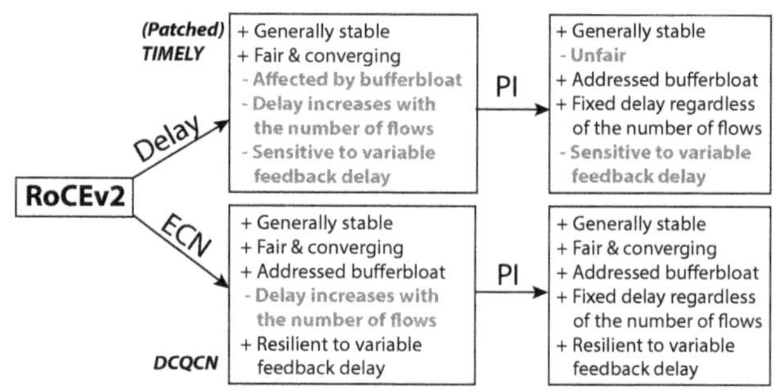

Figure 21: The design choices and desirable properties.

ECN marking is resilient to variable feedback transmission delay: Last but not the least, ECN marking is more resilient to the delay jitter during feedback transmission. After being generated at the bottleneck in the network, the congestion signal must be conveyed back to the sender. Any hardware jitter or additional congestion in this process can delay the arrival of ECN signal, or interfere round-trip delay measurement. Although DCQCN and TIMELY both attempt to mitigate this artifact, *e.g.,* by prioritizing feedback packets, the hardware jitter or feedback congestion on backward path cannot be completely eliminated in practice.

ECN marking is more resilient to this problem, because the queue length measurement at the bottleneck, and hence the feedback signal is not affected, it is just delayed (more). However, the variable delay of feedback directly injects noise in the TIMELY *feedback'* signal itself. This compounds the problem of congestion or variable delay on the reverse path: for delay based schemes you have delayed *and* noisy feedback, whereas for ECN based schemes you only have delayed feedback. Our simulation confirms this hypothesis. In Figure 20, we inject uniformed random jitter to the feedback delay of DCQCN (τ^*) and TIMELY (τ') models. With jitter of [0,100μs], TIMELY becomes unstable compared to the same scenario without the jitter (Figure 12(a)). In contrast, the same level of jitter does not impact DCQCN stability.

5.3 Summary

Based on the above three factors, *i.e.,* the faster feedback to the sources, the ability to simultaneously achieve fairness and bounded delay point, and the resilience to variable delay of congestion feedback transmission, we argue in favor of using ECN instead of delay for congestion control in a data center environment. We illustrate this in Figure 21.

Practical concerns: ECN can require creating per-flow state on the receiver, if ECN marks must be aggregated. DCQCN [31] does this, since RoCEv2 does not send per-packet ACKs for efficiency reasons. No matter which signal is used, the sender also needs to maintain per-flow state. This may not be scalable since RoCEv2 is implemented on the NIC. Detailed discussion of these issues is outside the scope of this paper.

While PI is not implemented in today's commodity switches, as shown in [14] it is a lightweight mechanism that requires less or comparable computational power as RED, which is supported by all modern switches. A variant of the PI controller (PIE) is being used to solve bufferbloat [23, 22] , and is part of DOCSIS 3.1 standard.

6. RELATED WORK

There is a vast amount of literature on congestion signals (drop, ECN, delay), congestion control algorithms and their analysis. See [27] for a succinct overview. Below, we discuss only a few representative papers.

In [3] and [4], Alizadeh et.al. analyze the DCTCP [2] and QCN [16] protocols that DCQCN is derived from. These papers served as useful guideposts during for our work.

Fluid model analysis of TCP under the RED AQM controller, and subsequent development of the PI controller was reported in [20, 14]. Our exploration of the PI controller for DCQCN and TIMELY is guided by results in [14].

A number of congestion control protocols where the bottleneck switch or a central controller plays a more active role have been proposed. For example, RCP [9] and XCP [19] require the switches to send more detailed feedback, while proposals like [29, 30, 24] use an omniscient central controller for fine grain scheduling and pFabric [5] is a timeout based congestion control that requires switches to sort packets. Comparison of these protocols to ECN and delay-based protocols is outside the scope of this paper.

7. CONCLUSION AND FUTURE WORK

We analyzed the behavior of two recently proposed congestion control protocols for data center networks; namely DCQCN (ECN based) and TIMELY (delay based). Using fluid models and control theoretic analysis we derived stability regions for DCQCN, which demonstrated a somewhat odd non-monotonic behavior of stability with respect to the number of contending flows. We verified this behavior via packet level simulations. We showed that DCQCN converges to a unique fixed point exponentially. In performing similar analysis for TIMELY, we discovered that as proposed the TIMELY protocol has infinite fixed points which could lead to unpredictable behavior and unbounded unfairness. We provide a simple fix to TIMELY to remedy this problem. The modified protocol is stable, and converges quickly.

However, for both protocols, the operating queue length grows with the number of contending flows, which can introduce significant latency. Using a PI controller on the switch to mark packets, we can guarantee bounded delay and fairness for DCQCN. However we demonstrate and prove a fundamental uncertainty result for delay-based protocols: if you use delay as the only feedback signal for congestion control, then you can either guarantee fairness or a fixed, bounded delay, but not both simultaneously. Based on this reason, the fact that ECN marking process on modern shared-buffer switches effectively excludes queuing delay from feedback loop, and that ECN is more robust to jitter in the feedback, we conclude that ECN is a better congestion signal in data center environment.

Future work: we are doing a full exploration of PI like controllers for congestion control protocols of RDMA in the data center, including a hardware implementation. Our analysis also suggests that DCQCN can be simplified considerably, to remove strange artifacts like the non-monotonic stability behavior.

We also plan to analyze problems that are not covered in the paper due to time and space limit. These include multiple bottleneck scenario, larger and realistic topolgoy and workload, and the impact of PFC-induced PAUSES on the two protocols. To capture these complicated behaviors, we will need to develop more analysis tools and improve the performance of DCQCN/TIMELY NS3 simulator [1].

8. ACKNOWLEDGEMENTS

The authors thank the anonymous reviewers and our shepherd, Michael Schapira, for their insightful feedback. Vishal Misra was supported in part by NSF Grant CNS-1618911. Any opinions, findings, and conclusions or recommendations expressed in this material are those of the authors and do not necessarily reflect the views of the NSF.

9. REFERENCES

[1] https://github.com/bobzhuyb/ns3-rdma.

[2] M. Alizadeh, A. Greenberg, D. Maltz, J. Padhye, P. Patel, B. Prabhakar, S. Sengupta, and M. Sridharan. Data Center TCP (DCTCP). In *SIGCOMM*, 2010.

[3] M. Alizadeh, A. Javanmard, and B. Prabhakar. Analysis of DCTCP: Stability, convergence and fairness. In *SIGMETRICS*, 2011.

[4] M. Alizadeh, A. Kabbani, B. Atikoglu, and B. Prabhakar. Stability analysis of QCN: the averaging principle. In *SIGMETRICS*, 2011.

[5] M. Alizadeh, S. Yang, S. Katti, N. McKeown, B. Prabhakar, and S. Shenker. Deconstructing datacenter packet transport. In *Proceedings of the 11th ACM Workshop on hot topics in networks*, pages 133–138. ACM, 2012.

[6] S. Athuraliya, D. E. Lapsley, and S. H. Low. An enhanced random early marking algorithm for internet flow control. In *Proceedings of IEEE INFOCOM 2000*, pages 1425–1434, 2000.

[7] A. Dragojevic, D. Narayanan, O. Hodson, and M. Castro. FaRM: Fast remote memory. In *NSDI*, 2014.

[8] N. Dukkipati. Rate control protocol (RCP): Congestion control to make flows complete quickly. In *PhD diss., Stanford University*, 2007.

[9] N. Dukkipati, N. McKeown, and A. G. Fraser. Rcp-ac: Congestion control to make flows complete quickly in any environment. In *INFOCOM 2006. 25th IEEE International Conference on Computer Communications. Proceedings*, pages 1–5. IEEE, 2006.

[10] S. Floyd and V. Jacobson. Random early detection gateways for congestion avoidance. *IEEE/ACM Transactions on Networking*, 1:397–413, 1993.

[11] J. Gettys and K. Nichols. Bufferbloat: Dark buffers in the internet. *Queue*, 9(11):40, 2011.

[12] M. Ghobadi, R. Mahajan, A. Phanishayee, J. Kulkarni, G. Ranade, N. Devanur, P.-A. Blanche, H. Rastegarfar, M. Glick, and D. Kilper. Projector: Agile

reconfigurable data center interconnect. In *sigcomm*, 2016.

[13] F. Golnarghi and B. C. Kuo. *Automatic control systems*. Wiely, 2009.

[14] C. Hollot, V. Misra, D. Towsley, and W.-B. Gong. On designing improved controllers for aqm routers supporting tcp flows. In *INFOCOM*, 2001.

[15] C. Hollot, V. Misra, D. Towsley, and W.-B. Gong. Analysis and design of controllers for aqm routers supporting tcp flows. *IEEE Transactions on Automatic Control*, 2002.

[16] IEEE. 802.11Qau. Congestion notification, 2010.

[17] IEEE. 802.11Qbb. Priority based flow control, 2011.

[18] Infiniband Trade Association. Supplement to InfiniBand architecture specification volume 1 release 1.2.2 annex A17: RoCEv2 (IP routable RoCE), 2014.

[19] D. Katabi, M. Handley, and C. Rohrs. Congestion control for high bandwidth-delay product networks. *ACM SIGCOMM Computer Communication Review*, 32(4):89–102, 2002.

[20] V. Misra, W.-B. Gong, and D. Towsley. Fluid-based analysis of a network of aqm routers supporting tcp flows with an application to red. In *ACM SIGCOMM Computer Communication Review*, volume 30, pages 151–160. ACM, 2000.

[21] R. Mitta, E. Blem, N. Dukkipati, T. Lam, A. Vahdat, Y. Wang, H. Wassel, D. Wetherall, D. Zats, and M. Ghobadi. TIMELY: RTT-based congestion control for the datacenter. In *SIGCOMM*, 2015.

[22] R. Pan, P. Natarajan, C. Piglione, M. S. Prabhu, V. Subramanian, F. Baker, and B. VerSteeg. https://tools.ietf.org/html/draft-pan-tsvwg-pie-00.

[23] R. Pan, P. Natarajan, C. Piglione, M. S. Prabhu, V. Subramanian, F. Baker, and B. VerSteeg. Pie: A lightweight control scheme to address the bufferbloat problem. In *HPSR*, pages 148–155. IEEE, 2013.

[24] J. Perry, A. Ousterhout, H. Balakrishnan, D. Shah, and H. Fugal. Fastpass: A centralized zero-queue datacenter network. In *Proceedings of the 2014 ACM conference on SIGCOMM*, pages 307–318. ACM, 2014.

[25] K. Ramakrishnan, S. Floyd, and D. Black. The addition of explicit congestion notification (ECN). RFC 3168.

[26] S. Shalunov, G. Hazel, J. Iyengar, and M. Kuehlewind. Low extra delay background transport (ledbat). Technical report, 2012.

[27] R. Srikant. *The mathematics of Internet congestion control*. Springer Science & Business Media, 2012.

[28] B. Stephens, A. Cox, A. Singla, J. Carter, C. Dixon, and W. Felter. Practical DCB for improved data center networks. In *INFOCOMM*, 2014.

[29] B. C. Vattikonda, G. Porter, A. Vahdat, and A. C. Snoeren. Practical tdma for datacenter ethernet. In *EuroSys*, pages 225–238. ACM, 2012.

[30] C. Wilson, H. Ballani, T. Karagiannis, and A. Rowstron. Better never than late: Meeting deadlines in datacenter networks. In *SIGCOMM*, 2011.

[31] Y. Zhu, H. Eran, D. Firestone, C. Guo, M. Lipshteyn, Y. Liron, J. Padhye, S. Raindel, M. H. Yahia, and M. Zhang. Congestion Control for Large-Scale RDMA Deployments. In *SIGCOMM*, 2015.

[32] The NS3 Simulator. https://www.nsnam.org/.

APPENDIX

A. DERIVING DCQCN CHARACTERISTIC EQUATION

We derive DCQCN characteristic equation by linearizing the system and Laplace transform.

Linearization. Below we denote $\delta R_C(t) = R_C(t) - R_C^*$, $\delta R_C(t) = R_C(t) - R_C^*$, $\delta p(t) = p(t) - p^*$, $\delta\alpha(t) = \alpha(t) - \alpha^*$, and $A = \left(\frac{1}{B} + \frac{1}{TR_C^*}\right)$. We again use Taylor series to simplify the expressions of a, b, c, d, e to handle the exponential forms like $(1-p)^x$. Due to lack of space, here we only just show the linearized expression for $\frac{d\delta R_C}{dt}$:

$$\begin{aligned}
&\tfrac{d\delta R_C}{dt} = -\tfrac{1}{2}(R_C^*)^2\alpha^*\delta p - \tfrac{1}{2}p^*R_C^*\alpha^*\delta R_C \\
&-\tfrac{1}{2}p^*R_C^*\alpha^*\delta R_C - \tfrac{1}{2}p^*(R_C^*)^2\delta\alpha \\
&+\tfrac{A}{2}\left(R_C^*\delta R_T - R_C^*\delta R_C + R_T^*\delta R_C - R_C^*\delta R_C\right) \\
&-\left(\tfrac{1}{2}+\tfrac{A}{4}\right)\left(p^*R_C^*\delta R_T - p^*R_C^*\delta R_C + p^*R_T^*\delta R_C\right) \\
&-\left(\tfrac{1}{2}+\tfrac{A}{4}\right)\left(p^*R_C^*\delta R_C - R_C^*R_T^*\delta p + (R_C^*)^2\delta p\right)
\end{aligned} \tag{33}$$

Laplace transform. We get the Laplace transform of the above linearized model:

$$\begin{aligned}
&sR_C(s) - \delta R_C(0) = \\
&\left(-\tfrac{1}{2}(R_C^*)^2\alpha^* - \left(\tfrac{1}{2}+\tfrac{A}{4}\right)R_C^*R_T^* + \left(\tfrac{1}{2}+\tfrac{A}{4}\right)(R_C^*)^2\right)e^{-s\tau*}p(s) \\
&+\left(-\tfrac{1}{2}p^*R_C^*\alpha^* - \tfrac{A}{2}R_C^* + \left(\tfrac{1}{2}+\tfrac{A}{4}\right)p^*R_C^*\right)e^{-s\tau*}R_C(s) \\
&+\left(-\tfrac{1}{2}p^*R_C^*\alpha^* - \tfrac{A}{2}R_C^* + \tfrac{A}{2}R_T^*\right)R_C(s) \\
&+\left(\left(\tfrac{1}{2}+\tfrac{A}{4}\right)p^*R_C^* - \left(\tfrac{1}{2}+\tfrac{A}{4}\right)p^*R_T^*\right)R_C(s) \\
&-\tfrac{1}{2}p^*(R_C^*)^2\alpha(s) \\
&+\left(\tfrac{A}{2}R_C^* - \left(\tfrac{1}{2}+\tfrac{A}{4}\right)p^*R_C^*\right)R_T(s)
\end{aligned} \tag{34}$$

With Laplace transform of the other equations, we can use $R_C(s)$ to express $R_T(s)$, $p(s)$ and $\alpha(s)$. We then derive the characteristic equation of $R_C(s)$. Finally we compute the phase margin values of the characteristic equation with different parameters, and show the results in Section 3.2.

B. PROOF OF DCQCN CONVERGENCE

Below we provide the additional details of our proof for Theorem 2. Figure 22 illustrates the variables we use.

Part I: The analysis of R_T. During the consecutive additive rate increase, *i.e.*, $\forall t \in (T_k + 1, T_{k+1}]$, $R_C^{(i)}$ and $R_T^{(i)}$ have following relationship according to DCQCN's definition:

$$R_C^{(i)}(t+1) = \frac{1}{2}\left(R_C^{(i)}(t) + R_T^{(i)}(t+1)\right) \tag{35}$$

$$R_T^{(i)}(t+1) = R_T^{(i)}(t) + R_{AI} \tag{36}$$

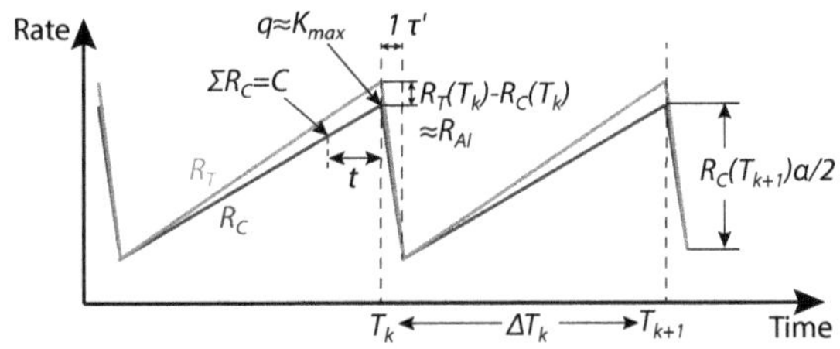

Figure 22: A more detailed view of DCQCN's AIMD-style updates of flow rate.

By (35)-$\frac{1}{2}\times$(36), we get:

$$\begin{aligned} & R_C^{(i)}(T_{k+1}) - R_T^{(i)}(T_{k+1}) + R_{AI} \\ & = \tfrac{1}{2}\left(R_C^{(i)}(T_{k+1}-1) - R_T^{(i)}(T_{k+1}-1) + R_{AI}\right) \\ & = \ldots = \left(\tfrac{1}{2}\right)^{\Delta T_k - 1}\left(R_C^{(i)}(T_k+1) - R_T^{(i)}(T_k+1) + R_{AI}\right) \end{aligned} \tag{37}$$

From this, we know that during a consecutive additive rate increase phase, $R_T^{(i)} - R_C^{(i)}$ will converge towards R_{AI} exponentially. In addition, at the beginning of the phase, $R_C^{(i)}(T_k + 1) = R_T^{(i)}(T_k)$ (Figure 6). Therefore:

$$R_T^{(i)}(T_k) = R_C^{(i)}(T_k) + \left(1 - (\frac{1}{2})^{\Delta T_k - 1}\right) R_{AI}, \forall k = 1, 2, \ldots \tag{38}$$

Part II: The lower bound of α. To prove Equation 19, we first need to estimate ΔT_k using α. In the period of ΔT_k, after the first time unit of rate decrease, the aggregated flow rates will climb back to $R_T(T_{k+1})$ by NR_{AI} every time unit. Thus we have:

$$\Delta T_k = 1 + \frac{\sum_{i=1}^{N}\left(R_T^{(i)}(T_{k+1}) - \left(1 - \alpha^{(i)}(T_k)/2\right) R_C^{(i)}(T_k)\right)}{NR_{AI}} \tag{39}$$

Suppose $\alpha^{(i)}(T_k)$ already converged to the same value $\alpha(T_k)$, as guaranteed by Equation 17. We simplify it as:

$$\begin{aligned} \Delta T_k & = 1 + \frac{\sum_{i=1}^{N} R_T^{(i)}(T_{k+1}) - (1-\alpha(T_k)/2)\sum_{i=1}^{N} R_C^{(i)}(T_k)}{NR_{AI}} \\ & \approx 1 + \frac{(C + tNR_{AI} + NR_{AI}) - (1-\alpha(T_k)/2)(C + tNR_{AI})}{NR_{AI}} \\ & = 2 + \left(\frac{t}{2} + \frac{C}{2NR_{AI}}\right)\alpha(T_k) \end{aligned} \tag{40}$$

Where t is the time it takes for the flows to build up queue and get packets ECN-marked, after the aggregated flow rates exceed link capacity C, as shown in Figure 6. We can estimate t by the queue being built up:

$$\begin{aligned} & N\tau'(R_{AI} + 2R_{AI} + \ldots + tR_{AI}) = Q_{ECN} \le K_{\max} \\ & \Rightarrow t \le \left(-1 + \sqrt{1 + \frac{8K_{\max}}{NR_{AI}\tau'}}\right)/2 \end{aligned} \tag{41}$$

Now, we prove Equation 19, where α^* is the solution of the following:

$$\alpha^* = (1-g)^{\Delta T^*}\left((1-g)\alpha^* + g\right) \tag{42}$$

Once Equation 19 is proved, $\alpha(T_k)$ has a non-zero lower bound, R_C will converge exponentially. We prove this by mathematical induction. The initial value of α is 1, as defined by DCQCN. So, $\alpha(T_0) > \alpha^* > 0$. Now assuming $\alpha(T_k) > \alpha^* > 0$, we prove $\alpha(T_k) > \alpha(T_{k+1}) > \alpha^*$. We define $f(\alpha)$ as the RHS of Equation 16:

$$f(\alpha) = (1-g)^{2 + \left(\frac{t}{2} + \frac{C}{2NR_{AI}}\right)\alpha}\left((1-g)\alpha + g\right) \tag{43}$$

By analyzing the derivative of $f(\alpha)$, it is not hard to see that with common parameter settings, $f(\alpha)$ is monotonically increasing. Therefore,

$$\alpha(T_{k+1}) = f(\alpha(T_k)) > f(\alpha^*) = \alpha^* \tag{44}$$

In addition, because $\alpha(T_k) > \alpha^* \Rightarrow \Delta T_k > \Delta T^*$, α^* satisfies:

$$\alpha^* > (1-g)^{\Delta T_k}\left((1-g)\alpha^* + g\right) \tag{45}$$

Subtract this from Equation 16, we see $\alpha(T_k)$ is exponentially converging towards α^*:

$$\alpha(T_{k+1}) - \alpha^* < (1-g)^{\Delta T_n}\left(\alpha(T_k) - \alpha^*\right) \tag{46}$$

Equation 44 and 46 lead to $\alpha^* < \alpha(T_{k+1}) < \alpha(T_k)$. □

Composite-Path Switching

Shay Vargaftik[1,2], Katherine Barabash[1], Yaniv Ben-Itzhak[1], Ofer Biran[1],
Isaac Keslassy[2,3], Dean Lorenz[1], Ariel Orda[2]
[1] IBM Research [2] Technion [3] VMware Research

ABSTRACT

Hybrid switching combines a high-bandwidth optical circuit switch in parallel with a low-bandwidth electronic packet switch. It presents an appealing solution for scaling datacenter architectures. Unfortunately, it does not fit many traffic patterns produced by typical datacenter applications, and in particular the skewed traffic patterns that involve highly intensive one-to-many and many-to-one communications.

In this paper, we introduce *composite-path switching* by allowing for composite circuit/packet paths between the two switches. We show how this enables the datacenter network to deal with skewed traffic patterns, and offer a practical scheduling algorithm that can directly extend any hybrid-switching scheduling algorithm. Through extensive evaluations using modern datacenter workloads, we show how our solution outperforms two recently proposed state-of-the-art scheduling techniques, both in completion time and in circuit utilization.

CCS Concepts

•**Networks → Bridges and switches; Data center networks; Packet scheduling; Hybrid networks;**

Keywords

hybrid networks; composite-path switching; OCS; EPS

1. INTRODUCTION

Hybrid switching has emerged in recent work as an appealing solution for scaling datacenter architectures [1–11]. As illustrated in Figure 1(a), a hybrid switch typically combines a low-bandwidth electronic packet switch (EPS) and a high-bandwidth optical circuit switch (OCS). The EPS system can send traffic from any port to any port simultaneously at a relatively low speed, and can therefore handle low-bandwidth densely-connected traffic. The OCS system can create arbitrary low-latency high-capacity circuits, using a relatively slow-to-reconfigure cross-board. It handles high-bandwidth flows that require sparse connections.

The hybrid switch has n senders and n receivers, corresponding to either ToR (Top of Rack) switches or individual servers. While the EPS and the OCS systems are modeled as single switches, they could be generalized to multi-layer networks of switches.

Unfortunately, these hybrid switches are not suited to many modern data-parallel datacenter applications, because they cannot efficiently switch their communication patterns. To simplify, these applications can be modeled using the *coflow* abstraction, as a collection of flows with a shared completion time [12–15]. The coflows consist of four main types: (a) *Many-to-many*, including a large number of low-bandwidth point-to-point communications, *e.g.,* data-parallel applications and dataflow pipelines [16, 17]; (b) *One-to-one*, involving a few high-bandwidth point-to-point flows, *e.g.,* distributed file systems [18, 19]; (c) One-to-many, *e.g.,* distributed data storage and backup, query traffic, etc. [16, 20, 21]; and (d) Many-to-one, *e.g.,* aggregation of data (*i.e.,* MapReduce, Partition-Aggregate, etc.) [16, 22–24]. The last two kinds (*i.e.,* (c) and (d)) are often more delay-sensitive [21].

The hybrid switch can deal well with the first two types of coflows: the EPS system with (a) low-bandwidth many-to-many, and the OCS system with (b) high-bandwidth one-to-one. However, (c) one-to-many and (d) many-to-one coflows achieve poor performance in hybrid switches. They are constrained by the low bandwidth of EPS switches and the high reconfiguration times of OCS switches. For instance, the black line in Figure 1(a) shows how a one-to-many coflow that exceeds the EPS capacity would need to use time-division multiplexing over the OCS system, and therefore would achieve a poor performance.

In practice, this poor performance with skewed one-to-many and many-to-one traffic is further compounded

CoNEXT '16, December 12-15, 2016, Irvine, CA, USA
© 2016 ACM. ISBN 978-1-4503-4292-6/16/12...$15.00
DOI: http://dx.doi.org/10.1145/2999572.2999610

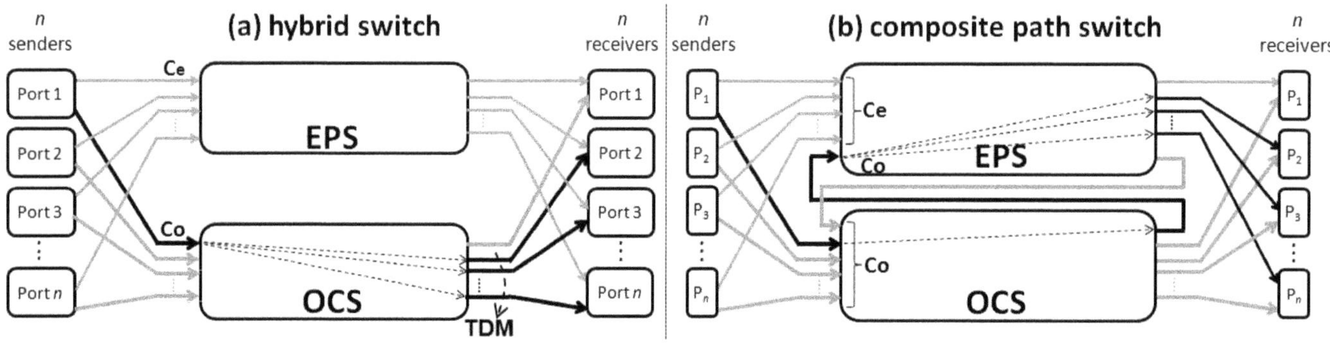

Figure 1: (a) The hybrid switch model vs. (b) the composite-path switch model. The black line shows one-to-many communication from the first sender to all the other receivers. In (a) the flows are serialized with Time Division Multiplexing (TDM), while in (b) the flows are sent through the OCS over the OCS/EPS composite-path, and then are efficiently demultiplexed by the Packet Switch.

by the fact that modern workloads are increasingly decomposed into micro-services, often implemented using a large number of identical containers, and interconnected using message brokers as barriers that receive messages from many service endpoints and deliver messages to many other service endpoints. As a result, this multi-component datacenter traffic is even more skewed than each of its components, and its performance acutely depends on the last flow to complete in each coflow [25,26].

In this paper, we introduce the *composite-path switch* (*cp-Switch*) to deal with skewed one-to-many and many-to-one coflows. As Figure 1(b) illustrates, we propose a small extension to the hybrid switch by interconnecting the EPS and OCS systems using *composite paths*. For instance, to schedule the same black one-to-many coflow, the scheduler can first forward the aggregate traffic though the OCS system, then through the one-to-many composite path to the EPS system. Finally, at the EPS system, the different flows of this coflow are switched to their respective destinations. Thus, this one-to-many coflow can be switched without a need for many costly OCS reconfigurations.

The goal of this paper is to extend hybrid Circuit/Packet switches and allow them to efficiently support modern datacenter workloads that include a large variety of traffic patterns and applications.

First, we introduce the composite-path switch architecture and explain how it can better serve skewed one-to-many and many-to-one datacenter traffic.

Next, we tackle the challenge of simplifying cp-Switch scheduling so as to leverage state-of-the-art hybrid switch scheduling techniques. We show how it is possible to build a reduced cp-Switch demand matrix using an additional column and row that would represent the composite paths. We also introduce intuition about traffic that would fit such composite paths, and deduce constraints on how to filter the demand matrix.

We are then able to apply hybrid-switch scheduling to our problem. However, we still need to process results in order to be able to schedule our cp-Switch. In particular, we explain how to schedule flows within a composite path and why we want to reserve EPS slots.

Finally, using extensive evaluation, we demonstrate that the composite-path switch is capable of accommodating more traffic patterns while significantly improving both the flow completion time and the circuit utilization metrics.

The rest of this paper is structured as follows: In Section 2 we present our composite path Circuit/Packet switching model, and formalize the translation of the known scheduling techniques to our new Circuit/Packet switching model. We follow up by describing our evaluation methodology and presenting the evaluation results in Section 3. In Section 4 we discuss possible extensions and present future research directions for the cp-Switch. Section 5 describes related work, and Section 6 concludes the paper.

2. COMPOSITE-PATH SWITCH

Our goal in this section is to provide a scheduling algorithm for our proposed composite-path switch.

2.1 Composite-Path Switch Model

We start by defining and modeling our composite-path switch, denoted *cp-Switch*. We largely follow the model for the hybrid switch, denoted *h-Switch* [1,2].

We already saw in Figure 1(b) how cp-Switch combines an EPS system and an OCS system to connect n input ports to n output ports. Both the EPS and OCS systems implement a matching between their respective input and output ports. While EPS can be reconfigured instantaneously, the circuits of the OCS can be reconfigured with a reconfiguration time penalty δ. Following [1,2], we assume that during the reconfiguration time no data can pass through the circuit switch.

In addition, EPS has a much lower capacity than OCS (*e.g.,* if the EPS link rate is C_e = 10 Gbps and the OCS link rate is C_o = 100 Gbps, there is a 1-to-10 ratio). Each sender implements per-receiver *Virtual Output Queues* (VOQs) [27, 28]. The occupancy of these VOQs can be used to build the demand matrix. EPS also implements input and output queues. We further classically assume that time is slotted and propagation times are negligible.

Composite OCS/EPS paths: The main addition in cp-Switch compared to h-Switch are the composite paths, *i.e.,* two high-bandwidth links connecting the output of each fabric to the input of the other fabric. As mentioned, these composite paths help us deal with skewed datacenter traffic, and especially with one-to-many and many-to-one traffic. These new composite paths require two main architectural abilities.

First, the dedicated use of an additional input/output port pair at each switch to inter-connect the EPS and the OCS systems. In particular, the cp-Switch needs the ability for the EPS fabric to deal with a higher-bandwidth input/output port of capacity C_o. Current switches are already offering heterogeneous port bandwidth, with many low-bandwidth and a few high-bandwidth ports. For instance, the Mellanox SN2410 switch [29] offers 48x25GbE and 8x100GbE ports; Arista 7280TR-48C6 [30] offers 48x10GbE and 6x100GbE ports; and Cisco 93180YC-EX [31] offers flexible 48x10/25-Gbps ports and 6x40/100-Gbps ports.

This is also generally related to the well-known issue of what to do with switches when upgrading the link speed.

Second, the ability to synchronize the transmission of subsets of hosts through the EPS upon the creation of a many-to-one composite path. To that end, Precision Time Protocol (PTP) [32] is commonly used in order to achieve sub-microsecond network-wide time synchronization. For instance, Fastpass [33] presents an implementation for fine-grain timing between endpoints and switches by using commodity NICs, which achieves a time accuracy of a few hundred nanoseconds across a multi-hop network. White Rabbit [34], which is used by CERN, provides a sub-nanosecond accuracy, by using a state-of-the-art FPGA-based implementation.

2.2 cp-Switch Demand Reduction

We would like to introduce a simple scheduling algorithm for cp-Switch that essentially follows the h-Switch scheduling algorithm approach. Unfortunately, cp-Switch scheduling is not so simple. In the h-Switch, the OCS and EPS configurations can be scheduled in a simple, pipeline-like manner. First, given an $n \times n$ demand matrix D, the scheduler decides on the OCS configurations and their respective duration. Next, it selects all unscheduled packets and schedules them through the EPS.

On the other hand, since cp-Switch has composite cross-platform paths, they induce a *strong dependency* between the two fabrics, such that the above pipelined scheme with separate decisions for OCS and EPS cannot be directly applied. As a result, a joint schedule for the EPS, the OCS and the composite paths seems significantly more complex to design.

To deal with this challenge, we pursue the ability to *translate* h-Switch scheduling to cp-Switch scheduling. In addition to making the approach more tractable, this would also enable us to leverage the existing body of research on h-Switch scheduling.

Demand Reduction: Our approach is to reduce the $n \times n$ input demand matrix D into a new $(n+1) \times (n+1)$ demand matrix D_I, such that D_I could be directly fed to a h-Switch scheduling algorithm, and the resulting schedule could be modified into a viable schedule for the cp-Switch.

To construct the new $(n+1) \times (n+1)$ matrix D_I, we augment the demand matrix D by adding a column that represents the one-to-many composite path and an additional row over D that represents the many-to-one composite path. Our scheduler then selects entries in D that it aggregates and puts in the new composite entries, while removing them from the non-composite entries. The new non-zero entries will be served by the composite paths, whereas the rest of the demand matrix is served by the regular EPS-EPS and OCS-OCS paths. Now, when D_I is fed to an h-Switch scheduling algorithm, the resulting permutation matrices can indicate both the creation of regular OCS-OCS circuits and the creation of composite paths (*i.e.,* when the last row or column has an entry of 1, it means that the corresponding sender or receiver has a composite path within the duration of this permutation matrix).

The above reduction helps us use h-Switch scheduling as a sub-routine in cp-Switch scheduling. However, it also introduces a new challenge: the scheduler now needs to decide which demand-matrix entries in D should be aggregated into composite-path entries in D_I. Of course, exhaustively considering all possibilities leads to an exponential complexity.

Demand Filtering: We adopt a heuristic approach motivated by the following intuition:

(a) The traffic along the composite paths should provide high utilization for the OCS while not overwhelming the EPS—*i.e.,* it should serve one-to-many or many-to-one patterns.

(b) The time to serve each individual entry by the OCS should not exceed too much the reconfiguration time penalty of the OCS.

The intuition for (a) is relatively straightforward. A demand-matrix row with 1-2 entries would not gain in being aggregated into a composite entry. It would be more efficient to simply service these entries one by one using either OCS or EPS. (b) was more surprising at first. It would seem that a row with several large entries would be a perfect candidate for composite aggregation. However, consider a demand-matrix row with 5 entries of 100 packets each. Scheduling it using a one-to-many composite path would take 100 slots, where at each slot 5 packets transfer first through the OCS, then through the composite path, and finally through the EPS (as in

Algorithm 1: cp-SwitchDemandReduction

Data: D, R_t, B_t.

$D_I = 0$;
$D_f = 0$;
$D_{low} = ZerosAboveB_t(D)$;
$rows = RowSums(Sign(D_{low})) \geq R_t$;
$cols = ColSums(Sign(D_{low})) \geq R_t$;
for *each* $(i, j) \in rows, (i, j) \notin cols$ **do**
  $D_f[i, j] = D[i, j]$;
  $D_I[i, n+1] += D[i, j]$;
for *each* $(i, j) \notin rows, (i, j) \in cols$ **do**
  $D_f[i, j] = D[i, j]$;
  $D_I[n+1, j] += D[i, j]$;
for *each* $(i, j) \in rows, (i, j) \in cols$ **do**
  $(x, y) = argmin(D_I[n+1, j], D_I[i, n+1])$;
  $D_f[i, j] = D[i, j]$;
  $D_I[x, y] += D[i, j]$;
$D_I[1:n, 1:n] = D - D_f$;
return (D_I, D_f)

Figure 1(b)). On the other hand, assuming a 1-to-10 link rate ratio, it would take $100/10 = 10$ slots for each of the 5 entries to go through the OCS, together with a reconfiguration time of 5δ, *i.e.*, $50 + 5\delta$. As long as $\delta \leq 10$, there is no point using the composite path.

Following (a) and (b), to find these specific patterns, we filter the input demand matrix D and obtain the filtered demand matrix D_f.

Specifically, we define two threshold parameters, B_t and R_t. First, following intuition (b), we filter the demand D by removing large entries, and assign zeros to each entry that is bigger than threshold B_t. Then, following intuition (a), we look for rows and columns that contain at least R_t non-zero entries. All entries that do not belong to such row or column are also set to zero.

We are left with a last challenge. Some entries could be assigned to either their row composite path or their column composite path. Intuitively, we try to load-balance such entries so that the sums of the composite paths will tend to equalize, and one composite path sum will not grow too large compared to the other.

Specifically, we greedily assign such entries to the less loaded composite path, and consider such entries in an arbitrary order.

Finally, Algorithm 1 (cp-SwitchDemandReduction) combines the demand reduction and filtering processes.

Demand Reduction and Filtering Example: Figure 2 illustrates a demand reduction and filtering example with $n = 6$, $B_t = 10$ and $R_t = 4$. The input matrix is D. First, we set to zero each entry in D that is greater than B_t=10. Then, we count the number of non-zero entries in each row and column. Each entry that does not belong to a row or column with a total of at least R_t=4 non-zero entries is set to zero as well. Thus, we receive the filtered matrix D_f, containing the entries we want to schedule using composite paths. Finally, the reduced demand D_I is equal to $D - D_f$ in the first $n \times n$ entries, representing traffic that is destined to be served by regular EPS-EPS and OCS-OCS paths. The last row and column of D_I represent the composite-path traffic.

Note that the orange entry $D_f[5, 2] = 3$ belongs to both a row and a column with at least 4 non-zero entries. Therefore, $D_f[5, 2]$ can be assigned to a composite path in either direction (*i.e.*, $D_f[5, 2]$ can be added to $D_I[5, n+1]$ and served by a one-to-many composite path given to input port 4. Alternatively, $D_I[5, 2]$ can be added to $D_I[n+1, 2]$ and served by the many-to-one composite path given to output port 1). After handling all other entries of D_f, $D_I[5, n+1] = 15$ and $D_I[n+1, 2] = 14$. Thus, we greedily add $D_f[5, 2] = 3$ to the smallest sum, *i.e.*, $D_I[n+1, 2]$.

2.3 cp-Switch Scheduling

Scheduling Interpretation: The scheduler can finally use the h-Switch scheduling algorithm as a subroutine. It feeds it with the new $(n+1) \times (n+1)$ demand matrix D_I, and receives a scheduling output, *i.e.*, a set of OCS permutation matrices with their respective duration.

Permutation matrices are treated as usual for entries that are not at the last row or column. When a permutation matrix contains an entry at the last row or column, it represents a port that receives a composite one-to-many or many-to-one path.

Scheduling Within a Composite Path: Upon the creation of a composite path with its respective duration, we still need to decide on the scheduling *within* this path. Specifically, we need to choose among the different sources or destinations to serve, and to decide on the duration of this service. In addition, the rate at which data can be transferred along such a path is restricted *asymmetrically*. On one hand, each particular source or destination is connected to the EPS and thus restricted by C_e. On the other hand, the path is connected to the OCS, and therefore the *total* rate is restricted by C_o. This reflects an inherent tradeoff in the cp-Switch between the benefits of data parallelism and of optical speedup. We choose to send data to all available sources or destinations simultaneously with a rate that respects both constraints.

The scheduler relies on Algorithm 2, denoted *CPSched*, to schedule within a composite path. CPSched receives an input or an output port p with a set of demands S and the path time duration t. The output is the remaining set R of demands after the duration of this path. Namely, examining $S - R$ reveals how much traffic is sent to or from each specific port along this path.

EPS Reservation: Since composite paths are asymmetric, their scheduling indirectly assumes that the EPS links involved in every particular one-to-many or many-to-one composite-path are reserved for its use when

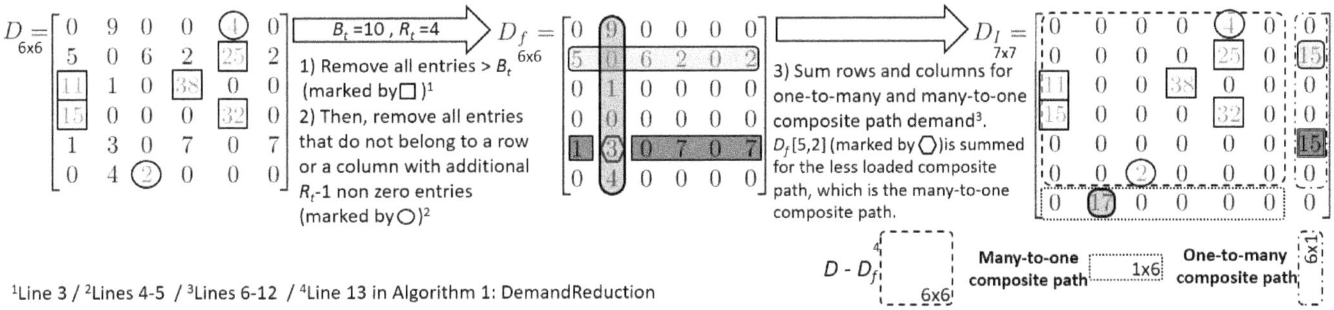

Figure 2: Demand reduction and filtering example with $B_t = 10$ and $R_t = 4$. In steps 1) and 2), the scheduler first filters demand matrix D to obtain the filtered demand matrix D_f, representing the entries that should be scheduled using composite paths. Then, in step 3), it assigns these entries to specific composite paths (*i.e.*, in the last row or column of D_I). The remaining entries of D_I in the other rows and columns will simply be scheduled in the OCS and EPS systems without using composite paths. Next, Figure 3 illustrates the final schedule computation using D_f and D_I.

Algorithm 2: CPSched

Data: S, t, C_o, C_e

```
τ = t ;
R = S ;
while τ > 0 do
    R_m = min{non-zero{R}} ;
    R_c = |non-zero{R}| ;
    t_max = max{R_m/C_e, R_m·R_c/C_o} ;
    t_curr = min{t_max, τ} ;
    for each d ∈ R do
        d = max{d − t_curr · min{C_e, C_o/R_c}, 0} ;
    τ = τ − t_curr ;
return R
```

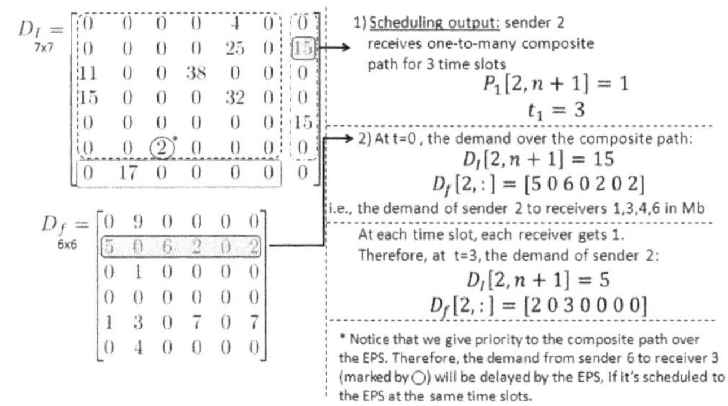

Figure 3: Example for CPSched. Assume that the scheduler needs to schedule the second one-to-many entry, illustrated in gray, for 3 time-slots. It can service up to 3 packets from each of the non-zero entries in the gray row. Only the first and third entries are left with packets at the end, *i.e.*, $5 - 3 = 2$ and $6 - 3 = 3$ packets respectively.

needed. This assumption may adversely impact short and delay-sensitive flows that want to concurrently use these EPS links.

To resolve this issue, we adopt a simple approach. The scheduler assigns a bandwidth budget $C_e^* \leq C_e$ to the composite paths on each *individual* EPS link when they are used. Then, the scheduler feeds Algorithm 2 with C_e^* instead of C_e to respect this budget. Such bandwidth management on the EPS links can be enforced by well-established traffic-shaping techniques, *e.g.*, [35–38], and bandwidth and resource-reservation techniques, *e.g.*, [39, 40].

DivideByType is the last sub-function in our scheduler, as presented in Algorithm 3. It receives an outputted permutation matrix for cp-Switch, and returns its decomposition into regular paths and composite paths with their respective port numbers.

Finally, as illustrated in Figure 4 and formally defined in Algorithm 4, *CPSwitchSched* forms the entire scheduling algorithm for cp-Switch. CPSwitchSched receives as an input the demand and the switch parameters. Its output is a full schedule for cp-Switch.

Algorithm 3: DivideByType

Data: P

```
P_h = P[1 : n, 1 : n] ;
row = argmax(P[:, n + 1] > 0) ;
if row ≠ NULL then
    S_row = P[row, :] ;
col = argmax(P[n + 1, :] > 0) ;
if col ≠ NULL then
    S_col = P[col, :] ;
return P_h, S_row, row, S_col, col
```

Complexity: We want to evaluate the complexity of the entire scheduling procedure. We begin by analyzing Algorithm 1 (cp-SwitchDemandReduction). Since this algorithm requires to go over the demand matrix

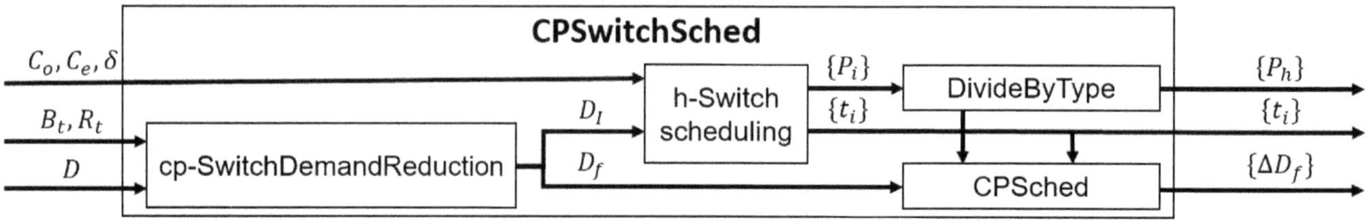

Figure 4: Diagram block for the cp-Switch scheduler CPSwitchSched. The initial demand matrix D is first reduced and filtered to obtain demand matrix D_I of size $(n+1) \times (n+1)$. D_I is then sent to an h-Switch scheduler, which outputs permutation matrices and their respective duration. But these permutations fit an OCS in the h-Switch, not in the cp-Switch. They need to be sent to DivideByType in order to obtain a decomposition into regular paths and composite paths with their respective port numbers. Finally, CPSched provides the specific scheduling time of each sender or receiver using a composite path.

Algorithm 4: CPSwitchSched

```
Data: D, C_o, C_e, C_e*, δ, R_t, B_t.
(D_I, D_f)=cp-SwitchDemandReduction(D,R_t,B_t) ;
sched=h-Switch-Scheduling(D_I, C_o, C_e, δ) ;
cpssched = {} ;
for each (P_i, t_i) ∈ sched do
    D_{f,prev} = D_f ;
    (P_h, S_r, r, S_c, c) = DivideByType(P_i) ;
    if r ≠ NULL then
        D_f[r,:] = CPSched(S_r, t_i, C_o, C_e*) ;
    if c ≠ NULL then
        D_f[:,c] = CPSched(S_c, t_i, C_o, C_e*) ;
    cpssched = cpssched ⋃ {P_h, t_i, D_{f,prev} − D_f} ;
return cpssched
```

a constant number of times (*i.e.,* 3 at most), we obtain a complexity of $O(n^2)$. Algorithm 2 (CPSched) can do no more than $n-1$ iterations (*i.e.,* the *while* loop) where in each such iteration it needs to update the remaining demand. Each such update is done efficiently in $O(\log n)$ by using a priority queue and two counters. Thus, the complexity of Algorithm 2 is $O(n \log n)$. Clearly, since Algorithm 3 requires examining the permutation matrix only once, its complexity is $O(n^2)$. Finally, putting it all together, the complexity of the *interpretation process* part of Algorithm 4 (CPSwitchSched) is $O(n^2)$ for each permutation matrix in the schedule. Thus the complexity of the entire algorithm is $O(\max\{m \cdot n^2, \text{h-Switch-Scheduling}\})$ where m is the number of OCS reconfigurations in the schedule (*i.e.,* the number of permutation matrices) and $O(\text{h-Switch-Scheduling})$ is the complexity of the h-Switch scheduler.

3. EVALUATION

In this section, we evaluate and compare h-Switch and cp-Switch with $C_e = 10$ Gbps and $C_o = 100$ Gbps (*i.e.,* 1/10 ratio), for radix (*i.e.,* number of ports) 32, 64 and 128. Two OCS types are considered throughout our evaluation: *Fast OCS* with $\delta = 20\mu s$ (2D MEMS wavelength selective switches, such as [4, 6, 41]), and *Slow OCS* with $\delta = 20ms$ (3D MEMS optical circuit switches, such as [3, 5, 42, 43]).

We evaluate different demands, which include a DCN traffic workload [44], one-to-many, and many-to-one traffic demands. For each evaluation, we define the demand model and produce 100 random demand matrices accordingly. Then, each such demand is evaluated for both h-Switch and cp-Switch, by the same order of the permutation matrices produced by the scheduling algorithms (termed *online execution*). Finally, the results of all the 100 random demands are averaged and compared between h-Switch and cp-Switch.

The demand reduction process for cp-Switch is configured with $R_t = 0.7 \cdot n$, and $B_t = 2Mb$ ($B_t = 200Mb$) for the Fast OCS (Slow OCS). Further discussion about R_t and B_t settings can be found in Section 4.

In the following we present the evaluation criteria in Section 3.1. Then, in Section 3.2 we evaluate a given one-to-many/many-to-one DCN demand example. We extend the demand model by adding typical background DCN demand in Section 3.3. In Section 3.4 we stress the schedulers with intensive background demand along with one-to-many and many-to-one demand. Finally, in Section 3.5 we stress the composite paths by increasing the one-to-many/many-to-one demands along with typical DCN traffic.

3.1 Evaluation Criteria

For our evaluation, we adopt two recent state-of-the-art scheduling algorithms optimized for h-Switch, Eclipse [1] and Solstice [2], which attempt to optimize two different metrics: fraction of demand over the OCS, and demand completion time, respectively.

Eclipse (Fraction of Demand over the OCS[1]): Eclipse identifies a submodularity structure [45] and leverages it to *guarantee* an efficiency of at least half of the optimal solution according to the associated op-

[1] Notice that for a similar demand and switch parameters (*i.e.,* n, C_e, C_o), increase of this metric corresponds to increase of the OCS utilization.

timization criterion, which is to maximize the fraction of demand over the OCS in a given time window. In our evaluation, Eclipse is used with a window period input of $1ms$ for the Fast OCS, and $100ms$ for the Slow OCS.
Solstice (Completion Time): Solstice takes advantage of the sparsity and skewness observed in real DCN traffic. The basic idea of Solstice is to *stuff* the demand into a bistochastic matrix and then efficiently decompose the demand by *slicing* it into permutation matrices with long duration. The guiding optimization criterion of Solstice is the completion run-time.

Each given demand matrix D is scheduled by Eclipse and Solstice, for both h-Switch and cp-Switch[2]. Then, we measure the corresponding metrics for the total demand. Notice that for cp-Switch the metrics include the demand that is assigned to the composite paths, which we also measure separately. Furthermore, for comparison purpose, we measure the metrics of the same demand (*i.e.,* assigned to the composite paths in the cp-Switch) for the h-Switch.
OCS Reconfigurations: We count the number of OCS configurations required by Solstice and Eclipse. This measurement has a strong correlation with the results. Namely, a large number of reconfigurations leads to both longer completion times and diminished OCS utilization, because of the idle time periods during the OCS reconfigurations.

3.2 One-to-Many/Many-to-One Demand Example

Our one-to-many and many-to-one demand model is based on previous work that presents DCN measurements, *e.g.,* DCTCP [23] and TCP Outcast [24].
One-to-Many/Many-to-One Demand Model: In this section, we start with a simple example in order to provide insight about the benefit of cp-Switch composite paths. We randomly choose a single sender for which we create one-to-many traffic and a single receiver for which we create many-to-one traffic. All other demands are zero. The number of destinations for the sender and the number of sources for the receiver are chosen randomly and uniformly in the range of $[0.7{\cdot}n, n]$. The demand towards each destination of the sender and each source of the receiver is chosen randomly and uniformly in the range of $[1, 1.3]$ Mb for Fast OCS and $[100, 130]$ Mb for Slow OCS.
Evaluation Results: Figure 5(a) and Figure 5(b) present the completion time of the total demand, and the demand that is assigned to the one-to-many and many-to-one composite paths (noted by *o2m* and *m2o*, respectively). Compared to h-Switch, cp-Switch results in a better completion time for the total, one-to-many, and many-to-one demands, for both the Fast and Slow OCSs. Furthermore, the relative completion time improvement of cp-Switch increases as the switch radix increases.

There are several reasons for the h-Switch completion time degradation: First, the total demand of the sender and the receiver exceeds the EPS port bandwidth due to the high number of destinations and sources, respectively. Second, Figure 5(c) presents the required number of OCS configurations. h-Switch serves the demand by many costly OCS reconfigurations, which increase with the switch radix. On the other hand, cp-Switch employs its one-to-many and many-to-one composite paths to serve the demand, without any OCS reconfigurations. Moreover, the completion time improvement of cp-Switch as compared to h-Switch is more significant for the Slow OCS, due to its higher reconfiguration penalty as compared to the time it takes to serve the demand.

Figure 6(a) presents the fraction of the demand that is served by the OCS, which corresponds to the OCS utilization. The objective of Eclipse is to maximize the OCS utilization, and therefore it prefers to schedule large entries over the OCS. Therefore, one-to-many and many-to-one demands are scheduled over the OCS with lower priority.

For switch radix 32, the one-to-many and many-to-one demands do not incur a severe bottleneck over the sender and the receiver, respectively; hence, Eclipse achieves the demand fraction over the OCS for both h-Switch and cp-Switch. However, as the switch radix increases, the sender and the receiver are overloaded by the one-to-many and many-to-one demand as it increases as well. Therefore, the cp-Switch results improve with the switch radix as compared to h-Switch.

Eclipse achieves a lower OCS utilization as the OCS reconfiguration penalty increases. Therefore, for the Slow OCS case, cp-Switch achieves much higher results as compared to h-Switch (Figure 6(b)). Figure 6(c) presents the required OCS configurations for h-Switch and cp-Switch with both Fast and Slow OCSs. Eclipse produces approximately the same number of OCS configurations independently of the switch radix. h-Switch with Fast OCS requires approximately 31-35 OCS configurations by Eclipse, where each re-configuration takes $20\mu s$. Therefore, the total reconfiguration penalty of the fast OCS equals $620\mu s$-$700\mu s$, out of its $1ms$ period window.

3.3 Typical DCN with One-to-Many/Many-to-One Demand Example

Our demand model consists of both typical data center demand as background traffic, and one-to-many and many-to-one traffic patterns. The typical DCN demand is based on the aforementioned works on data center traffic; and the one-to-many and many-to-one demand is based on our demand model described in Section 3.2.

[2]For cp-Switch, we employ the demand reduction and filtering, then we employ Eclipse or Solstice, respectively, for the new demand D_I, and finally produce cp-Switch scheduling (*i.e.,* we employ Algorithm 4).

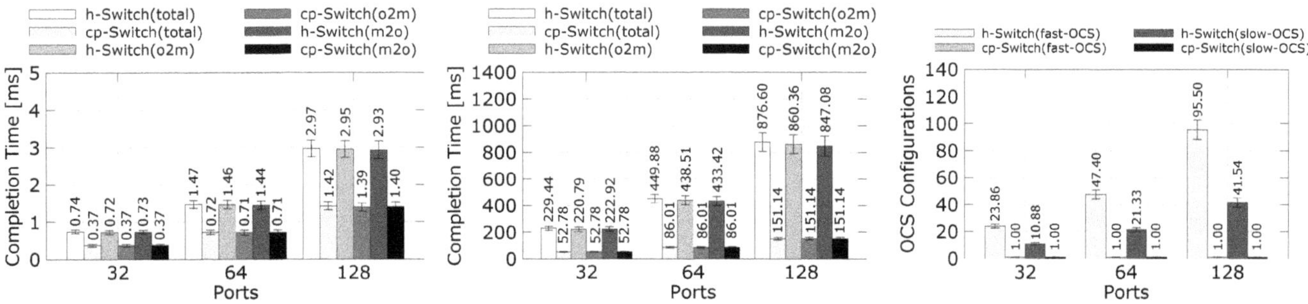

(a) Completion time with Fast OCS. (b) Completion time with Slow OCS. (c) OCS configurations.

Figure 5: One-to-Many/Many-to-One Demand Example - Completion Time (Based on Solstice). The cp-Switch advantage over h-Switch increases with the switch radix. This is due to the increased number of reconfigurations required by h-Switch as the switch radix increases; while cp-Switch does not require any reconfiguration. The number of reconfigurations for h-Switch is proportional to the increased number of sources and destinations in the many-to-one and one-to-many traffic, respectively.

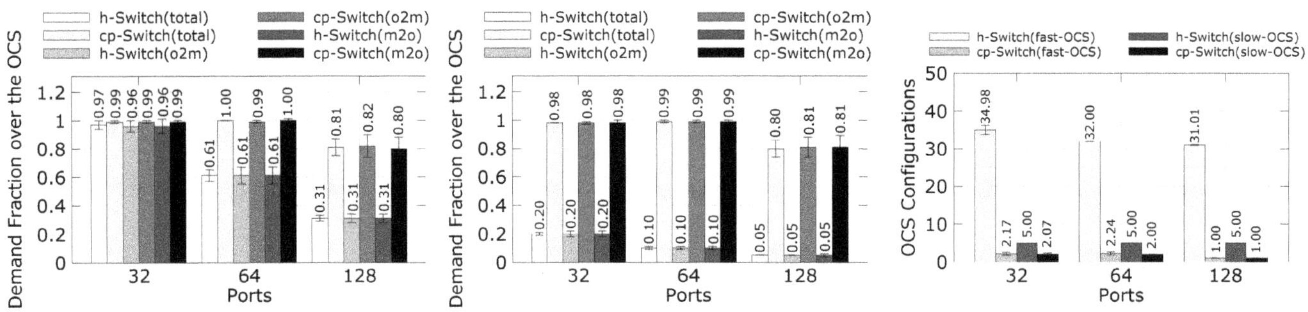

(a) Fast OCS. Window of 1 ms. (b) Slow OCS. Window of 100 ms. (c) OCS configurations.

Figure 6: One-to-Many/Many-to-One Demand Example - Fraction of Demand Served by the OCS (Based on Eclipse). There is a significant degradation of the OCS utilization for h-Switch that is proportional to the switch radix. On the contrary, cp-Switch demonstrates high utilization for 32 and 64 ports, and only a slight degradation for 128 ports. This is because h-Switch with fast OCS spends more than half of the time window on reconfigurations, and with slow OCS more than 80%. On the other hand, cp-Switch requires at most 1-2 reconfigurations on average.

Our Typical Background Demand Modeling: Our typical background demand modeling is based on the DCN measurements presented in [44], and is constructed similarly to the demand used in Eclipse [1] and Solstice [2]. Some of the input ports have four big flows (a.k.a. elephant flows, 30Mb and 3Gb for Fast OCS and Slow OCS, respectively) and 12 small flows (a.k.a. mice flows, 3Mb and 300Mb for Fast OCS and Slow OCS, respectively), where the big flows carry 70% of the demand. The destination of the flows is chosen randomly and uniformly. We refer to this demand as *typical background traffic*.

Evaluation Results: Figures 7(a) and 7(b) present the completion time of the total demand, and the demand that is assigned to the one-to-many and many-to-one composite paths (noted by *o2m* and *m2o*, respectively). The cp-Switch with Fast OCS results in completion time reduction of 15%-70% for the one-to-many and many-to-one demands, and of 9%-37% for the total demand; and the cp-Switch with Slow OCS results in completion time reduction of 11%-75%, and 4%-49%, respectively. The results fit with the number of OCS configurations presented in Figure 7(c); *i.e.*, more OCS configurations result in higher completion time.

Figure 8(a) indicates that the fraction of the demand that is served by the Fast OCS within the $1ms$ period window is 2-3 times higher for cp-Switch, as compared to h-Switch. Figure 8(b) shows that cp-Switch with Slow OCS results in improvements that are 5.4-10 times higher, within the $100ms$ period window. Similarly to the results in Section 3.2, Figure 8(c) shows that Ecplise results in approximately the same number of OCS configurations, independently of the switch radix. Again, the h-Switch with the Fast OCS incurs significant penalty by the OCS reconfigurations, which consumes 62%-72% of its $1ms$ period.

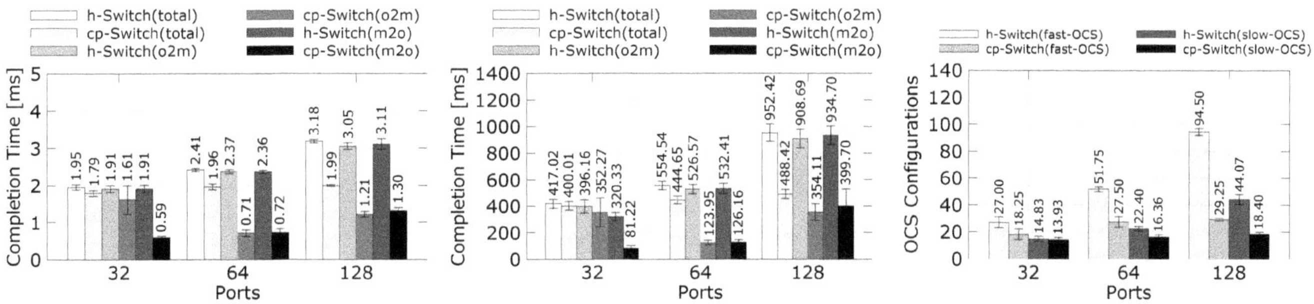

(a) Completion time with Fast OCS. (b) Completion time with Slow OCS. (c) OCS configurations.

Figure 7: Typical DCN with One-to-Many/Many-to-One Demand Example - Completion Time (Solstice Based). In addition to the significantly faster completion time for one-to-many and many-to-one traffic, the completion time of the entire demand decreases by up to 37% and 49% for fast and slow OCS, respectively.

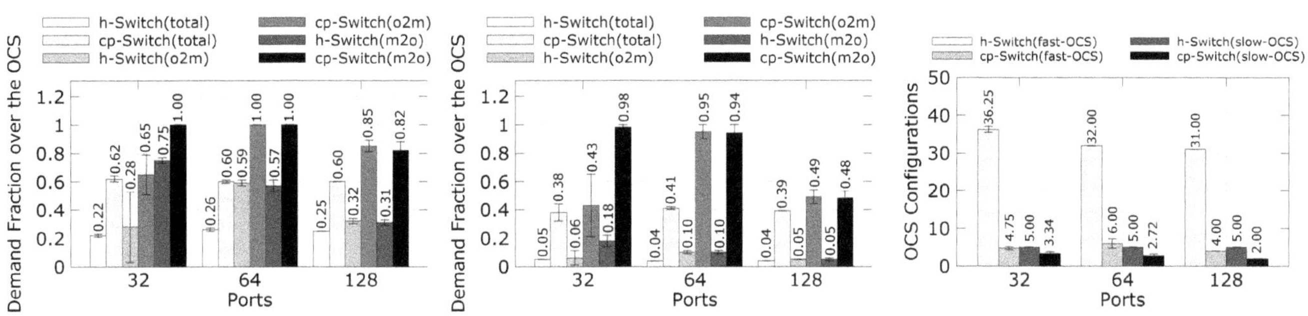

(a) Fast OCS. Window of 1 *ms*. (b) Slow OCS. Window of 100 *ms*. (c) OCS configurations.

Figure 8: Typical DCN with One-to-Many/Many-to-One Demand Example - OCS Utilization (Eclipse Based). The OCS utilization of both h-Switch and cp-Switch for the total demand is similar for each switch radix. The cp-Switch improves the OCS utilization by up to 800%, as compared to h-Switch.

The completion time (by Solstice) and fraction of demand over the OCS (by Eclipse) are improved by cp-Switch over h-Switch for both the total and one-to-many and many-to-one demands. The improvements of the one-to-many and many-to-one demands by cp-Switch clearly result from the use of the composite paths. On the other hand, the improvements of the total demand stem from the following reasons: First, the lower number of OCS reconfigurations as indicated by Figures 7(c) and 8(c). Second, both Solstice and Eclipse perform better when the demand matrix is more sparse and contains similar traffic patterns (*i.e.,* our empirical results that correspond to [1] and [2] show that such matrices are more efficiently decomposed into a smaller set of permutation matrices with a longer duration). It allows both algorithms to use less configurations with a larger duration; hence providing better utilization of the OCS and reducing the completion time of the total demand. Specifically, in these experiments the mean number of non-zero entries in the reduced demand matrix for cp-Switch is lower by $1.63 \cdot n$. Hence, it results in a better scheduling.

3.4 Intensive Typical DCN and One-to-Many/Many-to-One Demand

In this section, in order to stress the cp-Switch scheduler, we create a one-to-many/many-to-one demand (as defined in Section 3.2) together with an intensive typical background demand. To that end, similarly to Solstice scheduler stressing tests, we increase the density of the demand matrix (*i.e.,* non-zero entries) by a factor of four.

Figures 9(a) and 9(b) present the completion time of the total demand, and the demand that is assigned to the one-to-many and many-to-one composite paths (noted by *o2m* and *m2o*, respectively). It can be seen that for switch radix 32, the differences of the completion times between h-Switch and cp-Switch are within 5%. This result stems from the heavy background demand, which dictates the completion time for both switches. In addition, the number of OCS reconfigurations is almost identical, as indicated by Figure 9(c)—causing the completion time of the one-to-many and many-to-one demand to increase as well due to the expensive OCS idle periods. As the switch radix increases

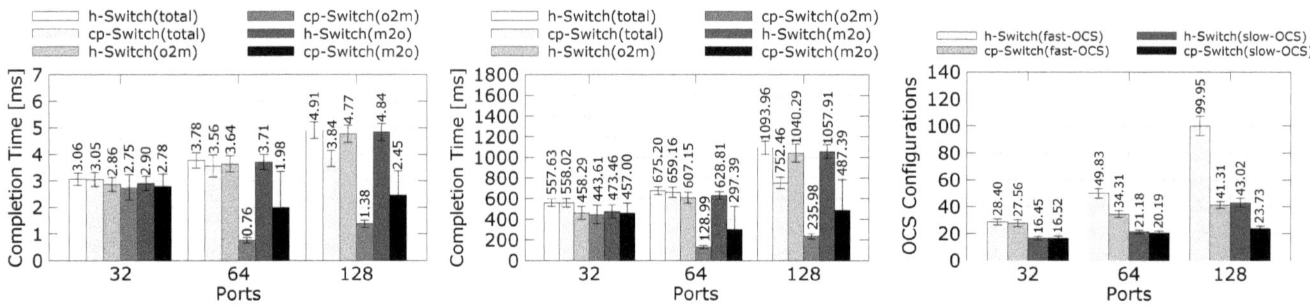

(a) Completion time with Fast OCS. (b) Completion time with Slow OCS. (c) OCS configurations.

Figure 9: Intensive Typical DCN and One-to-Many/Many-to-One Demand - Completion Time (Solstice Based). For 32 and 64 ports, the completion time is similar since it is dominated by the intensive background traffic. However, for 128 ports the completion time of the total demand for cp-Switch decreases by up to 7% and 27% for the fast and slow OCS, respectively.

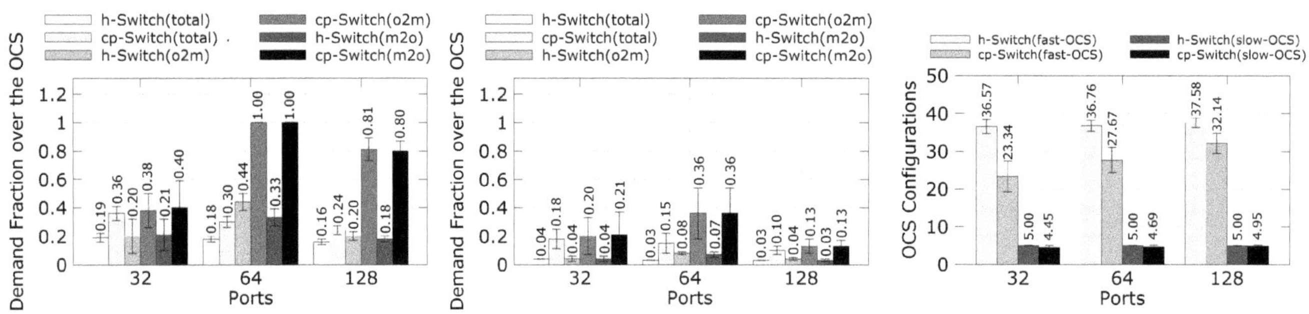

(a) Fast OCS. Window of 1 ms. (b) Slow OCS. Window of 100 ms. (c) OCS configurations.

Figure 10: Intensive Typical DCN and One-to-Many/Many-to-One Demand - OCS Utilization (Eclipse Based). cp-Switch improves the OCS utilization by up to 400%, as compared to h-Switch.

to 64 and 128, cp-Switch improves the completion time of the total demand, as compared to h-Switch, by 6% and 27%, respectively. The improvement stems from the increased number of OCS reconfigurations of h-Switch, as shown in Figure 9(c). On the other hand, cp-Switch significantly improves the completion time of the one-to-many and many-to-one demand by 46%-80%.

Figure 10 demonstrates the same OCS utilization improvement trend as shown in Figure 8. Therefore, we demonstrate the stability of our scheduler, which results in the same improvements also when it is stressed by a higher density demand matrix.

3.5 Typical DCN Traffic and Intensive One-to-Many/Many-to-One Demand

In this section, we create a typical background demand (as defined in Section 3.2) together with a varying one-to-many/many-to-one demand. Specifically, we increase the number of senders and receivers with one-to-many and many-to-one demand from one to six, respectively. These demands are generated such that they are chosen to be served by the composite paths, according to the filtering parameters employed by algorithm 1 for the demand reduction process. We seek the point at which the composite paths are overloaded; *i.e.*, how many one-to-many/many-to-one demand ports can cp-Switch bear?

Figure 11 presents the completion time of the total demand, and the demands that are assigned to the one-to-many and many-to-one composite paths, for switch radix 32, 64, and 128.

For switch radix 128 and more than four ports with one-to-many/many-to-one demand, cp-Switch results in a higher completion time as compared to h-Switch. In such scenarios, enforcing too many one-to-many/many-to-one demand ports over the composite paths results in performance degradation for cp-Switch.

There are several solutions to mitigate the following performance degradation of cp-Switch: First, tuning the filter parameters to select a lower number of ports with one-to-many/many-to-one demand (*i.e.*, increasing R_t and/or decreasing B_t). Second, we can revise the cp-Switch scheduler to limit the number of served one-to-many/many-to-one demand ports over the composite paths. Third, we can increase the number of composite paths in cp-Switch (Further discussed in Section 4).

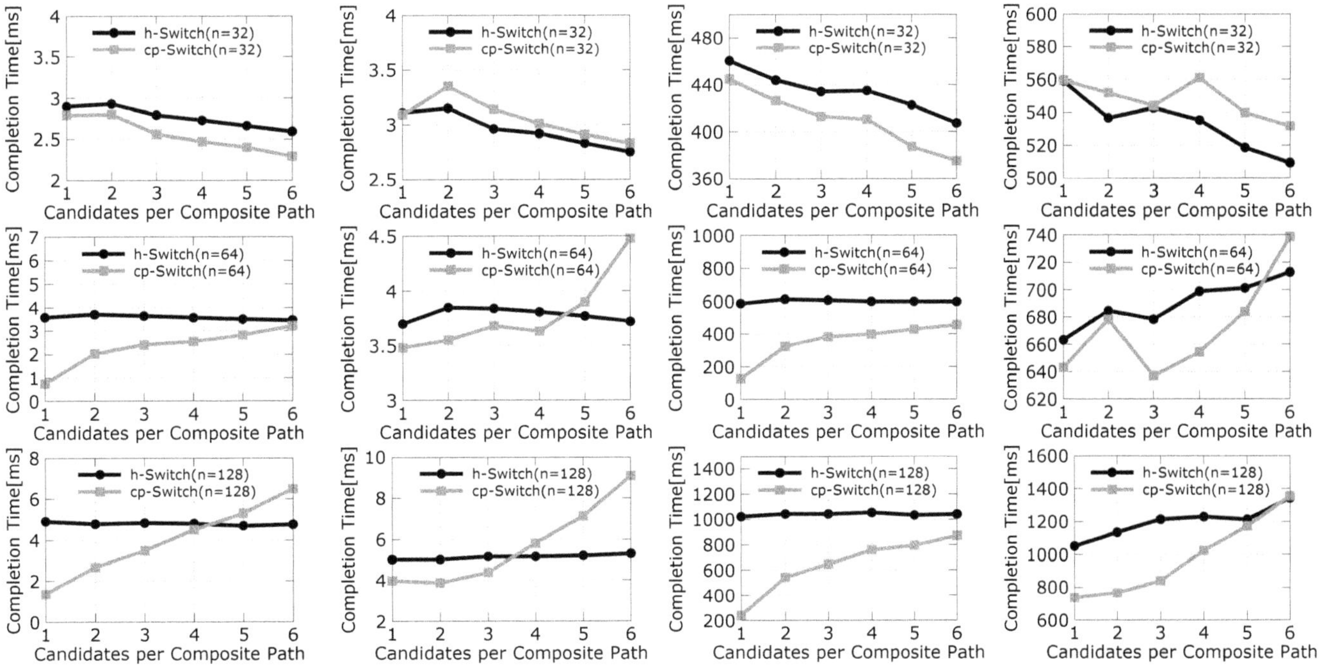

(a) Fast OCS. One-to-many and many-to-one ports. (b) Fast OCS. Total demand completion time. (c) Slow OCS. One-to-many and many-to-one ports. (d) Slow OCS. Total demand completion time.

Figure 11: Typical DCN Traffic and Increasing One-to-Many/Many-to-One Demand. The advantage in favor of cp-Switch decreases as the composite one-to-many and many-to-one paths are overloaded.

4. DISCUSSION AND FUTURE WORK

In this section we discuss possible extensions and future directions for composite-path switching.

Binding the cp-Switch and h-Switch Scheduling Run Times: We want to provide an efficient way to extend a given h-Switch algorithm to cp-Switch scheduling, and thus to *bind* the scheduling feasibility of both systems. Accordingly, in our evaluation, we found that the complexity of CPSwitchSched is dominated by the used h-Switch scheduling algorithm, i.e., Eclipse or Solstice[3]. Specifically, for all switch sizes we test (*i.e.,* 32, 64, 128), the h-Switch scheduling sub-routine takes at least 88% of the cp-Switch algorithm run time. Moreover, as the switch radix grows, this percentage increases and reaches more than 99% for 128 ports under moderate load.

We summarize the comparison between h-Switch and cp-Switch scheduling algorithms run-time in Tables 1 and 2. Since our absolute running times are not optimized (we use a high-level Python implementation for our controller), we emphasize the ratio between h-Switch and cp-Switch algorithms run-time which also corresponds to the theoretical analysis.

[3] In our implementation, the complexity of Eclipse is $(O(n^3 log(n) \cdot \frac{W}{\delta}))$ where W is the time window for the schedule and there are at least n non-zero entries in D. The complexity of Solstice is $O(n^3 log^2(n))$.

n/Ev.	Typical (Figure 7)			Intensive (Figure 9)		
	h-Switch	cp-Switch	**Ratio**	h-Switch	cp-Switch	**Ratio**
32	7.1, 16.5	8.2, 11.1	**0.86, 1.49**	8.3, 14.6	9.2, 14.2	**0.9, 1.03**
64	35.7, 97	31.1, 41.3	**1.48, 2.35**	35.4, 75.5	32.2, 56	**1.1, 1.35**
128	222, 453	111, 154	**2, 2.94**	244, 456	132, 243	**1.85, 1.87**

Table 1: Comparing h-Switch and cp-Switch scheduling run-times using Solstice. Each entry presents the run-time in milliseconds for slow and fast OCS pair, *i.e.,* (slow, fast).

n/Ev.	Typical (Figure 8)			Intensive (Figure 10)		
	h-Switch	cp-Switch	**Ratio**	h-Switch	cp-Switch	**Ratio**
32	15.1, 97.2	9.4, 102	**1.6, 0.95**	146, 1070	86, 480	**1.7, 2.38**
64	55.3, 330	25, 40.2	**2.22, 8.2**	310, 3310	341, 2643	**0.91, 1.25**
128	210, 1350	70, 133	**3, 10.15**	1370, 9340	1020, 6782	**1.35, 1.38**

Table 2: Comparing h-Switch and cp-Switch scheduling run-times using Eclipse. Each entry presents the run-time in milliseconds for slow and fast OCS pair, *i.e.,* (slow, fast).

As can be seen in Tables 1 and 2, in all our experiments, the run time of the scheduling algorithm for cp-Switch was at most 14% slower than for h-Switch when both scheduling algorithms produce similar number of permutation matrices, and mostly much faster, up to an order of magnitude, when the produced number of permutation matrices for cp-Switch is significantly lower. The reason for this is the strong dependence of the scheduling run time in the number of produced permutation matrices, which is consistently lower for cp-Switch, especially as the switch radix grows.

Tuning Heuristic: In our evaluation we set the filtering parameters B_t and R_t according to the intuition provided in Section 2.2. Specifically, B_t and R_t are set to: (1.) capture traffic that utilizes the OCS links of composite paths without overwhelming the corresponding EPS links of each particular source or destination port within these paths; and (2.) make sure that the time to serve each individual entry does not exceed to much the reconfiguration penalty of the OCS—namely, by aggregating such entries to the composite entries, we want to avoid multiple OCS reconfigurations with potentially low utilization.

(1.) R_t is set to filter one-to-many and many-to-one demands with large fan-out relative to the switch radix (*i.e.,* large number of destination/sources, respectively). Hence, we set R_t to be $\beta \cdot n$, where n is the switch radix and β is a factor variable ($0 < \beta \leq 1$). Specifically, in our evaluations we use $\beta = 0.7$, such that the fan-out is high enough to guarantee that the OCS is fully utilized when serving the demand over the composite paths.

(2.) B_t is set to filter demand entries which are suitable for the composite paths, which aggregation avoids the OCS configurations penalty by utilizing the EPS through the composite paths. To that end, such demand entries should be below certain value, in order to sustain the EPS ports bandwidth, and to avoid frequent OCS reconfigurations. Since R_t is already set to utilize the OCS, B_t is set to be proportional to the OCS configuration penalty. Specifically, any demand below a certain value over the OCS results in inefficient utilization and expensive OCS reconfiguration penalty. Therefore, we set B_t to $\alpha \cdot (\delta \cdot C_o)$, where α is a proportion factor. In our evaluations we use $\alpha = 1$ ($B_t = 2Mb$) and $\alpha = 0.1$ ($B_t = 200Mb$) for the Fast OCS and Slow OCS, respectively.

Optimal Tuning: In this work, we did not exhaustively search for the best B_t and R_t. We chose the specific (α, β) pair heuristically according to the provided intuition and by examining the workload. Generally, we have found that providing the best (α, β) pairs to an arbitrary demand is challenging since there is a strong coupling between the algebraic structure of the demand matrix, the switch parameters (*i.e.*, n, C_e, C_o) and the performance of the scheduling algorithms (*i.e.*, some matrices are more easily decomposed to a smaller set of permutation matrices as previously indicated by [1, 2]). Thus, we leave a further study of (α, β) tuning to future work.

Offline Execution: During our work, we have also examined possible reorderings of the permutation matrices execution. Clearly, nor the total completion time neither the average OCS utilization in a given time window are affected by such reordering. In addition, we have found that such a reordering also has a negligible impact on the average completion time of one-to-many and many-to-one traffic in h-Switch (such traffic patterns require multiple OCS reconfigurations to be served via the OCS. Thus, even such a change in the order of execution is limited by the total high penalty of constant reconfigurations and lack of bandwidth of the EPS links to serve such demand). On the contrary, such reordering can reduce the completion time of one-to-many and many-to-one demand in cp-Switch. Specifically, consider a single input port with a demand of a single big flow and many small flows, each sent to a different destination. Then, the scheduler can schedule the big flow over the OCS repeatedly, before the one-to-many traffic has been satisfied. Therefore, in such a case of mixed *big* single flow demand and one-to-many/many-to-one demand, reordering of the permutation matrices can reduce the completion time (termed *offline execution*).

Additional Composite Paths: The tradeoff of having more or less composite paths in cp-Switch is between having the ability to handle more one-to-many and many-to-one traffic on one hand, and under-utilizing high bandwidth EPS ports in the absence of such traffic on the other. Thus the choice of how many composite paths lead to the best performance/price tradeoff is dependent both on the switch radix and on the workload. We examined the benefit of having a single composite path in each direction. However, for high-radix switches it may be beneficial to have more than a single composite path in each direction. In Section 3.5 we demonstrate that for intensive one-to-many/many-to-one demand, cp-Switch might underperform, due to lack of composite paths. To that end, the demand reduction (Algorithm 1) and cp-Switch scheduler (Algorithm 4) should be extended.

Specifically, the desired extension to handle k composite paths in each direction should preserve the ability of using h-Switch scheduling technique as a subroutine in order to make cp-Switch scheduling more tractable and leverage state-of-the-art evolving h-Switch scheduling techniques to cp-Switch scheduling.

To that end, the reduced demand matrix D_I has additional k rows and k columns to represent the composite paths (*i.e.,* a row for each many-to-one composite-path and a column for each many-to-one composite-path). Then, we need to decide during the demand filtering process (Algorithm 1) how to balance the traffic among the k composite paths. This is achieved by extending lines 7, 10 and 13 in Algorithm 1 to consider the minimal composite entry so far. This can be done efficiently by using priority queues to hold the minimal composite entries among the different paths. Thus, the resulting complexity of Algorithm 1 is $O(log(k) \cdot (n + k)^2)$. The extensions to Algorithms 2, 3 and 4 are straightforward resulting in a total complexity of $O(\max\{m \cdot (n + k)^2, \text{h-Switch-Scheduling}\})$ for Algorithm 4.

Scaling: As depicted in Figure 1, cp-Switch is composed of both EPS and OCS planes; therefore, one should scale both of the planes in order to scale the cp-Switch. First, scaling the EPS plane can be done using different multi-layer topologies (*e.g.,* , Folded-Clos or Fat-Tree). Furthermore, current electronic packet switches already offer for example 128 ports of 25 Gbps [46], and their radix is regularly increased. Second, OCS systems also offer a higher radix either using switches with a high radix (*e.g.,* of about 1,000 ports [47]), or using Folded-Clos optical cross-connect fabrics that can scale incrementally to tens of thousands of ports [48].

Augmenting Hybrid Architectures: Current hybrid architectures present topologies with a hard separation between the OCS and the EPS switching planes. As we showed in this work, integrating between the two fabrics using composite paths has the potential to better support modern data center traffic and provide better flow completion times and better link utilization. For example: (a) a leaf-spine hybrid solution such as [3] can be extended by connecting among the OCS and the EPS spines. Clearly, the exact number of the suggested connections is highly dependent on the number of OCS and EPS spines as well as on the typical workload. (b) Three tier hybrid solutions such as [5] can be extended by connecting the OCS to the aggregation layer switches on top of the ToR switches, thus allowing composite-paths among them.

Additional Use Cases: As mentioned, cp-Switches can be used to connect among servers and/or among ToR switches. As such, they can handle more traffic patterns. In addition, cp-switches can be used for special uses such as ToRs in specific racks that require one-to-many and many-to-one traffic support that nowadays cannot be served efficiently by a hybrid switch, *e.g.,* storage racks and especially object storage [49].

5. RELATED WORK

Hybrid Switching: One of the very first comprehensive works that advocated OCS for the DCN [50] has considered HPC workloads with static or semi-static traffic patterns. Such traffic patterns naturally benefit from offloading the long lived one-to-one data transfers to high capacity optical circuits, while sending the rest of the traffic over traditional EPS. Follow up works, *e.g.,* Helios [3] and c-Through [5], have refined the approach and presented different methods for identifying big one-to-one flows, heuristics for circuits scheduling, and control planes for sending the traffic over EPS and OCS paths. REACToR [6] leveraged a microsecond scale Mordia [51] optical circuit switch and proposed a control plane which synchronizes end host transmissions with end-to-end circuit assignments over a hybrid network. Their control plane is designed to react to rapid, bursty changes in the traffic from end hosts on a time scale of 100s of microseconds. XFabric [41] suggested a *rack-scale* network that reconfigures the topology and uplink placement using a circuit-switched physical layer over which System-on-Chips perform packet switching.

Free Space Optics: FireFly [52] suggested free-space optics (FSO) as a potential technology to provide flexible wireless interconnect throughout the data center network. An additional advancement was made by ProjecTor [53] that suggested to use digital micromirror devices (DMDs), instead of the Galvo or switchable mirrors used by Firefly, which enable a single transmitter to reach high fan-out and a microseconds scale reconfiguration time periods.

In a sense, an FSO system can be logically viewed as a high radix distributed OCS, thus shares its scheduling disadvantages. Accordingly, we believe that FSO can also benefit from composite-paths. Consider a rack producing one-to-many coflows. Then in a pure FSO system, such traffic, in order to be served quickly can repeatedly occupy multiple DMDs for short time periods causing poor circuit utilization due to the reconfiguration penalties, or alternatively suffer from large completion times waiting for multiple reconfigurations of fewer DMDs. Such an FSO system can reach higher utilization when augmented by low-bandwidth EPS system with fewer high-bandwidth EPS ports reachable by DMDs.

6. CONCLUSIONS

In this work, we introduced the *composite path switch* to deal with skewed one-to-many and many-to-one coflows. We explained how it efficiently extends hybrid circuit/packet switches and allows them to efficiently support modern datacenter workloads.

We also tackled the challenge of simplifying cp-Switch scheduling so as to leverage state-of-the-art hybrid-switch scheduling techniques, by building a reduced demand matrix, filtering irrelevant traffic, scheduling flows within a composite path and reserving specific packet-switching slots. Finally, using extensive evaluation, we demonstrated that the composite-path switch is capable of accommodating more traffic patterns while improving significantly both the flow completion time and the circuit utilization metrics.

Looking forward, our results open new opportunities for leveraging the reconfiguration capabilities of contemporary optical circuit switches for scaling modern data center networks and modern application workloads.

7. ACKNOWLEDGMENTS

The authors would like to thank Eitan Zahavi, Tal Mizrahi, our shepherd Paolo Costa and our anonymous reviewers for their helpful comments. The research leading to results published in this paper was partially supported by the European Community's Seventh Framework Programme (FP7/2001-2013) under grant agreement number 619572, in the context of the COSIGN Project, as well as by the Hasso Plattner Institute Research School, the Technion Fund for Security Research, the Gordon Fund for Systems Engineering, and the Israel Ministry of Science and Technology.

8. REFERENCES

[1] Shaileshh Bojja, Mohammad Alizadeh, and Pramod Viswanath. Costly circuits, submodular schedules and approximate Carathéodory theorems. *ACM Sigmetrics*, 2015.

[2] He Liu, Matthew K Mukerjee, Conglong Li, et al. Scheduling techniques for hybrid circuit/packet networks. *ACM CoNEXT*, 2015.

[3] Nathan Farrington et al. Helios: a hybrid electrical/optical switch architecture for modular data centers. *ACM SIGCOMM Computer Communication Review*, 2011.

[4] George Porter, Richard Strong, Nathan Farrington, et al. *Integrating microsecond circuit switching into the data center.* ACM SIGCOMM, 2013.

[5] Guohui Wang, David G Andersen, Michael Kaminsky, et al. c-Through: Part-time optics in data centers. *ACM SIGCOMM Computer Communication Review*, 2011.

[6] He Liu, Feng Lu, Alex Forencich, Rishi Kapoor, et al. Circuit switching under the radar with reactor. In *ACM/USENIX NSDI*, 2014.

[7] Christoforos Kachris, Konstantinos Kanonakis, and Ioannis Tomkos. Optical interconnection networks in data centers: recent trends and future challenges. *Communications Magazine, IEEE*, 2013.

[8] Nathan Farrington, George Porter, Yeshaiahu Fainman, George Papen, and Amin Vahdat. Hunting mice with microsecond circuit switches. In *Proc. ACM Workshop on Hot Topics in Networks*, 2012.

[9] Bin Wu and Kwan L Yeung. Nxg05-6: Minimum delay scheduling in scalable hybrid electronic/optical packet switches. In *Global Telecommunications Conference, 2006. GLOBECOM'06. IEEE*, pages 1–5. IEEE, 2006.

[10] Shoaib Kamil, Ali Pinar, Daniel Gunter, et al. Reconfigurable hybrid interconnection for static and dynamic scientific applications. In *Proceedings of the 4th international conference on Computing frontiers*, 2007.

[11] Howard Wang, Yiting Xia, Keren Bergman, TS Ng, Sambit Sahu, and Kunwadee Sripanidkulchai. Rethinking the physical layer of data center networks of the next decade: Using optics to enable efficient*-cast connectivity. *ACM SIGCOMM Computer Communication Review*, 2013.

[12] Mosharaf Chowdhury, Yuan Zhong, and Ion Stoica. Efficient coflow scheduling with varys. In *ACM SIGCOMM Computer Communication Review*, 2014.

[13] Yangming Zhao, Kai Chen, Wei Bai, et al. Rapier: Integrating routing and scheduling for coflow-aware data center networks. In *Computer Communications (INFOCOM), 2015 IEEE Conference on*, 2015.

[14] Zhen Qiu, Cliff Stein, and Yuan Zhong. Minimizing the total weighted completion time of coflows in datacenter networks. In *Proceedings of the 27th ACM on Symposium on Parallelism in Algorithms and Architectures*, 2015.

[15] Mosharaf Chowdhury and Ion Stoica. Coflow: A networking abstraction for cluster applications. In *Proceedings of the 11th ACM Workshop on Hot Topics in Networks*, 2012.

[16] Michael Isard et al. Dryad: distributed data-parallel programs from sequential building blocks. In *ACM SIGOPS Operating Systems Review*, 2007.

[17] Grzegorz Malewicz, Matthew H Austern, Aart JC Bik, et al. Pregel: a system for large-scale graph processing. In *ACM SIGMOD*, 2010.

[18] Dhruba Borthakur. The hadoop distributed file system: Architecture and design. *Hadoop Project Website*, 2007.

[19] Mosharaf Chowdhury, Srikanth Kandula, and Ion Stoica. Leveraging endpoint flexibility in data-intensive clusters. In *ACM SIGCOMM Computer Communication Review*, 2013.

[20] Matei Zaharia, Mosharaf Chowdhury, Tathagata Das, et al. Resilient distributed datasets: A fault-tolerant abstraction for in-memory cluster computing. In *Proceedings of the 9th USENIX conference on Networked Systems Design and Implementation*, 2012.

[21] Christo Wilson, Hitesh Ballani, Thomas Karagiannis, and Ant Rowtron. Better never than late: Meeting deadlines in datacenter networks. In *ACM SIGCOMM Computer Communication Review*, 2011.

[22] Jeffrey Dean and Sanjay Ghemawat. Mapreduce: simplified data processing on large clusters. *Communications of the ACM*, 2008.

[23] Mohammad Alizadeh, Albert Greenberg, David A Maltz, et al. Data center tcp (dctcp). In *ACM SIGCOMM computer communication review*, 2010.

[24] Pawan Prakash, Advait Dixit, Y Charlie Hu, and Ramana Kompella. The tcp outcast problem: exposing unfairness in data center networks. In *Proceedings of the 9th USENIX conference on Networked Systems Design and Implementation*, 2012.

[25] Mosharaf Chowdhury, Matei Zaharia, Justin Ma, Michael I Jordan, and Ion Stoica. Managing data transfers in computer clusters with orchestra. *ACM SIGCOMM Computer Communication Review*, 2011.

[26] Fahad R Dogar, Thomas Karagiannis, Hitesh Ballani, and Antony Rowstron. Decentralized

task-aware scheduling for data center networks. In *ACM SIGCOMM Computer Communication Review*, 2014.

[27] Nick McKeown, Martin Izzard, Adisak Mekkittikul, William Ellersick, and Mark Horowitz. Tiny tera: a packet switch core. *Micro, IEEE*, 1997.

[28] Balaji Prabhakar and Nick McKeown. On the speedup required for combined input-and output-queued switching. *Automatica*, 1999.

[29] Mellanox SN2410 Switch System. http://www.mellanox.com/related-docs/prod_eth_switches/PB_SN2410.pdf.

[30] Arista 7280R Series Data Center Switch Router. https://www.arista.com/assets/data/pdf/Datasheets/7280R-DataSheet.pdf.

[31] Cisco Nexus 93180YC-EX Switch. http://www.cisco.com/c/en/us/products/collateral/switches/nexus-93108tc-ex-switch/datasheet-c78-736651.html.

[32] IEEE Standard for a Precision Clock Synchronization Protocol for Networked Measurement and Control Systems. *IEEE Std 1588-2008 (Revision of IEEE Std 1588-2002)*, pages 1–269, July 2008.

[33] Jonathan Perry, Amy Ousterhout, Hari Balakrishnan, Devavrat Shah, and Hans Fugal. Fastpass: A centralized zero-queue datacenter network. In *ACM SIGCOMM Computer Communication Review*, volume 44, pages 307–318. ACM, 2014.

[34] Pedro Moreira et al. White rabbit: Sub-nanosecond timing distribution over ethernet. In *2009 International Symposium on Precision Clock Synchronization for Measurement, Control and Communication*, pages 1–5. IEEE, 2009.

[35] Steven Blake, David Black, Mark Carlson, Elwyn Davies, Zheng Wang, and Walter Weiss. An architecture for differentiated services. 1998.

[36] CCITT Recommendation. I. 371: Traffic control and congestion control in b-isdn. *Geneva, Study Group*, 13, 1992.

[37] Cisco Tech Notes. Comparing traffic policing and traffic shaping for bandwidth limiting. *Document ID*, 19645:22–42.

[38] ITUT SGI. Traffic control and congestion control in b-isdn. *ITU-T Rec*, 1.

[39] John William Evans and Clarence Filsfils. *Deploying IP and MPLS QoS for Multiservice Networks: Theory & Practice*. Morgan Kaufmann, 2010.

[40] Cisco DocWiki. Resource Reservation Protocol. http://docwiki.cisco.com/wiki/Resource_Reservation_Protocol.

[41] Sergey Legtchenko, Nicholas Chen, Daniel Cletheroe, et al. Xfabric: a reconfigurable in-rack network for rack-scale computers. In *13th USENIX Symposium on Networked Systems Design and Implementation (NSDI 16)*, 2016.

[42] Kai Chen et al. OSA: An Optical Switching Architecture for Data Center Networks With Unprecedented Flexibility. *Networking, IEEE/ACM Transactions on*, 2014.

[43] Polatis 6000n Protection Services Switch Data Sheet. http://www.polatis.com/datasheets/products/Polatis_6000n_Protection_Services_Switch_Data_Sheet.pdf.

[44] Theophilus Benson, Aditya Akella, and David A Maltz. Network traffic characteristics of data centers in the wild. In *Proceedings of the 10th ACM SIGCOMM conference on Internet measurement*, 2010.

[45] Yossi Azar and Iftah Gamzu. Efficient submodular function maximization under linear packing constraints. In *Automata, Languages, and Programming*. 2012.

[46] High-Density 25/100 Gigabit Ethernet StrataXGS Tomahawk Ethernet Switch Series. https://www.broadcom.com/products/ethernet-communication-and-switching/switching/bcm56960-series.

[47] Dan Alistarh, Hitesh Ballani, Paolo Costa, Adam Funnell, Joshua Benjamin, Philip Watts, and Benn Thomsen. A high-radix, low-latency optical switch for data centers. In *ACM SIGCOMM Computer Communication Review*, 2015.

[48] SDN-Enabled All-Optical Circuit Switching: An Answer to Data Center Bandwidth Challenges. https://www.sdxcentral.com/wp-content/uploads/2015/02/Polatis-SDN-Enabled-All-Optical-Circuit-Switching.pdf.

[49] Mike Mesnier, Gregory R Ganger, and Erik Riedel. Object-based storage. *IEEE Communications Magazine*, 2003.

[50] Kevin J Barker, Alan Benner, Ray Hoare, et al. On the feasibility of optical circuit switching for high performance computing systems. In *Proceedings of the 2005 ACM/IEEE conference on Supercomputing*. IEEE Computer Society, 2005.

[51] George Porter, Richard Strong, Nathan Farrington, Alex Forencich, et al. Integrating microsecond circuit switching into the data center. In *Proc. ACM SIGCOMM.*, 2013.

[52] Navid Hamedazimi, Zafar Qazi, Himanshu Gupta, et al. Firefly: a reconfigurable wireless data center fabric using free-space optics. *ACM SIGCOMM Computer Communication Review*, 2015.

[53] Monia Ghobadi, Ratul Mahajan, Amar Phanishayee, et al. Projector: Agile reconfigurable data center interconnect. In *ACM SIGCOMM*, 2016.

Source Accountability with Domain-brokered Privacy

Taeho Lee, Christos Pappas, David Barrera, Pawel Szalachowski, Adrian Perrig
ETH Zürich
{kthlee, pappasch, david.barrera, psz, adrian.perrig}@inf.ethz.ch

ABSTRACT

In an ideal Internet, every packet would be attributable to its sender, while host identities and transmitted content would remain private. Designing such a network is challenging because source accountability and communication privacy are typically viewed as conflicting properties. In this paper, we propose an architecture that guarantees source accountability and privacy-preserving communication by enlisting ISPs as accountability agents and privacy brokers. While ISPs can link every packet that originates from their network to their customers, customer identity remains unknown to the rest of the Internet. In our architecture, network communication is based on Ephemeral Identifiers (EphIDs)—cryptographic tokens that can be linked to a source only by the source's ISP. We demonstrate that EphIDs can be generated and processed efficiently, and we analyze the practical considerations for deployment.

1. INTRODUCTION

The commercialization of the Internet and its integral role in our daily lives have spawned a debate on privacy and accountability—a long-standing discussion about two properties that are typically considered conflicting. Unfortunately, today's Internet does not provide native support for either. We propose an architecture that resolves the accountability-privacy tussle and guarantees network-level *source accountability* without forfeiting end-to-end *communication privacy*.

On one end of the spectrum, source accountability protects the integrity of the source's identity and holds the source responsible for any traffic that it originates. The lack of source accountability has become a Pandora's box for Internet security. Attackers spoof their addresses and launch massive reflection attacks exhausting the available network resources. IP spoofing makes it impossible to identify the actual attacker and renders traffic filtering ineffective, not to mention the collateral damage when incorrectly blocking benign hosts.

On the other end of the spectrum is privacy. Recent revelations of pervasive monitoring and mass surveillance [1–3] have increased users' interest in communication privacy. Users know that their identities and network traffic are being systematically collected by state-level entities. The lack of native support for private communication in the Internet forces users to rely on overlay networks and specialized applications to obtain privacy guarantees [4, 5]. These solutions are complex to install and manage, and degrade application performance.

To date, the research community has mainly investigated approaches that favor either privacy or accountability, typically offering one at the expense of the other. To our knowledge, the Accountable and Private Internet Protocol (APIP) is the main proposal that has aimed to find a balance between the two properties at the network layer [6]. However, the privacy guarantees are constrained to source anonymity; data privacy is not addressed but delegated to conventional protocols, such as IPsec [7] and its key-exchange protocol (IKE [8]) that in themselves do not explicitly address a critical problem: certificate management (e.g., issuance, revocation) at Internet-scale.

In this paper, we propose an Accountable and Private Network Architecture (APNA) that provides source accountability guarantees *and* privacy-preserving communication. Our notion of communication privacy covers host privacy (for the source and destination) and data privacy—host privacy means that the identity of the host (e.g., IP address) remains private and data privacy means that the transmitted data remains secret from unintended recipients.

To provide such properties, we enlist Internet Service Providers (ISPs) as a fundamental component of our architecture for several reasons. First, we build on past efforts to hold Autonomous Systems (ASes) accountable for malicious traffic generated within their domain [9, 10]. Second, we believe ISPs have business incentives to provide privacy features to their customers, especially in light of recent revelations regarding global surveillance. In APNA, ISPs facilitate connection establishment between communicating hosts, but traffic encryption is still performed directly by communica-

CoNEXT '16, December 12–15, 2016, Irvine, CA, USA.
© 2016 ACM. ISBN 978-1-4503-4292-6/16/12...$15.00
DOI: http://dx.doi.org/10.1145/2999572.2999581

tion endpoints, keeping communication content hidden even from their ISPs.

In our scheme, network communication is based on Ephemeral IDentifiers (EphIDs) instead of long-lived network addresses, such as IP addresses. ASes issue EphIDs and assign them to their customer hosts as tokens of approval for communication. EphIDs are designed to mask the host address in the network, providing host privacy, while still functioning as a return address. In addition, EphIDs are bound to short-lived and domain-certified public/private key pairs. These keys are used by hosts to mutually authenticate each other and to negotiate a shared secret key, which allows native payload secrecy through network-layer traffic encryption.

The privacy architecture proposed in this paper, which establishes shared keys based on EphIDs, by default encrypts all payload data. Pervasive encryption frustrates large-scale surveillance by obfuscating all communicated content. Moreover, the encryption scheme provides Perfect Forward Secrecy (PFS) such that an adversary that obtains all long-term keys cannot decrypt the content of previous communication sessions.

EphIDs are cryptographically linked to the identity of a host and serve as accountability units. ISPs issue and assign EphIDs only to their authenticated customers, thus bootstrapping source accountability. We argue that ISPs are the natural accountability agents in today's Internet since they already know the identities of their customers. Furthermore, we describe a shutoff protocol [11], which is a common security mechanism relying on source accountability. A complaining destination host instructs an ISP to block outgoing traffic from a customer-host that is associated with an EphID. The accountable identifiers allow an ISP to first verify that a customer has indeed sent traffic to a certain destination and then to prohibit any further communication.

Contributions: This paper proposes a cohesive architecture, the Accountable and Private Network Architecture (APNA), that simultaneously guarantees accountability and protects privacy by involving ASes as accountability agents and privacy brokers. In particular, APNA achieves the following properties:

- Source accountability by linking every packet in the network to its originating source.
- Host privacy by hiding the host's identity from every entity except the host's AS.
- Data privacy by supporting network-layer encryption with perfect forward secrecy.
- Support for a shutoff protocol that terminates unwanted communication sessions.

2. PROBLEM DEFINITION

Our goal is to design a network architecture that simultaneously supports source accountability while preserving communication privacy. This section describes the necessary requirements to realize these seemingly conflicting goals, the security properties we strive to achieve, and the adversary model we consider.

2.1 Source Accountability

Source accountability refers to an unforgeable link between the identity of a sender host and the sent packet. Thus, accountability ensures that a source cannot deny having sent a packet and a host cannot be falsely accused of having sent a packet which it did not send.

Achieving source accountability in practice translates to two fundamental requirements. First, a strong notion of host identity is necessary so that hosts cannot create multiple identities nor impersonate other hosts. Second, a link between the source's identity and all of its traffic must be established. This link must be established (or at least confirmed) by a third-party (e.g., source AS) that is not the sender itself, since senders themselves can be malicious. To this end, the third party must observe all of the sender's traffic such that every packet in the network can be linked to a specific sender.

Adversary Model: The goal of the adversary is to break source accountability by creating a packet that is attributed to someone else in the network. We assume that the adversary can reside in multiple ASes and that she can see all packets within those ASes. Specifically, the adversary can eavesdrop on all control and data messages in the network, but cannot compromise the secret keys of the ASes that it resides in.

2.2 Communication Privacy

Our first goal with respect to privacy at the network layer is host privacy. To achieve host privacy, the identity of a host must be hidden from any other host in the source AS that is not in the same broadcast domain as the host (e.g., on the same WiFi network or LAN segment), any transit network that forwards traffic, as well as the destination AS (including the communication peer). A host cannot hide from its AS, since the AS knows the identity and network attachment point of every customer; and, a host cannot hide from other hosts in the same broadcast domain, since the layer-2 address is visible. We address host privacy at the network layer, which means that network-layer headers should not leak identity information. A host's identity may still leak at higher layers (e.g., HTTP cookies); however, these aspects are out of scope for this paper.

In addition, our notion of host privacy includes sender-flow unlinkability [12]: simply by observing packet contents (both headers and payloads) of any number of flows originating from the same AS, the source(s) of the flows are no more and no less related after the observation than they were before the observation.

Our second goal is data privacy through pervasive end-to-end encryption. Transmitted data should be hidden from unintended recipients, including the source and destination ASes. To this end, the architecture must natively (i.e., without relying on upper-layer protocols) provide secure key establishment between hosts and protection against Man-in-the-Middle (MitM) attacks.

Moreover, our notion of data privacy includes perfect forward secrecy (PFS): disclosure of long-term secret keying material does not compromise the secrecy of exchanged keys from past sessions and thus data privacy of prior communication sessions is guaranteed [13, p. 496].

Adversary Model: Breaking *host privacy* means that an adversary can determine the identity of a sender, or can determine if two flows from the same source AS originate from the same host. We assume that the adversary can control any entity in the Internet except for the source host, hosts that are in the same broadcast domain as the source host, and the source AS itself. The adversary can observe packet headers and content, but we do not consider timing analysis techniques, such as inter-packet arrival times.

We argue that the architecture should provide only the basic building blocks to achieve host privacy at the network layer; stronger privacy guarantees (e.g., resiliency against timing analysis) should be provided by protocols at a higher layer (e.g., transport protocol). For instance, a transport protocol could implement a packet scheduling algorithm that alters timing between packets to mitigate traffic identification based on inter-packet timing analysis [14–17]. Our argument is grounded by the fact that strong privacy guarantees often come at the expense of network performance, and not every user (or application) requires strong privacy guarantees. Hence, protocols that offer stronger privacy guarantees are left to upper layers so that users can choose the appropriate protocol based on their requirements.

An adversary can try to compromise *data privacy* by decrypting the communication content exchanged between two hosts. To this end, we assume that the adversary can control any entity in the Internet except for the two communicating hosts and one of the two ASes that the hosts reside in.

2.3 Additional Goals

Shutoff Functionality: An accountability architecture can provide security mechanisms that build on top of accountable addresses. A shutoff mechanism is commonly used to terminate any active communication session flagged for misbehavior. The architecture must ensure that the shutoff mechanism does not create other attack vectors, such as denial-of-service through non-permitted shutoff requests.

Support for Network Feedback: The architecture must allow the network to communicate back to the source without revealing the identity of the source. Feedback from the network is crucial for network-diagnostic and management tools, such as ICMP.

3. APNA OVERVIEW

This section describes the components of our Accountable and Private Network Architecture (APNA), beginning with the role of the ASes (Section 3.1), followed by the use of ephemeral identifiers (Section 3.2), and ending with an end-to-end communication example (Section 3.3).

3.1 Role of ASes

In APNA, ASes act both as accountability agents and as privacy brokers due to their position in the network. Since ASes already know the identity and the physical attachment point of their customers, they naturally act as *accountability agents*. At the same time, ASes mask their customers' identities from all other entities, and thus act as *host-privacy brokers*. In addition, ASes certify their customer-related information (e.g., public keys), which is then used to generate keys for pervasive data encryption at the network layer; thus ASes act as *data-privacy brokers*.

Accountability Functions: As an accountability agent, the AS performs the following functions.

First, the AS creates a strong notion of host identity. To this end, the AS ensures that subscribers do not create and use multiple unauthorized identities for their communication. ASes already authenticate their customers and are thus selected as accountability agents.

Second, the AS creates a link between the identity of the source and the sent packet. To this end, the AS can store every packet or insert a cryptographic mark into every packet. Regardless of the implementation, the AS is on the forwarding path of all the traffic originating from its customers and is therefore selected to establish this link. Using any other third party, which is not on the traffic path, as an accountability agent would require additional mechanisms to report every packet to the third party [6].

Third, the AS realizes the shutoff functionality by accepting (and validating) shutoff requests and blocking the corresponding flows. An AS is in a strategic position to block malicious traffic since it is close to the source and can stop traffic before it leaves its network.

Privacy Functions: As a privacy broker, the AS performs the following functions.

First, the AS issues an Ephemeral IDentifier (EphID) that a host uses to mask his identity by using it as the source address. This identifier serves as a privacy-preserving return address and thus does not break bidirectional communication. However, EphIDs must be bound to specific hosts; and, since ASes know the identities of the hosts, they are well suited to perform this binding and act as host-privacy brokers. We provide more details on EphIDs in the following section.

Second, the AS acts as a certificate issuer, certifying that a public key indeed belongs to a host in the AS's network. More specifically, the AS certifies the binding between an ephemeral identifier that is issued to a host and a public key that is bound to the identifier. Hence, the AS becomes a data-privacy broker without revealing the identity of its customers.

3.2 Ephemeral IDs

At the heart of our proposal is the use of ephemeral identifiers instead of addresses. An EphID is an identifier associated with the identity of a host, yet it does not leak identity information. Since ASes know the identities of their customers, issuing EphIDs to their connected hosts enables the hosts to hide their identity without sacrificing accountability.

EphID as an Accountability Unit: As an accountability unit, an EphID is an authorization token for communication that is issued by the AS to its customer hosts. Issuing these tokens requires strong host authentication: the host must first prove its identity to the AS and only then EphIDs can be issued.

In APNA, a host is represented to its AS through a Host Identifier (HID). An HID could be a hash of the host's public key or a number that is assigned by the AS to the host (e.g., IPv4 address). We do not specify how an AS assigns HIDs, but require that HIDs be unique within the AS's boundary. There can be multiple EphIDs that are associated with an HID, and the EphIDs are cryptographically bound to the HID such that only the host's AS can determine the binding. Furthermore, an EphID serves as the accountability unit for shutoff requests. A shutoff request against an EphID terminates all flows of the host that use that EphID as the source identifier. In other words, flows with the same source EphID are fate-sharing with respect to the shutoff protocol. Blacklisting source EphIDs instead of source and destination EphID pairs forces hosts to carefully manage their pool of assigned EphIDs.

EphID as a Privacy Unit: The EphID has two roles as a privacy unit: it hides the identity of a host and provides a tool to achieve sender-flow unlinkability. An EphID is meaningful only to the issuing AS and opaque to all other parties. It reveals no information about the host's identity to other hosts inside the same AS nor to the peer host that the host is communicating with.

EphIDs alone are insufficient for routing packets to a destination, since location information is missing; and, in APNA, the location information is provided at the granularity of ASes. Hence, a host is fully addressed by an AS Identifier (AID) and EphID tuple (i.e., AID:EphID) where the AID identifies the AS in which the host resides (e.g., Autonomous System Number), and the EphID is the ephemeral identifier issued to the host by the corresponding AS. Hence, the only leaked information is the AS where the host resides; the host's anonymity set becomes the size of the AS in terms of number of hosts.

In addition, decoupling the identity from the address provides a means to achieve sender-flow unlinkability. A host can be issued multiple EphIDs and can use them at will, e.g., a single EphID for all flows or a different EphID for every flow. We do not impose any requirements on how EphIDs are used. We discuss different granularities of EphIDs in Section 8.1.

3.3 Communication Example

We describe the high-level workflow for communication between two hosts (Figure 1). The protocol details are provided in Section 4.

An AS needs to manage its hosts; issue and manage EphIDs; and authenticate packets that its hosts send. For these tasks, the following logical entities are present in every AS:

- **Registry Service (RS)**: authenticates and bootstraps hosts in the AS.
- **Management Service (MS)**: issues EphIDs to the hosts.
- **Border Router (BR)**: handles incoming and outgoing packets based on the AID:EphID tuple.
- **Accountability Agent (AA)**: handles shutoff requests against the hosts in the AS.

In Figure 1, a host in AS_A initiates communication with a host in AS_B. Communication proceeds in four steps:

1. **Host Bootstrapping:** the host authenticates to the RS of its AS and receives bootstrapping information.
2. **EphID Issuance:** the host contacts the MS of its AS to obtain an EphID.
3. **Connection Establishment:** the hosts know each other's AID:EphID identifiers and establish a shared key that will be used for network-layer data encryption. The shared key is derived from public keys that are associated with the EphIDs. In Section 7.1, we describe how hosts can obtain the necessary communication information through DNS.
4. **Encrypted Communication:** the hosts proceed with the actual communication by using their AID:EphID tuples instead of network addresses and by encrypting every packet with their shared symmetric key.

4. APNA PROTOCOL DETAILS

To construct a lightweight and efficient architecture, APNA is built under consideration of the following design choices:

- Symmetric encryption is used to cryptographically link EphIDs with HIDs; this allows an AS to efficiently obtain the HID from the EphID without a mapping table, which can be large.
- Proof of sending a packet is embedded in the packet, avoiding large amounts of stored state at ASes.
- Forwarding devices perform only symmetric cryptographic operations, guaranteeing high forwarding performance.

We begin by stating our assumptions and proceed with the details of the steps that are shown in our communication example (Section 3.3). Table 1 summarizes the notation we use throughout the protocol description.

4.1 Assumptions

- *We assume that the cryptographic primitives we use are secure.* For instance, we assume that authenticated encryption is used for encrypting data communication, securing data communication against chosen-ciphertext attacks (i.e., CCA-secure). We also require that the generation of EphIDs to be CCA-secure; in Section 5.1.1, we describe an efficient CCA-secure encryption scheme for generating EphIDs.
- *Participating parties can retrieve and verify the public keys of ASes.* For example, a scheme such as RPKI [18] can be used to verify the public keys of the corresponding ASes. For simplicity, ASes use the same public/private key pairs for 1) signing messages, and 2) key exchanges. In a real-world deployment, these two keys would be different, and the key used for signing messages would be registered with RPKI.

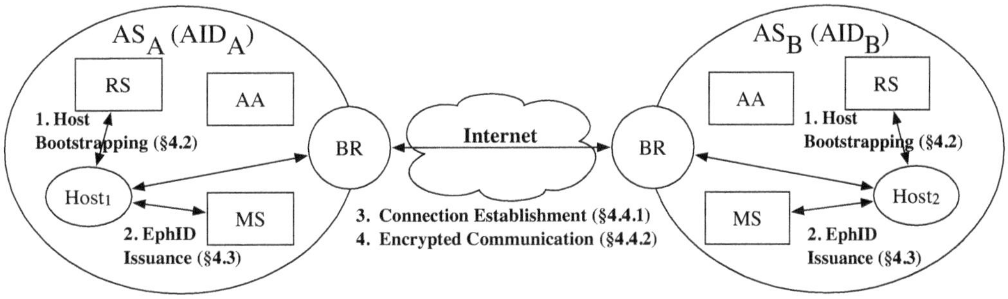

Figure 1: An end-to-end communication example.

Table 1: Notation.

k_{A_i}	Symmetric key of AS_i that is known among the infrastructure (e.g., routers, RS, MS, AA).
$k_{H_iA_i}$	Symmetric key shared between host H_i and its AS (AS_i).
$k_{E_iE_j}$	Symmetric key generated for the EphID pair E_i and E_j.
HID_i	Host identifier (HID) assigned to host H_i.
$EphID_h$	An EphID issued to host H.
C_{EphID_i}	Certificate for EphID $EphID_i$.
K_E^+, K_E^-	Public, private key of entity E for both DH Exchange and Digital Signatures.
$MAC_k(M)$	Message M and MAC of M using symmetric key k.
$\{M\}_{K^-}$	Message M and Signature of M using private-key K^-.
$E_k(M)$	Symmetric encryption of M with key k.
$E_k^{-1}(C)$	Symmetric decryption of C with key k.

- *Hosts do not use connection sharing devices (e.g., NAT).* We discuss how to relax this assumption in Section 7.2.

4.2 Host Bootstrapping

A host authenticates to its AS using a well-established authentication protocol [19, 20]. For example, when a user subscribes to an Internet provider, the provider creates the authentication credentials and these credentials are preconfigured into an Internet access device (e.g., cable or DSL modem). The device performs the authentication protocol when the user connects it to the network.

The host (or his access device) creates a symmetric key k_{HA} that serves two purposes: encrypting EphID request and reply messages (Section 4.3), and authenticating every packet that the host transmits to the network.[1] During the authentication procedure, the host securely sends k_{HA} to the RS by encrypting it using AS's public key (K_{AS}^+).

Once the host has successfully authenticated, the Registry Service (RS) of the AS performs the bootstrapping procedure (Figure 2). During this procedure, the host receives information about its AS's services that are necessary to (later) establish communication sessions; and to support these communication sessions, the infrastructure of the AS gets updated with the host's information. We require that all bootstrapping messages are authenticated in order to avoid modifications en route.

First, the RS creates a *control* EphID ($EphID_h^{ctrl}$) for the host. Control EphIDs are used to access AS's internal services, e.g., to request data-plane EphIDs from a Management Service (MS). Both control and data-plane EphIDs are constructed identically so that all communication is based on EphIDs. However, control EphIDs have longer lifetime (e.g., DHCP lease time) than data-plane EphIDs. In addition, control EphIDs cannot be used for data communication—unlike data-plane EphIDs, certificates are not issued for control EphIDs (see Section 4.3). We use the term EphIDs to refer to the data-plane EphIDs.

The RS returns the following information to the host: the control EphID ($EphID_h^{ctrl}$) with its expiration time ($ExpTime$), and the EphIDs for the MS ($EphID_{ms}$) and the DNS ($EphID_{dns}$) within the AS. The host uses $EphID_h^{ctrl}$ as the source address, and $EphID_{ms}$ and $EphID_{dns}$ as the destination addresses to access the respective services.

Finally, the RS sends the host information (HID, k_{HA}) to infrastructure entities in the AS (e.g., routers, MS, AA); the entities store the information in their database ($host\_info$). The infrastructure of the AS must learn the host information in order to handle packets that are originating from and destined to this host. Specifically, the entities need to learn the HID of the host (HID) and the shared key (k_{HA}) with the host so that they can verify the authenticity of the packets that originate from the host.

4.3 Ephemeral ID Issuance

An EphID is an encrypted token using the AS's secret key (k_A); it contains the host's HID and an expiration time that indicates the validity period for the EphID (i.e., $EphID = E_{k_A}(HID, ExpTime)$). Note that the use of encryption enables the issuing AS to obtain the HID and expiration time from an EphID in a stateless fashion, without an additional mapping table.

Every EphID is associated with a public/private key pair (K_{EphID}^+, K_{EphID}^-), which serves three purposes: 1) to mutually authenticate with a peer host, 2) to create a shared key with a peer host for data encryption (Section 4.4.1), and 3) to authenticate shutoff requests (Section 4.5). To keep the data encryption key secret from the AS, the host (not the AS)

[1] In practice, two keys (one for encryption and the other for authentication) are derived from k_{HA}, but for simplicity, we refer to both keys as k_{HA} throughout the protocol description.

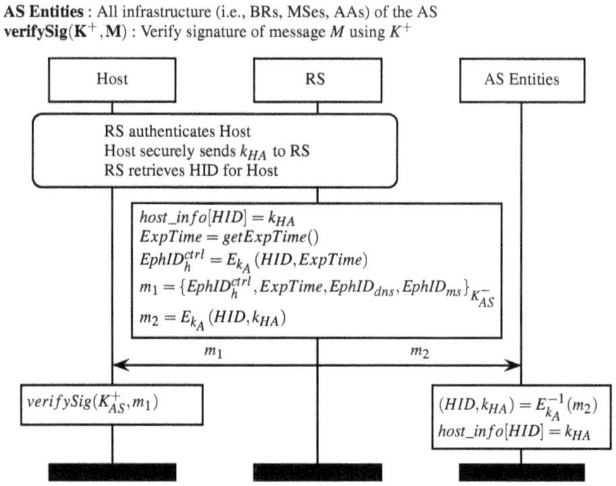

Figure 2: Procedure for Host Bootstrapping.

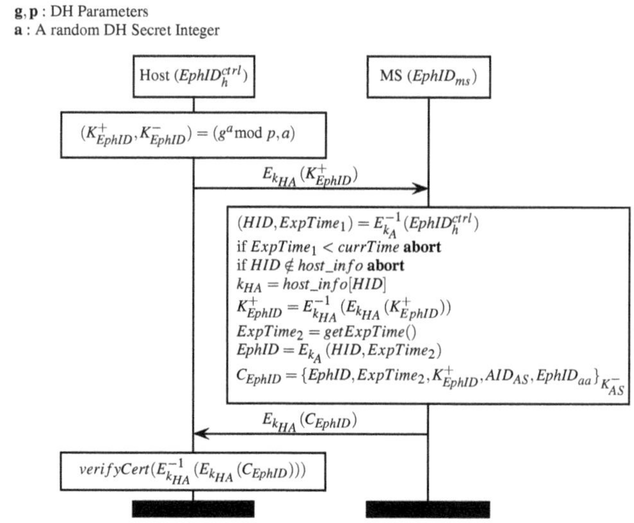

Figure 3: Procedure for EphID Issuance.

generates the key pair and the private key is never revealed to the AS.

The AS certifies the binding between an EphID and a public/private key pair by issuing a short-lived certificate (C_{EphID}) that has the same expiration time as the EphID. From the certificate, a peer host learns the public key (K_{EphID}^+) that is associated to the EphID as well as the EphID expiration time. The certificate additionally contains information about the issuing AS—the AID and the EphID of the accountability agent ($EphID_{aa}$). $EphID_{aa}$ is used by a peer host (with which the requesting host communicates) to initiate the shutoff protocol when necessary (Section 4.5).

To obtain an EphID, the host creates and sends an EphID request message to the MS (Figure 3). Specifically, the host first generates the public/private key pair (K_{EphID}^+, K_{EphID}^-) for the EphID and includes K_{EphID}^+ in the request message. In addition, the host uses $EphID_h^{ctrl}$ as the source address for the request message and encrypts the message using the shared key with the AS (k_{HA}). The message is encrypted to hide it from other entities in the AS that are not part of the AS infrastructure.

If an adversary trying to compromise sender-flow unlinkability (see Section 2.2 for the adversary model) sees the content of EphID request packets, she can identify a common sender across multiple flows at the level of $EphID_h^{ctrl}$. The adversary first learns the ($EphID_h^{ctrl}$, K_{EphID}^+) pair from the EphID request packets; then, the adversary sees the K_{EphID}^+s from the connection establishment packets (see Section 4.4.1), allowing the adversary to identify the common sender of multiple connections. Note that the adversary has not compromised the host identity since only the host's AS can extract host identity from $EphID_h^{ctrl}$. Nonetheless, she has successfully identified a common sender across multiple flows. In APNA, encrypting the EphID request message prevents such attacks.

Upon receiving the request, the MS validates the authenticity of the request; decrypts the source EphID ($EphID_h^{ctrl}$); and performs the following checks: 1) $EphID_h^{ctrl}$ has not expired, 2) the client's identifier (HID) is valid (i.e., has not been revoked), and 3) the message is valid (i.e., the message can be decrypted successfully). If any one of the checks fails, the request is dropped.

Then, the MS proceeds with the EphID issuance: it generates an EphID and creates the short-lived certificate (C_{EphID}) for the EphID. Finally, the MS encrypts the certificate and sends it to the requesting host. The certificate is encrypted for the same reason as encrypting the EphID request packets.

4.4 Data Communication

To communicate, two hosts mutually authenticate each other using each other's certificates and generate a shared symmetric key for their communication session. This key is then used to encrypt all traffic that belongs to this communication session. We emphasize that two hosts can create multiple communication sessions and each session has a different symmetric key to ensure that disclosure of one encryption key does not compromise data privacy of other communication sessions.

4.4.1 Connection Establishment

For every connection establishment between a pair of hosts, the two hosts perform the following tasks: 1) verify each other's EphID certificate that is issued by their corresponding ASes, and 2) establish a shared key via a DH key exchange to encrypt their communication.

Consider two hosts, A and B, with EphIDs $EphID_a$[2] and $EphID_b$, respectively, that are establishing a connection. Assume that the hosts have obtained each other's EphID and the associated certificate (we discuss obtaining EphIDs through DNS in Section 7.1). Using the short-lived certificate of $EphID_b$ and the public-private key pair associated with $EphID_a$, A derives a shared key ($k_{E_aE_b}$) between $EphID_a$ and $EphID_b$. Similarly, B computes the same shared key, completing the

[2]We use small 'a' to denote the EphID issued to A (i.e., $EphID_a$) to emphasize that there can be many EphIDs that are issued to a host.

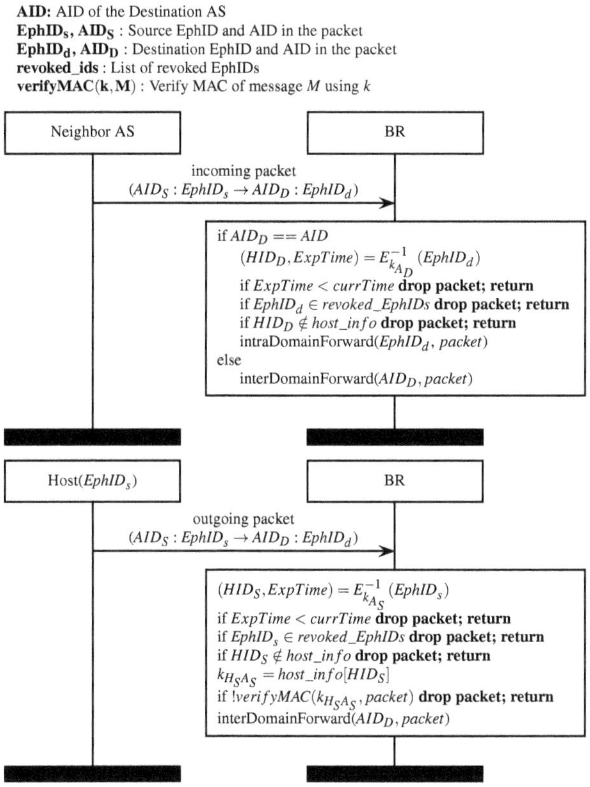

Figure 4: Procedures for Data Packet Forwarding at Border Routers for Incoming (Top) and Outgoing (Bottom) Packets.

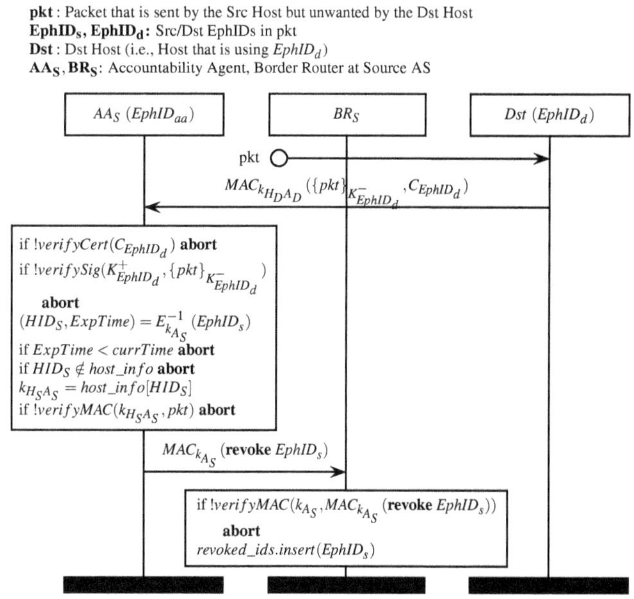

Figure 5: Procedure for Shutoff Protocol.

connection establishment. This symmetric shared key is then used to encrypt data packets between the two hosts.

4.4.2 Encrypted Communication

After the connection establishment, communication is based on symmetric cryptographic operations. First, the host uses the symmetric key that it shares with the peer to encrypt the packets to the peer. Any existing CCA-secure encryption scheme can be used for the encryption. Second, the host computes a MAC for every packet that it sends, using the symmetric key that it shares with its AS (k_{HA}). This allows the host's AS to link every packet to its source and to drop packets from (potentially) malicious hosts.

4.4.3 Data Forwarding

A border router in the source AS ensures that only packets from authenticated hosts and authorized EphIDs leave the AS; and a border router in the destination AS forwards packets to the correct host based on the destination EphID. Transit ASes do not perform additional operations and simply forward packets to the next AS on the path. As per our design choice, to achieve high-performance data forwarding, only symmetric cryptographic operations are used.

Communication end-points are specified as AID:EphID tuples. For inter-domain forwarding, border routers use only AID to forward packets (Figure 4). Specifically, for external packets entering the AS, a border router checks whether the packet has arrived at the destination AS. If not, the packet is forwarded to the neighboring AS towards the destination AS. At the destination AS, the border router checks the following conditions: 1) the destination EphID ($EphID_d$) is valid (i.e., has not expired and has not been revoked), and 2) HID_D is valid (i.e., is registered and non-revoked).

If all conditions are satisfied, then the packet is forwarded to the destination host: border routers derive the corresponding HID from the EphID and then forward the packet; we assume that intra-domain routers forward packets based on HIDs (e.g., IP addresses).

For outgoing packets, a border router forwards the packets to a neighboring AS only if all of the following conditions are satisfied: 1) the source EphID ($EphID_s$) is valid (i.e., has not expired and has not been revoked), 2) HID_S is valid, and 3) the MAC in the packet is correct.

To verify the MAC in the packet, a border router retrieves the shared key (k_{HA}) between the source host and the AS by searching the host information database (*host_info*) using the *HID* of the source host as the key. These checks ensure that only authenticated packets leave the source AS.

4.5 Shutoff Protocol

Shutoff protocols are designed to allow hosts to selectively block traffic from specific source hosts. In our architecture, an accountability agent (AA) checks the validity of a shutoff request and then blocks the source EphID. More specifically, the AA checks whether a customer-host has actually sent the specific packet that the requesting party reports and whether the party is authorized to make the request (e.g., the requesting host was indeed the recipient of the specific packet). The AA checks the validity of the request since, if misused, the shutoff protocol can be used to launch DoS attack against a benign source. Note that the AA does not examine the intent of the source nor tries to determine whether the packet is malicious.

Figure 5 shows the procedure for the shutoff request: the destination host (D) that owns $EphID_d$ is attempting to block traffic coming from the source host (S) that owns $EphID_s$ after receiving a specific packet. The destination host creates a shutoff request message with the following information: 1) the received packet, 2) a signature over the unwanted packet using the private key of $EphID_d$ ($K^-_{EphID_d}$), and 3) the certificate of $EphID_d$. This information serves as evidence that S has indeed sent traffic to D and that the shutoff request is not rogue. Then, D sends the request message to the AA of S.

Upon receiving the request, the AA verifies the certificate of $EphID_d$ and the signature in the request message to confirm that the request has indeed been made by D who owns $EphID_d$. Then, to ensure that the packet has been really generated by S that owns $EphID_s$, the AA checks the authenticity of the packet using the shared key ($k_{H_S A_S}$) with S. Finally, the AA instructs the border routers to revoke $EphID_s$ by putting it into their *revoked_ids* list.

5. IMPLEMENTATION & EVALUATION

We present the implementation and performance evaluation of the architecture's core components—EphID management server and border router.

5.1 EphID Management Server

The EphID Management Server (MS) is responsible for generating EphIDs and for assigning them to hosts. The EphID generation must be efficient since our architecture should even support per-flow EphIDs. We describe the EphID structure, the MS implementation, and then evaluate the performance of the EphID generation procedure.

5.1.1 EphID Structure

We engineer the EphID length to optimize processing for the AES block cipher; it is the only cipher with widespread hardware support, which enables high performance.

An EphID requires the HID of the host and an expiration time (*ExpTime*). AES operates on 16-byte (B) blocks, and we use 4 B for the HID, which are sufficient to uniquely represent all hosts even in large ASes. The expiration time is 2 B long, which is sufficiently large to express one day in two-second granularity.

Recall that the security requirement for EphIDs is a CCA-secure encryption scheme. To this end, we use a generic composition called Encrypt-then-MAC [21] that combines a symmetric encryption with a message authentication code (MAC) (Figure 6). The concatenation of *HID* and *ExpTime* is first encrypted using AES in counter mode. Secure operation of this mode requires a unique initialization vector (IV) for every encryption (i.e., for every EphID). Moreover, the use of the IV allows us to generate multiple EphIDs for a single *HID*. Note that the plaintext data is shorter than a single

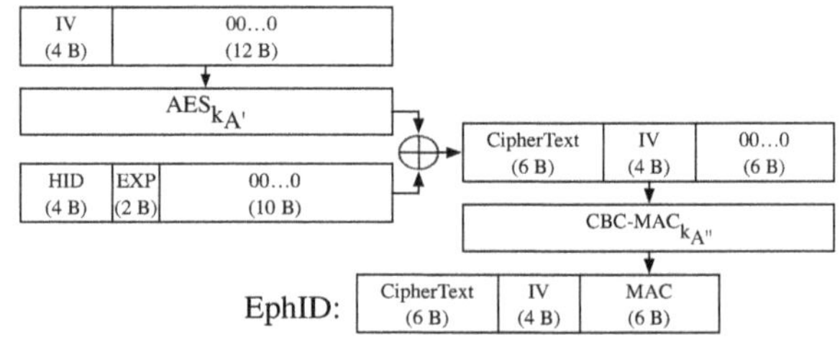

Figure 6: EphID Construction, where ExpTime is EXP.

AES block (16 B) and thus the input must be padded to 16 B; the one-block plaintext requires a single AES operation.

Next, a MAC is computed. The MAC is computed over the first 6 B of the previously generated ciphertext and the IV that was used in that encryption. We use CBC-MAC based on AES to generate the MAC, which is secure as we have a fixed input length.

Finally, the EphID is constructed from the 6 B of the ciphertext, 4 B IV, and 6 B of the MAC; the total length is 16 B. Note that the keys used for encryption ($k_{A'}$) and authentication ($k_{A''}$) are different; however, they are derived from the secret key of the AS (k_A).

5.1.2 MS Implementation

The MS generates EphIDs according to the procedure in Figure 3. For asymmetric cryptography, we use cryptographic primitives based on Curve25519 [22], which offers high performance and features small public-keys (32 B) and small signatures (64 B). Key exchange is done using the elliptic-curve variant of Diffie-Hellman (ECDH). To create digital signatures for certificates, we use the Ed25519 signature scheme [23] and the Ed25519 SUPERCOP REF10 implementation.[3] For symmetric cryptographic operations, we leverage Intel's AES-NI encryption instruction set [24]. Furthermore, we implement the host database (*host_info*) that stores the shared keys between hosts and the AS as a hash table using HID as the key.

As an optimization, we parallelize the EphID generation by using four processes to simultaneously handle EphID requests. The parallelization is straightforward since the generation does not require any coordination between the processes (e.g., shared memory or inter-process communication). However, no other optimizations were performed (e.g., optimizing the Ed25519 REF10 implementation).

5.1.3 MS Performance Evaluation

We demonstrate the efficiency of generating per-flow EphIDs. To this end, we need statistics for the peak flow generation rate inside an AS.

We use a 24-hour packet trace of HTTP(S) traffic from SWITCH.[4] The trace contains over 104 million entries for HTTP traffic and 74 million entries for HTTPS traffic. Each entry contains a timestamp and anonymized source/destination

[3]http://bench.cr.yp.to/supercop.html

[4]The Swiss academic ISP (www.switch.ch).

Field	Length
Source AID	4 Bytes
Source EphID	16 Bytes
Dest AID	4 Bytes
Dest EphID	16 Bytes
MAC	16 Bytes
Total	56 Bytes

Field	Length
HID	4 Bytes
ExpTime	4 Bytes
IV	4 Bytes
MAC	4 Bytes
Total	16 Bytes

Figure 7: APNA Header Information and EphID Field Lengths.

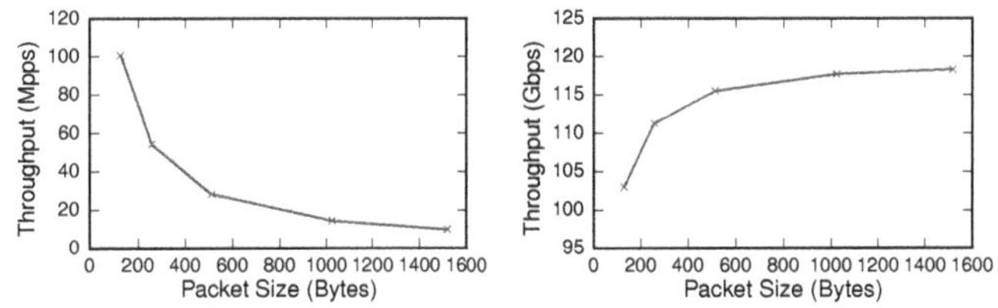

(a) (b)

Figure 8: Forwarding performance expressed as (a) packet-rate and (b) bit-rate.

IDs. We identify 1,266,598 unique hosts generating a peak rate of 3,888 active HTTP(S) sessions per second.

We test our implementation on a desktop machine with an Intel Core i5-3470s CPU (4 cores, 2.9GHz) and 4 GB of DDR3 memory. For 500,000 EphID requests, our implementation runs for 6.87 seconds. On average, 13.7 µs are needed for a single EphID generation, translating to a generation rate of 72.8k EphIDs/sec—over 18 times higher than the request rate. Our experiment shows that even a low-end desktop machine can keep up with the traffic demands of a real AS that has over 1.2 million hosts.

5.2 Border Router

We describe our border router prototype starting with the structure of the network header. Then, we describe the border router implementation and evaluate the forwarding performance.

5.2.1 APNA Header Information

The network header information (Figure 7) contains the source and destination end points (expressed as AID:EphID tuples) and a MAC over the packet's content. We use 4 B to express the AID since 4 B are used for AS numbers in the Internet; the EphID field requires 16 B as described in Section 5.1.1; the MAC field requires 16 B. The fields in the packet header sum up to 56 B.

5.2.2 Border Router Implementation

Our border router performs additional processing compared to traditional IPv4/IPv6 forwarding (Figure 4). Namely, the border router additionally performs one decryption, two table lookups, and one MAC verification. For MAC computation, we use Cipher-based Message Authentication Code (CMAC) that is secure for variable-length inputs [25].

We use DPDK [26] as our packet processing platform, which allows us to implement the required functionality in userspace. The decryption of the EphID in the packet is implemented through Intel AES-NI [24].

5.2.3 Forwarding Performance Evaluation

We evaluate the forwarding performance on a commodity server with two Intel Xeon E5-2680 CPUs and two non-uniform memory access (NUMA) nodes; each NUMA node has four banks of 8 GB DDR3 RAM. The server is equipped with 6 dual-port 10 GbE NICs, providing a total capacity of 120 Gbps. To generate traffic, we use Spirent-SPT-N4U-220 [27] connected back-to-back with the server. The server receives the traffic, processes it, and sends it back to the generator.

We perform a throughput experiment for 5 different packet sizes—128, 256, 512, 1024, and 1518-byte packets. The results (Figure 8) confirm that we are able to perform the required additional processing without incurring a throughput penalty. The measured performance matches the theoretical maximum performance; we omit this performance line for demonstration purposes since the two lines match. Figure 8(a) shows that even for small packet sizes (i.e., high packet-rates), the border router performs optimally. Figure 8(b) shows that as packet sizes increase, we saturate the capacity of 120 Gbps. The border router performs optimally because the additional operations are lightweight. The border router's CPUs have adequate capacity to perform this processing without degrading performance for the given packet rates. Under higher packet rates, the heavier load would start to degrade forwarding performance slightly.

6. SECURITY ANALYSIS

We demonstrate how APNA prevents attacks that undermine source accountability and data privacy.

6.1 Attacking Source Accountability

An adversary attacking source accountability (Section 2.1) has three attack vectors at hand.

EphID Spoofing: The adversary can attempt to use an EphID that is issued to another host (the spoofed victim). For instance, an adversary that shares the same access port with the victim can sniff traffic and observe valid EphIDs that are in use. However, using such an EphID is not sufficient since every outgoing packet has to contain a MAC that is computed with the shared key between the host and the host's AS. Without the corresponding shared key, the adversary cannot create valid MACs, resulting in spoofed packets that are dropped by the host's AS (additionally making the attack visible). Obtaining the shared key requires compromising the host or the AS; our adversary model does not account for such compromises.

An active adversary can attempt to obtain an EphID by pretending to be another host. However, such an attack is infeasible: the adversary not only needs to learn the control EphID ($EphID_h^{ctrl}$) of the victim, but also needs to learn the shared key between the victim and the source AS.

Unauthorized EphID Generation: The adversary can attempt to create an unauthorized EphID. However, such an attempt is not feasible since the EphID construction (Figure 6) is CCA-secure.

We achieve a CCA-secure encryption scheme through two primitives. First, we use symmetric encryption in counter mode with a fresh IV for every encryption; this encryption is secure under a chosen plaintext attack. Second, we use a CBC-MAC scheme to authenticate the concatenation of the ciphertext and the IV. Note that our use of the CBC-MAC is secure since the input length to the CBC-MAC is fixed to 16 B.[5] The combination of these two primitives results in a CCA-secure encryption scheme [21].

Identity Minting: A common attack against systems that provide accountability is identity minting, whereby a malicious host attempts to create multiple (unauthorized) identities. In APNA, a host can at most have one HID at any moment; and, a new HID invalidates previous HID and all associated EphIDs.

Unauthorized Shutoff Requests: The shutoff protocol can be misused to perform a DoS attack against a host. To prevent unauthorized shutoff requests, three measures are implemented. First, only the destination host and destination AS are authorized to issue a shutoff request. Furthermore, the shutoff requester has to present the unwanted packet, which proves that the source has indeed sent the packet. Since every packet has been cryptographically marked by the source AS, the destination cannot issue a shutoff request with a rogue packet. Lastly, the shutoff requester must present its authorization credentials—it needs to sign the request message with the private key associated with the destination EphID, and include the corresponding short-lived certificate in the request message, proving that it is an authorized party.

6.2 Attacking Privacy

An adversary attacking data privacy can attempt to eavesdrop on communication data or store it and decrypt it once she obtains the encryption keys. In APNA, traffic is encrypted by default and our scheme achieves perfect forward secrecy: The symmetric key that is used for data encryption is bound to the EphID (and the public/private key pair for that EphID) that is used for the corresponding communication session. This key pair is not used to derive other encryption keys and is not derived from other long-term private keys (K_{AS}^{-}). Hence, only the compromise of a private key for an EphID compromises data privacy and only for the communication session that uses this EphID.

Alternatively, an AS-level adversary can actively try to compromise data privacy of a customer host through a MitM attack. The malicious AS can perform a MitM attack during the shared key establishment between the victim ($EphID_v$) and a peer host ($EphID_p$). In this attack the malicious AS replaces the certificate for the EphID of the victim host (C_{EphID_v}) with another (fake) certificate, pretending to be the victim host to the peer host; the peer host accepts C_{EphID_v}. However, the AS cannot deceive the victim by pretending to be the peer host because it cannot generate the certificate for $EphID_p$ (C_{EphID_p}) that is signed by the private key of the peer host's AS. Consequently, the connection is not established and the adversary cannot read any communication of the hosts. The MitM attack is only possible if the source and destination ASes collude, which we do not consider.

For communication between two hosts in the same AS (i.e., intra-domain communication), APNA does not provide any privacy guarantee from the AS: the identities of the two hosts are already known to the AS (compromising host privacy), and the AS can perform MitM attacks to decrypt communication between the hosts (compromising data privacy) as the AS can fake both certificates for the EphIDs that the hosts use. The two hosts can use security protocols at higher layers (e.g., TLS) to encrypt their communication or use onion routing, such as Tor [5], to make a detour.

7. PRACTICAL CONSIDERATIONS

7.1 DNS Registration

Today, the names of publicly accessible services (e.g., an online shopping website) are typically registered to public DNS servers. In APNA, the servers that host public services publish the EphID to a DNS server, and the DNS server returns the EphID with the corresponding certificate for a requested domain name. To this end, the server performs two tasks: 1) it requests an EphID and the associated certificate from its AS; and 2) it registers the certificate under the domain name to DNS;[6] the registered EphID will be used as the destination address in future communication.

Publishing certificates to the DNS raises a problem: a shutoff request against a published EphID would terminate any ongoing communication sessions that use this EphID. A naïve solution is to update the DNS entry with a new EphID whenever the published EphID becomes invalid. However, this would become burdensome for the DNS infrastructure, if attackers continuously issue shutoff requests against a domain.

Our solution is to define *receive-only EphIDs*—EphIDs that are used only to receive packets and are never used as the source EphIDs. Since they are never used as the source identifier, they cannot become the target of shutoff requests. To avoid using receive-only EphIDs as the source identifier, the communication establishment to a server needs to be changed (i.e., the server does not respond to the client using the receive-only EphID).

Client-Server Connection Establishment: To support receive-only EphIDs by the server, the connection establishment procedure in Section 4.4.1 is extended. To simplify the narrative, assume that the client uses $EphID_c$ to connect to the server, and that the server uses $EphID_r$ as the receive-only EphID and $EphID_s$ to serve the client.

After obtaining $EphID_r$ from DNS, the client contacts the

[5]CBC-MAC is insecure for variable-length messages [25].

[6]We assume DNSSec to authenticate DNS records.

server using $EphID_c$ and $EphID_r$ as the source and destination EphIDs, respectively. The server verifies the short-lived certificate of $EphID_c$ and computes a shared key that will be used to encrypt data packets between the client and the server. However, instead of using the short-lived certificate of $EphID_r$, the server uses the short-lived certificate of $EphID_s$ to compute the shared key. Then, in the response message to the client, the server includes the short-lived certificate of $EphID_s$ to inform the client that $EphID_s$ will be used by the server to serve the client.

The client verifies the short-lived certificate of $EphID_s$ and computes the shared key using the certificates for $EphID_s$ and $EphID_c$. Then, the client uses $EphID_s$ as the destination EphID to communicate to the server.

Protecting DNS Queries: If the DNS server is operated by the host's AS, the AS can compromise the privacy of the DNS query—the AS knows the identity of the host from the EphID and retrieves the content of the query from the DNS server. To prevent such a compromise, the host can use a DNS server that he trusts and that is not operated by the AS that he resides in.

7.2 Deployment in today's Internet

Our ideas are not restricted to a certain Internet architecture, thus APNA could be used in today's Internet: IPv4 addresses of hosts serve as HIDs; IPv4 addresses of APNA routers in ASes serve as AIDs; Generic Routing Encapsulation (GRE) [28] is used to insert the APNA header into IPv4 packets; and, APNA gateways mediate between IPv4 and the APNA protocol, leaving the host's operating system unchanged. The following paragraphs summarize the deployment strategy in the Internet; our technical report [29] contains more detailed descriptions.

For intra-domain forwarding in the source AS, the source host puts its IP address and the IP address of an APNA router in the source AS as the source and destination addresses in the IPv4 header (that comes before the GRE header), respectively. For intra-domain forwarding in the destination AS, an APNA router 1) decrypts the destination EphID in the APNA header to get the HID (i.e., IPv4 address) of the destination host; and, 2) replaces the destination IPv4 address of the IPv4 header with the HID.

This intra-domain forwarding has a privacy implication. Within the source and destination ASes, the addresses of the hosts are visible; hence, it is not possible to provide any privacy guarantee against an adversary who observes packets within the ASes. However, once an AS fully deploys APNA (i.e., all routers forward packets based on EphIDs), this privacy leakage can be mitigated.

For inter-domain forwarding in the source AS, an APNA router replaces the addresses in the IPv4 header of the APNA packet with its IPv4 address and the destination AID as the new source and destination addresses, respectively. For all transit ASes, the packet is forwarded based on the destination address in the IPv4 header.

We leverage the GRE protocol to interconnect two APNA entities (e.g., border routers) over the IPv4 network. This enables encapsulation of the APNA header after the GRE tunnel header; a protocol number assigned by IANA and used for the *Protocol Type* field in the GRE header would indicate that the encapsulated protocol is APNA.

Furthermore, gateways are used to bridge between today's Internet and APNA, without having to update the host network stack. The role of the gateway is two-fold: 1) as an APNA host, it runs the protocols described in Section 4; and 2) as a packet translator, it converts between native IPv4 and APNA packets.

Hosts Behind NAT Devices. In order to support NATs, the NAT acts as a small AS for its hosts, while it acts as a single host for the AS network. Thus, the NAT acts as a RS, a MS, a router, and an accountability agent on behalf of its clients. As a RS, the NAT bootstraps the hosts into the AP's internal network. As an MS, the NAT makes EphID requests on behalf of its hosts to the AS. As a router, the NAT implements the data forwarding procedures described in Figure 4. The NAT plays these roles following the same protocols as described for an AS, only with minor differences [29].

As an accountability agent, the NAT identifies the misbehaving hosts based on EphIDs. Since the hosts behind a NAT are not visible to the AS and since the AS issues EphIDs to the NAT not to the hosts, the AS holds the NAT accountable for misbehaving EphIDs. Then, the NAT determines the host that is using the misbehaving EphID.

8. DISCUSSION

8.1 Ephemeral ID Granularity

Thus far, we have argued that APNA does not impose the granularity at which EphIDs should be used and we have shown that the EphIDs can be generated at high speed (see Section 5.1.3). In this section, we present four granularities at which EphIDs can be used.

Per-Flow Ephemeral ID: We expect this to be the typical use case where a host uses different EphIDs for different flows. There are two advantages to per-flow EphIDs. First, it prevents an observer's attempt to identify a common sender of multiple flows by inspecting the content of the packets (i.e., APNA header and payload). Second, shutoff incidents have limited impact on a host. It terminates the flow that uses the reported EphID as the source; however, all other flows remain intact. The disadvantage of this case is that a host needs to acquire and manage EphIDs for every new flow.

Per-Host Ephemeral ID: A host uses a single EphID for all packets. The advantage of this model is that a host only needs to acquire and manage one EphID. However, there are two drawbacks. Since all packets have the same source EphID, all packets are linked to a common sender; and, a shutoff request terminates all connections from the host.

Per-Packet Ephemeral ID: A host could use a different EphID for each packet so that it is difficult to link packets to a single flow. This provides the strongest privacy guarantee; however, additional mechanisms are necessary for the destination host to demultiplex packets into flows [30].

Per-Application Ephemeral ID: An EphID can be used to represent all packets that are generated by an application or a service that is running on the host. This EphID granularity facilitates managing traffic that is generated by an application. For example, if an AS enforces its hosts to use per-application EphIDs, the AS and its hosts could collaboratively identify malicious applications (e.g., a bot) running at the hosts. The network identifies malicious activities (e.g., flooding attacks) to a source EphID and inform the host about the EphID; then, the host identifies the application that uses the EphID and takes appropriate actions.

8.2 Support for Network Feedback

In APNA, an on-path intermediate node (e.g., router) can send messages (e.g., ICMP) back to the source host.

Assume that router R is attempting to send an ICMP message to the source host S. To send an ICMP message to S, R uses the source EphID (i.e., $EphID_s$) from the received packet (that has prompted the ICMP message), and uses one of its EphIDs (i.e., $EphID_r$) as the destination and source EphIDs, respectively. Hence, APNA protects the identity of R from the source host while holding R accountable for the ICMP message.

8.3 Parameter Considerations

Expiration Time for EphIDs: If EphIDs are used per flow, the expiration time can be set to 15 minutes as 98% of the flows in the Internet last less than 15 minutes [31]. Alternatively, the EphID issuance protocol (Section 4.3) can be extended to allow hosts to express their choice of expiration time. For instance, an AS may specify three categories (short-term, medium-term, long-term EphIDs) to accommodate diverse flow duration times.

Managing Revoked EphIDs: EphIDs can be preemptively revoked before they expire: a host could revoke an EphID that is no longer needed, or an EphID could have been subjected to a shutoff incident. Regardless of the reason for revoking EphIDs, border routers in the ASes need to store a list of revoked EphIDs (i.e., *revoked_EphIDs* in Figure 4). If there are too many revocations in an AS, it burdens the border routers since the size of the *revoked_EphIDs* would become large.

There are methods to limit the size of the *revoked_EphIDs* list. First, an AS can rotate its secret key (k_A) periodically; the rotation invalidates all previously issued EphIDs. Second, since EphIDs will expire over time and packets using expired EphIDs are dropped, the expired EphIDs can be removed from *revoked_EphIDs*. Third, if too many EphIDs of a host are revoked, the AS should view it as a sign of malicious activity by the host. In such an event, the AS revokes the HID of the host invalidating all EphIDs that are issued to the host and it assigns a new HID to the host. In addition, the AS can contact the host for corrective measures. Such approaches are already in use, e.g., ISPs that participate in the Copyright Alert System (CAS) [32].

8.4 Handling Replay Attacks

A malicious entity that aims to "harm" a source host may replay packets of the source. In the short-term, replayed packets may induce shutoff incidents against the source host, disrupting communication of the source; and in the long-term, the AS of the source host may take retributive action against the source host for repeated shutoff incidents.

Replay attacks can be prevented by making every packet unique. That is, a nonce field is added to the APNA header (Figure 7), and a source host puts a unique number for each generated packet. Then, the destination host performs replay detection based on the nonces in the packets and discards all duplicate packets.

Ideally, replayed packets should be filtered near the replay location, but this requires routers in the network to perform replay detection. Designing a practical in-network replay detection mechanism that does not affect routers' forwarding performance is not trivial; it is our future work to design such a mechanism.

8.5 Governments and Privacy

Although generally perceived as a threat on communication privacy, there are legitimate reasons for governments to subvert communication privacy (e.g., to monitor terrorist activities). In fact, many governments by law mandate ISPs to keep a record of their traffic (e.g., source and destination IP addresses, packet content, etc).

APNA protects communication privacy by making mass surveillance difficult; however, at the same time, it allows entities, such as a government, to deanonymize communication when necessary. With the cooperation of an AS, a government can deanonymize the identity of hosts from EphIDs. Furthermore, if the government has cooperation from the ASes in which communicating hosts reside, the AS could decrypt ongoing communication by performing a MitM attack. However, the government cannot observe communication by simply collecting packets since packets are encrypted, which makes mass surveillance difficult. In addition, since APNA achieves perfect forward secrecy, governments cannot decrypt past communication sessions of a host even if the long-term public key of the host is disclosed.

9. RELATED WORK

Persona [33] seeks to balance privacy and accountability at the network layer. The source ISP replaces the IP address of each outgoing packet with another address from an assigned pool. This approach hides the source's identity, but it breaks the notion of flow and prevents the destination from demultiplexing connections.

Accountable and Private Internet Protocol (APIP) [6] proposes an architecture that balances accountability and privacy at the network layer. In APIP, the source address in the network header is replaced with the address of an *accountability delegate* that vouches for the source's packets. The return address can then be specified at a higher layer—invisible from the network—protecting the source's privacy.

Senders are expected to brief each packet to their accountability delegate such that on-path devices can request a "vouching proof" from the corresponding delegate.

APIP balances privacy and accountability at the network layer, but it comes with certain limitations. APIP's notion of privacy is limited to sender-flow unlinkability, leaving data privacy and the associated challenges (e.g., key distribution, management, and establishment) unaddressed. Our proposal presents a holistic architecture that addresses these drawbacks and by default supports data privacy. Furthermore, the design of APIP precludes every packet from being accounted for in the network: it is possible for a malicious host to omit reporting packets to its accountability delegate when the flow for those packets has been "whitelisted".[7] In APNA, every packet is linked to its sender since a MAC is computed using the shared key between the AS and the host for every packet (Section 4.4). Second, masking the return address complicates getting messages from the network back to the source—the messages must be redirected through the accountability delegate of the source; the complexity of this functionality remains unaddressed. APNA allows the network to send messages directly to the source while preserving host privacy and the accountability properties (Section 8.2).

Source Accountability: The Accountable Internet Protocol (AIP) [11] treats source accountability as a central principle. In AIP, self-certifying IDs and a shutoff protocol (implemented by smart Network Interface Cards) are used to identify and block malicious sources. Our architecture uses self-certifying IDs in an anonymity-preserving way and delegates the shutoff functionality to the source domain.

In Passport [34], OPT [35] and ICING [36], MACs are used for each AS on the end-to-end path, allowing on-path ASes to verify the authenticity of packets. In APNA, such mechanisms can be used to strengthen the shutoff mechanism [29].

Bender et al. [37] were first to introduce the concept of accountability agents in their Accountability-as-a-Service (AaaS) proposal. However, AaaS does not address privacy considerations and requires symmetric keys between all AS pairs.

Host Privacy and Anonymity: Raghavan et al. [38] propose ISP-wide NATs to hide the hosts' identities from entities in other ASes. We borrow their motivation that the size of today's large ISPs provides sufficiently large anonymity sets. Onion routing [4] and Mix Networks [39] by design provide anonymity at the cost of source accountability.

Han et al. [40] propose a cross-layer design that uses pseudonyms to hide the user's identity. Similar to APNA, the proposal allows the user to choose the level of anonymity and it uses encryption to mask the identity of the host in network addresses. However, the proposal falls short of being a complete architecture that balances between accountability and privacy: it does not consider pervasive data encryption and the associated challenges, such as certificate management, and does not consider source accountability.

[7]Verifiers do not verify flows that have been "whitelisted," and a sender does not brief packets unless it is asked by its accountability delegate under the recursive verification method (Section 5 in APIP [6]).

Data Privacy: Farrell and Tschofenig [1] argue that pervasive monitoring—defined as the widespread and often covert surveillance through intrusive gathering of communication information—is a widespread attack on privacy. In response, Kent [41] proposes pervasive encryption as a countermeasure against pervasive monitoring. In a related effort, the Let's Encrypt[8] organization encourages the use of encrypted web traffic by issuing free TLS certificates for web servers. Our proposal does not replace transport-layer encryption, but rather promotes pervasive encryption to a fundamental design tenet of the network layer. In addition, we propose a concrete solution for key distribution, establishment, and management.

MinimaLT [42] proposes an architecture that supports pervasive data encryption and achieves PFS at low latency; however, MinimalLT does not consider source accountability. In Section 4.4.1, we show how our architecture supports data privacy with PFS while enforcing source accountability.

10. CONCLUSIONS

We propose APNA, an architecture that resolves the accountability-privacy tussle by enlisting ISPs as accountability agents and privacy brokers. As accountability agents, ISPs authenticate hosts and their packets; and as privacy brokers, ISPs anonymize the identities of communicating parties and assist in the establishment of shared keys for end-to-end data encryption. Even with additional tasks that an AS has to perform, we have demonstrated that our architecture can be implemented on commodity hardware and scale to large networks without adding substantial overhead.

By facilitating (and by enabling by default) pervasive encryption between endpoints, APNA can help frustrate adversaries conducting indiscriminate mass surveillance. At the same time, APNA can assist in lawful, targeted requests for subscriber communications, since ISPs can comply with data retention laws by storing customer to EphID bindings as well as the packets. However, abuse of such requests for information are minimized due to the perfect forward secrecy of our scheme.

11. ACKNOWLEDGMENTS

We would like to thank Yue-Hsun Lin for the initial discussion; and the anonymous reviewers and our shepherd, Roya Ensafi, for their insightful feedback and suggestions. The research leading to these results has received funding from the European Research Council under the European Union's Seventh Framework Programme (FP7/2007-2013)/ERC grant agreement 617605; and from the Institute for Information & communications Technology Promotion (IITP) grant funded by the Korean government (MSIP)/No.B0717-16-0040. We also gratefully acknowledge support by ETH Zürich and by Intel for their equipment donation that enabled the high-capacity experiments.

[8]https://letsencrypt.org

12. REFERENCES

[1] S. Farrell and H. Tschofenig, "Pervasive Monitoring Is an Attack," RFC 7258, IETF, 2014.

[2] "NSA Spying," https://www.eff.org/nsa-spying.

[3] K. McCarthy, "World's Largest Internet Exchange Sues Germany over Mass Surveillance," http://www.theregister.co.uk/2016/09/16/ixp_sues_german_govt_surveillance/.

[4] M. G. Reed, P. F. Syverson, and D. M. Goldschlag, "Anonymous Connections and Onion Routing," *Selected Areas in Communications, IEEE J. on*, 1998.

[5] R. Dingledine, N. Mathewson, and P. Syverson, "Tor: The Second-generation Onion Router," in *Proc. of USENIX Security Symposium*, 2004.

[6] D. Naylor, M. K. Mukerjee, and P. Steenkiste, "Balancing Accountability and Privacy in the Network," in *Proc. of ACM Conference on SIGCOMM*, 2014.

[7] S. Kent and K. Seo, "Security Architecture for the Internet Protocol," RFC 4301, IETF, 2005.

[8] C. Kaufman, "Internet Key Exchange (IKEv2) Protocol," RFC 4306, IETF, 2005.

[9] B. Rowe, D. Wood, D. Reeves, and F. Braun, "The Role of Internet Service Providers in Cyber Security," http://goo.gl/t7f7NA, 2011.

[10] D. G. Lichtman, "Holding Internet Service Providers Accountable," *University of Chicago Coase-Sandor Working Paper Series in Law and Economics*, 2004.

[11] D. G. Andersen, H. Balakrishnan, N. Feamster, T. Koponen, D. Moon, and S. Shenker, "Accountable Internet Protocol (AIP)," in *Proc. of ACM Conference on SIGCOMM*, 2008.

[12] A. Pfitzmann and M. Hansen, "Anonymity, Unobservability, and Pseudonymity: A Consolidated Proposal for Terminology," http://goo.gl/GExcmQ, Jul 2000.

[13] A. J. Menezes, P. C. v. Oorschot, and S. A. Vanstone, *Handbook of Applied Cryptography*, fifth printing ed. CRC Press, 2001.

[14] V. Shmatikov and M.-H. Wang, "Timing Analysis in Low-latency Mix Networks: Attacks and Defenses," in *Proc. of European Conference on Research in Computer Security (ESORICS)*, 2006.

[15] K. P. Dyer, S. E. Coull, T. Ristenpart, and T. Shrimpton, "Peek-a-Boo, I Still See You: Why Efficient Traffic Analysis Countermeasures Fail," in *Proc. of IEEE Symposium on Security and Privacy (S&P)*, 2012.

[16] M. Juarez, M. Imani, M. Perry, C. Diaz, and M. Wright, "Toward an Efficient Website Fingerprinting Defense," in *Proc. of European Conference on Research in Computer Security (ESORICS)*, 2016.

[17] J. Hayes and G. Danezis, "k-fingerprinting: A Robust Scalable Website Fingerprinting Technique," in *Proc. of USENIX Security Symposium*, 2016.

[18] ARIN, "Resource Public Key Infrastructure," http://bit.ly/1EJCQoT.

[19] C. Rigney, S. Willens, A. Rubens, and W. Simpson, "Remote Authentication Dial In User Service (RADIUS)," RFC 2865, IETF, 2000.

[20] V. Fajardo, J. Arkko, J. Loughney, and G. Zorn, "Diameter Base Protocol," RFC 6733, IETF, 2012.

[21] M. Bellare and C. Namprempre, "Authenticated Encryption: Relations among Notions and Analysis of the Generic Composition Paradigm," in *Advances in Cryptology—ASIACRYPT*, 2000.

[22] D. J. Bernstein, "Curve25519: New Diffie-Hellman Speed Records," in *Public Key Cryptography (PKC)*, 2006.

[23] D. J. Bernstein, N. Duif, T. Lange, P. Schwabe, and B.-Y. Yang, "High-speed High-security Signatures," *J. of Cryptographic Engineering*, 2012.

[24] S. Gueron, "Intel Advanced Encryption Standard (AES) New Instruction Set," Mar 2010.

[25] M. Bellare, J. Kilian, and P. Rogaway, "The Security of the Cipher Block Chaining Message Authentication Code," *J. of Computer and System Science*, 2001.

[26] "Data Plane Development Kit," http://dpdk.org.

[27] "Spirent SPT-N4U-220 Chassis," http://www.spirent.com/Ethernet_Testing/Platforms/N4U_Chassis.

[28] D. Farinacci, T. Li, S. Hanks, D. Meyer, and P. Traina, "Generic Routing Encapsulation (GRE)," RFC 2784, IETF, 2000.

[29] T. Lee, C. Pappas, D. Barrera, P. Szalachowski, and A. Perrig, "Source Accountability with Domain-brokered Privacy," https://arxiv.org/abs/1610.00461, 2016.

[30] T. Lee, C. Pappas, P. Szalachowski, and A. Perrig, "Communication Based on Per-Packet One-Time Address," in *Proc. of IEEE Conference on Network Protocols (ICNP)*, 2016.

[31] N. Brownlee and K. Claffy, "Understanding Internet Traffic Streams: Dragonflies and Tortoises," *IEEE Communication Magazine*, 2002.

[32] "The Copyright Alert System," http://goo.gl/I9GsOl.

[33] Y. Mallios, S. Modi, A. Agarwala, and C. Johns, "Persona: Network Layer Anonymity and Accountability for Next Generation Internet," *IFIP Advances in Information and Communication Technology*, 2009.

[34] X. Liu, A. Li, X. Yang, and D. Wetherall, "Passport: Secure and Adoptable Source Authentication," in *Proc. of USENIX Conference on Networked Systems Design and Implementation (NSDI)*, 2008.

[35] T. H.-J. Kim, C. Basescu, L. Jia, S. B. Lee, Y.-C. Hu, and A. Perrig, "Lightweight Source Authentication and Path Validation," in *Proc. of ACM Conference on SIGCOMM*, 2014.

[36] J. Naous, M. Walfish, A. Nicolosi, D. Mazières, M. Miller, and A. Seehra, "Verifying and Enforcing Network Paths with ICING," in *Proc. of ACM Conference on Emerging Networking EXperiments and Technologies (CoNEXT)*, 2011.

[37] A. Bender, N. Spring, D. Levin, and B. Bhattacharjee, "Accountability as a Service," in *Proc. of USENIX Worskhop on Steps to Reducing Unwanted Traffic (SRUTI)*, 2007.

[38] B. Raghavan, T. Kohno, A. C. Snoeren, and W. David, "Enlisting ISPs to Improve Online Privacy: IP Address Mixing by Default," in *Proc. of Privacy Enhancing Technologies Symposium (PETS)*, 2009.

[39] D. L. Chaum, "Untraceable Electronic Mail, Return Addresses, and Digital Pseudonyms," *Communications of the ACM*, 1981.

[40] S. Han, V. Liu, Q. Pu, S. Peter, T. Anderson, A. Krishnamurthy, and D. Wetherall, "Expressive Privacy Control with Pseudonyms," in *Proc. of ACM Conference on SIGCOMM*, 2013.

[41] S. Kent, "Pervasive Encryption as a Countermeasure to Pervasive Monitoring," draft-kent-pervasive-encryption-00, IETF, 2014.

[42] M. W. Petullo, X. Zhang, J. A. Solworth, D. J. Bernstein, and T. Lange, "MinimaLT: Minimal-latency Networking Through Better Security," in *Proc. of ACM Conference on Computer & Communications Security (CCS)*, 2013.

A NEaT Design for Reliable and Scalable Network Stacks

Tomas Hruby Cristiano Giuffrida Lionel Sambuc Herbert Bos Andrew S. Tanenbaum
Vrije Universiteit Amsterdam
thruby@few.vu.nl,{giuffrida,lionel.sambuc,herbertb,ast}@cs.vu.nl

ABSTRACT

Operating systems provide a wide range of services, which are crucial for the increasingly high reliability and scalability demands of modern applications. Providing both reliability and scalability at the same time is hard. Commodity OS architectures simply lack the design abstractions to do so for demanding core OS services such as the network stack. For reliability and scalability guarantees, they rely almost exclusively on ensuring a high-quality *implementation*, rather than a reliable and scalable *design*. This results in complex error recovery paths and hard-to-maintain synchronization code.

We demonstrate that a simple and structured design that strictly adheres to two principles, *isolation* and *partitioning*, can yield reliable and scalable network stacks. We present NEaT, a system which partitions the stack across isolated process replicas handling independent requests. Our design principles intelligently partition the state to minimize the impact of failures (offering strong recovery guarantees) and to scale comparably to Linux without exposing the implementation to common pitfalls such as synchronization errors, poor locality, and false sharing.

1. INTRODUCTION

Building reliable and scalable OS services such as the network stack is a daunting task. Even when opportunities for reliability [43] and scalability [19] exist at the interface level, producing a reliable and scalable implementation is notoriously challenging [11, 14, 29]. This problem is exacerbated by the dominant *"build-and-fix"* model adopted in commodity OSes, which generally attempts to retrofit reliability and scalability in legacy implementations. This strategy—*reliability and scalability of implementation*—misses important opportunities to address key problems at design time and has trouble scaling with the fast-paced evolution of modern hardware and software [11].

This paper presents a new coordinated approach to the reliability and scalability of the network stack—one of the most demanding and dependability-sensitive subsystems. Our approach relies on two well-known key principles—*isolation* and *partitioning*. That means, we break large entities into smaller ones and isolate them from each other in such a way that they cannot unexpectedly interfere with execution of each other. What is new is that we apply them to an extreme degree in our design, demonstrating that such a strategy can (i) allow reliability and scalability to coexist and symbiotically improve with the number of available cores and (ii) greatly simplify and improve the longevity of the final implementation. To substantiate our claims, we present NEaT, a reliable and scalable componentized network stack implemented using a "clean slate" approach on top of the NewtOS microkernel-based architecture [37]. NEaT embraces our principles to isolate individual threads of execution in separate processes and transparently partition the network state (and user requests) across N independent network stack *replicas*, while preserving application-level sharing and standard BSD socket interfaces. Thanks to its replicated design, NEaT: (i) survives run-time failures with minimal service disruption, (ii) scales comparably to the Linux' network stack, and (iii) minimizes code explicitly dealing with reliability and scalability concerns—making it easier to maintain in the face of constant hardware and software changes.

We do not claim that our design (and its implementation) is the only one possible for a reliable and scalable network stack, let alone for generic operating system services. Rather, our goal is to demonstrate that reliability and scalability are not conflicting requirements and can be both effectively addressed at design time using well-defined principles. Experience shows that the alternative—reliability and scalability of implementation—is increasingly unsustainable, threatening the growing reliability and scalability demands of modern applications.

CoNEXT '16, December 12 - 15, 2016, Irvine, CA, USA

 ISBN 978-1-4503-4292-6/16/12...$15.00

DOI: http://dx.doi.org/10.1145/2999572.2999579

The Linux kernel is a case in point. With its code base growing from the original few thousand lines of code (LoC) to the millions of LoC and dozens of architectures today [42], maintaining high reliability and scalability standards has become increasingly prohibitive despite huge community efforts. For instance, replacing the big kernel lock with fine-grained locking and lockless data structures took more than 8 years [3]. In addition, the new synchronization mechanisms have been updated several times since then, after repeatedly exhausting their scalability opportunities on contemporary hardware [16]. Further, as the size and complexity of the kernel dramatically increase, so does the rate of faults in the code, with an average fault lifespan of around 1 year even for high-impact faults that can bring the system to a halt [51].

While NEaT is a research prototype and it may not be fair to compare it to full-featured and highly optimized systems such as Linux, its replicated network stack design based on isolation and partitioning does structurally solve many of the recurring implementation issues described above (§2). Similarly, while prior work has considered principles such as isolation and partitioning before—in different forms—for either reliability [29, 23, 38, 63, 43, 37, 21] or scalability [11, 14, 66, 26, 10], our design rigorously combines these principles together to address both reliability and scalability to demonstrate their effectiveness in a BSD-compliant network stack.

Contributions. To summarize, our contributions are:

- We present a new approach to design reliable and scalable network stacks based on the rigorous application of two principles— *isolation* and *partitioning*—and analyze the opportunities to solve challenging implementation problems in existing systems.

- We present the principle-based design and implementation of NEaT, a BSD-compliant network stack that rigorously isolates and partitions its individual components across N independent network stack replicas running on top of a microkernel-based architecture. We show that NEaT only marginally relies on the implementation to obtain the desired reliability and scalability properties. Furthermore, the full decoupling between replicas allows NEaT to assign independent user requests to a random replica, ensuring load balancing and, as a by-product, location unpredictability, resulting in improved security against emerging memory error attacks [13, 57]. NEaT demonstrates that supporting reliability and scalability (and enhanced security) by design is possible and, to our knowledge, is the first network stack of its kind.

- We evaluate NEaT using a representative web server application (lighttpd). Our results show that NEaT can handle up to 13-35% more requests than Linux, despite the underlying microkernel design being traditionally perceived as a major limiting factor to compete with commodity OS architectures.

Outline. The remainder of the paper is laid out as follows. §2 provides background information, highlighting problems in existing OS and network stack designs and comparing our approach to reliability and scalability with prior work. §3 and §4 present the design and implementation of the NEaT network stack. §5 compares to other userspace network stacks and §6 presents experimental results, assessing the reliability and scalability properties of our NEaT prototype and §7 concludes the paper.

2. BACKGROUND

Shaping the design of reliable and scalable systems using *isolation* and *partitioning* makes intuitive sense: (i) they enforce fault containment and conflict-free failure recovery for reliability purposes; (ii) they enforce data locality and conflict-free parallelism for scalability purposes. The vast majority of commodity operating systems—whose original design dates back to the single core computing era—however, opt for a monolithic architecture, where multiple threads typically coexist in a single address space. This design naturally induces a "*shared everything*" model, with no implicit isolation nor partitioning and, as a result, no reliability and scalability of design. In the next subsections, we develop this intuition further and highlight the fundamental limitations of this model and reliability and scalability of implementation in general.

2.1 Reliability

Reliability of Implementation. The lack of *isolation* in monolithic architectures complicates the implementation of effective fault containment mechanisms: a single fault can arbitrarily propagate throughout the kernel, corrupt arbitrary data structures, and lead the entire operating system to fail. To mitigate this problem, commodity operating systems such as Linux adopt a pragmatic approach to reliability, relying on dedicated error-handling logic or killing the offending process when a fault is detected (kernel *oops* [68]). Unfortunately, the former approach may also result in the introduction of a large amount of complex but trusted recovery code, which is often untested [8]—thus creating a vicious circle [29]—while the latter approach provides weak reliability with the inability to detect (or recover from) global error propagation—recently estimated to occur in more than 25% of the cases [68]. To improve fault containment, researchers have devised a number of techniques to retrofit isolation guarantees in existing kernel extensions and, in particular, device drivers. Some approaches rely on hardware-based isolation [63, 27, 17], others on language- [69] or compiler-based strategies [40, 18], yet others on virtualization techniques [61]. While such approaches are generally effective in containing faults in untrusted components, they are typically limited to relatively small OS subsystems—recovery techniques for subsystems comparable to the network stack do exist, but at the cost of more complex recovery code [62]—and may fail to guarantee full isolation when the subsystem interacts with the rest of the kernel using nonstandard interfaces [40].

Furthermore, when a fault is detected, recovery actions are necessary to ensure that the system is in a globally consistent state. The lack of explicit state *partitioning* in monolithic architectures, however, induces "*hidden*" cross-thread dependencies that significantly complicate this process. For this reason, commodity operating systems generally have to resort to a best-effort failure recovery model [68]. To mitigate this problem, researchers have proposed manual state reconstruction [23]—which, however, introduces pervasive and hard-to-maintain recovery code—or software transactional memory-like schemes to selectively rollback all the threads that yield conflicting state changes with the faulting thread [43]—which, however, greatly limits the performance and scalability of the system [29]. Techniques that retrofit partitioning into monolithic kernels using virtualized domains have also been recently attempted [49], but at the cost of greatly limiting application-level sharing and cooperation.

Reliability of Design. A vast body of research has been devoted to principles supporting reliability of design. Isolation, in particular, is a well-established design principle in reliable OS architectures. Microkernel-based operating systems such as QNX [34], MINIX 3 [4], Sawmill [28], and Singularity [38], in particular, are structured around a number of hardware- or software-isolated processes communicating via message passing to support fault containment by design. NEaT is based on the partitioned network stack of NewtOS [37], a variant of MINIX 3, and supports different configurations. Unlike these systems, NEaT generally provides much stronger isolation guarantees—no multithreading—and relies on isolation to also support scalability by design, not only reliability. In addition, unlike NEaT, these systems do not generally partition or replicate state across components, with important scalability but also reliability drawbacks. For example, prior work demonstrated that most of these systems fail to recover from any failure in their stateful components [21]. Techniques devised to address this problem rely on state replication [21] or checkpointing [29]. Thanks to its state partitioning strategy, in contrast, NEaT can gracefully recover from failures by restarting the faulty replica, with no impact on the other replicas and thus minimal network state loss. Our recovery strategy is inspired by replication-based fault tolerance, a common design pattern in reliable distributed systems [30].

2.2 Scalability

Scalability of Implementation. To scale to the increasing number of available cores, network stacks in monolithic kernel architectures have grown to become massively threaded in modern implementations [67]. Although multithreading is a widely accepted strategy to achieve parallelism—and potentially scalability—the lack of *isolation* between threads comes at the cost of subordinating scalability to the implementation of complex synchronization mechanisms that grant safe access to shared data structures. Implementing provably correct synchronization primitives is challenging due to the complexity of modern hardware and compilers [24]. Implementing such primitives in a scalable way is even more challenging and also heavily dependent on the particular hardware [22].

Even widely deployed fine-grained locking primitives such as Linux' ticket spinlocks have been recently found plagued with scalability problems, with researchers showing that more scalable implementations such as MCS locks [46] are necessary to avoid dramatic performance drops on many-core architectures [16]. More scalable alternatives to locking include lockless data structures or lightweight synchronization mechanisms such as RCU [45]. While increasingly popular in the Linux kernel and especially in its network stack, RCU indirectly exemplifies the difficulties of implementing scalable and general-purpose synchronization primitives: it can only satisfy less than 8% of the entire kernel (9,000 uses) [6] and only provide scalable read-side semantics.

Further, monolithic architectures structured around a single address space allow all their threads to implicitly share arbitrary data structures. While a common programming abstraction, this approach enforces no explicit state *partitioning* and comes at the cost of subordinating scalability to the implementation's ability to limit sharing and preserve optimal data locality. In modern cache-coherent multicore architectures, this is crucial to prevent shared data from frequently (and unnecessarily) traveling between caches and hindering scalability. This is, for example, a well-known scalability bottleneck in many common synchronization primitive implementations [16].

To mitigate this problem, monolithic architectures strive to maintain data structures local to the core where they are most frequently used. Such implementation-driven strategies are, however, insufficient, since data structures still follow processes that migrate across cores—due to load balancing—and threads still share common data structures within the same process. A particularly insidious threat is *false sharing*, where different data structures that are not logically shared happen to reside on the same cache line, unnecessarily causing frequent—but silent—cache line bouncing [44]. gcc's controversial `__read_mostly` attribute exemplifies the difficulties of addressing this scalability problem at the implementation level: its adoption in the Linux kernel required 1554 annotations to group all the "*read-mostly*" variables together—preventing conflicts with frequently modified cachelines—but only to raise concerns that many remaining "*write-often*" variables may then increase cache line sharing—ultimately degrading write-side scalability [7].

Scalability of Design. While scalability of implementation is still a realistic—but already cumbersome—option today [15], many researchers have recognized the need for principles supporting scalability of design before, without, however, applying them in a radical way or also addressing reliability concerns. Tornado [26] and K42 [10] first argued for "*partitioning, distributing,* and *replicating*" data across independent (but not isolated) objects to improve locality on shared-memory multiprocessors. In a similar direction, Corey [14] proposes granting applications the ability to limit sharing of OS data structures and improve scalability. In all these systems, however, multithreading and sharing are still the norm, greatly limiting the opportunities offered by true isolation and partitioning. Corey [14] partitions the network stack state across multiple per-core replicas. Unlike NEaT, however, Corey's library OS-based design imposes strict partitioning at the application level as well, greatly limiting application-level sharing. More recent solutions such as IX [12] and Arrakis [53]— building on top of Dune and Barrelfish [11] multikernel architectures (respectively)—share similar issues imposed by the underlying library OS model.

Unlike all these systems, we will demonstrate that, in the context of a network stack in particular, a more radical design based on even stricter isolation and partitioning—no implicit or explicit sharing—is realistic and effective, with important scalability, but also reliability benefits. More recently, fos [66] also assessed the potential utility of replicating core OS services across cores, but without considering its reliability benefits or evaluating scalability at high bit and request rates. Finally, recent work advocates reconsidering scalability as a property of the interfaces rather than of the implementation, proposing a *commutativity rule* to assess the scalability of high-level operations [19]. Our work is similar in that we advocate for reconsidering the drive for scalability of implementation, but also complementary in that we investigate scalability at the design rather than at the interface level.

Finally, scalable network stacks such as IsoStack [58], MegaPipe [31], and mTCP [39] focus solely on scalability with no emphasis on reliability. They also take a less radical approach to scalability with limited isolation and partitioning as their main goal is to circumvent the performance limitations imposed by monolithic architectures. However, the userspace library stacks such as mTCP can also run in a multiserver OS on top of a microkernel with similar benefits and limitations as in a monolithic system.

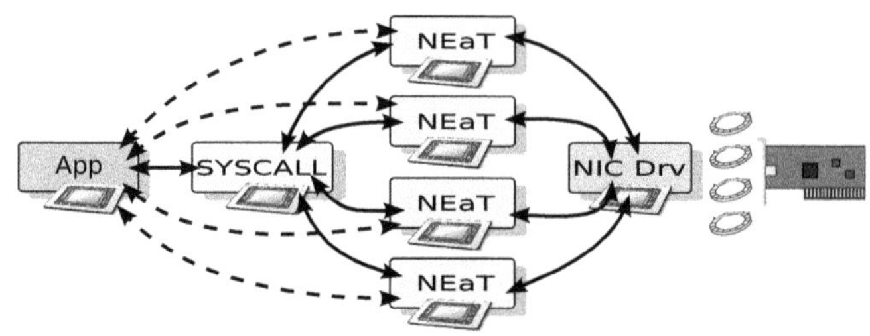

Figure 1: NEaT: a 4-replica example.

3. A RELIABLE AND SCALABLE NETWORK STACK

We present NEaT, the first network stack designed from the ground up for reliability and scalability. To enforce isolation of its components, NEaT relies on a microkernel-based architecture with all the core OS components running as event-driven and hardware-isolated processes. Thanks to such isolation guarantees, each component of the network stack can be provided with fault containment capabilities and also assigned its own core. While beneficial for reliability, this design is highly unsatisfactory for scalability purposes.

The key scalability problem of a system executing as a set of isolated processes is that any of its components may easily get overloaded, even when assigned an entire CPU core for itself. We rule out having multithreaded components spanning multiple cores as this strategy would impose the same scalability limitations evidenced in monolithic architectures. For this reason, NEaT opts for a radically different design, that is partitioning the network state across a number of isolated processes replicated from the original components of the network stack (replicas).

NEaT's design eliminates *implicit* synchronization and sharing both within the individual processes (by disallowing threading) and across generic OS processes (by allowing communication only via message passing). The latter guarantees that each process always modifies only its own data structures—except the messaging queues. At the same time, NEaT's design also eliminates *explicit* synchronization and sharing across stack replicas (by disallowing communication) so that the network stack can both scale and simplify failure recovery. A failing replica does not prevent other replicas from continuing running undisturbed, causing minimal service disruption and state loss.

3.1 Overview

Figure 1 presents the high-level overview of NEaT, which internally partitions the network state across several replicas (4 in the example). Each replica communicates with each NIC driver and, by default, applications communicate with all the replicas of the network stack as though only one logical instance were present—although it is possible to configure NEaT differently. This is

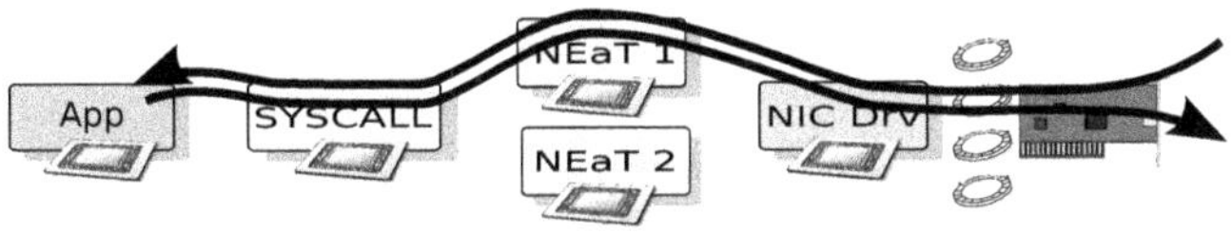

Figure 2: A dedicated path for packets of each connection.

transparent to the application programmer, since all the blocking system calls are routed through a dedicated system call server (SYSCALL). Our socket implementation (§3.2), however, allows applications to largely bypass the SYSCALL server and communicate directly with the assigned replica of the network stack (dashed lines in Figure 1). This complexity is hidden by our user-space POSIX library. The individual OS processes are assigned dedicated cores, allowing fast communication between OS components without intervention of the microkernel, an idea previously explored in the original NewtOS' network stack [37].

With no data sharing or synchronization across replicas, NEaT allows each network socket to live only in a single instance of the network stack. This is especially important for TCP, as each TCP connection requires the stack to maintain a large amount of state and NEaT must ensure that every packet of each connection uses the same path through the network stack (Figure 2). The applications (libraries), the SYSCALL server, and the network devices are responsible for selecting the network stack replica to handle each socket. fos proposes using a fleet coordinator for similar replica selection problems [66]. NEaT, in contrast, allows no process with a special role, since the intention is to avoid explicit communication between the processes of the network stack. Our solution is to delegate part of the data plane functionality to the hardware, similar, in spirit, to Arrakis [53] and IX [12]. In contrast to both projects, NEaT does not aim at separating independent instances of library systems or userspace stacks used by different applications. NEaT aims at separating collections of replicas that form a single network stack accessed by multiple applications.

Contemporary network devices already have the ability to match incoming packets by a set of rules, split the traffic, and steer packets to the intended network stack replica using multiple internal NIC queues. The NIC driver can thus dispatch the packets to the right replica based on the receive queue of the NIC. Although these modern features were originally motivated by the design of monolithic systems and virtualization, NEaT successfully exploits them to implement replica-aware connection management.

3.2 Sockets

While adhering to the POSIX API, NewtOS refrains from using a traditional implementation of network sockets for scalability reasons. Our socket implementation, which we described in detail in [35], requires the network stack and the applications to run on different hardware threads. While applications occasionally communicate with the SYSCALL server, NEaT resolves the vast majority of the system calls within the application itself, exposing socket buffers to the application level similar to user-space message queues.

The socket design makes the replication transparent to the applications as once a socket is open and the system establishes the corresponding shared-memory channel, an application can automatically communicate with the right network stack replica without exact knowledge of the particular replica on the other end. This makes the fast path completely agnostic to the number of network stack replicas, ensuring scalability to a large number of network stacks (and cores).

In contrast to monolithic systems, multiserver systems have a key and a little counterintuitive CPU load distribution difference. Our experience when running a loaded server on Linux—also confirmed by others [39]—indicates that it is realistic to expect approximately 70-80% of the execution to happen within the operating system (the kernel). If an application in Linux uses 30% of overall cycles, this is exactly equivalent to the same application using all cycles of 30% of all cores in NewtOS. The conclusion is that while NEaT reduces the number of cores normally available to the applications, the load distribution has generally no negative impact on the end-to-end networked application performance.

3.3 TCP Connections

We focus our analysis on TCP as UDP and other protocols build on top of it are fairly simple to handle as they are stateless, however, most Internet traffic uses the more challenging stateful TCP protocol. TCP raises interesting challenges by maintaining per-connection state. When initiating a client connection, the socket library selects the network stack replica to handle the connection, while, when accepting a TCP connection from a remote client, the NIC decides based on hashes or filtering rules, as it is the first component to process each packet. Once the decision on the replica responsible to handle the connection is made, both the NIC and the libraries must honor the choice. This process is transparent to the application programmer and hidden by the provided libraries (§4).

To be able to accept a connection through different network stack replicas, the listening TCP sockets are the only types of sockets that are replicated across all the possible stacks. Binding listening sockets to a single replica would otherwise force NEaT to assign all the incoming connections to the same replica, resulting in load imbalance (and less unpredictability, i.e., security). Note that listening sockets are replicated across all the network stacks only at `listen()`-time, given that there is no general way of knowing whether a socket will be a listening socket at creation time. `listen()` call tells the library to create a socket per each replica of the stack, they all listen at the same address and are not visible to the application. Each "*subsocket*" remains then fully isolated in a single replica, with the user library hiding the underlying replication from the application itself. Applications can simply use the original file descriptor obtained at socket creation time, allowing the library to perform the necessary socket-subsocket mapping operations behind the scenes if needed. The `accept` implementation, for instance, checks for any subsocket with an available incoming connection and simply "*accepts*" the connection from it. This also allows the loopback devices to be implemented by each of the replicas. After a connection is accepted with a new socket number, the new socket is independent of all other sockets with its own communication set up. This is fully transparent to the application and the library. Neither needs to be aware of which replica owns a particular socket. The library only translates between socket numbers and the internal communication channels. Therefore, there is no need for synchronization. Details of the communication, notifications and buffer mappings are described in [35].

Since connections are naturally spread across several different isolated replicas, NEaT can easily allow for accepting connections in parallel and in a conflict-free way. In a system with a single instance of the listening socket, in contrast, there is contention when multiple threads attempt to access the socket simultaneously. Recent work has sought to directly address this particular problem on Linux [31, 52]. Unlike these systems, NEaT eliminates the need for synchronizing access to the subsockets residing in different network stack replicas altogether, allowing different application threads to accept from a single subsocket while "stealing" connections from others for load balancing purposes with synchronization limited to the application.

3.4 Scaling Up and Down

By default, NEaT runs with a static number of replicas to enforce stable and predetermined reliability guarantees. In settings where a limited number of cores is available and reducing reliability guarantees is an option, we describe how NEaT can fulfill more dynamic scalability requirements by scaling the number of replicas in use up and down depending on the current load and the performance required by the applications. For example, when certain parts of the system are not needed, it is possible to place multiple components on a single core, for example idle NIC drivers.

The system boots with at least one replica, depending on the redundancy requirements. When NEaT becomes overloaded, it automatically spawns a new network stack replica. Since the NIC has rules for the existing connections, their distribution remains intact as long as each connection exists. The new connections are assigned across all the replicas. This may lead to initial imbalance in load distribution after reconfiguration. We expect the system to rebalance itself as soon as existing connections terminate and new connections appear.

When the load drops again, NEaT can also scale down and terminate some network stack replicas. Since the connections are in a general case likely distributed across all the replicas, simply shutting down a single replica would result in abruptly terminating all the TCP connections handled by it—similar to the effect caused by an unexpected failure. Migrating connections from a replica in termination state to another replica in nontermination state, however, would require handing off TCP-related state and in-flight data of currently non-idle connections. NEaT would also need to change the filtering rules in the NIC. This strategy is overly complicated and also violates NEaT's isolation principles, potentially introducing subtle reliability and scalability issues. For these reasons, NEaT adopts a different strategy, which (i) marks the necessary replicas as in termination state and makes the corresponding cores available to the applications; (ii) instructs the NIC to distribute new connections only to replicas in nontermination state but continue to serve packets on existing connections across all the replicas; (iii) garbage collects replicas in termination state as soon as their connection count drops to zero. This approach implements an effective lazy termination strategy without breaking any of the existing connections. The trade off is a slower scaling down phase, which, however, only results in short-lived resource overcommitment periods and can actually better handle load fluctuations—that is quickly scaling up again whenever necessary.

In general, creating and terminating network stack replicas incurs latency and management overhead. In addition, the number of replicas the applications can indirectly use is limited by the ratio of cores dedicated to the system compared to those dedicated to the applications. Many modern CPUs, however, support several hardware threads on each core, for example the SPARC T7 processor features 8 threads per core. This allows NEaT to use significantly more replicas than cores while preserving fast user-space communication, given that each replica maintains its own hardware context. Interestingly, as shown in §6, this strategy allows NEaT to use available cores more efficiently, given that a single process can hardly use up all the core's cycles due to the latency of main memory [50]. We conclude that scaling down the number of replicas is not always necessary and, when hyper-threading is available, a better scale-down strategy is to relocate the replicas.

3.5 Scaling NIC Drivers

The only performance-sensitive component that NEaT does not actively scale up is the NIC driver, since none of our tests demonstrated the driver to be a potential performance bottleneck and also other researchers [54] have reported 10G line rate processing on a single core. From a reliability point of view, previous research has demonstrated the ability to seamlessly recover NIC drivers without replication [33].

Figure 3: A replica of the multi-component network stack

3.6 Reliability

Isolation and partitioning of the network stack are key to the reliability of NEaT. The individual replicas are isolated and do not interact with each other, preventing a failure in one of the replicas from having any direct or indirect reliability impact on all the other replicas. Currently, NEaT opts for a completely stateless failure recovery strategy: when a replica crashes, a new replica is created and all the TCP-related state associated to the failed replica is lost. While supporting more complex stateful recovery policies is possible, this simple approach fully embraces our state partitioning strategy and ensures minimal state loss with all the other replicas continuing to serve existing and new connections with no interference or global service disruption. During the (short) recovery phase, the driver does not pass any packets to the recovering replica until it announces itself again. This strategy eliminates the need to reconfigure the device.

3.7 Multi-component Network Stack

Although each network stack replica can run as a single process, NEaT can also be configured (at compile time) to vertically split each replica into multiple isolated processes for increased reliability. Although this strategy requires more cores and internal communication, it also yields improved reliability since it can fully isolate faults in smaller network components. Excluding TCP, the other components are essentially stateless (or pseudostateless) and thus more easily amenable to application-transparent recovery even with a stateless recovery strategy. When adopting more heavyweight stateful recovery strategies such as the one described in [29], our state partitioning strategy effectively decreases the state surface to recover and reduces the likelihood of state corruption. Figure 3 presents a simplified version of a multi-component network stack replica, showing only the IP and TCP components used for TCP processing, but additional UDP and packet filter components are also present and isolated from the rest of the stack.

3.8 Security

Replication has been previously proposed for security purposes, using synchronized multivariant execution to detect arbitrary memory error attacks [20, 55, 56]. Unlike these approaches—which incur high run-time overhead—NEaT pursues the less ambitious goal of enforcing *address space re-randomization* [59] across user connections. NEaT naturally enforces this security defensive mechanism as part of its design at no extra cost. This is simply done by binding each connection to a random replica, while creating each replica independently and with ASLR [1] enabled. The latter strategy yields completely different memory layouts across (semantically equivalent) replicas, resulting in consecutive user connections being handled by processes with *unpredictably* different memory layouts. Albeit not our primary focus here, our design can support such address space re-randomization strategy in a natural and inexpensive way, effectively countering recent memory error attacks that rely on a stable memory layout across user connections [13, 57].

4. HARDWARE SUPPORT

NEaT requires certain hardware features for an efficient implementation. For example, the current implementation of our fast user-space communication channels relies on the `MWAIT` x86 instruction that allows NEaT to halt a core and enables a process running on another core to wake up the first core using a simple memory write. This eliminates kernel assistance for expensive interprocessor interrupts and process halting. Note that NEaT actually switches to such slower communication channels as needed automatically, in particular when the load is low and allowing the scheduler to colocate processes on shared cores—thus freeing up the dedicated ones—becomes an appealing option. To share the cores more efficiently, NEaT also exploits hardware multithreading, which results in increased parallelism, coalescing replicas on fewer cores, and the ability to leverage `MWAIT`-based communication channels. We evaluate the benefits of hardware multithreading in §6.

Efficiently scaling the network stack replicas requires dedicated NIC support to split the packet flow. Commonly available NICs feature many pairs of transmit and receive queues. NEaT uses one pair of queues to direct packets to each network stack replica. The controller can place the packets on different queues based on different criteria, using protocol fields to uniquely identify each flow. In contrast to the number of cores, the number of queues is not a limiting factor. In particular, modern network cards can already classify and steer packets to different endpoints (i.e., different processes and/or virtual machines) based on a hash of a 5-element tuple including destination, source addresses, ports, and protocol number, or also use precise filters over the same fields. For example, Intel 10G cards can hold up to 8 thousand filters. Software is, however, responsible for configuring the filters, which makes issuing frequent updates impractical with hundreds of thousands of connections per second. The NIC programming interface, in particular, requires many read-write transactions across the PCI bus to configure the filters, which can negatively impact network processing [25]. For instance, the Intel ixgbe driver on Linux can optionally use TCP packet sampling, which sets up the NIC's filters to track locality of connections [15]—hence offloading the work done by receive flow steering (RFS [32]). Due to performance concerns, the driver only samples every 20th packet.

Since the NIC already inspects packets in its local memory, we believe a much more practical solution—which, however, requires extensions not yet available in contemporary commodity hardware—is adding extra logic into the NIC and creating "tracking" filters based on the packets the NIC handles. Such filters would simply instruct the NIC to ensure all the corresponding packets of each flow follow the same route.

On contemporary hardware, it is theoretically possible to implement the missing connection tracking features in the NIC driver itself (mimicking a smart NIC). We, however, felt this was a step in the wrong direction, when compared to the much more realistic option of offloading such support to the hardware, similar to TCP segmentation (TSO), large receive (LRO), and other similar features which eventually made their way into modern hardware. For this reason—but also not to introduce artificial overhead moving forward—we opted for a different solution in our experiments, compensating for the missing hardware features by limiting our evaluation to server applications, while still relying on contemporary NIC's hash functions to randomly distribute the inbound connections.

Summarizing, similar to Arrakis [53] and IX [12], our scalability design strongly advocates for the devices taking over part of the system data plane while the operating system acts only as a control plane managing its settings, for instance the TCP `TIME_WAIT` timeout. We can also look at the NIC as an additional processing core that runs certain parts of the stack very efficiently, while lacking the huge flexibility of a generic core. Therefore, dedicating a core of a truly many-core system might be an option. We believe that, as modern NICs have already evolved to match the requirements of monolithic systems, reliability and scalability of design can effectively initiate similar developments or may lead to a renaissance of programmable network cards. If the programmable NIC were to offer the same interface as the network driver (as we have done previously [36]), there would be no need for the drivers and we could free their cores.

5. COMPARISON WITH OTHER USERSPACE NETWORK STACKS

As discussed in §2, the literature documents many existing efforts to build user-mode network stacks. The primary motivation to implement a network stack in user space is to bypass and eliminate the overhead imposed by the operating system, typically implemented as a monolithic kernel that runs its own network stack in privileged mode and exposes it to user applications. The most common examples of such an operating system architecture are Linux, BSD, and Windows.

Unlike traditional user-mode network stacks, NEaT's goal is not to bypass the operating system itself, but to implement a generic network stack that is presented by the operating system to the applications through a standard and widely used POSIX interface. NEaT is a user-mode stack by definition, as all parts of the NewtOS operating system itself are implemented as unprivileged code running on top of a microkernel. We believe that any microkernel such as L4 or a multikernel such as Barrelfish could offer similar IPC mechanisms the NewtOS kernel provides. We also believe that even a monolithic kernel such as Linux could provide such mechanisms, and even though the NEaT design does not naturally map to a monolithic system design, it can represent a scalable and reliable alternative to the native network stack of monolithic operating systems.

Userspace stacks such as mTCP [39], MegaPipe [31], and OpenOnload [5] target low latencies by avoiding system calls and interacting directly with the devices. These stacks are linked directly against a given application to bypass the operating system. Thereby, they are not generally available to other applications on the system to facilitate sharing and cooperation. This strategy minimizes various overheads that a generic network stack cannot afford ignoring and hence applications that use such a network stack outperform applications that use the good-for-all stack provided by the operating system. NEaT and NewtOS draw inspiration from these projects and their sockets (§3.2 and [35]) are implemented in a nearly system-call-less fashion. Similarly, the networks stacks of Arrakis [53] and IX [12] are tuned for low latency and low overhead, closer to a library OS design rather than a general-purpose stack like NEaT.

On the reliability side, userspace network stacks increase the overall reliability of the system, as a fault in the network stack does not affect applications that do not use it. However, there is no isolation between the stack and its application. Nevertheless, such network stacks are useful in certain domains and it is, in fact, plausible to allow particular applications in NewtOS to use such a design next to other applications that use NEaT within the same system.

6. EVALUATION

We evaluated NEaT using two different multicore machines: (i) a 12-core AMD Opteron 6168 (1.9 GHz) and (ii) a dual-socket quad-core Intel Xeon E5520 (2.26 GHz). The AMD machine has more physical cores, but the Xeon machine features 2 hardware threads per core (hyperthreading). For our experiments, we used a 10G Intel i82599 network card in each machine. This network card implements some features required in order to steer incoming network traffic to different replicas, as well as TSO (TCP Segment Offloading) which greatly improves performance and allows smaller configurations to reach a full 10Gb/s throughput utilization. The two machines are connected through a 10GbE DAC—Direct Attach

Option Tuned	kreq/s
defaults	184.118
sched+eth+irqAff+rxAff	186.667
sched+eth+irqAff+rxAff+serv	**223.987**

Table 1: Request rate breakdown per option tuned, with 12 concurrent httperf instances, each opening 1000 connections, with 1000 requests for a 20 byte file per connection. *sched* refers to the scheduler policy set to deadline, *eth* turns off auto-negotiation and uses TSO, *irqAff* sets IRQ affinities, *rxAff* sets receive queues affinity, *serv* denotes lighttpd being pinned to cores.

Copper—SFP+ cable. Depending on the experiment they alternate roles between system under test and load generator.

6.1 Linux

For comparison purposes, we selected Ubuntu Server 14.04 LTS as our Linux reference system. We configured our installation with default settings except for the fine tuning presented in Table 1 to yield the highest possible performance. Likewise, we used a default lighttpd configuration, except for the two following changes: (i) we allowed up to a thousand (1000) requests per TCP connection, and (ii) we ran each lighttpd server on a different TCP port. This section provides details on tuning Linux on the AMD machine.

Table 1 presents a breakdown of options we tuned in order to improve as much as possible the performance of our Linux baseline to ensure a fair comparison. We first evaluated the out-of-the-box performance (defaults) on our testbed, then we changed the scheduler policy to earliest deadline. Next, we used `ethtool` to turn auto-negotiation off and TSO on. As shown in the table, we obtained the first substantial gains when setting the IRQs affinities (irqAff). We observed, in turn, that the request rate drops when we manually set the receive queues affinity (reqAff), most likely explained by the lighttpd processes being scheduled on different cores than where the related receive queues are pinned. The best performing configuration is when we also pin the lighttpd processes to a specific core (serv). Using RFS did not result in observable benefits and as such was not considered in the final configuration.

In each case, we used 12 httperf processes —one per client machine's core— each targeted at one specific, different port. For each port we started a different lighttpd server.

Httperf dismisses from the request rate and throughput any connection which has an error. Given that errors might happen at any time during the connection, the actual bandwidth is higher than reported when connection errors occur. Figure 4 shows a clear correlation between the number of requests issued and the evolution of latency. As soon as we switch to moderately large files (between 100K - 1M), the latency dramatically increases,

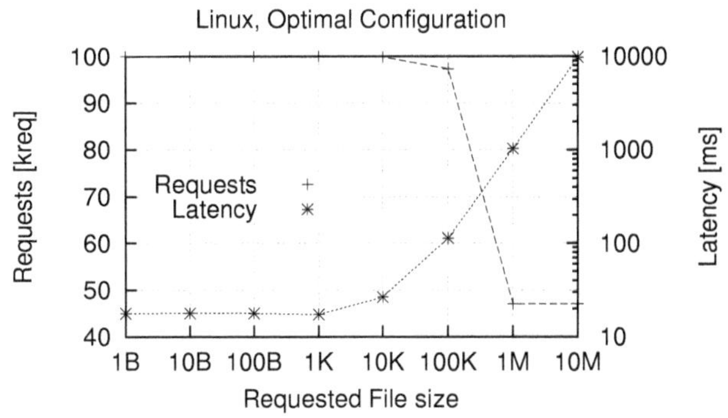

Figure 4: Latency and total number of requests vs. file size

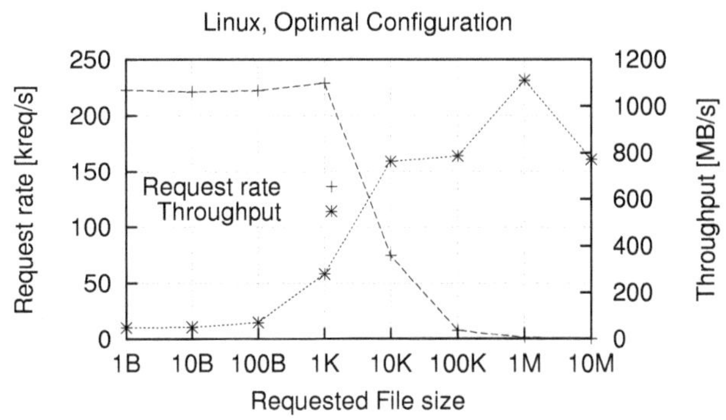

Figure 5: Throughput and request rate vs. file size

the number of requests drops, as the link bandwidth becomes the limiting factor. Figure 5 shows the relationship between the *successful* request rate and bandwidth. As soon as the link bandwidth reaches saturation, we see a high variance in the number of successful transfers. For file sizes between 100KB, 1MB and 10MB, the bandwidth fluctuates heavily as connection errors start appearing —timeouts and connection resets mainly— forcing httperf to discard results in its reports, lowering the scores. As figure 5 shows, as soon as the file size exceeds 7KB, the 10Gb/s bandwidth becomes the bottleneck. This is why, in all the following experiments, we used a very small size of 20 bytes for the requests as this is what stresses the most the network stack, the least the web server and other components of the OS, and also guarantees that the hardware doesn't introduces limitation other than CPU-bound issues.

6.2 Scalability

Evaluating the scalability of NEaT required us to select a representative server application, known to efficiently scale to a large number of CPUs and thus able to expose scalability deficiencies in the underlying network stack. As we wanted to evaluate the stack by itself, the actual application is not really important, as long as it "does as little as possible", lest we (partially) measure the application or other subsystems rather than the net-

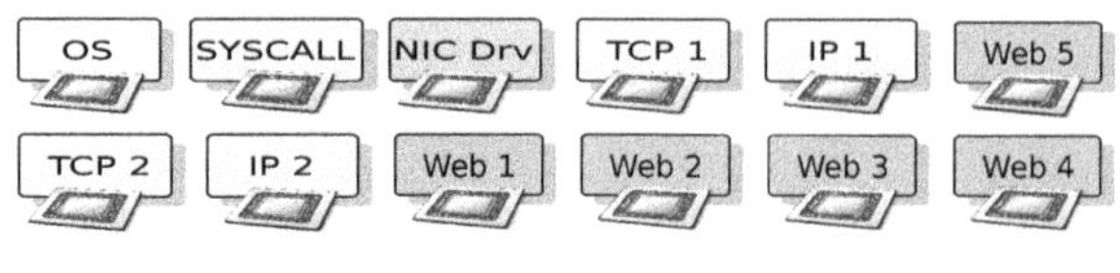

(a) Multi-component stacks

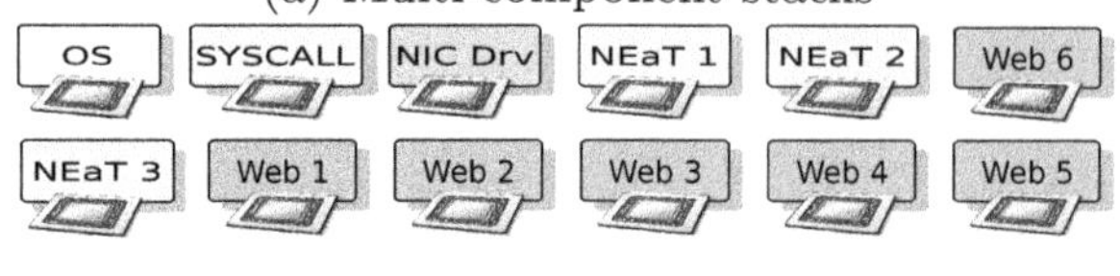

(b) Single-component stacks

Figure 6: AMD - The best configurations - all 12 cores

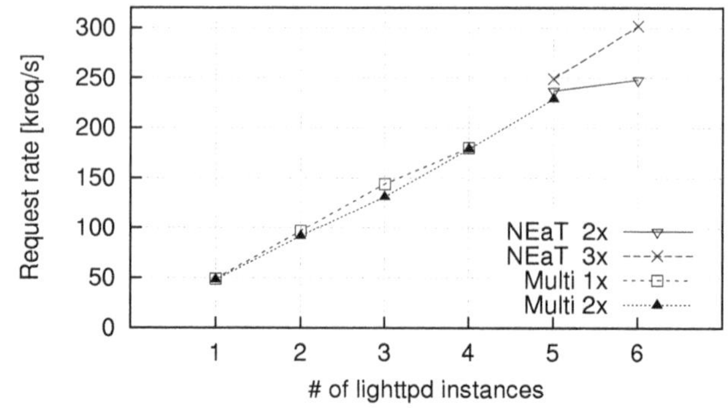

Figure 7: AMD - Scaling lighttpd and the network stack

work stack. For our purposes, we selected lighttpd, an efficient web server application, and made it serve only static files cached in memory to minimize interference with other operating system subsystems.

We evaluated NEaT both in single- and multi-component configurations. In the figures, we denote such configurations as NEaT Nx and Multi Nx respectively, where N refers to the number of replicas used. We also refer to a particular replica R as NEaT R and TCP R (or IP R).

To evaluate the scalability, we used the *httperf* benchmarking utility to repeatedly open persistent connections and request a small 20-byte file 100× per connection. This workload stresses the network stack without taking advantage of NIC offloading features, while allowing us to scale up the number of servers freely. A lighttpd instance serving just 8 or more simultaneous connections can drive the application cores close to 100% utilization. At the same time, repeatedly requesting small files stresses the network stack as it must handle many requests from the network as well as the applications.

6.3 Scalability on a 12-core AMD

We first present results on the 12-core AMD. The number of available cores allows us to compare both single- and multi-component configurations. Figure 6 illustrates both configurations in their best-performing setups and Figure 7 presents scalability results for the different configurations of NEaT. In our experiments, we dedicated one of the cores to all the remaining operating system processes (OS) and one of the cores to the SYSCALL server, which generally needs its own core for low-latency messaging when the load is relatively low, but its role is crucial to ramp up the load for testing purposes. As the load grows, the core becomes increasingly idle, since the applications can bypass it with our mostly system-call-less socket design.This leaves our test machine with 10 cores available for the network stack and lighttpd. As Figure 7 shows, a configuration consisting of a single replica of the multi-component stack can scale fairly linearly up to 4 lighttpd instances. At that point, the stack becomes overloaded, but 3 cores remain completely unused. Adding one more replica can use up 2 (TCP, IP) of the 3 remaining cores, allowing the throughput to scale further, up to 5 lighttpd instances. Although the CPU usage suggests that NEaT could effectively scale further, no more cores are available to scale up our multi-component stack with more replicas or applications. While we do not have more cores at our disposal, we believe NEaT would in fact scale to larger numbers with no restrictions. The single-component version of NEaT, on the other hand, scales further. In particular, *NEaT 2x* performs comparably to its multi-component counterpart when serving up to 5 lighttpd instances. With an additional replica (*NEaT 3x*), NEaT perfectly scales up to 6 lighttpd instances. Similar to *Multi 2x*, NEaT is not overloaded yet.

We have conducted similar experiments for lighttpd running on Linux on the same hardware. When using all 12 cores, in the best performing configuration, lighttpd handled 224 kilo-requests per second (krps). With 3 single-component replicas, NEaT reached 302 krps (i.e., 34.8% more requests per second).

6.4 Scalability on a 8-core Xeon

Current trends suggest that the number of cores will keep growing (for example, Intel announced a new 72-core version of Knight's Landing [2] and SPARC T7 has 256 threads on a die) and, above all, as other researchers have suggested [41, 48, 60, 65], cores will become more heterogeneous and specialized. Nevertheless, our experience demonstrates that NEaT can replace cores by hardware threads—which are much cheaper—allowing NEaT's processes to use the available cores more efficiently. The general intuition is that hyper-threading allows NEaT to efficiently colocate relatively idle processes—which need their own context—like the SYSCALL server. Although a hardware thread is not the same as a fully-fledged core, the threaded setup can handle more load and provide redundancy. To confirm this intuition, we present our scalability results on a Xeon with hyper-threading.

Figure 8 depicts an example of using hyper-threading to reduce the number of cores that 2 NEaT replicas normally require in core-only configurations (a). For example, NEaT can colocate the NIC driver with the SYSCALL server, since as the driver's thread becomes

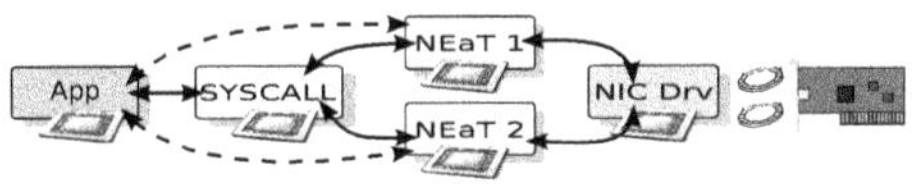

(a) All components on dedicated cores

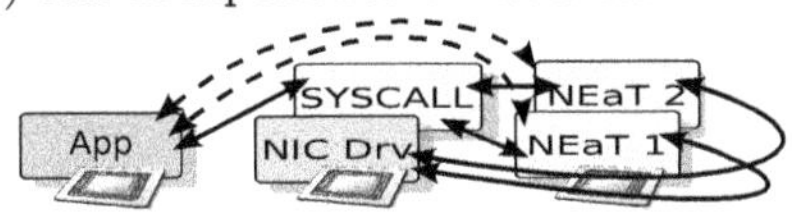

(b) Colocated components using hyper-threading

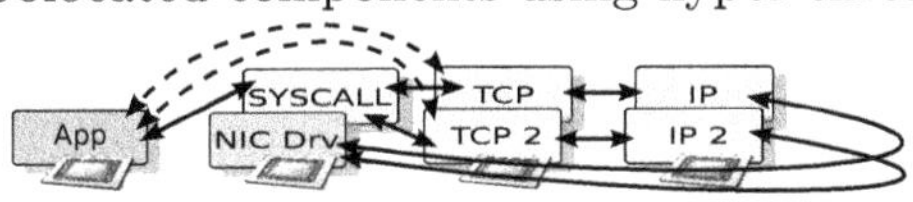

(c) Colocated multi-component configuration of NEaT

Figure 8: Reducing the used number of cores with threads

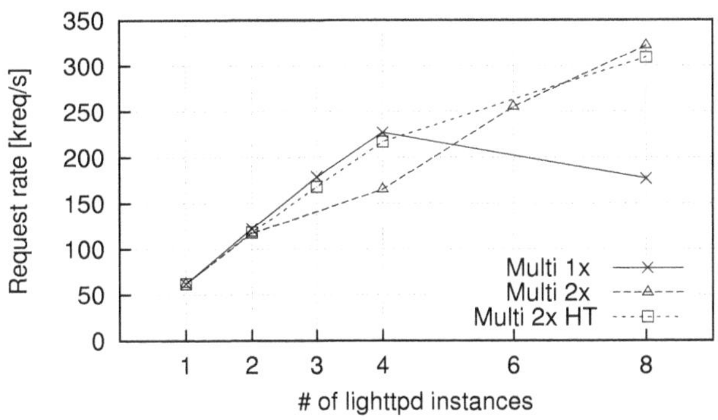

Figure 9: Xeon - Scaling the multi-component stack

more loaded, the SYSCALL's thread gets less loaded, ensuring little interference between the two processes. NEaT can also successfully place multiple NIC drivers on the same core. Similarly, the multi-component configuration of NEaT can use only 3 cores instead of the 6 cores used in the original configuration (Figure 8c). We use HT to denote the NEaT configurations that use hyper-threading.

In contrast to the AMD, deploying the TCP and IP processes leaves only 4 cores available for lighttpd. NEaT can now, however, take advantage of hyper-threads to run 8 instances. Figure 9 shows that similar to the AMD case, the throughput of the network stack peaks when using 4 lighttpd instances.

To scale further, we ran a second replica (*Multi 2x*), which leaves only 2 cores for lighttpd. Using all 4 threads of those cores reported similar performance to the 3-application-instance scenario in the previous test. This is expected, since the network stack is not the bottleneck and the 33% speedup (2 cores instead of 3) of the application is within the bounds of the benefits of hyper-threading. Further scaling up—denoted by points 6 and 8 in Figure 9—uses threads on the cores occupied by the network stack itself, first using both TCP (6 lighttpd instances) and then both IP cores (8 lighttpd

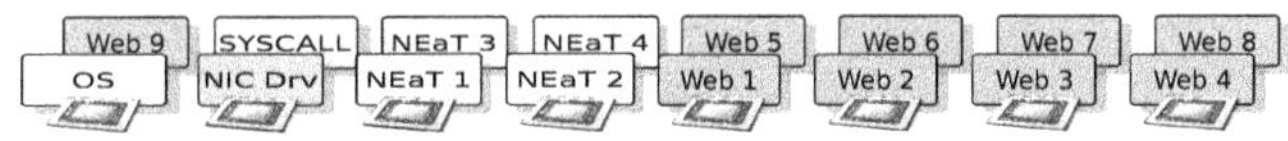

Figure 10: Xeon - The best-performing configuration of the NEaT, fully exploiting hyper-threading.

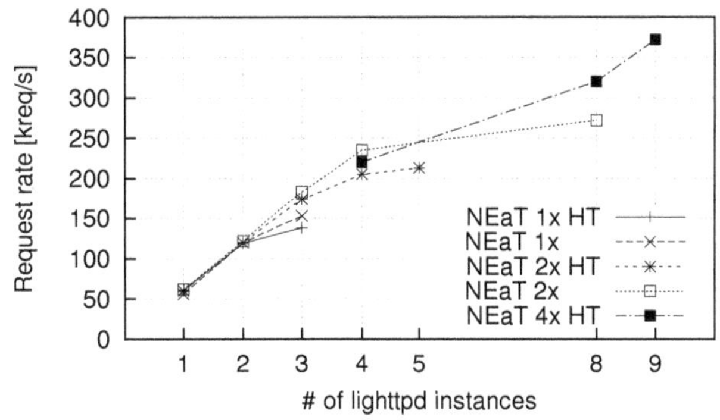

Figure 11: Xeon - Scaling the single-component stack

instances). In the latter configuration, Figure 9 shows the throughput peaking at 322 krps.

Finally, we colocated two replicas on different threads from the same cores (*Multi 2x HT*, Figure 8c)—enforcing this policy for both TCP and IP replicas. As expected, 4 lighttpd instances yielded similar performance to the 1-replica configuration, since the stack is not the bottleneck and—while using the same number of cores as in the 1-replica configuration—can handle 8 lighttpd instances (4 cores, both threads).

When evaluating single-component configurations, we used up to 4 replicas, as shown in Figure 10. The labels (*NEaT*x and *WebX*) illustrate the order in which we scaled up NEaT and lighttpd. We present the results in Figure 11. Note that once NEaT becomes overloaded, it can spawn another replica and keep processing the growing load. As the figure shows, *NEaT 4x* can sustain the load of 372 krps, using all cores up to 100%. This is a 13.4% improvement over 328 krps maximum we measured for the best Linux configuration on the Xeon, running 16 lighttpd instances on each of the 8 cores / 16 threads.

6.5 Impact of Different Configurations

Finally, we evaluated the impact of the different configurations of NEaT and compared their overhead in detail. We used a modified test issuing only a single request per connection, which significantly increases the load on the network stack itself. We evaluated 5 different configurations of the network stack using the 12-core AMD and different workloads. We deployed (i) 1 lighttpd instance processing 8 to 64 simultaneous connections, (ii) 2 instances processing 32 simultaneous connections, and (iii) 4 instances processing 64 simultaneous connections. Figure 12 reports our results, demonstrating that when the load is relatively low, using only a single replica of the multi-component stack to handle 8 connections is better than using 2 such replicas. This is primarily

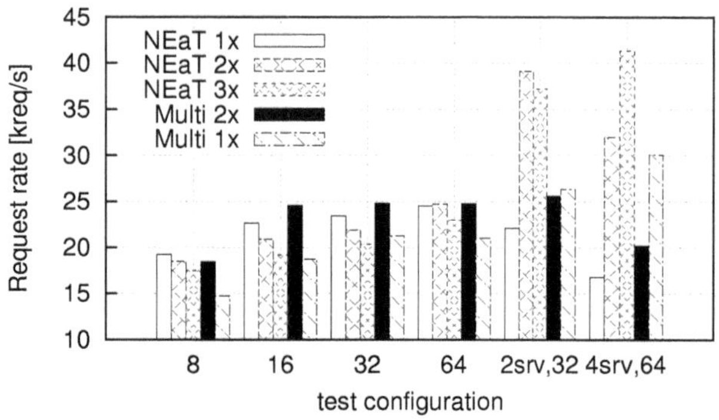

Figure 12: 12-core AMD - Comparing performance of different configurations stressed by the same workload.

CPU load	Active in kernel	Polling	Web krps
6%	33.3%	51.8%	3
60%	14.2%	27.9%	45
88%	5.4%	19.7%	90
97%	0.1%	7.4%	242

Table 2: 10G driver CPU usage breakdown on Xeon.

due to the fact that lightly loaded components often sleep, which introduces latency that is more evident in the multi-component stack. At higher loads, having multiple network stack replicas becomes more obviously beneficial.

Table 2 presents samples collected using statistical profiling of the NIC driver under a range of loads serving 3 replicas. A mostly idle driver spends a significant portion of the active time suspending/resuming in the kernel (as Intel's `MWAIT` is a privileged instruction), polling the 3 stacks and the NIC queues. The "wasted" time shrinks with increasing load. When the core's usage is close to 100%, the driver almost never enters the kernel and uses more than 90% of its time processing. Other components show similar behavior. Note that the CPU usage grows sharply, but levels off as the driver trades more of the "wasted" time for useful processing. While the CPU load is 60% when the lighttpd handles 45 krps, the load is only 88% when the number of requests doubles and still lower than 100% when the number of requests increases almost 5-fold.

6.6 Reliability

To thoroughly assess the reliability properties of our design, we first performed fault injection experiments on the different components of a NEaT replica. For our purposes, we developed a fault injection tool inspired by similar tools adopted in prior work to evaluate fault-tolerant designs [64, 47]. In our experiments, we injected faults into various (randomly selected) parts of the code in the network stack and monitored their impact on the execution. We ignored runs without any visible crash within a minute from the injection (e.g., runs with no fault activation) and collected results from 100 failing runs. We restarted the system after every run to clean up. For our experiments, we used the same test workload as the one used for our scalability evaluation.

Fully transparent recovery	53.8%
TCP connections lost	46.2%

Table 3: Fault injection experiment results.

Table 3 shows the recovery success rate in our fault injection experiments. In more than 50% cases, we observed fully transparent failure recovery—applications nor the users notice—with no manual intervention needed and the effect on network traffic being no worse than a packet delay or loss. Since packet losses happen regularly on the Internet, we expect the impact of (infrequent) failure recovery to be negligible in practice—even under heavy load conditions. In all the other cases, the faults caused a crash in the TCP component, which resulted in the abrupt termination of all the open TCP connections (and loss of TCP state in general). After recovery, however, the TCP server was always reachable and, as expected, ready to establish new client connections.

Our fault injection results directly derive from the properties of our stack implementation, which, for drivers, IP, UDP, and packet filter component, maintain no or little read-mostly state which can thus be preserved in an independent data store, configuration file, or just recreated at restart time. In contrast, our TCP component maintains significant per-connection read/write state, read/write control state, and in-flight data. As a result, only TCP faults can cause visible state loss (and failures) in a single replica of our stack. In addition, thanks to the state partitioning and isolation strategy used by NEaT, only the TCP connections (and state) of the failing replica are lost while the connections managed by other replicas are completely unaffected. In other words, the larger the number of replicas, the lower the fraction of state lost after failures and thus the higher the reliability guarantees.

We discuss the reliability of a single replica experiment in more detail in our previous work [37]. Due to the complete isolation of the replicas, the fact that we run multiple replicas of the same multi-component network stack side by side has no impact on the fault recovery capabilities of each replica independently. We verified each replica can recover from a crash of its components without any interference with the other replicas. More interestingly, the overall resiliency of a network stack that consists of multiple replicas grows with the number of replicas.

To estimate the concrete reliability benefits of our replicated design, Figure 13 shows the expected fraction of state preserved after a failure against the maximum throughput across all the different configurations we

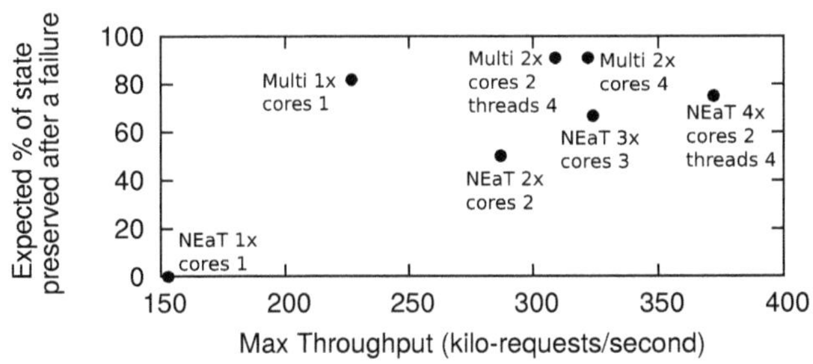

Figure 13: Expected fraction of state preserved after a failure vs. max throughput across network stack setups.

evaluated on the Xeon. We used the code size (proportional to code coverage for our test workload) of each component to estimate the probability that a single component fails when a failure occurs within the network stack—assuming uniform failure probability throughout the code—and the resulting expected fraction of state preserved after a failure. We also assumed the simple stateless TCP recovery strategy used in NEaT, which results in (only) the TCP state being always irrecoverable—after a TCP failure—as evidenced earlier. To further improve reliability, an option is to rely on checkpointing techniques [9] to support a (TCP) stateful recovery strategy allowing existing connections to survive failures. However, such techniques typically incur nontrivial run-time and recovery-time overhead (other than being generally unable to recover from a corrupted state), trading off performance for reliability. In contrast, as shown in the figure, NEaT's performance and reliability both increase with the number of replicas across all our configurations, confirming that our design allows reliability and scalability to effectively coexist with no compromises. In addition, as the figure demonstrates, given any fixed number of available cores (and HTs), NEaT's single- and multi-component configurations yield different performance-reliability tradeoffs, opening up interesting research opportunities on fine-grained isolation and allocation policies.

7. CONCLUSION

Reliability and scalability are commonly perceived as largely independent—and possibly conflicting— requirements concerning the implementation of operating system services. This paper challenged the common belief, demonstrating that two key design principles, isolation and partitioning, can effectively address reliability and scalability of a core OS service such as the network stack at the same time, and both with constant returns with respect to the number of available CPUs on modern multicore architectures. The principles we employ also demonstrated that not only is reliability and scalability of design possible, but represents a realistic and far superior alternative to reliability and scalability of implementation, plagued with problems and increasingly unable to "scale" to the complexity of modern hardware and software systems. Using such principled design, we implemented NEaT, a reliable and scalable network stack that isolates and partitions its state across multiple and truly independent replicas. Thanks to the design principles, NEaT can outperform Linux both in terms of reliability—withstanding failures and reducing service disruption as the number of replicas increases—and scalability—up to 13-35% higher throughput in our benchmark with 4 replicas—while retaining full compatibility with the BSD socket API and supporting full sharing and cooperation at the application level.

8. ACKNOWLEDGEMENT

We would like to thank the anonymous reviewers and our shepherd Olivier Bonaventure for their valuable feedback. This work was supported by the European Commission through project H2020 ICT-32-2014 "SHARCS" under Grant Agreement No. 64457 and the Netherlands Organisation for Scientific Research (NWO) through the grant 639.023.309 VICI "Dowsing".

9. REFERENCES

[1] ASLR: Leopard versus Vista. http://blog.laconicsecurity.com/2008/01/aslr-leopard-versus-vista.html.

[2] Intel's "knights landing" xeon phi coprocessor detailed. http://www.anandtech.com/show/8217/intels-knights-landing-coprocessor-detailed.

[3] Killing the Big Kernel Lock. http://lwn.net/Articles/380174/.

[4] MINIX 3. http://www.minix3.org.

[5] OpenOnload. http://www.openonload.org.

[6] RCU Linux Usage. http://www.rdrop.com/users/paulmck/RCU/linuxusage.html.

[7] RFC: remove __read_mostly. http://lwn.net/Articles/262557.

[8] The "too small to fail" memory-allocation rule. http://lwn.net/Articles/627419/.

[9] CRIU. http://criu.org/, 2015.

[10] J. Appavoo, D. D. Silva, O. Krieger, M. Auslander, M. Ostrowski, B. Rosenburg, A. Waterland, R. W. Wisniewski, J. Xenidis, M. Stumm, and L. Soares. Experience Distributing Objects in an SMMP OS. *ACM Trans. Comput. Syst.*, 2007.

[11] A. Baumann, P. Barham, P.-E. Dagand, T. Harris, R. Isaacs, S. Peter, T. Roscoe, A. Schüpbach, and A. Singhania. The Multikernel: A New OS Architecture for Scalable Multicore Systems. In *Proceedings of the ACM Symposium on Operating Systems Principles*, pages 29–44, 2009.

[12] A. Belay, G. Prekas, A. Klimovic, S. Grossman, C. Kozyrakis, and E. Bugnion. IX: A Protected Dataplane Operating System for High Throughput and Low Latency. In *Proceedings of the USENIX Symposium on Oper. Sys. Design and Impl.*, Oct. 2014.

[13] A. Bittau, A. Belay, A. Mashtizadeh, D. Mazieres, and D. Boneh. Hacking Blind. In *Proceedings of the IEEE Symposium on Security and Privacy*, 2014.

[14] S. Boyd-Wickizer, H. Chen, R. Chen, Y. Mao, F. Kaashoek, R. Morris, A. Pesterev, L. Stein, M. Wu, Y. Dai, Y. Zhang, and Z. Zhang. Corey: An Operating System for Many Cores. In *Proceedings of the USENIX*

Symposium on Oper. Sys. Design and Impl., pages 43–57, 2008.

[15] S. Boyd-Wickizer, A. T. Clements, Y. Mao, A. Pesterev, M. F. Kaashoek, R. Morris, and N. Zeldovich. An Analysis of Linux Scalability to Many Cores. In *Proceedings of the USENIX Symposium on Oper. Sys. Design and Impl.*, pages 1–8, 2010.

[16] S. Boyd-Wickizer, M. F. Kaashoek, R. Morris, and N. Zeldovich. Non-scalable locks are dangerous. In *Proceedings of the Linux Symposium*, July 2012.

[17] S. Boyd-Wickizer and N. Zeldovich. Tolerating Malicious Device Drivers in Linux. In *Proceedings of the USENIX Annual Technical Conference*, page 9, 2010.

[18] M. Castro, M. Costa, J.-P. Martin, M. Peinado, P. Akritidis, A. Donnelly, P. Barham, and R. Black. Fast Byte-granularity Software Fault Isolation. In *Proceedings of the ACM Symposium on Operating Systems Principles*, pages 45–58, 2009.

[19] A. T. Clements, M. F. Kaashoek, N. Zeldovich, R. T. Morris, and E. Kohler. The scalable commutativity rule: Designing scalable software for multicore processors. In *Proceedings of the ACM Symposium on Operating Systems Principles*, pages 1–17, 2013.

[20] B. Cox, D. Evans, A. Filipi, J. Rowanhill, W. Hu, J. Davidson, J. Knight, A. Nguyen-Tuong, and J. Hiser. N-variant systems: A secretless framework for security through diversity. In *Proceedings of the USENIX Security Symposium*, pages 105–120, 2006.

[21] F. M. David, E. M. Chan, J. C. Carlyle, and R. H. Campbell. CuriOS: Improving Reliability Through Operating System Structure. In *Proceedings of the USENIX Symposium on Oper. Sys. Design and Impl.*, pages 59–72, 2008.

[22] T. David, R. Guerraoui, and V. Trigonakis. Everything you always wanted to know about synchronization but were afraid to ask. In *Proceedings of the ACM Symposium on Operating Systems Principles*, pages 33–48, 2013.

[23] A. Depoutovitch and M. Stumm. Otherworld: Giving Applications a Chance to Survive OS Kernel Crashes. In *Proceedings of the European Conference on Computer Systems*, pages 181–194, 2010.

[24] M. Desnoyers, P. E. McKenney, and M. R. Dagenais. Multi-core Systems Modeling for Formal Verification of Parallel Algorithms. *SIGOPS Oper. Syst. Rev.*, 47(2):51–65, 2013.

[25] M. Flajslik and M. Rosenblum. Network Interface Design for Low Latency Request-Response Protocols. In *Proceedings of the USENIX Annual Technical Conference*, pages 333–346, 2013.

[26] B. Gamsa, O. Krieger, J. Appavoo, and M. Stumm. Tornado: Maximizing Locality and Concurrency in a Shared Memory Multiprocessor Operating System. In *Proceedings of the USENIX Symposium on Oper. Sys. Design and Impl.*, pages 87–100, 1999.

[27] V. Ganapathy, M. J. Renzelmann, A. Balakrishnan, M. M. Swift, and S. Jha. The Design and Implementation of Microdrivers. In *Proceedings of the International Conference on Architectural Support for Programming Languages and Operating Systems*, pages 168–178, 2008.

[28] A. Gefflaut, T. Jaeger, Y. Park, J. Liedtke, K. J. Elphinstone, V. Uhlig, J. E. Tidswell, L. Deller, and L. Reuther. The SawMill Multiserver Approach. In *Proceedings of the ACM SIGOPS European Workshop*, pages 109–114, 2000.

[29] C. Giuffrida, L. Cavallaro, and A. S. Tanenbaum. We Crashed, Now What? In *Proceedings of the Workshop on Hot Topics in System Dependability*, pages 1–8, 2010.

[30] R. Guerraoui and A. Schiper. Software-based Replication for fault Tolerance. *Computer*, 30(4):68–74, 1997.

[31] S. Han, S. Marshall, B.-G. Chun, and S. Ratnasamy. MegaPipe: A New Programming Interface for Scalable Network I/O. In *Proceedings of the USENIX Symposium on Oper. Sys. Design and Impl.*, 2012.

[32] T. Herbert. RFS: Receive Flow Steering. http://lwn.net/Articles/381955/, 2010.

[33] J. N. Herder, H. Bos, B. Gras, P. Homburg, and A. S. Tanenbaum. Failure Resilience for Device Drivers. In *Proceedings of the Annual IEEE/IFIP International Conference on Dependable Systems and Networks*, 2007.

[34] D. Hildebrand. An Architectural Overview of QNX. In *Proceedings of the Workshop on Micro-kernels and Other Kernel Architectures*, pages 113–126, 1992.

[35] T. Hruby, T. Crivat, H. Bos, and A. S. Tanenbaum. On sockets and system calls: Minimizing context switches for the socket api. In *Proceedings of the Conference on Timely Results in Operating Systems*, 2014.

[36] T. Hruby, K. van Reeuwijk, and H. Bos. Ruler: easy packet matching and rewriting on network processors. In *Symposium on Architectures for Networking and Communications Systems (ANCS'07)*, Orlando, FL, USA, December 2007.

[37] T. Hruby, D. Vogt, H. Bos, and A. S. Tanenbaum. Keep Net Working - on a Dependable and Fast Networking Stack. In *Proceedings of the Annual IEEE/IFIP International Conference on Dependable Systems and Networks*, pages 1–12, 2012.

[38] G. C. Hunt, J. R. Larus, D. Tarditi, and T. Wobber. Broad New OS Research: Challenges and Opportunities. In *Proceedings of the Workshop on Hot Topics in Operating Systems*, 2005.

[39] E. Jeong, S. Wood, M. Jamshed, H. Jeong, S. Ihm, D. Han, and K. Park. mTCP: a Highly Scalable User-level TCP Stack for Multicore Systems. In *Proceedings of the USENIX Symposium on Networked Systems Design and Implementation*, 2014.

[40] A. Kadav, M. J. Renzelmann, and M. M. Swift. Fine-grained Fault Tolerance Using Device Checkpoints. In *Proceedings of the International Conference on Architectural Support for Programming Languages and Operating Systems*, pages 473–484, 2013.

[41] Khubaib, M. A. Suleman, M. Hashemi, C. Wilkerson, and Y. N. Patt. MorphCore: An Energy-Efficient Microarchitecture for High Performance ILP and High Throughput TLP. In *Proceedings of the Annual IEEE/ACM International Symposium on Microarchitecture*, pages 305–316, 2012.

[42] O. Koren. A Study of the Linux Kernel Evolution. *SIGOPS Oper. Syst. Rev.*, 40(2):110–112, Apr. 2006.

[43] A. Lenharth, V. S. Adve, and S. T. King. Recovery Domains: An Organizing Principle for Recoverable Operating Systems. In *Proceedings of the International Conference on Architectural Support for Programming Languages and Operating Systems*, pages 49–60, 2009.

[44] T. Liu and E. D. Berger. SHERIFF: Precise Detection and Automatic Mitigation of False Sharing. In *Proceedings of the ACM International Conference on*

Object Oriented Programming Systems Languages and Applications, pages 3–18, 2011.
[45] P. E. Mckenney and J. D. Slingwine. Read-Copy Update: Using Execution History to Solve Concurrency Problems. In *Parallel and Distributed Computing and Systems*, pages 509–518, Oct. 1998.
[46] J. M. Mellor-Crummey and M. L. Scott. Algorithms for Scalable Synchronization on Shared-memory Multiprocessors. *ACM Trans. Comput. Syst.*, 9(1):21–65, Feb. 1991.
[47] W. T. Ng and P. M. Chen. The systematic improvement of fault tolerance in the rio file cache. In *Proceedings of the 29th Annual International Symposium on Fault-Tolerant Computing*, pages 76–83, 1999.
[48] E. B. Nightingale, O. Hodson, R. McIlroy, C. Hawblitzel, and G. Hunt. Helios: Heterogeneous Multiprocessing with Satellite Kernels. In *Proceedings of the ACM Symposium on Operating Systems Principles*, pages 221–234, 2009.
[49] R. Nikolaev and G. Back. Virtuos: An operating system with kernel virtualization. In *Proceedings of the ACM Symposium on Operating Systems Principles*, pages 116–132, 2013.
[50] K. Olukotun, L. Hammond, and J. Laudon. *Chip Multiprocessor Architecture: Techniques to Improve Throughput and Latency*. 2007.
[51] N. Palix, G. Thomas, S. Saha, C. Calvès, J. Lawall, and G. Muller. Faults in linux: Ten years later. In *Proceedings of the International Conference on Architectural Support for Programming Languages and Operating Systems*, pages 305–318, 2011.
[52] A. Pesterev, J. Strauss, N. Zeldovich, and R. T. Morris. Improving Network Connection Locality on Multicore Systems. In *Proceedings of European Conference on Computer Systems*, 2012.
[53] S. Peter, J. Li, I. Zhang, D. R. K. Ports, D. Woos, A. Krishnamurthy, T. Anderson, and T. Roscoe. Arrakis: The Operating System is the Control Plane. In *Proceedings of the USENIX Symposium on Oper. Sys. Design and Impl.*, Oct. 2014.
[54] L. Rizzo and G. Lettieri. iVALE, a Switched Ethernet for Virtual Machines. In *Proceedings of the International Conference on Emerging Networking Experiments and Technologies*, pages 61–72, 2012.
[55] B. Salamat, A. Gal, T. Jackson, K. Manivannan, G. Wagner, and M. Franz. Multi-variant Program Execution: Using Multi-core Systems to Defuse Buffer-Overflow Vulnerabilities. In *Proceedings of the International Conference on Complex, Intelligent and Software Intensive Systems*, pages 843–848, 2008.
[56] B. Salamat, T. Jackson, A. Gal, and M. Franz. Orchestra: Intrusion detection using parallel execution and monitoring of program variants in user-space. In *Proceedings of the European Conference on Computer Systems*, pages 33–46, 2009.
[57] J. Seibert, H. Okkhravi, and E. Söderström. Information leaks without memory disclosures: Remote side channel attacks on diversified code. In *Proceedings of the ACM SIGSAC Conference on Computer and Communications Security*, pages 54–65, 2014.
[58] L. Shalev, J. Satran, E. Borovik, and M. Ben-Yehuda. IsoStack: Highly Efficient Network Processing on Dedicated Cores. In *Proceedings of the USENIX Annual Technical Conference*, 2010.
[59] K. Z. Snow, F. Monrose, L. Davi, A. Dmitrienko, C. Liebchen, and A.-R. Sadeghi. Just-In-Time Code Reuse: On the Effectiveness of Fine-Grained Address Space Layout Randomization. In *Proceedings of the IEEE Symposium on Security and Privacy*, pages 574–588, 2013.
[60] R. Strong, J. Mudigonda, J. C. Mogul, N. Binkert, and D. Tullsen. Fast Switching of Threads Between Cores. *SIGOPS Oper. Syst. Rev.*, 43(2):35–45, Apr. 2009.
[61] Y. Sun and T.-c. Chiueh. SIDE: Isolated and Efficient Execution of Unmodified Device drivers. In *Proceedings of the Annual IEEE/IFIP International Conference on Dependable Systems and Networks*, pages 1–12, 2013.
[62] S. Sundararaman, S. Subramanian, A. Rajimwale, A. C. Arpaci-Dusseau, R. H. Arpaci-Dusseau, and M. M. Swift. Membrane: Operating System Support for Restartable File Systems. In *Proceedings of the USENIX Conference on File and Storage Technologies*, page 21, 2010.
[63] M. M. Swift, M. Annamalai, B. N. Bershad, and H. M. Levy. Recovering Device Drivers. *ACM Trans. Comput. Syst.*, 24(4):333–360, Nov. 2006.
[64] M. M. Swift, B. N. Bershad, and H. M. Levy. Improving the reliability of commodity operating systems. *ACM Transactions on Computer Systems*, 23(1):77–110, 2005.
[65] K. Van Craeynest, A. Jaleel, L. Eeckhout, P. Narvaez, and J. Emer. Scheduling Heterogeneous Multi-cores Through Performance Impact Estimation (PIE). In *Proceedings of the Annual IEEE/ACM International Symposium on Microarchitecture*, pages 213–224, 2012.
[66] D. Wentzlaff, C. Gruenwald, III, N. Beckmann, K. Modzelewski, A. Belay, L. Youseff, J. Miller, and A. Agarwal. An Operating System for Multicore and Clouds: Mechanisms and Implementation. In *Proceedings of the ACM Symposium on Cloud Computing*, pages 3–14, 2010.
[67] P. Willmann, S. Rixner, and A. L. Cox. An Evaluation of Network Stack Parallelization Strategies in Modern Operating Systems. In *Proceedings of the USENIX Annual Technical Conference*, 2006.
[68] T. Yoshimura, H. Yamada, and K. Kono. Is Linux Kernel Oops Useful or Not? In *Proceedings of the Workshop on Hot Topics in System Dependability*, page 2, 2012.
[69] F. Zhou, J. Condit, Z. Anderson, I. Bagrak, R. Ennals, M. Harren, G. Necula, and E. Brewer. SafeDrive: Safe and Recoverable Extensions Using Language-based Techniques. In *Proceedings of the USENIX Symposium on Oper. Sys. Design and Impl.*, pages 45–60, 2006.

ACACIA – Context-aware Edge Computing for Continuous Interactive Applications over Mobile Networks*

Junguk Cho
University of Utah
junguk.cho@utah.edu

Karthikeyan Sundaresan
NEC Labs America Inc.
karthiks@nec-labs.com

Rajesh Mahindra
NEC Labs America Inc.
rajesh@nec-labs.com

Jacobus Van der Merwe
University of Utah
kobus@cs.utah.edu

Sampath Rangarajan
NEC Labs America Inc.
sampath@nec-labs.com

ABSTRACT

There is widespread agreement that future continuous interactive (CI) applications will require edge computing capabilities from mobile networks. There is also widespread expectation that the emerging 5G network architecture, with its constituent technology components, will be the context in which this will be realized. Indeed many of the components that will be part of such an environment have been studied in standalone manner. However, the question of whether an end-to-end combination of these components would satisfy application requirements, or indeed, how these components would be combined into service offerings by mobile network providers, have not been meaningfully addressed. Towards addressing these challenges, we propose ACACIA-a service abstraction framework that enables CI applications on edge clouds in mobile networks. Evaluation of our prototype implementation shows that our holistic approach provides a 70% end-to-end application level latency reduction when compared with existing cloud and mobile solutions.

CCS Concepts

•**Networks** → **Mobile networks;** *Cloud computing; Wireless access networks;*

*Instructions for accessing an ACACIA profile in the PhantomNet testbed are available here: https://wiki.phantomnet.org/wiki/phantomnet/acacia

CoNEXT '16, December 12-15, 2016, Irvine, CA, USA

DOI: http://dx.doi.org/10.1145/2999572.2999604

Keywords

mobile network; service offerings; context-aware mobile edge computing; NFV/SDN

1. INTRODUCTION

Future continuous interactive (CI) applications, like augmented reality (AR), virtual reality (VR), autonomous driving, etc [45, 21, 23], will have network requirements that cannot be provided by existing mobile networks. CI applications might require very low end-to-end latencies (low tens of milliseconds or less) [19, 37], and might similarly require computational resources to be close to the network edge [47]. Current 4G mobile networks are incapable of providing such delays since the core mobile network itself incurs a substantial delay (high tens of milliseconds or more) [33, 52]. Further, current mobile networks provide basic communication service abstractions aimed at human-to-human and human-to-machine type communication. To effectively support future CI applications *both* the underlying mobile network technology as well as the service abstractions provided by the network need to evolve.

There is widespread expectation that the emerging 5G mobile network architecture will address these concerns, that cloud platforms in the form of mobile edge computing (MEC) will satisfy edge computing requirements and that localization and context discovery frameworks will provide the means for CI applications to be realized. Indeed many of these necessary components have been proposed and studied in standalone manner. Mobile edge computing has been the subject of both academic and industrial efforts [31, 51, 22, 43]. Computational offloading has also been studied to facilitate CI applications [48, 47, 34, 38, 32]. User localization [25, 41, 50, 29, 40] and context discovery [5, 7, 17] frameworks have been proposed in support of CI applications. However, the question of whether an end-to-end combination of these components would satisfy application requirements, or indeed, how these components would be combined into service offerings by mobile network providers, have not been meaningfully addressed. Given the real-time interactions between user, network and application, the key question we ask is *how should the three entities (user, network and application) be jointly orchestrated and combined in a service abstraction to deliver low latencies and enable CI applications in mobile networks?*

We answer this question through the design of our service abstraction framework called ACACIA. ACACIA enables CI applications on edge clouds in mobile networks. ACACIA leverages client context information through proximity service discovery to optimize network and application processing. ACACIA leverages SDN/NFV principles with LTE/EPC QoS mechanisms to steer CI application traffic, on demand, to closely located mobile edge clouds. We expect our work to inform the emerging 5G mobile network architecture, however, we note that the use of SDN and NFV mechanisms allow our approach to be readily realized with existing LTE/EPC mobile networks.

In designing ACACIA our key insight is that a user's context with respect to her environment is a critical factor in optimizing both the network and application aspects required by MEC-based CI applications. Specifically, a CI application using MEC-based services should be directed to an edge cloud instance in close proximity to the user where the required services are available (i.e., providing network level optimization). Similarly, the specific context of the user can be used to inform and optimize the application functionality. For example, a cognitive assistance face recognition AR application [30] might optimize its functionality by knowing where the user is (e.g., normal domestic environment vs. shopping mall) and knowing whether a person interacting with the user is someone the user interacted with before (i.e., family or friends in a domestic environment, vs. acquaintances associated with service outlets the user frequents). Similarly, a retail shopping AR application can benefit not only from knowing the relative location of a user (e.g., the appliance department), but also from knowing that the user is interested in a specific type of appliance (e.g., a microwave oven).

ACACIA leverages this insight to realize *Context-Aware MEC for CI applications over mobile networks*. Specifically, ACACIA leverages user context in the form of their interest in specific CI proximity "services" as well as proximity to landmarks to (i) create *on-demand* connections to MEC servers only when a client is interested in CI applications and MEC-based CI services are available, while maintaining an always-on connection to the core network, thus alleviating the control overhead in establishing such additional connections, (ii) automatically *classify* MEC traffic at the source (client) itself, and *re-direct* only the MEC traffic to the closest MEC server, thereby avoiding the need for traffic inspection and classification as well as the load of non-relevant traffic at the MEC server, and (iii) speed-up the application processing through *location-aware optimization*, that is especially useful in CI services like AR/VR.

We developed an end-to-end prototype of the ACACIA architecture, specifically using a software LTE/EPC platform, Open vSwitch, and an SDN controller to implement the decoupled control and data planes of ACACIA's LTE network function gateways, thus realizing a centralized control plane but a distributed data plane. Our prototype leveraged the LTE-direct D2D (Device-to-Device) [5] capabilities of commercial smartphones to provide the user context necessary to intelligently orchestrate and optimize the network as well as the CI service. With LTE-direct, ACACIA avoids incurring any infrastructure overhead and easily ties it to other components as a potential service offering by mobile carriers. While ACACIA can be applied to various low latency CI applications, to demonstrate its efficacy, we built a sample real-world AR application for engaged retail services that utilizes ACACIA's MEC and user-context optimization. Our retail application enables store owners to simply equip their sales people in different sections of the store with smartphones capable of LTE-direct, and customers are presented with an enriched shopping experience in real-time as they explore the store with their smartphones.

To our knowledge, ACACIA represents the first holistic end-to-end design to support CI applications in mobile networks. Using our prototype realization we performed extensive evaluation to validate our design. Our evaluations reveal that ACACIA provides a 70% end-to-end application level latency reduction when compared with existing cloud and mobile solutions, and a 60% reduction compared with a mobile edge cloud solution that only optimizes network latencies. We make the following specific contributions in this work:

- We design and build a service abstraction framework that leverages user context information, made available without any infrastructure support through LTE-direct capabilities, to intelligently orchestrate and optimize both the MEC network and CI service.
- Leveraging SDN/NFV with existing QoS bearer framework in LTE network, we empower an LTE core network (EPC) with MEC capabilities, without requiring any changes to LTE specifications, additional hardware/middleboxes and modifications to LTE base stations[1].
- We build and deploy an AR based interactive retail service on commercial smartphones which uses an existing LTE network enhanced with our framework.

2. RELATED WORK

Computation Offloading: To support mobile applications requiring heavy computation, several offloading frameworks have been proposed [48, 47, 34, 38, 32]. The Gabriel system [34] follows a long history of cloudlet related works [48, 47] and proposes a multi-tiered mobile offloading architecture in support of cognitive assistance applications. MAUI [32] proposed a system which supports fine-grained code offload from a smartphone to a server to maximize energy savings with minimal developer effort. OverLay [38] proposed a

[1]In the remainder of this paper we follow common practice by referring to current 4G long term evolution (LTE) radio access networks combined with evolved packet core (EPC), simply as "LTE" networks.

practical mobile augmented reality framework. It reduces the search space for computer vision algorithms based on human behavior and uses GPU processing to accelerate computation. These efforts have mainly focused on reducing application level computation latency and do not address the networking complexities that arise in realizing such offloading in mobile networks. ACACIA aims to enable these offloading solutions over mobile networks through a novel and practical mobile edge networking approach.

MEC: Several works [31, 51, 22, 43] have proposed mechanisms and architectures for Mobile Edge Computing (MEC) over mobile networks: (i) Traffic offload mechanisms located at the eNodeB or close to it (in middleboxes) can inspect traffic and route them to dedicated MEC servers [31, 51]. This approach incurs the cost of middlebox deployment and the processing overhead of traffic inspection and de/encapsulation of GTP tunnels. Further, deploying these solutions without modification to current LTE networks, requires monitors to sniff all control messages. (ii) Extension to small-cell home eNodeB deployments for local IP access (LIPA [8]) has been proposed to realize cloudlet [48] functionality in the home environment [22]. While this is conceptually similar to an MEC environment, it is not clear how (or whether) this approach generalizes beyond the home environment. (iii) The new industry initiative for MEC aims to develop an architecture and standards to allow flexible MEC realizations [43]. While details of their work are still emerging, their approach calls for the integration of computing elements with radio access network (RAN) equipment, which suggests the need for new standardized protocol interfaces to be developed. This in turn will require new equipment (or at best upgrades to existing equipment) before the approach can become reality. ACACIA's MEC approach differs from the above approaches in that it does not require new protocol interfaces, extra hardware or heavy-weight monitoring to realize MEC in current LTE networks. In addition, it provides low latencies for mobile users as well as reduced network overhead to effectively realize CI applications based on service availability and user interests.

Service Discovery: There are various proximity service discovery techniques [5, 7, 17] like LTE-direct [5], iBeacon [7], and Wifi-Aware [17] that can be used to provide user context. Further, there is a rich set of literature in indoor localization [25, 41, 50, 29, 40]. From a mobile provider's perspective, there is synergy in using LTE-direct as part of its service offerings. Hence, ACACIA employs LTE-direct for proximity service discovery and coarse indoor localization. However, ACACIA's focus extends beyond service discovery and localization to more importantly, optimize and enable context-aware CI applications.

While the above works clearly indicate active research in various areas (computation offloading, MEC, service discovery and localization) in isolation, it is not clear how these components need to be combined synergistically to provide an end-end service offering for CI applications. Addressing the challenges that arise from realizing this vision, is the objective of our work on ACACIA.

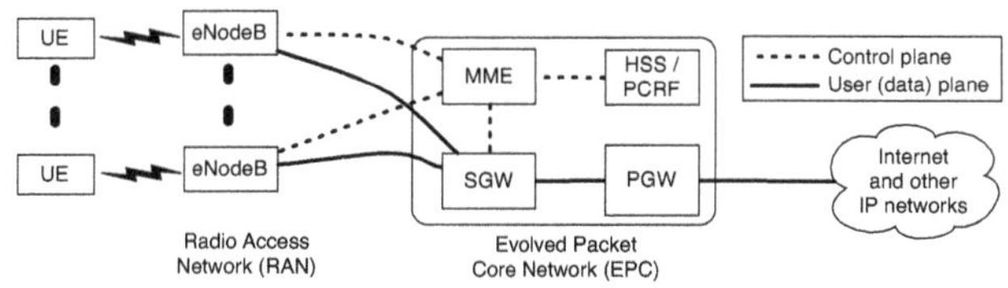

Figure 1: LTE/EPC Architecture

3. BACKGROUND

Acronym	Definition
EPC	Evolved Packet Core
eNodeB (eNB)	E-UTRAN Node B
UE	User Equipment
MME	Mobility Management Entity
HSS	Home Subscriber Server
PCRF	Policy and Charging Rule Function
SGW	Serving Gateway
PGW	Packet Data Network Gateway
GTP	GPRS Tunneling Protocol
TEID	Tunnel EndPoint Identifier
TFT	Traffic Flow Templates
QCI	QoS Class Identifier
MEC	Mobile Edge Computing
SCTP	Stream Control Transmission Protocol

Table 1: Frequently used acronyms

LTE/EPC Architecture. The 4G mobile network architecture consists of the Radio Access Network (RAN) and the Evolved Packet Core (EPC) as shown in Figure 1. While the RAN includes eNodeBs (base stations) that serve the user equipment (UEs), the EPC consists of both control-plane components that *manage* the devices and data-plane components that *forward* the data traffic. The control-plane components mainly consist of the MME (Mobility Management Entity), the HSS (Home Subscriber Server) and the PCRF (Policy and Charging Rule Function). The data-plane components consist of the Serving Gateway (SGW) and the Packet Data Network Gateway (PGW) which primarily perform forwarding of user data traffic. In addition, the SGW serves as an anchor point in case of handover between eNodeBs and contains buffers for paging functionality. The PGW acts as the Internet gateway for the data traffic and also enforces operator-defined policies (QoS), packet filtering and accounting. After a UE is attached to the mobile network, packets from the UE are forwarded from eNodeB to the two GWs and vice versa for traffic towards the UE.

Role of SDN/NFV in LTE Networks. With advances in Network Function Virtualization (NFV) and Software Defined Networking (SDN), it has been widely advocated [42, 46, 6] that the two GWs should be split into control-plane entities (GW-C) and user-plane entities (GW-U). The GW-Cs interact with other control-plane entities like MME using 3GPP standard interfaces and setup the forwarding paths

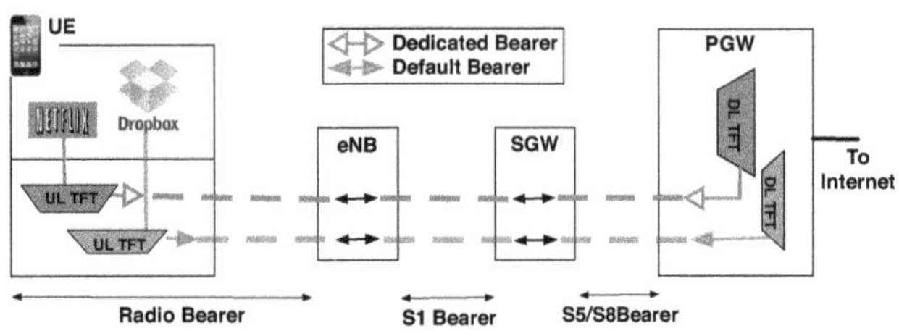

Figure 2: Bearers in LTE/EPC [49]

on the GW-U entities using OpenFlow. This split architecture has several advantages. It allows for (i) better scaling of control and data planes independently, (ii) fine-grained load balancing across the SGW-Us and the PGW-Us by the SGW-C and PGW-C and (iii) flexible management of multiple SGW-Us and PGW-Us (distributed across data centers) by logically or physically centralized SGW-C and PGW-C.

Bearers in LTE/EPC. When a UE registers with the network, a default data-path called a *default bearer* is created between the UE and the PGW to ensure always-on connectivity. Each bearer is composed of three segments: (i) radio bearer between UE and eNodeB, (ii) data bearer (S1 bearer) between eNodeB and SGW and (iii) data bearer (S5/S8 bearer) between SGW and PGW as shown in Figure 2. The data bearers are carried over GTP based UDP tunnels that are differentiated by a unique GTP Tunnel EndPoint Identifier (TEID). In addition to the default bearer, *dedicated* bearers can be set up for specific traffic flows, which are identified using traffic flow templates (TFTs) [3] in both up (in UE) and downstream (in PGW) directions (essentially a five-tuple packet filter). In addition to providing a basic connectivity abstraction, a bearer can also be associated with a QoS Class Identifier (QCI) [4], which specifies the priority, packet delay budget and packet loss rate associated with the bearer's traffic. Figure 2 shows an example instantiation with both default and dedicated bearers. In this example the dedicated bearer, with better QoS metrics, is associated with traffic flow for a Netflix application, while other traffic, e.g., associated with Dropbox, is carried on the default bearer.

LTE-direct. LTE-direct [5] is a proximity service discovery techniques using a device-to-device (D2D) paradigm. It employs *Publish* and *Subscribe* messages on the radio (LTE) channel to advertise and discover nearby services. It is particularly attractive owing to the ubiquitous availability of LTE on smart devices (no additional infrastructure required), and provides superior range and robustness. In addition, it leverages the eNB for timing information, resource allocation as well as user authentication without requiring explicit and complex initial setup procedures [5]. Resources for service discovery are allocated in the uplink part of the LTE spectrum, which is lightly loaded compared to the downlink. At periodic intervals (e.g., 5 or 10 sec), the eNB allocates resource blocks (RBs) for LTE-direct transmissions as part of its uplink frames. This has a negligible impact on the uplink capacity (utilizes $< 1\%$ of uplink resources [5]). All information related to service discovery is stored and handled in the LTE modem itself. While a service discovery message from a publisher is broadcasted on a periodic basis, application specific information (binary codes and their mask that express user's interest) stored at the subscriber is used for filtering and matching the service discovery message. If matching happens in the LTE modem, the service discovery message is forwarded to the appropriate application and translated by the application. Otherwise, it is filtered out in the LTE modem. Handling service discovery entirely in the modem allows for scalability (hundreds of devices [5]), security and fast discovery.

4. MOTIVATION

To understand the various factors impacting the latencies perceived by CI applications over mobile networks, we experimented with augmented reality (AR) as a representative CI application. AR-based applications overlay useful information like text, audio and video over the live scene of the user's current environment in real-time, and find numerous use-cases (object information in retail shops, navigation in museums, cognitive assistance, etc.). Hence, they require tight end-to-end latencies (low tens of ms) for satisfactory interactive user experience [22, 38].

Computation Offloading. We measure the latency incurred by running two important AR-related operations, namely feature detection and description (finding features (keypoints) from an image and describing them (descriptors) using the SURF algorithm [27]) and object matching (using keypoints and descriptors to compare them against in the database) by using the OpenCV [12] library. Figure 3(a) and Figure 3(b) show computation time for SURF detection and description and for object matching respectively as a function of image resolution on four different devices: (i) the latest One+ One smartphone device, (ii) a single i7 core server, (iii) an eight i7 core server and (iv) a server with a GeForce GTX TITAN GPU processor. When AR operations are executed on the smartphone, the computation time is quite high, e.g., 2 seconds even with the lowest image resolution, suggesting the unfeasibility of deploying the AR application on the smartphone itself. Running AR operations on the server on the average shows 36x (1-core), 182x (8-cores) and 1087x (GPU) reduction in latency for feature detection and description computation and 223x (1-core), 852x (8-cores) and 3284x (GPU) latency reduction for matching operations. These results indicate the necessity of using the offloading compute resources of CPU and GPU to realize the latencies demanded by AR applications.

Low Network Latency. The always-on, universal availability and stable operation of LTE in licensed spectrum make it a promising candidate for mobile devices to offload computation to the cloud. However, cloud servers being located far from mobile devices and centralized S/P-GWs employing hierarchical routing in the core network [33, 52] result in high and unpredictable latencies. For example, Figure 3(c) shows the round-trip-time (RTT) measurements in a commercial LTE network from a smartphone in the US midwest to Amazon EC2 servers in different locations. Consistent with previously reported LTE measurements [36], our

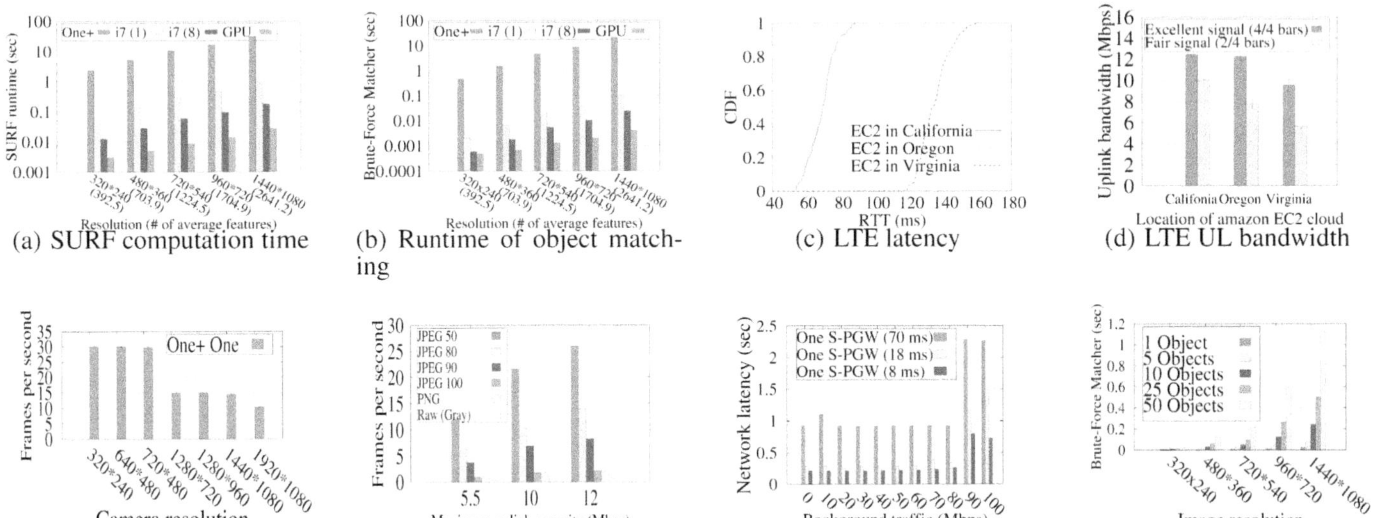

(a) SURF computation time

(b) Runtime of object matching

(c) LTE latency

(d) LTE UL bandwidth

(e) Preview FPS

(f) FPS based on network capacity and compression

(g) Latency by competing traffic and RTT between UE and a server

(h) Runtime of object matching according to database size

Figure 3: Factors impacting AR applications

measurements show the RTT between the smartphone and the EC2 server in California is the shortest and around 70 ms, with other EC2 servers delivering much higher median latencies. Considering human sensitivity to latencies higher than roughly 25-50 ms for AR applications, the LTE network latency warrants optimization and can account for a substantial portion of the end-to-end latency [22].

High Network Bandwidth. In addition to latency, network bandwidth is also important for AR applications. AR applications typically generate a large volume of data from a camera in a smartphone, which require high bandwidth to upload the data to the cloud. Figure 3(d) shows the measured uplink bandwidth from a smartphone connected to a commercial LTE network in the midwest US to Amazon EC2 servers in different locations. The highest uplink bandwidth between the smartphone and an EC2 server in California is about 12 Mbps, which is consistent with previous results [36]. We conducted an experiment to determine whether these data rates are sufficient for AR applications. First we measured the maximum frames per second (FPS) generated by the camera preview mode in a One+ One smartphone. Figure 3(e) shows FPS based on the configuration of camera resolution. At HD resolution (1920*1080), the device generates 10 FPS. Second, we calculated the (upload) frame rates (FPS) possible via the the current LTE network. The results are shown in Figure 3(f) for different image compression approaches and as a function of the available LTE network capacity. In uncompressed mode (Grayscale image) the smartphone cannot even send one frame per second, even with the highest uplink capacity. With a reasonable compression ratios, e.g., JPEG 90 (higher number indicates less compression), the device can send 8 frames per second, which is relatively close to the FPS generated from its camera for a HD scene. While one could resort to compression, this would significantly affect the accuracy of the object detection/matching component of the AR application due to lossy compression. This clearly indicates that without guaranteeing sufficient uplink bandwidth for AR-applications, one cannot realize the ideal FPS needed to run the AR applications satisfactorily.

We note that mobile edge computing aims to address computation offloading and latency reduction, and by bringing cloud processing to the edge of the mobile network might also positively impact network capacity constraints. However, as we consider below, other challenges remain.

Traffic Differentiation. MEC provides a means to bypass the core network bottleneck by handling the traffic closer to the wireless access. While proximity of the MEC server to the UE helps, it is equally important to control the traffic load that is directed to the MEC server and hence needs to be processed/classified by it. Figure 3(g) presents the network latencies observed as a function of the background traffic load that is handled by core network GWs serving the MEC server. Proximity of the server to the UE is varied by emulating different RTTs to the server. It can be seen that even for small RTTs (MEC server located close to the eNodeB), if the AR traffic competes with other background traffic, this can have a significant impact on the end-to-end network latency (e.g., in our experiment 90 Mbps of background traffic increased the end-to-end delay to approximately 800 ms which makes AR applications impractical.). Hence, it is critical to have mechanisms that differentiate between traffic, and identify only those that require the use of MEC resources and direct them to the appropriate MEC servers.

Control Overhead. The feasibility of creating dedicated bearers in LTE offers the potential to create such a bearer between the mobile device and an MEC server in the edge cloud. However, the creation of every such bearer incurs additional overhead in the form of control messages. This control overhead is exacerbated by the fact that LTE tears down the bearers associated with a device when the device goes idle (i.e., have no data to send for 11.576 seconds [35]), and then needs to reestablish the bearers when there is data activity (known as an LTE radio promotion event). The total number of control messages (and bytes) involved with such a "release and reestablish" sequence in an NFV/SDN LTE architecture is 15 messages (2914 bytes) in our testbed setup (Composed of: SCTP 7 (1138), GTPv2 protocol 4 (352), OpenFlow 4 (1424)). Assuming such a dedicated MEC bearer is established every time the default bearer is established, this could translate to 2.58MB of control traffic per day per device, assuming bearer creation based on the behavior of popular applications (i.e., 929 times per day) [24]. For a worst case (upper bound) scenario where bearers are recreated every time after LTE radio promotion event, this number can be as high as 20MB per device per day (i.e., 7200 times.) Thus, to keep such control overheads low, one has to be judicious in the creation of separate (additional) bearers (say, for MEC) only when it is warranted. Considering the huge number of mobile users, the overheads are not negligible.

Application Optimization. In addition to the network, often most CI applications involve heavy-weight operations that incur substantial latency even in a server machine. In the case of AR applications, this would correspond to the object detection/matching operations. Figure 3(h) indicates the latency incurred in searching for an object from a database of various sizes running on an eight i7 core server. It clearly shows that the impact of pruning the database can have a significant impact on the end-end latency, making it a critical component for optimization as well.

Thus, we find that to deliver the tight latencies demanded by CI applications at end users, one needs to not only optimize the network but also the application. In the next section, we demonstrate how to accomplish this by intelligently leveraging *user context* along with SDN/NFV capabilities of the network to realize our service abstraction framework called ACACIA.

5. ACACIA'S DESIGN

Figure 4 shows an overview of the ACACIA mobile edge computing (MEC) service framework for context-aware continuous interactive (CI) applications. As shown, ACACIA assumes a core mobile network consisting of both centralized network functions (e.g., using LTE nomenclature, standard evolved packet core (EPC) functions), as well as distributed mobile edge cloud instances. Following current technology trends, the mobile edge cloud instances, in addition to hosting application servers, are capable of realizing virtualized core network functions (i.e., NFV/SDN-based EPC functions). Finally, ACACIA uses the D2D-based LTE-direct proximity discovery functionality.

Given this context, ACACIA enables context-aware CI applications by orchestrating the following functional components: (i) *User context discovery:* The ACACIA device

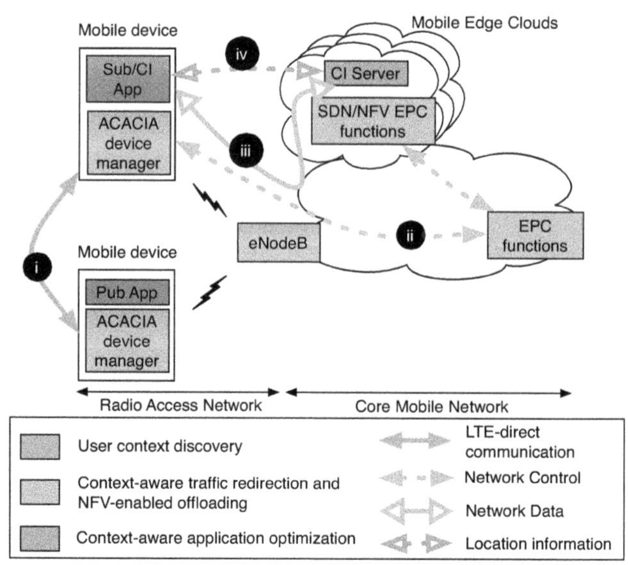

Figure 4: ACACIA Overview

manager enables applications on mobile devices to make use of the publish-subscribe capabilities of LTE-direct proximity services to advertise (publish) and learn about (subscribe) the availability of "services" that are of interest to users. The semantics of the messages associated with these service advertisements are application specific, but an "interest match" by a subscriber will trigger a CI application to provide the user with more information. (ii) *Context-aware traffic redirection:* When CI applications require mobile edge cloud resources to realize their functionality the ACACIA device manager will establish connectivity to the mobile edge cloud. The ACACIA device manager interacts with EPC functions in the mobile core network, which makes use of the proximity service discovery information to establish connectivity to the appropriate CI server on a mobile edge cloud that would satisfy the latency requirements of the CI application. (iii) ACACIA *Mobile Edge Network:* ACACIA combines existing LTE/EPC QoS bearer framework with novel SDN and NFV enabled mechanisms to realize the standards-compliant MEC data-plane offloading for only CI traffic. (iv) *Context-aware application optimization:* With connectivity to the mobile edge cloud in place, the ACACIA device manager provides location information for the CI application, which can be used to optimize its functionality. Thus, ACACIA is capable of enabling a variety of CI related use cases.

5.1 ACACIA Use Case

ACACIA can help various CI applications in significant ways. Consider an enriched retail shopping application as an example, where a retail shop uses ACACIA's service framework provided by a mobile operator. The service framework would encompass a number of components: First, an augmented reality (AR) server hosted in the mobile edge cloud. Second, the ability to use LTE-direct as a means to trigger access to the AR server. LTE-direct is used through a paired set of applications, one used by the retail store, the other used by customers.

When the sales personnel in the retail shop start work, they open the retail shop appplication in their smartphones and select their section or products from its User Interface (UI). As a result, their smartphones periodically publish the section or product information over the air with LTE-direct. Assume a customer, who wears Google glasses or has a smartphone, and comes to the shop to buy a laptop. When she enters the shop, she opens a retail shop application which has the same UI as that of salesmen and selects 'laptop' as her interests. (Note that in a more sophisticated setting, this information might be obtained based on the user's recent internet search activity.) Her device starts subscribing to laptop related information through LTE-direct. When she comes closer to the laptop section, her retail application receives the notification in the form of an alarm and a vibration (or a notification via her wearable device). It means the "service" which corresponds to her "interest" is available in this area of the store.

After the notification, her device runs an AR application. The AR application sends the live scene of her environment to an AR server in the mobile edge cloud closest to her. The AR server sends back information relevant to the scene such as prices, reviews, and current sales using text, audio or video. Using this information, she can make an informed decision and be aware of any current incentives (sales) available to her. While the AR application runs, it also sends information on nearby "sections" to the AR server based on messages it receives through LTE-direct from other publishers. This information is then transformed to approximate user "location" in the AR server, to optimize the latter's processing of the AR application.

In this context, the mobile carrier's service abstraction is realized via its LTE mobile network, its mobile edge cloud and the LTE-direct functionality. In addition, the mobile provider might provide libraries to use LTE-direct in the service application (e.g., a retail shop application in our example) and the ACACIA device manager to seamlessly orchestrate the service application, LTE networks and user contexts. The retail store would be responsible for developing the pair of applications (for customers and employees) using the LTE-direct libraries, as well as the server application running in the mobile edge cloud.

5.2 User Context Discovery

ACACIA leverages LTE-direct to discover nearby CI services based on user's interests. Publishers (any portable device with the LTE-direct feature) can publish any information relevant to their service called *service discovery message* through a small message and broadcast it periodically over the air. The service discovery message includes the service name (e.g., a retail shop name) and its detailed information (e.g., section/products) from a service application. Subscribers (any portable device with LTE-direct feature) can decide whether they want to receive such broadcasted service discovery message by selecting their interest in specific CI applications. Different LTE-direct publishers (e.g., different retail stores) will have different LTE-direct service names (managed by the mobile carrier providing LTE-direct services). This will allow LTE-direct subscribers to distinguish between different publishers.

5.3 Context-aware Traffic Redirection

ACACIA deploys a service or daemon called the ACACIA device manager that runs on mobile devices and plays two important roles. It first works as a proxy to transfer the service discovery message requests and responses between the CI applications and the LTE modem. More importantly, it is responsible for managing network connectivity of CI applications to use their CI servers in the mobile edge cloud on demand based on user contexts. When a user starts a CI application, the CI application first connects to the ACACIA device manager and registers itself. Then, the subscriber selects her specific interests (e.g., a laptop in our retail use case) through the UI of the CI application. When there is a match (of user interests) with the service discovery message received by the LTE modem for the CI application, the ACACIA device manager sends a request for network connectivity between the CI application and CI server to MEC Registration Server (MRS). The MRS is a core network component (i.e. Application Function (AF) in 3GPP terminology) in ACACIA, which manages the CI services and starts creating/deleting the network connectivity to the CI server in the mobile edge cloud instances. The first service discovery message from the ACACIA device manager, which has the information on the service, is used to locate the closest CI server in the MRS. When the user finishes using the CI application, the ACACIA device manager sends the request to delete network connectivity to the MRS, which results in the deletion of network connectivity for CI server in mobile network. Then it unregisters the ACACIA device manager, which deletes all relevant CI application information. The detailed procedure for network management between the CI application and its server is explained in Section 5.4.

The above design has two advantages. First, since the ACACIA device manager requests creation/deletion of network connectivity to the MRS based on user context *on demand*, it avoids maintaining two always-on bearers (default and dedicated), which would cause the unnecessary control overhead identified in Section 4. Second, it allows decoupling the CI application logic from MEC connectivity setup logic. Thus, application developers do not have to worry about provisioning the MEC connections closer to the UEs, as this is transparently handled by the ACACIA device manager, the MRS and mobile network components.

5.4 ACACIA Mobile Edge Network

ACACIA achieves the network connectivity between CI application and its server and selective CI traffic offloading to the appropriate CI server as shown in Figure 5. It leverages the user context-aware ACACIA device manager and the QoS bearer framework (i.e., a dedicated bearer) in LTE to selective steer traffic towards the MEC-based server. Specifically, traffic classification happens on the mobile device, where CI application traffic is sent on a dedicated bearer

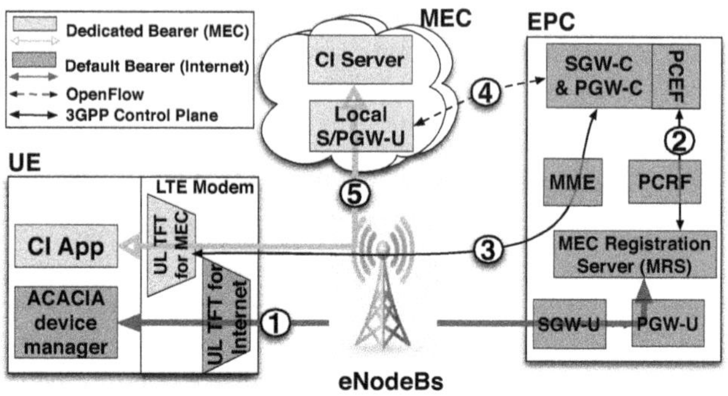

Figure 5: ACACIA Mobile Edge Network Architecture.

associated with the CI application and server. ACACIA uses split mobile GW functionality (i.e., GW-C and GW-U), to terminate the dedicated bearer on a set of GW-Us resident on the MEC. (This is realized using SDN and NFV functionality.) We denote GW-Us that serve the CI server and handle dedicated bearers as *local* GW-Us. Other GW-Us handle the default bearers, which connect UEs to the internet.

① *Request:* When the ACACIA device manager receives a match through LTE-direct, it sends a request to setup a dedicated bearer to MEC Registration Server (MRS) through the default bearer. The request includes the UE's IP address and service information.

② *Create:* Once the request is successful, the MRS signals the PCRF (Policy Control and Charging Rules Function) with the service ID, and flow information including IP addresses of UE and CI server corresponding to service information. The PCRF dynamically generates policy rules, which consist of service ID, QCI, and flow information from the MRS. The PCRF invokes the PCEF (Policy and Charging Enforcement Function) in PGW-C with the policy rules, which results in a network-initiated dedicated bearer activation [2].

③ *Set-up:* PGW-C, SGW-C, MME, eNB, and UE then exchange control messages to setup a dedicated bearer between these various components. To setup data plane for the dedicated bearer between *local* GW-Us, PGW-C and SGW-C should provide IP addresses of *local* GW-Us (not those of GW-Us serving default bearers) as the F-TEID (Fully Qualified Tunnel Endpoint Identifier) values in the *Create Bearer Request/Response* control messages. In addition, the MME sends the received IP address of the *local* SGW-U from SGW-C to eNB in the *Bearer Setup Request* control message, which ensures that only the MEC traffic is routed through eNB and *local* SGW-U. The eNB then sends the new Radio Bearer ID, Radio Bearer QoS, and IP address of the CI server as the TFT values in *RRC Connection Reconfiguration* control message to the UE. This ensures that the traffic for the MEC server uses a radio bearer (i.e., UE and eNB) that corresponds to the dedicated bearer, based on the traffic filtering function (UL TFT) that exists in the LTE modem.

④ *Route:* After successful exchange of control messages, SGW-C and PGW-C insert SDN (OpenFlow in our set-up) flow rules into the *local* SGW-U and PGW-U based on information such as TEID, and IP address of GW-Us and eNB from control messages. At this point the CI applications can use the local CI server (⑤).

ACACIA design presents a cleaner and more efficient solution than other MEC approaches explained in Section 2. It is a standards compatible and does not require the modifications to eNBs, standard LTE interfaces and protocols. Further, traffic classification happens in LTE modem through the LTE/EPC QoS bearer mechanism, which avoids the middlebox deployment for selective traffic offload in the network. ACACIA guarantees short latencies due to closer CI server and avoids the competing traffic between CI traffic and others in centralized GW-Us. In addition, in our ACACIA realization, the GW-Cs are decoupled into a 3GPP control plane and the OpenFlow control plane, thereby allowing them to scale independently.

5.5 Context-aware Application Optimization

While all CI applications benefit significantly from ACACIA's abilities explained in the previous sections, certain classes of CI applications, like AR, require further optimization of their application processing to meet their end-to-end latency requirements. As shown in Section 4, this arises from their need to *match* real-time scenes (e.g., faces, objects, etc.) from the client with a large database of apriori tagged images from the environment so as to provide relevant information back to the client in real-time. Towards addressing this latency, ACACIA leverages LTE-direct capabilities to help localize the client in the environment, and uses the client's location information to speed up the CI application.

Note that the requirements on localization accuracy are not very stringent, as the focus is to leverage location information for database pruning. For example, in a retail shop AR application, if the AR application server knows the approximate location of a user, say at the granularity of sections (e.g., clothes vs. shoes, etc.) this will be sufficient.

LTE-direct based Indoor Localization: LTE-direct provides received power (rxPower) level and signal to noise ratio (SNR) with a service discovery message when a subscriber receives it. We conduct a basic experiment to investigate the utility of such auxiliary information since there are no commercialized LTE-direct so far.

Choosing the right parameter: Figure 6(a) presents a map showing the locations of three landmarks (publishers) and the motion path of a subscriber. The landmarks periodically broadcast their distinct service messages over the air using LTE-direct. The subscriber registers with all three services in his CI application and then starts moving from landmark1 to landmark3. Figures 6(b) and 6(c) plot the measured SNR and rxPower values respectively. Figure 6(c) clearly shows the strong correlation between the rxPower and the subscriber's distance to the landmark, with the former peaking as the subscribers gets closer to each landmark. However, the SNR case does not exhibit such strong correlation, owing to the limited dynamic range that is used for decoding (i.e., 25 dB span compared to 50 dB span in rx-

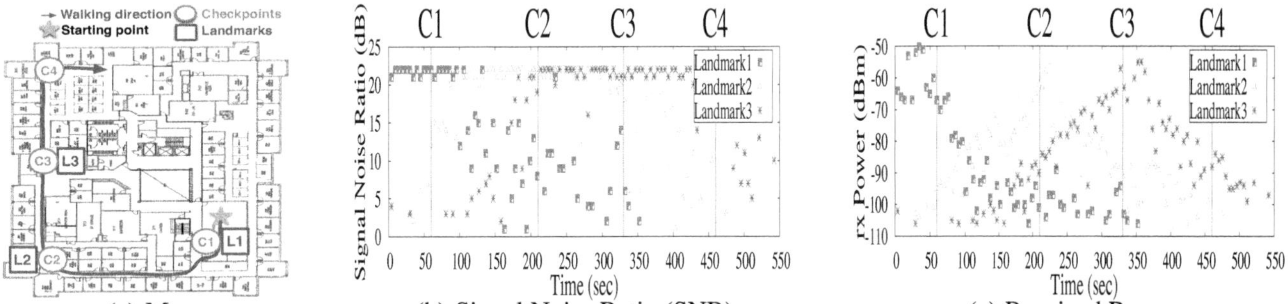

(a) Map (b) Signal Noise Ratio (SNR) (c) Received Power

Figure 6: LTE-direct

Power). Thus, ACACIA leverages rxPower as a more reliable parameter for indoor localization.

Tri-lateration: Once the rxPower values are obtained from the client through LTE-direct, ACACIA employs tri-lateration to localize the client. Tri-lateration requires the location of landmarks (e.g., (x,y) coordinates) and the distance between a subscriber and each of the landmarks as inputs, and returns the estimated coordinate of user's current location as output. While the location of the landmarks is known a-priori, the distance between a subscriber and each of the landmarks needs to be obtained. Here, a linear regression model for the path loss between a user and landmark is constructed for the given environment, which is a one-time overhead. When a subscriber gathers real-time rxPower information (through LTE-direct) from landmarks that it can hear from, the model is used to predict its distance from each of those landmarks. This information is then used by the tri-lateration algorithm [28] to predict the user's coordinates.

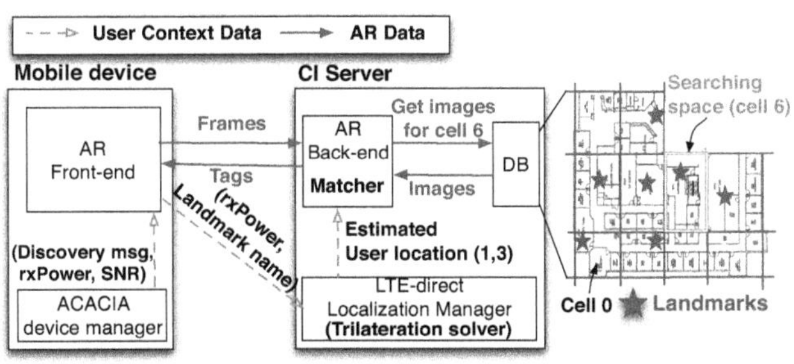

Figure 7: ACACIA CI application Architecture

Leveraging Fine-grained User Context: Figure 7 shows the interaction between the AR application on the user and CI server in the network. The AR front-end application on the user device continuously uploads frames from its camera to the AR back-end application on the CI server running on the mobile edge cloud in mobile network. In addition, whenever the front-end application receives a service discovery message from a landmark, it sends the rxPower and name of the corresponding landmark to the LTE-direct localization manager, also residing on the CI server. The LTE-direct localization manager aggregates such information from the user and uses it to estimate the user's current location by using Tri-lateration, which is then forwarded to the AR back-end application regularly. The AR back-end application maintains a geo-tagged database (Fig. 7), wherein the environment is geographically partitioned into different areas/segments, and the images/scenes from a particular segment (along with their AR-related information) are stored under the same geo-tag. On receiving the location information of the user, the back-end application determines the portion of the database (geo-tag) that covers the user's location. Then, it compares the frames uploaded from the user in real-time with only those from the database that have the identified geo-tag (e.g., cell 6 in Fig. 7). This significantly prunes the database and reduces the time required for matching images, thereby substantially decreasing the response time of the AR application. A noteworthy aspect of using such fine-grained user context (i.e., indoor location), enabled through LTE-direct capabilities of user devices, is the elimination of the need for any additional infrastructure.

6. IMPLEMENTING ACACIA

We have implemented a prototype of ACACIA on two different testbeds; the PhantomNet mobile testbed [26] as well as a private LTE testbed. Both testbeds were equipped with LTE-direct enabled One+ One smartphones (available with Release 12 LTE), Open vSwitch (OVS) [11], Ryu controller [14], OpenEPC-based LTE/EPC software [20] and eNodeBs. The main difference between the two testbeds is the eNodeB hardware. PhantomNet uses a small cell eNodeB from ip.access (scaling up to tens of users), while the private testbed uses a commercial grade eNodeB macrocell (scaling to a hundred users). We also build an AR-based retail application as a representative CI application.

6.1 Network Components

We use OpenEPC software [20] for LTE core network components (e.g., MME, GW-Cs, PCRF, PCEF, HSS and AF) and for processing 3GPP standard control plane. We use OVS as the GW-Us and the Ryu (SDN) controller to control the GW-Us by equipping them with GTP tunneling functions. The Ryu controller dynamically manages GTP flow rules with GW-Us with IP addresses and TEID from GW-Cs for GTP tunneling.

Dedicated bearer: *(i) MEC Registration Server (MRS) & PCRF:* We refactor the Client-RX module in OpenEPC as the MRS. We configure appropriate *policy rules* (e.g., application ID, QCI) for AR applications in the PCRF databases. *(ii) Control messages for dedicated bearer:* We extend the OpenEPC software to support dedicated bearers. We first extend the PCEF module in OpenEPC to distinguish between the default and dedicated bearer creation requests. Second, we modify each GW-Cs module by setting the IP addresses of MEC GW-Us in Fully Qualified Tunnel Endpoint Identifier (F-TEID) in dedicated bearer request messages to select the correct GW-Us for reaching the MEC server. Finally, we implement the generation of correct control messages (e.g., TFT, ARP), which pass from the MME to eNB, in the MME module.

SDN: *(i) Ryu controller:* We use Ryu OpenFlow controller to control the GW-Us. We extend the Ryu library to support GTP flow management, allowing the generation of GTP en/decapsulate flow rules. *(ii) Open vSwitch:* We use OVS 2.0 and extend it to work as GW-Us by adding GTP encapsulation/decapsulation mechanisms in kernel-space. We extend OVS to processes GTP packets in a kernel-resident fast-path once a packet is matched in the user-space using OpenFlow tables (called slow path in [44]). We use the logical port concept [39], which simplifies header manipulation in the OVS to process GTP packets.

6.2 ACACIA Device Manager

We implement the ACACIA device manager as an Android Service in the smartphone. It defines a *ServiceInfo* class, which implements the *Parcelable* interface [13] to exchange class instances between CI applications and ACACIA device manager. This allows for the expression of user interests (e.g., the landmark name) and discovery messages (landmark name, rxPower, SNR) corresponding to the class instance. To support this communication between the ACACIA device manager and CI applications, ACACIA uses the *Messenger* class [9], which is one of the interprocess communication methods in the Android operating system. In addition, it manages the creation/deletion of dedicated bearer requests to the MRS, when the first interest match is detected by LTE-direct or the user terminates the use of the CI application.

6.3 AR-based Retail Application

We have built a retail GUI application to interface with the ACACIA *device manager* and a prototype of an AR application which consists of a front-end Android application and a back-end object matching server by using OpenCV 2.4.10 [12].

(i) Service Discovery GUI application: The GUI application presents potential landmarks/services (e.g., sections or objects in a retail store) to users and records the user's interest in specific services and contains a localization handler which is connected to the LTE-direct localization manager at the CI server. When it is started, it first binds to the ACACIA device manager and communicates with it using the *ServiceInfo* class. When service discovery happens based on the user's interest, the ACACIA device manager returns the discovered information to the CI application. Then, the localization handler forwards the landmark's name and rxPower to the LTE-direct localization manager at CI server.

(ii) AR front-end: The AR front-end application continuously reads frames from the smartphone's camera. To reduce the latency in uploading frames to the AR back-end server and to save uplink bandwidth, it initially configures the frame size to an appropriate resolution to avoid resize computation overhead and encodes the grayscale frame with JPEG format.

(iii) LTE-direct Localization Manager: We implement a LTE-direct localization manager at the CI server by extending the trilateration solver [16]. When the manager starts, it reads the metadata from a file. This includes information on the number, location and names of landmarks, and the model parameters (α, β) for linear regression to convert rxPower values to distance between a user's location and each landmark. When it receives rxPower and landmark updates from a user, it runs the trilateration algorithm to estimate the user's current location. After estimating the user location, it passes this information to the AR back-end application to help prune the search space in the database.

(iv) AR back-end: The AR back-end server processes uploaded frames from the AR front-end and matches it with objects in its database. When it is started, it first reads the current database stored in YAML format [18]. Our database is populated with 105 objects emulating a retail store and is partitioned based on sections like food, toys and so on. Each object is stored in the database as a set of: object name, an annotated tag, SURF [27] keypoints and descriptors from the image of object. The AR back-end server first decodes an encoded frame from the AR front-end and runs the SURF algorithm to extract SURF feature keypoints and descriptors from it. Using this information, it starts the matching process with objects currently stored in the database. Here, the database is pruned based on the user's location information provided by the LTE-direct localization manager. During the matching procedure, it uses several steps to improve the matching accuracy even though it increases runtime. In each step, it compares the output with the threshold and then decides whether to proceed to the next step or return a "no-match" response. First, it performs the ratio test with the two best matches from a brute-force k-nearest matcher for the two images. Second, it performs the symmetry test to check whether the best matches from two brute-force k-nearest matchers are the same or not. If they are not the same, the best match is discarded. Last, it validates the matches using RANSAC (random sample consensus) to return the correct estimates (matches) as inliers and incorrect one as outliers.

7. EVALUATION

We first evaluate the various components in ACACIA in isolation, followed by the impact of their optimization on application latency.

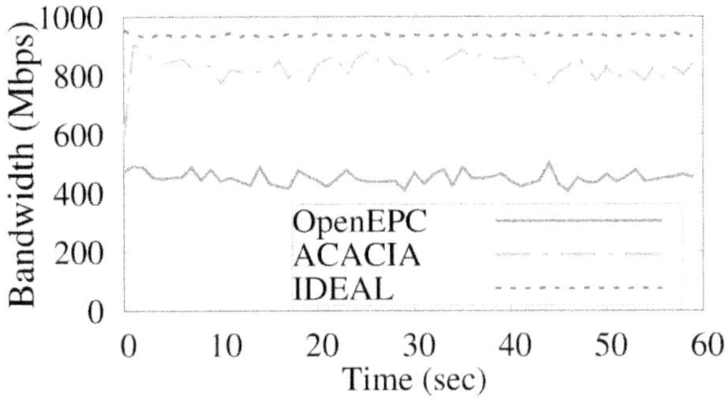

Figure 8: Data plane comparison

7.1 Micro-benchmarks

Validating ACACIA*'s standard compliance.* We verify ACACIA's standards compliance by testing its inter-operability with several closed source, standards based eNodeBs and UEs. Specifically, we successfully tested ACACIA against the following combinations: (i) eNodeB: ip.access small cell; UE: One+ One (Android 5.0), Nexus 5 (Android 4.4) and Huawei dongle (connected to a Ubuntu 14.01). (ii) eNodeB: commercial macrocell; UE: One+ One (Android 5.0), Nexus 6 (Android 5.0) and Pantech dongle (connected to Ubuntu 12.04). We test each combination with the QoS-based dedicated bearer provisioning for the MEC server in ACACIA. Our results illustrate the standards compliant operation of ACACIA. The time to set up a dedicated bearer in ACACIA depends on the location of the network components in the mobile core network.

SDN Data Plane. We compare our OVS-based GW-U implementation with a (non-split) OpenEPC GW implementation which executes entirely in user-space. (We used OpenEPC release 5 which does not have a functional split GW implementation.) Figure 8 shows the network throughput for ACACIA and the vanilla OpenEPC implementation when the GWs process GTP packets from Iperf TCP test on the mobile client. The figure also shows the maximum achievable throughput in this setup.

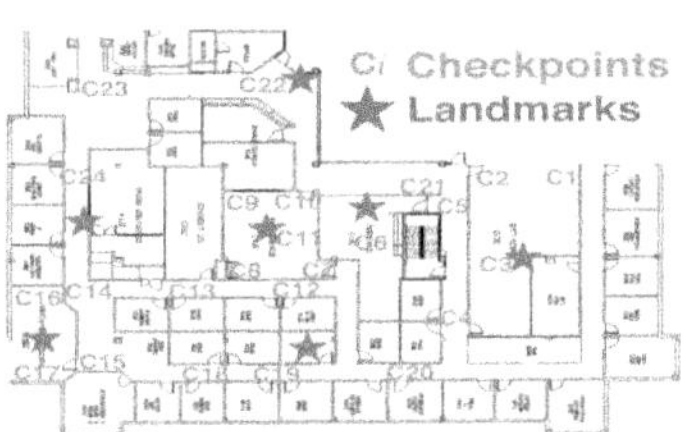

(a) Map with seven landmarks

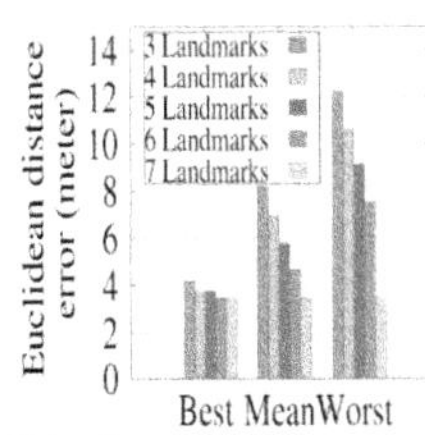

(b) Accuracy according to # of landmarks and positions

Figure 9: LTE-direct localization accuracy

LTE-direct based Device Localization. We conduct trace-based evaluations to study the accuracy of ACACIA's indoor localization component. The traces were collected from LTE-direct enabled One+ One smartphone devices. Figure 9(a) shows a map indicating the locations of seven landmarks (publishers) and several checkpoints (subscriber locations), which are used for location estimation. We employ Euclidean distance to evaluate localization accuracy error.

When a subscriber can hear several landmarks, it uses various combinations of signals from the landmarks to estimate the location. Figure 9(b) shows the results. As the number of landmarks increase, the accuracy of localization estimation increases, with seven landmarks showing the best accuracy. In addition, the position of landmarks, especially when the number of landmarks is small, impacts the accuracy of localization. This manifests in the large difference between the best and worst case errors in the case of small number of landmarks, and decreases considerably for a large number of landmarks. Thus, to obtain good accuracy, it is essential to either deploy a large number of randomly placed landmarks, or a small number of well-positioned landmarks.

Our localization error with LTE-direct is around 3 meter on average, which may be high for certain applications. However, note that, ACACIA leverages user's location information to track down the relevant segment of the store, which will in turn be used to prune the search space for computer vision based AR applications. While our current accuracies translate to appreciable application speed-up for AR applications (Section 7.3), ACACIA can benefit from other sophisticated fine-grained localization techniques.

7.2 Impact of Traffic Redirection

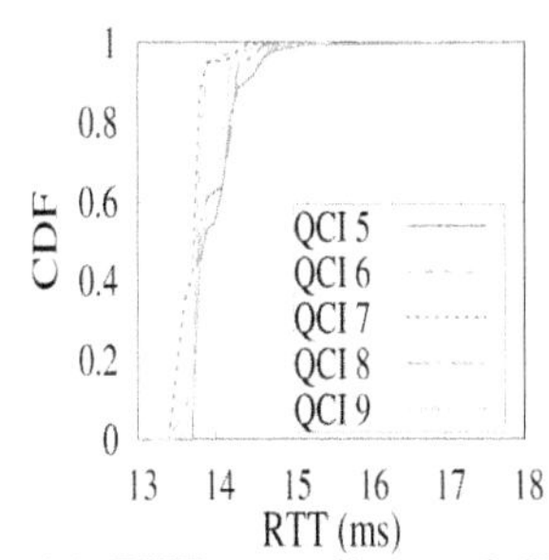

(a) RTT according to QCI

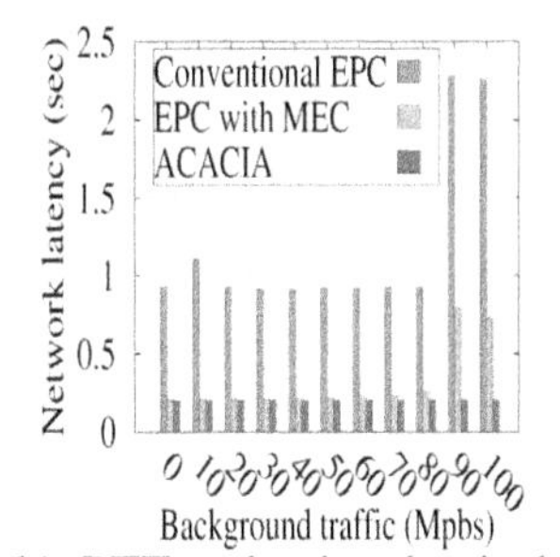

(b) RTT reduction by isolation

Figure 10: Redirection effects

RTT Reduction. To measure the RTT between a UE and MEC server, we use a One+ One smartphone as the UE, and LTE ip.access as the eNB with ACACIA's MEC platform (including GW-Us and MEC server). We use different QoS Class Identifier (QCI) [4] values when setting up a dedicated bearer for MEC server and measure RTT by using Ping command. All experiments are conducted with the best LTE signal (full signal bars) in One+ (signal strength: -70 dBm, -74 ASU).

Figure 10(a) shows the end-to-end RTT between UE and the MEC server. 95% of the RTTs are within 15 ms, with RTT between eNB and MEC accounting for a meagre 1.6 ms. Thus, latency is significantly reduced compared to the median latency over current LTE network (e.g., 70 ms) [36].

This makes the case for offloading the computation of CI applications from the smartphone in the presence of MEC.

RTT Reduction from Isolation of CI Traffic. We conduct experiments, where the AR application serves as the MEC/CI traffic, while Iperf is used for generating background traffic at varying rates. We also introduce controlled delays between eNB and SGW and between SGW and PGW to emulate network latencies between UE and MEC server under different core network architectures (conventional and MEC).

Figure 10(b) shows the combined benefit from (i) isolating and redirecting AR traffic (non-split vs. split control-data plane architecture), and (ii) location of the MEC server. (70 ms vs. 13 ms) The conventional core networks employ the non-split architecture, where all traffic from the UE goes through the same S-GW and P-GW. The results indicate that until the network capacity is saturated (around 90 Mbps), the location of the MEC server plays the dominant role in the end-end application latency. However, once the network capacity is saturated, the background traffic has a large impact to increase latency significantly in the conventional architecture. However, ACACIA's ability to isolate/redirect AR traffic helps maintain stable, low latencies for the AR application.

7.3 Impact of Application Optimization

AR front-end resize and compression. Given the volume of data, even when using grayscale images, our AR application uses compression. We measure compression time and the compression ratio. To compress raw grayscale images (1280*720, 960*720 and 720*480) with JPEG 90, on average takes 53ms, 38ms and 23 ms on the One+ One device and shows 5x, 5.8x, and 4.7x size reduction.

Application Search-space Optimization. We evaluate the reduction in the AR application search-space by leveraging user location information. We consider three schemes. *Naive* approach searches over all objects (in the entire floor) in the database. *rxPower* searches a smaller part of the database (e.g., sections in the floor) based on user's proximity to landmarks from which it received the highest and second-highest rxPower signals. Lastly, ACACIA uses LTE-direct based indoor localization and searches only a much smaller portion of the database (e.g., sub-sections in the floor) based on location information from *LTE-direct localization manager*.

We divide the floor into 5 sections and 21 subsections, as shown in Figure 9(a). Our AR database has 105 objects that are tagged at a sub-section level. We select 24 objects, which are located at checkpoints shown in Figure 9(a) and generate 5 frames per object from the AR application running on One+ One phones at those locations. For the last two approaches, we also measure rxPower from the 7 Landmarks at each of those checkpoints. We use i7 (8 cores) and Xeon processor (32 cores) as the AR server to see impact of processing capability with varying size of frames as inputs.

Figure 11(a) shows the average runtime latency for object matching alone in AR. Clearly, ACACIA incurs the shortest time by being able to reduce its search-space to 2-6 subsections out of 21 with the help of user location information.

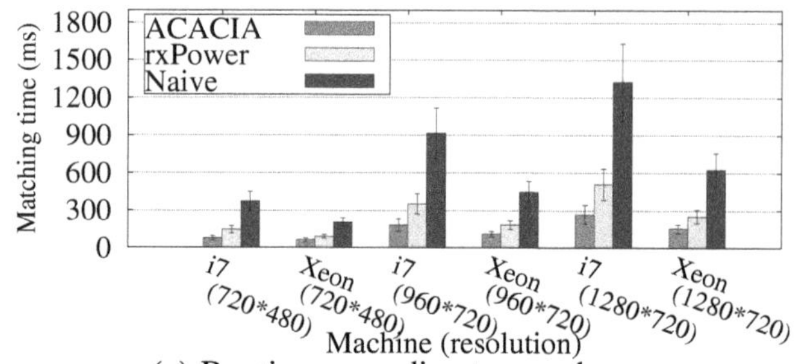

(a) Runtime according to search-space

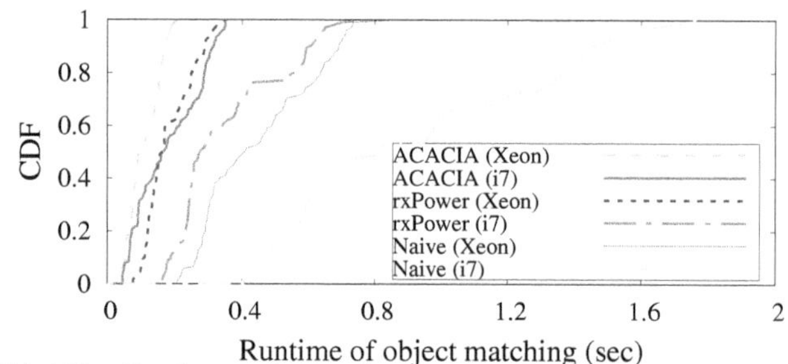

(b) Distribution of runtime according to search-space (960*720)

Figure 11: LTE-direct localization impact

ACACIA shows up to 5.02x and 1.93x reduction in average run-time for matching operations compared to *Naive* and *rxPower* respectively. In high resolution, ACACIA shows better performance than the other approaches since high resolution requires longer processing time for the matching operation. The Xeon processor, with a larger number of cores and OpenCV's support for parallel computations, shows a much better performance. Figure 11(b) shows the CDF of the runtime latency with 960*720 resolution. Without the help of user location information, matching takes over 1 second for some images on i7 (8 cores) processor.

Further, while ACACIA and *Naive* return correct matches in all instances, *rxPower* returns one false negative (object exists in DB, but is not matched/found) in boundary area (C13 in a map) from multiple landmarks as it only searches for objects in the database corresponding to the two landmarks that return the highest rxPower values.

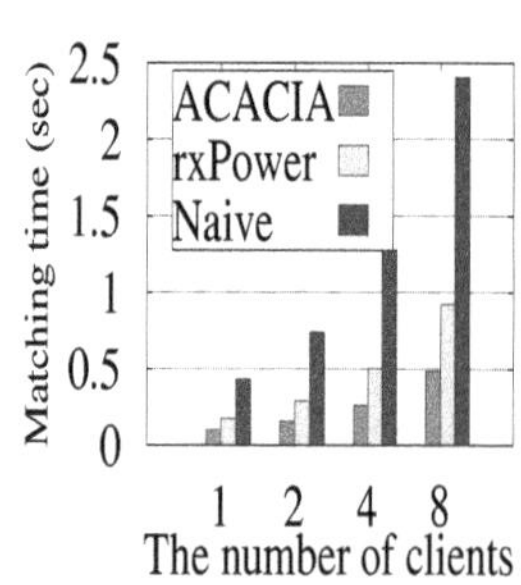

(a) With Xeon processor

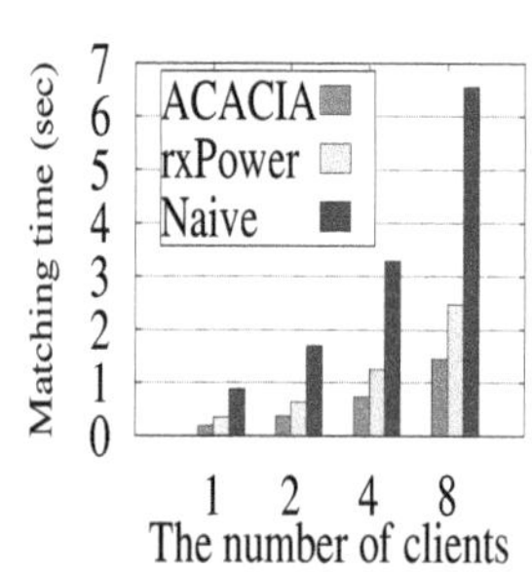

(b) With i7 processor

Figure 12: Runtime of object matching based on # of users

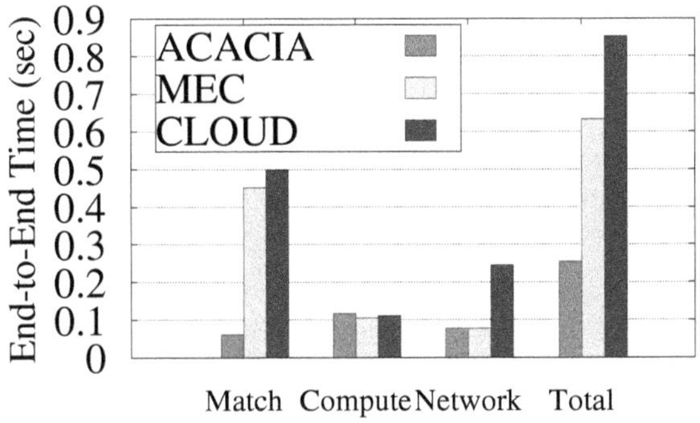

Figure 13: End-to-End comparison

Figure 12(a) and 12(b) show the runtime latency for object matching with 960*720 resolution frames as the number of clients increases with i7 and xeon processor respectively. As the number of clients increase, the runtime is almost doubled. So, ACACIA shows higher reductions compared to the other two cases as the number of clients increase. Experiments at other resolutions (720*480 and 1280*720) show the similar results.

In this experiment, the AR server does not show false negative or false positive since the server has 4 stages which improve accuracy.

7.4 End-to-end Evaluation

We conduct experiments to evaluate end-to-end latency. A One+ One device connects to an LTE ip.access eNodeB and we set the camera input to a 720*480 resolution in the AR application. We evaluate the end-to-end latency by using a subset of the objects in our image database.

In this experiment, we compare ACACIA with (i) an *MEC* implementation which does not have search-space optimization and (ii) *CLOUD* which is conventional EPC and without search-space optimization. Figure 13 shows the results. ACACIA shows a 7.7x reduction for match compared to the other approaches and a 3.15x reduction for network latency compared to *CLOUD*. *Compute* includes the compression of frames on the smartphone, and decompression and SURF computations of keypoints and descriptors in the AR server. There is no significant difference between the different approaches. *MEC* shows a 25% end-to-end reduction compared to *CLOUD*. ACACIA shows a 60% and a 70% end-to-end reduction compared to *MEC* and *CLOUD* respectively.

8. DISCUSSION

A real deployment of ACACIA. A realistic deployment of ACACIA would require Device-to-Device capability in eNodeBs and smartphones, e.g., in our implementation we use LTE-direct. We expect smartphones and eNodeBs to support this functionality in the near future since it is a part of 3gpp release 12 [1]. In addition, since LTE-direct works with smartphones supporting LTE, we expect ACACIA will not require significant additional infrastructure for either the mobile provider or service providers. In the core network side, ACACIA requires split mode GWs (GW-Cs and GW-Us), which differs from current centralized hardware-based GWs. While different GW realization will be needed, our approach does not require changes to the LTE/EPC interface (i.e., does not require 3gpp specification changes). Further, considering current trends [15, 10], we expect software-based split mode GWs will soon be deployed in mobile network. ACACIA does not require change the rest of the mobile core network components (e.g., MME, PCRF, etc.).

We expect that the ACACIA architecture will be able to support a variety of business models. A possible mapping could involve the mobile provider offering an infrastructure service to service providers, including the ACACIA device manager, a device-to-device library and MEC clouds. A service provider could then use this infrastructure to provide different services and/or applications, e.g., retail AR applications and servers as in our prototype.

Other proximity discovery techniques with ACACIA. ACACIA can use other proximity service discovery techniques, e.g., bluetooth ibeacon [7] and WiFi Aware [17]. These technologies also use a pub-sub model and provide similar features like service discovery messages and power level information. To support these technologies, the ACACIA device manager will need to be extended with similar approaches to what we use for LTE-direct.

ACACIA *without proximity service discovery.* It is possible for ACACIA to function without proximity service discovery. In this case ACACIA would need a different trigger to request network connectivity to an appropriate MEC server. For example, launching a specific application might serve as the trigger to activate ACACIA functionality.

9. CONCLUSION

We identified the critical need for edge computing as well its synergistic optimization with both the user and application, towards enabling continuous interactive (CI) applications in mobile networks. To this end, we proposed ACACIA - a service abstraction framework that adopts a holistic end-to-end approach to enabling low latency CI services over mobile networks offered by mobile network providers. ACACIA leverages client context information, namely proximity to landmarks and user interests, along with the SDN/NFV capabilities of the core network, to optimize both network and application processing latencies. The benefits of ACACIA are showcased through a highly-responsive augmented reality based retail service application. Our results show significant improvement over existing mobile networks, and even over a basic mobile edge cloud approach. This validates our holistic optimization strategy. At the same time our results suggest the need for further improvements, likely for both radio access network latencies as well device computational power, before scalable CI applications will be feasible.

Acknowledgements: We would like to thank our shepherd Vijay Sivaraman and our reviewers for their feedback on earlier versions of this paper. This work was initiated when the primary author was an intern at NEC Labs America, and is supported in part by the National Science Foundation under grant numbers 1343713 and 1305384.

10. REFERENCES

[1] 3GPP Release 12. http://www.3gpp.org/specifications/releases/68-release-12.

[2] 3GPP TS 23.401. http://www.3gpp.org/DynaReport/23401.htm.

[3] 3GPP TS 24.008. http://www.3gpp.org/DynaReport/24008.htm.

[4] 3GPP TS 24.008. http://www.3gpp.org/DynaReport/24008.htm.

[5] Creating a Digital 6th Sense with LTE Direct. http://tinyurl.com/jj9tdg4.

[6] Flexible and Elastic User-data Plane with OpenFlow v1.4.0. http://www.openepc.com/specials-and-tooling/cpup-split-with-openflow/.

[7] Getting Started with iBeacon. https://developer.apple.com/ibeacon/Getting-Started-with-iBeacon.pdf.

[8] Local IP Access and Selected IP Traffic Offload (LIPA-SIPTO). http://www.3gpp.org/ftp/Specs/html-info/23829.htm.

[9] Messenger Class. http://developer.android.com/reference/android/os/Messenger.html.

[10] NEC Virtualized Evolved Packet Core. http://tinyurl.com/nuefq28.

[11] Open vSwitch. http://openvswitch.org/.

[12] OpenCV. http://opencv.org/.

[13] Parcelable Interface. http://developer.android.com/reference/android/os/Parcelable.html.

[14] Ryu controller, a component-based software-defined networking framework. http://osrg.github.io/ryu/.

[15] The Journey to Packet Core Virtualization. http://resources.alcatel-lucent.com/asset/174234.

[16] Trilateration. https://github.com/lemmingapex/Trilateration.

[17] Wi-Fi Aware. http://www.wi-fi.org/discover-wi-fi/wi-fi-aware.

[18] XML/YAML Persistence. http://tinyurl.com/jzc5fdr.

[19] The tactile internet - itu-t technology watch report. http://www.itu.int/dms_pub/itu-t/oth/23/01/T23010000230001PDFE.pdf, Aug 2014.

[20] OpenEPC. http://www.openepc.com/, 2015.

[21] 5GPPP. 5G Vision - The 5G Infrastructure Public Private Partnership: the next generation of communication networks and services. https://5g-ppp.eu/wp-content/uploads/2015/02/5G-Vision-Brochure-v1.pdf, 2015.

[22] Agarwal, S., Philipose, M., and Bahl, P. Vision: the case for cellular small cells for cloudlets. In *Proceedings of the fifth international workshop on Mobile cloud computing & services* (2014), ACM, pp. 1–5.

[23] Alliance, N. 5g white paper-executive version. *White Paper, December* (2014).

[24] Aucinas, A., Vallina-Rodriguez, N., Grunenberger, Y., Erramilli, V., Papagiannaki, K., Crowcroft, J., and Wetherall, D. Staying online while mobile: The hidden costs. In *Proceedings of the ninth ACM conference on Emerging networking experiments and technologies* (2013), ACM, pp. 315–320.

[25] Bahl, P., and Padmanabhan, V. N. Radar: An in-building rf-based user location and tracking system. In *INFOCOM 2000. Nineteenth Annual Joint Conference of the IEEE Computer and Communications Societies. Proceedings. IEEE* (2000), vol. 2, Ieee, pp. 775–784.

[26] Banerjee, A., Cho, J., Eide, E., Duerig, J., Nguyen, B., Ricci, R., Van der Merwe, J., Webb, K., and Wong, G. Phantomnet: Research infrastructure for mobile networking, cloud computing and software-defined networking. *GetMobile: Mobile Computing and Communications 19*, 2 (2015), 28–33.

[27] Bay, H., Tuytelaars, T., and Van Gool, L. Surf: Speeded up robust features. In *Computer vision–ECCV 2006*. Springer, 2006, pp. 404–417.

[28] Borenstein, J., Everett, H. R., Feng, L., and Wehe, D. Mobile robot positioning-sensors and techniques. Tech. rep., DTIC Document, 1997.

[29] Chen, Y., Lymberopoulos, D., Liu, J., and Priyantha, B. Fm-based indoor localization. In *Proceedings of the 10th international conference on Mobile systems, applications, and services* (2012), ACM, pp. 169–182.

[30] Chen, Z., Jiang, L., Hu, W., Ha, K., Amos, B., Pillai, P., Hauptmann, A., and Satyanarayanan, M. Early implementation experience with wearable cognitive assistance applications. In *Proceedings of the 2015 Workshop on Wearable Systems and Applications* (New York, NY, USA, 2015), WearSys '15, ACM, pp. 33–38.

[31] Cho, J., Nguyen, B., Banerjee, A., Ricci, R., Van der Merwe, J., and Webb, K. Smore: Software-defined networking mobile offloading architecture. In *Proceedings of the 4th workshop on All things cellular: operations, applications, & challenges* (2014), ACM, pp. 21–26.

[32] Cuervo, E., Balasubramanian, A., Cho, D.-k., Wolman, A., Saroiu, S., Chandra, R., and Bahl, P. Maui: making smartphones last longer with code offload. In *Proceedings of the 8th international conference on Mobile systems, applications, and services* (2010), ACM, pp. 49–62.

[33] Dong, W., Ge, Z., and Lee, S. 3g meets the internet: Understanding the performance of hierarchical routing in 3g networks. In *Teletraffic Congress (ITC), 2011 23rd International* (Sept 2011), pp. 15–22.

[34] Ha, K., Chen, Z., Hu, W., Richter, W., Pillai, P., and Satyanarayanan, M. Towards wearable cognitive assistance. In *Proceedings of the 12th annual international conference on Mobile systems, applications, and services* (2014), ACM, pp. 68–81.

[35] Huang, J., Qian, F., Gerber, A., Mao, Z. M., Sen, S., and Spatscheck, O. A close examination of performance and power characteristics of 4g lte networks. In *Proceedings of the 10th international conference on Mobile systems, applications, and services* (2012), ACM, pp. 225–238.

[36] Huang, J., Qian, F., Guo, Y., Zhou, Y., Xu, Q., Mao, Z. M., Sen, S., and Spatscheck, O. An in-depth study of lte: effect of network protocol and application behavior on performance. In *ACM SIGCOMM Computer Communication Review* (2013), ACM, pp. 363–374.

[37] ITU. Tactile Internet. http://www.itu.int/en/ITU-T/techwatch/Pages/tactile-internet.aspx.

[38] Jain, P., Manweiler, J., and Roy Choudhury, R. Overlay: Practical mobile augmented reality. In *Proceedings of the 13th Annual International*

Conference on Mobile Systems, Applications, and Services (2015), ACM, pp. 331–344.

[39] KEMPF, J., JOHANSSON, B., PETTERSSON, S., LUNING, H., AND NILSSON, T. Moving the mobile evolved packet core to the cloud. In *Wireless and Mobile Computing, Networking and Communications (WiMob), 2012 IEEE 8th International Conference on* (2012), IEEE, pp. 784–791.

[40] KOTARU, M., JOSHI, K., BHARADIA, D., AND KATTI, S. Spotfi: Decimeter level localization using wifi. In *Proceedings of the 2015 ACM Conference on Special Interest Group on Data Communication* (2015), ACM, pp. 269–282.

[41] LAU, E.-E.-L., AND CHUNG, W.-Y. Enhanced rssi-based real-time user location tracking system for indoor and outdoor environments. In *Convergence Information Technology, 2007. International Conference on* (2007), IEEE, pp. 1213–1218.

[42] LI, L. E., MAO, Z. M., AND REXFORD, J. Toward software-defined cellular networks. In *Proceedings of the 2012 European Workshop on Software Defined Networking* (Washington, DC, USA, 2012), EWSDN '12, IEEE Computer Society, pp. 7–12.

[43] PATEL, M., NAUGHTON, B., CHAN, C., SPRECHER, N., ABETA, S., NEAL, A., ET AL. Mobile-edge computing introductory technical white paper. *White Paper, Mobile-edge Computing (MEC) industry initiative* (2014).

[44] PFAFF, B., PETTIT, J., AMIDON, K., CASADO, M., KOPONEN, T., AND SHENKER, S. Extending networking into the virtualization layer. In *Hotnets* (2009).

[45] RODRIGUEZ, J., Ed. *Fundamentals of 5G Mobile Networks*. John Wiley & Sons, 2015.

[46] SAID, S. B. H., SAMA, M. R., GUILLOUARD, K., SUCIU, L., SIMON, G., LAGRANGE, X., AND BONNIN, J. M. New control plane in 3gpp lte/epc architecture for on-demand connectivity service. In *Cloud Networking (CloudNet), 2013 IEEE 2nd International Conference on* (Nov 2013), pp. 205–209.

[47] SATYANARAYANAN, M. A brief history of cloud offload: A personal journey from odyssey through cyber foraging to cloudlets. *GetMobile: Mobile Comp. and Comm. 18*, 4 (Jan. 2015), 19–23.

[48] SATYANARAYANAN, M., BAHL, P., CACERES, R., AND DAVIES, N. The case for vm-based cloudlets in mobile computing. *IEEE Pervasive Computing 8*, 4 (Oct 2009), 14–23.

[49] STEFANIA, S., ISSAM, T., AND MATTHEW, B. Lte-the umts long term evolution: From theory to practice. *A John Wiley and Sons, Ltd* (2009).

[50] VARSHAVSKY, A., DE LARA, E., HIGHTOWER, J., LAMARCA, A., AND OTSASON, V. Gsm indoor localization. *Pervasive and Mobile Computing 3*, 6 (2007), 698–720.

[51] WANG, K., SHEN, M., CHO, J., BANERJEE, A., VAN DER MERWE, J., AND WEBB, K. Mobiscud: A fast moving personal cloud in the mobile network. In *Proceedings of the 5th Workshop on All Things Cellular: Operations, Applications and Challenges* (2015), ACM, pp. 19–24.

[52] ZARIFIS, K., FLACH, T., NORI, S., CHOFFNES, D., GOVINDAN, R., KATZ-BASSETT, E., MAO, Z. M., AND WELSH, M. Diagnosing path inflation of mobile client traffic. In *Proceedings of the 15th International Conference on Passive and Active Measurement - Volume 8362* (New York, NY, USA, 2014), PAM 2014, Springer-Verlag New York, Inc., pp. 23–33.

Lying Your Way to Better Traffic Engineering

Marco Chiesa
Universitè catholique de Louvain
marco.chiesa@uclouvain.be

Gábor Rétvári
MTA-BME Information Systems Research Group
retvari@tmit.bme.hu

Michael Schapira
Hebrew University of Jerusalem
schapiram@cs.huji.ac.il

ABSTRACT

To optimize the flow of traffic in IP networks, operators do traffic engineering (TE), i.e., tune routing-protocol parameters in response to traffic demands. TE in IP networks typically involves configuring static link weights and splitting traffic between the resulting shortest-paths via the Equal-Cost-MultiPath (ECMP) mechanism. Unfortunately, ECMP is a notoriously cumbersome and indirect means for optimizing traffic flow, often leading to poor network performance. Also, obtaining accurate knowledge of traffic demands as the input to TE is elusive, and traffic conditions can be highly variable, further complicating TE. We leverage recently proposed schemes for increasing ECMP's expressiveness via carefully disseminated bogus information ("lies") to design COYOTE, a readily deployable TE scheme for robust and efficient network utilization. COYOTE leverages new algorithmic ideas to configure (static) traffic splitting ratios that are optimized with respect to all (even adversarially chosen) traffic scenarios within the operator's "uncertainty bounds". Our experimental analyses show that COYOTE significantly outperforms today's prevalent TE schemes in a manner that is robust to traffic uncertainty and variation. We discuss experiments with a prototype implementation of COYOTE.

1. INTRODUCTION

To adapt the routing of traffic to the demands network operators do traffic engineering (TE), i.e., tune routing-protocol parameters so as to influence how traffic flows in their networks [1–3]. Today's prevalent scheme for TE within an organizational IP network is based on configuring static link-weights into shortest-path protocols such as OSPF [4] and splitting traffic between the resulting shortest-paths via ECMP [5]. Traditional TE with ECMP significantly constrains both route-computation and traffic splitting between multiple paths in two crucial ways: (1) traffic from a source to a destination in the network can only flow along the shortest paths between them (for the given configuration of link weights), and (2) traffic splitting between multiple paths (if multiple shortest paths exist) can only be done in very specific manners (see Section 2.1 for an illustration).

CoNEXT '16, December 12 - 15, 2016, Irvine, CA, USA

 ISBN 978-1-4503-4292-6/16/12. . . $15.00

DOI: http://dx.doi.org/10.1145/2999572.2999585

ECMP's lack of expressiveness makes traffic engineering with ECMP a notoriously hard task that often results in poor performance. Indeed, not only does ECMP's inflexibility imply that traffic flow might be arbitrarily far from the global optimum [6], but even choosing "good" link weights for TE with ECMP is infeasible in general [7]. Beyond ECMP's deficiencies, today's dominant TE schemes also suffer from other predicaments, e.g., obtaining an accurate view of traffic demands so as to optimize TE is elusive, as most networks lack the appropriate measurement infrastructure. Also, traffic can be highly variable and routing configurations that are good with respect to one traffic scenario can be bad with respect to another. We thus seek a TE scheme that is backwards compatible with legacy routing infrastructure (i.e., OSPF and ECMP), yet *robustly* achieves high performance even under uncertain or variable traffic conditions.

Introducing COYOTE: optimized, OSPF/ECMP-compatible TE. We leverage recently introduced approaches for enriching ECMP's expressiveness without changing router hardware/software to design COYOTE (COmpatible Yet Optimized TE). Recent studies show that by injecting "lies" into OSPF-ECMP (specifically, information about fake links and nodes), OSPF and ECMP can support much richer traffic flow configurations [8, 9]. We exploit these developments to explore how OSPF-ECMP routing can be extended to achieve consistently high performance even under great uncertainty about the traffic conditions and high variability of traffic. To accomplish this, COYOTE relies on new algorithmic ideas to configure (static) traffic splitting ratios at routers/switches that are optimized with respect to *all* (even *adversarially* chosen) traffic scenarios within operator-specified "uncertainty bounds".

We view COYOTE as an important additional step in the recent exploration of how SDN-like functionality can be accomplished without changing today's networking infrastructure (see [8,9]). Our experimentation with COYOTE on real network topologies shows that COYOTE indeed consistently and robustly achieves good performance even with very limited (in fact, sometimes even no) knowledge about the traffic demands and, in particular, exhibits significantly better performance than (optimized) traditional TE with ECMP. Our experiments with a prototype implementation of COYOTE also demonstrate its performance benefits. We briefly discuss below the algorithmic challenges facing the design of COYOTE and how these are tackled.

New algorithmic framework: destination-based oblivious routing. A rich body of literature in algorithmic theory investigates "(traffic-demands-)oblivious routing" [10–12], i.e., how to compute provably good routing configurations with limited (possibly even no) knowledge of the traffic demands. Past studies [11, 13] show that, even though lacking accurate information about the traffic demands, demands-oblivious routing algorithms yield remarkably close-to-optimal performance on real-world networks. Unfortunately, the above-mentioned algorithms involve forwarding packets based on both source and destination and are so inherently incompatible with destination-based routing via OSPF-ECMP. In addition, realizing these schemes in practice entails either excessive use of (e.g., MPLS) tunneling/tagging in traditional IP networks [11, 14], or the ubiquitous deployment of per-flow routing software-defined networking infrastructure [15].

Our design of COYOTE relies on a novel algorithmic framework for demands-oblivious IP routing. We initiate the study of optimizing oblivious routing under the restriction that forwarding is destination-based. In light of the recent progress on enhancing OSPF-ECMP's expressiveness, we view the algorithmic investigation of destination-based oblivious routing as an important and timely research agenda. We take the first steps in this direction. Our first result establishes that, in contrast to unconstrained oblivious routing, computing the optimal destination-based oblivious routing configuration is computationally intractable. We show how, via the decomposition of this problem into sub-problems that are easier to address with today's mathematical toolkit, and by leveraging prior research, good routing configurations can be generated. We regard our algorithmic results along these lines as a first, yet promising, step en route to better TE in IP networks, and leave the reader with many interesting open questions in Section 6.

2. COYOTE: OVERVIEW AND DESIGN

We next motivate COYOTE through a simple example, present the algorithmic challenges facing COYOTE's design, and explain how these are tackled.

2.1 Motivating Example

Consider the toy example in Fig. 1a. Two network users, s_1 and s_2, wish to send traffic to target t. Suppose that each user is expected to send between 0 and 2 units of flow and each link is of capacity 1. Suppose also that the network operator is oblivious to the actual traffic demands or, alternatively, that traffic is variable and user demands might drastically change over time. The operator aims to provide robustly good network performance, and thus has an ambitious goal: configuring OSPF-ECMP routing parameters

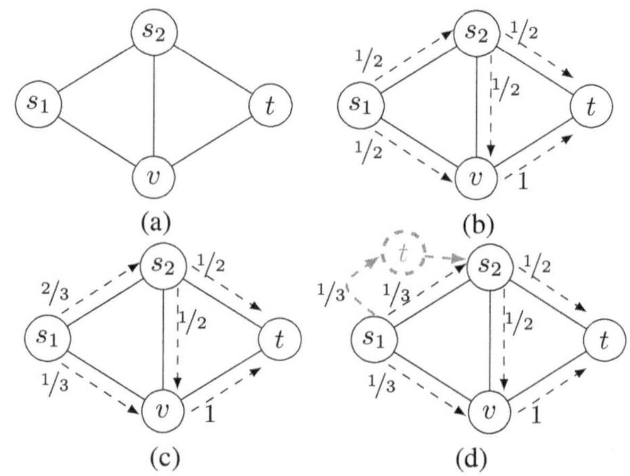

Figure 1: A sample network: (a) topology with unit capacity links; (b) per-destination ECMP routing (oblivious performance ratio $3/2$); (c) COYOTE (oblivious performance ratio $4/3$); and (d) COYOTE implementation with a fake node inserted at s_1 for realizing the required splitting ratio.

so as to minimize link over-subscription across *all* possible combinations of traffic demands within the above-specified uncertainty bounds.

Consider first the traditional practice of splitting traffic equally amongst the next-hops on shortest-paths to the destination (i.e., traditional TE with ECMP, see Fig. 1b), where the shortest path DAG towards t is depicted by dashed arrows labelled with the resulting flow splitting ratios. Observe that if the actual traffic demands are 2 and 0 for s_1 and s_2, respectively, routing as in Fig. 1b would result in link (over-)utilization that is $3/2$ higher than that of the optimal routing of these specific demands (which can send all traffic without exceeding any link capacity). Specifically, routing as in Fig. 1b would result in $3/2$ units of traffic traversing link (v, t), whereas the total flow could be optimally routed without at all exceeding the link capacities by equally splitting it between paths $(s_1\ s_2\ t)$ and $(s_1\ v\ t)$. One can actually show that this is, in fact, the *best* guarantee achievable for this network via traditional TE with ECMP, i.e., for *any* choice of link weights, equal splitting of traffic between shortest paths would result in link utilization that is $3/2$ higher than optimal for *some* possible traffic scenario. Can we do better?

We show that this is indeed possible if more flexible traffic splitting than that of traditional TE with ECMP is possible. One can prove that for *any* traffic demands of the users, per-destination routing as in Fig. 1c results in a maximum link utilization at most $4/3$ times that of the optimal routing [1]. We explain later how COYOTE realizes such uneven per-destination load balancing without any modification to legacy OSPF-ECMP.

[1]In fact, even the routing configuration in Fig. 1c is not optimal in this respect. Indeed, COYOTE's optimization techniques, discussed in Section 2.3, yield configurations with better guarantees (see [16]).

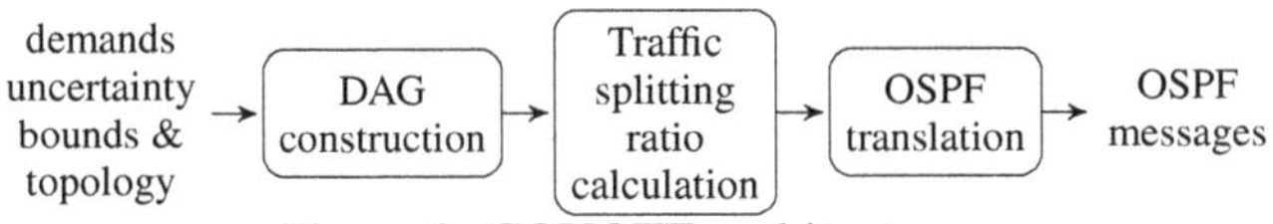

Figure 2: COYOTE architecture.

2.2 Challenges

Realizing hop-by-hop destination-based traffic engineering boils down to computing, for each destination, (1) a Directed Acyclic Graph (DAG) rooted in that destination (so as to guarantee loop-free packet forwarding) along which traffic is to be forwarded, and (2) the splitting of traffic within each DAG (c.f., Fig. 1c). Thus, the optimization problem that underlies COYOTE is the following: compute per-destination DAGs and traffic splitting ratios so as to minimize the worst-case link utilization (also referred to as congestion in TE literature [1, 2]) across *all* possible traffic scenarios (within the operator-specified uncertainty bounds). Our first (and negative) result shows that this is, in fact, intractable. The proof is omitted due to space constraints and is available in [16].

THEOREM 1. *Given a capacitated network graph $G = (V, E)$ and a set $\mathcal{D}$ of possible traffic demands between nodes, computing the optimal combination of DAGs and traffic splitting ratios with respect to minimizing the worst-case link utilization is NP-hard.*

Hence, efficiently computing the *optimal* selection of DAGs *and* in-DAG traffic splitting ratios is beyond reach. We next describe how COYOTE's design addresses this challenge. COYOTE's flow-computation decomposes the task of computing destination-based oblivious routing configurations into two sub-problems, and tackles each independently. First, COYOTE applies a simple heuristic to compute destination-oriented DAGs. Then, COYOTE optimizes in-DAG traffic splitting ratios through a combination of optimization techniques, including iterative geometric programming. We show in Section 3 that COYOTE's routing algorithm empirically exhibits good network performance.

2.3 COYOTE Design

Figure 2 presents an overview of the COYOTE architecture. COYOTE gets as input the (capacitated) network topology and the so-called "uncertainty bounds", i.e., for every two nodes (routers) in the network, i and j, a real-valued interval $[d_{ij}^{min}, d_{ij}^{max}]$, capturing the operator's uncertainty about the traffic demand from i to j or, alternatively, the potential variability of traffic. COYOTE then uses this information first to compute a forwarding DAG rooted in each destination node, and then to optimize traffic splitting ratios within each DAG. Lastly, the outcome of this computation is converted into OSPF configuration by injecting "lies" into routers. We next elaborate on each of these components.

Computing DAGs. Theorem 1 implies that computing DAGs so as to support optimal routing (through the appropriate in-DAG traffic splitting) is intractable. In COYOTE, DAGs rooted in different destinations are not coupled in any way, allowing network operators to specify any set of DAGs. We show in Section 3, however, that COYOTE significantly outperforms TE with ECMP even when the underlying DAGs are selected with the following simple heuristic: (1) compute, for each destination, the shortest-path DAG rooted in that destination when the link weights are the inverse capacities, and then (2) augment each DAG with additional links by orienting each link that does not appear in the shortest-path DAG towards the incident node that is closer to the destination, breaking ties lexicographically (suppose that the nodes are numbered). Revisiting our running example in Fig.1a, observe that while the shortest-path DAG rooted at t does *not* contain link (s_2, v) if all links have the same weight, the augmented forwarding DAGs will also utilize this link (in some direction).

Computing traffic splitting ratios for each DAG. The second fundamental building block of COYOTE is an algorithm that receives as input a set of per-destination DAGs and optimizes traffic splitting within these DAGs, with the objective of minimizing the worst-case congestion (link utilization) over a given set of possible traffic demands. Whether this problem can be solved optimally in a computationally-efficient manner remains an open question (see Section 6. This seems impossible within the familiar mathematical toolset of TE, namely, integer and linear programming. We found that a different approach is, however, feasible: casting the optimization problem as a geometric program (in fact, a mixed linear-geometric program [17]).

Stating COYOTE's traffic splitting optimization as a geometric program is not straightforward and involves careful application of various techniques (convex programming, monomial approximations, LP duality). We provide an intuitive exposition of some of these ideas below using the running example in Fig. 1 (more details in in [16]).

Again, s_1 and s_2 send traffic to t, let the DAG for t be as in Fig. 1c, and suppose that the capacity on links (s_1, s_2), (s_1, v), and (s_2, v) is infinite (that is, arbitrarily large) and on (s_2, t) and (v, t) is 1. We are given a set of possible traffic demands $\{d_{s_1}, d_{s_2}\}$ for the two users and our goal is to find the traffic splitting ratios ϕ so that the worst-case link utilization across all demands is minimized. A simplified mathematical program for this problem would take the following form (see explanations below):

$$\min \alpha \tag{1}$$

$$\frac{d_{s_1}\phi(s_1,s_2)\phi(s_2,t)+d_{s_2}\phi(s_2,t)}{\text{capacity}(s_2,t)} \le \alpha \quad \forall d_{s_1}, d_{s_2} \tag{2}$$

$$\frac{d_{s_1}(1-\phi(s_1,s_2)\phi(s_2,t))+d_{s_2}(1-\phi(s_2,t))}{\text{capacity}(v,t)} \le \alpha \quad \forall d_{s_1}, d_{s_2} \tag{3}$$

The objective is to minimize α, which represents worst-case link utilization, i.e., the load (flow divided by capacity) on the most utilized link across all the admissible traffic demands. Each variable $\phi(x, y)$ denotes the fraction of the incoming flow at vertex x that is routed on link (x, y). Constraints (2) and (3) force α to be at least the value of the link utilization of links (s_2, t) and (s_1, s_2), respectively. For the sake of simplicity, we do not show the link utilization constraints for the remaining links. Now, consider constraint (2) for link (s_2, t). Observe that from user s_1 the fraction of traffic sent through (s_2, t) equals the fraction of s_1's traffic through (s_1, s_2) (i.e., $\phi(s_1, s_2)$) times the fraction sent through (s_2, t) by s_2 (i.e., $\phi(s_2, t)$). The fraction of s_2's traffic through (s_2, t) is simply $\phi(s_2, t)$. Accordingly the total flow on (s_2, t) equals $d_{s_1} \cdot \phi(s_1, s_2) \cdot \phi(s_2, t) + d_{s_2} \cdot \phi(s_2, t)$. Hence, the link utilization of (s_2, t) is this expression divided by the capacity of (s_2, t), and the corresponding constraint (2) requires that this utilization be at most α for *all* demands d_{s_1}, d_{s_2}. Constraint (3) states the same for link (v, t), where the fraction of traffic sent by s_1 (s_2) to t through (v, t) is equal to 1 minus the fraction of flow sent from s_1 (s_2) to t through (s_2, t).

Two difficulties with these constraints immediately arise: one is that it is *universally quantified* over an entire set of traffic demands, possibly of infinite cardinality, and the other is that it involves a *product of unknowns*, namely, $\phi(s_1, s_2) \cdot \phi(s_2, t)$, and such products do not fit into the framework of standard linear and integer programming. For a discrete demand set we can handle the first problem by stating (2) and (3) for each individual demand. Otherwise (if the set of demands is of infinite size) the elegant dualization technique from [11] can be used. To handle the second issue, however, we need a small trick from geometric programming [17]. Let $d_{s_1} = 1$ and $d_{s_2} = 1$ and consider constraint (2):

$$\phi(s_2, t) + \phi(s_1, s_2) \cdot \phi(s_2, t) \leq \alpha \ .$$

Now, substitute for new variables, $\widetilde{\phi}(s_1, s_2) = \log \phi(s_1, s_2)$ and $\widetilde{\phi}(s_2, t) = \log \phi(s_2, t)$, and take the logarithm of both sides:

$$\log \left(e^{\widetilde{\phi}(s_2,t)} + e^{\widetilde{\phi}(s_1,s_2)+\widetilde{\phi}(s_2,t)} \right) \leq \log \alpha \ .$$

This constraint is now a logarithm of a sum of exponentials of linear functions and so is convex, opening the door to using standard convex programming. Our implementation uses a convex program based on the above ideas and others delicate techniques to compute the traffic splitting ratios. The reader is referred to our technical report for a detailed explanation [16].

Translation to OSPF-ECMP configuration. As explained above, using OSPF and ECMP for TE constrains the flow of traffic in two significant ways: (1) traffic only flows on shortest-paths (induced from operator specified link weights), and (2) traffic is split equally between multiple next-hops on shortest-paths to a destination. Recent studies show how OSPF-ECMP's expressiveness can be significantly enhanced by effectively deceiving routers. Specifically, Fibbing [8, 9] shows how *any* set of per-destination forwarding DAGs can be realized by introducing fake nodes and virtual links into an underlying link-state routing protocol, thus overcoming the first limitation of ECMP. [18] shows how ECMP's equal load balancing can be extended to much more nuanced traffic splitting by setting up virtual links alongside existing physical ones, thus relaxing the second of these limitations.

We revisit our running example to show how COYOTE exploits these techniques. Consider Fig. 1d. Inserting a fake advertisement at s_1 into the OSPF link-state database can "deceive" s_1 into believing that, besides its available shortest paths via s_2 and v , destination t is also available via a third, "virtual" forwarding path. The forwarding adjacency in the fake advertisement is mapped to s_2, so that out of s_1's three next-hops to t node s_2 will appear *twice* while v only appears once. Consequently, the traffic is *effectively* split between s_2 and v in a ratio ⅔ to ⅓. Beyond changing how traffic is split *within* a given shortest-path DAG, as illustrated in Fig. 1d, fake nodes/links can be injected into OSPF so to as change the forwarding DAGs themselves at the per-IP-destination-prefix granularity, as shown in [9]. COYOTE leverages the techniques in [9] and in [18] to carefully craft "lies" so as to generate the desired per-destination forwarding DAGs and approximate the optimal traffic splitting ratios with ECMP. Section 3 that highly optimized TE is achievable even with the introduction of few virtual nodes and links.

3. EVALUATION

We experimentally evaluate COYOTE in order to quantify its performance benefits and its robustness to traffic uncertainty and variation. Importantly, our focus is solely on destination-based TE schemes (i.e., TE schemes that can be realized via today's IP routing). We show below that COYOTE provides significantly better performance than ECMP even when *completely* oblivious to the traffic demands. Also, COYOTE's increased path diversity does not come at the cost of long paths: the paths computed by COYOTE are on average only a factor of 1.1 longer than ECMP's. We also discuss experiments with a prototype implementation of COYOTE.

While the reader might think that COYOTE's performance benefits over traditional TE with ECMP are merely a byproduct of its greater flexibility in selecting DAGs and in traffic splitting, our results show that this intuition is, in fact, false. Specifically, we show that, similarly to unconstrained (i.e., source and destination based) oblivious routing [11], even the *optimal* routing with respect to *estimated* traffic demands, which can unevenly split traffic, fares much worse than COYOTE if the *actual* traffic demands are not very "close" to the estimated demands. Hence, COYOTE's good performance should be attributed not only to its expressiveness but also, in large part, to its built-in algorithms for optimizing performance in the presence of uncertainty, as discussed in Section 2.3.

3.1 Simulation Framework

We use the set of 16 backbone Internet topologies from the Internet Topology Zoo (ITZ) archive [19] to assess the performance of COYOTE and ECMP. When available, we use the link capacities provided by ITZ. Otherwise, we set the link capacities to be inversely-proportional to the ITZ-provided ECMP weights (in accordance with the Cisco-recommended default OSPF link configuration [20]). When neither ECMP link weights nor capacities are available we use

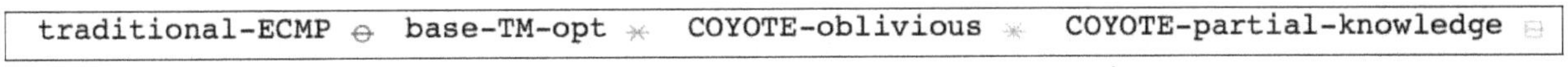

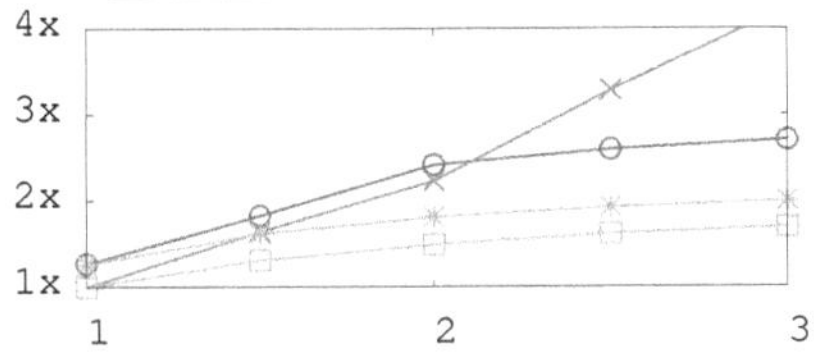

Figure 3: Geant, gravity model.

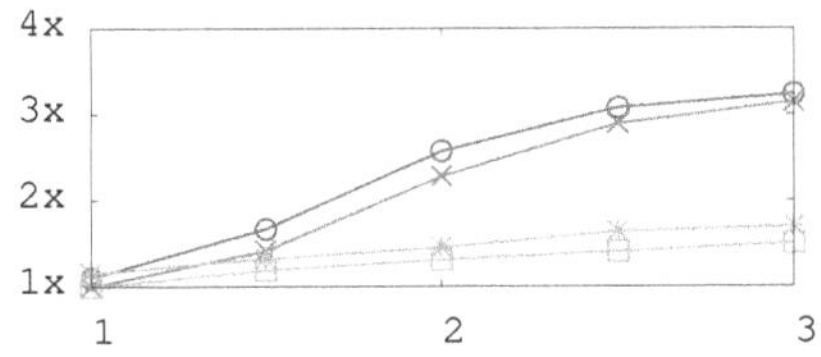

Figure 4: Digex, gravity model.

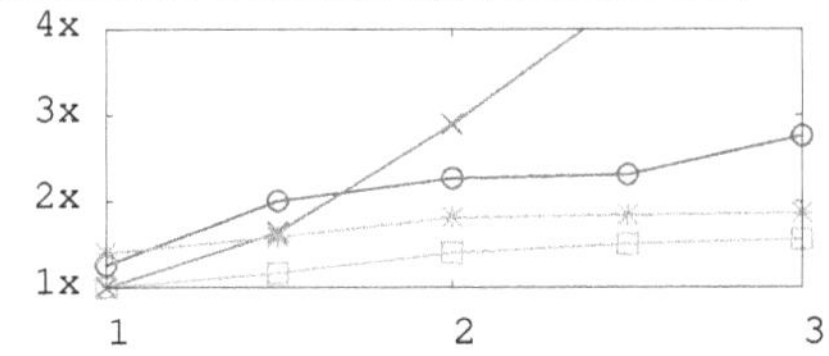

Figure 5: AS 1755, bimodal model

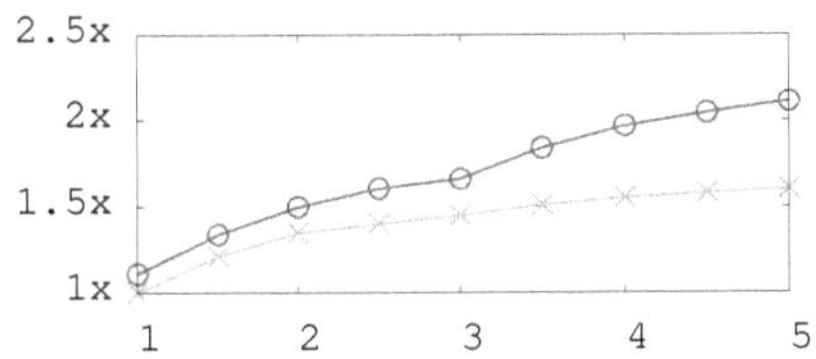

Figure 6: Abilene, optimized-ECMP.

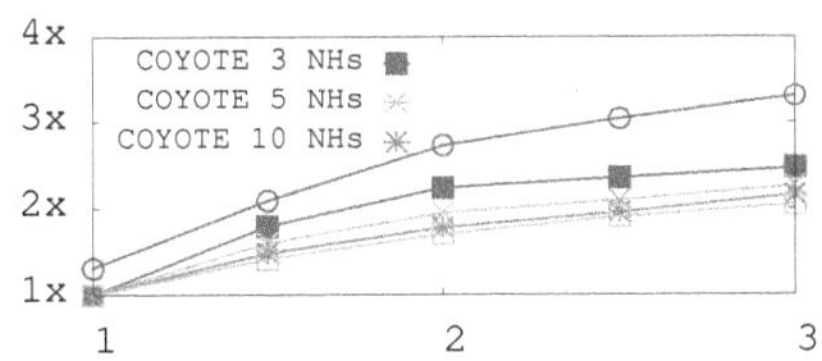

Figure 7: Approximation.

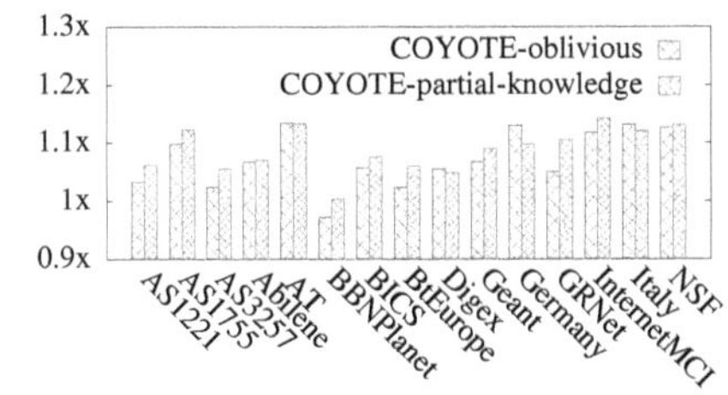

Figure 8: Average stretch.

unit capacities and link weights. We evaluate COYOTE against ECMP using two simple DAG-construction heuristics: (1) constructing augmented shortest-path DAGs as explained in Section 2 with the link weights provided in the ITZ archive, and (2) optimizing the link weights using the local greedy algorithm of Altin et al [12]. In both cases, we augment the shortest path DAGs as explained in Section 2.

To compute COYOTE's in-DAG traffic splitting ratios (see Section 2), we use AMPL [21] as the problem formulation language and MOSEK [22], a non-linear convex optimization solver. The running time with our current single-threaded proof-of-concept implementation ranges from few minutes (for small networks) to few days (for large networks).

While we are currently working on improving the running times, we would like to point out that the computation of the in-DAG traffic splitting ratios needs only be performed once or on a daily/weekly-base, as routing in COYOTE is not dynamically adjusted, and that routing configurations for failure scenarios (e.g., every single link/node failure) can be precomputed.

We measure performance in terms of the worst-case link utilization (referred to as "congestion" in TE literature [1, 2]), i.e., the performance of (multicommodity) flow of traffic f is $\max_l \frac{f(l)}{c_l}$, where $f(l)$ is the flow traversing link l and c_l is link l's capacity.

3.2 Network Performance

We compare COYOTE to ECMP for both DAG-construction heuristics described above and for two types of base traffic demands: (1) *gravity* [23], where the amount of flow sent from router i to router j is proportional to the product of i's total outgoing capacity and j's total outgoing capacity, and (2) *bimodal* [24], where a small fraction of all pairs of routers exchange large quantities of traffic, and the other pairs send small flows.

We first present our results with respect to the ITZ [19] link weights and an ideal version of COYOTE capable of arbitrarily fine-grained traffic splitting. We then show that a close approximation of the optimal splitting ratios can be obtained with the introduction of a limited number of additional virtual links. Fig. 3 and Fig. 4 describe our results for two networks (Geant and Digex, respectively), the gravity model, and augmented shortest path DAGs based on the ITZ link weights. The x-axis represents the "uncertainty margin": let $d_{i,j}$ be the amount of flow from router i to router j in the base traffic demands (namely, gravity), a margin of uncertainty of x means that the actual flow from i to j can be any value between $\frac{d_{i,j}}{x}$ and $x \cdot d_{i,j}$. We increase the uncertainty margin in increments of 0.5 from 1 (no uncertainty whatsoever) to 3 (fairly high uncertainty). The y-axis specifies how far the computed solution is from the *demands-aware* optimum within the same DAGs.

We plot four lines, corresponding to the performance of four different protocols: (1) traditional TE with ECMP, (2) the optimal demands-aware routing for the base gravity model (with no uncertainty), which can be obtained with linear programming techniques [25], (3) COYOTE (oblivious) with traffic splitting optimized with respect to *all* possible traffic demands (i.e., assuming *nothing* about the demands), (4) COYOTE (partial-knowledge) optimized with respect to the traffic demands within the uncertainty margin. Observe that both variants of COYOTE provide significantly better performance than TE with ECMP and, more surprisingly, both COYOTE and (sometimes) ECMP outperform the optimal base routing, whose performance quickly degrades even with little demands uncertainty. Our results thus show that COYOTE's built-in robustness to traffic uncertainty, in the form of optimization under specified uncertainty margins, indeed leads to superior performance in the face of inaccurate knowledge about the traffic demands or, alternatively, variable traffic conditions.

We observe the same trends when the base traffic demands are sampled from the bimodal model, as shown in Fig. 5.

We now discuss our results with respect to our second DAG-construction heuristic, which is based on the heuristic of Altin et al. [12] for oblivious ECMP routing configuration. Specifically, [12] presents a heuristic that starts from the link weights provided by the ITZ dataset, and applies a local-search heuristic that greedily changes one link weight if this change improves the worst-case ECMP link utilization across all the admissible traffic demands. We use the output of this procedure as the ECMP configuration and augment it with additional links to obtain COYOTE's per destination DAGs, as explained in Section 2. Fig. 6 presents a comparison of COYOTE and ECMP using the bimodal model as the base traffic demands. We use the above heuristic to compute, for each uncertainty margin in the range $1-5$, increasing in 0.5 increments, the (traditional) ECMP configuration and COYOTE DAGs with respect to the bimodal-based traffic demands. We then compare the worst-case link utilization of the two, again, normalized by the *demands-aware* optimum within the same (augmented) DAGs. We note that ECMP is, on average, almost 80% times further away from the optimum than COYOTE.

Approximating the optimal traffic splitting. We evaluated above COYOTE under the assumption that arbitrarily fine-grained traffic splitting is achievable, yet in practice, the resolution of traffic splitting is derived from the number of virtual links introduced. Clearly, an excessive number of virtual links should be avoided for at least two reasons: (a) each virtual next-hop is installed into the finite-sized Forwarding Information Base (FIB), and (b) injecting additional information into OSPF comes at the cost of additional computational overhead. Our results, illustrated in Fig. 7 for AS 1755 network's topology (all other topologies exhibit the same trend), show that even with just 3 additional virtual links per router interface, COYOTE achieves a 50% improvement over traditional TE with ECMP. We observe that with 10 virtual links the computed routing configuration closely approximates the ideal solution.

Average path lengths. COYOTE augments the shortest path DAG with additional links so as to better utilize the network. Consequently, traffic can potentially traverse longer paths. We show, however, that COYOTE's increased path redundancy does not come at the expense of long paths. Specifically, the average stretch (increase in length) of the paths in COYOTE is typically bounded within a 10% factor with respect to the OSPF/ECMP paths. Fig. 8 plots the average stretch across all pairs for a margin of 2.5. Similar results are obtained for all different margins between 1 to 5. Observe that the DAGs computed by COYOTE rely on shortest-path computation with respect to the link weights, whereas the stretch is measured in terms of the number of hops. Thus, it is possible for the stretch to be less than 1, as is the case, e.g., for BBNPlanet.

4. PROTOTYPE IMPLEMENTATION

We implemented and experimented with a prototype of the COYOTE architecture, as described in Section 2. Our prototype extends the Fibbing controller code, written in Python and provided by Vissicchio et al. [9], and uses the code of Nemeth et al. from [18] for approximating the splitting ratios. We plan to make our code public in the near future.

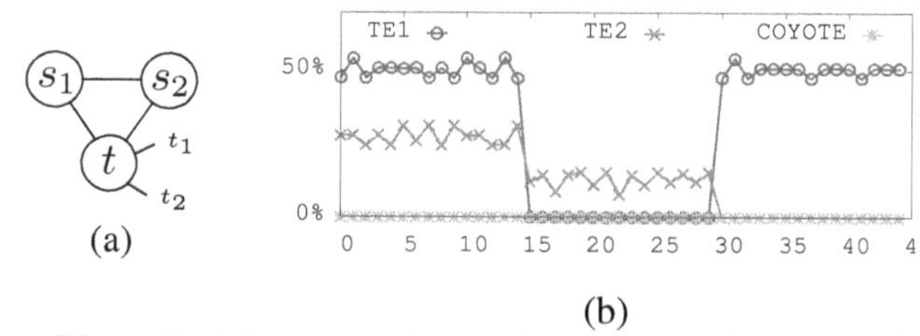

Figure 9: Mininet topology (a) and packet drop rate (b).

We next illustrate the benefits of COYOTE over traditional TE, as reflected by an evaluation of our prototype via the mininet [26] network emulator.

Consider the example in Fig 9a: a target node t advertises two IP prefixes t_1 and t_2 and two sources, s_1 and s_2, generate traffic destined for these IP prefixes. As in traditional TE with ECMP, the network operator must use the same forwarding DAG for each destination, this forces either s_1 or s_2 to route all of its traffic only on the direct path to the destination. Thus, three forwarding DAGs are possible: (1) both s_1 and s_2 route all traffic on their direct paths to t (TE1), (2) s_1 equally splits its traffic between t and s_2, and s_2 forwards all traffic on its direct link to t (TE2), and (3) same as the previous option, but s_1 and s_2 swap roles (TE3).

We evaluate these three TE configurations in mininet with links of bandwidth 1Mbps. We measure the cumulative packet drop rate towards two IP destinations, t_1 and t_2, for three 15-seconds-long traffic scenarios, where traffic is UDP generated with `iperf3` and units are in Mbps: $(s_1-t_1, s_2-t_2) = (0,2)$, $(s_1-t_1, s_2-t_2) = (1,1)$, $(s_1-t_1, s_2-t_2) = (2,0)$.

Fig 9b plots the results of this experiment for each of the TE schemes, described above (excluding TE3, which is symmetric to TE2). The x-axis is time (in seconds) and the y-axis is the measured packet loss rate, i.e., the ratio of traffic received to traffic sent (observe that sent traffic is 30 megabits in all scenarios). During the first 15 seconds the experiment emulates the first traffic scenario described above, in the next 15 seconds the second traffic scenario is emulated, and in the last 15 seconds the third scenario is emulated.

Observe that each of the TE schemes (TE1-3) achievable via traditional TE with ECMP leads to a significant packet-drop rate (25%-50%) in at least one of traffic scenarios. COYOTE, in contrast, leverages its superior expressiveness to generate different DAGs for each IP prefix destination, as follows: traffic to for destination t_1 is evenly split at node s_1 and traffic to destination t_2 is evenly split at s_2. This is accomplished by injecting a lie to s_2 so as to attracts half of its traffic to t_2 to the (s_2, s_1) link. Consequently, as seen in Fig 9b, the rate of dropped packets is significantly reduced.

5. RELATED WORK

TE with ECMP. TE with ECMP is today's prevalent approach to TE (see surveys in [1, 2]). Consequently, this has been the subject of extensive research and, in particular, selecting good link weights for ECMP TE has received much attention [6, 7, 12, 27–30]. To handle uncertainty about traffic demands and variation in traffic, past studies also examined the optimization of ECMP configuration with respect to multiple expected traffic demands [6, 30, 31], or even with no knowledge of the traffic demands [11]. Unfortunately, while careful and delicate optimizations of ECMP configuration can be close-to-optimal in some networks [30], this approach is fundamentally plagued by the intrinsic limitations of ECMP, specifically, routing only on shortest paths and equally splitting traffic at each hop, and can hence easily result in poor network performance. Worse yet, this scheme suffers from inherent computational intractability, as shown in [7, 27].

Lying for more expressive OSPF-ECMP routing. The first technique to approximate unequal splitting through ECMP via the introduction of virtual links was introduced by Nemeth et al. in [18] (see also [32]). [18], however, was still limited to shortest-path routing and, consequently, coarse-grained traffic flow manipulation. Recently, Fibbing [8, 9] showed how any set of destination-based forwarding DAGs can be generated through the injection of fake nodes and links into the underlying link-state protocol (e.g., OSPF).

Adaptive TE schemes. One approach to overcoming ECMP's limitations is dynamically adapting the routing of traffic in response to changes in traffic conditions as in, e.g., [27]. Adaptive schemes, however, typically require frequently gathering fairly accurate information about traffic demands, potentially require new routing or measurement infrastructure, and can be prone to routing instability [33], slow convergence, packet reordering, and excess control plane burden [3] (especially in the presence of failures). COYOTE, in contrast, reflects the exact opposite approach: optimizing the *static* configuration of traffic flow so as to simultaneously achieve good network performance with respect to *all*, even adversarially chosen, traffic demands within specified "uncertainty bounds".

Demands-oblivious routing. A rich body of literature on algorithmic theory investigates so-called "(demand-)oblivious routing" [10–12]. Breakthrough algorithmic results by Räcke established that the static (non-adaptive) routing can be optimized so as to be within an $O(\log n)$ factor from the optimum (demands-aware) routing with respect to *any* combination of traffic demands [10]. Applegate and Cohen [11] showed that when applied to actual (ISP) networks, such demand-oblivious routing algorithms yield remarkably close-to-optimal performance. Kulfi [13] uses semi-oblivious routing to improve TE in wide-area networks. Unfortunately, all the above demand-oblivious algorithms involve forwarding packets based on both the source and destination, these immediately hit a serious deployability barrier in traditional IP networks (e.g., due to extensive tunneling [28]). COYOTE, in contrast, is restricted to OSPF-based destination-based routing, and so tackles inherently different (and new) algorithmic challenges and techniques, as discussed in Sect. 2.

6. CONCLUSION

We presented COYOTE, a new OSPF-ECMP-based TE scheme that efficiently utilizes the network even with little/no knowledge of the traffic demands. We showed that COYOTE significantly outperforms today's prevalent TE schemes while requiring no changes whatsoever to routers. We view COYOTE as an important additional step in the recent exploration [8, 9] of how SDN functionality can be accomplished without changing today's networking infrastructure. We next discuss two important directions for future research.

Further exploring destination-based oblivious routing. To efficiently utilize the network in an OSPF-ECMP-compatible manner, COYOTE leveraged new algorithmic insights about destination-based oblivious routing. We believe that further progress on optimizing such routing configurations is key to improving upon COYOTE. We next mention two interesting research questions in this direction: (1) We showed in Section 2 that computing the optimal oblivious IP routing configuration is NP-hard. Can the optimal configuration be provably *well-approximated*? (2) COYOTE first computes a forwarding DAG rooted in each destination node, and then computes traffic splitting ratios within each DAG. The latter computation involves nontrivial optimizations, e.g., via iterative geometric programming, yet, it remains unclear whether traffic splitting within a given set of DAGs is, in fact, efficiently and optimally solvable.

Evaluating COYOTE under real-world network conditions. Our experimental evaluation of COYOTE combined simulations on 16 backbone Internet topologies from the Internet Topology Zoo (ITZ) archive [19] with small-scale experiments on the mininet network emulator [26]. An important direction for future research is experimenting with COYOTE on empirically-derived traffic traces, e.g., data collected from the Internet2 Network [34], and running larger-scale experiments with our prototype implementation of COYOTE on mininet and on SDN-capable network testbeds such as [35].

Acknowledgements

We thank the anonymous reviewers of the CoNEXT PC and Walter Willinger for their valuable comments. We thank Francesco Malandrino for useful discussions about the geometric programming approach, and Olivier Tilmans and Stefano Vissicchio for guiding us through the Fibbing code. This research is (in part) supported by European Union's Horizon 2020 research and innovation programme under the ENDEAVOUR project (grant agreement 644960). The 1st and 3rd authors are supported by the Israeli Center for Research Excellence in Algorithms. The 2nd author is with the Department of Telecommunications and Media Informatics, Budapest University of Technology and Economics.

7. REFERENCES

[1] B. Fortz, J. Rexford, and M. Thorup. Traffic engineering with traditional IP routing protocols. *Communications Magazine, IEEE*, 40(10):118–124, 2002.

[2] Ning Wang, Kin Ho, G. Pavlou, and M. Howarth. An overview of routing optimization for internet traffic

engineering. *Communications Surveys Tutorials, IEEE*, 10(1):36–56, 2008.

[3] Andrew R. Curtis, Jeffrey C. Mogul, Jean Tourrilhes, Praveen Yalagandula, Puneet Sharma, and Sujata Banerjee. DevoFlow: Scaling Flow Management for High-performance Networks. In *SIGCOMM 2011*.

[4] John Moy. OSPF version 2. RFC 2328, 1998.

[5] C. Hopps. Analysis of an ECMP Algorithm. RFC 2992, 2000. www.ietf.org/rfc/rfc2992.txt.

[6] Bernard Fortz and Mikkel Thorup. Increasing Internet Capacity Using Local Search. *Computational Optimization and Applications*, 29(1):13–48, 2004.

[7] Marco Chiesa, Guy Kindler, and Michael Schapira. Traffic Engineering with Equal-Cost-MultiPath: An Algorithmic Perspective. In *INFOCOM'14*, pages 1590–1598, 2014.

[8] Stefano Vissicchio, Laurent Vanbever, and Jennifer Rexford. Sweet little lies: Fake topologies for flexible routing. In *HotNets-XIII*, pages 1–7, 2014.

[9] Stefano Vissicchio, Olivier Tilmans, Laurent Vanbever, and Jennifer Rexford. Central control over distributed routing. In *SIGCOMM 2015*.

[10] Harald Räcke. Optimal Hierarchical Decompositions for Congestion Minimization in Networks. In *STOC '08*, pages 255–264, 2008.

[11] D. Applegate and E. Cohen. Making Routing Robust to Changing Traffic Demands: Algorithms and Evaluation. *Networking, IEEE/ACM Transactions on*, 14(6):1193–1206, 2006.

[12] Ayşegül Altin, B. Fortz, and Hakan Ümit. Oblivious OSPF Routing with Weight Optimization Under Polyhedral Demand Uncertainty. *Netw.*, 60(2):132–139, 2012.

[13] Praveen Kumar, Yang Yuan, Chris Yu, Nate Foster, Robert D. Kleinberg, and Robert Soulé. Kulfi: Robust traffic engineering using semi-oblivious routing. *CoRR*, abs/1603.01203, 2016.

[14] David Applegate and Mikkel Thorup. Load optimal MPLS routing with N+M labels. In *Proceedings IEEE INFOCOM 2003*.

[15] Nick McKeown, Tom Anderson, Hari Balakrishnan, Guru Parulkar, Larry Peterson, Jennifer Rexford, Scott Shenker, and Jonathan Turner. Openflow: Enabling innovation in campus networks. *SIGCOMM Comput. Commun. Rev.*, 38(2):69–74, March 2008.

[16] Marco Chiesa, Gábor Rétvári, and Michael Schapira. Lying Your Way to Better Traffic Engineering. *CoRR*, abs/1610.02728, 2016.

[17] S. Boyd, S. Kim, L. Vandenberghe, and A. Hassibi. A Tutorial on Geometric Programming. *Optimization and Engineering*, 8(1):67–127, 2007.

[18] K. Németh, A. Körösi, and G. Rétvári. Optimal OSPF traffic engineering using legacy Equal Cost Multipath load balancing. In *IFIP Networking Conference 2013*.

[19] Internet Topology Zoo. www.topology-zoo.org, 2010.

[20] Configuring OSPF Cisco. http://www.cisco.com/c/en/us/support/docs/ip/open-shortest-path-first-ospf/7039-1.html, 2005.

[21] R. Fourer, D. M. Gay, and B. W. Kernighan. *AMPL: A Modeling Language for Mathematical Programming*. Duxbury-Thomson, 2003.

[22] Mosek ApS. www.mosek.com, 2015.

[23] M. Roughan, A. Greenberg, C. Kalmanek, M. Rumsewicz, J. Yates, and Y. Zhang. Experience in Measuring Backbone Traffic Variability: Models, Metrics, Measurements and Meaning. In *Proc. Workshop on Internet Measurment*, IMW '02, 2002.

[24] A. Medina, N. Taft, K. Salamatian, S. Bhattacharyya, and C. Diot. Traffic Matrix Estimation: Existing Techniques and New Directions. *SIGCOMM Comput. Commun. Rev.*, 32(4):161–174, August 2002.

[25] D. G. Cantor and M. Gerla. Optimal routing in a packet-switched computer network. *IEEE Trans. Comp.*, 23(10):1062–1069, 1974.

[26] Brandon Heller, Nikhil Handigol, Vimalkumar Jeyakumar, Bob Lantz, and Nick McKeown. Reproducible network experiments using container based emulation. In *CoNEXT*, 2012.

[27] Bernard Fortz and Mikkel Thorup. Internet Traffic Engineering by Optimizing OSPF Weights. In *INFOCOM'00*, pages 519–528, 2000.

[28] Yufei Wang, Zheng Wang, and Leah Zhang. Internet traffic engineering without full mesh overlaying. In *INFOCOM'01*, volume 1, pages 565–571, 2001.

[29] Ashwin Sridharan, R. Guerin, and C. Diot. Achieving near-optimal traffic engineering solutions for current OSPF/IS-IS networks. *Networking, IEEE/ACM Transactions on*, 13(2):234–247, 2005.

[30] B. Fortz and M. Thorup. Optimizing OSPF/IS-IS weights in a changing world. *IEEE Journal of Selected Areas in Communications*, 20(4):756–767, 2002.

[31] M. Ericsson, M.G.C. Resende, and P.M. Pardalos. A Genetic Algorithm for the Weight Setting Problem in OSPF Routing. *Journal of Combinatorial Optimization*, 6(3):299–333, 2002.

[32] Junlan Zhou, Malveeka Tewari, Min Zhu, Abdul Kabbani, Leon Poutievski, Arjun Singh, and Amin Vahdat. WCMP: weighted cost multipathing for improved fairness in data centers. In *EuroSys 2014*.

[33] D. P. Bertsekas. Dynamic Behavior of Shortest Path Routing Algorithms for Communication Networks. *IEEE Trans. on Automatic Control*, 27:60–74, 1982.

[34] Internet2 NOC. http://noc.net.internet2.edu/, 2016.

[35] OCEAN. http://ocean.cs.illinois.edu/, 2016.

EYEORG: A Platform For Crowdsourcing Web Quality Of Experience Measurements

https://eyeorg.net/

Matteo Varvello[†], Jeremy Blackburn[†], David Naylor[•], Kostantina Papagiannaki[‡*]
[†]Telefónica Research, [•]Carnegie Mellon University, [‡]Google Inc.

ABSTRACT

Tremendous effort has gone into the ongoing battle to make webpages load faster. This effort has culminated in new protocols (QUIC, SPDY, and HTTP/2) as well as novel content delivery mechanisms. In addition, companies like Google and SpeedCurve investigated how to measure "page load time" (PLT) in a way that captures *human perception*. In this paper we present Eyeorg [12], a platform for crowdsourcing web quality of experience measurements. Eyeorg overcomes the scaling and automation challenges of recruiting users and collecting consistent user-perceived quality measurements. We validate Eyeorg's capabilities via a set of 100 *trusted* participants. Next, we showcase its functionalities via three measurement campaigns, each involving 1,000 *paid* participants, to 1) study the quality of several PLT metrics, 2) compare HTTP/1.1 and HTTP/2 performance, and 3) assess the impact of online advertisements and ad blockers on user experience. We find that commonly used, and even novel and sophisticated PLT metrics fail to represent actual human perception of PLT, that the performance gains from HTTP/2 are imperceivable in some circumstances, and that not all ad blockers are created equal.

CCS Concepts

•**Human-centered computing** → **Web-based interaction;** •**Networks** → *Application layer protocols; Network measurement;*

Keywords

Web measurements; Crowdsourcing; Quality of Experience; HTTP/2; Adblockers

*Work done while K. Papagiannaki was with Telefónica Research.

CoNEXT '16, December 12-15, 2016, Irvine, CA, USA
© 2016 ACM. ISBN 978-1-4503-4292-6/16/12...$15.00
DOI: http://dx.doi.org/10.1145/2999572.2999590

1. INTRODUCTION

Improving Quality of Experience (QoE) on the Web remains a hot topic. One obvious aspect of QoE, page load time (PLT), heavily impacts revenue for web-based companies [2]. It is no surprise, then, that there are many recent efforts to decrease PLT from both industry (e.g., QUIC, SPDY, and HTTP/2) and academia [10, 17, 24]. To evaluate the effectiveness of such techniques, we need quantitative measures of their impact on QoE. Unfortunately, this is difficult because QoE is hard to define and even harder to measure.

Perhaps surprisingly, this is true even for PLT, which seems straightforward to define and measure. The typical PLT metric, the browser's "onload" event, denotes when "all of the objects in the document are in the DOM, and all the images, scripts, links and sub-frames have finished loading" [1]. OnLoad is not a perfect proxy for *user-perceived page load time* (UserPerceivedPLT) for two reasons: first, the user may only care how quickly the *visible* portion of the content loads ("above-the-fold" render time), meaning OnLoad might be an overestimate. Second, scripts might continue loading objects after OnLoad fires, in which case it may be an underestimate. To address this problem, new PLT metrics attempt to bridge the gap between OnLoad and UserPerceivedPLT. For example, SpeedIndex[1] defines PLT as the average time at which above-the-fold content is displayed. Unfortunately, even this is not perfect: the user may consider the page ready to interact with even before some above-the-fold content (e.g., ads) loads.

Ideally, we want a direct assessment of a user's experience on a webpage. This is difficult for the following reasons. First, a large number of people need to be recruited and surveyed. Second, participants need to be shown consistent views of a page loading. Third, we need to design experiments that lead to *quantitative* results about a technique's impact on QoE. In some studies [5, 6], participants are shown a page load in person in a controlled environment and give qualitative feedback to interviewers. Clearly, this approach neither scales nor yields quantitative results.

[1]https://sites.google.com/a/webpagetest.org/docs/using-webpagetest/metrics/speed-index

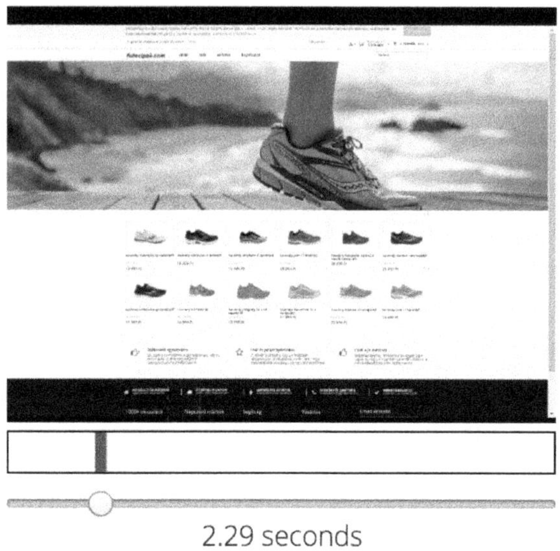

(a) Timeline of UserPerceivedPLT responses.

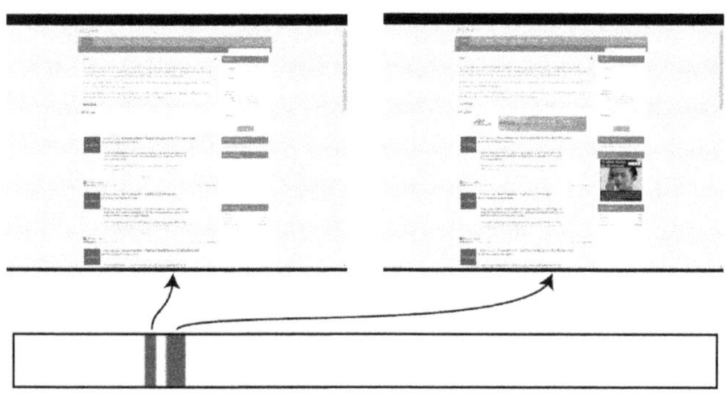

(b) Some sites exhibit multiple modes; here, some participants consider the site "ready" before the ads load.

Figure 1: Exploring responses with Eyeorg's visualization tools.

We take a different approach with Eyeorg, a system for crowdsourcing Web QoE measurements. Eyeorg allows researchers to test the impact of changes to how a page is structured or delivered. Eyeorg uses crowdsourced participants to scale (we currently integrate with two popular services, Microworkers and CrowdFlower); it shows *videos* of pages loading to provide a consistent experience to all participants, regardless of their network connections and device configurations; and its surveys are designed to provide quantifiable feedback (e.g., participants are asked to pick the point on a timeline when they consider a page loaded). With this approach, we maintain full control of experimental conditions and we can recruit any participant with a modern web browser, without requiring special hardware or software.

We present two kinds of results. First, we validate that Eyeorg can produce good quality results; to do so, we recruit 100 *trusted* participants and compare the quality of their answers with those of 100 *paid* participants. We find that we can reliably identify unreliable participants, flagging about 20% of the participants in our experiments as "low performers" whose results should be discarded. The speed with which crowdsourced participants can be recruited outweighs this overhead (e.g., 1 hour rather than 10 days in this specific experiment).

Next, we use Eyeorg to 1) study how people perceive PLT, 2) compare HTTP/1.1 and HTTP/2 performance, and 3) compare the QoE impact of three popular ad blockers: AdBlock, Ghostery and uBlock. For each measurement "campaign," we recruited 1,000 paid participants to which we showed 5,000 page load videos (selected from 100 sites). Each campaign required 1.5 days to hit the 1,000 participants target. Our analysis shows that people find the HTTP/2 version of a website faster and that Ghostery outperforms its competitors. We also show that existing PLT metrics only partially match participants responses.

To help understand the PLT data, we built a visualization tool that displays the UserPerceivedPLT responses as a timeline next to the video, as shown in Figure 1(a). Using this tool, we uncovered patterns in responses; for example, many videos have two modes, one for participants who consider the pages "ready" when the primary content is in place and one for those who wait for auxiliary content like ads (Figure 1(b)). The user-perceived PLT data we crowdsourced from 1,000 people is available at [12].

2. RELATED WORK

2.1 Latency and Human Perception

Bouch, Kuchinsky, and Bhatti performed one of the earliest in-depth studies to understand user perceptions and web page load time [9]. They approached the problem from an HCI perspective by designing a controlled experiment where a small ($N = 30$) set of users were given an e-commerce related task to perform on the web. They artificially introduced delay for each of the pages that the task required visiting and asked users to respond with a qualitative assessment ("high", "average" , "low", and "unacceptable") of page performance. While they had many interesting findings, the one most relevant to Eyeorg was that a mapping between subjective and objective PLT measurements was possible. Eyeorg takes the next step by greatly increasing the scale of responses as well as being a more general platform for conducting experiments.

Arapakis, Bai, and Cambazoglu investigated the impact of search engine response latency and user behavior in [5]. Although their work was focused primarily on how latency affects user interaction and behavior for search engines, they provide some insight into how user perceived page load times might be measured. In particular, in controlled experiments in a laboratory environment they asked participants to give an estimation of how long a page took to load. They found that although individual responses did not match the controlled ground truth, the average of the estimates was quite close to the real values. Although they used relatively coarse grained latency intervals (250 ms steps), their results indicate that aggregating human responses is a reasonable way to measure UserPerceivedPLT.

Egger et al. [11] investigate the relationship between user perceived PLT and "application" PLT.[2] To do so, they ask participants to mark the time at which they considered a page loaded. The outcome of their study is that user-perceived PLT largely departs from application PLT: in most cases, users perceived a page as loading substantially faster than the application-reported PLT. Their methodology differs significantly from ours, however. In their study, participants browsed five different pages while link bandwidth and delay were manipulated. In contrast, we show video captures of pages loading to thousands of study participants which might have subtle effects on their responses. For example, our participants are able to precisely pinpoint the frame that they feel a page has loaded, fine-tuning their choice until satisfied. We also measure a binary "which is faster" choice, which was not explored at all in [11].

2.2 Page Load Time

While the research community has focused on understanding the consequences of, and how to improve, page load time, it seems that understanding how to measure it is a mostly overlooked problem. The greater "web community," instead, has invested a lot into figuring out how to tell how fast their pages are being delivered to users. These efforts range from blog posts discussing how to measure PLT [21], to ebooks explaining how to make your page load faster [22], to repositories of tools for measuring performance [15], to full on commercial measurement offerings [16]. Even though there are serious business consequences associated with page performance, unfortunately, there is little science behind most of these efforts.

Regardless, it is worth exploring the efforts made in a bit more detail. SpeedCurve [16] is a comprehensive suite of tools for web developers to gain a deeper understanding into page performance. They provide instrumentation that extracts some of the metrics we use in this paper in addition to allowing the definition of custom metrics. One interesting feature is that they provide developers a head-to-head benchmark comparing the developer's site with other, similar sites. Ultimately, however, SpeedCurve blindly PLT metrics without any scientific justification that they are meaningful. Determining the validity of computer-generated metrics is a primary goal of Eyeorg.

In the scholarly community, "onload" has been the de facto PLT metric (e.g., [10, 17, 24])—until recently. Bocchi, De Cicco, and Rossi performed a preliminary study comparing different page load metrics [8]. They focused on evaluating two proposed metrics that are similar to SpeedIndex but are computationally less expensive. Their most salient result is that correlating these metrics with real human perception is incredibly difficult, which is what Eyeorg tries to address.

[2]To the best of our knowledge, this is the browser reported "onLoad" time.

Nikravesh et al. [18] measured web performance from 80 crowdsourced mobile devices using their library Mobilyzer. They found a large degree of variability between PLT and what they call the "page interaction time" (similar to SpeedIndex). The SpeedPerception[3] project has adopted a methodology similar to Eyeorg's; in particular the idea of a human supplied response to a "head-to-head" matchup of page performance. At the time of this writing, there are a few significant implementation differences: 1) SpeedPerception's A/B tests[4] ask users to provide a decision on two *different* sites and 2) the way that SpeedPerception implements A/B tests differs from Eyeorg's (§3.2).

3. EYEORG

Eyeorg [12] is a platform for crowdsourcing web quality of experience measurements; the goal of Eyeorg is to measure improvements to user experience on the web. Both research and industry have expended great effort exploring different techniques for building and delivering web pages. Popular examples are content optimization techniques like "inlining" (putting CSS styles and JavaScript code directly in HTML) and "spriting" (putting collection of images in a single image). More far-fetched solutions are shandian [26], klotski [10], and polaris [17] which aim at optimizing content delivery based on how it gets displayed from a browser.

To understand when and how to use these techniques, we need to be able to *measure their impact*. Doing this in an automated and quantitative way is hard. First, "quality of experience" is amorphous and ill-defined—it is not obvious what to measure, let alone how. Second, even aspects of Web experience that seem straightforward, like PLT, are difficult for machines to measure: ultimately, how *humans* perceive performance is what matters.

Eyeorg takes a new approach to quantifying quality of experience by allowing experimenters to directly test the impact of web page design or delivery techniques on real users in a controlled fashion at large scale. Experimenters can use Eyeorg to answer questions like, "Does changing the order in which objects load impact UserPerceivedPLT", "Does the presence of advertisements on a page negatively impact user experience?", or "Which demographics are more sensitive to PLT speedup?".

Experimenters can use Eyeorg to draw responses from various classes of users, such as invited participants (e.g., friends or colleagues), paid crowdsourced workers, or general visitors to the Eyeorg site. Eyeorg provides tools to design experiments, recruit users, filter low-quality responses, and visualize results. The rationale behind Eyeorg is that computer generated PLT metrics only partially capture how people perceive the web. The human perception data gathered by Eyeorg can be used to augment and evaluate computer-generated PLT metrics.

[3]http://speedperception.meteorapp.com/

[4]SpeedPerception currently only supports A/B tests.

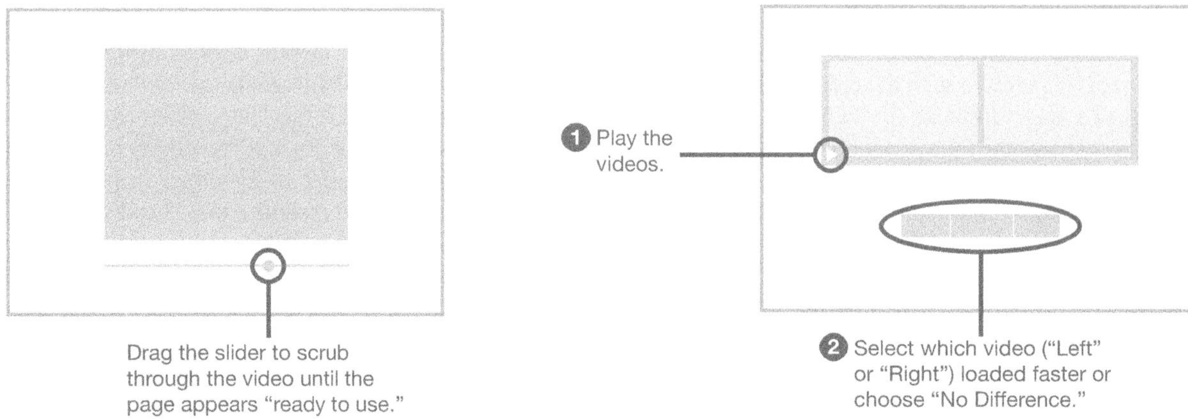

(a) **Timeline Test.** Participants "scrub" the slider to the point where they consider the page "ready to use."

(b) **A/B Test.** Participants watch side-by-side page load videos and indicate which load is faster.

Figure 2: Eyeorg**'s experiment types.**

In the remainder of this section we describe the design and rationale behind Eyeorg. In particular, we discuss how we address the following three challenges:

1. **How do we present page loads to participants? (§3.1)** Variations in load time caused by a particular participant's device or network could mask variations due to the technique being tested. Furthermore, experimenters might want to test the impact of protocols or browser extensions that participants' browsers do not support.

2. **How do we ask questions about quality of experience (and get quantitative answers)? (§3.2)** For example, how can participants indicate to us when a page "seems loaded" (particularly non-technical participants)?

3. **How do we get lots of trustworthy responses? (§3.3)** Drawing meaningful conclusions requires a large sample size; at the same time, recruiting participants not invested in the experiments could yield careless, sloppy responses.

3.1 Providing a Controlled Experience

Apart from the engineering challenge to build Eyeorg, a more fundamental challenge lies in dealing with real people. Testing participants' reactions to a web experience "in the wild" and at scale is difficult for several reasons. First, differences between participants' browsers could impact results. Second, in many cases the outcome we want to test (like PLT) is dependent on network conditions, but we have no control over the quality of participants' network access. Third, experimenters may want to test the impact of protocols (e.g., HTTP/2 or SPDY) that some participants' browsers may not support, or browser extensions (e.g., AdBlockers) that some participants may not have installed. In short, we want to guarantee the same experience for each participant.

To ensure that all participants base their responses on identical experiences, Eyeorg uses *video*. This allows us to fully control what participants see—we pick the browser, network conditions, protocols, and plugins—regardless of individual participants' configurations.

We built a tool, webpeg, to record videos of web pages loading. Pages are loaded with Chrome because: 1) unlike headless browsers like PhantomJS[5], Chrome provides rapid (and optimized) support for new technologies like SPDY and HTTP/2 and 2) Chrome offers better support for instrumentation than Firefox or Safari. We use Xvfb[6] (the X virtual frame buffer) so we can run webpeg on machines without displays (e.g., EC2 instances) and we capture videos in the webm format[7] (which offers small file sizes) using ffmpeg.[8]

We designed webpeg to be highly customizable. We use Chrome's command line options to control things like protocol (HTTP/1.1 or HTTP/2) and appearance (kiosk mode) and Chrome's remote debugging protocol[9] to enable device and network emulation. The remote debugging interface also gives us detailed information about the page load (as an HTTP Archive, or HAR), including when each object loaded, which protocol was used, and when the onload event fired. An alternative to using Chrome's remote debugging interface would have been to use the Navigation Timing API.[10] However, the Navigation Timing API is designed to be accessed by web "applications" themselves via JavaScript. To avoid *any* impact our methodology might have on performance, we thus chose to use the asynchronous debugging protocol. In the future, we will explore performant uses of the NT API when expanding Eyeorg to other browsers. Fi-

[5]http://phantomjs.org/

[6]https://www.x.org/archive/X11R7.7/doc/man/man1/Xvfb.1.xhtml

[7]https://www.webmproject.org/

[8]https://ffmpeg.org/

[9]https://developer.chrome.com/devtools/docs/debugger-protocol

[10]https://developer.mozilla.org/en-US/docs/Web/API/Navigation_timing_API

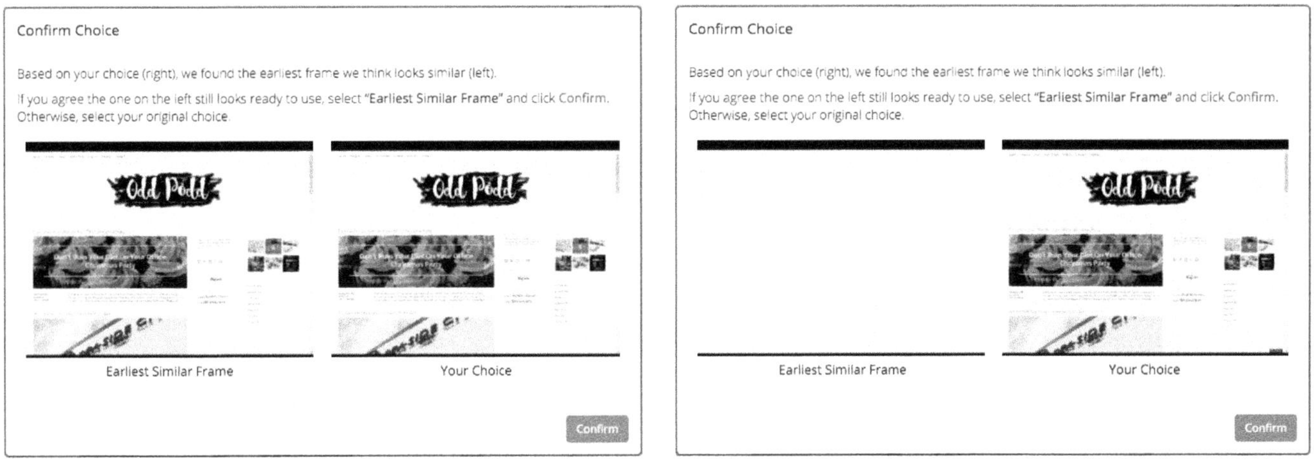

(a) Standard frame selection helper.

(b) Control frame selection helper.

Figure 3: Frame selection helper. Eyeorg helps participants adjust their selected PLT by giving them the option to choose the earliest visually similar frame to the one they chose (left). To ensure participants do not blindly accept the "rewind" frame, as a control we occasionally show a drastically different frame (right).

nally, webpeg directly modifies Chrome's preference file to enable/disable extensions and turn off distracting messages like "Would you like to translate this page?".

To capture videos, the experimenter supplies a list of URLs, how many loads to perform per site, and how many seconds to record after onload (since there is no automatic way for webpeg to know when the page has finished loading—if there were, Eyeorg would be unnecessary!). A fresh browser state is ensured by deleting Chrome's local state after each load. As in [23], before testing a new website, an initial "primer" load is performed. The primer ensures that all needed DNS records are cached at the ISP's DNS resolver before the first real trial (to prevent a cache miss from skewing the load time results). Local content and DNS caches are disabled and each request carries a cache-control header instructing network caches not to respond.

3.2 Designing Experiments with Eyeorg

Despite its subjective nature, we would like to run quantitative experiments measuring how QoE is impacted by various content or delivery optimizations. To demonstrate how Eyeorg can be used to do this, we picked one aspect of user experience, page load time, and designed two initial types of experiments to study it: timeline and A/B.

Timeline In a timeline experiment, we present the participant with a page load video and ask them to choose the point when they consider the page "ready to use." The naive way to design this test is to let the participant play the video and ask them to pause it when the page is loaded; however, since they may not be familiar with the page, they will likely wait until they are sure no more content will load, overshooting and pausing too late. Instead, we disable the standard HTML5 video controls and present participants with a slider they use to "scrub" through the video (Figure 2(a)). Even with the slider, in early tests we observed that (both trusted and paid) participants still overshot, choosing times well beyond onload. We suspect this is due to a combination of two reasons. First, browsers often only preload a small portion of the video at a time, so when participants seek quickly, they may see a blank screen and assume the *page in the video* has not loaded yet, when in reality the *video* has not loaded yet. By the time the video catches up, they have overshot. To address this, for timeline tests we force the browser to preload the entire video before the test begins, only then enabling the slider. Second, to correct for simple sloppiness, we add one final step: after the participant chooses a time, we show them the frame they chose and the earliest similar frame (no more than 1% different in a pixel-by-pixel comparison (Figure 3(a)). The participant can either accept our "rewind frame" or stick with their original choice.

We use timeline tests to compare participants' perceived load time with other metrics like onload and SpeedIndex. Since these metrics are frequently used to evaluate techniques for improving PLT, it is important to understand how closely they match user-perceived load time. Our tests use page load videos for a sample of 100 of the Alexa top 1M sites that fully support HTTP/2 [3]. For each experiment configuration, we repeat each load five times and use the video with the median onload time. Results are described in §5.

A/B The timeline test is tricky; "ready to use" is subjective and participants are not always sure how to decide what time to pick. However, for some experiments, it is not important to choose precisely *when* a page is loaded; it may be useful simply to indicate which of two page loads is *faster*. For these cases, Eyeorg uses A/B experiments. Participants watch two page load videos simultaneously and pick which loaded faster or "No Difference" (see Figure 2(b)). Video pairs are shown in a random order (i.e., "A" is not always on the left and "B" is not always on the right). There is no guarantee that two videos in a browser stay perfectly synchronized; for instance, lost packets might momentarily stall one video while the other continues playing. To ensure the videos stay synchronized, we splice them into a single video file. If playback stalls, both sides are affected equally.

We demonstrate A/B test's versatility with two experiments: 1) comparing the speed of HTTP/1.1 vs. HTTP/2, and 2) comparing the impact of ad blockers on PLT. For HTTP/1.1 vs. HTTP/2, we capture videos of the same 100 websites above while loading over HTTP/1.1 and HTTP/2. For the ad blocker analysis, we use data from [3] to identify 10,000 websites that display ads. From this list, we sample 100 websites and make videos of page loads through Chrome using one of three popular ad block extensions: AdBlock, uBlock, and Ghostery. In this case we do not control the protocol, which means Chrome will default to HTTP/2 if the target website supports it. For each experiment configuration (e.g., "HTTP/2" or "Ghostery"), we repeat each load five times and keep the video with the median onload time. Results are described in §5.

3.3 Crowdsourcing & Response Validation

For large sample sizes, Eyeorg turns to crowdsourcing. While many crowdsourcing services offer built-in tools for creating and hosting tests, we chose to build our own infrastructure. First, the built-in facilities tend to be limited and are not flexible enough to implement our timeline and A/B tests. Second, we did not want to tie Eyeorg to one particular crowdsourcing service; we wanted the ability to draw from a larger, more diverse participant pool, including those not registered as crowd workers, like friends and colleagues. Eyeorg currently supports Microworkers[11] and CrowdFlower[12] and can easily be extended to integrate with other platforms.

Using crowdsourced participants poses a challenge: we need to verify that responses are meaningful, e.g., that paid participants do not just blindly click through our tests to get paid (there are indications that workers from well known services like Mechanical Turk[13] do not always perform as well as desired [13]).

While there is no standardized methodology to determine the quality of a crowd worker, we draw on existing research in the field to detect unreliable responses (using a combination of test-time mechanisms and after-the-fact filtering).

Hard Rules Participants are given a set of clear instructions for each test, defining a set of *hard rules* they must follow for the system to allow them to complete the test. For example, in A/B tests, participants must choose "Left," "Right," or "No Difference" in order to move to the next video. Because we are interested in *human perception*, we also use Google's "I'm not a robot" service to verify "humanness" before participants take tests.

Soft Rules These are rules that, while not strictly enforced by the system, can reflect the conscientiousness of the workers [19]. Eyeorg does not force participants to watch a video before answering our questions, but failure to do so is a sign of low quality.

Engagement High quality workers tend to be "active." While the total amount of time a worker spends on a task is a rough indication of the quality of their work [20], it is not enough. On the one hand, a short time might indicate an unengaged worker whose only goal is finishing the task as fast as possible; on the other hand, a long time might be due to a distracted worker. We track how long participants spend reading the instructions, how much time they spend on each video, how many times they play it (if at all), how much of the video they watch, how often they seek, and whether they switch to different tabs or windows during a test. We also capture information about the participant's system, like browser, OS, and how large the video was on their screen.

Control Questions A common technique in crowdsourcing experiments is to randomly insert *control questions*—questions to which the answer is known [14]. For timeline tests, we want to verify that participants do not blindly accept the rewind frame we suggest, so we occasionally suggest a nearly-blank rewind frame (Figure 3(b)) and check that the participant continues with their original choice. For A/B tests, we occasionally show two copies of the same video with one side artificially delayed by three seconds and check that the participant picks the non-delayed side.

Wisdom of the Crowd A classic problem in crowdsourcing is the lack of ground truth, meaning the quality of responses is difficult to evaluate. However, if most participants are reasonably good, ground truth can be built using the average or majority vote of all responses [25, 7]. Participants whose responses deviate wildly from this pseudo-ground truth can be dropped. We also leverage the crowd to improve the system: participants can report broken videos; a video flagged by 5 different workers is automatically banned and manually inspected by our team.

4. VALIDATING EYEORG'S RESULTS

In this section, we validate the quality of the crowdsourced responses that Eyeorg collects. We introduce the data sets we have collected (§4.1) and present an analysis of various techniques for throwing away unreliable responses (§4.2), which leads us to our final "cleaning" procedure (§4.3).

[11]https://microworkers.com
[12]https://www.crowdflower.com
[13]https://www.mturk.com/mturk/welcome

	Type	Participants	Male/Female	Duration	Cost	# Sites	Engagement	Soft	Control
Validation									
PLT	timeline	Paid	76/24	1 hour	$12	20	16	2	7
PLT	timeline	Trusted	79/21	10 days	-	20	10	-	1
H1-H2	A/B	Paid	77/23	1 hour	$12	20	9	5	2
H1-H2	A/B	Trusted	84/16	10 days	-	20	1	2	1
Final									
PLT	timeline	Paid	685/315	1.5 days	$120	100	151	45	54
H1-H2	A/B	Paid	697/303	1.5 days	$120	100	98	56	82
ADS	A/B	Paid	716/284	1.5 days	$120	100	128	34	57

Table 1: Summary of data collected. Engagement, Soft, and Control indicate the number of participants filtered out by the techniques described in Section 4.3.

4.1 Data Sets

Before exploring methods for detecting low quality workers (§3.3), we define a "pseudo-ground truth" baseline using responses from a set of trusted participants. We evaluate the effectiveness of different filtering techniques by comparing filtered paid participant responses against these baseline trusted participant responses.

To gather the baseline, we ran two small-scale campaigns, one A/B[14] and one timeline, with 20 videos each. For each campaign, we recruited 100 *paid* participants on CrowdFlower and 100 *trusted* participants via email and social media. On CrowdFlower, we requested only workers that are "historically trustworthy," which comes at the cost of a longer recruitment time. For the trusted participants, we carefully selected friends and colleagues who promised full commitment to the task. We asked each participant to watch six videos (*i.e.,* we served 600 videos in total per experiment and each video has, on average, responses from 30 different participants).

The top of Table 1 summarizes the validation data set. For both timeline and A/B campaigns, it took about one hour to recruit paid participants (cost: $12) compared to 10 days for the trusted participants (at no cost). Both participant sets exhibit a roughly 75/25% male/female gender split. Paid participants are located in 30 countries (Venezuela being the most popular); trusted participants came from 12 countries (the U.S. being the most popular).

4.2 Evaluating Filtering Techniques

Based on the high-level techniques presented in §3.3, our goal is to design a strategy for filtering out low-quality responses. We validate each technique by comparing paid responses after filtering to the trusted baseline.

Engagement Figure 4(a) shows the Cumulative Distribution Function (CDF) of the time (minutes) each participant spent on Eyeorg broken down both by participant type (paid and trusted) and experiment type (timeline and A/B). The time spent on site is computed as the sum of the time spent evaluating each video, which in turn is computed as the difference between the time a response was submitted and the time the page loaded.

Figure 4(a) shows that, for both experiment types, the CDFs for paid and trusted participants are quite similar, though paid participants tend to take slightly longer than trusted participants (e.g., the median grows from 2.5 to 3 minutes for the timeline experiment). This result is counter-intuitive, as one would expect paid participants to skim through the videos faster in an attempt to increase their earnings by completing more tasks. Further analysis indicates that this is the result of two things: more "out of focus" time (Figure 5) where Eyeorg is in the background and longer video transfer times. The figure also suggests that the timeline test requires more effort than the A/B test; it takes 3x longer on average. This is primarily because 1) the timeline experiment requires more interaction with the video (Figure 4(b)) to complete the task and 2) the timeline experiment requires the video to be fully loaded before the participant can begin the task (§3.2).

Taking a closer look, Figure 5 shows the CDF of the time a participant did not have the Eyeorg browser tab in the foreground. We do not plot results for trusted participants in the A/B experiments since only one participant switched tabs during that test. For the timeline experiment (paid participants) we also differentiate by how long the video took to load (L). Overall, Figure 5 shows that participants tend to get more distracted the longer the video takes to load—we see about 10% more distracted users when the video takes up to 100 seconds to load compared to less than 2 seconds. A/B campaign participants are, overall, as distracted as timeline campaign participants for whom the video took less than 2 seconds to play. Since in the A/B campaign participants can click play right away and let the video load in the background, this further indicates that long video preloading time in the timeline campaign is responsible for the (understandable) engagement drop. In addition, the higher complexity of the timeline campaign might also have a role,

[14]The A/B campaign is HTTP/1.1 vs HTTP/2.

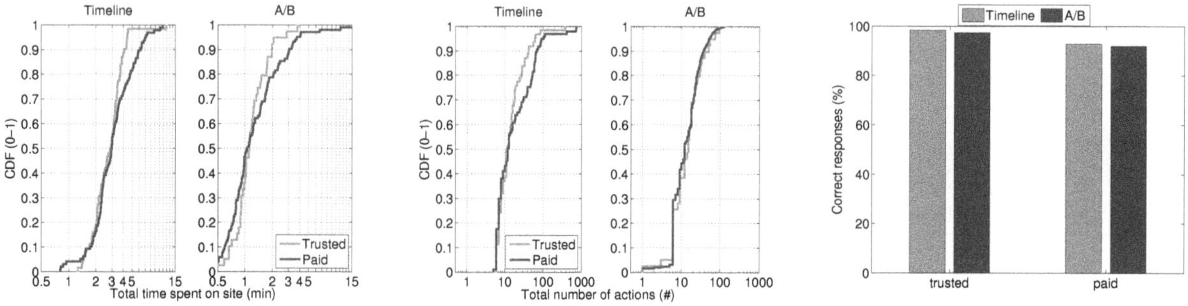

(a) Time spent on site

(b) Number of actions on site

(c) Percentage of correct responses to control questions.

Figure 4: Participant behavior. Comparing the behavior of paid and trusted participants.

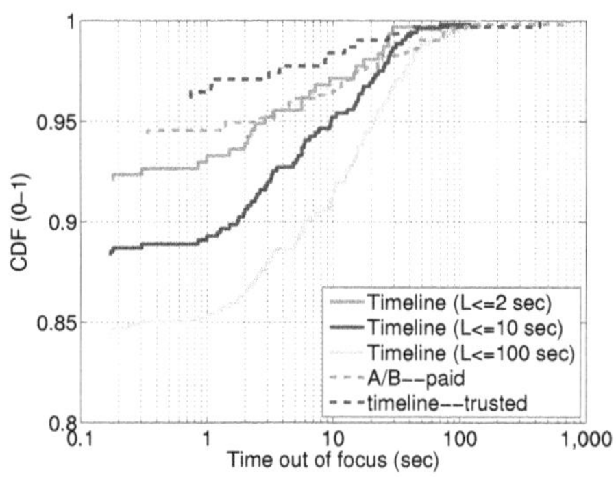

Figure 5: Out of focus time. L = video load time.

as suggested by 4% of the trusted participants also getting distracted for several seconds.

Next, we investigate how participants interact with each video; Figure 4(b) shows the CDF of the total number of actions (play, pause, and seek), again broken down by participant type and experiment type. The figure shows, overall, very similar CDFs, which indicates that paid and trusted participants are more similar in terms of actions performed than time spent on site. This further confirms the impact of external factors, such as long video load times, on the slower responses from paid participants. This result also shows Eyeorg's ability to equalize participant feedback despite heterogeneous network conditions, which would be impossible if participants were asked to, for example, navigate to a given website and provide feedback.

The tail of Figure 4(b) shows two users performing 714 and 724 actions (seek); this is twice as many actions as the most active trusted participant (369 seek actions). Nevertheless, these participants finished in 2 and 4 minutes, respectively, meaning that despite the large number of actions, they rank in the fastest 15% and fastest 70% of participants overall. Such frenetic behavior looks extremely suspicious, but, from our data, we could not figure out what causes it. We doubt it it is a realistic human interaction, and we conjecture a browser extension might have been used.

Soft Rules Though Eyeorg does not enforce it, we set a soft rule that participants should watch each video before submitting a response (§3). Although hard to see due to log scale, Figure 4(b) shows that trusted participants always interact with each video, seeking (timeline) or hitting play (A/B) at least once. By contrast, 1–2% of the paid participants speed through the test without interacting with the video at all.

Control Figure 4(c) shows the percentage of correct responses to control questions. Overall, we notice no major difference between the two control types (timeline versus A/B) for both paid and trusted participants, suggesting both control types were well designed. It is important to note, however, that paid participants tend to fail control questions at a higher rate (5%), suggesting that there are some random clickers. Nevertheless, we found one distracted participant per campaign in the trusted user-set as well.

Wisdom of the Crowd Finally, we investigate whether we can use consensus among paid participants as a proxy for ground truth in the absence of a trusted baseline, starting with the timeline experiment. To build intuition, Figure 6(a) shows the CDF of paid participants' UserPerceivedPLT for four representative websites. The wisdom of the crowd effect is clearly visible: the majority of the responses are concentrated around one (or a few) UserPerceivedPLT values, e.g., 6.2 and 9.5 seconds for video-2. We further discuss sites with multiple modes (like the one shown in Figure 1) in §6. The figure also shows fairly long heads/tails, indicating that, while most participants agree, some strongly disagree with the rest of the crowd. One possible explanation for this is that these participants simply scroll to the beginning or end of the video in an attempt to finish the test and get paid as soon as possible.

We generalize this observation to the entire timeline campaign by using the standard deviation of the UserPerceivedPLT for each website as a measure of agreement among participants—the tighter the distribution, the more in agreement the responses are. By removing outliers at the ends of each distribution (e.g., keeping only responses between the 10th and 90th percentiles of each site's UserPerceivedPLT distri-

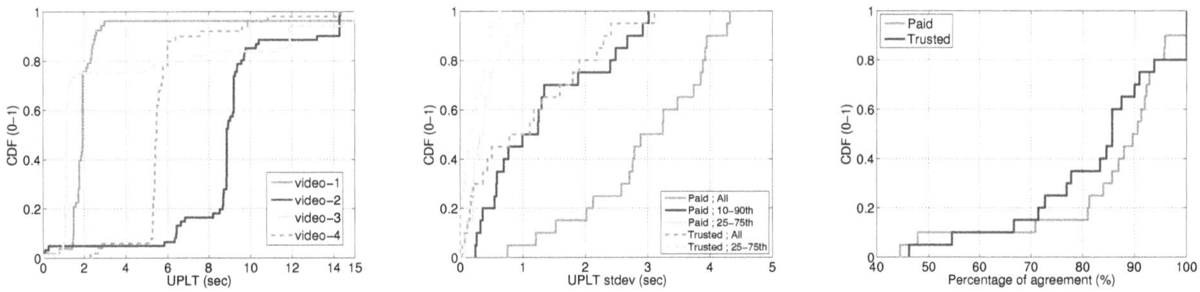

(a) Sample UserPerceivedPLT CDFs (b) Timeline experiments (c) A/B experiments

Figure 6: Wisdom of the crowd. With appropriate filtering, the responses of paid participants demonstrate a consistent majority opinion; furthermore, paid responses are in line with those of trusted participants.

bution), we arrive at a set of high-quality responses in relatively tight agreement. Figure 6(b) shows CDFs of standard deviations across all videos in the validation data set. First, without any filtering, the "Paid All" and "Trusted All" show wide standard deviations, which comes as no surprise based on the tails in Figure 6(a)). Second, the gap between the "Paid All" and "Trusted All" curves demonstrates the overall lower quality of the paid participants. Third, as we apply filtering, we see that the standard deviation of UserPerceivedPLT drops quickly, indicating most participants are in agreement. Finally, when restricted to responses between the 25th and 75th percentiles, results for paid and trusted participants are in line, which confirms that the wisdom of the paid crowd is a reasonable pseudo-ground truth in the absence of a trusted baseline.

Next, we extend this analysis to the A/B experiment. In this case, the analysis is simpler as the user input is restricted to three discrete values—left was faster, right was faster, or there was no difference—rather than the continuous set of values for the timeline experiment. Accordingly, Figure 6(c) shows the CDF of participant "agreement" for each video for paid and trusted participants. We define agreement as the fraction of responses matching the most popular answer, independent of what that answer is. For example, an agreement of 80% indicates that 80% of the votes went to one choice and the remaining 20% were split, somehow, between the other two.

Figure 6(c) shows no dramatic difference between trusted and paid participants in term of overall agreement. Likely, this is due to the ease of the A/B task compared to the timeline task, as previously discussed. The figure also shows a high level of agreement, e.g., more than 85% of participants converge to the same response for 60% of the videos and 10–20% of the videos have a 100% agreement. In addition, we never saw a completely split response (33% agreement)—the minimum level of agreement in the figure is 45%. Paid participants tend to agree more than trusted participants. Coupled with a lower rate of "no difference" responses, this might indicate that trusted participants are more cautious about their choices.

4.3 Final Filtering Strategy

Based on the analysis above, we arrive at the following methodology for filtering low-quality responses. Table 1 (last three columns) summarizes the number of participants dropped per campaign according to the methods below.

Engagement The previous analysis suggests that the time spent on site (Figure 4(a)) is not a reliable way to filter unengaged participants as it can be impacted by external factors like network connectivity. Instead, we use the following two engagement metrics. First, a large number of video interactions (Figure 4(b)) is a good indicator of suspicious activity, so we introduce a simple rule dropping paid participants with 50% more video interactions than the most active trusted participant (369 seeks). This filtering is very minor; it applied to only two paid participants in the validation data-set and three paid participants[15] in the final data-set (§5.1). Second, we apply a more aggressive filter based on the amount of time a participant is distracted, with the caveat that longer video load times may understandably cause participants to briefly switch to other tabs. Accordingly, we filter participants who switch away from the Eyeorg tab for more than 10 seconds so long as the video was delivered within those 10 seconds. Table 1 shows that this removes 10–15% of the paid participants.

Soft Rules We discard responses from participants who skipped (*i.e.,* did not play or scrub) even just one video. This removes 2–5% of both trusted and paid participants (apart from the trusted timeline campaign, where no participant broke this rule).

Control We discard participants who failed any control question. This amounts to 2–8% of participants, with no consistent trend between campaign types (more timeline participants fail the control in the validation set, whereas more A/B participants fail in the final data set). Only one trusted participant failed a control question in each campaign, which

[15]These paid participants managed to perform between 912 and 1931 seek actions in 5 minutes.

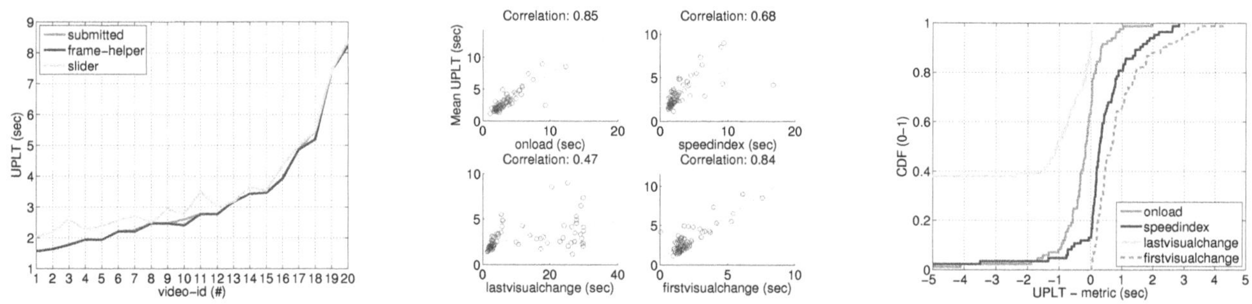

(a) Comparison of submitted UserPerceivedPLT with slider selection and frame-helper suggestion.

(b) Scatter-plot of UserPerceivedPLT and PLT metrics.

(c) CDF of difference between UserPerceivedPLT and PLT metrics.

Figure 7: Timeline Results.

gives us confidence our control mechanisms do not introduce false positives.

Wisdom of the Crowd For timeline campaigns, we only keep responses between the 25th and 75th percentiles for each video.

5. PAGE LOAD TIME RESULTS

This section summarizes our findings from using Eyeorg to study page load time (PLT), an important aspect of QoE. Specifically, we answer three questions: 1) to what extent do existing PLT metrics represent user perception, 2) do users perceive a speed difference between HTTP/1.1 and HTTP/2, and 3) what impact do ad blockers have on PLT?

5.1 Data Set

To answer these questions, we ran three campaigns, summarized in the *Final* section in Table 1. Each campaign consisted of 100 videos and targeted 1,000 paid participants (again, recruited from CrowdFlower's "most trustworthy" pool). Each participant watched six videos, meaning we served 6,000 videos in total per campaign and each video has, on average, responses from 60 different participants.

Overall, it took about 1.5 days per campaign to recruit 1,000 participants at a cost of $120. Across all three campaings, 70% of the participants are male and 30% are female. Participants are located in 76 distinct countries, with Venezuela being the most popular.

5.2 User Perception and PLT

We compare UserPerceivedPLT against four existing, automatically computable metrics:

OnLoad refers to the time it takes for the JavaScript "onLoad" event to fire. This event fires once the page's *embedded* resources have been downloaded, but not necessarily before, e.g., objects loaded via scripts are retrieved. OnLoad is the simplest and most used metric in practice.

SpeedIndex "is the average time at which visible parts of the page are displayed" (the average is over all above-the-fold pixels). Imagine a curve plotting the percentage of pixels that are "visually complete" (*i.e.,* match their final state) over time as the page loads; SpeedIndex is the area *above* this curve (smaller values better—the load feels faster the more "up and to the left" the curve is).

FirstVisualChange/LastVisualChange are the times at which the first pixels are drawn and the last pixels stop changing on the user's screen.

Figure 7 summarizes the results from the timeline campaign. For each video, we compute the UserPerceivedPLT as the mean of the filtered participant responses. To start, we investigate the impact of the frame selection helper (§3.2). Figure 7(a) compares participants' final UserPerceivedPLT choices ("submitted") with their original choices ("slider") and the one proposed by the frame selection dialog ("frame-helper"). For visibility, we only show results for the 20 videos used for validation in Section 4. For most videos, the submitted UserPerceivedPLT matches the value proposed by the frame selection helper, suggesting that most participants agree with Eyeorg's suggestions for fine-tuning their responses. On average, the submitted UserPerceivedPLT differs from the original value selected with the slider by 300 ms and up to a maximum of 1.6 s. In the remainder of the PLT analysis, we only consider the submitted UserPerceivedPLT and extend to the full video pool.

Are existing metrics related to UserPerceivedPLT at all? Figure 7(b) shows how UserPerceivedPLT correlates with each of the four PLT metrics. OnLoad and FirstVisualChange highly correlate with UserPerceivedPLT (0.84–0.85), while SpeedIndex, despite its higher complexity, has a lower correlation with UserPerceivedPLT (0.68). LastVisualChange provides almost no indication of when participants consider a page to be loaded (0.47). Though a non negligible number of responses (7%) exactly match LastVisualChange, most participants indicate that the pages are "ready enough" to be used way earlier.

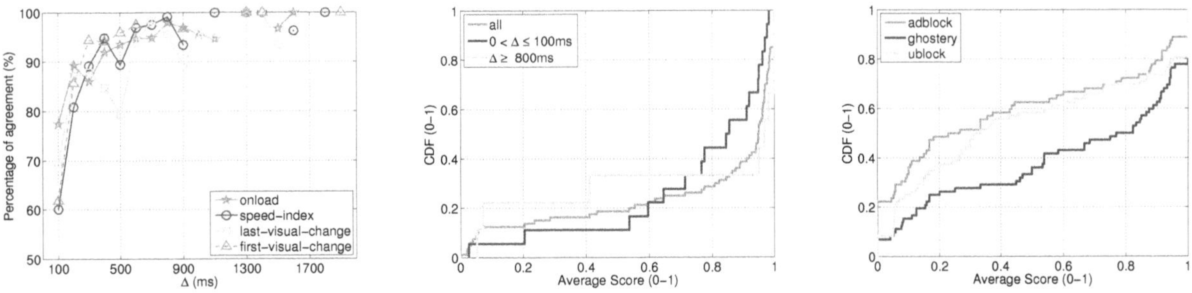

(a) Agreement as a function of PLT Δ. (b) HTTP/1.1 vs HTTP/2. (c) Comparison of ad blockers.

Figure 8: A/B Results.

Are existing metrics able to predict the* value *of UserPerceivedPLT? While correlation gives a rough picture of how each metric relates to UserPerceivedPLT, it is also important to show how close the actual values are. Figure 7(c) shows a CDF of the difference between UserPerceivedPLT and each PLT metric, *i.e.,* a negative number indicates that participants selected a time *before* that metric indicated the page had loaded. Overall, OnLoad was within 100 ms of the mean UserPerceivedPLT for 30% of the sites compared to just 7% for SpeedIndex. Also note that 60% of the UserPerceivedPLT values are smaller than OnLoad—that is, OnLoad tends to over-estimate. Unsurprisingly, FirstVisualChange and LastVisualChange under- and over-estimate, respectively.

Can existing metrics at least tell us "which is faster"? Finally, we quantify how good the existing PLT metrics are at identifying a difference in load time between two page loads using data from the HTTP/1.1 vs HTTP/2 A/B campaign. Intuitively, choosing which site in an A/B test is faster becomes easier as the absolute difference between the "true" load times for A and B (Δ) increases. Therefore, we can use the level of participant agreement as a proxy for Δ—the more the participants agree, the larger Δ likely was.

Based on this reasoning, 1) if a PLT metric is good, we expect to see agreement increase monotonically as the measured Δ for that metric increases, and 2) the higher the agreement for a particular Δ-value for a particular metric, the more confidence we have that when we measure a Δ of that size in the future, it represents a meaningful difference in UserPerceivedPLT. Figure 8(a) shows the median agreement (as previously defined in §4.2 Figure 4(c)) among participants for HTTP/1.1/HTTP/2 video pairs as a function of each metric's Δ. Overall, Figure 8(a) shows that as Δ increases, participants tend to agree more, which matches our intuition. While there is no clear winner among the PLT metrics, the figure shows that OnLoad better captures small loading time differences ($\Delta \leq 200$ ms) whereas SpeedIndex and FirstVisualChange do a better job in the medium range ($200 < \Delta \leq 800$ ms). The figure also shows that LastVisualChange and SpeedIndex do not exhibit a monotonic increase in agreement as Δ grows, meaning that small variations in LastVisualChange and SpeedIndex measurements are less significant.

5.3 HTTP/1.1 vs HTTP/2

Do users perceive a speed difference between HTTP/1.1 and HTTP/2? In this section, we examine the responses from our HTTP/1.1 vs HTTP/2 A/B campaign. Figure 8(b) shows the CDF of the average "score" per website; 0 means the HTTP/1.1 version was faster, 0.5 is a "split" decision, and 1 means the HTTP/2 version was faster. We plot scores for 1) all websites, 2) websites with similar HTTP/1.1 and HTTP/2 PLTs ($\Delta \leq 100$ ms), and 3) websites that loaded much faster over one protocol than the other ($\Delta \geq 800$ ms). To build these subsets, we compute PLT using SpeedIndex.

Figure 8(b) shows that 70% of the websites have an average score of 0.8 or higher; this means that 70 out of 100 websites "feel" faster using HTTP/2 than HTTP/1.1. Conversely, 12% of the websites have an average score of 0.2 or lower and thus feel faster using HTTP/1.1. The remaining 18% of websites create some disagreement. Note that the score here does not take into account the "No Difference" responses. These websites with scores in the 0.2–0.8 range also have twice as many No Difference responses compared to the other websites. This further indicates that participants are just not sure which version was actually faster.

Next, we focus on the subset of websites with similar PLTs ($\Delta \leq 100$ ms). The figure shows that participant indecision grows, with more scores in the 0.2–0.8 range. This is to be expected based on the results from Figure 8(a). On the other hand, when $\Delta \geq 800$ ms, participants mostly agree on which version was faster. This result indicates that, while aiming at reducing loading time of a webpage is overall beneficial, many users are not able to appreciate the difference when only few hundred milliseconds are saved.

5.4 Ad Blocker Comparison

How do popular ad blockers impact PLT? We compare three popular ad blockers, AdBlock, Ghostery, and uBlock. Figure 8(c) shows the CDF of the average "score" obtained by each website where 0 means the original version with ads was faster and 1 means the ad-blocked version was faster.

The figure shows that 30–40% of the websites have scores in the 0.2–0.8 range, *i.e.,* participants did not agree on which version was faster. This is about 15% more compared to when participants were asked to evaluate HTTP/1.1 versus HTTP/2. Based on feedback collected on Eyeorg, we believe this is due to the fact that the two versions of the websites are now not perfectly equal, which makes deciding which was faster harder. Nevertheless, the figure shows Ghostery is a clear favorite; for example, for 50% of sites, participants strongly agreed (≥ 0.8) that the Ghostery version of the page was faster compared to just 25% for AdBlock and uBlock.

6. DISCUSSION

What Does "Ready" Mean? In our timeline tests, we ask participants to "drag the slider to the point where you consider the site 'ready to use.'" We intentionally left the wording open to individual interpretations of "ready," since *what humans consider "ready" is exactly what we're trying to learn.* If, for example, we instructed participants to "pick the point where content stops changing," we would simply be asking them to reproduce LastVisualChange.

To see if participants have consistent definitions of "ready," we look at the UserPerceivedPLT distributions for different sites. Three rough patterns emerge (Figure 9). 1) Some sites exhibit a single, clear peak in UserPerceivedPLT choices. After manually inspecting the associated videos, these sites tend to be characterized by "fast" loads (in the sense that the span of time between FirstVisualChange and LastVisualChange is very short). These cases are relatively cut-and-dry; not much is open to interpretation, and participants are pretty consistent with the times they choose. 2) Some sites have a much wider distribution. These sites tend to have a much longer gap between FirstVisualChange and LastVisualChange, giving participants more freedom to choose different "ready" times. 3) Some sites exhibit *multiple* peaks. In some cases, this appears to be due to auxiliary content, like social media widgets and ads—some participants consider the page ready after the main content has loaded, while others wait for the auxiliary content to load.

Comments we collected from trusted participants help shed light on this. The first two comments confirm that auxiliary content does impact some participants' responses:

> *"Sometimes my choice may not be ... due to the [order] in which the content loaded. I selected the one where the main content loaded first, not necessarily which one finished loading everything [first]."*

> *"Ads/like buttons/etc. usually load last; it's a little unclear whether 'ready to use' should include those or not. I start using sites before all of the ads loaded, but when I do that, I know that the page isn't totally done loading—I just don't care."*

In conjunction with Figure 9 these comments are particularly interesting in light of new features in HTTP/2 like push and priority that could be exploited to ensure the optimal delivery order for *specific* users (similar to Klotski [10]).

The following two comments echo the first two, but also point out some limitations of our methodology. First, some participants' responses are affected by their familiarity with a site. They are easily able to identify when the important content is loaded if the site is familiar (*i.e.,* they will think the page is loaded "faster"), whereas with an unfamiliar site they might wait until every piece of content loads. Second, some participants look for more than just visual cues, e.g., when an element on the page becomes responsive to user input. Eyeorg's page load videos fail to capture these cues.

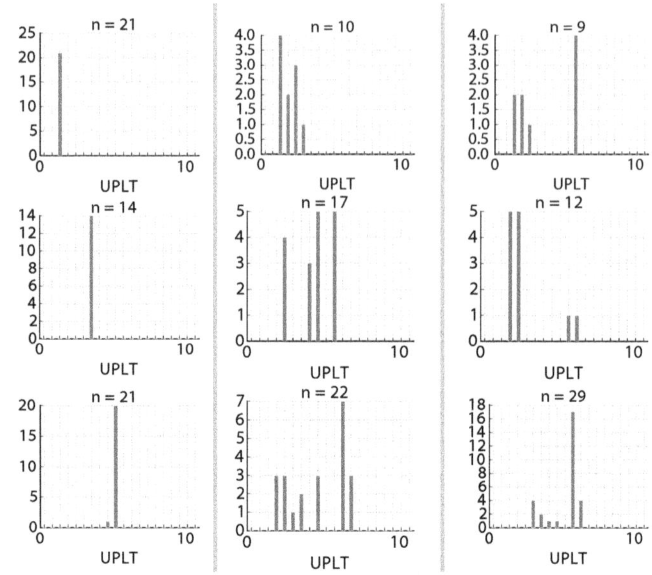

Figure 9: UserPerceivedPLT **Distributions:** Sites typically had one of three types of distributions: single mode and tight (left column), single mode and spread out (center column), or multi-modal (right column).

> *"Sometimes how early I feel the site is ready to use depends on what I want to use the site for. For example, if I am looking for articles, I don't care if the ads have loaded. So usually I consider the webpage ready when the part I want has loaded. However, there are other cases, like I don't know what is on the site, when I want to wait for everything to load. There is also the case where the links move when other parts load and for those cases, I commonly have to wait for the whole page to load because it's too easy to click where the link used to be and click something else instead."*

> *"It is difficult to say when a site becomes 'usable' without knowing whether the search bar is responsive. For many sites I consider it usable the instant the search bar becomes responsive."*

Extending Eyeorg In this paper, we only scratched the surface of what can be done with Eyeorg. Many *existing* features of Eyeorg that enable rich experimentation, e.g., (mobile) device and network emulation, have not been discussed at all. Similarly, although we have provided an extensive analysis into understanding how humans perceive PLT, we are fully aware that *many* open questions remain. We believe that the community at large can leverage Eyeorg as a platform to enable high quality, novel research that answers these and other questions. Eyeorg can be used to measure the impact of a variety of changes to the web; e.g., TCP vs. QUIC, TLS 1.2 vs TLS 1.3, HTTP/2 push/priority strategies, web design techniques like domain sharding or image spriting, browser plugins, or even in-network services like Google's Flywheel compression proxy [4].

Data Collection and Privacy Eyeorg collects data from human participants, so we have to take care we collect and use this data responsibly. (Note that paid participants may also provide data directly to the crowdsourcing services Eyeorg uses; this data is not shared with us and is subject to those services' privacy policies.)

We collect three types of data. First, we ask participants to provide standard demographic information like gender, age, country, and self-assessed technical ability. We collect this information at a coarse enough granularity there is no danger of identifying individual people. Next, we collect activity data like how long a participant spends reading instructions, when they play/pause a video, and whether they switch away from the Eyeorg tab during an experiment. (Note that we only collect information about the Eyeorg tab; if they switch away, we have no information about what they do.) We use this data to filter out uncommitted participants. We do *not* use this data to discriminate (e.g., refuse payment) against participants.Finally, we collect participant responses to our QoE questions (e.g., "when is this page ready to use" or "which video is faster"). Clearly this data is needed, as it is what Eyeorg seeks to measure to begin with.

7. CONCLUSION

This work presented Eyeorg, a platform for crowdsourcing web quality of experience measurements. Eyeorg collects *quantitative* QoE measurements from real users *at scale*. Eyeorg relies on *videos* to ensure each participant sees a consistent view of the page loading; our video collection tool control parameters like device type, protocol, network conditions, and more. We validate the responses collected from crowdsourced workers by comparing them to responses from a controlled set of 100 trusted users. Next, we conduct three measurements campaigns involving 1,000 participants each; our campaigns investigate the quality of existing PLT metrics, compare HTTP/1.1 vs HTTP/2 performance, and assess the impact of online advertisements on user experience. Going forward, we plan to extend Eyeorg with a broader set of capabilities for conducting web QoE experiments. In particular, we plan to make Eyeorg a platform that any researcher can use to test web content or delivery optimizations easily, without worrying about the challenges of designing a user study from scratch.

Acknowledgements

This project has received funding from the European Union's Horizon 2020 research and innovation programme under grant agreement No 688421. The opinions expressed and arguments employed reflect only the authors' view. The European Commission is not responsible for any use that may be made of that information.

8. REFERENCES

[1] Globaleventhandlers.onload. https://developer.mozilla.org/en/docs/Web/API/GlobalEventHandlers/onload.

[2] How One Second Could Cost Amazon $1.6 Billion In Sales. http://www.fastcompany.com/1825005/how-one-second-could-cost-amazon-16-billion-sales.

[3] Is the Web HTTP/2 Yet? http://isthewebhttp2yet.com.

[4] AGABABOV, V., BUETTNER, M., CHUDNOVSKY, V., COGAN, M., GREENSTEIN, B., MCDANIEL, S., PIATEK, M., SCOTT, C., WELSH, M., AND YIN, B. Flywheel: Google's data compression proxy for the mobile web. In *Proc. USENIX NSDI* (Oakland, CA, USA, May 2015).

[5] ARAPAKIS, I., BAI, X., AND CAMBAZOGLU, B. B. Impact of response latency on user behavior in web search. In *Proc. ACM SIGIR* (Gold Coast, Queensland, AU, July 2014).

[6] BARREDA-ÁNGELES, M., ARAPAKIS, I., BAI, X., CAMBAZOGLU, B. B., AND PEREDA-BAÑOS, A. Unconscious physiological effects of search latency on users and their click behaviour. In *Proc. ACM SIGIR* (Santiago, Chile, Aug. 2015).

[7] BLACKBURN, J., AND KWAK, H. STFU NOOB! Predicting Crowdsourced Decisions on Toxic Behavior in Online Games. In *Proc. WWW* (Seoul, Korea, Apr. 2014).

[8] BOCCHI, E., DE CICCO, L., AND ROSSI, D. Measuring the quality of experience of web users. In *In Proc. LANCOMM* (Florianopolis, Brazil, Aug. 2016).

[9] BOUCH, A., KUCHINSKY, A., AND BHATTI, N. Quality is in the eye of the beholder: Meeting users' requirements for internet quality of service. In *CHI* (The Hague, The Netherlands, Apr. 2000).

[10] BUTKIEWICZ, M., WANG, D., WU, Z., MADHYASTHA, H. V., AND SEKAR, V. Klotski: Reprioritizing web content to improve user experience on mobile devices. In *Proc. USENIX NSDI* (Oakland, CA, USA, May 2015), NSDI'15.

[11] EGGER, S., REICHL, P., HOBFELD, T., AND SCHATZ, R. "time is bandwidth"? narrowing the gap between subjective time perception and quality of experience. In *Proc. IEEE ICC* (Ottawa, Canada, June 2012).

[12] EYEORG. A platform for crowdsourcing web quality of experience measurements. https://eyeorg.net.

[13] HARRIS, A. Dropping mechanical turk helps our customers get the best results, Jan. 2014. https://speedcurve.com.

[14] HOSSFELD, T., KEIMEL, C., HIRTH, M., GARDLO, B., HABIGT, J., DIEPOLD, K., AND TRAN-GIA, P. Best practices for qoe crowdtesting: Qoe assessment with crowdsourcing. *Trans. Multi. 16*, 2 (Feb. 2014).

[15] LIDSKOG, T. browsertime. https://github.com/tobli/browsertime.

[16] LIMITED, S. Speedcurve. https://speedcurve.com.

[17] NETRAVALI, R., GOYAL, A., MICKENS, J., AND BALAKRISHNAN, H. Polaris: Faster page loads using fine-grained dependency tracking. In *Proc. USENIX NSDI* (Santa Clara, CA, USA, Mar. 2016).

[18] NIKRAVESH, A., YAO, H., XU, S., CHOFFNES, D., AND MAO, Z. M. Mobilyzer: An open platform for controllable mobile network measurements. In *Proc. ACM MobiSys* (Florence, Italy, May 2015).

[19] RAINER, B., WALTL, M., AND TIMMERER, C. *A Web based Subjective Evaluation Platform*. Klagenfurt am Worthersee, Austria, July 2013.

[20] RZESZOTARSKI, J. M., AND KITTUR, A. Instrumenting the crowd: Using implicit behavioral measures to predict task performance. In *UIST* (Santa Barbara, California, USA, May 2011).

[21] SHULL, M. Measuring performance, Apr. 2015. https://davidwalsh.name/measuring-performance.

[22] STEFANOV, S. Book of speed. http://www.bookofspeed.com/chapter2.html.

[23] VARVELLO, M., SCHOMP, K., NAYLOR, D., BLACKBURN, J., FINAMORE, A., AND PAPAGIANNAKI, K. Is the web http/2 yet? In *Proc. PAM* (Crete, Greece, Mar. 2016).

[24] WANG, X. S., KRISHNAMURTHY, A., AND WETHERALL, D. Speeding up web page loads with shandian. In *Proc. USENIX NSDI* (Santa Clara, CA, USA, Mar. 2016).

[25] WELINDER, P., BRANSON, S., PERONA, P., AND BELONGIE, S. J. The multidimensional wisdom of crowds. In *Advances in Neural Information Processing Systems* (2010).

[26] XIAO SOPHIA, W., ARVIND, K., AND DAVID, W. Speeding up web page loads with shandian. In *Proc. USENIX NSDI* (Santa Clara, CA, USA, Mar. 2016).

GRETEL: Lightweight Fault Localization for OpenStack

Ayush Goel* IBM Research

Sukrit Kalra* IBM Research

Mohan Dhawan IBM Research

ABSTRACT

Like any other distributed system, cloud management stacks such as OpenStack, are susceptible to faults whose root cause is often hard to diagnose and may take hours or days to fix. We present GRETEL, a system that leverages non-intrusive system monitoring, to expedite root cause analysis of both operational and performance faults manifesting in OpenStack operations. GRETEL uses unique operational fingerprints to quickly identify faulty operations at runtime. GRETEL is accurate in its diagnosis, and achieves >98% precision in identifying the faulty operation with very few false positives even under conditions of stress. GRETEL is lightweight and orders of magnitude faster than prior work, sustaining a throughput of ~77 Mbps.

Keywords

Fault localization; Network monitoring; OpenStack

1. INTRODUCTION

Cloud management stacks (or CMSes) like Apache's CloudStack [1], VMware's vSphere [19] and OpenStack [9] are complex distributed systems. Current operational and performance fault localization is both heavyweight and time consuming, even for skilled developers/operators. Recent faults [4,5,10–12,18] in Rackspace's OpenStack based cloud offering took hours and days to fix. In this paper, we focus on the problem of fast and lightweight fault localization and expedited root cause analysis in OpenStack.

Software and human issues are one of the major reasons for faults arising in cloud systems [31]. Most of the prior art [20, 21, 25–29, 33, 34, 37, 38, 41–45, 47] focuses either on active software instrumentation, passive monitoring or log analysis to detect and diagnose problems. All these techniques offer low-level diagnosis, typically reporting errors in specific API executions or listing dependencies on possible softwares or operations. However, all these solutions are often slow in reporting the fault and are not real time. For example, log analysis requires collation of event logs and subsequent parsing to reveal the exceptions or errors occurring at runtime; all of which takes significant time. Further, state of the art passive monitoring systems report an operational latency of the order of several seconds [43]. Lastly, the above systems mostly target operational faults, i.e., faults in API executions, and do not consider diagnosis of performance issues.

We present the design and implementation of GRETEL—a system for fast and lightweight fault localization of both operational and performance issues in OpenStack. GRETEL monitors relevant network communication and distributed system state, and systematically analyzes the information for fault diagnosis. Specifically, GRETEL builds a precise sequence of APIs, which identify an operation (called the operational fingerprint), of possible administrative tasks in OpenStack a priori, and leverages it to detect operations with faults. It then combines this knowledge of the faulty operations with additional passively collected system state to expedite fault analysis at runtime. GRETEL is novel because it (a) detects root cause of failures (both operational and performance) without requiring any expensive system modification, (b) identifies the high-level administrative operation responsible for the fault, and (c) requires no change even on introduction of new system components.

GRETEL builds upon the key observation that the various OpenStack components interact using a finite set of API interfaces. Note that additions or updates to these APIs is very infrequent, even across different OpenStack versions. Thus, for all practical purposes, there exist a finite set of high-level administrative operations. Furthermore, this set of operations is effectively captured in the OpenStack integration tests, which exercise several real world and relevant combinations of OpenStack APIs. GRETEL leverages these integration tests to create, a priori, a fingerprint for all these OpenStack operations, which build a sequence of REST and RPC invocations for each high-level administrative task. Thus, faults in OpenStack API invocations not covered by the operational fingerprints will not be diagnosed.

GRETEL localizes operational faults by analyzing relevant

*Both authors contributed equally.

CoNEXT '16, December 12-15, 2016, Irvine, CA, USA

© 2016 ACM. ISBN 978-1-4503-4292-6/16/12...$15.00

DOI: http://dx.doi.org/10.1145/2999572.2999600

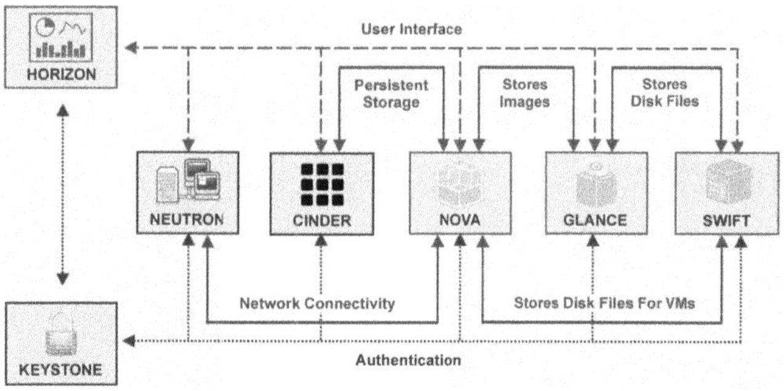

Figure 1: OpenStack architecture.

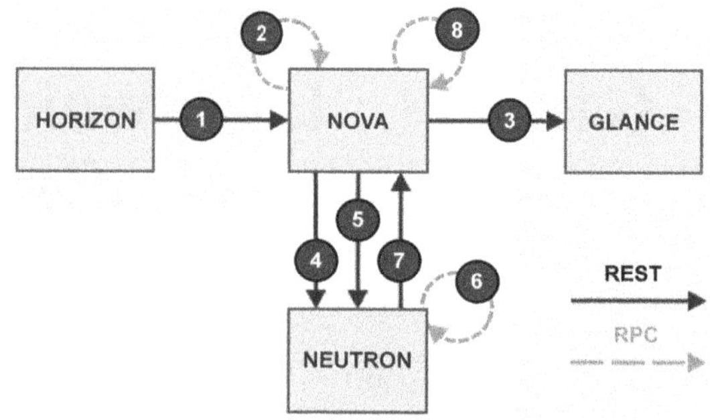

Figure 2: Workflow for launching a new instance.

OpenStack REST and RPC messages for API return errors and anomalous API latencies. To do so, GRETEL leverages the set of operational fingerprints to determine the high-level administrative task and subsequently, the OpenStack component that caused the fault. GRETEL then analyzes each network interaction amongst the various components decorated with operational and performance metadata, like per-API latency, availability of external dependencies, and resource utilization, for anomalies to expedite root cause analysis of the fault. Note that abnormal resource utilization that does not affect API latencies is not identified as a fault.

We have built a prototype of GRETEL for OpenStack LIBERTY. GRETEL's use of well defined patterns to detect API error codes for operational faults, and passive monitoring to detect API latencies, makes it compatible with all OpenStack versions, and potentially other cloud orchestration platforms as well. We evaluated GRETEL on a physical setup with 3 compute nodes, using OpenStack's Tempest integration test suite [15] with over 1600 real world scenarios, and exercised 470 faulty high-level administrative tasks in our setup. We further stress tested GRETEL and observed that for a fault frequency of 1 in $2K$ messages, it can process about 50K REST/RPC events per second of control traffic, or ~77 Mbps, which is orders of magnitude higher than prior work [43].

This paper makes the following contributions:

(1) We present GRETEL—a system that analyzes relevant network messages and distributed system state to localize faults and expedite root cause analysis in OpenStack operations, without requiring any system modifications. GRETEL also determines the high-level administrative task in progress that potentially led to the fault.

(2) We list scenarios (§ 3 and § 7) where existing tools are slow or mislead even skilled developers and operators.

(3) We provide a practical design for GRETEL (§ 4 and § 5), which leverages precise operational fingerprints to identify the faulty operation even at high throughputs.

(4) We apply GRETEL on OpenStack (§ 6), and evaluate it (§ 7) to demonstrate its accuracy, precision and speed, even under conditions of stress.

2. BACKGROUND

OpenStack is a state of the art cloud management stack, written in over 2.5 million lines of Python. It is a complex distributed system, where each high-level administrative task involves several cross component interactions.

Fig. 1 shows a conceptual architecture of a basic OpenStack deployment, where each of these services run on different nodes with distinct IP addresses, and provide a command-line interface (CLI) to enable access to their APIs via REST calls. **Horizon** is OpenStack's web-based dashboard, and provides an administrative interface to other services. **Keystone** is OpenStack's identity service, which provides authentication for all other OpenStack services. **Neutron** provides virtual networks as a service between devices managed by other OpenStack services. It allows users to create their own networks and then link them to the devices of their choice. **Cinder** is OpenStack's block storage service that provides persistent storage for VMs hosted on the cloud. **Nova** provides a controller for orchestrating cloud computing tasks for OpenStack, and supports a variety of virtualization technologies, including KVM, Xen, etc. **Glance** provides image services for OpenStack, such as a catalog and a repository for VM images using REST calls. **Swift** is an object/blob store, which enables creation, modification, and retrieval of objects via REST APIs.

COMMUNICATION. OpenStack mandates that all inter-service communication, such as those between Nova and Neutron happen via well defined REST calls. Thus, each OpenStack component has a corresponding HTTP client that enables access to its REST APIs. In contrast, all intra-service communication takes place exclusively through RPCs. Since OpenStack services could be distributed across several nodes, all RPC messages are routed through the RabbitMQ broker. For example, communication between the Nova controller and Nova agents on the compute nodes happens via RPCs channeled through the RabbitMQ broker.

DEPENDENCIES. All data processed or operated upon by OpenStack services is stored and managed by MySQL. OpenStack has communication dependencies on Python-based HTTP clients for REST calls, and Python's `oslo` messaging module for RPC invocations using RabbitMQ. Lastly, OpenStack relies upon virtualization solutions like KVM and Xen, and mandates that all nodes be NTP synchronized. If any of these dependencies are not satisfied, administrative operations in OpenStack would experience either operational or performance faults, or both.

2.1 Example: Launch a new VM

We now briefly describe the sequence of interactions amongst the various OpenStack component services to launch a new VM instance from the dashboard. Fig. 2 shows a schematic workflow for the same. For the sake of brevity, we omit all invocations to Keystone for authentication.

(1) When an administrator initiates the launch of a VM from the dashboard, Horizon issues an HTTP `POST` to Nova (using the `novaclient`) to create a VM for the specified tenant.

(2) At this instant, the control migrates from the Nova controller to the `nova-compute` service on the compute node, where it initiates RPCs to build the instance.

(3) Nova then leverages the `glanceclient` to issue an HTTP `GET` request to Glance to fetch the desired VM image and initiates the boot process.

(4) Concurrently, Nova issues a series of `GET` requests to the Neutron controller node (leveraging the `neutronclient`) to determine the existing network, port and security group bindings for the specified tenant.

(5) Nova temporarily halts the boot process, and invokes Neutron APIs requesting it to create and attach a new port for the VM instance. Nova sends the desired VM and network identifiers within the `POST` request body to Neutron.

(6) Neutron immediately responds with the newly created port identifier for the VM. Subsequently, Nova makes the request to attach the port to the VM and blocks the boot process while waiting for a callback from Neutron, indicating that it has plumbed in the virtual interface.

(7) Upon completing port attachment to the VM, Neutron sends out a `POST` to Nova using the `novaclient`.

(8) Nova boots the VM when all events have been received.

3. MOTIVATION

Faults may arise in OpenStack operations due to incorrect component configuration, third party dependencies, request/response latencies, resource exhaustion, etc. In this paper, we consider a *fault* as a manifestation of deviant system behavior, whether operational or performance or both. Operational faults include API error responses, while performance faults include abnormal API latencies that impact currently executing OpenStack operations. Operational faults are detected using lightweight regular expression checks, while inordinate API latencies are detected using online anomaly detection tools. Note that we do not consider operational or performance issues arising in VM instances booted atop OpenStack, as faults.

FAULT LOCALIZATION. OpenStack operations involve complex interactions amongst its distributed components. While API errors or anomalous performance metadata are indicative of some fault, they can often be misleading [43]. Further, in several scenarios, these fault notifications may even be absent altogether, forcing developers/operators to mine the system logs to determine the actual source of the problem. Moreover, the actual root cause may be further upstream than the component exhibiting the fault.

ROOT CAUSE ANALYSIS USING METADATA. While it is imperative to detect what operation resulted in failure, mere fault isolation does not reveal the exact cause of the problem. Moreover, debugging the component involved requires extensive domain knowledge. However, we observe that faults afflicting OpenStack operations, typically perturb some state on the physical node, atop which the OpenStack component is running. These perturbations in system state can often provide evidence of the root cause of failure.

Root cause analysis either through log analysis or software instrumentation [22, 27, 29, 33, 34] often requires complete knowledge of the entire system. Moreover, its success depends on the intrusiveness of the implementation. Effectiveness of log analysis is limited by the verbosity and precision of the log level, while software instrumentation often requires source level changes, with subsequent compilation and deployment.

3.1 Representative Scenarios

We now illustrate the effectiveness of GRETEL's approach with the help of three representative scenarios. We show how GRETEL's root cause analysis using metadata, assists developers and operators. We also argue why state of the art log analysis and passive monitoring tools, such as HANSEL [43], do not suffice for root cause analysis in production environments on the scenarios discussed.

3.1.1 VM create

In a particular VM create scenario, with no compute nodes available, we observed that Horizon first schedules the VM for creation and then abruptly reflects a "No valid host was found" error on the dashboard.

DIAGNOSIS WITH EXISTING TOOLS. Analysis of the Nova logs with log level set to `ERROR` reveals no errors. However, setting the log level to `WARNING` simply reflects the same error as on the dashboard. We next used HANSEL and observed that it identifies a chain of messages that led to the error [43]. Specifically, HANSEL traces that the `POST` request from Horizon to Nova succeeds, but the subsequent `GET` to determine the status of the VM fails with the error mentioned above. However, HANSEL's diagnosis stops at that stage and does not reveal the true reason for the error.

GRETEL'S DIAGNOSIS. GRETEL leverages its set of operational fingerprints to detect that the failed operation corresponded to a VM creation. HANSEL, in contrast, does not indicate the operation; it merely detects the sequence of API invocations. GRETEL, then systematically leverages the available distributed state (as will be discussed in § 5.4) to indicate that the `nova-compute` service on all the compute hosts is down, which is the true reason for the error.

3.1.2 API bottlenecks

When creating several VM instances in parallel, we observed significant delays in the completion of the operation. The operation eventually succeeds but is delayed, and thus constitutes a performance fault.

DIAGNOSIS WITH EXISTING TOOLS. Log analysis yields no information even with `TRACE` level logging enabled across all OpenStack services. Since the operation succeeds and does not raise any operational error, HANSEL is not even invoked. Thus, neither of the above approaches indicate any performance issue with the operation.

GRETEL'S DIAGNOSIS. Latency anomalies are detected for two Neutron RPCs—`get_devices_details_list` and security_group_info_for_devices—and thus reports a performance fault. It then leverages its operational fingerprints to identify the operation as a VM instance creation. Lastly, GRETEL checks the resource utilization on every node in the deployment and confirms anomalous CPU usage on the Neutron server, thereby isolating the performance bottleneck in the operation.

3.1.3 Multiple parallel operations

Production deployment of OpenStack may have several similar operations executing in parallel. For example, a client could invoke multiple VM creation operations. Even if one of those create operation fails, the administrator must accurately pinpoint the offending operation.

DIAGNOSIS WITH EXISTING TOOLS. Log analysis could identify the failed operation, only if log levels are set to WARNING or below. Recall that log level set to ERROR may not capture all failed operations. Furthermore, log analysis is slower than other runtime solutions. In contrast, parallel operations present the worst case scenario for HANSEL, which would end up reporting every operation (as per its operation stitching algorithm). Furthermore, HANSEL keeps a buffer window of 30s to avoid out-of-order or delayed messages, and also stitches operations on receipt of every message, both of which significantly increase the stitching and reporting time for faulty operations.

GRETEL'S DIAGNOSIS. GRETEL's operational fingerprints can quickly determine the failed operation, in spite of the several parallel invocations. Since GRETEL invokes operation detection only upon faults, it is not affected by any number of successful parallel operations.

4. FAULT DETERMINATION

Precise root cause analysis of an OpenStack operation requires that given a (sub)set of API invocations and a fault, we must accurately identify the high-level administrative task responsible for the fault.

MODEL. We model OpenStack as a closed system, where all operations would continue to completion without any operational or performance issues, unless the system is acted upon by external factors, like software and resource dependencies. Software dependencies involve the set of third-party software binaries that are required for correct execution of the OpenStack operation. Resource dependencies include the system-level resources that could potentially affect execution of the operation, such as CPU load, free memory, network throughput, etc. In such a scenario, any operational and/or performance issue can be attributed to external factors.

Given the above operating model, root cause analysis can be expedited by systematic analysis of external factors. Thus, the fault determination problem reduces to correctly determining the OpenStack operation responsible for the fault. To do so, GRETEL leverages operational fingerprints available a priori, and determines the closest match to a given (sub)set of API invocations containing the fault.

COMPOSITE OPERATIONS. We consider each OpenStack operation as a temporally related sequence of REST and RPC API invocations. Like other distributed systems, OpenStack pieces together several basic REST and RPC invocations to build more complex administrative tasks. In a typical OpenStack deployment, all such complex, administrative tasks originate at the dashboard or CLI, and use relevant REST directives to initiate it. These starting REST directives then initiate further sequences of REST and RPC invocations to complete the operation.

Operations from a particular OpenStack component, say Nova, may perform similar functionality, like launching or deleting a VM instance. All such operations leverage similar set of APIs. If each API is denoted by a literal, then OpenStack operations can be represented by a context free grammar (CFG). Let S_1 be the operation to snapshot a VM instance, and S_2 be the operation to create a volume. Since VM snapshotting subsumes volume creation, the two operations could be represented as shown below:

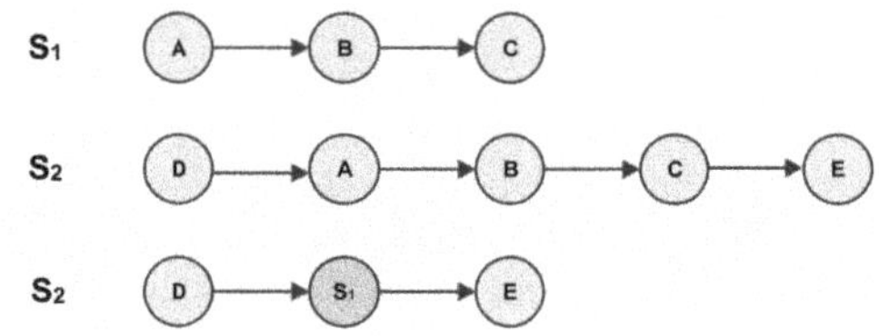

We note that S_2 is completely subsumed by S_1. Hence, their CFG representation will have a common operation preceded or succeeded (or both) by terminals corresponding to additional operations, i.e., $S_2 \rightarrow DS_1E$.

CHALLENGE. Determining the single operation responsible for the fault, however, gets exacerbated in OpenStack primarily because several REST and RPC APIs may be used across multiple high-level administrative tasks. Occurrence of simultaneous OpenStack operations makes it challenging to segregate them.

5. GRETEL

GRETEL leverages two key observations to enable fast and precise root cause analysis in OpenStack operations.

(1) There exist a finite set of OpenStack APIs (both REST and RPC), and subsequently, only a finite set of high-level administrative tasks are possible.

(2) Since OpenStack is a closed system, faults afflicting its operations must be a result of some perturbations of the system state on the physical node, atop which the OpenStack component is running.

GRETEL leverages the first observation to build a precise fingerprint of each OpenStack operation. It uses the second observation to systematically combine (in real time) any API faults (both operational and performance) along with per component OpenStack activity, operational fingerprints, and fine-grained metadata about per node resource utilization, for fault localization and subsequent root cause analysis.

Fig. 3 shows a schematic architecture for GRETEL, which consists of a distributed setup of monitoring agents and a central analyzer service. GRETEL analyzes network messages flowing across different components in OpenStack to (a) list constituent APIs per operation, (b) gather per

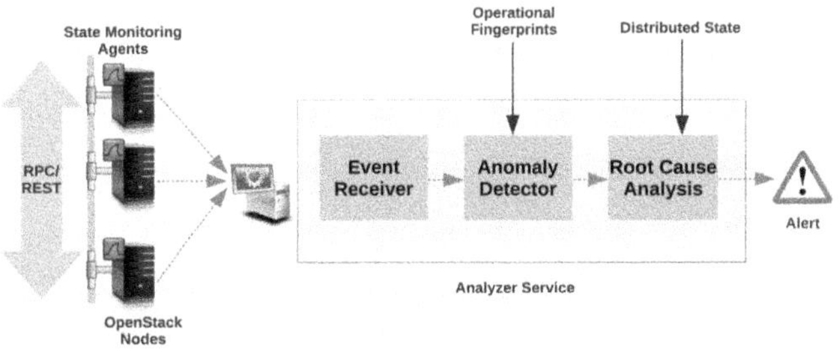

Figure 3: Schematic architecture of GRETEL.

GET_OPERATIONAL_FINGERPRINT($\mathbb{T}$)
Input: $\mathbb{T}$: List of traces for an operation.
Output: $\mathbb{R}$: Regular expression representation of the operation.

$\mathbb{T}$ = SORT_BY_TRACE_LENGTH($\mathbb{T}$);
$\mathbb{F}$ = FILTER_NOISE($\mathbb{T}$[0]);
foreach *($\tau \in \mathbb{T}$)* **do**
    τ = FILTER_NOISE(τ);
    $\mathbb{F}$ = GET_LONGEST_COMMON_SUBSEQUENCE($\mathbb{F}$, τ);
end
$\mathbb{R}$ = "";
// Iterate over all the APIs in the fingerprint.
foreach *($f \in \mathbb{F}$)* **do**
    if *(*GET_API*(f) ∈ {*POST, PUT, DELETE*})* **then**
        $\mathbb{R}$ = $\mathbb{R}$ + GET_SYMBOL(f);
    else
        $\mathbb{R}$ = $\mathbb{R}$ + GET_SYMBOL(f) + "*";
    end
end
return $\mathbb{R}$;

Algorithm 1: GRETEL's fingerprint generation.

API latency, and (c) determine API return errors, if any (for root cause analysis). Since, GRETEL sits transparently underneath the existing deployment, it does not affect the *safety* or *liveness* of the distributed system.

Several third-party dependencies, like `libvirt` and Python-REST clients are loaded dynamically when required by an operation. Thus, GRETEL leverages administrative help to list each of the dynamically loaded software dependencies touched upon, when executing the operation under consideration. This involves listing out the services installed during the installation of OpenStack. In the absence of such a list, GRETEL may be unable to pinpoint the root cause of faults arising from these services. Other software dependencies for OpenStack, like NTP, RabbitMQ and MySQL, are typically standard across all operations and components. GRETEL also works seamlessly with third-party vendor specific plugins as long as an agent for these plugins is provided in OpenStack.

FINGERPRINTING OPERATIONS. To fingerprint operations, GRETEL executes OpenStack in a controlled setting to avoid interference and determine the list of all APIs and set of software dependencies per operation.

GRETEL analyzes relevant OpenStack network packets, i.e., traffic corresponding to REST and RPC communication, to determine the most precise sequence of APIs that identify an operation (also known as the fingerprint).

Routine OpenStack operations typically involve several messages, both REST and RPC, that do not contribute in any meaningful way to segregate user-level operations at run time. These messages include heartbeat and status update RPCs, common REST invocations involving Keystone, and repeat occurrences of idempotent REST actions for a specific URI. GRETEL identifies such messages and removes them from the operational fingerprint to improve its quality. GRETEL further prunes the fingerprint by re-executing each operation several times and considering only those common APIs as the operational fingerprint that occur in each of the successful iterations. This mechanism removes any inadvertently captured transient REST or RPC invocations. If the re-execution of an operation leads to a different set of API invocations, GRETEL only considers the common set of APIs as a fingerprint of the operation. As will be discussed later in § 5.3.1, GRETEL prioritizes state change operations to improve the precision of the fingerprints being generated. Algorithm 1 briefly lists these steps.

5.1 Distributed State Monitoring

GRETEL uses monitoring agents at each OpenStack node in the deployment to monitor (a) relevant OpenStack REST and RPC communication, (b) resource utilization, and (c) health of OpenStack dependencies at each node. The network monitoring agents determine the observed network latency between request and response for each network message. The resource monitoring agents periodically poll the host nodes for CPU, memory, network throughput, storage, and disk read/write behavior. Additionally, GRETEL maintains watchers on third-party software dependencies.

5.2 Event Receiver

The event receiver receives relevant OpenStack traffic from every node, and forwards them to an anomaly detector to detect operational and performance faults in operations. Complex OpenStack tasks are essentially a combination of simpler operations consisting of REST and RPC messages, which must occur in a specified order to complete the task. Thus, while messages may be interleaved across different operations or delayed, they will not occur out of order for a successful operation. Further, TCP connections from network monitoring agents to GRETEL ensure that order of messages along a TCP stream is preserved.

5.3 Anomaly Detector

The anomaly detector has two main tasks. First, it analyzes each message to determine an anomaly. Second, based on that anomaly, it determines the operation which potentially contains the offending message.

DETECTING FAULTS. An API error return value signifies an operational error, while an inordinate API latency indicates a performance issue. Detecting operational faults is straightforward for RESTs, where errors are indicated in the HTTP response header. For RPCs, however, diagnosing faulty messages requires domain-specific knowledge of OpenStack so that error patterns are accurately identified in the message body. To ensure that anomaly detection for operational faults remains lightweight, GRETEL does not parse the JSON formatted message body and simply uses regular expressions to identify error codes in the message.

API latencies are computed based on timestamps

associated with each message, and GRETEL leverages available online outlier detection tools to detect performance faults. REST latencies are computed by pairing request and response messages based on TCP connection metadata, like IP and port, while RPC latencies are computed using IP and message identifier that is unique to each pair. With such lightweight message analysis, anomaly detection proceeds at high throughput rates.

5.3.1 Operation detection

GRETEL maintains a sliding window of size α to isolate the possible faulty OpenStack operation. We define α as

$$\alpha = 2 * max\{FP_{max}, P_{rate} \times t\}$$

FP_{max} is the size of the largest fingerprint across all OpenStack operations, while P_{rate} is the rate of the incoming message stream in packets per second and t is the time in seconds. The choice of a small time interval t is shadowed by FP_{max}, whereas a bigger value of t ensures that the sliding window is big enough to determine the largest operation given a high P_{rate}. On detection of an anomaly, GRETEL slides the window ahead by $\alpha/2$ messages and waits for the event receiver to fill the remainder $\alpha/2$ of the window. This mechanism helps GRETEL to have a snapshot of both the past and the future of the faulty message, and effectively determine the operations in progress at the time of the fault.

Once the sliding window is full, GRETEL spawns a new thread to detect the faulty operations in progress. To do so, GRETEL first determines the set of operations that include the offending message in their API sequences and then uses regular expressions for these operations (derived from the CFGs as per § 4) to detect a match in the snapshot.

If at least one such match is detected, the anomaly detector forwards the (a) set of operations that matched the snapshot, (b) set of messages (both REST and RPC) corresponding to these matched operations, and (c) source and destination IPs for all the error messages, to the root cause analysis engine.

PROBLEM. The sliding window may, however, include APIs from multiple different operations, where every API can potentially be part of several other administrative tasks. Thus leveraging the entire sliding window to narrow down the faulty operation may yield poor results.

SOLUTION. GRETEL, therefore, uses a context buffer atop this sliding window that dynamically adjusts itself to determine the minimum context required for identifying the OpenStack task and prune away any noise that could affect precise operation determination. Specifically, GRETEL starts with a small fixed size window $\beta = c_1\alpha$ and determines the precision θ of matching with the operational fingerprint, where c_1 is empirically determined.

We define GRETEL's precision θ of detecting unique operations per fault as:

$$\theta = (N - n)/(N - 1)$$

where N is the total number of operational fingerprints, and n is the actual count reported by GRETEL's operation detection mechanism. A precision of one, i.e., $\theta = 1$, indicates that the

```
GET_FAILED_OPERATIONS(𝔹, 𝔸)
Input: 𝔹: List of packets inside the context buffer.
Input: 𝔸: The offending API.
Output: 𝔽: The set of failed operations.
// Get the operations that contain the failed operation
𝕆 = GET_POSSIBLE_OFFENDING_OPERATIONS(𝔸);
𝕆 = TRUNCATE_OPERATION_FINGERPRINTS(𝕆, 𝔸);
ℙ = "";
// Build the pattern to match the fingerprints against
foreach (b ∈ 𝔹) do
  | ℙ = ℙ + GET_SYMBOL(b);
end
𝔽 = {};
foreach (o ∈ 𝕆) do
  if (REGEX_MATCH(o, ℙ)) then
    | 𝔽 = 𝔽 ∪ o;
  end
end
return 𝔽;

TRUNCATE_OPERATION_FINGERPRINTS(𝕆, 𝔸)
Input: 𝕆: Set of operations to truncate.
Input: 𝔸: The offending API.
Output: 𝕋: The given set of operations with truncated fingerprints.
𝕋 = {};
foreach (o ∈ 𝕆) do
  i = FIND_LAST_OCCURENCE(o, 𝔸);
  𝕋 = 𝕋 ∪ o[0 : i];
end
return 𝕋;
```

Algorithm 2: GRETEL's anomaly detection.

fault has been correctly narrowed down to a single operation. A value of $n > 1$ degrades the precision, with $\theta = 0$ for $n = N$.

At each iteration, GRETEL increments the context buffer β by $\delta = c_2\alpha$ messages on either side of the fault, where c_2 is empirically determined. GRETEL stops these iterations as soon as the precision θ drops. This also ensures that a false negative is not returned unless one of the APIs characterizing the operation is not contained within the sliding window. GRETEL starts with a small value of β so as to minimize the number of operations matched and then rapidly increases the buffer size by δ on each side of the fault to make sure that the whole sliding window α is covered as fast as possible.

IMPROVING PRECISION. Errors manifesting in RPC invocations are typically communicated back to the dashboard or CLI via REST calls. To avoid processing duplicate snapshots, GRETEL initiates the snapshot mechanism only when it detects an error in REST messages. However, all REST and RPC errors present in the snapshot are together analyzed to detect the root cause of the fault.

In case of performance faults, the operation will proceed to completion, and the snapshot is likely to match APIs even beyond the point of the observed fault. GRETEL, therefore, makes use of the entire context buffer to detect a match with the operational fingerprints. However, in case of operational errors the entire sequence of operations may not complete (due to the failed operation), and the snapshot may not match any regular expression. Thus, GRETEL truncates the regular expressions corresponding to operations that contain the offending API till its last occurrence in the fingerprint. The intuition is that the snapshot would match with one or more of these truncated regular expressions, which identifies

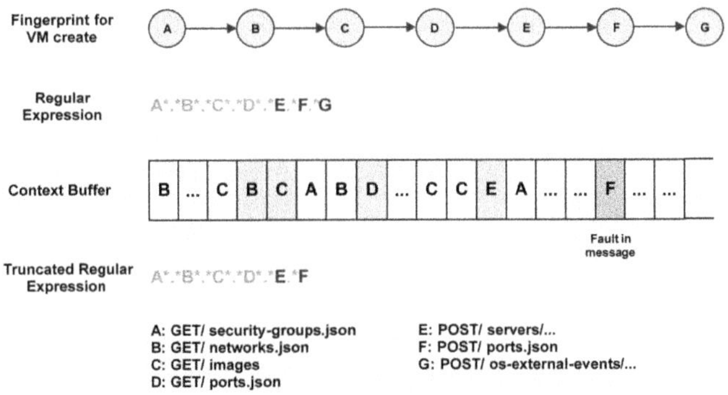

Figure 4: GRETEL's operation detection mechanism. We omit RPCs for brevity. State change APIs are marked in dark.

the potential faulty operations executing in the system. Algorithm 2 briefly lists these steps.

GRETEL also prioritizes matching of literals in the regular expression corresponding to state change operations, such as REST APIs with `POST`, `PUT` and `DELETE` modifiers and RPCs. Thus if the fault is in a state change operation, which is more likely in a dynamic system, then GRETEL generates regular expressions that are simpler and, hence, faster to match.

OpenStack is in the process of introducing a correlation identifier [8] to tie together requests and responses from different services pertaining to a single operation. When fully implemented, GRETEL can exploit these correlation identifiers to increase its precision by reducing the number of packets against which a fingerprint is matched.

EXAMPLE. The operational fingerprint for the VM create operation involves 7 REST and 3 RPC invocations. Fig. 4 lists this fingerprint, but omits the RPCs for brevity. If Nova's `POST ports.json` call to Neutron (node F) for creating and attaching a port to the VM instance fails, i.e., step 6 in § 2.1, GRETEL then creates a snapshot of the messages in its context buffer (which sits atop the sliding window) and initiates the operation detection procedure. Specifically, GRETEL converts the regular expressions corresponding to the operational fingerprints and the snapshot into strings, where each symbol represents a REST or RPC API, and isolates all fingerprints that contain the symbol F. It then truncates these regular expressions till the last seen occurrence of the symbol F. GRETEL uses these truncated regular expressions to match against the snapshot.

Due to several concurrent operations in the system, it is possible that some of the symbols even in the truncated regular expression are not captured in the snapshot. Thus, GRETEL further relaxes the notion of a fingerprint match, such that a regular expression matches the snapshot if the sequence of symbols corresponding to the state change operations, i.e., RPCs and `POST`, `PUT` and `DELETE` REST calls, is preserved. Fig. 4 presents the mechanism for the detection of a faulty VM create operation. Note that even though symbol A is missing from the context buffer, the truncated regular expression still matches as it preserves the order of E and F, corresponding to `POST servers` and `POST ports.json` invocations from Nova to Neutron.

GRETEL limits itself to analyzing request and response headers alone, and does not parse the JSON formatted

```
GET_ROOT_CAUSE(𝕆, 𝔸)
Input: 𝕆: Operation under consideration.
Input: 𝔸: Set of all dependencies.
Output: ℝ: Root cause.
Initialize: ℝ = {}
ϕ = Get_List_Of_Error_Messages_For_Operation(𝕆);
ℕ = Get_List_Of_Nodes_For_Operation(𝕆);
[nodes] = Get_Error_Nodes(ℕ, ϕ);
ℝ += Find_Root_Cause([nodes], 𝔸);
if (True == Is_Empty(ℝ)) then
   [remaining_nodes] = Get_Remaining_Nodes_In_Operation(ℕ,
[nodes]);
   ℝ += Find_Root_Cause([remaining_nodes], 𝔸);
return ℝ;

FIND_ROOT_CAUSE(ℕ, 𝔸)
Input: ℕ: List of nodes.
Input: 𝔸: Set of all dependencies.
Output: faulty: Return value indicating root cause.
Initialize: faulty: { }.
// Determine anomalies in metadata
foreach (ψ ∈ ℕ) do
    𝕄 = 𝔸['resource'][ψ];
    𝕊 = 𝔸['software'][ψ];
    foreach (ρ ∈ 𝕄) do
        if (True == Is_Anomalous(ψ, ρ)) then
            faulty += ρ;
    end
    foreach (η ∈ 𝕊) do
        if (True == Is_S/W_Dependency(𝕊, ψ, η)) then
            sw = Get_Offending_S/W(𝕊, ψ, η);
            faulty += sw;
    end
end
return faulty;
```

Algorithm 3: GRETEL's root cause analysis.

payload for extracting rich operation metadata. As a result, it may miss out on matching certain operations that change their fingerprints according to the data in the payload. While GRETEL should leverage payload for more precise operation tagging, we leave this improvement for future work.

5.4 Root Cause Analysis

GRETEL leverages (a) the error metadata forwarded by the anomaly detector, and (b) the knowledge of the distributed state obtained from polling individual nodes, within the duration of events captured in the context buffer (as passed on by the anomaly detector) to detect the root cause.

Algorithm 3 briefly lists the steps. Specifically, GRETEL analyzes all operations containing the offending error message (as forwarded by the anomaly detector), and uses the operational fingerprints to determine the set of nodes in the OpenStack deployment that correspond to the particular high-level administrative task. GRETEL focuses on the source and destination nodes (as passed on by the anomaly detector for the offending message), and determines anomalous resource or software usage that could potentially affect the operation. In case no anomalous values are detected on the nodes analyzed, GRETEL expands its search to other possible nodes that participate in the operation (as per the fingerprint). This is imperative since the root cause of the error in the operations may manifest upstream from the actual node where the fault arose. We further describe, in detail, the utility of this approach in § 7.2.

IMPROVING PRECISION. OpenStack deployments typically install each of its component services on separate nodes for scalability and fault isolation. GRETEL leverages this observation to further improve the accuracy of its root cause detection. This distinction enables GRETEL to accurately track API level performance metadata per node, for every operation. Note that even if the component services share IP addresses, GRETEL would only require the various OpenStack HTTP clients to report the source service as an HTTP request header to identify the start of an operation. No further changes would be needed in the core deployment. By annotating each packet with the service name, GRETEL remains unaffected by hardware failures or upgrades that may typically change low level information about the deployment. In other words, this small change will make GRETEL oblivious to the underlying deployment.

6. IMPLEMENTATION

We have implemented a prototype of GRETEL for OpenStack LIBERTY based on the design described in § 4 and § 5. We built GRETEL's distributed state monitoring infrastructure using Bro [2, 39] and `collectd` [7]. We augmented Bro with a custom protocol parser for the RabbitMQ messaging protocol (60 LOC in C++), and leveraged Python-bindings for Broccoli [3] (Bro's communication library) to send events from the OpenStack nodes to GRETEL's analyzer service, written in ~1600 LOC in Python. We additionally installed and configured `collectd` on all OpenStack nodes to capture system metrics and send them to the analyzer service. We now briefly describe a few salient features of our implementation.

(1) **System state monitoring**. GRETEL performs a comprehensive check about the status of the dependencies and the resources utilized. Specifically, GRETEL analyzes `collectd` generated snapshots of the system resource usage. Additionally, GRETEL also has watchers to detect TCP-level reachability to MySQL, RabbitMQ and NTP servers, and other nodes in the deployment.

(2) **Anomaly detection**. GRETEL detects operational faults by analyzing the error packets, which involves lightweight regular expression checks over the message payload. However, to determine performance anomalies, GRETEL leverages Python-bindings for the R `tsoutliers` package [16]. Specifically, GRETEL uses the LS (Level Shift) mode in the `tsoutliers` to detect the outliers in the continuous stream of API latencies and resource utilization received at the analyzer. The LS mode ensures that GRETEL adapts to the underlying system changes and does not report many false alarms. Note that outlier detection in GRETEL is pluggable and administrators can leverage any sophisticated detection mechanism for the same.

OPTIMIZATIONS. GRETEL detects currently executing OpenStack operations using regular expressions. Since the number of unique OpenStack APIs is 643, we use Unicode encoding to assign a symbol to each API. However, matching hundreds of regular expressions against a Unicode-encoded message snapshot is slow. Thus, GRETEL removes symbols corresponding to RPC messages to speed up operation detection. The intuition here is that an RPC error message must also be captured in the REST message(s) to the dashboard or CLI. To further speed up operation detection, GRETEL offloads all regular expression matching to a Perl process.

Lastly, GRETEL leverages a dual buffer to receive and process the incoming REST and RPC messages. It speeds up the snapshotting process using a combination of two pointers in the dual buffer separated by α messages, where α is the size of the sliding window. Whenever an error is encountered in the message stream, GRETEL freezes the messages between these two pointers to create a snapshot.

7. EVALUATION

We now present an evaluation of GRETEL. In § 7.1, we characterize OpenStack operations and build their fingerprints, which can be used to identify operations at high throughput rates. In § 7.2, we present case studies highlighting GRETEL's utility in root cause analysis for OpenStack operations. In § 7.3, we use Tempest to evaluate GRETEL for its precision in uniquely identifying the possible operations for every fault introduced because there exists no publicly available trace, representative of real OpenStack workloads. Lastly, in § 7.4, we measure GRETEL's network and system overhead under conditions of stress.

EXPERIMENTAL SETUP. Our physical testbed consists of 7 servers (including 3 compute nodes) connected to 14 switches (IBM RackSwitch G8264) arranged in a three-tiered design with 8 edge, 4 aggregate, and 2 core switches. All servers are IBM x3650 M3 machines having 2 Intel Xeon x5675 CPUs with 6 cores each (12 cores in total) at 3.07 GHz, and 128 GB of RAM, running 64-bit Ubuntu v14.04. We installed OpenStack LIBERTY with each component on a different server. The inter-component OpenStack traffic and Bro-to-analyzer service communication was isolated to avoid any performance penalties. `collectd` frequency to poll for resource utilization was set to 1s.

EMPIRICAL DETERMINATION OF THRESHOLDS. We empirically determine the values of the thresholds used by the anomaly detector. We use Bro to determine the value of P_{rate}, which is the only dynamic parameter affecting the value of α and in turn β. As will be shown later in § 7.1, the maximum fingerprint size FP_{max} was 384 across all OpenStack operations. P_{rate} for our deployment with 400 concurrent operations was observed to be ~150 pps and we chose the value of parameter t as 1s. Thus, we set the sliding window size α to be 768 (recall § 5.3.1). We empirically determined c_1 as 0.1 and c_2 as 0.04 and thus, the start value of the context buffer β was set at 80, while δ was set at 30.

7.1 OpenStack Characterization

We characterize OpenStack by developing fingerprints for all possible operations. Specifically, we leveraged OpenStack's Tempest integration test suite [15], which includes an exhaustive set of tests representative of actual

Category	Tests	Unique APIs		Events		Avg. Fingerprint	
		RPC	REST	RPC	REST	w/ RPC	w/o RPC
Compute	517	61	195	77.2K	87.8K	100	56
Image	55	10	38	0.9K	4.8K	18	15
Network	251	24	70	20.2K	18.5K	31	16
Storage	84	11	40	3.5K	6.2K	17	15
Misc.	293	11	20	9.1K	14.1K	16	11
Total	1200	-	-	110.9K	131.4K	-	-

Table 1: Characterization of the Tempest test suite.

administrative tasks in OpenStack. We executed each Tempest test (applicable for our setup) in isolation and monitored the sequence of REST and RPC APIs reported by GRETEL, along with the software dependencies required at every node in the OpenStack deployment (per § 5.1).

WHY TEMPEST? Tempest has an extensive battery of tests for OpenStack API validation, real-world scenarios testing the integration between different OpenStack services, and other specific tests useful in validating an OpenStack deployment. Further, Tempest is designed to run against any OpenStack deployment, irrespective of the scale, the environment setting or the underlying services that the deployment uses. Since Tempest can run on large deployments, it provisions running its test cases in parallel to stress the OpenStack deployment close to the degree that it would endure during peak usage cycles.

All tests that Tempest runs and validates are tasks that a tenant or administrator can execute in a real-world setting via OpenStack APIs. Further, Tempest's functional and integration tests are complex operations, derived from actual, real-world use cases occurring daily in fully operational OpenStack deployments. Typically, these scenarios involve a series of steps for testing OpenStack functionality spanning single or multiple nodes, where complicated state requiring multiple services is set up, exercised, and torn down.

GRETEL's fingerprint generation is an offline process since these fingerprints are independent of the scale of the deployment. Hence, GRETEL does not require learning atop production environments and can be trained on test environments. Unlike operational anomalies which leverage these fingerprints generated offline, performance anomaly detection is an online process and makes use of mechanisms described earlier in § 5.3 and § 6.

TEST SUITE CHARACTERIZATION. The latest Tempest test suite has 1645 tests of which 1200 executed successfully on our setup. The rest were not applicable for our setup and thus skipped by the test harness. We further classified these tests based on the nature of the operations. All tests that include creation, migration, etc., of instances, were classified under Compute. Tests that operate upon network configuration, ports, routers, etc., were classified under Network, while those involving VM images were categorized under Image. Tests operating upon VM storage were grouped under Storage. All other tests, such as those involving management tasks, like querying for key pairs, availability zones, etc., were grouped as Miscellaneous.

We executed each of the applicable 1200 Tempest tests in isolation using GRETEL, and report our findings for each

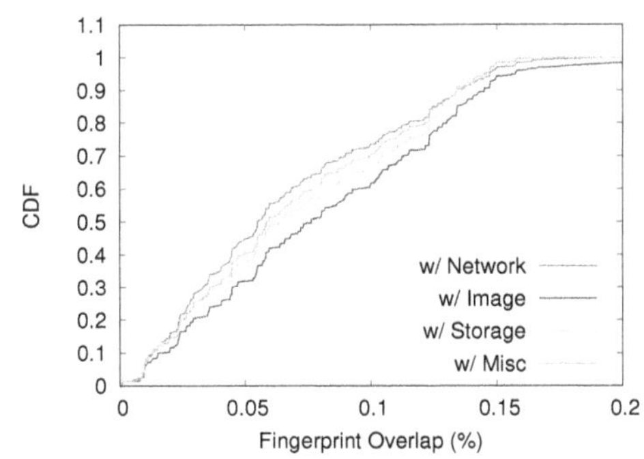

Figure 5: CDF for Compute operations.

category as described above in Table 1. TESTS indicates the count of tests executed per category. UNIQUE APIS indicate the number of unique RESTs and RPCs observed across all tests in the corresponding category. The REST and RPC events column indicate the network messages processed by GRETEL. These messages also include periodic updates, heartbeats, etc., which GRETEL prunes. The last column indicates the average fingerprint size for each category, both with and without RPCs.

We observe some overlap across operations within the same category. This overlap stems from the fact that operations belonging to the same category tend to leverage a small set of APIs provided by a single OpenStack service. However, GRETEL's fingerprints are substantially unique across operations of different categories. We select 70 representative Compute operations and plot their overlap across all other categories in Fig. 5. We note that ~90% of the representative Compute operations have <15% overlap across all categories.

LIMITATION. While Tempest aims to be exhaustive in its API coverage, we note that it is not sufficient to fingerprint 'all' possible OpenStack operations. Specifically, OpenStack components expose a total of 643 public APIs through their REST clients and CLIs. However, our characterization reveals that Tempest tests utilizes only a subset of these APIs across all its operations. Therefore, our characterization must be augmented to cover scenarios not included in the Tempest test suite.

7.2 Accuracy

We now present representative scenarios highlighting GRETEL's utility in root cause analysis of OpenStack operations. While the scenarios presented here are far from being exhaustive, they are indicative of (a) typical OpenStack operations and the nature of cross-component communications involved, and (b) GRETEL's effectiveness in isolating and identifying the root cause of faults.

7.2.1 Failed image uploads

We observed that uploading new VM images failed with Horizon showing a "Unable to create new image" error. Analysis of Glance logs revealed no entries. However, GRETEL discovered a REST 413 "Request Entity Too Large" error issued from Glance to Horizon for the `PUT` method of the `v2/images/<UUID>/file` API and

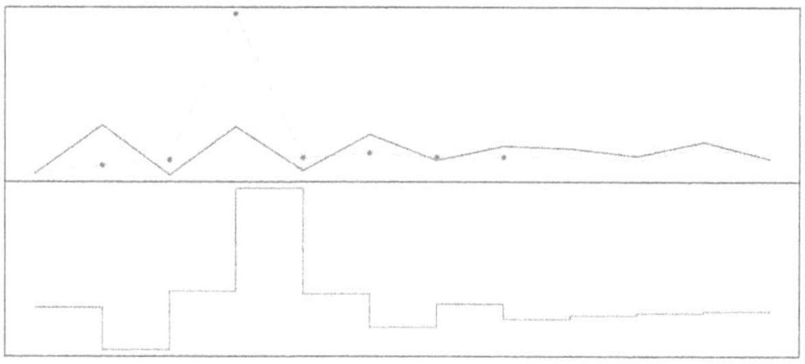

Figure 6: Anomalous latency for Neutron's GET /ports.json.

narrowed down the number of possible operations to just one, which was the Image upload operation. Subsequently, GRETEL's root cause analysis engine detected a resource issue on the Glance server, specifically low free disk space. After clearing up space and restarting the Glance service, subsequent image upload operations succeeded.

7.2.2 Neutron API latency increase

VM instance creation is one of the most common and significant operation in OpenStack, and any increase in its latency will have an adverse effect on overall system performance. During a run of 400 concurrent operations, we observed an increase in the latency of Neutron's `v2.0/ports.json` API as shown in Fig. 6. The original and adjusted time series are plotted in gray and blue respectively, while the level shift corresponding to the anomalous behavior is marked in red.

GRETEL was able to recognize this anomalous API latency increase and initiated the root cause analysis, which focuses on both Neutron and Nova controller nodes to determine the reason for the performance fault. GRETEL detects no issues with Nova, but observes a surge in the CPU utilization on the Neutron server during the execution of the operation. GRETEL attributed the increased latency to the high CPU usage. Other Neutron APIs like `v2.0/quotas/{ID}` and `v2.0/networks.json` that are part of the same VM create operation also experienced similar API latency increase.

7.2.3 Linux bridge agent failure

Neutron's layer 2 Linux bridge agent plugin configures a Linux bridge to realize the various Neutron abstractions. This plugin is deployed on all compute nodes and in event of its failure, the VM creation operation fails since it is not able to provide a network to the newly created instance. When launching an instance from the dashboard, we observed that Horizon reported a "No valid host was found. There are not enough hosts available." error. However, a subsequent listing of Nova's services showed that there was a compute node enabled and up and running. There were no errors on the Nova compute host, while the controller's logs showed the same error as the one on the Horizon dashboard.

GRETEL characterized this operation as a failed VM create operation and started the root cause analysis, which found no resource related anomalies on any of the servers involved in the operation. Subsequently, GRETEL checked for failures in software dependencies and found that the `neutron-plugin-linuxbridge-agent` on the compute host had crashed and reported that as a possible reason for the failure. Manual debugging revealed service misconfiguration, and fixing it completed the operation.

7.2.4 NTP failure

OpenStack requires the presence of NTP agents on each server that is part of the deployment to properly synchronize services amongst nodes. While doing a `cinder list` on the controller node, we noticed that the operation failed with the error "Unable to establish connection to Keystone". Log analysis found no error logs on the Keystone service and Cinder logs showed a "Timeout is too large" error; none of which were useful in identifying the root cause.

GRETEL identified a 401 Unauthorized error being relayed from Keystone to Cinder. Our root cause analysis engine checked the node hosting Keystone for both resource anomalies and software issues and found none. The engine then checked for resource related issues on the Cinder node and found no anomalies, but checking the software dependencies listed out the stopped NTP agent as a possible cause of the issue, and upon restarting the NTP agent on the host, the cinder client started working.

7.3 Precision

PARALLEL WORKLOAD. We evaluate GRETEL's precision in a controlled setting with several parallel operations. We randomly select non-faulty Tempest tests proportional to their distribution in the test suite, and execute them concurrently with a specified number of faulty test cases. These faulty operations included erroneous APIs only from the Compute and Network category, which form over 80% of all REST API invocations in the test suite (per Table 1). We ignore all performance faults for these tests, and evaluate them separately. Since each test spans several distinct operations, this setup is representative of real world, parallel operations, and is particularly challenging for our characterization that considered only individual operations executing in isolation.

We measure GRETEL's precision with varying number of parallel tests from 100 to 400 in increments of 100. For each scenario, we varied the number of operational faults injected (1, 4, 8 and 16) and plot the precision in Fig. 7a. Each fault additionally invokes operation detection against entire set of the 1200 fingerprints (corresponding to all OpenStack operations) in our characterization set.

In all scenarios, GRETEL reports a precision of >98%. We also observe that as we increase the load and the faults injected, GRETEL's precision increases only marginally. We attribute this small increase in precision to the availability of more operational context, which increases due to increase in size of the context buffer (β). Note that an increase in the number of parallel operations increases the number of interleavings between subsequent calls of the same operation. Thus, GRETEL increases the size of the context buffer (β), which forces a more precise match with the truncated regular expressions for the operational fingerprints (per § 5.3.1).

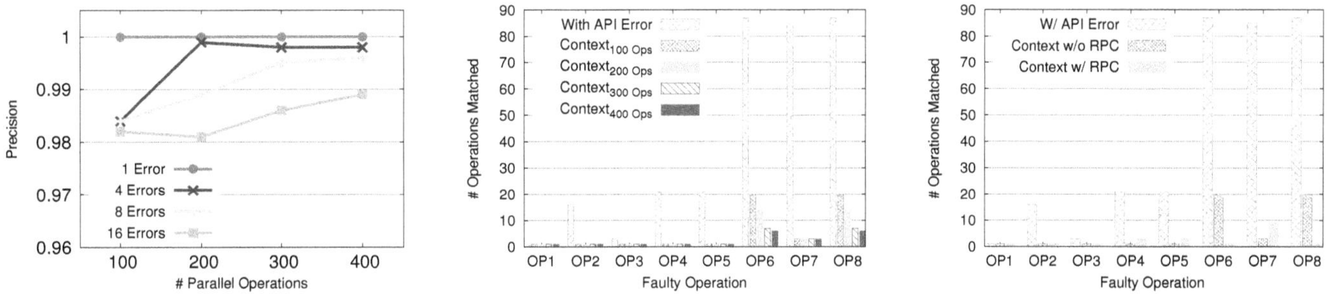

(a) Precision for parallel workload. **(b)** Operations matched w/ increasing context. **(c)** Operations matched w/ and w/o RPCs.

Figure 7: GRETEL's precision.

(1) False positives: A false positive for GRETEL occurs when it cannot narrow down the sequence of messages in its context buffer to just a single OpenStack operation. This is possible since majority of OpenStack operations involve cross-service interactions (e.g VM create, VM migrate etc.). Further, as discussed in § 7.1, GRETEL's fingerprints are substantially unique for composite operations and hence, a larger snapshot results in lower number of false positives.
Fig. 7b plots the variation in operations matched when executing 100, 200, 300 and 400 concurrent operations along with 8 faulty operations. "With API error" indicates the number of operations matched based on just the REST error API, without using the snapshot from the context buffer. We note that as the parallelism grows, GRETEL's precision improves marginally. We attribute this improvement primarily to an increase in the context buffer, whose size increases with increased parallelism in the system to improve precision (per § 5.3.1).
(2) Pruning RPCs in fingerprint: As a performance optimization, GRETEL prunes the operational fingerprint to match upon only the set of REST APIs in the operation (recall § 6). We executed 100 tests concurrently along with 8 injected faulty operations. Fig. 7c plots the number of operations matched with the fingerprint with and without RPCs included. 'With API error' indicates the count of operations matched on just the REST error API, without using the snapshot from the context buffer. We observe that the use of RPCs only marginally improves precision for some scenarios, which is possible due to a richer context available for matching with the operational fingerprints.
(3) Multiple parallel faults: We measure the number of operations matched when executing 16 parallel instances of the same faulty operation, along with varying number of concurrently executing tests from 100 to 400 in increments of 100. Fig. 8a plots the results. We observe that the average number of operations with which the fault matches decreases steadily as the concurrency increases. This is primarily due to the increase in the context buffer, where a larger context buffer size helps to match the operational fingerprint and subsequently improve precision (per § 5.3.1).
(4) Performance faults: We determine the performance faults reported for anomalous API latencies observed for Glance's `v2/<ID>/images` REST API when executing 200 Tempest operations concurrently, which took ~20 mins to complete. The `v2/<ID>/images` API is one of the most frequently invoked APIs by OpenStack services to retrieve metadata for the specified image ID. We used `tc` [13] to inject a 50 ms latency in all communication to/from the Glance server for 10 mins, starting at the 5 min mark.
Fig. 8b plots the original (in gray) and adjusted time series (in blue), and the level shift (in red) corresponding to the anomalous behavior. We observe that GRETEL raises 18 alarms during the 10 min duration and is also corroborated by the level shifts reported during the corresponding time period. Note that the adaptive nature of LS raises alarms only when there is a sudden spike in the time series values. LS does not raise alerts even if latency variations are smaller than the initial observed spike.

7.4 Performance

7.4.1 Throughput

Since the 1200 tests chosen from the Tempest test suite may not stress our deployment, we perform a synthetic evaluation of GRETEL's fault testing mechanism at scale using a large number of concurrent operations. We measure the steady throughput achieved by GRETEL for fault frequencies of 1 fault per 100, 500, 1K, 1.5K and 2K messages. We use tcpreplay [14] to generate RPC events at varying rates from the Bro agents, and plot the results in Fig. 8c. We observe that for 1 fault per 100 messages, GRETEL reports a throughput of ~7.5 Mbps. On reducing the error rate to 1 fault per 1K messages, GRETEL processes messages at near line rates. Thus, GRETEL's snapshotting mechanism is not a bottleneck.

We limit the maximum packets per second (pps) rate for tcpreplay to 50K, since higher pps results in several packet retries, which affect throughput calculations. Further, GRETEL took a maximum duration of <2 seconds to report the faults even with 400 concurrent operations. In contrast, HANSEL [43] achieves a peak throughput of only 1.6K REST messages per second, and introduces a latency of 30 seconds to account for delayed or out-of-order messages.

7.4.2 System Overhead

We ran 100 Tempest tests in parallel, which took ~6 mins

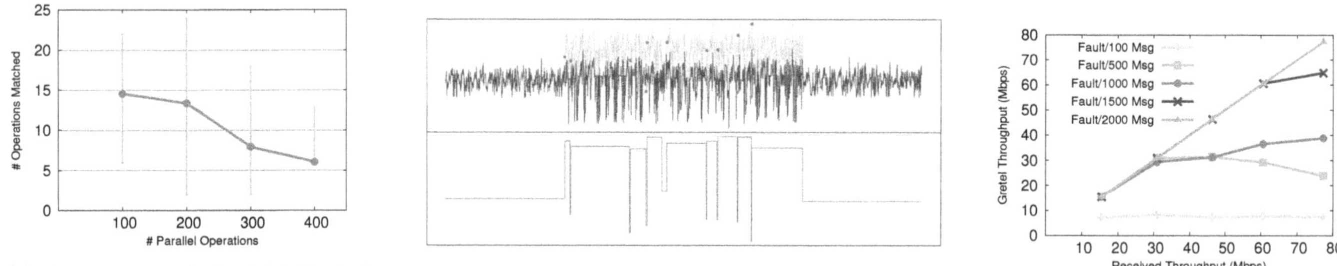

(a) Operations matched w/ 16 identical concurrent operations.

(b) Performance faults observed w/ parallel workload.

(c) GRETEL's throughput.

Figure 8: GRETEL's evaluation.

to complete, and monitored all nodes for CPU and memory consumption by the analyzer and the Bro agents. Note, we disabled our watchers for passive state monitoring for this experiment. The analyzer reported peak CPU usage of ~4.26% and memory consumption of ~123 MB. We observed that peak CPU usage for Bro-based monitoring agents was <12.38%, while their memory usage was ~1 GB.

8. LIMITATIONS

(**1**) GRETEL's accuracy is contingent upon the message context available in the sliding window used to determine the faulty operation. A small snapshot may include only a partial fingerprint resulting in no operation match.
(**2**) GRETEL requires the presence of a REST or RPC error message for detection of faults, and may miss out on faulty operations that do not generate any tangible operational or performance errors, like a stuck VM create
(**3**) GRETEL leverages regular expression checks to detect operational faults. Faults that do not match any regular expression may be potentially missed. For performance faults, GRETEL relies upon its watchers. Thus, transient changes resulting in performance issues, may be missed if not polled at a finer granularity.
(**4**) GRETEL's use of fingerprints for all OpenStack operation governs the precision of operation detection. Thus, more number of test scenarios would improve the fingerprint. In its present form, GRETEL may miss on operations that are not captured in the Tempest test suite, i.e., it is predicated on the completeness of the test suite.
(**5**) GRETEL cannot detect root cause of errors that manifest due to interfering operations, such as those that have causal dependencies upon each other. This limitation is, however, present across most prior art, including log analysis systems.
(**6**) GRETEL does not handle asynchronous calls that occur in the middle of an operation and lead to a branched fingerprint. Currently, GRETEL's re-execution of operations removes truly asynchronous APIs from the fingerprint.
(**7**) Enhancements to OpenStack or its APIs require building additional fingerprints for the newly introduced operations.
(**8**) GRETEL currently requires manual input to determine software dependencies for each operation, and the accuracy of its root cause analysis is contingent upon the correctness of the characterization provided.

9. RELATED WORK

9.1 Software instrumentation

Causal dependencies can be derived by comprehensively instrumenting all software, including any middleware, for communication, scheduling, and synchronization to record interaction amongst the various different components in the distributed system. Such systems [21, 25–29, 33, 37, 41, 42, 44, 45, 47] often integrate end-to-end tracing of all component interaction within the distributed system operations themselves.

X-trace [29], BorderPatrol [37], Pip [41], Webmon [30], Pinpoint [27], vPath [45] and Ju *et al.* [33], actively instrument the network stream along the software stack to uniquely tag all network operations. Popular industry implementations, like Zipkin [17] Dapper [44], and Htrace [6], also take a similar approach towards end-to-end tracing. In contrast, X-ray [21] instruments application binaries and uses dynamic information flow tracking to estimate the root cause of performance issues.

While being useful, the above systems have implementation and deployment limitations. Not only do they require exhaustive knowledge of the entire system, their success primarily depends on the intrusiveness of the implementation. Further, whole system instrumentation to track faults, requires modification of the entire source code, recompilation and subsequent deployment, which may not be possible in some deployments. Thus, GRETEL, unlike prior work, does not rely on any instrumentation. Instead, GRETEL employs a combination of precise operational fingerprints of OpenStack operations and passive monitoring of resources and dependencies to identify root cause of operational and performance issues.

9.2 Passive monitoring

GRETEL, like prior work [20, 34, 38, 43], utilizes passive monitoring of the deployment (without any knowledge of node internals or message semantics) to infer causal sequences of actions leading to faults. However, unlike prior work, GRETEL employs a learning phase to build a precise operational fingerprint of OpenStack operations, and combines it with statistical inferences from system metrics to determine the root cause of faults.

Sherlock [22], SCORE [36], NetMedic [34], dFault [40],

FChain [38] and HANSEL [43] exploit dependency graphs representing the complex chain of dependencies that exists in services, analyze symptoms from the network, and output a candidate set of root causes for the faults. Even though GRETEL requires a training phase to build its operational fingerprints, it operates at high throughput rates and reports no lag or loss of packets (per § 7.4.1).

COMPARISON WITH HANSEL. GRETEL is similar in spirit to HANSEL [43]. However, there exists significant differences between the two systems, as described below:

(1) GRETEL detects both operational and performance anomalies and provides a potential root cause of such errors. In contrast, HANSEL merely detects operational faults without providing a possible reason for the error.

(2) GRETEL classifies a faulty operation as a high level administrative task. In contrast, HANSEL merely provides the administrator with a low-level sequence of operations for each task that failed.

(3) GRETEL processes messages as they arrive and requires no buffering. Thus, it provides a more scalable design as compared to HANSEL, which employs time buckets to avoid any dropped packets.

(4) GRETEL triggers its error reporting only when it detects a fault. HANSEL, in contrast, leverages a heavy duty stitching logic that is triggered on every message, which coupled with the time buckets, increases its error reporting latency to almost 30s for zero dropped packets.

(5) HANSEL analyzes the request and response payloads to extract meaningful identifiers. However, common identifiers, like tenant ID, etc., may cause a faulty operation to link with several successful operations. In contrast, GRETEL is precise and detects only the faulty operation.

(6) GRETEL may fail to report the faulty operation if the sequence of packets fails to match a fingerprint. On the other hand, HANSEL does not suffer from this limitation and will always a report a chain of events leading to the fault.

(7) GRETEL does not handle failures in asynchronous calls in OpenStack operations. In contrast, HANSEL can still provide a chain of events leading to the fault.

9.3 Log analysis

Tracing systems [24, 35, 46, 48, 49] leverage log analysis to determine causal relationships among events. Such tools, however, are limited by the verbosity of the logs, and employ probabilistic data mining approaches.

Magpie [23] and ETE [32] rely on the distributed system's event semantics, and use temporal join-schemas on custom log messages. However, effectiveness of log analysis is limited by the comprehensiveness of the system logs and their debug level. Moreover, production systems typically have very lightweight logging enabled. Thus, GRETEL does not depend on log analysis, but can augment its root cause analysis using logs, if available.

Log analysis approaches induce a delay since determination of causal relations takes time until all the logs are collected and analyzed. In contrast, GRETEL can operate at high network speeds.

10. CONCLUSION

We present GRETEL, a fast fault detection and diagnosis system for OpenStack, which leverages non-intrusive system monitoring to systematically combine different system states and identify root cause of operational and performance faults in OpenStack. GRETEL uses unique operation fingerprints to quickly identify faulty operations at runtime. GRETEL is lightweight and precise even under stress.

11. ACKNOWLEDGEMENT

We thank our shepherd, Nedeljko Vasic, and Vijay Mann and the anonymous reviewers for their valuable comments.

12. REFERENCES

[1] Apache CloudStack. https://goo.gl/1S3K9W.

[2] Bro. https://www.bro.org/.

[3] Broccoli. https://goo.gl/4NUdFi.

[4] Cloud block storage issues. https://goo.gl/E6BPxG.

[5] Cloud servers issues. https://goo.gl/yg9gFB.

[6] Cloudera HTrace. https://goo.gl/Pz3lQu.

[7] collectd. https://collectd.org/.

[8] Correlation id in python-glanceclient. https://goo.gl/UyFDOr.

[9] OpenStack. https://www.openstack.org/.

[10] Rackspace Issue 1. https://goo.gl/2tdjHB.

[11] Rackspace Issue 2. https://goo.gl/CnqSTl.

[12] Rackspace Issue 3. https://goo.gl/JVVpX0.

[13] tc: Traffic Control in the Linux kernel. http://goo.gl/f8YDaH.

[14] Tcpreplay. http://tcpreplay.synfin.net/.

[15] Tempest. http://goo.gl/OZiXTV.

[16] tsoutliers. https://goo.gl/aVxsSJ.

[17] Twitter Zipkin. https://goo.gl/bHtUKc.

[18] VM build intermittent failure. https://goo.gl/s3VP3j.

[19] VMware vSphere. http://goo.gl/kNAR0f.

[20] M. K. Aguilera et al. Performance Debugging for Distributed Systems of Black Boxes. In *SOSP'13*.

[21] M. Attariyan et al. X-ray: Automating Root-cause Diagnosis of Performance Anomalies in Production Software. In *OSDI'12*.

[22] P. Bahl et al. Towards Highly Reliable Enterprise Network Services via Inference of Multi-level Dependencies. In *SIGCOMM'07*.

[23] P. Barham et al. Using Magpie for Request Extraction and Workload Modelling. In *OSDI'04*.

[24] L. Bitincka et al. Optimizing Data Analysis with a Semi-structured Time Series Database. In *SLAML'10*.

[25] A. Chanda et al. Whodunit: Transactional Profiling for Multi-tier Applications. In *SOSP'07*.

[26] M. Y. Chen et al. Path-based Failure and Evolution Management. In *NSDI'04*.

[27] M. Y. Chen et al. Pinpoint: Problem Determination in Large, Dynamic Internet Services. In *DSN'02*.

[28] R. Fonseca et al. Experiences with Tracing Causality in Networked Services. In *INM/WREN'10*.

[29] R. Fonseca et al. X-trace: A Pervasive Network Tracing Framework. In *NSDI'07*.

[30] T. Gschwind et al. Webmon: A Performance Profiler for Web Transactions. In *WECWIS'02*.

[31] H. S. Gunawi et al. What Bugs Live in the Cloud?: A Study of 3000+ Issues in Cloud Systems. In *SOCC'14*.

[32] J. L. Hellerstein et al. ETE: A Customizable Approach to Measuring End-to-end Response Times and their Components in Distributed Systems. In *ICDCS'99*.

[33] X. Ju et al. On Fault Resilience of OpenStack. In *SOCC'13*.

[34] S. Kandula et al. Detailed Diagnosis in Enterprise Networks. In *SIGCOMM'09*.

[35] S. P. Kavulya et al. Draco: Statistical Diagnosis of Chronic Problems in Distributed Systems. In *DSN'12*.

[36] R. R. Kompella et al. IP Fault Localization via Risk Modeling. In *NSDI'05*.

[37] E. Koskinen et al. BorderPatrol: Isolating Events for Black-box Tracing. In *Eurosys'08*.

[38] H. Nguyen et al. FChain: Toward Black-box Online Fault Localization for Cloud Systems. In *ICDCS'13*.

[39] V. Paxson. Bro: A System for Detecting Network Intruders in Real-time. In *USENIX Security'98*.

[40] P. Prakash et al. dFault: Fault Localization in Large-scale Peer-to-peer Systems. In *Middleware'10*.

[41] P. Reynolds et al. Pip: Detecting the Unexpected in Distributed Systems. In *NSDI'06*.

[42] R. R. Sambasivan et al. Diagnosing Performance Changes by Comparing Request Flows. In *NSDI'11*.

[43] D. Sharma et al. HANSEL: Diagnosing Faults in OpenStack. In *CoNEXT'15*.

[44] B. H. Sigelman et al. Dapper: A Large-scale Distributed Systems Tracing Infrastructure. *Google Research*, 2010.

[45] B. C. Tak et al. vPath: Precise Discovery of Request Processing Paths from Black-Box Observations of Thread and Network Activities. In *ATC'09*.

[46] J. Tan et al. Visual, Log-based Causal Tracing for Performance Debugging of MapReduce Systems. In *ICDCS'10*.

[47] E. Thereska et al. Stardust: Tracking Activity in a Distributed Storage System. In *SIGMETRICS'06*.

[48] W. Xu et al. Detecting Large-scale System Problems by Mining Console Logs. In *SOSP'09*.

[49] D. Yuan et al. SherLog: Error Diagnosis by Connecting Clues from Run-time Logs. In *ASPLOS'10*.

FlexRAN: A Flexible and Programmable Platform for Software-Defined Radio Access Networks

Xenofon Foukas
The University of Edinburgh
x.foukas@ed.ac.uk

Navid Nikaein
Eurecom
Navid.Nikaein@eurecom.fr

Mohamed M. Kassem
The University of Edinburgh
M.M.M.Kassem@sms.ed.ac.uk

Mahesh K. Marina
The University of Edinburgh
mahesh@ed.ac.uk

Kimon Kontovasilis
NCSR "Demokritos"
kkont@iit.demokritos.gr

ABSTRACT

Although the radio access network (RAN) part of mobile networks offers a significant opportunity for benefiting from the use of SDN ideas, this opportunity is largely untapped due to the lack of a software-defined RAN (SD-RAN) platform. We fill this void with FlexRAN, a flexible and programmable SD-RAN platform that separates the RAN control and data planes through a new, custom-tailored southbound API. Aided by virtualized control functions and control delegation features, FlexRAN provides a flexible control plane designed with support for real-time RAN control applications, flexibility to realize various degrees of coordination among RAN infrastructure entities, and programmability to adapt control over time and easier evolution to the future following SDN/NFV principles. We implement FlexRAN as an extension to a modified version of the OpenAirInterface LTE platform, with evaluation results indicating the feasibility of using FlexRAN under the stringent time constraints posed by the RAN. To demonstrate the effectiveness of FlexRAN as an SD-RAN platform and highlight its applicability for a diverse set of use cases, we present three network services deployed over FlexRAN focusing on interference management, mobile edge computing and RAN sharing.

1. INTRODUCTION

Mobile data traffic has seen a dramatic rise in recent times due to the rapid adoption of smartphones and their support for data-hungry services like video streaming. This trend is expected to continue into the foreseeable future, posing a major challenge for future mobile networks. Besides, the need to support newer communication paradigms like machine-to-machine (M2M) and device-to- device (D2D) makes the problem more challenging as they are characterized by high control signaling-to-data ratios, not the regime for which current mobile networks are designed for.

CoNEXT '16, December 12-15, 2016, Irvine, CA, USA

DOI: http://dx.doi.org/10.1145/2999572.2999599

The aforementioned observations have become driving factors behind the impending evolution of mobile networks to the 5G era. Key 5G requirements include: 1000x increase in peak data rate, support of 100x more devices, sub-millisecond round-trip communication latency and the reduction of energy/cost through the optimized network management [10]. These requirements are necessitating innovation in various dimensions ranging from scaling capacity (via ultra densification, new radio access technologies and spectrum bands) to newer, more flexible mobile network architectures.

Software Defined Networking (SDN) is among the key technologies considered in the context of evolving mobile networks. SDN has gained significant traction over the past decade, mainly in the context of data centers and wired networks. This is brought about by paradigm shifting ideas underlying SDN, which are the separation of the control from the data plane through a well-defined API (e.g., OpenFlow), the consolidation of the control plane and the flexibility introduced to the network through its programmability. These fundamental SDN ideas can contribute towards addressing various challenges faced by current and future mobile networks. Not surprisingly, there has been considerable research interest on software-defined mobile networks in recent years with much of the early work focusing on mobile core given its similarity to wired networks (e.g., [24],[29]).

The radio access network (RAN) part of mobile networks, both the costliest and the most complex part of the mobile network infrastructure, arguably offers even greater opportunities to benefit from SDN ideas. One reason is that strategies and technologies being adopted to improve spectrum efficiency and scale system capacity — cell densification, use of multiple radio access technologies (e.g., LTE and WiFi), use of advanced PHY techniques like Coordinated Multipoint (CoMP), etc. — require a high level of coordination among base stations, which SDN can naturally enable. As another reason, softwarization of control in mobile networks, especially in the RAN, not only allows easier evolution to the future through programmability but also enables a wide range of use cases and novel services (as we will discuss later). At the same time, a software-defined RAN (SD-RAN) design is challenging given the unique nature of wireless resources to be managed and the stringent timing constraints associated with some key RAN control operations (e.g., MAC scheduling). As discussed in Section 2, existing SD-RAN work, although abundant (e.g., [22], [9], [17], [40]), is largely conceptual with no implemented solution that researchers can use as a reference to evaluate their SD-RAN designs and to assess the benefit of new SD-RAN enabled services.

In this paper, we develop FlexRAN that to the best of our knowledge is the first open-source SD-RAN platform, thereby filling the above mentioned void. FlexRAN incorporates an API to separate control and data planes that is tailored for the mobile RAN. FlexRAN controller design and implementation factors in the need to make real-time RAN control applications feasible. Moreover, FlexRAN is designed with flexibility, programmability and ease of deployment in mind. FlexRAN offers a great degree of flexibility to easily and dynamically realize different degrees of coordination among base stations reflecting centralized to fully distributed modes of operation. It offers programmability at two levels, one in the form of RAN control/management applications that can be built over the FlexRAN controller and the other within the controller to be able to update the implementation of any control function on the fly. FlexRAN is also transparent to the end-devices, aiding easier deployment and evolution.

Specifically, we make the following contributions:

- (Sections 3 and 4) Realizable SD-RAN design in the form of FlexRAN. FlexRAN incorporates an API (FlexRAN Agent API) for clean separation of control and data planes in the RAN. Its hierarchical master-agent controller architecture is well suited for real-time RAN control operations while allowing reprogrammability and reconfigurability via its features of virtualized control functions and control delegation following Network Functions Virtualization (NFV) principles.
- (Sections 4 and 5) Implementation of FlexRAN over the OpenAirInterface (OAI) LTE platform [31] is shown to be efficient to the extent the use of FlexRAN is imperceptible to an end user device compared to using vanilla OAI, even when considering the time critical MAC scheduling operations. We also thoroughly characterize the FlexRAN performance behavior under different network conditions, varying number of UEs, and in presence of control delegation.
- (Section 6) We show results from using FlexRAN in a diverse set of use cases relevant to current and future mobile networks, namely interference management, mobile edge computing and RAN sharing. This demonstrates the ease with which new applications and services can be realized with FlexRAN, thereby its effectiveness as an SD-RAN platform. We also discuss additional use cases that FlexRAN can enable.

2. RELATED WORK

Software-defined control of mobile networks has received substantial attention from the research community in recent years with both academia and industry recognizing its benefits and proposing ways to integrate SDN principles to operational mobile networks [27]. Owing to the similarity between mobile core and wired networks much of the cellular SDN research till date focuses on the core part of mobile networks. The focus of this body of work [24],[29], [13], [33], [32], [28], [20] is on novel control designs based on SDN and NFV to address key core network issues of traffic and mobility management, and enable mobile networks to scale in the presence of high volumes of traffic.

While the scope of some of the above mentioned works includes the RAN, none of them address radio resource management, a vital aspect of the RAN and the focus of our work. RAN radio resource management is unique in the type of resources managed and the stringent timing constraints associated with some of the key functions (e.g., scheduling). In the last few years, there have been *several high-level conceptual works on SD-RANs* that do consider the radio resource management aspect [22], [9], [17], [40], [39], [8], [12]. SoftRAN [22] is among the earliest of these works. It introduced the idea of a big base station abstraction aimed at turning dense network deployments into sparse ones through the separation of the control and the data plane. In SoftRAN, control functions are *statically* separated into central and distributed ones based on their time criticality and their requirement for a centralized network view (e.g., centralized handovers and distributed downlink scheduling). Later works outline several potential SD-RAN designs, targeting different applications and settings. Similarly to SoftRAN, these works consider the tradeoffs between cost and efficiency for the control of the RAN and accordingly propose designs that follow either a hierarchical approach as in SoftRAN (e.g., [9], [17], [40]), where different layers of controllers are responsible for different operations based on their time criticality, or a fully centralized approach (e.g., [39], [8], [12]) where all the processing (L1/2/3) is performed centrally at a cloud data center.

A common and key limitation of the aforementioned SD-RAN works, which serves as the main motivation of our work, is that none of them have been implemented (and thus do not consider the associated challenges such as real-time control in their designs) nor do they tackle the issue of separating the control and data planes in the RAN in a practical and concrete manner. Moreover, none of these works offer mechanisms to make control in the RAN adaptive and flexible by allowing a dynamic functional split (e.g., centralized to distributed scheduling and vice versa) depending on the deployment scenario and the constraints posed by the underlying network conditions at any given point in time. Finally, not all of the proposed SD-RAN architectures are transparent to the UEs, with some designs proposing the introduction of programmability even at the UE-level (e.g., [40], [15]), raising backward compatibility concerns for legacy devices.

There are also works in the literature that are relevant from a RAN programmability perspective but can be viewed as complementary to our focus on a SD-RAN platform capable of performing radio resource management. For example, RadioVisor [25] deals with the challenge of radio resource virtualization in the RAN, allowing individual SD-RAN controllers to manage their own isolated slices. OpenRadio [14] and PRAN [38] deal with data plane programmability and how new wireless protocols can be implemented on-the-fly programmatically. Finally, the work of Tsagkaris et al. [36] proposes a software-defined framework for self organizing networks (SON) that simplifies the management of SON functions via a controller based on SDN principles.

3. FlexRAN OVERVIEW

This section gives a high-level overview of the FlexRAN SD-RAN platform, the key contribution of this paper. We present FlexRAN in the context of LTE for concreteness and to match with its current implementation, using the LTE terminology of eNodeBs and UEs for base stations and mobile devices. It is however important to note that there is nothing LTE-specific that FlexRAN assumes, thus its design is general and equally suitable for future mobile RAN architectures.

Fig. 1 provides a high-level schematic of the FlexRAN platform, which is made up of two main components: **FlexRAN Control Plane** and **FlexRAN Agent API**. The control plane follows a hierarchical design and is in turn composed of a **Master Controller** that is connected to a number of **FlexRAN Agents**, one for each eNodeB. The agents can either act as local controllers with a limited network view and handling control delegated by the master, or in concert with other agents and the master controller. The control and data plane separation is provided by the FlexRAN Agent API which acts as the southbound API (*a la* OpenFlow) with FlexRAN control plane on one side and eNodeB data plane on the other side.

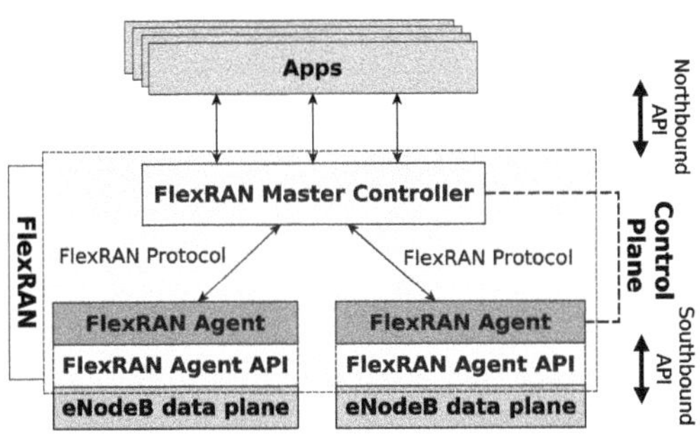

Figure 1: High-level schematic of the FlexRAN platform.

The FlexRAN **Protocol** facilitates communication between the master controller and the agents by allowing a two-way interaction between them. In one direction, the agent sends relevant messages to the master with eNodeB statistics, configurations and events, while in the other direction the master issues control commands that define the operation of the agents. In contrast to typical SDN controllers found in the wired domain, the FlexRAN controller has been designed with support for time critical RAN operations (e.g., MAC scheduling) in mind. Due to this real-time aspect and in order to fully utilize the power of FlexRAN, in the ideal case the communication channel between the agents and the master would be a high-bandwidth and low-latency channel (e.g., optical fiber path). However it should be noted that this is not a hard constraint, as the system provides flexibility to operate in non-ideal networking conditions with a small impact on its performance and capabilities (see Section 4.3.1).

Note that Fig. 1 does not include a UE, reflecting the fact that FlexRAN is transparent to UEs. The FlexRAN agent ensures that any command issued by the master that would affect the operation of a UE will be passed to the eNodeB, which will in turn apply the modification using the RAN technology standard in use (LTE protocol in our implementation). This transparency ensures the evolvability of the system, since new LTE and FlexRAN protocol extensions can be implemented at the RAN without causing backwards compatibility issues for users and without disrupting the use of their devices with constant updates to enable support of new network features. As long as a UE adheres to the LTE standard, it will be fully compatible with the FlexRAN platform.

On top of the master controller lies a northbound API, which allows RAN control and management applications to modify the state of the network infrastructure (eNodeBs and UEs) based on the statistics and events gathered from the eNodeBs in the FlexRAN control plane. Such applications could vary from simple monitoring applications that obtain statistics reporting which can be used by other apps (e.g., mobile edge computing app) to more sophisticated applications that modify the state of the RAN (e.g., MAC scheduler).

4. FlexRAN DESIGN & IMPLEMENTATION

4.1 Design Challenges

Based on the discussion of Sections 1 and 2 we identified a number of challenges that FlexRAN should resolve in order to be an effective SD-RAN platform:

- Separation of the control from the data plane in a clean and programmable way (Section 4.2).
- Adaptive and flexible RAN control with support for a dynamic control function placement depending on the deployment scenario and the constraints posed by the underlying network conditions (Sections 4.3.1 and 4.3.2).
- Support for the deployment of network applications over the controller, considering critical real-time applications (e.g. a MAC scheduler) (Sections 4.3.3 and 4.4).

In the following subsections, we describe the way that we overcame these challenges through the detailed description of the components that make up the FlexRAN platform (Fig. 1) as well as their implementation details over the OpenAirInterface LTE software platform. We present our design in a bottom-up manner, starting with the FlexRAN Agent API.

4.2 FlexRAN Agent API

All the access stratum protocols of LTE (RLC/MAC, PDCP, RRC) can be decomposed into two parts; the control part that makes the decisions for the radio link and the action part that is responsible for applying those decisions. For example, the control part of the MAC makes scheduling decisions (resource block allocation, modulation and coding

Call Type	Description	Target	Example outcomes of function calls
Configuration (Synchronous)	Get/Set configurations of target	eNodeB/Cell/UE/ Logical Channel	eNodeB ID, Number of cells, Cell id, UL/DL bandwidth, Number of antenna ports, RNTIs, UE transmission mode
Statistics (Asynchronous)	Request/reply statistics reporting.	List of cells/UEs	Transmission queue size, CQI measurements, SINR measurements
Commands (Synchronous)	Apply control decisions	Agent Control Modules (See Section 4.3.1)	Scheduling decisions, DRX commands, Handover initiation
Event-triggers (Asynchronous)	Notify control plane about changes in the data plane	Master Controller	Initiation of Transmission Time Interval, UE attachment, Random access attempt, Scheduling requests
Control Delegation (Synchronous)	Push control functions and modify their behavior at the agent side	Agent Control Modules (See Section 4.3.1)	Swap DL scheduler or mobility manager, Modify threshold of signal quality for handover initiation

Table 1: Type of function calls in FlexRAN Agent API.

scheme etc), while the action part applies them. Similarly, part of the logic of the RRC protocol decides on UE handovers, while the actual handover operation requires RRC to perform the corresponding action. Based on this taxonomy, FlexRAN separates the RAN control plane from the data plane by detaching the control logic from the action and consolidating all the control operations in a logically centralized controller, which in FlexRAN comprises of Master Controller and Agents interacting via the FlexRAN Protocol (see Fig. 1). As a result, eNodeBs only handle the data plane to perform all the action-related functions (e.g., applying scheduling decisions, performing handovers, applying DRX commands, (de)activating component carriers in carrier aggregation).

To control and manage the eNodeB data plane, we introduce the FlexRAN Agent API, which defines a set of functions that constitute the southbound API of FlexRAN and are the primary enabler for software-defined control of the RAN. These functions allow the control plane to interact with the data plane in five ways: (1) to obtain and set configurations like the UL/DL bandwidth of a cell; (2) to request and obtain statistics like transmission queue sizes of UEs and SINR measurements of cells; (3) to issue commands to apply control decisions (e.g., calls for applying MAC scheduling decisions, performing handovers, activating secondary component carriers); (4) to obtain event notifications like UE attachments and random access attempts; and (5) to perform a dynamic placement of control functions to the master controller or the agent (e.g. centralized scheduling at the master controller or local scheduling at the agent-side). These API calls can be invoked either by the master controller through the FlexRAN protocol using the message handler and dispatcher entity residing at the agent side (Figure 2) or directly from the agent if control for some operation has been delegated to it. The API calls are currently defined using the C language. A detailed list of the function call types is shown in Table 1.

Through the FlexRAN Agent API it becomes possible to develop two types of applications: (1) applications related to the control and management of the RAN resources like schedulers, interference and mobility managers etc. (e.g. by controlling resource block allocations, modulation and coding schemes, handovers and DRX cycles) and (2) applications relying on the monitoring of the RAN resources to make more sophisticated decisions (e.g. adaptive video streaming based on channel quality, resource-block allocations for RAN sharing etc) (see Sections 6 and 7.1). It should be noted that FlexRAN does not deal with the control of flows in the wired domain and therefore does not directly support related applications like routing. To enable this, FlexRAN should be coupled with corresponding flow-control solutions, like an OpenFlow-based SDN controller.

4.3 FlexRAN Controller Architecture

4.3.1 *FlexRAN Agent*

In this subsection, we elaborate on the different subcomponents of the FlexRAN Agent architecture shown in Fig. 2.

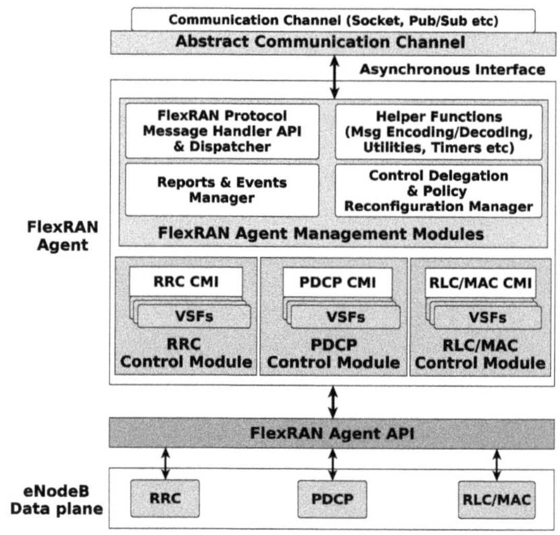

Figure 2: The architecture of a FlexRAN Agent.

Virtualized Control Functions. To allow flexible and programmable control of the RAN infrastructure, the FlexRAN Agent provides a number of eNodeB *Control Modules* as illustrated in Fig. 2. These modules reflect a logical separation of the control operations that an eNodeB in the standard LTE architecture has to perform on the radio side and can be seen as a set of individual control subsystems, each targeting a specific area of control. Since the LTE standard (the technology supported by our current implementation) already provides a precise definition and scope for such control operations through the Access Stratum protocols (RRC, MAC/RLC, PDCP), FlexRAN adopts the same structure for the agent's control modules, with each module providing functionality according to the scope of its corresponding LTE protocol (e.g., MAC/RLC control module for scheduling, RRC control module for the radio resource control).

Each control module is in turn composed of a well-defined set of functions called *Virtual Subsystem Functions (VSFs)*. The VSFs implement the action that needs to be taken by the agent during a corresponding operation. As an example, consider the MAC control module which is broadly responsible for various scheduling operations of the eNodeB. For each of the scheduling operations (e.g., UE specific downlink and uplink scheduling, broadcast scheduling), FlexRAN defines a VSF that designates how the agent should behave for the corresponding operation. For instance, the UE specific downlink scheduling VSF could designate that the agent should forward the scheduling decision sent by the master controller to the data plane or that the agent should make its own decision based on a higher-level policy defined by the master.

The number and type of VSFs that each control module supports is defined through a well-defined *Control Module Interface (CMI)*, which essentially allows the agent to abstract the set of operations of each control module from their corresponding implementations. In this way, the agent reacts to a specific event (e.g., time for downlink scheduling) without having to worry about the underlying implementation of the operation. Through this design decision, the FlexRAN agent becomes very flexible, programmable and extensible since new operations can be introduced simply by extending the CMI, while at the same time the functionality of these operations can easily be redefined in a technology-agnostic manner via the abstract FlexRAN Agent API. As already discussed, a message handler and dispatcher entity residing at the agent side (see Fig. 2) is responsible to receive FlexRAN protocol messages from the FlexRAN master controller and forward them to be handled by the appropriate VSF of the corresponding control module using the FlexRAN Agent API.

Control Delegation. FlexRAN allows the master controller to assume control of the underlying infrastructure and orchestrate its operation by making and pushing control decisions at a very fine time granularity (per subframe). While this is a feature that is essential when considering centralized time-critical applications (e.g., coordinated remote scheduling of eNodeBs), such fine grained control is not always desirable nor even possible. For example, FlexRAN enabled small cells may not all be connected to the master via a high-speed backhaul (e.g., optical fiber link), making the exchange of all the required FlexRAN protocol messages (MAC statistics, scheduling decisions, event notifications, etc.) at a subframe granularity a very challenging task. In such cases, it is preferable to let the individual agents make time-critical decisions as per the policy specified by the master.

A naive way to achieve this would be to identify a set of hardcoded policies at the agent for each delegated operation. For example, the agent might offer a local scheduler with two policies (round-robin and proportional fair) to choose from. If the master chooses to delegate scheduling to an agent due to an unsuitable master-agent communication channel (e.g., high latency), it would have to choose among the available hardcoded policies. However, such a mechanism can be very limiting since it does not allow the modification of the agent's behavior at runtime nor its extension with new functionality in the future. FlexRAN avoids this via two complementary mechanisms: **VSF updation** and **policy reconfiguration**.

VSF updation This mechanism exploits the control function virtualization feature described above and allows the master to modify the behavior of the VSFs of a control module on-the-fly by "pushing" new code to the agent over the FlexRAN protocol. This code is actually a callback assigned to one of the CMI function calls that corresponds to a specific control module - VSF pair. The callback function is able to access and modify the underlying eNodeB data plane using the FlexRAN agent API discussed in Section 4.2. A VSF update FlexRAN protocol message designates the name of the control module and the VSF that the new code is intended for and contains the actual code in the form of a shared library that has been compiled against the agent architecture. The pushed code is initially stored in a cache memory at the agent-side until the master decides to modify the behavior of the corresponding VSF. The agent cache can store many different implementations for a specific VSF, which the master can swap at runtime. As an example, considering the case of the downlink UE scheduling VSF, the master could push two schedulers to the agent, a local proportional fair scheduler and a stub for a centralized remote scheduler, which it could switch at runtime (e.g., based on the network conditions).

Policy reconfiguration This mechanism is complementary to VSF updation since it allows the master to swap the agents' VSFs and reconfigure their parameters at runtime. A policy reconfiguration FlexRAN protocol message indicates the VSFs to be modified using YAML syntax (Fig. 3). At the top level, the control module name is indicated, followed by a sequence of VSFs to be modified, each composed of two (optional) sections; *behavior* and *parameters*. The *behavior* section is used for swapping VSFs, i.e., it is an instruction to the agent to link a specific CMI function call to one of the callbacks stored at its cache through the VSF updation mechanism. The *parameters* section indicates a list of parameters that can be modified for the specific VSF. These parameters act as a public API that the controller can modify and can either refer to a single value or a sequence of values (e.g., an array). The available parameters depend on the VSF implementation (e.g., two scheduler implementations could have different sets of parameters based on their functionality).

```
<Control Module Name>:
  - <VSF Name1>:
        behavior: <callback name>
        parameters:
            parameter<i>: val
  - <VSF Name2>:
        behavior: <callback name>
        parameters:
            parameter<j>: [val1, val2, val3]
```

Figure 3: Structure of a policy reconfiguration message.

The control delegation capabilities through the virtualization of control functions offered by FlexRAN follow the NFV principles and indeed bring runtime service function chaining capabilities to the RAN by adding a virtualization layer over the RAN infrastructure and allowing the flexible placement of RAN control functions closer or further away from the base station based on the networking conditions, the available computing resources and the requirements of the operator in terms of performance. However, it should be noted that such capabilities relevant to the RAN are yet to be considered by NFV standards specifications, like that of ETSI NFV.

An important issue when considering control delegation via the above mechanisms is concerned with the security implications that might arise from pushing new VSFs to the agent which modify the behavior of the eNodeB. One way to deal with this is to force the agent to accept only code that is signed from a trusted authority, similarly to how third-party device drivers for an operating system need to be verified before installation. Since FlexRAN targets a critical part of the mobile infrastructure, getting certification from trusted authorities is expected to become a common practice for developers of VSFs; one could also envision an online VSF store similar to mobile app stores. Another measure to limit the effects of unwanted behavior from the VSFs is to allow the control modules of the agent to run in a sandboxed mode, where each VSF will need to ask for permissions to use the various parts of the FlexRAN agent API, similarly to how Android apps request the permission of the user to access different services of their device. In this way, the network operator could quickly identify VSFs that present an unexpected behavior.

eNodeB Report and Event Management. One of the responsibilities of the FlexRAN agent is to provide statistics reports and event notifications to the master for the various control modules (e.g., transmission queue sizes and random access attempts for the MAC module, radio bearer statistics and reference signal received power measurements for the RRC module). The master can use the FlexRAN protocol to make asynchronous requests for such reports and notifications and the FlexRAN agent is responsible to register these requests and to notify the master through the Reports & Events Manager (illustrated in Fig. 2) once the results are available.

FlexRAN supports three types of reports: *one-off*, *periodic* and *triggered*. A *one-off* report is sent by the agent to the master only once as a reply to its initial request, while a *periodic* report is sent at fixed intervals that are designated in the initial request sent by the master, using the TTI as a time reference for the length of the interval. A *triggered* report is sent by the agent aperiodically and only when there is a change in the contents of the requested report. Similarly, the master can choose whether or not to be notified for a specific event occurring at the eNodeB by registering for it at the agent using the FlexRAN protocol. These statistics reports offer high level of flexibility in tuning the level of interaction between the agents and the master, thereby the degree of coordination. For example, triggered reports of MAC statistics is required for a remote scheduler deployed at the master. However, if the scheduling application of the controller is intended to be used as a non-real time application at a more coarse-grained timescale as a hypervisor of a local agent-side scheduler, the master can only request periodic or even one-off reports.

Extending OpenAirInterface with FlexRAN. We implement the FlexRAN platform over OpenAirInterface (OAI) [31]. OAI to our knowledge is the most complete open-source LTE software implementation. As such, it provides the right base to realize FlexRAN. Recall that the focus of FlexRAN is to achieve software based control of a mobile RAN that is totally decoupled from the data plane. Since we use LTE as the concrete setting for our implementation, it essentially involves using the implementation of FlexRAN as the LTE RAN control plane over the data plane implementation that is retained from the base OAI. To achieve this, we had to bypass the control plane of OAI, which does not clearly separate control and data planes, and then interface it with FlexRAN via the newly defined FlexRAN Agent API. This clean separation offered by FlexRAN simplifies the development of control applications, which now appear as modules completely separated from the data plane (based on OAI in the current implementation); this is not possible with the standard LTE RAN and therefore even with vanilla OAI. Although in our implementation the FlexRAN Agent resides over OAI eNodeB data plane, it is important to note that FlexRAN as a whole (including the FlexRAN Agent) is a separate entity allowing the agent to be realized even on a physically different machine.

All the FlexRAN Agent Management Modules (Fig. 2) and the FlexRAN Agent API were implemented from scratch, creating a basic agent stub that could be enriched with functionality through the implementation of the FlexRAN Control Modules identified earlier in this section. For our prototype the focus was on the RLC/MAC control module, due to the significant challenges that it presents in terms of its stringent time constraints. For this module, the proper CMI was identified and the corresponding scheduling VSFs were implemented. Even though the functionality related to these VSFs was already present in OAI, the involved control and data plane operations were tightly coupled, which was counter to the intention behind FlexRAN. To overcome this, the OAI eNodeB source code was refactored to allow the separation of the eNodeB data plane from the control logic as per the design of FlexRAN and all the required function calls were added to the FlexRAN Agent API to support this separation. For example, function calls were added to the API to obtain data plane MAC/RLC related information like transmission queue sizes of UEs, along with calls for applying scheduling decisions. To better highlight the effort required for this prototype implementation, more than 10000 lines of code were written for the agent management modules and Agent API and more than 6000 lines of original OAI code were refactored to support the control and data plane separation.

The FlexRAN agent API, as well as the CMIs are written in C, while the whole eNodeB/agent implementation currently supports x64 and ARM Linux systems. As a consequence, any VSF written for an OAI FlexRAN agent currently needs to be implemented in C and compiled against this architecture. The agent is multi-threaded with one thread responsible for the management of reports and events, one for dispatching the incoming protocol messages to the control modules and calling the corresponding VSFs, and two for the asynchronous network communication with the master controller.

4.3.2 FlexRAN Protocol

The abstract communication channel is another feature of

the FlexRAN agent (Fig. 2) for the interactions of the agent with the master. The main FlexRAN agent components communicate and exchange protocol messages with the master through an asynchronous interface that abstracts the communication operations. The communication channel implementation can vary (socket-based, pub/sub etc) depending on the master that the agent is interfacing with. It should be noted that the interface between the master and the agent needs to be asynchronous as the agent may need to perform certain operations in specific time intervals (e.g., a scheduling decision per TTI) while protocol messages from the master can arrive in asynchronously (e.g., receiving a request for a measurement report). In the current implementation, TCP is used for the communication of the agents with the master and the exchange of protocol messages. The protocol messages are implemented using Google Protocol Buffers [1], which provides an optimized platform-neutral serialization mechanism and allows the expression of protocol messages in a language-agnostic manner. Detailed specification of the protocol messages are omitted due to space constraints.

4.3.3 FlexRAN Master Controller

The master controller (Fig. 4) constitutes the brain of the FlexRAN control plane as it manages the operation of the FlexRAN agents. In FlexRAN, we employ a custom design for the master instead of using a conventional OpenFlow-based one and this is for two reasons: (1) the nature of control in the RAN is tied to a significant extent to the control of radio resources which cannot be effectively captured by the flow abstraction; (2) the RAN presents a requirement for the support of real-time applications with very quick reaction times, a feature not essential for SDN control in the wired domain.

Management of network information. The RAN Information Base (RIB) is a key component that maintains all the statistics and configuration related information about the underlying network entities, i.e. UEs, eNodeBs and FlexRAN agents. The RIB is always loaded in memory for improved performance and is structured as a forest graph. The root node of each tree in this forest is an agent associated with the master, while the nodes of the second level are the cells associated with a specific agent/eNodeB. Finally, the leaves of the trees are the UEs associated to a specific (primary) cell. It should be noted that the current implementation of the RIB does not provide any high-level abstraction for the stored information, revealing raw data to the northbound API.

Support for real-time applications. The applications as well as the Events Notification Service of the master consult the RIB to perform any operation, but they do not modify the RIB directly. Instead they issue control commands through the northbound interface, which indirectly affect the RIB state through the modifications performed to the eNodeB data plane and the agent state. These modifications are reflected back to the master through the statistics reports and event notifications sent by the agents. Only the RIB Updater component of the master can update the RIB with the information received from the agents (Fig. 5). This design decision improves the support of real-time applications (e.g., MAC scheduler) that must be non-blocking in order to meet their time constraints (e.g., a TTI for the scheduler). Allowing all components to modify the RIB could give rise to write conflicts, negatively affecting the system performance. Having just a single writer (the RIB Updater) and multiple readers helps avoid this problem. The update frequency of the RIB depends on the way the FlexRAN agent reporting and event notification mechanism is configured by the master.

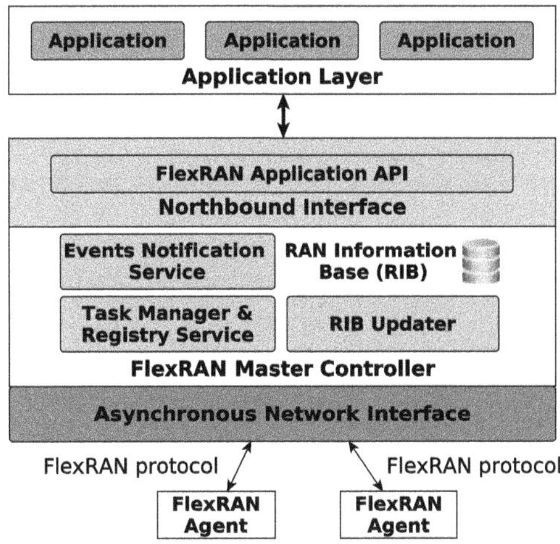

Figure 4: Components of the FlexRAN master controller and its interface to the application layer.

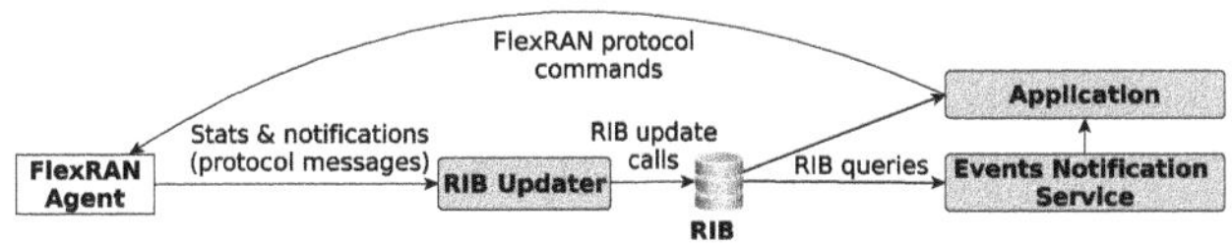

Figure 5: Flow of information for updating the RIB.

Since the FlexRAN controller is designed to support real-time RAN applications, a Task Manager is responsible for handling all the tasks (both applications and core management modules) running on the master. More specifically, it is responsible to start, stop and pause applications; to assign priorities to running services and to allow them to execute based on their time constraints. For example, the Task Manager would assign a very high priority to a centralized MAC scheduler running on the master, whereas a non time-critical monitoring application would get a lower priority. To support real-time control, the Task Manager is implemented as a non-preemptive thread running in an infinite loop and operating in cycles of length equal to a TTI, where each cycle is composed of two slots — one for the execution of the RIB Updater (e.g., 20% of the TTI) and the other for the execution of the applications as well as the Event Notification Service threads (e.g., 80% of the TTI). This guarantees the mutual exclusion of the reads and writes in the RIB and allows the applications to operate in a non-blocking mode while accessing the RIB, ensuring the real-time operation of the controller.

Master controller implementation. The master controller is implemented from scratch using C++ and currently supports x64 Linux systems (kernel >= 3.14 for support of real-time applications). The master can operate in a non real-time mode, supporting only applications that are not time-critical, with the advantage of being more lightweight. The Task Manager in the non-real time mode does not enforce a strict duration of the cycle as tasks are not scheduled with a real-time priority and thus could take longer than a TTI.

4.4 Northbound API and Applications

RAN control and management applications in the application layer communicate with the master through the northbound interface (Fig. 4), which allows the applications to monitor the infrastructure through the information obtained from the RIB and apply their control decisions through the agent control modules. The applications run as threads and use the FlexRAN Application API (currently in C++) to register with the Registry Service of the master, access the RIB and send control messages to the agents. Applications can be broadly divided into two categories: (*periodic* or *event-based*). Periodic applications employ a periodic execution pattern (e.g,, a periodic scheduler) whereas the execution of event-based applications is triggered by specific events (e.g., a mobility manager that expects changes in the received signal strength of a UE to react). The Events Notifications Service of the master controller notifies the applications (mainly of the event-based type) about any changes that might have occurred on the agent side. Some applications could fall into both categories and it is ultimately the application developer who would choose the appropriate execution pattern.

5. SYSTEM EVALUATION

In this section we evaluate the engineering decisions and the design choices behind FlexRAN. For the experiments, a FlexRAN master controller was deployed, in which one or more agent-enabled eNodeBs (depending on the experiment) were connected through dedicated Gigabit Ethernet connections. Each eNodeB was also connected to a machine acting as the EPC, running the corresponding EPC software implementation (openair-cn [2]). All the test machines were equipped with quad-core Xeon CPUs at 3.4GHz and 16GB of RAM. Depending on the experiment, the testbed was used either in emulation mode (emulated PHY layer and emulated UEs) or with a real RF front-end (Ettus B210 USRP) and a COTS UE (Nexus 5 smartphone). All the experiments were conducted with the same eNodeB configuration, namely FDD with transmission mode 1 and 10MHz bandwidth in band 5.

5.1 Comparison to Vanilla OAI

We begin by investigating the overhead introduced to an eNodeB by the addition of the FlexRAN agent in terms of memory and CPU utilization (Fig. 6a) comparing a vanilla OAI eNodeB and a FlexRAN-capable eNodeB in two cases; one with the system in idle state and one with a COTS UE connected and performing a speedtest. As we can observe, there is a very slight increase in the memory footprint and the CPU utilization in the FlexRAN case, due to the threads used for the operation of the agent and the protocol messages exchanged with the FlexRAN master controller. Despite the aforementioned overhead incurred from the FlexRAN agent, the communication of the eNodeB with the UE is fully transparent, with the UE experiencing the same service quality in its connection as with the vanilla OAI (Fig. 6b).

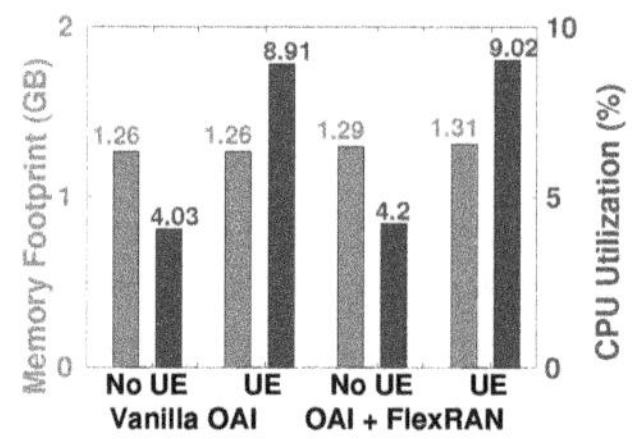

(a) Normalized CPU utilization (8-processors) and memory footprint with(out) UE

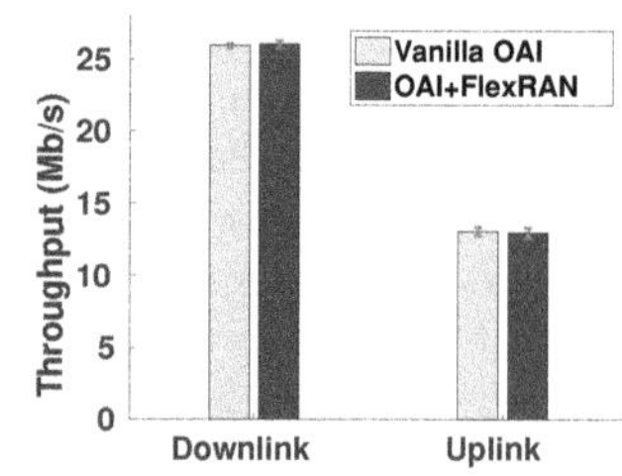

(b) Downlink and Uplink throughput comparison

Figure 6: Comparison of Vanilla OAI to FlexRAN .

5.2 Scalability

Next, we evaluate how FlexRAN scales as the number of eNodeBs and UEs increases. For these experiments we used OAI in emulation mode with the PHY layer abstracted in order to perform tests with a large number of UEs. It is noted that this choice has a minimum effect in the obtained results, since the focus of our evaluation was in operations occurring above the PHY which were unaffected by the emulation.

5.2.1 Controller-agent signaling overhead

One very important element regarding the scalability of FlexRAN is the network overhead incurred by the FlexRAN protocol, especially when support for real-time applications is required. For this, we measured the signaling overhead between the agent and the master in the demanding case of deploying a centralized scheduling application and for a varying number of UEs. To study the system's scalability, we tested a scenario with the worst case configuration signaling-wise, where statistics reports were sent from the agent to the master every TTI, the centralized scheduler undertook all scheduling decisions at a TTI granularity and the master was fully synchronized with the agent at a TTI level using the appropriate FlexRAN protocol synchronization messages. During the experiment uniform downlink UDP traffic was generated for all the UEs, in order to force the centralized scheduler to frequently send scheduling decisions to the agent.

The agent-to-master network overhead for 50 UEs can reach 100 Mb/s (Fig. 7a). The main source of this overhead are the periodic statistics reports (buffer status reports, CQI measurements etc.) followed by the master-agent synchronization messages, with the overhead of the agent management related messages being negligible. One important thing to notice is that the agent-to-master signaling overhead increases sublinearly with the number of connected UEs due to the aggregation of relevant information in the FlexRAN protocol messages (e.g. list of UE status reports) and their optimized serialization by the Google Protocol Buffers library.

In the case of the master-to-agent signaling (Fig. 7b), the overhead is much lower compared to the previous case (less than 4Mb/s) and comes almost entirely from the scheduling

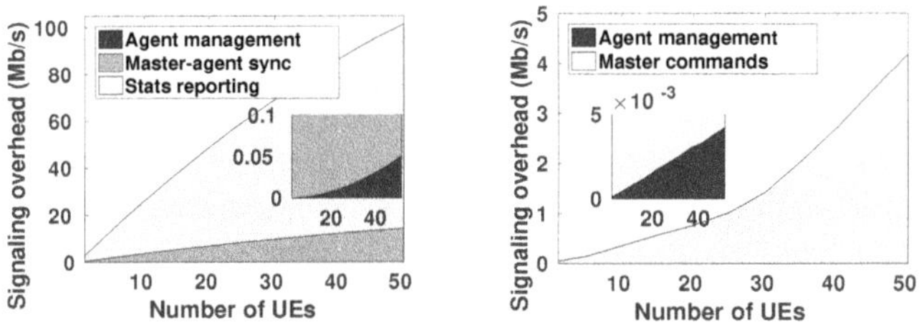

(a) Agent-to-master (b) Master-to-agent

Figure 7: Signaling overhead for the communication between the master and the agent using the FlexRAN protocol.

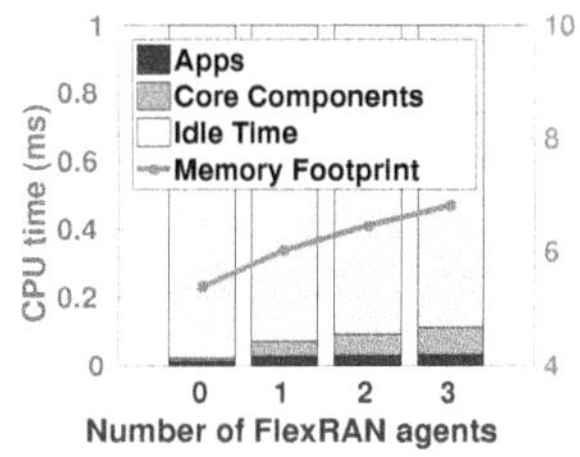

Figure 8: Utilization of master TTI cycle and memory footprint (16 UEs/eNodeB).

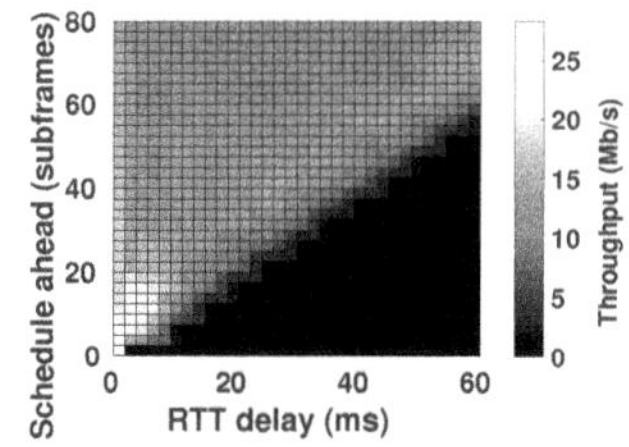

Figure 9: Effect of latency and scheduling ahead time on downlink throughput.

decisions sent by the centralized scheduler. In contrast to the previous case, this overhead is increasing with a higher rate as the number of UEs goes up. The reason is that the larger the number of UEs, the less resources are available for scheduling each UE and therefore more TTIs will be required for scheduling, leading to an increase in the overall number of scheduling decisions sent by the controller to the agent.

The aforementioned results show that FlexRAN is suitable even in demanding scenarios like multi-cell scheduling on a per-TTI basis, where depending on the deployment (macro or small-cell) the agent can be connected to the master either through a dedicated high-bandwidth channel (e.g. optical fibers) or through a lower bandwidth channel (e.g. a VDSL connection). In practice, the controller will apply policies or delegate the scheduling to the agent, which will significantly reduce the network overhead. This overhead could be further reduced through agent configuration changes. For example, by setting the periodicity of the MAC reports to 2 TTIs, this overhead could be reduced to almost half without any significant impact in the system's performance. Other methods that could be considered to reduce this overhead could be compression algorithms for the protocol messages or event-triggered instead of periodic message transmissions.

5.2.2 *Master controller resources*

Using the previous setup, we measured (Fig. 8) the requirements of the master in computing resources and memory for a varying number of connected agents (16 UEs/eNodeB). As already discussed, the master operates in TTI cycles, where part of each cycle is allocated to the execution of applications (80% in this experiment) and the rest to the execution of the core components of the master. As we can observe, the operation of the master is lightweight, with only a small fraction of the total cycle being actually utilized. The execution time of the core components increases as we add more agents, mainly due to the increase in the updates that need to be performed by the RIB updater. The memory footprint of the master is also very small and its increase is mainly related to the increase of the RIB size.

5.3 Control channel latency impact

One very important aspect for real-time control in FlexRAN is the impact of the control channel latency between the master and the agent. To test its effect we used a COTS UE scheduled in the downlink by a centralized scheduling application running at the master. The scheduler was implemented so that it could be parametrized to make scheduling decisions n subframes ahead of time, meaning that the scheduler would observe the MAC state (transmission queue sizes of UEs, signal quality etc) at subframe x and would issue a scheduling decision that should be applied by the data plane in subframe $x + n$. The scheduling decision will be valid and can be applied by the agent only if its designated time is greater than the latency in the master-agent control channel.

Based on this setup we modified the schedule ahead parameter of the application and the latency in the control channel using the *netem* tool [3] and measured the UE downlink throughput for various configurations (Fig. 9). As we can observe, the lower triangular region of the figure depicts a throughput of 0, indicating that for these configurations the UE was unable to complete network attachment. This is due to the one-way delay of the control channel being greater than the schedule ahead time, meaning that scheduling decisions always miss their deadline. Moreover, the control channel delay affects the synchronization between the master and the agent, since the agent subframe reported to the master is always outdated by an offset equal to half the RTT delay. Since the scheduler relies to this outdated value to make a scheduling decision, the scheduling ahead time should take it into account. Assuming a symmetrical RTT delay, the schedule ahead time should be set to a value that is at least equal to it; half to make up for the outdated subframe value reported by the agent and half to ensure that the scheduling decision will be valid at the time it arrives to the agent.

In the upper triangular region we have all the cases in which the controller application successfully manages to schedule the UE. In this case the application is able to schedule the UE even for a control channel with a very high latency, as long as the schedule ahead parameter is configured properly. As the RTT delay and the schedule ahead time increases, the throughput gradually drops. One reason for this is that higher RTT delays make the information stored in the RIB (e.g. CQI measurements) more outdated, leading to wrong scheduling decisions (e.g. due to a bad modulation and coding scheme choice) that could affect the throughput. Moreover, for increased values of the schedule ahead parameter, the scheduler needs to make predictions further into the future, while making assumptions about the outcome of previous transmissions for which it has not yet received any feedback. Depending on the use case and on the scheduling performance requirements, one could choose to either use approximation methods like scheduling ahead of time to mitigate the effect of latency or to delegate control to the agents for the time critical functions that are affected by this latency as long as coordinated operation among the eNodeBs is not a hard constraint.

5.4 Control delegation performance

Since control delegation is one of the most important features of FlexRAN we evaluated the mechanisms of VSF updation and policy reconfiguration in terms of efficiency and service continuity. For this experiment we used the same setup as in Section 5.3, starting with a centralized scheduler running as an application at the master. At the same time, we built an equivalent (in terms of functionality) local scheduler, as a VSF for the MAC control module of the agent, using the FlexRAN agent API. The experimental scenario involved the pushing of this code to the agent using the FlexRAN protocol and the dynamic switching between the local and the remote scheduler through the policy reconfiguration mechanism.

Using this setup, we tested the downlink throughput of the attached UE, while swapping the local and the remote schedulers with various frequencies down to the TTI level (1ms), and observed the same application performance of 25 Mb/s (figure not included for brevity). The code is pushed to the agent-side only once and is stored in its local cache meaning that no additional overhead is incurred for the control delegation. Moreover, the absolute VSF load time required to swap between the local and remote scheduler is very small (~103ns) and therefore does not disrupt service continuity as it only forms an insignificant fraction of the overall TTI.

6. FlexRAN USE CASES

Till date, the lack of an implemented SD-RAN platform meant that there was no way to actually study SD-RAN benefits and use cases. To demonstrate the usefulness of FlexRAN towards this end, we now present diverse use cases that SD-RANs in general and FlexRAN in particular can enable.

6.1 Interference Management

One of the ways to cope with the requirement for higher throughput in the RAN is the creation of Heterogeneous Networks (HetNets) composed of multiple small cells within the area of a macro cell. However, such dense network deployments are more susceptible to interference. One proposed solution is the enhanced Inter-Cell Interference Coordination (eICIC) [21] that introduces the concept of Almost-Blank Subframes (ABS) during which the macro cells are muted to allow small-cells to transmit user traffic. Even though eICIC is one effective way to manage interference, the semi-static configuration of ABSs can lead to an underutilization of the radio resources when small cells are idle. To remedy this, we consider an optimized eICIC mechanism that allows the macro-cell to exploit periods of inactivity of the small-cells to transmit to UEs even during ABSs as long as no small-cell is transmitting at the same time. Such a mechanism requires a high-level of coordination among cells which cannot be easily achieved using the traditional X2 interface [18] [11]. To deal with this, we build a downlink UE scheduling application over FlexRAN that exploits its consolidated control plane to implement this optimized eICIC mechanism.

Specifically, we implemented a centralized scheduler application on top of the master and two different types of local agent-side downlink schedulers, one for the macro-cell and one for the small-cells of a region. During a non-ABS, the macro-cell eNodeB performs the scheduling using its agent-side scheduler, while the agent-side schedulers of the small-cells remain inactive exactly as in a normal eICIC case. However, during an ABS the centralized scheduler at the master performs a coordinated UE scheduling of all cells and decides whether the macro or the small cells should be scheduled, always giving priority to the small-cells. The scheduling decisions are then pushed to the agents using the FlexRAN protocol and are applied by the agent-side schedulers that during an ABS act as stubs of the centralized scheduler.

Two agent-enabled OAI eNodeBs were used, one acting as a macro-cell and one as the small-cell, both running in emulation mode over the same physical machine. The reason we resorted to emulation over the same machine is that eICIC requires a microsecond-level synchronization of eNodeBs, which was not supported by our hardware. Moreover, due to a limitation of the current OAI implementation, the association of UEs over different eNodeBs is not supported in emulation mode when the PHY is abstracted. This forced us to use the more computationally intensive full-PHY emulation mode of OAI (that involves convolution of the real PHY signal with an emulated-channel in real time) and to limit the number of emulated UEs used for this experiment to 4.

One UE was associated with the small-cell and three were associated with the macro-cell. Downlink UDP traffic was generated uniformly for all the UEs and the overall network throughput was measured (Fig. 10a) in three cases: (i) an uncoordinated case, where each eNodeB performed scheduling independently, (ii) a simple eICIC use case with 4 ABSs and (iii) the optimized eICIC use case with the same ABS configuration as case (ii). The optimized eICIC use case almost doubled the overall network throughput over the uncoordinated scenario and had an improvement of about 22% over the simple eICIC scenario. The reason for the difference between the two eICIC use cases is that while the small-cell throughput remains the same (Fig. 10b), the throughput of the macro-cell increases under optimized eICIC because the ABSs not used by the small-cell are assigned by the centralized scheduling application to the macro-cell.

6.2 Mobile Edge Computing

For our second use case, we consider FlexRAN as a deployment platform for Mobile Edge Computing (MEC) applications. MEC allows developers and content providers to deploy their services over the network edge. This presents many benefits including ultra-low latency, high bandwidth and real-time access to radio network information which can be used by applications for optimization purposes [23]. Such applications are expected to be deployed in a centralized manner and therefore doing this using the conventional LTE architecture becomes a challenging task. Moreover, their de-

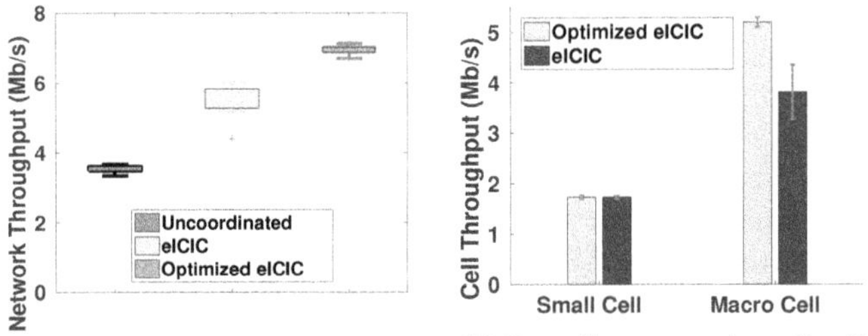

(a) Downlink network throughput in uncoordinated, simple and optimized eICIC.

(b) Overall macro and small cell downlink throughput for simple and optimized eICIC.

Figure 10: Throughput benefits of optimized eICIC.

ployment assumes the existence of a programmable network, which is naturally enabled by FlexRAN.

In this context, we show how the consolidated control plane and the real-time network information provided by FlexRAN can be beneficial for services such as video streaming. To show this, we used the DASH [34] streaming service and studied the effects of fluctuating a mobile's signal strength to the video streaming bitrate adaptation performed by the DASH reference client [4]. The idea of the experiment is that the channel quality reported by the UEs to the eNodeB through a Channel Quality Indicator (CQI) value (in the range [0,15]) indicates the modulation and coding scheme that the scheduler should use for the data transmissions of a UE and therefore has a direct impact in its highest achievable throughput. Knowing this can allow the streaming service to make smarter decisions regarding the optimal bitrate compared to a case when only transport layer information is available.

In order to obtain reproducible results, we emulated the fluctuations of the channel quality between the eNodeB and the UE and measured the maximum achievable TCP throughput of a COTS UE for various fixed CQI values. Moreover, for the same CQI values, we used the reference DASH client and the available test videos that it offered, to measure the maximum sustainable bitrate of a video stream (i.e. a bitrate that would never lead to buffer freezes) for the offered bitrate levels. The measurement results (Table 2) indicate that the TCP throughput needs to be greater (even double) than the video bitrate in order to always maintain a high quality; this is consistent with related observations in the literature [37].

CQI	TCP Throughput (Mb/s)	Max sustainable bitrate (Mb/s)
2	1.63	1.4
3	2.2	2
4	3.3	2.9
10	15	7.3

Table 2: Measurements of max TCP throughput and max sustainable bitrate of video stream for various CQI levels.

We used FlexRAN to implement a simple MEC application that uses the RIB to obtain real-time information about the CQI values of the attached UEs. The application computes an exponential moving average of the UE CQI and maps it to the optimal video bitrate based on the measurements of Table 2. The bitrate is then forwarded through an out-of-band channel to a modified version of the DASH reference client where it is used to adapt the video stream's quality. To simplify things, we performed the experiment in an ideal setting, where the channel quality fluctuation was the only cause for a change in the bitrate (a single UE attached to the network with the DASH video being the only source of traffic).

For our experiment, we considered two cases. In the first, we used a video [5] with three bitrates (1.2, 2 and 4 Mbps) and we introduced a small variation in the CQI value (from 3 to 2 and vice versa). In the second, we used a 4K video [6] with six available bitrates (2.9, 4.9, 7.3, 9.6, 14.6 and 19.6 Mbps) in which the CQI value was changed drastically (from 10 to 4 and vice versa). In both cases, we measured the bitrate selected by the default and the FlexRAN-assisted players in comparison to the maximum achievable TCP throughput, as well as their buffer sizes (Fig. 11). In the first case (Fig. 11a), the default player always kept the bitrate at the lowest value (1.2 Mb/s), even in times when the available throughput increased by 40%, meaning that the change in channel quality did not become apparent to the transport layer. On the other hand, the FlexRAN-assisted player exploited the information obtained by the RAN and managed to better adapt to the changing network conditions. Therefore, even though neither player experienced buffer freezes, the default player underutilized the available resources. In the second case (Fig. 11b), the default player aggressively attempts to increase the bitrate when the CQI increases, setting it to 19.6 Mb/s, even though the maximum achievable throughput is 15 Mb/s. This quickly results in TCP congestion, leading the player to significantly lower the bitrate (lower than the max sustainable bitrate) in order to adapt. At the same time this leads to frequent and sometimes long buffer freezes (e.g. sec 5-30). On the other hand, the MEC application running over FlexRAN can quickly identify the maximum sustainable bitrate (7.3 Mb/s) given the CQI measurements observed at the RIB and does not follow the same aggressive behavior as the default player, leading to a more stable and overall higher video quality.

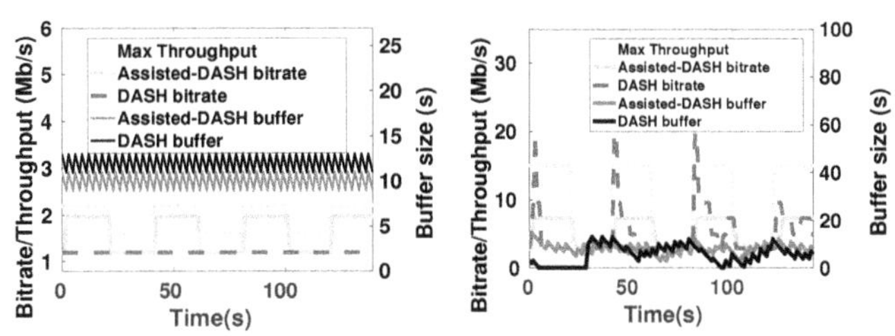

(a) Low throughput variability

(b) High throughput variability

Figure 11: Rate adaptation of DASH vs FlexRAN assisted DASH and corresponding buffer sizes.

6.3 RAN Sharing & Virtualization

A side effect from the densification of cells is the increase of the infrastructural CAPEX and OPEX. This leads to the creation of new business models, where multiple Mobile Network Operators (MNOs) share the same *passive* infrastructure such as masts and backhaul links in order to save costs. On top of that, a second level of *active* sharing can happen, where MNOs share the network equipment as well as provide wholesale access to Mobile Virtual Network Operators (MVNOs), allowing them to provide voice and data services using part of the available resources [19]. However, this can pose a significant challenge for the management of the RAN, since the requirements of operators in terms of the radio resources and the applied policies of scheduling and mobility management can constantly change based on the needs of their subscribers and the underlying setting. The control and management of such operations can be greatly simplified through the introduction of programmability in the RAN.

Based on this, we used FlexRAN as an enabler of active RAN sharing and on-demand resource allocation over an LTE network. More specifically, exploiting the virtualization capabilities of FlexRAN , we implemented a downlink UE scheduler for the agent-side that supports the dynamic introduction of new MVNOs to the RAN and the on-demand modification of the scheduling policy per operator. An application running at the master exploits the policy reconfiguration mechanism of FlexRAN to modify the parameters of the agent-side scheduler (scheduling policy and number of resource blocks per MVNO). To test this and in order to be able to support a large number of UEs, we used a single agent-enabled OAI eNodeB in emulation mode with the PHY abstraction enabled. We configured the agent-based scheduler to support one MVNO that shared the available resources with the RAN's MNO.

For our first experiment, each operator was assigned 5 UEs for which uniform UDP downlink traffic was generated, while the percentage of radio resource blocks allocated to each operator was dynamically adjusted based on their requirements. The results in terms of the total throughput per operator are illustrated in Fig. 12a. Initially, the MNO was allocated 70% of the radio resources and the MVNO was allocated the remaining 30%. At 10s, the master controller application sent a policy reconfiguration message, setting the available resources of the MNO to 40% and of the MVNO to 60%, simulating a brief requirement for additional resources for the MVNO. Then, at 140s, the application sent a second policy reconfiguration message that re-adjusted the radio resources so that 80% were allocated to the MNO.

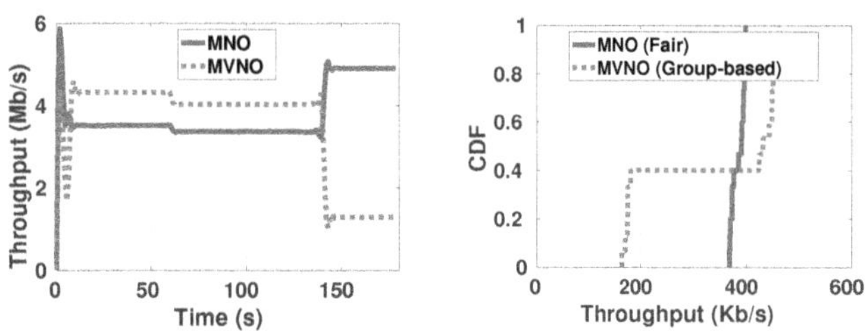

(a) Dynamic allocation of resources

(b) CDF of UE throughput based on scheduling type

Figure 12: Policy reconfiguration for MVNO management

As a second experiment, we implemented an agent-side scheduler supporting a fair scheduling policy and a group-based policy of premium and secondary users, with 70% of the resources allocated to the premium users and the rest to the secondary. One MNO and one MVNO was employed, where the MNO was assigned the fair policy and the MVNO the group-based one. Each operator was allocated half of the available radio resources and was assigned 15 UEs. In he group-based MVNO case, nine UEs belonged to the premium group and the remaining six acted as secondary users. We generated uniform UDP downlink traffic for all the UEs and measured the throughput of each UE per operator. The results are illustrated in the CDFs of Fig. 12b. In the case of the MNO, all the UEs had a throughput of about 380Kb/s due to their fair scheduling policy. On the other hand, in the case of the MVNO, UEs assigned to the premium group had a throughout of about 450Kb/s, while the UEs of the secondary group achieved a throughput of less than 200Kb/s.

7. DISCUSSION

7.1 Other Example Use Cases

Here we make a brief discussion on a non-exhaustive list of further use cases that were currently not implementable due to the limitations posed either by the OAI platform underlying FlexRAN or by the current LTE specifications.

Mobility Management. In current practice, handover decisions mainly rely on the signal strength of mobile devices. However, the centralized network view offered by FlexRAN could enable more sophisticated mobility management mechanisms that consider additional factors, e.g., the load of cells or use-driven resource requirements of mobile devices, leading to an optimization of the device-network associations.

Network Slicing. Future 5G networks are envisioned to support a wide range of vertical segments with a diverse set of performance and service requirements through the Slicing of the physical network into multiple isolated logical networks [30] [7]. Among the key features required to achieve network slicing is the existence of an end-to-end management and orchestration framework (e.g. [35]) and the means to virtualize the network resources. FlexRAN can be seen as a key enabler of virtualization in the RAN, providing a simple and flexible platform for the dynamic control and allocation of radio resources based on the needs of the deployed services.

Device Centric Networking. Another interesting application of FlexRAN could be in the domain of device-centric networking [16]. In this, the association of mobile devices is decoupled from the cell, e.g. by using different cells for control and data traffic, simplifying the adoption of new communication paradigms like D2D. While realizing such a paradigm would also require changes in the physical layer, its deployment could greatly be simplified through the centralized control of FlexRAN, as it inherently involves the coordinated control of multiple network nodes, e.g. control traffic through one cell and data traffic through another.

Spectrum Sharing. Shared spectrum access is seen as a promising solution that allows operators to cope with the high increase of mobile data traffic. One spectrum sharing mechanism that is of particular interest to MNOs is Licensed Shared Access (LSA) [26]. It enables incumbents not concerned with civilian wireless and mobile data communications to authorize other users (e.g. the MNOs) to access all or part of the spectrum allocated to them for designated periods of time and in designated places based on some agreement. An LSA controller dynamically manages the access to the shared spectrum based on these agreements. Such an operation could easily be implemented as an application on top of FlexRAN.

7.2 Adaptability Beyond LTE

As already discussed in Section 3, FlexRAN was presented in the context of LTE for concreteness and to match its current implementation. However, the design and the mechanisms supported by FlexRAN are not LTE-specific and are therefore equally suitable for future mobile RAN architectures. More specifically, the mechanisms of virtualized control functions and control delegation are technology-agnostic and use API calls and protocol messages that are completely decoupled from the underlying technology. The main difference that these mechanisms would present in the context of another technology is that the number and type of the control modules and VSFs on the agent side would change to reflect the capabilities and needs of the new technology (e.g. no PDCP module for WiFi). However, the mechanisms of policy reconfiguration and VSF updation make no assumption about the exact type and structure of the control modules at the agent side, allowing the controller to designate it on the fly based on the underlying implementation (see Fig. 3).

Apart from the technology agnostic part of the agent API, FlexRAN also requires a number of technology specific API calls. For example, LTE requires scheduling commands which are not applicable and therefore are not required in the WiFi domain. This means that for FlexRAN to be fully compliant with other technologies, the FlexRAN Agent API needs to be extended with additional function calls specifically tailored for the domain of interest, closely resembling the idea of device drivers found in operating systems. The more extended the API is for a specific technology, the more capabilities are offered for the control of the underlying radio access technology (RAT). It should also be noted that the FlexRAN protocol has been structured in such a way that it could be easily extended to support new messages that are technology specific without affecting the functionality of the existing ones.

Another important issue is the extensibility of FlexRAN in future 5G fronthaul architectures where base stations are expected to adopt a distributed design, with Remote Radio Units (RRUs) decoupled from the Baseband Unit (BBU) and connected through a fronthaul link (e.g. optical fibers) [18]. In such an architecture, the functional split between the RRU and the BBU is expected to play a significant role, depending on the capacity and the latency of the fronthaul link. The design of FlexRAN could be adopted in such an architecture, where the data plane and the agents could be placed on the RRU side and the control plane could be consolidated at the master residing at the BBU. Based on the quality of the fronthaul link, the control delegation features of FlexRAN could be exploited to perform a dynamic and adaptive functional split of the control operations while retaing the realtime deadlines. For example, in case of a high latency fronthaul link, the master could delegate control of the time critical PHY and MAC operations to the RRU, while in case of a low latency link all operations could be residing at the BBU side.

7.3 Issues for Future Work

Here we outline several extensions and aspects for future work on FlexRAN. Firstly, a conflict resolution mechanism ensuring state consistency becomes valuable when third-party network applications need to be supported. For example, such a mechanism should prohibit the deployment of multiple applications that may simultaneously issue scheduling decisions for the same resource blocks, effectively leading to conflicts. Secondly, a significant issue is related to control delegation, where the VSF code pushed to the agents by the controller needs to be compiled against the processor architecture of the target agent using the programming language of the FlexRAN agent API (currently in C). Introducing a high-level domain-specific language that would make the development of VSFs technology-agnostic would greatly simplify this process, especially in cases where the underlying infrastructure is heterogeneous in terms of the agent implementation. Another issue that needs to be further considered is related to the security concerns of the VSF updation mechanism, which could cause complications for the deployment of third-party applications (see Sec. 4.3.1). Furthermore, as already discussed, FlexRAN does not currently employ any high-level abstractions in the northbound API and instead reveals raw information. Therefore, introducing abstractions for control and for RIB access could greatly simplify the development of control and management applications. Finally, improving the scalability of FlexRAN for wide area settings by introducing another layer of control and broadening its scope to go beyond the control and management of the radio resources in the cellular RAN by considering other domains like the core network and multi-RAT settings would provide a more holistic SDN solution for future mobile networks.

8. CONCLUSIONS

In this paper we have presented FlexRAN, a flexible and programmable SD-RAN platform. FlexRAN enables the separation of the control from the data plane through a custom-tailored southbound API, while providing inherent support for real-time RAN applications. FlexRAN offers significant benefits to the RAN, including the flexibility to dynamically modify the degree of coordination among base stations to realize both distributed and centralized modes of operation and the programmability to adapt control over time turning the RAN into an evolvable network. All these while being transparent to end-devices, simplifying its deployment and promoting innovation both for the industrial and the academic research community. The implementation of FlexRAN over the OpenAirInterface LTE platform and our evaluation results confirm the feasibility of its deployment even when considering time critical operations like MAC scheduling. The effectiveness of FlexRAN as an SD-RAN platform was highlighted through a diverse set of use cases in the context of current 4G and future 5G networks, focusing on interference management, mobile edge computing and RAN sharing.

Acknowledgments

We thank our shepherd Wenjun Hu and the anonymous reviewers for their helpful suggestions on improving the paper. This work was partly funded by the European FP7 FLEX project (612050) and H2020 COHERENT project (671639).

9. REFERENCES

[1] https://developers.google.com/protocol-buffers/.

[2] https://gitlab.eurecom.fr/oai/openair-cn.

[3] http://www.linuxfoundation.org/collaborate/workgroups/networking/netem.

[4] http://dashif.org/reference/players/javascript/v2.1.1/samples/dash-if-reference-player/index.html.

[5] http://dash.edgesuite.net/dash264/TestCases/2a/qualcomm/1/MultiResMPEG2.mpd.

[6] http://dash.edgesuite.net/akamai/streamroot/050714/Spring_4Ktest.mpd.

[7] 5G PPP Architecture Working Group. View on 5G Architecture, 2016.

[8] I. F. Akyildiz et al. SoftAir: A software defined networking architecture for 5G wireless systems. *Computer Networks*, 85:1–18, 2015.

[9] H. Ali-Ahmad et al. CROWD: an SDN approach for DenseNets. In *Second European Workshop on Software Defined Networks (EWSDN)*, pages 25–31. IEEE, 2013.

[10] J. G. Andrews et al. What will 5G be? *IEEE Journal on Selected Areas in Communications*, 32(6):1065–1082, 2014.

[11] A. Apostolaras et al. Evolved User Equipment for Collaborative Wireless Backhauling in Next Generation Cellular Networks. In *12th Annual IEEE International Conference on Sensing, Communication, and Networking (SECON)*, pages 408–416. IEEE, 2015.

[12] M. Arslan et al. Software-Defined Networking in Cellular Radio Access Networks: Potential and Challenges. *Communications Magazine, IEEE*, 53(1):150–156, 2015.

[13] A. Banerjee et al. Scaling the LTE Control-Plane for Future Mobile Access. In *Proceedings of the 11th ACM CoNEXT*. ACM, 2015.

[14] M. Bansal et al. OpenRadio: A Programmable Wireless Dataplane. In *Proceedings of the 1st workshop on Hot topics in Software Defined Networks*, pages 109–114. ACM, 2012.

[15] C. Bernardos et al. An Architecture for Software Defined Wireless Networking. *Wireless Communications, IEEE*, 21(3):52–61, 2014.

[16] F. Boccardi et al. Five Disruptive Technology Directions for 5G. *Communications Magazine, IEEE*, 52(2):74–80, 2014.

[17] T. Chen et al. SoftMobile: Control Evolution for Future Heterogeneous Mobile Networks. *Wireless Communications, IEEE*, 21(6):70–78, 2014.

[18] I. Chih-Lin et al. Recent Progress on C-RAN Centralization and Cloudification. *Access, IEEE*, 2:1030–1039, 2014.

[19] X. Costa-Pérez et al. Radio Access Network Virtualization for Future Mobile Carrier Networks. *Communications Magazine, IEEE*, 51(7):27–35, 2013.

[20] S. Costanzo et al. OpeNB: A framework for Virtualizing Base Stations in LTE Networks. In *IEEE International Conference on Communications (ICC)*, pages 3148–3153. IEEE, 2014.

[21] S. Deb et al. Algorithms for Enhanced Inter Cell Interference Coordination (eICIC) in LTE HetNets. *IEEE/ACM Transactions on Networking (TON)*, 22(1):137–150, 2014.

[22] A. Gudipati et al. SoftRAN: Software Defined Radio Access Network. In *Proceedings of the second ACM SIGCOMM workshop on Hot topics in software defined networking*, pages 25–30. ACM, 2013.

[23] Y. C. Hu et al. Mobile Edge Computing - A Key Technology Towards 5G. *ETSI White Paper*, 11, 2015.

[24] X. Jin et al. SoftCell: Scalable and Flexible Cellular Core Network Architecture. In *Proceedings of the 9th ACM CoNEXT*, pages 163–174. ACM, 2013.

[25] S. Katti and L. E. Li. RadioVisor: A Slicing Plane for Radio Access Networks. In *Open Networking Summit 2014 (ONS 2014)*, 2014.

[26] J. Khun-Jush et al. Licensed shared access as complementary approach to meet spectrum demands: Benefits for next generation cellular systems. In *ETSI Workshop on reconfigurable radio systems*, 2012.

[27] L. E. Li et al. Toward Software-Defined Cellular Networks. In *European Workshop on Software Defined Networking (EWSDN)*, pages 7–12. IEEE, 2012.

[28] T. Mahmoodi and S. Seetharaman. Traffic Jam: Handling the Increasing Volume of Mobile Data Traffic. *Vehicular Technology Magazine, IEEE*, 9(3):56–62, 2014.

[29] M. Moradi et al. SoftMoW: Recursive and Reconfigurable Cellular WAN Architecture. In *Proceedings of the 10th ACM CoNEXT*, pages 377–390. ACM, 2014.

[30] NGMN Alliance. 5G White Paper, 2015.

[31] N. Nikaein et al. OpenAirInterface: A flexible platform for 5G research. *ACM SIGCOMM CCR*, 44(5):33–38, 2014.

[32] K. Pentikousis et al. MobileFlow: Toward Software-Defined Mobile Networks. *Communications Magazine, IEEE*, 51(7):44–53, 2013.

[33] Z. A. Qazi et al. KLEIN: A Minimally Disruptive Design for an Elastic Cellular Core. In *Proceedings of the 2nd ACM SIGCOMM Symposium on Software Defined Networking Research*. ACM, 2016.

[34] I. Sodagar. The MPEG-DASH Standard for Multimedia Streaming Over the Internet. *IEEE MultiMedia*, pages 62–67, 2011.

[35] A. Syed and J. Van der Merwe. Proteus: A network service control platform for service evolution in a

mobile software defined infrastructure. In *Proceedings of the 22nd Annual International Conference on Mobile Computing and Networking*, pages 257–270. ACM, 2016.

[36] K. Tsagkaris et al. SON Coordination in a Unified Management Framework. In *77th IEEE Vehicular Technology Conference (VTC Spring)*, pages 1–5. IEEE, 2013.

[37] B. Wang et al. Multimedia Streaming via TCP: An Analytic Performance Study. *ACM Transactions on Multimedia Computing, Communications, and Applications (TOMM)*, 4(2):16, 2008.

[38] W. Wu et al. PRAN: Programmable Radio Access Networks. In *Proceedings of the 13th ACM Workshop on Hot Topics in Networks*, page 6. ACM, 2014.

[39] M. Yang et al. OpenRAN: A Software-defined RAN Architecture Via Virtualization. *ACM SIGCOMM Computer Communication Review*, 43(4):549–550, 2013.

[40] V. Yazıcı et al. A new control plane for 5G network architecture with a case study on unified handoff, mobility, and routing management. *Communications Magazine, IEEE*, 52(11):76–85, 2014.

Leveraging Electromagnetic Polarization in a Two-Antenna Whiteboard in the Air

Longfei Shangguan[†] and Kyle Jamieson[†,‡]
[†]Princeton University, [‡]University College London
{longfeis, kylej}@cs.princeton.edu

ABSTRACT

Wireless sensing, tracking, and drawing technologies are enabling exciting new possibilities for human-machine interaction. They primarily rely on measurements of backscattered phase, amplitude, and Doppler signal distortions, and often require many measurements of these quantities—in time, or from multiple antennas. In this paper we present the design and implementation of PolarDraw, the first whiteboard in the air that sends differentially-polarized wireless signals to glean more precise tracking information from a tag. Leveraging information received from each polarization angle, our novel algorithms infer orientation and position of an RFID-tagged pen using just two antennas, when the user writes in the air or on a physical whiteboard. An experimental comparison in a cluttered indoor office environment compares two-antenna PolarDraw with recent state-of-the-art object tracking systems that use double the number of antennas, demonstrating comparable centimeter-level tracking accuracy and character recognition rates (88–94%), thus making a case for the use of polarization in many other tracking systems.

Keywords

RFID; Tracking; Electromagnetic Polarization

1. INTRODUCTION

We are rapidly moving toward a pervasively-sensed wireless world where most of our interactions with machines will be accomplished via gestures [3, 31] and writing in the air [38], and machines will be able to recognize our activities and pinpoint our location [1, 2, 16, 46]. On the industrial side, recent efforts include both short-range [12] and medium-range [11] indoor radar technologies, as well as mo-

CoNEXT '16 December 12-15, 2016, Irvine, CA, USA

ACM ISBN 978-1-4503-4292-6/16/12.

DOI: http://dx.doi.org/10.1145/2999572.2999601

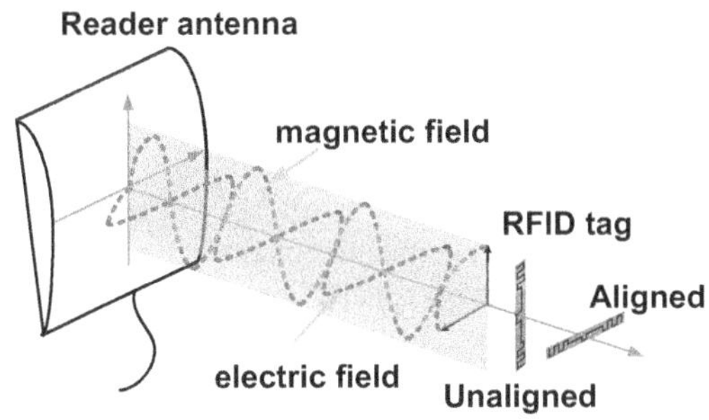

Figure 1— Linearly-polarized electromagnetic waves propagate with a fixed electric field angle, exciting antennas or tags in proportion to alignment with this angle.

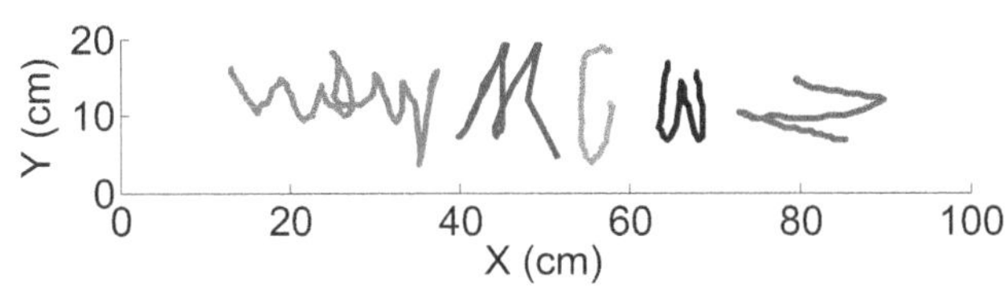

Figure 2— Recovered trajectory: *WoW, M, C, W, Z.*

re mature electronic whiteboard technologies based on ultrasound/infrared [25] and laser curtains [24]. While the use cases are compelling, the real-world utility of these sensing systems depends on several factors:

1. Infrastructure requirements— Systems that use angle-of-arrival information generally require a significant number of physically-separated antennas [3, 50], reducing deployability. Other systems require the simultaneous use of multiple widely-separated carrier frequencies [41], requiring simultaneous or added communication on these frequencies.

2. Pointing equipment— Some systems achieve millimeter accuracy, but require expensive ($100) styluses in order to interact with ultrasound and infrared receivers [25].

3. Location and orientation estimation— In many cases, estimating the orientation of an object or person helps improve accuracy or activity recognition.

Electromagnetic wave *polarization* is a fundamental property of a wireless transmission, and refers to the orientation

Table 1— Infrastructure cost comparison. For a fair comparison of reader hardware, we include comparable products in the same product line as the ThinkMagic RFID reader hardware module that RF-IDraw used.

Item	Unit cost	Quantity	Total cost
Reader (2-port) [39]	$ 285	1	$ 285
Antenna [20]	79	2	158
PolarDraw's system cost			443
Reader (4-port) [40]	398	1	398
Antenna [53]	135	4	540
Tagoram's system cost			938
Reader (4-port) [40]	398	2	796
Antenna [6]	89	8	712
RF-IDraw's system cost			1508

of the electrical field in the plane transverse to the wave's propagation, as shown in Figure 1. In the context of mobile devices, polarization has received the most attention in recent years as increasing smartphone usage in an orientation facing the user (roughly level with the ground) has resulted in a loss of signal strength from a vertically-polarized transmissions, both indoors and outdoors [33]. Outdoors, the horizontally- and vertically-polarized paths from base station to mobile (of length *ca.* 2 mi.) are very different [21] due to differing reflectors. Indoors, for smaller Wi-Fi cell sizes, the same is true for longer non-line-of-sight paths, but shorter paths tend to share similar reflectors (and a more dominant line-of-sight path) when viewed from orthogonal polarizations [34].

It is well known among RFID practitioners that tag orientation affects RFID read rate, and prior academic work has leveraged these electromagnetic polarization differences to infer RFID tag orientation [17]. Our key observation in this work is that the similarity between horizontally- and vertically-polarized paths at modest ranges presents a unique opportunity for wireless motion tracking systems to leverage polarization for better location tracking accuracy. We use a simple RFID reader as a test case, but replace the reader's standard circularly polarized antennas with linearly polarized antennas as shown in Figure 1, resulting in the linearly polarized transmission shown.

In this paper, we present the design and implementation of PolarDraw, the first motion tracking system that can accurately reproduce handwritten letters in the air or on a whiteboard with just *two* nearby antennas. Compared with the prior state-of-the-art system Tagoram, PolarDraw reduces the infrastructure cost by half (see Table 1), hence setting a new standard for minimal supporting infrastructure[1]. PolarDraw estimates both the position and orientation of an RFID-tagged whiteboard pen, adding just pennies to the cost of each item to be used as a stylus. Thus PolarDraw meets each of the three preceding objectives for a practical and highly-deployable motion tracking system.

In brief, PolarDraw works as follows. Our system uses RFID antennas to measure the phase and amplitude of an RFID tag at a rate of *ca.* 100 Hz. Variations in the angle between tag and reader antenna result in fluctuations of power received from the tag, but as our feasibility study next (§2) shows, symmetry properties result in equal power changes when the tag rotates left or right. PolarDraw uses a second, linearly-polarized antenna to view the rotation from a 30° shift in perspective, thus overcoming this *rotational ambiguity* problem (§3.3). Rotation is just part of what determines the pen's true trajectory, however. PolarDraw also estimates the displacement of the pen on the whiteboard using phase difference readings across both time and space (§3.4). Since they do not attempt to discriminate polarization, current trajectory tracing systems have not yet explored how best to fuse the above phase readings (which estimate pen displacement) with power readings (which estimate pen rotation), and doing so carefully is key to getting highly accurate results. We describe our novel algorithm, which incorporates a simple Viterbi-based probabilistic search (§3.5), to complete the design of PolarDraw.

Contributions. Although using polarization to infer tag orientation has been studied before, PolarDraw is the first system we are aware of that uses a power-orientation model to track a pen's movement trajectory. The techniques introduced here introduce a new source of position information, and thus have the potential to be applied to many other indoor radar and indoor localization systems to enhance their accuracy. PolarDraw is also the first radio-based system we are aware of that simultaneously models changes in the pen's displacement and orientation. As our experimental evaluation shows, PolarDraw benefits from the pen orientation estimation.

Experimental results.. Our experiments measure:

1. Word recognition accuracy.
2. Letter recognition accuracy.
3. The general precision of tracking arbitrary writing.

Our experimental evaluation (§5) tests PolarDraw's performance against the two leading motion tracking systems in the research literature mentioned above, RF-IDraw and Tagoram, with all three systems running in the same experimental environment. Our results in this cluttered, real-world office environment show two-antenna PolarDraw achieves median 10 cm accuracy, versus 8 cm for four-antenna RF-IDraw and Tagoram. Further microbenchmark experiments justify parameter choices and test the experimental limits of our system as tag to reader distance increases and writing size decreases.

Roadmap. The rest of this paper is organized as follows: §2 presents initial microbenchmark-style measurements in a cluttered office environment to establish the basic experimental possibility of measuring orientation through polarized transmissions. §3 presents the design of PolarDraw, after which we present our implementation (§4) and experimental results (§5). The remainder of the paper consists of related work (§6), discussion (§7) and conclusion (§8).

[1] PolarDraw's evaluation actually uses a much cheaper antenna ($ 14 unit price) but we use a conservative cost estimation here for a generally-fair cost comparison.

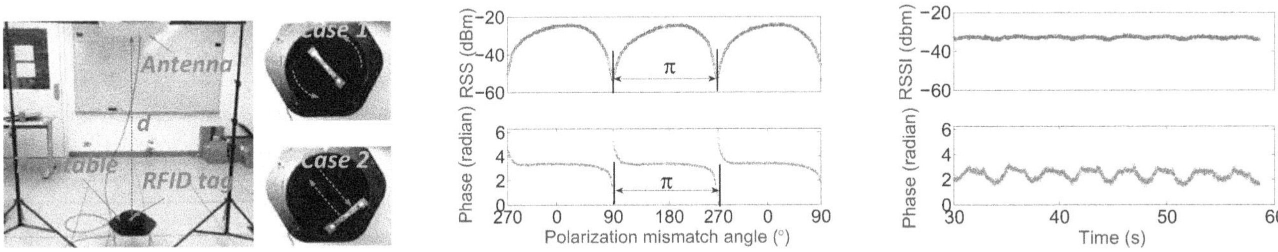

(a)— Feasibility study hardware setup. **(b)**— Rotating a tag (Case 1). **(c)**— Moving a tag (Case 2).

Figure 3— An initial feasibility study experimental setup and experimental results.

2. MEASURING POLARIZATION

To determine whether we can measure polarization in a real indoor environment where multipath is prevalent, we first describe emprical feasibility study, using the hardware setup shown in Figure 3(a). We situate an ImpinJ RFID reader connected to a linearly polarized antenna 2.5 m above an RFID tag placed on a turntable below, as shown in the picture.[2] In the first experiment, the tag rotates at a constant angular velocity on the turntable. In the second experiment, we manually translate the tag back and forth, keeping its orientation fixed. Figure 3(b) shows the received signal strength (RSS) and phase measured at the RFID reader during the tag's rotation. As expected, RSS changes periodically during the tag's rotation. It peaks at -24 dBm when the tag and the reader antennas are aligned, and drops gradually as the polarization mismatch angle between the two increases. Finally, the tag fails to acquire any power and there is no RSS reading when the orientation of the tag is perpendicular to the polarization angle of the reader antenna. On the other hand, since tag-to-antenna distance does not change during the tag's rotation, the phase reading stays roughly constant. We note that the phase reading jumps when the polarization mismatch angle is around 90° and 270°: this is because the tag fails to acquire energy from the line-of-sight path due to the polarization mismatch. Nonetheless, it acquires energy along non-line-of-sight signal propagation paths, where the signal bounces off nearby objects, changing the measured phase angle. PolarDraw's data pre-processing (§3.1) is designed to cope with and overcome these *spurious* readings from differently-polarized reflection paths.

Figure 3(c) shows RSS and phase during the tag's back-and-forth movement over a distance of 8 cm. We observe a roughly constant RSS value, as expected since RSS is insensitive to small changes in distance over the tag-to-antenna link. In contrast, we can see the phase reading increases when the tag moves in one direction, remains stable when the tag stands still, and decreases when the tag moves back.

We conclude from the above empirical results:

1. At moderate distances in our line-of-sight indoor environment, RSS is sensitive to the polarization mismatch, yet it is insensitive to small changes in the length of the tag-to-antenna link.

[2]Our hardware setup is more completely described in §4.

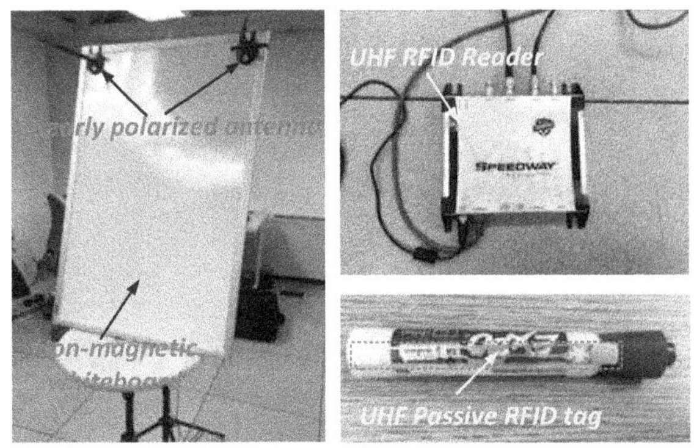

Figure 4— PolarDraw's high-level design: Two linearly-polarized antennas are mounted above a whiteboard or free space; users draw with RFID-tagged whiteboard pens.

2. With the exception of a "spurious" corner case when the tag antenna and reader antenna are orthogonal to each other, phase measurements are insensitive to polarization mismatch, yet are extremely sensitive to small changes in the length of the tag-to-antenna link.

Combining these two findings, we can conclude that in our experimental setup, separate measurements of RSS and phase can respectively estimate rotational and translational movement of the pen, with a reasonable degree of reliability. In the next section, we describe a design that extracts a high degree of reliability from these two signals.

3. DESIGN

PolarDraw comprises a UHF RFID reader connected to two linearly-polarized antennas mounted on a whiteboard as shown in Figure 4, or alternatively, simply tracking a "virtual whiteboard" in the air. Figure 5 shows PolarDraw's data processing workflow: first, PolarDraw controls the RFID hardware to interrogate the tag collecting the phase and amplitude readings of each backscattered signal. These data are then delivered to the pre-processing module for data smoothing and spurious data rejection (§3.1). After that, the filtered data are fed into the tracking module, where PolarDraw uses a writing model (§3.2) to estimate pen moving direction (§3.3) and distance (§3.4). These pen moving direction and distance estimates finally feed into a Hidden Markov Model (HMM) for pen trajectory estimation (§3.5).

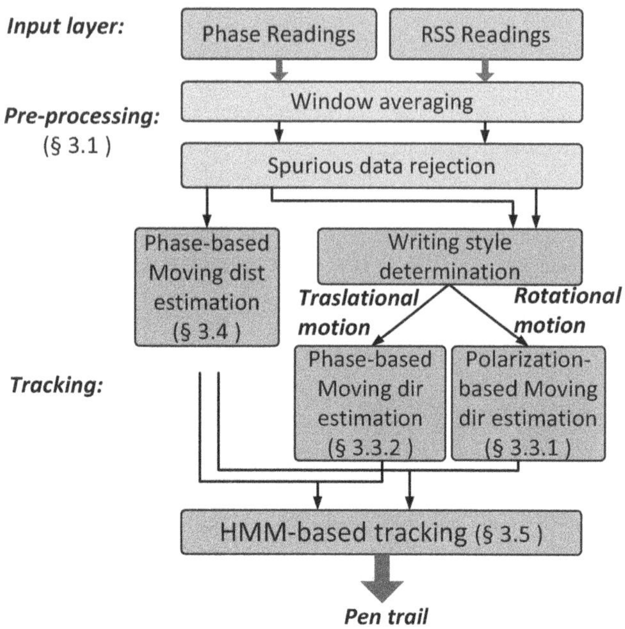

Figure 5— PolarDraw's high-level design: Separate modules handle data input, pre-processing and pen tracking.

3.1 RFID data pre-processing

The pre-processing module contains two steps: data smoothing and spurious data rejection. In the first step, data smoothing aims to improve the stability of amplitude and phase samples by averaging away the phase and amplitude noise affecting the raw data. PolarDraw first divides time into windows of length 50 ms.[3] Within each window, PolarDraw averages together the amplitude and phase readings belonging to that window. These averaged data form a new amplitude and phase series, indexed by the timestamp.

In the second step, PolarDraw rejects the spurious phase data desribed in §2 by comparing phase readings of adjacent windows. If the absolute value of their difference is larger than a threshold, PolarDraw rejects the readings at current window. Following the experimental setup in §2, we rotate the tag on the turntable at different speeds and test for the presence of spurious phase readings. Based on the result, we empirically set this angle threshold to 0.2 radians. The filtered data are then fed into the tracking module.

3.2 Modeling pen movement

A *pen trajectory* is composed of a set of discrete trajectory *fragments*, each of which can be characterized by a movement direction and distance on the (virtual or real) whiteboard. When a user is writing on a whiteboard, wrist movements tend to cause azimuthal rotations clockwise when the pen moves to the right, and counterclockwise when the pen moves to the left. The pen is of course free to rotate in three-space, and so we define the angular measurements of the pen's elevation from the X–Z plane and azimuthal rotation measured from the X-axis and projected onto the X–Z plane summarized in Table 2 and illustrated in Figure 6.

[3]We chose this averaging window size based on an empirical sensitivity analysis.

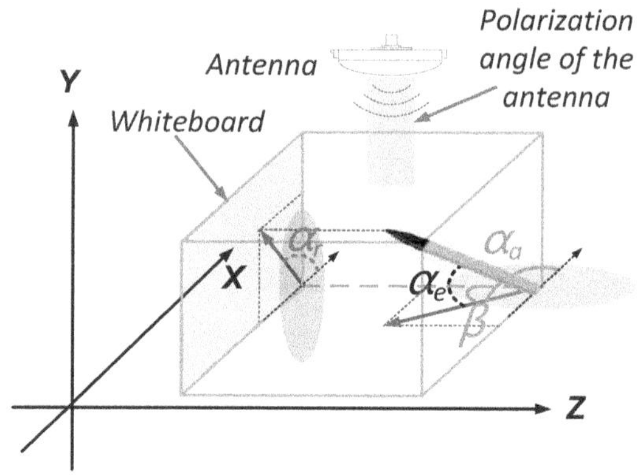

Figure 6— Modeling pen movement during writing.

α_e:	Pen *elevation angle*, from the X–Z plane,
α_r:	Pen *rotation angle*, as projected on the X–Y plane,
α_a:	Pen *azimuthal angle*, as projected on the X–Z plane.

Table 2— Pen angle as illustrated in Figure 6.

3.3 Estimating pen movement direction

PolarDraw estimates pen direction using both rotational and translational pen movements. PolarDraw's rotational direction estimation estimates left-right directions only, and its translational direction estimation estimates movement in all four board directions. At each 50 ms timestep, PolarDraw first detects the dominant type of movement (translational or rotational) by observing the RSS trend: if the change in RSS reaches above some threshold δ,[4] then PolarDraw infers primarily rotational movement and tracks α_a (§3.3.1) to determine its direction. Otherwise, PolarDraw infers significant translational movement and instead inspects changes in phase to determine the pen's direction of movement (§3.3.2).

3.3.1 Rotational movement direction estimation

The main idea behind rotational movement direction is as follows. We continuously estimate α_r, the pen rotation angle projected onto the whiteboard, and estimate a pen moving direction perpendicular to α_r, as illustrated in Figure 7.

The problem then reduces to the estimation of α_r. PolarDraw translates α_a to the pen rotation angle α_r using the following equation relating the angles shown in Figure 6:

$$\alpha_r = \pi - \arctan\left(-\frac{\sin\alpha_e}{\cos\alpha_e\cdot\cos\alpha_a}\right). \qquad (1)$$

Since the antennas are directly above the pen, we can estimate α_a based on polarization mismatch (we describe this process next). There remains another variable free in Equation 1 however, α_e, the elevation angle. For simplicity of

[4]We test various thresholds, and empirically set δ =2 dBm, which optimizes the overall performance.

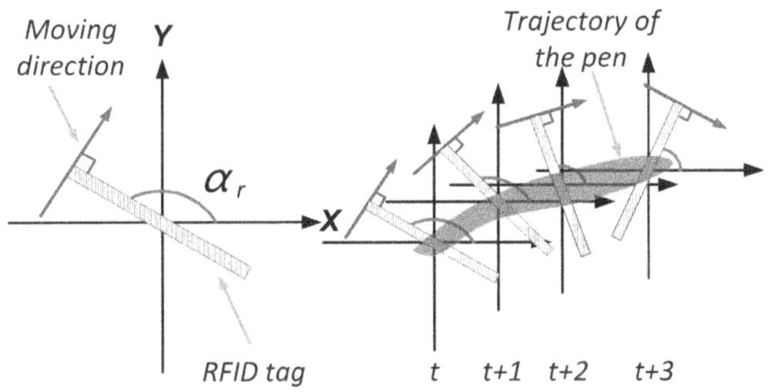

Figure 7— Tracking pen rotation and translation.

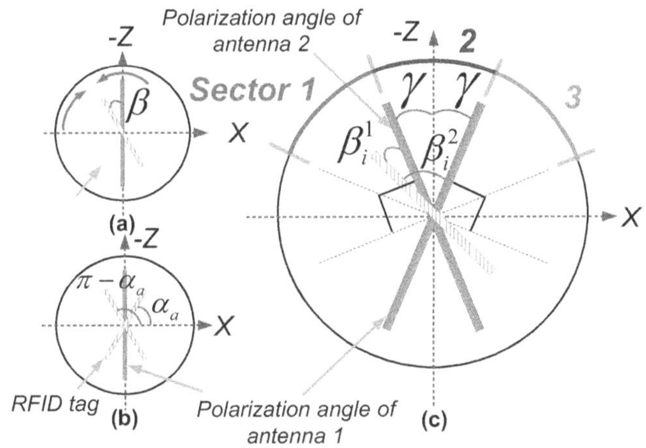

Figure 8— Polarization angle mismatch. The thick blue line indicates the polarization angle of the reader antenna. (a): rotation direction ambiguity. (b): azimuthal angle ambiguity. (c): breaking the rotation ambiguity by spatially separated antennas.

design we take a pragmatic approach: since pen elevation angle changes only slightly when rotating left to right while writing, we set α_e to be a constant determined by experiments described in §5.4.1 (there we also show that accuracy is insensitive to choice of α_e). Equation 1 can then be solved for α_r and hence pen movement direction.

The problem now reduces to the estimation of α_a. In designing PolarDraw's α_a estimation algorithm, we face the following two challenges. Firstly, as Figure 8(a) shows, both a clockwise and a counterclockwise rotation could result in an identical polarization mismatch angle β, hence the same end RSS. Consequently, we are unable to differentiate the rotation direction by simply observing the end RSS value alone. We term this challenge the *rotation direction ambiguity*. Secondly, as Figure 8(b) shows, within the range $[0, 180°]$, there are always two azimuthal angles that result in the same RSS value. Therefore, we are also unable to estimate the azimuthal angle based on RSS alone. We term this challenge the *azimuthal angle ambiguity*.

Breaking ambiguities. An intuitive way is to refer to the tag's location. However, the tag's location is undetermined since the two-antenna based hyperbolic positioning scheme will yield multiple symmetric hyperbolas, and the tag's location could be anywhere on any of these hyperbolas. In PolarDraw, we address the above challenges by jointly analyzing RSS trends from the two antennas. As Figure 8(c) shows, we orient the antennas so that their angles with the Z-axis are equal, denoting that measure γ. Let β_i^j denote the polarization mismatch angle between the tag and antenna j at time i. Then the antenna directions together with their perpendiculars naturally separate the rotation plane into three *sectors* 1, 2, and 3, as shown in Figure 8(c). During normal writing, pen azimuthal rotations are small relative to γ, and so we assume the azimuthal angle α_a is well within the union of these three sectors. Therefore, if we can determine in which sector the current α_a is, then we can break the azimuthal angle ambiguity.

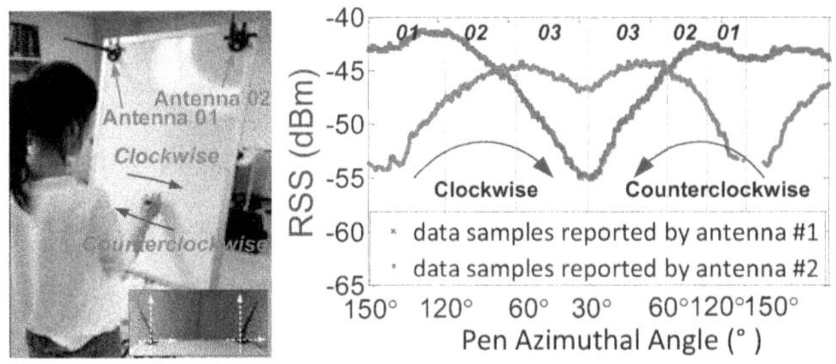

Figure 9— Writing motion RSS trends ($\gamma = 30°$).

Table 3— RSS trend. ("–" means don't care.)

Area	Direction	RSS trend	RSS changing rate
Sector 1	⇒	$s_i^1 \uparrow$ $s_i^2 \uparrow$	$\lvert\Delta s_i^1\rvert < \lvert\Delta s_i^2\rvert$
	⇐	$s_i^1 \downarrow$ $s_i^2 \downarrow$	$\lvert\Delta s_i^1\rvert < \lvert\Delta s_i^2\rvert$
Sector 2	⇒	$s_i^1 \downarrow$ $s_i^2 \uparrow$	–
	⇐	$s_i^1 \uparrow$ $s_i^2 \downarrow$	–
Sector 3	⇒	$s_i^1 \downarrow$ $s_i^2 \downarrow$	$\lvert\Delta s_i^1\rvert > \lvert\Delta s_i^2\rvert$
	⇐	$s_i^1 \uparrow$ $s_i^2 \uparrow$	$\lvert\Delta s_i^1\rvert > \lvert\Delta s_i^2\rvert$

Figure 9 shows RSS trends reported by the two antennas when a user writes on the whiteboard. Let s_i^j be the RSS reading reported by antenna j at time i, and $\Delta s_i^j = s_{i+1}^j - s_i^j$. As indicated in this figure, when the pen rotates in different direction within different sectors, the polarization mismatch angle β_i^1 and β_i^2 changes in a different way, which leads to a different direction of change as well as a different rate of change of RSS—Table 3 summarizes the result. From the table we find that by jointly analyzing RSS trends and changing rates, we can successfully estimate the moving direction of the pen as well as the range of the current azimuthal angle α_a that the pen points to, thereby solving both the rotation direction ambiguity and the azimuthal angle ambiguity.

Continuous azimuthal angle tracking.. Let α_a^i be the azimuthal angle of the pen at time i. When the user begins writing, PolarDraw estimates in which sector the pen points and in which direction the pen points. Based on these, Polar-

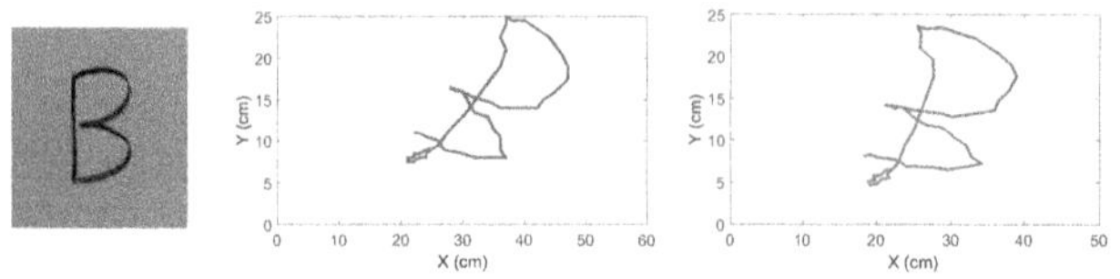

Figure 10— Ground-truth **(a)**, and recovered pen trajectory before and after azimuthal angle correction.

Table 4— Phase changing trends during pen movement.

Pen:	Up	Down	Left	Right
Phase:	$\theta_i^1\downarrow, \theta_i^2\downarrow$	$\theta_i^1\uparrow, \theta_i^2\uparrow$	$\theta_i^1\downarrow, \theta_i^2\uparrow$	$\theta_i^1\uparrow, \theta_i^2\downarrow$

Draw assigns an initial azimuthal angle as follows:

$$\alpha_a^0 = \begin{cases} \pi-\gamma, & \text{if clockwise and in Sector 1,} \\ \frac{\pi}{2}+\gamma, & \text{if clockwise and in Sector 2,} \\ \frac{\pi}{2}-\gamma, & \text{if clockwise and in Sector 3,} \\ \frac{\pi}{2}+\gamma, & \text{if counterclockwise and in Sector 1,} \\ \frac{\pi}{2}-\gamma, & \text{if counterclockwise and in Sector 2,} \\ \gamma, & \text{if counterclockwise and in Sector 3.} \end{cases} \quad (2)$$

PolarDraw then tracks α_a^i at each time i as follows:

$$\alpha_a^i = \begin{cases} \alpha_a^{i-1}-\Delta\beta, & \text{if clockwise rotation,} \\ \alpha_a^{i-1}+\Delta\beta, & \text{if counterclockwise rotation.} \end{cases} \quad (3)$$

where $\Delta\beta$ is a variable, indicating the average changing rate of the azimuthal angle over each 50 ms time window when human writes on the whiteboard. The assignment of $\Delta\beta$ is as follows:

$$\Delta\beta = \begin{cases} 6^\circ, & \text{if } |\Delta s_i^1| > \delta \text{ and } |\Delta s_i^2| > \delta, \\ 0, & \text{otherwise.} \end{cases} \quad (4)$$

We perform a sensitivity analysis of both δ and $\Delta\beta$, and set $\delta = 1.5$ dBm, $\Delta\beta = 6^\circ$, which jointly maximize overall system performance.

Initial azimuthal angle correction.. In the tracking process, the initial azimuthal angle we assigned will likely deviate from its true value by some amount $\tilde{\alpha}_a$. Consequently, later azimuthal angle estimates suffer from this error $\tilde{\alpha}_a$ as well, resulting in an inaccurate tracking result.

PolarDraw corrects $\tilde{\alpha}_a$ based on detecting when the azimuthal angle of the pen crosses over the boundary of two sectors. Suppose at time i PolarDraw detects that the pen crosses over the boundary of two neighboring sectors based on the principle shown in Table 3. The azimuthal angle of the pen at time i should be approximately equal to the azimuthal boundary angle of these two sectors, denoted as $\hat{\alpha}_a^i$. Hence the difference between $\hat{\alpha}_a^i$ and α_a^i (the estimated azimuthal angle) indicates the initial azimuthal angle error $\tilde{\alpha}_a$. PolarDraw corrects the estimated azimuthal angles by subtracting $\tilde{\alpha}_a$ from all α_a^i, thus achieving a more accurate result. Figure 10 shows a snapshot of our system's output before and after azimuthal angle error correction.

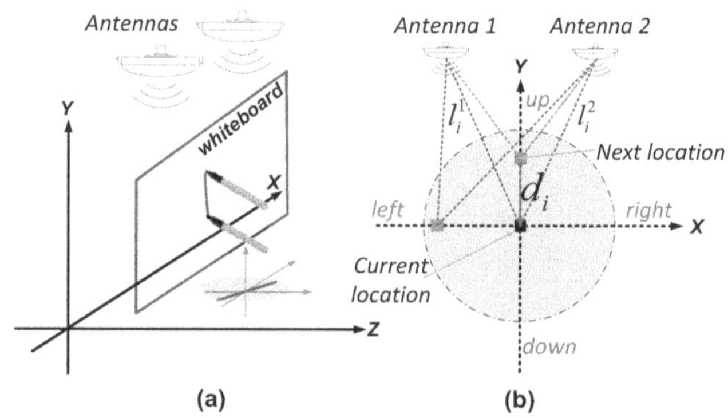

Figure 11— Writing without rotation. (a): the user writes on the whiteboard with a constant rotation angle; (b): geometry relationship of moving directions;

3.3.2 *Translational movement direction estimation*

Writing movement varies from moment to moment, and so sometimes the pen may move with negligible rotation, translation dominating its path, as shown in Figure 11(a). Consequently, the azimuthal angle α_a fails to reflect the true moving direction of the pen. When the pen moves in this primarily translational manner, PolarDraw quickly (within a 50 ms timestep) switches to exploit phase changes to estimate the pen's direction of movement. Specifically, we denote the distance between reader antenna j and the tag at time i as l_i^j. Let θ_i^j be the unwrapped phase reading reported by the antenna j at time i. As Figure 11(b) shows, when the pen moves up, both l_i^1 and l_i^2 decrease, resulting in $\theta_i^1\downarrow$ and $\theta_i^2\downarrow$. Conversely, when the pen moves down, both l_i^1 and l_i^2 increase, leading to $\theta_i^1\uparrow$ and $\theta_i^2\uparrow$. Table 4 shows measured phase trends when the pen moves in different directions, allowing us to decode four rough movement directions over the small timestep. In the next section, we describe how we determine the magnitude of this estimated movement.

3.4 Pen movement distance estimation

PolarDraw again exploits phase trends to estimate the moving distance of the pen. Our approach is based on an assumption that the moving distance during consecutive tag readings is within a half wavelength ($\lambda/2 \approx 16$ cm), where λ is the wavelength of the backscattered signal. This assumption holds in practice since our processing timestep is 50 ms, yielding a maximum detectable speed of 3.2 m/s—significantly exceeding normal writing speed.

Moving distance bounds.. Let d_i be the moving distance of the pen at timestep i, and l_i^j be the distance between the pen and reader antenna j at the same timestep. Since phase cycles completely over a distance of λ, the change in distance between the pen and a reader antenna $\Delta l_i^j = l_{i+1}^j - l_i^j$ can be computed as follows:

$$\Delta l_i^j = (\theta_{i+1}^j - \theta_i^j)\cdot\lambda/(4\pi). \quad (5)$$

By the triangle inequity, $d_i \geq \max\{|\Delta l_i^1|, |\Delta l_i^2|\}$. Next, we denote the maximum moving speed of the pen as v_{max} (we

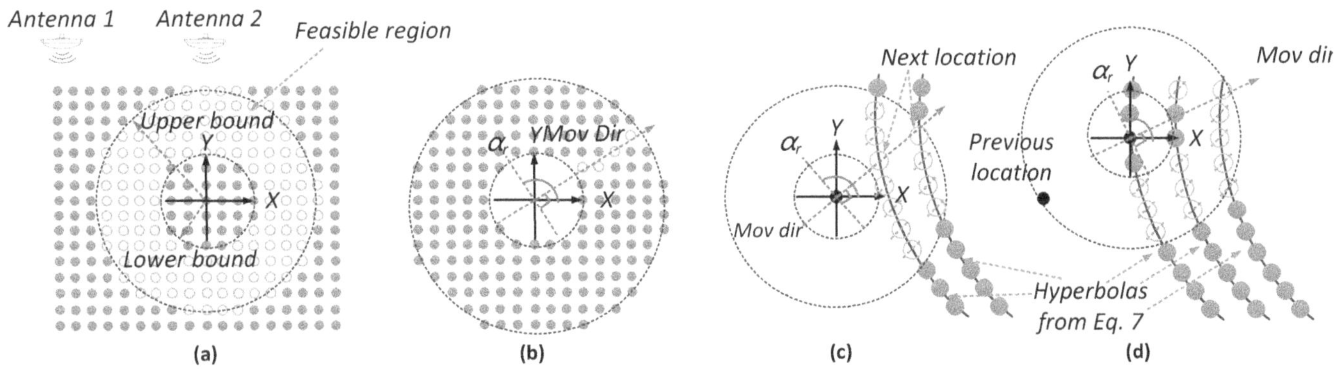

Figure 12— Moving distance inference; (a): Under the lower and upper distance bound. (b). Under the moving direction constraint; (c): Under the hyperbola constraint. (d): Tracking the second trajectory segment of the pen.

set v_{max} to 0.2 m/s in the experiment, which leads to empirically acceptable tracking accuracy.). Then an upper bound of the displacement is $v_{max}\Delta t$, where Δt is the 50 ms timestep.

Based on the foregoing analysis, we know the pen moving distance d_i should be within an annulus: $\max\{|\Delta l_i^1|, |\Delta l_i^2|\} \leq d_i \leq v_{max}\Delta t$ (as shown in Figure 12(a)), which we term the *feasible region*. Within the feasible region, the line segment between the current location and each block forms the displacement *candidate set*. Since the pen's next location should be aligned with the pen's current moving direction, we eliminate a large portion of infeasible locations in the feasible region, as shown in Figure 12(b). However, a large moving distance uncertainty still remains, as many blocks are aligned with the pen moving direction.

Antenna difference measurements.. We also exploit the inter-antenna phase difference $\theta_i^2 - \theta_i^1$ to further reduce the uncertainty in our pen movement distance estimate. The relationship between phase readings and the tag-to-antenna distance can be formulated as follows:

$$\begin{cases} \theta_i^1 + 2k_1\pi = 4\pi l_i^1/\lambda \\ \theta_i^2 + 2k_2\pi = 4\pi l_i^2/\lambda \end{cases} \tag{6}$$

Subtracting the above equations and dropping subscripts:

$$\Delta l_i^{2,1} = \frac{\lambda}{4\pi}(\Delta\theta_i^{2,1} + 2k\pi), \tag{7}$$

where k is an unknown integer, $\Delta\theta_i^{2,1} = \theta_i^2 - \theta_i^1$ and $\Delta l_i^{2,1} = l_i^2 - l_i^1$. Let (x_1, y_1) and (x_2, y_2) be the location of two antennas, $\Delta l_i^{2,1}$ be the distance difference of these two antenna-to-tag links, we can construct a hyperbola with the two foci at the location (x_1, y_1) and (x_2, y_2) as our location estimation. Due to the phase ambiguity, there are multiple candidate hyperbolas. PolarDraw makes its movement distance estimate by intersecting the candidate hyperbolas with the location candidates already acquired, as shown in Figure 12(c) for the case of rotational moving direction estimation (we take an analogous approach for the case of translational moving direction estimation).

3.5 Tracking pen trajectory

Our design so far focuses on how to track the moving direction and the moving distance of the pen, separately. Now we put them together and show how to leverage moving direction and the moving distance to infer the pen's trajectory fragment at each timestamp.

We approach the pen trajectory tracking problem as a discrete-time state estimation problem, where the state of the system at time t, X_t, is the location of the pen at that time. The measurements at time t, Y_t, are the phase and RSS readings reported by the two antennas. PolarDraw employs an HMM to find the most likely sequence of pen trajectory segments. The HMM consists of a set of interconnected states, each of which emits an observable output. The HMM is characterized by two probabilities: the *transition probability* between states and the *emission probability* over the position estimate.

Modeling the state transition probability.. We divide the whiteboard into equal-sized blocks, denoted $B_{i,j}$. Then the state space of HMM consists of all blocks on the whiteboard. We consider the transitions between consecutive states to have equal probabilities.[5] This state transition probability $Pr(X_{t+1} = (x_1, y_1)|X_t = (x_0, y_0))$ is defined as:

$$\begin{cases} \frac{1}{M}, & \text{if} \quad \max\{|\Delta l_t^1|, |\Delta l_t^2|\} \leq \sqrt{(x_1 - x_0)^2 + (y_1 - y_0)^2} \\ & \qquad \leq v_{max}\Delta t, \\ 0, & \qquad \text{otherwise,} \end{cases} \tag{8}$$

where M is the the number of blocks within the feasible region (*i.e.*, gray circles in Figure 12(a)).

Modeling emission probability.. At timestep t, the observation Y_t is represented as a tuple of phase and RSS readings: $[\theta_t^1, \theta_t^2, s_t^1, s_t^2]$. The emission probability for a given state represents the likelihood of seeing the pen located at the block conditioned on Y_t. We model emission probability by jointly considering both the moving direction constraint (Figure 12(b)) and the hyperbola constraint (Figure 12(c)). Let (x_0, y_0) and α_r^t be the location and the rotation angle of the pen at time t, respectively. We construct the line passing through (x_0, y_0) with slope equal to the estimated pen moving direction to describe the approximate trajectory of the pen:

$$y = -\cot(\alpha_r^t) \cdot (x - x_0) + y_0. \tag{9}$$

[5]We leave more sophisticated motion modeling, such as the Kalman and Particle filters, for future work.

The pen's next location is likely on this trajectory. On the other hand, the pen's next location should also be on the hyperbolas we estimated based on the inter-phase difference of two antennas $\Delta\theta_t^{1,2}$. Equation 11 in the Appendix on p. , combines the moving direction and the hyperbola constraint to define the emission probability $Pr(X_{t+1} = (x_1, y_1)|Y_t = \theta_t^1, \theta_t^2, s_t^1, s_t^2)$.

Initial location estimation. PolarDraw finds the initial location of the tag using hyperbolic positioning. Since two antennas will determine multiple hyperbolas, PolarDraw randomly chooses a point on one of these hyperbola to bootstraps the relative location.

Trajectory Rotation. PolarDraw leverages Viterbi decoding to find the most likely pen trajectory. The computational complexity of Viterbi decoding is linear in the number of states and the number of observed variables, hence can be computed in real-time even with an embedded mini PC. As mentioned in §3.3, the initial azimuthal angle may have an error $\tilde{\alpha}_a$. Hence after the trajectory tracking, PolarDraw corrects the azimuthal angle error to acquire a more accurate pen trajectory. Let $\mathbb{P} = \{P_{x_1,y_1}, P_{x_2,y_2,...,P_{x_T,y_T}}\}$ be pen's trajectory recovered by the Viterbi algorithm, where P_{x_t,y_t} is the location of the pen on time t. PolarDraw eliminates the impact of $\tilde{\alpha}_a$ on pen's trajectory as follows:

$$\hat{\mathbb{P}} = \mathbb{P} \cdot \begin{bmatrix} \cos\tilde{\alpha}_r & -\sin\tilde{\alpha}_r \\ \sin\tilde{\alpha}_r & \cos\tilde{\alpha}_r, \end{bmatrix} \tag{10}$$

where $\hat{\mathbb{P}}$ is the new trajectory of the pen; $\tilde{\alpha}_r$ is the rotational angle error induced by the azimuthal angle error.

4. IMPLEMENTATION

PolarDraw's front-end hardware consists of an ImpinJ Speedway R420 RFID reader [15], two Laird tilt RF linearly polarized antennas [19], and an Avery Dennison AD-227m5 UHF passive RFID tag [7]. The passive tag is attached on a standard whiteboard pen. PolarDraw's software components control the RFID reader to interrogate the RFID tag and process the tag readings for pen trajectory tracking. The tag interrogation module, implemented in Java, collects tag readings through the Low Level Reader Protocol (LLRP) [23] which the C#-based pen trajectory tracking module then processes.

Modulation scheme selection.. A typical EPC GEN 2 reader supports different modulation schemes, with varying levels of robustness to background noise. PolarDraw round-robins all available modulation schemes, selecting the first with the standard deviation of phase variances at most 0.1 rad^2 for tag interrogation. We have conducted a sensitivity analysis to test other thresholds, and find this choice of phase variance threshold optimizes performance.

5. EVALUATION

In this section, we first present our experimental methodology (§5.1), after which we conduct end-to-end experiments in a laboratory environment to evaluate PolarDraw's performance (§5.2). We then compare PolarDraw with two state-of-the-art motion tracking systems, Tagoram and RF-IDraw.

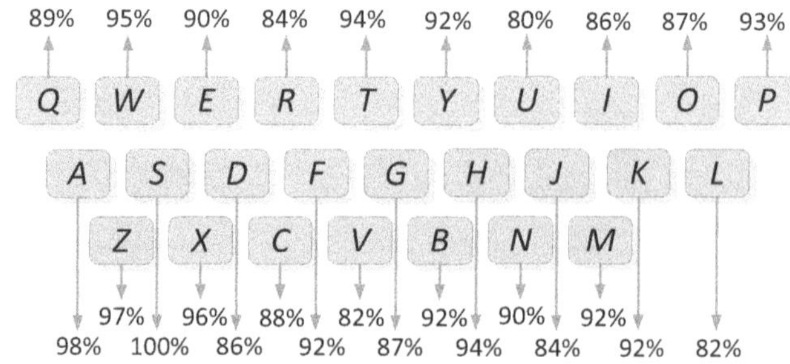

Figure 13— PolarDraw's letter recognition accuracy.

Finally, we present micro-benchmark experiments that provide additional insight into which factors most impact PolarDraw's performance (§5.4).

5.1 Methodology

To determine ground truth, we photograph the user's writing on the whiteboard and leverage edge detection algorithm to extract writing trajectories. We use LipiTk [13] for hand writing recognition.

Performance metrics.. We use the following metrics:

1. *Recognition Accuracy*: the fraction of successful character recognitions over the total number of characters.
2. *Similarity*: the *Procrustes distance* between the recovered trajectory and the ground truth trajectory. This metric determines a linear transformation (translation, rotation, and scaling) of the points in one trajectory that results in the closest match with to the points in another. The goodness-of-fit criterion is the sum of squared errors between the two trajectories.
3. *Confusion matrix*: each row shows the actual character and each column shows the estimated character.

Compared schemes. We compare PolarDraw with two other 2D tracking algorithms: RF-IDraw [45] and Tagoram [52]. RF-IDraw uses eight spatially separated antennas for RFID tag localization and tracking. Most COTS RFID reader support four antennas apiece, so we compare a four-antenna version of RF-IDraw with PolarDraw, for equal hardware resources. Tagoram adopts four antennas to locate and track an RFID tag based on the phase readings: our implementation uses two or four antennas, the former comparing Tagoram against PolarDraw with equal hardware resources.

5.2 End-to-end performance

We first present end-to-end results of studies in an office environment. The algorithm parameters are set according to the results in §5.4.

5.2.1 Character recognition accuracy

We first examine character recognition accuracy over the English alphabet. In these experiments, we invite a volunteer to write all 26 characters 100 times. The result is shown in Figure 13. PolarDraw achieves 93.6% recognition accuracy on average. Specifically, 15 out of 26 characters are correctly recognized with a probability higher than 90%. 21 out of 26 characters are correctly recognized with a probability higher than 85%. The remaining five characters have

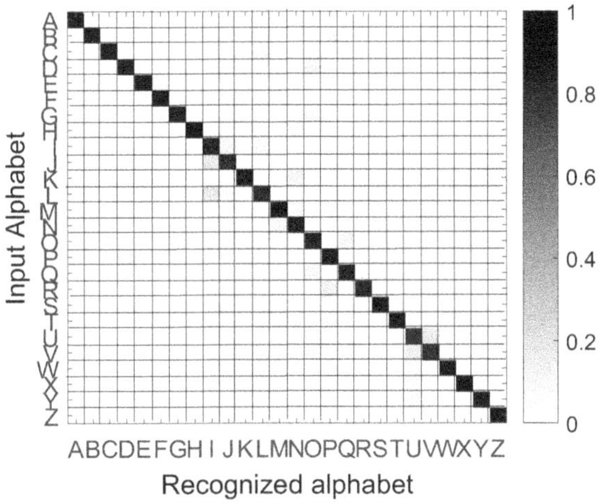

Figure 14— PolarDraw's letter confusion matrix.

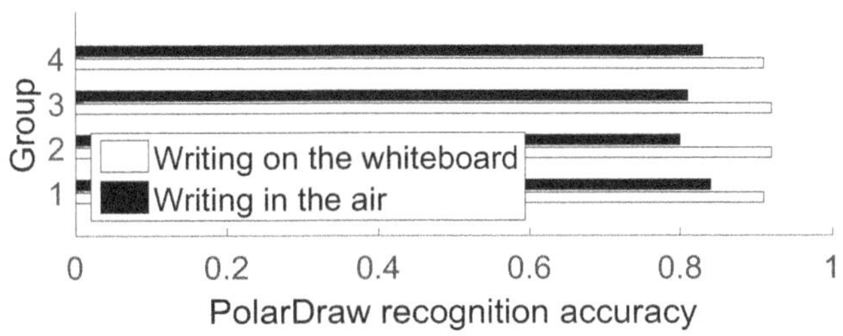

Figure 15— Writing in air *v.* on the whiteboard.

a much lower recognition accuracy. However, their recognition accuracies are still above 80%. We believe by applying natural language processing techniques, we can further increase recognition accuracy.

5.2.2 *Character recognition confusion matrix*

To quantify whether character recognition performance is better for some characters over others, we present the character confusion matrix in Figure 14. The darker areas represent a higher rate of classification of the particular character. We observe from this figure that the rate of misclassifications varies for different ground truth characters. A large portion of errors is usually associated with to those letters that share a very similar writing style. For example, the characters L and V are prone to be incorrectly recognized as I and U. We also note that recognition accuracy also varies with the complexity of the character. For example, those characters that can be written in a single stroke usually achieve a higher recognition accuracy.

5.2.3 *Performance of in-air writing*

We next remove the whiteboard and let the user write in the air. We conduct four groups of experiments here. In each group, we randomly choose 10 letters and let the user write each letter 10 times in air. For comparison, this user is also required to repeat these experiments but write on the whiteboard. Figure 15 shows the resulting recognition accuracy. As the result shows, PolarDraw performs consistently when the user is writing on the whiteboard, achieving a recognition accuracy around 91% on average. In contrast, PolarDraw's performance declines about 8% when the user writes in the air. The reason is that without the whiteboard, writing is not confined to a two-dimensional plane, which leads to errors in the pen moving distance inference. However, PolarDraw still achieves over 80% recognition accuracy in this case.

Table 5— Recognition accuracy *v.* tag-reader distance.

Distance (cm)	**20**	**40**	**60**	**80**	**100**	**120**	**140**
Accuracy (%)	77	83	87	90	91	90	88

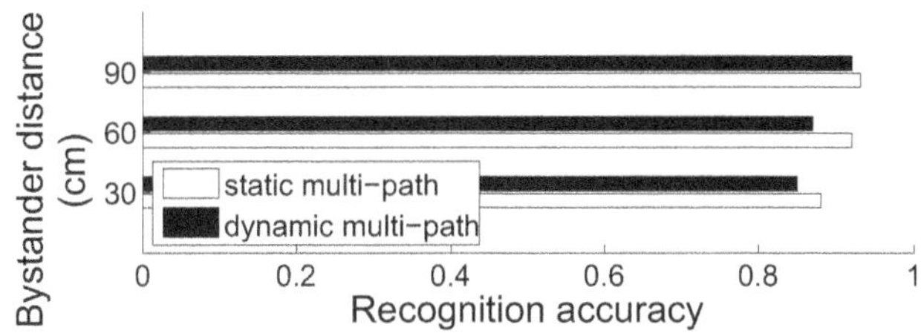

Figure 16— Impact of both dynamic and static multipath on PolarDraw's performance.

5.2.4 *Effect of tag-to-reader distance*

Here we examine the impact of the tag-to-reader distance on PolarDraw's trajectory tracking performance. In these experiments, we vary this distance distance from 20 cm to 140 cm, with a step of 20 cm. Table 5 shows the recognition accuracy at each distance. Somewhat surprisingly, accuracy is relatively low (77%) when the tag is close to the reader antenna (*e.g.*, 20 cm spacing)—this is because in this regime both polarization angle mismatch and the tag movement contribute to the RSS change. But as we increase the tag-reader distance, RSS becomes less sensitive to pen translational movements and PolarDraw accuracy increases. Recognition accuracy only slightly drops as we further expand the tag-to-reader distance from 100 cm to 120 cm and further to 140 cm. One possible explanation may be that the backscattered signal bounces off nearby objects and changes the polarization angle, which leads to an unusual RSS trend during human writing. We plan to investigate the use of more directional antennas to increase range in future work.

5.2.5 *Effect of nearby interfering human motion*

To examine the effect of multipath reflections on PolarDraw's pen tracking accuracy, we invite a volunteer to write on the whiteboard, while another person stands nearby or walks around the whiteboard to generate static or dynamic multipath interference on the backscattered signal. Figure 16 shows the recognition accuracy of PolarDraw under these different multipath conditions, as a function of the distance of the interfering user ("bystander") from the whiteboard. As the results show, PolarDraw's performance is insensitive to both dynamic and static multipath when the bystander is 90 cm away from the whiteboard. As the bystander stands or walks even closer nearby (60 cm and 30 cm), PolarDraw's performance only slightly decreases—PolarDraw still achie-

Table 6— Recognition accuracy of PolarDraw with and without polarization information.

Algorithm	PolarDraw	w/o polarization
Accuracy (%)	91	23

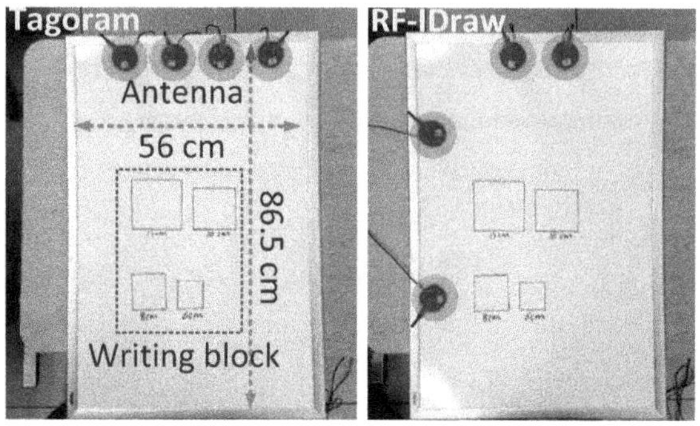

Figure 17— Tagoram/RF-IDraw experimental setup.

ves 83% and 87% recognition accuracy in these dynamic and static multipath regimes, respectively, demonstrating strong robustness.

5.2.6 *Gain of using polarization*

To drill down into the benefit of polarization on tracking accuracy, we implement a version of PolarDraw that tracks pen trajectory without polarization angle estimation. Table 6 presents the letter recognition accuracy of PolarDraw with and without polarization angle estimation. The data show that PolarDraw benefits substantially from polarization angle estimation—by a factor of around 4× in terms of letter recognition accuracy.

5.3 Comparison v. RF-IDraw and Tagoram

We now compare PolarDraw directly against Tagoram and RF-IDraw. The hardware setup is shown in Figure 17.

5.3.1 *Word recognition accuracy*

We compare these three algorithms' ability on written words recognition. We divide the test words into four groups according to the word length. Within in each group, we randomly select 10 words from the Oxford English Dictionary (O.E.D) [28]. Figure 18 shows the word recognition accuracy of PolarDraw, Tagoram and RF-IDraw. When the word contains two characters, PolarDraw achieves a similar performance with both RF-IDraw and Tagoram, with a recognition accuracy over 91%. As the number of characters in the word increases, the performance of all three algorithms drops slightly. The performance of PolarDraw degrades slightly more than the other two algorithms, but with just two antennas, the minimum recognition accuracy of PolarDraw remains above 75%. With natural language processing techniques, we believe the recognition accuracy can be improved further. Furthermore, we find that the recognition accuracy of RF-IDraw here is lower than reported in [45]. This is due to the lesser number of antennas used in this experiments.

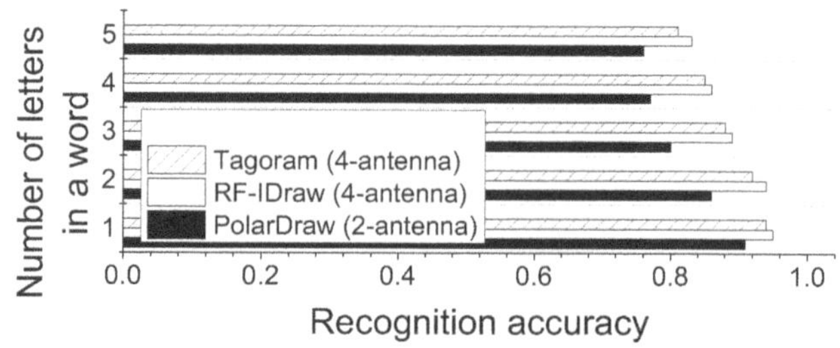

Figure 18— Recognition accuracy for various words.

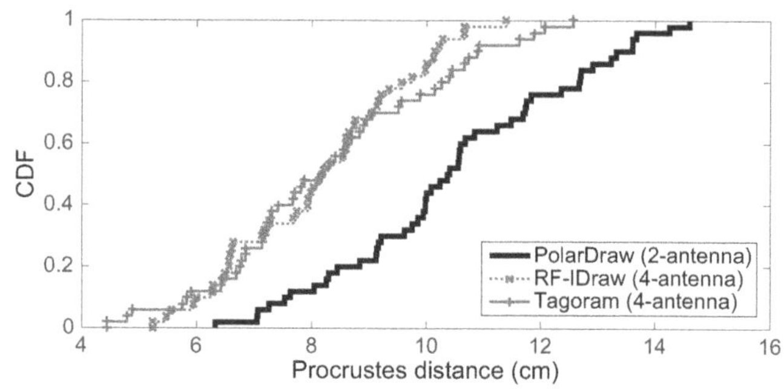

Figure 19— The CDF of the Procrustes distance between the groundtruth and the trajectory recovered by algorithms.

5.3.2 *Trajectory similarity*

Here we directly examine the trajectory similarity of handwritten letters recovered by these three algorithms. We randomly choose five letters and invite one volunteer to write each letter 10 times with a 20 cm writing size. Figure 19 shows the cumulative distribution function (CDF) of the Procrustes distance between the recovered trajectories and the ground truth. The four-antenna versions of Tagoram and RF-IDraw achieve similar performance, with 90th percentile errors of 11.3 cm and 10.2 cm, respectively. PolarDraw's two-antenna performance is comparable at 13.8 cm.

We present examples of the pen trajectories recovered by the three algorithms in Figure 20. Compared with ground truth, we can see that all the recovered trajectories are stretched or rotated due to the localization and tracking errors. Comparing the trajectories recovered by these three algorithms, we find that these trajectories are distinct from each

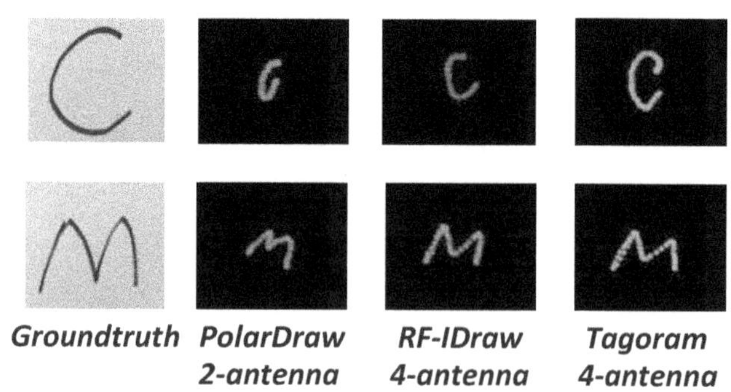

Figure 20— Pen trajectory recovered by three algorithms.

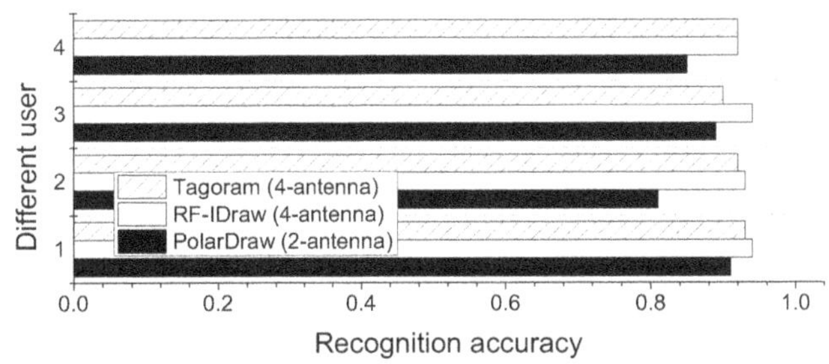

Figure 21— Recognition accuracy across users: User 2 writes with a "stiff" style, rotating the pen only slightly.

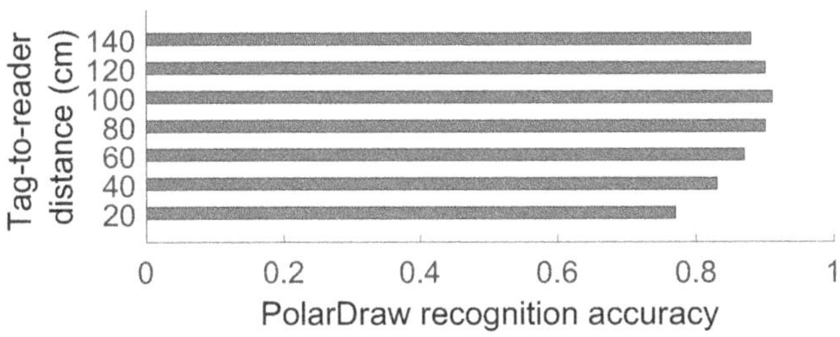

Figure 22— PolarDraw's recognition accuracy over different tag-to-reader distance settings.

other, especially at the beginning and the ending part of the pen trajectory. Nevertheless, all of them preserve the basic profile of the handwritten letters.

5.3.3 Recognition accuracy across users

In this experiment we examine the recognition accuracy over different users. Figure 21 shows the resulting recognition accuracy. As the results show, PolarDraw, Tagoram and RF-IDraw all achieve roughly consistent and high performance for all four users, with two-antenna PolarDraw approaching the other two systems' accuracies for User 1. To test the limits of PolarDraw's performance, one of the users (User 2) was instructed to write in an unnaturally "stiff" style on the whiteboard. While slightly diminished, the resulting accuracy of PolarDraw remains at a comparably high level with just two antennas, demonstrating graceful degradation.

5.3.4 Impact of the tag-to-reader distance

We further examine the impact of the tag-to-reader distance on the trajectory tracking performance. In these experiments, we vary the tag-to-reader distance from 20 cm to 140 cm, with a step of 20 cm. Figure 22 shows the recognition accuracy at each distance. The recognition accuracy is relatively low (around 78%) when the tag is close to the reader antenna (*e.g.*, 20 cm spacing). This is because both the polarization angle mismatch and the tag movement contribute to the RSS change. Hence PolarDraw less often correctly estimates the pen's direction of movement. As we increase the spacing between tag and the reader, the RSS tends to be less sensitive to the pen translation movement. Hence, PolarDraw could accurately estimate the pen moving direction, which results in an increased recognition accuracy, as shown in the result. The recognition accuracy drops as

Table 7— PolarDraw's recognition accuracy *v.* α_e.

α_e (°)	**−45**	**−30**	**−15**	**15**	**30**	**45**
Accuracy (%)	91	91	92	91	93	90

Table 8— PolarDraw's recognition accuracy *v.* γ.

γ (°)	**15**	**30**	**45**	**60**	**75**
Accuracy (%)	92	90	91	85	80

we further increase the tag-to-reader distance from 100 cm to 120 cm and further to 140 cm. A possible explanation may be that the backscatter signal bounces off nearby objects and changes the polarization angle, which leads to an unpredictable RSS trend during human writing. We plan to investigate that use of more directional antennas to even further increase range in future work.

5.4 Microbenchmarks

These microbenchmark experiments aim to give further insight into PolarDraw's performance. In particular, we seek to understand which factors will most affect tracking performance as we tune various operating parameters, to better understand how polarization angle mismatch helps to improve the pen trajectory tracking accuracy. The hardware setup of our microbenchmarks is shown in Figure 4. In the following experiments, we randomly choose 10 letters from the English alphabet, invite a volunteer to write each letter 10 times under different parameter settings, and measure the resulting letter recognition accuracy.

5.4.1 Choosing elevation angle

We first perform a sensitivity analysis examining how the pen elevation angle α_e (defined in §3.2) affects accuracy. Table 7 shows letter recognition accuracy for different pen elevation angles. As the result shows, PolarDraw achieves similar performance under different α_e settings. Based on these data we set $\alpha_e = 30°$ in all other experiments.

5.4.2 Choosing inter-antenna angle

We now examine how the inter-antenna angle γ (defined §3.3) affects accuracy. In this experiment, we manually align the antenna orientation using a protractor. Table 8 shows letter recognition accuracy under different γ settings. PolarDraw achieves similar recognition accuracy when γ is relatively small (*e.g.*, $\gamma = 15$, 30, and 45°). This is because the pen is prone to cross over the border of neighboring sectors (as shown in Figure 8) when the user writes on the whiteboard, which improves PolarDraw's accuracy. As expected, when γ increases, the probability that the pen crosses over the border of neighboring sectors decreases, resulting in a lower recognition accuracy. Informed by these experimental results, we set $\gamma = 15°$ in all other experiments.

6. RELATED WORK

In this section we compare PolarDraw to prior work in multiple areas, chiefly whiteboard transcription systems, RF-

ID-based systems, and inertial sensor-based systems.

Whiteboard transcription systems.. These use cameras to record a whiteboard's contents [10, 14, 51]. While they function well in a controlled lecture theater setting where infrastructure can be permanently installed, they depend on sufficient ambient light, and require a mostly unobstructed line of sight from a camera placed at a sufficient distance from the whiteboard, precluding deployment in some scenarios and complicating deployment in most. In contrast, PolarDraw can be deployed simply with two small antennas attached to a whiteboard. Electronic whiteboard technologies based on ultrasound-infrared [25] and laser curtains [24] also exist, but require expensive styluses in comparison with RFID tags, which cost cents apiece. Finally, the whiteboard transcription systems do not generalize to writing in the air, as we have experimentally demonstrated for PolarDraw.

RFID positioning and tracking systems.. Initial attempts in RFID positioning have used the RSS to estimate the distance between the reader and the tag. *PinIt* [44] localizes RFID tags in a non-line of sight environment by exploiting the multipath profile of each tag. *STPP* [37] uses RFID to spatially order tags without localizing them. However, the localization error of these two systems is relatively high (around 12 cm for PinIt, and 8 cm for STPP), hence they are unsuitable for motion tracing. Later work exploits fine-grained phase information of the backscattered signal for more accurate tag localization. *BackPos* [22] is a hyperbolic-based positioning system that requires at least three RFID antennas, but only achieves *ca.* 13 cm accuracy, which is unsuitable for tracking writing. *Tagoram* [52] introduces a holography-based tag tracking algorithm that achieves an accuracy of around 12 cm[6] based on four reader antennas. In contrast, PolarDraw requires only two antennas and achieves comparable or better accuracy, depending on the number of antennas Tagoram operates with. *RF-IDraw* [45] is a pen-tracking scheme that achieves high accuracy via a nonlinear spaced RFID antenna array, but requires a significant number (eight) of physically-separated antennas and rigid placement of antenna locations, reducing deployability. In contrast, PolarDraw requires minimal supporting infrastructure yet achieves high tracking accuracy.

Gesture recognition systems.. *E-Gesture* [30] employs the gyroscope and accelerometer to characterize eight kinds of predefined hand gestures. Similarly, *RisQ* [29] recognizes smoking gestures by using the accelerometer and gyroscope readings from a smart wristband. However, both systems only recognize simple and pre-defined hand gestures like "throw," "draw," "smoking" *& c.*, and so are not applicable to fine-grained finger motion or writing tracking.

Fine-grained motion tracking systems.. *PhonePoint Pen* [4] enables in-air human writing by tracking a smartphone's motion with the gyroscope and accelerometer. *MoLe* [43] designs a inference algorithm to detect and identify the human typing through smart watch gyroscope and accelerometer readings. However, it requires a large amount of user data for model training. *WiDraw* [38] enables device-free in-air writing by exploiting changes in the AoA spectrum measured at many nearby Wi-Fi devices caused by human arm motion. However, to achieve five cm accuracy, WiDraw requires the support of 30 neighboring Wi-Fi devices and human writing 25 cm in width, considerably larger than PolarDraw. A Wi-Fi band software-defined radio based system by Chen *et al.* [9] passively tracks keystrokes adapting to interfering environmental motion, but requires five nearby antennas for best accuracy.

FingerIO [27] uses sound to track finger motion without the need for added RFID tags or any mobile device present, to a fine-grained precision of 8 mm. However when there is an interfering bystander in the environment at a range of 50 cm, the authors' experimental results show an increase in FingerIO's motion tracking error from 8 mm to 15 cm. On the other hand, our results in §5.2.5 demonstrate that PolarDraw suffers no significant degradation of tracking precision in the presence of interfering human motion at a lesser standoff distance (30 cm). *AAMouse* [55] uses acoustic ranging to track a smartphone's trajectory with an median error of around 1.4 cm, but high frequency acoustic noises, especially sounds emitted by other smartphone-based styluses interfere with the system. The three-antenna *mTrack* system [48] uses one millimeter-wave transmit antenna and two receive antennas to track a pen with a 90th. percentile error below 8 mm, if background motion interference is not present, but accuracy degrades by almost a factor of two to 1.2 cm in the presence of an interfering person walking at a two meter range or standing still at a one meter range [7]. In contrast, our experiments show that PolarDraw can handle interfering walking-speed motion at a 30 cm range, hence demonstrate more robustness than the mTrack results. Besides, a back of the envelope calculation shows it will cost at least $7k to implement and is thus not cost effective.

Compared to both acoustic and millimeter-wave tracking, our experiments demonstrate greater range (§5.2.4) and more robustness to nearby interfering motion (§5.2.5).

Wi-Fi localization and tracking.. Many of these proposals achieve meter-level localization accuracy [8, 26, 32, 54], hence are unable to recognize fine-grained human writing. Although later schemes achieve centimeter-level localization accuracy [2, 16, 18, 35, 36, 50, 56], they generally rely on software-defined radio and Wi-Fi chipsets on the mobile, and require more infrastructure than PolarDraw.

Human activity recognition.. *E-eyes* [47] detects and classifies different kinds of human activity at home through the use of commercial Wi-Fi APs. *WiHear* [42] recognizes human speech by analyzing the CSI pattern of Wi-Fi signals reflected by human lips. *WiKey* [5] decodes user input on keyboards by matching Wi-Fi signal patterns to fingerprints. These systems only work for predefined coarse-grained ac-

[6]When the device's location track is unknown *a priori*. When the device's future path is known beforehand, Tagoram achieves one cm accuracy, but this does not apply to writing.

[7]mTrack's experiments did not study closer writing to motion interference ranges.

tivities, and hence cannot be directly applied to fine-grained motion tracking and writing recognition since writing style varies from person to person.

7. DISCUSSION AND FUTURE WORK

We discuss limitations and opportunities for improvement.

Trade-off between infrastructure cost and performance. Prior systems such as Tagoram and RF-IDraw require four and eight antennas for tag motion tracking, respectively. In contrast, PolarDraw requires only two antennas to operate, hence reducing the system cost by half compared to Tagoram. While the recognition accuracy of PolarDraw decreases slightly compared to both Tagoram and RF-IDraw, we believe by applying natural language processing techniques, we can further increase recognition accuracy. Furthermore, Tagoram requires a relatively close antenna spacing, so that the tag is within the coverage area of all four antennas. In contrast, since PolarDraw relies on just two antennas, it can cover much larger geographical area and potentially reduce the deployment cost, *e.g.*, classroom whiteboard.

Extending to multi-user case. Although our experiments are conducted in the single-user case, we believe it can be easily extended to multiple users by separating phase readings of each tag. This would involve examining the tag ID and rejecting dynamic multipath phase readings caused by nearby user writings. We leave this for our future work.

Scaling to abrupt hand motions. We assume a smooth hand movement and a relative stable tilt angle, which may not true for all users. We believe with lightweight inertial sensors on the tag (*e.g.*, WISP [49]), it is possible to detect tile angle changes and fetch this angle into the HMM model for a more accurate trail estimation. The tag attached on the pen responds to the reader all the time, hence PolarDraw is unable to distinguish the words from a sentence. However, it is possible to detect whether the pen is touching the whiteboard or not by examining the accelerometer readings of this sensor-based tag. We leave this problem for our future work.

8. CONCLUSION

We have presented the design of PolarDraw, the first motion tracking system that can accurately reproduce and recognize handwritten letters in the air or on a whiteboard with just two nearby antennas. Our experimental results show that compared with other state-of-the-art multi-antenna tracking systems, PolarDraw reduces the infrastructure cost in half with a slightly degraded performance.

Acknowledgements

We sincerely thank our shepherd Prof. Neil Spring and the anonymous reviewers for their insightful comments. This material is based upon work supported by the National Science Foundation under Grant No. 1617161 and European Research Council under the European Union's Seventh Framework Programme (FP/2007-2013) / ERC Grant Agreement No. 279976.

APPENDIX

Modeling the HMM emission probability.. By jointly considering pen moving direction and the hyperbola constraint, we define the emission probability in Equation 11. In this equation, $\Delta\theta_{x_1,y_1}^{1,2}$ is the theoretical inter-phase difference of two antennas on location (x_1, y_1). d_{max} is the maximum moving distance of the pen within the feasible region. This equation takes into account the likelihood that the location (x_1, y_1) is on the hyperbolas computed from $\Delta\theta_i^{1,2}$ and the likelihood that the location (x_1, y_1) is on the pen trajectory:

$$Pr(X_{t+1} = (x_1, y_1)|Y_t) = \left(1 - \frac{\left|\Delta\theta_t^{1,2} - \Delta\theta_{x_1,y_1}^{1,2}\right|}{4\pi}\right) \cdot \left(1 - \frac{|-\cot(\alpha_r^t)\cdot x_1 - y_1 + \cot(\alpha_r^t)\cdot x_0 + y_0|}{d_{max}\cdot\sqrt{\cot^2(\alpha_r^t)+1}}\right) \quad (11)$$

References

[1] F. Adib, Z. Kabelac, D. Katabi. Multi-person localization via rf body reflections. *NSDI*, 2015.

[2] F. Adib, Z. Kabelac, D. Katabi, R. Miller. 3D Tracking via body radio reflections. *NSDI*, 2014.

[3] F. Adib, D. Katabi. See through walls with Wi-Fi! *SIGCOMM*, 2013.

[4] S. Agrawal, I. Constandache, S. Gaonkar, R. Roy Choudhury, K. Caves, F. DeRuyter. Using mobile phones to write in air. *MobiSys*, 2011.

[5] K. Ali, A. X. Liu, W. Wang, M. Shahzad. Keystroke recognition using WiFi signals. *MobiCom*, 2015.

[6] An-900lh antenna (http://rf-links.com/newsite/pdf/an900lh.pdf).

[7] Avery-Dennison UHF RFID inlay *AD-227m5*.

[8] P. Bahl, V. N. Padmanabhan. RADAR: An in-building RF-based user location and tracking system. *Infocom*, 2000.

[9] B. Chen, V. Yenamandra, K. Srinivasan. Tracking keystrokes using wireless signals. *MobiSys*, 2015.

[10] P. Dickson, W. Adrion, A. Hanson. Automatic capture and presentation creation from multimedia lectures. *Frontiers in Education Conf.*, 2008.

[11] Emerald (http://emeraldforhome.com).

[12] Google Project Soli.

[13] LipiTk: online hand writing recognition toolkit.

[14] L. He, Z. Zhang. Real-time whiteboard capture and processing using a video camera for remote collaboration. *IEEE Trans. on Multimedia*, **9**(1), 198–206, 2007.

[15] ImpinJ Speedway R420 reader.

[16] K. Joshi, D. Bharadia, M. Kotaru, S. Katti. WiDeo: Fine-grained device-free motion tracing using RF backscatter. *NSDI*, 2015.

[17] R. Krigslund, P. Popovski, G. Petersen. Orientation sensing using multiple passive RFID tags. *IEEE*

Antennas and Wireless Prop. Letters, **11**, 176–179, 2012.

[18] S. Kumar, S. Gil, D. Katabi, D. Rus. Accurate indoor localization with zero start-up cost. *MobiCom*, 2014.

[19] Laird antenna 915MHZ 1/2WV-7 RA RPSMA.

[20] Laird pa9-12 antenna (https://www.atlasrfidstore.com/laird-pa9-12-lp-outdoor-rfid-antenna-fcc/).

[21] W. Lee, Y. Yeh. Polarization diversity system for mobile radio. *IEEE Trans. on Commms.*, **20**(5), 912–923, 1972.

[22] T. Liu, L. Yang, Q. Lin, Y. Guo, Y. Liu. Anchor-free backscatter positioning for RFID tags with high accuracy. *Infocom*, 2014.

[23] LLRP Toolkit.

[24] MimioProjector Touch Projector.

[25] MimioTeach Interactive Whiteboard.

[26] A. Musa, J. Eriksson. Tracking unmodified smartphones using Wi-Fi monitors. *SenSys*, 2012.

[27] R. Nandakumar, V. Iyer, D. Tan, S. Gollakota. FingerIO: Using Active Sonar for Fine-Grained Finger Tracking. *CHI*, 2016.

[28] Oxford English Dictionary.

[29] A. Parate, M.-C. Chiu, C. Chadowitz, D. Ganesan, E. Kalogerakis. Risq: Recognizing smoking gestures with inertial sensors on a wristband. *MobiSys*, 2014.

[30] T. Park, J. Lee, I. Hwang, C. Yoo, L. Nachman, J. Song. E-gesture: a collaborative architecture for energy-efficient gesture recognition with hand-worn sensor and mobile devices. *SenSys*, 2011.

[31] Q. Pu, S. Gupta, S. Gollakota, S. Patel. Whole-home gesture recognition using wireless signals. *MobiCom*, 2013.

[32] A. Rai, K. K. Chintalapudi, V. N. Padmanabhan, R. Sen. Zee: Zero-effort crowdsourcing for indoor localization. *MobiCom*, 2012.

[33] T. Rappaport. *Wireless Communications: Principles and Practice*. Prentice Hall, second edn., 2002.

[34] T. Rappaport, D. Hawbaker. Wide-band microwave propagation parameters using circular and linear polarized antennas for indoor wireless channels. *IEEE Trans. on Comms.*, **40**(2), 240–245, 1992.

[35] S. Sen, R. R. Choudhury, B. Radunovic, T. Minka. Precise indoor localization using PHY layer information. *MobiSys*, 2011.

[36] S. Sen, B. Radunovic, R. R. Choudhury, T. Minka. You are facing the Mona Lisa: Spot localization using PHY layer information. *MobiSys*, 2012.

[37] L. Shangguan, Z. Yang, A. X. Liu, Z. Zhou, Y. Liu. Relative localization of RFID tags using spatial-temporal phase profiling. *NSDI*, 2015.

[38] L. Sun, S. Sen, D. Koutsonikolas, K.-H. Kim. WiDraw: Enabling hands-free drawing in the air on commodity WiFi devices. *MobiCom*, 2015.

[39] Thinkmagic micro embeded rfid reader module (https://www.atlasrfidstore.com/thingmagic-micro-embedded-rfid-reader-module/).

[40] Thinkmagic m6e micro embeded rfid reader module (https://www.atlasrfidstore.com/thingmagic-m6e-embedded-rfid-reader-module/).

[41] D. Vasisht, S. Kumar, D. Katabi. Decimeter-level localization with a single WiFi access point. *NSDI*, 2016.

[42] G. Wang, Y. Zou, Z. Zhou, K. Wu, L. M. Ni. We can hear you with Wi-Fi! *MobiCom*, 2014.

[43] H. Wang, T. Lai, R. Choudhury. MoLe: Motion leaks through smartwatch sensors. *MobiCom*, 2015.

[44] J. Wang, D. Katabi. Dude, where's my card? RFID positioning that works with multipath and non-line of sight. *SIGCOMM*, 2013.

[45] J. Wang, D. Vasisht, D. Katabi. RF-IDraw: Virtual touch screen in the air using RF signals. *SIGCOMM*, 2014.

[46] W. Wang, A. Liu, M. Shahzad, K. Ling, S. Lu. Understanding and modeling of WiFi signal based human activity recognition. *MobiCom*, 2015.

[47] Y. Wang, J. Liu, Y. Chen, M. Gruteser, J. Yang, H. Liu. E-eyes: device-free location-oriented activity identification using fine-grained WiFi signatures. *MobiCom*, 2014.

[48] T. Wei, X. Zhang. mTrack: High-precision passive tracking using millimeter wave radios. *MobiCom*, 2015.

[49] Wisp 5 (https://wisp5.wikispaces.com/wisp+home).

[50] J. Xiong, K. Jamieson. ArrayTrack: A fine-grained indoor location system. *NSDI*, 2013.

[51] D. Xu, R. Yi. A computer vision based whiteboard capture system. *IEEE WACV*, 2008.

[52] L. Yang, Y. Chen, X.-Y. Li, C. Xiao, M. Li, Y. Liu. Tagoram: Real-time tracking of mobile RFID tags to high precision using COTS devices. *MobiCom*, 2014.

[53] Yap-100cp antenna (http://sbrfid.com/yap100cp.pdf).

[54] M. Youssef, A. Agrawala. The Horus WLAN location determination system. *MobiSys*, 2005.

[55] S. Yun, Y.-C. Chen, L. Qiu. Turning a mobile device into a mouse in the air. *MobiSys*, 2015.

[56] Y. Zhu, Y. Zhu, B. Zhao, H. Zheng. Reusing 60GHz radios for mobile radar imaging. *MobiCom*, 2015.

Maximizing Broadcast Throughput Under Ultra-Low-Power Constraints

Tingjun Chen[†], Javad Ghaderi[†], Dan Rubenstein[‡], Gil Zussman[†]
[†] Electrical Engineering, [‡] Computer Science, Columbia University
{tingjun@ee, jghaderi@ee, danr@cs, gil@ee}.columbia.edu

ABSTRACT

Wireless object tracking applications are gaining popularity and will soon utilize emerging ultra-low-power device-to-device communication. However, severe energy constraints require much more careful accounting of energy usage than what prior art provides. In particular, the available energy, the differing power consumption levels for listening, receiving, and transmitting, as well as the limited control bandwidth must all be considered. Therefore, we formulate the problem of maximizing the throughput among a set of heterogeneous broadcasting nodes with differing power consumption levels, each subject to a strict ultra-low-power budget. We obtain the oracle throughput (i.e., maximum throughput achieved by an oracle) and use Lagrangian methods to design EconCast – a simple asynchronous distributed protocol in which nodes transition between sleep, listen, and transmit states, and dynamically change the transition rates. We also show that EconCast approaches the oracle throughput. The performance is evaluated numerically and via extensive simulations and it is shown that EconCast outperforms prior art by 6x – 17x under realistic assumptions. Finally, we implement EconCast using the TI eZ430-RF2500-SEH energy harvesting nodes and experimentally show that in realistic environments it obtains 57% – 77% of the achievable throughput.

CCS Concepts

•Networks → Network protocol design; Network performance analysis; Wireless local area networks; •Mathematics of computing → Probabilistic algorithms;

Keywords

Ultra-low-power networking; Wireless networks; Sleep-wake protocols

CoNEXT '16, December 12 - 15, 2016, Irvine, CA, USA

 ISBN 978-1-4503-4292-6/16/12...$15.00

DOI: http://dx.doi.org/10.1145/2999572.2999608

1. INTRODUCTION

Object tracking and monitoring applications are gaining popularity within the realm of Internet-of-Things [3]. One enabler of such applications is the growing class of ultra-low-power wireless nodes. An example is active tags that can be attached to physical objects, harvest energy from ambient sources, and communicate tag-to-tag toward gateways [20, 41]. Relying on node-to-node communications will require less infrastructure than traditional (RFID/reader-based) implementations. Therefore, as discussed in [7, 20, 34, 56], it is envisioned that such ultra-low-power nodes will facilitate tracking applications in healthcare, smart building, assisted living, manufacturing, supply chain management, and intelligent transportation.

A fundamental challenge in networks of ultra-low-power nodes is to schedule the nodes' sleep, listen/receive, and transmit events without coordination, such that they communicate effectively while adhering to their strict power budgets. For example, energy harvesting tags need to rely on the power that can be harvested from sources such as indoor-light or kinetic energy, which provide between $0.01\,\mathrm{mW}$ and $0.1\,\mathrm{mW}$ [21, 22] (for more details see the review in [51] and references therein). These power budgets are much lower than the power consumption levels of current low-power wireless technologies such as Bluetooth Low Energy [2] and ZigBee/802.15.4 [32] (usually at the order of $1 - 10\,\mathrm{mW}$). On the other hand, Bluetooth Low Energy and ZigBee are designed to support data rates (up to a few Mbps) that are higher than required by the applications our work envisages supporting (less than a few Kbps).

In this paper, we formulate the problem of *maximizing broadcast throughput among energy-constrained nodes*. We design, analyze, and evaluate EconCast: **E**nergy-**con**strained Broad**Cast**. EconCast is an asynchronous distributed protocol in which nodes transition between sleep, listen/receive, and transmit states, while maintaining a power budget. The nodes and network we focus on have the following characteristics:

Broadcast: A transmission can be heard by all listening nodes in range.

Severe power constraints: The power budget is so limited that each node needs to spend most of its time in sleep state and the supported data rates can be of a few Kbps [22]. Traditional approaches that spend energy in order to improve

coordination (e.g., accurate clocks, slotting, synchronization) or form some sort of structure (e.g., routing tables and clusters) are too expensive given limited energy and bandwidth.
Unacquainted: Nodes do not require pre-existing knowledge of their environment (e.g., properties of neighboring nodes). This can result from the restricted power budget or from unanticipated environment changes due to altered energy sources and/or node mobility.
Heterogeneous: The power budgets and the power consumption levels can differ among the nodes.

Efficiently operating such structureless and ultra-low-power networks requires nodes to make their sleep, listen, or transmit decisions in a distributed manner. Therefore, we consider the fundamental problem of maximizing the rate at which the messages can be delivered (the actual content of the transmitted messages depends on the application). Namely, we focus on maximizing the broadcast throughput and consider two alternative definitions:

- **Groupput** – the total rate of successful bit transmissions to *all the receivers* over time. Groupput directly applies to tracking applications in which nodes utilize a neighbor discovery protocol to identify neighbors which are within wireless communication range [8,27,29,42,49,53,57,60]. In such applications, broadcasting information to all other nodes in the network is important, allowing the nodes to transfer data more efficiently under the available power budgets. Groupput can also be applied to data flooding applications where the data needs to be collected at all the nodes in a network.
- **Anyput** – the total rate of successful bit transmissions to *at least one receiver* over time. It applies to delay-tolerant environments that utilize gossip-style methods to disseminate information. In traditional gossip communication, a node selects a communication partner in a deterministic or randomized manner. Then, it determines the content of the message to be sent based on a naive store-and-forward, compressive sensing [4,23,37,38,47,48], or decentralized coding [15,28]. As another example, in delay-tolerant applications, data transmission may get disrupted or lost due to the limits of wireless radio range, sparsity of mobile nodes, or limited energy resources, a node may wish to send its data to any available receiver.

First, we derive oracle throughput (i.e., maximum throughput achieved by an oracle). This is done both for the groupput and anyput and it is shown that the value can be efficiently computed. Then, we use Lagrangian methods and a Q-CSMA (Queue-based Carrier Sense Multiple Access) approach to design EconCast. The protocol has variants that maximize both groupput and anyput. In both of them, nodes dynamically adapt their transition rates between sleep, listen, and transmit states based on (i) the energy available at the node and (ii) the number (or existence) of other active listeners. To support the latter, a listening node emits a low-cost informationless "ping" which can be picked up by other listening nodes, allowing them to estimate the number (or existence) of active listeners. We briefly discuss how this method helps increasing the throughput and the implementation aspects. We analyze the performance of EconCast and prove that, in theory, it converges to the oracle throughput.

We evaluate EconCast numerically and via extensive simulations under a wide range of power budgets, and listen/transmit power consumption levels, and for various heterogeneous nodes. Specifically, numerical results show that EconCast outperforms prior art (Panda [42], Birthday [43], and Searchlight [5]) by a factor of 6x – 17x under realistic assumptions. In addition to throughput, we consider the performance in terms of burstiness and latency.

We implement EconCast using the TI eZ430-RF2500-SEH energy harvesting nodes and experimentally show that in practice it obtains $57\% - 77\%$ of the achievable throughput. Moreover, we compare the throughput obtained experimentally to analytical results for Panda [42] (where the analytical results are usually better than the experimental performance) and show that, for example, EconCast outperforms Panda by 8x – 11x.

We note that the design of EconCast does not assume a specific topology (nodes do not know anything about their neighbors). Yet, in this paper, we mainly focus on a clique topology (i.e., nodes are within the communication range of each other), since it lends itself to analysis. We briefly extend the analytic results to non-clique topologies and also evaluate the performance for such networks.

To summarize, the main contributions of this paper are: (i) a distributed asynchronous protocol for a heterogeneous collection of energy-constrained wireless nodes, that can obtain throughput that approaches the maximum possible, (ii) efficient methods to compute the oracle throughput, (iii) extensive performance evaluation of the protocol.

The rest of the paper is organized as follows. We discuss related work in Section 2 and formulate the problem in Section 3. In Section 4, we present methods to compute the oracle throughput. We present EconCast in Section 5 and outline the proof of the main theoretical result in Section 6. We evaluate EconCast numerically and via simulations and compare to related work in Section 7. In Section 8, we discuss the experimental implementation and evaluation. We conclude in Section 9. Due to space constraints, some of the proofs are omitted and can be found in the technical report [12].

2. RELATED WORK

There is vast amount of related literature in sensor networking and neighbor discovery that tries to limit energy consumption. Within this large body of work, most of the protocols do not explicitly account for different listen and transmit power consumption levels of the nodes [5,6,8,9,16, 26,43,46,49,50,52–54,59,60], or do not account for different power budgets [14, 17, 52–54, 59]. They mostly use a duty cycle during which nodes sleep to conserve energy and when nodes are simultaneously awake, a pre-determined listen-transmit sequence with an unalterable power consumption level is used. However, for ultra-low-power nodes constrained by severe power budgets, the appropriate amount

$\mathcal{N}$, N	Set of nodes, number of nodes
L_i, $\mathbf{L}$	Node i's listen power consumption (W), $\mathbf{L} = [L_i]$
X_i, $\mathbf{X}$	Node i's transmit power consumption (W), $\mathbf{X} = [X_i]$
ρ_i, $\boldsymbol{\rho}$	Node i's power budget (W), $\boldsymbol{\rho} = [\rho_i]$
b_i	Energy storage level of node i (J)
$\mathbf{w}$, $\mathcal{W}$	Network state, the set of collision-free states
α_i, $\boldsymbol{\alpha}$	Fraction of time node i listens, $\boldsymbol{\alpha} = [\alpha_i]$
β_i, $\boldsymbol{\beta}$	Fraction of time node i transmits, $\boldsymbol{\beta} = [\beta_i]$
γ, $\hat{\gamma}$	Indicator if existing some nodes listening, its estimated value
c, $\hat{c}$	Number of nodes listening, its estimated value
ν	Indicator if there is exactly one node transmitting
$\pi_{\mathbf{w}}$, $\boldsymbol{\pi}$	Fraction of time the network is in $w \in \mathcal{W}$, $\boldsymbol{\pi} = [\pi_{\mathbf{w}}]$
$\mathcal{T}_g$, $\mathcal{T}_a$	Groupput and Anyput of the network
$\mathcal{T}_{\mathbf{w}}$	Throughput of state $\mathbf{w} \in \mathcal{W}$
$\mathcal{T}^*$	Oracle throughput
η_i, $\boldsymbol{\eta}$	Lagrangian multiplier of node i, $\boldsymbol{\eta} = [\eta_i]$

Table 1: Nomenclature

of time a node sleeps should explicitly depend on the relative listen and transmit power consumption levels. These prior approaches achieve throughput levels which are much below optimal (and hence much below what EconCast can achieve). Additionally, there are protocols that often require some explicit coordination (e.g., slotting [14, 43, 46, 59], or explicitly require exchange of parameters [42], which are not suitable for emerging ultra-low-power nodes.

From the theoretical point of view, our approach is inspired by the prior work on network utility maximization (e.g., [13, 30, 35, 36]), and queue-based CSMA literature (e.g., [18, 19, 25, 33, 40, 58]). However, the problem considered in this paper is not a simple extension of the prior work for two reasons. First, in the past work on CSMA and network utility maximization, nodes or links make decisions based on the relative sizes of queues. Often, a queue is a backlog of data to send or the available energy. Prior work that considers the latter (e.g., [10, 31, 39]) uses the energy only for transmission, while listening is "free", which is a very different paradigm than the one considered in this paper. Second, in our setting, the queue "backlogs" energy but there is no clear mapping as previously assumed from energy to successful transmission. A node's listen or transmit events will relieve the backlog, but *do not* increase utility (throughput) unless other nodes are appropriately configured (i.e., transmitting when no listening nodes exist or listening when no transmitting nodes exist does not increase the throughput). This coordination of state among nodes to utilize their energy makes the considered problem more challenging.

Finally, we note that our approach should be amenable to emerging physical layer broadcast methods such as backscatter [34, 44].

3. MODEL AND PROBLEM FORMULATION

We consider a network of N energy-constrained nodes whose objective is to distributedly maximize the broadcast throughput among them. The set of nodes is denoted by $\mathcal{N}$. Table 1 summarizes the notations.

3.1 Basic Node Model

Power consumption: A node $i \in \mathcal{N}$ can be in one of three states: *sleep* (s), *listen/receive*[1] (l), and *transmit* (x), and the respective power consumption values are 0, L_i (W), and X_i (W).[2] These power consumption levels are based on hardware characteristics.

Power budget: Each node i has a *power budget* of ρ_i (W). This budget can be the rate at which energy is harvested by an energy harvesting node or a limit on the energy spending rate such that the node can maintain a certain lifetime. In practice, the power budget may vary with time [21, 22] and the distributed protocol should be able to adapt. For simplicity, we assume that the power budget is constant with respect to time. However, the analysis can be easily extended to the case with time-varying power budget with the same constant mean. Each node i also has an energy storage (e.g., a battery or a capacitor) whose level at time t is denoted by $b_i(t)$.

Severe Power Constraints: Intermittently connected energy-constrained nodes cannot rely on complicated synchronization or structured routing approaches.

Unacquainted: Low bandwidth implies that each node i must operate with very limited (i.e., no) knowledge regarding its neighbors, and hence, does not know or use the information (ρ_j, L_j, X_j) of the other nodes $j \neq i$.

3.2 Architecture Assumptions

We assume that there is only *one frequency channel* and *a single transmission rate* is used by all nodes in the transmit state. Similar to CSMA, nodes perform *carrier sensing* prior to attempting transmission to check the availability of the medium. Energy-constrained nodes can only be awake for very short periods, and therefore, the likelihood of overlapping transmissions is negligible.

We also assume that *a node in the listen state can send out low-cost, informationless "pings"* which can be picked up by other listening nodes, allowing them to estimate the number (or existence) of active listeners. We explain in Section 5 how this property will help us develop a distributed protocol and in Section 8, we provide practical means by which such estimates can be obtained.

3.3 Model Simplifications

At any time t, the network state can be described as a vector $\mathbf{w}(t) = [w_i(t)]$, where $w_i(t) \in \{s, l, x\}$ represents the state of node i. While the distributed protocol EconCast (described in Section 5) can operate in general scenarios, for analytical tractability, we make the following assumptions:

- The network is a *clique*.[3]
- Nodes can perform *perfect carrier sensing* in which the propagation delay is assumed to be zero.

These assumptions are suitable in the envisioned applications where the distances between nodes are small. Under these assumptions, the network states can be restricted to

[1]We refer the *listen* and *receive* states synonymously as the power consumption in both states is similar.

[2]The actual power consumption in the *sleep* state, which may be non-zero, can be incorporated by reducing ρ_i, or increasing both L_i and X_i, by the sleep power consumption.

[3]We also investigate non-clique networks in Section 4.3.

the set of *collision-free* states, denoted by $\mathcal{W}$ (i.e., states in which there is *at most* one node in transmit state). This reduces the size of the state space from 3^N to $(N+2)2^{N-1}$.

Let $\gamma_{\mathbf{w}} \in \{0,1\}$ indicate whether there *exists* some nodes listening in state $\mathbf{w}$ and let $c_{\mathbf{w}}$ be the number of listeners in state $\mathbf{w}$. We use $\nu_{\mathbf{w}} \in \{0,1\}$ as an indicator which is equal to 1 if there is *exactly* one transmitter in state $\mathbf{w}$ and is 0 otherwise. Based on these indicator functions, two measures of broadcast throughput, *groupput* and *anyput*, and the throughput of a given network state $\mathbf{w}$ are defined below.

DEFINITION 1 (GROUPPUT). *The groupput, denoted by $\mathcal{T}_g$, is the aggregate throughput of the transmissions received by all the receivers, where each transmitted bit is counted once per receiver to which it is delivered, i.e.,*

$$\mathcal{T}_g = \lim_{T\to\infty} \frac{1}{T} \int_{t=0}^{T} \nu_{\mathbf{w}(t)} c_{\mathbf{w}(t)} dt. \quad (1)$$

DEFINITION 2 (ANYPUT). *The anyput, denoted by $\mathcal{T}_a$, is the aggregate throughput of the transmissions that are received by at least one receiver, i.e.,*

$$\mathcal{T}_a = \lim_{T\to\infty} \frac{1}{T} \int_{t=0}^{T} \nu_{\mathbf{w}(t)} \gamma_{\mathbf{w}(t)} dt. \quad (2)$$

DEFINITION 3 (NETWORK STATE THROUGHPUT). *The throughput associated with a given network state $\mathbf{w} \in \mathcal{W}$, denoted by $\mathcal{T}_{\mathbf{w}}$, is defined as*

$$\mathcal{T}_{\mathbf{w}} = \begin{cases} \nu_{\mathbf{w}} c_{\mathbf{w}}, & \textit{for Groupput} \\ \nu_{\mathbf{w}} \gamma_{\mathbf{w}}, & \textit{for Anyput} \end{cases} \quad (3)$$

Note that without energy constraints, the oracle (maximum) groupput is $(N-1)$ and is achieved when some node always transmits and the remaining $(N-1)$ nodes always listen and receive the transmission. Similarly, the oracle (maximum) anyput without energy constraints is 1 and is achieved when some node always transmits and some other node always listens and receives the transmission.

3.4 Problem Formulation

Define $\pi_{\mathbf{z}}$ as the fraction of time the network spends in a given state $\mathbf{z} \in \mathcal{W}$, i.e.,

$$\pi_{\mathbf{z}} = \lim_{T\to\infty} \frac{1}{T} \int_{t=0}^{T} \mathbf{1}_{\{\mathbf{w}(t)=\mathbf{z}\}}\, \mathrm{d}t, \quad (4)$$

where $\mathbf{1}_{\{\mathbf{w}(t)=\mathbf{z}\}}$ is the indicator function which is 1, if the network is with state $\mathbf{z}$ at time t, and is 0 otherwise. Correspondingly, denote $\boldsymbol{\pi} = [\pi_{\mathbf{w}}]$.

Below, we define the *energy-constrained throughput maximization problem* (P1) where the fractions of time each node spends in sleep, listen, and transmit states are assigned while the node maintains the power budget. Define variables $\alpha_i, \beta_i \in [0,1]$ as the fraction of time node i spends in listen and transmit states, respectively. The fraction of time it spends in sleep state is simply $(1-\alpha_i-\beta_i)$. In view of (1) – (4), (P1) is given by

$$\text{(P1)} \quad \max_{\boldsymbol{\pi}} \ \sum\nolimits_{\mathbf{w}\in\mathcal{W}} \pi_{\mathbf{w}} \mathcal{T}_{\mathbf{w}} \quad (5)$$

$$\text{subject to} \quad \alpha_i L_i + \beta_i X_i \le \rho_i, \ \forall i \in \mathcal{N}, \quad (6)$$

$$\alpha_i = \sum\nolimits_{\mathbf{w}\in\mathcal{W}_i^l} \pi_{\mathbf{w}}, \ \beta_i = \sum\nolimits_{\mathbf{w}\in\mathcal{W}_i^x} \pi_{\mathbf{w}}, \quad (7)$$

$$\sum\nolimits_{\mathbf{w}\in\mathcal{W}} \pi_{\mathbf{w}} = 1, \ \pi_{\mathbf{w}} \ge 0, \ \forall \mathbf{w} \in \mathcal{W}, \quad (8)$$

where $\mathcal{W}_i^l$ and $\mathcal{W}_i^x$ are the sets of states $\mathbf{w} \in \mathcal{W}$ in which $w_i = l$ and $w_i = x$, respectively. Each node is constrained by a power budget, as described in (6), and (8) represents the fact that at any time, the network operates in one of the collision-free states $\mathbf{w} \in \mathcal{W}$.

Based on the solution to (P1), the maximum throughput is achievable by an *oracle* that can schedule nodes' sleep, listen, and transmit periods, in a centralized manner. Therefore, we define the maximum value obtained by solving (P1) as the *oracle throughput*, denoted by $\mathcal{T}^*$. Respectively, we define the *oracle groupput* and *oracle anyput* as $\mathcal{T}_g^*$ and $\mathcal{T}_a^*$.

To evaluate EconCast, it is essential to compare its performance to the oracle throughput. However, (P1) is a Linear Program (LP) over an exponentially large number of variables (i.e., $|\mathcal{W}|$ is exponential in N) and is computationally expensive to solve. In Section 4, we show how to convert (P1) to another optimization problem with only a linear number of variables. Note that the solution to (P1) only provides the optimal fraction of time each node should spend in sleep, listen, and transmit states, but *does not* indicate how the nodes can make their individual sleep, listen, and transmit decisions locally. Therefore, in Section 5, we focus on the design of EconCast that makes these decisions based on (P1).

4. ORACLE THROUGHPUT

In this section, we present an equivalent LP formulation for (P1) in a clique network which only has a linear number of variables. We also derive both an upper and a lower bound for the oracle groupput in non-clique topologies which will be used later for evaluating the performance of EconCast in non-clique topologies.

Recall that α_i and β_i are the fraction of time node i spends in listen and transmit states, respectively. We can rewrite the constraints in (P1) as follows

$$\alpha_i L_i + \beta_i X_i \le \rho_i, \quad \forall i \in \mathcal{N}, \quad (9)$$

$$\alpha_i + \beta_i \le 1, \quad \forall i \in \mathcal{N}, \quad (10)$$

$$\sum\nolimits_{i\in\mathcal{N}} \beta_i \le 1. \quad (11)$$

Specifically, (9) is the usual power budget constraint on each node $i \in \mathcal{N}$, and (10) is due to the fact that a node can only operate in one state at any time. We remark that energy-constrained nodes can only be awake for very small fractions of time (i.e., $\alpha_i + \beta_i \ll 1$), and therefore (10) may be redundant. Finally, collision-free operation in a clique network when *at most* one transmitter can be present at any time imposes (11) which bounds the sum of the transmit fractions by 1.

4.1 Oracle Groupput in a Clique

To maximize the groupput (1), it suffices that any node only listens when there is another transmitter, since listening when no one transmits wastes energy. Namely, the fraction of time node i listens cannot exceed the aggregate fraction of time all other nodes transmit, i.e.,

$$\alpha_i \leq \sum\nolimits_{j \neq i} \beta_j, \ \forall i \in \mathcal{N}. \qquad (12)$$

Since a node only listens when there exists *exactly one* transmitter, every listen counts as a reception, and the groupput of a node (i.e., the throughput it receives from all other nodes) is simply the fraction of time it spends in listen state α_i. Therefore, the groupput in a clique network simplifies to $\sum_{i \in \mathcal{N}} \alpha_i$. The *oracle groupput*, denoted by $\mathcal{T}_g^*$, can be obtained by solving the following maximization problem

$$(\mathsf{P2}) \quad \mathcal{T}_g^* := \max_{\boldsymbol{\alpha}, \boldsymbol{\beta}} \ \sum\nolimits_{i \in \mathcal{N}} \alpha_i \qquad (13)$$
$$\text{subject to} \quad (9) - (12).$$

(P2) is an LP consisting of $2N$ variables and $(3N+1)$ constraints (i.e., solving for $\boldsymbol{\alpha}$ and $\boldsymbol{\beta}$ given inputs of N, $\boldsymbol{\rho}$, $\mathbf{L}$, and $\mathbf{X}$). On a conventional laptop running Matlab, this computation for thousands of nodes takes seconds. Moreover, we show that the oracle groupput obtained by solving (P2) is indeed *achievable* by an oracle which can schedule nodes' listen and transmit periods. This result is summarized in the following lemma and the proof is in [12].

LEMMA 1. *The (rational-valued) solution $(\boldsymbol{\alpha}^*, \boldsymbol{\beta}^*)$ to (P2) can be feasibly scheduled by an oracle in a fixed-size slotted environment via a periodic schedule, (perhaps) after a one-time energy accumulation interval.*

For the case of *homogeneous* nodes (i.e., $\rho_i = \rho$, $L_i = L$, $X_i = X$, $\forall i \in \mathcal{N}$) where nodes are sufficiently energy-constrained (i.e., (9) dominates (10)), the closed-form solution to (P2) (note that the equalities hold for equations (9) and (12)[4]) is given by

$$\beta^* = \rho/(X + (N-1)L), \ \alpha^* = (N-1)\beta^*, \ \mathcal{T}_g^* = N\alpha^*.$$

4.2 Oracle Anyput in a Clique

The oracle anyput is obtained based on the observation that a transmission only occurs when there is *at least* one listener. We define additional variables $\chi_{i,j}$ as the fraction of time node j receives a transmission from node i, for the following two constraints

$$\beta_i \leq \sum\nolimits_{j \neq i} \chi_{i,j}, \quad \forall i \in \mathcal{N}, \qquad (14)$$

$$\alpha_j = \sum\nolimits_{i \neq j} \chi_{i,j}, \quad \forall j \in \mathcal{N}. \qquad (15)$$

The *oracle anyput*, denoted by $\mathcal{T}_a^*$, can be obtained by solving the following maximization problem

$$(\mathsf{P3}) \quad \mathcal{T}_a^* := \max_{\boldsymbol{\alpha}, \boldsymbol{\beta}} \ \sum\nolimits_{i \in \mathcal{N}} \beta_i \qquad (16)$$
$$\text{subject to} \quad (9) - (11), (14), \text{and } (15).$$

[4]This can be proved by contradiction. The details can be found in [12].

First, (14) ensures that when node i transmits, there is always *at least* one other node than can receive this transmission. Then, (15) makes sure that in the optimal schedule, the fraction of time node j listens is large enough to cover all the transmissions it receives. Therefore, (P3) maximizes the anyput by ensuring that every transmission is received by *at least* one node.

For the case of homogeneous nodes, the closed-form solution to (P3) is given by

$$\beta^* = \alpha^* = \rho/(X + L), \ \mathcal{T}_a^* = N\beta^*.$$

4.3 Oracle Groupput in Non-cliques

The problem formulations (P1) – (P3) so far have assumed a clique network. Obtaining the exact maximum groupput for non-cliques (denoted by $\mathcal{T}_{\text{nc}}^*$) is difficult. This is because a node may receive simultaneous transmissions from two nodes which are not within communication range of each other. As explained before, listen and transmit events are rare within energy-constrained nodes. Therefore, the likelihood of simultaneous transmissions is small and it is expected to have minimal impact on the throughput.

We present both an upper bound $\overline{\mathcal{T}_{\text{nc}}^*}$ and a lower bound $\underline{\mathcal{T}_{\text{nc}}^*}$ on the maximum groupput in non-clique topologies. In the scenarios where $\overline{\mathcal{T}_{\text{nc}}^*}$ and $\underline{\mathcal{T}_{\text{nc}}^*}$ are the same, the exact maximum groupput $\mathcal{T}_{\text{nc}}^*$ can be obtained. The lower bound $\underline{\mathcal{T}_{\text{nc}}^*}$ is obtained by solving (P2) but replace constraint (12) by

$$\alpha_i \leq \sum\nolimits_{i \in \mathcal{N}(i)} \beta_j, \ \forall i \in \mathcal{N},$$

where $\mathcal{N}(i)$ is the set of neighboring nodes of node i. This ensures that the fraction of time node i listens cannot exceed the sum of its neighboring nodes' fractions of transmissions. The upper bound $\overline{\mathcal{T}_{\text{nc}}^*}$ is obtained by solving (P2) in which the constraint (11) is removed. This allows overlapping transmissions which can possibly happen in non-cliques. Numerical results show that with certain topologies, $\overline{\mathcal{T}_{\text{nc}}^*} = \underline{\mathcal{T}_{\text{nc}}^*}$ holds, resulting in the exact maximum groupput $\mathcal{T}_{\text{nc}}^*$. In Section 7.5, we compute $\mathcal{T}_{\text{nc}}^*$ and evaluate the performance of EconCast in such scenarios.

5. DISTRIBUTED PROTOCOL

In this section, we describe EconCast from the perspective of a single node that transitions between sleep, listen, and transmit states, under a power budget. Since we focus on a single node i, in parts of this section, we drop the subscript i of previously defined variables for notational compactness.

5.1 A Simple Heterogeneous Example

To better understand the challenges faced in designing EconCast, consider a simple example of 4 nodes, all having identical listen and transmit costs $L_i = X_i = 1\,\text{mW}$ ($i = 1, 2, 3, 4$), but different power budgets ρ_i, as indicated in Table 2. Table 2 also shows the percentage of time each node spends in listen and transmit states (α_i^*, β_i^*) ($i = 1, 2, 3, 4$) such that the groupput is maximized by solving (P1). It also shows the percentage of time each node spends in transmit state *when awake* (i.e., $\frac{100 \cdot \beta_i^*}{\alpha_i^* + \beta_i^*}\%$).

Node	1	2	3	4
Power Budget: ρ_i(mW)	0.005	0.01	0.05	0.1
Awake(%): $\alpha_i^* + \beta_i^*$	0.5	1.0	5.0	10.0
Transmit when Awake(%)	20.0	22	53.6	65.7

Table 2: A simple example in a heterogeneous network.

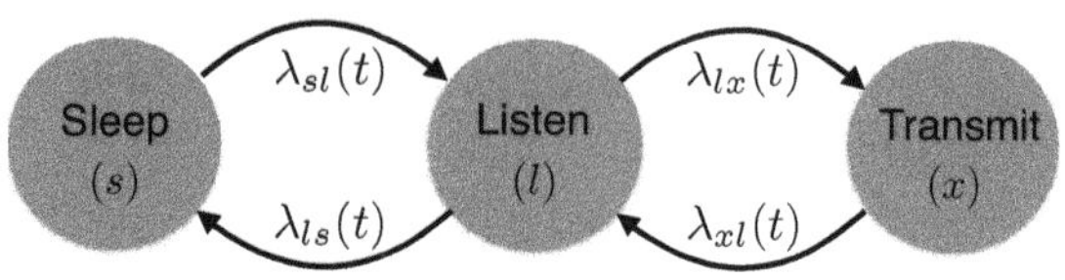

Figure 1: The node's states and transition rates.

If, instead, all nodes have the same power budget of $\rho_i = 0.1\,\text{mW}$, the percentage of time each node spends in transmit state when awake is 25% (with $\alpha_i^* = 0.075$, $\beta_i^* = 0.025$, $i = 1, 2, 3, 4$). Note that in the above example, the power budget of node 4 remains unchanged but changes in other nodes' power budgets shift the percentage of time it should transmit when awake from 25% to 65.7%. This clearly shows that the partitioning of a node's power budget among listen and transmit states is highly dependent on other nodes' properties. *However, we will show that if a node does not know the properties of its neighbors, an optimal configuration can be obtained without explicitly solving (P1).*

5.2 Protocol Description

To clearly present EconCast, we start from a theoretical framework and slowly build on it to address practicalities. As mentioned in Section 3, a node can be in one of three states: sleep (s), listen (l), and transmit (x). As depicted in Figure 1, it must pass through the listen state to transition between sleep and transmit states. The time duration a node spends in a given state u before transitioning to state v is exponentially distributed with rate $\lambda_{uv}(t)$. These *transition rates* can be adjusted over time. We remark that sending packets with exponentially distributed length (i.e., a node transitions from transmit state to listen state with a rate λ_{xl}) is impractical. However, it can be shown that this is equivalent to continuously transmitting back-to-back unit-length packets with probability $(1 - \lambda_{xl})$ if $\lambda_{xl} \in [0, 1]$, which is indeed the case in EconCast.

The throughput (5) as a function of π_{w} is controlled by appropriately adjusting the transition rates between different states of each node. EconCast determines in a distributed manner how these adjustments are performed over time. Roughly speaking, each node adjusts its transition rates $\lambda_{uv}(t)$ based on limited information that can be obtained in practice, which includes

- Its power consumption levels, L and X, and energy storage level $b(t)$.
- A sensing of transmit activity of other nodes over the channel (CSMA-like carrier sensing).
- A count of other active listeners (for groupput maximization), $c(t)$, or an indicator of whether there are any active listeners (for anyput maximization), $\gamma(t)$. In practice, $c(t)$ and $\gamma(t)$ may not be accurate, and we denote $\hat{c}(t)$ and $\hat{\gamma}(t)$ as their estimated values.

We note that in EconCast, unlike in previous work such as Panda [42], each node *does not* need to know the number of nodes in the network, N, and the power budgets and power consumption levels of other nodes. Furthermore, a node does not need to know its power budget ρ explicitly (e.g., in the case of energy harvesting [41]), although this knowledge can be incorporated, if available.

Under EconCast, a node sets $\lambda_{sl}(t)$ as an increasing function of the available stored energy, $b(t)$, to more aggressively exit sleep state. Furthermore, it sets $\lambda_{lx}(t)$ as an increasing function of the number of listeners, $\hat{c}(t)$, to enter transmit state more frequently when more nodes are listening. We will describe how these functions are chosen in Section 5.5.

5.3 Estimating Active Listeners: Pings

As described above, an important input to EconCast is the number of active listeners $c(t)$ (for groupput) or the indicator of existence of active listeners $\gamma(t)$ (for anyput). We now discuss the estimation of $\hat{c}(t)$ or $\hat{\gamma}(t)$. Recall from Section 3 that nodes can send out periodic *pings* that any other listener can receive. The pings need not carry any explicit information and are potentially significantly cheaper and shorter than control packet transmissions (e.g., an ACK). Therefore, they consume less power and take much less time than a minimal data transmission.

Consider the case in which all nodes are required to send pings at a pre-determined rate and the power consumption is accounted for in the listening power consumption L. In such a case, a fellow listener detecting such pings (e.g., using a simple energy detector) can use the count of such pings in a given period of time, or the inter-arrival times of pings, to estimate the number of active listeners $c(t)$. Estimating $\gamma(t)$ is even easier by detecting the existence of any ping. In general, the estimates do not need to be accurate for EconCast to function, although poor estimates are expected to reduce throughput.

5.4 Two Variants of EconCast

We now address the incorporation of the estimates $\hat{c}(t)$ and $\hat{\gamma}(t)$ into EconCast. We present two versions of EconCast which only differ when a node is in transmit state:

- EconCast-C (the capture version): a node may "capture" the channel and transmit for an exponential amount of time (i.e., several back-to-back packets). When each packet transmission is completed, the transmitter listens for pings for a fixed-length *pinging interval*. Each successful recipient of the transmission initiate one ping at time chosen uniformly at random on this interval. The transmitter then estimates $\hat{c}(t)$ or $\hat{\gamma}(t)$ based on the count of pings received and adjusts $\lambda_{xl}(t)$ (as described in Section 5.5). In Section 8.3, we discuss the experimental implementation of this process.
- EconCast-NC (the non-capture version): a node always releases the channel after one packet transmission. Each

node continuously pings and receives pings from other nodes when listening, estimates $\hat{c}(t)$ or $\hat{\gamma}(t)$, and adjusts $\lambda_{lx}(t)$ (as described in Section 5.5).

EconCast-C is significantly easier to implement since the estimates are only needed for the transmitter right after each packet transmission. The probability that the same transmitter will continue transmitting depends on the estimates $\hat{c}(t)$ or $\hat{\gamma}(t)$. Therefore, our implementation and experimental evaluations in Section 8 focus on EconCast-C.

5.5 Setting Transition Rates

Consider a node running EconCast. Time is broken into intervals of length τ_k ($k = 1, 2, \cdots$). The k-th interval is from time t_{k-1} to time t_k and we let $t_0 = 0$. EconCast takes input of two internal variables:

- η is a multiplier which is updated at the beginning of each time interval. Let $b[k]$ ($k = 0, 1, \cdots$) denote the energy storage level at the end of the k-th time interval. Let $(\cdot)^+$ denote $\max(0, \cdot)$ and $\eta[k]$ is updated as follows

$$\eta[k] = \left(\eta[k-1] - \frac{\delta_k}{\tau_k} \cdot (b[k] - b[k-1])\right)^+, \quad (17)$$

  in which $\delta_k \in (0, 1)$ is a step size and $b[k] = b(t_k)$. We use square brackets here to imply that the multiplier $\eta[k]$ remains constant for $t \in [t_k, t_{k+1})$.
- $A(t)$ is the carrier sensing indicator of a node, which is 1 when the node does not sense any ongoing transmission, and is 0 otherwise. Carrier sensing forces a node to "stick" to its current state. When receiving an ongoing transmission, a node in listen state will not exit the listen state until it finishes receiving the full transmission, and a node in sleep state will not leave the sleep state (i.e., it enters the listen state but immediately leaves when it hears the ongoing transmission by performing carrier sensing).

The transition rates are described as follows (the superscripts C and N denote EconCast-C and EconCast-NC). For grouppput maximization, at any time t in the k-th interval,

$$\lambda_{sl}(t) = A(t) \cdot \exp[-\eta[k]L/\sigma)], \quad (18a)$$
$$\lambda_{ls}(t) = A(t), \quad (18b)$$
$$\lambda_{lx}^C(t) = A(t) \cdot \exp[\eta[k](L - X)/\sigma], \quad (18c)$$
$$\lambda_{lx}^N(t) = A(t) \cdot \exp[\eta[k](L - X)/\sigma + \hat{c}(t)/\sigma], \quad (18d)$$
$$\lambda_{xl}^C(t) = \exp[-\hat{c}(t)/\sigma], \quad (18e)$$
$$\lambda_{xl}^N(t) = 1. \quad (18f)$$

For anyput maximization, $\hat{c}(t)$ is replaced with $\hat{\gamma}(t)$. Theorem 1 below states the main result of this paper. We outline the proof and explain the intuition behind the protocol in Section 6.

THEOREM 1. *Let $\sigma \to 0$ and select parameters δ_k and τ_k properly (e.g., $\delta_k = 1/[(k+1)\log(k+1)]$ and $\tau_k = k$). Under perfect knowledge of $c(t)$ or $\gamma(t)$, the average throughput of EconCast ($\mathcal{T}_g$ or $\mathcal{T}_a$) converges to the oracle throughput ($\mathcal{T}_g^*$ or $\mathcal{T}_a^*$) given by (P1).*

5.6 Stability and Choice of σ, δ_k, and τ_k

EconCast is adaptive and, as expected, it must deal with the tradeoff of "adapting quickly but poorly" to "adapting optimally but slowly". This adaptation manifests itself into the parameters σ, δ_k, and τ_k. When σ is increased, the throughput is less bursty (nodes transition from transmit state to listen state more frequently). However, the resulting throughput also decreases with respect to increased σ, as we will describe in Section 6.

Under a given value of σ, each node continuously adjusts the rates $\lambda_{uv}(t)$ based on its multiplier η according to (17), which is a function of the ratio δ_k/τ_k. Small δ_k/τ_k ratios make smaller changes of η over time, and lead to longer convergence time to the "right" multiplier values. In contrast, larger δ_k/τ_k ratios make η oscillate more wildly near the optimal value, such that the performance of EconCast is further from the optimal. Although the guaranteed convergence requires careful choices of the parameters (as stated in Theorem 1), in practice, we can choose $\delta_k = \delta$ and $\tau_k = \tau$ for some small constant δ and large constant τ.

6. PROOF OUTLINE OF THEOREM 1

In this section we provide an outline of the proof of Theorem 1. The complete proof can be found in [12]. The proof is based on a Markov Chain Monte Carlo (MCMC) approach [18, 25, 40] from statistical physics.

First, note that if the vector of multipliers $\boldsymbol{\eta} = [\eta_i]$ freezes, EconCast generates the network state distribution described in the following lemma.

LEMMA 2. *With fixed $\boldsymbol{\eta}$, the network Markov chain, resulted from overall interactions among the nodes according to the transition rates (18), has the steady state distribution*

$$\pi_{\mathbf{w}}^{\boldsymbol{\eta}} = \frac{1}{Z^{\boldsymbol{\eta}}} \exp\left[\frac{1}{\sigma}\left(\mathcal{T}_{\mathbf{w}} - \sum_{i:w_i=l} \eta_i L_i - \sum_{i:w_i=x} \eta_i X_i\right)\right], \quad (19)$$

where $Z^{\boldsymbol{\eta}}$ is a normalizing constant so that $\sum_{\mathbf{w}\in\mathcal{W}} \pi_{\mathbf{w}}^{\boldsymbol{\eta}} = 1$.

PROOF. The proof is followed by checking that the steady state distribution (19) satisfies the detailed balance equations of the network Markov chain. Details can be found in [12]. □

We then present an optimization problem (P4) as follows

$$\text{(P4)} \max_{\boldsymbol{\pi}} \sum_{\mathbf{w}\in\mathcal{W}} \pi_{\mathbf{w}} \mathcal{T}_{\mathbf{w}} - \sigma \sum_{\mathbf{w}\in\mathcal{W}} \pi_{\mathbf{w}} \log \pi_{\mathbf{w}} \quad (20)$$
$$\text{subject to} \quad (6), (7), \text{and } (8),$$

where σ is the positive constant used in EconCast (the counterpart in statistical physics is the temperature in systems of interacting particles). Note that (P4) is a concave maximization problem and as $\sigma \to 0$, the optimal value of (P4) approaches that of (P1). To solve (P4), consider the Lagrangian function $\mathcal{L}(\boldsymbol{\pi}, \boldsymbol{\eta})$ formulated by moving the energy constraint (6) into the objective (20) with a Lagrange multiplier $\eta_i \geq 0$ for each node i, i.e.,

$$\mathcal{L}(\boldsymbol{\pi}, \boldsymbol{\eta}) = \sum_{\mathbf{w}\in\mathcal{W}} \pi_{\mathbf{w}} \mathcal{T}_{\mathbf{w}} - \sigma \sum_{\mathbf{w}\in\mathcal{W}} \pi_{\mathbf{w}} \log \pi_{\mathbf{w}} - \sum_{i\in\mathcal{N}} [\eta_i(\alpha_i L_i + \beta_i X_i - \rho_i)]. \quad (21)$$

Algorithm 1 Gradient Descent Algorithm

Input parameters: σ, $\boldsymbol{\rho}$, $\mathbf{L}$, and $\mathbf{X}$
Initialization: $\alpha_i(0) = \beta_i(0) = \eta_i(0) = 0$, $\forall i \in \mathcal{N}$
1: **for** $k = 1, 2, \cdots$ **do**
2: $\quad\delta(k) = 1/k$, compute $\boldsymbol{\pi}(k)$ from (19) using $\boldsymbol{\eta} = \boldsymbol{\eta}(k)$
3: $\quad$**for** $i = 1, 2, \cdots, N$ **do**
4: $\quad\quad$Update $\eta_i(k)$, $\alpha_i(k)$, and $\beta_i(k)$ according to (23), (24)

In view of (7) and (8), given a vector of multipliers $\boldsymbol{\eta}$, it can be shown that the optimal $\boldsymbol{\pi}^{\boldsymbol{\eta}} = [\pi^{\boldsymbol{\eta}}_{\mathbf{w}}]$ that maximizes $\mathcal{L}(\boldsymbol{\pi}, \boldsymbol{\eta})$ is exactly given by (19). Thus if EconCast knows the optimal choice of Lagrange multipliers, it can start with the optimal choice and the steady state distribution generated by EconCast will converge to the optimal solution to (P4).

Next, to find the optimal Lagrange multipliers $\boldsymbol{\eta}^*$, consider the dual $\mathcal{D}(\boldsymbol{\eta}) := \mathcal{L}(\boldsymbol{\pi}^{\boldsymbol{\eta}}, \boldsymbol{\eta})$ over $\boldsymbol{\eta} \succeq \mathbf{0}$ (here $\mathbf{0}$ is an N-dimensional zero vector and $\succeq$ denotes component-wise inequality). Interestingly, it can be shown that the partial derivative of $\mathcal{D}(\boldsymbol{\eta})$ with respect to η_i is simply given by

$$\partial\mathcal{D}/\partial\eta_i = \rho_i - (\alpha_i L_i + \beta_i X_i), \tag{22}$$

which is the difference between the power budget ρ_i and the average power consumption of node i. Therefore, the dual can be minimized by using a gradient descent algorithm with inputs of step size $\delta_k > 0$, $\boldsymbol{\rho}$, $\mathbf{L}$, and $\mathbf{X}$, which generates a state probability $\boldsymbol{\pi}(k)$ $(k = 1, 2, \cdots)$. This algorithm is described in Algorithm 1 along with the following equations

$$\eta_i(k) = [\eta_i(k-1) - \delta_k(\rho_i - \alpha_i(k)L_i - \beta_i(k)X_i)]^+, \tag{23}$$

$$\alpha_i(k) = \sum\nolimits_{\mathbf{w}\in\mathcal{W}_i^L} \pi^{\boldsymbol{\eta}(k)}_{\mathbf{w}},\ \beta_i(k) = \sum\nolimits_{\mathbf{w}\in\mathcal{W}_i^X} \pi^{\boldsymbol{\eta}(k)}_{\mathbf{w}}. \tag{24}$$

Hence, with the right choice of step size δ_k (e.g., $\delta_k = 1/k$), $\boldsymbol{\pi}(k)$ converges to the optimal solution to (P4).

Finally, to arrive at a distributed solution, instead of computing the quantities α_i and β_i directly according to (24) (which is centralized with high complexity), we can approximate the difference between the power budget and the average power consumption (22) by observing the dynamics of the energy storage level at each node. Specifically, each node i can update its Lagrange multiplier $\eta_i(k)$ based on the difference between its energy storage levels at the end and the start of an interval of length τ_k, divided by τ_k, as described by (17). Therefore η_i is updated according to a "noisy" gradient descent. However, it follows from stochastic approximation (with Markov modulated noise) that by choosing step sizes and interval lengths as given in Theorem 1, these noisy updates will converge to $\boldsymbol{\eta}^*$ as $k \to \infty$ (see e.g., Theorem 1 of [24]). As mentioned in Section 5.6, the choice of parameters σ, δ_k, and τ_k will affect the tradeoff between convergence time and the performance of EconCast.

7. NUMERICAL RESULTS

In this section, we consider various heterogeneous networks and numerically show that the throughput approaches the oracle throughput $\mathcal{T}^*$ as σ decreases. In the special case of homogeneous networks, we explore the sensitivity of the throughput to various power consumption levels, and compare to related work. Then, via simulations, we study the burstiness and latency of EconCast, and evaluate its performance in non-clique topologies.

Our general conclusions with respect to anyput performance are quite similar as to groupput. Therefore, we focus on the *groupput performance achieved by EconCast-C* throughout this section. For brevity, we omit the subscript for groupput and use the following notation: (i) $\mathcal{T}^*$ is the oracle groupput obtained by solving (P1) or, equivalently, (P2), (ii) $\mathcal{T}^\sigma$ is the achievable groupput of EconCast with a given value of σ obtained by solving (P4), and (iii) $\widetilde{\mathcal{T}^\sigma}$ is the groupput of EconCast obtained via simulations with a given value of σ.

7.1 Setup

We consider $\sigma \in \{0.1, 0.25, 0.5\}$. The nodes' power budgets and consumption levels correspond to energy harvesting budgets and ultra-low-power transceivers in [21,22,45]. Unless stated otherwise, we use a power budget of $\rho = 10\,\mu\text{W}$ and power consumption levels $L = X = 0.5\,\text{mW}$. This results in a ratio of 50 between the transceiver power consumption and the budget. Note that the performance of EconCast only depends on the *ratio* between the listen or transmit power and the power budget. For example, nodes with $\rho = 10\,\mu\text{W}, L = X = 0.5\,\text{mW}$ behave exactly the same as nodes with $\rho = 1\,\text{mW}, L = X = 50\,\text{mW}$. Therefore, the oracle throughput applies and EconCast can operate in very general settings.

Recall that we assume that there are not simultaneous transmissions and collisions. We also assume that the packet length is 1 ms and that nodes have accurate estimate of the number of listeners, i.e., $\hat{c}(t) = c(t)$.

Our simulation results show that $\widetilde{\mathcal{T}^\sigma}$ perfectly matches $\mathcal{T}^\sigma$ for $\sigma \in \{0.25, 0.5\}$. For $\sigma = 0.1$, $\widetilde{\mathcal{T}^\sigma}$ does not converge to $\mathcal{T}^\sigma$ within reasonable time due to the bursty nature of EconCast, as will be described in Section 7.4. Therefore, we evaluate the throughput performance of EconCast by comparing $\mathcal{T}^\sigma$ to $\mathcal{T}^*$ with varying σ in both heterogeneous and homogeneous networks. Specifically, *homogeneous networks* consist of nodes with the same power budget and consumption levels, i.e., $\rho_i = \rho, L_i = L, X_i = X, \forall i \in \mathcal{N}$.

7.2 Heterogeneous Networks – Throughput

One strength of EconCast is its ability to deal with *heterogeneous* networks. Figure 2 shows the throughput achieved by EconCast normalized to the corresponding oracle throughput (i.e., $\mathcal{T}^\sigma/\mathcal{T}^*$) for heterogeneous networks with $N = 5$ and $\sigma \in \{0.1, 0.25, 0.5\}$. The results are obtained by solving (P1) for $\mathcal{T}^*$ and (P4) for $\mathcal{T}^\sigma$ with a given value of σ. Intuitively, higher values of $\mathcal{T}^\sigma/\mathcal{T}^*$ indicate better performance of EconCast.

Along the x-axis, the *network heterogeneity*, denoted by h, is varied from 10 to 250 at discrete points. The relationship between the network heterogeneity and the values of h is as follows: (i) for each node i, L_i and X_i are indepen-

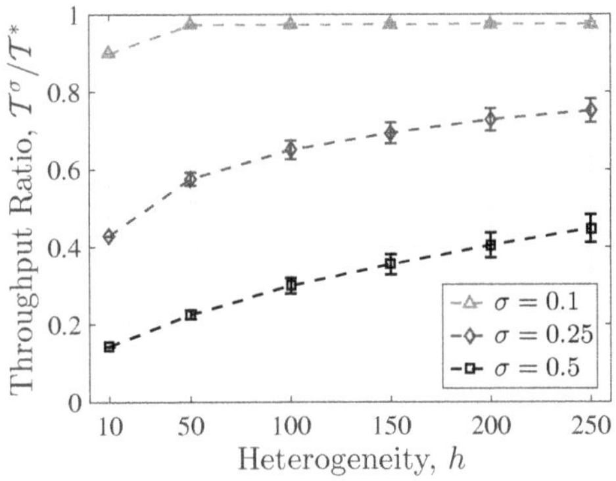

Figure 2: Sensitivity of the achievable throughput normalized to the oracle throughput, $\mathcal{T}^\sigma/\mathcal{T}^*$, to the heterogeneity of the power budget, ρ, and consumption levels, L and X.

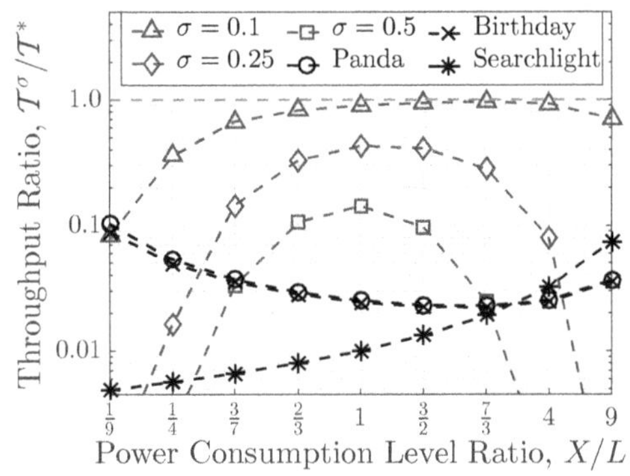

Figure 3: Throughput performance of various protocols (all normalized to the oracle throughput $\mathcal{T}^*$) with $N = 5$, $\rho = 10\,\mu\text{W}$, and $L + X = 1\,\text{mW}$, as a function of X/L.

dently selected from a uniform distribution on the interval $[510 - h, 490 + h]$ (μW), (ii) for each node i, a variable h' is first sampled from the interval $[-\log \frac{h}{100}, \log h]$ uniformly at random, and then ρ_i is set to be $\exp(h')$. Therefore, the energy budget ρ_i varies from $100/h$ to h (μW). As a result, for any h, L_i and X_i have mean values of $0.5\,\text{mW}$. ρ_i has median of $10\,\mu\text{W}$ but its mean increases as h increases. Note that a homogeneous network is represented by $h = 10$.

The y-axis indicates for each value of h, the mean and the 95% confidence interval of the ratios $\mathcal{T}^\sigma/\mathcal{T}^*$ averaged over 1000 heterogeneous network samples. Figure 2 shows that $\mathcal{T}^\sigma/\mathcal{T}^*$ approaches 1 as σ decreases, illustrating the results in Section 6. Furthermore, with increased heterogeneity of the network, $\mathcal{T}^\sigma/\mathcal{T}^*$ has little dependency on the heterogeneity but heavy dependency on σ. Since larger h values impose higher power budgets, the corresponding oracle throughput $\mathcal{T}^*$ increases as well.

7.3 Homogeneous Networks – Comparison to Related Work

We now evaluate the performance of EconCast in *homogeneous* networks with repest to different power consumption levels, and compare to related work which assumes homogeneity across nodes. We consider three protocols: *Panda* [42], *Birthday* [43], and *Searchlight* [5], which operate under stricter assumptions than EconCast. In particular:

- The probabilistic protocols Panda and Birthday both require a homogeneous set of nodes and a priori knowledge of the number of nodes, N. The throughput of Panda and Birthday is computed as described in [42] and [43], respectively.
- The deterministic protocol Searchlight is designed for minimizing the worst case pairwise discovery latency, which does not directly address multi-party communication across a shared medium. However, the discovery latency is closely related to the throughput, since the inverse of the average latency is the throughput. Hence, maximizing throughput is equivalent to minimizing the average discovery latency. We derive an upper bound on the throughput of Searchlight by multiplying the pairwise throughput by $(N - 1)$. This is assuming that all other $(N - 1)$ nodes will be receiving when one node transmits. However, in practice the throughput is likely to be lower unless all the nodes are synchronized and coordinated.

Figure 3 presents the throughput achieved by various protocols normalized to the oracle throughput $\mathcal{T}^*$ as a function of the ratio X/L, with $N = 5$, $\rho = 10\,\mu\text{W}$, and $L + X = 1\,\text{mW}$. The protocols considered are: EconCast with $\sigma \in \{0.1, 0.25, 0.5\}$, Panda, Birthday, and Searchlight.[5] The horizontal dashed line at 1 represents the oracle throughput. Note that with $L = X = 0.5\,\text{mW}$, the ratio $\mathcal{T}^\sigma/\mathcal{T}^*$ achieved by EconCast outperforms that of Panda by 6x and 17x with $\sigma = 0.5$ and $\sigma = 0.25$, respectively. The simulation results, which will be discussed later, also verify this throughput improvement.

Figure 3 shows that with $\sigma = 0.1$, $\mathcal{T}^\sigma$ is very close to the oracle throughput $\mathcal{T}^*$ unless $X \ll L$. As σ is increased, the ratio $\mathcal{T}^\sigma/\mathcal{T}^*$ drops as expected (see Section 6) but still significantly outperforms that of prior art for $X \approx L$. However, the performance of EconCast degrades with extreme values of X/L. This is because with small X/L values, nodes enter transmit state infrequently, since listen is expensive and they must pass the listen state to enter the transmit state. On the other hand, with large X/L values, nodes waste their energy to transmit even when there is no other nodes listening (e.g., $\hat{c}(t) = 0$). We believe that any distributed protocol will suffer from such performance degradation since, unlike Panda, Birthday, and Searchlight, nodes in a fully distributed setting *do not* have any information about the properties of other nodes in the network.

7.4 Burstiness and Latency

The results until now suggest allowing $\sigma \to 0$. While reducing σ improves throughput, it considerably increases the communication *burstiness*, as described in Section 5. In general, increased burstiness means that the long term throughput can be achieved with given power budgets but the vari-

[5]For Searchlight we compare its throughput upper bound to $\mathcal{T}^*$, as described in Section 7.3.

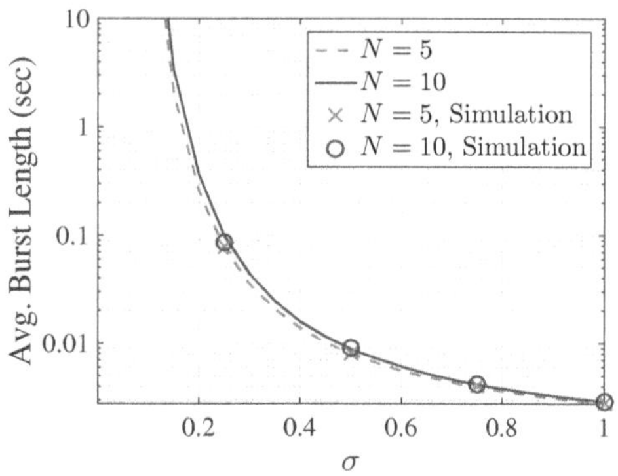

Figure 4: Average burst length obtained analytically (curves) and via simulation (markers) with $N \in \{5, 10\}$, $\sigma \in \{0.25, 0.5\}$, $\rho = 10\,\mu\text{W}$, and $L = X = 500\,\mu\text{W}$.

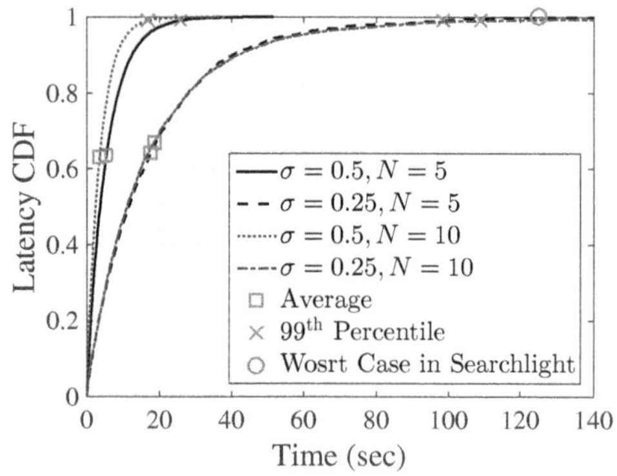

Figure 5: The CDF, mean, and 99th percentile latency of EconCast obtained via simulation with $N \in \{5, 10\}$, $\sigma \in \{0.25, 0.5\}$, $\rho = 10\,\mu\text{W}$, and $L = X = 500\,\mu\text{W}$, compared to the pairwise worst case latency of Searchlight.

ance is more significant during short term intervals. Recall from Section 7.1 that the packet length is 1 ms, we therefore measure the average burst length compared to this unit packet length.

Figure 4 shows the average burst length received by the nodes in homogeneous networks with $N \in \{5, 10\}$, $\rho = 10\,\mu\text{W}$, $L = X = 500\,\mu\text{W}$, and varying σ. Values are extracted using an analytical formula (curves) derived from the solution of (P4) and contrasted with simulations at specific values of σ (markers). Aside from showing that the simulation results and the analytical results are well matched, Figure 4 also demonstrates how reducing σ dramatically increases burstiness. For example, with $\sigma = 0.25$ and $N = 10$, a node has an average received burst length of 85 ms, and this value is increased to 4.5×10^5 ms with $\sigma = 0.1$. This explains why $\widetilde{\mathcal{T}^{\sigma}}$ cannot be obtained with $\sigma = 0.1$ (see Section 7.1) and we remark that reducing the communication burstiness is a subject of future work.

A second metric we consider is the communication *latency*. It is defined as the time interval between consecutive bursts received by a node from some other node where the interval includes *at least* one sleep period. We focus on this metric because nodes receiving longer bursts consume

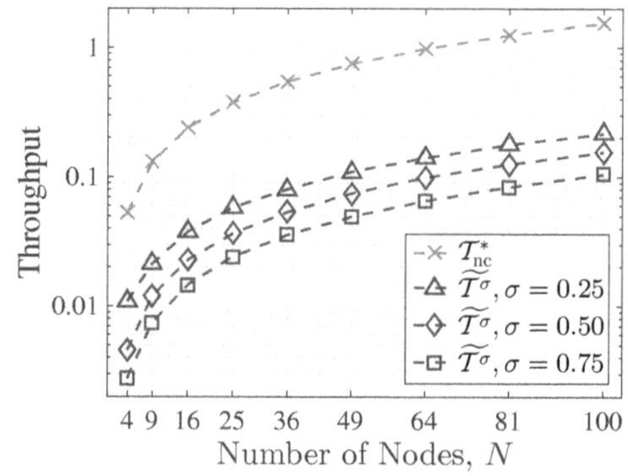

Figure 6: The oracle throughput in non-clique topologies, $\mathcal{T}^*_{\text{nc}}$, and the throughput of EconCast obtained via simulations, $\widetilde{\mathcal{T}^{\sigma}}$, in grid topologies with varying N and σ.

more energy, and therefore, need to sleep for longer periods of time. It is possible for a node to receive multiple bursts in one listen period. Figure 5 presents the CDF of communication latency obtained via simulations, for $N \in \{5, 10\}$ and $\sigma \in \{0.25, 0.5\}$, and indicates both the average and the 99th-percentile latency values. It also shows the pairwise worst case latency of Searchlight computed from [5] under the same power consumption level and power budget.[6]

Figure 5 shows that (i) as σ decreases, the latency increases since nodes suffering from long bursts will sleep longer, and (ii) larger value of N results in lower latency, since it is more likely to receive when more nodes exist. As an example, with $\sigma = 0.5$ and $N = 5$, a node receives bursts from some other node on average every 5 seconds. In addition, for all parameters considered, the 99th-percentile latency is within 120 seconds, outperforming the Searchlight pairwise worst case latency bound of 125 seconds. Note that although EconCast has a non-zero probability of having any latency, in most cases (over 99%), its latency is below the worst case latency of Searchlight.

7.5 Evaluation in Non-clique Topologies

We now compute the oracle throughput for non-clique topologies (derived in Section 4.3) and evaluate the throughput of EconCast in such scenarios. Operating in a distributed manner, EconCast can be easily adapted to non-clique topologies: if a node hears two simultaneous transmissions from two nodes, it does not count any of the transmissions as throughput. Recall from Section 3 that nodes always check the channel utilization before waking up, simultaneous transmission can only happen if two nodes are not within communication range of each other.

We use grid topologies with varying number of nodes, N, in which a node can only have at most 4 neighbors. For example, $N = 25$ represents a 5×5 grid. For each value of N, we compute the oracle throughput (groupput). Figure 6 presents the oracle throughput, $\mathcal{T}^*_{\text{nc}}$, for grid topologies, and the throughput achieved by EconCast via simulations with

[6]This is computed with slot length of 50 ms and a beacon (packet) length of 1 ms as was done in [49].

with varying σ. Note that for all the grid topologies considered, the upper and lower bounds of $\mathcal{T}_{\mathrm{nc}}^*$ (see Section 4.3) are the same, providing the exact oracle throughput.

Figure 6 shows that EconCast achieves $14\% - 22\%$ of the maximum throughput $\mathcal{T}_{\mathrm{nc}}^*$ with $\sigma = 0.25$. Although increasing σ leads to lower throughput, it can be observed that as N increases, the throughput approaches 10% of $\mathcal{T}_{\mathrm{nc}}^*$ with $\sigma = 0.5$. Although we cannot obtain the throughput for $\sigma = 0.1$, achieving $10\% - 20\%$ of $\mathcal{T}_{\mathrm{nc}}^*$ is remarkable given the fact that EconCast works in a distributed manner in which each node does not have any information of the properties of other nodes.

8. EXPERIMENTAL EVALUATION

To experimentally evaluate the performance of EconCast-C,[7] we implement it using the Texas Instruments eZ430-RF2500-SEH node [1].[8] In this section, we first describe the energy measurements performed on the nodes running EconCast. Then, we describe the method by which nodes can estimate the number of listening nodes. Finally, we experimentally evaluate the performance of EconCast.

8.1 Experimental Setup

The TI eZ430-RF2500-SEH node is equipped with: (i) an ultra-low-power MSP430 microcontroller and a CC2500 wireless transceiver operating at 2.4 GHz at 250 Kbps, (ii) a solar energy harvester (SEH-01) that converts ambient light into electrical energy, and (iii) a 1 mF capacitor to power up the transceiver board. Despite its drawbacks which will be discussed below, it can be used for evaluation by extending the length of the shortest allowable data transmission.

We consider power budgets of $\rho \in \{1\,\mathrm{mW}, 5\,\mathrm{mW}\}$. From our measurements, a node spends $L = 67.08\,\mathrm{mW}$ in the listen state and $X = 56.29\,\mathrm{mW}$ in the transmit state.[9] The power consumption levels are very similar from node to node. Recall from Section 7 that the performance of EconCast depends on the ratio between the power consumption levels and budget. Therefore, our experimental results will be similar to experiments when both the power consumption levels and budget are scaled down (e.g., a network of nodes with $\rho \in \{10\,\mu\mathrm{W}, 50\,\mu\mathrm{W}\}$, $L = 0.67\,\mathrm{mW}$, and $X = 0.56\,\mathrm{mW}$).

Each node is programmed with its ρ, L, and X as the input of EconCast-C. The nodes' main drawbacks include (i) inaccurate readings of the energy storage level (i.e., the voltage of the on-board capacitor) which are sensitive to the environment, and (ii) the fact that the 1 mF capacitor cannot support multiple packet transmissions. Due to these drawbacks, we implement (via software) a virtual battery at each node. The virtual battery emulates the node's energy storage level based on its sleep, listen, and transmit activities, and is used for updating the Lagrange multiplier according to (17). We show in the following section that in practice, a node running EconCast-C using this virtual battery is indeed consuming power at a rate close to its power budget.

8.2 Energy Consumption Measurements

To accurately measure the power consumption of the nodes, we disable the on-board solar cell, and attach a large pre-charged capacitor ($C_{\mathrm{cap}} = 5\,\mathrm{F}$) that stores energy in advance (similar power consumption measurements were used in [55]). The energy consumed is computed by

$$E_{\mathrm{consumed}} = 0.5 C_{\mathrm{cap}} \cdot \left(V_{t_0}^2 - V_{t_1}^2\right), \qquad (25)$$

where V_{t_0} and V_{t_1} are the measured power voltage values of the capacitor at t_0 and t_1. The empirical average power consumption, $\overline{P}(\mathrm{mW})$, is then computed by

$$\overline{P} = E_{\mathrm{consumed}} / \left(t_1 - t_0\right). \qquad (26)$$

Note that even with such a big capacitor, a node with a power budget of 1 mW (5 mW) has a lifetime of only 135 (27) minutes with $V_{t_0} = 3.6\,\mathrm{V}$ and $V_{t_1} = 3.0\,\mathrm{V}$, which represent its stable working voltage range.

To measure the power consumption of the nodes, we charge the capacitor to $V_{t_0} = 3.6\,\mathrm{V}$ and log the readings of V_{t_1} after 30 minutes using a multimeter. The empirical average power consumption is computed from (25) and (26) for $\sigma \in \{0.25, 0.5\}$ and is averaged using 60 runs. Because L and X do not account for some additional energy usage,[10] the *actual power consumption*, $\overline{P}$, is in fact a small fraction higher than the *target power budget*, ρ. Irrespective of σ, the measurement results show that $\overline{P}$ exceeds ρ by 11% for $\rho = 1\,\mathrm{mW}$, and by 4% for $\rho = 5\,\mathrm{mW}$.

Observing the empirical power consumption of the nodes, we compute the achievable throughput by solving (P4) using both the actual power consumption, $\overline{P}$, and the target power budget, ρ, denoted by $\overline{\mathcal{T}^{\sigma}}$ and $\mathcal{T}^{\sigma}$, respectively. In Section 8.4, we compare the experimental throughput to both $\overline{\mathcal{T}^{\sigma}}$ and $\mathcal{T}^{\sigma}$. Having verified the power consumption of the nodes, we replace the capacitor with AAA batteries,[11] allowing the experiments to run for longer times.

8.3 Practical Pinging

To enable practical pinging in EconCast-C, a short, fixed-length *pinging interval* is introduced after each packet transmission. During this interval, the transmitter listens for pings and recipients of the previous packet send a short ping at a random time uniformly distributed within the interval. The transmitter then estimates the number of listeners, $\hat{c}(t)$, by counting the pings it receives, and adjusts the transition rate, $\lambda_{xl}^{C}(t)$, according to (18e).

Ideally, each ping should be much shorter than both the pinging interval and the packet length in order to reduce the collisions between pings, as well as for the transmitter to

[7]See Section 5.4 the reasons for only implementing EconCast-C.

[8]A demonstration of the testbed is presented in [11].

[9]This corresponds to a $-16\,\mathrm{dBm}$ transmission power, at which nodes within the same room typically have little or no packet loss.

[10]The additional energy usage includes the energy consumed in powering up the regulator circuitry, etc.

[11]The constant voltage of AAA batteries limits the ability to measure the power consumption of the nodes.

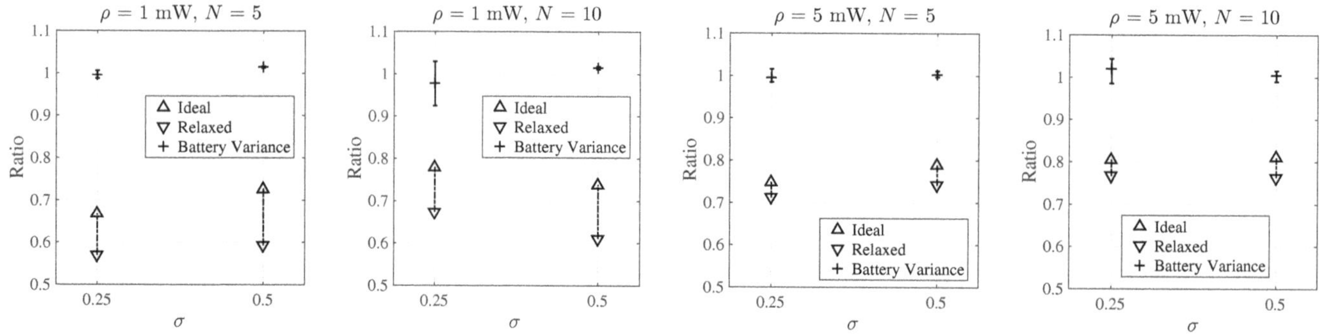

Figure 7: Points marked as "Ideal" ("Relaxed") represent ratio of experimental throughput normalized to the achievable throughput obtained by using the target power budget (actual power consumption) and points marked as "Battery Variance" present the average, minimum, and maximum ratios of power consumption normalized to target power budget, with $N \in \{5, 10\}$, $\rho \in \{1\,\text{mW}, 5\,\text{mW}\}$, and $\sigma \in \{0.25, 0.5\}$.

successfully receive it. Therefore, we use pings of length 0.4 ms, which is the shortest packet that can be sent by a node. Based on this, we empirically set the pinging interval to 8 ms and each data packet to 40 ms.

8.4 Performance Evaluation

We consider homogeneous networks of size $N \in \{5, 10\}$, power budgets $\rho \in \{1\,\text{mW}, 5\,\text{mW}\}$, $\sigma \in \{0.25, 0.5\}$, and nodes that are all located in proximity. One additional listening node (a 6th or 11th node) is also present but only as an observer and is connected to a PC via a USB port. Each data packet contains the node ID and information about the number of packets it has received from each other node. The observer node reports all received packets to the PC for storage and post processing. Each experiment is conducted for up to 24 hours. The experimental throughput is computed by dividing the duration of successful transmissions by the experiment duration.

Throughput evaluation: Figure 7 presents the ratio of the experimentally obtained throughput, $\widetilde{\mathcal{T}^\sigma}$, normalized to the achievable throughput $\mathcal{T}^\sigma$ and $\overline{\mathcal{T}^\sigma}$ (see Section 8.2). Separate charts represent the results for differing power budget, ρ, and number of nodes, N. Points marked "Ideal" show the experimental throughput normalized to the achievable throughput computed by solving (P4) with the target power budget ρ (i.e., $\widetilde{\mathcal{T}^\sigma}/\mathcal{T}^\sigma$). Points marked "Relaxed" show the experimental throughput normalized to the achievable throughput computed by solving (P4) with the actual power consumption $\overline{P}$ (i.e., $\widetilde{\mathcal{T}^\sigma}/\overline{\mathcal{T}^\sigma}$). As expected, $\overline{\mathcal{T}^\sigma}$ is higher than $\mathcal{T}^\sigma$, resulting in a lower throughput ratio.

Figure 7 shows that despite the practical limitations (e.g., packet collisions and inaccurate clocks) faced when running EconCast-C on real hardware, the ratio $\widetilde{\mathcal{T}^\sigma}/\overline{\mathcal{T}^\sigma}$ is between $57\% - 77\%$ ($\widetilde{\mathcal{T}^\sigma}/\mathcal{T}^\sigma$ is between $67\% - 81\%$) for all settings considered. Moreover, Table 3 shows the improvement of EconCast-C over the throughput of Panda computed according to [42], denoted by $\mathcal{T}_{\text{Panda}}$, under the same power consumption levels and budget, with $\sigma = 0.25$. It can be seen that with power budget of $\rho = 1$ mW, the experimental throughput of EconCast-C outperforms the analytically computed throughput of Panda by 8x – 11x.

$(N, \rho(\text{mW}))$	$(1, 5)$	$(1, 10)$	$(5, 5)$	$(5, 10)$
$\widetilde{\mathcal{T}^\sigma}/\mathcal{T}^\sigma$ (%)	66.78	77.96	74.84	80.53
$\mathcal{T}_{\text{Panda}}/\mathcal{T}^\sigma$ (%)	6.24	9.64	19.35	35.63
$\widetilde{\mathcal{T}^\sigma}/\mathcal{T}_{\text{Panda}}$	10.76	8.09	3.87	2.26

Table 3: Experimental throughput of EconCast-C compared to computed throughput of Panda (all normalized to the achievable throughput $\mathcal{T}^\sigma$), with $\sigma = 0.25$ and varying (N, ρ).

We remark that getting a higher experimental throughput ratio is limited by the following reasons. First, there is an 8 ms pinging interval (see Section 8.3) after each packet transmission which effectively reduces the number of bits delivered. Second, collisions of pings or failed decodings of pings result in inaccurate estimates of the number of listeners. Third, the low-power clock used by a node during its sleep state drifts and additionally can be affected by its environment.

Power consumption: Recall that in the power consumption measurements described in Section 8.2, we show that the power consumption of the virtual battery is valid for evaluating the actual power consumption of the node. Table 3 also presents the mean, minimum, and maximum power consumption of the virtual battery normalized to the target power budget ρ. Specifically, a value of 1 means that a node consumes power on average at the rate of its power budget throughout the experiment, and a higher value means that a node consumes power at the rate which is higher than its power budget.

The results show that nodes running EconCast-C consume power at rates which are within 7% and 3% of the target power budget with $\sigma = 0.25$ and $\sigma = 0.5$, respectively. This is because smaller value of σ increases the communication burstiness (see Section 7.4), resulting in larger variance of the nodes' virtual battery levels.

Collection of Pings: An important input to EconCast-C is the estimates of number of active listeners, $\hat{c}(t)$, based on which the transmitter decides the probability to continuously transmit. Larger values of $\hat{c}(t)$ lead to longer average burst length and can potentially significantly increase the throughput. For example, receiving 1 ping, the transmit-

# of Listeners	0	1	2	3	4
$\rho = 1\,\mathrm{mW}(\%)$	89.03	9.69	1.28	0.00	0.00
$\rho = 5\,\mathrm{mW}(\%)$	59.21	31.22	8.22	1.24	0.11

Table 4: Distribution of number of pings (active listeners) received after each packet transmission with $N = 5$, $\sigma = 0.25$, and varying ρ.

ter continuously transmits a packet with probability 0.8647 with $\sigma = 0.5$. This probability increases to 0.9817 with $\sigma = 0.25$, which substantially increases the burstiness. Also, with lower power budget, a successful transmission happens more rarely and it becomes harder to collect pings.

Table 4 presents the distribution of number of pings (equivalently, number of active listeners) received by the transmitter after each packet transmission, during experiments of $N = 5$, $\sigma = 0.25$, and $\rho \in \{1\,\mathrm{mW}, 5\,\mathrm{mW}\}$. It can be shown that with a higher power budget, the nodes are more active and the transmitter has higher probability to receive more pings. On the other hand, with lower power budget, the transmitter almost never receives more than 3 pings in a 5 nodes experiment, resulting in lower throughput as illustrated in Figure 7.

9. CONCLUSION

In this paper, we considered the problem of maximizing the broadcast groupput and anyput among a set of energy-constrained nodes with heterogeneous power budgets and listen and transmit power consumption levels. We provided methods to obtain oracle groupput and oracle anyput for a given set of heterogeneous nodes.

We developed the EconCast-C and EconCast-NC distributed protocols that control the nodes' transitions among sleep, listen, and transmit states. We analytically showed that heterogeneous nodes using the protocols (without any a priori knowledge regarding the number of nodes, power consumption levels, and budgets) can achieve the oracle groupput and anyput in a limiting sense (when $\sigma \to 0$).

Through simulations we evaluated EconCast and compared it to the state of the art. We also considered the tradeoffs in its design as a function of σ, where low values increase both burstiness and throughput, while high values reduce both of them. Finally, we experimentally evaluated EconCast using commercial-off-the-shelf nodes, thereby demonstrating its practicality.

There are several open future research directions. In particular, future research will focus on extending the analysis to non-clique toplogies. Moreover, evaluation with custom designed ultra-low-power nodes (e.g., [41]), that have improved energy awareness compared to the TI eZ430-RF2500-SEH nodes, would enable to better assess the tradeoffs related to the protocol design. Finally, considering unique application characteristics and their relation to groupput and anyput is an open problem.

10. ACKNOWLEDGMENTS

This research was supported in part by ARO grant 9W911NF-16-1-0259, NSF grant ECCS-1547406, and the People Programme (Marie Curie Actions) of the European Union's Seventh Framework Programme (FP7/2007-2013) under REA grant agreement n°[PIIF-GA-2013-629740].11.

11. REFERENCES

[1] Texas Instruments eZ430-RF2500-SEH solar energy harvesting development tool user's guide, 2013.

[2] Texas Instruments CC2640 SimpleLink Bluetooth smart wireless MCU, 2015.

[3] L. Atzori, A. Iera, and G. Morabito. The internet of things: A survey. *Computer Networks*, 54(15):2787 – 2805, 2010.

[4] W. Bajwa, J. Haupt, A. Sayeed, and R. Nowak. Compressive wireless sensing. In *Proc. ACM/IEEE IPSN'06*, 2006.

[5] M. Bakht, M. Trower, and R. H. Kravets. Searchlight: Won't you be my neighbor? In *Proc. ACM MobiCom'12*, 2012.

[6] S. A. Borbash, A. Ephremides, and M. J. McGlynn. An asynchronous neighbor discovery algorithm for wireless sensor networks. *Ad Hoc Netw.*, 5(7):998 – 1016, 2007.

[7] M. Buettner, B. Greenstein, and D. Wetherall. Dewdrop: an energy-aware runtime for computational RFID. In *Proc. USENIX NSDI'11*, 2011.

[8] L. Chen, R. Fan, K. Bian, M. Gerla, T. Wang, and X. Li. On heterogeneous neighbor discovery in wireless sensor networks. *arXiv preprint arXiv:1411.5415*, 2014.

[9] L. Chen, Y. Gu, S. Guo, T. He, Y. Shu, F. Zhang, and J. Chen. Group-based discovery in low-duty-cycle mobile sensor networks. In *Proc. IEEE SECON'12*, 2012.

[10] S. Chen, P. Sinha, N. B. Shroff, and C. Joo. A simple asymptotically optimal joint energy allocation and routing scheme in rechargeable sensor networks. *IEEE/ACM Trans. Netw.*, 22(4):1325–1336, 2014.

[11] T. Chen, G. Chen, S. Jain, R. Margolies, G. Grebla, D. Rubenstein, and G. Zussman. Demo abstract: Power-aware neighbor discovery for energy harvesting things. In *Proc. ACM SenSys'16*, 2016.

[12] T. Chen, J. Ghaderi, D. Rubenstein, and G. Zussman. Maximizing broadcast throughput under ultra-low-power constraints. *arXiv preprint arXiv:1610.04203*, 2016.

[13] M. Chiang, S. H. Low, J. C. Doyle, et al. Layering as optimization decomposition: A mathematical theory of network architectures. *Proc. IEEE*, 95(1):255–312, 2007.

[14] S. Cui, A. J. Goldsmith, and A. Bahai. Energy-efficiency of MIMO and cooperative MIMO techniques in sensor networks. *IEEE J. Sel. Areas Commun.*, 22(6):1089–1098, 2004.

[15] A. G. Dimakis, V. Prabhakaran, and K. Ramchandran. Ubiquitous access to distributed data in large-scale sensor networks through decentralized erasure codes. In *Proc. ACM/IEEE IPSN'05*, 2005.

[16] P. Dutta and D. Culler. Practical asynchronous neighbor discovery and rendezvous for mobile sensing applications. In *Proc. ACM SenSys'08*, 2008.

[17] A. El-Hoiydi and J.-D. Decotignie. Wisemac: an ultra low power MAC protocol for the downlink of infrastructure wireless sensor networks. In *Proc. IEEE ISCC'04*, 2004.

[18] J. Ghaderi, S. Borst, and P. Whiting. Queue-based random-access algorithms: Fluid limits and stability issues. *Stochastic Systems*, 4(1):81–156, 2014.

[19] J. Ghaderi and R. Srikant. On the design of efficient CSMA algorithms for wireless networks. In *Proc. IEEE CDC'10*, 2010.

[20] M. Gorlatova, P. Kinget, I. Kymissis, D. Rubenstein, X. Wang, and G. Zussman. Challenge: ultra-low-power energy-harvesting active networked tags (EnHANTs). In *Proc. ACM MobiCom'09*, 2009.

[21] M. Gorlatova, J. Sarik, G. Grebla, M. Cong, I. Kymissis, and G. Zussman. Movers and shakers: Kinetic energy harvesting for the internet of things. *IEEE J. Sel. Areas Commun.*, 33(8):1624–1639, 2015.

[22] M. Gorlatova, A. Wallwater, and G. Zussman. Networking low-power energy harvesting devices: Measurements and algorithms. *IEEE Trans. Mobile Comput.*, 12(9):1853–1865, Sept. 2013.

[23] J. Haupt, W. U. Bajwa, M. Rabbat, and R. Nowak. Compressed sensing for networked data. *IEEE Sigal Process Mag.*, 25(2):92–101, 2008.

[24] L. Jiang and J. Walrand. Convergence and stability of a distributed CSMA algorithm for maximal network throughput. In *Proc. CDC'09*, 2009.

[25] L. Jiang and J. Walrand. A distributed CSMA algorithm for throughput and utility maximization in wireless networks. *IEEE/ACM Trans. Netw.*, 18:960–972, 2010.

[26] A. Kandhalu, K. Lakshmanan, and R. R. Rajkumar. U-connect: A low-latency energy-efficient asynchronous neighbor discovery protocol. In *Proc. ACM/IEEE IPSN'10*, 2010.

[27] S. Katti, S. Gollakota, and D. Katabi. Embracing wireless interference: Analog network coding. In *Proc. ACM SIGCOMM'07*, 2007.

[28] L. Keller, E. Atsan, K. Argyraki, and C. Fragouli. Sensecode: Network coding for reliable sensor networks. *ACM Trans. Sens. Netw.*, 2013.

[29] L. Keller, M. J. Siavoshani, C. Fragouli, K. Argyraki, and S. Diggavi. Identity aware sensor networks. In *Proc. IEEE INFOCOM'09*, 2009.

[30] F. P. Kelly, A. K. Maulloo, and D. K. Tan. Rate control for communication networks: shadow prices, proportional fairness and stability. *J. Operational Research Society*, 49(3):237–252, 1998.

[31] M. Khouzani, S. Eshghi, S. Sarkar, N. B. Shroff, and S. S. Venkatesh. Optimal energy-aware epidemic routing in DTNs. In *Proc. ACM MobiHoc'12*, 2012.

[32] J.-S. Lee, Y.-W. Su, and C.-C. Shen. A comparative study of wireless protocols: Bluetooth, UWB, ZigBee, and Wi-Fi. In *Proc. IEEE IECON'07*, 2007.

[33] J. Liu, Y. Yi, and A. Proutiere. Towards utility-optimal random access without message passing. *Wireless Commun. Mobile Comput.*, 10:115–128, 2010.

[34] V. Liu, A. Parks, V. Talla, S. Gollakota, D. Wetherall, and J. R. Smith. Ambient backscatter: wireless communication out of thin air. In *Proc. ACM SIGCOMM'13*, 2013.

[35] S. H. Low and D. E. Lapsley. Optimization flow control - I: basic algorithm and convergence. *IEEE/ACM Trans. Netw.*, 7(6):861–874, 1999.

[36] S. H. Low and R. Srikant. A mathematical framework for designing a low-loss, low-delay internet. *Networks and Spatial Economics*, 4(1):75–101, 2004.

[37] C. Luo, F. Wu, J. Sun, and C. W. Chen. Compressive data gathering for large-scale wireless sensor networks. In *Proc. ACM MobiCom'09*, 2009.

[38] J. Luo, L. Xiang, and C. Rosenberg. Does compressed sensing improve the throughput of wireless sensor networks? In *Proc. IEEE ICC'10*, 2010.

[39] Z. Mao, C. E. Koksal, and N. B. Shroff. Cross-layer resource allocation in energy harvesting sensor networks. In *Rechargeable Sensor Networks: Technology, Theory, and Application: Introducing Energy Harvesting to Sensor Networks*. 2014.

[40] P. Marbach and A. Eryilmaz. A backlog-based CSMA mechanism to achieve fairness and throughput-optimality in multihop wireless networks. In *Proc. Allerton Conf.*, 2008.

[41] R. Margolies, M. Gorlatova, J. Sarik, G. Stanje, J. Zhu, P. Miller, M. Szczodrak, B. Vigraham, L. Carloni, P. Kinget, et al. Energy-harvesting active networked tags (EnHANTs): Prototyping and experimentation. *ACM Trans. Sens. Netw.*, 11(4):62, 2015.

[42] R. Margolies, G. Grebla, T. Chen, D. Rubenstein, and G. Zussman. Panda: Neighbor discovery on a power harvesting budget. In *Proc. IEEE INFOCOM'16*, 2016.

[43] M. J. McGlynn and S. A. Borbash. Birthday protocols for low energy deployment and flexible neighbor discovery in ad hoc wireless networks. In *Proc. ACM MobiHoc'01*, 2001.

[44] P. V. Nikitin, S. Ramamurthy, R. Martinez, and K. Rao. Passive tag-to-tag communication. In *Proc. IEEE RFID'12*, 2012.

[45] K. Philips. Ultra low power short range radios: Covering the last mile of the IoT. In *Proc. IEEE ESSCIRC'14*, 2014.

[46] A. Purohit, B. Priyantha, and J. Liu. WiFlock: Collaborative group discovery and maintenance in mobile sensor networks. In *Proc. ACM/IEEE IPSN'11*, 2011.

[47] M. Rabbat, J. Haupt, A. Singh, and R. Nowak. Decentralized compression and predistribution via randomized gossiping. In *Proc. ACM/IEEE IPSN'06*, 2006.

[48] T. Srisooksai, K. Keamarungsi, P. Lamsrichan, and K. Araki. Practical data compression in wireless sensor networks: A survey. *J. Netw. Comput. Appl.*, 35(1):37–59, 2012.

[49] W. Sun, Z. Yang, K. Wang, and Y. Liu. Hello: A generic flexible protocol for neighbor discovery. In *Proc. IEEE INFOCOM'14*, 2014.

[50] W. Sun, Z. Yang, X. Zhang, and Y. Liu. Energy-efficient neighbor discovery in mobile ad hoc and wireless sensor networks: A survey. *IEEE Commun. Surveys Tuts.*, 16(3):1448–1459, 2014.

[51] S. Ulukus, A. Yener, E. Erkip, O. Simeone, M. Zorzi, P. Grover, and K. Huang. Energy harvesting wireless communications: A review of recent advances. *IEEE J. Sel. Areas Commun.*, 33(3):360–381, Mar. 2015.

[52] S. Vasudevan, M. Adler, D. Goeckel, and D. Towsley. Efficient algorithms for neighbor discovery in wireless networks. *IEEE/ACM Trans. Netw.*, 21(1):69–83, 2013.

[53] S. Vasudevan, J. Kurose, and D. Towsley. On neighbor discovery in wireless networks with directional antennas. In *Proc. IEEE INFOCOM'05*, 2005.

[54] S. Vasudevan, D. Towsley, D. Goeckel, and R. Khalili. Neighbor discovery in wireless networks and the coupon collector's problem. In *Proc. ACM MobiCom'09*, Sept. 2009.

[55] J. Wang, H. Hassanieh, D. Katabi, and P. Indyk. Efficient and reliable low-power backscatter networks. In *Proc. ACM SIGCOMM'12*. ACM, 2012.

[56] J. Wang and D. Katabi. Dude, where's my card?: RFID positioning that works with multipath and non-line of sight. In *Proc. ACM SIGCOMM'13*, 2013.

[57] Y. Wu, P. Chou, S.-Y. Kung, et al. Minimum-energy multicast in mobile ad hoc networks using network coding. *IEEE Trans. Commun.*, 53(11):1906–1918, 2005.

[58] K. Xu, O. Dousse, and P. Thiran. Self-synchronizing properties of CSMA wireless multi-hop networks. In *Proc. ACM SIGMETRICS'10*, 2010.

[59] W. Ye, J. Heidemann, and D. Estrin. Medium access control with coordinated adaptive sleeping for wireless sensor networks. *IEEE/ACM Trans. Netw.*, 12(3):493–506, 2004.

[60] Y. Zeng, K. A. Mills, S. Gokhale, N. Mittal, S. Venkatesan, and R. Chandrasekaran. Robust neighbor discovery in multi-hop multi-channel heterogeneous wireless networks. *arXiv preprint arXiv:1505.00267*, 2015.

Measuring Latency Variation in the Internet

Toke Høiland-Jørgensen
Dept of Computer Science
Karlstad University, Sweden
toke.hoiland-jorgensen@kau.se

Bengt Ahlgren
SICS
Box 1263, 164 29 Kista
Sweden
bengta@sics.se

Per Hurtig
Dept of Computer Science
Karlstad University, Sweden
per.hurtig@kau.se

Anna Brunstrom
Dept of Computer Science
Karlstad University, Sweden
anna.brunstrom@kau.se

ABSTRACT

We analyse two complementary datasets to quantify the latency variation experienced by internet end-users: (i) a large-scale active measurement dataset (from the Measurement Lab Network Diagnostic Tool) which shed light on long-term trends and regional differences; and (ii) passive measurement data from an access aggregation link which is used to analyse the edge links closest to the user.

The analysis shows that variation in latency is both common and of significant magnitude, with two thirds of samples exceeding 100 ms of variation. The variation is seen within single connections as well as between connections to the same client. The distribution of experienced latency variation is heavy-tailed, with the most affected clients seeing an order of magnitude larger variation than the least affected. In addition, there are large differences between regions, both within and between continents. Despite consistent improvements in throughput, most regions show no reduction in latency variation over time, and in one region it even increases.

We examine load-induced queueing latency as a possible cause for the variation in latency and find that both datasets readily exhibit symptoms of queueing latency correlated with network load. Additionally, when this queueing latency does occur, it is of significant magnitude, more than 200 ms in the median. This indicates that load-induced queueing contributes significantly to the overall latency variation.

Keywords

Latency; Bufferbloat; Access Network Performance

CoNEXT '16 December 12-15, 2016, Irvine, CA, USA

ACM ISBN 978-1-4503-4292-6/16/12.

DOI: http://dx.doi.org/10.1145/2999572.2999603

1. INTRODUCTION

As applications turn ever more interactive, network latency plays an increasingly important role for their performance. The end-goal is to get as close as possible to the physical limitations of the speed of light [25]. However, today the latency of internet connections is often larger than it needs to be. In this work we set out to quantify how much. Having this information available is important to guide work that sets out to improve the latency behaviour of the internet; and for authors of latency-sensitive applications (such as Voice over IP, or even many web applications) that seek to predict the performance they can expect from the network.

Many sources of added latency can be highly variable in nature. This means that we can quantify undesired latency by looking specifically at the *latency variation* experienced by a client. We do this by measuring how much client latency varies above the minimum seen for that client. Our analysis is based on two complementary sources of data: we combine the extensive publicly available dataset from the Measurement Lab Network Diagnostic Tool (NDT) with a packet capture from within a service provider access network. The NDT data, gathered from 2010 to 2015, comprises a total of 265.8 million active test measurements from all over the world. This allows us to examine the development in latency variation over time and to look at regional differences. The access network dataset is significantly smaller, but the network characteristics are known with greater certainty. Thus, we can be more confident when interpreting the results from the latter dataset. These differences between the datasets make them complement each other nicely.

We find that significant latency variation is common in both datasets. This is the case both within single connections and between different connections from the same client. In the NDT dataset, we also observe that the magnitude of latency variation differs between geographic regions, both between and within continents. Looking at the development over time (also in the NDT dataset), we see very little change in the numbers. This is in contrast to the overall throughput that has improved significantly.

Table 1: Total tests per region and year (millions).

Reg.	2010	2011	2012	2013	2014	2015
AF	0.65	0.63	0.79	0.72	0.76	0.57
AS	7.79	7.45	6.55	5.75	5.83	4.57
EU	35.00	31.12	27.96	22.40	21.23	16.82
NA	11.70	8.51	7.90	7.01	7.06	8.00
SA	2.68	1.73	2.83	2.94	2.05	1.26
OC	1.33	1.33	0.79	0.55	0.65	0.57
Total	59.22	50.81	46.87	39.43	37.60	31.79

One important aspect of latency variation is the correlation between increased latency and high link utilisation. Queueing delay, in particular, can accumulate quickly when the link capacity is exhausted, and paying attention to such scenarios can give insight into issues that can cause real, if intermittent, performance problems for users. We examine queueing delay as a possible source of the observed latency variation for both datasets, and find strong indications that it is present in a number of instances. Furthermore, when queueing latency does occur it is of significant magnitude.

The rest of the paper is structured as follows: Section 2 introduces the datasets and the methodology we have used to analyse them. Section 3 discusses the large-scale variations in latency over time and geography, and Section 4 examines delay variation on access links. Section 5 presents our examination of load-induced queueing delay. Finally, Section 6 discusses related work and Section 7 concludes the paper.

2. DATASETS AND METHODOLOGY

The datasets underlying our analysis are the publicly available dataset from Measurement Lab (M-Lab), specifically the Network Diagnostic Tool (NDT) data [1], combined with packet header traces from access aggregation links of an internet service provider. This section presents each of the datasets, and the methodology we used for analysis.

2.1 The M-Lab NDT data

The M-Lab NDT is run by users to test their internet connections. We use the 10-second bulk transfer from the server to the client, which is part of the test suite. When the test is run, the client attempts to pick the nearest server from the geographically distributed network of servers provided by the M-Lab platform. The M-Lab servers are globally distributed[1], although with varying density in different regions.

The server is instrumented with the Web100 TCP kernel instrumentation [21], and captures several variables of the TCP state machine every 5 ms of the test. Data is available from early 2009, and we focus on the six year period 2010–2015, comprising a total of 265.8 million test runs. Table 1 shows the distribution of test runs for the years and regions we have included in our analysis.

Since the NDT is an active test, the gathered data is not a representative sample of the traffic mix flowing through the internet. Instead, it may tell us something about the *links* being traversed by the measurement flows. Looking at links under load is interesting, because some important effects can be exposed in this way, most notably bufferbloat: Loading up the link causes any latent buffers to fill, adding latency that might not be visible if the link is lightly loaded. This also means that the baseline link utilisation (e.g., caused by diurnal usage patterns) become less important: an already loaded link can, at worst, result in a potentially higher baseline latency. This means that the results may be biased towards showing lower latency variation than is actually seen on the link over time. But since we are interested in establishing a lower bound on the variation, this is acceptable.

For the base analysis, we only exclude tests that were truncated (had a total run time less than 9 seconds). We use the TCP RTT samples as our data points, i.e., the samples computed by the server TCP stack according to Karn's algorithm [23], and focus on the *RTT span*, defined as the difference between the minimum and maximum RTT observed during a test run. However, we also examine a subset of the data to assess what impact the choice of min and max observed RTT has on the data when compared to using other percentiles for each flow (see Section 3.3).

[1]See http://www.measurementlab.net/infrastructure for more information on the server placements.

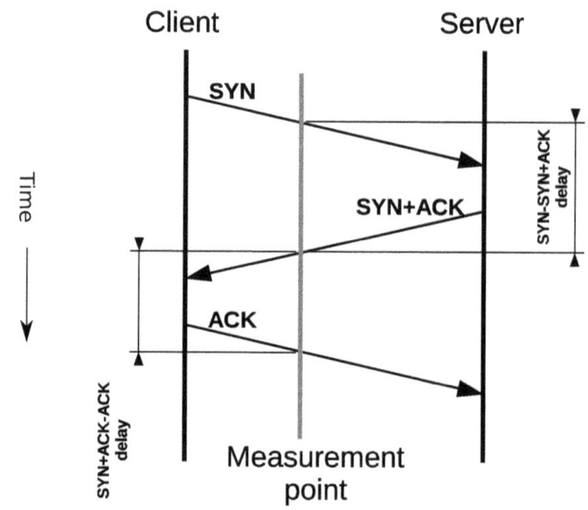

Figure 1: Delays computed from the TCP connection setup.

2.2 The access aggregation link data

The second dataset comes from two access aggregation links of an internet service provider. The links aggregate the traffic for about 50 and 400 clients, respectively, and connect them to the core network of the service provider. The traffic was captured passively at different times distributed over an eight-month period starting at the end of 2014. The average loads on the 1 Gbps links were, respectively, about 200 and 400 Mbit/s during peak hours. This dataset is an example of real internet traffic, since we are not generating any traffic.

We analyse the delay experienced by the TCP connection setup packets in this dataset. The TCP connection setup consists of a three-way handshake with SYN, SYN+ACK, and ACK packets, as illustrated in Figure 1.

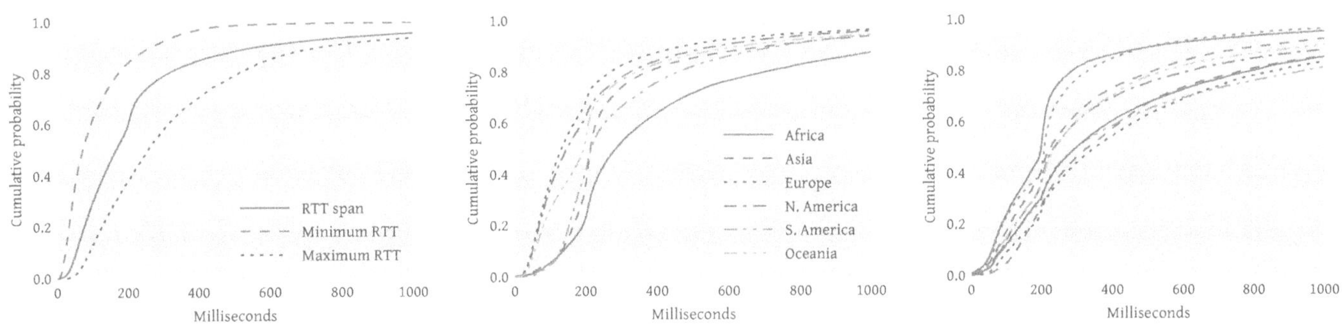

(a) (b) (c)

Figure 2: RTT values computed over individual flows. (a) Min and max RTT and the span between them, for all flows. (b) Distribution of per-flow RTT span per continent (2015 data). (c) Distribution of per-flow RTT span per country in Africa (2015 data for countries with $n > 10,000$).

For the purpose of this paper, we study the client side of connections made to the public internet. That is, we study the path from the client, over the access link, to the measured aggregation link. This allows us to examine increased delays due to excess queuing in consumer equipment, and ensures that the path we measure is of known length.

We examine the data for outgoing connections, i.e., connections that are initiated from the access side and connect to the public internet, which means we compute the round-trip delay between the SYN+ACK packet and the first ACK packet in the three-way handshake. The variation in these delay values is likely to be caused by queueing, since connection endpoints normally respond immediately. We also compute the instantaneous load at each sample and examine the correlation between delay and load for a few clients.

2.3 Sources of latency variation

Naturally, the observed latency variation can have several causes [6]. These include queueing delay along the path, delayed acknowledgements, transmission delay, media access delays, error recovery, paths changing during the test and processing delays at end-hosts and intermediate nodes. For the main part of our analysis, we make no attempt to distinguish between different causes of latency variation. However, we note that latency variation represents latency that is superfluous in the sense that it is higher than the known attainable minimum for the path. In addition, we analyse a subset of each dataset to examine to what extent queueing latency is a factor in the observed latency variation.

We believe that the chosen datasets complement each other nicely and allow us to illuminate the subject from different angles, drawing on the strengths of them both. The NDT dataset, being based on active measurements, allows us to examine connections that are being deliberately loaded, and the size of the dataset allows us to examine temporal and geographic trends. The access network dataset, on the other hand, has smaller scope but the examined path is known; and so we can rule out several sources of delay and be more confident when interpreting the results.

3. LATENCY VARIATION OVER TIME AND GEOGRAPHY

In this section, we analyse the M-Lab NDT dataset to explore geographic differences, and also look at the development of the RTT span over time. For an initial overview, Figure 2a shows the distribution of the RTT span in the whole M-Lab NDT dataset, along with the minimum and maximum RTTs it is derived from. This shows a significant amount of extra latency: two thirds of samples exceed 100 ms of RTT span, with the 95th percentile exceeding 900 ms.

3.1 Geographic differences

Figure 2b shows the RTT span distributed geographically per continent for the 2015 data. This shows a significant difference between regions, with the median differing by more than a factor of two between the best and the worst region. Looking within these regions, Figure 2c shows the per-country distributions within Africa. Here, the heavy tail of latencies above one second affects as much as 20% of the samples from the country with the highest latency. These high latencies are consistent with previous studies of African internet connections [8]. The data for Europe (omitted due to space constraints) shows that the difference among European countries is of the same magnitude as the difference among continents.

3.2 Development over time

Figure 3a shows the minimum RTT and the RTT span for each of the years in the dataset. While the minimum RTT has decreased slightly over the years, no such development is visible for the span. This is striking when compared to the development in throughput, which has increased consistently, as shown in Figure 3b. Some of this increase in average throughput may be due to other factors than increase in link capacity (e.g. protocol efficiency improvements). Even so, the disparity is clear: while throughput has increased, RTT span has not decreased, and the decrease in minimum RTT is slight.

Looking at this development for different continents, as shown in Figure 3c, an increase in latency span over the

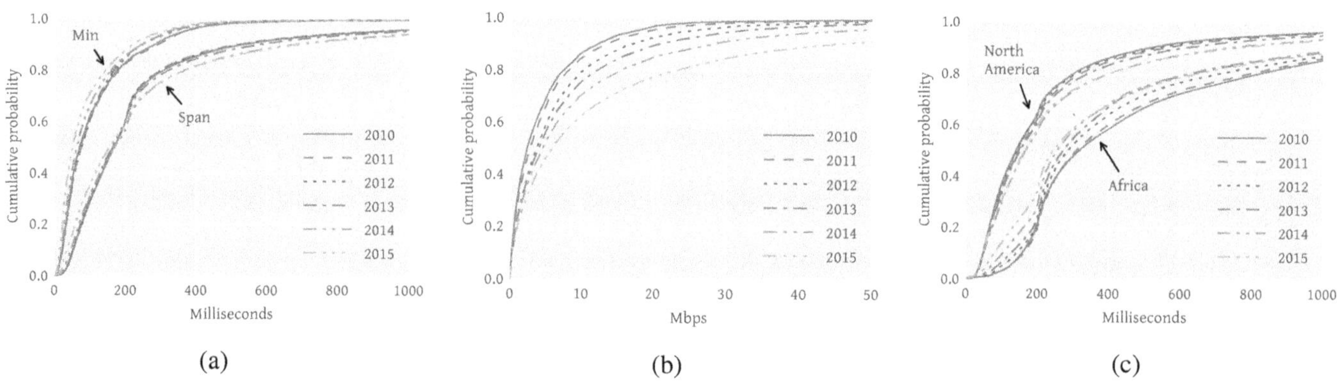

Figure 3: Development over time of per-flow latency and throughput in the NDT dataset. (a) Min RTT and RTT span, per year. (b) Per-flow average throughput, per year. (c) The development in latency span over time for North America and Africa.

years is seen in North America while Africa has seen a consistent, but small, reduction in latency span over time. This latter development is most likely due to developments in infrastructure causing traffic to travel fewer hops, thus decreasing the potential sources of extra latency.

3.3 Different measures of latency span

The way the NDT dataset is structured makes the per-flow min and max RTT values the only ones that are practical to analyse for the whole dataset. To assess what effect this choice of metric has on the results, we performed a more detailed analysis for a subset of the data. Figure 4a shows the latency span distribution for the data from August 2013 when using percentiles of the per-flow RTT measurements ranging from 90 to 99 in place of the max. We see that in this case the median measured RTT span drops to between 151 ms and 204 ms, from 250 ms when using the max — a drop of between 17% and 40%. It is not clear that the max is simply an outlier for all flows; but for those where it is, our results will overestimate the absolute magnitude of the RTT span. However, the shape of the distribution stays fairly constant, and using the max simply leads to higher absolute numbers. This means that we can still say something about trends, even for those flows where the max RTT should be considered an outlier.

4. LATENCY VARIATION IN THE ACCESS NETWORK

In this section we analyse the latency variation of TCP 3-way handshakes in the access network dataset. Figure 4b shows the distribution of the per-client RTT variation, computed as the span between the per-client minimum delay and the respective percentiles of samples to that client. To ensure that we do not mistakenly use a too low minimum delay value, only handshakes which did not have any SYN+ACK retransmissions are considered when computing the minimum.

For about half of the client population covered by the link shown in Figure 4b, delay increases substantially over the minimum at times. For example, 20% of the clients experience increased delays of more than about 80 ms, at least 5% of the time. The second link shows similar behaviour, but has *more* clients that are affected by increased delay.

Another interesting feature of the data is that there is a significant difference in the magnitude of the latency span depending on which percentile of latency measurements one looks at. That is, if we consider the per-user 99th percentile of latency rather than the 95th, suddenly more than half the users experience latency variations in excess of 100 ms for the first link, and more than 80% for the second link. This underscores the fact that delay spikes can be a very transient problem, but one that is of significant magnitude when it does occur.

Comparing with the NDT dataset, the analysis of the access link data shows a lower frequency of latency variation, as well as a lower magnitude of the variation when it does occur. However, both datasets show that significant latency variation occurs for a considerable fraction of users. We attribute the difference in magnitude to the difference in measurement methods: the NDT measurements are taken while the link is deliberately loaded, while not all measurements from the access network are taken from saturated links.

5. EXAMINING QUEUEING LATENCY

As mentioned in Section 2.3, latency variations can have many causes, and without having insight into the network path itself it can be difficult to identify which are the most prevalent. However, experience from more controlled environments (such as experiments performed to evaluate AQM algorithms [14]) suggests that queueing delay can be a significant source. Due to the magnitude of the variation we see here, we conjecture that this is also the case in this dataset. To examine this further, in this section we present an analysis of the queueing delay of a subset of the traffic in both datasets. We aim to perform a conservative analysis, and so limit ourselves to tests for which it is possible to identify queueing latency with high certainty.

5.1 Latency reductions after a drop

Our analysis is based upon a distinct pattern, where the sample RTT increases from the start of a flow until a congestion event, then sharply decreases afterwards. An exam-

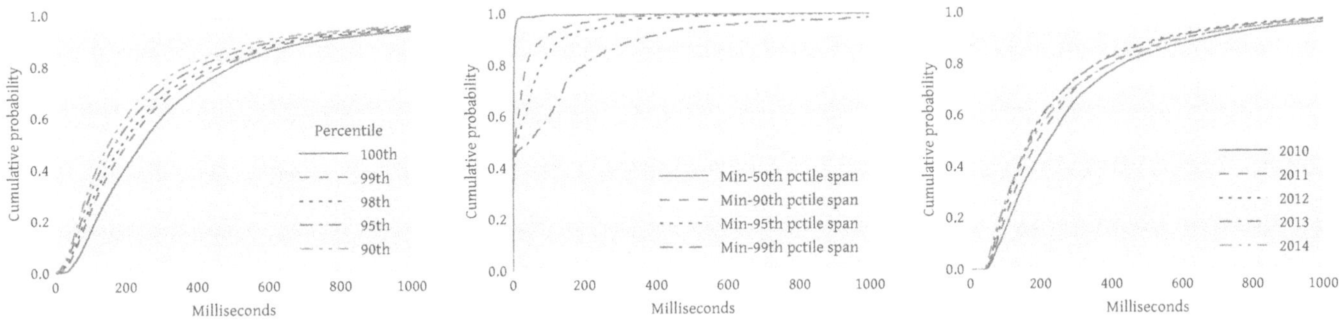

(a) (b) (c)

Figure 4: (a) Latency span for all flows in August 2013 when using different percentiles to determine the max RTT. NDT dataset. (b) Client side round trip delay percentiles over all clients relative to the minimum delay. A full day of the first aggregation link in the access network dataset. (c) Distribution of the magnitude of detected queueing delay, per year. Flows with detected queueing latency, NDT dataset.

ple of this pattern is seen in Figure 5. This pattern is due to the behaviour of TCP: The congestion control algorithm will increase its sending rate until a congestion event occurs, then halve it. If a lot of packets are queued when this happens, the queue has a chance to drain, and so subsequent RTT samples will show a lower queueing delay. Thus, it is reasonable to assume that when this pattern occurs, the drop in RTT is because the queue induced by the flow dissipates as it slows down. So when we detect this sharp correlation between a congestion event and a subsequent drop in RTT, we can measure the magnitude of the drop and use it as a lower bound on queueing delay.

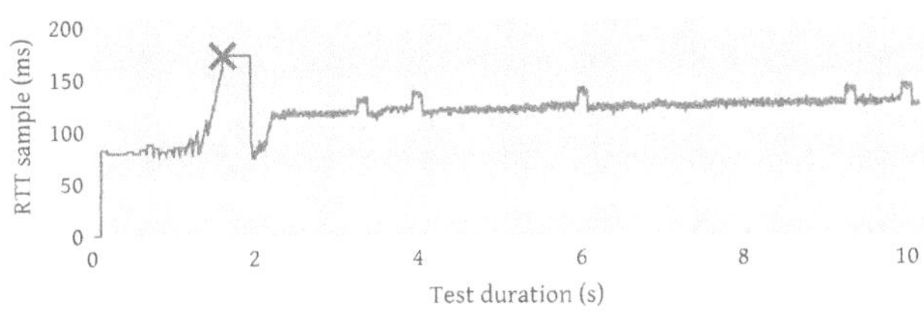

Figure 5: Example of the drop in RTT after a congestion event. The red cross marks the congestion event.

We limit the analysis to flows that have exactly one congestion event, and spend most of its lifetime being limited by the congestion window. Additionally, we exclude flows that are truncated or transfer less than 0.2 MB of data. For the remaining flows, we identify the pattern mentioned above by the following algorithm:

1. Find three values: *first_rtt*, the first non-zero RTT sample; *cong_rtt*, the RTT sample at the congestion event; and *cong_rtt_next*, the first RTT sample after the event that is different from *cong_rtt*.
2. Compute the differences between *first_rtt* and *cong_rtt* and between *cong_rtt* and *cong_rtt_next*. If both of these values are above 40 ms,[2] return the difference between *cong_rtt* and *cong_rtt_next*.

We add a few minor refinements to increase the accuracy of the basic algorithm above:[3]

1. When comparing *first_rtt* and *cong_rtt*, use the median of *cong_rtt* and the two previous RTT samples. This weeds out tests where only a single RTT sample (coinciding with the congestion event) is higher than the baseline.
2. When comparing *cong_rtt* and *cong_rtt_next*, use the minimum of the five measurements immediately following *cong_rtt_next*. This makes sure we include cases where the decrease after the congestion event is not instant, but happens over a couple of RTT samples.
3. Compute the maximum span between the largest and smallest RTT sample in a sliding window of 10 data samples over the time period following the point of *cong_rtt_next*. If this span is higher than the drop in RTT after the congestion event, filter out the flow.

By applying the algorithm to the data from 2010 through 2014[4], we identified a total of 5.7 million instances of the RTT pattern, corresponding to 2.4% of the total number of flows. While this is a relatively small fraction of the flows, in this section we have aimed to be conservative and only pick out flows where we can algorithmically identify the source of the extra latency as queueing delay with a high certainty. This does not mean, however, that queueing delay cannot also be a source of latency variation for other flows.

Figure 4c shows the distribution of the magnitude of the detected queueing delay. We see that this follows a similar heavy-tailed distribution as the total latency variation. In

[2]The threshold is needed to exclude naturally occurring variation in RTT samples from the detection. We found 40 ms empirically to be a suitable conservative threshold: It is the lowest value that did not result in a significant number of false positives.

[3]The full code and dataset is published at http://www.cs.kau.se/tohojo/measuring-latency-variation/

[4]The Measurement Lab dataset was restructured in the middle of 2015, making it difficult to apply the detailed analysis for the 2015 data. For that reason, we have not included 2015 in these results.

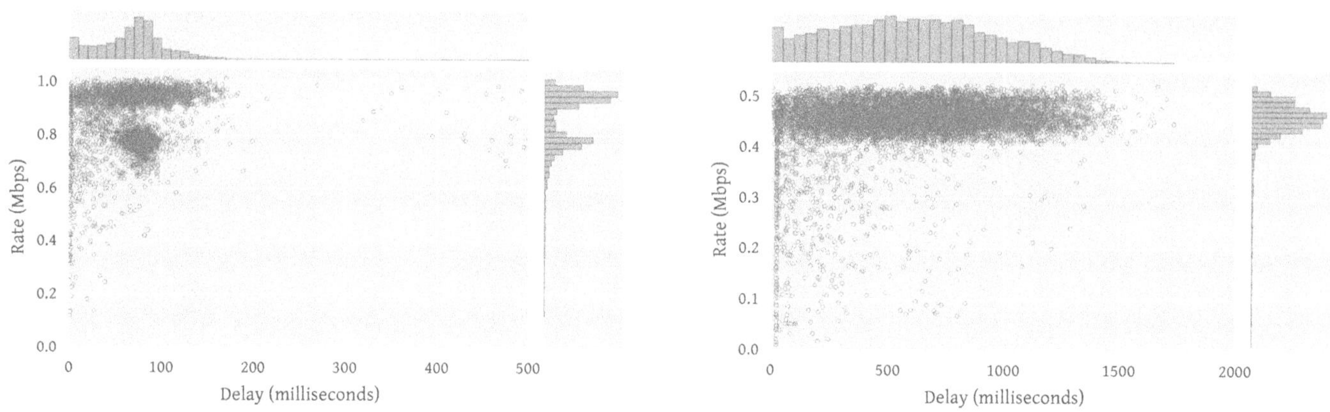

(a) (b)

Figure 6: Delay and instantaneous outbound rate for two clients in the access network dataset. The histograms on the axes show the marginal distributions for the rate and delay samples.

addition, of those tests that our algorithm identifies as experiencing self-induced queueing, a significant percentage see quite a lot of it: 80% is above 100 ms, and 20% is above 400 ms. We see a downward trend in the queueing delay magnitude from 2010 to 2012/13, with a slight increase in 2014.

Based on our analysis of this subset of the whole dataset, we conclude that (i) queueing delay is present in a non-trivial number of instances and that (ii) when it does occur, it is of significant magnitude.

5.2 Delay correlated with load

A network is more likely to exhibit queueing delay when it is congested. Thus, delay correlated with load can be an indication of the presence of queueing delay. When analysing the access network dataset, we identified several cases where strong correlation between delay and load existed. In this section we look at two examples of this behaviour.

Figures 6a and 6b show the correlation between client side delay and the instantaneous outbound load during the 200 ms just preceding each delay sample. The sample period is one hour during peak time (20.30–21.30).

For the first client, we see two clusters of delay/load values, indicating two kinds of behaviour. There is one cluster just under a performance ceiling of 1 Mbit/s, but with increased round-trip delays up to almost 200 ms. This behaviour clearly indicates a saturated uplink where the upstream bottleneck limits the throughput and induces queueing latency. The other cluster is centred around about 0.8 Mbit/s and 80 ms increase in round-trip delay. This indicates an equilibrium where the outbound capacity is not the primary bottleneck, and so doesn't induce as much queueing delay. In addition to these clusters, there are some scattered data points up to just over 3 s increase in round-trip delay (not all of which are visible on the figure). The second client is clearly limited by a low uplink capacity, resulting in very large delays — up to about 1.5 s, which is consistent with the low capacity resulting in large queue drain times.

Together, the behaviour of these two client links (along with additional clients we have examined but not included here) clearly show that load-induced queueing delay is one source of the latency variation we have observed in the analysis of the whole dataset. According to the service provider, the access network otherwise does not have the amount of buffering needed for the delays we see in our measurements, pointing to large buffers in consumer equipment as the likely culprit.

5.3 Discussion

The analysis presented in this section indicates that excess queueing latency (i.e., bufferbloat) is indeed a very real and routinely occurring phenomenon. While we do not claim to have a means of accurately quantifying bufferbloat in all instances, we have sought to compensate for the lack of accuracy by erring on the side of caution in identifying bloat. And the fact that signs of bufferbloat so readily appears in both datasets constitutes a strong indicator that bufferbloat is indeed prevalent in real networks.

Another finding is that in the cases where bufferbloat does appear, it tends to be significant: most often on the order of several hundreds of milliseconds. This means that when bufferbloat does appear, it is quite noticeable and a considerable inconvenience for the end-user.

6. RELATED WORK

Several other studies have looked at the latency characteristics of internet traffic. These fall roughly into three categories: studies based on large-scale active measurements, studies based on targeted active measurements of a more limited scope, and passive measurements performed at various vantage points in the network. In this section we provide an overview of each of these categories in turn.

6.1 Large-scale active measurements

The *speedtest.net* measurement tool and the Netalyzr test suite are popular performance benchmark tools in wide use.

Canadi et al [7] perform a study based on 54 million test runs from the former which shows very low baseline (unloaded) latencies, but considers neither latency variation nor development over time. Kreibich et al [18] base their study on 130,000 tests from the latter, and show queueing latency on the order of hundreds of milliseconds, but does not consider differences over time or between regions.

Another approach to large-scale active measurements is taken by the BISMark and SamKnows measurement platforms, both of which provide instrumented gateways to users. A study based on this data by Sundaresan et al [26] measures baseline and under-load latency and shows significant buffering in head-end equipment. Chetty et al [8] also use BISMark data (as well as other sources) to measure broadband performance in South Africa. Consistent with our results for this continent, they find that latencies are generally high, often on the order of several hundred milliseconds.

Another large-scale active measurement effort is the Dasu platform [24], which is a software client users install on their machines. This study does not focus on latency measurements, but it includes HTTP latency figures which indicate a large regional variation, not unlike what we observe.

Finally, the M-Lab Consortium has studied ISP interconnections [19] using the same data as we use. However, this study only considers aggregate latency over large time scales.

6.2 Targeted active measurements

Dischinger et al [11] and Choy et al [10], both use active probing of residential hosts to measure network connections. The former study finds that queueing delay in the broadband equipment is extensive, while the latter finds that a significant fraction of users experience too high latency to run games in the cloud. Bischof et al [5] perform a slightly different type of measurements, piggy-backing on the BitTorrent protocol, and find a majority of the users see median last-mile latency between 10 and 100 ms, with the 95th percentile of seeing several hundred milliseconds. A similar conclusion, but specifically targeted at assessing queueing latency, is reached in [9], which estimates that 10% of users experience a 90th percentile queueing latency above 100 ms.

Another type of targeted active measurements are performed by clients under the experimenters' control to examine the access network. These types of experiments are performed by, e.g., Jiang et al [17] and Alfredsson et al [3] to measure bufferbloat in cellular networks. Both studies find evidence of bufferbloat on the order of several hundred ms.

6.3 Passive measurements

Several studies perform passive measurements of backbone or other high-speed links between major sites [12, 15, 16]. They generally find fairly low and quite stable latencies, with the backbone link experiencing latencies dominated by the speed of light, and the others generally seeing median latencies well below 100 ms. Jaiswal et al [15] additionally measure RTT variations and find that the median variation is around 2–300 ms and the 95th percentile variation is on the order of several seconds. In addition, Pathak et al [22] perform passive measurement of latency inflation in MPLS overlay networks and find that inflation is common, mostly due to path changes in the underlying tunnels.

Another technique for passive measurements consists of taking captures at the edge of a network and analysing that traffic. Aikat et al [2] and Allman [4] both employ this technique to analyse the RTT of TCP connections between hosts inside and outside the network where the measurement is performed. Both studies analyse the latency variation, Aikat et al finding it to be somewhat higher than Allman.

Another vantage point for passive measurements is at edge networks. Such studies are performed by Vacirca et al [27] and Maier et al [20] for mobile and residential networks, respectively. The former study finds that RTT can vary greatly over connections, while the latter finds that the baseline latency of the TCP handshake is dominated by the client part.

Finally, Hernandez-Campos and Papadopouli [13] compares wired and wireless traffic by means of passive packet captures. They find that wireless connections experience a much larger RTT variation than wired connections do.

7. CONCLUSIONS

We have analysed the latency variation experienced by clients on the internet by examining two complementary datasets from active measurement tests and from traffic captures from an ISP. In addition, we have analysed a subset of the data to attempt to determine whether load-induced queueing delay in the network can be part of the reason for the large variations. Based on our analysis, we conclude:

– Latency variation is both common and of significant magnitude, both within single connections and between connections to the same client. This indicates that it has a large potential to negatively affect end-user perceived performance.

– The worst affected clients see an order of magnitude larger variation than the least affected, and the choice of per-client percentile for the measured latency significantly affects the resulting conclusions. This indicates that latency spikes are transient and non-uniformly distributed.

– While throughput has increased over the six years we have examined, both minimum latency and latency variation have remained stable, and even increased slightly. This indicates that the improvements in performance afforded by the development of new technology are not improving latency.

– We find that in both datasets load-induced queueing delay is an important factor in latency variation, and quite significant in magnitude when it does occur. This indicates that load-induced queueing does in fact contribute significantly to the variation we see in overall latency behaviour.

8. ACKNOWLEDGEMENTS

We wish to thank Matt Mathis and Collin Anderson for suggesting we look at the Measurement Lab dataset, and for their helpful comments and technical expertise. We also wish to thank Henrik Abrahamsson for the use of his tools for computing instantaneous load from the access link data.

This work was in part funded by The Knowledge Foundation (KKS) through the SIDUS READY project.

9. REFERENCES

[1] NDT test methodology. Wiki page: https://goo.gl/KrqtbQ, 2015.

[2] J. Aikat, J. Kaur, F. D. Smith, and K. Jeffay. Variability in TCP round-trip times. In *3rd ACM SIGCOMM conference on Internet measurement*. ACM, 2003.

[3] S. Alfredsson, G. Del Giudice, J. Garcia, A. Brunstrom, L. De Cicco, and S. Mascolo. Impact of tcp congestion control on bufferbloat in cellular networks. In *IEEE 14th International Symposium and Workshops on a World of Wireless, Mobile and Multimedia Networks (WoWMoM)*, 2013.

[4] M. Allman. Comments on bufferbloat. *ACM SIGCOMM Computer Communications Review*, January 2013.

[5] Z. S. Bischof, J. S. Otto, and F. E. Bustamante. Up, down and around the stack: Isp characterization from network intensive applications. *ACM SIGCOMM Computer Communication Review*, 2012.

[6] B. Briscoe, A. Brunstrom, A. Petlund, D. Hayes, D. Ros, I.-J. Tsang, S. Gjessing, G. Fairhurst, C. Griwodz, and M. Welzl. Reducing internet latency: A survey of techniques and their merits. *Communications Surveys Tutorials, IEEE*, 2014.

[7] I. Canadi, P. Barford, and J. Sommers. Revisiting broadband performance. In *2012 ACM conference on Internet measurement*. ACM, 2012.

[8] M. Chetty, S. Sundaresan, S. Muckaden, N. Feamster, and E. Calandro. Measuring broadband performance in south africa. In *4th Annual Symposium on Computing for Development*. ACM, 2013.

[9] C. Chirichella and D. Rossi. To the moon and back: are internet bufferbloat delays really that large? In *Computer Communications Workshops (INFOCOM WKSHPS), 2013 IEEE Conference on*. IEEE, 2013.

[10] S. Choy, B. Wong, G. Simon, and C. Rosenberg. The brewing storm in cloud gaming: A measurement study on cloud to end-user latency. In *11th annual workshop on network and systems support for games*. IEEE Press, 2012.

[11] M. Dischinger, A. Haeberlen, K. P. Gummadi, and S. Saroiu. Characterizing residential broadband networks. In *Internet Measurement Conference*, 2007.

[12] C. Fraleigh, S. Moon, B. Lyles, C. Cotton, M. Khan, D. Moll, R. Rockell, T. Seely, and S. C. Diot. Packet-level traffic measurements from the sprint ip backbone. *Network, IEEE*, 2003.

[13] F. Hernandez-Campos and M. Papadopouli. Assessing the real impact of 802.11 wlans: A large-scale comparison of wired and wireless traffic. In *14th IEEE Workshop on Local and Metropolitan Area Networks*. IEEE, 2005.

[14] T. Høiland-Jørgensen, P. Hurtig, and A. Brunstrom. The Good, the Bad and the WiFi: Modern AQMs in a residential setting. *Computer Networks*, Oct. 2015.

[15] S. Jaiswal, G. Iannaccone, C. Diot, J. Kurose, and D. Towsley. Inferring tcp connection characteristics through passive measurements. In *INFOCOM 2004*. IEEE, 2004.

[16] H. Jiang and C. Dovrolis. Passive estimation of tcp round-trip times. *ACM SIGCOMM Computer Communication Review*, 2002.

[17] H. Jiang, Y. Wang, K. Lee, and I. Rhee. Tackling bufferbloat in 3g/4g networks. In *2012 ACM conference on Internet measurement*. ACM, 2012.

[18] C. Kreibich, N. Weaver, B. Nechaev, and V. Paxson. Netalyzr: illuminating the edge network. In *10th ACM SIGCOMM conference on Internet measurement*. ACM, 2010.

[19] M. Lab. ISP interconnection and its impact on consumer internet performance. Technical report, Measurement Lab Consortium, October 2014.

[20] G. Maier, A. Feldmann, V. Paxson, and M. Allman. On dominant characteristics of residential broadband internet traffic. In *9th ACM SIGCOMM conference on Internet measurement*. ACM, 2009.

[21] M. Mathis, J. Heffner, and R. Raghunarayan. TCP Extended Statistics MIB. RFC 4898 (Proposed Standard), May 2007.

[22] A. Pathak, M. Zhang, Y. C. Hu, R. Mahajan, and D. Maltz. Latency inflation with mpls-based traffic engineering. In *2011 ACM SIGCOMM conference on Internet measurement*. ACM, 2011.

[23] V. Paxson, M. Allman, J. Chu, and M. Sargent. Computing TCP's Retransmission Timer. RFC 6298 (Proposed Standard), June 2011.

[24] M. A. Sánchez, J. S. Otto, Z. S. Bischof, D. R. Choffnes, F. E. Bustamante, B. Krishnamurthy, and W. Willinger. Dasu: Pushing experiments to the internet's edge. In *NSDI*, 2013.

[25] A. Singla, B. Chandrasekaran, P. Godfrey, and B. Maggs. The internet at the speed of light. In *13th ACM Workshop on Hot Topics in Networks*. ACM, 2014.

[26] S. Sundaresan, W. De Donato, N. Feamster, R. Teixeira, S. Crawford, and A. Pescapè. Broadband internet performance: a view from the gateway. In *ACM SIGCOMM computer communication review*. ACM, 2011.

[27] F. Vacirca, F. Ricciato, and R. Pilz. Large-scale RTT measurements from an operational UMTS/GPRS network. In *First International Conference on Wireless Internet*. IEEE, 2005.

LossRadar: Fast Detection of Lost Packets in Data Center Networks

Yuliang Li* Rui Miao† Changhoon Kim‡ Minlan Yu*
*Yale University †University of Southern California ‡Barefoot Networks

ABSTRACT

Packet losses are common in data center networks, may be caused by a variety of reasons (e.g., congestion, blackhole), and have significant impacts on application performance and network operations. Thus, it is important to provide fast detection of packet losses independent of their root causes. We also need to capture both the locations and packet header information of the lost packets to help diagnose and mitigate these losses. Unfortunately, existing monitoring tools that are generic in capturing all types of network events often fall short in capturing losses fast with enough details and low overhead. Due to the importance of loss in data centers, we propose a specific monitoring system designed for loss detection. We propose LossRadar, a system that can capture individual lost packets and their detailed information in the entire network on a fine time scale. Our extensive evaluation on prototypes and simulations demonstrates that LossRadar is easy to implement in hardware switches, achieves low memory and bandwidth overhead, while providing detailed information about individual lost packets. We also build a loss analysis tool that demonstrates the usefulness of LossRadar with a few example applications.

1. INTRODUCTION

Packet losses are common in data center networks and can happen for a variety of reasons. For example, Jeff Dean's keynote [7] indicates on average in a production data center for one year, up to 40-80 machines can experience packet losses, 4 network maintenance jobs can cause 30-minute random connectivity losses, and 3 router failures can cause immediate traffic blackholing for an hour. Such losses can significantly affect application tail latency and throughput especially when applications often view losses as a signal of congestion. It also takes operators tens of hours to diagnose the root causes of losses and recover from them.

It is important to detect losses *fast* and *independent of the loss types* (e.g., congestion, blackholes). With fast loss detection, operators have enough time to diagnose their root causes and mitigate the impact of losses. Being independent of loss types, we can capture all kinds of losses, especially unexpected ones such as those caused by hardware and software errors. Moreover, to diagnose the root causes, operators often need the detailed location on where losses happen, and the packet header information on what kind of packets get lost, the timing of losses, and other loss patterns.

Unfortunately, existing monitoring tools that are generic in capturing all types of network events often fall short in capturing losses fast with enough details and low overhead. End-host based solutions [37, 25, 12] cannot provide the exact location information on where losses happen. Packet mirroring [38, 13] either incurs large bandwidth overhead of mirroring all the traffic, or selectively mirrors some packets and thus miss capturing all types of losses. Some counters at switches (e.g., SNMP counters) can report a few loss types (e.g., ACL drops) but often miss the other losses that are harder to capture (e.g., caused by hardware and software errors). Flow-based monitoring tools (e.g., FlowRadar [21], NetFlow [26]) keep counters for individual flows and compare them across hops to identify losses, which do not have the timing and sequence patterns of losses and have an overhead associated with the number of flows (which can be large in large data centers [33]). One common theme of these approaches is to detect loss by keeping records of ongoing flows and identify the missing ones.

Due to the importance of loss in data centers, we propose a specific monitoring system designed for loss detection. Instead of keeping records whose overhead is proportional to the ongoing traffic or flows, we propose to keep records whose overhead is proportional to the number of losses.

We propose LossRadar, a lightweight packet loss detection service that quickly reports the locations and 5-tuple flow information of individual lost packets in 10s of milliseconds. The very basic component we introduce for LossRadar is a meter, a light-weight traffic digest generation logic. We place several meters at various vantage points in a network. Then, each meter periodically generates small digests summarizing all the traffic passing through itself and exports the digests

CoNEXT '16, December 12-15, 2016, Irvine, CA, USA

DOI: http://dx.doi.org/10.1145/2999572.2999609

to a remote collector. The collector then decodes the digests exported by the meters. The way collector performs such analysis is inspired by the flow conservation rule in graph theory (and the current conservation rule in electrical-circuit theory as well). Given any segments (a link, switch, or group of switches) in a network and all uni-directional flows passing through the segment, the collector compares between the traffic digests generated by all the meters surrounding the segment. Any mismatch across the digests indicates packet losses, and the collector decodes the digest mismatch further to restore the identifiers of each lost packet. We also introduce an analyzer that can identify several (but not all) types of root causes of packet losses.

We design a Bloom-filter based data structure to collect traffic digests at each meter in real time with three key benefits: (1) Its memory requirement only grows linearly with the number of lost packets instead of all the transferred packets. (2) It keeps all the details of the lost packets such as 5 tuples, timing, and sequences of packets. (3) These traffic digests are generic to capture all types of losses and can be easily implemented in today's commodity switches.

Our extensive testbed evaluations with open vSwitch based prototype and large-scale packet-level simulations show that LossRadar uses only 1.4% of memory usage compared to the state-of-the-art approach when the loss rate is lower than 0.1%, and 0.5% of the bandwidth overhead of full mirroring, while providing detailed information for all the lost packets.

2. PACKET LOSS IN DATA CENTERS

Packet losses not only significantly affect application performance but also make network management tasks such as traffic engineering and diagnosis hard [12]. In this section, we first discuss the key requirements of loss detection: fast detection to minimize the impact of losses, generic detection of all types of losses, and capturing the locations and the headers of lost packets to help diagnosis. Next, we discuss existing tools in data centers which fall short in supporting these requirements of loss detection with low overhead.

2.1 Requirements on loss detection

We summarize three key requirements on loss detection: (1) We need to detect packet losses *fast* to minimize their impact. (2) We need a generic approach to capture all types of packet losses ranging from congestion losses to random losses. (3) We need to know the locations and all the details of lost packets (e.g., header fields) to infer their root causes.

Fast detection. Packet losses are common in data center networks. Studies have shown that, on average in a production data center for one year, up to 40-80 machines can experience up to 50% packet loss rates, four network maintenance jobs can cause 30-minute random connectivity losses, and three router failures can cause immediate traffic blackholing for an hour [7]. Microsoft also reports one to ten new blackholes every day in a data center [12].

Packet losses often have significant impacts on application performance and network operations. Just a few non-

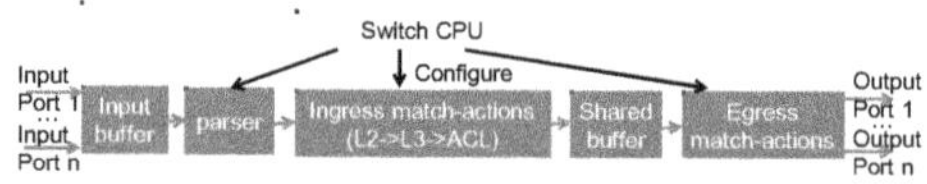

Figure 1: Switch packet processing pipeline

congestion-related losses can cause significant tail latency increase and throughput drop (especially because TCP treats them as congestion signals) [23, 30], leading to violations of service level agreements (SLAs) and revenue drops of online services [8, 35]. Moreover, it often takes operators tens of hours to identify whether a failure or performance problem is caused by packet losses, where losses happen, which flows are affected, and finally identify the root causes of losses and figure out fixes [1, 2].

Instead, we need a loss detection solution that can identify losses and narrow down their root causes fast (e.g., in tens of milliseconds). In this way, we can give operators enough time to identify their root causes or take actions to eliminate these losses, in order to minimize their impact on applications and network operations.

Generic detection of all loss types. Losses can be related to different components in the network (Figure 1) and be caused by different reasons. It is impossible to enumerate all types of losses, so we highlight a few common ones normally reported in data centers to illustrate the diversity of losses.

Congestion: Congestion loss happens at the output buffer and is caused by multiple flows competing for the same output port, and the total rate exceeds the capacity of that port.

Persistent blackholes: The persistent blackhole is a kind of problem that drops all packets matching a certain "pattern" at a switch [12, 38]. Persistent blackholes could be caused by match-actions table corruptions [12, 38] or the controller misconfiguring the rules.

Transient blackholes: The transient blackhole is similar to the persistent blackhole, but only during a short period. Transient blackholes could be caused by non-atomic rule updates [19] or network-wide inconsistent updates [14].

Random drops: The random drop is a type that the switch persistently drops packets randomly without reporting [12, 38]. Random drops could be caused by component problems such as not-well-seated linecards or faulty links [12].

Of course, there are many other losses we have not mentioned here. Such a diversity of losses demands a tool that can detect all losses regardless of the types.

Capturing location information. The first step to diagnose a packet loss is to identify the location of it—which switch, NIC, or host that incur the packet loss. Knowing the location, we can take quick actions (e.g., reboot the switch, reroute the traffic) to quickly mitigate the impact [36] or analyze the flows at the location to help diagnose the root causes [12].

Capturing packet header information. We need to distinguish different types of losses to identify the best solution to mitigate these losses (Table 1). For example, if there are

Loss types	Example error places	Mitigation	Details
Congestion	Buffer	Re-schedule flows	Flows, timing
Persistent blackholes	Switch match-action tables, Controller	Reboot, fix config	Flows, sequences
Transient blackholes	Controller, switch software	Debug controller or switch software	Flows, sequences, timing
Random drops	switch hardware	direct traffic away	Flows, timing

Table 1: Example types of packet losses

congestions, operators can re-schedule the flows to avoid congested links or move the applications to other servers. For persistent blackholes, we need to reboot the switches to fix table corruptions, or to correct the misconfigurations at the controller. If there is a transient blackhole, it helps operators to identify and fix the bugs in the controllers or switch softwares. If there are silent random drops, operators have to shut down and RMA (return merchandise authorization) the faulty components [12].

To distinguish different types of losses and understand the impacts of losses, we need different types of details. (1) flow information such as 5 tuples (source, destination IP addresses, ports, and protocol). Different flows may have different loss patterns, so it is important to know the 5 tuples. Also, such 5-tuple information can indicate the applications affected by the losses and allow operators to take fine-grained actions to help these applications. (2) Timing information. Many types of losses are very short, such as congestions or transient blackholes, so it is good to know the timing of each individual loss, which can help identify the temporal pattern of the losses. (3) Loss pattern. It is also important to identify the loss pattern, because different types of losses have different loss patterns (e.g., blackhole losses are continuous, while others may not be).

2.2 Existing monitoring tools

In data centers, there have already been a lot of monitoring tools. Some of them can be used for detecting packet losses. However, we now show that these solutions fall short in achieving the above goals. Due to the importance of loss detection in data centers, we need a new monitoring tool that is specifically designed for packet losses.

End host based solutions. End host based solutions [37, 25] can capture losses at the TCP level or by inspecting packets at the hypervisors. Although these solutions can capture all the details of lost packets independent of their types, it is hard to pinpoint the exact location of packet losses.

Pingmesh [12] can infer the location of packet losses through all-to-all probing, but cannot identify the exact switch that causes the problem within the leaf or spine groups. However, it does not track the packet losses of the actual applications. Moreover, its probing frequency is at least 10 seconds to reduce its overhead. Thus, it may miss many transient losses that happen between probes.

Packet mirroring at switches. Everflow [38] selectively mirrors packets to the collector, so the operators can know the traces of packets matching pre-selection filters and can detect losses by identifying those packets that do not have complete traces to reach the destination. However, it is not good at capturing most types of losses, and it is unclear if the packets get lost or if the report to the collectors gets lost.

Counters at switches. Switch vendors provide various counters (e.g., SNMP) to indicate the health conditions and operations at switches, some of which are related to losses. However, due to the diversity of loss types, it is difficult to identify and implement the right set of counters.

FlowRadar [21] captures per-flow counters at each switch at a fine time scale (e.g., 10s of milliseconds). One can use FlowRadar to detect packet losses by comparing the counters at two nearby hops. However, since it is hard to synchronize the counters to capture the same batch of packets, we often have to wait for a flow ends (or a flowlet ends with enough idle time after it [3]). The memory usage for FlowRadar is proportional to the number of flows we need to capture.

2.3 LossRadar Design

Instead of relying on generic monitoring tools which often fall short in loss detection, we propose to build a monitoring tool specific to loss detection given the prevalence and importance of packet losses in data centers. We propose to design a new loss detection solution that can capture all types of losses that happen at anywhere anytime and identify individual lost packets, while keeping the overhead low.

Generic to all types of losses. To detect losses regardless of their types and root causes, our key idea follows the *Flow Conservation Rule*: The set of packets that comes into any network domain (a link, a switch module, a switch, or an area of network devices) should be equal to the set of packets that leaves the domain, as long as the domain does not include any packet sources and sinks (e.g., middleboxes, hosts)[1].

Fast detection of losses and their locations. Based on the Flow Conservation Rule, we design LossRadar as shown in Figure 2. LossRadar installs *meters* to capture unidirectional traffic before it enters and after it leaves a domain in the network (called *upstream* and *downstream meters*). Each meter encodes the unique identifiers for individual packets into a traffic digest, and periodically reports traffic digests

[1]We recognize that a network switch can occasionally behave as a packet source or sink for certain types of packets (e.g., routing protocol messages, switch management protocol messages). Those packets, however, can be easily and unambiguously distinguished and hence can be filtered out from the LossRadar mechanism.

Loss detection tools	Detection time	Generic	Location	packet header info	Overhead
Host monitoring [37, 25]	10s of ms	Yes	No	Yes	Host CPU
Pingmesh [12]	10s of seconds	Only persistent losses	Infer	No	Host CPU
Mirroring [38]	10s of ms	Miss congestion	Yes	Yes	B/w prop. to # packets
Flow-level counters [21]	After a flow(let) ends	Yes	Yes	Only per-flow info	Memory prop. to # flows
LossRadar	10s of ms	Yes	Yes	Yes	Memory prop. to # losses

Table 2: State-of-the-art datacenter monitoring solutions

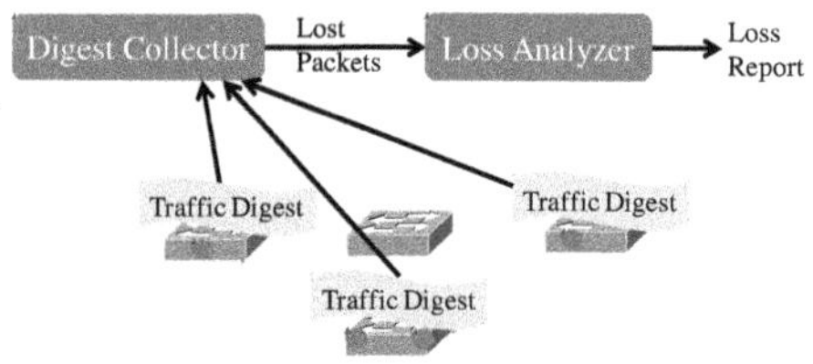

Figure 2: LossRadar architecture (Red circles are meters)

to a central LossRadar collector. LossRadar collector compares traffic digests from upstream and downstream meters, detects violations of the Flow Conservation Rule, and reports detailed information of lost packets.

Capture packet header information with low overhead. We want to store detailed information (e.g., 5 tuples, timing, sequences) to help the diagnosis of lost packets. However, switches have limited memory (only tens of MB for all the counters and match-action tables). Thus, it is important to capture important information about packet losses in limited memory. Rather than keeping information about all the traffic (e.g., FlowRadar [21]), we propose to build a traffic digest whose size is proportional to the number of packet losses independent of the total traffic or flows in the system.

With LossRadar, operators only need to provision the switch memory based on the number of losses they expect and the amount of details they need. When the number of losses goes beyond the expected number, LossRadar can still report the total number of losses at each location but may miss the detailed information such as 5 tuples for some losses. This is reasonable because when there is a large number of losses at a place, it is more important to reboot the entire switch or direct traffic away from it.

To collect more useful details of unknown lost packets, operators may also choose to pre-filter expected losses (e.g., those packets dropped by access control list) by specifying the right set of packets that LossRadar needs to keep in its traffic digests.

Challenges: There are three key challenges in building LossRadar:

Small size digests: To capture individual lost packets and their detailed information with low overhead, we proposed data structures that can capture all the packets in the digest while keeping the digest small enough to reduce the storage, bandwidth, and processing overhead. The key insight is we leverage coding techniques[10] to only keep information about lost packets. (Section 3)

Meter placement: To locate where losses happen in the network, we identify the right places to install meters that can cover the entire network. In some networks where we cannot deploy meters at all places, we can still install the meters at some locations that can narrow down the potential location of losses. (Section 4)

Loss analyzer: Given the details of losses, we design temporal and spatial loss analysis algorithms that can quickly identify some root causes such as blackholes, congestions and random drops. Moreover, we develop algorithms that can identify the set of rules that may cause the blackhole. (Section 5)

3. LossRadar TRAFFIC DIGESTS

In this section, we describe the design of traffic digests with low memory overhead and the benefits of our design, and then discuss the challenges in collecting the digests.

3.1 Capturing losses with small digests

We observe that although the number of packets in the network is too large for the meters to keep track of, the number of lost packets are much smaller. Thus if we can only keep track of the lost packets rather than all packets, we can reduce the overhead a lot. The question is how to track lost packets? Our idea is to keep traffic digests at an upstream meter and a downstream meter. When we compare the two meters, the same packets at both digests will cancel out, so only the packets that do not appear at the downstream (i.e., lost packets) remain in the result. In this way, the digest size only needs to be large enough for the number of losses, not the total number of packets.

We build traffic digests using Invertible Bloom Filter (IBF) [10], as shown in Figure 3. The digest has an array of cells. Each cell contains two values: $xorSum$ and $count$. When a packet x arrives, we insert it into k cells. Each cell is updated as $xorSum = xorSum \oplus x.sig$, $count = count + 1$. The $x.sig$ denotes x's *signature*, which includes the immutable header fields that can uniquely identify the packet (e.g. 5-tuple and IP_ID) and other information about the packet, which we will discuss in Section 3.2. The k cells are indexed by k hash functions ($h_1 \ldots h_k$) calculated on $x.sig$.

Figure 3 (a) and (b) shows two traffic digests, each of which is taken at the upstream meter UM and the downstream meter DM respectively. The upstream digest contains four packets from two flows, and the downstream one contains only one packet – the other three are lost.

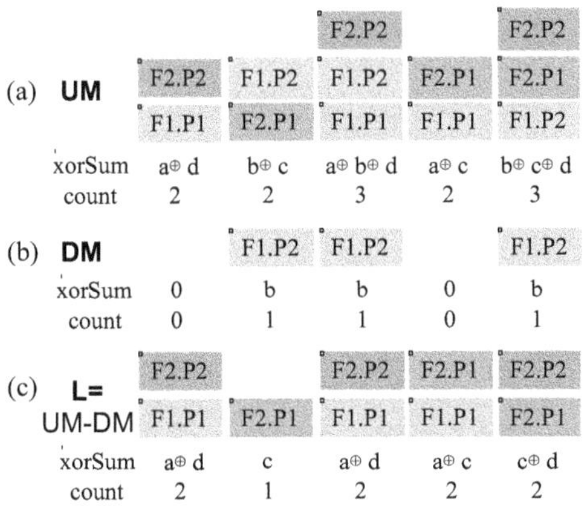

Figure 3: Traffic digests to get individual lost packets. (a) two flows, each with two packets at the upstream meter, indicated as a (F1.P1), b (F1.P2), c (F2.P1), d(F2.P2); (b) only F1.P2 is received at the downstream meter; (c) the result of the subtraction contains only lost packets

To identify lost packets, the digest collector subtracts each cell i in DM's digest from the corresponding one in UM's digest. That is: $L_i.xorSum = UM_i.xorSum \oplus DM_i.xorSum$; $L_i.count = UM_i.count - DM_i.count$. We can decode lost packets from the digest difference L as follows: We first find the cells of L that contain exactly one packet (i.e., $count = 1$) which are called *pure cells*. The $xorSum$ of a pure cell is exactly the signature of the packet in it. We then remove the packet from all the k cells in which the packet was hashed into. Once this is done, some other pure cells may appear, and we repeat the same process for them. By doing this iteratively, we can retrieve all packets in L with a very high probability (we will explain this in Section 3.2). For example, in Figure 3 (c), we first identify a pure cell whose count is 1 (F2.P1). After removing F2.P1, we get the packet F1.P1 (the 4th cell's updated count is 1); and finally after removing F1.P1, we decode F2.P2.

3.2 Benefits of digests

There are two benefits of the digests.

The size of the digest in the meter is proportional to the number of lost packets, but not the total number of packets that go through the meter. Suppose both UM and DM have n_{cell} cells. Then L, as a result of the subtraction, also has n_{cell} cells. Because L only needs to be large enough to decode the n_{loss} lost packets, n_{cell} is determined by the n_{loss}. Existing works have shown that n_{cell} only needs to be proportional to n_{loss} (i.e., $c = \frac{n_{cell}}{n_{loss}}$ is a constant) to achieve a high success rate for decoding all losses[2]. Eppstein et al. [10] shows empirically that $c = 1.3$ to achieve a 99% success rate when $n_{loss} > 1000$ for $k = 3$. Thus, we only need to set the size of the digest in data plane with a small c times the expected number of losses to achieve a high success rate.

Because packet loss rate is very low (less than 0.01%) in data centers [12], we only need small sized digests. Thus we set our digest size small enough to capture lost packets based on an upper bound of expected loss rate R (e.g., 0.1%). When the loss rate is below R, we can decode individual lost packets with high probability (e.g., >99%). When the loss rate is above R, however, we can still detect the total number of lost packets per port, but may fail to identify individual lost packets. This is because the digest may have so many lost packets in each cell, and thus the occurrence of pure cells become progressively less probable. Note, however, this may be still be quite acceptable for most network admins because, when the loss rate is this high, it is much more crucial to take urgent action to fix the problem (e.g., shut down the link or the switch) than to diagnose the problem or to account for individual losses to particular applications that are affected.

We can include a lot of details we are interested in of each lost packet. The basic setting is to include two pieces of information in the signature of a packet. (1) Flow-level information. We store the 5-tuple information to provide enough details of individual packets. (2) Packet identifier. We use the IP_ID field because the IP_ID field is consecutive within each 5-tuple, so it can be used to uniquely identify a packet. In case the IP_ID field is not sufficient (e.g., if more than 64K packets from a single flow are monitored in a single monitoring window), we can include other fields such as fragment offset, TCP sequence number or a small fraction of the payload in the signature. In the basic setting, each signature is 120 bits[3].
Additionally, operators can configure to include any other fields of a packet that they are interested in (e.g., TCP flags). Note that if the field changes across hops, we need to consider that. For example, if we want to include TTL, and the TTL will decrement h in between, operators need to configure the DM to insert TTL + h instead of TTL into the digest. Operators can also include other metadata that are related to but not part of the packet, such as the timestamp when the packet arrives at the UM. In this case, the UM needs to tag the metadata in the packet header, so that the DM can use the same value. Including other fields require more bits in the signature. For example, if we include the TCP-SYN bit, TTL (only need 1 bit to distinguish zero and non-zero) and timestamp, we need to extend the signature by 16 bits[4], which are used in our loss root cause analysis (Section 5).

3.3 Digest configuration

With LossRadar, operators only need to provision the switch memory based on the number of losses they expect and the amount of details they need. When the number of losses goes beyond the expected number, LossRadar can still report the total number of losses at each location but may miss the detailed information such as 5 tuples for some losses. This is reasonable because when there is a large number of

[2]A success for decoding all losses means we can always find a pure cell until all lost packets are decoded.

[3]104 bits for 5-tuple, and 16 bits for IP_ID.

[4]1 bit for TCP-SYN, 1 bits for TTL, and 14 bits for microsecond-level timestamp in 10 ms (2^{14}us>10ms).

losses at a place, it is more important to reboot the entire switch or direct traffic away from it.

To collect more useful details of unknown lost packets, operators may also choose to pre-filter expected losses (e.g., those packets dropped by access control list) by specifying the right set of packets that LOSSRADAR needs to keep in its traffic digests. Recent programmable switches can export information of which packets they decide to drop because of access control lists or buffer overflow (e.g., using negative mirroring, which is presented at P4 workshop). With these techniques, we can also exclude the lost packets known by switches, and thus focus LOSSRADAR digests on those losses the switches cannot diagnose.

3.4 Measurement batch

To capture packet losses in near real time, we capture packets in batches at both upstream and downstream. So the operator needs to ensure the same packet goes to the same batch in both the upstream meter and the downstream meter.

To report packet losses in near real time, meters should keep collecting traffic digests for a small batch of packets every T (e.g., 10 ms) and immediately report the digests to the central collector as soon as the batch is over. To compare traffic digests correctly across meters, however, we need to ensure that a pair of upstream and downstream meters must agree on the boundary of batches so that they can put the same packet in the same batch. Otherwise, digests will always end up with mismatches. Unfortunately, relying on time-synchronization protocols or devices (e.g., NTP [27], PTP [32], GPS) to let meters agree on batch boundaries has fundamental limitations: no matter how accurate the time-sync protocol can ensure, there could always be packets on the fly, i.e. packets that leave the upstream meter, but have not arrived at the downstream meter. Hence, if we rely on the time-sync protocols, batch disagreement is inevitable.

Another possible solution is to use signal packets to synchronize the starting and ending times of a pair of upstream and downstream batches. However, if the signal packet is dropped or gets reordered, some packets may be classified into the wrong batch.

To work with packet losses and reordering, we propose to let each packet carry a batch identifier to tell the downstream meter which upstream batch the packet belongs to. Thus which batch at the downstream a packet belongs to is not based on the packet's arrival time, but the batch_ID it carries. If there is no packet reordering, a downstream batch can be terminated when a packet with a new batch_ID arrives. However, if there is reordering (e.g., due to different priority queues), packets from different batches may interleave at the downstream meter, so multiple downstream batches have to coexist. As a result, we set the lifetime of a downstream batch to $T + timeout$, starting at the first packet's arrival of this batch. The downstream batch is $timeout$ longer than the upstream batch, which is for the delay in between. The operator can set the value of $timeout$ based on their expectation of the maximum delay.

There is one question raised that how many downstream batches can coexist at the same time, which is related to the memory consumption. In data centers, the RTT is a few hundreds of microseconds [4], and per-hop delay should be shorter, so for $T > 1ms$, there will be at most two batches coexist at a downstream meter.

4. NETWORK WIDE DEPLOYMENT

In this section, we discuss where to install the meters to detect packet losses that happen at any place in the network, and pinpoint the exact loss locations. We consider two cases: When we have access to all the devices in the network, or we only have access to some switches.

4.1 Cover the entire network

We need to install meters to meet two goals: (1) Each pair of meters covers a segment of paths where packets have a unique path. In this way, we can easily compare the traffic digests taken at a pair of meters (upstream and downstream) to identify lost packets; (2) All pairs of meters together cover the entire network. In this way, we would not miss any packet loss event.

The high-level idea is to install one upstream meter at each output port of every switch, and one downstream meter at each input port of every switch as shown in Figure 4(a). In this way, both directions of every link are covered. Note that although we do not draw in Figure 4(a), there is also traffic from S2 to S1, so actually we also need an upstream meter at S2's output port connected to S1, and a downstream meter at S1's input port connected to S2. In fact, we need two pairs of upstream meter and downstream meter for each bidirectional link. We only draw one pair in Figure 4(a) for conciseness.

Then, given the packet processing pipeline of a switch, we need to figure out at which stages to install the meters. Considering that losses could happen at any stage of the pipeline, we need to make sure the meters cover every part of the data plane. We choose to put the meters at the end of the ingress pipeline of tables, and before the shared buffer, as shown in Figure 4(b). And, we put the upstream meters before the downstream meters within a switch, rather than the other way around, so that the segments between the upstream meters and downstream meters are also covered. In addition, we install meters for each network interface at hosts.

We choose this place to install meters for 2 reasons. First, at the place where upstream meters are installed, the decision of which output port(s) a packet goes to need to have been made, so that the switch knows which upstream meter (output port) to insert the packet into. Thus, the meters must be after all the ingress pipeline of tables, because the decision could be made at any of the ingress tables. Note, by doing so, we can handle multicast by inserting the packet into the upstream meters of all the output ports it goes to. Second, the timestamp collected at this stage is the closest to the time a packet is enqueued, so the timestamp can be used to describe the temporal pattern of congestion losses. By doing so, we make the most use of the timestamp of the packet.

4.2 Incremental deployment

We do not expect LOSSRADAR to be deployed at all the switches in data centers at once. Now we consider the incre-

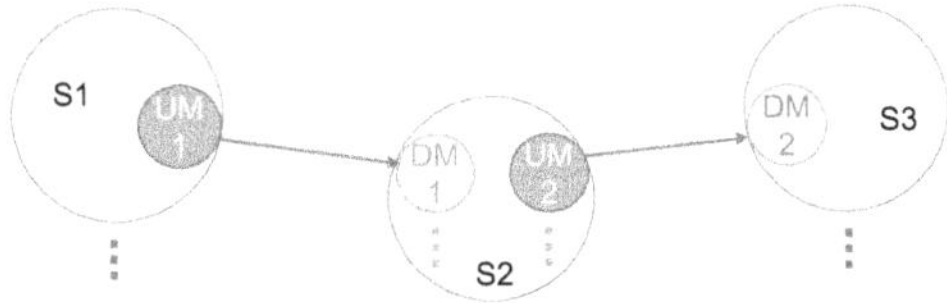

(a) Full deployment at all the switches

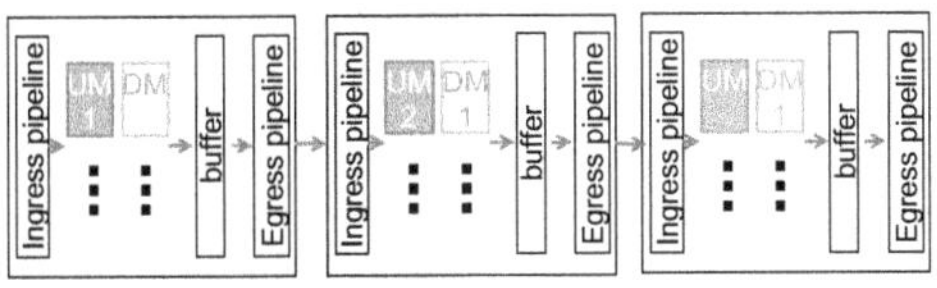

(b) Meter deployment details inside switches

Figure 4: Placing meters to cover the entire network (solid and empty circles are respective upstream and downstream meters)

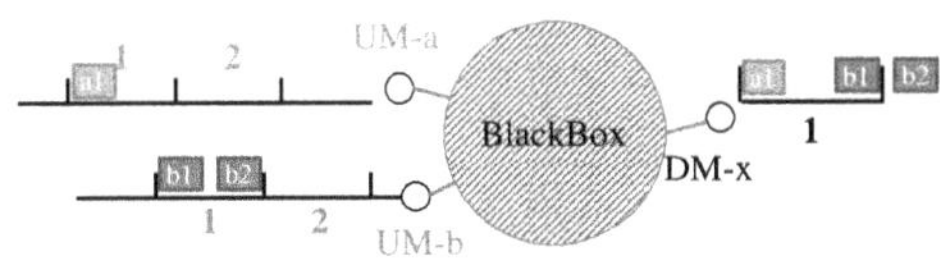

(a) Sync. Issue for blackbox

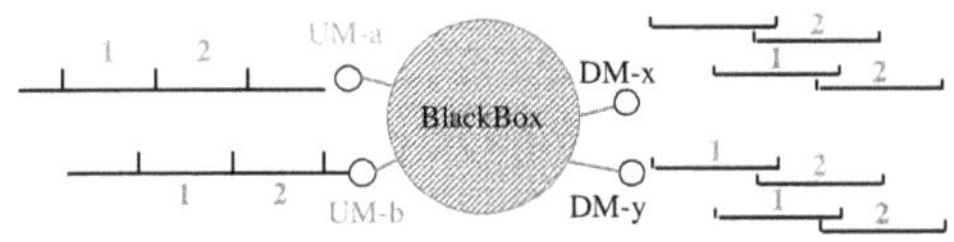

(b) Solution for blackbox case

Figure 5: Challenge and solution to blackbox case

mental deployment case where only a subset of the switches support LOSSRADAR. We define blackboxes as those areas where we cannot install the meters. The strawman approach is to install one meter at each port of the blackbox and compare across meters. When meters do not have synchronized clocks, we propose to let each meter maintain multiple small digests instead of one. Moreover, our solution can reduce the memory usage of the strawman approach by almost 2 times.

Strawman approach. Intuitively, we can insert an upstream meter at each entrance to the blackbox, and a downstream meter at each exit of the blackbox. Each upstream meter and downstream meter maintains one digest. To retrieve the losses, we can add up the digests at all upstream meters and the digests at all downstream meters respectively, and compare the two sums. Here adding up two digests a and b means for each corresponding cell i, $a_i.xorSum \oplus b_i.xorSum$, $a_i.count + b_i.count$. So the sum is also a digest of the same size with a and b.

The memory usage of each digest in this case is larger than in a non-blackbox case. The reason is as follows. Let us call the size of a digest in a non-blackbox case as *normal size*. Suppose there are n upstream meters and n downstream meters. During the comparison of the two sums, the total number of losses could be n times of the number of lost packets from a single upstream meter. Thus, the size of the sum digest has to be n times of the normal size. As a result, the size of the digest at each meter has to be the same with the sum, which is n times of the normal size.

Handle unsynchronized clock across meters. The problem with the strawman solution is that if the clocks of the upstream meters are not well synchronized, packets from the same batch of the same upstream meter may arrive at different batches at one downstream meter. For example (Figure 5(a)), UM-a's batch 1 is earlier than UM-b's batch 1. The packet a1 from UM-a's batch 1 goes to DM-x, and starts the downstream batch 1. The packets from UM-b's batch 1 also goes to DM-x. The packet b1 from the *early* part of UM-b's batch 1 arrives at the *late* part of DM-x's batch 1, since DM-x's batch 1 has already started for a while. The packet b2, however, arrives after DM-x's batch 1 ended. So b1 and b2 are in the same upstream batch, but end up in different downstream batches.

As long as the clocks of the upstream meters are not accurately synchronized, there is always a chance of batch disagreement.

Solution. Our solution is that each downstream meter maintains separate digests for each upstream meter, as shown in Figure 5(b). To detect the packet losses, we can add up all the digests for the same upstream meter across all the downstream meters (e.g., the digests for UM-a's batch 1 at DM-x and DM-y respectively), and compare the sum with the digest at the upstream meter (e.g., UM-a's batch 1). Thus, we can identify all the lost packets between one upstream meter and all its downstream meters.

Note that the downstream meters do not always know which upstream meter a packet comes from. Our solution is to let each upstream meter mark its meter ID in the packet header. This solution has another benefit that it reduces the memory usage. In the strawman approach, the size of each digest (no matter at an upstream or a downstream) is n times of normal size. In our solution, however, we compare one upstream digest with the sum of its corresponding downstream digest, so the total number of losses in each comparison is just the number of lost packet from one upstream meter, not all upstream meters. So the size of each digest only needs to be normal size. Thus, although each downstream meter maintains n separate digests, the total size is still n times of normal size. But for each upstream meter, the total size is only normal size, which is reduced by n times.

In practice, each port of a blackbox can be both entrance and exit, so each switch connects to the blackbox need to install both upstream meter and downstream meter. In this case, the memory usage reduction is $2n/(n+1)$ per switch, which is almost 2 times.

5. LOSS ANALYZER

Using the detailed information of lost packets, we build an analyzer to classify the causes of packet losses by analyzing traffic digests across the network over time. The loss analyzer consists of (1) a root cause analyzer, which uses only the loss information from LossRadar to analyse the root causes of the losses, and (2) an ACL rule corruption analyzer as an application of the root cause analyzer, which can infer the corrupted rules of an ACL table based on the correct version of the ACL (from controller) and the blackhole losses from the root cause analyzer.

5.1 Root cause analyzer

The root cause analyzer classifies the reasons for the losses on each individual switch. In a short time (e.g. 10 ms) at one switch, we assume losses are dominated by one reason, so we can identify the root causes by recognizing the unique patterns of different types of losses, given the details collected by LossRadar. We then relax the assumption to handle multiple problems all causing losses.

5.1.1 Classification based on loss patterns

We can classify the losses based on the unique patterns of different types of losses, given the details such as 5 tuples, IP_ID, TTL, timestamps and TCP flags. We list the common types of losses here. For other uncommon types, we classify them as unknown. However, after diagnosis, we can extract patterns of them based on the details we have, and use the patterns for future classification.

Congestion. We observed that *the congestion losses are bursty, and the gap between back-to-back losses is only a few microseconds.* The TCP sends a batch of packets every RTT, and the flows that experience losses will shrink their congestion windows, so in the next RTT congestion is much less likely to happen. Thus the congestion losses are bursty. The gap between back-to-back losses is only a few microseconds because the transmission time of a packet is microsecond level. For 10G link, the transmission time of a 1500B packet is 1.2us. Thus, even if the total receiving rate is only 10% higher than the sending rate of an output port, there will be one loss every 11 packets, which is one loss every 13.2us.

Blackholes. We observed three different loss patterns.

(1) Bursty and consecutive losses within a flow. If a blackhole happens and affects ongoing large flows (e.g., file transferring, video delivering), the affected ongoing large flows have consecutive lost packets, and the losses are bursty.

(2) Non-bursty and consecutive losses within a flow. If a blackhole happens and affects some ongoing small flows, which only carries small pieces of data (e.g., sending messages), the affected ongoing small flows have consecutive, but non-bursty losses.

(3) Only a SYN packet loss from each flow. In the above two cases, each flow has multiple losses, but there are cases some flows only have one loss for more than a few seconds. After further investigation, we found that these lost packets are mostly SYN or SYN-ACK. This means that for the new flows, their handshake packets are dropped, so there are no follow-up packets until the retransmission of the SYN packet, which waits for a few seconds (normally 3 seconds for the first retransmission, then the waiting time doubles).

Random drops. *The random drops are evenly distributed over time.* This is because random drops are caused by problematic hardware components of a switch, which randomly drops packets passing it with certain drop rates.

Loop. *Packets dropped by loops have TTL = 0.* So we can use the TTL field to detect the losses caused by loops.

5.1.2 Root cause inference algorithms

There is still a small chance that during a given time period, there may be multiple types of losses together, which blurs the patterns. Thus, we design the root cause inference algorithms based on two principles. **(1) Identify bursty losses first**. We identify bursty losses first because other types of losses have long term patterns (e.g. random drops are evenly distributed over time, and the SYN packets dropped by blackholes should represent a large fraction of losses), which can be blurred by the burst of losses. **(2) It is fine to correctly classify only one type of losses when multiple types are mixed**. This is because we can fix the problems for one type of losses first. Moreover, if the missed types are caused by persistent problems, we can detect them in the future when they are not mixed. **(3) Keep the false alarm rate low for blackholes and random drops**, because both of them require human involvement: operator needs to check the switch configuration for blackholes, and hardware components for random drops. Thus, when blackholes/random drops are mixed with congestion, we believe classifying the losses as congestion losses is better[5].

Before performing the inference algorithm, we first exclude the expected losses such as packets dropped by ACL tables. All the expected losses can be pre-filtered by programmable switches. If the switch does not support pre-filtering, the collector can easily identify this kind of losses by matching the lost packets against the table rules. We also exclude losses with TTL = 0, which could be dropped by loops, or are expected by the applications (e.g., traceroute). We can map the 5-tuple of the lost packets to the application to decide if the loss is expected or not.

The algorithm has two steps on different time scales: (1) For each new batch, we classify the bursty losses; (2) Every $long\_term\_interval$ (e.g. 100 ms), we classify the remaining losses (from multiple batches) into non-bursty types. We now describe the algorithm.

Analysis of bursty losses. We first perform an analysis of bursty losses for each new batch at each port (Algorithm 1). A burst is identified by at least n_{burst} losses with gaps less than t_{gap} between back-to-back losses. A burst of losses may be caused by either congestion or blackholes. If a flow's losses are non-consecutive in this burst, it cannot be caused by a blackhole, so we know there is congestion. In this case, according to the design principle (3), we classify the whole burst as congestion losses (Line 15 to 20). If all losses are consecutive, we only classify the flows that lost almost one

[5]We understand that different networks have different requirements, so operators may use other principles if necessary.

congestion window ($\#losses > n_{bb}$[6]) as blackhole losses, and the rest as congestion losses (Line 21 to 24).

Our idea to measure the consecutiveness is to examine the IP_ID of the lost packets. In current Linux, the IP_ID of each 5-tuple is consecutive [5], so we can use the IP_ID to determine if the losses are consecutive or not.

We should set t_{gap} large enough and n_{burst} small enough to detect slight and short congestion, but still keep the probability of randomly dropping n_{burst} packets with less than t_{gap} back-to-back gap low. n_{bb} should be set slightly lower than the bandwidth-delay product for flows with still-growing windows, while large enough to keep the probability of congestion dropping n_{bb} consecutive packets of a flow low.

Long term analysis. Every $long\_term\_interval$ (e.g. 100 ms), we classify the rest of the losses (Algorithm 2).

We first classify the consecutive losses within a flow as blackhole losses (Line 2 to 6), because its per-flow pattern is not affected by other types of losses, and after removing these losses, the pattern of other losses are clearer. We set a small threshold n_{nb}[7] (line 3) for the length of the consecutive losses. n_{nb} needs to be large enough to keep the probability of randomly dropping n_{nb} consecutive packets of a flow low.

After that, for the rest of the packets, we first classify SYN losses as blackhole losses (line 8 to 11) if the fraction of SYN packets in an interval is large ($> p_{syn}$). p_{syn} should be set large enough to keep false alarm rate low. Finally, we measure the distribution of the rest of the losses over time (line 12 to 14). We divide the time interval into n (number of losses) equal bins, and count the fraction of non-empty bins (bins with at least one loss) in all bins. We empirically estimate this fraction using a simple experiment: we randomly throw m balls into m bins following even distribution, and count the fraction of non-empty bins. The fraction is around 0.63 for different m. This fraction gives an upper bound of p_{rand}, because in practice packets' arrivals are non-uniform.

In practice, we should set $n_{burst} \leq n_{nb}$, because otherwise if a congestion loss burst of n packets where $n < n_{burst}$ contains $\geq n_{nb}$ consecutive losses of a flow, the losses of that flow would be classified as blackhole losses.

5.2 Rule corruption detection

For blackhole losses, after confirming with the configuration, we can determine if there are misconfigurations or not. If not, there must be rule corruptions. We develop algorithms that can locate the set of rules whose corruption may cause the blackhole. We take the access control list (ACL) table as an example. Given the list of blackhole losses and ACLs, we need to identify the rule that may get corrupted. For simplicity, we only consider one bit flip in the table, which is the most common case. There are three cases for unexpected losses: (a) a deny rule's match field corrupted, so it denies flows originally not covered by it; (b) an accept rule's match field corrupted, and the flows originally covered by it now match other deny rules; (c) an accept rule's action changes to deny. We enumerate all three cases. For case (a), we enumerate all deny rules in the correct ACL table, and find the candidates whose match field corrupted by one bit would match all unexpected loss. For case (b) and (c), we check if all unexpected loss all match the same rule in the correct ACL table. If so, then this rule is a candidate. Our evaluation

[6]bb stands for Bursty Blackhole

[7]nb stands for Non-bursty Blackhole

Algorithm 1: LossRadar bursty loss analysis

1 **Function** `bursty_loss_analysis` (*B: a new batch of losses*)
2   Mark the types of all losses in B as unknown;
3   burst = find_next_burst(B);
4   **while** *burst != Null* **do**
5   classify_burst(burst);
6   burst = find_next_burst(B);
7   **end**
8 **Function** `find_next_burst` (*B*)
9   Find the next $B_{i...j}$ that $B_{k+1}.time - B_k.time < t_{gap}$, and the gap before B_i and after B_j is larger than t_{gap};
10   **while** $j - i + 1 < n_{burst}$ **do**
11   Find the next $B_{i...j}$;
12   **end**
13   return $B_{i...j}$;
14 **Function** `classify_burst` (*burst*)
15   **foreach** *flow f in burst* **do**
16   **if** *f's lost packets have non-consecutive IP_ID* **then**
17   Mark all losses in $burst$ as congestion;
18   Return;
19   **end**
20   **end**
21   **foreach** *flow f that has more than n_{bb} losses in burst* **do**
22   Mark all losses of f as blackhole;
23   **end**
24   Mark losses in $burst$ whose types are unknown as congestion;

Algorithm 2: LossRadar root cause inference

1 **Function** `long_term_analysis` (*L: all losses at a port in* $long\_term\_interval$)
2   **foreach** *flow f in L* **do**
3   **if** *f's lost packets have consecutive IP_ID and #(unclassified losses) >= n_{nb}* **then**
4   Mark losses in f whose types are still unknown as blackhole;
5   **end**
6   **end**
7     $rest$ = all the losses in L whose types are still unknown;
8   **if** *fraction of SYN packets in rest > p_{syn}* **then**
9   Mark all the SYN packets' types in $rest$ as blackhole;
10   Remove the SYN packets from $rest$;
11   **end**
12   **if** *random_distribution(rest)* **then**
13   Mark all packets' types in $rest$ as random;
14   **end**
15 **Function** `random_distribution` (*L*)
16   n = number of losses in L;
17   Divide the time period of L into n equal time interval $T_{1...n}$;
18   Count the number of losses in each T_i;
19   **if** *fraction of T_i that has losses > p_{rand}* **then**
20   return True;
21   **end**
22   return False;

in Section 7.5 shows that this algorithm often narrows down the candidate rule set of 2-2.5 rules and always successfully cover the corrupted rules.

6. IMPLEMENTATION

We implemented LossRadar in both Open vSwitch [28] and P4 behavioral model [29].

6.1 Open vSwitch implementation

We modify Open vSwitch to support traffic digest collection. We direct all the packets to the user space and collect traffic digests there. We create a sending thread which sends digests at the end of each batch to a digest collector via a persistent TCP connection. Each time the collector receives both the traffic digests from a pair of upstream meter (UM) and downstream meters (DM), it runs the decoding process to report lost packets.

6.2 P4 implementation

At a high level, we put LossRadar's functions in two tables, at the end of the ingress pipeline. The first table is for updating UMs, and the second is for DMs. We now inspect the different components needed by LossRadar.

Storing traffic digests. LossRadar's traffic digest is implemented on the $register$ in P4. We defined two arrays of registers for $xorSum$ and $count$ respectively. The width of each register in the $xorSum$ array is set to the total number of bits in a packet's $signature$ (5-tuple, IP_ID, TTL, TCP flag, timestamp, etc.). The lengths of the arrays are the number of cells n_{cell}, which is defined by users according to their expected number of losses.

Each port of a switch has a UM and a DM. Each meter keeps two digests for different batches of packets. We put all $2n_{port}$ upstream digests in an array[8], and all $2n_{port}$ downstream digests in another array. The i-th cell in the b-th batch of the p-th port is indexed by $i + (b \cdot n_{port} + p) \cdot n_{cell}$.

Updating digests. This includes calculating hash values based on the packets' $signatures$, and updating the cells indexed by these hash values. We define 3 hash functions, calculated on a $field\_list$ that is defined to include the $signature$ of each packet. The $signature$ is a bit different for UM and DM. The mutable part of the $signature$ (e.g. timestamp and TTL) for the DM should be the same as the part for the UM at the *previous hop*. So each UM uses the timestamp at this hop, and each DM uses the timestamp carried by the packet. The DM uses TTL+1 instead of TTL to cancel out the decrement between hops.

Getting timestamps. LossRadar uses timestamps when packets are inserted into the UM. In current P4 behavioral model [29], among the timestamps exposed, the closest to our need is the timestamp when the switch starts processing the packet ($ingress\_global\_timestamp$). This choice sacrifices the time spent in the ingress pipeline, which, however, is stabler and smaller (sub-microsecond) than the queuing delay, so it is also useful for congestion detection. We believe in future programmable switch design, exposing timestamp at arbitrary stages in the pipeline is possible.

Pre-filtering. In P4, every packet go through the whole pipeline, including the ones dropped by tables. So we can pre-filter the table-dropped packets by inserting them into only the DM (not the UM). In this way, these packets will cancel out with the UM in the previous hop, without affecting decoding other lost packets. We add a metadata $drop$ with a default value 0 for each packet, and update it to 1 in the dropping actions of the tables. At the UM, we use a matching field to filter out packet with $drop = 1$.

Header modification. LossRadar needs the header to carry batchID and optionally the timestamp and meterID (if in a blackbox case). We either store these data in unused header fields (e.g. VLAN, DSCP) or add a header, and modify parsers or add a parser for these data accordingly.

Each hop needs to modify the batchID and timestamp in the header to the ones the UM uses. However, this modification cannot be performed before or at the UM, because after the UM, the DM needs the previous hop's batchID and timestamp, which is carried by the header. Thus, we store the new batchID and timestamp in a metadata at the UM, and copy the metadata to the header after the DM finishes the update.

7. EVALUATION

Our evaluation focuses on answering five key questions:

1. What is the memory and bandwidth usage of LossRadar, and how they compare to other solutions such as FlowRadar [21] and full packet mirroring [38, 13]? We test them with a single pair of switches with traffics of different loads and different loss rates. We use simulation to test up to 100G traffic load. The result shows that LossRadar always uses less memory than FlowRadar in large data centers where the number of flows is large and less bandwidth than full mirroring.

2. Under realistic network traffic, how effective are the detection and the root cause inference of LossRadar? We run a network with 80 switches and 128 hosts in ns-3 simulations and evaluate LossRadar with different traffic, different loss patterns and loss rates. The result shows that we only need a few KB per digest to capture more than 99.99% lost packets. Our root cause inference algorithm can capture all the root causes within a few 100s ms.

3. What is the memory usage per switch for different deployments? We evaluate a full deployment and different types of blackboxes cases, based on the same topology, traffic and loss problems in the previous question. The result shows that the memory usages per switch in blackbox cases are higher than in a full deployment, but are still acceptable.

4. How fast is the loss detection? Our result in a testbed with Open vSwitch [28] on a FatTree topology shows that the detection delay is only 12 ms.[9]

5. Is the information LossRadar provides useful? We show two applications that use the loss details to improve performance and identify corrupted rules.

[8]For brevity, we conceptually treat the two arrays for respective $xorSum$ and $count$ as one array.

[9]We evaluate the delay with Open vSwitch rather than P4 behavior model due to performance concerns.

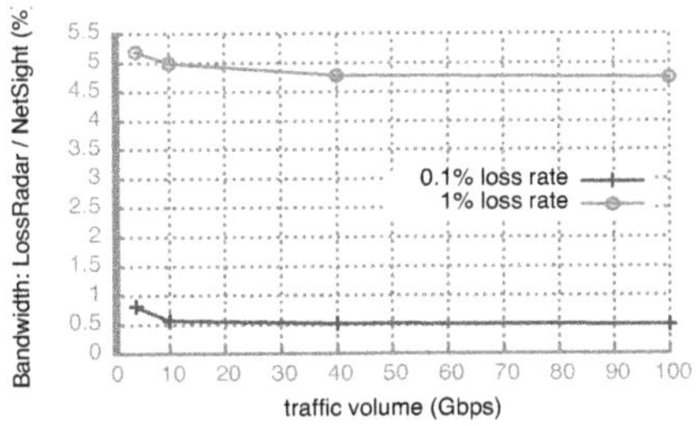

Figure 6: Bandwidth usage: LOSSRADAR vs. NetSight

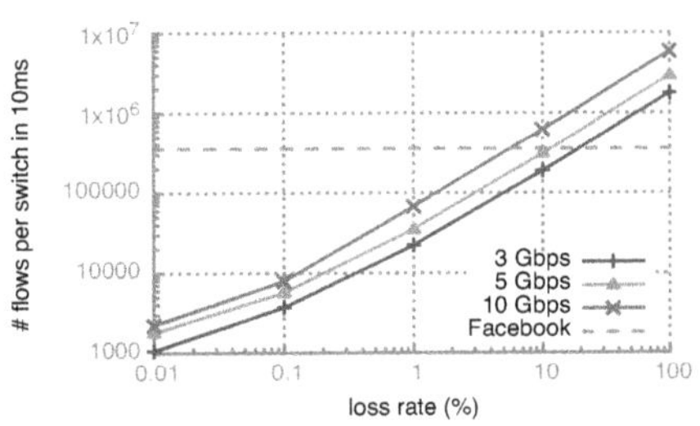

Figure 7: Memory usage: LOSSRADAR vs. FlowRadar.

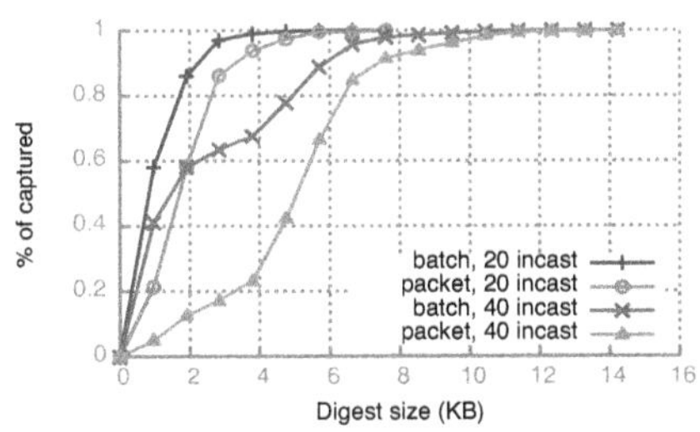

Figure 8: Memory usage under realistic traffic

7.1 Bandwidth and memory overhead

We set up a simulation with a simple topology where there are two switches. By default, we use 10G traffic, and the average packet size is 175B according to Facebook's data center traffic [33]. We change the traffic volume and the number of concurrent flows during the experiment for comparison with different state-of-the-art solutions. For LOSSRADAR, each meter in LOSSRADAR reports the digests every 10ms. Because it is possible that we fail to decode a digest, the size of the digest we tested is large enough so that it can decode all losses with 99% probability.

Bandwidth usage of LOSSRADAR is much less than full packet mirroring. Both Everflow [38] and NetSight [13] capture packets at every hop in the entire network and sends them to a centralized analyzer. While Everflow mirrors raw packets, NetSight introduces compression to reduce the overhead. Thus we compare with NetSight's best compression (Van Jacobson style compression plus gzip compression), which is reported 10Bytes per packet. In order to detect every loss, we configure it to capture every packet.

We evaluated the bandwidth usage with different traffic volume from 4Gbps to 100Gbps, and two loss rates 0.1% and 1%, and show the percentage of LOSSRADAR bandwidth usage to full packet mirroring bandwidth usage in Figure 6. The result shows that LOSSRADAR saves 95% and 99.5% of the bandwidth usage, for 1% and 0.1% loss rates respectively. For example, for 10Gbps traffic, full packet mirroring uses 513Mbps, while LOSSRADAR only uses 2.9Mbps for 0.1% loss rate, and 25.6Mbps for 1% loss rate.

LOSSRADAR saves memory when the number of concurrent flow is large or loss rate is low, compared with FlowRadar. FlowRadar [21] maintains per-flow counters at switches. It can get the loss counter by comparing the packet counters across hops. Its memory usage is proportional to the number of concurrent flows.

We perform experiments to find the number of concurrent flows, loss rate and throughput at which LOSSRADAR and FlowRadar need the same amount of memory, and plot the curves in Figure 7. The red, orange and blue curves are for 3 Gbps, 5 Gbps and 10 Gbps (which is also a 40G link at 25% utilization) throughput respectively. In the area above the curves LOSSRADAR uses less memory; below the curves FlowRadar uses less memory.

We also calculate and plot the average number of flows in 10ms at a cluster switch in Facebook. In Facebook, each server talks to 250 different racks in 5ms on average, and a cluster has 4 cluster switches and at least 64 racks. Thus, assuming each rack has 44 hosts (assuming the top of rack switch has 48 ports, 4 of which is connected to cluster switches), the total number of concurrent flows on average could be 352K in 10ms at a cluster switch. The green dotted line represents this number. This means that as long as the loss rate <5% at 10 Gbps, LOSSRADAR uses less memory than FlowRadar. At a lower throughput, LOSSRADAR can even support a higher loss rate (up to 10% and 20% for 5 Gbps and 3Gbps) while using less memory than FlowRadar.

7.2 Detection and inference effectiveness

We evaluate the fraction of losses being detected given different amounts of memory and the accuracy of the root cause inference, under realistic traffic with injected random drops and blackholes.

We run larger networks and higher link speed in the ns-3 simulator. We simulate a k=8 FatTree topology, which includes 16 core switches, 8 pods (8 switches per pod), and 128 hosts, all connected with 10G links. The simulated switch per-packet processing time is 5 us (not including queueing delay). We deploy 1536 meters in total at switches and hosts. To get realistic packet inter-arrival times, traffic distribution across switches, and realistic loss patterns, we implement DCTCP [4] and ECMP in the simulator. We take the same workload distribution from production data center [4], but add 1000 partition-aggregate queries per second to generate incast-related congestion losses. We set the default incast degree (i.e., the number of senders to one receiver in a query) as 20. The query traffic characteristics also follow the study in [4]. By default, we set the total traffic volume as 40% of the input bandwidth (i.e., 40% $\times$ 1280Gbps in our topology), and a network-wide loss rate of 0.1%. (Note that the per switch port loss rate can go much higher.)

We also inject blackhole and random drops. We select 3 bidirectional links to have 1% random drops, one for each layer (host to ToR, ToR to Aggr, Aggr To Core). We also select 3 switches (a ToR, an Aggr and a Core) to have blackholes. The blackhole is blocking a randomly selected specific destination IP address. Both the random drops and the blackholes are

	t_{gap} (us)	n_{burst}	n_{bb}	n_{nb}	p_{syn}	p_{rand}
Default	20	5	30	5	0.9	0.5
Range	[10,30]	[3,5]	[20,50]	[5,10]	[0.85,0.95]	[0.45,0.55]

Table 3: Root cause inference parameter settings

inserted in the middle of the simulation (not at the beginning). Moreover, we choose the time to inject the blackholes so that they will drop some ongoing large flows, in order to have all types of loss patterns (discussed in section 5.1.1).

7.2.1 Loss detection accuracy

LOSSRADAR needs a small digest size to capture most losses. We evaluate different digest sizes and show the percentage of lost packets being captured in Figure 8 for different incast degrees. A captured lost packet means the packet is retrieved from the digest. With a 20 incast degree, we just need 2KB digest size to capture around 90% of lost packets. Note that LOSSRADAR can still get the right number of losses at each switch, but only provide details for 90% of these packets. We need 7.6 KB to capture the details for more than 99.99% of the lost packets. With a 40 incast degree, the network-wide loss rate grows from 0.1% to 0.3%. Thus we need 14.25 KB to capture more than 99.99% of the lost packets.

LOSSRADAR can capture most batches successfully with a small digest. We also evaluate the percentage of batches where *all* lost packets in the digest of that batch are successfully retrieved (Figure 8) as compared with all the batches with at least one loss here. With a 40 incast degree, we need 6 KB per digest to capture around 90% of the batches. The percentage of captured batches is more than the percentage of captured lost packets because LOSSRADAR sometimes fails to decode some packets when there are too many lost packets in a batch. For these batches, it is ok to just get the total numbers of losses because they have large numbers of losses and operators should inspect the entire switch port.

7.2.2 Root cause inference accuracy

We run our root cause inference on all the losses we get from the trace, and classify each loss into congestion loss, random drop, blackhole loss, or unknown reason. We set the digest size to 7.6 KB according to section 7.2.1. We set the parameters according to the guideline described in Section 5.1.2, as shown in Table 3. We compare the inference result with the ground truth, and show the precision and recall of the three types of losses in Figure 9. We also vary each parameter within a range while keeping other parameters with default values; the error bars in the figure shows the range of the precisions and recalls over all these different settings.

The precision is close to 100%. We design the algorithm to keep the false alarm rates of blackholes and random drops low. The high precision shows our algorithm achieves this goal. The precision of blackholes is 100%, which means there is no false alarm.
With different parameter settings, the precisions of random

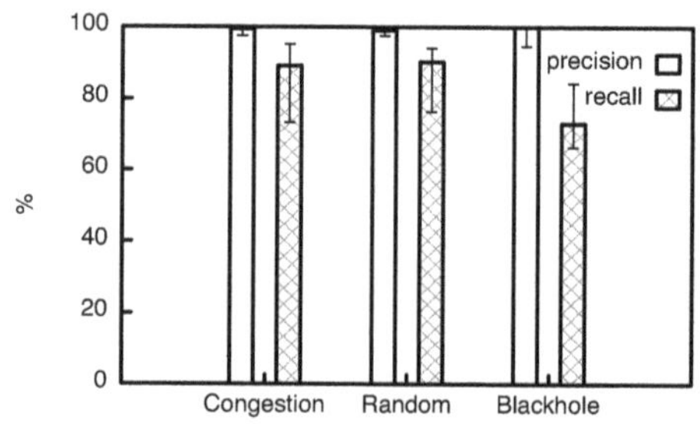

Figure 9: Root cause inference accuracy

drops are all above 97.6%. The precision of blackhole losses are almost all 100%, except when $n_{bb} = 20$ it becomes 94.7%. We inspect this case, and find that all false positives are 27 consecutive losses of a flow in a congestion. The reason for such long consecutive losses is similar to the outcast problem [31]. However, this phenomenon is exaggerated in simulation because all delays are deterministic.

Every injected problem is captured. We correctly classify 90.3% of the random drops and 73.1% of the blackhole losses. The missed blackhole losses are all short bursts (e.g. 5 losses) of consecutive losses, so they are classified as congestion losses. The missed random drops have two types: (1) a small number of random drops happen closely (e.g. 3 random drops with gaps less than 10 ms), so they are classified as congestion losses; (2) during some intervals, there are other losses being classified as unknown together with random drops, so the distribution is uneven, and we classify all the losses in these intervals as unknown. However, because the blackholes and the random drops are all persistent, we always correctly classify the losses caused by them in the next few intervals. Thus, the classified losses are sufficient for us to detect all problems.
With different parameter settings, most losses of each type are correctly classified, and we detect all problems as well.

7.3 Memory usage in partial deployments

We evaluate the memory usage per switch in different deployment scenarios based on the same topology, traffic pattern and injected problem in Section 7.2.
With a full deployment, we need 243.2 KB for all the digests in each switch[10]. We also evaluate the memory usage when we do not have access to some parts of the network, which is treated as blackboxes. In data centers, upgrading a ToR switch requires notifying applications or tenants running under the ToR on the planned downtime, or migrating the applications or tenants to other racks. On the other hand, upgrading an aggregation or a core switch is easier, because the traffic can be automatically rerouted to other paths when the switch is shut down without affecting applications.
Thus we evaluate the case that we have access to aggregation and core switches but treat ToR switches as blackboxes. We

[10]7.6 KB for each digest, two digests (batches) per meter, two meters (UM and DM) per port and eight ports.

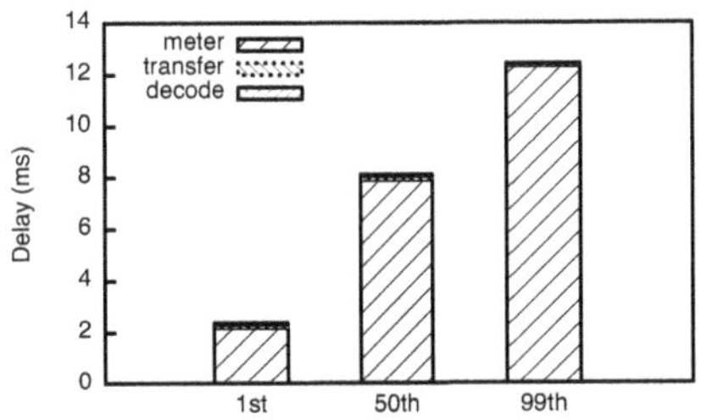

Figure 10: Breakdown of loss detection latency

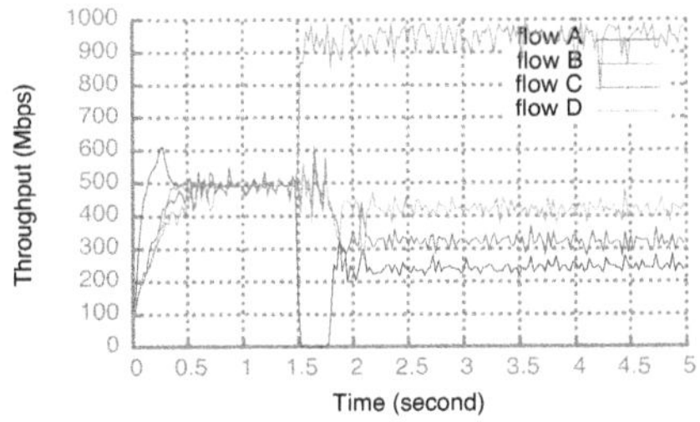

Figure 11: Recovery from blackhole

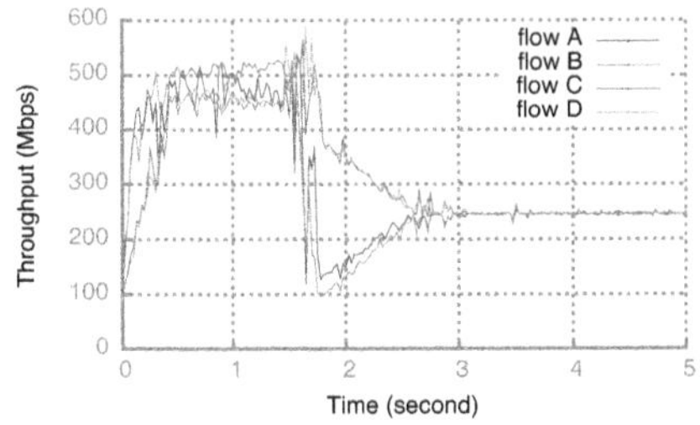

Figure 12: Recovery from random drops

deploy more meters at the devices around the ToR switches. On an aggregation switch, each of the 4 ports that connect to ToR switches receives packets from the 4 hosts under the ToR switch, which requires 4 downstream meters; each port that connects to a core switch only needs 1 downstream meter. So each aggregation switch needs 20 downstream meters, plus 8 upstream meters (one per port). We need 425.6 KB for all the digests in each aggregation switch.

We also evaluate other scenarios. If each aggregation switch is a blackbox, we need 608 KB in each core switch and each ToR switch. If each core switch is a blackbox, we need 608 KB in each aggregation switch.

7.4 Detection latency

We evaluate the detection latency in a testbed. We build a topology of k=4 FatTree in Deterlab [9] with our modified version of Open vSwitch [28] that supports LossRadar. Every 10 ms the upstream switch sends a batch to the collector. The downstream switch keeps each batch for 12 ms ($Timeout = 2$ ms). The size of each digest is set to 5 KB.

Detection latency is bound by the batch length plus the timeout. We break down the detection delay into meter waiting time, transfer time and decoding time (Figure 10). The meter waiting time dominates, during which the packets dropped, but its digest has not been sent out. The transfer time and the decoding time is negligible. For the waiting time, the 99th percentile of packets are close to 12 ms, bound by the waiting time at the downstream.

7.5 LossRadar applications

Improving flow throughput. We run four iperf flows (A, B, C, D) through two ECMP paths in our FatTree testbed, with two flows on each path. The two paths share the same edge and aggregation switches but differ at the core. We inject two types of losses. One is blackholing flow A (Figure 11). LossRadar quickly identifies that flow A is experiencing blackhole, and installs an entry matching flow A at the aggregation switch to moves A's path to the other. The throughput recovers after 250ms. The other case is randomly dropping 1% packets on A and B's link (Figure 12). LossRadar detects random drops on this link, so it moves both flows to the other path.

Correlating lost packets with ACLs. We use ClassBench ACL rules [34] and staggered data center traffic matching these rules as used in [24]. ClassBench has been shown to generates rules representative of real-world access control with accept and deny actions. The traffic is created by first generating staggered traffic for VMs and then assigning VMs with IP address ranges that match the ACL rules. The details are described in [24]. We take four rule sets of 50K, 100K, 150K, and 200K rules. We run the experiment 100 times by flipping a different random bit each time. We install the rules at a single switch, and send the traffic through the switch.

We compare the upstream and downstream traffic digests collected to get the set of lost packets. Given the set of lost packets, our loss analyzer first excludes the intended drops based on the correct set of rules, and then runs flow space correlation algorithm to narrow down the set of candidate rules that may cause the loss. The whole process takes 0.7-2.5ms. Our result shows that we have zero false negatives (i.e., the rule with flipped bit is always in our reported set). From 50K to 200K rules, we narrow down to 2-2.5 candidate rules that may get bit flip. Sometimes a high priority rule which covers all the losses is treated as a candidate rule but sometimes it is not the corrupted rule.

8. DISCUSSION

Avoid modifying packet header fields. It is possible to avoid tagging headers with the batch ID (section 3.4) and the meter ID (section 4.2), by tolerating on-the-fly packets.

Without the batch ID and the meter ID to synchronize batches, an on-the-fly packet would appear in two different batches at the upstream meter and the downstream meter, so it would appear as a difference in both the two batches' subtractions. Thus, we need to compare the results across batches and identify the true losses (only appear once not twice). The number of batches to compare depends on the time a packet takes from the upstream to the downstream, which is less than an RTT—100s of microseconds in data centers. Thus, as long as the batch length $T > 1$ ms, we only need to wait for one more batch to conclude a packet is lost or on-the-fly. Now the downstream digest is no longer a subset of the upstream digest. We leverage the original IBF design [10], which can handle two-way set difference. We also need larger digests, because the difference also include the on-the-fly packets besides the losses. The new trend of more synchronized clocks across switches (e.g. down to sub-microsecond level [20]) can help reduce the extra size. We leave how to further reduce the size to future works.

Improving root cause inferences. Our root cause inference algorithms take the first step in identifying root causes for packet losses. There are a few ways to improve the inference: One way is to use machine learning instead of threshold-based conditions to better classify different types of losses with dynamics. Another way is to incorporate the header patterns of blackholes (e.g. specific 5-tuple or specific dest IP) to help better distinguishing blackhole losses from other types. In addition, when a previously unknown type of losses happen, how the analyzer correctly reports the existence of an unknown type is an open question.

Reducing memory usage for incremental deployment cases. In a blackbox case, each downstream meter needs to maintain one digest for each upstream meter, and the size of each downstream digest has to be equal to the size of an upstream digest, which results in a high memory usage per switch. If we can partition the the upstream digest based on which downstream each packet goes to, the downstream digests can be smaller. This requires path-awareness at the upstream; we leave it to future works.

9. RELATED WORK

We discussed host passive mirroring [37, 25], Pingmesh [12], Mirroring [38], and FlowRadar [21] in Section 2.2. FlowRadar is the closest work to LOSSRADAR, but differs in four aspects: (1) FlowRadar collects per-flow counters at each switch, which can also be used for counting the aggregated number of losses per flow. In contrast, LOSSRADAR provides details of individual losses. (2) The memory usage of FlowRadar is proportional to the number of flows, while LOSSRADAR's is proportional to the number of losses. Thus, the memory usage of LOSSRADAR is lower than FlowRadar when the loss rate is low, as shown in Section 7.1. (3) To detect loss, FlowRadar needs to compare flow counters between two switches, and thus has to wait till an idle reporting interval (at least 10ms) to synchronize the two counters. In contrast, LOSSRADAR immediately detects the packet loss soon after a reporting interval. (4) FlowRadar uses Invertible Bloom Lookup Table [11] which also uses multiple hash functions per item and has a similar decoding process to IBF [10]. The key difference is that LOSSRADAR utilizes the subtraction operation to cancel out the packets between upstream and downstream meters. FlowRadar cannot use the subtraction, because each flow's 5-tuple would cancel out in the subtraction, resulting in useless data.

Some other research solutions are available for loss detection. LDA [18] leverages packet counters to identify losses, but cannot identify individual lost packets and their flow information. NetSight [13] can detect packet loss by sending the packet headers of all the packets at each hop to a centralized controller, but incurs significant bandwidth overhead. In contrast, LOSSRADAR provides detailed loss information with low memory and bandwidth overhead.

Many research works on network verification [15], [16], [17] performs static analysis of forwarding tables, and thus can detect blackholes caused by misconfiguration. Complementary to network verification, LOSSRADAR capture all lost packets in the network in real time.

The paper [6] allows the switch to send to end hosts the packet header information of those packets that are dropped due to congestion. Rather than focusing on one type of losses (misconfiguration or congestion), LOSSRADAR is generic to all types of packet losses.

Our traffic digest is inspired by Invertible Bloom Filters (IBFs). IBFs were introduced in [10] to identify *two-way* set differences for application-layer systems such as peer-to-peer networks and link-state databases. Our loss detection is a *one way* set difference problem, where one set is always a subset of the other. Therefore, we simplify the IBF design with XOR-based codes and counters, but store more flow information in the XOR-based codes. Moreover, because our data structure is used at switches with high-speed links, we face new challenges of synchronizing the data collection across nodes, and identifying the lost packets among multiple upstream and downstream meters around a blackbox. Counter Braids [22] are novel data structures to store *estimated* flow-based counters with low memory usage, but does not work for loss detection because it does not provide accurate counts and does not store flow information with counters.

10. CONCLUSION

With diverse types of packet losses in data center networks, and their significant impact on application performance and network operations, it is important to detect these losses in time and with detailed information of individual lost packets. We presented LOSSRADAR, a generic, light-weight loss detection system that can identify individual lost packets, their locations, and the flows they belong to in near real time. LOSSRADAR is easy to implement with programmable switch hardware, and can capture all the individual lost packets with small memory and bandwidth overhead. We also propose root cause inference algorithms based on the loss information from LOSSRADAR.

11. ACKNOWLEDGEMENT

We thank our shepherd Marco Canini and CoNEXT reviewers for their helpful feedbacks. We thank Sylvia Ratnasamy, George Varghese and Ori Rottenstreich for inspiring discussions. We thank Antonin Bas for the help on the P4 implementation. This paper is partially supported by the NSF grants CNS-1453662, CNS-1423505 and CNS-1413972.

References

[1] https://aphyr.com/posts/288-the-network-is-reliable.

[2] http://www.eweek.com/cloud/amazon-us-east-cloud-goes-down.html.

[3] Mohammad Alizadeh, Tom Edsall, Sarang Dharmapurikar, Ramanan Vaidyanathan, Kevin Chu, Andy Fingerhut, Vinh The Lam, Francis Matus, Rong Pan, Navindra Yadav, and George Varghese. "CONGA: Distributed Congestion-aware Load Balancing for Datacenters". In: *SIGCOMM*. 2014.

[4] Mohammad Alizadeh, Albert Greenberg, David A. Maltz, Jitendra Padhye, Parveen Patel, Balaji Prabhakar, Sudipta Sengupta, and Murari Sridharan. "Data Center TCP (DCTCP)". In: *SIGCOMM*. 2010.

[5] Weifeng Chen, Yong Huang, Bruno F. Ribeiro, Kyoungwon Suh, Honggang Zhang, Edmundo de Souza e Silva, Jim Kurose, and Don Towsley. "Exploiting the IPID Field to Infer Network Path and End-system Characteristics". In: *PAM*. 2005.

[6] Peng Cheng, Fengyuan Ren, Ran Shu, and Chuang Lin. "Catch the Whole Lot in an Action: Rapid Precise Packet Loss Notification in Data Centers". In: *NSDI*. 2014.

[7] Jeff Dean. "Designs, Lessons and Advice from Building Large Distributed Systems". In: *LADIS keynote*. 2009.

[8] G. DeCandia, D. Hastorun, M. Jampani, G. Kakulapati, A. Lakshman, A. Pilchin, S. Sivasubramanian, P. Vosshall, and W. Vogels. "Dynamo: Amazon's highly available key-value store". In: *SIGOPS*. 2007.

[9] *DeterLab*. https://www.isi.deterlab.net/.

[10] D. Eppstein, M. Goodrich, F. Uyeda, and G. Varghese. "What's the Difference? Efficient Set Difference without Prior Context". In: *SIGCOMM*. 2011.

[11] Michael T. Goodrich and Michael Mitzenmacher. "Invertible Bloom Lookup Tables". In: *arXiv:1101.2245v2*. 2011.

[12] Chuanxiong Guo, Lihua Yuan, Dong Xiang, Yingnong Dang, Ray Huang, Dave Maltz, Zhaoyi Liu, Vin Wang, Bin Pang, Hua Chen, Zhi-Wei Lin, and Varugis Kurien. "Pingmesh: A Large-Scale System for Data Center Network Latency Measurement and Analysis". In: *SIGCOMM*. 2015.

[13] Nikhil Handigol, Brandon Heller, Vimalkumar Jeyakumar, David Mazières, and Nick McKeown. "I Know What Your Packet Did Last Hop: Using Packet Histories to Troubleshoot Networks". In: *NSDI*. 2014.

[14] Xin Jin, Hongqiang Harry Liu, Rohan Gandhi, Srikanth Kandula, Ratul Mahajan, Ming Zhang, Jennifer Rexford, and Roger Wattenhofer. "Dynamic Scheduling of Network Updates". In: *SIGCOMM*. 2014.

[15] Peyman Kazemian, George Varghese, and Nick McKeown. "Header Space Analysis: Static Checking for Networks". In: *NSDI*. 2012.

[16] Peyman Kazemian, Michael Chang, Hongyi Zeng, George Varghese, Nick McKeown, and Scott Whyte. "Real Time Network Policy Checking Using Header Space Analysis". In: *NSDI*. 2013.

[17] Ahmed Khurshid, Xuan Zou, Wenxuan Zhou, Matthew Caesar, and P. Brighten Godfrey. "VeriFlow: Verifying Network-Wide Invariants in Real Time". In: *NSDI*. 2013.

[18] R. Kompella, K. Levchenko, A. Snoeren, and G. Varghese. "Every Microsecond Counts: Tracking Fine-Grain Latencies with a Loss Difference Aggregator". In: *SIGCOMM*. 2009.

[19] Maciej Kuźniar, Peter Perešíni, and Dejan Kostić. "What You Need to Know About SDN Flow Tables". In: *PAM*. 2015.

[20] Ki Suh Lee, Han Wang, Vishal Shrivastav, and Hakim Weatherspoon. "Globally Synchronized Time via Datacenter Networks". In: *SIGCOMM*. 2016.

[21] Yuliang Li, Rui Miao, Changhoon Kim, and Minlan Yu. "FlowRadar: A Better NetFlow for Data Centers". In: *NSDI*. 2016.

[22] Yi Lu, Andrea Montanari, Balaji Prabhakar, Sarang Dharmapurikar, and Abdul Kabbani. "Counter Braids: A Novel Counter Architecture for Per-Flow Measurement". In: *SIGMETRICS*. 2010.

[23] Matthew Mathis, Jeffrey Semke, Jamshid Mahdavi, and Teunis Ott. "The Macroscopic Behavior of the TCP Congestion Avoidance Algorithm". In: *SIGCOMM Comput. Commun. Rev.* 1997.

[24] Masoud Moshref, Minlan Yu, Abhishek Sharma, and Ramesh Govindan. "Scalable Rule Management for Data Centers". In: *NSDI*. 2013.

[25] Masoud Moshref, Minlan Yu, Ramesh Govindan, and Amin Vahdat. "Trumpet: Timely and Precise Triggers in Data Centers". In: *SIGCOMM*. 2016.

[26] *NetFlow*. http://www.cisco.com/go/netflow/.

[27] *NTP FAQ*. http://www.ntp.org/ntpfaq/NTP-s-algo.htm#Q-ACCURATE-CLOCK.

[28] *Open vSwitch*. http://openvswitch.org/.

[29] *P4 behavioral model*. https://github.com/p4lang/behavioral-model/blob/master/targets/simple_switch/simple_switch.cpp.

[30] *Packet loss impact on TCP throughput in ESNet*. http://fasterdata.es.net/network-tuning/tcp-issues-explained/packet-loss/.

[31] Pawan Prakash, Advait Dixit, Y. Charlie Hu, and Ramana Kompella. "The TCP Outcast Problem: Exposing Unfairness in Data Center Networks". In: *NSDI*. 2012.

[32] *Precision time protocol*. http://www.ieee1588.com/.

[33] Arjun Roy, Hongyi Zeng, Jasmeet Bagga, George Porter, and Alex C. Snoeren. "Inside the Social Network's (Datacenter) Network". In: *SIGCOMM*. 2015.

[34] D. E Taylor and J. S Turner. "ClassBench: A Packet Classification Benchmark". In: *Transactions on Networking* 15.3 (2007).

[35] W. Vogels. *Performance and Scalability*. http://www.allthingsdistributed.com/2006/04/performance_and_scalability.html. 2009.

[36] Xin Wu, Daniel Turner, Chao-Chih Chen, David A. Maltz, Xiaowei Yang, Lihua Yuan, and Ming Zhang. "NetPilot: Automating Datacenter Network Failure Mitigation". In: *SIGCOMM*. 2012.

[37] Minlan Yu, Albert Greenberg, Dave Maltz, Jennifer Rexford, Lihua Yuan, Srikanth Kandula, and Changhoon Kim. "Profiling Network Performance for Multi-tier Data Center Applications". In: *NSDI*. 2011.

[38] Yibo Zhu, Nanxi Kang, Jiaxin Cao, Albert Greenberg, Guohan Lu, Ratul Mahajan, Dave Maltz, Lihua Yuan, Ming Zhang, Ben Y. Zhao, and Haitao Zheng. "Packet-Level Telemetry in Large Datacenter Networks". In: *SIGCOMM*. 2015.

Demystifying and Puncturing the Inflated Delay in Smartphone-based WiFi Network Measurement

Weichao Li[1], Daoyuan Wu[2], Rocky K. C. Chang[1], and Ricky K. P. Mok[3] †
[1]The Hong Kong Polytechnic University, [2]Singapore Management University, [3]CAIDA/UCSD
{csweicli|csrchang}@comp.polyu.edu.hk[1], dywu.2015@smu.edu.sg[2],
cs.rickymok@connect.polyu.hk[3]

ABSTRACT

Using network measurement apps has become a very effective approach to crowdsourcing WiFi network performance data. However, these apps usually measure the *user-level* performance metrics instead of the *network-level* performance which is important for diagnosing performance problems. In this paper we report for the first time that a major source of measurement noises comes from the periodical SDIO (Secure Digital Input Output) bus sleep inside the phone. The additional latency introduced by SDIO and Power Saving Mode can inflate and unstablize network delay measurement significantly. We carefully design and implement a scheme to wake up the phone for delay measurement by sending just enough warm-up and background traffic. Our evaluation results show that the overall median delay overheads can be kept within 3ms, regardless of the actual network delay.

CCS Concepts

•Networks → Network measurement; Mobile networks; Wireless local area networks;

Keywords

Network measurement; Accuracy; WiFi; Android

1. INTRODUCTION

To manage and operate a reliable WiFi network, it is necessary to monitor the WiFi network performance, such as network delay, effectively and accurately. However, network delay cannot be obtained directly from the common wireless access points (APs). Moreover, existing passive monitoring methods, including sniffer-based methods [40, 14, 25] and methods based on AP hacking [33, 28, 29], are not flexible and scalable to deploy.

A promising approach to monitor mobile network performance is to use smartphone apps which have gained popularity in recent years. These speedtest-like services are available on Android [1, 2, 10], iOS [8, 9], and Windows Phone [7, 11]. Besides, the research community has deployed measurement apps (e.g., Netalyzr [6], MobiPerf [4], and the recent MopEye [5]) to analyze and diagnose various network performance issues [35, 36, 26, 38].

These measurement apps usually measure user-level performance, because they are implemented in the user space. While they are useful for characterizing the user experience, they cannot be used to reliably infer the network-level performance which is important for many reasons, such as for operators to know their network performance and for users to diagnose whether the network or their phone is responsible for performance degradation. As shown in [23], the network round-trip times (nRTTs) measured by apps in WiFi networks are all inflated, and the amount of inflation varies across smartphone models, measurement methods, and the actual nRTT. As CDN and cloud services continue to reduce the end-to-end delay, this delay inflation will significantly over-estimate the actual nRTT. Although it is shown that part of the delay inflation can be mitigated, the remaining overhead, which is not negligible, is still not understood.

In this paper, as the first main contribution, we discover and demonstrate that the energy-saving mechanisms—the Secure Digital Input Output (SDIO) bus sleeping and the IEEE 802.11 Power Saving Mode (PSM)—are the main sources of the delay inflation. Specifically, the SDIO bus sleeping inflates the nRTT internally, whereas the PSM externally, between the phone and AP. To the best of our knowledge, this paper is the first to report the effect of SDIO bus sleeping on the nRTT measurement. Our analysis also shows that the delay inflation is dependent on the WiFi chipset utilized by the smartphone. Therefore, two different smartphones may obtain quite different nRTTs for same network path.

In our second contribution, we propose to mitigate the

†This work was done when the author worked at the Hong Kong Polytechnic University.

We thank Dr. Dan Pei for shepherding our paper and the anonymous reviewers for their valuable comments. This work is partially supported by a grant (ref. no. G-YBAK) from The Hong Kong Polytechnic University and a grant (ref. no. H-ZL17) from the Joint Universities Computer Centre of Hong Kong.

CoNEXT '16, December 12-15, 2016, Irvine, CA, USA

DOI: http://dx.doi.org/10.1145/2999572.2999595

impact of the energy-saving mechanisms by enforcing the smartphones to operate in the wake-up mode during the delay measurement. Our approach is the first to mitigate the effect of SDIO bus sleeping. Although the impact of PSM have been studied by many works [13, 17, 30, 31], their focus is more on scheduling the packets on the AP side to achieve a better balance between energy consumption and network delay. Sui et al. [34] propose `ping2` to measure the network delay from the server side and try to avoid the additional delays introduced by the energy-saving mechanisms. However, `ping2` can be used only for network paths with short nRTT and cannot remove the inflations completely, because, when nRTT is long, the device could fall back to the inactive state again before it receives the response packet and starts the second ping.

We have implemented our approach in AcuteMon, an Android app prototype run on unrooted phones and requiring no system customization, such as kernel recompilation and customized ROM. We carefully design AcuteMon, so that the packets sent out to keep the phone in the wake-up state is minimal. We have conducted testbed experiments to validate our approach using five smartphones equipped with different WiFi chipsets and Android systems. The median additional delay is kept within 3ms for most of the tests, regardless of the actual nRTTs, and the delay variations are smaller than 3ms. To the best of our knowledge, this is the most accurate delay measurement that can be achieved on Android phones to this date without hacking the underlying system.

In §2 next, we first introduce our approach to evaluate the accuracy of the nRTT measurement. In §3, we illustrate the delay inflation problems caused by SDIO and PSM, and perform root-cause analysis. We describe AcuteMon in §4 and evaluate its performance. After highlighting the related works in §5, we conclude this paper in §6.

2. BACKGROUND

2.1 A model for nRTT measurement

The nRTT measurement can be inflated inside or outside the phones. For the internal factors, we use *delay overhead*, denoted by Δd, to evaluate the (in)accuracy of delay measurement [22, 23]. As shown in Fig. 1, the reported *user-level RTT* is computed by $d_u = t_u^i - t_u^o$, where t_u^o is the send time of the probe packet and t_u^i is the receive time of the response packet at the measurement app. However, due to various processing layers in the system, they are delivered to the air at t_n^o and received at t_n^i. Therefore, the delay overhead is computed as

$$\Delta d = d_u - d_n = (t_u^i - t_u^o) - (t_n^i - t_n^o). \quad (1)$$

Here we do not consider the processing delay introduced by the server, because the additional delay is in microsecond level for TCP data packets [24]. Since the delay overhead is accumulated at various layers of the system, it is necessary to record the timestamp at each vantage point to understand the sources of the overhead. Besides the timestamps reported by the app (t_u^o and t_u^i), Fig. 1 also shows the timestamps

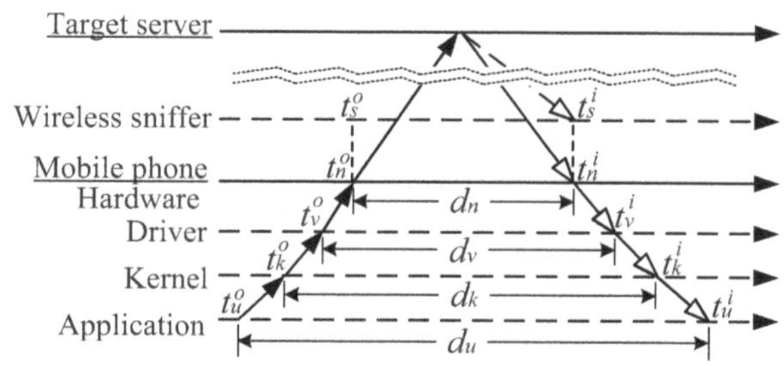

Figure 1: Measurement flow for Android apps.

in kernel space (t_k^o, t_k^i), WNIC (wireless NIC) driver (t_v^o, t_v^i), and network adapter (t_n^o, t_n^i). The kernel timestamps can be recorded with `bpf` and `libpcap`. Since the system usually does not provide any API to obtain the timestamps in the driver, we modify the driver to obtain them (see §3.2.1). As for t_n^o and t_n^i, we can estimate them through external wireless sniffers for WiFi networks [23]. In addition to d_u and d_n, we define *kernel-level RTT* as $d_k = t_k^i - t_k^o$ and *driver-level RTT* as $d_v = t_v^i - t_v^o$. To clarify where and how the delay inflation occurs, we also break down the overall delay overhead into three types of overheads:

- *User-kernel overhead*: $\Delta d_{u-k} = d_u - d_k$.
- *Kernel-driver overhead*: $\Delta d_{k-v} = d_k - d_v$.
- *Driver-phy overhead*: $\Delta d_{v-n} = d_v - d_n$.

Similarly, we can define *kernel-phy overhead* (Δd_{k-n}) as the difference between d_k and d_n ($= d_k - d_n$) or the sum of Δd_{k-v} and Δd_{v-n}.

Based on [23] and others, Δd_{u-k} is now better understood and can be mitigated. In particular, the overhead incurred in the DVM (i.e., Δd_{u-k}) can be mitigated by executing a pre-compiled native C program. In this paper, we focus on understanding and mitigating the inflated delay between PHY and the kernel space, because mitigating only the user-kernel overhead is not sufficient to obtain accurate nRTT.

Besides, the IEEE 802.11 PSM (see §3.2.2) can inflate the nRTT between an AP and smartphone, because the AP does not always send the received packets to the smartphone immediately. Although this additional delay looks like an external factor, we still treat it delay overhead, mainly because this inflation occurs only when the device is in dormancy and can vary across different smartphone models and at different times. Therefore, excluding this PSM-induced delay can facilitate a more accurate and stable nRTT.

2.2 A multiple-sniffer testbed in WiFi network

Our testbed, as shown in Figure 2, consists of a measurement server, which is equipped with a 1.86GHz Intel Core 2 Duo processor (E6320) and 2GB memory, and an IEEE 802.11g compatible wireless AP, NETGEAR WNDR3800. In §4.3 and §4.4, a load generator and a load server are added to the testbed to generate cross traffic. The three sniffers are wire-connected to the measurement server through the AP and a switch. The sniffers are three desktop PCs equipped with Intel 7260 WNIC. In particular, the smartphone is connected to one of the sniffer via USB cable, so that `adb` (Android Debug Bridge) and automation scripts can be run on the phone.

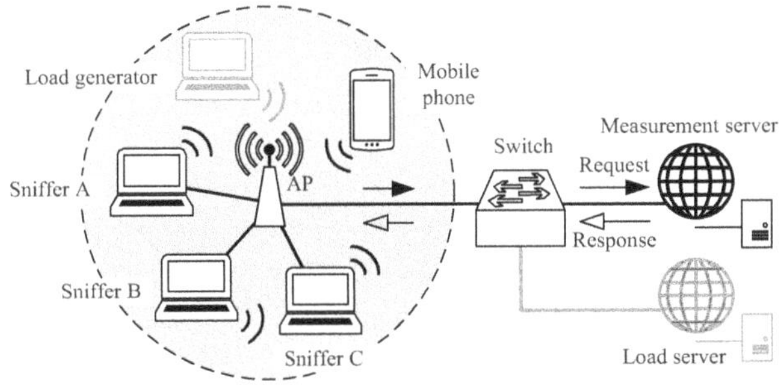

Figure 2: The testbed setup where the packet sniffers, smartphone, and wireless AP are placed within a distance of 0.5m.

3. DELAY OVERHEAD CAUSED BY ENERGY-SAVING MECHANISMS

3.1 Effect of packet sending interval

Our root-cause analysis begins with an ICMP ping experiment conducted in the testbed described in §2.2. We run a `ping` program through `adb shell` for 100 times with two packet sending intervals, a small interval of 10ms and larger default of 1s, measuring the nRTTs between the smartphones under test and the measurement server. In this paper, we test five different smartphones in Table 1. For the root-cause analysis, we use only Google Nexus 4 and Nexus 5, because they employ the WNIC chipsets manufactured by Qualcomm (WCN 3660) and Broadcom (BCM 4339), respectively. As most smartphones employ the WNIC chipsets provided by these two manufacturers [32], and these chipsets usually share the same source code for the same manufacturer, any delay overhead caused by these chipsets and drivers could be captured by these two phones. Given the fact that the average latency of broadband service for each monitored ISP in US ranges from 14ms to 52ms [16], we set the nRTT to 30ms and 60ms with `tc` command on the server side to emulate the real Internet environment.

Table 1: The smartphones used in the testbed evaluation.

Models	Ver.	CPU (core)	RAM	WNIC†
Google Nexus 5	4.4.2	2.26GHz (4)	2GB	BCM4339
Google Nexus 4	4.4.4	1.5GHz (4)	2GB	WCN3660
HTC One	4.2.2	1.7GHz (4)	2GB	WCN3680
Sony Xperia J	4.0.4	1GHz (1)	512MB	BCM4330
Samsung Grand	4.1.2	1.2GHz (2)	1GB	BCM4329

Note: †: WNIC model numbers with prefix BCM/WCN are manufactured by Broadcom/Qualcomm, respectively.

Table 2 summarizes the result of the multi-layer delay measurement. The measurement for both phones consistently report smaller and consistent d_u when the packet sending interval is small. Moreover, the RTTs captured by `tcpdump` (i.e., d_k) and the external wireless sniffers (i.e., d_n) show that both are very close to d_u. However, as the sending interval is increased to 1s, both phones are observed with significant delay increase. In particular, Nexus 4 shows two different patterns. With the emulated RTTs of 60ms, the nRTT for Nexus 4 is inflated mainly in the network. But when the emulated RTT is 30ms, the inflation occurs inside and outside the phone. On the other hand, Nexus 5's nRTT is mainly inflated inside the phone. The reasons will be given in §3.2.2.

Table 2: RTTs measured at different layers (mean with 95% confidence interval in ms).

Phone	RTT	Intv.	d_u	d_k	d_n
Google Nexus 4	30ms	10ms	33.16 ±0.96	32.46 ±0.04	31.29 ±0.35
		1s	48.15 ±3.88	48.10 ±3.88	42.58 ±4.28
	60ms	10ms	63.91 ±0.73	63.86 ±0.73	62.32 ±0.46
		1s	136.33 ±7.64	136.66 ±7.66	130.03 ±7.52
Google Nexus 5	30ms	10ms	33.38 ±0.58	33.27 ±0.59	31.22 ±0.45
		1s	43.21 ±1.29	43.03 ±1.29	31.78 ±1.01
	60ms	10ms	64.18 ±0.68	64.08 ±0.67	61.61 ±0.35
		1s	81.98 ±2.04	81.83 ±2.05	62.35 ±0.42

To better visualize the distribution of the delay overheads, we employ box-and-whisker plots to present Δd_{k-n} in Figure 3(a) and 3(c) and Δd_{u-k} in Figure 3(b) and 3(d). In each plot, the mark inside the box is the median and the top and bottom are the 75th and 25th percentile. The upper and lower whiskers are the maximum and minimum, respectively, after excluding the outliers. Figure 3(a) and 3(c) clearly show that Nexus 4 and 5 experience comparably small Δd_{k-n}, which are smaller than ~4ms, when the packet sending interval is small. With the interval of 1s, Nexus 5 has a much larger Δd_{k-n} than Nexus 4 (~18ms vs. ~6ms in median for emulated RTT of 60ms, and ~12ms vs. ~6ms for emulated RTT of 30ms). On the other hand, since Δd_{u-k} is very close to 0 for both Nexus 4 and 5, Δd_{u-k} is not a major source of delay inflation. Moreover, some values of Δd_{u-k} are negative due to the low resolution of the reported `ping` results. For example, ping on Nexus 4 reports RTT in integer when RTTs are larger than 100ms. Therefore, the fractional part could be truncated and the round-down RTT could be smaller than the `tcpdump` measurement.

3.2 Root cause analysis

3.2.1 *Effect of SDIO bus sleep*

We first analyze the source code of the WNIC driver in Nexus 5. The WiFi chipset used by Nexus 5 (Broadcom BCM 4339) connects to the system through SDIO bus and adopts the "bcmdhd" driver [1]. This driver also supports other Broadcom WNIC chipsets, such as BCM 4329, 4330, 4335, and others. Therefore, the finding here is also applicable to other phones equipped with Broadcom WiFi chipset, especially those with FullMAC MLME (MAC Sublayer Management Entity).

We trace the function calls in the packet sending and receiving directions. For packet sending, the kernel function `dev_queue_xmit()` maps to driver function `dhd_start_xmit()`. As shown in Figure 4(a), this function further

[1]In "`drivers/net/wireless/bcmdhd`".

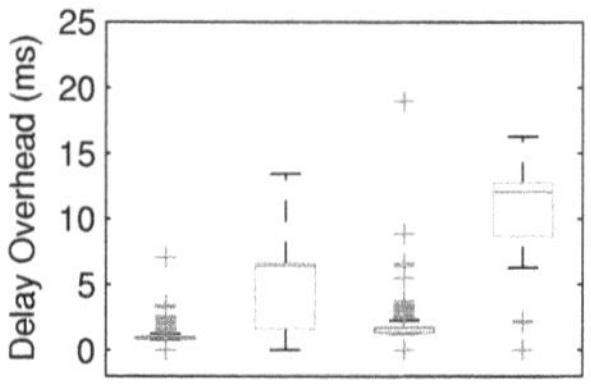

(a) Δd_{k-n} (30ms).

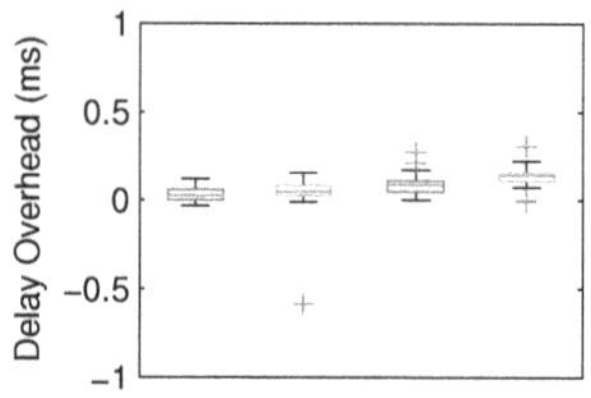

(b) Δd_{u-k} (30ms).

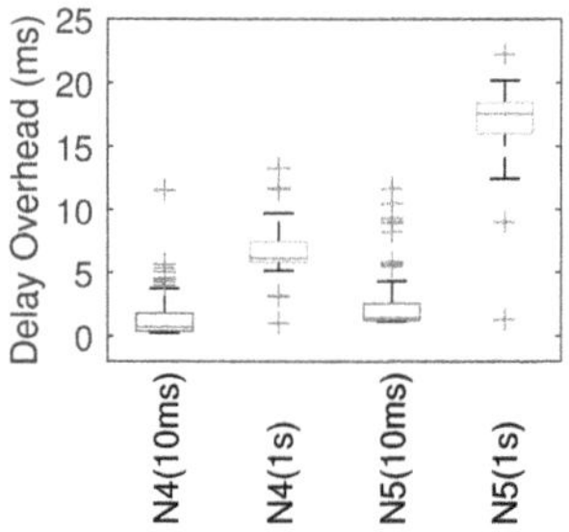

(c) Δd_{k-n} (60ms).

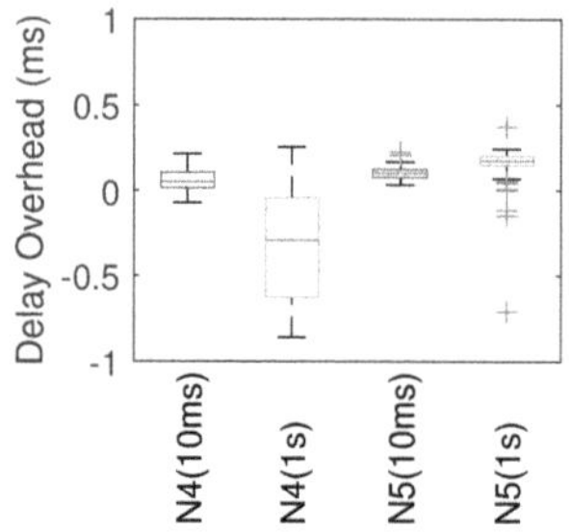

(d) Δd_{u-k} (60ms).

Figure 3: Kernel-phy delay overhead (Δd_{k-n}) and User-kernel delay overhead (Δd_{u-k}) for Google Nexus 4 and 5 when the emulated RTTs are 30ms and 60ms, respectively.

calls `dhd_sched_dpc()`, registering a packet sending task in a kernel thread, `dpc`. The `dpc` maintains a `while(1)` loop in its sub-function `dhdsdio_dpc()`. Before the `dpc` thread can send packets (③ in Figure 4(b)), `dhdsdio_dpc()` needs to check the status of SDIO bus and the readiness of backplane clock (① and ②, respectively). Eventually, function `dhdsdio_txpkt()` is executed, and the data are written to the bus.

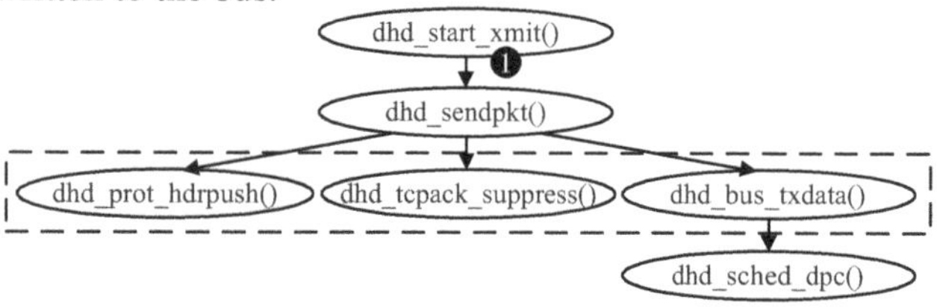

(a) In function `dhd_start_xmit()`.

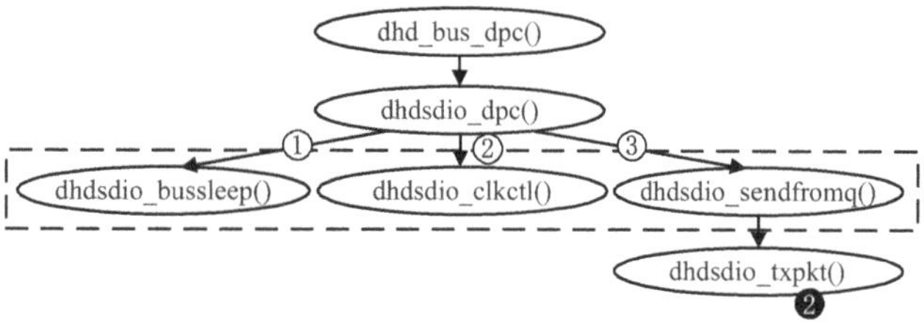

(b) In `dpc` thread.

Figure 4: Key WNIC driver functions for packet sending.

For packet receiving, the `dpc` thread is also responsible for data processing. As shown in Figure 5(a), the interrupt handling function `dhdsdio_isr()` first registers a task in the `dpc` thread. Similar to packet sending, the `dpc` thread also needs to check the status of SDIO bus and backplane clock (i.e., ① and ② in Figure 5(b)), and then receives frames from the bus with function `dhdsdio_readframes()`. After the frames are queued using `dhd_rxf_enqueue()`, another kernel thread `rxframe` invokes `netif_rx_ni()` to deliver the packets to the system.

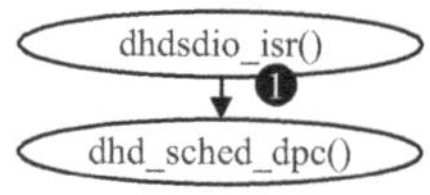

(a) In function `dhdsdio_isr()`.

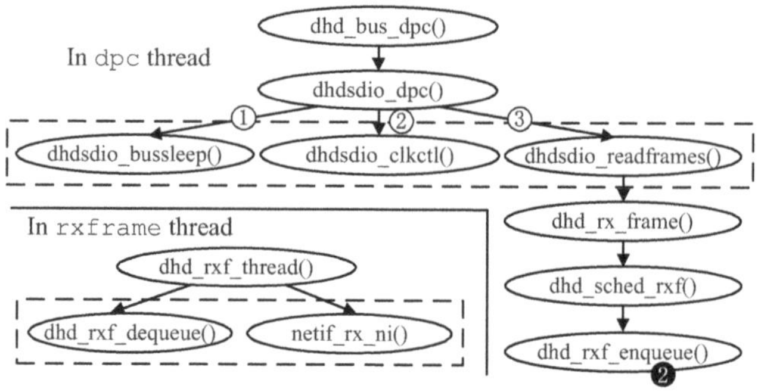

(b) In `dpc` and `rxframe` thread.

Figure 5: Key WNIC driver functions for packet receiving.

We enable the driver debug message by re-compiling the Android kernel. The kernel log information shows that the driver puts the SDIO bus into sleeping state frequently if the data transmission rate is not high. When there is a packet sending request or a packet arrival interrupt, it takes time for the driver to bring up the bus. We modify the source code by timestamping at the entrances of functions `dhd_start_xmit()` and `dhdsdio_txpkt()` (i.e., ❶ and ❷ in Figure 4), so that we can measure the delay when the driver sends out a packet, denoted by d_{vsend}. Similarly, the delay d_{vrecv} for the driver to receive a packet can be measured by timestamping `dhdsdio_isr()` and `dhd_rxf_enqueue()` (i.e., ❶ and ❷ in Figure 5). We re-build the kernel to measure d_{vsend} and d_{vrecv} in Nexus 5.

To evaluate the effect of bus sleep, we also disable the sleep feature in `dhdsdio_bussleep()`. Table 3 presents the minimum, mean, and maximum values of d_{vsend} (d_{vrecv}) when sending out (receiving) 100 ICMP packets with the two packet sending intervals (10ms and 1s). After disabling the bus sleep feature, both d_{vsend} and d_{vrecv} drop closely to 1ms, regardless of the packet transmission rate. Otherwise, the mean value can be as high as 14ms when the packet sending interval is 1s. As a result, we have verified that the SDIO bus sleep is the main component in d_{k-n}.

Table 3: d_{vsend} and d_{vrecv} measured by Nexus 5 with SDIO bus sleep mode enabled or disabled (in ms). The delay for waking up the bus could go up to ~14ms.

Type	Bus sleep	Packet interval	Min	Mean	Max
d_{vsend}	Enabled	10ms	0.096	0.321	10.184
		1000ms	0.139	10.151	13.547
	Disabled	10ms	0.092	0.229	0.836
		1000ms	0.139	0.720	0.858
d_{vrecv}	Enabled	10ms	0.314	1.635	2.827
		1000ms	0.368	12.754	14.224
	Disabled	10ms	0.311	1.589	2.651
		1000ms	0.362	1.756	2.088

We also investigate the criteria that trigger the bus sleep mode. Our driver analysis shows that the driver maintains a counter *idlecount*. For every *dhd_watchdog_ms*, whose default value is 10ms, the driver increases this counter by 1 if the hardware is idle. When the counter reaches a threshold $idletime$ (5 by default), the driver will instruct the bus to sleep. Therefore, the default idle period is 50ms. Both $idletime$ and $dhd\_watchdog\_ms$ are configurable when the driver is loaded. Our experiments also confirm that the idle period (demotion timer, T_{is}) for Nexus 5 is 50ms.

The "wcnss" driver used by Qualcomm WNIC chipsets shares similar mechanism, although the chipsets connect to the system via SMD interface instead of SDIO. To simplify our presentation, we refer also this energy-saving mechanism to SDIO bus sleep mode.

3.2.2 *Effect of Power Save Mode*

The PSM allows WNIC to switch from *active* state (a.k.a. Constantly Awake Mode, CAM) to *sleep* state (a.k.a. Power Save Mode, PSM) in order to reduce energy consumption and prolong battery lifetime. In PSM, the WiFi station (STA) and AP agree upon a *listen interval*, which is the number of *beacon intervals* that the STA will ignore before turning on the receiver. Right before the end of the listen interval, the STA wakes up and listens for the beacon frame. Only when there are packets buffered on the AP will the STA stay in CAM to receive them.

PSM can be further classified into *static PSM* and *adaptive PSM*. As static PSM could lead to RTT round-up effect and degrade network performance [19], adaptive PSM is usually adopted by smartphones today [15, 30, 31]. The adaptive PSM allows STA to stay in CAM for a pre-defined idle period (PSM timeout, T_{ip}), preventing the STA from immediately going to sleep after data transmission.

However, adaptive PSM could still inflate the nRTT. Let d_p and d_n be the measured and actual network delay, respectively. If d_n is larger than T_{ip}, the STA has already turned off its receiver when the response packet arrives at the AP. Only after the STA listens to the beacon frame can it change the state to CAM and receive the packet. As a result, d_n could be inflated by up to $I_B * (L + 1)$, where I_B is the *beacon interval* with a value of 100 TUs (Time Units, 1.024ms per TU), and L is the listen interval.

We measure the PSM timeout value (T_{ip}) by carefully sending out packets with increased packet sending interval. Table 4 shows that T_{ip} is smartphone-dependent. As an extreme case, Nexus 4 enters PSM in 40ms when the WNIC is idle. Therefore, there is a higher possibility for Nexus 4 to report an inaccurate result when measuring a network path longer than 40ms. This is why Nexus 4 is observed with significant increase of network delay when the emulated RTT is set to 60ms in §3.1. On the other hand, the values of the listen interval determines how much nRTT can be inflated by PSM. Although STA announces a default listen interval during the *association period* (1 for "wcnss" driver and 10 for "bcmhd" driver by default), we find that the smartphones do not adopt this default value. The actual listen interval for the phones are all 0, meaning that its length is 1 beacon cycle which is 102.4ms. Thus, the adaptive PSM can inflate the nRTT by over 100ms.

Table 4: PSM timeout values (T_{ip}) and initial listen intervals (L) of the smartphones under test.

Phone	T_{ip}	L (associated)	L (actual)
Google Nexus 4	~40ms	1	0
Google Nexus 5	~205ms	10	0
Samsung Grand	~45ms	10	0
HTC One	~400ms	1	0
Sony Xperia J	~210ms	10	0

4. A BETTER PRACTICE

In this section, we present an effective approach to mitigate the delay overhead in the WiFi network measurement. We have implemented our approach in AcuteMon, an Android app prototype running on unrooted phones and requiring no system modification and customization, such as kernel recompilation and customized ROM. Although AcuteMon is designed mainly for WiFi networks, it can be easily extended to cellular environment, mitigating the effect of RRC (Radio Resource Control) state transition.

4.1 Implementation details

As illustrated in Figure 6, AcuteMon consists of two concurrent threads—background traffic thread (BT) and measurement thread (MT). The goal of the BT is to keep the smartphone in the wake-up state (i.e., SDIO bus awake mode and CAM in WiFi) during nRTT measurement. The process starts with a *warm-up phase* where the BT sends a warm-up packet to a warm-up server. According to §3, a smartphone enters CAM immediately when sending out packets, but it has to wait a period of time (promotion delay, T_{prom}) for the SDIO bus to wake up. After being activated, it remains in the SDIO bus awake mode for T_{is} and CAM for T_{ip}, where T_{is} and T_{ip} are the demotion timeout value for SDIO bus sleep and PSM, respectively. Therefore, the warm-up time d_{pre} should meet $T_{prom} < d_{pre} < \min(T_{is}, T_{ip})$.

In the subsequent *measurement phase*, the BT periodically sends lightweight background traffic with an inter-packet interval of d_b. With a proper choice of d_b ($d_b < \min(T_{is}, T_{ip})$), the background traffic can reset the state demotion timers to prevent any state demotion. Here we assign both d_{pre} and d_b to 20ms. Our evaluation in §4.2 shows that the empirical values work effectively. For example, d_b of 20ms is also appropriate for the smartphones employing "wcnss" driver. AcuteMon ignores the response packets of warm-up and background packets by setting the TTL (time-to-live) value of the warm-up packets to 1, so that the packets will be dropped at the first-hop router.

The MT, on the other hand, sends K measurement probes to measure the nRTT between the phone and a target server. In the current version, AcuteMon uses TCP control messages (TCP SYN/ACK packets) and TCP data packets (HTTP request and response) to measure nRTT to any TCP servers. The implementation can be easily extended to UDP and ICMP packets. We implement the MT as a pre-compiled C binary (instead of running within the Android runtime) to mitigate the user-kernel delay overheads [23].

In our prototype of AcuteMon, d_{pre} and d_b were assigned with empirical values. Although they work well in our testbed evaluation (§4.2-§4.4), they could be inappropriate for some

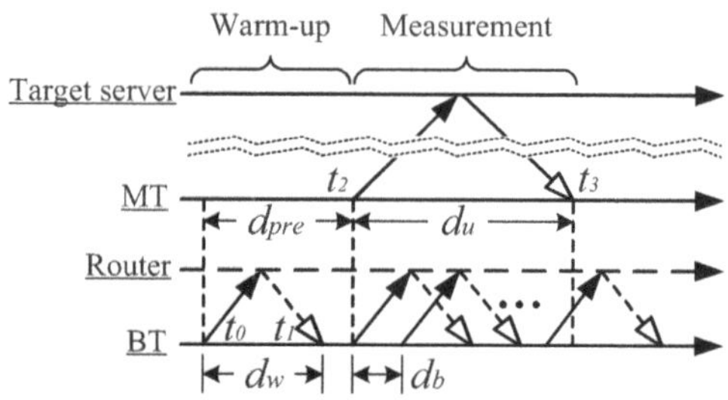

Figure 6: Measurement process of AcuteMon.

smartphone models, because both T_{is} and T_{ip} are tunable. However, inferring the actual T_{is} and T_{ip} of a particular smartphone is challenging. A simple solution is training the program to obtain suitable values. Another possible workaround is to collect the configurations by modelling and building a database. This will be our future work.

AcuteMon consumes very low battery, because it sends out very few additional packets in the measurement phase, and will not affect the energy-saving mechanisms when there are no measurement tasks. Moreover, the warm-up and background packet(s) are dropped in the first hop and will not burden the remaining part of a network path. Supposing that AcuteMon sends five probe packets ($K = 5$) to measure a path with nRTT of 100ms, the BT will send only around 25 packets to the gateway for the nRTT measurement. Our evaluation in §4.4 shows that the impact of the background traffic on the measurement results is negligible.

4.2 Performance evaluation

We evaluate the performance of AcuteMon in the testbed mentioned in §3.1. For each test, we run AcuteMon on the smartphone to measure the nRTT between the phone and the measurement server by sending out 100 TCP probes ($K = 100$). We introduce additional delays on the server side to emulate four different nRTTs: 20ms, 50ms, 85ms, and 135ms. Since the experiments are performed in an ideal environment without other mobile devices and cross traffic, introducing additional delays on the server side can be considered as controlling the length of the network path.

4.2.1 *Actual nRTT*

Table 5 presents the means and 95% confidence intervals of the actual nRTTs (d_n) measured by the external sniffers. For all five smartphones, d_ns are very close to their emulated values. In fact, no significant nRTT inflation can be observed, and most of the deviations are kept within 3ms, implying that the measurement packets have not been delayed at the AP. Our further analysis of the raw `pcap` files also confirms that no PSM activity can be detected when the smartphone receives response packets. Compared with the results shown in Table 2, AcuteMon successfully prevents the smartphones from entering PSM.

4.2.2 *Delay overheads*

Next we analyze the measurement accuracy of AcuteMon in terms of delay overhead. We use box plots to present Δd_{u-k} and Δd_{k-n} introduced by AcuteMon in Figure 7. On the x-axis, we use (u) and (k) after the RTT to denote Δd_{u-k} and Δd_{k-n}, respectively. Due to the page limit, we only show three of the five smartphones tested, because the rest have very similar results.

The previous study [23] has shown that executing the measurement logic as a native Linux program can mitigate the delay overheads caused in the DVM. The measurement results support this claim. We observe very small Δd_{u-k} for all the phones, most of which are smaller than 0.5ms. Even for the two smartphones with relatively low hardware configurations (i.e., Sony Xperia J and Samsung Grand), their Δd_{u-k}s are smaller than 1ms.

On the other hand, Δd_{k-n} accounts for the majority of the delay overhead. Although Δd_{k-n} is much larger than Δd_{u-k}, their medians are all less than 2ms, and the upper bounds are still less than 3ms (except for Sony Xperia J, whose upper bounds can be 4ms). For the smartphones equipped with Qualcomm's WNIC chipsets (Google Nexus 4 and HTC One), Figure 7(c) shows that the medians of Δd_{k-n} can be as small as ~0.8ms. As a result, the overall median delay overheads are kept within 3ms.

Another important observation is that the delay overheads for AcuteMon are independent of nRTTs, and the values of the overheads are much more stable. Therefore, the true value can be obtained by performing calibration.

Table 5: The actual nRTTs (d_n) measured by external sniffers (mean with 95% confidence interval, in ms).

Phone	Emulated RTT (ms)			
	20	50	85	135
Google Nexus 5	22.461 ±0.545	51.683 ±0.168	87.198 ±0.387	137.090 ±0.320
Sony Xperia J	21.584 ±0.184	51.597 ±0.149	86.868 ±0.275	136.79 ±0.178
Samsung Grand	22.020 ±0.382	52.614 ±0.485	86.675 ±0.177	137.0 ±0.217
Google Nexus 4	21.680 ±0.181	51.673 ±0.202	86.888 ±0.358	137.98 ±1.101
HTC One	21.874 ±0.200	51.786 ±0.198	86.810 ±0.192	136.850 ±0.154

4.3 Comparison with other tools

We compare AcuteMon with three other popular tools, including ICMP ping, `httping` [18], and MobiPerf, on Google Nexus 5. Since we have evaluated the delay overhead caused by AcuteMon in §4.2.2, here we compare only the RTTs measured by these tools in the same testbed. For httping, we download and cross-compile its source code, so that it can run on Android. As for MobiPerf, it supports three measurement methods: 1) invoking the ping program, employing Java classes 2) `InetAddress`, and 3) `HttpURLConnection`. In fact, the second and third methods are very similar, both of which utilize TCP control messages (SYN/RST vs. SYN/SYN ACK). Since MobiPerf cannot configure the number of probe packets, we implement its second method in our own test app, called Java ping.

In comparing the four tools, we introduce an additional delay of 30ms on the server side. During the measurement, each tool sends out 100 probes ($K = 100$). We consider

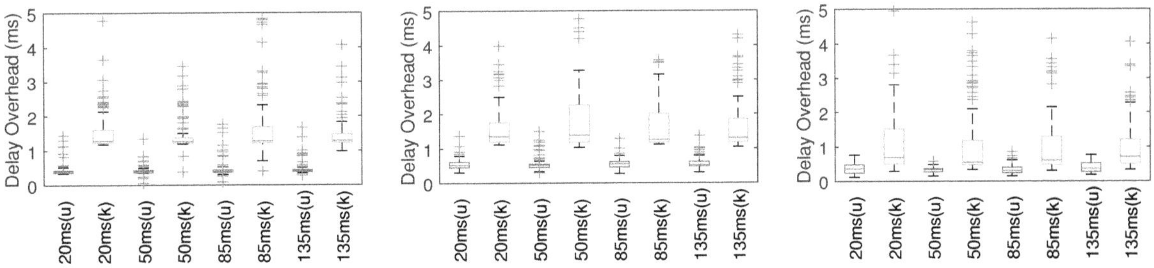

(a) Google Nexus 5. (b) Samsung Grand. (c) Google Nexus 4.

Figure 7: Box plots of Δd_{u-k} and Δd_{k-n} obtained by AcuteMon.

two scenarios, with and without cross traffic. The objective of introducing cross traffic is to congest the WiFi network. We use `iPerf` [3] to generate a large volume of data between a wireless load generator and a fixed load server. The load generator establishes 10 connections to the server, and each connection sends out UDP packets at a sending rate of 2.5Mbps. According to [37], the actual throughput for UDP traffic in an IEEE 802.11g WLAN is usually smaller than 20Mbps. Therefore, the introduced cross traffic can overload the network. In our test, we find that the maximum throughput is only around 10Mbps.

Figure 8 plots the CDF of the RTTs measured by the four tools. The figure clearly shows that AcuteMon outperforms the other three significantly in both scenarios. When the network is free of cross traffic, almost 90% of the RTTs measured by AcuteMon are smaller than 35ms. The differences between AcuteMon and the other three are almost larger than 10ms. In the congested network case, the measured RTTs are all increased, and AcuteMon still gives the smallest measured RTTs.

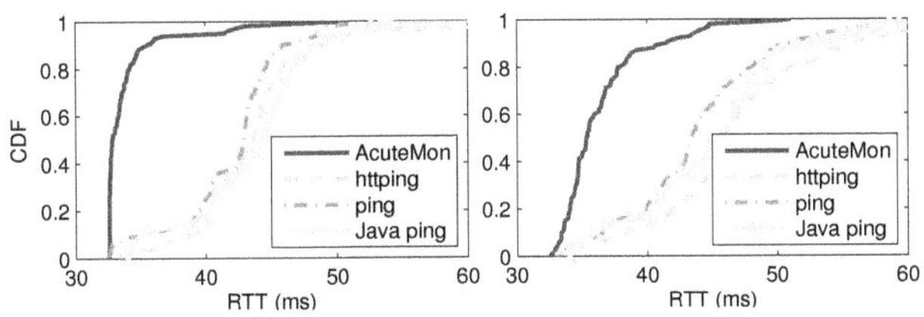

(a) Without cross traffic. (b) With cross traffic.

Figure 8: CDF plots of RTT measured by AcuteMon and other popular measurement tools.

4.4 Effect of background traffic

We further study whether the background traffic sent by AcuteMon will affect the measurement results in a congested WiFi network. We apply the same settings of emulated RTT and cross traffic described in §4.3 to the testbed. For a fair comparison, we disable the SDIO bus sleep function by modifying the driver, so that AcuteMon will stay in the wake-up mode without sending background traffic. Moreover, since the emulated RTT (30ms) is smaller than Nexus 5's PSM timeout value (~205ms), the smartphone will also stay in the CAM during the measurement. As shown in Figure 9, the difference between with and without background traffic for AcuteMon is very small, showing that the effect of sending just enough background traffic is slight. Compared to the result obtained when the network is not congested, the RTT increase here is mainly caused by the cross traffic, but not the background traffic.

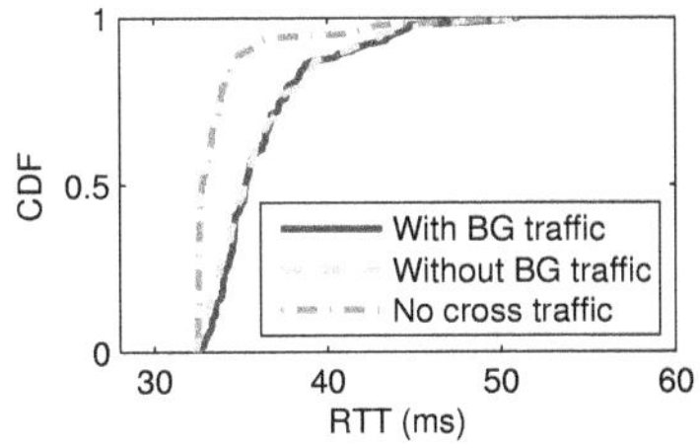

Figure 9: CDF plot of RTTs measured by AcuteMon with and without sending background traffic.

5. RELATED WORKS

The performance of Android system has been well studied and evaluated in the past, especially on the performance impact of DVM on Android apps [27], and the comparison between native C/JNI and Java applications in DVM [12, 21]. However, these works seldom study the relationship between system delay and network delay measurement. Although some other studies apply cross-layer analysis [39] and intercept system events [20], they do not analyze the network behavior systematically nor study the device driver. Li et al. [23] study the delay overhead in WiFi network and propose to mitigate the user-level overhead by using native C implementation. In this paper, we systemically investigate the delay overhead caused by energy-saving mechanisms for WiFi networks.

6. CONCLUSION

In this paper we considered the problem of measuring network RTT from smartphones. We presented AcuteMon, a network measurement app in Android, to mitigate all major sources of delay inflation for WiFi networks. We first reported and demonstrated that the energy-saving mechanisms (SDIO and PSM) employed in smartphones are the main sources of the delay inflation. Based on our driver code analysis and empirical evaluations, we proposed to keep the phone in the wake-up state during the delay measurement through a carefully timed sending of warm-up and periodic background traffic. Our testbed experiment results show that our approach can effectively mitigate the delay overheads and achieve very accurate network RTT.

7. REFERENCES

[1] Internet Speed Test 3G,4G,Wifi on Google Play. https://play.google.com/store/apps/details?id=uk.co.broadbandspeedchecker.

[2] Internet Speed Test on Google Play. https://play.google.com/store/apps/details?id=pl.speedtest.android.

[3] iPerf - the ultimate speed test tool for TCP, UDP and SCTP. https://iperf.fr/.

[4] MobiPerf on Google Play. https://play.google.com/store/apps/details?id=com.mobiperf.

[5] MopEye: Speed test & sniffer. https://play.google.com/store/apps/details?id=com.mopeye.

[6] Netalyzr on Google Play. https://play.google.com/store/apps/details?id=edu.berkeley.icsi.netalyzr.android.

[7] Network Speed Test on Windows Store. http://www.windowsphone.com/en-us/store/app/network-speed-test/9b9ae06b-2961-41ef-987d-b09567cffe70.

[8] Speedtest X HD WiFi & Mobile Speed Test on App Store. https://itunes.apple.com/us/app/speedtest-x-hd-wifi-mobile/id366593092.

[9] Speedtest.net on App Store. https://itunes.apple.com/us/app/speedtest.net-mobile-speed/id300704847.

[10] Speedtest.net on Google Play. https://play.google.com/store/apps/details?id=org.zwanoo.android.speedtest.

[11] Speedtest.net on Windows Store. http://www.windowsphone.com/en-us/store/app/speedtest-net/4fcd4de1-050b-44dc-b123-a786808eb49b.

[12] L. Batyuk, A.-D. Schmidt, H.-G. Schmidt, A. Camtepe, and S. Albayrak. Developing and benchmarking native Linux applications on Android. In *Proc. Mobilware*, 2009.

[13] Y. Bejerano, J. Ferragut, K. Guo, V. Gupta, C. Gutterman, T. Nandagopal, and G. Zussman. Scalable WiFi multicast services for very large groups. In *Proc. ICNP*, 2013.

[14] Y.-C. Cheng, J. Bellardo, P. Benkö, A. C. Snoeren, G. M. Voelker, and S. Savage. Jigsaw: Solving the puzzle of enterprise 802.11 analysis. In *Proc. ACM SIGCOMM*, 2006.

[15] N. Ding, A. Pathak, D. Koutsonikolas, C. Shepard, Y. Hu, and L. Zhong. Realizing the full potential of PSM using proxying. In *Proc. IEEE INFOCOM*, 2012.

[16] FCC. 2015 measuring broadband America fixed report. https://www.fcc.gov/reports-research/reports/measuring-broadband-america/measuring-broadband-america-2015, 2015.

[17] Y. He and R. Yuan. A novel scheduled power saving mechanism for 802.11 wireless LANs. *Mobile Computing, IEEE Transactions on*, 8(10):1368–1383, Oct 2009.

[18] F. Heusden. httping. http://www.vanheusden.com/httping/.

[19] R. Krashinsky and H. Balakrishnan. Minimizing energy for wireless web access with bounded slowdown. *Wireless Network*, 11:135–148, Jan. 2005.

[20] J.-C. Kuester and A. Bauer. Monitoring real android malware. In *Proc. Runtime Verification*, 2015.

[21] S. Lee and J. W. Jeon. Evaluating performance of Android platform using native C for embedded systems. In *Proc. IEEE ICCAS*, 2010.

[22] W. Li, R. Mok, R. Chang, and W. Fok. Appraising the delay accuracy in browser-based network measurement. In *Proc. ACM/USENIX IMC*, 2013.

[23] W. Li, R. Mok, D. Wu, and R. Chang. On the accuracy of smartphone-based mobile network measurement. In *Proc. IEEE INFOCOM*, 2015.

[24] X. Luo, E. Chan, and R. Chang. Design and implementation of TCP data probes for reliable network path monitoring. In *Proc. USENIX ATC*, 2009.

[25] R. Mahajan, M. Rodrig, D. Wetherall, and J. Zahorjan. Analyzing the MAC-level behavior of wireless networks in the wild. In *Proc. ACM SIGCOMM*, 2006.

[26] A. Nikravesh, D. Choffnes, E. Katz-Bassett, Z. Mao, and M. Welsh. Mobile network performance from user devices: A longitudinal, multidimensional analysis. In *Proc. PAM*, 2014.

[27] H.-S. Oh, B.-J. Kim, H.-K. Choi, and S.-M. Moon. Evaluation of Android Dalvik virtual machine. In *Proc. JTRES*, 2012.

[28] A. Patro, S. Govindan, and S. Banerjee. Observing home wireless experience through WiFi APs. In *Proc. ACM MobiCom*, 2013.

[29] C. Pei, Y. Zhao, G. Chen, R. Tang, Y. Mengy, M. Ma, K. Ling, and D. Pei. WiFi can be the weakest link of round trip network latency in the wild. In *Proc. IEEE INFOCOM*, 2016.

[30] A. J. Pyles, X. Qi, G. Zhou, M. Keally, and X. Liu. SAPSM: Smart adaptive 802.11 PSM for smartphones. In *Proc. ACM UbiComp*, 2012.

[31] E. Rozner, V. Navda, R. Ramjee, and S. Rayanchu. NAPman: Network-assisted power management for Wifi devices. In *Proc. ACM MobiSys*, 2010.

[32] B. Shaffer. Broadcom and Qualcomm battle for WLAN IC leadership. https://technology.ihs.com/517658/broadcom-and-qualcomm-battle-for-wlan-ic-leadership, November 2014.

[33] V. Shrivastava, S. Rayanchu, S. Banerjee, and K. Papagiannaki. PIE in the sky: Online passive interference estimation for enterprise WLANs. In *Proc. USENIX NSDI*, 2011.

[34] K. Sui, M. Zhou, D. Liu, M. Ma, D. Pei, Y. Zhao, Z. Li, and T. Moscibroda. Characterizing and improving WiFi latency in large-scale operational networks. In *Proc. ACM MobiSys*, 2016.

[35] N. Vallina-Rodriguez, N.Weaver, C. Kreibich, and V. Paxson. Netalyzr for Android: Challenges and opportunities. In *Proc. Workshop on Active Internet Measurements (AIMS)*, 2014.

[36] N. Vallina-Rodriguez, S. Sundaresan, C. Kreibich, N. Weaver, and V. Paxson. Beyond the radio: Illuminating the higher layers of mobile networks. In *Proc. ACM MobiSys*, 2015.

[37] A. L. Wijesinha, Y. tae Song, M. Krishnan, V. Mathur, J. Ahn, and V. Shyamasundar. Throughput measurement for UDP traffic in an IEEE 802.11g WLAN. In *Proc. SNPD/SAWN*, 2005.

[38] D. Wu, W. Li, R. Chang, and D. Gao. MopEye: Monitoring per-app network performance with zero measurement traffic. In *Proc. ACM CoNEXT Student Workshop*, 2015.

[39] L. Xue, C. Qian, and X. Luo. Androidperf: A cross-layer profiling system for Android applications. In *Proc. IEEE IWQoS*, 2015.

[40] J. Yeo, M. Youssef, and A. Agrawala. A framework for wireless LAN monitoring and its applications. In *Proc. ACM WiSe*, 2004.

Network Innovators Community Event (GENI NICE 2016)

Mark Berman
Raytheon BBN Technologies
10 Moulton Street
Cambridge, MA 02138
+1 (617) 873-3675
mberman@bbn.com

Ibrahim Matta
Boston University
111 Cummington Mall
Boston, MA 02215
+1 (617) 358-1062
matta@bu.edu

Violet R. Syrotiuk
Arizona State University
P.O. Box 878809
Tempe, AZ 85287
+1 (480) 965-7034
syrotiuk@asu.edu

Vicraj Thomas
Raytheon BBN Technologies
Park Place East, Ste. 630
5775 Wayzata Blvd.
St. Louis Park, MN 55416
+1 (952) 545-5713
vthomas@bbn.com

ABSTRACT
The Network Innovators Community Event (GENI NICE) is the premier event for researchers to demonstrate and present research results and to discuss work in progress related to the NSF's Global Environment for Network Innovations (GENI) and related advanced cyberinfrastructure testbeds.

Growing out of the strong experiment- and demonstration-driven tradition of the GENI Engineering Conferences (GECs), NICE specializes in direct experimenter-to-experimenter interaction and information exchange. NICE 2016 represents the second year of NICE, and its first year being held in conjunction with CoNEXT.

Keywords
GENI; Future Internet; Next generation networking; Future Internet testbeds; Distributed cloud computing, Edge cloud, Edge computing; Cellular research networks; Software-defined exchanges; Software-defined infrastructure.

1. The NICE Community
The Network Innovators Community Event (GENI NICE) provides a venue for a free and rapid exchange of information among researchers, educators, system builders, and IT professionals who make, sustain, and use advanced research cyberinfrastructure testbed environments. These include the Global Environment for Network Innovations (GENI), as well as related future Internet and distributed cloud (FIDC) testbeds and research infrastructures.

NICE brings together multiple interconnected segments of this dynamic and growing community. In an environment of shared, distributed cyberinfrastructure, effective and collaborative interaction among these groups is vital to sustaining rapid research progress.

End users: Researchers and educators who use advanced research cyberinfrastructure testbeds in their work.

Testbed builders: Systems researchers and builders who design and develop new research cyberinfrastructure concepts.

Infrastructure owners and operators: Chief information officers (CIOs) and information technology professionals who own and operate research cyberinfrastructure on behalf of end users.

CoNEXT '16, December 12-15, 2016, Irvine, CA, USA
ACM 978-1-4503-4292-6/16/12.
DOI: http://dx.doi.org/10.1145/2999572.3004860

2. The NICE Agenda
This year's event, NICE 2016, takes place at a particularly exciting time for this community. As the GENI project begins its transition to a broader management paradigm, a new, research-driven consortium is forming to play a key role both in GENI oversight and in driving the vision of new cyberinfrastructure research.

This is also a time of great potential for new developments in advanced research cyberinfrastructure testbeds, as researchers and sponsors are increasingly converging on key areas to pursue. As an example, the recent "Looking Beyond the Internet" report [1] identifies several promising areas for research testbed investment. One of these areas, city-scale wireless research testbeds, is addressed in a recently announced White House initiative, spearheaded by the NSF.

The NICE community is ideally positioned both to provide input to and to derive benefit from these important developments, and this year's event agenda draws heavily on these topics.

Sessions for NICE 2016 include the following.

Opening Session: In addition to the keynote presentation, this session includes an update on the Future Cyberinfrastructure Consortium, including the consortium's mission and goals, as well as how the community can participate in the consortium.

Session chair: Mark Berman (GENI project office).

Software-Defined Exchanges: This session explores recent developments and upcoming research in software-defined exchanges (SDXs) and software-defined infrastructure (SDI). These interrelated approaches apply software-defined networking concepts and technology to facilitate the sharing and exchange of networking and heterogeneous cyberinfrastructure resources.

Session chairs: Russ Clark (Georgia Institute of Technology) and Tom Lehman (University of Maryland).

Non-IP Experiments: One of the motivations of Future Internet and Distributed Cloud (FIDC) testbeds is the ability to conduct experiments using network protocols that are not compatible with the standard Internet protocol (IP) or transmission control protocol (TCP). This session reports on experiments in future Internet architectures and other research that explore this research space.

Session chairs: Nirmala Shenoy (Rochester Institute of Technology) and Ibrahim Matta (Boston University).

Wireless Experiments: This session addresses recent application work at campuses using 4G LTE technology. Areas addressed include heterogeneous vehicular networking, cloud-based radio processing and voice over LTE (VO-LTE) for public safety.

Session chairs: Abhimanyu Gosain (GENI project office) and Ivan Seskar (Rutgers University).

Joint Panel Session "Picking the Right Testbed for Your Experiment": This joint panel brings together participants from the NICE community as well as the co-located Cloud-Assisted Networking (CAN) workshop and CoNEXT student workshop to discuss the relative benefits of different advanced cyberinfrastructure research testbeds and comparable commercial offerings.

Session chairs: Mike Zink (University of Massachusetts, Amherst) and Murat Yuksel (University of Central Florida).

Evening demo session: The demo session is a longstanding tradition extended from the GECs to NICE. It provides an informal opportunity for information exchange in a style that matches the experiment- and demonstration-driven culture of the NICE community. (See Figure 1.)

3. ACKNOWLEDGMENTS

GENI and NICE are supported by the National Science Foundation and the GENI Project Office. Any opinions, findings, conclusions or recommendations expressed in this material are the authors' and do not necessarily reflect the views of the NSF.

Our thanks to the organizers of CoNEXT 2016 for welcoming NICE to the CoNEXT community.

4. REFERENCES

[1] NSF CISE Looking Beyond the Internet Steering Group. 2016. "Final Report: Looking Beyond the Internet."

Figure 1: Demo Session at NICE 2015

ACM CoNEXT 2016 Student Workshop

Rocky K. C. Chang
The Hong Kong Polytechnic University, Hong Kong
csrchang@comp.polyu.edu.hk

Hulya Seferoglu
University of Illinois at Chicago
Chicago, IL
hulya@uic.edu

Laurent Vanbever
ETH Zurich
Zurich, Switzerland
lvanbever@ethz.ch

ABSTRACT

The ACM CoNEXT 2016 Student Workshop is held in Irvine, California, USA on December 12, 2016 and co-located with the ACM 12th International Conference on emerging Networking Experiments and Technologies (CoNEXT 2016). The main objective of the workshop is to provide a platform for graduate students in the area of computer networks and communications to present their ongoing research efforts. The workshop is also a unique opportunity for students to network with other junior researchers as well as more experienced ones, receive constructive feedback, guidance, tips, and learn about cutting-edge research problems being tackled by the community. We have constructed an exciting program of 24 refereed presentations and posters, and an invited keynote talk (by Prof. Lixia Zhang, UCLA) that will give participating students an opportunity to hear from a senior researcher.

1. INTRODUCTION

This workshop is organized to provide a platform for graduate students in the area of computer networks and communications to present their ongoing research efforts. The workshop also represents a unique opportunity for students to network with other junior researchers as well as more experienced ones, receive constructive feedback, guidance, tips, and learn about cutting-edge research problems being tackled by the community.

The theme of ACM CoNEXT 2016 Student Workshop is broad and covers all aspects of networking research. Example topics include (but not limited to):

- Mobile, ad hoc, wireless, and cellular data networks
- Energy-efficient computing and networking
- Mobile data and computation offloading
- Augmented reality, cyber-physical systems, Internet of things
- Future Internet protocols and architectures
- Network applications and services
- Network measurement and modeling
- QoE measurement of network services
- Traffic measurement, analysis, and engineering
- Information/content-centric networks
- Data center networks and cloud computing
- SDN and network programming
- Network economics and networked markets
- Online social networks
- Security, trust, and privacy in fixed and mobile networks
- Network function virtualization, middleboxes
- Topics at the interface between networking, communications, and information theory

CoNEXT '16 December 12-15, 2016, Irvine, CA, USA

ACM ISBN 978-1-4503-4292-6/16/12.

DOI: http://dx.doi.org/10.1145/2999572.3004861

2. WORKSHOP OBJECTIVES

The main objective of the workshop is to provide a platform for graduate students in the area of computer networks and communications to present their ongoing research efforts. The workshop is also a unique opportunity for students to network with other junior researchers as well as more experienced ones, receive constructive feedback, guidance, tips, and learn about cutting-edge research problems being tackled by the community.

3. WORKSHOP PROGRAM FORMAT

The workshop is a one-day workshop. We received and reviewed 48 submissions, and accepted 24 papers. All of the accepted papers will be presented as posters. Furthermore, 17 out of these 24 papers will be presented during the workshop plenary session. The workshop includes an invited keynote talk (by Prof. Lixia Zhang, UCLA) that will give participating students an opportunity to hear from a senior researcher.

4. WORKSHOP ORGANIZERS

Rock K. C. Chang received the bachelor's degree from Virginia Tech and Vincennes University, and the M.Sc. and Ph.D. degrees from the Rensselaer Polytechnic Institute. He received his post-doctoral training with the Computer Science Department, IBM Thomas J. Watson Research Center. He is currently serving as an Associate Professor with the Department of Computing, The Hong Kong Polytechnic University (PolyU). He is leading an Internet Infrastructure and Security Research Laboratory, addressing network measurement, network security, and network operations and management problems. He also leads a Research Group on Internet Services Monitoring and Diagnostics with the Division of Smart Cities under PolyU's Research Institute for Sustainable Urban Development. He is a KTP Visiting Fellow at the University of Technology, Sydney in 2006.

Hulya Seferoglu is an Assistant Professor in the Electrical and Computer Engineering Department of University of Illinois at Chicago. She received the B.S. degree in Electrical Engineering from Istanbul University, Turkey, in 2003, M.S. degree in Electrical Engineering and Computer Science from Sabanci University, Turkey in 2005, and Ph.D. degree in Electrical and Computer Engineering from University of California, Irvine in 2010. She worked as a Postdoctoral Associate in the Laboratory of Information and Decision Systems (LIDS) at Massachusetts Institute of Technology during 2011-2013. She worked as a summer intern at AT&T Labs Research, Docomo USA Labs, and Microsoft Research Cambridge in 2010, 2008, and 2007, respectively. Her research interests are in the area of networking: design, analysis, and optimization of network protocols and algorithms. She is particularly interested in network optimization, network coding, and multimedia streaming.

Laurent Vanbever received the Ph.D. degree in computer science from the University of Louvain, Belgium, in 2012. From 2012 to 2014, he was a Post-Doctoral Research Associate at Princeton University where he collaborated with Prof. J. Rexford. He is currently an Assistant Professor at ETH Zurich, where he leads the Networked Systems Group since 2015. He won several awards for his research, including the ACM SIGCOMM 2015 Best Paper Award, the ACM SIGCOMM Doctoral Dissertation Award (runner-up), the University of Louvain Best Thesis Award, the ICNP 2013 Best Paper Award, and three Internet Society Applied Networking Research Prizes for his work on inter-domain routing and software-defined networking.

5. PROGRAM COMMITTEE

- Navid Abedini, *Qualcomm*
- Ozgu Alay, *Simula Research*
- Mustafa Arslan, *NEC Labs*
- Ioannis Avramopoulos, *National Technical University of Athens*
- Kai Bu, *Zhejiang University*
- Ignacio Castro Queen Mary, *University of London*
- Amogh Dhamdhere, *CAIDA*
- Benoit Donnet, *Universite de Liege*
- Kensuke Fukuda, *National Institute of Informatics, Japan*
- Polly Huang, *National Taiwan University*
- Hongqiang Liu, *Microsoft Research*
- Hung X. Nguyen, *The University of Adelaide*
- Rubens Merz, *Swisscom*
- Srinivas Narayana, *Princeton University*
- Damien Saucez, *INRIA*
- Narseo Vallina-Rodriguez, *University of California, Berkeley*
- Balajee Vamanan, *University of Illinois at Chicago*

Acknowledgments

We would like to thank all authors who submitted their papers and the program committee members for their excellent reviews of the papers. We are also very grateful for the invited keynote speaker Prof. Lixia Zhang for her presentation in the workshop.

Author Index